Sci/

A Dictionary of
Scientists

Oxford Paperback Reference

The most authoritative and up-to-date reference books for both students and the general reader.

Abbreviations
ABC of Music
Accounting
Archaeology*
Architecture*
Art and Artists
Art Terms*
Astronomy
Bible
Biology
Botany
Buddhism*
Business
Card Games
Chemistry
Christian Church
Classical Literature
Classical Mythology*
Colour Medical Dictionary
Colour Science Dictionary
Computing
Dance*
Dates
Earth Sciences
Ecology
Economics
Engineering*
English Etymology
English Folklore*
English Grammar
English Language
English Literature
English Place-Names
Euphemisms
Film*
Finance and Banking
First Names
Food and Nutrition
Fowler's Modern English Usage
Geography
King's English
Law
Linguistics

Literary Terms
Mathematics
Medical Dictionary
Medicines*
Modern Quotations
Modern Slang
Music
Nursing
Opera
Paperback Encyclopedia
Philosophy
Physics
Plant-Lore
Plant Sciences
Political Biography
Politics
Popes
Proverbs
Psychology*
Quotations
Sailing Terms
Saints
Science
Scientists
Shakespeare
Ships and the Sea
Sociology
Superstitions
Theatre
Twentieth-Century Art*
Twentieth-Century World History
Twentieth-Century Poetry
Weather Facts
Who's Who in Opera*
Who's Who in the Twentieth Century
Women Writers
Word Games
World Mythology
Writers' Dictionary
Zoology

*forthcoming

A Dictionary of

Scientists

Oxford   New York

OXFORD UNIVERSITY PRESS

1999

Oxford University Press, Great Clarendon Street, Oxford OX2 6DP

Oxford   New York
Athens   Auckland   Bangkok   Bogota   Bombay   Buenos Aires
Calcutta   Cape Town   Dar es Salaam   Delhi
Florence   Hong Kong   Istanbul   Karachi
Kuala Lumpur   Madras   Madrid   Melbourne
Mexico City   Nairobi   Paris   Singapore
Taipei   Tokyo   Toronto   Warsaw

and associated companies in
Berlin   Ibadan

Oxford is a trade mark of Oxford University Press

First published 1993 by the Institute of Physics as the
Encyclopedia of Scientists
This abridged and updated edition published as an
Oxford University Press paperback 1999

British Library Cataloguing in Publication Data

Data available

Library of Congress Cataloging in Publication Data

Data available

ISBN 0 19 280086 8

10 9 8 7 6 5 4 3 2 1

Typeset by Market House Books Ltd
Printed in Great Britain by
Cox & Wyman Ltd
Reading, Berkshire

Preface

This book is a shortened and updated version of *An Encyclopedia of Scientists*, published by the Institute of Physics in 1993. In compiling this edition we have followed the intention of the original editors – to say as much about science as about the scientists who have created it.

All the entries contain basic biographical data – place and date of birth, posts held, etc. – but do not give exhaustive personal details about the subject's family, prizes, honorary degrees, etc. Most of the space has been devoted to their main scientific achievements and the nature and importance of these achievements. This has not always been easy; in particular, it has not always been possible to explain in relatively simple terms work in the higher reaches of abstract mathematics or modern theoretical physics.

Perhaps the most difficult problem was compiling the entry list. We have attempted to include people who have produced major advances in theory or have made influential or well-known discoveries. A particular difficulty has been the selection of contemporary scientists, in view of the fact that of all scientists who have ever lived, the vast majority are still alive. In this we have been guided by lists of prizes and awards made by scientific societies and we have included all Nobel prizewinners in physics, chemistry, and physiology or medicine. A full list of Nobel prizewinners is given in the back of the book. We have to a great extent concentrated on what might be called the traditional pure sciences – physics, chemistry, biology, astronomy, and the earth sciences. We also give a more limited coverage of medicine and mathematics and have included a selection of people who have made important contributions to engineering and technology. A few of the entries cover workers in such fields as anthropology and psychology, and a small number of philosophers are represented.

Where appropriate, entries contain cross-references to other relevant entries. These are given in small capital letters. We have also included an index of key topics in science.

JD
DG
1998

General editors	John Daintith BSc, PhD
	Derek Gjertsen BA
Market House editors	John Clark BSc
	Elizabeth Martin MA
	Anne Stibbs BA
	Fran Alexander BA
	Jonathan Law BA
	Peter Lewis BA DPhil
	Mark Salad
	Elizabeth Tootill BSc, MSc
	Sarah Mitchell BA
Contributors	Eve Daintith BSc
	Rosalind Dunning BA
	Garry Hammond BSc
	Robert Hine BSc, MSc
	Valerie Illingworth BSc, MPhil
	Susan O'Neill BSc
	W. J. Palmer MSc
	Roger F. Picken BSc, PhD
	Carol Russell BSc
	W. J. Sherratt BSc, MSc, PhD
	Jackie Smith BA
	B. D. Sorsby BSc, PhD
	P. Welch D Phil
	Anthony Wootton

Abbe, Cleveland (1838–1916) *American meteorologist*

Abbe was born in New York City and educated there at City College; he later taught at the University of Michigan. He then spent two years (1864–66) in Russia at the Pulkovo Observatory under Otto Struve. On his return to America he worked as director of the Cincinnati Observatory (1868–70).

Abbe was the first official weather forecaster in America. He was appointed, in 1871, chief meteorologist with the weather service, which was later formed into the US Weather Bureau (1891), and remained in this organization for the rest of his life. He was one of the first scientists to see the revolutionary role the telegraph had to play in weather forecasting and used reports conveyed to him from all over the country.

Abbe published over 300 papers on meteorology and from 1893 he was in charge of the journals published by the US Weather Bureau. He was also responsible for the division of America into time zones in 1883.

Abbe, Ernst (1840–1905) *German physicist*

Abbe, who was born in Eisenach (now in Germany), came from poor parents but managed to become a lecturer at the University of Jena, where in 1886 he collaborated with Carl Zeiss, a supplier of optical instruments to the university, to improve the quality of microscope production. Up till then, this had been an empirical art without rigorous theory to aid design. Abbe's contribution was his knowledge of optical theory. He is known for the *Abbe sine condition* – a necessary condition for the elimination of spherical aberration in an optical system; such a system he described as aplanatic. He also invented the apochromatic lens system (1886), which eliminated both primary and secondary color distortions and the *Abbe condenser* (1872) – a combination of lenses for converging light onto the specimen in microscopes.

The partnership between Abbe and Zeiss was a productive combination of Zeiss's practical knowledge and Abbe's mathematical and theoretical ability. After Zeiss's death, Abbe became the sole owner of the Zeiss company.

Abegg, Richard (1869–1910) *German physical chemist*

Abegg was born in the German port of Danzig (now Gdańsk in Poland); he studied chemistry at Kiel, Tübingen, and Berlin. He graduated in 1891 as a pupil of Wilhelm Hofmann. Initially an organic chemist, he was attracted by the advances being made in physical chemistry, and in 1894 moved to Göttingen as an assistant to Hermann Nernst. Here, he worked on electrochemical and related problems and with G. Bodländer produced an important paper on valence, *Die Elektronaffinität* (1899; Electron Affinity). He is remembered for *Abegg's rule* (partially anticipated by Dmitri Mendeleev), which states that each element has two valences: a normal valence and a contravalence, the sum of which is eight. In 1899 he became a professor at Breslau (now Wrocław in Poland) and was about to become the director of the Physico-Chemical Institute there when he was killed in a ballooning accident.

Abel, Sir Frederick Augustus (1827–1902) *British chemist*

Abel was born in London, the son of a well-known musician and the grandson of a court painter to the grand duke of Mecklenberg-Schwerin. Despite this artistic background, Abel developed an early interest in science after visiting his uncle A. J. Abel, a mineralogist and pupil of Berzelius. In 1845 he was one of the first of the pupils to study at the Royal College of Chemistry under August von Hofmann, remaining there until 1851. After a brief appointment as a chemical demonstrator at St. Bartholomew's Hospital, London, he succeeded Michael Faraday in 1852 as a lecturer in chemistry at the Royal Military Academy at Woolwich. In 1854 he became ordnance chemist and chemist to the war department.

Abel's career was thus devoted exclusively to the chemistry of explosives. New and powerful explosives, including guncotton and nitroglycerin, had recently been invented but were unsafe to use. Abel's first achievement was to show how guncotton could be rendered stable and safe. His method was to remove all traces of the sulfuric and nitric acids used in its manufacture by mincing, washing in soda until all the acid had been removed, and drying. In 1888 he was appointed president of a government committee to find new high explosives. The two existing propellants, Poudre B and ballistite, had various defects, most important of which was a tendency to deteriorate during storage. Together with Sir James Dewar, Abel introduced the new explosive, cordite, in 1889. This was a mixture of guncotton and nitroglycerin with camphor and petroleum added as stabilizers and preservatives.

Abel was honoured for his services by being made a knight in 1891 and a baronet in 1893.

Abel, John Jacob (1857–1938) American biochemist

Abel was born in Cleveland, Ohio, the son of a farmer. He was educated at the University of Michigan and Johns Hopkins University. He spent the years 1884–90 in Europe studying at Leipzig, Heidelberg, Würzburg, Vienna, Bern, and Strasbourg, where he gained an MD in 1888. On his return to America he worked briefly at the University of Michigan before being appointed in 1893 to the first chair of pharmacology at Johns Hopkins, a post he retained until his retirement in 1932.

Abel approached biology with a first-rate training in chemistry and with the conviction that the study of molecules and atoms was as important as the observation of multicellular tissues under the microscope. He thus began by working on the chemical composition of various bodily tissues and fluids and, in 1897, succeeded in isolating a physiologically active substance from the adrenal glands, named by him epinephrine, also known as adrenalin. This extract was actually the monobenzoyl derivative of the hormone. It was left to Jokichi Takamine to purify it in 1900.

As early as 1912 Abel clearly formulated the idea of an artificial kidney and in 1914 isolated for the first time amino acids from the blood. He was less successful with his search (1917–24) for the pituitary hormone, being unaware that he was dealing with not one but several hormones. His announcement in 1926, that he had crystallized insulin met with considerable skepticism, especially regarding its protein nature. This work was not generally accepted until the mid 1930s.

After his retirement Abel devoted himself to a study of the tetanus toxin.

Abel, Niels Henrik (1802–1829) Norwegian mathematician

Abel was born in Froland, the son of a poor pastor; he was educated in mathematics at the University of Christiania (Oslo). After the death of his father, Abel had to support a large family; he earned what he could by private teaching and was also helped out by his teacher. He was eventually given a grant by the Norwegian government to make a trip to France and Germany to visit mathematicians. In Germany he met the engineer and mathematician August Crelle, who was to be of great assistance to him. Crelle published Abel's work and exerted what influence he could to obtain him a post in Germany. Tragically Abel died just when Crelle had succeeded in getting him the chair in mathematics at Berlin.

With Evariste Galois (whom he never met), Abel founded the theory of groups (commutative groups are known as *Abelian groups* in his honor), and his early death ranks as one of the great tragedies of 19th-century mathematics. One of Abel's first achievements was to solve the longstanding problem of whether the general quintic (of the fifth degree) equation was solvable by algebraic methods. He showed that the general quintic is not solvable algebraically and sent this proof to Karl Gauss, but unfortunately Gauss threw it away unread, having assumed that it was yet another unsuccessful attempt to solve the quintic.

Abel's greatest work was in the theory of elliptic and transcendental functions. Mathematicians had previously focused their attention on problems associated with elliptic integrals. Abel showed that these problems could be immensely simplified by considering the inverse functions of these integrals – the so-called 'elliptic functions'. He also proved a fundamental theorem, *Abel's theorem*, on transcendental functions, which he submitted to Augustin Cauchy (and unfortunately fared no better than he did with Gauss). The study of elliptic functions inaugurated by Abel was to occupy many of the best mathematicians for the remainder of the 19th century. He also made very important contributions to the theory of infinite series.

Abelson, Philip Hauge (1913–) American physical chemist

Abelson, who was born in Tacoma, was educated at Washington State College and at the University of California at Berkeley, where he obtained his PhD in 1939. Apart from the war years at the Naval Research Laboratory in Washington, he spent most of his career at the Carnegie Institution, Washington, serving as the director of the geophysics laboratory from 1953, and as president from 1971 to 1978. He subsequently became the editor of a number of scientific journals including the important periodical *Science*, which he edited from 1962 to 1985.

In 1940 he assisted Edwin McMillan in creating the first transuranic element, neptunium, by bombardment of uranium with neutrons in the Berkeley cyclotron. Abelson next worked on separating the isotopes of uranium. It was clear that a nuclear explosion was possible only if sufficient quantities of the rare isotope uranium–235 (only 7 out of every 1000 uranium atoms) could be obtained. The method Abelson chose was that of thermal diffusion. This involved circulating uranium hexafluoride vapor in a narrow space between a hot and a cold pipe; the lighter isotope tended to accumulate nearer the hot surface. Collecting sufficient uranium–235 involved Abelson in one of those massive research and engineering projects only possible in war time. In the Philadelphia Navy Yard, he constructed a hundred or so 48-foot (15-meter) precision-engineered pipes through which steam was pumped. From this Abelson was able to obtain uranium enriched to 14 U-235 atoms per 1000.

Although this was still too weak a mixture for a bomb, it was sufficiently enriched to use in other separation processes. Consequently a bigger plant, consisting of over 2000 towers, was constructed at Oak Ridge, Tennessee, and provided enriched material for the separation process from which came the fuel for the first atom bomb.

After the war Abelson extended the important work of Stanley Miller on the origin of vital biological molecules. He found that amino acids could be produced from a variety of gases if carbon, nitrogen, hydrogen, and oxygen were present. He was also able to show (1955) the great stability of amino acids by identifying them in 300-million-year-old fossils and later (1956) identified the presence of fatty acids in rocks.

Adams, John Couch (1819–1892)
British astronomer

Adams was born in the small Cornish town of Launceston, where his father was a tenant farmer. He developed an early interest in astronomy, constructing his own sundial and observing solar altitudes, and pursuing his astronomical studies in the local Mechanics Institute. He graduated brilliantly from Cambridge University in 1843, and became Lowndean Professor of Astronomy and Geometry there in 1858; in 1860 he was appointed director of the Cambridge Observatory.

His fame rests largely on the dramatic events surrounding the discovery of the planet Neptune in 1846. Astronomers had detected a discrepancy between the observed and predicted positions of Uranus and thus it appeared that either Newton's theory of gravitation was not as universal as had been supposed, or there was an as yet undetected body exerting a significant gravitational influence over the orbit of Uranus. There is evidence that Adams had decided to work on this problem as early as 1841. He had a general solution to the problem by 1843 and a complete solution by September, 1845. It was then that he payed a visit to George Airy, the Astronomer Royal, with the exact position of the new planet.

Airy payed little attention to it and was moved to action only when, in June 1846, the French astronomer, Urbain Leverrier, also announced the position of a new planet. It was within one degree of the position predicted by Adams the previous year. Airy asked James Challis, director of the Cambridge Observatory, to start looking for the new planet with his large 25-inch (63.5-cm) refractor. Unfortunately Challis decided to cover a much wider area of the sky than was necessary and also lacked up-to-date and complete charts of the area. His start was soon lost and Johann Galle in Berlin had no difficulty in discovering the planet on his first night of observation. All the fame, prizes, and honors initially went to Leverrier.

When it was publicly pointed out, by Challis and John Herschel, that Adams's work had priority over Leverrier's, the shy Adams wanted no part of the controversy that followed. In fact he seemed genuinely uninterested in honors. He declined both a knighthood and the post of Astronomer Royal, which was offered him after Airy's retirement in 1881. He later worked on the perturbations of the planets (1866), and on the secular variation of the mean motion of the Moon (1852), both difficult questions of mathematical astronomy. His scientific papers were published by his brother in two volumes, in 1876 and 1901.

Adams, Walter Sydney (1876–1956)
American astronomer

Adams was born in Antioch (now in Turkey). He was the son of missionaries working in Syria, then part of the Ottoman Empire, who returned to America in 1885. Adams graduated from Dartmouth College in 1898 and obtained his AM from the University of Chicago in 1900. After a year in Munich he began his career in astronomy as assistant to George Hale in 1901 at the

Yerkes Observatory. He moved with Hale to the newly established Mount Wilson Observatory in 1904 where he served as assistant director, 1913–23, and then as director from 1923 until his retirement in 1946.

At Mount Wilson Adams was able to use first the 60-inch (1.5-m) and from 1917 the 100-inch (2.5-m) reflecting telescopes in whose design and construction he had been closely associated. His early work was mainly concerned with solar spectroscopy, when he studied sunspots and solar rotation, but he gradually turned to stellar spectroscopy. In 1914 he showed how it was possible to distinguish between a dwarf and a giant star merely from their spectra. He also demonstrated that it was possible to determine the luminosity, i.e. intrinsic brightness, of a star from its spectrum. This led to Adams introducing the method of spectroscopic parallax whereby the luminosity deduced from a star's spectrum could be used to estimate its distance. The distance of many thousands of stars have been calculated by this method.

He is however better known for his work on the orbiting companion of Sirius, named Sirius B. Friedrich Bessel had first shown in 1844 that Sirius must have a companion and had worked out its mass as about the same as our Sun. The faint star was first observed telescopically by Alvan Clark in 1862. He succeeded in obtaining the spectrum of Sirius B in 1915 and found the star to be considerably hotter than the Sun. Adams realized that such a hot body, just eight light-years distant, could only remain invisible to the naked eye if it was very much smaller than the Sun, no bigger in fact than the Earth. In that case it must have an extremely high density, exceeding 100,000 times the density of water. Adams had thus discovered the first 'white dwarf' – a star that has collapsed into a highly compressed object after its nuclear fuel is exhausted.

If such an interpretation was correct then Sirius B should possess a very strong gravitational field. According to Einstein's general theory of relativity, this strong field should shift the wavelengths, of light waves emitted by it toward the red end of the spectrum. In 1924 Adams succeeded in making the difficult spectroscopic observations and did in fact detect the predicted red shift, which confirmed his own account of Sirius B and provided strong evidence for general relativity.

Adhemar, Alphonse Joseph
(1797–1862) *French mathematician*

Adhemar, who was born and died in Paris, France, was a private mathematics tutor who also produced a number of popular mathematical textbooks.

His most important scientific work was his *Les Revolutions de la mer* (1842) in which he was the first to propose a plausible mechanism by which astronomical events could produce ice ages on Earth. It had been known for some time that while the Earth moved in an elliptical orbit around the Sun it also rotated about an axis that was tilted to its orbital plane. Because the orbit is elliptical and the Sun is at one focus, the Earth is closer to the Sun at certain times of year. As a result, the southern hemisphere has a slightly longer winter than its northern counterpart. Adhemar saw this as a possible cause of the great Antarctic icesheet for, as this received about 170 hours less solar radiation per year than the Arctic, this could just be sufficient to keep temperatures cold enough to permit the ice to build up.

Adhemar was also aware that the Earth's axis does not always point in the same direction but itself moves around a small circular orbit every 26,000 years. Thus he postulated a 26,000-year cycle developing in the occurrence of glacial periods, but his views received little support.

Adler, Alfred (1870–1937) *Austrian psychologist*

Adler was born in Penzing, Austria, the son of a corn merchant, and was educated at the University of Vienna, where he obtained his MD in 1895. After two years at the Vienna General Hospital he set up in private practice in 1898.

In about 1900 Adler began investigating psychopathology and in 1902 he became an original member of Sigmund Freud's circle, which met to discuss psychoanalytical matters. His disagreements with Freud began as early as 1907 – he dismissed Freud's view that sexual conflicts in early childhood cause mental illness – and he finally broke away from the psychoanalytic movement in 1911 to form his own school of individual psychology. Adler tended to minimize the role of the unconscious and sexual repression and instead to see the neurotic as overcompensating for his or her 'inferiority complex', a term he himself introduced. His system was fully expounded in his *Practice and Theory of Individual Psychology* (1927). In 1921 Adler founded his first child-guidance clinic in Vienna, which was to be followed by over 30 more before the Nazi regime in Vienna forced their closure in 1932. From 1926 onward he began to spend more and more time in America, finally settling there permanently in 1932 and taking a professorship of psychiatry at the Long Island College of Medicine, New York, a post he retained until his death from a heart attack while lecturing in Aberdeen in Scotland.

Adrian, Edgar Douglas, Baron Adrian of Cambridge (1889–1977)
British neurophysiologist

Adrian, a lawyer's son, was born in London and studied at Cambridge University and St. Bartholomew's Hospital, London, where he obtained his MD in 1915. He returned to Cambridge in 1919, was appointed professor of physiology in 1937, and became the master of Trinity College, Cambridge, in 1951, an office he retained until his retirement in 1965. He was raised to the British peerage in 1955.

Adrian's greatest contribution to neurophysiology was his work on the nerve impulse. When he began it was known that nerves transmit nerve impulses as signals, but knowledge of the frequency and control of such impulses was minimal. The first insight into this process came from Adrian's colleague Keith Lucas, who demonstrated in 1905 that the impulse obeyed the 'all-or-none' law. This asserted that below a certain threshold of stimulation a nerve does not respond. However, once the threshold is reached the nerve continues to respond by a fixed amount however much the stimulation increases. Thus, increased stimulation, although it stimulates more fibers, does not affect the magnitude of the signal itself.

It was not until 1925 that Adrian advanced beyond this position. By painstaking surgical techniques he succeeded in separating individual nerve fibers and amplifying and recording the small action potentials in these fibers. By studying the effect of stretching the sternocutaneous muscle of the frog, Adrian demonstrated how the nerve, even though it transmits an impulse of fixed strength, can still convey a complex message. He found that as the extension increased so did the frequency of the nerve impulse, rising from 10 to 50 impulses per second. Thus, he concluded that the message is conveyed by changes in the frequency of the discharge. For this work Adrian shared the 1932 Nobel Prize for physiology or medicine with Charles SHERRINGTON.

Agassiz, Jean Louis Rodolphe
(1807–1873) *Swiss-American biologist*

Generally considered the foremost naturalist of 19th-century America, Agassiz was born in Motier-en-Vuly, Switzerland. He was educated at the universities of Zurich, Heidelberg, and Munich, where he studied under the embryologist Ignaz Döllinger. At the instigation of Georges Cuvier, he cataloged and described the fishes brought back from Brazil by C. F. P. von Martius and J. B. von Spix (*Fishes of Brazil*, 1929), following this with his *History of the Freshwater Fishes of Central Europe* (1839–42) and an extensive pioneering work on fossil fishes, which eventually ran to five volumes: *Recherches sur les poissons fossiles* (1833–43; Researches on Fossil Fishes). These works, completed while Agassiz was professor of natural history at Neuchâtel (1832–46), established his reputation as the greatest ichthyologist of his day. Agassiz's best-known discovery, however, was that of the Ice Ages. Extensive field studies in the Swiss Alps, and later in America and Britain, led him to postulate glacier movements and the former advance and retreat of ice sheets; his findings were published in *Etudes sur les glaciers* (1840; Studies on Glaciers).

A successful series of lectures given at Boston, Massachusetts, in 1846 led to his permanent settlement in America. In 1847 he was appointed professor of zoology and geology at Harvard, where he also established the Museum of Comparative Zoology (1859). Agassiz's subsequent teachings introduced a departure from established practice in emphasizing the importance of first-hand investigation of natural phenomena, thus helping to transform academic study in America. His embryological studies led to a recognition of the similarity between the developing stages of living animals and complete but more primitive species in the fossil record. Agassiz did not, however, share Darwin's view of a gradual evolution of species, but, like Cuvier, considered that there had been repeated separate creations and extinctions of species – thus explaining changes and the appearance of new forms. Unfortunately, one of Agassiz's most influential pronouncements was that there were several species, as distinct from races, of man: an argument used by slavers to justify their subjugation of the negroes as an inferior species. His ambitious *Contributions to the Natural History of the United States* (4 vols. 1857–62) remained uncompleted at his death.

Agricola, Georgius (1494–1555)
German metallurgist

Agricola's true name was Georg Bauer but, as was the custom of the day, he latinized it (Agricola and Bauer both mean 'farmer'). Beyond his place of birth – Glauchau (now in Germany) – little is known about him until his entry into the University of

Leipzig in 1514. He later pursued his studies of philosophy and medicine in Italy at Bologna, Padua, and Venice (1523–27). In 1527 he was engaged as physician to the Bohemian city of Joachimsthal – the center of a rich mining area – moving in 1534 to another celebrated mining town, Chemnitz, near his birthplace. Here he became burgomaster in 1545. He wrote seven books on geological subjects but these were so illuminating of other subjects that he was known in his lifetime as 'the Saxon Pliny'.

His most famous work, *De re metallica* (1556), concentrates on mining and metallurgy with a wealth of information on the conditions of the time, such as management of the mines, the machinery used (e.g. pumps, windmills, and water power), and the processes employed. The book is still in print having the unique distinction of being translated and edited (1912) by a president of the United States, Herbert Hoover, with Lou Henry Hoover (his wife).

Agricola is often regarded as the father of modern mineralogy. In the Middle Ages, the subject was based on accumulated lore from the Orient, the Arabs, and antiquity. Stones were believed to come in male and female form, to have digestive organs, and to possess medicinal and supernatural powers. Agricola began to reject these theories and to provide the basis for a new discipline. Thus in his *De ortu et causis subterraneorum* (1546; On the Origin and Cause of Subterranean Things) he introduced the idea of a lapidifying juice (or *succus lapidescens*) from which stones condensed as a result of heat. This fluid was supposedly subterranean water mixed with rain, which collects earthy material when percolating through the ground.

Agricola also, in *De natura fossilium* (1546), introduced a new basis for the classification of minerals (called 'fossils' at the time). Although far from modern, it was an enormous improvement on earlier works. Agricola based his system on the physical properties of minerals, which he listed as color, weight, transparency, taste, odor, texture, solubility, combustibility, and so on. In this way he tried to distinguish between earths, stones, gems, marbles, metals, building stone, and mineral solutions, carefully describing his terms, which should not be assumed to be synonymous with today's terms, in each case.

Airy, Sir George Biddell (1801–1892)
British astronomer

Airy, the son of a tax collector, was born in Alnwick in the north-east of England. He attended school in Colchester before going to Cambridge University in 1819. He met with early success, producing a mathematical textbook in 1826 and numerous papers on optics. He became Lucasian Professor of Mathematics at Cambridge in 1826 and two years later was made Plumian Professor of Astronomy and director of the Cambridge Observatory. In 1835 he was appointed Astronomer Royal, a post he held for 46 years.

Airy was a very energetic, innovative, and successful Astronomer Royal. He re-equipped the observatory, installing an altazimuth for lunar observation in 1847, a new transit circle and zenith tube in 1851, and a 13-inch (33-cm) equatorial telescope in 1859. He created a magnetic and meteorological department in 1838, began spectroscopic investigations in 1868, and started keeping a daily record of sunspots with the Kew Observatory heliograph in 1873. In optics he investigated the use of cylindrical lenses to correct astigmatism (Airy was astigmatic) and examined the disklike image in the diffraction pattern of a point source of light (in an optical device with a central aperture) now called the *Airy disk*. Also named for him is his hypothesis of isostasy: the theory that mountain ranges must have root structures of lower density, proportional to their height, in order to maintain isostatic equilibrium.

Despite his many successes he is now mainly, and unfairly, remembered for his lapses. When John Adams came to him in September, 1845, with news of the position of a new planet, Airy unwisely ignored him, leaving it to others to win fame as the discoverers of Neptune. He also dismissed Michael Faraday's new field theory.

Aitken, Robert Grant (1864–1951)
American astronomer

Born in Jackson, California, Aitken obtained his AB in 1887 and his AM in 1892 from Williams College, Massachusetts. He began his career at the University of the Pacific, then in San Jose, as professor of mathematics from 1891 until 1895 when he joined the staff of Lick Observatory, Mount Hamilton, California. He remained at Lick for his entire career, serving as its director from 1930 until his retirement in 1935.

Aitken did much to advance knowledge of binary stars, i.e. pairs of stars orbiting about the same point under their mutual gravitational attraction. He described over 3000 binary systems and published in 1932 the comprehensive work *New General Catalogue of Double Stars Within 120° of the North Pole*. He also produced the standard work *The Binary Stars* (1918).

Al-Battani (or Albategnius) (c. 858–929) Arab astronomer

Al-Battani was the son of a maker of astronomical instruments in Harran (now in Turkey). He worked mainly in Raqqah on the Euphrates (now ar-Raqqah in Syria) and was basically a follower of Ptolemy, devoting himself to refining and perfecting the work of his master. He improved Ptolemy's measurement of the obliquity of the ecliptic (the angle between the Earth's orbital and equatorial planes), the determination of the equinoxes, and the length of the year. He also corrected Ptolemy in various matters, in particular in his discovery of the movement of the solar perigee (the Sun's nearest point to the Earth) relative to the equinoxes. His work was widely known in the medieval period, having been translated by Plato of Tivoli in about 1120 as De motu stellarum (On Stellar Motion), which was finally published in Nuremberg in 1537.

Alcmaeon (fl. 450 BC) Greek philosopher and physician

Alcmaeon was born in Croton (now Crotone in Italy). Details of his work come from the surviving fragments of his book and through references by later authors, including Aristotle. He was probably influenced by the school of thought founded by Pythagoras in Croton and originated the notion that health was dependent on maintaining a balance between all the pairs of opposite qualities in the body, i.e. wet and dry, hot and cold, etc. Imbalance of these qualities resulted in illness. This theory was later developed by Hippocrates and his followers.

Alcmaeon performed dissections of animals and possibly of human cadavers also. He demonstrated various anatomical features of the eye and ear, including their connections with the brain, and correctly asserted that the brain was the control center of bodily functions and the seat of intelligence.

Alder, Kurt (1902–1958) German organic chemist. See DIELS, OTTO.

Alembert, Jean Le Rond d' See D'ALEMBERT, JEAN LE ROND.

Alfvén, Hannes Olof Gösta (1908–1995) Swedish physicist

Alfvén, who was born in Norrkoeping, Sweden, was educated at the University of Uppsala where he received his PhD in 1934. He subsequently worked at the Royal Institute of Technology, Stockholm, where he served as professor of the theory of electricity (1940–45), professor of electronics (1945–63), and professor of plasma physics (1963–73).

Alfvén is noted for his pioneering theoretical research in the field of magnetohydrodynamics – the study of conducting fluids and their interaction with magnetic fields. This work, for which he shared the 1970 Nobel Prize for physics with Louis Néel, was mainly concerned with plasmas; i.e. ionized gases containing positive and negative particles. He investigated the interactions of electrical and magnetic fields and showed theoretically that the magnetic field, under certain circumstances, can move with the plasma. In 1942 he postulated the existence of waves in plasmas; these Alfvén waves were later observed in both liquid metals and ionized plasmas.

Alfvén also applied his theories to the motion of particles in the Earth's magnetic field and to the properties of plasmas in stars. In 1942, and later in the 1950s, he developed a theory of the origin of the solar system. This he assumed to have formed from a magnetic plasma, which condensed into small particles that clustered together into larger bodies. His work is also applicable to the properties of plasmas in experimental nuclear fusion reactors. Alfvén's books include Cosmical Electrodynamics (1950), which collects his early work, On the Origin of the Solar System (1954), and On the Evolution of the Solar System (1976, with G. Arrhenius).

In his later years Alfvén argued against the current orthodoxy of the big-bang theory of the origin of the universe. Space, he argued, is full of immensely long plasma filaments. The electromagnetic forces produced have caused the plasma to condense into galaxies. As for the expansion of the universe, he attributed this to the energy released by the collision of matter and antimatter. Whereas Alfvén's critics charged him with vagueness, he responded by arguing that cosmologists derive their theories more from mathematical considerations than from laboratory experiments.

Alhazen (or Abu Ali Al-Hassan Ibn Al Haytham) (c. 965–1038) Arabian scientist

Born in Basra (now in Iraq), Alhazen was one of the most original scientists of his time. About a hundred works are attributed to him; the main one was translated into Latin in the 12th century and finally published in 1572 as Opticae thesaurus (The Treasury of Optics). This was widely studied and extremely influential. It was the first authoritative work to reject the curious Greek view that the eye sends out rays to the object looked at. Alhazen also made detailed measurements of angles of incidence and refraction. He studied spherical and parabolic mirrors, the camera obscura, and the role of the lens in vision. While the Greeks had had a good understanding of the formation of an image in a plane mirror, Alhazen tackled the much more difficult problem of the formation of images in spherical and parabolic mirrors and offered geometrical solutions. It is difficult to think of any other writer who had surpassed the Greeks in any branch of the exact sciences by the 14th let alone the 11th century. He was, however, unfortunate in his relationship with the deranged caliph al-Hakim. Having rashly claimed that he could regulate the flooding of the Nile, he was forced to simulate madness to escape execution until the caliph died in 1021.

Al-Khwarizmi, Abu Ja'far Muhammad Ibn Musa (c. 800–c. 847) *Arab mathematician, astronomer, and geographer*

Al-Khwarizmi takes his name from his birthplace, Khwarizm (now Khiva in Uzbekistan). His importance lies chiefly in the knowledge he transmitted to others. Very little is known about his life except that he was a member of the academy of sciences in Baghdad, which flourished during the rule (813–33) of caliph al-Ma'mun. Al-Khwarizmi's main astronomical treatise and his chief mathematical work, the *Algebra*, are dedicated to the caliph. The *Algebra* enlarged upon the work of Diophantus and is largely concerned with methods for solving practical computational problems rather than algebra as the term is now understood. Insofar as he did discuss algebra, al-Khwarizmi confined his discussion to equations of the first and second degrees.

His astronomical work, *Zij al-sindhind*, is also based largely on the work of other scientists. As with the *Algebra*, its chief interest is as the earliest Arab work on the subject still in existence.

Al-Khwarizmi's other main surviving works are a treatise on the Hindu system of numerals and a treatise on geography. The Hindu number system, with its epoch-making innovations, for example the incorporation of a symbol for zero, was introduced to Europe via a Latin translation (*De numero indorum*; On the Hindu Art of Reckoning) of al-Khwarizmi's work. Only the Latin translation remains but it seems certain that al-Khwarizmi was the first Arab mathematician to expound the new number system systematically. The term 'algorithm' (a rule of calculation) is a corrupted form of his name. His geographical treatise marked a considerable improvement over earlier work, notably in correcting some of the influential errors and misconceptions that had gained currency owing to Ptolemy's *Geography*.

Allen, Edgar (1892–1943) *American endocrinologist*

Allen, the son of a physician, was born in Canon City, Colorado, and educated at Brown University. After war service he worked at Washington University, St. Louis, before being appointed (1923) to the chair of anatomy at the University of Missouri. In 1933 he moved to a similar post at Yale and remained there until his death.

In 1923 Allen, working with Edward Doisy, began the modern study of the sex hormones. It was widely thought that the female reproductive cycle was under the control of some substance found in the corpus luteum, the body formed in the ovary after ovulation. Allen thought rather that the active ingredient was probably in the follicles surrounding the ovum. To test this he made an extract of the follicular fluid and found that on injection it induced the physiological changes normally found only in the estrous cycle. Allen had in fact discovered estrogen although it was only identified some six years later by Adolf Butenandt.

Allen, James Alfred Van See VAN ALLEN, JAMES ALFRED.

Alpher, Ralph Asher (1921–) *American physicist. See* GAMOW, GEORGE; DICKE, ROBERT.

Altman, Sidney (1939–) *American chemist*

Born in Montreal, Canada, Altman was educated at the University of Colorado, Boulder, where he obtained his PhD in 1967. He moved to Yale in 1971, becoming professor of biology in 1980 and a naturalized US citizen in 1984.

In 1982 Thomas CECH at Colorado had shown that RNA sometimes served as a biocatalyst – a role previously thought to be exclusive to protein enzymes. Cech's work was on a reaction in which the RNA was a self-catalyst. Altman set out to investigate other catalytic activity of RNA.

He worked with ribonuclease-P, an enzyme composed of both RNA and a protein, which catalyzes the processing of transfer RNA (tRNA). For the enzyme to work at the cellular level, it was thought that both protein and RNA were needed. It could, however, be possible that the RNA was merely a kind of structural support for the protein enzyme. Altman found that, *in vitro*, ribonuclease-P alone could splice the tRNA molecule at the correct place; the unaccompanied protein displayed no such activity.

Final proof came when a recombinant DNA template was used to produce only the RNA part of the ribonuclease-P. The artificial RNA still catalyzed the appropriate activity without any associated protein whatsoever. Altman had thus helped to break down the previously unquestioned dogma that molecules could either carry information, like RNA, or catalyze chemical reactions, like proteins, but they could not do both. The discovery could also throw light on the puzzle that if proteins are needed to assemble RNA, and RNA to assemble proteins, then how did the process ever get started? The answer could lie in the catalytic activity of RNA itself.

For his work on ribonuclease-P Altman shared the 1989 Nobel Prize for chemistry with Thomas CECH.

Alvarez, Luis Walter (1911–1988)
American physicist

Alvarez, the son of a research physiologist, was born in San Francisco and educated at the University of Chicago where he gained his PhD in 1936. He moved soon after to the University of California, Berkeley. Apart from wartime work on radar at the Massachusetts Institute of Technology Radiation Laboratory (1940–43) and on the Manhattan Project at Los Alamos (1943–45), Alvarez spent his entire career at Berkeley, serving as professor of physics from 1945 until his retirement in 1978.

In 1938 Alvarez reported his first major discovery, namely, the phenomenon of orbital electron capture. In 1936 Hans Bethe had argued that an excited nucleus could decay by capturing one of its own orbiting electrons, a process known as K-capture as the electron is taken from the innermost (K) electron shell. Alvarez succeeded in detecting the process experimentally by identifying the characteristic x-rays emitted during K capture as a result of electrons moving from outer orbits into the vacant K orbit.

Alvarez followed this by making (1939) the first measurement, with Felix BLOCH, of the neutron's magnetic moment. He also demonstrated that hydrogen-3 (tritium) was radioactive, work which proved to be of significance in the later development of the hydrogen bomb.

While working on radar during the war Alvarez had what he later described as one of his most valuable ideas. If radar could be used to track approaching aircraft then, he argued, the same information should be adequate to guide a pilot to a safe landing in bad weather. There were many obstacles to be overcome before GCA (Ground Controlled Approach) could be adopted. By early 1943, however, Alvarez was able to talk down a distant plane he could follow only on radar.

Soon after he moved to Los Alamos where he worked on the problem of detonating the bomb. It was necessary for 32 detonators to fire simultaneously. Alvarez was an observer in a follow-up plane of the Hiroshima bomb.

After the war Alvarez remained as creative as ever. His most important work was in the field of particle physics. By the early 1950s experimentalists had begun to find it difficult to track particles. Cloud chambers took too long to operate, emulsions could only pick up charged particles and consequently much was being missed. In April 1953 Alvarez was introduced by Donal GLASER to the idea that particles passing through a small glass bulb containing diethyl ether would produce bubble tracks. The chamber operated by suddenly reducing the pressure causing the liquid to 'boil' and leave a bubble track where a particle had passed.

Alvarez immediately began to design a much larger bubble chamber using liquid hydrogen as a fluid. After a few test runs with some small chambers Alvarez proposed to build a 72-inch model at a cost of 2.5 million dollars. It first came into operation in March, 1959, and was used to discover a large number of elementary particles. For his work in this field Alvarez was awarded the 1968 Nobel Prize for physics.

Alvarez also investigated other phenomena. In 1977 his son Walt, a geologist, showed him a rock from Gubbio in the Italian Apennines. It was aged 65 million years and consisted of two layers of limestone, one from the Cretaceous, the other from the Tertiary, separated by a thin clay strip. During the rock's formation the dinosaurs had flourished and passed into extinction.

Alvarez was intrigued by the presence in the clay of unusually high concentrations of iridium. No more than about 0.03 parts per billion are normally to be found in the Earth's crust. The geologists, however, reported that there was 300 times as much iridium in the clay layer than in the surrounding limestone samples (an example of what is now known as the 'iridium anomaly'). The clay, it was calculated, had formed over a mere 1000 years, and was located in time at the KT boundary (K = *Kreide*, German for Cretaceous, T = Tertiary). Could the thin strip of clay and its iridium content throw any light on the mass extinctions that were taking place during its formation?

He first suggested that the iridium could have come from a nearby supernova explosion. This was soon rejected after a fruitless search in the clay for traces of plutonium–244, another supernova byproduct. Alvarez began to consider another possibility, namely, a collision with a large asteroid. It would certainly bring along with it the observed iridium, but it was not immediately apparent how the asteroid could produce a global extinction. Further reflection suggested that an asteroid 10 kilometers in diameter would throw sufficient dust into the atmosphere to darken the sky for several years. This in turn would prevent photosynthesis, destroy plant life and, along the way, all other dependent creatures.

Alvarez published his theory in 1980 and spent much of the remaining decade of his life explaining and defending his views. Some geologists objected that dinosaurs had become extinct some 20,000 years before the iridium layer was deposited. Others claimed that prolonged darkness would have been as damaging to marine as to terrestrial life, whereas marine life suffered no comparable mass extinction. Despite these and other objections Alvarez's impact theory survived the 1980s as the most favored account of the death of the dinosaurs.

Alvarez left a vivid account of his life in his *Alvarez, Adventures of a Physicist* (1987).

Alzheimer, Alois (1864–1915) German psychiatrist

Alzheimer was born in Markbreit in Germany and studied medicine at the universities of Würzburg and Berlin. After working in hospitals in Frankfurt and Heidelberg, he joined the Munich Psychiatric Clinic of Emil Kraepelin (1856–1926) as head of the anatomy department. He worked in Munich from 1904 until 1912 when he was appointed professor of psychiatry and neurology at the University of Breslau (now Wrocław in Poland).

In 1907 Alzheimer treated a 51-year-old woman with a growing memory loss. Her condition rapidly deteriorated into severe dementia. On autopsy, he identified a number of pathological conditions including shrinking of the cortex and the presence of neurofibrillary tangles and neuritic plaques. The plaques and tangles were distinctive enough to warrant a diagnosis of senile dementia or, as it later became known, *Alzheimer's disease*.

Amagat, Emile Hilaire (1841–1915) French physicist

Born at Saint-Satur, Amagat obtained his doctorate in 1872 from Paris and became a professor of physics at the Faculté Libre des Sciences at Lyons and eventually a full member of the French Academy of Sciences.

He is noted for his work on the behavior of gases. He started work plotting isotherms of carbon dioxide at high pressures, expanding the results of Thomas AN-DREWS; this research was published in 1872 as his doctoral thesis. In 1877 followed a publication on the coefficient of compressibility of fluids, showing conclusively that this decreased with an increase in pressure, a result contradicting the results of other scientists. Between 1879 and 1882 Amagat investigated a number of gases, publishing data on isotherms and reaching the limit of pressures obtainable using glass apparatus – about 400 atmospheres. To get yet further Amagat invented a hydraulic manometer that could produce and measure up to 3200 atmospheres. (This manometer was later used in firearms factories for testing purposes.)

Ambartsumian (or Ambartsumyan), Viktor Amazaspovich (1908–1996) Armenian astrophysicist

Ambartsumian was born in Tbilisi (now in Georgia), the son of a distinguished Armenian philologist. He graduated from the University of Leningrad in 1928 and did graduate work at Pulkovo Observatory, near Leningrad, from 1928 to 1931. He was professor of astrophysics from 1934 to 1946 at Leningrad and held the same post from 1947 at the State University at Yerevan in Armenia. In 1946 he organized the construction, near Yerevan, of the Byurakan Astronomical Observatory, having been appointed its director in 1944. He remained as director until 1988.

Ambartsumian's work was mainly concerned with the evolution of stellar systems, both galaxies and smaller clusters of stars, and the processes taking place during the evolution of stars. The idea of a stellar 'association' was introduced into astronomy by Ambartsumian in 1947. Associations are loose clusters of hot stars that lie in or near the disk-shaped plane of our Galaxy. They must be young, no more than a few million years old, as the gravitational field of the Galaxy will tend to disperse them. This must mean that star formation is still going on in the Galaxy.

He also argued in 1955 that the idea of colliding galaxies proposed by Rudolph Minkowski and Walter Baade to explain such radio sources as Cygnus A would not produce the required energy. Instead, he proposed that the source of energy was gigantic explosions occurring in the dense central regions of galaxies and these would be adequate to provide the 10^{55} joules emitted by the most energetic radio sources.

Amontons, Guillaume (1663–1705)
French physicist

Amontons, a Parisian, who had been deaf since childhood, invented and perfected various scientific instruments. In 1687 he made a hygrometer (an instrument for measuring moisture in the air); in 1695 he produced an improved barometer; and in 1702–03 a constant-volume air thermometer. In 1699 he published the results of his studies on the effects of change in temperature on the volume and pressure of air. He noticed that equal drops in temperature resulted in equal drops in pressure and realized that at a low enough temperature the volume and pressure of the air would become zero – an early recognition of the idea of absolute zero. These results lay largely unnoticed and the relationship between temperature and pressure of gases was not reexamined until the next century (by scientists such as Jacques Charles).

Amontons also published in 1699 the results of his studies on friction, which he considered to be proportional to load.

Ampère, André Marie (1775–1836)
French physicist and mathematician

Ampère was born in Lyons, France, where his father was a wealthy merchant. He was privately tutored, and to a large extent self-taught. His genius was evident at an early age. He was particularly proficient at mathematics and, following his marriage in 1799 he was able to make a modest living as a mathematics teacher in Lyons. In 1802 he moved first to Bourg-en-Bresse to take up an appointment, then to Paris as professor of physics and chemistry at the Ecole Centrale.

His first publication was on the statistics of games of chance *Considérations sur la théorie mathématique de jeu* (1802; Considerations on the Mathematical Theory of Games) and his work at Bourg led to his appointment as professor of mathematics at the Lyceum of Lyons, and then in 1809 as professor of analysis at the Ecole Polytechnique in Paris. His talents were recognized

by Napoleon, who in 1808 appointed him inspector general of the newly formed university system – a post Ampère held until his death.

Ampère's most famous scientific work was in establishing a mathematical basis for electromagnetism. The Danish physicist Hans Christian Oersted had made the important experimental discovery that a current passing through a wire could cause the movement of a manetic compass needle. Ampère witnessed a demonstration of electromagnetism by François Arago at the Academy of Science on 11 September, 1820. He set to work immediately on his own investigations, and within seven days was able to report the results of his experiments.

In a succession of presentations to the academy in the next four months, he developed a mathematical theory to explain the interaction between electricity and magnetism, to which he gave the name 'electrodynamics' (now more commonly: electromagnetism) to distinguish it from the study of stationary electric forces, which he christened 'electrostatics'.

Having recognized that electric currents in wires caused the motion of magnets, and that a magnet can affect another magnet, he looked for evidence that electric currents could similarly influence other electric currents. The simplest example of this interaction is found by arranging for currents to flow through two parallel wires. Ampère discovered that if the currents passed in the same direction the wires were attracted to each other, but if they passed in opposite directions the wires were repelled. From this he went on to consider more complex configurations of closed loops, helices, and other geometrical figures, and was able to provide a mathematical analysis that allowed quantitative predictions.

In 1825 he had been able to deduce an empirical law of forces (*Ampère's law*) between two current-carrying elements, which showed an inverse-square law (the force decreases as the square of the distance between the two elements, and is proportional to the product of the two currents). By 1827 he was able to give a precise mathematical formulation of the law, and it was in this year that his most famous work *Mémoirs sur la théorie mathématique des phénomènes electrodynamiques uniquement déducte de l'expérience* (Notes on the Mathematical Theory of Electrodynamic Phenomena, Solely Deduced from Experiment) was published.

Besides explaining the macroscopic effects of electromagnetism, he attempted to construct a microscopic theory that would fit the phenomenon, and postulated an electrodynamic molecule in which electric-fluid currents circulated, giving each molecule a magnetic field.

In his honor, the unit of electric current is named for him, and in fact the ampere is defined in terms of the force between two parallel current-carrying wires.

Anaxagoras of Clazomenae
(*c*. 500 BC–*c*. 428 BC) *Greek philosopher*

Anaxagoras left his birthplace in Asia Minor (now Turkey) in about 480 BC and taught in Athens during its most brilliant period under Pericles, who was himself one of Anaxagoras's pupils. In about 450 BC he was exiled to Lampsacus after being prosecuted for impiety by the enemies of Pericles.

Although he wrote a book, *On Nature*, only fragments of his writings survive; his work is known through later writers, notably Aristotle and Simplicius, and is open to contradictory interpretations. The difficulty consists in reconciling his principle of homoemereity, which states that matter is infinitely divisible and retains its character on division, with his statement "there is a portion of everything in everything." His work can be seen as a criticism of the Eleatic school of Parmenides and Zeno of Elea, who had argued against plurality and even motion.

Anaxagoras's astronomy was more rational than that of his predecessors; he stated that the Sun and stars were incandescent stones, that the Moon derived its light from the Sun, and he gave the modern explanation for eclipses of the Sun and Moon.

Anaximander of Miletus (*c*. 611 BC–*c*. 547 BC) *Greek philosopher*

Anaximander, who was born and died in Miletus (now in Turkey), belonged to the first school of natural philosophy and was the pupil of Thales. He wrote one of the earliest treatises but none of his writings survive and his work is known only through later writers, notably Aristotle and Theophrastus.

Anaximander criticized Thales's idea that water was the basic element of the universe by pointing out that no one element gains the upper hand and that "they pay the penalty and retribution to one another... according to the ordering of time." From this he deduced that the primal matter was what he called the *apeiron* or the indefinite. This idea was later developed by the atomists. He was the first to realize that the Earth did not have to float on water or be supported in any way; he stated that it was

in equilibrium with the other bodies in the universe.

Anaximander was the first philosopher to speculate on the origin of man. He is also credited with the first determinations of the solstices and equinoxes and the production of the first map of the world as he knew it. He was the first to recognize that the Earth's surface is curved but believed it was curved only in the north–south direction and consequently represented the Earth as a cylinder.

Anaximenes of Miletus (*fl*. 546 BC)
Greek philosopher

Anaximenes was the last of the great Milesian philosophers. He was probably a pupil of Anaximander of Miletus and, like Thales before him, he identified one of the tangible elements as the primal substance. For Anaximenes this was air, which by processes of condensation and rarefaction could produce every other kind of matter. He used the rather mystical argument that since air is the breath of life for man it must also be the main principle of the universe.

Anderson, Carl David (1905–1991)
American physicist

Anderson, the son of Swedish immigrants, was born in New York City and educated at the California Institute of Technology where he obtained his PhD in 1930 and where he remained for his entire career, serving as professor of physics from 1939 until his retirement in 1978.

Anderson was deeply involved in the discovery of two new elementary particles. In 1930 he began to study cosmic rays by photographing their tracks in a cloud chamber and noted that particles of positive charge occurred as abundantly as those of negative charge. The negative particles were clearly electrons but those of positive charge could not be protons (the only positive particles known at the time) as they did not produce sufficient ionization in the chamber. Eventually Anderson concluded that such results "could logically be interpreted only in terms of particles of a positive charge and a mass of the same order of magnitude as that normally possessed by a free negative electron." It was in fact the positron or positive electron, whose existence he announced in September 1932. In the following year his results were confirmed by Patrick BLACKETT and Giuseppe OCCHIALINI and won for Anderson the 1936 Nobel Prize for physics.

In the same year Anderson noted some further unusual cosmic-ray tracks. As they appeared to be made by a particle more massive than an electron but lighter than a proton it was at first thought to be the particle predicted by Hideki Yukawa that was thought to carry the strong nuclear force and hold the nucleus together. The particle was initially named the 'mesotron' or 'yukon'. However, this identification proved to be premature, as its interaction with nucleons was found to be so infrequent that it could not possibly perform the role described by Yukawa. From 1938 the particle became known as the meson, and the confusion was partly dispelled in 1947 when Cecil Powell discovered another and more active meson, to be known as the pi-meson or pion to distinguish it from Anderson's mu-meson or muon.

Anderson, Philip Warren (1923–1995)
American physicist

Anderson was born in Indianapolis and obtained his BS (1943), MS (1947), and PhD (1949) at Harvard University, doing his doctoral thesis under John Van Vleck. The period 1943–45 was spent at the Naval Research Laboratory working on antenna engineering. Upon receiving his doctorate, Anderson joined the Bell Telephone Laboratories at Murray Hill, New Jersey, where he worked until his retirement in 1984.

Anderson's main research was in the physics of the solid state, incorporating such topics as spectral-line broadening, exchange interactions in insulators, the Josephson effect, quantum coherence, superconductors, and nuclear theory. Under Van Vleck he worked initially on elucidating the phenomenon of pressure broadening of lines in microwave, infrared, and optical spectroscopy. In 1959 he developed a theory to explain 'superexchange' – the coupling of spins of two magnetic atoms in a crystal through their interaction with a nonmagnetic atom located between them. He went on to develop the theoretical treatments of antiferromagnetics, ferroelectrics, and superconductors.

In 1961 Anderson conceived a theoretical model to describe what happens where an impurity atom is present in a metal – now widely known and used as the *Anderson model*. Also named for him is the phenomenon of *Anderson localization*, describing the migration of impurities within a crystal. In the 1960s Anderson concentrated particularly on superconductivity and superfluidity, predicting the existence of resistance in superconductors and (with Pierre Morel) pointing out the nature of the possible superfluid states of ^{3}He. In 1971 he returned to disordered media, working on low-temperature properties of glass and later studying spin glasses.

Along with his Harvard tutor Van Vleck and the British physicist Nevill Mott, Anderson shared the 1977 Nobel Prize for physics "for their fundamental theoretical investigation of the electronic structure of magnetic and disordered systems."

Besides his post at Bell Laboratories (where he was consulting director for physics research) Anderson worked as a part-time visiting professor in England at Cambridge and from 1975 held a professorship at Princeton.

In the late 1980s Anderson became a controversial figure in the physics community by arguing before Congress that the proposed SSC (Superconducting Super Collider) to be built in Texas at a cost of $8 billion would yield neither practical benefits nor any fundamental truths that could not be gained elsewhere and more cheaply. When Congress killed the plan in 1993 Anderson commented that he was only sorry that Congress had allowed the project to go on so long.

Andrews, Roy Chapman (1884–1960)
American naturalist and paleontologist

Andrews was born in Beloit, Wisconsin, and was educated there at Beloit College. After graduating, he took up a post at the American Museum of Natural History, New York, after graduating. His early interest lay in whales and other aquatic mammals, and these he collected assiduously on a number of museum-sponsored expeditions to Alaska, North Korea, and the Dutch East Indies (Indonesia) between 1908 and 1913. It was largely through Andrews's efforts that the collection of cetaceans at the American Museum of Natural History became one of the most complete in the world.

Andrews is best known for his discovery of previously unknown Asiatic fossils. Most of his findings were made on three expeditions to Asia, which he led as chief of the Asiatic Exploration Division of the American Museum of Natural History. The first of these was to Tibet, southwestern China, and Burma (1916–17); he then visited northern China and Outer Mongolia (1919), and central Asia (1921–22 and 1925). The third Asian expedition produced major finds of fossil reptiles and mammals, including remains of the largest known land mammal, the Paraceratherium (formerly called Baluchitherium), an Oligocene relative of the modern rhinoceros, which stood some 17–18 feet (5.5 m) at the shoulder. In Mongolia, Andrews discovered the first known fossil dinosaur eggs. He was also able to trace previously unknown geological strata, and unearthed evidence of primitive human life on the central Asian plateau.

Andrews was appointed director of the American Museum of Natural History in 1935, but resigned in 1942 in order to devote himself entirely to writing about his travels and discoveries.

Andrews, Thomas (1813–1885) *Irish physical chemist*

The son of a linen merchant from Belfast (now in Northern Ireland), Andrews studied chemistry under Thomas Thomson at Glasgow, under Jean Dumas in Paris, and under Justus von Liebig at Giessen. He also studied medicine at Edinburgh and obtained his MD in 1835. He practiced medicine in Belfast before becoming vice-president of Queen's College, Belfast, in 1845 and professor of chemistry in 1849.

Andrews made experimental studies on the heat evolved in chemical reactions and also showed that ozone is an allotrope of oxygen. He was a brilliant experimentalist and his work on the liquefaction of gases brought order to a confused subject. Andrews performed a famous series of experiments on the variation of the volume of carbon dioxide gas with pressure. He studied the behavior of the gas at different temperatures, and showed that there was a certain temperature – the critical temperature – above which the gas could not be liquefied by pressure alone. This work, which was published as *On the Continuity of the Liquid and Gaseous States of Matter* (1869) led to the liquefaction of those gases previously held to be 'permanent' gases.

Anfinsen, Christian Boehmer

(1916–1995) *American biochemist*

Born in Monessen, Pennsylvania, Anfinsen was educated at Swarthmore College, the University of Pennsylvania, and Harvard, where he obtained his PhD in 1943. He taught at Harvard Medical School from 1943 to 1950, when he moved to the National Heart Institute at Bethesda, Maryland, where from 1952 to 1962 he served as head of the laboratory of cellular physiology. In 1963 Anfinsen joined the National Institute of Arthritis and Metabolic Diseases at Bethesda, where he was appointed head of the laboratory of chemical biology. In 1982 he became professor of biology at Johns Hopkins University.

By 1960 Stanford Moore and William Stein had fully determined the sequence of the 124 amino acids in ribonuclease, the first enzyme to be so analyzed. Anfinsen, however, was more concerned with the

shape and structure of the enzyme and the forces that permit it always to adopt the same unique configuration. The molecule of ribonuclease – a globular protein – consists of one chain twisted into a ball and held together by four disulfide bridges. By chemical means, the sulfur bridges can be separated so that the enzyme becomes a simple polypeptide chain with no power to hydrolyze ribonucleic acid, i.e. it becomes denatured. Once the bridges are broken they can be reunited in any one of 105 different ways. Anfinsen found that the minimum of chemical intervention – merely putting the enzyme into a favorable environment – was sufficient to induce the ribonuclease to adopt the one configuration that restores enzymatic activity.

The important conclusion Anfinsen drew from this observation was that all the information for the assembly of the three-dimensional protein must be contained in the protein's sequence of amino acids – its primary structure. He went on to show similar behavior in other proteins. For this work Anfinsen shared the 1972 Nobel Prize for physiology or medicine with Moore and Stein.

Ångstrom, Anders Jonas (1814–1874) *Swedish physicist and astronomer*

Ångstrom was born the son of a chaplain in Lögdö, Sweden. He studied and taught physics and astronomy at the University of Uppsala, where he obtained his doctorate (1839) and later became professor of physics (1858), a position he held up to his death.

Ångstrom was one of the pioneers of spectroscopy. His most important work was *Optiska Undersökningar* (1853; Optical Investigations), in which he published measurements on atomic spectra, particularly of electric sparks. He noted spectral lines that were characteristic of both the gas and the electrodes used. Ångstrom applied Euler's theory of resonance to his measurements and deduced that a hot gas emits light at precisely the same wavelength at which it absorbs light when it is cool. In this he anticipated the experimental proof of Gustav Kirchhoff. He was also able to show the composite nature of the spectra of alloys.

Having established the principles of spectroscopy in the laboratory, Ångstrom turned his attention to the Sun's spectrum, publishing *Recherches sur le spectre solaire* (1868; Researches on the Solar Spectrum) in which he made the inference that hydrogen was present in the Sun. In this work he also reported the wavelengths of some 1000 Fraunhofer lines measured to six significant figures in units of 10^{-8} centimeter.

Since 1905 his name has been officially honored as a unit of length used by spectroscopists and microscopists; 1 Ångstrom = 10^{-8} cm. His map of the *Normal Solar Spectrum* (1869) became a standard reference for some 20 years. Ångstrom was also the first to examine the spectrum of the aurora borealis and to measure the characteristic bright yellow–green light sometimes named for him.

Antoniadi, Eugène Michael
(1870–1944) *Greek–French astronomer*

Antoniadi was born in Constantinople (now Istanbul, Turkey). He established quite early a reputation as a brilliant observer and in 1893 was invited by Camille Flammarion to work at his observatory at Juvisy near Paris. From 1909 he worked mainly with the 33-inch (84-cm) refracting telescope at the observatory at Meudon. He became a French citizen in 1928.

In his two works *La Planète Mars* (1930) and *La Planète Mercure* (1934), Antoniadi published the results of many years' observations and presented the best maps of Mars and Mercury to appear until the space probes of recent times. With regard to Mars he took the strong line: "Nobody has ever seen a genuine canal on Mars," attributing the "completely illusory canals," seen by astronomers such as Percival Lowell and Flammarion, to irregular natural features of the Martian surface. Antoniadi also observed the great Martian storms of 1909, 1911, and 1924 noting after the last one, that the planet had become covered with yellow clouds and presented a color similar to Jupiter.

On Mercury his observations made between 1914 and 1929 seemed to confirm Giovanni Schiaparelli's rotation period of 88 days, identical with the planet's period of revolution around the Sun. The effect of this would be for Mercury always to turn the same face to the Sun, in the same way as the Moon always turns the same face to the Earth. Antoniadi cited nearly 300 observations of identifiable features always in the same position, as required by the 88-day rotation period.

However radar studies of Mercury in 1965 revealed a 59-day rotation period for Mercury. This time is however very close to half the synodic period of Mercury (116 days) so that when the planet returns to the same favorable viewing position in the sky, at intervals of 116 days, it does present the same face to observers.

Antoniadi also wrote on the history of astronomy, publishing *L'Astronomie Égyptienne* in 1934.

Apollonius of Perga (*c*. 262 BC–
c. 190 BC) *Greek mathematician*

Apollonius moved from his birthplace Perga (now in Turkey) to study in the Egyptian city of Alexandria, possibly under pupils of Euclid. Later he taught in Alexandria himself. One of the great Greek geometers, Apollonius's major work was in the study of conic sections and the only one of his many works to have survived is his eight-book work on this subject, the *Conics*. Apollonius's work on conics makes full use of the work of his predecessors, notably Euclid and Conon of Samos, but it is a great advance in terms of its thoroughness and systematic treatment. The *Conics* also contains a large number of important new theorems that are entirely Apollonius's creation. He was the first to define the parabola, hyperbola, and ellipse. In addition, he considered the general problem of finding normals from a given point to a given curve (i.e. lines at right angles to a tangent at a point on the curve).

Apart from the geometrical work that has survived, Apollonius is known to have contributed to optics – in particular to the study of the properties of mirrors of various shapes. This work, however, is now lost.

Appel, Kenneth (1932–   ) *American mathematician*

Appel, who was born in Brooklyn, New York City, was educated at the University of Michigan, where he completed his PhD in 1959. After working for two years at the Institute for Defense Analysis at Princeton, he joined the faculty of the University of Illinois, Urbana, where he served as professor of mathematics from 1991 to 1993. He then took up the chairmanship of the mathematics department at the University of New Hampshire.

In 1976, in collaboration with **Wolfgang Haken** (1928–   ), Appel announced the solution to one of mathematics long-standing unsolved problems, the four-color map problem. In 1852 Francis Guthrie had noticed that it seemed to be possible to color any map, assuming countries with common borders were colored differently, with no more than four colors. Guthrie was sufficiently intrigued by the point to raise it with the mathematician de Morgan and ask for a proof of the conjecture. De Morgan found the problem unexpectedly difficult, as did succeeding generations of mathematicians.

Appel and Hagen used a variation of a method first tried by Arthur Kempe in 1879. It depends on the fact that maps must contain certain unavoidable configurations –

Appel and Hagen recognized 1482 of these. They then used a computer to show that all of these could be reduced to four-color configurations. They began work in 1972, but it was not until 1976 that they were satisfied with their analysis and their program. It took more than 1200 hours of computer time to prove the theorem.

Appleton, Sir Edward Victor
(1892–1965) *British physicist*

Appleton was born in Bradford and studied physics at Cambridge University from 1910 to 1913. During World War I, while he was serving in the Royal Engineers, he developed the interest in radio that was to influence his later research. After the war he returned to Cambridge and worked in the Cavendish Laboratory from 1920. In 1924 he was appointed Wheatstone Professor of Experimental Physics at King's College, London.

Here, in his first year, he used a BBC transmitter to conduct a famous experiment, which established beyond doubt the presence of a layer of ionized gas in the upper atmosphere capable of reflecting radio waves. The existence of such a layer had been postulated by Oliver HEAVISIDE and Arthur KENNELLY to explain Marconi's transatlantic radio transmissions. By varying the frequency of a transmitter in Bournemouth and detecting the signal some 140 miles (225 km) away in Cambridge, he showed that interference occurred between direct (ground) waves and waves reflected off the layer (sky waves). Furthermore, the experiment measured the height of the layer, which he estimated at 60 miles (96 km). He proceeded to do theoretical work on the reflection or transmission of radio waves by an ionized layer and found, using further measurements, a second layer above the Heaviside–Kennelly layer. The *Appleton layer* undergoes daily fluctuations in ionization and he established a link between these variations and the occurrence of sunspots.

In 1936 he became the Jacksonian Professor of Natural Philosophy at Cambridge, and during the war years until 1949 he was secretary of the department of scientific and industrial research, in which period he led research into radar and the atomic bomb.

For his great achievements in ionospheric physics he was knighted in 1941 and in 1947 won the Nobel Prize for physics. From 1949 until his death he was principal of Edinburgh University.

Arago, Dominique François Jean
(1786–1853) *French physicist*

Born in Estagel, France, Arago was educated at the Ecole Polytechnique in Paris and then spent some years in Spain, where he accompanied Jean Baptiste Biot on a measurement of an arc of meridian. On his return to Paris in 1809 he was elected to the Académie des Sciences and received the chair of analytical geometry at the Ecole Polytechnique. In 1830 he succeeded J. B. J. Fourier as the permanent secretary of the Ecole Polytechnique. Arago worked in a number of branches of physics.

His first investigations concerned the polarization of light and in 1811 he discovered chromatic polarization. He was a vigorous defender of A. J. Fresnel's wave theory of light against the criticisms of Laplace and Biot, who both supported the corpuscular theory. In 1838 he described an experiment to decide the issue by comparing the speed of light in air with that in a denser medium. Shortly before Arago's death, Léon Foucault and Armand Fizeau proved that the experiment supported the wave theory.

Arago also worked on electromagnetism, showing that a coil of wire carrying a current could act as a magnet. He also found that a rotating copper disk could deflect a magnetic needle suspended above it. (This arrangement, known as *Arago's disk*, depends on magnetic induction.)

In astronomy, Arago discovered the Sun's chromosphere. He also played a part in the discovery of Neptune by Urbain Leverrier.

Arago was a fierce republican and, from 1830 onward, he was involved in political life as deputy for the Pyrenées Orientales. In 1848 he became a government minister and, among other measures, abolished slavery in the French colonies.

Arber, Werner (1929–) *Swiss microbiologist*

Arber, who was born in Gränichen, Switzerland, graduated from the Swiss Federal Institute of Technology in 1953 and gained his PhD from the University of Geneva in 1958. He spent a year at the University of Southern California before returning to Geneva where he became professor of molecular genetics in 1965. In 1971 Arber moved to Basel to take the chair of molecular biology.

In the early 1950s Giuseppe Bertani reported a phenomenon he described as 'host-controlled variation' in which phage (the viruses that infect bacteria) successfully growing on one host found it difficult to establish themselves on a different bacterium. In 1962, he proposed that bacteria possess highly specific enzymes capable of destroying invading phage by cutting up their DNA. The existence of such 'restriction enzymes' as they came to be called was later established by Hamilton SMITH.

It turned out that, as Arber had proposed, the enzymes attack the invading DNA at a specific site, always cutting them at exactly the same place. It was this property that endowed restriction enzymes with such interest for if strands of DNA could be so manipulated to be cut at particular known points, it only needed the power to join such strands together in desired combinations for genetic engineering to be a reality. As restriction enzymes were found to leave DNA strands 'sticky' and ready to combine with certain other 'sticky' strands it was soon apparent to molecular biologists that genetic engineering was at last a practical proposition.

For his work on restriction enzymes Arber shared the 1978 Nobel Prize for physiology or medicine with Smith and Daniel NATHANS.

Archimedes (287 BC–212 BC) *Greek mathematician*

Archimedes' father was an astronomer and he himself inherited an interest in the subject. He was educated in Alexandria and spent most of the rest of his life in his birthplace, Syracuse, under the patronage of King Hieron. Archimedes was without question the greatest mathematician and scientist that classical Greek civilization produced and is usually considered to be one of the greatest mathematicians of all time. He was held in very high regard even by his contemporaries, and Karl Friedrich Gauss thought that only Isaac Newton was Archimedes' equal as a mathematician. Archimedes was as much an applied mathematician as a pure mathematician. He was very much interested in putting his theoretical discoveries to practical use and is known to have been skilled in making his own equipment and carrying out his own experiments. It is no exaggeration to describe Archimedes as the creator of the science of mechanics. Naturally before his time many isolated facts had been discovered, but it was only with him that mechanics became a unified body of theory capable of yielding new and unexpected practical applications.

Archimedes was able to find methods for determining the center of gravity of a variety of bodies. He also gave the first general theory of levers, and organized a practical demonstration to show how, with a suitable series of levers, a very small force is capable of moving a very large weight. He amazed his contemporaries by arranging for the king of Syracuse to move a large ship simply by pressing a small lever. In connection with his work on levers Archimedes made one of his famous statements, "Give me a firm place to stand on and I will move the Earth." Archimedes also had a practical interest in optics, although no writings of his on the subject have come down to us. He put all this newfound theoretical knowledge to deadly effect when Syracuse was besieged by the Romans, by designing and building a variety of war machines. Among these were enormous mirrors to focus the Sun's rays and set fire to the Roman ships, and a variety of catapults.

Archimedes also successfully applied his scientific discoveries in hydrostatics. He designed all sorts of pumps, and the Archimedean water-screw is still widely used. But his most famous practical success was in solving a problem presented to him by King Hieron. Hieron wished to know whether a newly made crown, which was supposed to be of pure gold was, as he suspected, partly silver. Archimedes solved the problem by grasping the concept of relative density. By immersing successively the crown itself and pieces of gold and silver of equal weight in full containers of water and observing the amount of water each displaced, Archimedes was able to show that the crown was indeed not made of pure gold. One of the famous stories associated with Archimedes tells how this occured to him when he was getting into his bath and observed how the more of his body was immersed the more water overflowed from the bath. He saw instantly how to solve his problem, leaped from the bath, and rushed through the streets, stark naked, shouting "Eureka!" (I have found it).

Archimedes' work in applied mathematics and science ensured his great contemporary fame, but some of his greatest work was probably in his more esoteric researches in pure mathematics. Like all Greek mathematicians, his interest was primarily concentrated on geometry. Arithmetic was greatly hampered by a very cumbersome system of notation. Although Archimedes himself invented a much improved system for notation of very large numbers, algebra had yet to be invented, in Europe at least. Archimedes' most profound achievement was to perfect the 'method of exhaustion' for calculating the areas and volumes of curved figures. The method involves successively approximating the figure concerned by inscribed and circumscribed polygons. This method essentially used the concept of limit – a concept that took some time for later European mathematicians to grasp. Archimedes used this method to determine an approximate value for π, which was not to be improved on for many centuries.

Archimedes was put to death by a Roman soldier when the Romans, under general Marcellus, finally successfully besieged Syracuse. The killing was against the orders of Marcellus who respected Archimedes and wished for him to be protected. Archimedes was apparently drawing mathematical symbols in the sand when killed.

Argelander, Friedrich Wilhelm August (1799–1875) *German astronomer*

Born in the Baltic port of Memel (now Klaipeda in Lithuania), Argelander was the son of a wealthy Finnish merchant and a German mother. He was educated at Königsberg, where his interest in astronomy was aroused by the lectures of Friedrich Bessel. Argelander began his career in 1820 as an assistant in Bessel's Königsberg Observatory. In 1823 he moved to the Åbo Observatory in Finland, then part of Russia. The observatory burned down in 1827 and Argelander began the design and construction of a new observatory in Helsinki, which was completed in 1832. In 1836 he was appointed professor of astronomy at Bonn. Here Friedrich Wilhelm IV built for Argelander an impressive new observatory. They were in fact old friends. In 1806, following Prussia's defeat by Napoleon, Friedrich Wilhelm, then the crown prince, had sought refuge in the Argelander home in Memel, East Prussia.

Argelander's name continues to be known by astronomers for his compilation of the *Bonner Dorchmusterung* (1859–63; 3 vols; Bonn Survey), still the largest and most comprehensive of pre-photographic catalogs. Under Bessel he had begun a survey of the sky from 15°S to 45°N. This was extended at Bonn to an area from 90°N to 2°S and when complete listed the positions of 324,198 stars down to the ninth magnitude. His work was continued by his successor, E. Schonfeld, who in the *Southern Bonner Dorchmusterung* (1886) added a further 133,659 stars located in the southern skies (2°S–23°S).

Aristarchus of Samos (*c.* 320 BC– *c.* 250 BC) *Greek astronomer*

Little is known of the life of Aristarchus, but Archimedes reported that Aristarchus had proposed that, while the Sun and the fixed stars are motionless, the Earth moves around the Sun on the circumference of a circle. Just what led Aristarchus to this view and how firmly he held it is not known. It received no support until the late medieval period.

One short work of Aristarchus has survived – *On the Sizes and Distances of the Sun and Moon.* In this work he calculated that the Earth is about 18 times further away from the Sun than from the Moon. His method was to use the fact that when the Moon is exactly in the second quarter it will form a right-angled triangle with the Earth and the Sun, and the relative lengths of the sides of the triangle can be determined by angular measurement. Although Aristarchus's method is correct, his measurement was inaccurate (the Sun is roughly 400 times further away). Despite the size of the error it was nevertheless the first attempt to come to grips with astronomical distances by something more sophisticated than revelation or guesswork.

Aristotle (384 BC–322 BC) *Greek philosopher, logician, and scientist*

Aristotle, the son of Nicomachus, physician at the court of Mayntas II of Macedon, was born in Chalcis and moved to Athens in 367 BC, where he was a member of the academy until Plato's death in 347. For the next 12 years he worked in Assos in Asia Minor, Mytilene on Lesbos, and, from 342 until 335, in Macedon as the tutor of the young Alexander the Great. Unfortunately little is known of this legendary relationship apart from the fact that Alexander took with him on his campaigns a copy of Homer's *Iliad* annotated by Aristotle. Also, Plutarch quotes a letter from Alexander rebuking his former tutor for publishing his *Metaphysics* and revealing to all what had been privately and, he assumed, exclusively taught to him. Following Alexander's accession to the throne of Macedon in 335 Aristotle returned to Athens to found his own school, the Lyceum. When, however, Athens, with little cause to love the power of Macedon, heard of the death of Alexander (323) they turned against Aristotle and accused him, as they had Socrates earlier in the century, of impiety. To prevent Athens from "sinning twice against philosophy" he moved to Chalcis where he died the following year.

Aristotle not only developed an original and systematic philosophy but applied it in a deliberate manner to most areas of the knowledge of his day. The resulting treatises on such subjects as physics, cosmology, embryology, and mineralogy acquired a considerable authority, becoming for medieval scholars if not the last word on any subject then invariably the first. Aristotelian science was not overthrown until the great scientific revolution of the 16th and 17th centuries.

In cosmology Aristotle basically accepted the scheme in which the Earth was at the center of the universe with the planets and fixed stars moving around it with uniform speed in perfectly circular orbits. (He also believed, on empirical grounds, that the Earth was round.) But Aristotle was not content simply to construct models of the universe and faced the problem of how to account for the various forms of motion. He began by accepting that matter was composed of the four elements of Empedocles – earth, water, fire, and air. Left to themselves the elements would either fall freely, like earth and water, or rise naturally like air and fire. This for Aristotle was natural motion, self-explanatory and consisting simply of bodies freely falling or rising to their natural place in the universe. For a stone to fall to the ground no one had to push or pull it but merely to remove all constraints for it to fall in a straight line to the Earth.

But the heavenly bodies do not move up or down in straight lines. Therefore, Aristotle concluded, they must consist of a fifth element, aether (or *quinta essentia* to the medieval schoolmen) whose natural motion was circular. Thus, in the Aristotelian universe different bodies obey different laws; celestial and terrestrial bodies move differently because the laws of motion are different in the heavens from those operating below the Moon. Nor was this the only distinction. For Aristotle the heavens were, with their supposed regularity, incorruptible, without change or decay; such processes were only too apparent on the Earth.

Aristotle also produced a number of volumes on biological problems. In particular his *De partibus animalium* (On the Parts of Animals) and his *De generatione animalium* (On the Generation of Animals) show a detailed knowledge of the fauna of the Mediterranean world and a concern to understand their anatomy and physiology. Over 500 species of animal are referred to by Aristotle. He was also a keen observer and had obviously made empirical investigations on the development of the chick embryo for example, noting the appearance of its heart on the fourth day. In fact some of his observations were only confirmed by zoologists in the 19th century and had for long been thought to be as erroneous as his physics.

In embryology he was also able to refute by dissection the prevailing view that the sex of an embryo is determined by its site in the womb. He also argued against the doctrine of pangenesis, that the seed comes from the whole of the body, as he also did against the classical version of preformationism, that the embryo contains all parts already preformed. His physiology, which could not be obtained so readily from simple dissection, was less acute. Respiration was thought to cool the body, an exercise unnecessary for fish who could cool themselves merely by drawing water through their gills.

He, further, produced a rudimentary taxonomy that went to some length to show that divisions based on number of limbs turned out to be obviously arbitrary. Instead, he proposed that mode of reproduction be used. This gave him the basic division between viviparous (exclusively mammalian) and the oviparous, subdivided into birds and reptiles laying proper eggs and the fishes laying 'imperfect eggs'. He added the insects, who lay no eggs at all but simply produce larvae.

If Aristotle had produced only his *Organon* – works on logic – he would have been considered a prolific and powerful thinker. His style of logic lasted unchallenged even longer than his physics for it was not until 1847 that George Boole laid the foundations of a more modern logic and it was not until the present century that non-Aristotelian logics were systematically developed.

Arrhenius, Svante August (1859–1927) *Swedish physical chemist*

Arrhenius was born in Wijk, near Uppsala, Sweden. He originally went to Uppsala University to study chemistry, changing later to physics. Finding the standard mediocre, he transferred to Stockholm in 1881 to do research under the physicist Erik Edlund, working initially on electrical polarization and then on the conductivity of solutions (electrolytes).

At the time it was known that solutions of certain compounds conduct electricity and that chemical reactions could occur when a current was passed. It was thought that the current decomposed the substance. In 1883 Arrhenius proposed a theory that substances were partly converted into an active form when dissolved. The active part was responsible for conductivity. In the case of acids and bases, he correlated the strength with the degree of decomposition on solution. This work was published as *Recherches sur la conductibilité galvanique des electrolytes* (1884; Researches on the Electrical Conductivity of Electrolytes) and submitted as his doctoral dissertation. The paper's great merit was not recognized by the Swedish authorities and he was awarded only a fourth-class doctorate. Arrhenius sent his work to several leading physical chemists, including Jacobus van't Hoff, Friedrich Ostwald, and Rudolf Clausius, who were immediately impressed. This led to a period of travel and work in various European laboratories in the period 1885–91.

In 1887 van't Hoff showed that although the gas law ($pV = RT$) could be applied to the osmotic pressure of solutions, certain solutions behaved as if there were more molecules than expected. Arrhenius at once realized that this was due to dissociation – a conclusion confirmed by further experimental work and published in the classic paper *Über die Dissociation der in Wasser gelösten Stoffe* (1887; On the Dissociation of Substances in Water). The idea that electrolytes were dissociated even without a current being passed proved difficult for many chemists but the theory has stood the test of time.

This work won Arrhenius a high international reputation but only limited acclaim in Sweden. Despite this he returned to Stockholm in 1891 as lecturer at the Technical Institute and in 1895 became professor there. In 1903 he was awarded the Nobel Prize for chemistry and in 1905 he became the director of the Nobel Institute, a post he held until shortly before his death.

Arrhenius was a man of wide-ranging intellect and besides developing his work on solutions, in later life he worked on cosmogony and on serum therapy, being especially interested in the relation between toxins and antitoxins. He also investigated the greenhouse effect by which carbon dioxide regulates atmospheric temperature and calculated the changes that would have been necessary to have produced the Ice Ages.

Astbury, William Thomas (1889–1961)
British x-ray crystallographer and molecular biologist

Astbury was born in Longton, where his father was a potter. In 1916 he won a scholarship to Cambridge University, to study chemistry, physics, and mathematics, and graduated in 1921 after spending two years of the war doing x-ray work for the army. He then joined William Henry Bragg's brilliant group of crystallographers, first at University College, London, and from 1923 at the Royal Institution. In 1945 Astbury was appointed to the new chair of biomolecular structure at Leeds.

Astbury's early structural studies were carried out on tartaric acid but in 1926

Bragg asked him to prepare some x-ray photographs of fibers for his lectures. The results stimulated an interest in biological macromolecules that Astbury retained for the rest of his life. In 1928 he moved to the University of Leeds as lecturer in textile physics and by 1930 had produced an explanation of the extensibility of wool in terms of two keratin structures: α-keratin in which the polypeptides were hexagonally folded (unextended wool) and β-keratin in which the chain was drawn out in zigzag fashion. A popular account of this work was given in *Fundamentals of Fibre Structure* (1933).

The keratin structure established his reputation, and he quickly extended his studies to other fibers and proteins. He showed that the globular proteins consisted of three-dimensionally folded chains that could be denatured and drawn out into protein fibers. This work laid the foundation for the x-ray structural investigations of hemoglobin and myoglobin. The hexagonal α-keratin structure dominated British crystallographic protein studies until 1951, when it was shown to be incorrect by Linus Pauling who demonstrated the α-helical structure of polypeptide chains.

In 1935 Astbury began to study nucleic acids by x-ray crystallography, and in 1938 he and his research student Florence Bell produced the first hypothetical structure of DNA.

Aston, Francis William (1877–1945)
British chemist and physicist

Aston was born in Harborne, England, the son of a metal merchant. He was educated at Mason College, the forerunner of Birmingham University, where he studied chemistry. From 1898 until 1900 he did research under P. F. FRANKLAND on optical rotation. He left Birmingham in 1900 to work in a Wolverhampton brewery for three years. During this time he continued with scientific research in a home laboratory, where he worked on the production of vacua for x-ray discharge tubes. This work came to the notice of J. H. Poynting of the University of Birmingham who invited Aston to work with him. He remained at Birmingham until 1910 when he moved to Cambridge as research assistant to J. J. Thomson. He became a research fellow at Cambridge in 1920 and stayed there for the rest of his life, apart from the war years spent at the Royal Aircraft Establishment, Farnborough. Aston's main work, for which he received the Nobel Prize for chemistry in 1922, was on the design and use of the mass spectrograph, which was used to clear up several outstanding problems and became one of the basic tools of the new atomic physics.

Thomson had invented an earlier form of spectrograph in which a beam of positive rays from a discharge tube passed through a magnetic and an electric field, which deflected the beam both horizontally and vertically. All particles (ions) with the same mass fell onto a fluorescent screen in a parabola. Aston improved the design by using a suitable magnetic field, so that ions of the same mass were focused in a straight line rather than a parabola. Different ions were deflected by different amounts, and the spectrograph produced a photographic record of a series of lines, each corresponding to one type of ion. The deflections allowed accurate calculation of the mass of the ions.

Aston's first spectrograph was ready in 1919 and with it he was soon able to throw light on one outstanding problem about the nature of the elements. In 1816 William Prout had put forward his hypothesis that all elements are built up from the hydrogen atom and that their atomic weights are integral multiples of that of hydrogen. Although receiving considerable support it was eventually rejected when it was found that many elements have non-integral weights (e.g. chlorine: 35.453). Frederick Soddy in 1913 had introduced the idea of isotopes; that is, the same chemical element in different forms having differing weights. Aston established that isotopes are not restricted to radioactive elements but are common throughout the periodic table. He also saw that they could explain Prout's hypothesis. Thus he found that neon was made from the two isotopes ^{20}Ne and ^{22}Ne in the proportion of 10 to 1. This will give a weighted average of 20.2 for a large number of neon atoms. The value of 35.453 for chlorine can be similarly explained. The whole-number rule is his principle that atoms have a mass that is equivalent to a whole number of hydrogen atoms.

Aston then went on to determine as many atomic weights as accurately as his instruments would allow. His first spectrograph was only suitable for gases but by 1927 he had introduced a new model capable of dealing with solids. From 1927 to 1935 he resurveyed the atomic weights of the elements with his new instrument.

In the course of this activity he found some minor discrepancies with the whole-number rule. Thus the atomic weight of hydrogen is given not as 1 but 1.008, of oxygen-16 as 15.9949 and of oxygen-17 as 16.99913. Aston attempted to show why these values are so tantalizingly close to the integral values of Prout – why the isotopes of oxygen are not simple 16 and 17 times as massive as the hydrogen atom. He argued that the missing mass is in fact, by the mass–energy equivalence of Einstein, not really missing but present as the binding energy of the nucleus. By dividing the missing mass by the mass number and multiplying by 10,000, Aston went on to calculate what was later called the 'packing fraction' and is a measure of the stability of the atom and the amount of energy required to break up or transform the nucleus.

Thus, contained in Aston's work were the implications of atomic energy and destruction and he believed in the possibility of using nuclear energy – he also warned of the dangers. He lived just long enough to see the dropping of the first atomic bomb in August 1945.

Atanasoff, John Vincent (1904–1995)
American physicist and computer pioneer

Atanasoff was born in Hamilton, New York, and educated at the universities of Florida, Iowa, and Wisconsin, where he gained his PhD in 1930. He taught at the Iowa State University from 1930 until 1942, when he moved to the Naval Ordnance Laboratory at White Oak, Maryland. After World War II, Atanasoff worked for various technical companies, eventually serving as president of Cybernetics Inc from 1961 until 1982.

The son of a Bulgarian immigrant who was an electrical engineer, Atanasoff was introduced to calculation at the age of nine when his father gave him a slide rule. This was of little use when, in 1930, he was trying to complete his thesis on the electrical properties of helium. Not even a desk calculator could significantly lighten the extensive computations. He began to think about how things could be improved. By 1937 he had opted for a machine that operates digitally, uses capacitors to store binary numbers, and calculates by logic circuits. Working with his assistant, Clifford Berry, Atanasoff built a prototype in 1939 of the suitably named ABC (Atanasoff-Berry Computer). This was good enough to raise sufficient funds to build an operating machine, which was completed in 1942.

Although the ABC was the first device to incorporate a number of key notions, it was unsatisfactory as a working machine. It was slow, could not be programmed, had to be controlled at all times, and suffered from a number of systematic errors. Clearly, it could be improved but the outbreak of war in 1942 took Atanasoff away to other duties. By the time he was free to work on the ABC other workers had seized the initiative. Atanasoff's work long lay forgotten.

This was corrected in a 1973 court case involving two American companies. Sperry Rand had bought the patent to ENIAC and were seeking to charge royalties to other computer manufacturers. Honeywell Inc resisted, claiming that ENIAC was derived from the ABC and from information passed to ENIAC's designer, John MAUCHLY, by Atanasoff in the early 1940s. Atanasoff gave evidence and the judge found that ENIAC was not the first "automatic electronic digital computer," and that it was "derived from one Dr. John Vincent Atanasoff."

Audubon, John James (1785–1851)
American ornithologist and naturalist

The illegitimate son of a French sea captain and his Creole mistress, Audubon was born in Les Cayes on the Caribbean island of Haiti and was brought up in Nantes in his father's family. He studied painting in Paris, spending six months in the studio of Jacques Louis David. In 1803, to escape conscription into Napoleon's army, Audubon was sent to Pennsylvania where his father owned a farm. Neither the farm nor any of Audubon's other business interests flourished and he was declared bankrupt in 1819 and imprisoned.

No doubt one cause of Audubon's commercial failure was the time spent hunting and observing birds and other animals in the wild. The first hint that his skills as an artist and naturalist could be combined to make money came in 1810 when Alexander Wilson passed through Louisville, Louisiana, where Audubon was operating a general store. Wilson was looking for subscribers to his lavishly illustrated *American Ornithology* (9 vols; 1808–14).

By 1820 Audubon had decided to publish his own collection of animals and birds. He spent a further four years traveling through Louisiana and Mississippi shooting specimens. As no American publisher appeared to be interested in his work, Audubon took his paintings to Britain in 1826. He eventually found a printer in Edinburgh willing to work on his 'double elephant size' engravings (39″ × 29″). Sets of five plates were sold to subscribers for 2 guineas to finance the next set. In this way 200 full sets of *Birds of America* (1827–38) were published in Britain in 87 parts with 435 plates. Full sets are rarely available for sale – when auctioned they are unlikely to raise less than a million dollars.

Audubon returned to America in 1839, where he bought an estate on the Hudson and began to prepare his *Viviparous Quadrupeds of North America* (3 vols; 1845–48).

Auer, Karl, Baron von Welsbach
(1858–1929) *Austrian chemist*

Auer was born in Vienna, the son of the director of the Imperial Printing Press. He was educated at the Vienna Polytechnic and at Heidelberg University, where he was a pupil of Robert Bunsen.

In 1885 he made a major contribution to knowledge of the lanthanoid (rare-earth) elements. In 1840, Carl Mosander had isolated a new 'element' called didymium. Auer showed (1885) that this contained, on fractionation, green and rose-red portions. He named them *praseodymia* ('green twin') and *neodymia* ('new twin').

Auer was also one of the first to find some use for the rare-earth elements. Gas had been in use as an illuminant since the beginning of the century and, although an improvement on the early oil lamps, it had many disadvantages of its own. It was expensive, hot, smoky, and smelly. Auer realized that it would be better to use the gas to heat a solid that would itself provide light, rather than use the luminosity of the flame. He used a mantle over the flame, impregnated with thorium oxide and a small amount of cerium. The *Welsbach mantle*, patented in 1885, delayed the end of gas lighting for a few years. Unfortunately for Auer, his invention was too late for, in 1879, Edison had managed to burn an electric bulb for 40 continuous hours.

Later, in 1898, Auer tried to improve the electric lamp by replacing its carbon filament by metallic osmium, which has a melting point of 2700°C. Once more he failed, for the future lay with tungsten, which has a higher melting point of 3410°C.

He was more successful with the so-called *Auer metal* – an alloy consisting mainly of cerium with other lanthanoid elements. It is also called Mischmetal (German: mixed metal) and is used for flints in cigarette lighters.

Auger, Pierre Victor (1899–1993)
French physicist

Auger was born in Paris and educated there at the Ecole Normale Supérieure, where he obtained his doctorate in 1926. He was later appointed to the staff of the University of Paris and after serving there as professor of physics from 1937 became director of higher education for France in 1945. From 1948 until 1960 he was director of the science department of UNESCO; he left UNESCO to become president of the French Space Commission but in 1964 he took the post of director-general of the European Space and Research Organization, a post he retained until his retirement in 1967.

Auger worked mainly on nuclear physics and cosmic rays. In 1925 he discovered the *Auger effect* in which an excited atom emits an electron (rather than a photon) in reverting to a lower energy state. In 1938 Auger made a careful study of 'air showers', a cascade of particles produced by a cosmic ray entering the atmosphere and later known as an *Auger shower*. Auger had an interest in the popularization of science. He also published volumes of poetry.

Averroës (or Abu Al-Walid Muhammad Ibn Ahmad Ibn Rushd)

(1126–1198) *Spanish–Muslim physician and philosopher*

Averroës, also known simply as 'The Commentator' to the Latin West, or Ibn Rushd, came from a family of jurists and was born in Cordoba in Moorish Spain. He himself trained in law and medicine and later served as *qadi* or judge in Seville and Cordoba. In 1182 he was appointed physician to the court of caliph Abu Ya'qub Yusuf in Marrakesh and to his son, Abu Yusuf Ya'qub, in 1195 but was recalled shortly before his death.

In the field of medicine Averroës produced his *Kulliyat fi al tib* (General Medicine) between 1162 and 1169. He is however better known for his great commentaries on Aristotle but, above all, for his *Tahafut al-Tahafut* (The Incoherence of the Incoherence), a strong attack on the Muslim philosopher al-Ghazzali's *Tahafut al-Falasifah* (The Incoherence of the Philosophers). The work was more influential in the Latin Christian West than in the Muslim East, and its contents paved the way for the medieval separation of faith and reason.

Avery, Oswald Theodore (1877–1955)

American bacteriologist

Avery was born in Halifax, the capital of Nova Scotia, Canada. Educated at Colgate University, he received his AB in 1900 and his medical degree in 1904. After a time at the Hoagland Laboratory, New York, as a lecturer and researcher in bacteriology, he joined the Rockefeller Institute Hospital (1913–48). While investigating the pneumococcus bacteria responsible for causing lobar pneumonia, Avery found that the bacteria produced soluble substances, derived from the cell wall and identified as polysaccharides, that were specific in their chemical composition for each different type of pneumococcus. This work provided a basis

for establishing the immunologic identity of a cell in biochemical terms.

In 1932 Avery started work on the phenomenon of transformation in bacteria. It had already been shown that heat-killed cells of a virulent pneumococcus strain could transform a living avirulent strain into the virulent form. In 1944 Avery and his colleagues Maclyn McCarty and Colin MacLeod, extracted and purified the transforming substance and showed it to be deoxyribonucleic acid (DNA). Previously it had been thought that protein was the hereditary material and thus Avery's work was an important step toward the eventual discovery, made nine years later by James Watson and Francis Crick, of the chemical basis of heredity.

Avogadro, Lorenzo Romano Amedeo Carlo, count of Quaregna and Cerreto (1776–1856) *Italian physicist and chemist*

Avogadro was born in Turin in northern Italy and came from a long line of lawyers. He too was trained in law and practiced for some years before taking up the study of mathematics and physics in 1800. His early work was carried out in the field of electricity, and in 1809 he became professor of physics at the Royal College at Vercelli. He was professor of mathematical physics at Turin from 1820 until 1822 and from 1834 to 1850.

His fame rests on his paper *Essai d'une manière de determiner les masses relatives des molecules des corps et les proportions selon lesquelles entrent dans cet combinaisons* (1811; On a Way of Finding the Relative Masses of Molecules and the Proportions in which They Combine), published in the *Journal de Physique*. This states the famous hypothesis that equal volumes of gases at the same temperature and pressure contain equal numbers of molecules. It follows from the hypothesis that relative molecular weights can be obtained from vapor densities and that the proportion by volume in which gases combine reflects the combining ratio of the molecules. Using this theory, Avogadro showed that simple gases such as hydrogen and oxygen are diatomic (H_2, O_2) and assigned the formula H_2O to water, whereas John Dalton had arbitrarily assumed that the simplest compound of two elements would have the formula HO.

Avogadro's work provided the essential link between Gay-Lussac's law of combining volumes and Dalton's atomic theory. This was not, however, realized at the time and, as a consequence, the determination of a self-consistent set of atomic weights was delayed for 50 years. The French physicist André Ampère was one of the few who accepted the theory and for many years it was taken to be Ampère's own.

Avogadro's contribution to chemisty was not appreciated in his own lifetime. The importance and truth of the theory was unrecognized until 1860 when his fellow Italian, Stanislao CANNIZZARO, forcefully restated it at the Karlsruhe Conference and demonstrated that it was the key needed to unlock the problem of atomic and molecular weights. The number of particles in one mole of a substance was named *Avogadro's constant* or *number* in his honor. It is equal to $6.022\,52 \times 10^{23}$.

Axelrod, Julius (1912–   ) *American neuropharmacologist*

Axelrod was born in New York City and educated there at the City College. Unable to finance a medical career, Axelrod worked from 1935 to 1945 as a technician in a laboratory of industrial hygiene that had just been set up in New York. But still with an ambition for a career in scientific research, and after some years at the Goldwater Memorial Hospital and the National Heart Institute, he took a year off in 1955, obtained a PhD from George Washington University, and moved to the National Institute of Mental Health as chief of the pharmacology section. He held this post until his retirement in 1984, while also continuing to work in the cell biology laboratory at the NIMH.

Axelrod has thrown much light on the action of the catecholamines, the neurotransmitters of the sympathetic nervous system. The most important of these is norepinephrine, first identified as a neurotransmitter by Ulf VON EULER in 1946. Axelrod realized that once the molecule had interacted with its target cell some mechanism must come into action to switch it off.

Later he was able to describe the role of two enzymes, catechol-o-methyltransferase (COMT) and monoamine oxidase (MAO), which degrade the catecholamines.

However, studies with radioactive norepinephrine showed its persistence in the sympathetic nerves for some hours. This led Axelrod to propose that norepinephrine is taken up into, as well as released from, sympathetic nerves. This recapture inactivates the neurotransmitter.

For work on the catecholamines Axelrod shared the 1970 Nobel Prize for physiology or medicine with von Euler and Bernard KATZ.

Axelrod has also worked on the role of the pineal gland in the control of circadian rhythms, and the neuropharmacology of schizophrenia.

Ayala, Francisco José (1934–   ) *Spanish–American biologist*

Ayala, who was born in Madrid, began his higher education there at the University of Madrid, moved to America in 1961, and obtained his PhD from Columbia in 1964. He worked initially at Rockefeller before joining the Davis campus of the University of California in 1971, where he was later appointed professor of genetics in 1974. He was professor of biology at the University of California, Irving, from 1987 to 1989, when he became Donald Bren Professor of Biological Sciences.

Ayala has worked extensively in the field of molecular evolution. He has also sought to measure genetic variation in natural populations, rates of evolution, and the amount of genetic change needed to produce new species. Many of his results were published in his *Molecular Evolution* (1976) and in a work he coauthored in 1977 entitled *Evolution*. He has written a number of other books including *Molecular Genetics* (1984).

Baade, Wilhelm Heinrich Walter
(1893–1960) *German–American astronomer*

Baade, born the son of a schoolteacher in Schröttinghausen, Germany, was educated at the universities of Münster and Göttingen, where he obtained his PhD in 1919. He worked at the University of Hamburg's Bergedorf Observatory from 1919 to 1931, when he moved to America. He spent the rest of his career at the Mount Wilson and Palomar Observatories, retiring in 1958.

In 1920 Baade discovered the minor planet Hidalgo, whose immense orbit extends to that of Saturn. He was also, in 1949, to detect the minor planet Icarus, whose orbit, which lies within that of Mercury, can bring it very close to Earth. In the 1930s he did important work with Fritz Zwicky on supernovae, with Edwin Hubble on galactic distances, and with his old Hamburg colleague, Rudolph Minkowski, on the optical identification of radio sources.

Baade's most significant work however began in 1942. As he was of German origin he was precluded from the general induction of scientists into military research, being allowed to spend the war observing the heavens. In early 1943 he was blessed with ideal viewing conditions. Los Angeles was blacked out because of wartime restrictions and, for a short while, the air was calm and the temperature constant. Under these near-perfect conditions Baade took some famous photographs with the 100-inch (2.5-m) reflecting telescope of the central region of the Andromeda galaxy. To his great excitement he was able to resolve stars in the inner region where Hubble before him had found only a blur of light.

These observations allowed Baade to introduce a fundamental distinction between types of stars. The first type, Population I stars, he found in the spiral arms of the Andromeda galaxy. They were young hot blue stars as opposed to the Population II stars of the central part of the galaxy, which were older and redder with a lower metal content. This distinction, now much expanded, has played a crucial role in theories of galactic evolution.

Some of the stars that Baade observed in the Andromeda galaxy were Cepheid variables, stars that vary regularly in brightness. His realization that there were two kinds of Cepheids had an immediate impact. The relationship between period and luminosity of Cepheids, had been discovered by Henrietta Leavitt in 1912 and put into a quantified form by Harlow Shapley so that it could be used in the determination of stellar distances of great magnitude. In the 1920s Hubble had found Cepheids in the outer part of the Andromeda galaxy, and, using the period-luminosity rule, had calculated its distance as 800,000 light-years. Since then the relationship had been used by many astronomers.

Baade, by 1952, was able to show that the original period-luminosity relationship was valid only for Population II Cepheids whereas Hubble's calculation involved Population I Cepheids. Baade worked out a new period-luminosity relationship for these Cepheids and found that the Andromeda galaxy was two million light-years distant.

The distance to the Andromeda galaxy had been used by Hubble to estimate the age of the universe as two billion years. Baade's revised figure gave the age as five billion years. This result was greeted with considerable relief by astronomers as Hubble's figure conflicted with the three to four billion years that the geologists were demanding for the age of the Earth. Further, with Baade's revision of the distance of the Andromeda galaxy without any change in its luminosity, it was now clear that its size must also be increased together with the size of all the other galaxies for which it had been a yardstick. Baade was thus able to establish that while our Galaxy was somewhat bigger than normal it was not the largest, as Hubble's work had implied.

Babbage, Charles (1792–1871) *British mathematician*

Babbage, whose father was a banker, was born in Teignmouth and studied at Cambridge. He played a major role in ending the isolationist attitudes prevalent in British mathematical circles in the early 19th century. In 1815 he helped to found the Analytical Society, which aimed to make the work of Continental mathematicians better known in Britain. Babbage's interest in stimulating British scientific activity was by no means confined to mathematics. In 1820 he was a founder of the Royal Astronomical Society and in 1834 of the Statistical Society, and he continued to attack the British public for their lack of interest in science. Among his inventions were a speedometer, and the locomotive 'cowcatcher'. Babbage also did mathematical work that contributed to the setting up of the British postal system in 1840. From 1828 to 1839 he was Lucasian Professor of Mathematics at Cambridge University.

Babbage is best known for his work in designing and attempting to build three mechanical computers. He had been struck by the discrepancies found in mathematical tables, and the persistence of error. "I wish to God these calculations had been executed by steam," he lamented in 1821. Mechanical execution, he argued, would eliminate error. Consequently he began work in 1823 on the machine later known as his Difference Engine No. 1. It operated by the method of finite differences and thus allowed values of functions to be obtained by addition rather than by multiplication. The engine was an analog decimal machine in which numbers were represented by the rotation of various wheels. After a decade of work the project was abandoned when Babbage's credit ran out. It had cost £17,000, was 8 feet high, and was made from 25,000 parts.

He later designed a simpler version, Difference Engine No. 2, with only a third of the number of parts. Plans were drawn up in 1847 and offered to an uninterested government in 1852. Without financial support Babbage never saw the project develop beyond the design stage.

The more ambitious analytical engine, first described in 1834, was similarly unsuccessful. Unlike the Difference Engine, this was to be a general computing machine in the manner of a modern computer, and was intended to be programmed with punched cards. One of Babbage's more enthusiastic supporters in this work was Ada BYRON, Countess of Lovelace.

In 1985, Doron Swade and his colleagues at the Science Museum in London set out to build a full-size Babbage computer based upon his original designs. They chose to work on No. 2 and hoped to have it ready for Babbage's bicentenary in 1992. The construction was carried out in full public view on the floor of the museum. It was completed in May 1991 and has worked satisfactorily ever since.

Babbage was influential in a number of other areas. His *Reflections on the Decline of Science in England* (1830) began the move to the professionalization of British science. In his *On the Economy of Machinery and Manufactures* (1832), a work closely studied by Marx, Babbage argued that industry could only flourish by adopting a scientific approach to both technical and commercial

matters. He also campaigned against street noises and was largely responsible for 'Babbage's Bill' of 1864, restricting the rights of street musicians. The subject was sufficiently important to him to form a chapter in his revealing *Passages from the Life of a Philosopher* (1864).

Babcock, Harold Delos (1882–1968)
American astronomer. See BABCOCK, HORACE WELCOME.

Babcock, Horace Welcome (1912–)
American astronomer

Babcock was born in Pasadena, California, the son of **Harold Delos Babcock**, a distinguished American astronomer who spent a lifetime observing at the Mount Wilson Observatory. Horace Babcock graduated in 1934 from the California Institute of Technology and obtained his PhD in 1938 from the University of California. He worked initially at Lick Observatory from 1938 to 1939 and at the Yerkes and McDonald observatories from 1939 to 1941. He then engaged in war work at the radiation laboratory at the Massachusetts Institute of Technology (1941–42) and at Cal Tech (1942–45). In 1946 Babcock returned to astronomy and joined his father at Mount Wilson where they began an enormously profitable collaboration. Babcock later served from 1964 until his retirement in 1978 as director of the Mount Wilson and Palomar Observatories, which became known in 1969 as the Hale Observatories.

In 1908 George Hale had detected splitting of the spectral lines in the light from sunspots. Such an effect results from the presence of a magnetic field, an effect first described by Pieter Zeeman in 1896. The fields observed by Hale were of considerable strength, ranging up to some 4000 gauss. The field of the Earth by contrast is less than one gauss. The question then arose as to whether the Sun itself possessed a general magnetic field distinct from fields associated with sunspots. The problem facing early investigators was how to detect weak fields and was not overcome until 1948 when the Babcocks successfully developed their magnetograph, permitting them to measure and record the Zeeman effect continuously and automatically. By the late 1940s they were able to report the presence of weak magnetic fields on the Sun, about one gauss in strength and restricted to latitudes greater than 55°. Further unexpected features were changes in polarity discovered in the 1950s: when examined in 1955 the north solar pole possessed positive polarity, the south negative polarity; by 1958 the situation was completely reversed.

In 1948 the Babcocks announced the further major discovery of stellar magnetic fields. By 1958 they had established the presence of magnetic fields in some 89 stars. The fields tended to be strong, of the order of several thousand gauss, and seemed to belong mainly to stars of spectral types O and B. Attempts to explain the presence of such fields were made considerably more difficult by the realization that some stars were 'magnetic variables': the field of the brighter component of the binary star Alpha Canes Venatici was found to vary, with reversing polarity, from +5000 to −4000 gauss in 5.5 days. Such studies have done much to stimulate work on magneto-hydrodynamics.

Babcock, Stephen Moulton (1843–1931) *American agricultural chemist*

A farmer's son from New York State, Babcock gained his AB degree from Tufts College, Massachusetts, in 1866 and after a period of farming became a chemistry assistant and (from 1875) instructor at Cornell University. In 1879 he gained his doctorate under Hans Hübner at Göttingen, Germany. After a further spell at Cornell on his return, he became chemist at the New York Agricultural Station in 1882, where he worked on the analysis of milk.

In 1888 Babcock became professor of agricultural chemistry at the University of Wisconsin. Here, in 1890, he devised an efficient test (the *Babcock test*), which quickly became standard, for measuring the butterfat content of milk. Studies followed on rennet, fermentation, metabolic water, and animal nutrition. In 1907 Babcock's associates began studies in which cattle were fed balanced diets derived from a single source – corn, wheat, or oats. The results obtained provided further evidence for the existence of accessory food factors and Babcock's school played an important part in the vitamin studies that followed.

Babinet, Jacques (1794–1872) *French physicist*

Babinet, who was born in Lusignan, France, studied in Paris at the Ecole Polytechnique and from 1820 he was a professor at the Collège Louis le Grand. He was elected to the Académie des Sciences in 1840.

His major work was devoted to the diffraction of light; he used diffraction to measure wavelengths more accurately than before, and did theoretical work on general diffraction systems. The *Babinet theorem* states that there is an approximate equivalence between the diffraction pattern of a large system and that of the complementary system, which is opaque where the original system is transparent and vice versa.

Furthermore he showed an interest in the optical properties of minerals, developing new instruments for the measurement of angles and polarizations. He also studied meteorological phenomena, especially those of an optical nature, investigating rainbows and the polarization of skylight. Babinet was the first to suggest (1829) that the wavelength of a given spectral line could be used as a fundamental standard of length. The idea was adopted in 1960, when the meter was defined as 1 650 763 73 wavelengths of the radiation emitted by an atom of krypton–86 in a specified transition. (This definition was changed in 1983 to the distance traveled by light in a certain fraction of a second.)

Backus, John (1924–) *American computer scientist*

Backus was born in Philadelphia. After graduating from Columbia University, New York, he joined the staff of IBM in 1952 and remained with them until his retirement in 1991. From 1959 until 1963 he worked at the IBM Research Center, Yorktown Heights, New York, and thereafter as an IBM Fellow at the IBM Research Laboratory, San Jose, California.

Backus has reported on the state of programming when he joined IBM. It was, he noted, "a black art, a private arcane matter." All programming was done using machine or assembly language. There were no compilers, no index registers, and the programmer spent most of his time debugging the program and feeding it into the computer. The programmers actually cost more than the computer. Backus commented, "They dismissed as foolish plans to make programming accessible to a larger population," it was inconceivable "that any mechanical process could possibly perform the mysterious feats of invention required to write an efficient program."

In 1954 Backus led an IBM team determined to free computer programming from the professional élite. As the speed of computers increased it made no sense to have them standing idle while a programmer struggled to operate them. The problem was made more pressing by the development of the new and more powerful IBM 704. By late 1954 some of the main details of the high level language FORTRAN (from Formula Translation) had been established. Backus defined his aim as "to design a language which would make it possible for engineers and scientists to write programs for the 704." The language itself was available in 1957 and soon became the most widely used programming language.

Baekeland, Leo Hendrik (1863–1944)
Belgian–American industrial chemist

Baekeland was born in Ghent and educated at the university there, graduating in 1884. He was professor of physics and chemistry at Bruges in 1887 and returned to Ghent the next year as assistant professor of chemistry. But Baekeland grew impatient with academic life and in 1889 a honeymoon tour took him to America where he settled.

Baekeland worked at first as a photographic chemist and in 1891 he opened his own consulting laboratory. In 1893 he began to manufacture a photographic paper, which he called Velox, and six years later his company was bought out by the Kodak Corporation for one million dollars. Now financially independent, Baekeland returned to Europe to study at the Technical Institute at Charlottenburg.

On his return to America, Baekeland began to investigate, as a synthetic substitute for shellac, the phenol–formaldehyde resins discovered by Karl BAEYER in 1871. Since nothing remotely like shellac emerged, he began to look for other uses for this material. By choosing suitable reaction conditions he produced a hard amber-like resin, which could be cast and machined and which had excellent durability and electrical properties. Bakelite was finally unveiled in 1909, when Baekeland set up the General Bakelite Corporation.

In 1922 Baekeland's company merged with two rivals and in 1939 it became a subsidiary of the Union Carbide and Carbon Corporation. Baekeland continued to produce scientific papers throughout this period. He received many honors and held many professional posts, including that of president of the American Chemical Society.

Baer, Karl Ernst von (1792–1876)
German–Estonian biologist, comparative anatomist, and embryologist

Baer is generally considered the father of modern embryology. He was born on his family's estate in Piep, Estonia, and received private tutoring and schooling before entering Dorpat University to study medicine. He graduated in 1814 and then studied comparative anatomy at the University of Würzburg, where he was introduced to embryology by Ignaz Döllinger. In 1817 Baer became professor of zoology at Königsberg

and in 1834 was appointed academician and librarian of the Academy of Sciences at St. Petersburg.

It was prior to his move to St. Petersburg that Baer did most of his pioneering work in laying the foundation of comparative embryology as a separate discipline. In distinguishing the mammalian ovum within the Graafian follicle he established that all mammals, including man, develop from eggs. He also traced the development of the fertilized egg and the order in which the organs of the body appear and develop, showing that similar (homologous) organs arise from the same germ layers in different animals, thus extending the work of Kaspar Wolff and the German anatomist Christian Pander. His expounding of the 'biogenetic law', demonstrating the increasing similarity and lack of specialization in the embryos of different animals as one investigates younger and younger embryos, provided Darwin with basic arguments for his evolutionary theory. Baer was, however, opposed to the idea of there being a common ancestor for all animal life, although he conceded that some animals and some races of man might have had common ancestry. His other notable discoveries included the mammalian notochord and the neural folds as the precursors of the nervous system. Baer intended his embryological work to be, at least partly, a means of improving animal classification by demonstrating vertebrate affinities. Indeed modern zoological classification is now based partly on biogenetic principles. His great work on the mammalian egg, *De ovi mammalium et hominis genesi* (1827; On the Origin of the Mammalian and Human Ovum) was followed (1828–37) by *Über Entwickelungsgeschichte der Tiere* (On the Development of Animals), in which he surveyed all existing knowledge of vertebrate development.

A man of wide interests, Baer did much work in other scientific disciplines. He was instrumental in founding the German Anthropological Society and helped to found the Russian Geographical and Entomological Societies.

Baeyer, Johann Friedrich Adolph von (1835–1917) *German organic chemist*

Baeyer's father was a member of the Prussian General Staff and his mother was the daughter of a celebrated jurist and literary historian. Born in Berlin, Baeyer went to Heidelberg in 1856 to study chemistry with Robert Bunsen. Here he met August Kekulé, who had a profound influence on his development as a chemist and gave him the theoretical foundation for his work. After obtaining his PhD (1858) Baeyer took up a teaching position in 1860 at a small technical school, the Gewerbe-Institut, in Berlin. In 1872 he was appointed professor of chemistry at Strasbourg and in 1875 succeeded Liebig as professor of chemistry at Munich, where he remained for the rest of his life.

In 1864, continuing the work of Wöhler, Liebig, and Schlieper on uric acid, Baeyer characterized a related series of derivatives including alloxan, parabanic acid, hydantoin, and barbituric acid. In 1871 he discovered the phthalein dyes, phenolphthalein and fluorescein, by heating phenols with phthalic anhydride. In the course of this work he discovered the phenol–formaldehyde resins, which were later developed commercially by BAEKELAND. The centerpiece of Baeyer's prolific researches, however, was his work on indigo, which started in 1865 and lasted for 20 years.

In 1883 he gave a structure of indigo that was correct except for the stereochemical arrangement of the double bond, which was later shown to be *trans* by x-ray crystallography (1928). Baeyer's syntheses proved too costly for commercial manufacture and he took no part in the industrial development of indigo, terminating his work in 1885. Commercial synthetic indigo was eventually produced in 1890. Baeyer's work also led to the production of many other new dyes.

From indigo Baeyer turned to the polyacetylenes, compounds whose explosive properties led him to consider the stability of carbon–carbon bonds in unsaturated and ring compounds. He formulated the *Baeyer strain theory*, stating that compounds are less stable the more their bond angles depart from the ideal tetrahedral arrangement. Baeyer's other researches included work on oxonium compounds; on the reduction of aromatic compounds, in which he observed a loss of aromaticity on reduction; and on terpenes, including the first synthesis of a terpene in 1888.

The strain theory was one of Baeyer's few theoretical contributions; he was a virtuoso of test-tube chemistry at a time when this could produce extraordinary results. In 1905 he received the Nobel Prize for chemistry for his work on indigo and aromatic compounds.

Bahcall, John Noris (1934–   ) *American physicist*

Bahcall was born in Shreveport, Louisiana, and educated at the universities of California, Chicago, and Harvard, where he obtained his PhD in 1961. He immediately moved to the faculty of the California Institute of Technology, and remained there until 1971 when he was appointed to the Institute of Advanced Studies, Princeton.

In the 1960s Bahcall began to consider the emission of neutrinos from the Sun. One of the apparent early triumphs of nuclear physics was the light it threw on the internal workings of the Sun. Theorists such as Hans Bethe had proposed the existence of a number of cyclic fusion reactions producing vast amounts of energy, heavier elements, and a certain number of neutrinos. As neutrinos have a low probability of interacting with other particles, some solar neutrinos should be received at the Earth's surface. Bahcall calculated that one event per second for every 10^{36} target atoms, one solar neutrino unit (SNU), should be detectable. The matter was put to the test by Ray DAVIS who used a detector consisting of a tank of 100,000 gallons of cleaning fluid in a one-mile-deep mine.

Bahcall predicted that Davis would observe a flux of about 8 SNU. In fact, from 1967 onwards, Davis recorded a flux of about 2 SNU. The burden was placed upon the theorists to account for the anomalous results, or to revise the theory in ways that would make the results acceptable. This is the *solar neutrino problem*.

A number of options have been considered by Bahcall. Perhaps, the Sun is passing through a quiet phase and over long periods of time neutrino output will agree with theory. The issue will eventually be resolved when the abundance of radioactive technetium, produced by interactions deep in the Earth between neutrinos and molybdenum, has been accurately measured.

Or, perhaps, our solar model is wrong. This, Bahcall points out, leads nowhere. Alternative solar models agree with the standard model in the rate of neutrino production. Other theorists have challenged generally accepted physical principles. Thus, Bahcall considered the possibility that neutrinos could decay before they reach the Earth. As there seems to be nothing a neutrino can decay into, the suggestion has been dropped.

As a number of new and more sensitive detectors are being built, theorists seem inclined to await fresh data before judging between competing theories. Until then, Bahcall notes, physicists will dismiss the problem as a matter of astronomy while astronomers will attribute the anomaly to the failings of physics.

Baird, John Logie (1888–1946) *British inventor*

Baird, who was born in Helensburgh, Scotland, studied electrical engineering at the Royal Technical College in Glasgow and then went to Glasgow University. His poor health prevented him from active service during World War I and from completing various business enterprises in the years following the war.

After a breakdown in 1922 he retired to Hastings and engaged in amateur experiments on the transmission of pictures. Using primitive equipment he succeeded in transmitting an image over a distance of a couple of feet, and in 1926 he demonstrated his apparatus before a group of scientists. Recognition followed, and the next year he transmitted pictures by telephone wire between London and Glasgow. In the same year he set up the Baird Television Development Company. He continued to work on improvements and on 30 September, 1929, gave the first experimental BBC broadcast. Synchronization of sound and vision was achieved a few months later. In 1937, however, the Baird system of mechanical scanning was ousted by the all-electronic system put forward by Marconi–EMI. Baird was at the forefront of virtually all developments in television and continued research into color, stereoscopic, and big-screen television until his death.

Bakker, Robert (1945–   ) *American paleontologist*

The son of an electrical engineer, Bakker was born in Ridgewood, New Jersey, and educated at Yale and at Harvard, where he completed his PhD in 1976. After teaching for eight years at Johns Hopkins University, Baltimore, he moved to Boulder, Colorado, in 1984 to work as an independent paleontologist.

In the early 1970s, while still a graduate student, Bakker argued that traditional views on the nature of dinosaurs were misguided. Dinosaurs, he claimed, were warmblooded, like mammals, and not cold-blooded like reptiles. In support Bakker offered three main arguments derived from comparative anatomy, latitudinal zonation, and ecology.

Anatomically the bones of endotherms (warm-blooded creatures) are rich in blood vessels and show no growth rings. Precisely these features are found in mammals, birds, and, Bakker noted, dinosaurs as well. They are lacking in cold-blooded reptiles (ectotherms).

Further, endotherms can cope with most temperature variations and can be found in temperate, arctic, and equatorial zones. Large reptiles, however, cannot survive cool winters. Yet, during the Cretaceous, dinosaurs could have been found in the far north of Canada, well within the Arctic Circle.

Finally Bakker points to predator–prey ratios. The Komodo dragon, the largest living lizard, consumes its own weight every 60 days, a lion in only eight days. Such are the demands of endothermy. As a consequence a community can support fewer warm-blooded predators than cold-blooded predators. The predator–prey ratio, Bakker argued, is a constant characteristic of the predator's metabolism. Calculations revealed that a given biomass can support a warm-blooded predator biomass of 1–3%, and a cold-blooded predator biomass of up to 40%. Given that some fossil deposits yield remains of thousands of individuals, their predator–prey ratio should be measurable. And Bakker did find that amongst the reptiles of the Permian (285–225 million years ago) the ratio was very high (35–60%), while the dinosaurs of the Triassic (225–195 million years) had a ratio of only 1–3%.

Bakker's work called for a revision of vertebrate systematics. In traditional classifications birds and dinosaurs are seen as collateral descendants of thecodonts, that is, animals with teeth set in sockets. Bakker, however, has proposed that birds are descended from dinosaurs. Such views, vigorously and frequently expressed, have made Bakker a controversial and well-known figure.

Bakker has sought to reach an even wider public with his *Raptor Red* (1995), a novel dealing with a year in the life of *Utahraptor*, a much bigger version of the *Velociraptor* of *Jurassic Park*.

Balard, Antoine-Jérôme (1802–1876) *French chemist*

Balard was born in Montpellier in southern France, and studied there at the School of Pharmacy. After graduating in 1826, he remained at Montpellier as a demonstrator in chemistry. In 1825, while investigating the salts contained in seawater, he discovered a dark red liquid, which he proved was an element with properties similar to chlorine and iodine. Balard proposed the name 'muride' but the editors of *Annales de chimie* preferred 'brome' (because of the element's strong odor, from the Greek for 'stink') and the element came to be called bromine. Balard also (1834) discovered dichlorine oxide (Cl_2O) and chloric(I) acid (HClO).

In 1833 he became professor at Montpellier and in 1843 succeeded Louis Thenard at the Sorbonne as professor of chemistry. In 1854 he was appointed professor of general chemistry at the Collège de France, where he remained until his death.

Balfour, Francis Maitland (1851–1882) *British zoologist*

The younger brother of the British statesman Earl Balfour, Francis Balfour's career was cut short when, while convalescing from typhoid fever in Switzerland, he died attempting an ascent of the Aiguille Blanche, Mont Blanc. Balfour, who was born in Edinburgh, held the position of animal morphologist at the Naples Zoological Station and in 1882 was appointed to the specially created post of professor of animal morphology at Cambridge University. Much influenced by the work of Michael Foster, with whom he wrote *Elements of Embryology* (1883), Balfour showed the evolutionary connection between vertebrates and certain invertebrates, both of which have a notochord (a flexible rod of cells extending the length of the body) in their embryonic stages. Similar research was being conducted at that time by Aleksandr Kovalevski. Balfour proposed the term Chordata for all animals possessing a notochord at some stage in their development, the Vertebrata (backboned animals) being a subphylum of the Chordata. He was an early exponent of recapitulation – the theory that ancestral forms are repeated in successive embryonic stages undergone by modern species. Balfour also did pioneer work on the development of the kidneys and related organs, as well as the spinal nervous system. His other important publications include *On the Development of Elasmobranch Fishes* (1878) and *Comparative Embryology* (1880–81) published in two volumes (invertebrates and vertebrates), the latter forming the basis of modern embryological study.

Balmer, Johann Jakob (1825–1898) *Swiss mathematician*

Born in Lausanne, Switzerland, Balmer was not a professional scientist but worked as a school teacher in Basel from 1859. In 1885 he discovered that there was a simple mathematical formula that gave the wavelengths of the spectral lines of hydrogen – the *Balmer series*. This formula proved to be of great importance in atomic spectroscopy and in developing the atomic theory. Balmer arrived at his result purely from empirical evidence and was unable to explain why it yielded correct answers. Not until the further development of the atomic theory by Niels BOHR and others was this possible.

Baltimore, David (1938–) *American molecular biologist*

Baltimore was born in New York City and studied chemistry at Swarthmore College. He continued with postgraduate work at the Massachusetts Institute of Technology, and at Rockefeller University, where he obtained his PhD in 1964. After three years at the Salk Institute in California, he returned to MIT in 1968 where, in 1972, he became professor of biology.

Francis Crick had formulated what came to be known as the Central Dogma of molecular biology, namely, that information could flow from DNA to RNA to protein but could not flow backward from protein to either DNA or RNA. Although he had not actually excluded the passage of information from RNA to DNA it became widely assumed that such a flow was equally forbidden. In June 1970 Baltimore and, quite independently, Howard TEMIN announced the discovery of an enzyme later to be known as reverse transcriptase, which is capable of transcribing RNA into DNA. Apparently certain viruses, like the RNA tumor viruses used by Baltimore, could produce DNA from an RNA template. For this work Baltimore shared the 1975 Nobel Prize for physiology or medicine with Temin and Renato DULBECCO. A few years later their work took on an added significance when GALLO and MONTAGNIER identified a retrovirus as the cause of AIDS.

Earlier (1968) Baltimore had done important work on the replication of the polio virus. He revealed that the RNA of the virus first constructed a 'polyprotein' (or giant protein molecule), which then split into a number of smaller protein molecules. Two of these polymerized further RNA while the remainder formed the protein coat of the new viral particles.

In 1982 Baltimore became founding director of the Whitehead Institute, Cambridge, Massachusetts, a research biomedical foundation backed by the industrialist E. C. Whitehead. While at Whitehead, in collaboration with D. Schatz, he identified two antibody genes, RAG-1 and RAG-2. In 1990 Baltimore was appointed president of Rockefeller University; it was not to prove a fruitful or happy time. Many staff opposed the appointment and Baltimore became involved in a bitter controversy. It had been claimed that a paper co-authored by Baltimore and published in 1986 in *Cell* was based on falsified data. Although Baltimore withdrew his name from the paper, the public controversy persisted in Congressional hearings and the correspondence columns of *Nature*. Baltimore resigned the presidency in 1992 and returned to MIT in 1994 as professor of molecular biology.

Banks, Sir Joseph (1743–1820) *British botanist*

The son of William Banks of Revesby Abbey, Lincolnshire, Joseph Banks inherited a large fortune when he came of age, and later used this money to finance his scientific expeditions. Born in London, he studied botany at Oxford, graduating in 1763, and three years later traveled abroad for the first time as naturalist on a fishery-protection vessel heading for Labrador and Newfoundland. On the voyage he was able to collect many new species of plants and insects and, on his return, was elected a fellow of the Royal Society.

In London Banks learned that the Royal Society was organizing a voyage to the South Pacific to observe the transit of Venus across the Sun. In 1768 James Cook set sail in the *Endeavour* and Banks, together with a team of artists and the botanist Daniel Solander, accompanied him. Cook landed in Australia, a continent with a flora and fauna different from any found elsewhere. Banks found that most of the Australian mammals were marsupials, which are more primitive, in evolutionary terms, than the placental mammals of other continents.

After three years with the *Endeavour* Banks returned, with a large collection of unique specimens, to find himself famous. George III, interested in hearing a first-hand account of Banks's travels, invited him to Windsor. This visit was the start of a long friendship with the king, which helped Banks establish many influential contacts – possibly a factor in his election as president of the Royal Society in 1778, a post that he held until his death.

Throughout his life Banks retained his interest in natural history and in the specimens collected on the many expeditions mounted during that period. As honorary director of Kew Gardens he played a major part in establishing living representatives of as many species as possible at Kew and in providing a center for advice on the practical use of plants. He initiated many successful projects, including the introduction of the tea plant to India from its native China and the transport of the breadfruit from Tahiti to the West Indies. By George III's request, he also played an active role in importing merino sheep into Britain from Spain.

The British Museum (Natural History) now houses Banks's library and herbarium, both regarded as major collections.

Banting, Sir Frederick Grant (1891–1941) *Canadian physiologist*

Banting, a farmer's son from Alliston, Ontario, began studying to be a medical missionary at Victoria College, Toronto, in 1910. During his studies he concentrated increasingly on medicine and graduated MD in 1916, whereupon he immediately joined the Canadian Army Medical Corps. In 1918 he was awarded the Military Cross for gallantry in action and was invalided out of the army.

Banting then returned to Toronto and worked for a time studying children's diseases before setting up practice in London, Ontario, in 1920. He also began work at the London Medical School, specializing in studies on the pancreas, particularly the small patches of pancreatic cells known as the islets of Langerhans. Earlier work had shown a connection between the pancreas and diabetes mellitus and Banting wondered if a hormone was produced in the islets of Langerhans that regulated glucose metabolism. In 1921 he approached John MacLeod, professor of physiology at Toronto University, who was initially skeptical. Feeling that Banting needed help in physiological and biochemical methods, Macleod suggested the assistance of a young research student, Charles Best, and eventually merely granted Banting and Best some laboratory space during the vacation, while he went abroad.

Over the next six months Banting and Best devised a series of elegant experiments. They tied off the pancreatic ducts of dogs and made extracts of the islets of Langerhans free from other pancreatic substances. These extracts, called 'isletin', were found to have some effect against diabetes in dogs. Prior to trials on humans, Macleod asked a biochemist, James Collip, to purify the extracts and the purification method for what was now known as insulin were patented by Banting, Best, and Collip in 1923. They allowed manufacturers freedom to produce the hormone but required a small royalty to be paid to finance future medical research.

The pharmaceutical firm Eli Lilley began industrial production of insulin in 1923 and in the same year Banting was awarded the chair of medical research at Toronto University and a government annuity of $7000. The Nobel Prize for physiology or medicine was awarded jointly to Banting and Macleod in 1923; Banting was furious that Best had not been included in the award and shared his part of the prize money with him. Macleod shared his portion with Collip. In 1930 the Banting and Best Department was opened at the University of

Toronto and Banting became its director. Under Best's guidance, it became the center of medical research in Canada. His own later researches were into cancer and also the function of the adrenal cortex.

Banting was knighted in 1934. When war broke out in 1939 he joined an army medical unit and worked on many committees linking Canadian and British wartime medical research. His bravery was much in evidence at this time, particularly his personal involvement in research into mustard gas and blackout problems experienced by airmen. In 1941 on a flight from Gander, Newfoundland, to Britain his plane crashed and he died in the snow.

Bárány, Robert (1876–1936) *Austro-Hungarian physician*

Bárány was born in Vienna and educated at the university there, graduating in medicine in 1900. After studying at various German clinics, he returned to Vienna to become an assistant at the university's ear clinic. In 1909 he was appointed lecturer in otology. Through his work at the clinic he devised a test, now called the *Bárány test*, for diagnosing disease of the semicircular canals of the inner ear by syringing the ear with either hot or cold water. For this he was awarded the 1914 Nobel Prize in physiology or medicine. At this time he was being held as a prisoner of war in Siberia, but through the offices of the Swedish Red Cross he was released for the presentation.

In 1917 Bárány was appointed professor at Uppsala University, where he continued his investigations on the inner ear and the role of the cerebellum in the brain in controlling body movement. *Bárány's pointing test* is used to test for brain lesions.

Bardeen, John (1908–1991) *American physicist*

Bardeen, the son of a professor of anatomy, was born in Madison, Wisconsin, and studied electrical engineering at the University of Wisconsin. He obtained his PhD in mathematical physics at Princeton in 1936. Bardeen began work as a geophysicist with Gulf Research and Development Corporation, Pittsburgh, in 1931 but in 1935 entered academic life as a junior fellow at Harvard, moving to the University of Minnesota in 1938. He spent the war years at the Naval Ordnance Laboratory, followed by six creative years from 1945 until 1951 at the Bell Telephone Laboratory, after which he was appointed professor of physics and electrical engineering at the University of Illinois, a post he held until 1975.

Bardeen is remarkable as a recipient of two Nobel Prizes for physics. The first, awarded in 1956, he shared with Walter BRATTAIN and William SHOCKLEY for their development of the point-contact transistor (1947), thus preparing the way for the development of the more efficient junction transistor by Shockley.

Bardeen's second prize was awarded in 1972 for his formulation, in collaboration with Leon COOPER and the American physicist **John Schrieffer** (1931–), of the first satisfactory theory of superconductivity – the so-called BCS theory. In 1911 Heike Kamerlingh-Onnes had discovered that mercury lost all electrical resistance when its temperature was lowered to 4.2 K. Superconductivity was also shown to be a property of many other metals, yet despite much effort to understand the phenomenon, a full explanation was not given until 1957. The basic innovation of the BCS theory was that the current in a superconductor is carried not by individual electrons but by bound pairs of them, later known as *Cooper pairs*. The pairs form as a result of interactions between the electrons and vibrations of the atoms in the crystal. The scattering of one electron by a lattice atom does not change the total momentum of the pair, and the flow of electrons continues indefinitely. The success of the BCS theory led to an enormous revival of interest in both the theory of superconductors and their practical application.

Barkhausen, Heinrich Georg (1881–1956) *German physicist*

After attending the gymnasium and engineering college in his native city of Bremen, Barkhausen gained his PhD in Göttingen and in 1911 became professor of electrical engineering in Dresden. Here he formulated the basic equations governing the coefficients of the amplifier valve.

In 1919 he discovered the *Barkhausen effect*, observing that a slow continuous increase in the magnetic field applied to a ferromagnetic material gave rise to discontinuous leaps in magnetization, which could be heard as distinct clicking sounds through a loudspeaker. This effect is caused by domains of elementary magnets changing direction or size as the field increases.

In 1920, with K. Kurz he developed an ultrahighfrequency oscillator, which became the forerunner of microwave-technology developments. After World War II he returned to Dresden to aid the reconstruction of his Institute of High-Frequency Electron-Tube Technology, which had been destroyed by bombing, and remained there until his death.

Barkla, Charles Glover (1877–1944)
British x-ray physicist

Barkla was born in Widnes in the north-west of England. After taking his master's degree in 1899 at Liverpool, Barkla went to Trinity College, Cambridge but, because of his passion for singing, he transferred to King's College to sing in the choir. At King's College he started his important research on x-rays. In 1902 he returned to Liverpool as Oliver Lodge Fellow and in 1909 became Wheatstone Professor at King's College, London. From 1913 onward he was professor of natural philosophy at Edinburgh University.

His scientific work, for which he received the 1917 Nobel Prize for physics, concerned the properties of x-rays – in particular, the way in which they are scattered by various materials. He showed in 1903 that the scattering of x-rays by gases depends on the molecular weight of the gas. In 1904 he observed the polarization of x-rays – a result that indicated that x-rays are a form of electromagnetic radiation like light. Further confirmation of this was obtained in 1907 when he performed certain experiments on the direction of scattering of a beam of x-rays as evidence to resolve a controversy with William Henry Bragg who argued, at the time, that x-rays were particles.

Barkla also demonstrated x-ray fluorescence, in which primary x-rays are absorbed and the excited atoms then emit characteristic secondary x-rays. The frequencies of the characteristic x-rays depend on the atomic number of the element, as shown by Henry MOSELY, who could well have shared Barkla's Nobel Prize but for his untimely death.

From about 1916, Barkla became isolated from modern physics with an increasingly dogmatic attitude, a tendency to cite only his own papers, and a concentration on untenable theories.

Barnard, Edward Emerson
(1857–1923) American astronomer

Although Barnard was born into a poor family in Nashville, Tennessee, and received little formal education, he developed a great interest in astronomy and also became familiar with photographic techniques from his work in a portrait studio. He managed both to study and instruct at Vanderbilt University from 1883 to 1887. From 1888 he worked at the Lick Observatory until in 1895 he became professor of astronomy at Chicago and was thus able to work at the newly established Yerkes Observatory.

Barnard was a keen observer and had detected more than ten comets by 1887 and several more in subsequent years. In 1892 he became the first astronomer after Galileo to discover a new satellite of Jupiter, subsequently named Amalthea, which lay inside the orbits of the four Galilean satellites and was much smaller and fainter. In 1916 he discovered a nearby red star with a very pronounced proper motion of 10.3 seconds of arc per year: in 180 years it will appear to us to have moved a very considerable distance, equal to the diameter of the Moon. The star is now called *Barnard's star*.

Barnard's other discoveries included various novae, variable stars, and binary stars. He was also one of the first to appreciate that dark nebulae were not areas of the sky containing no stars at all (as William Herschel had thought) but, as Barnard and Max Wolf demonstrated, were enormous clouds of dust and gas that shielded the stars behind them from our view. By 1919 he had discovered nearly 200 such nebulae.

Barr, Murray Llewellyn (1908–)
Canadian geneticist and anatomist

Barr was born in Belmont, Ontario, and was educated at the University of Western Ontario, gaining his BA in 1930, MD in 1933, and MSc in 1938. His association with Western Ontario was continued with his appointment as an instructor in 1936. He subsequently became professor of microscopical anatomy (1952), professor of anatomy and head of the anatomy department (1964), and emeritus professor (1979).

Barr is best known for his discovery, made in 1949 in conjunction with Ewart Bertram, of the densely staining nuclear bodies present in the somatic cells of female humans and other female mammals. These are called sex chromatin or *Barr bodies*. Later studies by Barr and others revealed that the single Barr body in normal cells is one of the two X-chromosomes in a highly condensed and genetically inactive state. The other X-chromosome is in the diffuse state and is genetically active.

Their discovery enabled Barr and his co-workers to devise a relatively simple diagnostic test for certain genetic abnormalities, in which cells rubbed from the lining of the mouth cavity (a buccal smear) were stained and examined microscopically. For instance, individuals suffering from Turner's syndrome, which usually affects females, have only one X-chromosome and lack Barr bodies. In contrast, males affected by Klinefelter's syndrome possess an extra X-chromosome and exhibit Barr bodies in their cells.

Besides his work in cytogenetics and inherited human disorders, Barr is also noted for his descriptions of nervous-system anatomy. His publications include *The Human Nervous System: an Anatomical Viewpoint* (1972; 5th edn. (with J. A. Kiernan) 1988).

Barrow, Isaac (1630–1677) *British mathematician*

Born the son of a prosperous London linen draper, Barrow was educated at Cambridge University. Because of his royalist sympathies he was rejected, on Cromwell's instructions, as a candidate for the professorship of Greek. Consequently he began in 1655 an extensive tour of Europe. With the restoration of Charles II, he returned to Britain in 1660 and was finally elected professor of Greek at Cambridge. In 1663 he accepted the newly created Lucasian Professorship of Mathematics, a post he resigned from in 1669.

The claim has often been made that Barrow resigned his chair in favor of his pupil, Isaac Newton. In reality Newton was not the pupil of Barrow and, while he appreciated Newton's mathematical genius and saw to it that Newton succeeded him, Barrow was more interested in advancing his own career. He was appointed chaplain to Charles II in 1669 and in 1673 returned to Cambridge as Master of Trinity College, an office in the gift of the king. He died soon after in 1677 from, according to John Aubrey, an overdose of opium, an addiction that he had acquired in Turkey.

Barrow is best known for his *Lectiones opticae* (1669) and *Lectiones geometricae* (1670), both edited by Newton, and the posthumously published *Lectiones mathematicae* (1683). Unfortunately for Barrow's reputation, his work in both optics and mathematics was soon overshadowed by Newton's own publications.

Bartholin, Erasmus (1625–1698) *Danish mathematician*

Bartholin, the son of Caspar and brother of Thomas Bartholin, who were both distinguished anatomists, was born in Roskilde, Denmark, and educated in Leiden and Padua, where he obtained his MD in 1654. After further travel in France and England he returned to Denmark in 1656 and held chairs in mathematics and medicine at the University of Copenhagen from 1657 until his death.

Bartholin worked on the theory of equations and with Olaus Romer made an unsuccessful attempt to calculate the orbits of the comets prominent in the late 1660s. He is however best remembered for his discovery of double refraction announced in his *Experimenta crystalli Islandici disdiaclastici* (1669). In it he described how Icelandic feldspar (calcite) produces a double image of objects observed through it. This discovery greatly puzzled scientists and was much discussed by Newton and Christiaan Huygens, who tried unsuccessfully to incorporate the strange phenomenon into their respective theories of light.

Double refraction proved remarkably recalcitrant to all proposed explanations for well over a century and it was only with the work of Etienne Malus on polarized light in 1808, and that of Augustin Fresnel in 1817, that Bartholin's observations could at last be understood.

Bartlett, Neil (1932–) *British–American chemist*

Bartlett was born in Newcastle upon Tyne and educated at the University of Durham, where he obtained his PhD in 1957. He taught at the University of British Columbia, Canada, and at Princeton before being appointed to a chemistry professorship in 1969 at the University of California, Berkeley.

Bartlett was studying metal fluorides and found that the compound platinum hexafluoride (PtF_6) is extremely active. In fact it reacted with molecular oxygen to form the novel compound $O_2{}^+PtF_6{}^-$. This was the first example of a compound containing the oxygen cation. At the time it was an unquestioned assumption of chemistry that the noble gases – helium, neon, argon, krypton, and xenon – were completely inert, incapable of forming any compounds whatsoever. Further, there was a solid body of valence theory that provided good reasons why this should be so. So struck was Bartlett with the ability of PtF_6 to react with other substances that he tried, in 1962, to form a compound between it and xenon. He knew that the ionization potential of xenon was not too much greater than the ionization potential of the oxygen molecule. To his and other chemists' surprise xenon fluoroplatinate ($XePtF_6$) was produced – the first compound of a noble gas. Once the first compound had been detected xenon was soon shown to form other compounds, such as xenon fluoride (XeF_4) and oxyfluoride ($XeOF_4$). Krypton and radon were also found to form compounds although the lighter inert gases have so far remained inactive.

Barton, Sir Derek Harold Richard (1918–1998) *British chemist*

Barton was born in Gravesend and was educated at Imperial College, London, where he obtained his PhD in 1942. After doing some industrial research he spent a year as visiting lecturer at Harvard before being appointed reader (1950) and then professor (1953) in organic chemistry at Birkbeck College, London. Barton moved to a similar chair at Glasgow University in 1955 but returned to Imperial College in 1957 and held the chair of chemistry until 1978, when he became director of the Institute for the Chemistry of Natural Substances at Gif-sur-Yvette in France. In 1986 he became a distinguished professor at Texas Agricultural and Mechanical University.

In 1950 Barton published a fundamental paper on conformational analysis in which he proposed that the orientations in space of functional groups affect the rates of reaction in isomers. Barton discussed six-membered organic rings, particularly, following the earlier work of Odd HASSELL, the 'chair' conformation of cyclohexane and explained its distinctive stability.

This was done in terms of the distinction between equatorial conformations, in which the hydrogen atoms lie in the same plane as the carbon ring, and axial, where they are perpendicular to the ring. He confirmed these notions with further work on the stability and reactivity of steroids and terpenes.

It was for this work that he shared the 1969 Nobel Prize for chemistry with Hassell. Barton's later work on oxyradicals and his predictions about their behavior in reactions helped in the development of a simple method for synthesizing the hormone aldosterone.

Basov, Nikolai Gennediyevich
(1922–) *Russian physicist*

Basov, who was born in Voronezh in western Russia, served in the Soviet army in World War II, following which he graduated from the Moscow Institute of Engineering Physics (1950). He studied at the Lebedev Institute of Physics of the Soviet Academy of Sciences in Moscow, gaining his doctoral degree in 1956 and going on to become deputy director (1958) and later director (1973). In 1989 he became director of the quantum radiophysics division.

Basov's major contribution was in the development of the maser (microwave amplification by stimulated emission of radiation), the forerunner of the laser. From 1952 he had been researching the possibility of amplifying electromagnetic radiation using excited atoms or molecules. His colleague at the Lebedev Institute, Aleksandr

PROKHOROV, was involved in the microwave spectroscopy of gases, with the aim of creating a precise frequency standard, for use in very accurate clocks and navigational systems. Their work led to theories and experiments designed to produce a state of 'population inversion' in molecular beams, through which amplification of radiofrequency radiation became possible.

Together Basov and Prokhorov in 1955 developed a generator using a beam of excited ammonia molecules. This was the maser, developed simultaneously but independently in America by Charles TOWNES. Basov, Prokhorov, and Townes received the 1964 Nobel Prize for physics for this work.

The first masers used a method of selecting the more excited molecules from a beam, but a more efficient method was proposed by Basov and Prokhorov in 1955, the so-called 'three-level' method of producing population inversion by 'pumping' with a powerful auxilliary source of radiation. The next year the method was applied by Nicolaas Bloembergen in America in a quantum amplifier.

Basov went on to develop the laser principle, and in 1958 introduced the idea of using semiconductors to achieve laser action. In the years 1960–65 he realized many of his ideas in practical systems. He has since done considerable theoretical work on pulsed ruby and neodymium-glass lasers, which are now in common use, and on the interaction of radiation with matter. In particular, he has studied the production of short powerful pulses of coherent light.

Bates, Henry Walter (1825–1892)
British naturalist and explorer

The son of a stocking-factory owner in the central English town of Leicester, Bates left school at 13 and was apprenticed to a hosiery manufacturer, but still found time for indulging his hobby of beetle collecting. In 1844 he met Alfred Wallace and stimulated the latter's interest in entomology. This led, three years later, to Wallace suggesting they should travel together to the tropics to collect specimens and data that might throw light on the evolution of species.

In May 1848 they arrived at Pará, Brazil, near the mouth of the Amazon. After two years collecting together they split up, and Bates spent a further nine years in the Amazon basin. By the time he returned to England in 1859, he estimated he had collected 14,712 species, 8000 of which were new to science.

While collecting Bates had noted startling similarities between certain butterfly species – a phenomenon later to be termed *Batesian mimicry*. He attributed this to natural selection, since palatable butterflies that closely resembled noxious species would be left alone by predators and thus tend to increase. His paper on this, *Contributions to an Insect Fauna of the Amazon Valley, Lepidoptera: Heliconidae* (1861) provided strong supportive evidence for the Darwin–Wallace evolutionary theory published three years earlier.

Darwin persuaded Bates to write a book on his travels, which resulted in the appearance of *The Naturalist on the River Amazon* (1863), an objective account of the animals, humans, and natural phenomena Bates encountered. Although one of the best and most popular books of its kind, Bates was to comment that he would rather spend a further 11 years on the Amazon than write another book. He became assistant secretary of the Royal Geographic Society in 1864.

Bateson, William (1861–1926) *British geneticist*

Born in the coastal town of Whitby in northeast England, Bateson graduated in natural sciences from Cambridge University in 1883, having specialized in zoology. He then traveled to America, where he studied the embryology of the wormlike marine creature *Balanoglossus*. He discovered that, although its larval stage resembles that of the echinoderms (e.g. starfish), it also has gill slits, the beginnings of a notochord, and a dorsal nerve cord, proving it to be a primitive chordate. This was the first evidence that the chordates have affinities with the echinoderms.

Back at Cambridge Bateson began studying variation within populations and soon found instances of discontinuous variation that could not simply be related to environmental conditions. He believed this to be of evolutionary importance, and began breeding experiments to investigate the phenomenon more fully. These prepared him to accept Mendel's work when it was rediscovered in 1900, although other British scientists were largely skeptical of the work. Bateson translated Mendel's paper into English and set up a research group at Grantchester to investigate heredity in plants and animals.

Through his study of the inheritance of comb shape in poultry, Bateson demonstrated that Mendelian ratios are found in animal crosses (as well as plants). He turned up various deviations from the normal dihybrid ratio (9:3:3:1), which he rightly attributed to gene interaction. He also found that certain traits are governed by two or more genes, and in his sweet-pea crosses showed that some characters are not inherited independently. This was the first hint that genes are linked on chromosomes, but Bateson never accepted T. H. Morgan's explanation of linkage or the chromosome theory of inheritance.

In 1908 Bateson became the first professor of the subject he himself named – genetics. However he left Cambridge only a year later and in 1910 became director of the newly formed John Innes Horticultural Institution at Merton, Surrey, where he remained until his death. He was the leading proponent of Mendelian genetics in Britain and became involved in a heated controversy with supporters of biometrical genetics such as Karl Pearson. The views of both sides were later reconciled by the work of Ronald Fisher. Bateson wrote a number of books, including the controversial *Materials for the Study of Variation* (1894) and *Mendelian Heredity – A Defence* (1902); he also founded, with R. C. Punnett, the *Journal of Genetics* in 1910.

Bauer, Georg *See* AGRICOLA, GEORGIUS.

Bawden, Sir Frederick Charles (1908–1972) *British plant pathologist*

Bawden was born in North Tawton, England, and was educated at Cambridge University, receiving his MA in 1933. From 1936 to 1940 he worked in the virus physiology department at Rothamsted Experimental Station, becoming the head of the plant pathology department in 1940. He was director of the station from 1958 until his death.

In 1937 Bawden discovered that the tobacco mosaic virus (TMV) contains ribonucleic acid, this being the first demonstration that nucleic acids occur in viruses. With Norman Pirie, Bawden isolated TMV in crystalline form and made important contributions to elucidating the structure of viruses and the ways in which they multiply. Bawden's work also helped in revealing the mechanisms of protein formation.

Bayer, Johann (1572–1625) *German astronomer*

Born in Rhain in Germany, Bayer was a lawyer by profession. In 1603 he published *Uranometria*, the most complete catalog of pretelescopic astronomy. To Tycho Brahe's catalog of 1602, he added nearly a thousand new stars and twelve new southern constellations. The catalog's main importance, however, rests on Bayer's innovation of naming stars by letters of the Greek alphabet. Before Bayer, prominent stars were given proper names, mainly Arabic ones such as Altair and Rigel. If not individually named, they would be referred to by their position in the constellation. Bayer introduced the scheme, which is still used, of referring to the brightest star of a constellation by 'alpha', the second brightest by 'beta', and so on. Thus, Altair, which is the brightest star in the constellation Aquila, is systematically named Alpha Aquilae. If there were more stars than letters of the Greek alphabet, the dimmer ones could be denoted by letters of the Roman alphabet and, if necessary, numbers.

Bayer's other proposed innovation – to name constellations after characters in the Bible – was less successful.

Bayliss, Sir William Maddock
(1860–1924) *British physiologist*

Bayliss was the son of a wealthy iron manufacturer in Wolverhampton. In 1881 he entered University College, London, as a medical student but when he failed his second MB exam in anatomy he gave up medicine to concentrate on physiology. He graduated from Oxford University in 1888, then returned to University College, where he worked for the rest of his life, holding the chair of general physiology from 1912. Bayliss was elected a fellow of the Royal Society in 1903 and was knighted in 1922.

He was chiefly interested in the physiology of the nervous, digestive, and vascular systems, on which he worked in association with his brother-in-law, Ernest Starling. Their most important work, published in 1902, was the discovery of the action of a hormone (secretin) in controlling digestion. They showed that in normal digestion the acidic contents of the stomach stimulate production of the hormone secretin when they reach the duodenum. Secretin is transported in the bloodstream to initiate secretion of digestive juices by the pancreas. In 1915 Bayliss produced what became a standard textbook on physiology, *Principles of General Physiology*.

Beadle, George Wells (1903–1989)
American geneticist

Beadle was born in Wahoo, Nebraska, and graduated from the University of Nebraska in 1926; he gained his PhD from Cornell University in 1931. He then spent two years doing research in genetics under T. H. Morgan at the California Institute of Technology. Beadle was a professor at the California Institute of Technology from 1946 until 1961 and was president of the University of Chicago from 1961 until 1968. In 1937 Beadle

went to Stanford University, where in 1940 he began working with Edward TATUM on the mold *Neurospora*. They used nutritional mutants, which were unable to synthesize certain essential dietary compounds, to determine the sequence of various metabolic pathways. Substances similar to the missing compound were added to the mutant mold cultures to find whether or not they could substitute for the lacking chemical. If the culture survived then it could be assumed that the mold could convert the substance into the chemical it needed, showing that the nutrient was likely to be a precursor of the missing chemical.

From this and similar work Beadle and Tatum concluded that the function of a gene was to control the production of a particular enzyme and that a mutation in any one gene would cause the formation of an abnormal enzyme that would be unable to catalyze a certain step in a chain of reactions. This reasoning led to the formulation of the one gene–one enzyme hypothesis, for which Beadle and Tatum received the 1958 Nobel Prize for physiology or medicine, sharing the prize with Joshua LEDERBERG, who had worked with Tatum on bacterial genetics.

Beaufort, Sir Francis (1774–1857)
British hydrographer

Beaufort was born in Navan in Ireland; his father was a cleric of Huguenot origin who took an active interest in geography and topography, publishing in 1792 one of the earliest detailed maps of Ireland. Beaufort joined the East India Company in 1789 and enlisted in the Royal Navy the following year, remaining on active service until 1812.

He proposed, in 1806, the wind scale named for him. This was an objective scale ranging from calm (0) up to storm (13) in which wind strength was correlated with the amount of sail a full-rigged ship would carry appropriate to the wind conditions. It was first used officially by Robert Fitzroy in 1831 and adopted by the British Admiralty in 1838. When sail gave way to steam the scale was modified by defining levels on it in terms of the state of the sea or, following George SIMPSON, wind speed.

In 1812 Beaufort surveyed and charted the Turkish coast, later writing his account of the expedition, *Karamania* (1817). He was appointed hydrographer to the Royal Navy in 1829. In this office Beaufort commissioned voyages to survey and chart areas of the world, such as those of the *Beagle* with Charles Darwin and the *Erebus* with Joseph Hooker. The sea north of Alaska was named for him.

Beaumont, (Jean Baptiste Armand Léonce) Elie de (1798–1874) *French geologist*

Beaumont, who was born and died in Canon, France, was educated at the Ecole Polytechnique and the School of Mines, Paris, and taught at the School of Mines from 1827, later becoming professor of geology there (1835). He is remembered chiefly for his theory on the origin of mountains. He published his views in 1830 in his *Revolutions de la surface du globe*, in which he argued that mountain ranges came into existence suddenly and were the result of distortions produced by the cooling crust of the Earth. Such a view fitted in well with the catastrophism of such zoologists as Georges CUVIER. Beaumont summarized his theories in his *Notice sur les systèmes des montagnes* (1852; On Mountain Systems).

Beaumont served as engineer-in-chief of mines for the period 1833–47. He also collaborated with Ours Pierre Dufrénoy in compiling the great geological map of France, published in 1840.

Beche, Sir Henry Thomas de la *See* DE LA BECHE, SIR HENRY THOMAS.

Becquerel, Antoine Henri (1852–1908) *French physicist*

Becquerel was born in Paris; his early scientific and engineering training was at the Ecole Polytechnique and the School of Bridges and Highways, and in 1876 he started teaching at the Polytechnique. From 1875 he researched into various aspects of optics and obtained his doctorate in 1888. In 1899 he was elected to the French Academy of Sciences, continuing the family tradition as his father and grandfather, both renowned physicists, had also been members. He held chairs at the Ecole Polytechnique, the Museum of Natural History, and the National Conservatory of Arts and Crafts, and became chief engineer in the department of bridges and highways.

Becquerel is remembered as the discoverer of radioactivity in 1896. Following Wilhelm Röntgen's discovery of x-rays the previous year, Becquerel began to look for x-rays in the fluorescence observed when certain salts absorb ultraviolet radiation. His method was to take crystals of potassium uranyl sulfate and place them in sunlight next to a piece of photographic film wrapped in black paper. The reasoning was that the sunlight induced fluorescence in the crystals and any x-rays present would penetrate the black paper and darken the film.

The experiments appeared to work and his first conclusion was that x-rays were present in the fluorescence. The true explanation of the darkened plate was discovered by chance. He left a plate in black paper next to some crystals in a drawer and some time later developed the plate. He found that this too was fogged, even though the crystals were not fluorescing. Becquerel investigated further and discovered that the salt gave off a penetrating radiation independently, without ultraviolet radiation. He deduced that the radiation came from the uranium in the salt.

Becquerel went on to study the properties of this radiation; in 1899 he showed that part of it could be deflected by a magnetic field and thus consisted of charged particles. In 1903 he shared the Nobel Prize for physics with Pierre and Marie CURIE.

Bednorz, Johannes Georg (1950–) *German physicist*

Bednorz was educated at the Federal Institute of Technology, Zurich, where he gained his PhD in 1982. He immediately joined the staff of the IBM Research Center in Zurich.

Here he was invited by his senior colleague, Alex MULLER, to collaborate in a search for superconductors with higher critical temperatures. Little progress had been made in this area for a decade and, as a young unknown scientist, Bednorz's decision to work in such an unpromising field appeared to many to be somewhat rash. Success, however, came relatively quickly and in 1986 Bednorz and Muller found a mixed lanthanum, barium, and copper oxide that had a critical temperature of 35 K ($-238°C$), which was significantly higher than that of any other superconductor known at the time. Their work was quickly recognized and in 1987 Muller and Bednorz were awarded the Nobel Prize for physics.

Behring, Emil Adolf von (1854–1917) *German immunologist*

Behring was born in Hansdorf in Germany. He graduated in medicine at Berlin University and entered the Army Medical Corps before becoming (in 1888) a lecturer in the Army Medical College, Berlin. In 1889 he moved to Robert Koch's Institute of Hygiene and transferred to the Institute of Infectious Diseases in 1891, when Koch was appointed its chief.

In 1890, working with Shibasaburo KITASATO, Behring showed that injections of blood serum from an animal suffering from tetanus could confer immunity to the disease in other animals. Behring found that the same was true for diphtheria and this led to the development of a diphtheria antitoxin for human patients, in collaboration with Paul Ehrlich. This treatment was first used in 1891 and subsequently caused a dramatic fall in mortality due to diphtheria.

Behring's success brought him many prizes, including the first Nobel Prize in physiology or medicine, awarded in 1901. He was appointed professor of hygiene at Halle University in 1894 and one year later moved to a similar post at Marburg. In 1913 he introduced toxin–antitoxin mixtures to immunize against diphtheria, a refinement of the immunization technique already in use. He also devised a vaccine for the immunization of calves against tuberculosis.

Beilstein, Friedrich Konrad
(1838–1906) *Russian organic chemist*

Born to German parents in the Russian city of St. Petersburg, Beilstein studied chemistry in Germany under Bunsen, Liebig, and Wurtz and gained his PhD under Wöhler at Göttingen (1858). He was lecturer at Göttingen (1860–66) and from 1866 professor of chemistry at the Technological Institute at St. Petersburg.

Beilstein's many researches in organic chemistry included work on isomeric benzene derivatives. He is better remembered, however, for his monumental *Handbuch der organischen Chemie* (1880–82; Handbook of Organic Chemistry), in which he set out to record systematically all that was known of every organic compound. He produced the second (1886) and third (1900) editions, after which the work was assigned to the Deutsch Chemische Gesellschaft, who have published it ever since.

Békésy, Georg von (1899–1972)
Hungarian–American physicist

Békésy, the son of a diplomat in the Hungarian capital, Budapest, studied chemistry at the University of Bern and physics at Budapest University, where he obtained his PhD in 1923. He immediately joined the research staff of the Hungarian Telephone Laboratory where he remained until 1946 while simultaneously holding the chair of experimental physics at Budapest University from 1939. He left Hungary in 1947, via the Swedish Karolinska Institute, for America, where he served first as a senior fellow in psychophysics at Harvard from 1949 to 1966 and finally as professor of sensory science at the University of Hawaii from 1966 until his death.

Békésy first worked on problems of long-distance telephone communication before moving to the study of the physical mechanisms of the cochlea within the inner ear. When he began this study it was generally thought, following the work of Hermann von Helmholtz, that sound waves entering the ear selectively stimulated a particular fiber of the basilar membrane; this in turn stimulated hairs of the organ of Corti resting on it, which transferred the signal to the auditory nerve.

Using the techniques of microsurgery, Békésy was able to show that a different mechanism is involved. He found that when sound enters the cochlea, a traveling wave sweeps along the basilar membrane. The wave amplitude increases to a maximum, falling sharply thereafter; it is this maximum point to which the organ of Corti is sensitive. For this insight into the mechanism of hearing, Békésy was awarded the 1961 Nobel Prize for physiology or medicine.

Bel, Joseph Achille Le *See* LE BEL, JOSEPH ACHILLE.

Bell, Alexander Graham (1847–1922)
British inventor

Bell's family were practitioners in elocution and speech correction and he himself trained in this. Born in Edinburgh, as a child he was taught mainly at home. For a short time he attended Edinburgh University and University College, London, after which he taught music and elocution at a school in Elgin, Scotland. It was in Elgin that he carried out his first studies on sound.

From 1868 Bell worked in London as his father's assistant, but after the death of his two brothers from tuberculosis, the family moved to Canada, where Alexander, who had also become ill, recovered. In 1871 he went to Boston where he gave lectures on his father's method of 'visible speech' – a system of phonetic symbols for teaching the deaf to speak. A year later he opened a school for teachers of the deaf. In 1873 he became professor of vocal physiology at Boston University.

With financial help from two of his deaf students, Bell experimented with the transmission of sound by electricity, aided by Thomas Watson, his technician. His multiple telegraph was patented in 1875 and, in 1876, the patent for the telephone was also granted. Bell's wife Mabel Hubbard, whom he married in 1877, was deaf. Later she founded the Aerial Experiment Association.

In 1880 he received the Volta Prize from France and the money was used to fund the laboratories in which an improved form of the gramophone was invented by Thomas Edison. Although best known as the inventor of the telephone, Bell investigated a wide range of related technical subjects, including sonar and various equipment for the deaf. In 1885 he bought land and established laboratories and a summer home on Cape Breton Island.

Bell, John Stuart (1928–1990) *British physicist*

Born into a poor family in the Northern Irish capital of Belfast, Bell was encouraged by his mother to continue his education after leaving school at sixteen. Consequently, after working for a year as a laboratory assistant in the physics department of Queen's University, Belfast, he enrolled as a student and graduated in 1949. Rather than pursue a PhD and burden his family further, Bell began work immediately at the Atomic Energy Research Establishment at Harwell. He worked initially on the design of CERN's first accelerator, the Proton Synchrotron. He was also given a year's leave of absence to work on a doctorate at Birmingham University. On his return to Harwell he turned to the theoretical study of elementary particles. Bell moved to CERN in Geneva in 1960 where he remained for the rest of his life. He was accompanied by his wife, Mary Bell, also a physicist, who worked at CERN on accelerator design.

In 1964 Bell published what for many has become the single most important theoretical paper in physics to appear since 1945; it was entitled *On the Einstein Podolsky Rosen Paradox*. The title referred to a thought experiment proposed by Einstein and others in 1935 sharply challenging the basis of quantum theory. He proposed a principle of reality stating that: "If, without in any way disturbing a system we can predict with certainty ... the value of a physical quantity then there exists an element of physical reality corresponding to this physical quantity." For example, electrons have a spin that can take one of two values, conveniently classed as positive or negative. Spin, like angular momentum, is conserved. Consequently, if a particle with zero spin decays into an electron/positron (e^-/p^+) pair, the two particles must have equal and opposite spins. Knowing, for example, that the electron has a negative spin, it can be inferred that the positron must have a positive spin.

But this, according to Einstein, gives us a way to measure the spin of a particle without disturbance. If the $p+$ spin is measured and found to be positive, the measurement may well disturb the $p+$, but on this basis the spin of the e^- can be concluded to be negative without in any way disturbing the

e^-. It follows from Einstein's reality principle that the negative spin of e^- is a real property of the electron. This view, however, conflicts with the usual interpretation of quantum mechanics, which sees the spin of the electron as a superposition of both spin states, a condition only resolved when the electron is observed and the wave function collapses. Nor can it be said that the state of the electron is in any way influenced by the outcome of the observation of the positron's spin for, as no signal can travel faster than the speed of light, instantaneous communication between separated particles is impossible.

The theoretical physicist is therefore presented with an uncomfortable choice. He or she can accept that electrons have intrinsic spin, in accordance with the reality principle and against quantum mechanics, or adopt what Einstein scornfully termed a "spooky action at distance." One weekend in 1964 Bell saw a way in which the matter could be resolved.

The spin of a particle is complicated in that it can be independently measured along three coordinates x, y, and z at right angles to each other. Further, a measurement of the electron's spin in the x direction will influence the spin of the positron in the x direction also; it will, however, have no effect on measurements along the y and z directions. Similar rules apply to measurements along the y and z axes. Bell argued that, if the reality principle is correct, then one would expect to find for a large number of observations:

$$x^+y^+ < (x^+z^+ + y^+z^+)$$

That is, the number of particles with a positive spin along the x and y axes, is smaller than the number found on both the x^+z^+ and y^+z^+ axes. The result is known variously as *Bell's inequality* and *Bell's theorem*. Although it proved impossible to test Bell's inequality in terms of the reactions described in the 1964 paper, later workers have produced equivalent formulations that are testable. The most convincing of these, the *Aspect experiment* performed by Alain Aspect of the Institute of Optics at the University of Paris in 1982, using correlations between polarized photons, established that the inequality did not hold. The conclusion seemed to be that nature preferred to act 'spookily' at a distance rather than using Einstein's reality principle.

At first Bell's five-page paper was ignored. Only when experimentalists such as John Clauser at Berkeley in 1969 took his work up did Bell's argument become widely known. Bell's views on his own work, more tentative and less extreme than those of many of his followers and popularizers, were collected in his *Speakable and Unspeakable in Quantum Mechanics* (1987).

Bell Burnell, (Susan) Jocelyn

(1943–) *British astronomer*

Born in Belfast, Northern Ireland, the daughter of the architect who designed the Armagh planetarium, Jocelyn Bell developed an early interest in radioastronomy. She was advised by Bernard LOVELL to study physics first and consequently found herself the only woman in a class of 50 physics students at Glasgow University. After graduating from Glasgow she moved to Cambridge, where she completed her PhD in 1969.

As part of her duties she visited the Mullard Radio Astronomy Laboratory each day, filled the inkwells and monitored the 100-foot length of paper chart produced daily by the 4.5-acre telescope. The sky was scanned every four days and, with little computer power available at that time, the data had to be analyzed by hand. One day she identified a strange signal. As it meant nothing to her, Bell simply put a question mark against it. When she noticed it again she drew it to the attention of her supervisor, Antony HEWISH. But nothing more was seen for a month. Perhaps, Hewish suggested, it had been a one-off event, a flare which had been and gone.

But after a month it reappeared. On examination Bell found the signals were equally spaced out at intervals of about 1.3 seconds. It was soon established that the signal was genuine and not an instrumental malfunction; nor was it produced by satellites or any terrestrial interference. The source was shown to lie outside the solar system and to have a sidereal motion. A more detailed examination of the signals revealed a regular sequence of pulses at intervals of 1.337 301 13 seconds with an accuracy better than one part per hundred million. Bell discovered a second signal coming from a different part of the sky in December, and a third and fourth the following month.

Once it had been decided that no LGMs, or 'Little Green Men', were involved in the signals, Hewish made the discovery public in 1968. The name 'pulsar' was soon coined and soon after Thomas GOLD proposed that the signals were emitted by a small, rapidly rotating neutron star. In an earlier age the first pulsar would have been known as *Bell's Star*; today it carries number CP 1919. Bell's work helped Hewish to gain the 1974 Nobel Prize for physics.

Bell herself married and became Bell Bur-

nell and was appointed in 1968 to a research fellowship at the University of Southampton, where she worked on gamma rays. In 1973 she moved to the Mullard Space Science Laboratory in London to work on x-ray astronomy. Bell moved again in 1982 to head the James Clerk Maxwell Telescope project at the Royal Observatory, Edinburgh. In 1991 she was appointed professor of physics at the Open University, Milton Keynes.

Belon, Pierre (1517–1564) *French naturalist*

Belon was born in Le Mans, France, and studied medicine in Paris. In 1540 he went to Germany to study botany, becoming a leading figure in the 16th-century revival of natural history that followed the great voyages, the invention of printing, and the new artistic realism of the Renaissance.

Between 1546 and 1549 Belon traveled in the eastern Mediterranean countries, comparing the animals and plants he observed with their descriptions by classical authors. The results were published as *Les Observations des plusieurs singularitez et choses mémorables trouvées en Grèce, Asie, Judée, Egypte, Arabie et autre pays éstranges* (1553; Observations of Many Singularities and Memorable Items in Greece, Asia, Judea, Egypt, Arabia, and Other Foreign Countries). On his travels, Belon was in the habit of investigating the birds and fishes that came to market, and in England he met the Venetian Daniel Barbaro, who had made many drawings of Adriatic fishes. From these sources Belon produced two books on fishes: *L'Histoire naturelle des éstranges poissons marins* (1551; The Natural History of Foreign Sea Fish) and *De aquatilibus* (1553). The first is notable for its dissertation on the dolphin, in which he identified the common Atlantic species with the dolphin of the ancients and distinguished it from the porpoise.

Belon's principal achievement is a history of birds, *L'Histoire de la nature des oyseaux* (1555; The Natural History of Birds). An illustrated book of the kind inspired by the drawings of Albrecht Dürer and Leonardo da Vinci, it describes about 200 birds, mostly of European origin. He drew attention to the correspondence between the skeletons of birds and man, an early hint of the discipline of comparative anatomy.

Belon was also interested in geology and botany and is reputed to have introduced the cedar of Lebanon into western Europe. He also established two botanical gardens in France and suggested that many exotic plants might be acclimatized and grown in temperate regions. In many ways a typical figure of the Renaissance, Belon's end was all too typical of that time, for he was murdered in the Bois de Boulogne in 1564.

Belousov, Vladimir Vladimirovich
(1907–) *Russian geologist and geophysicist*

Belousov, a Muscovite by birth, became head of the department of geodynamics at the Soviet Academy of Sciences, Moscow, in 1942 and was later (1953) made professor of geophysics at Moscow University. His main work has concentrated on the structure and development of the Earth's crust. In 1942 he put forward his theory on Earth movements, in which he proposed that the Earth's material has gradually separated according to its density and this is responsible for movements in the crust. He at first rejected theories on continental drift.

Belousov became chairman of the Soviet Joint Geophysical Committee in 1961. His works include *Principles of Geotectonics* (1975).

Benacerraf, Baruj (1920–) *American immunologist*

Benacerraf, who was born in the Venezuelan capital of Caracas, was brought up in France but moved to America in 1940, becoming naturalized in 1943. He studied at Columbia and the University of Virginia where he obtained his MD in 1945. He worked first at the Columbia Medical School before spending the period 1950–56 at the Hospital Broussais in Paris. He returned to America in 1956 to the New York Medical School where he served from 1960 to 1968 as professor of pathology. After a short period at the National Institute of Allergy and Infectious Diseases at Bethesda, Maryland, Benacerraf accepted the chair of comparative pathology at Harvard in 1970, a position he held until his retirement in 1991.

In the 1960s, working with guinea pigs, Benacerraf began to reveal some of the complex activity of the H2 system, described by George SNELL. In particular he identified the Ir (immune response) genes of the H2 segment as playing a crucial role in the immune system. This was achieved by injecting simple, synthetic, and controllable 'antigens' into his experimental animals and noting that some strains responded immunologically while others were quite tolerant. Such differential responses have so far indicated there are over 30 Ir genes in the H2 complex.

Later work began to show how virtually all responses of the immune system, whether to grafts, tumor cells, bacteria, or viruses, are under the control of the H2 region. Benacerraf and his colleagues continued to explore its genetic and immunologic properties and also to extend their work to the analogous HLA system in humans. This work may well be important in the study of certain diseases, such as multiple sclerosis and ankylosing spondylitis, which have been shown to entail defective immune responses.

In 1980 Benacerraf was awarded for this work, together with George Snell and Jean DAUSSET, the Nobel Prize for physiology or medicine.

Bentham, George (1800–1884) *British botanist*

Bentham, son of the naval architect Samuel Bentham, was born in the southwestern English county of Devon; he first became interested in botany at the age of 17, while living in France with his parents. There he read Augustin Pyrame de Candolle's revision of J. B. Lamarck's *Flore Française* and was much impressed with its analytical keys for plant identification. Thus began his consuming interest in plant taxonomy, on which he consistently worked during his leisure time.

From 1826 to 1832 he was secretary to his uncle, the famous jurist and philosopher, Jeremy Bentham, and studied for the bar at Lincoln's Inn. However, in 1833 he abandoned law for his growing botanical collection and library, which he generously presented to the Royal Botanic Gardens, Kew, in 1854. He then worked at Kew for the rest of his life.

His first botanical work, *Catalogue des plantes indigènes des Pyrénées et du bas Languedoc* (Catalog of the Indigenous Plants of the Pyrenees and lower Languedoc), was published in Paris in November, 1826. On his return to England he published *Outlines of a New System of Logic* (1827). Then beginning in the early 1830s, Bentham turned his attention more to botany and his first important work in this field, *Labiatarum Genera et Species*, appeared between 1832 and 1836. While at Kew he published his popular *Handbook of the British Flora* (1858) and contributed to the Kew series of colonial floras with his *Flora Hongkongensis* (1861) and the seven-volume *Flora Australiensis* (1863–78). In collaboration with Joseph HOOKER he produced his greatest work, the *Genera Plantarum* (1862–83), which remains a standard in plant classification.

Berg, Paul (1926–) *American molecular biologist*

Berg was born in New York City and educated at Pennsylvania State University and Western Reserve, where he obtained his PhD in 1952. He taught first at the School of Medicine at Washington University, St. Louis, moving to the University of Stanford in California in 1959, where he was professor of biochemistry from 1959 to 1970, and Willson professor of biochemistry from 1970.

In 1955 Francis Crick proposed his adaptor hypothesis, in which he argued that amino acids did not interact directly with the RNA template but were brought together by an adaptor molecule. Crick offered little information on the nature of such molecules, merely arguing that they were unlikely to be large protein molecules and suggesting that there might well be a specific adaptor for each of the 20 amino acids. In 1956 Berg successfully identified such an adaptor, later known as transfer RNA, even though he was then unaware of Crick's hypothesis. He found a small RNA molecule that appeared to be quite specific to the amino acid methionine.

Berg's name later became known to a much wider public with the publication in *Science* (24 July, 1974) of the 'Berg letter', written with the backing of many leading molecular biologists, in which he gave clear warning of the dangers inherent in the uncontrolled practice of recombinant DNA experiments. It had become possible, Berg stated, to excise portions of DNA from one organism, using specialized enzymes, and to insert them into the DNA of another organism. For example, the harmless microorganism *Escherichia coli*, found in all laboratories, could be implanted with active DNA from the tumor-causing virus SV 40 and perhaps allowed to spread throughout a human population with quite unpredictable results. Berg consequently proposed an absolute voluntary moratorium on certain types of experiment and strict control on a large number of others. An international conference was held in Asilomar, California, followed by the publication of strict guidelines by the National Institutes of Health in 1976. That such agreement could be reached and maintained, it has been claimed, was largely a result of the integrity and authority of Berg. Ironically Berg was awarded the Nobel Prize for chemistry in 1980 for the large part he played in developing the splicing techniques that made recombinant DNA techniques possible in the first place.

Berger, Hans (1873–1941) *German psychiatrist*

Berger was born in Neuses, Germany, and studied medicine at the University of Jena; having joined the university psychiatric clinic in 1897 as an assistant, he eventually served as its director and professor of psychiatry (1919–38). In his early work, he attempted to correlate physical factors in the brain, such as blood flow and temperature, with brain function. Disappointing results in this area made Berger turn to investigating the electrical activity of the brain. In 1924 he made the first human electroencephalogram by recording, as a trace, the minute changes in electrical potential measured between two electrodes placed on the surface of the head. Berger subsequently characterized the resultant wave patterns, including alpha and beta waves, and published his findings in 1929. The technique of electroencephalography is now used to diagnose such diseases as brain tumors and epilepsy. It is also used in psychiatric research and in diagnosing brain death.

Bergeron, Tor Harold Percival (1891–1977) *Swedish meteorologist*

Bergeron, who was born in Stockholm, studied at the universities of Stockholm and Leipzig. During the period 1925–28 he worked at the famous Geophysical Institute at Bergen before taking a teaching appointment at Oslo University (1929–35). He held various appointments in the Swedish Meteorological Institute and was elected to the chair of meteorology at Uppsala in 1947.

Bergeron is best known for his work on cloud formation and in 1935 published the fundamental paper *On the Physics of Clouds and Precipitation*. Clouds consist of minute drops of water, but these drops will only fall as rain when they coalesce to form sufficiently large drops. Bergeron considered various processes, such as electric attraction and collisions caused by turbulence, but dismissed these as being too slow and inefficient. He therefore proposed a mechanism in which both ice crystals and water droplets are present in clouds. The water droplets tend to evaporate and the vapor then condenses onto the crystals. These fall, melt, and produce rain. Thus all rain, according to Bergeron, begins as snow and without the presence of ice crystals in the upper reaches of clouds there can be no rain. This theory was supported by the experimental and observational work of Walter Findeisen in 1939 and became known as the *Bergeron–Findeisen theory*. It does not explain precipitation from tropical clouds where temperatures are above freezing point.

Bergeron also produced important work on weather fronts, methods of weather forecasting, and the growth of ice sheets.

Bergius, Friedrich Karl Rudolph
(1884–1949) *German industrial chemist*

The son of a chemicals industrialist, Bergius, who was born in Goldschmieden, Poland, gained his doctorate at Leipzig (1907) and worked with Hermann Nernst at Berlin and Fritz HABER at Karlsruhe, where he became interested in high-pressure chemical reactions. He was a professor at the Technical University at Hannover (1909–14) and then worked for the Goldschmidt Organization until 1945.

He is noted for his development of the *Bergius process* – a method of treating coal or heavy oil with hydrogen in the presence of catalysts, so as to produce lower-molecular-weight hydrocarbons. The process was important as a German source of gasoline in World War II. After the war Bergius lived in Austria and Spain before settling in Argentina as a technical adviser to the government, working on the production of sugar, alcohol, and cattle feed from wood. He shared the Nobel Prize for chemistry with Carl BOSCH in 1931.

Bergman, Torbern Olaf (1735–1785)
Swedish chemist

Bergman, who was born in Katrineberg, Sweden, studied at the University of Uppsala, at first reading law and theology before turning to science and mathematics. He was a prolific scientist, working in physics, mathematics, and physical geography as well as chemistry. After graduating with a master's degree in 1758, he became professor of mathematics at Uppsala in 1761 and later professor of chemistry and pharmacy in 1767.

Bergman carried out many quantitative analyses, especially of minerals, and he extended the chemical classification of minerals devised by Axel Cronstedt. He remained an adherent of the phlogiston theory and although he firmly supported the doctrine of constant composition his analyses were not as solidly based as those of his later compatriot Jöns BERZELIUS. His most influential work was probably *Disquisitio de Attractionibus Electivis* (1785; A Dissertation on Elective Attractions). He compiled extensive tables listing relative chemical affinities of acids and bases. Bergman gave early encouragement to Karl Scheele, some of whose work he published.

Bergmann, Max (1886–1944) *German organic chemist and biochemist*

Bergmann, who was born in Fuerth in Germany, studied in Munich and Berlin and gained his PhD under Emil Fischer in 1911. He worked as Fischer's assistant in Berlin until the latter's death in 1919. From 1921 to 1934 he was director of the Kaiser Wilhelm Institute for Leather Research, Dresden, from which he resigned on Hitler's coming to power. He then emigrated to America where he worked as a member of the Rockefeller Institute for Medical Research.

Bergmann's research interests were those of his teacher, FISCHER: carbohydrates and amino acids. In 1932 he discovered the carbobenzoxy method of peptide synthesis, the greatest advance in this field since Fischer's first peptide synthesis in 1901. In this method the amino group of amino acids is 'protected' by the carbobenzoxy group during condensation to form the peptide linkage and later freed by hydrolysis. Following Bergmann's work, many other protective groups have been used in peptide syntheses.

In America Bergmann investigated the specificity of proteinase enzymes and discovered (1937) that enzymes like papain were capable of splitting quite small peptides at precise linkages. The last three years of his life were devoted mainly to problems connected with the war.

Bergström, Sune (1916–) *Swedish biochemist*

Bergström was born in Stockholm and educated at the Karolinska Institute there, where he obtained his MD in 1943. In 1947 he was appointed to the chair of biochemistry at Lund. In 1958 he moved to a comparable position at the Karolinska Institute, which he left in 1981.

In the 1930s Ulf von Euler found an active substance in human semen capable of lowering blood pressure and causing muscle tissue to contract. He named it prostaglandin on the assumption that it came from the prostate gland. It soon became clear that there was not one such substance but a good many closely related ones with a variety of important physiological roles, but as they were produced in small quantities and rapidly broken down by enzymatic action, they proved to be very difficult to isolate and analyze. From 100 kilograms of rams' seminal vesicles, Bergström was able to extract a minute dose. To his surprise, however, he found the prostaglandin "extraordinarily active in virtually non-existent doses."

In the 1950s Bergström succeeded in extracting the prostaglandins referred to as PGD_2, PGE_2, and PGF_2. He went on to demonstrate that they were derived from arachidonic acid ($C_{20}H_{36}O_2$), a fatty acid present in the adrenal gland, liver, and brain. Bergström's discovery opened up the study of prostaglandins by allowing them to be produced in the laboratory. For his pioneering work in this field he shared the 1982 Nobel Prize for physiology or medicine with John VANE and Bengt SAMUELSSON.

Bernal, John Desmond (1901–1971)
British crystallographer

Bernal's family were farmers in Nenagh, now in the Republic of Ireland; his mother was an American journalist. He was educated at Cambridge University, where his first work on crystallography was done as an undergraduate on the mathematical theory of crystal symmetry. William Bragg offered him a post at the Royal Institution, which he joined in 1922.

Bernal was one of the most influential scientists of his generation. He had decided early in his career that x-ray crystallography would turn out to be the most likely tool to reveal details of the structure of matter. In addition to his intellectual mastery of the subject, he also possessed the ability to transmit his own enthusiasm to others and to attract around him a large number of highly talented and ambitious colleagues. To this group he was always known as 'Sage'.

His first success came in 1924 when he worked out the structure of graphite. He also began to work on bronze. In 1927 Bernal moved to Cambridge to a newly created lectureship in structural crystallography. While at Cambridge he worked on the structure of vitamin B_1 (1933), pepsin (1934), vitamin D_2 (1935), the sterols (1936), and the tobacco mosaic virus (1937).

Much of this research came not from Bernal alone; in most of his Cambridge studies he collaborated closely with Dorothy HODGKIN and many others came to work with Bernal, including Max PERUTZ, Francis CRICK, and Rosalind FRANKLIN.

In 1937 he was appointed professor of physics at Birkbeck College, London. With the outbreak of war in 1939 he joined the Ministry of Home Security and carried out with Solly Zuckerman an important analysis of the effects of enemy bombing. Later in the war he served as scientific adviser to Lord Mountbatten, the Chief of Combined Operations. Bernal's main duties were connected with the planned Normandy landings. He spent much time establishing the physical condition of the beaches the Allies would land on in 1944. Maps, he soon discovered, were inaccurate. "Do you realize," he would tell his staff, "no one knows where France is?" He was one of the first to land on the beaches on D-day.

Bernal's duties were performed despite the fact that he was one of Britain's best known communists, having joined the party in 1924. While many of his friends abandoned the party at some stage of their life, some because of the Stalinist purges, others because of the Molotov pact, and most of those remaining because of the Hungarian uprising, Bernal remained with the party throughout his life. He traveled frequently in Eastern Europe, Russia, and China, and he was probably the only significant Western scientist to give permanent support to the work of Lysenko.

In 1963 Bernal suffered the first of several serious strokes. He became progressively less mobile and in the last two years of his life, unable to speak, he was confined to a wheelchair.

Bernard, Claude (1813–1878) *French physiologist*

Bernard, the son of a poor wine grower from St. Julien, began writing plays to earn money but turned to medicine on the advice of a literary critic. His first experiences of medicine were discouraging but, following his appointment as assistant to François Magendie at the Collège de France, he began a period of extremely productive research. He drew attention to the importance of the pancreas in producing secretions for breaking down fat molecules into fatty acid and glycerine and showed that the main processes of digestion occur in the small intestine and not, as was previously thought, in the stomach. In 1856 he discovered glycogen, the starchlike substance in the liver, whose role is to build up a reserve of carbohydrate, which can be broken down to sugars as required; normally the sugar content of the blood remains steady as a result of this interaction. The digestive system, he found, is not just catabolic (breaking down complex molecules into simple ones), but anabolic, producing complex molecules (such as glycogen) from simple ones (such as sugars).

Bernard also did valuable work on the vasomotor system, demonstrating that certain nerves control the dilation and constriction of blood vessels; in hot weather blood vessels of the skin expand, releasing surplus heat, contracting during cold to conserve heat. The body is thus able to maintain a constant environment separate from outside influences. Apart from elucidating the role of the red blood corpuscles in transporting oxygen, Bernard's investigation of the action of carbon monoxide on the blood proved that the gas combines with hemoglobin, the effect being to cause oxygen starvation. He also carried out important work on the actions of drugs, such as the opium alkaloids and curare (curarine), on the sympathetic nerves.

Bernard's health deteriorated from 1860 and he spent less time in the laboratory. He thus turned to the philosophy of science and in 1865 published the famous *Introduction à la médecine expérimentale* (An Introduction to the Study of Experimental Medicine, 1927). The book discusses the importance of the constancy of the internal environment, refutes the notion of 'vital force' to explain life, and emphasizes the need in planning experiments for a clear hypothesis to be stated, which may then be either proved or disproved. On the strength of this work he was elected to the French Academy in 1869.

Bernoulli, Daniel (1700–1782) *Swiss mathematician*

Daniel was a son of Johann I Bernoulli. Of all the Bernoulli family he was probably the most outstanding mathematician and certainly the one with the widest scientific interests. Daniel, who was born in Groningen in the Netherlands, studied at the universities of Basel, Strasbourg, and Heidelberg. His studies, which reflected his already wide interests, included logic, philosophy, and medicine in addition to mathematics.

In 1724 Daniel produced his first important piece of mathematical research – a work on differential equations, which sufficiently impressed the European scientific community to earn him an invitation to the St. Petersburg Academy of Sciences as a professor of mathematics. Once installed in Russia he continued to pursue his varied interests and obtained a post at the academy for his friend Leonhard Euler. In 1733 he left Russia to return to Switzerland to take up a chair in mathematics at Basel. Bernoulli's wide interests continued to occupy him and during his time at Basel he also held posts in botany, anatomy, physiology, and physics.

In Switzerland Daniel did the work for which he is best known, namely his virtual founding of the modern science of hydrodynamics using Isaac Newton's laws of force. He published these ideas in his *Hydrodynamica* (1738). Apart from his work in fluid dynamics Daniel made distinguished contributions to probability theory and differential equations in mathematics, and to electrostatics in physics. He also laid the basis for the kinetic theory of gases. Like his uncle, Jakob I Bernoulli, Daniel corresponded voluminously with many scholars throughout Europe, thus extensively disseminating his new ideas.

Bernoulli, Jakob (*or* Jacques) I (1654–1705) *Swiss mathematician*

Jakob I was the first of the Bernoulli family of scientists to achieve fame as a mathematician. As with the two other particularly outstanding Bernoullis – his brother, Johann I and nephew, Daniel – Jakob I played an important role in the development and popularization of the then recently invented integral and differential calculus of Isaac Newton and Gottfried Leibniz. His particular contribution to the calculus consisted in showing how it could be applied to a wide variety of fields of applied mathematics.

Jakob I, who was born in Basel, Switzerland, began studying theology and in 1676 traveled through Europe where he met many of the important scientists of the day, such as Robert Boyle in England. He returned to Basel in 1682 where he began lecturing on mechanics and held a chair in mathematics at Basel University from 1687 until his death. Apart from his mathematical work he was an influential figure in the European scientific community through his voluminous correspondence.

His most important contributions to mathematics were in the fields of probability and in the calculus of variations. His work on probability is contained in his treatise the *Ars conjectandi* (1713; The Art of Conjecturing) in which he made numerous important contributions to the subject, among which was his discovery of what is now known as the 'law of large numbers'. The law has a number of forms. In effect it says that for an event of probability P in a large number of trials n the number of actual events approaches $n\,P$ as n increases. *Ars conjectandi* also contains Bernoulli's work on permutations and combinations.

The Bernoulli family were always prone to rivalry and Jakob I and his younger brother, Johann I, became involved in a controversy over the problem of finding the shortest path between two points of a particle moving solely under the influence of gravity. The result of this vigorous dispute was the creation of the calculus of variations, a field that Leonhard Euler was later to develop. In addition to this Jakob I did important and useful work in the study of the catenary, which he applied to the design of bridges.

Bernoulli, Johann (*or* Jean) I (1667–1748) *Swiss mathematician*

Johann I was the brother of Jakob I Bernoulli and was born in Basel, Switzerland. As in the case of several of the Bernoulli family Johann I's father did not encourage him to make a career of mathematics and he graduated in medicine in 1694.

Once he had abandoned medicine for mathematics he became chiefly interested in applying the calculus to physical problems. He played an important role as a propagandist for the calculus in general and in particular as a champion of Gottfried Leibniz's priority over Isaac Newton. Johann I held a chair in mathematics at Groningen, Holland, from 1695 and returned to Switzerland to take up a chair in mathematics at Basel on the death of his brother in 1705. Johann I's interests ranged over many fields outside mathematics including physics, chemistry, and astronomy. His mathematical work also included particularly important contributions to optics, to the theory of differential equations, and to the mathematics of ship sails.

Berthelot, Pierre Eugène Marcellin
(1827–1907) *French chemist*

The Parisian-born son of a doctor, Berthelot studied medicine at the Collège de France but became interested in chemistry, becoming assistant to Antoine-Jérôme Balard in 1851. He was professor of organic chemistry at the Ecole Supérieure de Pharmacie (1859–76) and professor of chemistry at the Collège de France (1864–1907).

Alcohols were Berthelot's early research interest and he introduced the terms mono-, di-, and polyatomic alcohols. He showed that glycerin was a triatomic alcohol and in 1854 he synthesized fats from glycerin and fatty acids. He carried out a great deal of work on sugars, which he recognized as being both polyhydric alcohols and aldehydes.

Berthelot was one of the pioneers of organic synthesis. Before his time, organic chemists had mainly been concerned with degradations of natural products but Berthelot, in keeping with his logical systematic nature, began with the simplest molecules; his syntheses included methane, methanol, formic acid, ethanol, acetylene, benzene, naphthalene, and anthracene. His favored techniques were reduction using red-hot copper and the silent electric discharge. His methods were somewhat crude and the yields were low. Berthelot's work on organic synthesis was published as *Chimie organique fondée sur la synthèse* (1860).

Arising from his interest in esterification, Berthelot studied the kinetics of reversible reactions. In 1862, working with Péan de Saint Gilles, he produced an equation for the reaction velocity. This was incorrect but it inspired Cato Guldberg and

Peter Waage to enunciate the law of mass action (1864).

In 1864 Berthelot turned to thermochemistry. In his book *Mecanique chimique* (1879) he introduced the terms 'endothermic' and 'exothermic' to describe reactions that respectively absorb and release heat. He also introduced the bomb calorimeter for the determination of heats of reaction and investigated the kinetics of explosions.

Berthelot's interest in agricultural chemistry was stimulated by his discovery of nitrogen uptake by plants in the presence of an electrical discharge. In 1883 he established an agricultural station at Meudon, where fundamental work on the nitrogen cycle was carried out. He looked forward to the day when poverty and squalor would be eradicated by the application of synthetic chemistry and new sources of energy.

Berthelot was a pioneer of historical studies in chemistry. In this he was influenced by his friend, the scholar Renan. In later life he became increasingly involved in affairs of state, mostly concerned with education, and in 1895–96 he served as foreign minister.

Berthollet, Comte Claude-Louis
(1748–1822) *French chemist*

Born in Talloires, France, Berthollet studied medicine at Turin and gained his MD in 1768. He went to Paris in 1772 where he began publishing chemical researches in 1776 and was elected a member of the Académie Française in 1780. His Italian medical degree was not recognized in France so he obtained a Parisian degree in 1778.

When Berthollet published his important paper on chlorine, *Mémoire sur l'acide marin déphlogistique* (1785), he was the first French chemist to accept Antoine Lavoisier's new system. Unfortunately, he also accepted Lavoisier's erroneous idea that chlorine contains oxygen. In 1784 Berthollet became inspector of a dyeworks and he discovered and developed the use of chlorine as a bleach. He published a standard text on dyeing *Eléments de l'art de la teinture* (1791).

Berthollet was neither a great manipulator nor a persuasive lecturer, but he did original work in many fields. He analyzed ammonia (1785), prussic acid (hydrogen cyanide, 1787), hydrogen sulfide (1798), and discovered potassium chlorate (1787). Although a convert, he remained skeptical about Lavoisier's oxygen theory of acidity: his analyses showed no oxygen in prussic acid or hydrogen sulfide, despite their undoubted acidity. Berthollet attempted to use his newly discovered potassium chlorate in gunpowder but it proved too unstable, destroying a powder mill at Essones in 1788. More productive were his analyses of iron and steel, which resulted in better quality steel.

After the French Revolution of 1789 Berthollet was a member of various commissions and in 1795 he became a director of the national mint. In 1798 he was entrusted by Napoleon with the organization of scientific work on the expedition to Egypt and he established an Institute of Egypt. On his return to Paris in 1799 Berthollet bought a large house at Arcueil in the suburbs of Paris, where he set up a laboratory and subsequently founded the Société d'Arcueil, which included Pierre de Laplace, Alexander von Humboldt, Jean Biot, Louis Thenard, and Joseph-Louis Gay-Lussac. At Arcueil, Berthollet produced his magnum opus, the *Essai de statique chimique* (1803), in which he propounded a theory of indefinite proportions. By 1808, following the work of John DALTON, Jöns BERZELIUS, and GAY-LUSSAC, indefinite proportions was decisively rejected, but Berthollet's idea that mass influences the course of chemical reactions was eventually vindicated in the law of mass action of Cato Guldberg and Peter Waage (1864).

Berthollet was made a senator in 1804 and in his later years was regarded as the elder statesman of French science.

Berzelius, Jöns Jacob (1779–1848)
Swedish chemist

Born in Väversunda, Sweden, Berzelius's early life was marked by a struggle to obtain a satisfactory education. In 1796 he entered the University of Uppsala but his studies were interrupted because of lack of funds. He began his chemical experiments without any official encouragement and from 1799 he worked during the summers as a physician at Medevi Springs where he analyzed the waters. He finally obtained his MD degree in 1802 with a dissertation on the medical uses of the voltaic pile.

After graduating Berzelius moved to Stockholm where he did research with **Wilhelm Hisinger** (1766–1852), a mining chemist. Their first success came in 1803 with the isolation of cerium but they were anticipated in this by Martin Klaproth. Berzelius later discovered selenium (1817), thorium (1828), and his coworkers discovered lithium (1818) and vanadium (1830). In 1807 Berzelius was appointed professor at the School of Surgery in Stockholm (later the Karolinska Institute), and he was soon able to abandon medicine and to concentrate on chemistry.

Berzelius was a meticulous experimenter and systemizer of chemistry. His early work was on electrochemistry and he formed a 'dualistic' view of compounds, in which they were composed of positive and negative parts. He was an ardent supporter of John DALTON's atomic theory, but, like LAVOISIER, believed in the importance of oxygen – thus, he argued for many years that chlorine contained oxygen.

In 1810 Berzelius began a long series of studies on combining proportions that established Dalton's atomic theory on a quantitative basis. This work led to tables of atomic weights that were generally very accurate, but he never accepted Amedeo AVOGADRO's hypothesis and this led to some confusion. He was a prolific author with about 250 papers to his credit. His *Lärbok i kemien* (1808–1818; Textbook of Chemistry) subsequently passed through many editions and was translated into most languages except English. Pupils who came to study with him included Friedrich Wöhler, Leopold Gmelin, and Eilhard Mitscherlich. His ideas on chemical proportions and electrochemistry are set out in *Essai sur la théorie des proportions chimiques et sur l'influence chimique de l'électricité* (1819; Essay on the Theory of Chemical Proportions and on the Chemical Effects of Electricity).

Berzelius's work in organic chemistry was less fruitful than the rest of his work but he improved organic analysis by introducing a tube of calcium chloride for the collection of water and the use of copper(II) oxide as an oxidizing agent. From 1835 Berzelius's rigid adherence to the dualistic theory proved obstructive to progress in organic chemistry, although it was given a certain plausibility by Wöhler and Justus von Liebig's discovery of the benzoyl radical (1832).

Berzelius introduced much of the familiar chemical apparatus, including rubber tubing and filter paper, and the modern chemical symbols, although these were little used in his lifetime. He had a knack of coining words for phenomena and substances – 'catalysis', 'protein', and 'isomerism' were all introduced by him.

Bessel, Friedrich Wilhelm (1784–1846)
German astronomer

Bessel was born into a poor family in Minden, Germany, and started work as a clerk. His interest in and aptitude for astronomy brought him to the attention of Heinrich Olbers, who obtained a position for him in the observatory at Lilienthal. Four years later he was entrusted with the construction of the observatory at Königsberg and appointed its director.

Bessel made many advances in astronomy. He cataloged the position of 50,000 stars down to the ninth magnitude between 15°S and 45°N and, using James Bradley's results, achieved new levels of accuracy. He also made careful observations of 61 Cygni and was able to detect a parallax of 30 arc seconds and to calculate the star's distance – the first such determination – as 10.3 light years. (The distance is now known to be 11.2 light years.) Although Bessel was the first to announce the detection of parallax (1838), Thomas Henderson had in fact measured it in 1832 in his observations of Alpha Centauri.

Bessel's other great discovery came after observing a slight displacement in the proper motion of Sirius, which he explained as the effect of an orbit around an unseen star, and announced in 1844 that Sirius was a double star system having a dark companion. Sirius B was detected optically by Alvan Clark in 1862. Bessel made a similar claim for Procyon whose companion was discovered optically in 1895. He also noted irregularities in the motion of Uranus and suggested that they were caused by an unknown planet, but died just before the discovery of Neptune.

In mathematics Bessel worked on the theory of the functions, named for him, that he introduced to determine motions of bodies under mutual gravitation and planetary perturbations. They still have a wide application in modern physics.

Bessemer, Sir Henry (1813–1898)
British inventor and engineer

Bessemer was the son of a mechanical engineer who had fled from the French Revolution. After leaving the village school in Charlton, where he was born, he worked as a type-caster, until the family moved to London in 1830. At the age of 17 he set up his own business to produce metal alloys and bronze powder. In 1843 he had an idea that made his fortune. On purchasing some 'gold' paint (made of brass) for his sister he was horrified at its high price. He designed an automatic plant to manufacture the paint and made sufficient money to pursue a career as a professional inventor.

During the Crimean War (1853–56) Bessemer invented a new type of gun with a rifled barrel. To manufacture the gun he needed a strong metal that could be run into a mold in a fluid state. At that time cast iron (pig iron) contained carbon and silicon impurities, which made it brittle. Wrought iron, which was relatively pure,

was made by a laborious process of refining pig iron. The temperature of the furnace, while sufficient to melt the pig iron, was not sufficient to keep the purer iron molten. The refined metal was extracted in lumps after which it was 'wrought'. Bessemer proposed burning away the impurities by blowing air through the molten metal. The *Bessemer converter* that he invented is a cylindrical vessel mounted in such a way that it can be tilted to receive a charge of molten metal from the blast furnace. It is then brought upright for the 'blow' to take place. Air is blown in through a series of nozzles at the base and the carbon impurities are oxidized and carried away by the stream of air.

Bessemer announced his discovery in 1856. At first his idea was accepted enthusiastically and within weeks he obtained £27,000 in license fees. However, though the process had worked for him, elsewhere it failed dismally because of excess oxygen trapped in the metal, and because of the presence of phosphorus in the ores. (By chance Bessemer's ore had been phosphorus-free.) His invention was dropped and Bessemer found himself the subject of much ridicule and criticism. Bessemer established his own steelworks in Sheffield (1859) using imported phosphorus-free iron ore.

Robert Mushet (about 1856) solved the problem of the excess oxygen by the addition of an alloy of iron, manganese, and carbon to the melt. Bessemer's process then worked provided nonphosphoric ores were used, but it took much time and determination to convince ironworkers after the initial failure. The invention eventually reduced the price of steel to a fifth of its former cost, made it possible to produce it in large quantities, and made possible its use in a variety of new products. The problem of dealing with the phosphorus impurities was solved in 1878 by Sydney Gilchrist Thomas and Percy Carlyle Gilchrist. Bessemer retired a rich man in 1873.

Best, Charles Herbert (1899–1978)
American–Canadian physiologist

Best, who was born in West Pembroke, Maine, graduated in physiology and biochemistry from the University of Toronto in 1921. In the summer of that year he gave up a lucrative holiday playing professional football and baseball to begin work with Frederick BANTING. Together they isolated the hormone insulin, and showed its use in the treatment of diabetes mellitus. Banting was furious when Best was not awarded a share in the 1923 Nobel Prize for physiology or medicine for the discovery of insulin.

Best remained at the University of Toronto and gained his MB in 1925. He was made head of the physiology department in 1929 and became director of the Banting and Best Department of Medical Research when Banting was killed in 1941. He continued the work on insulin throughout these years and in an important paper published in 1936 he suggested the administration of zinc along with insulin to reduce its rate of absorption and make it more effective over a longer time. He also studied cardiovascular disease and established the clinical use of heparin as an anticoagulant for blood in the treatment of thrombosis. He discovered the vitamin choline, which prevents liver damage, and the important enzyme histaminase, which takes part in local inflammation reactions, breaking down histamine.

Bethe, Hans Albrecht (1906–)
German–American physicist

Bethe, the son of an academic, was born in Strasbourg in France and educated at the universities of Frankfurt and Munich, where he obtained his doctorate in 1928. He taught in Germany until 1933 when he moved first to England and, in 1935, to America. In America he held the chair of physics at Cornell from 1937 until his retirement in 1975, serving in the war as director of theoretical physics at Los Alamos from 1943 to 1946.

Bethe soon established a reputation for his impressive knowledge of nuclear reactions. This was, in part, based on three review articles on nuclear physics he published in 1936 and 1937, which have been described as the first presentation of this field as a branch of science and which are sometimes known as 'Bethe's Bible'.

In 1938 Bethe was invited by Edward Teller to contribute a paper on astrophysics for a conference he was organizing. Bethe at first pleaded ignorance of the subject but, under pressure from Teller, he finally agreed to search for a relevant topic. He noted that most astrophysicists seemed to be puzzling over the origin of the chemical elements. He therefore decided to consider another issue, namely, the sources of stellar energy. He managed to find, as he reported in his 1939 paper *Energy Production in Stars*, "...the only nuclear reaction which gives the correct rate of stellar energy production within the limits of the theory."

Bethe was referring to the carbon cycle (or CNO cycle). The cycle begins with a hydrogen nucleus or proton (^{1}H) and a carbon-12 atom; it has six stages:

$$^{12}C + {}^1H \rightarrow {}^{13}N + \gamma$$

$$^{13}N \rightarrow {}^{13}C + e^+ + \nu$$

$$^{13}C + {}^1H \rightarrow {}^{14}N + \gamma$$

$$^{14}N + {}^1H \rightarrow {}^{15}O + \gamma$$

$$^{15}O \rightarrow {}^{15}N + e^+ + \nu$$

$$^{15}N + {}^1H \rightarrow {}^{12}C + He^4$$

Here, γ is a gamma ray, e^+ a positron, and ν a neutrino. The net result of the cycle is to convert four protons ($4{}^1$H) into a helium nucleus (He^4), while the carbon-12 atom remains available after step 6 to repeat the cycle once more. In the process 27 MeV (million electron volts) are released.

Although the amount of energy produced per cycle is modest, the large amount of stellar matter involved is sufficient to generate the enormous energies met with inside stars. Bethe's CNO cycle, however, gives no indication of the origin of the carbon-12 that starts the cycle. It was left to Fred HOYLE and his colleagues to resolve this issue in the 1950s. Bethe did, however, contribute, with Ralph ALPHER to George GAMOW's famous 1948 alpha-beta-gamma paper on the origin of the elements and the big bang. Unfortunately their paper advanced no further than the isotopes of hydrogen and helium.

Bethe has also played a significant part in public affairs. He quarreled in the 1940s with Teller on the need to build the hydrogen bomb and in the 1980s over the viability of the US Strategic Defense Initiative (known as 'Star Wars'). In 1958 he served as a delegate to the Geneva Conference which negotiated the first test-ban treaty. He also worked for the 1963 ban on atmospheric testing. More recently, in 1992, Bethe called upon the US and Russia to reduce their nuclear arsenals to a thousand warheads each.

Bethe has also continued to work at physics in his retirement. He has collaborated with John BAHCALL on several papers dealing with the solar-neutrino problem. He has also begun to tackle the problem of explaining how stars explode. Modern computer models, he complains, lead to moderate explosions when compared with the massive eruptions of a supernova.

For his earlier work on the theory of nuclear reactions, and for his contributions to astrophysics, Bethe was awarded the 1967 Nobel Prize for physics.

Biela, Wilhelm von (1784–1856)
Austrian astronomer

Born in Rossia, Austria, Biela was an army officer and an amateur astronomer. In 1826 he observed a comet with a short period of

6.6 years. When *Biela's comet* reappeared in 1845 it had split into two parts. It was last seen in 1852 when it presumably broke up, for in November 1872 what was probably its remains was seen as a fantastic meteor shower, which caused a worldwide sensation. The shower can still be seen faintly in Andromeda in late November. The meteors are sometimes called the Bielids or, alternatively, the Andromedids.

Biffen, Sir Rowland Harry
(1894–1949) *British geneticist and plant breeder*

Biffen was born in Cheltenham and, after graduating in natural sciences from Cambridge in 1896, joined a team investigating rubber production in Mexico, the West Indies, and Brazil. On his return he was appointed lecturer in botany at Cambridge and patented a method for handling rubber latex.

Biffen was inclined more toward applied than pure botany and joined the Cambridge School of Agriculture shortly after its foundation in 1899. He began conducting cereal trials in order to select improved types, and when Gregor Mendel's laws of inheritance were rediscovered in 1900, he realized immediately that they could be applied to improving plant-breeding methods. Biffen speculated that physiological as well as morphological traits would prove to be inherited in Mendelian ratios, and in 1905 demonstrated that this was true for resistance to yellow rust, a fungal disease of wheat.

Little Joss and Yeoman, two wheat varieties bred by Biffen, were unequaled for many years. In 1912 Biffen became director of the Plant Breeding Institute at Trumpington, a newly formed research center established by the government to promote Biffen's work and the application of scientific principles to plant breeding. Biffen was also professor of agricultural botany at the university from 1908 to 1931 and was instrumental in setting up the National Institute of Agricultural Botany at Cambridge. He was knighted for his services to agriculture in 1925.

Binnig, Gerd (1947–) *German physicist. See* ROHRER, HEINRICH.

Biot, Jean Baptiste (1774–1862) *French physicist*

Biot, a Parisian by birth, grew up during the French Revolution and at the age of 18 he joined the army as a gunner. He left a year later to study mathematics at the Ecole Polytechnique in Paris. On leaving he taught at a school in Beauvais but soon returned to Paris to become a professor of physics at the Collège de France.

In 1804 Biot made an ascent in a balloon with Joseph Gay-Lussac. They reached a height of three miles and made many observations, including the fact that the Earth's magnetism was not measurably weaker at that height.

For the next few years Biot collaborated with François Arago in many fields of research and they traveled to Spain together to measure the length of an arc of meridian, in order to calibrate a standard unit of length. Biot later went on a number of other important expeditions.

His most famous work was on optical activity, for which, in 1840, he was awarded the Rumford medal of the Royal Society. He was the first to show that certain liquids and solutions, as well as solids, can rotate the plane of polarized light passing through them. Biot suggested that this is due to asymmetry in the molecules. From this idea grew the technique of polarimetry as a method of measuring the concentration of solutions.

Birkeland, Kristian Olaf Bernhard
(1867–1917) *Norwegian physicist and chemist*

Birkeland was born in the Norwegian capital, Christiania (now Oslo), and studied in Paris, Geneva, and Bonn where he was a pupil of Robert Bunsen. In 1898 he was appointed to the chair of physics in Oslo University. He is remembered today for his discovery of a means for the fixation of nitrogen (the *Birkeland–Eyde process*).

In 1898 William Crookes in his presidential address to the British Association had pointed out that, given the world demand for nitrogenous fertilizers, the deposits of nitrates would rapidly be exhausted. As there is a virtually unlimited supply of nitrogen in the atmosphere the obvious solution was to find some way in which it could be used. Birkeland, in collaboration with Samuel Eyde, solved the problem in 1903 by passing air through an electric arc to form oxides of nitrogen, which could then be absorbed in water to give nitric acid. This was mixed with lime to give calcium nitrate. The process is particularly useful in regions (as in Scandinavia) where there is a plentiful supply of hydroelectric power, although the Haber process is now the main industrial method of fixing nitrogen.

Birkeland also spent much time studying the aurora borealis, making several expeditions and establishing a geophysical laboratory as far north as 70°. In 1896 he was the first to suggest the correct explanation that the aurora borealis could be the result of charged rays emitted by the Sun and trapped in the Earth's magnetic field near the poles. He derived this idea from the resemblance between the newly discovered cathode rays and the aurora.

Birkhoff, George David (1884–1944)
American mathematician

Birkhoff, who was born in Overisel, Michigan, studied at the Lewis Institute (now the Illinois Institute of Technology) from 1896 to 1902, and subsequently at the University of Chicago and at Harvard. In 1907 he obtained his PhD from Chicago and took up a teaching post at the University of Wisconsin, moving to Princeton in 1909. In 1912 he became assistant professor at Harvard and, in 1919, professor there, a post he held until 1939.

Birkhoff's mathematical interests were wide, and among the many areas to which he made notable contributions were differential equations, celestial mechanics, difference equations, and the three-body problem. His main field of research was mathematical analysis, especially applied to dynamics. In the course of his work on dynamical systems Birkhoff obtained a famous proof of a conjecture made by Henri Poincaré in topology, usually known as Poincaré's last geometric theorem. The ergodic theorem, a result concerned with the formal mathematics of probability theory, that Birkhoff proved in 1931, is another of his outstanding achievements. Modern dynamics received an enormous impetus from Birkhoff's work, and he also worked on the foundations of relativity and quantum mechanics.

Bishop, John Michael (1936–   )
American microbiologist

Bishop attended Gettysburg College and studied medicine at Harvard University. In 1962 he secured an internship at Massachusetts General Hospital in Boston, and in 1964 he moved to the National Institutes of Health, Washington DC, as research associate in virology, later becoming senior investigator (1966) and assistant professor (1968). He was appointed professor of microbiology and immunology at the University of California Medical Center, San Francisco, in 1972, and in 1981 he became director of the G. W. Hooper Research Foundation.

Bishop, working in collaboration with Harold VARMUS, demonstrated for the first time that cancer-causing genes (*oncogenes*) carried by certain viruses are derived from normal genes present in the cells of their host, known as *proto-oncogenes*. This work by the team at the University of California, published in 1976, led to the discovery of many more such cellular genes, and represented a major advance in cancer research. In recognition of this, Bishop and Varmus were jointly awarded the 1989 Nobel Prize for physiology or medicine.

Bittner, John Joseph (1904–1961)
American experimental biologist

Bittner, who was born in Meadville, Pennsylvania, gained his doctorate at the University of Michigan and spent the greater part of his academic life involved in cancer research. He was George Chase Christian Professor of Cancer Research at the University of Michigan and director of cancer biology of the University of Minnesota's medical school (1942–57), and latterly professor of experimental biology.

While working at Ben Harbor Research Station, Maine (1936), Bittner found that some strains of mice were highly resistant to cancer, while others were very prone to it. If the young of cancer-resistant mice were transferred to cancer-prone mothers they became cancerous, apparently via the mothers' milk, whereas cancer-resistant parents induced resistance in cancer-prone young. Bittner's discovery of viruslike organisms in the milk of cancer-prone parents suggested that these organisms are the cause of the cancer. Bittner's findings followed, and may be linked with, those of Francis Rous, who made the controversial finding that other viruslike organisms are, perhaps, the cause of sarcomas (tumors originating in connective tissue) in chickens. Such work does not, of course, suggest that all cancers are caused by viruses or viruslike organisms, merely that some forms may be.

Bjerknes, Jacob Aall Bonnevie (1897–1975) *Norwegian meteorologist*

Bjerknes was the son of **Vilhelm Bjerknes** (1862–1951), a theoretical physicist who developed some of the first mathematical models of atmospheric and oceanic motions. Jacob followed the example of his father in studying meteorology. Born in the Swedish capital, Stockholm, he was educated at the University of Oslo, where he obtained his PhD in 1924, and worked at the Geophysical Institute at Bergen with his father from 1917, remaining there when Vilhelm moved to Oslo in 1926.

During World War I Bjerknes worked with his father in establishing a series of weather observation stations throughout Norway. From the data collected, and working with other notable meteorologists, including Tor Bergeron, they developed their theory of polar fronts, also known as the *Bergen theory* or the *frontal theory*. They had established that the atmosphere is composed of distinct air masses possessing different characteristics and applied the term 'front' to the boundary between two air masses. The polar front theory showed how cyclones (low-pressure centers) originated from atmospheric fronts over the Atlantic Ocean where a warm air mass met a cold air mass.

In 1939 Bjerknes moved to America and, unable to return to occupied Norway, became professor of meteorology at the University of California where he continued to study atmospheric circulation. In 1952 he became one of the first to use space techniques for meteorological research when he used photographs of cloud cover taken by research rockets for weather analysis.

Bjerknes, Vilhelm Friman Koren

(1862–1951) *Norwegian meteorologist. See* BJERKNES, JACOB.

Black, Sir James Whyte (1924–   )
British biochemist

Black graduated from St. Andrews University in 1946 and, after a number of academic posts, joined ICI as a pharmacologist (1958–64). After working with Smith, Kline and French he became professor of pharmacology at University College, London (1973–77), before joining Wellcome as Director of Therapeutic Research (1978–84). Since 1984 he has been professor of analytical pharmacology at King's College Hospital, London.

Black has been associated with two important advances in pharmacology. In the 1950s he isolated the first beta blockers. These are compounds that prevent the stimulation of certain nerve endings (beta receptors) in the sympathetic nervous system, thus reducing heart activity. Beta blockers are widely used to treat hypertension and angina. His subsequent work has been concerned with the control of gastric ulcers and his discovery of the drug cimetidine, which reduces acid secretion in the stomach and is used to treat ulcers in the stomach and duodenum. For this work and his earlier work on beta blockers he was awarded the 1988 Nobel Prize for physiology or medicine.

Black, Joseph (1728–1799) *British physician and chemist*

Black, the son of a wine merchant, was born in Bordeaux, France, and studied languages and natural philosophy, and later, medicine and chemistry at Glasgow University (1746–50). He moved to Edinburgh in 1751, where he presented his thesis in 1754. Black published very little and the thesis, expanded and published as *Experiments upon Magnesia Alba, Quicklime, and some other Alcaline Substances* (1756), contained his most influential work. The paper in fact marked the beginning of modern chemistry. Black investigated quantitatively the cycle of reactions: limestone → quicklime → slaked lime → limestone, and showed that the gas evolved ('fixed air' or carbon dioxide) is distinct from and a constituent of atmospheric air, and is the cause of the effervescence of limestone with acids. He proved that mild alkalis will become more alkaline when they lose carbon dioxide and they are converted back to mild alkalis through reabsorption of the gas.

Black's other great discovery was that of latent heat (the heat required to produce a change of state). The concept of latent heat came to him in 1757 and the experimental determination of the latent heat of fusion of ice was made in 1761. The next year he determined the latent heat of formation of steam. Black also distinguished the difference between heat and temperature and conceived the idea of specific heat.

Black was professor of medicine and lecturer in chemistry at Glasgow (1756–66) and then professor of chemistry at Edinburgh for the rest of his life. Black's lectures, which he gave for over 30 years, were immensely popular and were published in 1803.

Blackett, Patrick Maynard Stuart

(1897–1974) *British physicist*

Blackett, the son of a London stockbroker, attended the Royal Naval College at Dartmouth. After serving with the navy in World War I, during which he fought at the Battle of the Falklands and Jutland, he entered Cambridge University, resigned his commission, and decided to become a scientist. He worked in the 1920s with Ernest Rutherford at the Cavendish Laboratory and, in 1933, was appointed professor of physics at London University. In 1937 he moved to Manchester, returning to London in 1953 to take the chair at Imperial College where he remained until his retirement in 1963. During World War II he worked on numerous advisory bodies and from 1942 to 1945 was director of operational research at the admiralty.

Just as Blackett was beginning his research career RUTHERFORD had announced his discovery of the atomic transmutation of nitrogen into oxygen by bombardment with alpha particles. Blackett, using a cloud chamber, took some 23,000 photographs containing some 400,000 alpha particle tracks in nitrogen and found in 1925 just eight branched tracks in which the ejected proton was clearly separated from the newly formed oxygen isotope.

Blackett continued with the Wilson cloud chamber and began, in collaboration with the Italian physicist **Giuseppe Occhialini** (1907–   ), to use it to detect cosmic rays. As the appearance of cosmic rays is unpredictable it was standard practice to set up the chamber to take a photograph every 15 seconds, producing a vast amount of worthless material for analysis. To avoid this Blackett introduced in 1932 the counter-controlled chamber. Geiger counters were so arranged above and below the chamber that when a cosmic ray passed through both, it activated the expansion of the chamber and photographed the ion tracks produced by the ray. Using this device they confirmed in 1933 Carl ANDERSON's discovery of the positron. They also suggested that the positron was produced by the interaction of gamma rays with matter, in which a photon is converted into an electron–positron pair. The phenomenon is known as pair production.

After the war Blackett's research interests moved from cosmic rays to terrestrial magnetism. Using new sensitive magnetometers his group began a major survey of the magnetic history of the Earth. By 1960 they could report that there had been considerable change in the relative positions of the continents over the past 500 million years, thus providing further support for the doctrine of continental drift.

Blackett was also active in public affairs and a noted opponent of nuclear weapons. In 1948 he was awarded the Nobel Prize for physics for "his development of the Wilson cloud chamber and his discoveries therewith in the field of nuclear physics and cosmic radiation." He was raised to the British peerage as Baron Blackett in 1969.

Blackman, Frederick Frost (1866–1947) *British plant physiologist*

Blackman, born in London the son of a doctor, studied medicine at St. Bartholomew's Hospital there, and natural sciences at Cambridge University. He remained in Cambridge for the whole of his career where he served as head of plant physiology until his retirement in 1936.

Blackman is mainly remembered for his classic 1905 paper, *Optima and Limiting Factors*, in which he demonstrated that where a process depends on a number of independent factors, the rate at which it can take place is limited by the rate of the slowest factor. This paper was stimulated by the research of one of his students, who showed that raising the temperature only increased the rate of photosynthesis if the level of illumination was high. Increased temperatures had no effect at low light intensities.

He had earlier, in 1895, provided convincing experimental support for the long held view that gaseous exchange between the leaves and the atmosphere takes place through the stomata, the pores on the leaf's surface.

Blagden, Sir Charles (1748–1820) *English physician and chemist*

Blagden, born in Wotton under Edge, studied medicine at Edinburgh, where one of his professors was Joseph Black, and graduated in 1768. He became a medical officer in the British army in the same year and theoretically remained in that post until 1814. From 1782 to 1789 Blagden was assistant to Henry Cavendish, a post that involved him in the so-called 'water controversy', a dispute between James Watt, Cavendish, and Antoine Lavoisier concerning the priority of the discovery of the synthesis of water from its elements. Blagden was friendly with the great French scientists of the day, especially Claude Berthollet, and on a visit to Paris in 1783 he told Lavoisier of Cavendish's synthesis, an experiment that Lavoisier repeated in Blagden's presence. Blagden became secretary of the Royal Society soon afterward, in which capacity he published Watt's papers on the same subject. The dispute was largely artificial because the three men drew different conclusions from their work.

Blagden's own scientific work was concerned with the freezing of mercury, the supercooling of water, and the freezing of salt solutions. He discovered, in 1788, that the lowering of the freezing point of a solution is proportional to the concentration of the solute present. This became known as *Blagden's law*. Blagden was knighted in 1792.

Blakeslee, Albert Francis (1874–1954) *American botanist and geneticist*

Blakeslee was born at Geneseo in New York State and educated at the Wesleyan University, Connecticut, graduating in 1896. He taught science for four years before entering Harvard to do post-graduate research, gaining his PhD in 1904. In this year he discovered that the bread molds (*Mucorales*) exhibit heterothallism (self sterility) and spent the next two years in Germany making further investigations on the fungi.

From 1907 to 1914 Blakeslee was professor of botany at Connecticut Agricultural College. In 1915 he moved to the department of genetics at the Carnegie Institution, where he remained until 1941. In 1924 he began work on the alkaloid colchicine, which is found in the autumn crocus, and 13 years later he discovered that plants soaked in this alkaloid had multiple sets of chromosomes in their cells. Such plants, termed polyploids, often exhibit gigantism and this discovery proved of immediate use in the horticultural industry in producing giant varieties of popular ornamentals. More importantly, however, colchicine often converts sterile hybrids into fertile polyploids and is therefore an invaluable tool in crop-breeding research.

Other contributions made by Blakeslee to plant genetics include his study of inheritance in the jimson weed and his research on embryo culture as a method of growing hybrid embryos that would abort if left on the parent plant.

Bloch, Felix (1905–1983) Swiss–American physicist

Bloch was born in Zürich, Switzerland, and educated at the Federal Institute of Technology there and at the University of Leipzig, where he obtained his PhD in 1928. He taught briefly in Germany and in 1933 moved to America, via various institutions in Italy, Denmark, and Holland. In 1934 he joined the Stanford staff, remaining there until his retirement in 1971 and serving from 1936 onward as professor of physics. He also served briefly (1954–55) as first director of the international laboratory for high-energy physics in Geneva, known as CERN.

In 1946, Bloch and Edward PURCELL independently introduced the technique of nuclear magnetic resonance (NMR). This utilizes the magnetic property of a nucleus, which will interact with an applied magnetic field such that it takes certain orientations in the field (a quantum mechanical effect known as space quantization). The different orientations have slightly different energies and a nucleus can change from one state to another by absorbing a photon of electromagnetic radiation (in the radiofrequency region of the spectrum). The technique was used initially to determine the magnetic moment (i.e. the torque felt by a magnet in a magnetic field at right angles to it) of the proton and of the neutron. It has since, however, been developed into a powerful tool for the analysis of the more complex molecules of organic chemistry. The energy states of the nucleus are affected slightly by the surrounding electrons, and the precise frequency at which a nucleus absorbs depends on its position in the molecule. In 1952 Bloch shared the Nobel Prize for physics with Purcell for this work on NMR.

Bloch worked extensively in the field of solid-state physics developing a detailed theory of the behavior of electrons in crystals and revealing much about the properties of ferromagnetic domains.

Bloch, Konrad Emil (1912–)
German–American biochemist

Born in Neisse (now Nysa in Poland), Bloch was educated at the Technical University, Munich, and – after his emigration to America in 1936 – at Columbia University, New York, where he obtained his PhD in 1938. He then taught at Columbia until 1946, when he moved to the University of Chicago, becoming professor of biochemistry there in 1950. In 1954 Bloch accepted the position of Higgins Professor of Chemistry at Harvard, a post he retained until his retirement in 1978.

In 1940 the important radioisotope carbon-14 was discovered by Martin Kamen and Samuel Ruben. Bloch was quick to see that it could be used to determine the biosynthesis of such complex molecules as cholesterol, a basic constituent of animal tissues characterized by four rings of carbon atoms. Thus in 1942, in collaboration with David Rittenberg, Bloch was able to confirm the earlier supposition that cholesterol was partly derived from the two-carbon acetate molecule.

The many steps through which acetate develops into the 27-carbon cholesterol took years of analysis to establish. The breakthrough came in 1953, when Bloch and R. Langdon identified squalene as an intermediate in cholesterol synthesis. Squalene, a terpene with an open chain of 30 carbon atoms, initiates the folding necessary to produce the four rings of cholesterol. For this work Bloch shared the 1964 Nobel Prize for physiology or medicine with Feodor LYNEN.

Bloembergen, Nicolaas (1920–)
Dutch–American physicist

Bloembergen was born in Dordrecht in the Netherlands and was educated at the universities of Utrecht and Leiden, where he obtained his PhD in 1948. He moved to America soon afterward, joined the Harvard staff in 1949, and served from 1957 as Gordon McKay Professor of Applied Physics;

from 1974 to 1980 he was also Rumford Professor of Physics. He became Gerhard Gade university professor in 1980, a post he held until his retirement in 1990.

In the mid 1950s Bloembergen introduced a simple yet effective modification to the design of the maser. First built by Charles Townes in 1953, the early maser could only work intermittently: once the electrons in the higher energy level had been stimulated they would fall down to the lower energy level and nothing further could happen until they had been raised to the higher level once more. Bloembergen developed the three-level and multilevel masers, which were also worked on by Nikolai Basov and Aleksandr Prokhorov in the Soviet Union. In the three-level maser, electrons are pumped to the highest level and stimulated. They consequently emit microwave radiation and fall down to the middle level where they can once more be stimulated and emit energy of a lower frequency. At the same time more electrons are being pumped from the lowest to the highest level making the process continuous. Bloembergen has worked extensively on nonlinear optics – i.e. on effects produced by high intensities of radiation. He has particularly investigated the use of lasers to excite or break particular bonds in a chemical reaction. For his work he shared the 1981 Nobel Prize for physics with Arthur Schawlow (and Kai Siegbahn).

Bloembergen wrote *Nuclear Magnetic Relaxations* (1948) and *Nonlinear Optics* (1965).

Blumberg, Baruch Samuel (1925–)
American physician

Blumberg was born in New York City and studied physics and mathematics at Union College, Schenectady, and at Columbia, where, after a year, he changed to medical studies. He received his MD from Columbia in 1951 and his PhD in biochemistry from Oxford University in 1957. After working at the National Institutes of Health in Bethesda from 1957 until 1964 Blumberg was appointed professor of medicine at the University of Pennsylvania, a position he held until his retirement in 1994.

In 1963, while examining literally thousands of blood samples in a study of the variation in serum proteins in different populations, Blumberg made the important discovery of what soon became known as the 'Australian antigen'. He found in the blood of an Australian aborigine an antigen that reacted with an antibody in the serum of an American thalassemia patient. It turned out that the antigen was found frequently in the serum of those suffering from viral hepatitis, hepatitis B, and was in fact a hepatitis B antigen.

It was hoped that from this discovery techniques for the control of the virus would develop. It certainly made it easier to screen blood for transfusion for the presence of the hepatitis virus; it also permitted the development of a vaccine, from the serum of those with the Australian antigen. Blumberg has also suggested that the virus is involved in primary liver cancer.

For his work on the Australian antigen Blumberg shared the 1976 Nobel Prize for physiology or medicine with Carleton Gajdusek.

Bode, Johann Elert (1747–1826)
German astronomer

Born in Hamburg, Germany, Bode was the director of the Berlin Observatory and popularized a discovery made earlier in 1772 by Johann Titius of Wittenberg. This was a simple but inexplicable numerical rule governing the distance of the planets from the Sun measured in astronomical units (the mean distance of the Earth from the Sun). The rule, known as *Bode's law*, is to take the series 0, 3, 6, 12, 24 ..., add 4 to each member, and divide by 10. The result is the distance in astronomical units of the planets from the Sun. The law and its application can be tabulated and, provided that the asteroids are counted as a single planet, quite an impressive fit can be achieved. It breaks down for Neptune and is hopelessly wrong for Pluto. It played a role in the discovery of Neptune by Urbain Le Verrier in 1846. It is not known whether the law is simply a pure coincidence, or whether it is a consequence of the way in which the solar system formed.

Bodenstein, Max Ernst August
(1871–1942) *German physical chemist*

Bodenstein, who was born in Magdeburg, Germany, gained his doctorate at Heidelberg (1893). He subsequently worked with Wilhelm Ostwald at Leipzig before becoming a professor at Hannover (1908–23) and at the Institute for Physical Chemistry, Berlin (1923–36). He made a series of classic studies on the equilibria of gaseous reactions, especially that of hydrogen and iodine (1897). His technique was to mix hydrogen and iodine in a sealed tube, which he placed in a thermostat and held at a constant high temperature. The reaction eventually reached an equilibrium, at which the rate of formation of hydrogen iodide (HI) was equal to the rate of decomposition to the original reactants:

$$H_2 + I_2 \leftrightarrow 2HI$$

The equilibrium mixture of H_2, I_2, and HI was 'frozen' by rapid cooling, and the amount of hydrogen iodide present could be analyzed. Using different amounts of initial reactants, Bodenstein could vary the amounts present at equilibrium and verify the law of chemical equilibrium proposed in 1863 by Cato Guldberg and Peter Waage.

Bodenstein also worked in photochemistry and was the first to show how the large yield per quantum for the reaction of hydrogen and chlorine could be explained by a chain reaction.

Bohm, David Joseph (1917–1992)
American physicist

Bohm's father, an Austrian immigrant, ran a successful furniture business. Born in Wilkes-Barre, Pennsylvania, Bohm attended Penn State University before moving to the University of California, Berkeley, where he gained his PhD in 1943. After a period working on the development of the atomic bomb under the supervision of Oppenheimer at the Radiation Laboratory, Berkeley, Bohm joined the Princeton physics faculty in 1947. Here he ran into political trouble; called to testify before the House Un-American Activities Committee he pleaded the Fifth Amendment and refused to give evidence against his colleagues. He was cited for contempt and threatened with prison. When his Princeton position expired in 1951, Bohm found himself unemployable in the USA. Oppenheimer advised him to leave the country and he worked in Brazil at São Paulo University (1951–55) and in Israel at Haifa (1955–57). He then settled in Britain, working first at Bristol University as a research fellow before being appointed professor of theoretical physics at Birkbeck College, London (1961), a post he held until his retirement in 1983.

In 1951 Bohm published a much respected textbook, *Quantum Theory*. He was, however, unhappy with the traditional account of quantum theory. His concern lay not with its lack of determinism, but with the fact that "it had no place in it for an adequate notion of an independent actuality." Electrons could be both wave and particle and, because of Heisenberg's uncertainty principle, we can never simultaneously know an electron's position and momentum. One way around this difficulty is to suppose that quantum theory presents an imperfect view of nature, with a more complete and deterministic underlying reality. Such approaches, it was widely believed, had been shown by VON NEUMANN in 1931 to be incompatible with quantum theory. Against this

Bohm argued that von Neumann's proof was entirely mathematical and consequently based on axioms and presuppositions that were always open to question. In the 1950s he began to seek for the 'hidden variables', which would allow him better to understand quantum theory.

He proposed that the electron is a real particle with a definite position and momentum, but it is also connected with a 'pilot wave'. Bohm regarded this new wave as real and known only by its effects on the electron. Electrons, of course, in Bohm's theory still display wave–particle duality because of the effect of the pilot wave. As the wave reacts with both the electron and the environment, the wave–particle complex responds accordingly to a particular type of measurement. It is a necessary consequence of this view that signals can be conveyed instantaneously from the pilot wave to the electron.

In a later work, *Wholeness and the Implicate Order* (1980), Bohm sought to establish a more general position. Bohm was inspired by an analogy with a device that he saw at a science exhibition. Two concentric glass cylinders have a layer of glycerine between them. If a localized spot of ink is placed in the glycerine and one cylinder is rotated with respect to the other, the ink is smeared out and the spot of ink disappears (in Bohm's terminology, it is 'enfolded' or 'implicated'). Turning the cylinder in the opposite direction brings the ink back into a spot (it is 'unfolded' or 'explicate'). Thus, while order may appear to have been lost in a system, it may in fact be enfolded in the system, and could be unfolded under the right conditions.

Bohr, Aage Niels (1922–) *Danish physicist*

Bohr, the son of Niels Bohr, was born in the Danish capital, Copenhagen, and educated at the university there. After postgraduate work at the University of London from 1942 to 1945 he returned to Copenhagen to the Institute of Theoretical Physics, where he served as professor of physics from 1958 to 1981.

When Bohr began his research career the shell model of the nucleus of Maria GOEPPERT-MAYER and Hans Jensen had just been proposed in 1949. Almost immediately Leo James RAINWATER produced experimental results at odds with the predictions derived from a spherical shell model, and proposed that some nuclei were distorted rather than perfectly spherical.

Bohr, in collaboration with Ben MOTTELSON, followed Rainwater's work by proposing their collective model of nuclear structure (1952), so called because it was argued that the distorted nuclear shape was produced by the participation of many nucleons. For this work Bohr shared the 1975 Nobel Prize for physics with Rainwater and Mottelson.

Bohr, Niels Hendrik David

(1885–1962) *Danish physicist*

Niels Bohr came from a very distinguished scientific family in Copenhagen, Denmark. His father, Christian, was professor of physiology at Copenhagen and his brother Harald was a mathematician of great distinction. (His own son, Aage, was later to win the 1975 Nobel Prize for physics.) Bohr was educated at the University of Copenhagen where he obtained his PhD in 1911. After four productive years with Ernest Rutherford in Manchester, Bohr returned to Denmark becoming in 1918 director of the newly created Institute of Theoretical Physics.

Under Bohr (who after Albert Einstein was probably the most respected theoretical physicist of the century) the institute became one of the most exciting research centers in the world. A generation of physicists from around the world were to pass through it and eventually it was to bestow on the orthodox account of quantum theory the apt description of the 'Copenhagen interpretation'.

In 1913 Bohr published a classic paper, *On the Constitution of Atoms and Molecules*, in which he used the quantum of energy, h, introduced into physics by Max Planck in 1900, to rescue Rutherford's account of atomic structure from a vital objection and also to account for the line spectrum of hydrogen. The first problem Bohr faced was to explain the stability of the atom. Rutherford's 1911 model of the atom with electrons orbiting a central nucleus (the so-called planetary model) was theoretically unstable. This was because, unlike planets orbiting the Sun, electrons are charged particles, which, according to classical physics, should radiate energy and consequently spiral in toward the nucleus.

Bohr began by assuming that there were 'stationary' orbits for the electrons in which the electron did not radiate energy. He further assumed that such orbits occurred when the electron had definite values of angular momentum, specifically values $h/2\pi$, $2h/2\pi$, $3h/2\pi$, etc., where h is Planck's constant. Using this idea he was able to calculate energies E_1, E_2, E_3, etc., for possible orbits of the electron. He further postulated that emission of light occurred when an electron moved from one orbit to a lower-energy orbit; absorption was accompanied by a change to a higher-energy orbit. In each case the energy difference produced radiation of energy $h\nu$, where ν is the frequency. In 1913 he realized that, using this idea, he could obtain a theoretical formula similar to the empirical formula of Johannes Balmer for a series of lines in the hydrogen spectrum. Bohr received the Nobel Prize for physics for this work in 1922. The Bohr theory was developed further by Arnold SOMMERFELD.

Bohr also made other major contributions to this early development of quantum theory. The 'correspondence principle' (1916) is his principle that the quantum-theory description of the atom corresponds to classical physics at large magnitudes.

In 1927, Bohr publicly formulated the 'complementarity principle'. This argued against continuing attempts to eliminate such supposed difficulties as the wave–particle duality of light and many other atomic phenomena. His starting point was the impossibility to distinguish satisfactorily between the actual behavior of atomic objects, and their interaction with the measuring instruments that serve to define the conditions under which the phenomena appear. Examine light with one instrument, the argument went, and it undulates like a wave; select another and it scatters like a particle. His conclusion was that evidence obtained under different experimental conditions cannot be comprehended within a single picture, but must be regarded as complementary in the sense that only the totality of the phenomenon exhausts the possible information about the objects. It was a principle Bohr remained faithful to, even representing it on his coat of arms in 1947 with the motto *Contraria sunt complementa* above the Yin/Yang symbols. Together with the indeterminacy principle of Werner Heisenberg and the probability waves of Max Born, this principle emerged from the 1930 Solvay conference (the last one Einstein attended) as the most authoritative and widely accepted theory to describe atomic phenomena.

Bohr also made major contributions to the work on radioactivity that led to the discovery and exploitation of nuclear fission. Bohr's liquid-drop model of the nucleus, which was published in 1936, provided the basis for the first theoretical account of fission worked out in collaboration with John Wheeler in 1939. It was also Bohr who, in 1939, made the crucial suggestion that fission was more likely to occur with the rarer isotope uranium–235 than the more common variety uranium–238.

In 1943 Bohr, who had a Jewish mother, felt it necessary to escape from occupied Denmark and eventually made his way to Los Alamos in America where he served as a consultant on the atomic bomb project. He was quick to appreciate the consequences of using such weapons and in 1944 made an early approach to Roosevelt and Churchill proposing that such obvious danger could perhaps be used to bring about a rapprochement between Russia and the West. Scientists were in a unique position, he argued, in having the Soviet contacts and the knowledge to make the first approach. Much of Bohr's time after the war was spent working, among scientists, for adequate controls of nuclear weapons and in 1955 he organized the first Atoms for Peace conference in Geneva.

Bok, Bart Jan (1906–1983) *Dutch–American astronomer*

Bok, who was born at Hoorn in the Netherlands, studied at the universities of Leiden (1924–27) and Groningen (1927–29) and obtained his PhD from Groningen in 1932. He had moved to America in 1929, becoming naturalized in 1938, and served at Harvard from 1929 to 1957 with the appointment of professor of astronomy from 1947 onward. Bok spent the period 1957–66 in Australia as director of the Mount Stromlo Observatory, Canberra, and professor of astronomy at the Australian National University. He returned to America in 1966 to become director of the Steward Observatory, Arizona, until 1970 and professor of astronomy (from 1974 emeritus professor) at the University of Arizona, Tucson.

Bok's major interest was the structure of our galaxy, the Milky Way. With his wife, Priscilla, he published a survey of the subject: *The Milky Way* (1941). Although it had been long assumed that the Milky Way had a spiral structure it was not until Walter Baade identified in the 1940s the hot young O and B stars of the Andromeda galaxy as spiral markers that such a conjecture could be confirmed. The actual structure was first worked out in some detail by William MOR-GAN. The existence of 21-centimeter radio signals from clouds of neutral hydrogen in the galaxy was predicted by Hendrik VAN DE HULST and their discovery in 1951 provided a second tracer. It was clear to Bok by the late 1950s that the radio data, which were expected to support the optical picture, instead contradicted it. He consequently attempted to harmonize the two structures by modifying Morgan's somewhat elliptical arms, making them much more spherical, and giving more emphasis to the Carina–Centaurus arm.

Bok's name is also associated with his discovery in 1947 of small dark circular clouds visible against a background of stars or luminous gas and since known as *Bok globules*. Since they are thought to be precursors of stars, as Bok himself conjectured, they have received considerable attention in recent years.

Boltwood, Bertram Borden
(1870–1927) *American chemist and physicist*

Boltwood, the son of a lawyer, was born in Amherst, Massachusetts, and educated at Yale and the University of Munich. Apart from the period 1900–06, when he served as a private consultant, and the year 1909–10, which he spent in England with Ernest Rutherford at the University of Manchester, he devoted the whole of his academic career to Yale. He occupied the chair of physics (1906–10), the chair of radioactivity (1910–18), and the chair of chemistry from 1918 until his death by suicide in 1927.

Boltwood made a number of contributions to the study of radioactivity. The radioactivity of uranium and radium had been discovered in the 1890s by Henri BEC-QUEREL and Marie CURIE. Starting in 1902 RUTHERFORD and Frederick Soddy had shown that radium, uranium, and other radioactive elements broke down in a quite complicated sequence into other elements. Boltwood worked on the breakdown of uranium into radium, a process that Soddy had not found easy to demonstrate. Soddy had tried to obtain radium directly from uranium in 1904 and failed. Boltwood postulated that this was because uranium did not decay directly into radium but into some intermediate element, and began to search for it. After much effort Boltwood eventually found what he was looking for in 'actinium X', which, as it appeared different from anything else, he felt confident enough to claim as a new element and named it 'ionium' in 1907. This claim ran into trouble when ionium was found to behave very much like thorium and in 1908 it was shown by B. Keetman that if ionium and thorium are mixed together no chemical technique can separate them. Soddy decided the matter in 1913 when he was able to obtain a spectrograph of ionium and found it to be the same as thorium. Although he was wrong in detail, the general picture Boltwood had developed of the decay of uranium to radium was valid until superseded by Soddy's idea of the isotope.

One important byproduct of Boltwood's

work was his demonstration in 1905 that lead was always found in uranium and was probably the final stable product of its decay. He argued that in minerals of the same age the lead–uranium ratio would be constant, and in minerals of different ages the ratio would be different. He calculated some estimates of the ages of several rocks based on the estimates then accepted for decay rates and came up with some good results. This was the beginning of attempts to date rocks and fossils by radiation measurements and other physical techniques, which have so revolutionized geology and archeology.

Boltzmann, Ludwig Edward
(1844–1906) *Austrian theoretical physicist*

Boltzmann studied at the university in his native city of Vienna, where he received his doctorate in 1866. He held professorships in physics or mathematics at Graz (1869–73; 1876–79), Vienna (1873–76; 1894–1900; 1902–06), Munich (1889–93), and Leipzig (1900–02).

Boltzmann made important contributions to the kinetic theory of gases. He developed the law of equipartition of energy, which states that the total energy of an atom or molecule is, on average, equally distributed over the motions (degrees of freedom). He also produced an equation showing how the energy of a gas was distributed among the molecules (called the *Maxwell–Boltzmann distribution*).

Boltzmann also worked on thermodynamics, in which he developed the idea that heat, entropy, and other thermodynamic properties were the result of the behavior of large numbers of atoms, and could be treated by mechanics and statistics. In particular, Boltzmann showed that entropy – introduced by Rudolf Clausius – was a measure of the disorder of a system. *Boltzmann's equation* (1896) relates entropy (*S*) to probability (*p*): $S = k\log p + b$. The constant k is known as *Boltzmann's constant* and has the value $1.380\,54 \times 10^{-23}$ joule per kelvin. The equation is engraved on his gravestone.

Boltzmann's work in this field was heavily criticized by opponents of atomism, particularly Wilhelm Ostwald. It did however lead to the science of statistical mechanics developed later by Josiah Willard GIBBS and others. Boltzmann also worked on electromagnetism. He is further noted for a theoretical derivation of the law of radiation discovered by Josef STEFAN.

Toward the end of his life he suffered from illness and depression, and committed suicide in 1906.

Bolyai, Janos (1802–1860) *Hungarian mathematician*

Bolyai, who was born in Koloszvár (now Cluj) in Romania, was the son of Farkas Bolyai, a distinguished mathematician who had an obsession with the status of Euclid's famous parallel postulate and devoted his life to trying to prove it. Despite his father's warnings that it would ruin his health, peace of mind, and happiness, Janos too started working on this axiom until, in about 1820, he came to the conclusion that it could not be proved. He went on to develop a consistent geometry in which the parallel postulate is not used, thus establishing the independence of this axiom from the others. In 1882 Bolyai published an account of his non-Euclidean geometry. Although his discovery had been anticipated by Nikolai LOBACHEVSKY and Karl GAUSS he was unaware of their work.

The discovery of the possibility of non-Euclidean geometries had a tremendous impact on both mathematics and philosophy. In mathematics it opened the way for a far more general and abstract approach to geometry than had previously been pursued, and in philosophy it settled once and for all the arguments about the supposed privileged status of Euclid's geometry. Bolyai also did valuable work in the theory of complex numbers.

Bond, George Phillips (1825–1865) *American astronomer*

George Bond spent most of his early life assisting his father **William Bond**, whom he succeeded as director of the Harvard College Observatory in 1859. He thereafter contributed to most of his father's observational and photographic work, including their joint discovery of Hyperion in 1848, the first photograph of a star (Vega) in 1850, and the detection in 1850 of Saturn's third ring, the so-called 'crepe ring'. He is best known, however, for showing how stellar magnitude could be calculated from photographs. In 1857 he noted that the size of the image is relative to the brightness of the star and the length of the exposure. It is this basic fact that has been used by the compilers of the Astrographic Catalog to record measurements of stellar magnitudes. He was also the first to photograph a double star, Mizar, in 1857.

Bond, William Cranch (1789–1859)
American astronomer. See BOND, GEORGE PHILLIPS.

Bondi, Sir Hermann (1919–)

British–Austrian mathematician and
cosmologist. See HOYLE, SIR FRED.

Bonner, James Frederick (1910–   )
American biologist

Born at Ansley, Nebraska, Bonner graduated
in chemistry from the University of Utah
in 1931 but turned to biology under the
influence of Theodosius Dobzhansky. He received his PhD from the California Institute
of Technology in 1934, which was then becoming known as the main center for molecular biology. Here he became interested
in developmental biology and the question
of why only some genes of the chromosome
complement of an organism are expressed
in any one cell. He discovered that histone,
a protein that is found associated with the
chromosomes, is responsible for shutting
off gene activity, and that if the histone is
removed then the repressed genes become
functional again. He also discovered that
certain hormones act by repressing and
derepressing genes.

Bonner has in addition conducted research on the artificial synthesis of ribonucleic acid and studied ribosomes and
mitochondria. From 1946 to 1981 he was
professor of biology at Cal Tech, becoming
Professor Emeritus in 1981. He has written
many books, including *The Nucleohistones*
(1964) and *The Molecular Biology of Development* (1965).

Bonnet, Charles (1720–1793) *Swiss naturalist*

Born in Geneva, Switzerland, Bonnet studied law, gaining his doctorate in 1743. In the
same year he was elected a fellow of the
Royal Society for his work on regeneration
in lower animals and his demonstration of
breathing pores (stigmata or spiracles) in
caterpillars and butterflies. He is chiefly remembered however for discovering
parthenogenesis (reproduction without fertilization) in the spindle-tree aphid and for
the ideas on evolution he proposed following this observation.

Bonnet believed all organisms are preformed and that the germs of every subsequent generation are contained within the
female. Such thinking implied that species
remain constant, leaving Bonnet to explain
how species become extinct as evidenced by
fossil remains. He argued that the Earth
had experienced periodic catastrophes, each
destroying many life forms, but the remaining species all evolved to some degree.
(Bonnet was the first to use the term 'evolution' in a biological context.) Thus after the
next catastrophe apes progress to men, and
men become angels. The catastrophism the-

ory was adopted by Georges CUVIER, and
strongly influenced geological thinking
until the 1820s.

Boole, George (1815–1864) *British mathematician*

Boole came from a poor background in the
English city of Lincoln and was virtually
self-taught in mathematics. He discovered
for himself the theory of invariants. Before
he obtained an academic post Boole spent
several years as a school teacher, first in
Yorkshire and later at a school he opened
himself. In 1849 he became professor of
mathematics at Queen's College, Cork, Ireland.

Boole's main work was in showing how
mathematical techniques could be applied
to the study of logic. His book *The Laws of
Thought* (1854) is a landmark in the study of
logic. Boole laid the foundations for an axiomatic treatment of logic that proved essential for the further fundamental
developments soon to be made in the subject by such workers at Gottlob Frege and
Bertrand Russell.

Boole's own logical algebra is essentially
an algebra of classes, being based on such
concepts as complement and union of
classes. His work was an important advance
in considering algebraic operations ab-
stractly – that is, studying the formal properties of operations and their combinations
without reference to their interpretation
or 'meaning'. Fundamental formal properties like commutativity and associativity
were first studied in purely abstract terms
by Boole.

Boole's work led to the recognition of a
new and fundamental algebraic structure
the *Boolean algebra* alongside such structures as the field, ring, and group. The
study of Boolean algebras both in themselves and their application to other areas
of mathematics has been an important concern of 20th-century mathematics. Boolean
algebras find important applications in
such diverse fields as topology, measure theory, probability and statistics, and computing.

Boot, Henry Albert Howard
(1917–1983) *British physicist. See* RANDALL,
SIR JOHN TURTON.

Bopp, Thomas (1949–   ) *American astronomer*

Thomas Bopp was born in Denver, Colorado.
His interest in astronomy led him to join a
local informal group of amateur astronomers in the Phoenix area. Here, on
July 22nd 1995, he was the first to see a new

comet, now known as *Hale-Bopp*. The comet was independently found by the astronomer Alan HALE.

Bordet, Jules Jean Baptiste Vincent
(1870–1961) *Belgian immunologist*

Bordet was born in Soignies, Belgium, and graduated in medicine from Brussels University in 1892. In 1894 joined the Pasteur Institute, Paris, where he worked under the bacteriologist Elie Metchnikoff. In collaboration with Octave Gengou, Bordet discovered that in an immunized animal the antibodies produced by the immune response work in conjunction with another component of blood (which Bordet termed 'alexin' but which is now called 'complement') to destroy foreign cells that invade the body. This component, Bordet found, was present in both immunized and nonimmunized animals and was destroyed by heating to over 55°C. This work formed the basis of the *complement-fixation test*, a particularly sensitive means of detecting the presence of any specific type of cell or its specific antibody. A notable application of this was the test to detect syphilis devised by August von Wasserman.

In 1901 Bordet left Paris to found and direct the Pasteur Institute in Brussels and in 1907 he was appointed professor of pathology and bacteriology at Brussels University. In 1906 Bordet isolated the bacterium responsible for whooping cough, which is named after him: *Bordetella (Haemophilus) pertussis*. For his discovery of complement and other contributions to medicine, he was awarded the 1919 Nobel Prize in physiology or medicine.

Borelli, Giovanni Alfonso (1608–1679) *Italian mathematician and physiologist*

Borelli was born in Naples. His mathematical training – he was professor at Messina and Pisa – led him to apply mathematical and mechanical laws to his two main interests, astronomy and animal physiology. He rightly explained muscular action and the movements of bones in terms of levers, and also carried out detailed studies of the flight mechanism of birds. However, his extension of such principles to internal organs, such as the heart, stomach, and lungs, overlooked the essential chemical actions that take place in these organs. Borelli's *De motu animalium* (1680; On the Movement of Animals), which includes his theory of blood circulation, is thus in part erroneous.

In astronomy, in his *Theoricae mediceorum planetarum* (Theory of the Medicean Planets; 1666), Borelli presented a novel and influen-

tial account of the motions of the Medicean satellites around their parent plant Jupiter. He accounted for their elliptical orbits in terms of two distinct motions. The first, 'perpetual and uniform', whereby the satellite is attracted rectilinearly to Jupiter as iron moves in a straight line to a magnet; the second, and "directly contrary...continually decreasing," arises from the manner in which the satellite "is driven out from the sun by the force of its circular motion." Newton was aware of Borelli's work and appreciated the originality of his approach, in the use of elliptical orbits and also his appreciation that orbital motion was complex.

Borelli was also one of the first astronomers, in his *Del movimento della cometa di Decembre 1664* (1665), to propose, on the basis of observations and calculations, that comets also move in elliptical orbits. Earlier workers, including Kepler, had taken comets to be transient visitors passing through the solar system in a straight line. As the church opposed such views, Borelli chose to publish under the pseudonym Pier Maria Mutoli.

Borlaug, Norman Ernest (1914–   ) *American agronomist and plant breeder*

Borlaug was born in Cresco, Iowa, and graduated in forestry from Minnesota University in 1937, gaining his doctorate in plant pathology in 1941. He then spent three years with the Du Pont Chemical Company, testing the effects of chemicals on plants and plant diseases. In 1944 he joined the newly formed International Maize and Wheat Improvement Center in Mexico and began the breeding work that was to produce the highly adaptable dwarf wheats that played so large a part in the 'Green Revolution' of the late 1960s and early 1970s.

Borlaug's high-yielding cereals increased agricultural production in the developing countries to the extent that many became self-sufficient for grain. For his major role in temporarily alleviating world famine, Borlaug was awarded the Nobel Peace Prize in 1970.

Born, Max (1882–1970) *German physicist*

Born was the son of an embryologist, a professor of anatomy at the University of Breslau (now Wrocław) in Poland. He was educated at the university in his native city of Breslau, and at the universities of Heidelberg, Zurich, and Göttingen, where he obtained his PhD in 1907. From 1909 until 1933 he taught at Göttingen, being appointed professor of physics in 1921. With the rise of Hitler he moved to Britain, and from 1936 served as professor of natural philosophy at the University of Edinburgh, returning to Germany on his retirement in 1953.

Born's early work was on crystals, particularly the vibrations of atoms in crystal lattices. The *Born–Haber cycle* is a theoretical cycle of reactions and changes by which it is possible to calculate the lattice energy of ionic crystals. He is noted for his role in the development of the new quantum theory. Together with Pascual Jordan, he developed (1925) the matrix mechanics introduced by Werner HEISENBERG. He also showed how to interpret the theoretical results of Louis DE BROGLIE and the experiments of such people as Clinton J. DAVISSON, which showed that particles have wavelike behavior.

At the time, it was known that in some circumstances light, electrons, etc., behaved as waves whereas in others they acted like particles. (William Bragg once suggested using the corpuscular (particle) theory on Monday, Wednesday, and Friday, and the undulatory (wave) theory on Tuesday, Thursday, and Saturday.) Mathematical treatments could be used to predict behavior, but there was a problem in finding some accepted physical picture of how electrons, for instance, could act in this way. Erwin Schrödinger, who developed wave mechanics, interpreted particles as 'wave packets', but this was unsatisfactory because such packets would dissipate in time. Born's interpretation was that the particles exist but are 'guided' by a wave. At any point, the amplitude (actually the square of the amplitude) indicates the probability of finding a particle there.

An essential part of this idea of electrons, atoms, etc., is that it depends on probability – there is no predetermined way in which absolute predictions can be made, as in classical physics. A similar result is embodied in the uncertainty principle of Werner Heisenberg. Einstein, amongst others, could never accept this and Born corresponded with him on the subject (the *Born–Einstein letters* were published in 1971).

Born shared (with Walter BOTHE) the 1954 Nobel Prize for physics. He is buried in Göttingen, where his tombstone displays his fundamental equation of matrix mechanics:

$$pq - qp = h/2\pi i$$

Bosch, Carl (1874–1940) *German industrial chemist*

Born in Cologne, Germany, Bosch was trained as both metallurgist and chemist and gained his doctorate under Johannes Wislicenus at Leipzig (1898). He joined the large German dyestuffs company, Badische Anilin und Soda Fabrik (BASF), in 1899. Following Fritz Haber's successful small-scale ammonia synthesis in 1909, Bosch began to develop a high-pressure ammonia plant at Oppau for BASF. The plant was opened in 1912 – a successful application of the Haber process on a large scale. Bosch also introduced the use of the water-gas shift reaction as a source of hydrogen for the process:

$$CO + H_2O = CO_2 + H_2$$

After World War I the large-scale ammonia fertilizer industry was established and the high-pressure technique was extended by BASF to the synthesis of methanol from carbon monoxide and hydrogen in 1923. Bosch was chairman of BASF's successor, IG Farben (1935–40) and concurrently director of the Kaiser Wilhelm institutes. He shared the Nobel Prize for chemistry with Friedrich BERGIUS in 1931.

Bose, Sir Jagadis Chandra (1858–1937) *Indian plant physiologist and physicist*

Bose, who was born in Mymensingh (which is now in Bangladesh), began his studies in London as a medical student. He then won a scholarship to Cambridge University, from where he graduated in natural sciences in 1884. He was appointed professor of physical science at Presidency College, Calcutta, in 1885 and retained this post until 1915. In 1917 he founded and became director of the Bose Research Institute, Calcutta. He was knighted in 1917 and in 1920 became the first Indian to be elected a fellow of the Royal Society.

Bose's early research was on the properties of very short radio waves – work in which he showed their similarity to light. He also designed an improved version of Oliver Lodge's coherer, then used to detect radio waves, and as a result was able to put forward a general theory of the properties of contact-sensitive materials.

His most famous work concerned his investigations into plant physiology and the similarities between the behavioral response of plant and animal tissue. By devising extremely sensitive instruments he was able to demonstrate the minute movements of plants to external stimuli and to measure their rate of growth. While his experimental skill was widely admired, this work did not at the time gain universal acceptance.

Bose, Satyendra Nath (1894–1974) *Indian physicist*

Bose was educated at Presidency College, in his native Calcutta. Among his teachers was the eminent Indian physicist Jagadis Chandra Bose. Bose held the post of lecturer at the Calcutta University College of Science from 1917 until he left in 1921 to become a reader in physics at the new University of Dacca in East Bengal. His work ranged over many aspects of physics, among them statistical mechanics, the electromagnetic properties of the ionosphere, theories of x-ray crystallography, and unified field theory. However it is for his work in quantum statistics that he is best known.

Bose attracted the attention of Albert Einstein and other European physicists by publishing a paper in 1924 in which he was able to derive Max Planck's black body radiation law, but without using the classical electrodynamics as Planck himself had done. On the strength of this work Bose was able to get two years' study leave in Europe and during his visit he came into contact with many of the great physicists of the day, such as Louis de Broglie, Max Born, and Einstein. Einstein's generalization of Bose's work led to the system of statistical quantum mechanics now known as *Bose–Einstein* statistics. This system of statistics contrasts with the rival Fermi–Dirac statistics in that it applies only to particles not limited to single occupancy of the same state, i.e. particles (known as bosons) that do not obey the Pauli exclusion principle.

Bothe, Walther Wilhelm Georg Franz (1891–1957) *German atomic physicist*

Bothe, who was born in Oranienburg, Germany, studied at the University of Berlin under Max Planck and received his PhD in 1914. For the next few years, he was a prisoner of war in Russia but, on his return to Germany in 1920, he started teaching at Berlin and worked in Hans Geiger's radioactivity laboratory.

He devised the 'coincidence method' of detecting the emission of electrons by x-rays in which electrons passing through two adjacent Geiger tubes at almost the same time are registered as a coincidental event. He used it to show that momentum and energy are conserved at the atomic level. In 1929 he applied the method to the study of cosmic rays and was able to show that they consisted of massive particles rather than photons. For this research he shared the 1954 Nobel Prize for physics with Max Born.

By 1930 his reputation was established and he was appointed professor of physics at Giessen. The same year he observed a strange radiation emitted from beryllium when it was exposed to alpha particles. This radiation was later identified by Chadwick as consisting of neutrons.

While director of the Max Planck Institute in Heidelberg, Bothe supervised the construction of Germany's first cyclotron. This work was finished in 1943 and during World War II he led German scientists in their search for atomic energy. When the war ended he was given the chair of physics at Heidelberg, which he retained until his death.

Bouguer, Pierre (1698–1758) *French physicist and mathematician*

Bouguer, the son of a hydrographer and mathematician, was born in Le Croisic, France, and followed into his father's profession. He was a child prodigy and obtained a post as professor of hydrography at the remarkably early age of 15. The study of the problems associated with navigation and ship design was his chief interest. Bouguer took part in an extended expedition to Peru led by Charles de la Condamine to determine the length of a degree of the meridian near the equator. While on this expedition Bouguer also did a great deal of other valuable experimental work.

One of Bouguer's most successful inventions was the heliometer to measure the light of the Sun and other luminous bodies. Although it was not his chief interest the research for which Bouguer is now best remembered was on photometry. Here too he did much valuable experimental work and one of his major discoveries was of the law now named for him. This states that in a medium of uniform transparency the intensity of light remaining in a collimated beam decreases exponentially with the length of its path in the medium. The law is sometimes unjustly attributed to Johann Lambert. Bouguer's work in optics can be seen as the beginning of the science of atmospheric optics.

Bourbaki, Nicolas *French group of mathematicians*

'Bourbaki' is the collective *nom de plume* of a group of some of the most outstanding of contemporary mathematicians. The precise membership of Bourbaki, which naturally has changed over the years, is a closely guarded secret but it is known that most of the members are French.

Since 1939, Bourbaki has been publishing a monumental work, the *Eléments de mathématique* (Elements of Mathematics), of which over thirty volumes have so far appeared. In this Bourbaki attempts to expound and display the architecture of the whole mathematical edifice starting from certain carefully chosen logical and set-theoretic concepts. The emphasis throughout the *Eléments* is on the interrelationships to be found between the various structures present in mathematics, and to a certain extent this means that Bourbaki's exposition cuts across traditional boundaries, such as that between algebra and topology. Indeed for Bourbaki, pure mathematics is to be thought of as nothing other than the study of pure structure.

Since the members of Bourbaki are all working mathematicians, rather than pure logicians, in contrast to other foundational enterprises (e.g. those of Gottlob Frege, Bertrand Russell, and A.N. Whitehead) the influence of Bourbaki's writings on contemporary mathematicians and their conception of the subject has been immense.

Boveri, Theodor Heinrich (1862–1915)
German zoologist

Boveri was born in Bamberg, Germany, and graduated in medicine from Munich in 1885. He remained at Munich to do cytological research until his appointment as professor of zoology and comparative anatomy at Würzburg in 1893. In 1888, he coined the term 'centrosome' for the region of the cell that contains the centriole, first discovered by Edouard van Beneden. Boveri also proved Beneden's theory that equal numbers of chromosomes are contributed by the egg and the sperm to the zygote. Boveri accurately described the formation of the polar bodies following meiosis in the egg cell, and made pioneering studies of sperm formation (spermatogenesis), introducing a diagrammatic representation of the process (1892), which is still in use today.

Bovet, Daniel (1907–1992) *Swiss–Italian pharmacologist*

Bovet was born in Neuchâtel, Switzerland. In 1929 he gained a DSc in zoology and comparative anatomy from the University of Geneva where his father was professor of pedagogy. He continued research work at the Pasteur Institute in Paris, serving as director from 1936 until 1947 and following up the discoveries of Gerhard Domagk on prontosil. He and his coworkers were able to show that the sulfonamide group is responsible for the antibacterial action of prontosil. The drug is only active *in vivo* as the animals metabolize the parent drug into sulfanilamide, which is the antibacterial compound.

Prontosil was a dye, protected by patents and expensive. Sulfanilamide was colorless, freely available, cheap to manufacture, and equally as effective as a bactericide. Many analogs, known as sulfa-drugs, have been made and these are widely used against streptococcal infections such as pneumonia, meningitis, and scarlet fever.

These researches led Bovet to develop the earlier ideas of Paul Ehrlich, Emil Fischer, and Juda Quastel into a more refined 'antimetabolite hypothesis', which is one of the fundamental lines of approach in modern drug research. It is based on the idea that a chemical compound whose properties and molecular shape resemble those of a normal body metabolite may affect the functions of that metabolite. Just as a lock (a metabolic reaction) is opened by just one shape of key (a metabolite) so another slightly different shape of key (an antimetabolite) may jam the lock and prevent the new key from fitting. These ideas led Bovet to develop the antihistamine drug 933F in 1937 and this gave rise to a series of drugs that are useful for asthma and hay fever.

Later, after a trip to Brazil, Bovet became interested in the Indian nerve poison curare. The structure of curare had already been worked out and in 1946 Bovet began work on analogs, which led to the use of succinylcholine as a muscle relaxant in surgical operations.

In 1947 Bovet became head of pharmacology and chemotherapeutics at the Superior Institute of Health in Rome, where he remained until 1964, when he was appointed professor of pharmacology at the University of Sassari. He became an Italian citizen and in his later years carried out research work on tranquilizers and anesthetics. In 1971 he accepted the chair of psychobiology at the University of Rome, finally retiring in 1982. He was awarded the Nobel Prize for physiology or medicine in 1957 for his work on curare and antihistamines.

Bowen, Ira Sprague (1898–1973)
American astronomer

Bowen, who was born in Seneca Falls, New York State, graduated from Oberlin College, Chicago in 1919 and gained his PhD from the California Institute of Technology, Pasadena in 1926. He taught physics at Cal Tech from 1921 to 1945, serving from 1931 as professor. In 1946 he was made director of the Mount Wilson Observatory and in 1948 of the newly opened Palomar Observatory, posts he continued to hold until his retirement in 1964.

In 1928 Bowen tackled the problem of the strange lines first observed by William Huggins in the 1860s in the spectrum of planetary nebulae and the Orion nebula. The difficulty was, according to Bowen, that the strong lines had not been reproduced in the laboratory. Spectrographic evidence showed that such lines must be emitted by an element of low atomic weight. Talk of a new element, known as 'nebulium', that could produce the observed spectral lines was however dismissed by Bowen as nonsense.

Bowen was able to show that the lines were in fact due to radiation emitted from ionized atoms of oxygen and nitrogen as they decayed into more stable lower-energy levels. Specifically he was able to show that triply and doubly ionized oxygen as well as doubly ionized nitrogen would radiate at the wavelengths attributed to 'nebulium' but only in the highly rarefied conditions of nebulae where collisions between atoms are very infrequent. It is this radiation that contributes to the green and red colors observed in emission and planetary nebulae.

Boyd, William Clouser (1903–1984)
American biochemist. See LANDSTEINER, KARL.

Boyer, Herbert Wayne (1936–)
American biochemist

Boyer was born in Pittsburgh, Pennsylvania, and educated at St. Vincent College, Latrobe, and the University of Pittsburgh where he obtained his PhD in 1963. He joined the faculty of the University of California, San Francisco, shortly afterward in 1966 and served as professor of biochemistry from 1976 to 1991.

Much of Boyer's work has been concerned with developing some of the basic techniques of recombinant DNA, known more popularly as genetic engineering. Thus in 1973 he succeeded with Robert Helling, and independently of the work of Stanley Cohen and Annie Chang, in constructing functional DNA from two different sources. Such chimeras, as they became called, were initially engineered by splicing together segments from two different plasmids (extrachromosomal DNA found in some bacteria) from the *Escherichia coli* bacillus. The chimera was then inserted into *E. coli* and was found to replicate and, equally significant, to express traits derived from both plasmids.

Development after 1973 was so rapid that by 1976 it had occurred to Boyer and a number of other workers that recombinant DNA could be used to produce such important proteins as insulin, interferon, and growth hormone in commercial quantities. Consequently in 1976 he joined with financier Robert Swanson to invest $500 each to form the company Genentech, which went public in 1980.

Despite successfully developing techniques for the production of somastatin in 1977, insulin in 1978, and growth hormone in 1979, the position of Genentech was far from secure at the beginning of 1981 with the emergence of competition from a number of rival companies and legal problems concerned with the ownership of genes.

Boyer, Paul Delos (1918–) *American biochemist*

Boyer was educated at Brigham Young University and at the University of Wisconsin, where he gained his PhD in 1943. He then taught at the universities of Wisconsin, Stanford, and Minnesota before being appointed professor of biochemistry at UCLA in 1963.

A basic problem in biochemistry is explaining how the energy-rich compound adenosine triphosphate (ATP) is used to fuel cellular activities and how, once used, it is recovered. Work by Peter MICHELL had identified a difference in hydrogen-ion concentration across the cell's mitochondrial membrane. Further investigation revealed in broad outline that energy was derived from adenosine diphosphate (ADP) in a reaction catalysed by the enzyme ATP synthase. Energy is released when one of the phosphate bonds of ATP breaks and becomes available for such tasks as muscle contraction. ADP is then converted back to ATP through the action of ATP synthase.

Boyer, from the 1970s onwards, began to throw more light on this process. It was found that ATP synthase came in three parts: a wheel-like assembly in the mitochondrial membrane, an attached rod, and a cylinder joined to the rod's other end located within the mitochondria. Boyer proposed that the hydrogen ions spin the wheel as they pass through the mitochondrial membrane, turning the rod and cylinder at the same time. The rotation of the cylinder attracts ADP and phosphate groups in the first step to synthesizing ATP.

Further light has been thrown on the reaction by John WALKER and Jens SKOU, with whom Boyer shared the 1997 Nobel Prize for chemistry.

Boyle, Robert (1627–1691) *British chemist and physicist*

The son of the Earl of Cork, and born at Lismore Castle, now in the Republic of Ireland, Boyle was a member of an aristocratic and wealthy family. He spent four years at Eton College and from 1638 studied at Geneva, returning to London in 1644. He then retired to his estate at Stalbridge, Dorset, where he took up the life of a scientific 'virtuoso'.

In 1654 Boyle moved to Oxford, where he worked on pneumatics. In 1658–59 he had an air pump built for him by Robert Hooke, after the type invented by Otto von GUER-ICKE in 1654. Boyle was ably assisted by Hooke in various pioneering experiments in which he showed that air was essential for the transmission of sound, and for respiration and combustion – and that the last two processes exhausted only part of the air.

In Boyle's most famous experiment he took a U-shaped tube with a shorter closed end, and a longer open end into which he poured mercury, thus isolating a given volume of air in the shorter end. When the mercury was level in both 'limbs' the air was under atmospheric pressure, and by adding more mercury to the longer limb the pressure could be increased. Boyle found that the volume was halved if the pressure was doubled, reduced to a third if the pressure was tripled, and so on – and that this process was reversible. Boyle's work on the compressibility of air was published in *New Experiments Physico-Mechanicall, Touching the Spring of the Air and its Effects* (1660) but the famous law stating that the pressure and volume of air are inversely proportional was not stated explicitly until the second edition (1662). The law, known as *Boyle's law* in America and Britain but in Europe as *Mariotte's law*, can be expressed (where C is a constant) as $p \times V = C$; that is, the product of the pressure and volume of a gas remains constant if, as Edmé Mariotte noted, the temperature remains constant. This law (together with its companion gas law, that of Jacques CHARLES) is true only for ideal gases, but approximately holds for real gases at very low pressures and at high temperatures.

Boyle developed a mechanical corpuscular philosophy of his own, derived from the Greek tradition and the work of Galileo and Pierre Gassendi. In Boyle's conception all physical phenomena could be explained by corpuscules of different shapes, sizes, and motions, this corpuscular matter being capable of infinite transformations (which allowed the possibility of alchemy and excluded the existence of elements).

However, in *The Sceptical Chymist* (1661) Boyle proposed a view of matter that presaged modern views and certainly disposed effectively of the Aristotelian doctrine of the four elements. He supposed that all matter was composed of primary particles, some of which joined together to form semi-indivisible corpuscles and whose organization and motion explained all qualities of matter.

Boyle's main contribution to chemistry was his insistence on experiment, precision, and accurate observation. He devised many analytical tests including the use of vegetable dyes as acid–base indicators and of flame tests to detect metals. The chemist's concern for the purity of his materials began with Boyle. Although he prepared hydrogen by the action of acids on iron and observed the oxidation of mercury and its subsequent regeneration on further heating, the 'fixation' of gases in bodies remained unexplained in his work. Likewise, he observed the increase in weight of metals on calcination but attributed this to heat, which he sometimes regarded as material.

Boyle left Oxford for London in 1668 where, despite his scholarly nature and poor health, he was very much at the center of scientific life as a founder member of the Royal Society. He believed, like his hero Francis Bacon, that science could be put to practical use.

Boys, Sir Charles Vernon (1855–1944)
British physicist

The son of a clergyman, Boys was born in Wing in the eastern English county of Rutland and educated at the Royal School of Mines, London. He later taught at the Royal College of Science, South Kensington. Boys left the College in 1897 to take up the appointment of Metropolitan gas referee, a post that he held until 1939 when the job was abolished. The post was something of a sinecure, and required Boys to do little more than supervise the work of his assistants and to monitor methods used to test the quality of the gas the Board supplied to its customers. Boys also found time to establish himself as an expert witness, appearing in numerous patent and other technical disputes.

Boys is best known for his determination of the gravitational constant in 1897. The measurement was first made by Henry CAVENDISH in 1797 and was expressed in terms of the Earth's density. Newton had proposed a density between five and six in 1687; Cavendish found experimentally a density of 5.448.

Whereas Cavendish had used a six-foot beam in his torsion rod experiment, Boys opted for a mere nine inches. The decrease in size was made possible by using some exceedingly fine quartz fibers in the torsion balance. Boys drew these fine filaments by attaching the end of an arrow to a piece of molten quartz and firing it with a crossbow. As a result uniform temperatures were easier to maintain, and convection current disturbances were minimized. Boys calculated on the basis of his measurements that two 1 gram point masses 1 centimeter apart would attract each other with a force of $6.657\,6 \times 10^{-8}$ dyne, and consequently the density of the Earth would be $5.527\,\mathrm{gm/cm^3}$, figures which compare well with the modern figure of 6.670×10^{-8} dyne, and 5.517 $\mathrm{gm/cm^3}$.

There are a number of other instruments linked to Boys. Amongst these are an integraph (1881) for mechanical integration, a radiomicrometer (1890) for measuring stellar radiation, a rotating lens camera (1900) for photographing the flight of a bullet, and, in his capacity as gas referee, an improved calorimeter to measure the calorific value of gas (1905).

Brachet, Jean Louis Auguste
(1909–   ) *Belgian cell biologist*

Brachet was educated at the Free University in his native city of Brussels where his father, an embryologist, was rector. After gaining his MD in 1934 he joined the faculty as an anatomy instructor and in 1943 was appointed professor of general biology.

Brachet began his career by studying the then poorly understood nucleic acids. It had been thought that plant cells contain RNA and animal cells DNA but, in 1933, Brachet demonstrated that both types of nucleic acid occur in both plant and animal cells. He proved this by developing a cytochemical technique that made it possible to localize the RNA-containing structures in the cell. Brachet also noted that cells rich in RNA tend to be those actively engaged in protein synthesis. On this basis Brachet was led in 1942 to propose the important hypothesis that ribonucleoprotein granules could be the agents of protein synthesis. Such granules, later termed ribosomes, were indeed shown to function in this way by George Palade in 1956.

Later experiments, in which Brachet removed the nucleus from the cell, showed that although protein synthesis continued for a while the amount of RNA in the cytoplasm decreased until there was none left. This indicated that the production of RNA occurs in the nucleus and that it is then transported from the nucleus to the cytoplasm.

Bradley, James (1693–1762) *British astronomer*

Bradley was born in Sherborne in Dorset and educated at Oxford University. He was taught astronomy by his uncle, the Rev.

James Pound, who was also an astronomer. In 1721 Bradley became Savilian Professor of Astronomy at Oxford and in 1742 he succeeded Edmond Halley as Astronomer Royal. His astronomical career began with a determined effort to detect parallax – the angular displacement of a body when viewed from spatially separate positions (or, more significantly, one position on a *moving* Earth). He fixed a telescope in as vertical a position as possible to minimize the effects of atmospheric refraction and began to observe the star Gamma Draconis. He soon found that the star had apparently moved position but prolonged observation convinced him that it could not be parallax he had measured, for he found the greatest shift in position in September and March and not in December and June as it should have been if he was observing parallax. However, the change in position was so regular (every six months) that it could be due only to the observer being on a moving Earth. It took him until 1729 to find the precise cause of the change in position. He realized that as light has a finite speed it will therefore take some time, however small, to travel down the length of the telescope. While it is traveling from the top to the bottom of the telescope the bottom of the instrument will have been carried by the orbital motion of the Earth. The image of the star will therefore be slightly displaced. Bradley realized that he had at last produced hard observational evidence for the Earth's motion, for the finite speed of light, and for a new aberration that had to be taken into account if truly accurate stellar positions were to be calculated. He worked out the constant of aberration at between $20''$ and $20''.5$ – a very accurate figure. He also discovered another small displacement, which, because it had the same period as the regression of the nodes of the Moon, he identified as the result of the $5°$ inclination of the Moon's orbit to the ecliptic. This caused a slight wobble of the Earth's axis, which he called 'nutation'. Friedrich Bessel later used Bradley's observations to construct a catalog of unprecedented accuracy.

Bragg, Sir William Henry (1862–1942) *British physicist*

Bragg's father was a merchant seaman turned farmer. William Henry Bragg was born in Westwood in England and educated at a variety of schools before going as a scholar to Cambridge University. He graduated in 1884 and after a year's research under J. J. Thomson took the chair of mathematics and physics at the University of

Adelaide, Australia, in 1886. He returned to England as professor of physics at Leeds University in 1909, moving from there to University College, London, in 1915.

In Australia, Bragg concentrated on lecturing and started original research late in life (in 1904). He first worked on alpha radiation, investigating the range of the particles. Later he turned his attention to x-rays, originally believing (in opposition to Charles Barkla) that they were neutral particles. With the observation of x-ray diffraction by Max von Laue, he accepted that the x-rays were waves and constructed (1915) the first x-ray spectrometer to measure the wavelengths of x-rays. Much of his work was on x-ray crystallography, in collaboration with his son, William Lawrence BRAGG. They shared the Nobel Prize for physics in 1915.

During the war Bragg worked on the development of hydrophones for the admiralty. In some ways his most significant work was done at the Royal Institution, London, where he was director from 1923. Under James Dewar's directorship the research functions of the Royal Institution had virtually disappeared. Bragg recruited several young and brilliant crystallographers who shared with him a commitment to applying the new technique to the analysis of organic compounds. There was no reason to suppose there was much chance of success but as early as the 1920s Bragg was planning to investigate biological molecules with x-rays. His first attempts were made on anthracene and naphthalene in 1921.

Bragg, Sir William Lawrence (1890–1971) *British physicist*

William Lawrence Bragg was the son of William Henry BRAGG. Born in Adelaide, Australia, he was educated at the university there and at Cambridge University, where he became a fellow and lecturer. After the war, in 1919, he was appointed professor of physics at Manchester University. He succeeded Ernest Rutherford in 1938, after a short period in 1937 as director of the National Physical Laboratory, as head of the Cavendish Laboratory and Cavendish Professor at Cambridge. Finally, in 1953, he became director of the Royal Institution, London, a post his father had held previously and which he held until his retirement in 1961.

Success came very early to Bragg, who shared the Nobel Prize for physics with his father in 1915. Following Max von Laue's discovery of x-ray diffraction by crystals in 1912, Lawrence Bragg in the same year formulated what is now known as the *Bragg law*:

$$n\lambda = 2d\sin\theta$$

which relates the wavelength of x-rays (λ), the angle of incidence on a crystal θ, and the spacing of crystal planes d, for x-ray diffraction. n is an integer (1, 2, 3, etc.).

Bragg collaborated with his father in working out the crystal structures of a number of substances. Early in this work they showed that sodium chloride does not have individual molecules in the solid, but is an array of sodium and chloride ions. In 1915 the Braggs published their book *X-rays and Crystal Structure*.

Lawrence Bragg later worked on silicates and on metallurgy. He was responsible for setting up a program for structure determinations of proteins.

Brahe, Tycho (1546–1601) *Danish astronomer*

Tycho, whose father Otto was the governor of Helsingborg castle, was born in Knudstrup, Denmark. Kidnapped by and brought up by his uncle Jörgen, an admiral in the Danish navy, he was sent to Leipzig University in 1562 to study law. However, his interest in astronomy had already been kindled. He witnessed a partial solar eclipse in 1560 in Copenhagen whose predictability so impressed him that he began a serious study of Ptolemy's *Almagest*. He was allowed to continue with the formal study of astronomy and began a tour of the universities of northern Europe. It was while at Rostock in 1566 that, according to tradition, he became involved in a dispute with another young Danish nobleman over who was the better mathematician. The dispute led to a duel in which Tycho lost part of his nose. This he replaced with a mixture of gold, silver, and wax; the nose is clearly visible in contemporary engravings.

Tycho became aware that the successful solar-eclipse prediction of 1560 was not a typical index of the state of 16th-century astronomy. For instance, a conjunction of Jupiter and Saturn predicted by current tables was wrong by ten days. Tycho therefore began his long apprenticeship, traveling through northern Europe meeting the astronomers, instrument makers, and patrons who would support him later on.

His international reputation was made with the dramatic events that centered upon the nova of 1572 – ever since known as *Tycho's star*. Not since the days of Hipparchus (second century BC) had a new star visible to the naked eye appeared in the sky. In *De nova stella* (1573; On the New Star),

Tycho was able to demonstrate that the new star showed no parallax and therefore truly belonged to the sphere of the fixed stars. This was important cosmologically because according to Aristotle no change could take place in the heavens, which were supposed to be eternal and incorruptible; change could take place only in the sublunary sphere. By demonstrating that the new star of 1572 and the great comet of 1577 were changes in the heavens, Tycho was providing new evidence against the traditional Aristotelian cosmology.

In order to induce him to stay in Denmark, Tycho's monarch, Frederick II, offered him the island of Hven and unlimited funds to build an observatory there at Uraniborg. Tycho moved there in 1577, building an observatory/castle stocked with the best instruments then in existence, and constructing enormous quadrants and sextants. He became the greatest observational astronomer of the pretelescopic age. Before Tycho, astronomers tended to work with observations many centuries old. Copernicus would be more likely to use the tables of Ptolemy (second century AD) than to make his own observations. When modern tables, such as the *Prutenic Tables* of Erasmus Reinhold, were constructed, although based on the Copernican system, they were scarcely more reliable. Tycho changed all this. Twenty years' careful observation using accurate instruments enabled him to determine the positions of 777 stars with unparalleled accuracy. He did not, however, accept the Copernican heliocentric system. Instead he proposed a compromise between that and the Ptolemaic, suggesting that the Earth remains at the center, immobile; the Sun and Moon move round the Earth; and all other bodies move round the Sun. His system received hardly any support.

After the death of Frederick II in 1588, Tycho quarreled with his successor, Christian IV, on his coming of age. The last recorded observation made at Hven was on 15 March, 1596. Tycho set off once more on his travels, this time encumbered by his enormous instruments. Eventually he found a new patron, one even stranger than himself, the mad Holy Roman Emperor Rudolph II. Tycho was made Imperial Mathematician in 1599, given yet another castle at Benatek outside Prague, and, more important, given the young Johannes Kepler as an assistant. Although the relationship was a stormy one, both benefited enormously. Tycho died suddenly in 1601 after a short illness leaving Kepler to publish Tycho's *Rudolphine Tables* posthumously in 1627. His last words were: "Let me not seemed to have lived in vain." That such a

fear was groundless is witnessed on the title page of Kepler's great work, *Astronomia nova*:

"Founded on observations of the noble Tycho Brahe."

Brandt, Georg (1694–1768) *Swedish chemist*

Brandt was the son of an ironworker and former apothecary in Riddarhyta, Sweden, and from an early age he helped his father with metallurgical experiments. He studied medicine and chemistry at Leiden, and gained his MD at Rheims in 1726. He was later made warden of the Stockholm mint (1730), and professor of chemistry at the University of Uppsala.

In 1733 he systematically investigated arsenic and its compounds. He invented the classification of semimetals (now called metalloids), in which he included arsenic, bismuth, antimony, mercury, and zinc.

In 1735 Brandt postulated that the blue color of the ore known as smalt was due to the presence of an unknown metal or semimetal. He named this 'cobalt rex' from the Old Teutonic 'kobold', originally meaning 'demon', later applied to the 'false ores' that did not yield metals under the traditional processes. In 1742 Brandt isolated cobalt, and found it was magnetic and alloyed readily with iron. His results were confirmed in 1780 by Torbern Bergman, who first obtained fairly pure cobalt.

Brandt also, in 1748, experimented with the dissolution of gold in hot concentrated acid, and with its precipitation from solution. These experiments clarified some of the alleged transmutations of silver into gold. Indeed, Brandt devoted his later years to exposing fraudulent transmutations of metals into gold, and it was said of him that no chemist did more to combat alchemy.

Brans, Carl Henry (1935–) *American mathematical physicist*

Brans was born in Dallas, Texas, and graduated in 1957 from Loyola University, Louisiana. Having obtained his PhD from Princeton in 1961, he returned to Loyola in 1960 and in 1970 was appointed professor of physics.

Brans has worked mainly in the field of general relativity. He is best known for his production with Robert DICKE in 1961 of a variant of Einstein's theory in which the gravitational constant varies with time. A number of very accurate measurements made in the late 1970s has failed to detect this and some of the other predictions made by the *Brans–Dicke theory*.

Brattain, Walter Houser (1902–1987)
American physicist

Brattain, who was born in Amoy, China, was brought up on a cattle ranch. He was educated at Whitman College, at the University of Oregon, and at Minnesota, where he obtained his PhD in 1929. He immediately joined the Bell Telephone Company with which he worked as a research physicist until his retirement in 1967. After leaving Bell, Brattain taught at Whitman College doing research there on phospholipids.

Brattain's main field of work was the surface properties of semiconductors. It was known that a junction at a semiconductor would rectify an alternating current and that this effect was a surface property. Brattain was particularly interested in using semiconductors to amplify signals. Working with John BARDEEN, he investigated various arrangements for achieving this – originally studying silicon in contact with electrolytes, but later using germanium in contact with gold. Their first efficient point-contact transistor (1947) consisted of a thin wafer of germanium with two close point contacts on one side and a large normal contact on the other. It had a power amplification of 18. Bardeen and Brattain shared the 1956 Nobel Prize for physics with William SHOCKLEY for their development of the transistor.

Braun, Karl Ferdinand (1850–1918)
German physicist

Braun, who was born in Fulda, Germany, studied at Marburg and, in 1872, received a doctorate from the University of Berlin. He taught in various university posts. In 1885 he became professor of experimental physics at Tübingen and in 1895 he became professor of physics at Strasbourg.

In 1874, Braun observed that certain semiconducting crystals could be used as rectifiers to convert alternating to direct currents. At the turn of the century, he used this fact in the invention of crystal diodes, which led to the crystal radio. He also adapted the cathode-ray tube so that the electron beam was deflected by a changing voltage, thus inventing the oscilloscope and providing the basic component of a television receiver. His fame comes mainly from his improvements to MARCONI's wireless communication system and, in 1909, they shared the Nobel Prize for physics. Braun's system, which used magnetically coupled resonant circuits, was the main one used in all receivers and transmitters in the first half of the 20th century.

Braun went to America to testify in litigation about radio patents but, when the United States entered World War I in 1917, he was detained as an alien and died in New York a year later.

Braun, Wernher von *See* VON BRAUN, WERNHER MAGNUS MAXIMILIAN.

Breit, Gregory (1899–1981) *Russian–American physicist*

Although born in Nicholaev, Russia, Breit moved to America in 1915 and became a naturalized citizen in 1918. He studied at Johns Hopkins University, gaining his PhD in 1921. From 1921 until 1924 he worked successively at the universities of Leiden, Harvard, and Minnesota, before joining the Carnegie Institution, Washington (1924–29).

At Carnegie, Breit worked in the department of terrestrial magnetism as a mathematical physicist, and it was there that he conducted, with Merle A. Tuve, some of the earliest experiments to measure the height and density of the ionosphere. Their technique was to transmit short bursts of radio waves and analyze the reflected waves received. Their work is now seen as a significant step in the historical development of radar.

Besides his pioneering studies of the ionosphere, Breit also worked on quantum theory, nuclear physics, and quantum electrodynamics. In particular, he and Eugene Wigner were able to show that the experimental observations of the interactions of neutrons and protons indicated that the particles differed only in their charge and other electrical properties, and not in their nuclear forces. The *Breit–Wigner formula* is a formula for the energy dependence of the absorption cross-section of a compound nucleus in a nuclear reaction.

Between 1929 and 1973 Breit held professorial posts at the universities of New York, Wisconsin, and Yale, and the State University of New York, Buffalo.

Brenner, Sydney (1927–) *South African–British molecular biologist*

The son of a Lithuanian exile, Brenner was born in Germiston, South Africa, and educated at the universities of Witwatersrand and Oxford, where he obtained his DPhil in 1954. In 1957 he joined the staff of the Medical Research Council's molecular biology laboratory in Cambridge.

Brenner's first major success came in 1957 when he demonstrated that the triplets of nucleotide bases that form the genetic code do not overlap along the genetic material (DNA). The basic idea was that the amino-acid sequence of a protein is determined by the sequence of the four nucleotides – A, T, C, and G – in the DNA, with a specific amino acid being specified by a sequence of three nucleotides. Thus, in an *overlapping* code the sequence:

ATTAGTACGTCGA....

would yield the following triplets, ATT, TTA, TAG, AGT, GTA, etc., each of which specified a particular amino acid.

Brenner however pointed out that such a code imposed severe restrictions on the permitted order of bases. ATT, for example in an overlapping code, could be followed by the four bases TTA, TTT, TTC, and TTG only. This was relatively easy to test without in any way understanding the true nature of the code, and it was soon shown that such implied restrictions were frequently broken.

A greater triumph followed in 1961 when Brenner, in collaboration with Francis Crick and others, reported the results of careful experiments with the bacteriophage T4, which clearly showed that the code did consist of base triplets that neither overlapped nor appeared to be separated by 'punctuation marks'.

The same year also saw Brenner, this time in collaboration with François Jacob and Matthew Meselson, introducing a new form of RNA, messenger RNA (mRNA). With this came one of the central insights of molecular biology – an explanation of the mechanism of information transfer whereby the protein-synthesizing centers (ribosomes) play the role of nonspecific constituents that can synthesize different proteins, according to specific instructions, which they receive from the genes through mRNA.

Brewster, Sir David (1781–1868)
British physicist

Brewster, who was born in Jedburgh, Scotland, started by studying for the ministry at Edinburgh University but, after completing the course, he abandoned the Church for science. He earned his living by editing various journals and spent much time popularizing science.

Brewster published almost 300 papers, mainly concerning optical measurements. He was an early worker in spectroscopy, obtaining (1832) spectra of gases and of colored glass. His most famous work was on the polarization of light. In 1813 he discovered *Brewster's law*, which states that if a beam of light is split into a reflected ray and a refracted ray at a glass surface, then they are polarized, and the polarization is complete when the two rays are at right angles. The angle of incidence at which this occurs is called the *Brewster angle*. He is also known for his invention, in 1816, of the kaleidoscope.

Brewster was knighted in 1832. From 1859 he was principal of Edinburgh University.

Bridgman, Percy Williams (1882–1961) *American physicist*

Bridgman, the son of a journalist, was born in Cambridge, Massachusetts, and educated at Harvard where he obtained his PhD in 1908. He immediately joined the faculty, leaving only on his retirement in 1954 after serving as professor of physics from 1919 to 1926, professor of mathematics and natural philosophy from 1926 to 1950, and as Huggins Professor from 1950 to 1954.

Most of Bridgman's research has been in the field of high-pressure physics. When he began he found it necessary to design and build virtually all his own equipment and instruments. In 1909 he introduced the self-tightening joint and with the appearance of high tensile steels he could aim for pressures well beyond the scope of earlier workers. At the beginning of the century Emile Amagat and Louis Cailletet had attained pressures of some 3000 kilograms per square centimeter; Bridgman increased this enormously, regularly attaining pressures of 100,000 kg/cm^2.

Bridgman used such pressures to explore the properties of numerous liquids and solids. In the course of this work he discovered two new forms of ice, freezing at temperatures above 0°C. He also, in 1955, transformed graphite into synthetic diamond. Bridgman was awarded the 1946 Nobel Prize for physics for his work on extremely high-pressures.

He was also widely known as a philosopher of science and in his book *The Logic of Modern Physics* (1927) formulated his theory of 'operationalism' in which he argued that a concept is simply a set of operations. In his 70s Bridgman developed Paget's disease, which gave him considerable pain and little prospect of relief. He committed suicide in 1961.

Briggs, Henry (1561–1630) *English mathematician*

Born in Warley Wood, Briggs became a fellow of Cambridge University in 1588 and was later made a lecturer (1592) and a professor (1596) of geometry at Gresham College, London.

He is remembered chiefly for the modifications he made to John NAPIER's logarithms, which were first published in 1614. Napier had produced these to base *e* (natural logarithms) but Briggs considerably improved their convenience of use by introducing the base 10 (common logarithms). He also introduced the modern method of long division. Briggs became Savilian Professor of Geometry at Oxford in 1619.

Broca, Pierre Paul (1824–1880) *French physician and anthropologist*

Broca, who was born in Sainte-Fou-la-Grande, France, studied at the University of Paris and received his MD in 1849. In 1853 he was appointed assistant professor in the faculty of medicine. His specialty was the brain and, through surgical work and postmortem examination, he was able to demonstrate that damage to one particular region (the left inferior frontal gyrus, now also known as Broca's convolution) of the cortex was associated with impairment or loss of speech. This was one of the first conclusive demonstrations that control of different bodily functions resides in localized regions of the cerebral cortex.

Broca applied his knowledge of the brain to anthropology. He devised techniques of accurately measuring skulls to enable comparison between the different races of modern man and skulls unearthed at prehistoric sites. Broca's findings supported the then highly contentious theory of Charles Darwin that man, like other living things, had evolved from primitive ancestors. Broca helped found several notable anthropological institutions, including the Société d'Anthropologie de Paris (1859) and the Ecole d'Anthropologie (1876), thus helping to establish anthropology as a respectable branch of science.

Brockhouse, Bertram Neville (1918–   ) *Canadian physicist*

Brockhouse gained his PhD from the University of Toronto in 1950. He worked initially with the Atomic Energy Commission of Canada at the Chalk River Nuclear Laboratory, Ontario. In 1962 he moved to MacMaster University, Hamilton, Ontario, where he remained until his retirement in 1984.

The construction of nuclear reactors in Canada and the USA in the 1940s allowed physicists, once the war had ended, to use neutron beams to explore atomic structure. Neutrons are more effective probes than protons because they are electrically neutral and consequently do not interact with the orbiting electrons. As neutrons can behave as waves they produce diffraction patterns as a result of collisions with their target atomic nuclei. The effect is similar to that of x-ray diffraction, in which the crystal lattice acts as a diffraction grating for the particles. Neutron diffraction from crystals can be used to select beams of neutrons with the same energy. These 'monochromatic' beams can then be used in neutron-scattering experiments.

Brockhouse chose to study the inelastic scattering of neutrons as they bombarded atoms bound in a crystal lattice. In this procedure neutrons give up or gain energy from the atoms they collide with. Monochromatic neutron beams were directed at a crystal target and the energies of the scattered neutrons measured as they emerged. It was thus possible to determine how much energy had been gained or lost. With this data Brockhouse was able to obtain information about the vibration of atoms in the crystal and such important properties as its ability to conduct heat and electricity.

For his work on atomic structure Brockhouse shared the 1994 Nobel Prize for physics with Clifford SHULL.

Brodie, Bernard Beryl (1909–1989) *American pharmacologist*

Born in Liverpool, Brodie was educated at McGill University in Canada and at New York University, where he obtained his PhD in 1935. He worked at the Medical School there from 1943 to 1950 when he moved to the National Institutes of Health at Bethesda, Maryland, where he served as chief of the chemical pharmacology laboratory until 1970.

Brodie worked in a wide variety of fields including chemotherapy, anesthesia, drug metabolism, and neuropharmacology. In 1955 Brodie and his colleagues produced some results that once more raised the possibility of a chemical basis of mental disease. Basically they showed that the tranquilizer reserpine – an alkaloid extracted from the roots of *Rauwolfia* – can produce a profound fall in the level of serotonin, a naturally occurring monoamine in the brain. The question then arose as to whether the tranquilizing effect of reserpine is due to its reduction of too high a level of serotonin.

It was further shown that some of the actions of serotonin could be neutralized by the presence of the hallucinogen LSD. As the structure of the two molecules are somewhat similar the possibility arose that LSD could monopolize the enzyme that normally breaks down serotonin and thus permit the accumulation of unusually high levels of serotonin. It is perhaps this action that causes the hallucinogenic state and which, it has been argued, mimics the schizophrenic state.

In reality the speculations arising from Brodie's work have turned out to be surprisingly difficult to confirm or reject.

Broglie, Prince Louis Victor de See DE BROGLIE, PRINCE LOUIS VICTOR.

Bronsted, Johannes Nicolaus (1879–1947) *Danish physical chemist. See* LOWRY, THOMAS MARTIN.

Broom, Robert (1866–1951) *British–South African morphologist and paleontologist*

Broom, who was born in Paisley, Scotland, graduated in medicine from Glasgow University in 1889. He traveled to Australia in 1892 and in 1897 settled in South Africa where he practiced medicine, often in remote rural communities, until 1928. He also held posts as professor of geology and zoology (1903–10) at Victoria College, now Stellenbosch University, South Africa, and curator of paleontology at the Transvaal Museum, Pretoria from 1934 until his death.

Apart from studies of the embryology of Australian marsupials and monotremes, Broom's major contributions to science have been concerned with the evolutionary origins of mammals, including man. He excavated and studied the fossils of the Karroo beds of the Cape, and in the 1940s discovered numbers of Australopithecine skeletons in Pleistocene age quarries at Sterkfontein, Transvaal. These latter have proved of considerable importance in investigations of man's ancestry and Broom's account of their discovery is given in *Finding the Missing Link* (1950).

Brouncker, William Viscount (1620–1685) *English mathematician and experimental scientist*

Brouncker graduated from Oxford University in 1647 with a degree in medicine. He held a variety of official posts, including serving as member of parliament and president of Gresham's College. He was a friend of the eminent mathematician John Wallis and his own most notable work was also in mathematics. He was a founder and first president of the Royal Society (1662–77) and as such carried out experimental work. Brouncker usually contented himself with solving problems arising from the work of other mathematicians rather than doing creative work himself but was the first to use continued fractions. He was a friend of Samuel Pepys and frequently figures in Pepys's *Diary*. Apart from science, he had a lively interest in music.

Brouwer, Dirk (1902–1966) *Dutch–American astronomer. See* CLEMENCE, GERALD MAURICE.

Brouwer, Luitzen Egbertus Jan (1881–1966) *Dutch mathematician and philosopher of mathematics*

Born in Overschie in the Netherlands, Brouwer took his first degree and doctorate at the University of Amsterdam, where he became successively *Privatdozent* and professor in the mathematics department. From 1903 to 1909 he did important work in topology, presenting several fundamental results, including the fixed-point theorem. This is the principle that, given a circle (or sphere) and the points inside it, then any transformation of all points to other points in the circle (or sphere) must leave at least one point unchanged. A physical example is stirring a cup of coffee – there will always be at least one particle of liquid that returns to its original position no matter how well the coffee is stirred.

Brouwer's best-known achievement was the creation of the philosophy of mathematics known as *intuitionism*. The central ideas of intuitionism are a rejection of the concept of the completed infinite (and hence of the transfinite set theory of Georg Cantor) and an insistence that acceptable mathematical proofs be constructive. That is, they must not merely show that a certain mathematical entity (e.g. a number or a function) *exists*, but must actually be able to construct it. This view leads to the rejection of large amounts of widely accepted classical mathematics and one of the three fundamental laws of logic, the law of excluded middle (either p or not-p; a proposition is either true or not true).

Brouwer was able to re-prove many classical results in an intuitionistically acceptable way, including his own fixed-point theorem.

Brown, Alexander Crum See CRUM BROWN, ALEXANDER.

Brown, Herbert Charles (1912–　) *American chemist*

Brown moved from London, where he was born, to Chicago with his family when he was two years old. His father, originally a cabinet maker, ran a hardware store but Brown had to leave school to help support his mother and three sisters. When he finally did get to college, Crane Junior, it was forced to close in 1933 for lack of funds. He eventually made it to the University of Chicago where he obtained his doctorate in 1938. Brown then worked at Wayne University, Detroit from 1943 until 1947, when he moved to Purdue University, Indiana, where he served as professor of inorganic chemistry until his retirement in 1978.

Brown has become particularly noted for his work on compounds of boron. He discovered a method of making sodium borohydride ($NaBH_4$), a reagent used extensively in organic chemistry for reduction. He also found a simple way of preparing diborane (B_2H_6). By reacting diborane (B_2H_6) with alkenes (unsaturated hydrocarbons containing a double bond) he produced a new class of compounds, organoboranes, which are also useful in organic chemistry. Brown has also used addition compounds of amines with boron compounds to investigate the role of steric effects in organic chemistry. He received the 1979 Nobel Prize for chemistry.

Brown, Michael Stuart (1941–)
American medical biochemist and geneticist.
See GOLDSTEIN, JOSEPH LEONARD.

Brown, Robert (1773–1858) *British botanist*

Brown, a clergyman's son from Montrose, Scotland, studied medicine at Edinburgh University. He joined the Fifeshire Regiment of Fencibles in 1795 and served five years in Ireland as a medical officer. During a visit to London in 1798 he was introduced to Sir Joseph Banks. This led, two years later, to his being recommended by Banks for the post of naturalist on the *Investigator* in an expedition to survey the coast of New Holland (Australia) under the command of Matthew Flinders. Brown accepted the appointment and the *Investigator* set sail for the Cape of Good Hope and Australia in 1801. During his five years with the expedition Brown collected 4000 plant specimens, and on his return to England spent another five years classifying these. Rather than use Linnaeus's artificial classification, he followed Antoine de Jussieu's more natural system, adding his own modifications and using microscopic characters to help delimit species. By 1810 he had described 2200 species, over 1700 of which were new (including 140 new genera). He intended to produce an extensive treatise on Australian plants but the poor sales of the first volume, which appeared in 1810, led him to discontinue publication of the remainder.

In the course of his painstaking work Brown became very familiar with plant morphology, which led him to make many important observations. He found that in conifers and related plants the ovary around the ovule is missing, thus establishing the basic difference between these plants and flowering plants or between the gymnosperms and the angiosperms, as the two groups of seed-bearing plants were later named. He also observed and named the nucleus, recognizing it as an essential part of living cells.

In 1827, while examining a suspension of pollen grains in water, under a microscope, Brown observed that the grains were in continuous erratic motion. Initially he believed that this movement was caused by some life force in the pollen, but when he extended his observations to inanimate particles suspended in water he found the same effect. This phenomenon was named *Brownian motion* and remained unexplained until the kinetic theory was developed.

From 1806 to 1822 Brown was librarian of the Linnean Society; in 1810 he also became librarian and curator at Banks's Soho Square residence. Banks stipulated in his will that on his death Brown should take charge of his house, library, and herbarium. In 1820 Brown duly inherited this responsibility and in 1827 he donated Banks's library and herbarium to the British Museum on the understanding that the trustees established an independent botany department in the museum. Thus a botanical collection became accessible to the general public for the first time in Britain.

Brown-Séquard, Charles-Edouard (1817–1894) *British–French physiologist and neurologist*

Brown-Séquard was born in Port Louis, Mauritius, and studied medicine in Paris, graduating in 1846. He was professor of physiology and pathology at Harvard (1864–68) and in 1878 succeeded Claude Bernard as professor of experimental medicine at the Collège de France. The intervening years were spent in a variety of posts in New York, London, and Paris. He is perhaps best known for his work on the adrenal gland. In his experiments on hormonal secretions, he demonstrated the connection between excision of the adrenal glands and Addison's disease.

Continuing the work of Galen on dissection of the spinal cord, he discovered the *Brown-Séquard syndrome* (crossed hemiplegia), a condition of motor nerve paralysis resulting from the lesion of one side of the spinal cord. This produces an absence of sensation on the opposite side of the body to the nerve paralysis. Brown-Séquard also investigated the possibility of prolonging human life by the use of extracts prepared from the testes of sheep. The majority of his research findings were published as papers in the *Archives de physiologie*, of which he was one of the founders.

Bruce, Sir David (1855–1931) *British bacteriologist*

Bruce was a one-time colleague of Robert Koch in Berlin but spent the greater part of his career as a military physician. Born in Melbourne, Australia, he was educated at Edinburgh University. He was assistant professor of pathology at the Army Medical School, Netley (1889–94), and then commandant of the Royal Army Medical College, Millbank, where he was also director of research on tetanus and trench fever (1914–18). He undertook royal commissions of enquiry into various diseases of man and domestic animals in Malta and central Africa. In Malta he was able to trace the cause of Malta fever (brucellosis or undulant fever found in the milk of goats) to a bacterium later named for him as *Brucella melitensis*. Bruce also investigated the cause of nagana, a disease of horses and cattle in central and southern Africa, and found it to be transmitted by a trypanosome parasite carried by the tsetse fly. This work was of great help in his later research on sleeping sickness (trypanosomiasis), which he also proved to be transmitted by the tsetse fly. The recipient of many honors for his humanitarian work, Bruce was chairman of the War Office's Pathological Committee during World War I. He was knighted in 1908.

Brunel, Isambard Kingdom
(1806–1859) *British engineer*

Brunel's father, Marc Brunel (1769–1849), a French emigré and distinguished engineer, arrived in England in 1799. He sent his son to Paris in 1820 to learn mathematics and engineering. Brunel returned to England in 1822 to work for his father and in 1825 they began the construction of the Rotherhithe-Wapping tunnel underneath the Thames. Here Brunel quickly learned of the unpredictability of great engineering projects; the tunnel flooded in 1828 and Brunel nearly drowned.

While convalescing, he heard that the city of Bristol was considering building a bridge across the River Avon. A competition was to be held with Thomas Telford as the judge. Brunel submitted plans for a suspension bridge at Clifton. Telford rejected Brunel's design and proposed instead that he himself should build something more

appropriate. The selection committee, however, preferred Brunel's plans. Although work began in 1831 it was not until 1864, well after Brunel's death, that the bridge was opened. The span is still standing and remains, perhaps, Brunel's most durable monument.

While in the Bristol region other commissions came his way. In 1833 he was invited to build the Great Western Railway (GWR) to run between London and Bristol. He decided to adopt a 7-foot gauge rather than the 4 foot 8½-inch gauge introduced by George STEPHENSON at the beginning of the railway age. The broad gauge enabled trains to run faster and more comfortably. It did not, however, allow the GWR to link up easily with the rest of the growing network. The line was opened in 1841 and extended to Exeter by 1844. It was insisted, however, in the interest of establishing a unitary railway system, that after 1846 no more broad-gauge track could be laid down. The last of the track was removed in 1896.

Not all Brunel's projects were as successful – in particular, the 'atmospheric railway' that he built between Exeter and Newton Abbot in the 1840s. The idea was to eliminate the locomotive. A continuous pipe was laid between the rails and attached to the carriages by a suspended piston. Air was evacuated from the pipe by pumping engines located along the route. In practice, it proved too difficult to maintain the leather seal through which the connecting rod emerged; it was either eaten by rats, or made brittle by the sea air, or it froze in winter. The line was opened in November 1847 and closed the following year, having incurred enormous losses.

Brunel also turned his attention to steamships. The first Atlantic steam crossing had been accomplished by the American *Savannah* in 1819 using steam in combination with sail. Conventional wisdom held that to cross the Atlantic on steam alone would require so much coal as to leave no room for freight. Brunel calculated otherwise and dispelled this myth with his *Great Western* (1837; 2340 tons), a timber ship driven by paddles. It crossed the Atlantic in 15 days with 200 tons of coal unused in its bunkers.

Brunel went on to build the equally revolutionary *Great Britain* (1843; 3676 tons) with an iron hull and screw propellor, which continued in service for 30 years. His final work was the *Great Eastern* (1858; 32,000 tons) with its double iron hull, screws, and paddles; it was later used to lay the first transatlantic telegraph cable.

The struggle to complete the *Great Eastern* against considerable financial and engineering difficulties seems to have ruined Brunel's health and probably caused the stroke he suffered soon after his great ship had been finally launched. He died soon after.

Bruno, Giordano (1548–1600) *Italian philosopher*

The son of a soldier from Nola in Italy, Bruno entered the Dominican Order in 1565 but was forced to leave in 1576 for unspecified reasons. The following 15 years were spent traveling in France, England, and Germany before visiting Venice in 1591 where he was arrested and handed over to the Inquisition (1592). He was extradited by the Roman Inquisition in 1593. As details of the trial have been destroyed it is no longer known which eight heretical propositions he refused to recant. The results of his action are not however in any doubt: he was burned at the stake.

The exact role of Bruno in 16th-century intellectual history remains a matter of considerable controversy and he was clearly a man of many parts. He was first an expert on the art of mnemonics (memory), a renaissance 'science' long extinct, and he was also involved with a revival of the occult mystical philosophical system of hermeticism. More importantly Bruno was also a keen supporter of the heliocentric system of Nicolaus Copernicus and in his *Cena de le Ceneri* (1584; The Ash Wednesday Supper) added to some rather implausible arguments in defence of Copernicus's claims for the infinity of the universe. His championing of the then unorthodox heliocentric theory was certainly considered heretical and his unhappy end may well have influenced Galileo's actions before the Inquisition.

Buch, Christian Leopold von See VON BUCH, CHRISTIAN LEOPOLD.

Buchner, Eduard (1860–1917) *German organic chemist and biochemist*

Buchner studied chemistry under Adolf von Baeyer and botany in his native city of Munich, gaining his doctorate in 1888. He was Baeyer's assistant until 1893. In 1897, while associate professor of analytical and pharmaceutical chemistry at Tübingen, he observed fermentation of sugar by cell-free extracts of yeast. Following Pasteur's work (1860), fermentation had been thought to require intact cells, and Buchner's discovery of zymase was the first proof that fermentation was caused by enzymes and did not require the presence of living cells. The name 'enzyme' came from the Greek *en* = in

and *zyme* = yeast. Buchner also synthesized pyrazole (1889). He was professor of chemistry at the University of Berlin from 1898 and won the Nobel Prize for chemistry in 1907 for his work on fermentation. He was killed in Rumania, whilst serving as a major in World War I.

Buchner, Hans Ernst Angass (1850–1902) *German bacteriologist*

Buchner, the brother of Eduard Buchner, was born in Munich, Germany, and gained his MD from the University of Leipzig in 1874. He later worked at Munich University serving as professor of hygiene from 1894 until his death.

In 1888 George Nuttall had shown that the ability of blood to destroy invading bacteria lay in the serum. Buchner followed up his work and went on to demonstrate that the bacteriolytic power was lost when the serum was heated to 56°C. He therefore concluded that serum possessed a heat labile substance that he proposed to name alexin.

This work was soon extended by Jules Bordet and the alexins were later renamed 'complement' by Paul Ehrlich. Buchner also did basic work on gamma globulins and developed techniques to study anaerobic bacteria.

Buffon, Comte Georges Louis Leclerc de (1707–1788) *French naturalist*

The son of wealthy Burgundian landowners, Buffon was born in Montbard; he studied law at Dijon and medicine at Angers. After traveling in Italy and England, he inherited his mother's estate upon her death in 1732. The estate flourished under his direction, benefitting from Buffon's knowledge of sylviculture and the ironworks he installed, thus allowing him to concentrate upon scientific matters.

He began by translating S. Hales's *Vegetable Statics* (1735) and Newton's *The Method of Fluxions* (1740) into French. In 1739 he was appointed keeper of the Jardin du Roi, a post he occupied until his death. Buffon restored, extended, and embellished the institution, which was renamed as the Natural History Museum during the Revolution.

Buffon began work on his *Histoire naturelle*, a work that would dominate the rest of his life and which would eventually run to 44 volumes. The completed *Histoire* consisted of:

Vols. 1–15. *Quadrupeds*, 1749–67, with the assistance of Louis Daubenton who provided the anatomical details.

Vols. 16–24. *Birds*, 1770–83, with the assistance of the Abbé Bexon and G. de Mont-beillard.

Vols. 25–31. *Supplementary Volumes.* These deal mainly with the quadrupeds, but Vol. 5 (1778) contains Buffon's important *Epochs of Nature.*

Vols. 32–36. *Minerals,* 1783–88.

The final 8 volumes, *Reptiles* (2 vols., 1788–89), *Fish* (5 vols., 1798–1803), and *Cetacea* (1804) were prepared by E. de Lacepede.

Vol. 1 contained an influential *Preliminary Discourse.* Nature, Buffon argued, was a continuum, and any attempts to divide it into apparently natural classes such as cats and dogs were misguided. Only individuals existed in nature; the rest, genera, species, classes and orders were bogus. In accordance with such views Buffon moved in the *Histoire,* quite artificially, from the familiar to the unfamiliar. He began with Man and familiar domestic animals such as dogs, horses, and cows, before moving on to savage animals. The horse was followed by the dog, not the zebra.

In later volumes of the *Histoire* Buffon modified these initial extreme views. He conceded that "two animals belong to the same species as long as they can perpetuate themselves," and also accepted that there did seem to be, beneath superficial differences, "a single plan of structure" present in all quadrupeds. This did not, however, imply a common descent. If, he argued, the ass was derived from the horse, where were the intermediate forms?

Buffon took a bolder line in his *Epochs of Nature.* He argued against the traditional Biblical chronology of about 6000 years for the Earth's age, claiming instead a period of 78,000 years between the formation of the solar system and the emergence of humans. The estimates were based upon assumptions concerning the rate at which hot bodies of known size and temperature cooled. His calculations allowed him to go further and predict that temperatures will continue to fall, and when they reach 1/25th of the present temperature after 93,000 years, life on Earth will be extinguished.

Bullard, Sir Edward Crisp (1907–1980)
British geophysicist

Bullard was born in Norwich and educated at Cambridge University. After war service in naval research he returned to Cambridge as a reader in geophysics before accepting a post as head of the physics department of the University of Toronto (1948) and visiting the Scripps Institute of Oceanography, California, (1949). After a five-year spell as director of the National Physical Laboratory, he returned to Cambridge as a reader

and later, in 1964, professor of geophysics and director of the department of geodesy and geophysics. Here he remained until his retirement in 1974.

Bullard made a number of contributions to the revolution in the Earth sciences that took place in the 1950s and 1960s. He carried out major work on the measurement of the heat flow from the Earth. It had been assumed that as the ocean floor was less rich in radioactive material than the continental crust, it would be measurably cooler. The technical difficulties of actually measuring the temperature of the ocean floor were not overcome until 1950, and in 1954 Bullard was able to announce that there was no significant temperature difference between the continental crust and the ocean floor. This led Bullard to reintroduce the idea of convection currents.

In 1965 Bullard studied continental drift, using a computer to analyze the fit between the Atlantic continents. An excellent fit was found for the South Atlantic at the 500-fathom contour line. However, a reasonable fit could only be made for the North Atlantic if a number of assumptions, such as deformation and sedimentation since the continents drifted apart, were taken into account. Later, when independent evidence for these assumptions was obtained, it gave powerful support for the theory of continental drift.

Bullard was knighted in 1953.

Bullen, Keith Edward (1906–1976)
Australian applied mathematician and geophysicist

Bullen, the son of Anglo-Irish parents, was born in Auckland, New Zealand; he was educated at the universities of Auckland, Melbourne, and Cambridge, England. He began his career as a teacher in Auckland then lectured in mathematics at Melbourne and in England in Hull. In 1946 he became professor of applied mathematics at the University of Sydney.

Bullen made his chief contributions to science from his mathematical studies of earthquake waves and the ellipticity of the Earth. In 1936 he gave values of the density inside the Earth down to a depth of 3100 miles (5000 km). He also determined values for the pressure, gravitation intensity, compressibility, and rigidity throughout the interior of the Earth as a result of his mathematical studies. From the results on the Earth's density he inferred that the core was solid and he also applied the results to the internal structure of the planets Mars, Venus, and Mercury and to the origin of the Moon.

Bullen conducted some of his early work in collaboration with Harold Jeffreys on earthquake travel times. This resulted in the publication of the *Jeffreys–Bullen* (JB) *tables* in 1940.

Bunsen, Robert Wilhelm (1811–1899)
German chemist

Bunsen, the son of a professor of linguistics, gained his doctorate at the university in his native city of Göttingen (1830) with a thesis on hygrometers. After an extensive scientific tour in Europe, he became a lecturer at Göttingen in 1834. He was professor of chemistry at Kassel (1836), Marburg (1841), and Heidelberg (1852–89).

Bunsen carried out one great series of researches in organic chemistry, *Studies in the Cacodyl Series* (1837–42), after which he abandoned organic for analytical and inorganic chemistry. During his research on the highly toxic cacodyl compound he lost one eye in an explosion and twice nearly killed himself through arsenic poisoning. He prepared various derivatives of cacodyl (tetramethylarsine, $(CH_3)_2As_2(CH_3)_2$), including the chloride, iodide, fluoride, and cyanide, and his work was eagerly welcomed by Jöns Berzelius as confirmation of his theory that organic chemistry mirrored inorganic, the 'radical theory'.

Bunsen was a great experimentalist, an expert in gas analysis and glass blowing, and a pioneer of photochemistry and spectroscopy. He also worked in electrochemistry, devising an improved version of the Grove cell. At Heidelberg he used his new cell to produce metals by electrodeposition. The classic paper *Chemical Analysis through Observation of the Spectrum* (1860) by Bunsen and Gustav KIRCHHOFF ushered in the era of chemical spectroscopy. The spectroscope was an extremely sensitive analytical instrument. With it Bunsen discovered two new elements: rubidium and cesium.

The famous *Bunsen burner* was introduced by him in 1855, although a similar burner, used by Michael Faraday, did exist before Bunsen and the regulating collar was a later refinement. He greatly refined gas analysis and wrote a standard treatise on the subject, *Gasometrische Methoden* (1857, Methods in Gas Measurement).

Bunsen was a great teacher and at Heidelberg he became a legend. Chemists who came to study with him included Adolph Kolbe, Edward Frankland, Victor and Lothar Meyer, Friedrich Beilstein, and Johann Baeyer.

Burbank, Luther (1849–1926) *American plant breeder*

Burbank was brought up on a farm in Lancaster, Massachusetts, and received only an elementary education. He began breeding plants in 1870, when he bought a seven-hectare plot of land. After about a year he had developed the Burbank potato, which was introduced to Ireland to help combat the blight epidemics. By selling the rights to this potato he made $150, which he used to travel to California, where three of his brothers had already settled.

Burbank established a nursery and experimental farm in Santa Rosa, where the climate was especially conducive to fruit and flower breeding – his occupation for the next 50 years. He worked by making multiple crosses between native and introduced strains, using his remarkable skill to select commercially promising types. These were then grafted onto mature plants to hasten development, so that their value could be rapidly assessed. In this way he produced numerous new cultivated varieties of plums, lilies, and many other ornamentals and fruits.

The works of Charles Darwin, particularly *The Variation of Animals and Plants under Domestication*, greatly influenced Burbank. However his success in varying plant characters reinforced his belief in the inheritance of acquired characteristics, even though he knew of Gregor Mendel's research.

Burbidge, Eleanor Margaret (1922–) *British astronomer*

Born Margaret Peachey in Davenport, Burbidge studied physics at the University of London. After graduation in 1948 she joined the University of London Observatory where she obtained her PhD and served as acting director (1950–51). She then went to America as a research fellow, first at the Yerkes Observatory of the University of Chicago (1951–53) and then at the California Institute of Technology (1955–57). The period 1953–55 was spent in highly productive work at the Cavendish Laboratory in Cambridge. She returned to Yerkes in 1957, serving as associate professor of astronomy from 1959 to 1962 and then transferred to the University of California, San Diego, where she was professor of astronomy from 1964 until 1990 and emeritus professor from 1990. She also served (1979–88) as director of the Center for Astrophysics and Space Sciences.

Burbidge returned briefly to England in 1972 on leave of absence to become director of the Royal Greenwich Observatory, now situated at Herstmonceux Castle in Sussex. She declared her aim to be to strengthen optical astronomy in Britain. But as the 98-inch (2.5-m) Isaac Newton telescope at Herstmonceux was only a few hundred feet above sea level and sited above a marsh her opportunities for observation at the Royal Observatory were somewhat limited. A little over a year later, in October 1973, Burbidge resigned amid much speculation declaring simply that she preferred "to return to her own research work rather than devote a major part of her time to administrative matters."

In 1948 she married Geoffrey Burbidge a theoretical physicist, and began a highly productive partnership. They collaborated with Fred Hoyle and William Fowler in 1957 in publishing a key paper on the synthesis of the chemical elements in stars. They also produced one of the first comprehensive works on quasars in their *Quasi-Stellar Objects* (1967). She had earlier recorded the spectra of a number of quasars with the 120-inch (3-m) Lick reflector and discovered that their spectral lines displayed different red shifts, probably indicating the ejection of matter at very high speeds.

The first accurate estimates of the masses of galaxies were based on Margaret Burbidge's careful observation of their rotation.

Burbidge, Geoffrey (1925–) *British astrophysicist*

Born at Chipping Norton, Burbidge graduated in 1946 from the University of Bristol and obtained his PhD in 1951 from the University of London. In the period 1950–58 he held junior university positions at London, Harvard, Chicago, Cambridge (England), and the Mount Wilson and Palomar Observatories in California. He became associate professor at Chicago (1958–62) before being appointed associate professor (1962), then professor of physics (1963) at the University of California, San Diego. Burbidge was director of the Kitt Peak National Observatory, Arizona, from 1978 until 1984, when he moved to the University of California, San Diego, as professor of astronomy.

Burbidge began his research career studying particle physics but after his marriage in 1948 to Margaret Peachey, who was to become one of the world's leading optical astronomers, he turned to astrophysics and began a productive research partnership with his wife. The Burbidges worked on the mysterious quasars, first described by Allan Sandage in 1960, and produced in their *Quasi-Stellar Objects* (1967) one of the earliest surveys of the subject. Geoffrey Burbidge was far from convinced that quasars were 'cosmologically distant' in ac-

cordance with the orthodox interpretation of their massive red shifts. In 1965 he proposed with Hoyle that they were perhaps comparatively small objects ejected at relativistic speeds from highly active radio galaxies such as Centaurus A. The effect of this would be to place the main body of quasars only 3–30 million light years from our Galaxy and not the 3 billion light years or more demanded by the generally accepted view.

He was equally reluctant to accept without reservation that other emerging orthodoxy of the 1960s, the big-bang theory on the origin of the universe. In 1971 he published a paper in which he maintained that we still do not know whether the big-bang occurred and that much more effort must be devoted to cosmological tests. Although such views have found little favor, Burbidge has continued, like Hoyle, to be highly productive, rich in new ideas, and yet to remain outside and somewhat skeptical of prevailing cosmological and astrophysical orthodoxy.

Burkitt, Denis Parsons (1911–1993) *British surgeon*

Born in Enniskillen, now in Northern Ireland, Burkitt attended Dublin University, receiving his BA in 1933 and MB in 1935. Having become a fellow of Edinburgh's Royal College of Surgeons in 1938, Burkitt served in the Royal Army Medical Corps during World War II (1941–46). After the war he worked in Uganda as government surgeon (1946–64), being appointed senior consultant surgeon to the Ugandan Ministry of Health in 1961.

In the late 1950s, Burkitt began studying a form of lymphoma that affected children in his part of Africa. Typically these patients had malignant swellings of the facial bones, although tumors could also be found in the ovaries and abdominal lymph nodes. Burkitt demonstrated that all cases were characterized by infiltration of the affected tissues by lymphocytes, and that the various clinical manifestations were all part of the same cancerous condition, now known as *Burkitt's lymphoma*.

With his colleagues Edward Williams and Clifford Nelson, Burkitt undertook a geographical survey of the incidence of the disease and found it to be correlated with the same temperature and rainfall zones as malaria. This suggested that the occurrence of the disease may be linked with the distribution of certain insect carriers, as with malaria. Also, an association has now been established between the disease and Epstein-Barr virus, which is isolated from many cases. Burkitt's lymphoma survey is regarded as one of the pioneering studies of geographical pathology.

In later life, and drawing on his experiences of the contrasting diets of developed and developing countries, Burkitt did much to promulgate the benefits to health of a high-fiber diet, and argued that certain diseases of affluent societies, such as bowel cancer and appendicitis, are attributable to dietary fiber deficiency. His publications include *Burkitt's Lymphoma* (1970), *Refined Carbohydrate Foods and Disease* (1975), and *Western Diseases, Their Emergence and Prevention* (1981).

Burnet, Sir Frank Macfarlane (1899–1985) *Australian virologist*

Burnet's father, a bank manager, had emigrated to Australia from Scotland as a young man. Burnet was born in Traralgon and studied medicine at Melbourne University, gaining his MD in 1924. After a period abroad at the Lister Institute, London, where he gained his PhD in 1928, Burnet returned to Melbourne to work at the Walter and Eliza Hall Institute; he remained here until his retirement in 1965, having been its director since 1944.

From 1932 until 1933 Burnet worked with the Medical Research Council virology unit in London on influenza. He continued to work with the flu virus in Melbourne, searching for something more convenient than ferrets in which to cultivate the virus. Following the lead of Ernest Goodpasture, Burnet showed (1935) that flu virus could be grown in chick embryo (hen's eggs). While developing this new technique Burnet made an unexpected discovery. Adult hens could be infected with flu and, as was well known, develop antibodies against the virus. Yet the chicks born from the eggs used to grow the flu virus failed to develop any flu antibodies. It appeared that there was a period in development before which an organism was "immunologically illiterate"; it could not distinguish between its own tissue and alien tissue.

In 1949 Burnet drew the immunological conclusions from his work. If an antigen were injected into an animal before birth it should develop an immunological tolerance to that antigen, and consequently fail to produce antibodies if ever exposed later in life. But, Burnet discovered, this did not happen. While a young chick exposed to the antigen as an embryo would fail to develop antibodies, such chicks in adulthood display the usual intolerance and produce antibodies to the appropriate antigen. Burnet had failed to realise that the exposure to the antigen must be continuous for tolerance, not only to develop, but be maintained. The point was later established by Peter MEDAWAR and his colleagues in 1953. It was for this work that Burnet shared the 1960 Nobel Prize for physiology or medicine with Medawar.

Burnet himself found his work on antibodies more satisfying. How, he asked, are organisms able to respond so quickly and so effectively to antigens never before encountered? In 1957, in a paper entitled *Antibody Production Using the Concept of Clonal Selection*, Burnet argued that antibodies, or more accurately the lymphocytes that produce the antibodies, are so comprehensive in their diversity that there is likely to be an antibody in circulation to match any conceivable antigen. The lymphocytes are specialized cells and can respond to just one kind of antigen by producing the appropriately matching antibodies. Once stimulated, however, the lymphocytes will pump out vast numbers of antibodies indefinitely.

Burnet described his work on his clonal selection theory in his autobiography, *Changing Patterns* (1968).

Burnet, Thomas (1635–1715) *English cleric and geologist*

Burnet was born at Croft and was educated at Cambridge University, becoming a fellow of Christ's College in 1657. After a period as tutor to various noblemen he was appointed master of Charterhouse School in 1685. He was also appointed chaplain to William III in 1686 but was later forced to resign (1692) because of his controversial account of the history of the Earth.

In 1681 he published his *Telluris theoria sacra*, which was published in an English version as *The Sacred Theory of the Earth* in 1684 and revised and extended in 1691. In this he tackled the problem that was to face all geologists until this century – how to write a history of the Earth that was consistent with the account given in Genesis. His aim was to take the facts of scripture and show how they could be used to give a rational account of the development of the Earth.

His theory was that the Earth had once been entirely smooth, trapping beneath its shell a large volume of water. Owing to the action of the Sun this shell – the Earth's crust – cracked and released the flood of water; parts of the shattered crust remaining formed the mountains.

Burnet's attempt to explain the history of the Earth in natural terms met a torrent of opposition, both theological and scientific. The strongest argument against this explanation was the presence of marine fossils in mountains for, if the Earth's crust from which the mountains were formed was created before the flood, how could it have come to contain evidence of marine life?

Burt, Cyril Lodowic (1883–1971) *British psychologist*

The son of a London physician, Burt was educated at Oxford University where he studied classics and philosophy. He was introduced to psychology by Oxford's single psychologist, William McDougall. After a period of study in Germany, Burt was appointed to a lectureship in experimental psychology at Liverpool University in 1908. He returned to London in 1912 and remained there for the rest of his career, first as educational psychologist to the London County Council, and from 1932 until his retirement in 1950 as professor of psychology at University College, London.

Much of Burt's life was devoted to the study of intelligence. The statistician Charles Spearman had claimed in 1905 to be able to measure 'g', the factor of general intelligence, objectively. In this he was followed by Burt, who further insisted that intelligence was innate as well as general. The surest way to establish this would be, Burt realized, to measure the intelligence quotients of identical twins separated at birth. If intelligence really was inherited, then the IQ of separated twins should show a high degree of correlation, even though they would have been raised in different homes, and educated in different ways. Consequently, he began to collect data from 1912 onwards. By 1966 Burt had collected a sample of 53 identical separated pairs and the correlation of their IQs was the high figure of 0.771.

Soon after, the journalist Oliver Gillie and the psychologist L. J. Kamin began to raise questions about Burt's work. Not only could research collaborators not be found, but their very existence could not be established. Again, the correlation figure of 0.771 appeared to remain constant over the years, despite changes in sample size, a most unlikely statistical outcome. Further, it turned out that much of Burt's work was based not on measurement, but on estimates of home background and intelligence that he made at a distance. For these and other reasons, Burt's work in this field has been largely discounted.

Butenandt, Adolf Friedrich Johann (1903–1995) *German organic chemist and biochemist*

Butenandt, who was born at Bremerhaven-Lehe (now Wesermünde) in Germany, took his first degree in chemistry at the University of Marburg and gained his doctorate in 1927 under Adolf Windaus at Göttingen. He remained at Göttingen as *Privatdozent* until 1933. Following the work of Windaus on cholesterol, Butenandt investigated the sex hormones and in 1929 he isolated the first pure sex hormone, estrone, from the urine of pregnant women (the compound was also discovered independently by Edward Doisy). A search for the male sex hormone resulted in the isolation in 1931 of 15 milligrams of androsterone from 3960 gallons of urine.

In 1933 he became professor of organic chemistry at the Danzig Institute of Technology and here he demonstrated the similarities between the molecular structures of androsterone and cholesterol. His proposed structure for androsterone was confirmed by Leopold RUŽIČKA's synthesis in 1934. The male hormone testosterone was synthesized by Butenandt and Ružička only months after its isolation in 1935. Butenandt and Ružička were jointly awarded the Nobel Prize for chemistry in 1939 but Butenandt was forbidden to accept it by the Nazi government. Butenandt was also the first to crystallize an insect hormone, ecdysone, and found that this too was a derivative of cholesterol. Later he led research on the isolation and synthesis of the pheromones.

From 1936 to 1945 Butenandt was director of the Max Planck Institute for Biochemistry at Tübingen and from 1945 to 1956 professor of physiological chemistry there. He retained these posts when the institute moved to Munich in 1956, and in 1960 he succeeded Otto Hahn as president of the Max Planck Society, becoming honorary president in 1972.

Buys Ballot, Christoph Hendrik Diederik (1817–1890) *Dutch meteorologist*

Buys Ballot was the son of a minister from Kloetinge in the Netherlands. He was educated at the University of Utrecht, obtaining his PhD in 1844, and became professor of mathematics in 1847 and professor of physics in 1867. He did much to organize the observation and collection of meteorological data in the Netherlands and founded, in 1854, the Netherlands Meteorological Institute.

He is best remembered for the law on wind direction he formulated in 1857. This states that an observer facing the wind in the northern hemisphere has the lower pressure on his right and the higher pressure on his left; in the southern hemisphere this is reversed. Its justification is clearer if stated in the equivalent form: in the northern hemisphere winds circulate counterclockwise around low-pressure areas and clockwise around high-pressure ones.

Byron, Augusta Ada, Countess of Lovelace (1815–1852) *British computer pioneer*

Ada Lovelace was the daughter of Annabella Millbanke and the poet Lord Byron. Ada's mother left her husband after a month of marriage and Ada never saw her father. Born in London, she was educated privately, studying mathematics and astronomy in addition to the more traditional topics. She seems to have developed an early ambition to be a famous scientist. Her correspondence, however, with Mary Somerville and Augustus De Morgan, two of her informal teachers, show that her formal skills were very limited. De Morgan saw her as a talented beginner who could have become an original mathematician if given the chance to receive a rigorous formal Cambridge-style training. Such routes were not open to young Victorian women.

In 1834 she heard Charles BABBAGE lecture on his famous 'difference engine'. She offered Babbage her support and they became good friends. In 1842 she translated from French an account of Babbage's analytical engine by the Italian engineer, L. F. Manabrea. At Babbage's suggestion she added some explanatory notes. They constitute one of the primary sources of his work.

Other plans, such as a *Calculus of the Nervous System*, failed to mature – the obstacles in her way were simply too great. As a woman, for example, she was denied access to the Royal Society Library. Nor did her private life flourish. Her marriage in 1835 to Lord King, created the Earl of Lovelace in 1838, seemed merely to replace the guardianship of her mother with that of her husband. She began an affair in the 1840s with John Crosse, a gentleman who seemed to be as interested in her money as herself. She also took in later life to heavy gambling on horses and by Derby day 1851 she had run up losses of over £3000. Worse was to come, however, as cancer of the uterus had been diagnosed. She was buried beside her father's remains at Newstead Abbey in Nottinghamshire, having died, like him, at the age of 36. Ada Lovelace has been commemorated in the name of the high-level computer language (ADA).

Cagniard de la Tour, Charles
(1777–1859) *French physicist*

Born in Paris, France, Cagniard de la Tour was educated at the Ecole Polytechnique and then spent his time as an amateur inventor. In 1819 he invented the disk siren, in which the sound is produced by air blowing through holes in a rotating disk, the pitch being determined by the speed of rotation. He made his most famous discovery in 1822; when he heated certain liquids in sealed tubes he observed that at a particular temperature and pressure the meniscus dividing liquid from vapor disappeared. Under these conditions – known as the *critical state* – the densities of liquid and vapor become the same and the two are identical.

In the field of biology Cagniard de la Tour discovered, independently of Theodor Schwann, the role of yeast in alcoholic fermentation. He also studied the physics of the human larynx and the sounds produced by it and invented a machine for studying bird flight.

Cailletet, Louis Paul (1832–1913)
French physicist

Born in Chatillon-sur-Seine in France, the son of a metallurgist, Cailletet studied in Paris and then became a manager at his father's foundry.

He is most famous for his work on the liquefaction of gases. Cailletet realized that the failure of others to liquefy the permanent gases, even under enormous pressures, was explained by Thomas ANDREWS's concept of critical temperature. In 1877 he succeeded in producing liquid oxygen by allowing the cold, compressed gas to expand. This technique, depending on the effect discovered by Joule and Thomson, cooled the gas to below its critical temperature. In later experiments he liquefied nitrogen and air. Raoul PICTET, working independently, used a similar technique. In 1884 Cailletet was elected to the Paris Academy for his work. He is also the inventor of the altimeter and the high-pressure manometer.

Calvin, Melvin (1911–1997) *American chemist and biochemist*

Born in St. Paul, Minnesota, Calvin studied chemistry at the Michigan College of Mining and Technology and gained his BS degree in 1931. After obtaining his PhD from the University of Minnesota in 1935 he spent two years at Manchester working with Michael Polanyi. Here he became interested in chlorophyll and its role in the photosynthetic process in plants. Calvin began a long association with the University of California at Berkeley in 1937. From 1941 to 1945 he worked on scientific problems connected with the war, including two years on the Manhattan Project (the atomic bomb).

In 1946 Calvin became director of the Bio-organic Division of the Lawrence Radiation Laboratory at Berkeley, where he used the new analytical techniques developed during the war – ion-exchange chromatography, paper chromatography, and radioisotopes – to investigate the 'dark reactions' of photosynthesis, i.e. those reactions that do not need the presence of light. Plant cells were allowed to absorb carbon dioxide labeled with the radioisotope carbon–14, then immersed at varying intervals in boiling alcohol so that the compounds they synthesized could be identified. In this way the cycle of photosynthetic reactions (known as the *Calvin cycle*) was elucidated and shown to be related in part to the familiar cycle of cell respiration. This work, which was collected in *The Path of Carbon in Photosynthesis* (1957), earned Calvin the Nobel Prize for chemistry in 1961.

Calvin remained at Berkeley, as director of the Laboratory of Chemical Biodynamics (1960–63), professor of molecular biology (1963–71), and professor of chemistry (1971). He continued to work on problems of photosynthesis (especially on the role of chlorophyll in quantum conversion) and on the evolution of photosynthesis.

Camerarius, Rudolph Jacob (1665–1721) *German botanist*

Born the son of a professor of medicine at Tübingen (now in Germany), Camerarius was himself educated there and received his doctorate in 1687. He joined the staff at Tübingen and following his father's death in 1695 was appointed professor of medicine and director of the botanic gardens, posts he occupied until his death from TB in 1721.

In 1694 in *De sexu plantarum* (On the Sex of Plants) Camerarius produced clear experimental evidence for the sexuality of plants first proposed by John Ray and Nehemiah Grew. By isolating pistillate (female) dioecious plants from staminate (male) plants (dioecious referring to plant species where the male and female flowers are borne on separate plants), he was able to show that although the pistillate plants produced fruit, they lacked seeds. With monoecious plants (those that bear separate unisexual male and female flowers on the same plant, e.g. maize) he found that removing the male inflorescence also resulted in sterile fruit.

In his description of plant anatomy Camerarius identified the stamens as the male organ and the style and stigma as the female part. He also described the role of pollination.

Candolle, Augustin Pyrame de
(1778–1841) *Swiss botanist*

Candolle, who was born in Geneva, Switzerland, studied medicine for two years at the academy there before moving to Paris in 1796 to study both medicine and natural sciences. In Paris he met many distinguished naturalists, including Georges Cuvier and Jean Baptiste Lamarck, and quickly established his own reputation through the publication of many outstanding monographs on plants. He received his MD from the University of Paris in 1804 and, at the request of the French government, made a botanical and agricultural survey of France between 1806 and 1812.

In 1813 he published his famous *Théorie élémentaire de la botanique* (Elementary Theory of Botany), in which he introduced the term 'taxonomy' to mean classification. This work was based on the natural classificatory systems of Cuvier and Antoine Jussieu, and in it Candolle maintained that relationships between plants could be established through similarities in the plan of symmetry of their sexual parts. He realized that the symmetry could be disguised by fusion, degeneration, or loss of sexual organs, making structures with a common ancestry appear different. Candolle thus formulated the idea of homologous parts – a concept that lends much weight to the theory of evolution, but surprisingly he continued to believe in the immutability of species. Candolle's classification replaced that of LINNAEUS and was used widely until George Bentham and Joseph Hooker produced their improved system 50 years later.

Candolle also made important contributions to plant geography, realizing that the distribution of vegetation can be profoundly influenced by soil type. The relationships he described between plants and

soil were backed up by personal observations from his travels in Brazil, East India, and North China.

From 1808 to 1816 Candolle was professor of botany at Montpelier University, after which he returned to Geneva to take the chair of natural history at the Academy. On his arrival in Geneva he completely reorganized the gardens. Between 1824 and 1839 he published the first seven volumes of his huge *Prodromus Systematis Naturalis Regni Vegetabilis* (Guide to Natural Classification for the Plant Kingdom), an encyclopedia of the plant kingdom. His son, Alphonse de Candolle, saw to the publication of the remaining ten volumes after his father's death and also carried on many of his father's other schemes.

Cannizzaro, Stanislao (1826–1910)
Italian chemist

Born the son of a magistrate in Palermo, Sicily, Cannizzaro studied physiology in his native city and at Naples. He turned to organic chemistry after realizing the importance of chemical processes in neurophysiology, and from 1845 to 1847 worked as a laboratory assistant to R. Piria at Pisa. Cannizzaro was an ardent liberal and in 1847 he returned to Sicily to fight as an officer in the insurrection against the ruling Bourbon regime. Following the abortive revolution of 1848 he went into exile and returned to chemistry, working with Michel Eugène Chevreul in Paris (1849–51).

Cannizzaro returned to Italy in 1851 as professor of chemistry and physics at the Collegio Nazionale at Alessandria. In 1853 he discovered the reaction known as *Cannizzaro's reaction*, in which an aromatic aldehyde is simultaneously oxidized and reduced in the presence of concentrated alkali to give an acid and an alcohol.

In 1855 Cannizzaro moved to Genoa as professor of chemistry and here he produced the work for which he is chiefly remembered. His pamphlet *Sunto di un corso di filosofia chimica* (1858; Epitome of a Course of Chemical Philosophy) finally resolved more than 50 years of confusion about atomic weights. In 1860 a conference was held at Karlsruhe, Germany, to discuss the problem. No agreement was reached but Cannizzaro's pamphlet was circulated and soon afterwas widely accepted. In it Cannizzaro restated the hypothesis first put forward by Amedeo AVOGADRO, clearly defined atoms and molecules, and showed that molecular weights could be determined from vapor-density measurements.

Politics intervened once more in Cannizzaro's life and in the struggle to reunite Italy he returned to Palermo in 1860 to join Garibaldi. He was professor of inorganic and organic chemistry at Palermo until 1870, when he went to Rome to found the Italian Institute of Chemistry. The most notable research of this last period was that on santonin, a compound derived from species of *Artemisia* (wormwoods) that is active against intestinal worms, which Cannizzaro showed to be a derivative of naphthalene. He was widely honored and became a senator in 1871.

Cannon, Annie Jump (1863–1941)
American astronomer

Annie Cannon was the daughter of a Delaware state senator and was born in Dover in that state. She was one of the first girls from Delaware to attend university, being a student at Wellesley College from 1880 to 1884. After a decade spent at home, where she became deaf through scarlet fever, she entered Radcliffe College in 1895 to study astronomy. In 1896 she was appointed to the staff of the Harvard College Observatory, as it was the practice of the observatory, under the directorship of Edward Pickering, to employ young well-educated women to do calculations. She worked there for the rest of her career, serving from 1911 to 1932 as curator of astronomical photographs. In 1938, after nearly half a century of distinguished service, she was appointed William Cranch Bond Astronomer.

One of the main programs of the observatory was the preparation of the *Henry Draper Catalogue* of a quarter of a million stellar spectra. Stars were originally to be classified into one of the 17 spectral types, A to Q, which were ordered alphabetically in terms of the intensity of the hydrogen absorption lines. Cannon saw that a more natural order could be achieved if some classes were omitted, others added, and the total reordered in terms of decreasing surface temperature. This produced the sequence O, B, A, F, G, K, M, R, N, and S. Cannon showed that the great majority of stars can be placed in one of the groups between O and M. Her classification scheme has since only been slightly altered.

Cannon developed a phenomenal skill in cataloging stars and at the height of her power it was claimed that she could classify three stars a minute. Her classification of over 225,000 stars, brighter than 9th or 10th magnitude, and the compilation of the *Catalogue* took many years. It was finally published, between 1918 and 1924, as volumes 91 to 99 of the *Annals of Harvard College Obser-*

vatory. She continued the work unabated, later publications including an additional 47,000 classifications in the *Henry Draper Extension* (*Annals*, vol. 100, 1925–36). Even as late as 1936 when she was over 70 she undertook the classification of 10,000 faint stars submitted to her by the Cape of Good Hope Observatory.

Cannon, Walter Bradford (1871–1945)
American physiologist

Cannon, who was born in Prairie du Chien, Wisconsin, graduated from Harvard in 1896 and was professor of physiology there from 1906 to 1942. His early work included studies of the digestive system, in particular the use of x-rays to study stomach disorders. For this he introduced the *bismuth meal*. Most of his working life, however, was spent studying the nervous system, particularly the way in which various body functions are regulated by hormones. As early as 1915 he showed the connection between secretions of the endocrine glands and the emotions. In the 1930s he worked on the role of epinephrine in helping the body to meet 'fight or flight' situations. He also studied the way hormonelike substances are involved in transmitting messages along nerves.

Cantor, Georg Ferdinand Ludwig Philipp (1845–1918) *German mathematician*

The son of a prosperous merchant of St. Petersburg, at that time the capital of Russia, Cantor was educated at the University of Berlin where he completed his PhD in 1868. In 1870 he joined the faculty of the University of Halle and was appointed professor of mathematics in 1879. He spent his entire career at Halle, although it was a career repeatedly interrupted after 1884 by mental illness; he was a manic depressive and was hospitalized first in 1899 and several times thereafter. After 1897 he made no further contribution to mathematics and died of heart failure in 1918 in a mental institution.

Although Cantor's earliest work was concerned with Fourier series, his reputation rests upon his contribution to transfinite set theory. He began with the definition of infinite sets proposed by DEDEKIND in 1872: a set is infinite when it is similar to a proper part of itself. Sets with this property, such as the set of natural numbers are said to be 'denumerable' or 'countable'.

In 1874, Cantor published a remarkable paper in Crelle's *Journal*. Here he first showed that the rational numbers (numbers that can be expressed by dividing one integer by another: 1/2, 1/3, 1/4, 2/3, etc.) are denumerable – they can be put in a one-to-one correspondence with the natural numbers (1, 2, 3, etc.). The usual method of demonstrating this is to set up an array in which the first line contains all the rationals in which the denominator is 1 (1/1, 2/1, 3/1, etc.), the second line has all the rationals with a denominator 2 (1/2, 2/2, 3/2, etc.), and so on. It is then possible to 'count' all the fractions in the array by moving diagonally backwards and forwards through the array, and it is clear that every rational number can be put in one-to-one correspondence with an integer. This technique, known as *Cantor's diagonal procedure*, is not the one Cantor used in the 1874 paper, although he did give the diagonal demonstration later. The set of rational numbers and the set of natural numbers are said to have the same 'power'.

Cantor then went on to show that the set of all real numbers is not denumerable. He did this by a *reductio ad absurdum* method. First he assumed that all the real numbers between 0 and 1 are denumerable and expressed as infinite decimal fractions (e.g. $\frac{1}{3}$ = 0.333...). They are arranged in denumerable order:

$a_1 = 0. \, a_{11} \, a_{12} \, a_{13} \, a_{14} \, ...$

$a_2 = 0. \, a_{21} \, a_{22} \, a_{23} \, a_{24} \, ...$

etc.

Here, a_1 is the first real number and a_{11} the first digit, a_{12} the second, etc. The first digit of the second number a_2 is a_{21}, etc. Cantor then showed that it is possible to construct an infinite decimal that is not in the above set by taking the diagonal containing a_{11}, a_{22}, a_{33}, etc., and changing the digit to 9 if it is 1 and changing the digit to 1 for all other digits. This gives a number that is a real number between 0 and 1, yet is not in the above set. In other words, the real numbers are not denumerable – there is a sense in which there are 'more' real numbers than rational numbers or natural numbers. The set of real numbers has a higher power than the set of natural numbers.

Cantor designated the set of natural numbers, the smallest transfinite set, with the symbol $\aleph_0$ and the set of real numbers by the letter c, the number of the continuum. $\aleph$ is the first letter of the Hebrew alphabet, called 'aleph'. Cantor's symbol $\aleph_0$ is referred to as 'aleph nul'.

Cantor went on to show that there were in fact an infinite number of transfinite sets. The power set of a set S consists of the subsets of S. Thus let $S = (1,2)$, the power set of S, $P(S) = [(1), (2), (1,2), (\emptyset)]$, bearing in mind that every set is a member of itself, and that the empty set ($\emptyset$) belongs to every set. In general Cantor demonstrated that if a set S has n members then $P(S)$ will have 2^n members, that $P(S) > S$, a result since known as *Cantor's theorem*.

The theorem applies to all sets, infinite as well as finite. Thus the power set of $\aleph_0$ will be greater than $\aleph_0$ and the process can be continued with the power set of the power set of $\aleph_0$, and so on indefinitely. Cantor had shown that the set of natural numbers had a cardinality of $\aleph_0$, and the real numbers, c, had a cardinality of $2^{\aleph_0}$. This enabled him to pose in 1897 the hypothesis that $2^{\aleph_0} = \aleph_1$, or, that the continuum (c) is the next highest infinite number after $\aleph_0$. Cantor made little progress with the continuum problem. It remained for GODEL and COHEN to illuminate the issue many years later.

Cardano, Gerolamo (1501–1576)
Italian mathematician, physician, and astrologer

The work of Cardano constitutes a landmark in the development of algebra and yet in his own time he was chiefly known as a physician. He studied medicine at the University of Pavia, the city of his birth, and at the University of Padua, receiving his degree in 1526. He spent much of his life as a practicing physician, becoming professor of medicine at Pavia in 1543. One of his notable nonmathematical achievements was to give the first clinical description of typhus fever.

It was however in mathematics that Cardano's real talents lay. His chief work was the *Ars magna* (1545; The Great Skill) in which he gave ways of solving both the general cubic and the general quartic. This was the first important printed treatise on algebra. The solution of the general cubic equation was revealed to him by Niccolò TARTAGLIA in confidence and Cardano's publication aroused a bitter controversy between the two. Cardano's former servant, Lodovico Ferrari, had discovered the solution of the general quartic equation. In his later *Liber de ludo aleae* (Book on Games of Chance) Cardano did some pioneering work in the mathematical theory of probability.

Cardano's interests were not, however, limited to mathematics and medicine. He also indulged in philosophical and astrological speculation and this had the unfortunate consequence that in 1570 he was charged with heresy by the Church. He was briefly jailed but was soon released after the necessary recantation. As a result of this episode Cardano lost his post as a professor at the University of Bologna, which he had held since 1562.

Carnot, Nicolas Leonard Sadi
(1796–1832) *French physicist*

Carnot came from a distinguished Parisian political family; his father, Lazare, was a leading politician under Napoleon Bonaparte. He studied at the Ecole Polytechnique, from which he graduated in 1814. For the next few years he worked as a military engineer, but the political climate had changed with the fall of Bonaparte and, in 1819, he transferred to Paris and concentrated on scientific research.

The fruits of this work ripened in 1824 in the form of a book called *Réflexions sur la puissance motrice de feu* (On the Motive Power of Fire). The main theme of this masterpiece was an analysis of the efficiency of engines in converting heat into work. He found a simple formula depending only on the temperature differences in the engine and not on intermediate stages through which the engine passed. He also introduced the concept of reversibility in the form of the ideal *Carnot cycle*. Using these ideas he derived an early form of the second law of thermodynamics, stating that heat always flows from hot to cold. It became an inspiration, many years later, for Rudolf Clausius's formulations of thermodynamics. Carnot died of cholera at the age of 36.

Carothers, Wallace Hume (1896–1937)
American industrial chemist

Carothers, the son of a teacher, was born in Burlington, Iowa, and gained a BS degree from Tarkio College, Missouri (1920), after working his way through college. He gained his PhD in 1924 from the University of Illinois and was an instructor in chemistry at Illinois and Harvard before joining the Du Pont company at Wilmington, Delaware, as head of organic chemistry research in 1928.

Carother's early work was in the application of electronic theory to organic chemistry but at du Pont he worked on polymerization. His first great success was the production of the synthetic rubber, neoprene (1931). Working with acetylenes he discovered that the action of hydrochloric acid on monovinylacetylene produced 2-chloro-buta-1,3-diene (chloroprene), which polymerized very readily to give a polymer that was superior in some respects to natural rubber.

In a systematic search for synthetic analogs of silk and cellulose he prepared many condensation polymers, especially polyesters and polyethers. In 1935 one polyamide, produced by condensation of adipic acid and hexamethylenediamine, proved outstanding in its properties and

came into full-scale production in 1940 as Nylon 66. But Carothers did not live to see the results of his achievements; despite his brilliant successes he suffered from fits of depression and took his own life at the age of 41.

Carrel, Alexis (1873–1944) *French surgeon*

Carrel received his medical degree from the university in his native city of Lyons in 1900. In 1902 he started to investigate techniques for joining (suturing) blood vessels end to end. He continued his work at the University of Chicago (1904) and later (1906) at the Rockefeller Institute for Medical Research, New York. Carrel's techniques, which minimized tissue damage and infection and reduced the risk of blood clots, were a major advance in vascular surgery and paved the way for the replacement and transplantation of organs. In recognition of this work, Carrel was awarded the 1912 Nobel Prize for physiology or medicine.

During World War I, Carrel served in the French army. With the chemist Henry Dakin, he devised the Carrel–Dakin antiseptic for deep wounds. Returning to the Rockefeller Institute after the war, Carrel turned his attention to methods of keeping tissues and organs alive outside the body. He maintained chick embryo heart tissue for many years on artificial nutrient solutions and with the aviator Charles Lindbergh he devised a so-called artificial heart that could pump physiological fluids through large organs, such as the heart or kidneys.

In *Man, the Unknown* (1935), Carrel published his controversial views about the possible role of science in organizing and improving society along rather authoritarian lines. During World War II he founded and directed the Carrel Foundation for the Study of Human Problems under the Vichy government, in Paris. Following the Allied liberation, Carrel faced charges of collaboration but died before a trial was arranged.

Cartan, Elie Joseph (1869–1951) *French mathematician*

Cartan is now recognized as one of the most powerful and original mathematicians of the 20th century, but his work only became widely known toward the end of his life. Cartan, who was born in Dolomieu, France, studied at the Ecole Normale Supérieure in Paris and held teaching posts at the universities of Montpellier, Lyons, Nancy, and, from 1912 to 1940, Paris.

Cartan's most significant work was in developing the concept of analysis on differentiable manifolds, which now occupies a central place in mathematics. He began his research career with a dissertation on Lie groups – a topic that led him on to his pioneering work on differential systems. The most important innovation in his work on Lie groups was his creation of methods for studying their global properties. Similarly his work on differential systems was distinguished by its global approach. One of his most useful inventions was the 'calculus of exterior differential forms,' which he applied to problems in many fields including differential geometry, Lie groups, analytical dynamics, and general relativity. Cartan's son Henri is also an eminent mathematician.

Carter, Brandon (1942–) *British physicist*

Born in Sydney, Australia, Carter was educated at the University of St. Andrews and at Cambridge University, where he completed his PhD in 1968. He remained in Cambridge as a research fellow at the Institute of Astronomy until 1973. Carter then moved to France to join the Centre National de la Recherche Scientifique (CNRS), working from 1986 as director of research at the Paris-Meudon Observatory.

In 1974 Carter formulated what is known as the *anthropic principle*. The argument began with COPERNICUS whose heliocentric system is often thought to have removed man from any special privileged position in the universe. Carter, however, insisted that it is privileged to the extent that our location in the universe must be compatible with our existence as observers. That is, if the universe had differed significantly in its size, age, and character then intelligent life would not now be present to observe it. If, for example, the strength of the gravitational force differed by just one part in 10^{40} all stars would be either blue giants or red dwarves; with no Sun-like stars to nourish life, the universe would be without observers. The fact that it has observers, therefore, presupposes that the nuclear, gravitational, and electromagnetic forces all fall within some very narrow limits.

This is sometimes known as the 'weak form' of the anthropic principle. Carter advanced from this to the strong version with his claim that "The universe must have those properties which allow life to develop within it at some stage in its history." While some physicists have seen in the anthropic principle a profound key to the secrets of nature, others have dismissed it on the grounds that it is immune to falsifica-

tion, makes no significant predictions, and offers all its explanations after the event.

Carver, George Washington
(1864–1943) *American agricultural chemist*

Carver was born a slave in Diamond Grove, Missouri. Nevertheless, he managed to acquire some elementary education and went on to study at the Iowa State Agricultural College from which he graduated in 1892. He taught at Iowa until 1896, when he returned to the South to become director of the department of agricultural research at the Tuskegee Institute, Alabama. There he stayed despite lucrative offers to work for such magnates as Henry Ford and Thomas Edison.

His main achievement was to introduce new crops into the agricultural system of the South, in particular arguing for large-scale plantings of peanuts and sweet potatoes. He saw that such new crops were vital if only to replenish the soil, which had become impoverished by the regular growth of cotton and tobacco.

But he did much more than introduce new crops for he tried to show that they could be used to develop many new products. He showed that peanuts contained several different kinds of oil. So successful was he in this that by the 1930s the South was producing 60 million dollars worth of oil a year. Peanut butter was another of his innovations. In all he is reported to have developed over 300 new products from peanuts and over 100 from sweet potatoes.

Casimir, Hendrik Brugt Gerhard
(1909–) *Dutch physicist*

Born in the Dutch capital city, The Hague, Casimir studied at the universities of Leiden, Copenhagen, and Zurich, and held various research positions between 1933 and 1942.

He has published many papers in the fields of theoretical physics, applied mathematics, and low-temperature physics. His most notable work has been in the theory of the superconducting state. Following the work of W. Meissner, Casimir and his colleague Cornelis Gorter advanced a two-fluid model of superconductivity in 1934 in which a fraction of the electrons were regarded as superconducting, while the rest remained 'normal' electrons. They were successful in explaining the high degree of interrelationship between the magnetic and thermal properties of superconductors.

From 1942, Casimir has pursued a highly successful career with the Philips company, becoming director of the Philips Research Laboratories in 1946, and a member of the board of management (1957–72). He has supervised Philips's research activities in several countries.

Caspersson, Torbjörn Oskar
(1910–   ) *Swedish cytochemist*

Caspersson, who was born in Motala, Sweden, gained his MD from Stockholm University in 1936. He then joined the staff of the Nobel Institute serving as professor of medical cellular research and genetics from 1944 to 1977. In 1977 he was appointed professor and head of the medical cell research and genetics department at the Kungliga Karolinska Mediko-Kirurgiska Instituet in Stockholm.

In the late 1930s Caspersson spent a few years working on DNA. In 1936 with the Swiss chemist Rudolf Signer he made fundamental measurements of the molecule that suggested a molecular weight between 500,000 and a million, so showing the nucleic acids to be larger than protein molecules.

Further important data was collected by a photoelectric spectrophotometer developed by Caspersson. This allowed the movement of RNA in the cell to be followed by its characteristic absorption peak in the ultraviolet at 2600 angstroms and to establish that protein synthesis in the cell was associated with an abundance of RNA. Despite this Caspersson remained committed to the orthodox view that genes were proteins and believed nucleic acids to be a structure-determining supporting substance.

In 1970 Caspersson made a major breakthrough in the study of chromosomes. Before 1970 the only way to identify a chromosome was by its length. Caspersson argued that if genes differed in their concentration of the four bases (guanine, adenine, cytosine, and thymine), then they would be distributed differently in each chromosome. If a dye could be found that bound to one of the bases only, then a characteristic chromosomal pattern would be displayed. Precisely this happened when Caspersson found a quina-acrine mustard with an affinity for guanine. When illuminated with ultraviolet the now familiar pattern of bright and dark bands were displayed with startling clarity. Within a year Caspersson had used distinctive banding patterns to characterize all human chromosomes.

Cassini, Giovanni Domenico (1625–1712) *Italian–French astronomer*

Born in Perinaldo, Italy, Cassini was educated in Genoa and at the early age of 25 became professor of astronomy at Bologna.

He remained there until 1669 when he moved to France in order to take charge of Louis XIV's new Paris Observatory. He became a French citizen in 1673.

While still at Bologna he worked out, fairly accurately, the rotational periods of Jupiter and Mars. In 1668 he constructed a table of the movements of the Medici planets – the satellites of Jupiter discovered by Galileo. It was this table that allowed Ole Romer to calculate the speed of light. In Paris, using aerial telescopes up to 150 feet (45.7 m) long, he discovered four new satellites of Saturn – Iapetus in 1671, Rhea in 1672, and Dione and Tethys in 1684. In 1675 he discovered the gap that divides Saturn's rings into two parts and has since been called *Cassini's division*.

Cassini's most important work concerned the size of the solar system. Using data collected by Jean Richer in Cayenne, together with his own observations in Paris, he was able to work out the parallax of Mars and thus calculate the astronomical unit (AU) – the mean distance between the Earth and the Sun. His figure of 87 million miles (140 million km) may have been 7% too low, but compared with earlier figures of Tycho Brahe (5 million miles) and Johannes Kepler (15 million miles) his results gave mankind a realistic picture of the size of the universe for the first time. Cassini also made fundamental measurements on the size and shape of the Earth concluding, erroneously, that it was a prolate spheroid. He became blind in 1710 and was succeeded in the directorship of his observatory by both his son, Jacques Cassini, and his grandson, César François Cassini.

Castner, Hamilton Young (1858–1898) *American chemist*

Born in New York City, Castner studied at Brooklyn Polytechnic and at Columbia University, New York. He started as a chemical consultant in 1879 and moved to Britain in 1886 when he failed to gain any backing in America for his process for the production of sodium.

Henri Sainte-Claire Deville had developed a system in which caustic soda could be reduced to sodium with charcoal at high temperatures. However he ran into a variety of practical difficulties, which were satisfactorily cleared up by Castner. Castner intended to use the sodium for producing aluminum by reduction of aluminum chloride – at the time aluminum was a very expensive metal. A factory was opened in 1888 at Oldbury, Birmingham, to manufacture 100,000 lbs of aluminum per annum. But it was too late for, two years earlier, Charles Hall in America and Paul Héroult in France had independently discovered a cheap way to produce aluminum by electrolysis. Castner quickly had to invent some uses for his sodium, for which there was little demand at the time. One was the manufacture of sodium peroxide (by burning sodium in air), used as a bleach. By passing ammonia over molten sodium and charcoal he produced sodium cyanide, which was used in the extraction of gold.

By the early 1890s, with the growing demand for his products, his problem was an inability to produce enough sodium. He solved this with a new method of making sodium by the electrolysis of brine using a mercury cathode. The process had been anticipated by **Carl Kellner** (1851–1905) in Austria; rather than litigate the two chemists cooperated and in 1897 set up the Castner–Kellner Alkali Company in Runcorn, Cheshire, where there was a cheap and abundant supply of salt. In the year of his death it was already producing 20 tons of caustic soda a day with the production also of 40 tons of bleaching powder daily as a byproduct.

Cauchy, Baron Augustin Louis (1789–1857) *French mathematician*

Cauchy showed great mathematical talent at an early age and came to the attention of Joseph Lagrange and Pierre Laplace, who encouraged him in his studies. Born in Paris, France, he was educated at the Ecole Polytechnique, where he later lectured and became professor of mechanics in 1816, and worked briefly as an engineer in Napoleon's army. He held extreme conservative views in religion and politics, typical of which was the strong allegiance to the Bourbon dynasty that caused him to follow Charles X (who had ennobled Cauchy) into exile in 1830. Cauchy then became professor of mathematics at Turin, but returned to France in 1838 and resumed his post at the Ecole Polytechnique.

Cauchy was an extremely prolific mathematician who made outstanding contributions to many branches of the subject, ranging from pure algebra and analysis to mathematical physics and astronomy. He was also an outstanding teacher. His greatest achievements were in the fields of real and complex analysis in which he was one of the first mathematicians to insist on the high standards of rigor now taken for granted in mathematics. He gave the first fully satisfactory definitions of the fundamentally important concepts of limit and convergence.

Cavalieri, Francesco Bonaventura (1598–1647) *Italian mathematician and geometer*

Born in the Italian city of Milan, Cavalieri joined the Jesuits as a boy. He became interested in mathematics while studying Euclid's works and met Galileo, whose follower he became.

Cavalieri's fame rests chiefly on his work in geometry in which he paved the way for the development of the integral calculus by Isaac Newton and Gottfried Leibniz. In 1629 Cavalieri became professor of mathematics at Bologna, a post he held for the rest of his life. At Bologna he developed what he called his "method of indivisibles," published in his *Geometria indivisibilibus continuorum nova quadam ratione promota* (1635; A Certain Method for the Development of a New Geometry of Continuous Indivisibles), which had much in common with the basic ideas of integral calculus.

Cavalieri also helped to popularize the use of logarithms in Italy through the publication of his *Directorium generale uranometricum* (1632; A General Directory of Uranometry).

Cavalli-Sforza, Luigi Luca (1922–   ) *Italian geneticist*

Cavalli-Sforza, who was born in Genoa, Italy, was educated at the University of Pavia where he gained his MD in 1944. After working on bacterial genetics at Cambridge (1948–50) and Milan (1950–57) he has held chairs in genetics at Parma (1958–62) and Pavia (1962–70). In 1970 he was appointed professor of genetics at the University of Stanford, California, a position he held until his retirement in 1992.

Cavalli-Sforza has specialized mainly in the genetics of human populations, producing with Walter Bodmer a comprehensive survey of the subject in their *Genetics, Evolution and Man* (1976).

He has also done much to show how genetic data from present human racial groups could be used to reconstruct their past separations. This reconstruction, based on the analysis of 58 genes, yields a bifurcated evolutionary tree with Caucasian and African races in one branch and Orientals, Oceanians, and Amerinds in the other. The main division appeared, according to Cavalli-Sforza, some 35–40,000 years ago.

Cavendish, Henry (1731–1810) *English chemist and physicist*

Cavendish, who was born in Nice in the south of France, was the son of Lord Charles Cavendish, himself a fellow of the Royal Society and administrator of the

British Museum. Henry was educated at Cambridge University (1749–53), but left without a degree. Following this he devoted the rest of his life to science. He inherited from his uncle a vast fortune with which he built up a large library and financed his scientific interests. Throughout his life he was an eccentric recluse, appearing only rarely in public and then chiefly at scientific meetings. He communicated with his housekeeper by a system of notes and was such a misogynist that he ordered all his female domestics to keep out of his sight.

Cavendish's first published work was *Three Papers containing Experiments on Factitious Airs* (1766). In these he clearly distinguished hydrogen (inflammable air) and carbon dioxide (fixed air) as gases separate from common air. Some of the work on fixed air duplicated that of Joseph Black, little of which had been published, but Cavendish was the first to weigh gases accurately.

Much of Cavendish's work remained unpublished in his lifetime and he is now known to have anticipated or come very close to several major discoveries. His electrical studies, which were edited by Clerk Maxwell in 1879, following the discovery of his notebooks and manuscripts, included the clear distinction between electrical quantity and potential, the measurement of capacitance, and the anticipation of Ohm's law (1781). He had the concept of specific heat in 1765 but the work was not published. In 1778, working on the effect of water vapor on the compressibility of air, he arrived at what is essentially the law of partial pressures (*see* **John Dalton**). One important physical investigation that was published was the determination of the mean density of the Earth (1798) by means of the torsion balance in what became known as the *Cavendish experiment*.

In his chemical work Cavendish came close to the concepts of equivalent weights and multiple proportions but he was not a generalizer and the concepts only became explicit in the works of others. His most illustrious and controversial work was his synthesis of water. The paper *Experiments on Air* (1784) reported his researches on exploding hydrogen with oxygen and air. He concluded that air consisted of a mixture of oxygen and nitrogen in a ratio of 1:4 and that hydrogen and oxygen mixed in proportions of 2:1 yielded their own weight of water. This work was carried out in 1781, and although Cavendish's priority is quite clear a dispute ensued between James Watt, Antoine Lavoisier, and Cavendish. It was discovered from this work that water is not an element but a compound.

The reason for Cavendish's three-year delay in publishing his work on water was the persistent discovery of nitric acid (then called nitrous acid) in the water after sparking hydrogen and air. In further experiments he accomplished the conversion of nitrogen to nitric acid by sparking over alkali, which formed potassium nitrate. This synthesis was the basis of the commercial production of nitric acid until 1789. In the course of his work on gases Cavendish refined the eudiometer and his measurements of the oxygen content of air showed it to be the same everywhere.

On his death Cavendish left over a million pounds sterling to his relatives. From this the endowment of the famous Cavendish Laboratory was made to Cambridge University in 1871.

Cavendish, Margaret, Duchess of Newcastle (1623–1673) *British natural philosopher*

The daughter of a wealthy landowner, Margaret was born at St. John's, Colchester, in the eastern English county of Essex and inherited £10,000 on his death. She received a scant education from "an ancient decayed gentlewoman." With the outbreak of the civil war the family lost its estates, two brothers died fighting for the king, and in 1641 Margaret entered the royal court as a maid of honor to Henrietta Maria, wife to Charles I. In 1643 she fled with the queen to Paris and spent the next eighteen years in impoverished exile in Europe.

In 1645 she married William Cavendish, Duke of Newcastle. While in exile in Paris and in Antwerp she moved in circles where the ideas of Hobbes, Descartes, and Gassendi were frequently discussed. From such discussions Margaret was introduced to mechanical philosophy.

While in exile she began to write on topics in natural philosophy, producing her *Philosophical and Physical Opinions* (1655). She continued to write about science after her return from exile with the restored Charles II in 1660, publishing her *Observations upon Natural Philosophy* (1666). She was highly critical of the new science. Her main objection was the familiar one that not all natural phenomena could be explained by "the Dusty motion of Atoms." Consequently, she argued, every atom must be "animated with life and knowledge." She was also critical of the newly invented microscope, claiming that it distorted nature.

Much of her later life was spent in seclusion at Welbeck writing verse and plays as well as concerning herself with natural philosophy. She did, however, pay a well-documented visit to London in 1667 when she visited the Royal Society and witnessed experiments performed by Boyle and Hooke. But membership would remain closed to her or any other woman for a further three centuries.

Caventou, Jean Bienaimé (1795–1877) *French pharmacist and organic chemist. See* PELLETIER, PIERRE JOSEPH.

Cayley, Arthur (1821–1895) *British mathematician*

Born in Richmond, Cayley studied mathematics at Cambridge University, but before becoming a professional mathematician spent 14 years working as a barrister. He was forced to do this since he was unwilling to take holy orders – which at that time was a necessary condition of continuing his mathematical career at Cambridge. When this requirement was dropped, Cayley was able to return to Cambridge and in 1863 became Sadlerian Professor there.

Cayley was an extremely prolific mathematician. His greatest work was the creation of the theory of invariants, in which he worked closely with his friend James Joseph Sylvester. Cayley developed this theory as a branch of pure mathematics but it turned out to play a crucial role in the theory of relativity, as it is important in the calculation of space–time relationships in physics. He also developed the theory of matrices and made major contributions to the study of n-dimensional geometry. He went a considerable way toward unifying the study of geometry. Cayley also did important work in the theory of elliptic functions.

One of Cayley's notable nonmathematical achievements was playing a large role in persuading the University of Cambridge to admit women as students.

Cech, Thomas Robert (1947–) *American chemist*

Chicago-born Cech was educated at the University of California, Berkeley, where he gained his PhD in 1975. He then joined the faculty of the University of Colorado, Boulder, where he became professor of chemistry in 1983.

In 1977 Philip SHARP discovered long stretches of non-coding DNA, later called 'introns'. In 1982 Cech began to investigate how these supposedly redundant sequences could be removed from the RNA molecule after it had been copied from the DNA template. For such a complex process to happen

so rapidly it must, it seemed, be catalyzed by an enzyme. Since the first enzyme to be synthesized (by James SUMNER in 1926) had turned out to be a protein, and since all of the hundreds of other cellular enzymes had also turned out to be proteins, Cech confidently began to search for the protein enzyme responsible for snipping introns from RNA molecules.

He worked with ribosomal RNA (rRNA) of the protozoa *Tetrahymena thermophilia*. He began with some unspliced rRNA and some protozoa nuclei mixed together *in vitro*. He assumed that the nuclear enzymes would catalyze the splicing. But, although the RNA introns were indeed neatly snipped away, none of the nuclear enzymes appeared to have been used. At first Cech assumed that the RNA itself harbored the protein enzyme responsible. To eliminate this possibility Cech synthesized his own pre-rRNA from a recombinant DNA template. The result was a viable but artificial rRNA, which, never having been in contact with a cell, could not possibly contain any cellular splicing enzymes. Despite this the introns were still removed.

RNA, Cech concluded in 1982, must be self-splicing. It acted like an enzyme in catalyzing a specific reaction, at a greatly accelerated rate, yet, unlike an enzyme, it operated upon itself. To mark the difference Cech proposed the name 'ribozyme'.

Confirmation of Cech's researches soon came from the work of Sidney ALTMAN on ribonuclease. For this work, Cech and Altman shared the 1989 Nobel Prize for chemistry.

Celsius, Anders (1701–1744) *Swedish astronomer*

Celsius, the son of a mathematician, became professor of astronomy at the university in his native city of Uppsala, where he opened an observatory in 1740. In 1742 he devised a temperature scale in which the temperature of melting ice was taken as 100° and the temperature of boiling water was taken to be 0°. The modern *Celsius* (or *centigrade*) scale has the opposite fixed points (ice point 0°; steam point 100°C).

Cerenkov, Pavel Alekseyevich *See* CHERENKOV, PAVEL ALEKSEYEVICH.

Cesalpino, Andrea (1519–1603) *Italian physician and botanist*

Born at Arezzo in Italy, Cesalpino studied anatomy and medicine at the University of Pisa, where he graduated in 1551; in 1555 he became professor of medicine and director of the botanic garden there. In 1592 he became physician to Pope Clement VIII and professor at the Sapienza University.

He is most famous for his plant classification based on fruit and seed characteristics, which is described in his work, *De plantis* (1583; On Plants). This work also discusses the whole of theoretical botany and had great influence on later botanists.

Cesalpino also wrote a number of anatomical books in which he partly anticipated the theory of the circulation of the blood proposed by William Harvey.

Chadwick, Sir James (1891–1974)
British physicist

Chadwick was born in Macclesfield and was educated at the University of Manchester, where he graduated in 1911 and remained as a graduate student under Ernest Rutherford. In 1913 he went to Leipzig to work under Hans Geiger and found himself interned in 1914 near Spandau as an enemy alien. There he remained for the duration of the war, cold and hungry but permitted, with the help of Walther Nernst, to carry out rudimentary research.

On his return to England in 1919 he was invited by RUTHERFORD to accompany him to Cambridge University where, from 1922 until 1935, he served as assistant director of research at the Cavendish Laboratory. It was during this period that Chadwick, in 1932, made his greatest discovery – the neutron. Before this, physicists had accepted the existence of only two elementary particles: the proton (p) with a positive charge, and the electron (e) with a negative charge. It was however clear to all that these two particles could not account for all the atomic phenomena observed. The helium atom, for example, was thought to consist of four protons; that it only possessed a positive charge of two was due to the nucleus also containing two 'internal electrons', which neutralized the charge on two of the protons. The difficulty of such a view was the failure of a disintegrating nucleus to produce the electrons supposedly contained within it.

In 1920 Rutherford had provided an alternative solution by introducing the possibility of "an atom of mass 1 which has zero nuclear charge." Chadwick attempted unsuccessfully to discover such a particle in the 1920s by bombarding aluminum with alpha particles (helium nuclei). More promising, however, was the report in 1930 that the bombardment of beryllium with alpha particles yielded a very penetrating radiation. In 1932 Irène and Frédéric JOLIOT-CURIE found that this radiation could eject protons with considerable velocities from

matter containing hydrogen. They thought such radiation consisted of gamma rays – electromagnetic radiation of very short wavelength. Chadwick showed that the gamma rays would not eject protons, but that the result was explained if the particles had nearly the same mass as protons but no charge, i.e. the particles were neutrons. It was for this work that Chadwick was awarded the 1935 Nobel Prize for physics.

By 1936 a certain amount of friction had begun to appear between Chadwick, who wished to build a cyclotron at the Cavendish Laboratory, and Rutherford who initially was violently opposed to any such project. It was therefore with some relief that Chadwick decided in 1935 to accept the offer of the chair of physics at Liverpool University. There he built Britain's first cyclotron and was on hand at the outbreak of war to support the claims made by Otto Frisch and Rudolph Peierls on the feasibility of the atomic bomb. Chadwick consequently spent most of the war in America as head of the British mission to the Manhattan project.

For this service he was knighted in 1945. He returned to Cambridge in 1958 as Master of Gonville and Caius College, in which office he remained until his retirement in 1958.

Chain, Ernst Boris (1906–1979)
German–British biochemist

Chain, born the son of a chemist in Berlin, Germany, graduated in 1930 from the Friedrich-Wilhelm University with a degree in chemistry. He left Germany for England in 1933 and, after two years' research at Cambridge University, joined Howard FLOREY at Oxford. Here his brilliance as a biochemist was put to good use in the difficult isolation and purification of penicillin – work that Alexander FLEMING had been unable to carry out. He shared the 1945 Nobel Prize for physiology or medicine with Florey and Fleming for this achievement.

After 1945 he was professor of biochemistry at the Superior Institute of Health in Rome, returning to England in 1961 for the chair of biochemistry at Imperial College, London. During this time he discovered penicillinase – an enzyme that some bacteria can synthesize and so destroy the drug. He also worked on tumor metabolism and the mode of action of insulin in diabetes.

Chamberlain, Owen (1920–   )
American physicist

The son of a prominent radiologist, Edward

Chamberlain, Owen Chamberlain followed his father's interest in physics. Born in San Francisco, he graduated from Dartmouth College in 1941 and gained his doctorate in physics from the University of Chicago in 1949. From 1948 until 1950 he was an instructor in physics at the University of California at Berkeley, becoming associate professor in 1954, professor in 1958, and emeritus professor from 1989.

The onset of America's involvement in World War II interrupted his university studies, and he spent the years 1942–1946 under the leadership of Emilio SEGRÈ working on the Manhattan atom-bomb project at Los Alamos. There he investigated spontaneous fission of the heavy elements and nuclear cross sections. Later he worked with Enrico Fermi on neutron diffraction by liquids.

At Berkeley, Chamberlain experimented with the bevatron particle accelerator of the Lawrence Radiation Laboratory, and in 1955 (together with Segrè, C. Weigand, and T. Ypsilantis) discovered the antiproton – a particle with the same mass as the proton, but of opposite (negative) charge. For their discovery, Chamberlain and Segrè received the 1959 Nobel Prize for physics. The existence of antiparticles had been predicted by Paul Dirac's theory of 1926, and the first of these, the positive electron (or positron) had been found by Carl David Anderson in cosmic radiation in 1931.

Chamberlain's more recent work has been on the interaction of antiprotons with hydrogen and deuterium, the production of antineutrons from antiprotons, and the scattering of pions.

Chamberlin, Thomas Chrowder
(1843–1928) *American geologist*

Chamberlin came from a farming background in Mattoon, Illinois. His discovery of fossils in a local limestone quarry aroused his interest in geology, which he pursued at the University of Michigan. He worked for the Wisconsin Geological Survey from 1873, serving as chief geologist for the period 1876–82. From 1881 until 1904 he was in charge of the glacial division of the US Geological Survey. After a period as president of the University of Wisconsin (1887–92) he became professor of geology at the University of Chicago (1892–1918).

Apart from his work on the geological surveys, Chamberlin's most significant work was in the field of glaciation. Early work on glaciation had assumed that there had been one great ice age but James Geikie, in his *The Great Ice Age* (1874–84), had begun collecting evidence that there had

been several ice ages separated by nonglacial epochs. Chamberlin contributed the chapter on North America to Geikie's work. He showed that drift deposits are composed of at least three layers and went on to establish four major ice ages, which were named the Nebraskan, Kansan, Illinoian, and Wisconsin after the states in which they were most easily studied.

Together with the astronomer Forest Moulton, Chamberlin formulated, in 1906, the planetismal hypothesis on the origin of the planets in the solar system. They supposed that a star had passed close to the Sun causing matter to be pulled out of both. Within the gravitational field of the Sun this gaseous matter would condense into small planetesimals, and eventually into planets. The theory was published in *The Two Solar Families* (1928) but it has little support today as it cannot account for the distribution of angular momentum in the solar system.

Chance, Britton (1913–) *American biophysicist*

Chance was born an engineer's son in Wilkes-Barre, Pennsylvania; he was educated at the University of Pennsylvania, where he obtained his PhD in 1940 and where he served as E.R. Johnson Professor of Biophysics from 1949 to 1983.

In 1943 he carried out a spectroscopic analysis that provided firm evidence for the enzyme–substrate complex whose existence had been confidently assumed by biochemists since the beginning of the century. Working with the iron-containing enzyme peroxidase, which strongly absorbs certain wavelengths of light, he found that variations in light absorption could be precisely correlated with rates of production of the enzyme–substrate complex. This was seen as confirming the important work of Leonor Michaelis.

Chance has also contributed to one of the great achievements of modern biochemistry, namely the unraveling of the complicated maze through which energy is released at the cellular level. He found that the concentration of ADP (adenosine diphosphate), as well as the oxygen concentration, determined the oxidation and reduction states of the proteins in the respiratory (electron-transport) chain. His studies of changes in ADP concentration led to a better understanding of how glucose is used in the body.

Chandler, Seth Carlo (1846–1913)
American astronomer

Chandler, who was born in Boston, Massachusetts, graduated from Harvard in 1861 and then acted as assistant to Benjamin Gould, an astronomer with the US Coast Survey, from 1861 to 1864. He remained with the Survey until 1870 when he started work as an actuary, returning to scientific work with the Harvard Observatory in 1881. From 1885 he devoted himself to private research.

Chandler is best known for his discovery of the variation in the location of the geographic poles – and, hence, of the variation in latitude of points on the Earth's surface. In 1891 he announced the discovery of a 428-day cycle during which latitude varied by 0.3 second. This variation in the Earth's rotation became known as the *Chandler wobble* and was soon confirmed by the International Latitude Service, established in 1900.

Chandrasekhar, Subrahmanyan

(1910–1995) *Indian–American astrophysicist*

Chandrasekhar, who was born in Lahore, which is now in Pakistan, studied at the Presidency College, Madras, gaining his MA in 1930. He then went to Cambridge University, England, where in 1933 he both obtained his PhD and was elected to a fellowship. In 1936 he moved to America and has worked since 1937 at the University of Chicago and the Yerkes Observatory, serving as the Morton D. Hull Distinguished Service professor of Theoretical Astrophysics from 1952 to 1986, and as professor emeritus from 1986. He became an American citizen in 1953.

Chandrasekhar's major fields of study were stellar evolution and stellar structure and the processes of energy transfer within stars. It was known that stars could end their life either dramatically and explosively as a supernova or as an extremely small dense star of low luminosity known as a white dwarf. But what decided the particular path a star took was answered by Chandrasekhar in his *Introduction to the Study of Stellar Structure* (1939). He showed that when a star has exhausted its nuclear fuel, an inward gravitational collapse will begin. This will eventually be halted in most stars by the outward pressure exerted by a degenerate gas, i.e. a gas that is completely ionized, with the electrons stripped away from the atomic nuclei, and that is very highly compressed. The star will therefore have shrunk into an object composed of material so dense that a matchbox of it would weigh many tons.

Chandrasekhar showed that such a star would have the unusual property that the larger its mass, the smaller its radius. There

will therefore be a point at which the mass of a star is too great for it to evolve into a white dwarf. He calculated this mass to be 1.4 times the mass of the Sun. This has since become known as the *Chandrasekhar limit*. A star lying above this limit must either lose mass before it can become a white dwarf or take a different evolutionary path. In support of Chandrasekhar's theoretical work, it has been established that all known white dwarfs fall within the predicted limit.

In the 1970s Chandrasekhar devoted much time to the mathematical theory of black holes. He later made a detailed study of Newton's work and published his results in his *Newton's Principia for the Common Reader.*

For his numerous contributions to astrophysics, Chandrasekhar shared the 1983 Nobel Prize for physics with William FOWLER.

Chang, Min Chueh (1908–1991)
Chinese–American biologist

Chang, who was born in T'ai-yüan in China, was educated at the Tsinghua University in Peking, and at Cambridge, England, where he obtained his PhD in 1941. He emigrated to America in 1945 and joined the Worcester Foundation in Shrewsbury, Massachusetts, where he subsequently remained. From 1961 he also served as professor of reproductive biology at Boston University.

Chang carried out a number of major research projects from which emerged not only greater understanding of the mechanisms of mammalian fertilization, but also such practical consequences as oral contraceptives and the transplantation of human ova fertilized *in vitro* (by Robert Edwards and Patrick Steptoe in 1978). In 1951, at the same time as Colin Austin, Chang discovered that a "period of time in the female tract is required for the spermatozoa to acquire their fertilizing capacity," a phenomenon known later as capacitation. He further demonstrated, in 1957, that there is a decapacitation factor in the seminal fluid, which, although it can be removed by centrifugation, has resisted further attempts at identification.

Chang also made the important advance in 1959 of fertilizing rabbit eggs *in vitro* and transplanting them into a recipient doe. This was followed in 1964 by comparable work for the first time with rodents. It was also Chang who provided much of the experimental basis for Gregory Pincus's 1953 paper showing that injections of progesterone into rabbits could serve as a contraceptive by inhibiting ovulation.

Chapman, Sydney (1888–1970) *British mathematician and geophysicist*

Born in Eccles near Manchester, Chapman entered Manchester University in 1904 to study engineering. After graduating in 1907, his interest was diverted into more strictly mathematical areas, and he went to Cambridge to study mathematics, graduating in 1910. His first post was as chief assistant at the Royal Observatory, Greenwich, and his work there sparked off his lasting interest in a number of fields of applied mathematics, notably geomagnetism. In 1914 Chapman returned to Cambridge as a lecturer in mathematics, and in 1919 he moved back to Manchester as professor of mathematics, remaining there for five years. From 1924 to 1946 he was professor of mathematics at Imperial College, London. After working at the War Office during World War II he moved to Oxford to take up the Sedleian Chair in natural philosophy, from which he retired in 1953. However, his retirement meant no lessening in his teaching and research activity, which continued for many years at the Geophysical Institute, Alaska, and at the High Altitude Observatory at Boulder, Colorado.

The two main topics of Chapman's mathematical work were the kinetic theory of gases and geomagnetism. In the 19th century James Clerk Maxwell and Ludwig Boltzmann had put forward ideas about the properties of gases as determined by the motion of the molecules of the gas. Chapman's work, which he began in 1911, was the next major step in the development of a full mathematical treatment of the kinetic theory. The Swedish mathematician Enskog had been working, independently of Chapman, along similar lines, and the resulting theory is now generally known as the *Chapman–Enskog theory of gases*. While working in 1917 on mixtures of gases Chapman predicted the phenomenon of gaseous thermal diffusion. His subsequent work on the upper atmosphere was a practical application of his earlier more theoretical study of gases.

Highlights of Chapman's work on geomagnetism are his work on the variations in the Earth's magnetic field in periods of a lunar day (27.3 days) and its submultiples. This he showed to be the result of a small tidal movement set up in the Earth's atmosphere by the Moon. He also developed, in 1930, in collaboration with one of his students, what has become known as the *Chapman–Ferraro theory* of magnetic storms. In collaboration with Julius Bartels, Chapman wrote *Geomagnetism* (2 vols. 1940), which soon established itself as a standard work.

Chaptal, Jean Antoine Claude (1756–1832) *French chemist*

Chaptal, the son of an apothecary from Nogaret, France, studied medicine at Montpellier, graduating in 1777. He later switched to chemistry, becoming professor at Montpellier in 1781. During the French Revolution he was arrested but then released to manage the saltpeter works at Grenelle. He also helped to organize the introduction of the metric system and published a textbook, *Elémens de chimie* (1790–1803).

Chaptal is mainly remembered as an industrial chemist; he was the first to produce sulfuric acid commercially in France at his factory at Montpellier. His early paper on bleaching (1787) was translated and published in England in 1790 by Robert Kerr. In 1800 he proposed a new method of bleaching using vapor from a boiling alkaline liquor, which was soon introduced into England. Chaptal also wrote one of the first books on industrial chemistry, *Chimie appliquée aux arts* (1807; Chemistry Applied to the Arts).

Charcot, Jean-Martin (1825–1893) *French neurologist*

Parisian-born Charcot studied medicine in his native city and received his MD in 1853. His interest in disease of the nervous system led to his appointment, in 1862, to the Salpêtrière Hospital for nervous and mental disorders. This marked the beginning of a long and distinguished association. Charcot described the pathological changes associated with several degenerative conditions of the nervous system, including the disintegration of ligaments and joint surfaces (known as *Charcot's disease*) that occurs in advanced stages of locomotor ataxia. His studies of brain damage in cases of speech loss (aphasia) and epilepsy supported the findings of his contemporary, Paul Broca, that is, different bodily functions are controlled by different regions of the cerebral cortex.

In 1872, Charcot was appointed professor of pathological anatomy at the faculty of medicine and later (1882) became professor of neurology at the Salpêtrière. He was increasingly concerned with the link between mind and body in cases of hysteria and trauma. With his eloquent manner and a dramatic presentation of his lectures on a small stage, he became a widely celebrated teacher. Among many famous students was Sigmund Freud, who was influenced by Charcot's use of hypnosis on patients.

Charcot's son, Jean, became a famous polar explorer.

Chargaff, Erwin (1905–   ) *Austrian–American biochemist*

Chargaff, who was born at Czernowitz (now Chernovtsy in Ukraine), gained his PhD from the University of Vienna in 1928 and then spent two years at Yale University. He returned to Europe, working first in Berlin and then at the Pasteur Institute, Paris, before returning permanently to America in 1935.

Initially Chargaff's work covered a range of biochemical fields, including lipid metabolism and the process of blood coagulation. Later his attention became concentrated on the DNA molecule, following the announcement in 1944 by Oswald Avery that the factor causing the heritable transformation of bacteria is pure DNA. Chargaff reasoned that, if this were so, there must be many more different types of DNA molecules than people had believed. He examined DNA using the recently developed techniques of paper chromatography and ultraviolet spectroscopy and found the composition of DNA to be constant within a species but to differ widely between species. This led him to conclude that there must be as many different types of DNA as there are different species. However, some interesting and very important consistencies emerged. Firstly the number of purine bases (adenine and guanine) was always equal to the number of pyrimidine bases (cytosine and thymine), and secondly the number of adenine bases is equal to the number of thymine bases and the number of guanine bases equals the number of cytosine bases. This information, announced by Chargaff in 1950, was of crucial importance in constructing the Watson–Crick model of DNA.

Since 1935 Chargaff has worked at Columbia University, as professor of biochemistry from 1952 and as emeritus professor from 1974.

Charles, Jacques Alexandre César (1746–1823) *French physicist and physical chemist*

Born in Beaugency, France, Charles was a clerk in the finance ministry who developed an interest in science, especially in the preparation of gases. Eventually he became professor of physics at the Conservatoire des Arts et Métiers in Paris. He constructed the first hydrogen balloons, making an ascent to over 3000 meters (1.9 mi) in 1783. This feat brought him popular fame and royal patronage.

His name is chiefly remembered, however, for his discovery of *Charles's law*, which states that the volume of a fixed quantity of gas at constant pressure is inversely proportional to its temperature. Hence all gases, at the same pressure, expand equally for the same rise in temperature. Strictly speaking, the law holds only for ideal gases but it is valid for real gases at low pressures and high temperatures. Charles deduced the law in about 1787, working with oxygen, nitrogen, carbon dioxide, and hydrogen, but he did not publish it. He communicated his results to Joseph-Louis GAY-LUSSAC, who published his own experimental results in 1802, six months after Dalton had also deduced the law. The priority, as Gay-Lussac pointed out, belongs to Charles but Gay-Lussac's figures were more accurate (and thus the law is sometimes referred to as *Gay-Lussac's law*). This law and that formulated by Robert BOYLE comprise the gas laws.

Charpak, Georges (1924–   ) *French physicist*

Charpak, who was born in Dabrovica, Poland, was educated at the Ecole des Mines, Paris. He was imprisoned at Dachau from 1943 until 1945. He then worked in France on nuclear research, mainly at the Centre National de la Recherche Scientifique (CNRS). He moved in 1959 to CERN (Conseil Européen pour la Reserche Nucléaire; European Laboratory for Particle Physics), in Geneva, where he has since remained.

By the time Charpak arrived at CERN nuclear physicists had begun to search for ever-more-elusive particles. To detect their fleeting and rare appearances could require the examination of thousands of particle tracks. Yet the older particle detectors – bubble chamber, cloud chamber, etc. – could handle only a small proportion of the data pouring from the newer and more powerful accelerators.

In 1968 Charpak described his newly designed drift chamber in which charged wires are strung 1.2 mm apart, layer on layer, in a gas-filled container. A voltage is applied to the wires in such a way that the central wires are charged positively, and the outer ones negatively. If a charged particle enters the detector, it ionizes atoms of gas, and the ions drift to the central wires, triggering a signal. As the wires criss-cross through the chamber it is possible to reconstruct a three-dimensional picture of the ion's tracks from the signals obtained.

When linked to computers the drift chamber can handle a million nuclear events per second. It played a vital role in the 1983 discovery of the W and Z bosons by Carlo RUBBIA. It also won for Charpak the 1992 Nobel Prize for physics.

In more recent times Charpak has turned his attention to biochemical reactions.

Charpentier, Jean de (1786–1885)
Swiss geologist and glaciologist

Charpentier studied under Abraham Werner at the Mining Academy in his native city of Freiberg, where his father was also a professor. He worked as an engineer in the Silesian mines before being appointed director of the Bex salt mines in 1813.

He studied the problem of the widely scattered and impressively large erratic boulders and soon rejected the current theories of their origin. The theory that such boulders were meteorites was unlikely for they were identical in composition with other Alpine rocks. The flood theory, supported by Charles LYELL, supposed that they had been distributed by boulder-laden icebergs. However, this raised the problems of where the water had come from and where it had gone to.

Charpentier concluded that the agent responsible was glaciation and first presented his glacial theory publicly in Lucerne in 1835. He gained little support but did attract the attention of Louis Agassiz. In 1841 Charpentier published his results in his *Essai sur les glaciers* (Essay on Glaciers) but was anticipated by Agassiz's earlier publication, in 1840, of his *Etudes sur les glaciers* (Studies on Glaciers).

Chatelier, Henri Louis Le *See* LE CHATELIER, HENRI LOUIS.

Cherenkov (or Cerenkov), Pavel Alekseyevich (1904–1990) *Soviet physicist*

Cherenkov came from a peasant family in Voronezh, Russia, and was educated at the university there, graduating in 1928. From 1930 he was a member of the Lebedev Institute of Physics in Moscow, serving there from 1953 as professor of experimental physics.

In 1934 Cherenkov was investigating the absorption of radioactive radiation by water when he noticed that the water was emitting an unusual blue light. At first he thought it was due simply to fluorescence but was forced to reject this idea when it became apparent that the blue radiation was independent of the composition of the liquid and depended only on the presence of fast-moving electrons passing through the medium.

It was later shown in 1937 by the Russian physicists **Ilya Frank** (1908–1990) and **Igor Tamm** (1895–1971) that the radiation was caused by electrons traveling through the water with a speed greater than that of light in water (though not of course greater than that of light in a vacuum). This *Cherenkov radiation* can be produced by other charged particles and can be used as a method of detecting elementary particles. Cherenkov, Frank, and Tamm shared the Nobel Prize for physics in 1958.

Chevreul, Michel Eugène (1786–1889)
French organic chemist

One of the longest-lived of all chemists, Chevreul, who was born at Angers in France, studied at the Collège de France (1803). He was an assistant to Antoine François de Fourcroy (1809), assistant at the Musée d'Histoire Naturelle (1810), then professor of physics at the Lycée Charlemagne (1813–30).

In 1810 Chevreul began a great program of research into fats, which was published in his book *Recherches chimiques sur les corps gras d'origine animale* (1823; Chemical Researches on Animal Fats). By acidification of soaps derived from animal fats and subsequent crystallization from alcohol he was able to identify for the first time various fatty acids: oleic acid, margaric acid (a mixture of stearic and palmitic acids), butyric acid, capric and caproic acids, and valeric acid. He recognized that fats are esters (called 'ethers' in the nomenclature of the day) of glycerol and fatty acids and that saponification produces salts of the fatty acids (soaps) and glycerol. In 1825 Chevreul and Joseph Gay-Lussac patented a process for making candles from crude stearic acid. Other fats investigated by Chevreul were spermaceti, lanolin, and cholesterol.

In 1824 Chevreul became director of the dyeworks for the Gobelins Tapestry, where he did important work on coloring matters, discovering hematoxylin in logwood, quercetin in yellow oak, and preparing the reduced colorless form of indigo. He also investigated the science and art of color with special application to the production of massed color by aggregations of small monochromatic dots, as in the threads of a tapestry.

Chevreul's later appointments were professor of chemistry at the Musée d'Histoire Naturelle (1830) and director there (1864). His other work included the discovery of creatine (1832) and studies on the history of chemistry.

Chittenden, Russell Henry (1856–1943) *American physiologist and biochemist*

As part of his undergraduate course at Yale, Chittenden, who was born in New Haven,

Connecticut, was asked to investigate why scallops taste sweeter when reheated from a previous meal than when freshly cooked. This project led to his discovery of glycogen and glycine in the muscle tissue – the first demonstration of the free occurrence of glycine (or glycocoll as it was then known) in nature. The work attracted the attention of Willy Kühne at Heidelberg who invited Chittenden to his laboratory. Later collaboration between Chittenden (at New Haven) and Kühne (in Heidelberg) provided a strong foundation for studies in enzymology.

Chittenden also did important work in toxicology and on the protein requirements of man, showing that the so-called Voit standard, which recommended 118 grams of protein per day, was a vast overestimate, and that good health could be maintained on 50 grams a day. He played a major part in the establishment of physiological chemistry (biochemistry) as a science in its own right.

Chladni, Ernst Florens Friedrich
(1756–1827) *German physicist*

Born in Wittenberg in Germany, Chladni was forced to study law by his father and obtained his degree from Leipzig in 1782. When his father died, Chladni turned to science. He is noted for his work on acoustics, being the first to analyze sound in a rigorous mathematical way. For this he invented the sand-pattern technique, in which thin metal plates covered in sand are made to vibrate. The sand collects in the nodal lines producing symmetrical patterns (called *Chladni's figures*).

Chladni also had a great interest in music and designed two musical instruments: the euphonium and the clavicylinder. He also measured the speed of sound in gases other than air by filling organ pipes with the gas and measuring the change in pitch.

Chladni was one of the first scientists to believe that meteorites fell from the sky but his opinion was treated with disdain until Jean Baptiste Biot proved him to be correct in 1803.

Chu, Paul Ching-Wu (1941–) *American physicist*

Chu was born in Hunan, China, but his parents were members of the Nationalist Party and the family fled to Taiwan in 1949 for political reasons. After graduating in physics from Chengkung University, Chu moved to America in 1963 and gained his PhD in 1968 from the University of California, San Diego. After spending some time working for the company AT & T, Chu entered academic life, first at Cleveland State University, and since 1979 as professor of physics at the University of Houston.

Much of Chu's work has been in the field of superconductivity. A major breakthrough had been achieved in 1986 when Alex Muller had discovered some materials that become superconductive below the relatively high critical temperature of 35 K (−238°C). This temperature was still too low to be economic. The vital temperature was 77.4 K (−195.8°C) – the temperature below which nitrogen becomes liquid. The aim was to find materials that could be cooled to a superconducting state using relatively cheap liquid nitrogen, rather than the extremely expensive liquid helium (b.p. −268.9°C). Chu was determined that his Houston laboratory would be the first to find a superconductor with a critical temperature above 77.4 K.

The superconductor found by Muller was a ceramic material composed of barium, lanthanum, and copper oxide (Ba–La–CuO). Chu began by reproducing Muller's work. He next developed new methods of synthesis for this type of compound and began first to vary the ratio of elements in the compound. Initial results obtained by reducing the amount of copper were encouraging, but could not be repeated. However, at high pressures of 10,000 atmospheres it was possible to increase the critical temperature to about 40 K. Changing the proportions of the elements could raise the temperature to 52.5 K, but this was still at high pressures.

The original Muller compound contained three metals in the ratio 2:1:4. Many researchers concentrated on substituting other metals in the same ratio. Copper seemed to play a special bonding role and was judged by Chu to be indispensable. Chu decided to replace the lanthanum with other related lanthanoid elements. One he chose to work with was yttrium (Y). Finally, in January 1987, just a year after Muller's breakthrough, Chu found that the critical temperature of $Y_{1.2}Ba_{0.8}CuO_4$ was 93 K and that the effect was stable and permanent.

Chu, Steven (1948–) *American physicist*

Chu was educated at the University of California, Berkeley, where he obtained his PhD in 1976. He joined Bell Labs in 1978 and, in 1987, took up an appointment as professor of applied physics at Stanford University, California.

In their normal state atoms are subject to a constant random thermal motion which limits the precision of measurements of atomic states. Physicists have therefore sought to slow atoms down as much as possible.

One proposed way to cool atoms was demonstrated in the early 1970s by William PHILLIPS. Phillips had used a single laser and worked with beams of sodium atoms. Chu used six laser beams and worked with a hot gas of sodium atoms. He managed to cool and trap atoms in what he called 'optical molasses'. By 1985 he had cooled sodium atoms to a temperature of about 240 microkelvins – i.e. a 240 millionth of a degree above absolute zero. The atoms could be trapped in the laser beams for a period of about half a second.

For his work in this field Chu shared the 1997 Nobel Prize for physics with Phillips and Claude COHEN-TANNOUDJI.

Clairaut, Alexis Claude (1713–1765)
French mathematical physicist

The Parisian-born son of a mathematics teacher, Clairaut was introduced to the subject at an early age. By the age of ten he was studying L'Hôpital's work on conic sections and two years later he read a paper to the French Académie des sciences. He was elected to the Académie at the age of 18 following the publication in 1731 of his *Recherches sur les courbes à double courbes.*

Soon after, in 1736, he accompanied MAUPERTUIS on an expedition to Lapland to determine the length of 1° of a meridian within the Arctic circle. The aim of the expedition was to determine the shape of the Earth by measuring its curvature at the places where it differed most – the equator and poles. A similar expedition under the direction of La Condamine measured the equatorial curvature in the Andes. Behind the expeditions lay a crucial test of Newtonian mechanics that the Earth's rotation should cause it to bulge at the equator and flatten at the poles. Cartesian science predicted that the reverse position should hold. As Clairaut revealed in his *Théorie de la figure de la terre* (1743; Theory of the Shape of the Earth) the Earth had, as Newton had claimed, a larger diameter through the equator than through the poles, a shape known to geometers as an oblate spheroid.

In 1747 Clairaut turned his attention to the Moon and once again the issue was the accuracy of Newtonian mechanics. The motion of the lunar apogee – the point in the lunar orbit furthest away from the Earth – differed from Newton's predicted value by a factor of two. At first Clairaut was tempted to question the validity of Newton's inverse square law, but in 1749 he discovered that no such drastic step need be taken; several factors of the lunar orbit had been ignored. When these were included in Newton's lunar equations the correct value for the motion of the lunar apogee was obtained.

Clairaut was also involved in the dramatic events surrounding the return of Halley's comet. Halley had claimed that the comet of 1682 would return in 1758. Clairaut realized that if Newtonian mechanics was to be an exact science it must make a more precise prediction. He informed the Académie in November 1758 that the comet would be at perihelion on April 13, 1759; the actual date was March 13, just within the allowed-for margins of error.

Clairaut also collaborated with the Marquise du Châtelet in her French translation of Newton's *Principia.*

Clark, Alvan Graham (1832–1897)
American astronomer and instrument-maker

Clark, the son of the instrument-maker Alvan Clark, was born at Fall River, Massachusetts. He started life as a portrait painter but soon joined his father's firm and became a lens grinder, preparing the mirrors and lenses for some of the best telescopes of the late 19th century. In 1861 he had made a lens for Edward Barnard at the University of Mississippi. Testing it before parting with it he looked through it at Sirius and to his surprise observed a faint image near the star. It was, in fact, Sirius B, the famous companion predicted by Friedrich Bessel in 1844. Clark made many more observations, and discovered 16 double stars.

The Clark firm provided Simon Newcomb, head of the US Naval Observatory, with a 26-inch (66-cm) refractor. It was with this that the very small satellites of Mars, Phobos, and Deimos were detected by Asaph HALL in 1877. In 1888 Clark built the 36-inch (91-cm) refractor for the Lick Observatory and his final achievement, just before his death, was to install his 40-inch (101-cm) refractor in the Yerkes Observatory. A practical limit is reached in using lenses larger than this and after Clark's death astronomers put their faith in mirrors rather than lenses. For this reason the Yerkes 40-inch and the Lick 36-inch are still the largest and the second largest refractors in the world.

Clarke, Sir Cyril Astley (1907–   )
British physician

Clarke, who was born in Leicester, was educated at the University of Cambridge and Guy's Hospital, London, where he qualified in 1932. He remained at Guy's until 1936 when he engaged in life-insurance work before spending the war years in the Royal Navy. From 1946 Clarke worked as a consultant physician in Liverpool until 1958 when he joined the staff of the university. Here he later served as professor of medicine from 1965 to 1972 and also, from 1963 to 1972, as director of the Nuffield unit of medical genetics.

Although a consultant physician, Clarke was also a skilled amateur lepidopterist. In 1952 he became interested in the genetics of the wing colors of swallowtail butterflies and began a collaboration with Philip Sheppard, a professional geneticist who later became a colleague at Liverpool University. In particular, they worked on the inheritance of mimicry in the wing patterns of certain swallowtails. They noted that the gene controlling the wing pattern is actually a group of closely-linked genes behaving as a single unit – a supergene. They also found that even though the males also carry such supergenes, the patterns only show in the females.

At this point Clarke was struck by certain striking parallels between the inheritance of swallowtail wing patterns and human blood types. Above all it aroused his interest in Rhesus babies. This condition arises when an Rh-negative mother, that is someone whose blood lacks the Rh factor or antigen, and an Rh-positive father produce an Rh-positive child. Occasionally the fetus's blood leaks from the placenta into the mother's blood and stimulates the production of Rh antibodies. This will cause her to destroy unwittingly the red cells of any subsequent Rh-positive babies she may carry.

Clarke and Sheppard puzzled over how to prevent the mother producing the destructive Rh antibodies. The answer eventually came from Clarke's wife who in an inspired moment told him to inject the Rh-negative mothers with Rh-antibodies. As this is what destroys the blood of the fetus in the first place, the answer initially sounds absurd. However the Rh-antibodies should destroy incompatible Rh-positive cells before the mother's own antibody machinery acted, that is, before the mother could become sensitized to Rh-positive blood.

In 1964 Clarke and his colleagues were able to announce a major breakthrough in preventive medicine. Since then thousands of women have received injections of Rh-antibodies with only a few failures.

Claude, Albert (1898–1983) *Belgian–American cell biologist*

Claude, who was born at Longlier in Belgium, was educated at the University of Liège where he obtained his doctorate in 1928. He joined the staff of the Rockefeller Institute, New York, in 1929 and in 1941 adopted American citizenship. Claude returned to Belgium in 1948 to serve as director of the Jules Bordet Research Institute, a post he retained until his retirement in 1972.

In the 1930s Claude attempted to purify Peyton Rous's chicken sarcoma virus (RSV) using a centrifuge. He succeeded in producing a fraction with an enhanced sarcogenic power, noting that small granules containing nucleoprotein were present. Suspecting these granules to be the cause of the RSV, he was somewhat surprised to find similar granules present in centrifuged cells taken from uninfected chicken embryo.

Over the next 20 years, using electron microscopes as well as improved centrifuges, Claude began to chart the constitution of the protoplasm. Although the mitochondria had first been described as early as 1897, Claude could distinguish them from what he originally termed 'microsomes'. Among such microsomes he could make out a lacelike structure spread throughout the cytoplasm, a structure later named the endoplasmic reticulum. Another member of Claude's laboratory, George PALADE, went on to identify the ribosome.

For his work in opening up the study of cell structures Claude shared the 1974 Nobel Prize for physiology or medicine with Palade and Christian DE DUVE.

Clausius, Rudolf Julius Emmanuel (1822–1888) *German physicist*

Clausius, who was born in Köslin (now Koszalin in Poland), studied at the University of Berlin and obtained his doctorate from Halle in 1848. He was professor of physics at the Royal Artillery and Engineering School, Berlin (1850–55) and professor of mathematical physics at Zurich (1855–67). He then transferred to the University of Würzburg (1867) and, from there, moved to Bonn (1869).

He is noted for his formulation of what is now known as the second law of thermodynamics. Clausius arrived at this by considering the theorem of Sadi Carnot on heat engines and attempting to reconcile this with the mechanical theory of heat, which was developing at the time. In 1850 he published a famous paper *Uber die bewegende Kraft der Wärme* (On the Motive Force of Heat), in which he first introduced the principle that "it is impossible by a cyclic process to transfer heat from a colder to a warmer reservoir without net changes in other bodies." An alternative statement of this, the second law, is "heat does not flow spontaneously from a colder to a hotter body." The second law of thermodynamics was independently recognized by Lord KELVIN.

Clausius gave the law a mathematical statement in 1854 and published a number of papers on the topic over the next few years. In 1865 he introduced the term *entropy* as a measure of the availability of heat. The change in entropy of a system is the heat absorbed or lost at a given temperature divided by the temperature. An increase in entropy corresponds to a lower availability of heat for performing work.

The second law of thermodynamics is one of the fundamental principles of physics. It describes the fact that, although the total energy in a system is conserved, the availability of energy for performing work is lost. Clausius showed that in any nonideal (irreversible) process the entropy increased. The first and second laws of thermodynamics are encapsulated in his famous statement, "The energy of the universe is a constant; the entropy of the universe always tends toward a maximum."

Clausius also followed the work of James Joule on the kinetic theory of gases, introducing the ideas of effective diameter and mean free path (the average distance between collisions). A contribution to electrochemistry was his idea that substances dissociated into ions on solution. In the field of electrodynamics he produced a theoretical expression for the force between two moving electrons – a formula later used by Hendrik Lorentz.

Clemence, Gerald Maurice (1908–1974) *American astronomer*

Clemence, who was from Smithfield, Rhode Island, studied mathematics at Brown University, Rhode Island. After graduating he joined the staff of the US Naval Observatory in 1930 where he remained until 1963, serving as head astronomer and director of the Nautical Almanac from 1945 to 1958 and science director of the Observatory from 1958. In 1963 he was appointed senior research associate and lecturer at Yale, becoming professor of astronomy in 1966, a post he held until his death.

Clemence's work was primarily concerned with the orbital motions of the Earth, Moon, and planets. In 1951, in collaboration with Dirk Brouwer and W. J. Eckert, Clemence published the basic paper *Coordinates of the Five Outer Planets 1653–2060*. This was a considerable advance on the tables for the outer planets calculated by Simon Newcomb and George W. Hill 50 years earlier. Clemence and his colleagues calculated the precise positions of the outer planets at 40-day intervals over a period of 400 years. It was the first time that the influence of the planets on each other was calculated at each step instead of the prevailing custom of assuming that the paths of all except one were known in advance.

Such an ambitious scheme was only made possible by the emergence of high-speed computers, one of which was made available to them by IBM from 1948. For each step some 800 multiplications and several hundred other arithmetical operations were required and would, Clemence commented, have taken a human computer 80 years if he could have completed the work without committing any errors en route.

Clemence also conceived the idea that the Dutch–American astronomer **Dirk Brouwer** (1902–1966) named *Ephemeris Time*, by which time could be determined very accurately from the orbital positions of the Moon and the Earth. This followed the discovery that the Earth's period of rotation was not constant and should not therefore be used in the measurement of time. Ephemeris Time eventually came into use in 1958, although it has been superseded for most purposes by the more convenient and even more accurate atomic time scale.

Cleve, Per Teodor (1840–1905) *Swedish chemist*

Cleve, who was born in the Swedish capital Stockholm, became assistant professor of chemistry at the University of Uppsala in 1868 and was later made professor of general and agricultural chemistry there. He is mainly remembered for his work on the rare earth elements.

In 1874 Cleve concluded that didymium was in fact two elements; this was proved in 1885 and the two elements named neodymium and praseodymium. In 1879 he showed that the element scandium, newly discovered by the Swedish chemist **Lars Nilson** (1840–1899), was in fact the ekaboron predicted by Dmitri Mendeleev in his periodic table. In the same year, working with a sample of erbia from which he had removed all traces of scandia and ytterbia, Cleve found two new earths, which he named holmium, after Stockholm, and thulium, after the old name for Scandinavia. Holmium in fact turned out to be a mixture for, in 1886, Lecoq de Boisbaudran discovered that it also contained the new element dysprosium.

Cleve is also remembered as the teacher of Svante Arrhenius.

Cockcroft, Sir John Douglas (1897–1967) *British physicist*

Cockcroft, who was born at Todmorden in northern England, entered Manchester University in 1914 to study mathematics, but left the following year to join the army. After World War I he was apprenticed to the engineering firm Metropolitan Vickers, which sent him to read electrical engineering at the Manchester College of Technology. He later went to Cambridge University, graduated in mathematics, and joined Ernest Rutherford's team at the Cavendish Laboratory.

Cockcroft soon became interested in designing a device for accelerating protons and, with E. T. S. WALTON, constructed a voltage multiplier. Using this Cockcroft and Walton bombarded nuclei of lithium with protons and, in 1932, brought about the first nuclear transformation by artificial means:

$$^7_3\text{Li} + ^1_1\text{H} \rightarrow ^4_2\text{He} + ^4_2\text{He} + 17.2 \text{ MeV}$$

For this work Cockcroft and Walton received the 1951 Nobel Prize for physics. During World War II Cockcroft played a leading part in the development of radar. In 1940 he visited America as a member of the Tizard mission to negotiate exchanges of military, scientific, and technological information. In 1944 he became director of the Anglo-Canadian Atomic Energy Commission. He returned to Britain in 1946 to direct the new Atomic Energy Research Establishment at Harwell and remained there until 1959, when he was appointed master of Churchill College, Cambridge, a new college devoted especially to science and technology. Cockcroft received a knighthood in 1948.

Cockerell, Sir Christopher Sydney (1910–) *British engineer and inventor*

Cockerell was born in Cambridge and educated at Cambridge University, graduating in engineering in 1931. Initially he joined a small engineering firm, then returned to Cambridge to study electronics, and in 1935 he joined the Marconi Company as an electronics engineer. Here he worked on the development of airborne navigational equipment and on radar.

In 1950 he left Marconi to set up his own boat-hire business on the Norfolk broads. As an amateur yachtsman, Cockerell was interested in the effect of water drag on the hull of a boat. He had the idea of raising the boat above the water on a cushion of air. In 1954 he performed a crucial experiment using kitchen scales, tin cans, and a vacuum cleaner to show that a properly directed stream of air could produce the required lift. The next year he built a working model out of balsa wood, powered by a model-aircraft engine.

He was granted a patent on his idea in 1955 and in 1957 the Ministry of Supply commissioned a full-size craft from the company Saunders Roe. The first prototype, SR-N1, weighed 7 tons and was capable of 60 knots. It crossed the English Channel in 1959 (with Cockerell aboard). Hovercraft entered regular cross-channel service in 1968.

Cockerell was a consultant to Hovercraft Development Ltd. until 1979. He has also been interested in the development of wave-power generators.

Cohen, Paul Joseph (1934–) *American mathematician*

Cohen, who was born at Long Branch, New Jersey, was educated at Brooklyn College and at the University of Chicago, where he obtained his PhD in 1958. He spent a year at the Massachusetts Institute of Technology and two years at the Institute for Advanced Studies, Princeton, before moving to Stanford in 1961. He was appointed professor of mathematics in 1964.

Mathematicians had been introduced to transfinite arithmetic by Georg CANTOR from the 1870s onwards. Cantor had identified two distinct infinite sets, namely the set of natural numbers and the set of real numbers, represented by $\aleph_0$ and c respectively. He had also proved that there were an infinite number of infinite numbers, that following $\aleph_0$, there came $\aleph_1$, $\aleph_2$, $\aleph_3$... indefinitely. Where did c fit into this sequence? Cantor answered by proposing that $c = \aleph_1$, a supposition since known as the 'continuum hypothesis'. It was the first member on David Hilbert's 1900 list of outstanding unsolved mathematical problems.

Little progress was made upon the problem before 1938 when Kurt GÖDEL demonstrated that set theory remains consistent if the continuum hypothesis is added as an axiom. This did not, however, constitute a proof of the hypothesis, for set theory's own absolute consistency has never been proved. Nonetheless, Gödel's work did show that the continuum hypothesis could not be shown to be false within set theory.

In 1963 Cohen proposed to develop a non-Cantorian set theory that contained not the continuum hypothesis but its negation. He showed that no contradiction ensued and it seemed to follow that the continuum hypothesis was quite independent of set theory and that it could be neither proved nor disproved within any standard system of set theory.

Cohen, Seymour Stanley (1917–   )
American biochemist

Cohen was educated in his native New York, at the City College and at Columbia, where he obtained his PhD in 1941. He joined the University of Pennsylvania in 1943, serving as professor of biochemistry from 1954 until 1971, when he moved to the University of Denver, Colorado, as professor of microbiology. Cohen returned to New York in 1976 to take the chair of pharmaceutical sciences at the State University, Stony Brook, becoming emeritus professor in 1985.

In 1946 Cohen began a series of studies in molecular biology using the technique of radioactive labeling. The common microorganism *Escherichia coli* could be infected in the laboratory with the bacteriophage known as T2. Within a matter of minutes the bacterial cell would burst releasing several hundred replicas of the invading T2. The problem was to understand the process. It was known that phages were nucleoproteins consisting of a protein coat surrounding a mass of nucleic acid (DNA in the case of T2). But, as Cohen realized, nucleic acid differed from protein in containing measurable amounts of phosphorus. This could in theory be traced through any biochemical reaction by labeling it with the radioactive isotope phosphorus–32.

Cohen used this technique in a number of experiments in the late 1940s that suggested rather than demonstrated the vital role of DNA in heredity. It was not until 1952, when Alfred Hershey and Martha Chase used Cohen's labeling technique, that more substantial results were available.

Cohen, Stanley (1922–   ) American biochemist

A native New Yorker, Cohen was educated at Brooklyn and Oberlin colleges and at the University of Michigan, where he was appointed teaching fellow in the department of biochemistry in 1946. He moved to the University of Colorado School of Medicine in 1948, and in 1952 he took up the post of American Cancer Society postdoctoral fellow at Washington University, St. Louis. His long association with the Vanderbilt University School of Medicine, Nashville, began in 1959, with his appointment as assistant professor of biochemistry. He subsequently became associate professor (1962), professor (1967), and distinguished professor (1986).

Cohen's appointment to Washington University in 1952 marked the start of a fruitful collaboration with the Italian cell biologist, Rita LEVI-MONTALCINI, who had discovered a chemical produced by a culture of mouse tumor cells that influenced the number of nerve cells growing in chick embryos. Cohen set about trying to characterize this growth factor (later termed *nerve growth factor*), and found the same chemical in snake venom and in the salivary glands of adult male mice.

His findings led Cohen to investigate another growth factor that influences the embryological development of such tissues as those of eyes and teeth, which are derived from epidermis. He was able to identify a receptor on the cell membrane that was responsive to this epidermal growth factor. This was of great significance, suggesting a mechanism by which cells are able to interact with chemical messengers such as hormones, which control their growth or normal functions. Such cell-surface receptors are also a crucial element in the abnormal uncontrolled growth of cells in cancer.

For his work on growth factors and membrane receptors, Cohen was awarded the 1986 Nobel Prize for physiology or medicine, jointly with Levi-Montalcini.

Cohen-Tannoudji, Paul (1933–   )
French physicist

Cohen-Tannoudji was educated at the Ecole Normale Supéreure. In 1973 he was appointed professor of atomic and molecular physics at the Collège de France, Paris.

Cohen-Tannoudji, following on from the work of William PHILLIPS and Steven CHU, sought to understand and improve the process of optical cooling of single atoms. He proposed that laser traps operate by a process of what has since been called Sisyphus cooling. The laser beams, he argued, produce a series of standing waves of light polarized in different directions. As the atoms pass through the various fields their energy levels and thereby temperature is lowered.

Early efforts at cooling had found that laser traps unfortunately also tend to agitate atoms causing them to move out of the beam. One solution proposed by Cohen-Tannoudji allowed helium atoms to be cooled to 0.18 microkelvins. The method exploited the fact that atoms could occupy a particular combination of two distinct quantum states with different velocities, in which they remain invisible to any additional photons. Thus, once in this state, their energy cannot be increased by any further photon collisions.

For his work in this field Cohen-Tannoudji shared the 1997 Nobel Prize for physics with Chu and Phillips.

Cohn, Ferdinand Julius (1828–1898)
German botanist and bacteriologist

Cohn, who was born in Breslau (now Wrocław in Poland), was an extremely intelligent child and progressed through school rapidly, being admitted to the philosophy department at Breslau University at the early age of 14. He later developed an interest in botany but was prevented from graduating at Breslau by the university's anti-Semitic regulations. He therefore moved to Berlin, where he received his doctorate in botany in 1847.

Cohn returned to Breslau, becoming professor of botany there in 1872. He had long argued that the state should be responsible for the establishment of botanical research institutes, and as a result of his campaign the world's first institute for plant physiology was set up in Breslau in 1866. Cohn was director of this institute until his death and in 1870 he founded the journal *Beiträge zur Biologie der Pflanzen*, mainly for the purpose of publishing work carried out at Breslau.

Cohn's early research concentrated on the morphology and life histories of the microscopic algae and fungi, which led to his demonstration that the protoplasm of plant and animal cells is essentially similar. Later, stimulated by the work of Louis Pasteur, he became increasingly interested in bacteria. His classic treatise *Untersuchungen über Bacterien* (Researches on Bacteria), published in his journal in 1872, laid the foundations of modern bacteriology. In it he defined bacteria, used the constancy of their external form to divide them into four groups, and described six genera under these groups. This widely accepted classification was the first systematic attempt to classify bacteria and its fundamental divisions are still used in today's nomenclature.

Although Cohn did not believe in the theory of spontaneous generation he was aware that bacteria could develop in boiled infusions kept in sealed containers. He postulated the existence of a resistant developmental stage and through careful observation was able to demonstrate the formation of heat-resistant spores by *Bacillus subtilis*.

Through his book *Die Pflanze* (1872) and the printing of many of his popular lectures, Cohn presented the study of biology to a wide and appreciative public. He was also responsible for the publication of Robert Koch's important work on the life cycle of the anthrax bacillus.

Compton, Arthur Holly (1892–1962)
American physicist

Compton came from a distinguished intellectual family in Wooster, Ohio. His father, Elias, was a professor of philosophy at Wooster College while his brother, Karl, also a physicist, became president of the Massachusetts Institute of Technology. He was educated at Wooster College and at Princeton, where he obtained his PhD in 1916. He began his career by teaching at the University of Minnesota and, after two years with the Westinghouse Corporation in Pittsburgh, he returned to academic life when in 1920 he was appointed professor of physics at Washington University, St. Louis, Missouri. The main part of his career however was spent at the University of Chicago where he served as professor of physics from 1923 to 1945. Compton then returned to the University of Washington first as chancellor and then (1953–61) as professor of natural philosophy.

Compton is best remembered for the discovery and explanation in 1923 of the effect named for him for which, in 1927, he shared the Nobel Prize for physics with Charles T. R. Wilson. He was investigating the scattering of x-rays by light elements such as carbon, and found that some of the scattered radiation had an increased wavelength, an increase that varied with the angle of scattering. According to classical physics there should be no such change, for it is difficult to see how the scattering of a wave can increase its wavelength, and Compton was led to seek its explanation elsewhere.

He thus assumed that the x-rays also exhibited particle-like behavior. Hence they could collide with an electron, being scattered and losing some of their energy in the process. This would lead to a lowering of the frequency with a corresponding increase in the wavelength. Compton went on to work out the formula that would predict the change of wavelength produced in the secondary x-rays and found that his precise predictions were fully confirmed by measurements made of cloud–chamber tracks by Wilson. Significantly, this was to provide the first hard experimental evidence for the dual nature of electromagnetic radiation; that is, that it could behave both as a wave and a particle. This would be developed much further in the 1920s as one of the cornerstones of the new quantum physics.

In the 1930s Compton concentrated on a major investigation into the nature of cosmic rays. The crucial issue, following the work of Robert Millikan, was whether or not a variation in the distribution of cosmic rays with latitude could be detected. Such an effect would show that the rays were charged particles, deflected by the Earth's magnetic field, and not electromagnetic radiation. As a result of much travel and the organization of a considerable amount of the research and measurements of others Compton was by 1938 able to establish conclusively that there was a clearly marked latitude effect.

During the war Compton was an important figure in the manufacture of the atomic bomb as a member of the committee directing research on the Manhattan project. He also set up at Chicago the Metallurgical Laboratory, which acted as a cover for the construction of the first atomic pile under the direction of Enrico Fermi and took responsibility for the production of plutonium. Compton later wrote a full account of this work in his book *Atomic Quest* (1956).

Conon of Samos (*fl.* 245 BC) *Greek mathematician and astronomer*

Conon settled in Alexandria and was employed as court astronomer to the Egyptian monarch Ptolemy III. None of Conon's own writings survive and what is known of his work is through secondhand references to him by other Greek mathematicians. For example, Conon's work on conics was made use of by Apollonius of Perga in his famous treatise on conics.

Among Conon's activities as an astronomer was the compilation of tables of the times of the rising and setting of the stars, known as the *parapegma*. He was also responsible for naming a constellation of stars. The consort of Ptolemy III, Berenice II, presented her hair as an offering at the temple of Aphrodite. This disappeared and Conon claimed that the hair now hung as a new constellation of stars, which he named *Coma Berenices* ('Berenice's Hair').

Conon was known to have been a friend of Archimedes and it is probable that the Spiral of Archimedes, a mathematical curve, was in fact Conon's discovery.

Conway, John Horton (1937–   ) *British mathematician*

Born in Liverpool, Conway was educated at Cambridge where he obtained his PhD in 1964. He was appointed professor of mathematics at Cambridge in 1983. In 1988 he moved to America to become John von Neumann Professor of Mathematics at Princeton.

Conway's name became familiar to a large number of nonmathematicians through his invention of the 'game of life'

in 1970. The game is played on an infinite two-dimensional cellular array. Each cell has eight immediate neighbors, and can be in one of two states: on or off, occupied or empty, alive or dead. Two simple rules govern the outcome of any initial state:

1. A live cell will remain alive in the next generation if it has either two or three live neighbors.
2. An empty or dead cell will be occupied or come to life in the next generation if it has exactly three live neighbors. In all other situations living cells die and dead cells remain dead.

The game starts with an initial pattern of live cells and proceeds by a series of discrete changes – at each change all the cells change simultaneously to give a new pattern in the next generation.

Is there a general way, Conway asked, to determine the fate of any pattern? He also offered a $50 prize to anyone who could produce a pattern that grew indefinitely, or demonstrated that no such pattern could exist. The problem so intrigued computer operators that the search for interesting *Life* forms is thought to have cost millions of dollars in unauthorized computer time. The prize was awarded to a group at the Massachusetts Institute of Technology which discovered a pattern, a 'glider', which every thirty generations produced another glider. Conway used gliders to demonstrate in 1982 that there are patterns that behave like self-replicating animals. The snag is that spontaneous creations of such patterns would require a computer screen larger than the solar system.

Conway has also made major contributions to group theory and knot theory. Is it possible to classify all finite simple groups? These are groups which, in the manner of prime numbers, cannot be decomposed into smaller groups. While many groups fitted into clearly defined classes, several others, known as sporadic groups, fitted into no recognized class. Five such groups were identified by Mathieu in the 1860s. A sixth was discovered in 1965 and Conway identified a further three in 1968. By 1975 twenty-six sporadic groups were known. This completed the classification theorem, also called the 'Enormous Theorem', which classifies all finite simple groups and has been estimated to be 15,000 pages long.

One aim of knot theorists is to distinguish between different types of knots. This can be done by calculating the crossing number, that is, the number of points the string crosses itself. Unfortunately, many different knots can have the same crossing number, and the number itself may be difficult to calculate. In 1960 Conway introduced a new and simpler way to find cross-ing numbers. It allowed him to establish, for example, that there are at least 801 distinct knots with a crossing number no higher than 11.

Conway is also the author, along with E. Burkelamp and R. Guy, of a book on mathematics and games – *Winning Ways* (1982).

Cook, James (1728–1778) *British navigator and explorer*

Cook, the son of a Scottish farm laborer, was born at Marston in England. He was educated at the local village school and joined the Royal Navy as an able seaman in 1755. He became a ship's master in 1759, spending eight years on survey work before being appointed by the Royal Society to take command of the *Endeavour* in 1768 on its voyage to the islands of Tahiti. He made two further major voyages of discovery in 1772–75 and in 1776.

In many ways Cook's journeys were the first modern voyages. His voyage in 1768 was to be the first of the great scientific expeditions that were to become so common in the following century. One of his main duties was to carry Royal Society observers to Tahiti to watch the transit of Venus across the Sun; such transits of planets were valuable for determining the distance between the Earth and the Sun. The scientists on board included the distinguished naturalists Joseph Banks and his assistant, Daniel Solander, and the expedition also carried artists to maintain a visual record.

The voyage's second main objective was to discover the southern continent, Terra Australis, which was believed to exist. It was assumed that the northern land mass of Eurasia must be symmetrically balanced by a southern land mass. Cook found New Zealand and extensively charted this over a period of six months and then, continuing his voyage, sighted the southeast coast of Australia on 19 April, 1770. He continued up the east coast of Australia successfully navigating the treacherous Great Barrier Reef. The *Endeavour* returned to England with a vast collection of scientific observations. Cook also won fame for preventing any of his crew members from dying of scurvy by insisting on a diet that included forms of fresh fruit and vegetables.

Cook led a second expedition (1772–75) to the South Seas in the *Resolution* and the *Adventure* in which he circumnavigated the high latitudes and traveled as far south as latitude 72°. He discovered new lands, including New Caledonia and the South Sandwich Islands, but found no trace of the 'great southern continent'. It was also on the second voyage that the chronometer was used as a standard issue after its successful testing. Before 1772 navigators determined their longitude either by guesswork or by some very complicated calculations based on the Moon. Now, merely by noting the time and making comparatively simple calculations, it was possible to determine positions east or west of Greenwich. On his return he was made a fellow of the Royal Society and, for his paper on scurvy and its prevention, was awarded the Copley Medal.

Cook's third voyage (1776), again in the *Resolution*, ended in disaster. In trying to recover one of the ship's boats, which had been stolen by Polynesian islanders, Cook was attacked and killed by the natives on the beach of Kealakekua Bay.

Cooke, Sir William Fothergill (1806–1879) *British physicist. See* WHEATSTONE, SIR CHARLES.

Cooper, Leon Neil (1930–   ) *American physicist*

Cooper, who was born in New York City, was educated at Columbia where he obtained his PhD in 1954. After brief spells at the Institute for Advanced Study, Princeton, the University of Illinois, and Ohio State University, he moved in 1958 to Brown University, Providence, and was later (1962) appointed to a professorship of physics.

Cooper's early work was in nuclear physics. In 1955 he began work with John BARDEEN and John Robert SCHRIEFFER on the theory of superconductivity. In 1956 he showed theoretically that at low temperatures electrons in a conductor could act in bound pairs (now called *Cooper pairs*). Bardeen, Cooper, and Schrieffer showed that such pairs act together with the result that there is no electrical resistance to flow of electrons through the solid. The resulting BCS theory stimulated further theoretical and experimental work on superconductivity and won its three authors the 1972 Nobel Prize for physics.

Cooper has also worked on the superfluid state at low temperatures and, in a different field, on the theory of the central nervous system.

Copernicus, Nicolaus (1473–1543) *Polish astronomer*

Following the death of his father, a merchant of Torun, Poland, in 1484, Copernicus was brought up by his maternal uncle Lucas, the bishop of Ermeland. In 1491 he entered the University of Cracow where he became interested in astronomy. He went to Italy in 1496, studying law and medicine at the universities of Bologna and Padua and finally taking a doctorate in canon law at the University of Ferrara in 1503. By this time he had become, through a literal case of nepotism, a canon of Frauenburg, a post he was to hold until his death. In 1506 Copernicus returned home to serve his uncle as his doctor and secretary at Heinsberg castle. When his uncle died in 1512 Copernicus moved to Frauenburg to take up his modest duties as a canon.

Copernicus's pursuit of his interest in astronomy both brought him a distinguished reputation and led to a dissatisfaction with the prevailing system of astronomy. However his first statement of his revolutionary views, the *Commentariolus* (written between about 1510 and 1514) was circulated privately in manuscript form. The system Copernicus was rebelling against goes back to the Greece of Plato and received its fullest development in the *Almagest* of Ptolemy in the second century AD. It assumed that the Earth, unmoving, was at the center of the universe around which not only the Moon but the Sun and the other known planets revolved with perfect uniform circular motion. However, in order to fit the complicated movements of the planets into such a simple scheme, all kinds of compromises had to be made and complications brought in. Hence the introduction of such concepts as epicycles, eccentrics, and equants into the basically simple system. The second weakness was its failure to predict at all accurately the movement of the planets. Thus a conjunction of the major planets in 1503 predicted by the almanacs of the day was as much as ten days out. Copernicus, unlike Tycho Brahe, seemed unworried about the second point and, in all his writings, emphasized the urgency of a return to uniform circular motion. How, he asked himself in the *Commentariolus*, could this be achieved? It is at this point that he came up with his revolutionary hypothesis, "All the spheres revolve about the Sun as their midpoint and therefore the Sun is the center of the universe."

Copernicus then worked his system out in detail. His great work *De revolutionibus orbium coelestium* (On the Revolution of the Celestial Spheres), although finished by the early 1530s, was to be published only in the month of his death in 1543. Why Copernicus withheld his masterpiece from the world is a matter for speculation. News of his system seems to have spread quite widely. The popes Leo X and Clement VII refer to it without any obvious hostility although Luther makes an abusive reference to it. The publication of *De revolutionibus* was due to a young professor of mathematics from Wittenberg, Rheticus. Having heard of Copernicus's system and wishing to study it at first hand he turned up in Frauenburg bearing the typical gifts of the humanist scholar, the first printed editions of Euclid and Ptolemy. But Copernicus was still reluctant to publish and would only agree to Rheticus writing a description of the new system, which appeared as *Narratio prima* (1539; First Narrative). Copernicus finally agreed, under strong pressure from Rheticus and his friends, to Rheticus's copying and publishing his manuscript. Rheticus went to Nuremberg intending to see the work through the press, but before its completion he had to leave to take up a new appointment at Leipzig. The task of seeing the work through the press was left with Andreas Osiander, a Nuremburg theologian who added to the work a famous and unauthorized preface asserting that the heliocentric hypothesis was not intended to be a true description of the universe but was merely a useful supposition. He was presumably trying to avoid any church opposition. It was finally published in March, 1543. It is recorded by a friend of Copernicus's that "he only saw his completed book at the last moment, on the day of his death." The book did meet opposition from theologians who found that it conflicted with the Bible. The Aristotelians were opposed to it and to many it seemed simply absurd that the Earth could be flying through space. Even professional astronomers like Tycho found it unacceptable. A moving Earth ought to imply apparent movement in the fixed stars, but none could be observed. Acceptance of Copernicus's explanation – that the stars were too far away for parallax to be observed – would involve a radical change in the accepted size of the universe. Moreover, although the heliocentric theory explained the movements of the Moon and the planets in a much more elegant way than the Ptolemaic system, Copernicus's insistence on perfect circular orbits involved nearly as much complexity as was found in Ptolemy.

However, there was no real official opposition to *De revolutionibus* and the system outlined in it until it was placed on the index of those books banned by the Catholic Church in 1616 (from which it was not removed until 1835). But it did find acceptance with many humanist mathematicians and astronomers, so that by the end of the century the issue had switched from whether to accept Ptolemy or Copernicus, to how one should accept Copernicus – as a true description or a useful mathematical trick.

Corey, Elias James (1928–   ) *American chemist*

Born in Methuen, Massachusetts, Corey was educated at the Massachusetts Institute of Technology, where he originally intended to train as an electrical engineer. He switched to chemistry after attending a lecture course on organic chemistry. He obtained his doctorate in 1950 and, after a period at the University of Illinois, moved to Harvard in 1959 as professor of chemistry.

Corey is a synthetic chemist with over a hundred first syntheses to his credit. These include a number of substances used medicinally, such as ginkgolide B (a compound extracted from the ginkgo tree and used to treat asthma) and the synthetic prostaglandins (hormonelike compounds used to induce labor and to treat infertility).

Yet Corey has done much more than synthesize any number of complex molecules. He has also worked out and described in detail a new and fruitful systematic approach to synthetic chemistry. The difficulty facing the chemist presented with the problem of making a known complex compound is to determine which of several possible routes are worth pursuing.

Corey proposed a systematic scheme known as retrosynthetic analysis. In this, the targeted compound is broken in stages into smaller and smaller sub-units, at the same time ensuring that all the steps could be reversed at each stage. The starting point is a catalog of the main features of the compound in terms of chains, rings, branches, etc. Molecular complexity is then reduced by, for example, breaking chains and removing branches to obtain a set of rules that leads from compound to reactants and back to compound again.

Corey has given an account of his method in his book, *The Logic of Chemical Synthesis* (1989). He has also devised a computer program, LHASA (Logic and Heuristics Applied to Synthetic Analysis), to generate synthetic paths. For his work on retrosynthetic analysis Corey was awarded the 1990 Nobel Prize for chemistry.

Cori, Carl Ferdinand (1896–1984) *Czech–American biochemist*

Cori, who was born in the Czech capital of Prague, was educated at the gymnasium in Trieste, where his father was director of the Marine Biological Station, and at the University of Prague Medical School. He graduated in 1920, the year he married Gerty Radnitz, a fellow student who was to become his collaborator until her death in 1957. The Coris moved to America in 1922,

taking up an appointment at the New York State Institute for the Study of Malignant Diseases in Buffalo. In 1931 they both transferred to the Washington University Medical School, where Cori was successively professor of pharmacology and of biochemistry until his retirement in 1966.

The great French physiologist Claude Bernard had shown as long ago as 1850 that glucose is converted in the body into the complex carbohydrate glycogen. This is stored in the liver and muscle, ready to be converted back into glucose as the body needs a further energy supply. Just what steps are involved in this process was the fundamental problem the Coris began to tackle in the mid 1930s.

The first clue came in 1935, when they discovered an unknown compound in minced frog muscle. This was glucose-1-phosphate, in which the phosphate molecule is joined to the glucose 6-carbon ring at the standard position (1). It was next established that when this new compound, or *Cori ester* as it was soon called, was added to a frog or rabbit muscle extract, it was converted rapidly to glucose-6-phosphate by an enzyme that was named phosphoglucomutase, a process that was reversible. As only glucose itself can enter the cells of the body, glucose-6-phosphate must be converted to glucose by the enzyme phosphatase.

Although the actual pathway of glycolysis is much more detailed and took several years to elucidate, the value of the Coris' work is undeniable. Above all they pointed the way to the crucial role of phosphates in the provision of cellular energy, the details of which were soon to be worked out by Fritz Lipmann.

For their work the Coris shared the 1947 Nobel Prize for physiology or medicine with Bernardo HOUSSAY.

Cori, Gerty Theresa Radnitz (1896–1957) *Czech–American biochemist*

Gerty Radnitz was born in the Czech capital of Prague and graduated from the Medical School there in 1920, the year in which she married her lifelong collaborator Carl Cori. She moved with him to America, taking a post in 1922 at the New York State Institute for the Study of Malignant Diseases in Buffalo. In 1931 she went with her husband to the Washington University Medical School, where she became professor of biochemistry in 1947.

In 1947 the Coris and Bernardo HOUSSAY shared the Nobel Prize for physiology or medicine for their discovery of how glycogen is broken down and resynthesized in the body.

Coriolis, Gustave-Gaspard (1792–1843) *French physicist*

Coriolis, a Parisian by birth, studied and taught at the Ecole Polytechnique, becoming assistant professor of analysis and mechanics in 1816. He was the first to give precise definitions of work and kinetic energy in his work *Du calcul de l'effet des machines* (1829; On the Calculation of Mathematical Action) and he particularly studied the apparent effect of a change in the coordinate system on these quantities.

From this latter research grew his most famous discovery. In 1835, while studying rotating coordinate systems, he arrived at the idea of the *Coriolis force*. This is an inertial force which acts on a rotating surface at right angles to its direction of motion causing a body to follow a curved path instead of a straight line. This force is of particular significance to astrophysics, ballistics, and to earth sciences, particularly meteorology and oceanography. It affects terrestrial air and sea currents; currents moving away from the equator will have a greater eastward velocity than the ground underneath them, and so will appear to be deflected. The idea was developed independently by William Ferrel in America.

In 1838 Coriolis stopped teaching and became director of studies at the Polytechnique, but his poor health grew worse and he died five years later.

Cormack, Allan Macleod (1924–   ) *South African physicist*

Born in Johannesburg in South Africa, Cormack was educated at the University of Cape Town. He became interested in x-ray imaging at the Groote Schuur Hospital in Johannesburg, where he worked as a physicist in the radioisotopes department. In 1956 he moved to America where he served as professor at Tufts University, Massachusetts, until his retirement in 1994.

Cormack was the first to analyze theoretically the possibilities of developing a radiological cross-section of a biological system. Independently of the British engineer Godfrey HOUNSFIELD, he developed the mathematical basis for the technique of computer-assisted x-ray tomography (CAT), describing this in two papers in 1963 and 1964, and provided the first practical demonstration. X-ray tomography is a process by which a picture of an imaginary slice through an object (or the human body) is built up from information from detectors rotating around the body. The applica-

tion of this technique to medical x-ray imaging was to lead to diagnostic machines that could provide very accurate pictures of tissue distribution in the human brain and body. Hounsfield was unaware of the work of Cormack when he developed the first commercially successful CAT scanners for EMI in England.

Cormack also pointed out that the reconstruction technique might equally be applied to proton tomography, or to gamma radiation from positron annihilations within a patient, and he is investigating these as possible imaging techniques.

Cormack shared the 1979 Nobel Prize for physiology or medicine with Hounsfield for the development of CAT.

Cornforth, Sir John Warcup (1917–   ) *Australian chemist*

Cornforth was educated at the university in his native city of Sydney and at Oxford University, where he obtained his DPhil in 1941. He spent the war in Oxford working on the structure of penicillin before joining the staff of the Medical Research Council in 1946. In 1962 Cornforth moved to the Shell research center at Sittingbourne in Kent to serve as director of the Milstead Laboratory of Chemical Enzymology. In 1975 he accepted the post of Royal Society Research Professor at Sussex University, where he served until 1982.

In 1951 the American chemist Robert Woodward had succeeded in synthesizing the important steroid, cholesterol; Cornforth was interested in how the molecule is actually synthesized in the cell. Using labeled isotopes of hydrogen, he traced out in considerable detail the chemical steps used to form the $C_{27}H_{45}OH$ molecule of cholesterol from the initial CH_3COOH of acetic acid. It was for this work that he shared the 1975 Nobel Prize for chemistry with Vladimir PRELOG. Cornforth has also synthesized alkenes, oxazoles, and the plant hormone abscisic acid.

Correns, Karl Erich (1864–1933) *German botanist and geneticist*

Correns, the only child of the painter Erich Correns, was born in Munich, Germany. He studied at Tübingen University, where he began his research on the effect of foreign pollen in changing the visible characters of the endosperm (nutritive tissue surrounding the plant embryo). In some of his crossing experiments Correns used varieties of pea plants, following the ratios of certain characters in the progeny of these. After four generations he had gathered sufficient evidence to formulate the basic laws of inheritance. Not until he searched for relevant literature did he find that Gregor Mendel had reached the same conclusion a generation earlier. Correns' own work, published in 1900, thus only provided further proof for Mendel's theories. His later research concentrated on establishing how widely Mendel's laws could be applied. Using variegated plants he obtained, in 1909, the first conclusive evidence for cytoplasmic, or non-Mendelian, inheritance, in which certain features of the offspring are determined by the cytoplasm of the egg cell. Other contributions to plant genetics include his proposal that genes must be physically linked to explain why some characters are always inherited together. Correns was also the first to relate Mendelian segregation (the separation of paired genes, or alleles) to meiosis and the first to obtain evidence for differential fertilization between gametes. From 1914 until his death he was director of the Kaiser Wilhelm Institute for Biology in Berlin.

Coster, Dirk (1889–1950) *Dutch physicist.*
See HEVESY, GEORGE CHARLES VON.

Coulomb, Charles Augustin de
(1736–1806) *French physicist*

Coulomb, who was born in Angoulême, France, was educated in Paris and then joined the army, serving as an engineer. He spent nine years in Martinique designing and building fortifications, returning to France because of ill health. On his return he accepted several public offices but with the coming of the revolution he withdrew from Paris, spending his time quietly and safely at Blois and devoting himself to science. He returned to public life under Napoleon, serving as an inspector of public instruction from 1802.

He made an early reputation for himself by publishing work on problems of statics and friction. Some of the concepts that he introduced and analyzed are still used in engineering theory, for example, the notion of a *thrust line*. This describes how a building must be constructed if it is to control the oblique force arising from such items as roof members. Coulomb gave a general solution to the problem.

He is however most widely remembered for his statement of the inverse square laws of electrical and magnetic attraction and repulsion published in 1785. The secret of his work was the invention of a simple but successful torsion balance, which he used with great experimental skill. It was so sensitive that a force equivalent to about 1/100 000 of a gram could be detected. The balance consisted of a silken thread carrying a carefully balanced straw covered with wax. The straw, to which a charged sphere could be fixed, was free to rotate in a large glass tube that was marked in degrees around its circumference. He could now bring another charged ball within various distances of the rotatable straw and measure the amount of twist produced. By varying the distances involved and the nature and amount of the charge, Coulomb was able to deduce a number of laws. He stated his "fundamental law of electricity" as "the repulsive forces between two small spheres charged with the same sort of electricity is in the inverse ratio of the squares of the distances between the centers of the two spheres." That is, two like charged bodies will repel each other and the force of that repulsion will fall off with the square of the distance separating them: if a body moves twice as far away the repulsive force will be four times weaker, if the body moves thrice as far away the repulsive force will be nine times weaker, and so on for any distance between them. Coulomb went on to show that the same form of law applies to magnetic as well as electrical attraction and repulsion. What is surprising about Coulomb (and his contemporaries) was an inability to see any relationship between electricity and magnetism. Despite having demonstrated that the two phenomena obey basically the same laws he insisted that they consisted of two distinct fluids.

Coulomb was immortalized by having the unit of electric charge named in his honor: the quantity of electricity carried by a current of one ampere in one second is a *coulomb*.

Cournand, André Frederic (1895–
1988) *French–American physician*

Cournand, the son of a Paris physician, was educated at the Sorbonne and, after serving in World War I, at the University of Paris where he finally obtained his MD in 1930. He then went to America for postgraduate work, at Bellevue Hospital, New York, and began working in collaboration with the American physician **Dickinson Richards** (1895–1973). Cournand remained in America, became naturalized in 1941, and continued at Bellevue where he served as professor of medicine from 1951 until his retirement in 1964.

In 1941 Cournand, in collaboration with H. Ranges, continued the earlier work of Werner FORSSMANN and developed cardiac catheterization as a tool of physiological research. He found, contrary to expectation, that the technique did not lead to blood clotting and involved virtually no discomfort.

Cournand spent much time in attempting to determine the pressure drop across the pulmonary system. He investigated the effect of shock on cardiac function and assessed the consequences of various congenital heart defects. He also looked at the action of drugs, notably the digitalin type, on the heart.

In 1945 Cournand introduced an improved catheter with two branches through which simultaneous pressures in two adjacent heart chambers could be recorded. This led to greatly improved diagnoses of anatomical abnormalities, which consequently provided a better guide to treatment.

For his "discoveries concerning heart catheterization" Cournand shared the 1956 Nobel Prize for physiology or medicine with Forssmann and Richards.

Courtois, Bernard (1777–1838) *French chemist*

Courtois was the son of a saltpeter manufacturer from Dijon in France and as a small boy he worked in the plant showing an alert interest. He was later apprenticed to a pharmacist and subsequently studied at the Ecole Polytechnique under Antoine Fourcroy. During his military service as a pharmacist he became the first to isolate morphine in its pure form from opium.

Meanwhile his father's saltpeter business had been running into difficulties because the product could be manufactured more cheaply in India, and Courtois returned to help his father. Saltpeter was obtained from the seaweed washed ashore in Normandy; the ashes (known as 'varec') were leached for sodium and potassium salts. Courtois noticed that the copper vats in which the lye was stored were becoming corroded by some unknown substance. By chance, in 1811, during the process of extracting the salts, he added excess concentrated sulfuric acid to the lye (the solution obtained by leaching) and was astonished to see "a vapor of a superb violet color" that condensed on cold surfaces to form brilliant crystalline plates. Courtois suspected that this was a new element but lacked the confidence and the laboratory equipment to establish this and asked **Charles Bernard Désormes** (1777–1862), the discoverer in 1801 of carbon dioxide, to continue his researches. His discovery was announced in 1813, and Joseph-Louis Gay-Lussac and Humphry Davy soon verified that it was an element, Gay-Lussac naming it iodine (from the Greek for 'violet').

Crafts, James Mason (1839–1917)
American chemist. See FRIEDEL, CHARLES.

Craig, Lyman Creighton (1906–1974)
American biochemist

Born in Palmyra, Iowa, Craig was educated at Iowa State University where he obtained his PhD in 1931. After two years at Johns Hopkins University he moved to Rockefeller University, New York, in 1933 where he was appointed professor of chemistry in 1949.

Craig concentrated on devising and improving techniques for separating the constituents of mixtures. His development of a fractional extraction method named countercurrent distribution (CCD) proved to be particularly good for preparing pure forms of several antibiotics and hormones. The method also established that the molecular weight of insulin is half the weight previously suggested. Craig also used CCD to separate the two protein chains of hemoglobin.

During work on ergot alkaloids Craig, with W. A. Jacobs, isolated an unknown amino acid, which they named lysergic acid. Other workers managed to prepare the dimethyl amide of this acid and found the compound, LSD, to have considerable physiological effects.

Cram, Donald James (1919–)
American chemist

Born in Chester, Vermont, Cram was educated at the University of Nebraska and at Harvard, where he completed his PhD in 1947. He moved immediately to the University of California, Los Angeles, where he served as professor of chemistry from 1956 until 1995.

In 1963 Charles PEDERSEN announced his discovery of the first of the crown ethers. Cram, it was reported, spent the next 48 hours in his laboratory fiddling with model kits and making a variety of new structures. He soon came to see that crown ethers could be modified in such a way as to distinguish between different forms of chiral molecules, i.e. molecules and their mirror images. By 1973 he had succeeded in devising crown ethers that could identify optically active amino acids. Cram introduced the name 'host–guest' chemistry to describe such reactions.

For his work in this new field Cram shared the 1987 Nobel Prize for chemistry with Pedersen and J-M. LEHN.

Crick, Francis Harry Compton
(1916–) *British molecular biologist*

The son of a shoe manufacturer from

Northampton, Crick was educated at University College, London. After graduating in physics in 1938 he began his research career under E. N. Andrade working on the measurement of the viscosity of water. With the outbreak of war he was posted to the Admiralty to work on the design of acoustic and magnetic mines. Crick found himself at the end of the war at a loss what to do. He was drawn towards pure science and after reading Schrödinger's book *What is Life?* (1944), Crick decided that he wanted to work on a "major mystery – the mystery of life and the mystery of consciousness." With backing from the Medical Research Council (MRC) Crick began his odyssey in 1947 at the Strangeways Laboratory, Cambridge, working on tissue culture. Two years later he moved to the newly formed MRC unit at the Cavendish studying the structure of proteins by x-ray diffraction analysis.

In 1951 a young American student, James WATSON, arrived at the unit. Watson suggested to Crick that it was necessary to find the molecular structure of the hereditary material, DNA, before its function could be properly understood. Much was already known about the chemical and physical nature of DNA from the studies of such scientists as Phoebus Levene, Erwin Chargaff, Alexander Todd, and Linus Pauling. Using this knowledge and the x-ray diffraction data of Maurice WILKINS and Rosalind FRANKLIN, Crick and Watson had built, by 1953, a molecular model incorporating all the known features of DNA. Fundamental to the model was their conception of DNA as a double helix. Despite the significance of Crick's work on DNA he remained officially a graduate student. Consequently he returned to his work on protein structure and completed his PhD in 1953 at the age of 37.

Ten years' intensive research in many laboratories around the world all tended to confirm Crick and Watson's model. For their work, which has been called the most significant discovery of this century, they were awarded, with Wilkins, the 1962 Nobel Prize for physiology or medicine.

Crick, in collaboration with Sydney Brenner, made important contributions to the understanding of the genetic code and introduced the term 'codon' to describe a set of three adjacent bases that together code for one amino acid. He also formulated the adaptor hypothesis in which he suggested that, in protein synthesis, small adaptor molecules act as intermediaries between the messenger RNA template and the amino acids. Such adaptors, or transfer RNAs, were identified independently by

Robert Holley and Paul Berg in 1956. Crick is also known for his formulation of the Central Dogma of molecular genetics, which assumes that the passage of genetic information is from DNA to RNA to protein. David BALTIMORE was later to show that in certain cases, information can actually go from RNA to DNA.

In 1977 Crick moved to the Salk Institute, San Diego, California where he has since remained. While at Salk he worked on the second of the great mysteries he identified in 1947, namely, the nature of consciousness. At an early stage he rejected computer models of the mind and the neural Darwinism of G. EDELMAN. He went on to publish his mature views on the nature of mind in his *The Astonishing Hypothesis* (1994), in which he argued that "your joys and your sorrows, your memories and ambitions, your sense of personal identity and free will, are in fact no more than the behaviour of a vast assembly of nerve cells and their associated miracles." He had previously published in 1983, with Graeme Mitchinson, a novel account of dreams. "We dream in order to forget," he claims. Dreams allow the brain to eliminate the unwanted information collected during the day which would otherwise clog up the system.

Crick has also published his intellectual autobiography, *What Mad Pursuit* (New York, 1988).

Croll, James (1821–1890) *British geologist*

Croll, the son of a stonemason and crofter from Cargill in Scotland, started work as a millwright. He became caretaker at Anderson's College, Glasgow, in 1859, and was later made resident geologist in the Edinburgh office of the Geological Survey, where he remained until his retirement in 1880.

In 1864 he studied the work of A. J. Adhemar and began research into the idea of an astronomical causation of ice ages. He developed the theory that the answer lay in the orbital history of the Earth. Using work done by Urbain Leverrier in 1843, he found that the degree of eccentricity had been subjected to substantial change – 100,000 years ago it was highly eccentric while 10,000 years ago its eccentricity was quite small. He concluded that if winter occurred when the Earth was furthest away from the Sun in its precessional cycle and if the orbit of the Earth was at its most eccentric, then the two factors would produce an ice age. He followed ADHEMAR in seeing this as alternating between the two hemispheres and having a period of about 26,000 years.

This view was generally accepted by

other geologists, notably by James Geikie in his pioneering work *The Great Ice Age* (1874–84), but tests made on the theory were too rudimentary to be conclusive.

Croll's work was published in his *Climate and Time* (1875) and *Climate and Cosmology* (1885).

Cronin, James Watson (1931–)
American physicist

Cronin, who was born in Chicago, Illinois, was educated at the Southern Methodist University and at Chicago, where he obtained his PhD in 1955. After a period at the Brookhaven National Laboratory he moved to Princeton in 1958 and later served as professor of physics from 1965 until 1971 when he was appointed to a comparable chair at the University of Chicago.

In 1956 Tsung Dao LEE and Chen Ning YANG made the startling claim that parity (P) was not conserved in weak interactions. To the surprise of physicists their bold conjecture was confirmed in a matter of months. It was however widely assumed that in a reaction the combination of parity and a property called charge conjugation (C) was conserved. Cronin and Val FITCH, together with James Christenson and René Turlay, tested this CP conservation in 1964 by investigating the decay of neutral kaons. It was known that one type of kaon could decay into two pions; the other could not without violating CP conservation. Cronin and his colleagues discovered a small number of decays of the second type into two pions, clearly demonstrating that CP is violated.

The result is of fundamental interest for it is known that the combined properties of charge conjugation (C), parity (P), and time (T) are conserved – so that if CP is violated then the decay of the kaons is not symmetrical with respect to time reversal.

Cronin and Fitch shared the 1980 Nobel Prize for physics for this work.

Crookes, Sir William (1832–1919)
British chemist and physicist

Crookes studied at the Royal College of Chemistry in his native city of London, under August von Hofmann (1848). After working at the Radcliffe Observatory, Oxford, and the Chester College of Science, he returned to London in 1856, where, having inherited a large fortune, he edited *Chemical News* and spent his time on research.

Following the invention of the spectroscope by Robert Bunsen and Gustav Kirchhoff, Crookes discovered the element thallium (1861) by means of its spectrum. In investigating the properties and molecular

weight of thallium, he noticed unusual effects in the vacuum balance that he was using. This led him to investigate effects at low pressure and eventually to invent the instrument known as the *Crookes radiometer* (1875). This device is a small evacuated glass bulb containing an arrangement of four light metal vanes. Alternate sides of the vanes are polished and blackened. When radiant heat falls on the instrument, the vanes rotate. The effect depends on the low pressure of gas in the bulb; molecules leaving the dark (hotter) surfaces have greater momentum than those leaving the bright (cooler) surfaces. Although the instrument had little practical use, it was important evidence for the kinetic theory of gases.

Crookes went on to investigate electrical discharges in gases at low pressure, producing an improved vacuum tube (the *Crookes tube*). He also investigated cathode rays and radioactivity. *Crookes glass* is a type of glass invented to protect the eyes of industrial workers from intense radiation.

From about 1870, Crookes became interested in spiritualism and became one of the leading investigators of psychic phenomena.

Crum Brown, Alexander (1838–1922)
British organic chemist

The son of a Presbyterian minister in the Scottish capital Edinburgh, Crum Brown studied arts and then medicine and chemistry there, gaining an MA degree in 1858 and his MD in 1861. He was also awarded a doctorate from London University (1862) and worked with Robert Bunsen at Heidelberg and Hermann Kolbe at Marburg before returning to Edinburgh as a lecturer in 1863, becoming professor of chemistry in 1869.

Crum Brown was essentially a theoretician of organic chemistry and his structural formulae, introduced in his MD thesis *On the Theory of Chemical Combination* (1861) and taken up by Edward Frankland in 1866, are essentially the symbols used today. In 1867–68, with T.R. Fraser, he carried out pioneering work in what is now called structure/activity relationships in pharmacology. In 1892 (with J. Gibson) he proposed a rule (*Crum Brown's rule*) concerning the effect of substitution of an organic group into a benzene ring that already contains a group. The rule can be used to predict the position into which the existing group will direct the second group. Other research interests were physiology (the function of the semicircular canals in the ear), phonetics, mathematics, and crystallography.

Crutzen, Paul (1933–) *Dutch meteorologist*

Crutzen first worked in Sweden, at Stockholm University, moving in 1974 to the National Oceanic and Atmospheric Administration and the National Center for Atmospheric Research in Boulder, Colorado. In 1980 he moved to Germany, where he has since served as director of the Department of Atmospheric Chemistry at the Max Planck Institute for Chemistry, Mainz.

It began to be suspected in the 1950s that the concentration of ozone in the stratosphere was lower than expected. In 1970 Crutzen argued that nitrous oxide, arising from the use of nitrogen-rich fertilizers and the combustion of fossil fuels, could be responsible. As it was relatively unreactive, nitrous oxide could rise unchanged into the stratosphere, where, under the influence of ultraviolet radiation, it could initiate a series of reactions that would lead to the conversion of ozone into molecular oxygen.

Little notice was taken of Crutzen's argument – if only because it was felt that the amount of nitrous oxide produced was too insignificant to cause any noticeable depletion of the ozone layer. The debate, however, was revived by the growing fear in the early 1970s that a proposed armada of supersonic transport aircraft (SSTs) would emit large quantities of nitrous oxide from their exhausts. Consequently the anti-SST lobby seized upon Crutzen's work.

In fact, the SSTs were never constructed. Soon after, Crutzen's warnings were overshadowed by the greater threat from the chlorofluorocarbons (CFCs), first identified in 1974 by F. Sherwood ROWLAND and Mario MOLINA, with whom Crutzen shared the 1995 Nobel Prize for chemistry.

Crutzen was also one of the first scientists to warn of the dangers of a 'nuclear winter'. In 1982, two years before Carl SAGAN and his colleagues published their famous paper on the subject, Crutzen argued that fires lit by large nuclear explosions would be extensive enough to generate massive amounts of smoke, which, added to the dust produced by the bomb, would profoundly restrict the amount of sunlight reaching the ground.

Curie, Marie Skłodowska (1867–1934) *Polish–French chemist*

Marie Skłodowska's father was a physics teacher and her mother the principal of a girls' school in the Polish capital Warsaw. She acquired from her father a positivism and an interest in science although to aid the family finances she was forced, in 1885, to become a governess. She seems to have been on the fringe of nationalist revolutionary politics at a time when Polish language and culture were very much under Russian domination, but her main interest at this time appears to have been science. There was no way in which a girl could receive any form of higher scientific education in Poland in the 1880s, and so in 1891 she followed her elder sister to Paris. Living in poverty and working hard she graduated in physics from the Sorbonne in 1893, taking first place. She received a scholarship from Poland, which enabled her to spend a year studying mathematics; this time she graduated in second place.

In 1894 she met Pierre Curie and they married the following year. He was a physicist of some distinction, having already made several important discoveries, and was working as chief of the laboratory of the school of Industrial Physics and Chemistry. Marie was at this time looking for a topic for research for a higher degree. Her husband was in full sympathy with her desire to continue with research, by no means a common attitude in late 19th-century France. She was also fortunate in her timing and choice of topic – the study of radioactivity. In 1896 Henri BECQUEREL had discovered radioactivity in uranium. Marie Curie had reason to believe that there might be a new element in the samples of uranium ore (pitchblende) that Becquerel had handled, but first she needed a place to work and a supply of the ore. It was agreed that she could work in her husband's laboratory. Her first task was to see if substances other than uranium were radioactive. Her method was to place the substance on one of the plates of Pierre's sensitive electrometer to see if it produced an electric current between the plates. In a short time she found that thorium is also radioactive.

Her next discovery was in many ways the most fundamental. She tried to see whether different compounds of uranium or thorium would have differing amounts of radioactivity. Her conclusion was that it made no difference what she mixed the uranium with, whether it was wet or dry, in powder form or solution; the only factor that counted was the amount of uranium present. This meant that radioactivity must be a property of the uranium itself and not of its interaction with something else. Radioactivity had to be an atomic property; it would soon be recognized as an effect of the nucleus.

One further advance was made by Marie Curie in 1898; she found that two uranium minerals, pitchblende and chalcolite, were more active than uranium itself. She drew the correct conclusion from this, namely that they must contain new radioactive elements. She immediately began the search for them. By the end of the year she had demonstrated the existence of two new elements, radium and polonium, both of which were highly radioactive. No precautions were taken at this time against the levels of radiation, as their harmful effects were not recognized. (Indeed, her notebooks of this period are still too dangerous to handle.)

Her next aim was to produce some pure radium. The difficulty here was that radium is present in pitchblende in such small quantities that vast amounts of the ore were needed. The Curies managed to acquire, quite cheaply, several tons of pitchblende from the Bohemian mines thanks to the intercession of the Austrian government. As there was too much material for her small laboratory she was offered the use of an old dissecting room in the yard of the school. It was freezing in winter and unbearably hot in summer – Wilhelm Ostwald later described it as a cross between a stable and a potato cellar. The work was heavy and monotonous. The limitations of her equipment meant that she could only deal with batches of 20 kilograms at a time, which had to be carefully dissolved, filtered, and crystallized. This procedure went on month after month, in all kinds of weather. By early 1902 she had obtained one tenth of a gram of radium chloride. She took it to the French chemist **Eugene Demarçay** (1852–1904) who had first identified the new elements spectroscopically. He now had enough to determine its atomic weight, which he calculated as 225.93.

The crucial question arising from the discovery of these new elements was, what was the nature of the radiation emitted? It was thought that there were at least two different kinds of rays. One kind could be deflected by a magnetic field while the other was unaffected and would only travel a few centimeters before disappearing. (These were identified as the alpha and beta rays by Ernest RUTHERFORD.) A further question was the nature of the source of the energy. Pierre Curie showed that one gram of radium gave out about a hundred calories per hour. One further mystery at this time was the discovery of induced radioactivity – they had found that metal plates that had been close to, but not in contact with, samples of radium became radioactive themselves and remained so for some time.

The mysteries of radioactivity were explained not by the Curies but by Rutherford and his pupils. Although Marie Curie was no great theorist, she was an industrious experimentalist who with great strength and singlemindedness would pursue important but basically tedious experimental procedures for years. Her thesis was presented in 1903 and she became the first woman to be awarded an advanced scientific research degree in France. In the same year she was awarded the Nobel Prize for physics jointly with her husband and Becquerel for their work on radioactivity.

In 1904, when her husband was appointed professor at the Sorbonne, Marie was offered a part-time post as a physics teacher at a girls' Normal School at Sèvres. In the same year her second daughter Eve was born. It is also about this time that she first appears to have suffered from radiation sickness. Given all these distractions it is not surprising that for a few years after the completion of her thesis she had little time for research. In 1906 Pierre Curie died in a tragic accident. The Sorbonne elected her to her husband's chair and the rest of her life was largely spent in organizing the research of others and attempting to raise funds. She made two long trips to America in 1921 and 1929. On her first trip she had been asked what she would most like to have. A gram of radium of her own was her reply, and she returned from America with a gram, valued at $100,000. She also received $50,000 from the Carnegie Institution. In 1912 the Sorbonne founded the Curie laboratory for the study of radioactivity. It was opened in 1914 but its real work could only begin after the war, during which Marie Curie spent most of her time training radiologists. Later her laboratory, with its gram of radium, was to become one of the great research centers of the world.

Her position in France was somewhat odd. As a foreigner and a woman France was never quite sure how to treat her. She was clearly very distinguished for in 1911 she was awarded her second Nobel Prize, this time in chemistry for her discovery of radium and polonium. Her eminence was recognized by the creation of the Curie laboratory, yet at almost the same time she found herself rejected by the Académie des Sciences. She allowed her name to go forward in 1910 as the first serious female contender but was defeated. There is no doubt that this offended her. She refused to allow her name to be submitted for election again and for ten years refused to allow her work to be published in the proceedings of the Académie.

The following year, 1911, worse was to happen and she became the center of a major scandal. The physicist and former pupil of her husband, Paul Langevin was accused of having an affair with her.

Langevin had left his wife and four children, but although he was close to Madame Curie it is by no means clear that there were grounds for the accusations. Some of her letters to Langevin were stolen and published in the popular press and doubts were raised about Pierre Curie's death. Most of the attacks seem to have emanated from Gustave Téry, editor of *L'Oeuvre* and a former classmate of Langevin. Langevin retaliated by challenging Téry to a duel. Langevin faced Téry late in 1911 at 25 yards with a loaded pistol in his hand. Both refused to fire and shortly afterward the scandal died down.

Her major published work was the massive two-volume *Treatise on Radioactivity* (1910). The Curies' daughter Irène and her husband Frédéric Joliot-Curie continued the pioneering work on radioactivity and themselves received the Nobel Prize for physics.

Curie, Pierre (1859–1906) *French physicist*

Pierre Curie was the son of a Paris physician. He was educated at the Sorbonne where he became an assistant in 1878. In 1882 he was made laboratory chief at the School of Industrial Physics and Chemistry where he remained until he was appointed professor of physics at the Sorbonne in 1904. In 1895 he married Marie Skłodowska, with whom he conducted research into the radioactivity of radium and with whom he shared the Nobel Prize for physics in 1903.

His scientific career falls naturally into two periods, the time before the discovery of radioactivity by Henri BECQUEREL, when he worked on magnetism and crystallography, and the time after when he collaborated with his wife Marie CURIE on this new phenomenon.

In 1880 with his brother Jacques he had discovered piezoelectricity. 'Piezo' comes from the Greek for 'to press' and refers to the fact that certain crystals when mechanically deformed will develop opposite charges on opposite faces. The converse will also happen; i.e. an electric charge applied to a crystal will produce a deformation. The brothers used the effect to construct an electrometer to measure small electric currents. Marie Curie later used the instrument to investigate whether radiation from substances other than uranium would cause conductivity in air. Pierre Curie's second major discovery was in the effect of temperature on the magnetic properties of substances, which he was studying for his doctorate. In 1895 he showed that at a certain temperature specific to a substance it

will lose its ferromagnetic properties; this critical temperature is now known as the *Curie point.*

Shortly after this discovery he began to work intensively with his wife on the new phenomenon of radioactivity. Two new elements, radium and polonium, were discovered in 1898. The rays these elements produced were investigated and enormous efforts were made to produce a sample of pure radium.

He received little recognition in his own country. He was initially passed over for the chairs of physical chemistry and mineralogy in the Sorbonne and was defeated when he applied for membership of the Académie in 1902. He was however later admitted in 1905. The only reason he seems eventually to have been given a chair (in 1904) was that he had been offered a post in Geneva and was seriously thinking of leaving France. Partly this may have been because his political sympathies were very much to the left and because he was unwilling to participate in the science policies of the Third Republic.

Pierre Curie was possibly one of the first to suffer from radiation sickness. No attempts were made in the early days to restrict the levels of radiation received. He died accidentally in 1906 in rather strange circumstances – he slipped while crossing a Paris street, fell under a passing horse cab, and was kicked to death. The unit of activity of a radioactive substance, the *curie*, was named for him in 1910.

The Curies' daughter Irène JOLIOT-CURIE carried on research in radioactivity and also received the Nobel Prize for work done with her husband Frédéric.

Curl, Robert Floyd Jnr (1933–   ) *American chemist*

Curl was educated at Rice University, Texas, and the University of California, Berkeley, where he gained his PhD in 1957. After working at Harvard he returned to Rice in 1967 as professor of chemistry.

Curl's initial work was on small clusters of atoms of semiconductors, such as germanium and silicon. In 1984, under the influence of Harry KROTO, he became interested in the possibility of producing long-chain carbon molecules, and persuaded his colleague Richard SMALLEY to deploy the resources of his laboratory towards this end. Although they expected on theoretical grounds to discover linear chain clusters with up to 33 carbon atoms, they in fact came across an unexpected molecule with 60 carbon atoms and with a cage-like structure. The discovery of this new allotrope of carbon, later named buckminsterfullerene, opened up a new branch of materials science.

Curl shared the 1996 Nobel Prize for chemistry with Smalley and Kroto.

Curtis, Heber Doust (1872–1942)
American astronomer

Born in Muskegon, Michigan, Curtis obtained his AB (1892) and AM (1893) from the University of Michigan, where he studied classics. He moved to California in 1894 where he became professor of Latin and Greek at Napa College. There his interest in astronomy was aroused and from 1897 to 1900 he was professor of mathematics and astronomy after the college merged with the University (now the College) of the Pacific. After obtaining his PhD in 1902 from the University of Virginia he joined the staff of the Lick Observatory where he remained until 1920 when he became director of the Allegheny Observatory of the University of Pittsburg. Finally, in 1930 he was appointed director of the University of Michigan's observatory.

Curtis's early work was concerned with the measurement of the radial velocities of the brighter stars. From 1910 however he was involved in research on the nature of spiral nebulae and became convinced that these were isolated independent star systems. In 1917 he argued that the observed brightness of novae found by him and by George Ritchey on photographs of the nebulae indicated that the nebulae lay well beyond our Galaxy. He also maintained that extremely bright novae (later identified as supernovae) could not be included with the novae as distance indicators. He estimated the Andromeda nebula to be 500,000 light-years away.

Curtis's view was opposed by many, including Harlow Shapley who proposed that our Galaxy was 300,000 light-years in diameter, far larger than previously assumed, and that the spiral nebulae were associated with the Galaxy. In 1920, at a meeting of the National Academy of Sciences, Curtis engaged in a famous debate with Shapley over the size of the Galaxy and the distance of the spiral nebulae. Owing to incomplete and incorrect evidence the matter was not settled until 1924 when Edwin Hubble redetermined the distance of the Andromeda nebula and demonstrated that it lay well beyond the Galaxy.

Cuvier, Baron Georges Léopold Chrétien Frédéric Dagobert (1769–1832) *French anatomist and taxonomist*

Cuvier was born in Montbéliard (now in France) and as a child was greatly influenced by Georges Buffon's books. In 1795 he became assistant to the professor of comparative anatomy at the Museum of Natural History in Paris – then the world's largest scientific research establishment. During his lifetime he greatly enlarged the comparative anatomy section from a few hundred skeletons to 13,000 specimens. Cuvier extended Linnaeus's classification, creating another level, the phylum, into which he grouped related classes. He recognized four phyla in the animal kingdom and his work on one of these, the fishes, is recognized as the foundation for modern ichthyology. Together with Achille Valenciennes, Cuvier compiled the lengthy *Histoire des poissons*, nine volumes of which had appeared by his death. The fish families delimited in this work remain as orders or suborders in today's classification. Cuvier was the first to classify fossils and named the pterodactyl. His results from investigations of the Tertiary formations near Paris are published in four volumes as *Recherches sur les ossements fossiles des quadrupèdes* (1812).

In 1799 Cuvier became professor of natural history at the Collège de France and in 1802 was also made professor at the Jardin des Plantes. In his later life he became increasingly involved in educational administration and played a large part in organizing the new Sorbonne.

Daguerre, Louis-Jacques-Mandé

(1789–1851) *French physicist, inventor, and painter*

Born in Cormeilles near Paris, France, Daguerre, the inventor of the *daguerreotype* (the first practical photograph), first became interested in the effect of light on films from the artistic point of view. After working first as a tax officer he became a painter of opera scenery. Working with Charles-Marie Bouton he invented the diorama – a display of paintings on semitransparent linen that transmitted and reflected light – and opened a diorama in Paris (1822).

From 1826 Daguerre turned his attention to heliography and he was partnered in this by Joseph-Nicéphore Niepce until Niepce's death in 1833. Daguerre continued his work and in 1839 presented to the French Academy of Sciences the daguerreotype, which needed only about 25-minutes exposure time to produce an image, compared with over eight hours for Niepce's previous attempts. In the daguerreotype a photographic image was obtained on a copper plate coated with a light-sensitive layer of silver iodide and bromide.

Daimler, Gottlieb Wilhelm (1834–1900) *German engineer and inventor*

Daimler, who was born in Schorndorf, Germany, became a gunsmith's apprentice in 1848. He studied at Stuttgart technical school, worked for a period in an engineering works, and completed his education at Stuttgart Polytechnic. After traveling in England and France, he worked from 1863 in German engineering companies, beginning work on an internal-combustion engine in 1872.

In 1885 Daimler set up a company with Wilhelm Maybach and in 1883 and 1885 designs for an internal-combustion engine suitable for light vehicles were patented. In 1890 he founded the Daimler-Motoren-Gesellschaft company, which, in 1899, built the first Mercedes car.

Dale, Sir Henry Hallett (1875–1968) *British physiologist*

Educated at Cambridge University and St. Bartholomew's Hospital in his native city of London, Dale became, in 1904, director of the Wellcome Physiological Research Laboratories. His work there over the next ten years included the isolation (with Arthur Ewins) from ergot fungi of a pharmacologically active extract – acetylcholine – which he found had similar effects to the parasympathetic nervous system on various organs. It was later shown by Otto Loewi that a substance released by electrical stimulation of the vagus nerve was responsible for effecting changes in heartbeat. Following up this work, Dale showed that the substance is in fact acetylcholine, thus establishing that chemical as well as electrical stimuli are involved in nerve action. For this research, Dale and Loewi shared the 1936 Nobel Prize for physiology or medicine. Dale also worked on the properties of histamine and related substances, including their actions in allergic and anaphylactic conditions. He was the chairman of an international committee responsible for the standardization of biological preparations, and from 1928 to 1942 was director of the National Institute for Medical Research.

D'Alembert, Jean Le Rond

(1717–1783) *French mathematician, encyclopedist, and philosopher*

D'Alembert was the illegitimate son of a Parisian society hostess, Mme de Tenzin, and was abandoned on the steps of a Paris church, from which he was named. He was brought up by a glazier and his wife, and his father, the chevalier Destouches, made sufficient money available to ensure that d'Alembert received a good education although he never acknowledged that d'Alembert was his son. He graduated from Mazarin College in 1735 and was admitted to the Academy of Sciences in 1741.

D'Alembert's mathematical work was chiefly in various fields of applied mathematics, in particular dynamics. In 1743 he published his *Traité de dynamique* (Treatise on Dynamics), in which the famous *d'Alembert principle* is enunciated. This principle is a generalization of Newton's third law of motion, and it states that Newton's law holds not only for fixed bodies but also for those that are free to move. D'Alembert wrote numerous other mathematical works on such subjects as fluid dynamics, the theory of winds, and the properties of vibrating strings. His most significant purely mathematical innovation was his invention and development of the theory of partial differential equations. Between 1761 and

1780 he published eight volumes of mathematical studies.

Apart from his mathematical work he is perhaps more widely known for his work on Denis Diderot's *Encyclopédie* as editor of the mathematical and scientific articles, and his association with the philosophes. D'Alembert was a friend of Voltaire's and he had a lively interest in theater and music, which led him to conduct experiments on the properties of sound and to write a number of theoretical treatises on such matters as harmony. He was elected to the French Academy in 1754 and became its permanent secretary in 1772 but he refused the presidency of the Berlin Academy.

Dalén, Nils Gustaf (1869–1937) *Swedish engineer*

Born in Stenstorp, Sweden, Dalén graduated in mechanical engineering in 1896 from the Chalmers Institute at Göteborg and then spent a year at the Swiss Federal Institute of Technology at Zürich. For several years he researched and improved hot-air turbines, compressors, and air pumps and from 1900 to 1905 worked with an engineering firm, Dalén and Alsing. He then became works manager for the Swedish Carbide and Acetylene Company, which in 1909 became the Swedish Gas Accumulator Company with Dalén as managing director.

Dalén is remembered principally for his inventions relating to acetylene lighting for lighthouses and other navigational aids, and in particular an automatic light-controlled valve, for which he received the 1912 Nobel Prize for physics. The valve, known as 'Solventil', used the difference in heat-absorbing properties between a dull black surface and a highly polished one to produce differential expansion of gases, and thus to regulate the main gas valve of an acetylene-burning lamp. The lamp could thus be automatically dimmed or extinguished in daylight; this allowed buoys and lighthouses to be left unattended and less gas to be used. The system soon came into widespread use and is still in use today.

Another invention of Dalén's was a porous filler for acetylene tanks, 'Agamassan', that prevented explosions. It was ironic that in 1912 he was himself blinded by an explosion during the course of an experiment. This did not, however, deter him from continuing his experimental work up to his death.

Dalton, John (1766–1844) *British chemist and physicist*

The son of hand-loom weaver from Eaglesfield in the northwestern English county of Cumbria, Dalton was born into the nonconformist tradition of the region and remained a Quaker all his life. He was educated at the village school until the age of 11, and received tuition from Elihu Robinson, a wealthy Quaker, meteorologist, and instrument maker, who first encouraged Dalton's interest in meteorology. At the age of only 12, Dalton himself was teaching in the village. He then worked on the land for two years before moving to Kendal with his brother to teach (1781). In 1793 he moved to Manchester where he first taught at the Manchester New College, a Presbyterian institute. In 1794 he was elected to the Manchester Literary and Philosophical Society at which most of his papers were read.

From 1787 until his death Dalton maintained a diary of meteorological observations of the Lake District where he lived. His first published work, *Meteorological Observations and Essays* (1793), contained the first of his laws concerning the behavior of compound atmospheres: that the same weight of water vapor is taken up by a given space in air and in a vacuum. Both Dalton and his brother were color blind and he was the first to describe the condition, sometimes known as daltonism, in his work *Extraordinary Facts Relating to the Vision of Colours* (1794).

In 1801 Dalton read four important papers to the Manchester Philosophical Society. *On the Constitution of Mixed Gases* contains what is now known as the law of partial pressures and asserts that air is a mixture, not a compound, in which the various gases exert pressure on the walls of a vessel independently of each other. *On the Force of Steam* includes the first explanation of the dew point and hence the founding of exact hygrometry. It also demonstrates that water vapor behaves like any other gas. The third paper, *On Evaporation*, shows that the quantity of water evaporated is proportional to the vapor pressure. *On the Expansion of Gases by Heat* contains the important conclusion that all gases expand equally by heat. This law had been discovered by Jacques CHARLES in 1787 but Dalton was the first to publish.

During this time, Dalton was developing his atomic theory, for which he is best known. A physical clue to the theory was provided by the solubility of gases in water. Dalton expected to find that all gases had the same solubility in water but the fact that they did not helped to confirm his idea that the atoms of different gases had different weights. The first table of atomic weights was appended to the paper *On the Absorption of Gases by Water* read in 1802 but not printed until 1805. In another paper read in 1802 and printed in 1805 he showed that when nitric oxide is used to absorb oxygen in a eudiometer they combine in two definite ratios depending on the method of mixing. This was the beginning of the law of multiple proportions and led Dalton to much work on the oxides of nitrogen and the hydrocarbons methane and ethylene to confirm the law.

The atomic theory was first explicitly stated by Dalton at a Royal Institution lecture in December 1803 and first appeared in print in Thomas Thomson's *System of Chemistry* (1807). Dalton's own full exposition appeared in *A New System of Chemical Philosophy* (1808), with further volumes in 1810 and 1827. The basic postulates of the theory are that matter consists of atoms; that atoms can neither be created nor destroyed; that all atoms of the same element are identical, and different elements have different types of atoms; that chemical reactions take place by a rearrangement of atoms; and that compounds consist of 'compound atoms' formed from atoms of the constituent elements.

Using this theory, Dalton was able to rationalize the various laws of chemical combination (conservation of mass, definite proportions, multiple proportions) and show how they followed from the theory. He did, however, make the mistake of assuming "greatest simplicity": i.e. that the simplest compound of two elements must be binary (e.g. water was HO). His system of atomic weights was not very accurate (e.g. he gave oxygen an atomic weight of seven rather than eight). Dalton's theory remained open to dispute until 1858 when Stanislao Cannizzaro's rediscovery of Amedeo AVOGADRO's work removed the last objections to the theory. Dalton's symbols for atoms and molecules were spherical representations and he used wooden molecular models similar to the modern version.

Dam, Carl Peter Henrik (1895–1976)
Danish biochemist

Dam was born in Copenhagen and educated at the polytechnic and the university there, obtaining his doctorate in 1934. He taught at the university from 1923 until 1941, when – although stranded in America because of the war – he was appointed professor of biochemistry at the Copenhagen Polytechnic. From 1956 until 1963 Dam served as director of the Biochemical Division of the Danish Fat Research Institute.

From 1928 to 1930 Dam worked on the problem of cholesterol metabolism in chickens. Cholesterol, first analyzed by Heinrich Wieland, is a sterol with an important role in mammalian physiology. It was known that many mammals could readily synthesize it, but it was assumed that chickens lacked this ability. To test this assumption Dam began to rear chickens on a cholesterol-free diet enriched with vitamins A and D.

As it turned out he found that chickens could synthesize cholesterol but, more importantly, he also found that if kept on such a diet for two to three weeks the chickens developed hemorrhages under the skin, and blood removed for examination showed delayed coagulation. Supplementing the diet with fat, vitamin C, and cholesterol made no appreciable difference, so Dam concluded that the condition was due to lack of a hitherto unrecognized factor in the diet.

The missing factor, found to be present in green leaves and pig liver, was designated vitamin K by Dam in 1935 (K being the initial letter of 'koagulation', the Scandinavian and German form of the word). Using ether, Dam went on to extract the fat-soluble vitamin K from such sources as alfalfa, and in 1939 succeeded, with Paul KARRER, in isolating it. It was for this work that Dam shared the 1943 Nobel Prize for physiology or medicine with **Edward Doisy** (1893–1986), the American biochemist who had first synthesized vitamin K in 1940.

Dana, James Dwight (1813–1895)
American geologist, mineralogist, and zoologist

Dana was born at Utica in New York State and educated at Yale (1830–33) where he became interested in geology. He worked initially as assistant to Benjamin Silliman and published, in 1837, *A System of Mineralogy*, one of the major textbooks on the subject.

He sailed as geologist and naturalist on the Wilkes expedition (1838–42) visiting the Antarctic and Pacific. On his return, Dana published a series of research reports on the voyage during the period 1844–54, which established his reputation as an important scientist. These included *Zoophytes* (1846), *Geology* (1849), and *Crustacea* (1852).

In 1847 Dana formulated his geosynclinal theory of the origin of mountains. He introduced the term geosyncline to refer to troughs or dips in the Earth's surface that became filled with sediment. These huge deposits of sediment could then, Dana proposed, be compressed and folded into mountain chains.

He was appointed to the chair of natural history at Yale in 1856 and in 1864 to the chair of geology and mineralogy where he remained until his retirement in 1890. He published several important books while at Yale, including his most notable textbook, *Manual of Geology* (1863), and the synthesis of his work on coral reefs in *Corals and Coral Islands* (1872). In agreement with Charles Darwin's ideas, published in 1842, Dana argued that coral islands are the result of subsidence of the island together with the upward growth of corals.

Daniell, John Frederic (1790–1845)
British chemist and meteorologist

Daniell was the son of a London lawyer. He started work in the sugar-refining factory of a relative and, on the basis of early researches, he was elected to the Royal Society at the age of 23. He was appointed as first professor of chemistry at the newly opened King's College, London, in 1831.

Daniell invented a number of scientific instruments, including a hygrometer (1820) to measure humidity in the atmosphere. His theories on the atmosphere and wind movements were published in *Meteorological Essays and Observations* (1823). He also stressed the importance of moisture in hothouse management.

Daniell is best remembered for his introduction in 1836 of a new type of electric cell. The voltaic cell, introduced by Alessandro Volta in 1797, lost power once the current was drawn. This was due to bubbles of hydrogen collecting on the copper plate and producing resistance to the free flow of the circuit (polarization). With the growth of telegraphy there was a real need for a cell that could deliver a constant current over a long period of time. In the *Daniell cell* a zinc rod is immersed in a dilute solution of sulfuric acid contained in a porous pot, which stands in a solution of copper sulfate surrounded by copper. Hydrogen reacts with the copper sulfate. The porous pot prevents the two electrolytes from mixing, and at the positive (copper) electrode, copper is deposited from the copper sulfate.

Dansgaard, Willi (1922–) *Danish meteorologist*

Dansgaard was born in the Danish capital of Copenhagen and educated at the university there, obtaining his PhD in 1961. He has studied the applications of environmental isotopes to meteorological, hydrological, and glaciological problems, and in particular to the climate of the last 100,000 years. Oxygen is present in two stable isotopes – the normal oxygen–16 and a much smaller proportion of oxygen–18 with two extra neutrons in its nucleus. In 1947 Harold Urey demonstrated that the variation of the two

isotopes in sea water depended on temperature, i.e. the colder the temperature the smaller the oxygen–18 content of the seas. He had further established that a slight change of temperature would produce a measurable alteration in oxygen–18 levels.

In the early 1960s the US army drilled down into the Greenland icecap, producing an ice core 4600 feet (1400 m) long and with a 100,000-year history. Dansgaard realized that by making careful measurement of the core's varying oxygen–18 level he should be able to reconstruct the climatic history of the last 100,000 years. The most recent ice age, ending 10,000 years ago, was clearly marked, as was evidence of a weather cycle during the last 1000 years.

Dart, Raymond Arthur (1893–1988)
Australian anatomist

Born in Toowong, Australia, Dart was educated at the universities of Queensland and Sydney where he qualified as a physician in 1917. After a short period (1919–22) at University College, London, Dart moved to South Africa to serve as professor of anatomy at the University of the Witwatersrand, Johannesburg, a post he held until his retirement in 1958.

In 1924 Dart was privileged to make one of the great paleontological discoveries of the century, the Taung skull. For this he was indebted to his student Josephine Salmons who brought him in the summer of 1924 a fossil collected from a mine at Taung, Bechuanaland. Dart named it *Australopithecus africanus*, meaning southern African ape, and declared it to be intermediate between anthropoids and man. Such a claim was far from acceptable to many scholars at the time who, like Arthur Keith, dismissed the skull as that of a young anthropoid. Other and older australopithecine remains were later discovered by Robert Broom in South Africa, East Africa, and Asia, making it clear that they were in fact hominid. It is still however a matter of controversy whether *Australopithecus* lies in the direct line of descent to *Homo sapiens* or whether it represents a quite separate and unsuccessful evolutionary sideline.

Darwin, Charles Robert (1809–1882)
British naturalist

Darwin, who was born in Shrewsbury, began his university education by studying medicine at Edinburgh (1825), but finding he had no taste for the subject he entered Cambridge University to prepare for the Church. At Cambridge his interest in natural history, first stimulated by the geologist Adam Sedgwick, was encouraged by the professor of botany John Henslow. Their friendship led to Henslow's recommending Darwin to the admiralty for the position of naturalist on HMS *Beagle*, which was preparing to survey the coast of South America and the Pacific.

The *Beagle* sailed in 1831 and Darwin, armed with a copy of Charles Lyell's *Principles of Geology*, initially concerned himself more with the geological aspects of his work. However, his observations of animal species – particularly the way in which they gradually change from region to region – also led him to speculate on the development of life. He was particularly struck by the variation found in the finches of the Galápagos Islands, where he recorded some 14 different species, each thriving in a particular region of the islands. Darwin reasoned that it was highly unlikely that each species was individually created; more probably they had evolved from a parent species of finch on mainland Ecuador. Further considerations, back in England, as to the mechanism that brought this about resulted in probably the most important book in the history of biology.

On returning to England in 1836, Darwin first concerned himself with recording his travels in *A Naturalist's Voyage on the Beagle* (1839), which received the acclaim of Alexander von Humboldt. His interest in geology was reflected in *Structure and Distribution of Coral Reefs* (1842) and *Geological Observations on Volcanic Islands* (1844). These early works, which established his name in the scientific community and won the respect of Lyell, were fundamental to the development of his theories on evolution.

Early on Darwin had perceived that many questions in animal geography, comparative anatomy, and paleontology could only be answered by disregarding the theory of the immutability of the species (an idea widely held at the time) and accepting that one species evolved from another. The idea was not original but Darwin's contribution was to propose a means by which evolution could have occurred and to present his case clearly, backed up by a wealth of evidence. In 1838 he read Thomas Malthus's *An Essay on the Principle of Population* and quickly saw that Malthus's argument could be extended from man to all other forms of life. Thus environmental pressures, particularly the availability of food, act to select better adapted individuals, which survive to pass on their traits to subsequent generations. Valuable characteristics that arise through natural variability are therefore preserved while others with no survival value die out. If environmental conditions change, the population itself will gradually change as it adapts to the new conditions, and with time this will lead to the formation of new species. Darwin spent over 20 years amassing evidence in support of this theory of evolution by natural selection, so as to provide a buffer against the inevitable uproar that would greet his work on publication. In this period the nature of his studies was divulged only to close friends, such as Joseph HOOKER, T.H. HUXLEY, and Charles LYELL.

The stimulus to publish came in June 1858 when Darwin received, quite unexpectedly, a communication from Alfred Russel WALLACE that was effectively a synopsis of his own ideas. The question of priority was resolved through the action of Lyell and Hooker, who arranged for a joint paper to be read to the Linnean Society in July 1858. This consisted of Wallace's essay and a letter, dated 1857, from Darwin to the American botanist Asa Gray outlining Darwin's theories. Darwin later prepared an 'abstract' of his work, published in November 1859 as *On The Origin of Species by Means of Natural Selection*.

As expected the work made him many enemies among orthodox scientists and churchmen since beliefs in the Creation and divine guidance were threatened by Darwin's revelations. Darwin, a retiring man, chose not to defend his views publicly – a task left to (and seemingly immensely enjoyed by) Huxley, 'Darwin's bulldog', notably at the famous Oxford debate in 1860. Darwin continued quietly with his work, publishing books that extended and amplified his theories. One of these was *The Descent of Man* (1871), in which he applied his theory to the evolution of man from subhuman creatures. Many of his books are seen as pioneering works in various fields of biology, such as ecology and ethology.

Darwin was, however, troubled by one flaw in his theory – if inheritance were blending, i.e., if offspring received an average of the features of their parents (the then-held view of heredity), then how could the variation, so essential for natural selection to act on, come about? This problem was put in a nutshell by Fleeming Jenkin, professor of engineering at University College, London, who wrote a review of the *Origin* in 1867. In this Jenkin pointed out that any individual with a useful trait, assuming it mated with a normal partner, would pass on only 50% of the character to its children, 25% to its grandchildren, 12½% to its great-grandchildren, and so on until the useful feature disappeared. The logic of this drove Darwin to resort to Lamarckian ideas of inheritance (of acquired characteristics) as elaborated in his theory of pangenesis in the sixth edition of the *Origin*. The question was not resolved until the rediscovery, nearly 20 years after Darwin's death, of Gregor MENDEL's work, which demonstrated the particulate nature of inheritance.

Darwin was troubled through most of his life by continuous illness, which most probably was due to infection by the trypanosome parasite causing Chagas' disease, contracted during his travels on the *Beagle*. On his death he was buried, despite his agnosticism, in Westminster Abbey.

Darwin, Erasmus (1731–1802) *British physician*

Darwin was born at Elston. He studied medicine at the universities of Cambridge and Edinburgh, obtaining his MB from Cambridge in 1755. Darwin set up practice in Lichfield, where he soon established a reputation such that George III asked him to move to London to become his personal physician – an offer Darwin declined. He remained in Lichfield and founded, with friends, the Lunar Society of Birmingham – so called because of the monthly meetings held at members' houses. It included such eminent men as Joseph Priestley, Josiah Wedgwood, James Watt, and Matthew Boulton.

Darwin was something of an inventor, but is best remembered for his scientific writings, which often appeared in verse form. These were generally well received until the politician George Canning produced a very damaging parody of his work. This was part of a general campaign by the government against the Lunar Society for its support of the French and American revolutions, as well as its denouncement of slavery.

In his work *Zoonomia* (1794–96), Darwin advanced an evolutionary theory stating that changes in an organism are caused by the direct influence of the environment, a proposal similar to that put forward by Jean Baptiste Lamarck some 15 years later.

Darwin was the grandfather, by his first wife, of Charles Robert Darwin and, by his second wife, of Francis Galton.

Darwin, Sir George Howard (1845–1912) *British astronomer and geophysicist*

Darwin, the second son of the famous biologist Charles Darwin, was born at Down in England. He was educated at Clapham Grammar School, where the astronomer Charles Pritchard was headmaster, and Cambridge University. He became a fellow in 1868 and, in 1883, Plumian Professor of Astronomy, a post he held until his death. He was knighted in 1905.

His most significant work was on the evolution of the Earth–Moon system. His basic premise was that the effect of the tides has been to slow the Earth's rotation thus lengthening the day and to cause the Moon to recede from the Earth. He gave a mathematical analysis of the consequences of this, extrapolating into both the future and the past. He argued that some 4.5 billion years ago the Moon and the Earth would have been very close, with a day being less than five hours. Before this time the two bodies would actually have been one, with the Moon residing in what is now the Pacific Ocean. The Moon would have been torn away from the Earth by powerful solar tides that would have deformed the Earth every 2.5 hours.

Darwin's theory, worked out in collaboration with Osmond Fisher in 1879, explains both the low density of the Moon as being a part of the Earth's mantle, and also the absence of a granite layer on the Pacific floor. However, the theory is not widely accepted by astronomers. It runs against the Roche limit, which claims that no satellite can come closer than 2.44 times the planet's radius without breaking up; there are also problems with angular momentum. Astronomers today favor the view that the Moon has formed by processes of condensation and accretion. Whatever its faults, Darwin's theory is important as being the first real attempt to work out a cosmology on the principles of mathematical physics.

Dausset, Jean (1916–) *French physician and immunologist*

Dausset, the son of a doctor from Toulouse in southern France, gained his MD from the University of Paris in 1945 following wartime service in the blood transfusion unit. He was professor of hematology at the University of Paris from 1958 and professor of immunohematology from 1968. He was professor of experimental medicine at the Collège de France from 1977 to 1987.

Dausset's war experience stimulated his interest in transfusion reactions, and in 1951 he showed that the blood of certain universal donors (those of blood group O), which had been assumed safe to use in all transfusions, could nonetheless be dangerous. This was because of the presence of strong immune antibodies in their plasma, which develop following antidiphtheria and antitetanus injections. Donor blood is now systematically tested for such antibodies.

In the 1950s Dausset noticed a peculiar feature in the histories of patients who had received a number of blood transfusions: they developed a low white blood cell (leukocyte) count. He suspected that the blood transfused could well have contained antigens that stimulated the production of antibodies against the leukocytes. With insight and considerable courage Dausset went on to claim that the antigen on the blood cells, soon to be known as the HLA or human lymphocyte antigen, was the equivalent of the mouse H2 system, described by George SNELL.

The significance of Dausset's work was enormous. It meant that tissues could be typed quickly and cheaply by simple blood agglutination tests as opposed to the complicated and lengthy procedure of seeing if skin grafts would take. Such work made the technically feasible operation of kidney transplantation a practical medical option, for at last the danger of rejection could be minimized by rapid, simple, and accurate tissue typing. Further confirmation of Dausset's work was obtained when the specific regions of the HLA gene complex were later identified by J. van Rood and R. Ceppellini as a single locus on human chromosome 6.

Dausset later shared the 1980 Nobel Prize for physiology or medicine with Snell and Baruj BENACERRAF.

Davis, Raymond (1914–   ) American chemist

Born in Washington DC, Davis was educated at the universities of Maryland and Yale where he obtained his PhD in 1942. After serving four years in the USAAF, Davis took the post of senior chemist at the Brookhaven National Lab, New York, and remained there until his retirement in 1984. He has continued to work, however, as a research professor in the astronomy department of the University of Pennsylvania, Philadelphia.

For many years Davis, an experimentalist, has worked on the detection of neutrinos emitted by the Sun. In working out the reactions that power the Sun, theorists, such as John BAHCALL, predict that a certain number of neutrinos should be produced, and that a measurable number should be detectable on Earth.

The problem is that neutrinos have a very low probability of interaction with matter. Millions of them pass unimpeded through the Earth every second. The average time lapse for an interaction of a neutrino with an atom is 10^{36} seconds. To increase the probability of detecting a neutrino it was necessary to use a detector containing a large number of atoms. The result was a 100,000-gallon tank of cleaning fluid (tetrachloroethene), containing about 10^{30} atoms. To exclude confusing interactions with cosmic rays Davis deposited his tank in 1969 at the bottom of the one-mile-deep Homestake Mine at Lead, South Dakota.

Davis was looking for a specific reaction. Neutrinos can react with the isotope chlorine-37 (about a quarter of chlorine atoms) converting it into the radioactive argon-37. The argon atoms could be removed at regular intervals and counted. Theory predicted that Davis should observe 7.9±2.6 solar neutrinos per second, otherwise known as solar neutrino units (SNUs). Actually Davis began by observing about 2 SNUs, and after twenty years of continuous observation he is still observing no more than 2 SNUs.

Davis has sought to eliminate the possibility that the anomalous results are the products of a faulty experimental design. After twenty years spent refining his work, he remains convinced that any errors are unlikely to be traced to the experiment. Further, other workers have produced very similar results. This discrepancy between theory and experiment constitutes the *solar neutrino problem*.

Davis, William Morris (1850–1934)
American physical geographer

Davis, who was born in Philadelphia, Pennsylvania, was educated at Harvard. He returned to teach there in 1877 after a period as a meteorologist in Argentina and as an assistant with the North Pacific Survey. He became professor of physical geography in 1890 and of geology in 1898.

Davis is acknowledged as the founder of geomorphology, the study of landforms. In his *The Rivers and Valleys of Pennsylvania* (1889) he first introduced what later became known as the *Davisian systems* of landscape analysis. His aim was to provide an explanatory description of how landforms change in an ideal situation and his most important contribution to this was his introduction of the 'cycle of erosion' into geographical thought.

He proposed a complete cycle of youth, maturity, and old age to describe the evolution of a landscape. In youth rivers occupy steep V-shaped valleys while in old age the valleys are broad. The end product would be a flat featureless plain he called a 'peneplain'. This was an ideal cycle but in practice the cycle would invariably be interrupted by Earth movements. It was, nevertheless, strongly attacked by German geographers who objected to it on the grounds that it neglected such vital factors as weathering and climate in transforming the landscape. They also believed him to be undermining their argument that landforms could only be discovered by local fieldwork and the production of regional monographs.

Davis also produced an influential work, *Elementary Meteorology* (1894), which was used as a textbook for over 30 years, and, in 1928, published *The Coral Reef Problem*.

Davisson, Clinton Joseph (1881–1958)
American physicist

Davisson, who was born in Bloomington, Illinois, was educated at the University of Chicago and at Princeton, where he obtained his PhD in 1911. After working for a short period at the Carnegie Institute of Technology, Pittsburgh, Davisson joined the Bell Telephone Laboratory (then Western Electric) in 1917 and remained there until his retirement in 1946.

Davisson began his work by investigating the emission of electrons from a platinum oxide surface under bombardment by positive ions. He moved from this to studying the effect of electron bombardment on surfaces, and observed (1925) the angle of reflection could depend on crystal orientation. Following Louis de Broglie's theory of the wave nature of particles, he realized that his results could be due to diffraction of electrons by the pattern of atoms on the crystal surface.

In 1927 he performed a classic experiment with the American physicist **Lester Germer** (1896–1971) in which a beam of electrons of known momentum (p) was directed at an angle onto a nickel surface. The angles of reflected (diffracted) electrons were measured and the results were in agreement with de Broglie's equation for the electron wavelength ($\lambda = h/p$). In 1937 Davisson shared the Nobel Prize for physics with George Thomson for "their experimental discovery of the diffraction of electrons by crystals."

Davy, Sir Humphry (1778–1829) *British chemist*

The son of a small landowner and woodcarver, Davy went to school in his native town of Penzance and in Truro. At the age of 17 he was apprenticed to an apothecary and surgeon with a view to qualifying in medicine. He was self-reliant and inquisitive from an early age and taught himself chemistry from textbooks. In 1798 he was appointed to Thomas Beddoes's Pneumatic Institute at Clifton, Bristol, to investigate the medicinal properties of gases. Davy's first papers were published by Beddoes in 1799. In one he concluded, independently of Count Rumford, that heat was a form of motion; the other contained some fanciful speculations on oxygen, which he called

phosoxygen. Davy soon discovered the inebriating effect of nitrous oxide and his paper *Researches, Chemical and Philosophical; chiefly concerning Nitrous Oxide* (1800), and the subsequent fashion for taking the 'airs', made him famous. At Clifton he met many eminent people, including the poets William Wordsworth, Samuel Taylor Coleridge, and Robert Southey (Davy was himself a Romantic poet), and his flirtation with fashionable society began.

In 1801 Davy moved to London, to the Royal Institution, where his lectures were spectacularly successful. At Clifton he had begun to experiment in electrochemistry, following William Nicholson's electrolysis of water, and this was to prove his most fruitful field. In the early years at the Royal Institution, however, he did much work of an applied nature, for example on tanning and on agricultural chemistry. In his 1806 Bakerian Lecture to the Royal Society he predicted that electricity would be capable of resolving compounds into their elements and in the following year he was able to announce the isolation of potassium and sodium from potash and soda. This result cast doubts on Antoine Lavoisier's oxygen theory of acidity. Davy was essentially a speculative and manipulative chemist, not a theorist, and he reasoned incorrectly that ammonia (because of its alkaline properties), and hence nitrogen, might contain oxygen. He remained skeptical about the elementary nature of bodies for many years and tried to show that sulfur and phosphorus contained hydrogen.

Davy's work in the years immediately following the discovery of sodium was hindered by his social success and competition for priority with the French chemists Joseph Gay-Lussac and Louis Thenard. He prepared boron, calcium, barium, and strontium by electrolysis but his priority was disputed. In 1810 he published a paper on chlorine, which established that it contained no oxygen – another blow against the oxygen theory of acidity – and was in fact an element. The name 'chlorine' was proposed by Davy.

In 1812 Davy was knighted, married a wealthy widow, and published his book *Elements of Chemical Philosophy*. In 1813 he appointed Michael Faraday as his assistant and the Davys and Faraday visited France. Working in Michel Chevreul's laboratory, he established that iodine, discovered two years before by Bernard Courtois, was an element similar in many properties to but heavier than chlorine. On his return to England, Davy was commissioned to investigate the problem of firedamp (methane) explosions in mines. In 1816, only six months after beginning the investigation, he produced the famous safety lamp, the *Davy lamp*, in which the flame was surrounded by a wire gauze.

Davy became president of the Royal Society in 1820 and the rest of his life was much taken up by traveling on the Continent. Despite his successes there is something incomplete about his life. He never accepted the atomic theory of Dalton, his great contemporary. He had in fact more in common with his Romantic poet friends than he did with Dalton. Jöns Berzelius said of him that his work consisted of "brilliant fragments."

Dawkins, Richard (1941–) *British ethologist*

Dawkins was educated at Oxford University where he worked for his doctorate under Niko Tinbergen. He initially taught at the University of California, Berkeley, before returning to Oxford in 1970 as lecturer in animal behavior. He was appointed reader in zoology in 1989 and professor of public understanding of science in 1995.

In *The Selfish Gene* (1976) Dawkins did much to introduce the work of such scholars as William Hamilton, Robert L. Trivers, and John Maynard Smith to a wider public. He tried to show that such apparently altruistic behavior as birds risking their lives to warn the flock of an approaching predator can be seen as the 'selfish' gene ensuring its own survival (by ensuring the survival of the descendents and relatives of the 'heroic' bird) – indeed that such behavior is as relentlessly under the control of the selfish gene as the compulsive rutting of the dominant stag. The work was immensely successful, being translated into eleven languages and selling 150,000 copies in English alone.

In 1986 Dawkins published another successful work, *The Blind Watchmaker*. The title refers to the image used by William Paley in his *Natural Theology* (1802). If anyone were to find a watch he would be able to infer from its mechanism that it had a maker; equally with nature, where the mechanisms of hand, eye, heart, and brain demand the existence of a designer just as strongly. Dawkins accepted the argument but insisted that the watchmaker was merely the operation of natural selection. In case after case he argued that the same effects could be produced by natural selection a good deal more plausibly than by a divine watchmaker.

One of the most original features of Dawkins's work was his demonstration that with few simple recursive rules, and some

very simple starting points, various complex life forms or biomorphs were produced on his computer screen. And, he emphasized, the biomorphs were produced not by Dawkins as designer, he was as surprised as anyone else by the outcome, but by the application of simple rules to a large number of apparently random initial positions.

Dawkins has continued to write on evolutionary theory, most notably in his *Climbing Mount Improbable* (1996), where he shows how such unlikely candidates as a spider's web and the vertebrate eye can have evolved under the guiding power of natural selection.

Debierne, André Louis (1874–1949) *French chemist*

Born in Paris, France, Debierne was educated at the Ecole de Physique et Chemie. After graduation he worked at the Sorbonne and as an assistant to Pierre and Marie Curie, finally succeeding the latter as director of the Radium Institute. On his retirement in 1949 he in turn was succeeded by Marie Curie's daughter, Irène Joliot-Curie.

Debierne was principally a radiochemist; his first triumph came in 1900 with the discovery of a new radioactive element, actinium, which he isolated while working with pitchblende. In 1905 he went on to show that actinium, like radium, formed helium. This was of some significance in helping Ernest Rutherford to appreciate that some radioactive elements decay by emitting an alpha particle (or, as it turned out to be, the nucleus of a helium atom). In 1910, in collaboration with Marie CURIE, he isolated pure metallic radium.

De Broglie, Prince Louis Victor Pierre Raymond (1892–1987) *French physicist*

De Broglie was descended from a French family ennobled by Louis XIV. He was born in Dieppe, France, and educated at the Sorbonne. Originally a historian, he became interested in science in World War I when he was posted to the Eiffel Tower as a member of a signals unit. He pursued this interest after the war and finally obtained his doctorate in physics from the Sorbonne in 1924. He taught there from 1926, serving as professor of theoretical physics at the newly founded Henri Poincaré Institute (1928–62).

De Broglie is famous for his theory that particles (matter) can have wavelike properties. At the start of the 20th century physicists explained phenomena in terms of particles (such as the electron or proton) and electromagnetic radiation (light, ultraviolet radiation, etc.). Particles were 'matter' – conceived as discrete entities forming atoms and molecules; electromagnetic radiation was a wave motion involving changing electric and magnetic fields.

In 1905 two papers by Albert EINSTEIN began a change in this conventional view of the physical world. His work on the special theory of relativity led to the idea that matter is itself a form of energy. More specifically he explained the photoelectric effect by the concept that electromagnetic radiation (a wave) can also behave as particles (photons). Later, in 1923, Arthur COMPTON produced further evidence for this view in explaining the scattering of x-rays by electrons.

In 1924 de Broglie, influenced by Einstein's work, put forward the converse idea – that just as waves can behave as particles, particles can also behave as waves. He proposed that an electron, for instance, can behave as if it were a wave motion (a *de Broglie wave*) with wavelength h/p, where p is the momentum of the electron and h is Planck's constant. This revolutionary theory was put forward in de Broglie's doctoral thesis. Experimental support for it was obtained independently by George Thomson and by Clinton J. Davisson and the wavelike behavior of particles was used by Erwin Schrödinger in his formulation of wave mechanics.

The fact that particles can behave as waves, and vice versa, is known as wave–particle duality and has caused intense debate as to the 'real' nature of particles and electromagnetic radiation (*see* Niels BOHR, Max BORN, Erwin SCHRÖDINGER). De Broglie took the view that there is a true deterministic physical process underlying quantum mechanics – i.e. that the current indeterminate approach in terms of probability can be replaced by a more fundamental theory. He based his ideas on the concept of particles that are concentrations of energy guided through space by a real wave, and exchanging energy with a 'subquantum medium'.

De Broglie received the 1929 Nobel Prize for physics for his "discovery of the wave nature of the electron."

Debye, Peter Joseph William (1884–1966) *Dutch–American physicist and physical chemist*

Born at Maastricht in the Netherlands, Debye studied electrical engineering at Aachen and gained his PhD at Munich in 1910. He held chairs of physics at Zurich (1911–12 and 1919–27), Utrecht (1912–14), Göttingen (1914–19), and Leipzig. He was director of the Kaiser Wilhelm Institute for Theoretical Physics (1935–40) before emigrating to America where he was professor of chemistry at Cornell (1940–50).

Debye was essentially a theoretician and most of his work, although varied, had a common theme: the application of physical methods to problems of molecular structure. An early work was the derivation of a relation governing the change of the specific heat capacity of solids with temperature. In 1915 he gave a theoretical treatment of electron diffraction by gases, not realized in practice until 1930. At Göttingen, Debye and P. Scherrer discovered a method of producing x-ray diffraction patterns from powders. This was later extended to the production of diffraction patterns from simple molecules such as tetrachloromethane, CCl_4 (1928).

A major part of Debye's work was devoted to dipole moments, beginning in 1912. He used these to determine the degree of polarity of covalent bonds and to determine bond angles. Together with his x-ray work and results from rotational spectra, this enabled the precise spatial configuration of small molecules to be deduced. For example, the planarity of the benzene molecule was confirmed by dipole moment measurements. It was for his work on dipole moments and for work on the diffraction of x-rays and electrons in gases that Debye was awarded the 1936 Nobel Prize for chemistry. Debye is probably better known, however, for the *Debye–Hückel theory* of electrolytes (1923). This was a theory that could be applied to concentrated solutions of ionic compounds, and was a great advance on the theories of the time, which applied only to very dilute solutions. The Debye–Hückel theory takes account of the fact that an ion in solution tends to attract other ions of opposite charge.

Dedekind, (Julius Wilhelm) Richard (1831–1916) *German mathematician*

The son of an academic lawyer from Braunschweig, Germany, Dedekind was educated at the Caroline College there and at Göttingen, where he gained his doctorate in 1852. After four years spent teaching at Göttingen, he was appointed professor of mathematics at the Zürich Polytechnic. In 1862 he returned to Braunschweig to the Technical High School where he remained until his retirement in 1912.

In 1872 Dedekind published his most important work *Stetigkeit und Irrationale Zahlen* (Continuity and Irrational Numbers) in which he provided a rigorous definition of the irrational numbers. He began by 'cutting' or dividing the rational numbers into two non-empty disjoint sets A and B such that if x belongs to A and y to B, then $x < y$. If A has a greatest member A' then A' is a rational number; if B has a smallest number B' then B' will also be a rational number. But if A has no greatest number and B no smallest, then the cut defines an irrational number.

In the same work Dedekind gave the first precise definition of an infinite set. A set is infinite, he argued, when it is "similar to a proper part of itself." Thus the set N of natural numbers can be shown to be 'similar', that is, matched or put into a one-to-one correspondence with a proper part, in this case $2N$:

$$N \quad 1 \quad 2 \quad 3 \quad 4 \quad 5 \quad 6 \quad 7 \quad 8 \quad 9 \ldots$$
$$2N \quad 2 \quad 4 \quad 6 \quad 8 \quad 10 \quad 12 \quad 14 \quad 16 \quad 18 \ldots$$

Whereas the only thing a finite set can be matched with is the set itself.

In a later work, *Was sind und was sollen die Zahlen?* (What numbers are and should be, 1888) Dedekind demonstrated how arithmetic could be derived from a set of axioms. A simpler, but equivalent version, formulated by PEANO in 1889, is much better known.

De Duve, Christian René (1917–)
Belgian biochemist

De Duve was born at Thames Ditton in southern England and educated at the Catholic University of Louvain where he obtained his MD in 1941. After holding brief appointments at the Nobel Institute in Stockholm and at Washington University he returned to Louvain in 1947 and was appointed professor of biochemistry in 1951. From 1962 to 1988 he held a similar appointment at Rockefeller University in New York.

In 1949 de Duve was working on the metabolism of carbohydrates in the liver of the rat. By using centrifugal fractionation techniques to separate the contents of the cell, he was able to show that the enzyme glucose-6-phosphatase is associated with the microsomes – organelles whose role was only speculative until de Duve began this work. He also noted that the process of homogenization led to the release of the enzyme acid phosphatase, the amount of which seemed to vary with the degree of damage inflicted on the cells. This suggested to de Duve that the enzyme in the cell was normally enclosed by some kind of membrane. If true, the supposition would

remove a problem that had long troubled cytologists – namely how it was that such powerful enzymes did not attack the normal molecules of the cell. This question could now be answered by proposing a self-contained organelle, which neatly isolated the digestive enzymes. Confirmation for this view came in 1955 with the identification of such a body with the aid of the electron microscope. As its role is digestive or lytic, de Duve proposed the name 'lysosome'. The peroxisomes (organelles containing hydrogen peroxide in which oxidation reactions take place) were also discovered in de Duve's laboratory.

For such discoveries de Duve shared the 1974 Nobel Prize for physiology or medicine with Albert CLAUDE and George PALADE.

De Forest, Lee (1873–1961) *American physicist and inventor*

De Forest, who was born in Council Bluffs, Iowa, was interested in science from the age of 13. His father, a congregational minister, wanted him to study for the Church, but De Forest refused, going instead, in 1893, to the Sheffield Scientific School at Yale University. His PhD thesis, *Hertzian Waves from the Ends of Parallel Wires* (1899), was probably the first PhD thesis on radio in America, and drew on the work of Heinrich Hertz and Guglielmo Marconi. While working for the Western Electric Company in Chicago, he developed an electrolytic detector and an alternating-current transmitter.

In 1907 De Forest patented the Audion tube, a thermionic grid-triode vacuum tube that was a very sensitive receiver of electrical signals. This invention was crucial to the development of telecommunications equipment. In 1912 he had the idea of 'cascading' these to amplify high-frequency radio signals, making possible the powerful signals needed for long-distance telephones and for radio broadcasting. His invention formed the basis of radio, radar, telephones, and computers until the advent of solid-state electronics.

Throughout his career De Forest pushed for the acceptance of radio broadcasting. He was not a very good business manager, however, and had to sell many of his patents. Later he worked on a sound film system that was similar to the one eventually adopted. In the 1930s he designed Audion diathermy machines for medical use and during World War II he worked on military research at the Bell Telephone Laboratories.

De Geer, Charles (1720–1778) *Swedish entomologist*

De Geer was born in Finspang, Sweden, and educated in the classics at the University of Utrecht; he then studied under Linnaeus at Uppsala. His extensive *Mémoires pour servir à l'histoire des insectes* (7 vols. 1752–78; Contributory Notes on the History of Insects) include excellent drawings and probably the earliest published accounts of the maternal instinct in such nonsocial insects as the earwig *Forficula auriculara* and the shield bug *Elasmucha griseus*. He also initiated a system of insect classification based on the wings and mouthparts.

Dehmelt, Hans Georg (1922–   ) *American physicist*

Born at Gorlitz in Germany, Dehmelt left the Berlin Gymnasium in 1940 to join the German army. He was allowed for a time to study physics at Breslau University but, in 1945, he was taken prisoner by the Americans at Bastoigne. After the war he continued his education at Göttingen, gaining his PhD there in 1950. He went to America in 1952 as a postdoctoral student at Duke University, North Carolina, and remained there until 1955. He then moved to the University of Washington, Seattle, where he was appointed professor of physics in 1961, the same year he became a naturalized American citizen.

Dehmelt has worked for many years on the seemingly impossible task of imprisoning a single electron for an extended period in a suitable container. In this manner Dehmelt hoped to measure more accurately the magnetic moment (g) of the electron. Earlier experiments by H. R. Crane at Michigan University had involved passing a beam of electrons through a magnetic field. But the evidence gathered in this manner necessarily involves the interactions of other electrons.

In 1955 Dehmelt began work on what later become known as a *Penning trap*. In 1973 he succeeded in isolating a single electron and went on to show (1975) how accuracy could be further improved by 'cooling' the electron (i.e. decreasing its kinetic energy). In this way it proved possible to measure g with an accuracy of 4 parts in a trillion.

The Penning trap operates with a combination of electrical and magnetic fields. An electron in a uniform magnetic field cannot move across the field lines, but is able to escape by moving parallel to the field. To avoid this, an electric field is imposed upon the magnetic field. This field is produced by three electrodes – two negatively charged

end traps, and a positively charged encircling nickel ring.

For his work in this area Dehmelt shared the 1989 Nobel Prize for physics with Wolfgang PAUL and Norman RAMSEY.

De la Beche, Sir Henry Thomas (1796–1855) *British geologist*

De la Beche entered the army but at the end of the Napoleonic Wars he chose to devote himself to geology instead. After traveling extensively in Europe and Jamaica on his own research work, he became, in 1835, director of the Geological Survey of Great Britain, which had been recently formed largely on his initiative. He was also instrumental in setting up the Royal School of Mines in 1851, of which he was the first principal.

He wrote extensively on the geology of southwest England and Jamaica, publishing the first account of the geology of Jamaica in 1827 and his report on the geology of Devon during the period 1832–35.

In 1834, while working in Devon, he made his most significant discovery. He observed that some rock strata contained fossil plants similar to those of the Carboniferous system, discovered by William Conybeare in 1822, but did not contain any of the fossils of the preceding Silurian system, recently discovered by Roderick Murchison. The Silurian was believed to merge directly into the Carboniferous and De la Beche assumed the strata he had discovered came before the Silurian. However, William Lonsdale, librarian of the Geological Society, convincingly argued for a system, later named the Devonian, which overlay the Silurian and underlay the Carboniferous.

De la Beche wrote extensively on geology; his *A Geological Manual* (1831), *How to Observe* (1835), and *Geological Observer* (1851) were in part aimed at satisfying the growing popular interest in geology.

Delambre, Jean Baptiste Joseph (1749–1822) *French astronomer and mathematician*

Born in Amiens in northern France, Delambre was most unusual for a mathematician and astronomer in that he did not begin the serious study of his subject until he was well over 30 years old. As a student he had been interested in the classics and only turned to the exact sciences when he was 36. He published tables of Jupiter and Saturn in 1789 and of Uranus in 1792. He also measured an arc of the meridian between Dunkirk and Barcelona to establish a basis for the new metric system. He succeeded Joseph de Lalande as professor of astronomy at the Collège de France in 1795. In his later years he devoted himself to a monumental six-volume *Histoire de l'astronomie* (1817–27; History of Astronomy).

Delbrück, Max (1906–1981) *German-born American physicist and molecular biologist*

The son of a history professor, Delbrück trained as a physicist first in his native city of Berlin, and then at Tübingen, Bonn, and Göttingen, where he completed his doctorate in 1930. After spending the period from 1931 to 1933 in Copenhagen, Delbrück was appointed to the Kaiser Wilhelm Institute for Chemistry, Berlin. He left Germany for America in 1937, working first at the California Institute of Technology and from 1940 until 1947 at Vanderbilt University, Nashville. Delbrück returned to Cal Tech in 1947 and remained there as professor of biology until his retirement in 1976. He became a naturalized American citizen in 1945.

While at Copenhagen, under the influence of Niels Bohr, Delbrück's interest was diverted from atomic physics to questions about the nature of life. In the late 1930s he began to work with bacteriophages, the viruses discovered by D'Herelle that infect and destroy bacteria. They were relatively simple, reproduced quickly, and were easy to handle; an ideal organism, Delbrück argued, in which to study the mechanisms of replication and development.

In 1939, with E. Ellis, he first demonstrated the phenomenon of 'one-step growth'. Working with the phage T4 he found that "a virus particle enters a bacterial cell and after a certain period (between 13 and 40 minutes, depending on the virus, on the dot for any particular type), the bacterial cell is lysed and 100 particles are liberated." How can one particle, Delbrück asked, become 100 in a mere 20 minutes?

Soon after he began to collaborate with Salvador LURIA. In 1943 they published a paper, *Mutations of Bacteria from Virus Sensitivity to Virus Resistance.* How, they asked, do bacteria acquire resistance to lethal phage? Is it induced by contact, or does it arise from a fortunate mutation? Luria and Delbrück realized that the dynamics of bacterial growth would differ in each case. The number of resistant strains found in bacterial colonies exposed to phage should fluctuate more than if the resistance was induced. Delbrück worked out the statistics and Luria performed the experiment; the results clearly revealed that bacteria underwent mutations.

Delbrück went on to show in 1945, in collaboration with W. Bailey, that phage can reproduce sexually. They were working with the two viruses T2 and T4r, both of which could be bred in bacterium B. They found that:

T2 formed small colonies and attacked bacterium A.

T4r formed large colonies and attacked bacterium C.

When both T2 and T4r were bred together in B, the parent types produced two new strains:

Strain 1: formed small colonies and attacked bacterium C.

Strain 2: formed large colonies and attacked bacterium A.

Obviously, Delbrück concluded, "the parents had got together and exchanged something."

By this time Delbrück had begun to be recognized as the leader of what became known as the phage group. From 1945 onwards he ran an annual summer phage course at Cold Spring Harbour Laboratory, New York, which was attended over the years by most of the leading molecular biologists of the following decade. For Delbrück himself, however, the mid-1950s seemed to be a good time to move on. He turned to the study of sensory mechanisms in the fungus *Phycomyces*. It grew towards the light, against gravity, and into the wind. How did it sense these stimuli? What range of light did it respond to? These and other questions were tackled by Delbrück and his coworkers in what was soon called the Phycomyces group. His last published paper in 1981 was in this field and proposed that the chemical photoreceptor of *Phycomyces* was a flavin and not, as had been supposed, a carotene.

For his earlier work with the phage group Delbrück shared the 1969 Nobel Prize for physiology or medicine with Salvador Luria and Alfred HERSHEY.

D'Elhuyar, Don Fausto (1755–1833) *Spanish chemist and mineralogist*

Born in Logroño, Spain, D'Elhuyar studied mineralogy with his brother, Juan José, at the Freiberg Mining Academy under Abraham Werner. He then studied chemistry in Paris (1772–77). He returned to Spain shortly after and was sent to Mexico in 1788 to supervise mining operations. On his return to Spain in 1821 he was made director general of mines.

The D'Elhuyar brothers working together in 1783 discovered the element tungsten (formerly also known as wolfram). Two very dense minerals were known to chemists in the 18th century: 'tungsten'

(Swedish meaning 'heavy stone') and wolframite. In 1781 Carl Scheele had discovered that 'tungsten' (now known as scheelite) contained tungstic acid. The brothers proved that the same acid is present in wolframite, from which mineral they succeeded in isolating the element tungsten.

Del Rio, Andrès Manuel (1764–1849)
Spanish mineralogist

Del Rio was born in the Spanish capital Madrid and graduated in Spain in 1781 before going on to study in France, England, and Germany, where he was a pupil of Abraham Werner at the Freiberg Mining Academy. He had been chosen by Charles III to acquire the new scientific learning and to introduce it into the Spanish empire in order to develop and modernize the mining industry. Consequently he was sent to Mexico City to become, in 1794, professor of mineralogy at the School of Mines set up by Fausto D'Elhuyar. While in Mexico he published the *Elementos de orictognosia* (1795; Principles of the Science of Mining), which has some claim to being the first mineralogical textbook published in the Americas. He was forced into exile in the period 1829–34 after Mexico's war of independence but on his return he tried to reestablish the scientific tradition he had first introduced.

As a scientist he is best remembered for his independent discovery of the element vanadium in 1801. He had found what he took to be a new metal in some lead ore from the Mexican mines and named it 'erythronium' (from the Greek *erythros*, red) as its salts turned red when ignited. However, he failed to press his claim, being persuaded by other scientists that it was probably a compound of lead and chromium. The Swedish chemist **Nils Gabriel Sefström** (1787–1845) rediscovered the metal in 1830 and named it vanadium. Its identity with Del Rio's erythronium was demonstrated by Friedrich Wöhler in 1831.

De Luc, Jean André (1727–1817) *Swiss geologist and meteorologist*

De Luc came from an Italian family, which had moved to Switzerland from Tuscany in the 15th century; he was born in the Swiss lakeside city of Geneva. He initially concentrated on commercial activities with science as a side line but, in 1773, after the collapse of his business, he moved to England where he devoted himself to science. He was appointed as reader to Queen Charlotte, retaining that post until his death.

In a series of letters *Sur l'histoire de la terre* (On the History of the Earth) addressed to Queen Charlotte in 1779, James Hutton in 1790, and Johann Blumenbach in 1798, De Luc, following in the tradition of Thomas Burnet, tried to write a history of the Earth that took account of the advances in geology yet was still compatible with the Creation as described in Genesis.

De Luc proposed that the Earth itself was old though the flood was recent. The flood was caused by a collapse of the existing lands causing their inundation by the oceans and the emergence of the present continents. As these had been the prediluvial ocean floor it was only reasonable to suppose that they should contain marine fossils. De Luc thus explained one of the puzzles facing early geologists – the presence of marine fossils in the center of continents.

De Luc opposed Hutton's fluvial theory that such major terrestrial features as valleys are the result of the still continuing action of the rivers. He pointed out that many valleys contain no rivers, that rivers far from eroding actually deposit material, and that there seems to be no relation between the size of the river and the valley it is supposed to have created. His main objection was over downstream lakes, for in this case, when the enormous amount of material eroded from the valley is considered, De Luc argued that the lake should have been filled in long before. Hutton's unsatisfactory answer was that such infilling does take place but that the lakes are much younger than the rivers. This issue was not finally resolved until the crucial role of glaciation was established by Louis AGASSIZ some fifty years later.

De Luc was also a major figure in meteorological research. His two works, *Recherches sur la modification de l'atmosphère* (1772; Studies on Atmospheric Change) and *Idées sur la météorologie* (1786–87; Thoughts on Meteorology), made important suggestions for advances in instrumental design. His most important achievement was his formula, in 1791, for converting barometric readings into height, which provided the first accurate measurements of mountain heights.

Demarçay, Eugene Anatole (1852–1904) *French chemist. See* CURIE, MARIE SKŁODOWSKA.

Demerec, Milislav (1895–1966) *Croatian–American geneticist*

Demerec was born in Kostajnica in Croatia and graduated from the College of Agriculture in Krizevci in 1916. After a few years' work at the Krizevci Experimental Station, he moved to America. He gained his PhD in genetics from Cornell University in 1923 and then worked at the Carnegie Institution, Cold Spring Harbor, where he remained for most of his career, becoming director in 1943.

Demerec was concerned with gene structure and function, especially the effect of mutations. He found that certain unstable genes are more likely to mutate than others and that the rate of mutation is affected by various biological factors, such as the stage in the life cycle. He also demonstrated that chromosome segments that break away and rejoin in the wrong place may cause suppression of genes near the new region of attachment. This lent additional support to the idea of the 'position effect', first demonstrated by Alfred Sturtevant.

Demerec's work with the bacterium *Salmonella* revealed that genes controlling related functions are grouped together on the chromosome rather than being randomly distributed through the chromosome complement. Such units were later termed *operons*. His radiation treatment of the fungus *Penicillium* yielded a mutant strain producing much larger quantities of penicillin – a discovery of great use in World War II. He showed that antibiotics should be administered initially in large doses, so that resistant mutations do not develop, and should be given in combinations, because any bacterium resistant to one is most unlikely to have resistance to both.

Demerec greatly increased the reputation of Cold Spring Harbor while he was director there and also served on many important committees. He founded the journal *Advances in Genetics* and wrote some 200 scientific articles.

De Moivre, Abraham (1667–1754)
French mathematician

Although born at Vitry in France, as a Huguenot De Moivre was forced to flee to England to escape the religious persecution that flared up in 1685 after the revocation of the Edict of Nantes. In England he came to know both Isaac Newton and Edmond Halley, eventually becoming a fellow of the Royal Society of London himself in 1697.

De Moivre made important contributions to mathematics in the fields of probability and trigonometry. His interest in probability was no doubt stimulated by the fact that despite his abilities he was unable to find a permanent post as a mathematician and so was forced to earn his living by, among other things, gambling. De Moivre was the first to define the concept of statistical independence and to introduce analytical techniques into probability. His work

on this was published in *The Doctrine of Chances* (1718), later followed by *Miscellanea analytica* (1730; Analytical Miscellany). De Moivre also introduced the use of complex numbers into trigonometry. *De Moivre's theorem* is the relationship

$$(\cos A + i \sin A)^n = \cos nA + i \sin nA$$

Dempster, Arthur Jeffrey (1886–1950) *Canadian–American physicist*

Dempster was born in Toronto, Ontario, in Canada and educated at the university there. He emigrated to America in 1914, attended the University of Chicago, obtained his PhD in 1916, and began teaching in 1919. In 1927, he was made professor of physics.

He is noted for his early developments of and work with the mass spectrograph (invented by Francis W. Aston). In 1935, he was able to show that uranium did not consist solely of the isotope uranium–238, for seven out of every thousand uranium atoms were in fact uranium–235. It was this isotope, ^{235}U, that was later predicted by Niels Bohr to be capable of sustaining a chain reaction that could release large amounts of atomic fission energy.

Derham, William (1657–1735) *British physicist*

Born at Stoughton in Worcestershire, and educated at Trinity College, Oxford, Derham was ordained in 1682. He was appointed to the living of Upminister where he remained for the rest of his life.

Derham is best known for his attempt to measure the speed of sound. Martin MERSENNE in 1640 had claimed a value of 1038 ft. per sec. while Newton, in the first edition of *Principia* (1687), had calculated it to be 968 ft. per sec. In 1705 Derham observed from the tower of his Upminiser church the flash of cannons being fired 12 miles away across the Thames at Blackheath. By timing the interval between the flash and roar of the cannon he was able to calculate the speed of sound to be 1142 ft. per sec., a result in good agreement with the 1130 ft. per sec. at 20°C given in modern textbooks. In the second edition of his *Principia* (1713), Newton revised his calculation in the light of Derham's published results.

Derham was also the author of two immensely popular works: *Physico-theology* (1713) and *Astro-theology* (1715). Based on his Boyle lectures, they set out to show that the basic facts of Newtonian mechanics and cosmology were convincing evidence for the "being and attributes of God."

Also known as an editor, Derham published a number of posthumous works of

John Ray as well as *The Philosophical Experiments* (1726) of Robert Hooke.

Desargues, Girard (1591–1661) *French mathematician and engineer*

Little is known of the early life of Desargues except that he was born in Lyons in France. He did serve as an engineer at the siege of La Rochelle (1628) and later became a technical adviser to Cardinal de Richelieu and the French government. He is said to have known René Descartes.

Around 1630 Desargues joined a group of mathematicians in Paris and concentrated on geometry. In his most famous work, *Brouillon projet d'une atteinte aux événements des rencontres d'une cône avec un plan* (1639; Proposed Draft of an Attempt to deal with the Events of the Meeting of a Cone with a Plane), he applied projective geometry to conic sections. *Desargues' theorem* states that if the corresponding points of two triangles in nonparallel planes in space are joined by three lines that intersect at a single point, then the pairs of lines that are the extensions of corresponding sides will each intersect on the same line. Blaise PASCAL was greatly influenced by Desargues, whose contribution to projective geometry was not recognized until a handwritten copy of his work was found in 1845. This oversight probably arose because he used obscure botanical symbols instead of the better-known Cartesian symbolism.

Descartes, René du Perron
(1596–1650) *French mathematician, philosopher, and scientist*

Descartes was the son of a counselor of the Britanny *parlement*; his mother, who died shortly after his birth, left him sufficient funds to make him financially independent. Born at La Haye in France, he was educated by the Jesuits of La Flèche (1604–12) and at the University of Poitiers, where he graduated in law in 1616. For the next decade Descartes spent much of his time in travel throughout Europe and in military service, first with the army of the Prince of Orange, Maurice of Nassau, and later with the Duke of Bavaria, Maximilian, with whom he was present at the battle of the White Mountain outside Prague in 1620. In the years 1628–49 Descartes settled in the freer atmosphere of Holland. There, living quietly, he worked on the exposition and development of his system. Somewhat unwisely, he allowed himself to be enticed into the personal service of Queen Christina of Sweden in Stockholm in 1649. Forced to indulge the Queen's passion for philosophy by holding tutorials with her at 5 a.m. on icy Swedish mornings Descartes, who normally loved to lie thinking in a warm bed, died within a year from pneumonia and the copious bleeding inflicted by the enthusiastic Swedish doctors.

Descartes is in many ways, in mathematics, philosophy, and science, the first of the moderns. The moment of modernity can be dated precisely to 10 November, 1619, when, as later described in his *Discours de la méthode* (1637; Discourse on Method), he spent the whole day in seclusion in a *poêle* (an overheated room). He began systematically to doubt all supposed knowledge and resolved to accept only "what was presented to my mind so clearly and distinctly as to exclude all ground of doubt."

Descartes thus managed to pose in a single night the problem whose solution would obsess philosophers for the next 300 years. The same night also provided him with one of the basic insights of modern mathematics – that the position of a point can be uniquely defined by coordinates locating its distance from a fixed point in the direction of two or more straight lines. This was revealed in his *La Geométrie* (1637; Geometry), published as an appendix to his *Discourse*, and describing the invention of analytic or coordinate geometry, by which the geometric properties of curves and figures could be written as and investigated by algebraic equations. The system is known as a *Cartesian coordinate* system.

His theories on physics were published in his *Principia philosophiae* (1644; Principles of Philosophy). "Give me matter and motion and I will construct the universe," Descartes had proclaimed. The difficulty for him arose from his account of matter which, on metaphysical grounds, he argued, "does not at all consist in hardness, or gravity or color or that which is sensible in another manner, but alone in length, width, and depth," or, in other words, extension. From this initial handicap Descartes was forced to deny the existence of the void and face such apparently intractable problems as how bodies of the same extension could possess different weights. With such restrictions he was led to describe the universe as a system of vortices. Matter came in three forms – ordinary matter opaque to light, the ether of the heavens transmitting light, and the subtle particles of light itself. With considerable ingenuity and precious little concern for reality Descartes used such a framework within which he was able to deal with the basic phenomena of light, heat, and motion. Despite its initial difficulties it was developed by a generation of Cartesian disciples to pose as a viable alternative to the mechanics worked out later in the century by Newton. Unlike many less radical thinkers Descartes did not shrink from applying his mechanical principles to physiology, seeing the human body purely in terms of a physicomechanical system with the mind as a separate entity interacting with the body via the pineal gland – the supposed seat of the soul.

The fundamental impact of Descartes's work was basically one of demystification. Apart from the residual enigma of the precise relationship between mind and body, the main areas of physics and physiology had been swept clear of such talk as that of occult powers and hidden forms.

De Sitter, Willem (1872–1934) *Dutch astronomer and mathematician*

De Sitter, the son of a judge from Leiden in the Netherlands, studied mathematics and physics at the University of Groningen, his interest in astronomy being aroused by Jacobus Kapteyn. After serving at the Cape Town Observatory from 1897 to 1899 and, back at Groningen, as assistant to Kapteyn from 1899 to 1908, he was appointed to the chair of astronomy at the University of Leiden. He also served as director of Leiden Observatory from 1919 to 1934.

De Sitter is remembered for his proposal in 1917 of what came to be called the *de Sitter universe* in contrast to the Einstein universe. Einstein had solved the cosmological equations of his general relativity theory by the introduction of the cosmological constant, which yielded a static universe. But de Sitter, in 1917, showed that there was another solution to the equations that produced a static universe if no matter was present. The contrast was summarized in the statement that Einstein's universe contained matter but no motion while de Sitter's involved motion without matter.

The Russian mathematician Alexander Friedmann in 1922 and the Belgian George Lemaître independently in 1927 introduced the idea of an expanding universe that contained moving matter. It was then shown in 1928 that the de Sitter universe could be transformed mathematically into an expanding universe. This model, the *Einstein–de Sitter universe*, comprised normal Euclidean space and was a simpler version of the Friedmann–Lemaître models in which space was curved.

De Sitter also worked on celestial mechanics and stellar photometry. He spent much time trying to calculate the mass of Jupiter's satellites from the small perturbations in their orbits. The results were published in 1925 in his *New Mathematical Theory of Jupiter's Satellites*.

Desmarest, Nicolas (1725–1815) *French geologist*

Desmarest was the son of a school teacher from Soulaines-Dhuys in France. He first came to notice when he won a prize essay set by the Amiens Academy in 1751 on whether England and France had ever been joined together. Working for a while in Paris as an editor of scholarly works, he eventually started work for the department of commerce in 1757 investigating and reporting on various trades and industries. He served as inspector-general of manufactures (1788–91).

In 1763, following the work of Jean Guettard, he noticed large basalt deposits and traced these back to ancient volcanic activity in the Auvergne region. He mapped the area and worked out the geology of the volcanoes and their eruptions in great detail, publishing his work in the *Encyclopédie* of 1768. This work disproved the theory that all rocks were sedimentary by revealing basalt's igneous origins. He later produced an influential work, *Géographie physique* (1794; Physical Geography).

Désormes, Charles Bernard (1777–1862) *French chemist. See* COURTOIS, BERNARD.

Deville, Henri Etienne Sainte-Claire (1818–1881) *French chemist*

The son of a wealthy shipowner from the West Indies island of St. Thomas, Deville studied medicine in Paris but became interested in chemistry by attending Louis Thenard's lectures. He isolated toluene and methyl benzoate from tolu balsam and investigated other natural products before turning to inorganic chemistry, following his appointment as professor of chemistry at Besançon (1845).

Deville's first major discovery was that of nitrogen pentoxide (1849). Following this success he became professor of chemistry at the Ecole Normale Supérieure (1851) and also lectured at the Sorbonne from 1853. Deville is best known for his work on the large-scale production of aluminum. This had been obtained by Kaspar Wöhler in 1827 but had been produced only in small quantities. Deville developed a commercially successful process involving reduction of aluminum chloride by sodium; the first ingot was produced in 1855. Deville was an expert on the purification of metals and produced (among others) crystalline silicon (1854) and boron (1856), pure magnesium (1857), and pure titanium (1857; with Wöhler). He did much work on the purification of platinum and in 1872 was commissioned to produce the standard kilogram.

After his work on aluminum, Deville's most important researches were those on dissociation. Working with L. J. Troost, he discovered that many molecules were dissociated at high temperature, giving rise to anomalous vapor-density results. Deville's work explained these results and helped to confirm Amedeo Avogadro's hypothesis. His other work included the production of artificial gemstones and improved furnaces.

De Vries, Hugo (1848–1935) *Dutch plant physiologist and geneticist*

Born the son of a politician at Haarlem in the Netherlands, de Vries studied botany at Leiden and Heidelberg. He became an expert on the Netherlands flora and later turned his attention from classification to physiology and evolution. He entered Julius von Sachs's laboratory at Würzburg University, where he conducted important experiments on the water of plant cells. He demonstrated that the pressure (turgor) of the cell fluid is responsible for about 10% of extension growth, and introduced the term *plasmolysis* to describe the condition in nonturgid cells in which the cell contents contract away from the cell wall. His work in this field led to Jacobus van't Hoff's theory of osmosis.

During the 1880s, de Vries became interested in heredity. In 1889 he published *Intracellular Pangenesis*, in which he critically reviewed previous research on inheritance and advanced the theory that elements in the nucleus, 'pangenes', determine hereditary traits. To investigate his theories, he began breeding plants in 1892 and by 1896 had obtained clear evidence for the segregation of characters in the offspring of crosses in 3:1 ratios. He delayed publishing these results, proposing to include them in a larger book, but in 1900 he came across the work of Gregor MENDEL, published 34 years earlier, and announced his own findings. This stimulated both Karl Correns and Erich von Tschermak-Seysenegg to publish their essentially similar observations.

De Vries' work on the evening primrose, *Oenothera lamarckiana*, began in 1886 when he noticed distinctly differing types within a colony of the plants. He considered these to be mutants and formulated the idea of evolution proceeding by distinct changes such as those he observed, believing also that new species could arise through a single drastic mutation. He published his observations in *The Mutation Theory* (1901–03). It was later shown that his *Oenothera* 'mutants' were in fact triploids or tetra-

ploids (i.e. they had extra sets of chromosomes) and thus gave a misleading impression of the apparent rate and magnitude of mutations. However, the theory is still important for demonstrating how variation, essential for evolution, can occur in a species.

De Vries was professor of botany at Amsterdam from 1878 to 1918 and was elected a fellow of the Royal Society in 1905.

Dewar, Sir James (1842–1923) *British chemist and physicist*

Dewar, the son of a wine merchant, was born at Kincardine-on-Forth in Scotland. He was educated at Edinburgh University where he was a pupil of Lyon Playfair. In 1869 he was appointed lecturer in chemistry at the Royal Veterinary College, Edinburgh, and from 1873 also held the post of assistant chemist to the Highland and Agricultural Society of Scotland. In 1875 Dewar became Jacksonian Professor of Experimental Philosophy at Cambridge University and from 1877 he was also Fullerian Professor of Chemistry at the Royal Institution, London. He did most of his work in London where the facilities for experimental work were much better.

Dewar conducted his most important work in the field of low temperatures and the liquefaction of gases. In 1878 he demonstrated Louis CAILLETET'S apparatus for the liquefaction of oxygen and by 1891 he was able to produce liquid oxygen in quantity. In about 1872 he devised a double-walled flask with a vacuum between its highly reflective walls, the *Dewar flask*, and used this to store liquefied oxygen at extremely low temperatures. This vessel (the thermos flask) has come into everyday use for keeping substances either hot or cold.

Hydrogen had so far resisted liquefaction and Dewar now turned his attention to this. Using the Joule–Thomson effect together with Karl von Linde's improvements of this, he produced a machine with which he obtained temperatures as low as 14 K and he produced liquid hydrogen in 1898 and solid hydrogen in 1899. Only helium now resisted liquefaction; this was achieved by Heike KAMERLINGH-ONNES in 1908.

From about 1891 Dewar also studied explosives and with Frederick ABEL he developed the smokeless powder, cordite. He was knighted in 1904.

Dewar, Michael James Stuart (1918–) *British–American chemist*

Born at Ahmednagar in India, Dewar was educated at Oxford University where he obtained his DPhil in 1942. After research at

Oxford he worked in industry as a physical chemist for the Courtauld company from 1945 until his appointment in 1951 as professor of chemistry at Queen Mary College, London. In 1959 Dewar moved to America and served successively as professor of chemistry at the University of Chicago and from 1963 at the University of Texas. In 1990 he was appointed graduate research professor at the University of Florida.

Dewar is noted for his contributions to theoretical chemistry. In his *Electronic Theory of Organic Chemistry* (1949) he argued strongly for the molecular-orbital theory introduced by Robert Mulliken. He did much to improve molecular-orbital calculations and by the 1960s he was able to claim that he and his colleagues could rapidly and accurately calculate a number of chemical and physical properties of molecules.

D'Hérelle, Felix (1873–1949) *French–Canadian bacteriologist*

D'Hérelle, the son of a Canadian father and Dutch mother, was born in Montreal, Quebec, and went to school in Paris, later studying medicine at the University of Montreal. He worked as a bacteriologist in Guatemala and Mexico from 1901 until 1909, when he returned to Europe to take up a position at the Pasteur Institute in Paris. D'Hérelle moved to the University of Leiden in 1921 but after only a short stay resigned to become director of the Egyptian Bacteriological Service (1923). Finally, in 1926, d'Hérelle was appointed to the chair of bacteriology at Yale, a position he held until his retirement in 1933.

D'Hérelle is best known for his discovery of the bacteriophage – a type of virus that destroys bacteria. This work began in 1910 in Yucatan, when he was investigating diarrhea in locusts as a means of locust control. While developing cultures of the causative agent, a coccobacillus, d'Hérelle found that occasionally there would develop on a culture a clear spot, completely free of any bacteria. The cause of these clear spots became clear to him in 1915, while investigating a more orthodox form of dysentery in a cavalry squadron in Paris. He mixed a filtrate from the clear area with a culture of the dysentery bacilli and incubated the resulting broth overnight. The next morning the culture, which had been very turbid, was perfectly clear: all the bacteria had vanished. He concluded that this was the action of "a filterable virus, but a virus parasitic on bacteria."

A similar discovery of what d'Hérelle termed a 'bacteriolytic agent' was announced independently by Frederick Twort

in 1915. D'Hérelle published his own account first in 1917, followed by his monograph *The Bacteriophage, Its Role in Immunity* (1921). He spent the rest of his career attempting to develop bacteriophages as therapeutic agents. Thus, he tried to cure cholera in India in 1927 and bubonic plague in Egypt in 1926 by administering to the patients the appropriate phage. D'Hérelle himself claimed good results with his treatment, although in the hands of other workers the effect of phage on such diseases as cholera and plague appeared to be minimal. This conclusion d'Hérelle continued to resist until his death, claiming that no proper test using his methods had ever been carried out.

However, the importance of the bacteriophage as a research tool in molecular biology cannot be disputed. It was the so-called phage group, centered on Max Delbrück, that made many of the early advances in this discipline in the 1940s.

Dicke, Robert Henry (1916–   ) *American physicist*

Dicke, who was born in St. Louis, Missouri, graduated in 1939 from Princeton University and obtained his PhD in 1941 from the University of Rochester. He spent the war at the radiation laboratory of the Massachusetts Institute of Technology, joining the Princeton faculty in 1946. In 1957 he was appointed professor of physics and served from 1975 to 1984 as Albert Einstein Professor of Science. In 1984 he was appointed Albert Einstein Emeritus Professor of Science.

In 1964, unaware that he was repeating a line of thought pursued earlier by George Gamow, **Ralph Alpher**, and Robert C. Herman in 1948, Dicke began to think about the consequences of a big-bang origin of the universe. Assuming a cataclysmic explosion some 18 billion years ago with a temperature one minute after of about 10 billion degrees, then intense radiation would have been produced in addition to particles of matter. As the universe expanded this radiation would gradually lose energy. Could there still be any trace left of this 'primeval fireball'? It would in fact be detected as black-body radiation, characteristic of the temperature of the black body, which is a perfect emitter of radiation. At Dicke's instigation his colleague P. J. E. Peebles made the necessary calculations and concluded that the remnant radiation should now have a temperature of only about 10 K, later corrected to about 3 K, i.e. −270°C. At this temperature a black body should radiate a weak signal at microwave wavelengths from 0.05 millimeter to 50 centimeters with a peak at about 2 mm. Further, the signal should be constant throughout the entire universe.

Dicke began to organize a search for such radiation and had actually begun to install an antenna on his laboratory roof when he heard from Arno Penzias and Robert Wilson that they had detected background microwave radiation at a wavelength of 7 cm. It was this confluence of theory, calculation, and observation that really established the big-bang theory.

Another major area of study for Dicke is gravitation. In the 1960s he carried out a major evaluation of the experiment originally performed by Roland von Eötvös to confirm that the gravitational mass of an object is equal to its inertial mass. Dicke was able to establish the accuracy of the equivalence to one part in 10^{11}. This equivalence is basic to Einstein's theory of general relativity.

In 1961, following a suggestion of Paul Dirac in 1937, Dicke and Carl BRANS proposed that the gravitational constant was not in fact a constant, but slowly decreases at a rate of one part in 10^{11} per year. The resulting *Brans–Dicke theory* differs somewhat from Einstein's general relativity at a number of points. Thus while Einstein predicts that a ray of light should be deflected by the Sun's gravitational field 1.75 seconds (") of arc, the Brans–Dicke theory leads to a figure of 1.62"; such a difference is within the range of observational error and so is not readily detectable. Again the perihelion of Mercury should advance for Einstein by 43" per century, for Brans–Dicke a mere 39". A value of 43" has in fact been measured but Dicke maintained that part of this value, 4", could be explained by the Sun's nonspherical shape. It has however been claimed that very precise measurements of radio pulses from pulsars appear to favor Einstein. The theory was concurrently and independently developed by Pascual Jordan, and is thus sometimes known as the *Brans–Dicke–Jordan theory*. The idea of a changing gravitational constant was put forward by Paul DIRAC.

Diels, Otto Paul Hermann (1876–1954) *German organic chemist*

The son of Hermann Diels, a famous classical scholar, Diels was born in Hamburg, Germany. He gained his doctorate under Emil Fischer in Berlin (1899), becoming professor there in 1906. From 1916 until his retirement in 1948 he was professor at Kiel. In 1906 he made an extremely unexpected discovery, that of a new oxide of carbon, carbon suboxide (C_3O_2), which he prepared by

dehydrating malonic acid with phosphorus pentachloride. Diels's second major discovery was a method of removing hydrogen from steroids by means of selenium. He used this method in research on cholesterol and bile acids, obtaining aromatic hydrocarbons that enabled the structures of the steroids to be deduced.

In 1928 Diels and his assistant **Kurt Alder** (1902–1958) discovered a synthetic reaction in which a diene (compound containing two double bonds) is added to a compound containing one double bond flanked by carbonyl or carboxyl groups to give a ring structure. The reaction proceeds in the mildest conditions, is of general application, and hence of great utility in synthesis. It has been used in the synthesis of natural products, such as sterols, vitamin K, and cantharides, and of synthetic polymers. For this discovery Diels and Alder were jointly awarded the Nobel Prize for chemistry in 1950.

Diesenhofer, Johann (1943–   ) *German chemist*

Diesenhofer, who was born in Zusamaltheim, Germany, obtained his PhD from the Max Planck Institute for Biochemistry, at Martinsried near Munich, in 1974. He remained at the Institute until 1987 when he moved to America to work at the Howard Hughes Medical Institute, Dallas, Texas.

In 1982 Hartmut MICHEL had succeeded in crystallizing the membrane proteins of the photosynthetic reaction center. Clearly, to understand how photosynthesis worked at the molecular level it would be necessary to determine the structure of these proteins, and Michel invited his colleague Diesenhofer to tackle the problem. By 1985, using the well-established techniques of x-ray crystallography, Diesenhofer's group had managed to locate the position of more than 10,000 atoms.

Diesenhofer's analysis revealed complex protein structures holding a molecular cluster containing four chorophyll molecules, two pheophytins (molecules resembling chlorophyll), two quinones (dehydrogenizing agents), and a single iron atom. It has been possible to show how this center can transform energy from incident photons. On absorbing a photon, one of the chlorophyll molecules releases an electron. This is transferred by the pheophytins and quinones to the membrane's outer surface. At the same time, an adjoining cytochrome molecule donates an electron to one of the chlorophyll molecules and thus gains a positive charge. In this way the photon energy has been stored in the charge separation of the negative electron and the positive cytochrome. And so begins the molecular process of photosynthesis.

For this work Diesenhofer shared the 1988 Nobel Prize for chemistry with Hartmut Michel and his departmental head **Robert Huber** (1937–).

Diophantus of Alexandria (*fl.* 250)
Greek mathematician

Diophantus was one of the outstanding mathematicians of his era but almost nothing is known of his life and his writings survive only in fragmentary form. His most famous work was in the field of number theory and of the so-called *Diophantine equations* named for him. His major work, the *Arithmetica*, contained many new methods and results in this field. It originally consisted of 13 books but only 6 survived to be translated by the Arabs. However Diophantus was not solely interested in equations with only integral (whole number) solutions and also considered rational solutions. Diophantus made considerable innovations in the use of symbolism in Greek mathematics – the lack of suitable symbolism had previously hampered work in algebra.

Dioscorides, Pedanius (*c.* 40–*c.* 90 AD)
Greek physician

Little is known of the life of Dioscorides except that he was born in Anazarbus (now in Turkey) and became a surgeon to Emperor Nero's armies, having most probably learned his skills at Alexandria and Tarsus. Many writings are attributed to him but the only book for which his authorship is undisputed is *De materia medica* (On Medicine). This pharmacopeia remained the standard medical text until the 17th century, undergoing many revisions and additions and greatly influencing both Western and Islamic cultures. It describes animal derivatives and minerals used therapeutically but is most important for the description of over 600 plants, including notes on their habitat and the methods of preparation and medicinal use of the drugs they contain. Many of the common and scientific plant names in use today originate from Dioscorides, and the yam family, Dioscoreaceae, is named for him.

Dirac, Paul Adrien Maurice (1902–
1984) *British mathematician and physicist*

Dirac, whose father was Swiss, was born in Bristol. After graduating in 1921 in electrical engineering at Bristol University, Dirac went on to study mathematics at Cambridge University, where he obtained his PhD in 1926. After several years spent lecturing in America, he was appointed (1932) to the Lucasian Professorship of Mathematics at Cambridge, a post he held until his retirement in 1969. In 1971 he became professor of physics at Florida State University.

Dirac is acknowledged as one of the most creative of the theoreticians of the early 20th century. In 1926, slightly later than Max Born and Pascual Jordan in Germany, he developed a general formalism for quantum mechanics. In 1928 he produced his relativistic theory to describe the properties of the electron. The wave equations developed by Erwin SCHRÖDINGER to describe the behavior of electrons were nonrelativistic. A significant deficiency in the Schrödinger equation was its failure to account for the electron spin discovered in 1925 by Samuel GOUDSMIT and George Uhlenbeck. Dirac's rewriting of the equations to incorporate relativity had considerable value for it not only predicted the correct energy levels of the hydrogen atom but also revealed that some of those levels were no longer single but could be split into two. It is just such a splitting of spectral lines that is characteristic of a spinning electron.

Dirac also predicted from these equations that there must be states of negative energy for the electron. In 1930 he proposed a theory to account for this that was soon to receive dramatic confirmation. He began by taking negative energy states to refer to those energy states below the lowest positive energy state, the ground state. If there were a lower energy state for the electron below the ground state then, the question arises, why do some electrons not fall into it? Dirac's answer was that such states have already been filled with other electrons and he conjured up a picture in which space is not really empty but full of particles of negative energy. If one of these particles were to collide with a sufficiently energetic photon it would acquire positive energy and be observable as a normal electron, apparently appearing from nowhere. But it would not appear alone for it would leave behind an empty hole, which was really an absence of a negatively charged particle or, in other words, the presence of a positively charged particle. Further, if the electron were to fall back into the empty hole it would once more disappear, appearing to be annihilated together with the positively charged particle, or positron as it was later called.

Out of this theory there emerged three predictions. Firstly, that there was a positively charged electron, secondly, that it could only appear in conjunction with a normal electron, and, finally, that a collision between them resulted in their total common annihilation. Such predictions were soon confirmed following the discovery of the positron by Carl ANDERSON in 1932. Dirac had in fact added a new dimension of matter to the universe, namely antimatter. It was soon appreciated that Dirac's argument was sufficiently general to apply to all particles.

In 1937 Dirac published a paper entitled *The Cosmological Constants* in which he considered large-number coincidences, i.e. certain relationships that appear to exist between the numerical properties of some natural constants. An example is to compare the force of electrostatic attraction between an electron and a proton with the gravitational attraction due to their masses. The ratio of these is about 10^{40}:1. Similarly, it is also found that the characteristic 'radius' of the universe is 10^{40} times as large as the characteristic radius of an electron. Moreover, 10^{40} is approximately the square root of the number of particles in the universe.

These coincidences are remarkable and many physicists have speculated that these apparently unrelated things may be connected in some way. The ratios were first considered in the 1930s by Arthur EDDINGTON, who believed that he could calculate such constants and that they arose from the way in which physics observes and interprets nature. Dirac used the 10^{40} number above in a model of the universe. He argued that there was a connection between the force ratio and the radius ratio. Since the radius of the universe increased with age the gravitational constant, on which the force ratio depends, may decrease with time (i.e. it may not actually be a constant).

Above all else however Dirac was a quantum theorist. In 1930 he published the first edition of his classic work *The Principles of Quantum Mechanics*. In 1933 he shared the Nobel Prize for physics with Schrödinger.

Dirichlet, (Peter Gustav) Lejeune

(1805–1859) *German mathematician*

Born in Düren (now in Germany), Dirichlet studied mathematics at Göttingen where he was a pupil of Karl Gauss and Karl Jacobi. He also studied briefly in Paris where he met Joseph Fourier, who stimulated his interest in trigonometric series. In 1826 he returned to Germany and taught at Breslau and later at the Military Academy in Berlin. He then moved to the University of Berlin, which he only left 27 years later when he

returned to Göttingen to fill the chair left vacant by Gauss's death.

Dirichlet's work in number theory was very much inspired by Gauss's great work in that field, and Dirichlet's own book, the *Vorlesungen über Zahlentheorie* (1863; Lectures on Number Theory), is of comparable historical importance to Gauss's *Disquisitiones*. He made many very significant discoveries in the field and his work on a problem connected with primes led him to make the fundamentally important innovation of using analytical techniques to obtain results in number theory.

His stay in Paris had stimulated Dirichlet's interest in Fourier series and in 1829 he was able to solve the outstanding problem of stating the conditions sufficient for a Fourier series to converge. (The other problem of giving necessary conditions is still unsolved). Fourier also gave the young Dirichlet an interest in mathematical physics, which led him to important work on multiple integrals and the boundary-value problem, now known as the *Dirichlet problem*, concerning the formulation and solution of those partial differential equations occurring in the study of heat flow and electrostatics. These are of great importance in many other areas of physics. The growth of a more rigorous understanding of analysis owes to Dirichlet what is essentially the modern definition of the concept of a function.

Djerassi, Carl (1923–) *American chemist*

Djerassi was born in the Austrian capital of Vienna, the son of a Bulgarian physician and an Austrian mother. As both parents were Jewish, Djerassi emigrated to America in 1939. He was educated at Kenyon College, Ohio, and at the University of Wisconsin, where he completed his PhD in 1945, the same year in which he became an American citizen. From 1945 to 1949 he worked for the pharmaceutical company CIBA in Summit, New Jersey, as a research chemist. In 1949 Djerassi decided to join a new pharmaceutical company, Syntex, in Mexico City, to work on the extraction of cortisone from plants. At that time it was being produced from cattle bile at a cost of 200 dollars a gram.

Despite competition from other leading laboratories, Syntex were the first to extract cortisone ($C_{21}H_{28}O_5$) from a vegetable source, namely diosgenin ($C_{27}H_{42}O_3$), a steroid derived from a variety of wild Mexican yam.

Following their initial success Djerassi and his team turned their attention to the steroid hormone progesterone. Known as 'nature's contraceptive', the hormone inhibits ovulation. Why, then, could it not be taken as a simple, natural contraceptive?

The difficulty was that taken orally it lost most of its activity. Further, as hormones were extracted from such animal sources as human urine, bull's testicles, and sow's ovaries where they occur in small amounts, they tended to be very expensive. The first step was to produce progesterone synthetically. This was achieved at Syntex by Djerassi and others in the early 1950s, the price of progesterone dropped dramatically and it became available in large quantities.

Chemists were inhibited by the belief that steroid hormones were structure-specific; change the structure, the claim went, and the potency is lost. Djerassi was aware, however, that Max Ehrenstein had destroyed this myth a decade earlier and that it was at least conceivable that progesterone could be changed into an oral form without necessarily changing its potency.

Progesterone ($C_{21}H_{30}O_2$) contains four rings of carbon atoms. Following some hints in the literature Djerassi thought that the removal of the methyl group at position 19, thus forming 19-norprogesterone, would increase its potency. His hunch proved to be sound. He was also aware that an acetylene bond introduced into position 17 of the male hormone testosterone increased its oral activity, although known as 'ethisterone', it had found no use.

Djerassi's crucial step was to propose that ethisterone's potency could be enhanced, as with progesterone, by removing a methyl group. By October 1951 he had produced testosterone minus a methyl group, but with an added acetylene group. The precise result was 19-nor-17a-ethinyltestosterone, which proved to be a highly active oral progestational hormone. A patent was filed in November 1951. After the appropriate testing it received Federal approval in 1962 under the name Ortho-Novum. Djerassi received one dollar for the patent, a standard payment by a pharmaceutical company to its staff.

In 1951 Djerassi left Syntex for Wayne State University, Detroit, where he remained until 1959 when he was appointed professor of chemistry at Stanford. He continued to work for Syntex, as vice-president in charge of research (1957–69) and as president of research from (1969–72).

He has also served since 1968 with Zoecon, a company partly owned by Syntex and specializing in pest control by using natural juvenile hormones that prevent insects maturing and breeding. In 1977 Zoecon was taken over by Occidental Petroleum and was then sold in 1982 to Sandoz, a Swiss pharmaceutical company. Djerassi has remained as chairman of the board.

Djerassi's business interests have had little impact on his productivity, with over 600 papers to his credit. He has also published a novel (*Cantor's Dilemma*), a collection of verse, and his autobiography, *The Pill, Pigmy Chimps, and Degas' Horse* (1992).

Döbereiner, Johann Wolfgang
(1780–1849) *German chemist*

Born the son of a coachman in Hof an der Saale, Germany, Döbereiner had little formal education and had worked as an assistant to apothecaries in several places from the age of 14. He was largely self-taught in chemistry and was encouraged by Leopold Gmelin whom he met at Strasbourg. After several failures in business, he was appointed assistant professor of chemistry at Jena (1810).

In 1823 he discovered that hydrogen would ignite spontaneously in air over platinum sponge, and subsequently developed the *Döbereiner lamp* to exploit this phenomenon. Döbereiner was interested in catalysis in general and discovered the catalytic action of manganese dioxide in the decomposition of potassium chlorate. His law of triads (1829), based on his observation of regular increments of atomic weight in elements with similar properties, was an important step on the way to Dmitri Mendeleev's periodic table. Thus in triads such as calcium, strontium, and barium or chlorine, bromine, and iodine, the middle element has an atomic weight that is approximately the average of the other two. It is also intermediate in chemical properties between the other two elements. Döbereiner also worked in organic chemistry.

Dobzhansky, Theodosius (1900–1975)
Russian–American geneticist

Dobzhansky, who was born in Nemirov, in Ukraine, graduated in zoology from Kiev University in 1921; he remained there to teach zoology before moving to Leningrad, where he taught genetics. In 1927 he took up a fellowship at Columbia University, New York, where he worked with T. H. Morgan. Morgan was impressed by Dobzhansky's ability and, when the fellowship was completed, offered him a teaching post at the California Institute of Technology. Dobzhansky accepted and became an American citizen in 1937.

Dobzhansky studied the fruit fly (*Drosophila*) and demonstrated that the genetic variability within populations was far greater than had been imagined. The high frequency of potentially deleterious genes had previously been overlooked because their effects are masked by corresponding dominant genes. Dobzhansky found that such debilitating genes actually conferred an advantage to the organism when present with the normal type of gene, and therefore they tended to be maintained at a high level in the population. Populations with a high genetic load – i.e. many concealed lethal genes – proved to be more versatile in changing environments. This work profoundly influenced the theories on the mathematics of evolution and natural selection with regard to Mendelism.

In addition, Dobzhansky wrote many influential books, including *Genetics and the Origin of Species* (1937), a milestone in evolutionary genetics.

Doherty, Peter Charles (1940–)
Australian immunologist

Doherty was educated at Queensland and later at Edinburgh, where he gained his PhD in 1970. After serving at the Wistar Institute in Philadelphia, he was appointed in 1982 professor of experimental pathology at the Curtin Institute, Canberra. In 1988 Doherty moved to St Jude's Children's Research Hospital, Memphis, as chairman of the Immunology Department.

In 1974 Doherty, in collaboration with Rolf ZINKERNAGEL, began to consider the response of the mouse immune system to viral meningitis. It was commonly held at this time that the presence of bacterial or viral invaders were alone sufficient in themselves to initiate an immune response. Consequently, as expected, the infected cells were attacked by the mouse's own T lymphocytes. Yet, to their surprise, when T cells from one mouse strain were deployed against infected cells from another strain, the lymphocytes failed to respond. Clearly an additional factor was required to trigger the immune response.

They were aware, following the work of George SNELL and others, that major histocompatibility (MHC) antigens played a significant role in controlling the immune response to transplants. They consequently began to examine the role of MHC proteins in the immune response. Working with mice from various strains, they found that T cells from one strain could be provoked to attack infected cells only if the invaders shared at least one MHC antigen.

For his work in this field Doherty shared the 1997 Nobel Prize for physiology or medicine with Rolf Zinkernagel.

Doisy, Edward Adelbert (1893–1986)
American biochemist. See DAM, CARL PETER HENRIK.

Dokuchaev, Vasily Vasilievich (1846–1903) *Russian soil scientist*

Dokuchaev was born in Milyukovo near Smolensk, Russia, the son of the village priest. He too was originally trained for the priesthood but later turned to the study of science at St. Petersburg University where he graduated in 1871. He was immediately appointed to the faculty, initially as curator of the geological collection but he also served as professor of geology until poor health forced him to retire in 1897.

Dokuchaev made the first comprehensive scientific study of the soils of Russia, details of which are to be found in his *Collected Works* (9 vols. 1949–61). He also, in the 1890s, set up at the Kharkov Institute of Agriculture and Forestry, the first department of soil science in Russia.

In the West he is mainly known for his work on the classification of soils, his insistence that soil is a geobiological formation, and his use of soil to define the different geographical zones.

It is also owing to Dokuchaev that the Russian term *chernozem*, used to describe a black soil rich in humus and carbonates, has entered most languages.

Dollond, John (1706–1761) *British optician*

Dollond was born in London, the son of Huguenot refugees. He started life as a silk weaver but later joined his eldest son, Peter, in making optical instruments, and devoted years of experiment to developing an achromatic lens. The problem confronting lens makers at the time was chromatic aberration – the fringe of colors that surrounds and disturbs images formed by a lens. This put a limit on the power of lenses (and of refracting telescopes), for the stronger the lens, the more chromatically disturbed the images became. Chromatic aberration is caused by the different wavelengths that make up white light being refracted to different extents by the glass, each being focused at a different point.

In 1758 Dollond succeeded in making lenses without this defect by using two different lenses, one of crown glass and one of flint glass (one convex and one concave), so made that the chromatic aberration of one was neutralized by the aberration of the other. In fact he was not the first to make such a lens, since Chester Hall had already done so in 1753, but Dollond managed to patent the idea because he was the first to publicize the possibility.

In 1761 he was appointed optician to George III but died of apoplexy later that year.

Domagk, Gerhard (1895–1964) *German biochemist*

Domagk, who was born in Lagow, now in Poland, graduated in medicine from the University of Kiel in 1921 and began teaching at the University of Greifswald and later at the University of Münster. At this time he carried out important researches into phagocytes – special cells that attack bacteria in the body.

He became interested in chemotherapy and in 1927 he was appointed director of research in experimental pathology and pathological anatomy at the giant chemical factory I.G. Farbenindustrie at Wuppertal-Elberfeld. Pursuing the ideas of Paul Ehrlich, Domagk tested new dyes produced by the Elberfeld chemists for their effect against various infections. In 1935 he reported the effectiveness of an orange-red dye called prontosil in combating streptococcal infections. For the first time a chemical had been found to be active *in vivo* against a common small bacterium. Earlier dyes used as drugs were active only against infections caused by much larger protozoa.

The work was followed up in research laboratories throughout the world – Alexander Fleming neglected penicillin to work on prontosil in the early 1930s – but the most significant ramifications were discovered by Daniele Bovet and his co-workers. Prontosil and the sulfa drugs that followed were effective in saving many lives, including those of Franklin D. Roosevelt Jr., Winston Churchill, and Domagk's own daughter. In 1939 Domagk was offered the Nobel Prize for physiology or medicine. The Nazis forced him to withdraw his acceptance because Hitler was annoyed with the Nobel Committee for awarding the 1935 Peace Prize to a German, Carl von Ossietzky, whom Hitler had imprisoned. In 1947 Domagk was finally able to accept the prize. In his later years he undertook drug research into cancer and tuberculosis.

Donati, Giovanni Battista (1826–1873) *Italian astronomer*

After graduating from the university in his native city of Pisa, Donati joined the staff of the Florence Observatory in 1852, and was appointed director in 1864. He died from bubonic plague in 1873.

Much of his work was concerned with comets. He discovered six new comets, one of which, first appearing in June 1858 has since been known as *Donati's comet*. He went on in 1864 to make the first observations of a comet's chemical composition. Spectroscopic observation of the 1864 comet produced a line spectrum with three lines named alpha, beta, and gamma by Donati. The three lines were also seen in an 1866 comet by SECCHI. The lines were shown by HUGGINS in 1868 to be due to the presence of carbon.

Doppler, Christian Johann (1803–1853) *Austrian physicist*

Christian Doppler, the son of a stonemason from the Austrian city of Salzburg, studied mathematics at the Vienna Polytechnic. In 1835 he started teaching at a school in Prague and six years later was appointed professor of mathematics at the Technical Academy there.

Doppler's fame comes from his discovery in 1842 of the *Doppler effect* – the fact that the observed frequency of a wave depends on the velocity of the source relative to the observer. The effect can be observed with sound waves. If the source is moving toward the observer, the pitch is higher; if it moves away, the pitch is lower. A common example is the fall in frequency of a train's whistle or a vehicle siren as it passes. Doppler's principle was tested experimentally in 1843 by Christoph Buys Ballot, who used a train to pull trumpeters at different speeds past musicians who had perfect pitch.

Doppler also tried to apply his principle to light waves, with limited success. It was Armand Fizeau in 1848 who suggested that at high relative velocities the apparent color of the source would be changed by the motion: an object moving toward the observer would appear bluer; one moving away would appear redder. The shift in the spectra of celestial objects (the *Doppler shift*) is used to measure the rate of recession or approach relative to the Earth.

Dorn, Friedrich Ernst (1848–1916) *German physicist. See* RAMSAY, SIR WILLIAM.

Douglass, Andrew Ellicott (1867–1962) *American astronomer and dendrochronologist*

Douglass came from a family of academics in Windsor, Vermont, with both his father and grandfather being college presidents. He graduated from Trinity College, Hartford, Connecticut in 1889 and in the same year was appointed to an assistantship at Harvard College Observatory. In 1894 he went with Percival Lowell to the new Lowell Observatory in Flagstaff, Arizona, moving to the University of Arizona in 1906 as professor of astronomy and physics.

Douglass's first interest was the 11-year sunspot cycle. In trying to trace its history he was led to the examination of tree rings in the hope that he would find some identifiable correlation of sunspot activity with terrestrial climate and vegetation. Soon the tree rings became the center of his studies.

The only previously established method of dating the past, except by inscriptions, was the geological varve-counting technique, which was developed from 1878. But this was of no use if there were no varves (thin seasonally deposited layers of sediment in glacial lakes) to be found. Douglass soon found that he could identify local tree rings with confidence and use them in dating past climatic trends. He thus founded the field of dendrochronology. By the late 1920s he had a sequence of over a thousand tree rings with six thin rings, presumably records of a severe drought, correlated with the end of the 13th century. In 1929 he found some timber that contained the six thin rings and a further 500 in addition. This took him to the eighth century and over the years he managed to get as far as the first century. This was extended still further and by careful analysis scholars have now established a sequence going back almost to 5000 BC.

The dated rings of Arizona and New Mexico were found however not to correlate with sequences from other parts of the world: the tree-ring clock was a purely local one. The search for a more universal clock continued, and the method of radiocarbon dating was developed by Willard LIBBY in 1949.

Drake, Frank Donald (1930–)
American astronomer

Drake, who was born in Chicago, Illinois, graduated in 1952 from Cornell University and obtained his PhD in 1958 from Harvard. He worked initially at the National Radio Astronomy Observatory (NRAO), West Virginia (1958–63) and at the Jet Propulsion Laboratory, California (1963–64) before returning to Cornell and serving as professor of astronomy from 1964. He was appointed professor of astronomy at the University of California in 1984.

Although Drake has made significant contributions to radio astronomy, including radio studies of the planets, he is perhaps best known for his pioneering search for extraterrestrial intelligence. In April 1959 he managed to gain approval from the director at NRAO, Otto Struve, to proceed with his search, which was called 'Project Ozma'. The name was taken from the Oz stories of Frank Baum. Drake began in 1960, using the NRAO 26-meter radio telescope to listen for possible signals from planets of the Sunlike stars Tau Ceti and Epsilon Eridani, both about 11 light-years away. He decided to tune to the frequency of 1420 megahertz at which radio emission from hydrogen occurs. This would have considerable significance for any civilization capable of building radio transmitters.

No signals were received although at one time excitement was generated when signals from a secret military radar establishment were received while the antenna was pointed at Epsilon Eridani. In July 1960 the project was terminated to allow the telescope to fulfill some of its other obligations. Drake revived the project in 1975, in collaboration with Carl Sagan, when they began using the Arecibo 1000-foot (305-meter) radio telescope to listen to several nearby galaxies on frequencies of 1420, 1653, and 2380 megahertz. No contact was made nor was it likely, they declared, for "A search of hundreds of thousands of stars in the hope of detecting one message would require remarkable dedication and would probably take several decades." He has published a number of works on this issue including *Is Anyone There? The Search for Extra Terrestrial Intelligence* (1992).

Draper, Henry (1837–1882) *American astronomer*

Draper, the son of the distinguished physician and chemist John W. Draper, was born in Prince Edward County, Virginia. He studied at the City University of New York, completing the course in medicine in 1857 before he was old enough to graduate. He obtained his MD in 1858, spending the preceding months in Europe where his interest in astronomy was aroused by a visit to the observatory of the third earl of Rosse at Parsonstown, Ireland. On his return to New York he joined the Bellevue Hospital and was later appointed professor of natural science at the City University in 1860. Draper later held chairs of physiology (1866–73) and analytical chemistry (1870–82) and in 1882 succeeded his father briefly as professor of chemistry. He retired from the university in 1882 in order to devote himself to astronomical research but died prematurely soon after.

One of the most important events in Draper's life was his marriage in 1867 to Anna Palmer, daughter and heiress to

Courtlandt Palmer who had made a fortune in hardware and New York real estate. His wife's money allowed him to purchase a 28-inch (71-cm) reflecting telescope and to begin a 15-year research partnership.

Draper was interested in the application of the new technique of photography to astronomy. He started by making daguerrotypes of the Sun and Moon but in 1872 succeeded for the first time in obtaining a photograph of a stellar spectrum, that of Vega. In 1879 he found that dry photographic plates had been developed and that these were more sensitive and convenient than wet collodion. By 1882 he had obtained photographs of over a hundred stellar spectra plus spectra of the Moon, Mars, Jupiter, and the Orion nebula. He also succeeded in directly photographing the Orion nebula, first with a 50-minute exposure in 1880 and then, using a more accurate clock-driven telescope, with a 140-minute exposure. He thus helped to establish photographic astronomy as an important means of studying the heavens.

At the time of his death his widow hoped to continue his work herself, but with prompting from Edward Pickering at the Harvard College Observatory, she set up the Henry Draper Memorial Fund. It was with the aid of this fund that the famous *Henry Draper Catalogue*, some nine volumes with details of the spectra of 225,000 stars, was published from 1918 to 1924 through the labors of Pickering and Annie Cannon.

Draper, John William (1811–1882)
British–American chemist

Draper, who was born in St. Helens, Lancashire, was educated at University College, London, before he emigrated to America in 1833. He qualified in medicine at the University of Pennsylvania in 1836. After a short period teaching in Virginia he moved to New York University (1838) where he taught chemistry and in 1841 helped to start the medical school of which he became president in 1850.

Most of his chemical work was done in the field of photochemistry. He was one of the first scientists to use Louis Daguerre's new invention (1837) of photography. He took the first photograph of the Moon in 1840 and in the same year took a photograph of his sister, Dorothy, which is the oldest surviving photographic study of the human face. In 1843 he obtained the first photographic plate of the solar spectrum. He was also one of the first to take photographs of specimens under a microscope. On the theoretical level Draper was one of the earliest to grasp that only those rays

that are absorbed produce chemical change and that not all rays are equally powerful in their effect. He also, in a series of papers (1841–45), showed that the amount of chemical change is proportional to the intensity of the absorbed radiation multiplied by the time it has to act. Draper's work was continued and largely confirmed by the work of Robert Bunsen and Henry Roscoe in 1857. Draper's work also resulted in the development of actinometers (instruments to measure the intensity of light). He also wrote on a wide variety of other topics.

Draper's son Henry was an astronomer of note after whom the famous Harvard catalog of stellar spectra was named.

Driesch, Hans Adolf Eduard (1867–1941) *German biologist*

Born in Bad Kreuznach, in southwest Germany, Driesch held professorships at Heidelberg, Cologne, and Leipzig, and was visiting professor to China and America. A student of zoology at Freiburg, Jena, and Munich, he was for some years on the staff of the Naples Zoological Station.

Driesch carried out pioneering work in experimental embryology. He separated the two cells formed by the first division of a sea-urchin embryo and observed that each developed into a complete larva, thus demonstrating the capacity of the cell to form identical copies on division. He was also the first to demonstrate the phenomenon of embryonic induction, whereby the position of and interaction between cells within the embryo determine their subsequent differentiation.

Driesch is perhaps best known for his concept of entelechy – a vitalistic philosophy that postulates the origin of life to lie in some unknown vital force separate from biochemical and physiological influences. This also led him to investigate psychic research and parapsychology.

Dubois, Marie Eugène François Thomas (1858–1940) *Dutch physician and paleontologist*

Dubois was born in Eijsden in the Netherlands and studied medicine at the University of Amsterdam. After briefly working there as a lecturer in anatomy, he served as a military surgeon in the Dutch East Indies, now Indonesia, from 1887 to 1895. On his return to Amsterdam he held the chair of geology, paleontology, and mineralogy from 1899 until his retirement in 1928.

The decision to go to the Indies was no accident. Dubois was determined to find the 'missing link' and had reasoned that such a creature would have originated in proximity to the apes of Africa or the orangutan of the Indies. After several years fruitless search in Sumatra, Dubois moved to Java and in 1890 discovered his first humanoid remains (a jaw fragment) at Kedung Brubus. The following year, at Trinil on the Solo river, he found the skullcap, femur, and two teeth of what he was later to name *Pithecanthropus erectus*, more commonly known as Java man. He published these findings in 1894.

Although Dubois's estimate of the cranial capacity of *Pithecanthropus* was, at 850 cubic centimeters (later estimates ranged up to 940 cubic centimeters), on the low side for a hominid, the femur it had been found with indicated to Dubois that it must be a form with a very erect posture. However many doubted this, stating the usual objections that the remains belonged to different creatures, to apes or (Rudolf Virchow's view) to deformed humans. So irritated did Dubois become by this reception that he withdrew the fossils from view, keeping them locked up for some 30 years.

When they were again made available to scholars in 1923 and Peking man was discovered in 1926 it at last became widely agreed that *Pithecanthropus* was, as Dubois had earlier claimed, a link connecting apes and man. By this time however Dubois would have no part of such a consensus and began to insist the bones were those of a giant gibbon, a view he maintained until his death.

Du Bois-Reymond, Emil Heinrich
(1818–1896) *German neurophysiologist*

Of Swiss and Huguenot descent, Du Bois-Reymond was born in Berlin and educated at the university there and in Neuchâtel (Switzerland). He is famous as the first to demonstrate how electrical currents in nerve and muscle fibers are generated. He began his studies under the eminent physiologist Johannes Müller at Berlin with work on fish capable of discharging electric currents as an external shock (e.g. eels). Turning his attention to nerve and muscle activity he then showed (1843) that applying a stimulus to the nerve brings about a drop in the electrical potential at the point of stimulus. This reduction in potential is the impulse, which travels along the nerve as "waves of relative negativity." This variation in negativity is the main cause of muscle contraction. Du Bois-Reymond's pioneering research, for which he devised a specially sensitive galvanometer capable of measuring the small amounts of electricity involved, was published as *Untersuchungen über tierische Elektricität* (2 vols. 1848–84; Researches on Animal Electricity): a landmark

in electrophysiology, although subject to later elaboration. Du Bois-Reymond's collaboration with fellow physiologists Hermann von Helmholtz, Carl Ludwig, and Ernst von Brücke was of great significance in linking animal physiology with physical and chemical laws.

Du Bois-Reymond was elected a member of the Berlin Academy of Sciences in 1851 and succeeded Müller as professor of physiology at Berlin in 1858. He was also instrumental in founding the Berlin Physiological Institute, opened in 1877, then the finest establishment of its kind.

Dubos, René Jules (1901–1982) *French–American microbiologist*

Dubos was born in Saint Brice, France, and graduated in agricultural sciences from the National Agronomy Institute in 1921. After a period with the International Institute of Agriculture in Rome as assistant editor, he emigrated to America in 1924.

Dubos was awarded his PhD in 1927 from Rutgers University for research on soil microorganisms, continuing his work in this field at the Rockefeller Institute for Medical Research. Reports that soil microorganisms produce antibacterial substances particularly interested him and in 1939 he isolated a substance from *Bacillus brevis* that he named tyrothricin. This is effective against many types of bacteria but unfortunately also kills red blood cells and its medical use is therefore limited. However, the discovery stimulated such workers as Selman Waksman and Benjamin Duggar to search for useful antibiotics and led to the discovery of the tetracyclines. He won the 1969 Pulitzer Prize for his book *So Human an Animal.*

Du Fay, Charles François de Cisternay (1698–1739) *French chemist*

Du Fay, a Parisian by birth, started his career in the French army, rising to the rank of captain. He left to become a chemist in the Académie Française and in 1732 became superintendent of the Jardin du Roi. His great achievement was to discover the two kinds of electricity, positive and negative, which he named 'vitreous' and 'resinous'. This was based on his discovery that a piece of gold leaf charged from an electrified glass rod would attract and not repel a piece of electrified amber. This was the 'two-fluid theory' of electricity, which was to be opposed by Benjamin Franklin's 'one-fluid theory' later in the century.

Dujardin, Félix (1801–1860) *French biologist and cytologist*

Largely self-educated, Dujardin, who was born in Tours, France, studied geology, botany, optics, and crystallography while working variously as a hydraulics engineer, librarian, and teacher of geometry and chemistry at Tours. In 1839 he was elected to the chair of geology and mineralogy at Toulouse, and in the following year was appointed professor of botany and zoology and dean of the Faculty of Sciences at Rennes. As a skilled microscopist, Dujardin carried out extensive studies of the microorganisms (infusoria) occurring in decaying matter. These led him, in 1834, to suggest the separation of a new group of protozoan animals, which he called the rhizopods (i.e. rootfeet). He was the first to recognize and appreciate the contractile nature of the protoplasm (which he termed the *sarcode*) and also demonstrated the role of the vacuole for evacuating waste matter. Such studies enabled Dujardin to refute the supposition, reintroduced by Christian Ehrenberg, that microorganisms have organs similar to those of the higher animals. Dujardin also investigated the cnidarians (jellyfish, sea anemones, corals, etc.), echinoderms (sea-urchins, starfish, etc.), as well as the platyhelminths, or flatworms, the last mentioned providing the basis for subsequent parasitological investigations.

Dulbecco, Renato (1914–   ) *Italian–American physician and molecular biologist*

Born in Cantanzaro, Italy, Dulbecco obtained his MD from the University of Turin in 1936 and taught there until 1947 when he moved to America. He taught briefly at Indiana before moving to California in 1949, where he served as professor of biology (1952–63) at the California Institute of Technology. Dulbecco then joined the staff of the Salk Institute where, apart from the period 1971–74 at the Imperial Cancer Research Fund in London, he has remained.

Beginning in 1959 Dulbecco introduced the idea of cell transformation into biology. In this process special cells are mixed *in vitro* with such tumor-producing viruses as the polyoma and SV40 virus. With some cells a 'productive infection' results, where the virus multiplies unchecked in the cell and finally kills its host. However in other cells this unlimited multiplication does not occur and the virus instead induces changes similar to those in cancer cells; that is, the virus alters the cell so that it reproduces without restraint and does not respond to the presence of neighboring cells. A normal cell had in fact been transformed into a 'cancer cell' *in vitro*.

The significance of this work was to pro-

vide an experimental set-up where the processes by which a normal cell becomes cancerous can be studied in a relatively simplified form. It was for this work that Dulbecco was awarded the Nobel Prize for physiology or medicine in 1975, sharing it with Howard TEMIN and David BALTIMORE.

In March 1986 Dulbecco published a widely read paper in *Science*, entitled *A Turning Point in Science*, in which he argued that "if we wish to learn more about cancer, we must now concentrate on the cellular genome." The paper appeared shortly after various groups of scientists had held a meeting at Sante Fe to discuss sequencing the entire human genome. Dulbecco's timely paper publicized the project, gave it some authority, and linked it with a practical purpose.

Dulong, Pierre-Louis (1785–1838) *French chemist and physicist. See* PETIT, ALEXIS-THÉRÈSE.

Dumas, Jean Baptiste André (1800–1884) *French chemist*

Dumas was educated in classics at the college in his native city of Alais and intended to serve in the navy. However, after Napoleon's final defeat he changed his mind and became apprenticed to an apothecary. In 1816 he went to Geneva, again to work for an apothecary. His first research was in physiological chemistry, investigating the use of iodine in goiter (1818). He also studied chemistry in Geneva and was encouraged by Friedrich von Humboldt to go to Paris, where he became assistant lecturer to Louis Thenard at the Ecole Polytechnique (1823). He subsequently worked in many of the Parisian institutes, becoming professor at the Ecole Polytechnique (1835) and at the Sorbonne (1841).

Dumas's early work included a method for measuring vapor density (1826), the synthesis of oxamide (1830), and the discoveries of the terpene cymene (1832), anthracene in coal tar (1832), and urethane (1833). In 1834 Dumas and Eugène Peligot discovered methyl alcohol (methanol) and Dumas recognized that it differed from ethyl alcohol (ethanol) by one $-CH_2$ group. The subsequent discovery that Chevreul's 'ethal' was cetyl alcohol (1836) led Dumas to conceive the idea of a series of compounds of the same type (this was formalized into the concept of homologous series by Charles Gerhardt).

Dumas was both a prolific experimentalist and a leading theorist and he took a vigorous part in the many controversies that bedeviled organic chemistry at the time. He was originally an exponent of the 'etherin' theory (in which ethyl alcohol (ethanol) and diethyl ether were considered to be compounds of etherin (ethene) with one and two molecules of water, respectively). However, he was converted to the radical theory (an attempt to formulate organic chemistry along the dualistic lines familiar in inorganic chemistry) by Justus von Liebig in 1837. He then introduced his own theory – the substitution theory – which was his greatest work. It had been noticed that candles bleached with chlorine gave off fumes of hydrogen chloride when they burned. Dumas discovered that during bleaching the hydrogen in the hydrocarbon oil of turpentine became replaced by chlorine. This seemed to contradict Jöns Berzelius's electrochemical theory and the latter was bitterly opposed to the substitution theory. Liebig, too, was hostile at first. Dumas then prepared trichloroacetic acid (1838) and showed that its properties were similar to those of the parent acetic acid. This convinced Liebig but not Berzelius. Further work on this series of acids, combined with the substitution theory, led him to a theory of types (1840), essentially similar to the modern concept of functional groups, although the credit for this theory was disputed between Dumas and Auguste Laurent.

Dumas also carried out important work on atomic weights. He had been an early supporter of Amedeo Avogadro but he never properly distinguished between atoms and molecules and the problems this raised caused him to abandon the theory. He also supported William Prout's hypothesis that atomic weights were whole-number multiples of that of hydrogen. In 1840, working with Jean Stas, he obtained the figure 12.000 for carbon instead of the figure 12.24 in use at that time.

Following the revolution of 1848 Dumas became involved in administration, becoming minister of agriculture and commerce (1849–51), minister of education, and permanent secretary of the Academy of Sciences (1868).

Dunning, John Ray (1907–1975)
American physicist

Born in Shelby, Nebraska, Dunning was educated at the Wesleyan University, Nebraska, and at Columbia University, New York, where he obtained his PhD in 1934. He took up an appointment at Columbia in 1933, being made professor of physics in 1950.

Dunning was one of the key figures in the Manhattan project to build the first atomic bomb. It had been shown by Niels Bohr that the isotope uranium–235 would be more likely to sustain a neutron chain reaction than normal uranium. Only 7 out of every 1000 uranium atoms occurring naturally are uranium–235, which presents difficulties in extraction. Various techniques were tried and Dunning was placed in charge of the process of separation known as gaseous diffusion. This involved turning the uranium into a volatile compound (uranium hexafluoride, UF_6) and passing the vapor through a diffusion filter. As ^{235}U atoms are slightly less massive than the normal ^{238}U they pass through the filter a little faster and can thus be concentrated. The difference in mass is so small, however, that simply to produce a gas enriched with ^{235}U atoms required its passage through thousands of filters.

It was largely through gaseous diffusion that sufficient enriched uranium was made available for the bomb to be built.

Du Toit, Alexander Logie (1878–1949)
South African geologist

Du Toit, who was born at Rondebosch, near Cape Town in South Africa, studied at the South Africa College (now the University of Cape Town), the Royal Technical College, Glasgow, and the Royal College of Science, London.

After a short period teaching at Glasgow University (1901–03) he returned to South Africa and worked with the Geological Commission of the Cape of Good Hope (1903–20), during which he explored the geology of South Africa. For the next seven years he worked for the Irrigation Department and produced six detailed monographs on South African geology. He served as a consulting geologist to De Beers Consolidated Mines during the period 1927–41.

Following a visit to South America in 1923, du Toit became one of the earliest supporters of Alfred Wegener's theory of continental drift, publishing his observations in *A Geological Comparison of South America with South Africa* (1927). He noted the similarity between the continents and developed his ideas in *Our Wandering Continents* (1937), in which he argued for the separation of Wegener's Pangaea into the two supercontinents, Laurasia and Gondwanaland.

Dutrochet, René Joachim Henri (1776–1847) *French physiologist*

Born in Néon, France, Dutrochet began medical studies while serving in the army in Paris in 1802. After graduating in 1806 he served as an army surgeon in Spain. However, through illness he resigned his post in

1809 and thereafter devoted his time to natural science.

In 1814 he published his investigations into animal development, suggesting a unity of the main features during the early stages. Later research into plant and animal physiology led to his assertion that respiration is similar in both plants and animals. In 1832, Dutrochet showed that gas exchange in plants was via minute openings (stomata) on the surface of leaves and the deep cavities with which they communicate. He further demonstrated that only cells containing chlorophyll can fix carbon and thus transform light energy into chemical energy. Dutrochet studied osmosis and suggested it may be the cause of ascent and descent of sap in plants. Although sometimes lacking in accuracy, the importance of his work lies mainly in his endeavor to demonstrate that the vital phenomena of life can be explained on the basis of physics and chemistry.

Dutton, Clarence Edward (1841–1912)
American geologist

Born in Wallingford, Connecticut, Dutton graduated from Yale in 1860 and then entered the Yale Theological Seminary. He joined the army in 1862 during the Civil War and remained in the army although not always on active service. He became interested in geology and joined the Geographical and Geological Survey of the Rocky Mountains and the West in 1875.

The term 'isostasy' was introduced into geology by Dutton in 1889. This described a theory propounded by George Airy in which it is supposed that mountain ranges and continents rest on a much denser base. As mountains are eroded or snow melts from the continents the land rises while the settling sediment will compensate by depressing some other part of the Earth.

After his return to the army in 1890 Dutton turned to the study of earthquakes and volcanoes. His research was published in 1904 in his *Earthquakes in the Light of the New Seismology*.

Duve, Christian René de *See* DE DUVE, CHRISTIAN RENÉ.

Du Vigneaud, Vincent (1901–1978)
American biochemist

Born in Chicago, Illinois, Du Vigneaud graduated from the University of Illinois in 1923; he remained there to take his master's degree before going to the University of Rochester. There he studied the hormone insulin, gaining his PhD in 1927. The research on insulin marked the beginning of his interest in sulfur compounds, particularly the sulfur-containing amino acids – methionine, cystine, and cysteine.

In 1938 Du Vigneaud became head of the biochemistry department of Cornell University Medical College. Two years later he had isolated vitamin H (biotin) and by 1942 had determined its structure. He then went on to examine the hormones secreted by the posterior pituitary gland, especially oxytocin and vasopressin. He found oxytocin to be composed of eight amino acids, worked out the order of these, and in 1954 synthesized artificial oxytocin, which was shown to be as effective as the natural hormone in inducing labor and milk flow. This was the first protein to be synthesized and for this achievement Du Vigneaud received the Nobel Prize for chemistry in 1955.

Du Vigneaud's other work included research on penicillin and on methyl groups. He was professor of chemistry at Cornell University from 1967 to 1975 and subsequently emeritus professor of biochemistry there.

Dyson, Freeman John (1923–   )
British–American theoretical physicist

The son of Sir George Dyson, director of the Royal College of Music, Dyson was born at Crowthorne and educated at Cambridge University. During World War II he worked at the headquarters of Bomber Command. In 1947 he went on a Commonwealth Fellowship to Cornell University and in 1953 joined the Institute of Advanced Studies, Princeton, where he served as professor of physics until his retirement in 1994.

Dyson is best-known for his contribution to quantum electrodynamics. The observation in 1946 by Willis LAMB of a small difference between the lowest energy levels of the hydrogen atom was an experimental result against which such theories could be tested. In the period 1946–48 independent formulations of quantum electrodynamics were put forward by Julian SCHWINGER, Sin-Itiro TOMONAGA, and Richard FEYNMAN. Dyson showed that the three methods were all consistent and brought them together into a single general theory.

Dyson later became known to a wider public through his work on the nuclear test ban treaty and for his quite serious considerations of space travel and the 'greening of the galaxy'. He also reached a wider audience with the publication of his autobiography *Disturbing the Universe* (1980) and his 1985 Gifford Lectures, *Infinite in All Directions* (1988).

E

Eastman, George (1854–1932)
American inventor

Eastman, who was born in Waterville, New York, began his career in banking and insurance but turned from this to photography. In 1880 he perfected the dry-plate photographic film and began manufacturing this. He produced a transparent roll film in 1884 and in the same year founded the Eastman Dry Plate and Film Company. In 1888 he introduced the simple hand-held box camera that made popular photography possible. The Kodak camera with a roll of transparent film was cheap enough for all pockets and could be used by a child. It was followed by the Brownie camera, which cost just one dollar.

Eastman gave away a considerable part of his fortune to educational institutions, including the Massachusetts Institute of Technology. He committed suicide in 1932.

Eccles, Sir John Carew (1903–1997)
Australian physiologist

Born in Melbourne, Australia, Eccles was educated at the university there and at Oxford University. In Oxford he worked with Charles Sherrington on muscular reflexes and nervous transmission across the synapses (nerve junctions) from 1927 to 1937. He then worked in Australia at the Institute of Pathology from 1937 to 1943. After a period in New Zealand, as professor of physiology at the University of Otago from 1944 to 1951, Eccles returned to Australia to the Australian National University, Canberra, where he served as professor of physiology from 1951 to 1966. In 1966 Eccles moved to the USA, working first in Chicago and finally, from 1968 until his retirement in 1975, at the State University of New York, Buffalo.

While at Canberra Eccles carried out work on the chemical changes that take place at synapses, pursuing the findings of Alan HODGKIN and Andrew HUXLEY, with whom he subsequently shared the 1963 Nobel Prize for physiology or medicine. Eccles showed that excitation of different nerve cells causes the synapses to release a substance (probably acetylcholine) that promotes the passage of sodium and potassium ions and effects an alternation in the polarity of the electric charge. It is in this way that nervous impulses are communicated or inhibited by nerve cells. Eccles was the author of *Reflex Activity of the Spinal Cord* (1932) and *The Physiology of Nerve Cells* (1957).

After his retirement Eccles published a number of works on the mind-body problem. Notable among them are *The Self and the Brain* (1977), written in collaboration with Karl Popper, *The Human Mystery* (1979), and *The Creation of the Self* (1989).

Eddington, Sir Arthur Stanley
(1882–1944) *British astrophysicist and mathematician*

Born at Kendal, Eddington moved with his mother and sister to Somerset after the death of his father in 1884. He was a brilliant scholar, graduating from Owens College (now the University of Manchester) in 1902 and from Cambridge University in 1905. From 1906 to 1913 he was chief assistant to the Astronomer Royal at Greenwich after which he returned to Cambridge as Plumian Professor of Astronomy. He was knighted in 1930. Eddington was a Quaker throughout his life.

Eddington was the major British astronomer of the interwar period. His early work on the motions of stars was followed, from 1916 onward, by his work on the interior of stars, which was published in his first major book, *The Internal Constitution of the Stars* (1926). He introduced "a phenomenon ignored in early investigations, which may have considerable effect on the equilibrium of a star, viz. the pressure of radiation." He showed that for equilibrium to be maintained in a star, the inwardly directed force of gravitation must be balanced by the outwardly directed forces of both gas pressure and radiation pressure. He also proposed that heat energy was transported from the center to the outer regions of a star not by convection, as thought hitherto, but by radiation.

It was in this work that Eddington gave a full account of his mass-luminosity relationship, which was discovered in 1924 and shows that the more massive a star the more luminous it will be. The value of the relation is that it allows the mass of a star to be determined if its intrinsic brightness is known. This is of considerable significance since only the masses of binary stars can be directly calculated. Eddington realized that there was a limit to the size of stars: relatively few would have masses exceeding 10 times the mass of the Sun while any exceeding 50 solar masses would be unstable owing to excessive radiation pressure.

Eddington wrote a number of books for both scientists and laymen. His more popular books, including *The Expanding Universe* (1933), were widely read, went through many editions, and opened new worlds to many enquiring minds of the interwar years. It was through Eddington that Einstein's general theory of relativity reached the English-speaking world. He was greatly impressed by the theory and was able to provide experimental evidence for it. He observed the total solar eclipse of 1919 and submitted a report that captured the intellectual imagination of his generation. He reported that a very precise and unexpected prediction made by Einstein in his general theory had been successfully observed; this was the very slight bending of light by the gravitational field of a star – the Sun. Further support came in 1924 when Einstein's prediction of the reddening of starlight by the gravitational field of the star was tested: at Eddington's request Walter Adams detected and measured the shift in wavelength of the spectral lines of Sirius B, the dense white-dwarf companion of the star Sirius. Eddington thus did much to establish Einstein's theory on a sound and rigorous foundation and gave a very fine presentation of the subject in his *Mathematical Theory of Relativity* (1923).

Eddington also worked for many years on an obscure but challenging theory, which was only published in his posthumous work, *Fundamental Theory* (1946). Basically, he claimed that the fundamental constants of science, such as the mass of the proton and the mass and charge of the electron were a "natural and complete specification for constructing a universe" and that their values were not accidental. He then set out to develop a theory from which such values would follow as a consequence, but never completed it.

Edelman, Gerald Maurice (1929–)
American biochemist

Born in New York City, Edelman was educated at Ursinus College, the University of Pennsylvania, and Rockefeller University, where he obtained his PhD on human immunoglobulins in 1960. He remained at Rockefeller where he was appointed professor of biochemistry in 1966 and Vincent Astor Distinguished Professor in 1974. Edelman left Rockefeller in 1992 to set up and direct the Neuroscience Institute at the Scripps Research Institute, La Jolla, California.

Edelman was interested in determining the structure of human immunoglobulin. The molecule is very large and it was first necessary to break it into smaller portions, which was achieved by reducing and splitting the disulfide bonds. Following this, Edelman proposed that the molecule contained more than one polypeptide chain and, moreover, that two kinds of chain exist, light and heavy. Such studies helped Rodney PORTER propose a structure for the antibody immunoglobulin G (IgG) in 1962.

Edelman was more interested in attempting to work out the complete amino-acid sequence of IgG. As it contained 1330 amino acids it was by far the largest protein then attempted. By 1969 he was ready to announce the results of his impressive work, the complete sequence, and was able to show that while much of the molecule was unchanging the tips of the Y-like structure were highly variable in their amino-acid sequence. It thus seemed obvious that such an area would be identical with the active antigen binding region in Porter's structure and that such variability represented the ability of IgG to bind many different antigens. It was for this work that Edelman and Porter shared the 1972 Nobel Prize for physiology or medicine.

Edelman has also speculated on antibody formation and the mechanism behind the spurt in production after contact with an antigen. In the former area he argued in 1966 for a major modification of the clonal theory of Macfarlane Burnet. In the latter case he suggested, in 1970, that the signal to the immune system to increase production is set off by the change in shape of the antibody molecule as it combines with its antigen.

Following his biochemical successes Edelman turned to the neurosciences. In such works as *Neural Darwinism* (1987) and *Bright Air, Brilliant Mind* (1993), he produced a distinctive theory of the development and nature of the mind. We are, he claims, at the beginning of a neuroscientific revolution from which we will learn "how the mind works, what governs our nature, and how we know the world."

Edelman was struck by a number of similarities between the immune system and the nervous system. Just as a lymphocyte can recognize and respond to a new antigen, the nervous system can respond similarly to novel stimuli. Neural mechanisms are selected, he argued, in the same manner as antibodies. Although the 10^9 cells of the nervous system do not replicate, there is considerable scope for development and variation in the connections that form between the cells. Frequently used connections will be selected, others will decay or be diverted to other uses. There are two kinds of selection: developmental, which takes place before birth, and experiential. There are also innate 'values' – built in preferences for such features as light and warmth over the dark and the cold.

In Edelman's model, higher consciousness, including self-awareness and the ability to create scenes in the mind, have required the emergence during evolution of a new neuronal circuit. To remember a chair or one's grandmother is not to recall a bit of coded data from a specific location; it is rather to create a unity out of scattered mappings, a process called by Edelman a 'reentry'. Edelman's views have been dismissed by many as obscure; some neurologists, however, consider Edelman to have begun what will eventually turn out to be a major revolution in the neurosciences.

Edison, Thomas Alva (1847–1931)
American physicist and inventor

Edison was born in Milan, Ohio, and was taught at home by his mother – he had been expelled from school as 'retarded', perhaps because of his deafness. From the age of seven he lived in Port Huron, Michigan, and when he was twelve years old began to spend much of his time on the railroad between Port Huron and Detroit, selling candy and newspapers to make money. However, he was also fascinated by the telegraph system, designing his own experiments and training himself in telegraphy. He became a casual worker on telegraphy (1862–68), reading and experimenting as he traveled. At the age of 21 he bought a copy of Faraday's *Experimental Researches in Electricity* and was inspired to undertake serious systematic experimental work.

While Edison was living in a Wall Street basement (1869) he was called in to carry out an emergency repair on a new telegraphic gold-price indicator in the Gold Exchange. He was so successful that he was taken on as a supervisor. Later he remodeled the equipment and, soon after being commissioned to improve other equipment, his skill became legendary.

For a while Edison had a well-paid job with the Western Union Telegraph Company, but he gave it up to set up a laboratory of his own at Menlo Park, New Jersey. This he furbished with a wide range of scientific equipment, costing $40,000, and an extensive library. He employed 20 technicians and later a mathematical physicist. The laboratory was the first organized research center outside a university and produced many inventions. In 1877 Edison became known internationally after the phonograph was invented. His original instrument used a cylinder coated with tinfoil to record sounds, and was not commercially practical. In 1878, after seeing an exhibition of glaring electric arc lights, he declared that he would invent a milder cheap alternative that could replace the gas lamp. Because of his past successes, he managed to raise the capital to do this and the Edison Electric Light Company was set up. It took 14 months to find a filament material but by October 1879, Edison was able to demonstrate 30 incandescent electric lamps connected in parallel with separate switches. Three years later a power station was opened in New York and this was the start of modern large-scale electricity generation. Edison later merged his electric-light company with that of Joseph Swan who developed the carbon-filament light independently. Also in his work on incandescent filaments, Edison discovered that a current flows in one direction only between the filament and a nearby electrode. The use of this *Edison effect* in the thermionic valve was independently achieved by J. A. Fleming. In 1887 Edison's laboratory moved to larger premises in West Orange, now a national monument. In his lifetime he took out over 1000 patents covering a variety of applications, including telephone transmission, cinematography, office machinery, cement manufacture, and storage batteries. No other inventor has been so productive.

Egas Moniz, Antonio Caetanio de Abreu Freire (1874–1955) *Portuguese neurologist*

Egas Moniz was born at Avanca in Portugal and educated at the University of Coimbra, where he gained his MD in 1899. After postgraduate work in Paris and Bordeaux he returned to Coimbra, becoming a professor in the medical faculty in 1902. He moved to Lisbon in 1911 to a newly created chair of neurology, a post he retained until his retirement in 1944. At the same time he was pursuing a successful political career, being elected to the National Assembly in 1900. He served as ambassador to Spain in 1917 and in the following year became foreign minister, leading his country's delegation to the Paris Peace Conference.

Egas Moniz achieved his first major success in the 1920s in the field of angiography (the study of the cardiovascular system using dyes that are opaque to x-rays). In collaboration with Almeida Lima, he injected such radiopaque dyes into the arteries, enabling the blood vessels of the brain to be photographed. In 1927 he was able to show that displacements in the cerebral circulation could be used to infer the presence and location of brain tumors, publishing a detailed account of his technique in 1931.

Egas Moniz is better known for his introduction in 1935 of the operation of prefrontal leukotomy. It was for this work, described by the Nobel authorities as "one of the most important discoveries ever made in psychiatric therapy," that they awarded him the 1949 Nobel Prize for physiology or medicine.

The operation consisted of inserting a sharp knife into the prefrontal lobe of the brain, roughly the area above and between the eyes; it required the minimum of equipment and lasted less than five minutes. The technique was suggested to Egas Moniz on hearing an account (by John Fulton and Carlyle Jacobsen in 1935) of a refractory chimpanzee that became less aggressive after its frontal lobes had been excised. Egas Moniz believed that a similar surgical operation would relieve severe emotional tension in psychiatric patients. He claimed that 14 of the first 20 patients operated upon were either cured or improved. The operation generated much controversy, since the extent of the improvement in the patients' symptoms was not easy to judge and the procedure often produced severe side-effects. Today a more refined version of the operation, in which selective incisions are made in smaller areas of the brain, is still quite widely practiced.

Ehrlich, Paul (1854–1915) *German physician, bacteriologist, and chemist*

Born in Strehlen (now Strzelin in Poland), Ehrlich studied medicine at the universities of Breslau, Strasbourg, and Freiburg, gaining a physician's degree at Breslau in 1878. For the next nine years he worked at the Charité Hospital, Berlin, on many topics including typhoid fever, tuberculosis, and pernicious anemia. He was awarded the title of professor by the Prussian Ministry of Education in 1884 for his impressive work in these fields. In 1887 he became a teacher at the University of Berlin but was not paid because of the antisemitic feeling at the time – Ehrlich would not renounce his Jewish upbringing. As a result of his laboratory work he contracted tuberculosis and was not restored to health until 1890, when he set up his own small research laboratory at Steglitz on the outskirts of Berlin.

In 1890 Robert Koch announced the discovery of tuberculin and suggested its use in preventing and curing tuberculosis. He asked Ehrlich to work on it with him at the Moabit Hospital in Berlin. Ehrlich accepted and for six years studied TB and cholera. In 1896 he accepted the post of director of the new Institute for Serum Research and Serum Investigation at Steglitz and in 1899 moved to the Institute of Experimental Therapy in Frankfurt. Here he investigated African sleeping sickness and syphilis along with his other studies. In 1908 he was awarded the Nobel Prize for physiology or medicine for his work on immunity and serum therapy.

Two years later he announced his most famous discovery, Salvarsan – a synthetic chemical that was effective against syphilis – and until the end of his life he worked on the problems associated with the treatment of patients using this compound of arsenic.

Ehrlich is considered to be the founder of modern chemotherapy because he developed systematic scientific techniques to search for new synthetic chemicals that could specifically attack disease-causing microorganisms. Ehrlich sought for these 'magic bullets' by carefully altering the chemical structure of dye molecules that selectively stained the microorganisms observable in his microscope but did not stain cells in the host. He was persevering and optimistic – Salvarsan (compound number 606) was not 'rediscovered' until almost 1000 compounds had been synthesized and tried. He made and tested about 3000 compounds based on the structure of Salvarsan in an attempt to make a drug that was bacteriocidal to streptococci.

Eigen, Manfred (1927–) *German physical chemist*

Eigen, the son of a musician, was born at Bochum in Germany and educated at the University of Göttingen where he obtained his PhD in 1951. He joined the staff of the Max Planck Institute for Physical Chemistry at Göttingen in 1953 and has served as its director since 1964.

In 1954 Eigen introduced the so-called relaxation techniques for the study of extremely fast chemical reactions (those taking less than a millisecond). Eigen's general method was to take a solution in equilibrium for a given temperature and pressure. If a short disturbance was applied to the solution the equilibrium would be very briefly destroyed and a new equilibrium quickly reached. Eigen studied exactly what happened in this very short time by means of absorption spectroscopy. He applied disturbances to the equilibrium by a variety of methods, such as pulses of electric current, sudden changes in temperature or pressure, or changes in electric field.

The first reaction he investigated was the apparently simple formation of a water molecule from the hydrogen ion, H^+, and the hydroxide ion, OH^-. Calculations of reaction rates made it clear that they could not be produced by the collision of the simple ions H^+ and OH^-. Eigen went on to show that the reacting ions are the unexpectedly large $H_9O_4^+$ and $H_7O_4^-$, a proton hydrated with four water molecules and a hydroxyl ion with three water molecules. For this work Eigen shared the 1967 Nobel Prize for chemistry with George PORTER and Ronald NORRISH.

Eigen later applied his relaxation techniques to complex biochemical reactions. He has also become interested in the origin of nucleic acids and proteins; with his colleague R. Winkler he has proposed a possible mechanism to explain their formation. Much of this and subsequent work was described by Eigen in his *Laws of the Game: How Principles of Nature Govern Chance* (1982).

Eijkman, Christiaan (1858–1930) *Dutch physician*

Eijkman was born at Nijkerk in the Netherlands and qualified as a physician from the University of Amsterdam in 1883. He served as an army medical officer in the Dutch East Indies from 1883 to 1885, when he was forced to return to the Netherlands to recuperate from a severe attack of malaria. In 1886 he returned to the East Indies as a member of an official government committee to investigate beriberi. After the completion of the committee's work, Eijkman remained in Batavia (now Djakarta) as director of a newly established bacteriological laboratory. In 1896 he took up the post of professor of public health at the University of Utrecht.

Eijkman was responsible for the first real understanding of the nature and possible cure of beriberi. For this work he shared the 1929 Nobel Prize for physiology or medicine with Frederick Gowland HOPKINS. Beriberi is a disorder caused by dietary deficiency, producing fatal lesions in the nervous and cardiovascular systems. Physicians of the late 19th century, however, were not trained to recognize its cause: with the clear success of the germ theory recently demonstrated by Robert Koch it was difficult to realize that symptoms could be produced by the absence of something rather than by the more obvious presence of a visible pathogen.

Eijkman's discovery was prompted by the outbreak of a disease very similar to human beriberi among the laboratory chickens. Despite the most thorough search no causative microorganisms could be identified, and then, for no obvious reason, the disease disappeared.

On investigation, Eijkman discovered that the symptoms of the disease had developed during a period of five months in which the chickens' diet was changed to hulled and polished rice. With a return to their normal diet of commercial chicken feed the symptoms disappeared. Eijkman subsequently found that he could induce the disease with a diet of hulled and polished rice and cure it with one of whole rice. However, he failed to conclude that beriberi was a deficiency disease. He argued that the endosperm of the rice produced a toxin that was neutralized by the outer hull: by eating polished rice the toxin would be released in its unneutralized form.

Thus although Eijkman had clearly demonstrated how to cure and prevent beriberi it was left to Hopkins to identify its cause as a vitamin deficiency. It was not until the early 1930s that Robert Williams identified the vitamin as vitamin B_1 (thiamine).

Einstein, Albert (1879–1955) *German–Swiss–American theoretical physicist*

Einstein was born at Ulm in Germany where his father was a manufacturer of electrical equipment. Business failure led his father to move the family first to Munich, where Einstein entered the local gymnasium in 1889, and later to Milan. There were no early indications of Einstein's later achievements for he did not begin to talk until the age of three, nor was he fluent at the age of nine, causing his parents to fear that he might even be backward. It appears that in 1894 he was expelled from his Munich gymnasium on the official grounds that his presence was disruptive. At this point he did something rather remarkable for a fifteen-year-old boy. He had developed such a hatred for things German that he could no longer bear to be a German citizen. He persuaded his father to apply for a revocation of his son's citizenship, a request the authorities granted in 1896. Until 1901, when he obtained Swiss citizenship, he was in fact stateless.

After completing his secondary education at Aarao in Switzerland he passed the entrance examination, at the second attempt, to the Swiss Federal Institute of Technology, Zurich, in 1896. He did not appear to be a particularly exceptional student finding the process of working for examinations repellent. Disappointed not to be offered an academic post, he survived as a private tutor until 1902, when he obtained the post of technical expert, third class, in the Swiss Patent Office in Bern. Here he continued to think about and work on physical problems. In 1905 he published four papers in the journal *Annalen der Physik* (Annals of Physics) – works that were to direct the progress of physics during the 20th century.

The first, and most straightforward, was on Brownian motion – first described by Robert Brown in 1828. Einstein derived a formula for the average displacement of particles in suspension, based on the idea that the motion is caused by bombardment of the particles by molecules of the liquid. The formula was confirmed by Jean Perrin in 1908 – it represented the first direct evidence for the existence of atoms and molecules of a definite size. The paper was entitled *Über der von molekularkinetischen Theorie der Wärme gerförderte Bewegung von in ruhenden Flüssigkeiten suspendierten Teilchen* (On the Motion of Small Particles Suspended in a Stationary Liquid According to the Molecular Kinetic Theory of Heat).

His second paper of 1905 was *Über einen die Erzeugung und Verwandlung des Lichtes betreffenden heuristischen Gesichtspunkt* (On a Heuristic Point of View about the Creation and Conversion of Light). In this Einstein was concerned with the nature of electromagnetic radiation, which at the time was regarded as a wave propagated throughout space according to Clerk Maxwell's equations. Einstein was concerned with the difference between this wave picture and the theoretical picture physicists had of matter. His particular concern in this paper was the difficulty in explaining the photoelectric effect, investigated in 1902 by Philipp Lenard. It was found that ultraviolet radiation of low frequency could eject electrons from a solid surface. The number of electrons depended on the intensity of the radiation and the energy of the electrons depended on the frequency. This dependence on frequency was difficult to explain using classical theory.

Einstein resolved this by suggesting that electromagnetic radiation is a flow of discreet particles – quanta (or photons as they are now known). The intensity of the radiation is the flux of these quanta. The energy per quantum, he proposed, was $h\nu$, where ν is the frequency of the radiation and h is the constant introduced in 1900 by Max Planck. In this way Einstein was able to account for the observed photoelectric behav-

ior. The work was one of the early results introducing the quantum theory into physics and it won for Einstein the 1921 Nobel Prize for physics.

The third of his 1905 papers is the one that is the most famous: *Zur Elektrodynamik bewegter Körper* (On the Electrodynamics of Moving Bodies). It is this paper that first introduced the special theory of relativity to science. The term 'special' denotes that the theory is restricted to certain special circumstances – namely for bodies at rest or moving with uniform relative velocities.

The theory was developed to account for a major problem in physics at the time. Traditionally in mechanics, there was a simple procedure for treating relative velocities. A simple example is of a car moving along a road at 40 mph with a second car moving toward it at 60 mph. A stationary observer would say that the second car was moving at 60 mph relative to him. The driver of the first car would say that, relative to him, the second car was approaching at 100 mph. This common-sense method of dealing with relative motion was well established. The mathematical equations involved are called the Galilean transformations – they are simple equations for changing velocities in one frame of reference to another frame of reference. The problem was that the method did not appear to work for electromagnetic radiation, which was thought of as a wave motion through the ether, described by the equations derived by Maxwell. In these, the speed of light is independent of the motion of the source or the observer. At the time, Albert Michelson and Edward Morley had performed a series of experiments to attempt to detect the Earth's motion through the ether, with negative results. Hendrik Lorentz proposed that this result could be explained by a change of size of moving bodies (the Lorentz–Fitzgerald contraction).

Although Einstein was unaware of the Michelson–Morley experiment, he did appreciate the incompatibility of classical mechanics and classical electrodynamics. His solution was a quite radical one. He proposed that the speed of light *is* a constant for all frames of reference that are moving uniformly relative to each other. He also put forward his 'relativity principle' that the laws of nature are the same in all frames of reference moving uniformly relative to each other. To reconcile the two principles he abandoned the Galilean transformations – the simple method of adding and subtracting velocities for bodies in relative motion. He arrived at this rejection by arguments about the idea of simultaneity – showing that the time between two events depends on the motions of the bodies involved. In his special theory of relativity, Einstein rejected the ideas of absolute space and absolute time. Later it was developed in terms of events specified by three spacial coordinates and one coordinate of time – a space–time continuum.

The theory had a number of unusual consequences. Thus the length of a body along its direction of motion decreases with increasing velocity. The mass increases as the velocity increases, becoming infinitely large in theory at the speed of light. Time slows down for a moving body – a phenomenon known as time dilation. These effects apply to all bodies but only become significant at velocities close to the speed of light – under normal conditions the effects are so small that classical laws appear to be obeyed. However, the predictions of the special theory – unusual as they may seem – have been verified experimentally. Thus increase in mass is observed for particles accelerated in a synchrocyclotron. Similarly, the lifetimes of unstable particles are increased at high velocities.

In that same year of 1905 Einstein had one more fundamental paper to contribute: *Ist die Trägheit eines Körpers von seinem Energieinhalt abhängig?* (Does the Inertia of a Body Depend on its Energy Content?). It was in this two-page paper that he concluded that if a body gives off energy E in the form of radiation, its mass diminishes by E/c^2 (where c is the velocity of light) obtaining the celebrated equation $E = mc^2$ relating mass and energy.

Within a short time Einstein's work on relativity was widely recognized to be original and profound. In 1908 he obtained an academic post at the University of Bern. Over the next three years he held major posts at Zurich (1909), Prague (1911), and the Zurich Federal Institute of Technology (1912) before taking a post in Berlin in 1914. This was probably due in part to the respect in which he held the Berlin physicists, Max Planck and Walther Nernst.

By 1907 Einstein was ready to remove the restrictions imposed on the special theory showing that, on certain assumptions, accelerated motion could be incorporated into his new, general theory of relativity. The theory begins with the fact that the mass of a body can be defined in two ways. The inertial mass depends on the way it resists change in motion, as in Newton's second law. The gravitational mass depends on forces of gravitational attraction between masses. The two concepts – inertia and gravity – seem dissimilar yet the inertial and gravitational masses of a body are always the same. Einstein considered that

this was unlikely to be a coincidence and it became the basis of his principle of equivalence.

The principle states that it is impossible to distinguish between an inertial force (that is, an accelerating force) and a gravitational one; the two are, in fact, equivalent. The point can be demonstrated with a thought experiment. Consider an observer in an enclosed box somewhere in space far removed from gravitational forces. Suppose that the box is suddenly accelerated upward, followed by the observer releasing two balls of different weights. Subject to an inertial force they will both fall to the floor at the same rate. But this is exactly how they would behave if the box was in a gravitational field and the observer could conclude that the balls fall under the influence of gravity. It was on the basis of this equivalence that Einstein made his dramatic prediction that rays of light in a gravitational field move in a curved path. For if a ray of light enters the box at one side and exits at the other then, with the upward acceleration of the box, it will appear to exit at a point lower down than its entrance. But if we take the equivalence principle seriously we must expect to find the same effect in a gravitational field.

In 1911 he predicted that starlight just grazing the Sun should be deflected by 0.83 seconds (″) of arc, later increased to 1″.7, which, though small, should be detectable in a total eclipse by the apparent displacement of the star from its usual position. In 1919 such an eclipse took place; it was observed by Arthur Eddington at Principe in West Africa, who reported a displacement of 1″.61, well within the limits of experimental error. It was from this moment that Einstein became known to a wider public, for this dramatic confirmation of an unexpected phenomenon seemed to capture the popular imagination. Even the London *Times* was moved to comment in an editorial, as if to a recalcitrant government, that "the scientific conception of the fabric of the universe must be changed."

In 1916 Einstein was ready to publish the final and authoritative form of his general theory: *Die Grundlage der allgemeinen Relativitätstheorie* (The Foundation of the General Theory of Relativity). It is this work that gained for Einstein the reputation for producing theories that were comprehensible to the very few. Eddington on being informed that there were only three people capable of understanding the theory is reported to have replied, "Who's the third?" It is true that Einstein introduced into gravitational theory a type of mathematics that was then unfamiliar to most physicists thus presenting an initial impression of incomprehension. In his theory Einstein used the space–time continuum introduced by Hermann Minkowski in 1907, the non-Euclidean geometry developed by Bernhard Riemann in 1854, and the tensor calculus published by Gregorio Ricci in 1887. He was assisted in the mathematics by his friend Grossmann. The theory of gravitation produced is one that depends on the geometry of space–time. In simple terms, the idea is that a body 'warps' the space around it so that another body moves in a curved path (hence the notion that space is curved). Einstein and Grossmann in 1915 succeeded in deriving a good theoretical value for the small (and hitherto anomalous) advance in the perihelion of mercury. The theory was put to an early test. Because of perturbations in the orbit of Mercury produced by the gravitational attractions of other planets, its perihelion (point in the orbit closest to the Sun) actually precesses by a small amount (9′ 34″ per century). When these perturbation effects were calculated on the basis of Newtonian mechanics, they could only account for a precession rate of 8′ 51″ per century, a figure 43″ too small. In 1915 Einstein, while completing his 1916 paper on General Relativity, calculated Mercury's perihelion precession on the basis of his own theory and found that, without making any extra assumptions, the missing 43″ were accounted for. The discovery, Einstein later reported, gave him palpitations and "for a few days I was beside myself with joyous excitement."

The theory also predicted (1907) that electromagnetic radiation in a strong gravitation field would be shifted to longer wavelengths – the *Einstein shift*. This was used by Walter Adams in 1925 to explain the spectrum of Sirius B. In 1959 Robert Pound and Glen Rebka demonstrated it on Earth using the Mossbauer effect. They found that at a height of 75 feet (23 m) above the ground gamma rays from a radioactive source had a longer wavelength than at ground level. Physicists have been less successful, however, with the prediction in 1916 of the existence of gravitational waves. Despite an intensive search from 1964 onward by Joseph Weber and others, they have yet to be detected.

Einstein was less successful in applying his theory to the construction of a cosmological model of the universe, which he assumed to be uniform in density, static, and lacking infinite distances. He found himself forced to complicate his equations with a cosmological constant, λ. It was left to Aleksandr Friedmann in 1922 to show that the term could be dropped and a solution

found that yielded an expanding universe, a solution that Einstein eventually adopted. He later described the cosmological constant as "my greatest mistake."

By the early 1920s Einstein's great work was virtually complete. He wrote in 1921 that: "Discovery in the grand manner is for young people ... and hence for me a thing of the past." From the early 1920s he rejected quantum theory – the theory he had done much to establish himself. His basic objection was to the later formulation that included the probability interpretation. "God does not play dice," he said, and, "He may be subtle, but he is not malicious." He felt, like Louis de Broglie, that although the new quantum mechanics was clearly a powerful and successful theory it was an imperfect one, with an underlying undiscovered deterministic basis. For the last 30 years of his life he also pursued a quest for a unified field theory – a single theory to explain both electromagnetic and gravitational fields. He published several attempts at such a theory but all were inadequate. This work was carried out right up to his death.

Also, from about 1925 onward, Einstein engaged in a debate with Niels Bohr on the soundness of quantum theory. He would present Bohr with a series of thought experiments, which seemed undeniable even though they were clearly incompatible with quantum mechanics. The best known of these was presented in a paper written with Boris Podolsky and Nathan Rosen and entitled: *Can Quantum Mechanical Description of Physical Reality Be Considered Complete?* (1935). The *EPR experiment*, as it soon became known, assumed that, after interacting, two particles become widely separated. Quantum theory allows the total momentum of the pair (A, B) to be measured accurately. Thus if the momentum of B is also measured accurately, it is a simple matter, as momentum is conserved, to calculate the momentum of particle A. We can then measure the position of A with as much precision as is practically possible. It would therefore seem to follow that, without violating any laws of physics, both the position and momentum of particle A have been accurately determined. But, according to the uncertainty principle of Heisenberg, we are prevented from ever knowing accurately a particle's position and momentum simultaneously.

The paper troubled Bohr. He spent six weeks going through the text word by word and analyzing every possibility. Eventually he saw that the measurements of A's position and momentum are separate and distinct. The uncertainty principle insisted that no *single* measurement could determine a particle's precise position and momentum, and this central claim remained unchallenged by the EPR experiment. The EPR experiment has continued to trouble people interested in the fundamental principles of quantum mechanics. In 1964 the British physicist John BELL published an important theoretical paper indicating how the experiment might be done in practice. Einstein's correspondence with Bohr about quantum mechanics is published as the *Bohr–Einstein letters*.

Einstein was also involved in a considerable amount of political activity. When Hitler came to power in 1933 Einstein made his permanent home in America where he worked at Princeton. In 1939 he was persuaded to write to President Roosevelt warning him about the possibility of an atomic bomb and urging American research. He was, in later years, a convinced campaigning pacifist. He was also a strong supporter of Zionist causes and, on the death of Chaim Weizmann in 1952 was asked to become president of Israel, but declined.

Einthoven, Willem (1860–1927) *Dutch physiologist*

Einthoven, the son of a physician, was born at Semarang on the Indonesian island of Java and educated at the University of Utrecht in the Netherlands, where he gained his MD in 1885. In the following year he moved to Leiden as professor of physiology.

As early as 1887 the English physiologist Augustus Waller had recorded electric currents generated by the heart. He had used the capillary electrometer invented by Gabriel Lippmann in 1873, which – although sensitive to changes of a millivolt – turned out to be too complicated and inaccurate for general use. In 1901 Einthoven first described a recording system using a string galvanometer, which he claimed would overcome the inadequacies of Waller's device.

A string galvanometer consists of a fine wire thread stretched between the poles of a magnet. When carrying a current it is displaced at right angles to the directions of the magnetic lines of force to an extent proportional to the strength of the current. By linking this up to an optical system the movement of the wire can be magnified and photographically recorded. As the differences in potential developed in the heart are conducted to different parts of the body it was possible to lead the current from the hands and feet to the recording instrument to obtain a curve that was later called an *electrocardiogram* (ECG).

Having demonstrated the potentiality of such a machine, two further problems needed solution. Einthoven first had to standardize his ECG so that different machines or two recordings of the same machine would produce comparable readings. It was therefore later established that a 1 millivolt potential would deflect a recording stylus 1 centimeter on standardized paper. The second problem was how to interpret such a curve in order to distinguish normal readings from recordings of diseased hearts. By 1913 Einthoven had worked out the interpretation of the normal tracing and, by correlating abnormal readings with specific cardiac defects identified at post mortem, was able to use the ECG as a diagnostic tool.

For his development of the electrocardiogram Einthoven was awarded the 1924 Nobel Prize for physiology or medicine.

Ekeberg, Anders Gustaf (1767–1813) *Swedish chemist*

Ekeberg, who was born in the Swedish capital of Stockholm, graduated from the University of Uppsala in 1788 and, after traveling in Europe, began teaching chemistry at Uppsala in 1794. He was an early convert to the system of Antoine Lavoisier and introduced this new chemistry to Sweden. He was partially deaf from a childhood illness but the further loss of an eye (1801) caused by an exploding flask did not impede his work.

Ekeberg is remembered chiefly for his discovery of the element tantalum. In 1802, while analyzing minerals from Ytterby quarry, Sweden, he isolated the new metal. The name supposedly comes from its failure to dissolve in acid, looking like Tantalus in the waters of Hell. It was a long time before it was recognized as a separate element as it was difficult to distinguish from niobium, isolated by Charles Hatchett in 1801. Wollaston failed to distinguish between them and it was as late as 1865 that Jean Marignac conclusively demonstrated the distinctness of the two new metals.

Ekman, Vagn Walfrid (1874–1954) *Swedish oceanographer*

Ekman, the son of an oceanographer, was born in the Swedish capital of Stockholm and educated at the University of Uppsala, graduating in 1902. He worked at the International Laboratory for Oceanographic Research in Oslo (1902–08) before he moved to Lund, Sweden, as a lecturer in mathematical physics, being made a professor in 1910.

In 1905 Ekman published a fundamental paper, *On the Influence of the Earth's Rotation on Ocean Currents*. This work originated from an observation made by the explorer Fridtjof Nansen that in the Arctic drift ice did not follow wind direction but deviated to the right. He showed that the motion, since known as the *Ekman spiral*, is produced as a complex interaction between the force of the wind on the water surface, the deflecting force due to the Earth's rotation (Coriolis force), and the frictional forces within the water layers.

Ekman also studied the phenomenon of dead water, a thin layer of fresh water from melting ice spreading over the sea, which could halt slow-moving ships. This, he established, resulted from the waves formed between water layers of different densities. The *Ekman current meter*, invented by him, is still in use.

Elhuyar, Don Fausto D' *See* D'ELHUYAR, DON FAUSTO.

Elion, Gertrude B. (1918–) *American biochemist*

Gertrude Elion's father emigrated to the United States at the age of 12 and settled in New York City, where he graduated in dentistry. Her mother came from a part of Russia now in Poland. Gertrude was educated at Hunter College, where she studied chemistry. In 1939 she entered graduate school at New York University.

After graduating she took a teaching job, continuing to do research in the evenings and at weekends for a master's degree, which she obtained in 1941. After a period working in the food industry she eventually obtained a job as assistant to George HITCHINS. Here she extended her work from organic chemistry into biochemistry, pharmacology, immunology, and virology. She also studied for a doctorate at Brooklyn Polytechnic Institute.

Elion and Hitchins collaborated over many years on nucleic acid metabolism, developing a series of drugs that block nucleic acid synthesis in cancer cells and harmful organisms. In 1988 they shared (with James BLACK) the Nobel Prize for physiology or medicine.

Elsasser, Walter Maurice (1904–1991) *German–American geophysicist*

Elsasser was born in the German city of Mannheim and educated at the University of Göttingen, where he obtained his doctorate in 1927. He worked at the University of Frankfurt before leaving Germany in 1933 following Hitler's rise to power. He taught at the Sorbonne, Paris, before emigrating to America (1936) where he joined the staff of the California Institute of Technology. He became professor of physics at the University of Pennsylvania (1947–50) and at the University of Utah (1950–58). In 1962 he became professor of geophysics at Princeton and he was appointed research professor at the University of Maryland from 1968 until his retirement in 1974.

Elsasser made fundamental proposals on the question of the origin of the Earth's magnetic field. It had been known for some time that this could not be due to the Earth's iron core for its temperature is too high for it to serve as a simple magnet. Instead he proposed that the molten liquid core contains eddies set up by the Earth's rotation. These eddies produce an electric current that causes the familiar terrestrial magnetic field.

Elsasser also made predictions of electron diffraction (1925) and neutron diffraction (1936). His works include *The Physical Foundation of Biology* (1958) and *Atom and Organism* (1966).

Elton, Charles Sutherland (1900–1991) *British ecologist*

Born in Liverpool, Elton graduated in zoology from Oxford University in 1922. He was assistant to Julian Huxley on the Oxford University expedition to Spitzbergen (1921), where Elton carried out ecological studies of the region's animal life. Further Arctic expeditions were made in 1923, 1924, and 1930. Such experience prompted his appointment as biological consultant to the Hudson's Bay Company, for which he carried out investigations into variations in the numbers of fur-bearing animals, using trapper's records dating back to 1736. In 1932 Elton helped establish the Bureau of Animal Population at Oxford – an institution that subsequently became an international center for information on and research into animal numbers and their ecology. In the same year he became editor of the new *Journal of Animal Ecology*, launched by the British Ecological Society, and in 1936 was appointed reader in animal ecology as well as a senior research fellow by Oxford University.

Elton was one of the first biologists to study animals in relation to their environment and other animals and plants. His demonstration of the nature of food chains and cycles, as well as such topics as the reasons for differences in animal numbers, were discussed in *Animal Ecology* (1927). In 1930 *Animal Ecology and Evolution* was published in which he advanced the notion that animals were not invariably at the mercy of their environment but commonly, perhaps through migration, practiced environmental selection by changing their habitats. Work on the rodent population of Britain, and how it is affected by a changing environment, was turned to eminently practical account at the outbreak of World War II when Elton conducted intensive research into methods of controlling rats and mice and thus conserving food for the war effort. *Voles, Mice and Lemmings: Problems in Population Dynamics* was published in 1942, and *The Control of Rats and Mice* in 1954, the latter becoming accepted as the standard work on the subject.

Elvehjem, Conrad Arnold (1901–1962)
American biochemist

Elvehjem, the son of a farmer from McFarland, Wisconsin, graduated from and spent his whole career at the University of Wisconsin. He obtained his PhD in 1927, and served as professor of biochemistry from 1936 until 1958, when he became president of the university, a position held until his retirement in 1962.

In 1937, following discoveries by Casimir Funk and Joseph Goldberger, Elvehjem succeeded in producing a new treatment for pellagra. In the 1920s Goldberger had postulated that this disease was caused by a deficiency of 'P-P' (pellagra preventive) factor present in milk. In 1913 Funk, while searching for a cure for beriberi, came across nicotinic acid in rice husks. Although it was of little use against beriberi, Elvehjem found that even in minute doses it would dramatically remove the symptoms of blacktongue, the canine equivalent of pellagra. Tests on humans revealed the same remarkable effects on pellagra.

Elvehjem, a prolific author with over 800 papers to his credit, also worked on the role of trace elements in nutrition, showing the essential role played by such minerals as copper, zinc, and cobalt.

Embden, Gustav George (1874–1933)
German physiologist

Embden, the son of a lawyer from Hamburg, was educated at the universities of Freiburg, Munich, Berlin, and Strasbourg. From 1904 he was director of the chemical laboratory in the medical clinic of the Frankfurt hospital, becoming in 1907 director of the Physiological Institute (which evolved from the medical clinic) and in 1914 director of the Institute for Vegetative Physiology (which in its turn evolved from the Physiological Institute).

In 1918 Otto Meyerhof threw considerable light on the process of cellular metabolism by showing that it involved the breakdown of glucose to lactic acid. Embden spent much time in working out the precise steps involved in such a breakdown, as did many other chemists and physiologists. By the time of his death the details of the metabolic sequence from glycogen to lactic acid, later known as the *Embden–Meyerhof pathway*, had been worked out.

Embden's earlier work concentrated on the metabolic processes carried out by the liver. In his experiments he used a new perfusion technique to maintain the condition of the dissected livers. In this way he discovered the breakdown of amino acids by oxidative deamination, realized that abnormal sugar metabolism can lead to the formation of acetone and acetoacetic acid, and showed that sugar is synthesized from lactic acid.

Empedocles of Acragas (c. 490 BC–c. 430 BC) *Greek philosopher*

Empedocles was a poet and a physician as well as a philosopher. Born at Acragas in Greece, he was probably a pupil of Parmenides. Much legend surrounds what is known of his life. Styling himself as a god, he reputedly brought about his own death in an attempt to persuade his followers of his divinity by throwing himself into the volcanic crater of Mount Etna. Fragments of two poems by Empedocles survive: *On Nature* and *Purifications*. There is some difficulty in reconciling the two because the first is purely physical while the second deals with the progress of the soul from fall to redemption.

Empedocles is best known as the originator of the four-element theory of matter (earth, fire, air, and water), which had a persuasive influence until the beginning of modern chemistry in the 18th century. He was noted for his keen observation and was the first to demonstrate that air has weight.

Encke, Johann Franz (1791–1865)
German astronomer

The son of a Lutheran pastor from Hamburg, Encke was educated at Göttingen where he impressed Karl Gauss. In 1816 he was appointed to the staff of the Seeberg Observatory, Gotha, where he remained until 1825 when he moved to the Berlin Observatory as its director.

A faint comet had first been observed by P. Mechain in 1786. Over the years other reports were made in 1795, 1805, and 1818 of a series of faint comets. Although several astronomers suspected there was only one comet involved, it was Encke who provided in 1819 the necessary computations. He showed that *Encke's comet*, as it became known, had a period of 3.3 years and predicted that it would be at perihelion again on 24 May 1822. His prediction was accurate to within a few hours and Encke thus became, after Halley, only the second man to predict the return of a periodic comet successfully.

Enders, John Franklin (1897–1985)
American microbiologist

Enders, the son of a wealthy banker from West Hartford in Connecticut, was educated at Yale and Harvard where he obtained his PhD in 1930. His career was somewhat delayed by the war, in which he served as a flying instructor, and also by his initial intention to study Germanic and Celtic languages. This was upset by the influence of the bacteriologist Hans Zinsser who 'seduced' Enders into science in the late 1920s.

In 1946 Enders set up an Infectious Diseases Laboratory at the Boston Children's Hospital; it was here that he did the work to be later described as opening up a "new epoch in the history of virus research." This referred to his success, in collaboration with Thomas Weller and Frederick Robbins, in 1949 in cultivating polio virus in test tube cultures of human tissue for the first time. They further demonstrated that the virus could be grown on a wide variety of tissue and not just nerve cells.

This at last allowed the polio virus to be studied, typed, and produced in quantity. Without such an advance the triumphs of Albert Sabin and Jonas Salk in developing a vaccine against polio in the 1950s would have been impossible. In 1954 Enders, Weller, and Robbins were awarded the Nobel Prize for physiology or medicine.

By this time Enders had already begun to work on the cultivation of the measles virus. This time, working with T. Peebles, they followed up their success in cultivating the virus with, in 1957, the production of the first measles vaccine.

Engelmann, George (1809–1884)
American botanist

Born the son of a schoolmaster at Frankfurt in Germany, Engelmann was educated at the universities of Heidelberg, Berlin, and Würzburg where he obtained his MD in 1831. In the following year he visited America to invest in some land for a wealthy uncle and decided in 1835 to settle and practice medicine in St. Louis.

Engelmann was not only a plant collector of some importance; he also did much to initiate and organize major collecting expeditions of the flora of the West. It was thus through Engelmann that many of the newly collected specimens passed on their way to eastern scholars as Asa Gray at Harvard. Engelmann's role became more official with the setting up of the Missouri Botanical Garden in 1859 with the backing of the St. Louis businessman Henry Shaw.

He is also remembered for his demonstration that some stocks of American vine were resistant to the pest *Phylloxera*, which had begun to devastate the vineyards of Europe from 1863 onward.

Engelmann, Theodor Wilhelm (1843–1909) *German physiologist*

Engelmann, the son of a publisher, was educated at Jena, Heidelberg, and Göttingen, before obtaining his PhD from the university in his native city of Leipzig in 1867. He immediately joined the faculty of the University of Utrecht, serving there as professor of physiology from 1888 until 1897 when he returned to Germany to a similar chair at the University of Berlin, where he remained until his retirement in 1908.

Between 1873 and 1895 Engelmann published a number of papers on muscle contraction. By this time, following the work of such physiologists as William Bowman, the main anatomical details of striated muscle had been established. However an explanation was needed as to why the anisotropic or A bands refract polarized light quite differently to the isotropic or I bands. Engelmann had noted that in contraction the A bands increased in volume while the I bands decreased. He consequently proposed his 'imbibition' theory in which the contraction of striped muscle is attributed to a flow of fluid from the I to the A bands.

Engelmann also worked on the nature and mechanism of the heartbeat and in 1875 devised an experiment that proved the heartbeat is myogenic; that is, the contraction originates in the heart muscle and not from an external nerve stimulus. In 1881 he discovered the chemotactic response of certain bacteria to oxygen, and he also demonstrated that red and blue light is far more effective in stimulating plant chloroplasts during photosynthesis than other parts of the spectrum.

Eötvös, Baron Roland von (1848–1919) *Hungarian physicist*

Born in Budapest, Eötvös studied at the University of Königsberg and at Heidelberg where he obtained his PhD in 1870 for a thesis concerning a method of detecting motion through the ether by measuring light intensity. At Königsberg in 1886 he introduced the *Eötvös law* – an equation approximately relating surface tension, temperature, density, and relative molecular mass of a liquid.

He then started teaching at Budapest University, where he was appointed professor in 1872. His work from then on centered on gravitation. In 1888 he developed the *Eötvös torsion balance*, consisting of a bar with two attached weights, the bar being suspended by a torsion fiber. He argued that if the two weights were made from different materials, and if the inertial and gravitational forces were not equivalent, there would be a discernible twisting force, which would cause a slight rotation of the bar about a vertical axis. Observations were made with copper, aluminum, asbestos, platinum, and other materials. No torque was found and Eötvös concluded that the masses of different materials were equivalent to a few parts per billion. His experiments were repeated in the 1960s by Dicke and in 1970 by Braginsky, with results affirming the equivalence to 1 part per 100 billion and 1 part per trillion respectively. The experiment became one of the foundation stones of general relativity since, by failing to distinguish between inertial and gravitational mass experimentally, it supported Einstein's principle of equivalence.

Eötvös spent much of his time trying to improve the Hungarian education system and for a short time was minister of instruction. He was also an excellent mountain climber and a peak in the Dolomites is named for him.

Epicurus (*c.* 341 BC–270 BC) *Greek philosopher*

Epicurus, who was born on the Greek island of Samos, traveled to Athens when he was about 18 years old, and received military training. He then taught at Mytilene and Lampsacus before returning to Athens (305 BC) where he founded a school of philosophy and attracted a substantial following.

Epicurus revived Democritean atomism and was little influenced by his predecessors, Plato and Aristotle. His work is known through substantial fragments in the writings of Diogenes Laërtius and especially through the long poem, *De rerum natura* (On the Nature of Things), by his Roman disciple Lucretius. The Epicurean philosophy aimed at the attainment of a happy, though simple, life and used the atomic theory to sanction the banishment of the old fears and superstitions. Epicurus also made important additions to the atomic theory, asserting the primacy of sense-perception where Democritus had distrusted the senses, and he introduced the concept of random atomic 'swerve' to preserve free will in an otherwise deterministic system.

Epstein, Sir Michael Anthony
(1921–) *British virologist*

Epstein, a Londoner, was educated at Cambridge University and at the Middlesex Hospital Medical School in his native city. After serving in the Royal Army Medical Corps (1945–47), he returned to the Middlesex Hospital as an assistant pathologist. He left the Middlesex in 1965 and in 1968 he was appointed professor of pathology at Bristol University, a position he held until his retirement in 1985. He has continued to work in the Department of Clinical Medicine at Oxford.

In 1961 Epstein heard Denis Burkitt describe the distribution of a particularly savage lymphoma throughout Africa. Epstein saw that "anything which has geographical factors such as climate affecting distribution must have some kind of biological cause." That biological cause, Epstein suspected, for no very good reason, was a virus.

Although Epstein received tumor samples from Burkitt, he found them impossible to culture and saw no trace of any virus. After struggling unsuccessfully for two years, Epstein and his assistant Yvonne Barr developed a new approach. Instead of working with small tumor lumps they divided the pieces into single cells. The technique proved successful and for the first time ever human lymphocytes were being grown in a continuous culture.

Yet Epstein initially found no virus until he examined some cells under an electron microscope. The virus was named the *Epstein–Barr virus* and proved to be a member of the herpes family.

The virus turned out to have a worldwide distribution and was identified as the cause of mononeucleosis. Clearly, its presence alone is insufficient to cause lymphoma. For if most of us have the virus, why is lymphoma not distributed more widely? Epstein and Burkitt argued that only in cases in which malaria or some other chronic condition has suppressed a child's immature immune system, could the virus provoke lymphoid cells into malignant growth.

Erasistratus of Chios (*c.* 304 BC– *c.* 250 BC) *Greek anatomist and physician*

Erasistratus, who was born on the Greek island of Chios, came from a distinctly medical background and studied in Athens, Cos, and Alexandria. Following Herophilus he became the leading figure in the Alexandrian School of Anatomy.

It is possible with Erasistratus, unlike his contemporaries, to make out at least the outline of his physiological system. Every organ and part of the body was served by a 'three-fold network' of vein, artery, and nerve. Indeed he believed the body tissues were a plaiting of such vessels, which at their extremities became so fine as to be invisible. The veins carried blood and the nerves and arteries transported nervous and animal spirits respectively.

As an atomist he rejected all attractive and occult forces seeking instead to explain everything in terms of atoms and the void. He thus accounted for the bleeding of severed arteries by assuming the escaped pneuma left a vacuum that was filled by blood from adjoining veins.

One of the most interesting aspects of his thought was his unusual rejection of the humoral theory of disease which, formulated by the Hippocratics and authorized by Galen became the sterile orthodoxy of Western medicine for 2000 years. Instead he seems to have argued for a more mechanical concept of disease, attributing it to a 'plethora' of blood, vital spirit, or food, which produces a blocking and inflammation of the various vessels.

His objection to the humoral theory found little support and with the passing of Erasistratus the great innovative period of Alexandrian medicine came to an end.

Eratosthenes of Cyrene (c. 276 BC–c. 194 BC) Greek astronomer

Eratosthenes was born in Cyrene, now in Libya, and educated at Athens. He then taught in Alexandria where he became tutor to the son of Ptolemy III and librarian. He was prominent in history, poetry, mathematics, and astronomy and was known by the nickname 'beta' because, some say, he was the second Plato.

In number theory he introduced the procedure named for him to collect the prime numbers by filtering out all the composites. The method, called the *sieve of Eratosthenes*, was to write down a list of ordered numbers and to strike out every second number after 2, every third number after 3, every fourth number after 4, and so on. The numbers remaining are primes.

Eratosthenes achieved his greatest fame by using a most ingenious and simple method to measure the circumference of the Earth. He was aware that on a certain day the Sun at Syene (now Aswan) was exactly at its zenith (it was known to shine directly down a deep well on that day). He found that on the same day at Alexandria it was south of its zenith by an angle corresponding to 1/50 of a circle (7° 12′). He also knew that the distance between Syene and Alexandria was 5000 stadia – a distance that he estimated from the time it took a camel train to make the journey. Therefore, 5000 stadia must be 1/50 of the circumference of the Earth; that is, 250,000 stadia. (Since the exact length of a stade is not known it is impossible to work out exactly how accurate his measurement was but it has been thought to be within 50 miles of the presently accepted value.) Eratosthenes also established an improved figure for the obliquity of the ecliptic (the tilt of the Earth's axis) of 23°51′20″. Finally, he produced the first map of the world, as he knew it, based on meridians of longitude and parallels of latitude.

Erdös, Paul (1913–1996) Hungarian mathematician

The son of two mathematics teachers from the Hungarian capital of Budapest, Erdös devoted his life to mathematics to an unequalled degree. He was educated at the University of Budapest where he obtained his PhD in 1934. Sensing difficult political times ahead, Erdös moved to Manchester on a four-year fellowship. Shortly before the outbreak of war he left for America. At the height of the McCarthy era he was denied a reentry permit after attending a conference in Amsterdam. Erdös then settled in Israel for several years until, in the 1960s, he was allowed an American visa once more.

Erdös was something of an eccentric. With no official job and no family, he lived out of a suitcase and traveled from one mathematical center to another. His life was spent working up to 20 hours a day on mathematical problems, usually with colleagues. In the process he produced over 1000 papers. He lived on lecture fees, prizes, grants, and the hospitality of his wide circle of collaborators. He wrote up to 1500 letters a year and had more than 250 published collaborators.

Erlanger, Joseph (1874–1965) American neurophysiologist

Erlanger, the son of a German immigrant drawn to California in the gold rush, was born in San Francisco. He was educated at the University of California and at Johns Hopkins University in Baltimore, where in 1899 he obtained his MD. After working on the staff for a few years Erlanger moved to the University of Wisconsin (1906) to accept the chair of physiology. In 1910 he moved to

Washington University, St. Louis, where he held the chair of physiology in the Medical School until his retirement in 1944.

Between 1921 and 1931 Erlanger carried out some fundamental research on the functions of nerve fibers with his former pupil and colleague, Herbert GASSER. They investigated the transmission of a nerve impulse along a frog nerve kept in a moist chamber at constant temperature. Their innovation was to study the transmission with the cathode-ray oscillograph, invented by Ferdinand Braun in 1897, which enabled them to picture the changes the impulse underwent as it traveled along the nerve.

Erlanger and Gasser found that on stimulating a nerve, the resulting electrical activity indicating the passage of an impulse was composed of three waves, as observed on the oscillograph. They explained this by proposing that the one stimulus activated three different groups of nerve fibers, each of which had its own conduction rate. They went on to measure these rates, concluding that the fastest fibers (the A-fibers) conduct with a speed of up to 100 meters per second (mps) while the slowest (the C-fibers) could manage speeds of no more than 2 mps. The intermediate B-fibers conducted in the range 2–14 mps. Erlanger and Gasser were able to relate this variation to the thickness of the different nerve fibers, A-fibers being the largest.

It was a short step from this to the theory of differentiated function, in which it was proposed that the slender C-fibers carry pain impulses whereas the thicker A-fibers transmit motor impulses. But it was soon demonstrated that while such propositions may be broadly true the detailed picture is more complex.

Erlanger and Gasser produced an account of their collaboration in *Electrical Signs of Nervous Activity* (1937); they were awarded the 1944 Nobel Prize for physiology or medicine for their work.

Erlenmeyer, Richard August Carl Emil (1825–1909) *German chemist*

Born near Wiesbaden in Germany, Erlenmeyer studied at Giessen and practiced at first as a pharmacist. In 1855 he became a private pupil of August Kekulé at Heidelberg and later was appointed professor at the Munich Polytechnic (1868–83). He synthesized guanidine and was the first to give its correct formula (1868). He also synthesized tyrosine and formulated the *Erlenmeyer rule*, which states the impossibility of two hydroxy groups occurring on the same carbon atom or of a hydroxy group occurring adjacent to a carbon–carbon double

bond (chloral hydrate is an exception to this rule). His son F.G.C.E. Erlenmeyer introduced the Erlenmeyer synthesis of amino acids and synthesized cystine, serine, and phenylalanine.

Ernst, Richard Robert (1933–) *Swiss chemist*

Born at Winterthur in Switzerland, Ernst was educated at the Federal Institute of Technology, Zurich, where he obtained his PhD in 1962. He spent the period from 1963 until 1968 working as a research chemist for Varian Associates, Palo Alto, California, before returning to the Federal Institute where he was appointed professor of physical chemistry in 1976.

The technique of nuclear magnetic resonance (NMR) described by I. I. Rabi in 1944, and developed by Felix Bloch and Edward Purcell in the late 1940s, quickly became a recognized tool for the exploration of atomic nuclei. As nuclei possess a magnetic moment they will tend to align themselves with any strong magnetic field. If, however, nuclei are subjected to radiowaves of the appropriate frequency, they will be raised to a higher energy level, and align themselves in a different direction with respect to the field. With the removal of the radio signal, the nuclei will revert to their original energy state by emitting radiation of a characteristic frequency. The frequency of the radiation emitted allows nuclei to be identified, and the structure of certain molecules determined.

But, the process was time-consuming because, in order to find which radiofrequency a sample responded to, it was necessary to sweep the applied frequency through a range of frequencies. Ernst developed a technique in which the sample was subjected to a single high-energy radio pulse. In this way numerous nuclei would respond and emit an apparently jumbled signal. But Ernst showed that, with the aid of Fourier analysis and a computer, the signal could be unraveled into its separate components. Ernst's procedure considerably increased the sensitivity of NMR.

In 1970 Ernst made a further advance. He found that if he subjected his samples to a sequence of high-energy pulses instead of to a single pulse, it enabled him to use NMR techniques to study much larger molecules. Ernst's 'two-dimensional analysis', as it became known, opened the way to investigate complex biological molecules such as proteins. His work also laid the foundation for the development by Peter Mansfield and others of MRI (magnetic resonance imaging).

For his work on NMR Ernst was awarded the 1991 Nobel Prize for chemistry.

Esaki, Leo (1925–) *Japanese physicist*

Born in the Japanese city of Osaka, Esaki graduated in physics at the University of Tokyo in 1947, gaining his doctorate there in 1959. His doctoral work was on the physics of semiconductors, and in 1958 he reported an effect known as 'tunneling', which he had observed in narrow p–n junctions of germanium that were heavily doped with impurities. The phenomenon of tunneling is a quantum-mechanical effect in which an electron can penetrate a potential barrier through a narrow region of solid, where classical theory predicts it could not pass.

Esaki was quick to see the possibility of applying the tunnel effect, and in 1960 reported the construction of a device with diodelike properties – the tunnel (or *Esaki*) diode. With negative bias potential, the diode acts as a short circuit, while under certain conditions of forward bias it can have effectively negative resistance (the current decreasing with increasing voltage). Important characteristics of the tunnel diode are its very fast speed of operation, its small physical size, and its low power consumption. It has found application in many fields of electronics, principally in computers, microwave devices, and where low electronic noise is required. Esaki shared the Nobel Prize for physics in 1973 with Brian JOSEPHSON and Ivar GIAEVER.

Esaki worked for the computer firm International Business Machines at the Thomas J. Watson Research Center, Yorktown Heights, New York, until 1992, when he returned to Japan to become president of Tsukuba University, Ibaraki.

Eschenmoser, Albert (1925–) *Swiss chemist*

Born at Erstfeld in Switzerland, Eschenmoser was educated at the Federal Institute of Technology, Zurich, where he has taught since 1956 and where, in 1960, he was appointed professor of organic chemistry.

He is best known for his work in synthesizing a number of complex organic compounds. His first success came with colchicine – an alkaloid found in the autumn crocus – which has important applications in genetical research. He also collaborated with Robert Woodward on the synthesis of vitamin B_{12} (cyanocobalamin), which had first been isolated in 1948 by the American organic chemist **Karl Folkers** (1906–). Its empirical formula was soon established and in 1956 Dorothy Hodgkin established its structure. It took many years with samples passing between Zurich and Harvard before Eschenmoser and Woodward were finally able to announce its synthesis in 1965.

Euclid (*c.* 330 BC–*c.* 260 BC) *Greek mathematician*

Euclid is one of the best known and most influential of classical Greek mathematicians but almost nothing is known about his life. He was a founder and member of the academy in Alexandria, and may have been a pupil of Plato in Athens. Despite his great fame Euclid was not one of the greatest of Greek mathematicians and not of the same caliber as Archimedes.

Euclid's most celebrated work is the *Elements*, which is primarily a treatise on geometry contained in 13 books. The influence of this work not only on the future development of geometry, mathematics, and science, but on the whole of Western thought is hard to exaggerate. Some idea of the importance that has been attached to the *Elements* is gained from the fact that there have probably been more commentaries written on it than on the Bible. The *Elements* systematized and organized the work of many previous Greek geometers, such as Theaetetus and Eudoxus, as well as containing many new discoveries that Euclid had made himself. Although mainly concerned with geometry it also deals with such topics as number theory and the theory of irrational quantities. One of the most celebrated number theoretic results is Euclid's proof that there are an infinite number of primes. The *Elements* is in many ways a synthesis and culmination of Greek mathematics. Euclid and Apollonius of Perga were the last Greek mathematicians of any distinction, and after their time Greek civilization as a whole soon became decadent and sterile.

Euclid's *Elements* owed its enormously high status to a number of reasons. The most influential single feature was Euclid's use of the axiomatic method whereby all the theorems were laid out as deductions from certain self-evident basic propositions or axioms in such a way that in each successive proof only propositions already proved or axioms were used. This became accepted as the paradigmatically rigorous way of setting out any body of knowledge, and attempts were made to apply it not just to mathematics, but to natural science, theology, and even philosophy and ethics.

However, despite being revered as an almost perfect example of rigorous thinking for almost 2000 years there are considerable defects in Euclid's reasoning. A number of his proofs were found to contain mistakes, the status of the initial axioms themselves was increasingly considered to be problematic, and the definitions of such basic terms as 'line' and 'point' were found to be unsatisfactory. The most celebrated case is that of the parallel axiom, which states that there is only one straight line passing through a given point and parallel to a given straight line. The status of this axiom was long recognized as problematic, and many unsuccessful attempts were made to deduce it from the remaining axioms. The question was only settled in the 19th century when Janos Bolyai and Nicolai Lobachevski showed that it was perfectly possible to construct a consistent geometry in which Euclid's other axioms were true but in which the parallel axiom was false. This epoch-making discovery displaced Euclidean geometry from the privileged position it had occupied. The question of the relation of Euclid's geometry to the properties of physical space had to wait until the early 20th century for a full answer. Until then it was believed that Euclid's geometry gave a fully accurate description of physical space. No less a thinker than Immanuel Kant had thought that it was logically impossible for space to obey any other geometry. However when Albert Einstein developed his theory of relativity he found that the appropriate geometry for space was not Euclid's but that developed by Georg Riemann. It was subsequently experimentally verified that the geometry of space is indeed non-Euclidean.

In mathematical terms too, the discovery of non-Euclidean geometries was of great importance, since it led to a broadening of the conception of geometry and the development by such mathematicians as Felix Klein of many new geometries very different from Euclid's. It also made mathematicians scrutinize the logical structure of Euclid's geometry far more closely and in 1899 David Hilbert at last gave a definitively rigorous axiomatic treatment of geometry and made an exhaustive investigation of the relations of dependence and independence between the axioms, and of the consistency of the various possible geometries so produced.

Euclid wrote a number of other works besides the *Elements*, although many of them are now lost and known only through references to them by other classical authors. Those that do survive include *Data*, containing 94 propositions, *On Divisions*, and the *Optics*. One of his sayings has come down to us. When asked by Ptolemy I Soter, the reigning king of Egypt, if there was any quicker way to master geometry than by studying the *Elements* Euclid replied "There is no royal road to geometry."

Eudoxus of Cnidus (c. 400 BC–c. 350 BC)
Greek astronomer and mathematician

Born in Cnidus, which is now in Turkey, Eudoxus is reported as having studied mathematics under Archytas, a Pythagorean. He also studied under Plato and in Egypt. Although none of his works have survived they are quoted extensively by Hipparchus. Eudoxus was the first astronomer who had a complete understanding of the celestial sphere. It is only this understanding that reveals the irregularities of the movements of the planets that must be taken into account in giving an accurate description of the heavens. For Eudoxus the Earth was at rest and around this center 27 concentric spheres rotated. The outermost sphere carried the fixed stars, each of the planets required four spheres, and the Sun and the Moon three each. All these spheres were necessary to account for the daily and annual relative motions of the heavenly bodies. He also described the constellations and the changes in the rising and setting of the fixed stars in the course of a year.

In mathematics, Eudoxus is thought to have contributed the theory of proportion to be found in Book V of Euclid – the importance of this being its applicability to irrational as well as rational numbers. The method of exhaustion in Book XII is also attributed to Eudoxus. This tackled in a mathematical way for the first time the difficult problem of calculating an area bounded by a curve.

Euler, Ulf Svante von *See* VON EULER, ULF SVANTE.

Euler-Chelpin, Hans Karl August Simon von (1873–1964) *German–Swedish biochemist*

Euler-Chelpin was born at Augsburg in Germany and educated at the universities of Berlin, Strasbourg, and Göttingen and at the Pasteur Institute. In 1898 he moved to Sweden being appointed to the staff of the University of Stockholm, where in 1906 he became professor of general and inorganic chemistry. In 1929 he also became director of the Institute of Biochemistry where he remained until his retirement in 1941. Although he became a Swedish citizen in 1902 he served Germany in both world wars.

In 1904 important work by Arthur HARDEN had shown that enzymes contain an easily removable nonprotein part, a coenzyme. In 1923 Euler-Chelpin worked out the structure of the yeast coenzyme. He showed that the molecule is made up from a nucleotide similar to that found in nucleic acid. It was named diphosphopyridine nucleotide (now known as NAD).

Euler-Chelpin shared the 1929 Nobel Prize for chemistry with Harden for this work. His son, Ulf von Euler, was also a Nobel prizewinner.

Evans, Robley Dunglison (1907–)
American physicist

Born in University Place, Nebraska, Evans was educated at the California Institute of Technology where he obtained his PhD in 1932. He went to the Massachusetts Institute of Technology in 1934 and was appointed professor of physics there in 1945.

In 1940 Evans suggested that radioactive potassium–40 could be of use in geologic dating. It is widespread in the Earth's crust and has an exceptionally long halflife of over a thousand million years. It decays to the stable isotope argon–40 and determination of the ratio of ^{40}K to ^{40}Ar allows estimations of the age of potassium-bearing rocks ranging from 100,000 to about 10 million years. The technique proved to be particularly valuable as it permitted accurate dating beyond the limits of Willard LIBBY's carbon–14 technique.

Everett III, Hugh (1930–1982) *American physicist*

Everett was a doctoral pupil of John Wheeler in the 1950s at Princeton. In 1957 he published a famous paper on the foundations of quantum mechanics describing what has become known as the 'many worlds' interpretation. The paper was entitled *Relative State Formulation of Quantum Mechanics.*

The traditional Copenhagen interpretation of quantum mechanics applied only to the submicroscopic world. Everett broke away from this tradition and attempted to apply quantum mechanics to the universe. He established a universal wave function that could be applied to both microscopic entities and macroscopic observers. As a consequence, there is no collapse of the wave function and quantum paradoxes, such as Schrödinger's cat, are avoided.

This approach, however, is not without paradoxical conclusions of its own. In Everett's formulation, the result of a measurement is to split the universe into as many ways as to allow all possible outcomes of the measurement. Thus if an observer were to check the outcome of a die throw, the universe would split into six copies with each one containing one of the six pos-

sible outcomes of the throw. Everett proposed that each outcome is realized in a number of parallel universes between which there is no communication.

While Everett's work has inevitably been taken up by many science fiction writers, it has also been taken seriously by other scientists. GELL-MANN, for example, has tried to develop a version of quantum theory that eliminates the role of the observer, in the manner of Everett, but reduces the idea of 'many worlds' to one of possible histories of the universe to which a probability value can be assigned.

Ewing, Sir James Alfred (1855–1935)
British physicist

The son of a minister of the Free Church of Scotland, Ewing was educated at the University of Edinburgh where he studied engineering. He served as professor of engineering at the Imperial University, Tokyo, from 1878 until 1883 when he returned to Scotland to a similar post at the University of Dundee. In 1890 he was appointed professor of applied mechanics at Cambridge University, but in 1903 moved into higher levels of administration, first as director of naval education and from 1916 until his retirement in 1929 as principal and vice-chancellor of Edinburgh University.

In Japan he worked on problems in seismology and in 1883 published *Treatise on Earthquake Measurement.* However, his most notable achievement as a physicist was his work on hysteresis, first described by him in 1881. Hysteresis is an effect in which there are two properties, M and N, such that cyclic changes of N cause cyclic variations of M. If the changes of M lag behind those of N, there is hysteresis in the relation of M to N. Ewing came across the phenomena when working on the effects of stress on the thermoelectric properties of a wire. Hysteresis effects were later shown to apply to many aspects of the behavior of materials, in particular in magnetization.

Ewing was put in charge of the cryptologists at the Admiralty from 1914 to 1916. He described his work there in his book *The Man in Room 40* (1939).

Ewing, William Maurice (1906–1974)
American oceanographer

Ewing was born at Lockney in Texas and educated at the Rice Institute, Houston, obtaining his PhD in 1931. He taught at Lehigh University, Pennsylvania, from 1934 until moving in 1944 to Columbia University, New York, where he organized the new Lamont Geological Observatory into one of the most important research institutions in the world.

Ewing pioneered seismic techniques to obtain basic data on the ocean floors. He was able to establish that the Earth's crust below the oceans is only about 3–5 miles (5–8 km) thick while the corresponding continental crust averages 25 miles (40 km).

Although the Mid-Atlantic Ridge had been discovered when cables were laid across the Atlantic, its dimensions were unsuspected. In 1956 Ewing and his colleagues were able to show that the ridge constituted a mountain range extending throughout the oceans of the world and was some 40,000 miles (64,000 km) long. In 1957, working with Marie Tharp and Bruce Heezen, he revealed that the ridge was divided by a central rift, which was in places twice as deep and wide as the Grand Canyon.

His group found that the oceanic sediment, expected to be about 10,000 feet (3000 m) thick, was nonexistent on or within about 30 miles (50 km) of the ridge. Beyond this it had a thickness of about 130 feet (40 m) – much less than the depth of the corresponding continental sediment. All this seemed to be consistent with the new sea-floor spreading hypothesis of Harry H. Hess. Ewing was however reluctant to support it until Frederick Vine and Drummond H. Matthews showed how the magnetic reversals discovered by B. Brunhes in 1909 could be used to test the theory.

Ewing also proposed, with William Donn, a mechanism to explain the periodic ice ages. If the Arctic waters were icefree and open to warm currents this source of water vapor would produce greater accumulations of snowfall. This would increase the Earth's reflectivity and reduce the amount of solar radiation absorbed. Temperatures would fall and glaciers move south, but with the freezing of the Arctic seas the supply of water vapor would be cut off and the ice sheets would retreat. This would cause an increase in solar radiation absorbed and the cycle would begin again. No hard evidence has yet been found in support of the theory.

Eyring, Henry (1901–1981) *Mexican– American physical and theoretical chemist*

Eyring, a grandson of American missionaries who had become American citizens, was born at Colonia Juarez in Mexico. He thus first came to America in 1912 as a Mexican citizen and did not take American citizenship until 1935. He was educated at the University of Arizona and the University of California, where he obtained his PhD in 1927. He then held a number of junior appointments before joining the Princeton faculty in 1931, becoming professor of chemistry there in 1938. Eyring moved to a similar chair at the University of Utah, holding the post until his retirement in 1966.

Eyring, the author of 9 books and over 600 papers, was as creative a chemist as he was productive. His main work was probably in the field of chemical kinetics with his transition-state theory. Since the time of Sven Arrhenius it had been appreciated that the rate constant of a chemical reaction depended on temperature according to an equation of the form:

$$k = Ae^{-E/RT}$$

The constant A is the frequency factor of the reaction; E_A is the activation energy. The values of A and E_A can be found experimentally for given reactions. Eyring's contribution to the field was to develop a theory capable of predicting reaction rates.

In a reaction, the atoms move – i.e., molecules break and new molecules form. If the potential energy of a set of atoms is plotted against the distances between atoms for chosen arrangements, the result is a surface. Positions of low energy on the surface correspond to molecules; a reaction can be thought of as a change from a low-energy point, over a higher energy barrier, to another low-energy position.

A. Marcelin, in 1915, had shown that reactions could be represented in this way, and in 1928 Fritz London pointed out that it was possible to calculate potential surfaces using quantum mechanics. Eyring, with Michael Polyani, first calculated such a surface (1929–30) for three hydrogen atoms and Eyring later went on to calculate the potential surfaces for a number of reactions. The activation energy of the reaction is the energy barrier that the system must surmount.

Eyring later (1935) showed how to calculate the frequency factor (A). He assumed that the configuration of atoms at the top of the energy barrier – the 'activated complex' – could be treated as a normal molecule except for a vibrational motion in the direction of the reaction path. Assuming that the activated complex was in equilibrium with the reactants and applying statistical mechanics, Eyring derived a general expression for reaction rate. Eyring's theory, called absolute-rate theory, is described in his book (with Samuel Glasstone and Keith J. Laidler) *The Theory of Rate Processes* (1941).

Fabricius ab Aquapendente, Hieronymus (1537–1619) *Italian anatomist and embryologist*

Fabricius was born at Aquapendente in Italy and educated at the University of Padua where he studied under Gabriel Fallopius, succeeding him, in 1565, as professor of anatomy.

As an anatomist his most significant work was his *De venarum ostiolis* (1603; On the Valves of the Veins), which contains a clear and detailed description of the venous system and which exercised a considerable influence on his most famous pupil, William HARVEY. Fabricius himself entertained no such idea as the circulation of the blood, explaining the role of the valves as retarding the blood flow, thus allowing the tissues to absorb necessary nutriment.

He spent much time observing the development of the chick embryo and published two works *De formato foetu* (1600; On the Formation of the Fetus) and *De formatione ovi et pulli* (1612; On the Development of the Egg and the Chick). These were hailed as elevating embryology into an independent science but they still contain many incorrect assumptions.

Thus for Fabricius semen did not enter the egg but rather initiated the process of generation from a distance in some mysterious way. He also made a now totally unfamiliar distinction between what nourishes and what produces the embryo. Thus he believed both the yolk and albumen merely nourished the embryo. Having eliminated the sperm, yolk, and albumen, Fabricius claimed that the chalaza – the spiral threads holding the yolk in position – produces the chick.

It was while engaged upon this work that he discovered and described the *bursa of Fabricius*. This is a small pouch in the oviduct of the hen, which Fabricius thought to be a store for semen. In the 1950s however the young research student B. Glick showed that this obscure organ plays a key role in the immune system of chickens, and by implication of humans who must possess a comparable system.

Fahrenheit, (Gabriel) Daniel (1686–1736) *German physicist*

Possibly owing to a business failure, Fahrenheit emigrated to Amsterdam from his native Danzig (now Gdańsk in Poland) to become a glass blower and instrument maker. He specialized in the making of meteorological instruments, and proceeded to develop a reliable and accurate thermometer. Galileo had invented the thermometer in about 1600, using changes in air volume as an indicator. Since the volume of air also varied considerably with changes in atmospheric pressure liquids of various kinds were quickly substituted. Fahrenheit was the first to use mercury in 1714. He fixed his zero point by using the freezing point of a mixture of ice and salt as this gave him the lowest temperature he could reach. His other fixed point was taken from the temperature of the human body, which he put at 96°. Given these two fixed points the freezing and boiling points of water then work out at the familiar 32° and 212°. One advantage of the system is that, for most ordinary purposes, negative degrees are rarely needed.

Using his thermometer, Fahrenheit measured the boiling point of various liquids and found that each had a characteristic boiling point, which changed with changes in atmospheric pressure.

Fairbank, William (1917–1989) *American physicist*

Fairbank was born at Minneapolis in Minnesota and educated at Whitman College, Walla Walla, Washington, and at the University of Washington. He gained his PhD at Yale in 1948. He spent the war years at the Radiation Laboratory of the Massachusetts Institute of Technology. After working at Amherst, Maryland (1947–52) and Duke University, North Carolina (1952–59), Fairbank was appointed professor of physics at Stanford, a post he held until his death from a heart attack in 1989.

In 1977, Fairbank, in collaboration with George Larue, claimed to have experimental evidence for the existence of a quark. The concept of quarks, with an electric charge $-1/3$ or $+2/3$ the electron charge, had been proposed by Murray GELL-MANN in 1963 to explain the behavior of hadrons. It was known that it would be unlikely that quarks could be produced at the energies available in particle accelerators. However, it was possible that some might be created in the atmosphere as a result of high-energy cosmic rays. A number of physicists set up ingenious sensitive experiments to "hunt the quark."

Fairbank's technique was a much more sensitive and sophisticated version of Robert Millikan's oil-drop experiment for measuring the charge of the electron. A small sphere (0.25 millimeter diameter) of niobium was suspended between metal plates at a temperature close to absolute zero. The charge on the sphere could be measured by the electric field between the plates.

When Fairbank examined his results he found that in the case of one ball there was "a nonzero residual change of magnitude −0.37 ± 0.03." At first, Fairbank warned, the results did not necessarily imply the presence of a quark as there could well be spurious charge forces present. Consequently, Fairbank spent a good deal of time eliminating these and numerous other possible distortions from his experimental setup.

Theorists were suspicious of Fairbank's work because free quarks are thought to be impossible to produce – the doctrine of "quark confinement." Despite this, Fairbank announced in 1979 that, using modified apparatus, he had detected a second particle with a fractional charge.

While no-one has managed to reproduce Fairbank's experiments, he was sufficiently respected as a careful and skillful experimentalist for his work to be taken seriously. Consequently, for some particle physicists at least, the issue of quark confinement remains an open question.

Fajans, Kasimir (1887–1975) *Polish–American physical chemist. See* SODDY, FREDERICK.

Faraday, Michael (1791–1867) *British physicist and chemist*

Faraday's father was a blacksmith who suffered from poor health and could only work irregularly. Faraday, who was born in Newington, knew real poverty as a child and his education was limited for he left school at the age of 13. He began work for a bookseller and binder in 1804 and was apprenticed the following year. His interest in science seems to have been aroused by his reading the 127-page entry on electricity in an Encyclopaedia Britannica he was binding and this stimulated him to buy the ingredients to make a Leyden jar and to perform some simple experiments. He joined the City Philosophical Society, which he attended regularly, broadening his intellectual background still further. The turning point in his life came when he attended some lectures by Humphry Davy at the

Royal Institution in 1812. He took very full notes of these lectures, which he bound himself.

By now he was no longer satisfied with his amateur experiments and evening lectures and wanted desperately to have a full-time career in science. He wrote to the President of the Royal Society, Joseph Banks, asking for his help in obtaining any post but received no reply. Faraday now had a little luck. Davy had had an accident and needed some temporary assistance. Faraday's name was mentioned and proved acceptable. While working with Davy he showed him the lecture notes he had taken and bound. When a little later, in 1813, a vacancy for a laboratory assistant arose, Davy remembered the serious young man and hired him at a salary of a guinea a week (less than Faraday had been earning as a bookbinder).

Faraday was to spend the rest of his working life at the Royal Institution, from which he finally resigned in 1861. In 1815 he was promoted to the post of assistant and superintendent of the apparatus of the laboratory and meteorological collection. In 1825 he was made director of the laboratory and, in 1833, he was elected to the newly endowed Fullerian Professorship of Chemistry at the Royal Institution. He had earlier turned down the offer of the chair of chemistry at University College, London, in 1827.

The paucity of the salary paid him was made up by Faraday with consultancy fees and a part-time lectureship he held at the Royal Military Academy, Woolwich. These extra sources took up his time and in 1831, when he was working as hard as he could on his electrical experiments, he gave up all his consultancies. This left him in some financial difficulties and moves were made to arrange for a government pension. He called on the prime minister of the day, Lord Melbourne, who made some sneering remark about such pensions being, in his view, a "gross humbug." This was enough to make Faraday refuse the pension. In fact, Faraday was one of nature's great refusers. Apart from the pension and the chair at University College, he also refused a knighthood and, what must surely be a record, the presidency of the Royal Society, not once, but twice. Faraday also had strong views on awards – "I have always felt that there is something degrading in offering rewards for intellectual exertion, and that societies or academies, or even kings and emperors, should mingle in the matter does not remove the degradation." He had become a fellow of the Royal Society in 1824 but not without some friction between himself and the president, Davy. He was asked to withdraw his application by Davy. Just why Davy behaved in this way is not clear. Some have seen it as jealousy by Davy of someone whose talents so clearly surpassed his own. There is no evidence of this but it is reasonably clear that when Faraday insisted on going ahead with his application Davy voted against him.

Faraday's financial problems were solved when, in 1835, Melbourne apologized, enabling him to accept the pension. After his labors of the 1830s he suffered some kind of breakdown in 1841 and went into the country to rest. Just what was wrong is not known; he wrote in 1842 that he could see no visitors because of "ill health connected with my head." For two years he did no work at all until in 1844 he seemed to be able to resume his experiments. Faraday continued to work but by the 1850s his creativity was in decline. He gave his last childrens' lectures at the Royal Institution in 1860 and resigned from it the following year, taking up residence in a house at Hampton Court made available to him by Prince Albert in 1858.

Faraday's first real successes were made in chemistry. In 1823 he unwittingly liquefied chlorine. He was simply heating a chlorine compound in a sealed tube and noticed the formation of some droplets at the cold end. He realized that this was the result of both temperature and pressure and on and off over the years applied the method to other gases. In 1825 he discovered benzene (C_6H_6) when asked to examine the residue collecting in cylinders of illuminating gas; he called the new compound 'bicarburet of hydrogen' because he took its formula to be C_2H. As a working chemist Faraday was one of the best analysts of his day. All his working life he was working and publishing as a chemist but in 1820 he also turned to a new field that was to dominate his life.

Faraday had begun by accepting the view that electricity is composed of two fluids. It was common in the 18th century to see such phenomena as light, heat, magnetism, and electricity to be the result of weightless fluids. In 1820 Hans Christian OERSTED made a most surprising discovery: he had found that a wire carrying a current is capable of deflecting a compass needle; the direction in which the needle turned depended on whether the wire was under or over the needle and the direction in which the current was flowing. André Marie AMPÈRE found that two parallel wires attract each other if the current in each is traveling in the same direction but repel each other if the currents are moving in

opposite directions. Finally François ARAGO discovered that a copper disk rotating freely on its own axis would produce rotation in a compass needle suspended over it.

These phenomena were difficult to fit into fluid theories of electricity and magnetism. They enabled Faraday to make his first important discovery in 1821, that of electromagnetic rotation. A magnet was placed upright in a tube of mercury and secured firmly at the bottom with the pole of the magnet above the surface. A wire dipping into the mercury but free to rotate was suspended over the pole. When a current was passed through the mercury and through the wire, the wire rotated around the magnet. If the wire was secured and the magnet allowed to move, then the current caused the magnet to rotate. The first electric motor had been constructed.

When Faraday published his results they were to cause him much distress. William Wollaston had spoken of the possibility of such rotation and many concluded that Faraday had stolen his ideas. Faraday was only too aware of the stories about him but found there was little he could do about them. It may well have been this that Davy thought disqualified him from membership of the Royal Society.

In any case it was not really electromagnetic rotation that interested Faraday. All the new results involved the production of a magnetic force by an electric current and Faraday, with many others, was sure that it should also be possible to induce an electric current by magnetic action. He tried intermittently for ten years without success until in 1832 he hit upon an apparatus in which an iron ring was wound with two quite separate coils of wire. One was connected to a voltaic cell; the other to a simple galvanometer. He showed that on making and breaking the current in the cell circuit, the galvanometer momentarily registered the presence of a current in its circuit. The following few months were some of the most active of his life. He showed that the same results can be obtained without a battery: a magnet moved in and out of a coil of wire produced a current. A steady current could be produced by rotating a copper disk between the poles of a powerful magnet. His results were published in his *Experimental Researches in Electricity, first series* (1831).

Faraday found this deeply satisfying for it reinforced one of his strongest convictions about nature "that the various forms under which the forces of matter are made manifest have one common origin." That electricity and magnetism could interact made this view more plausible. At the time it was by no means clear that the various types of electricity – static, voltaic, animal, magnetic, and thermoelectric – were the same and Faraday spent the period 1833–34 on this problem publishing his results in the third series of his *Experimental Researches*.

Faraday had also continued the work of Davy on electrolysis – i.e., on the chemical reaction produced by passing an electric current through a liquid. He applied his ideas on the quantity of electricity to this chemical effect and produced what are now known as *Faraday's laws of electrolysis*. By careful analysis he showed that the chemical action of a current is constant for a constant quantity of electricity. This was his first law, that equal amounts of electricity produce equal amounts of decomposition. In the second law he found that the quantities of different substances deposited on the electrode by the passage of the same quantity of electricity were proportional to their equivalent weights.

In his explanations of magnetic and electrical phenomena Faraday did not use the fluid theories of the time. Instead he introduced the concept of lines of force (or tension) through a body or through space. (A similar earlier idea had been put forward by R. J. Boscovich with his picture of point atoms surrounded by shells of force.) Thus Faraday saw the connection between electrical and magnetic effects as vibrations of electrical lines communicated to magnetic lines. His experiments on induction were described in terms of the cutting of magnetic lines of force, which induces the electrical current. He explained electrical induction in dielectrics by the strain in 'tubes of induction' – and electrolysis was complete breakdown under such strain.

Faraday was no mathematician, relying instead on his wonderful experimental skill and his imagination. His lines of force were taken up by others more skillful mathematically. In the latter half of the century Clerk Maxwell developed Faraday's ideas into a rigorous and powerful theory, creating an orthodoxy in physics that lasted until the time of Einstein. Faraday's greatness rests in his courage and insight in rejecting the traditional physics and creating an entirely new one. Few can compete with Faraday at the level of originality.

One further effect discovered by Faraday lay in optics. His discovery of *Faraday rotation* in 1845 was one that gave him pleasure for it seemed to be further evidence for the unity of nature by showing that "magnetic force and light were proved to have a relation to each other." Here, he showed that if polarized light is passed through a transparent medium in a magnetic field its plane of polarization will be rotated.

Not the least of Faraday's achievements was as a lecturer and popularizer of science. In 1826 he started the famous Christmas lectures to children at the Royal Institution in London and gave 19 of these lecture courses. For most only the notes exist but a couple of lectures were taken down in shorthand and later published: *The Chemical History of a Candle* and *Lectures on Various Forces of Matter*. The children's Christmas lectures still continue to be given every year by eminent scientists.

Fermat, Pierre de (1601–1665) *French mathematician and physicist*

Fermat was one of the leading mathematicians of the early 17th century although not a professional mathematician. Born at Beaumont-de-Lomagne in France, he studied law and spent his working life as a magistrate in the provincial town of Castres. Although mathematics was only a spare-time activity, Fermat was an extremely creative and original mathematician who opened up whole new fields of enquiry.

Fermat's work in algebra built on and greatly developed the then new theory of equations, which had been largely founded by François Viète. With Pascal, Fermat stands as one of the founders of the mathematical theory of probability. In his work on methods of finding tangents to curves and their maxima and minima he anticipated some of the central concepts of Isaac Newton's and Gottfried Leibniz's differential calculus.

Another area of mathematics that Fermat played a major role in founding, independently of René Descartes, was analytical geometry. This work led to violent controversies over questions of priority with Descartes. Nor were Fermat's disagreements with Descartes limited to mathematics. Descartes had produced a major treatise on optics – the *Dioptrics* – which Fermat greatly disliked. He particularly objected to Descartes' attempt to reach conclusions about the physical sciences by purely *a priori* rationalistic reasoning without due regard for empirical observation. By contrast Fermat's view of science was grounded in a thoroughly empirical and observational approach, and to demonstrate the errors of Descartes' ways he set about experimental work in optics himself. Among the important contributions that Fermat made to optics are his discovery that light travels more slowly in a denser medium, and his formulation of the principle that light always takes the quickest path.

Fermat is probably best known for his work in number theory, and he made numerous important discoveries in this field. But he also left one of the famous problems of mathematics – *Fermat's last theorem*. This theorem states that the algebraic analog of Pythagoras's theorem has no whole number solution for a power greater than 2, i.e., the equation

$$a^n + b^n = c^n$$

has no solutions for n greater than 2, if a, b, and c are all integers. In the margin of a copy of a book *Arithmetica of Diophantos*, an early treatise on equations, he wrote: "To resolve a cube into the sum of two cubes, a fourth power into two fourth powers, or in general any power higher than the second into two of the same kind, is impossible; of which I have found a remarkable proof. The margin is too small to contain it."

Fermat never wrote down his "remarkable proof" and the equation was the subject of much investigation for over 350 years. In June 1993 the British-born mathematician Andrew WILES presented a proof to a conference at Cambridge in a lecture entitled "Modular forms, elliptic curves, and Galois representations." His proof ran to 1000 pages – rather more space than Fermat's margin – and it is generally believed that Fermat, given the mathematical techniques available at the time, must have been mistaken in believing that he had a proof of the conjecture.

Fermi, Enrico (1901–1954) *Italian–American physicist*

Fermi was without doubt the greatest Italian scientist since Galileo and in the period 1925–50 was one of the most creative physicists in the world. Unusually in an age of ever-growing specialization he excelled as both an experimentalist and a theoretician.

He was born in Rome and brought up in the prosperous home of his father who, beginning as a railroad official, progressed to a senior position in government service. Fermi's intelligence and quickness of mind were apparent from an early age and he had little difficulty in gaining admission in 1918 to the Scuola Normale in Pisa, a school for the intellectual élite of Italy. He later completed his education at the University of Pisa where he gained his PhD in 1924. After spending some time abroad in Göttingen and Leiden, Fermi returned to Italy where, after some initial setbacks, he was appointed to a professorship of physics at the University of Rome. This in itself was a considerable achievement for one so young, considering the traditional and bureau-

cratic nature of Italian universities. It was no doubt due to the reputation he had already established with the publication of some 30 substantial papers, and the support of O. M. Corbino, the most distinguished Italian physicist at the time and also a senator. Corbino was determined to modernize Italian physics and had the good sense to see that Fermi, despite his youth, was the ideal man to advance his cause.

Fermi began by publishing the first Italian text on modern physics, *Introduzione alla Fisica Atomica* (1928; Introduction to Nuclear Physics). Soon his reputation attracted around him the brightest of the younger Italian physicists. But the growth of fascism in Italy led to the dispersal of its scientific talent. By 1938 Fermi, with a Jewish wife, was sufficiently alarmed by the growing anti-Semitism of the government to join the general exodus and move to America.

However, before his departure, his period in Rome turned out to be remarkably productive, with major advances being made in both the theoretical and the experimental field. His experimental work arose out of attempts to advance the efforts of Irène and Frédéric JOLIOT-CURIE who had announced in 1934 the production of artificial radioactive isotopes by the bombardment of boron and aluminum with helium nuclei (alpha particles). Fermi realized that the neutron, discovered by James Chadwick in 1932, was perhaps an even better tool for creating new isotopes. Although less massive than an alpha particle, the neutron's charge neutrality allowed it to overcome the positive charge of a target nucleus without dissipating its energy.

Fermi reported that in 1934 he had impulsively and for no apparent reason interposed paraffin between the neutron source and the target. "It was with no advance warning, no conscious prior reasoning … I took some odd piece of paraffin" and placed it in front of the incident neutrons. The effect was to increase the activation intensity by a factor that ranged from a few tens to a few hundreds. Fermi had stumbled on the phenomenon of slow neutrons. What was happening was that the neutrons were slowing down as the result of collisions with the light hydrocarbon molecules. This in turn meant that they remained in the vicinity of the target nucleus sufficiently long to increase their chance of absorption.

The production of slow neutrons was later to have a profound impact in the field of nuclear energy, both civil and military. However, Fermi's immediate task was to use them to irradiate as many of the elements as possible and to produce and investigate the properties of a large number of newly created radioactive isotopes. It was for this work, for "the discovery of new radioactive substances ... and for the discovery of the selective power of slow neutrons" that Fermi was awarded the 1938 Nobel Prize for physics.

He did however miss one significant phenomenon. In the course of their systematic irradiation of the elements Fermi and his colleagues naturally bombarded uranium with slow neutrons. This would inevitably lead to nuclear fission, but Fermi thought that transuranic elements were being produced and in his Nobel address actually referred to his production of elements 93 and 94, which he named 'ausonium' and 'hesperium'. In 1938 Otto Frisch and Lise Meitner first realized that nuclear fission was taking place in such reactions.

On the theoretical level Fermi's major achievement while at Rome was his theory of beta decay. This is the process in unstable nuclei whereby a neutron is converted into a proton with the emission of an electron and an antineutrino ($n \rightarrow p + e^- + v$). Fermi gave a detailed analysis which introduced a new force into science, the so-called 'weak' force. An account was published in Italian in 1933 as an original English version was rejected by the journal *Nature* as being too speculative.

In America Fermi soon found himself caught up in the attempt to create a controlled nuclear chain reaction. In 1942 he succeeded in building the first atomic pile in the stadium of the University of Chicago at Stagg Field. Using pure graphite as a moderator to slow the neutrons, and enriched uranium as the fissile material, Fermi and his colleagues began the construction of the pile. It consisted of some 40,000 graphite blocks, specially produced to exclude impurities, in which some 22,000 holes were drilled to permit the insertion of several tons of uranium. At 2.20 p.m. on 2 December 1942, the atomic age began as Fermi's pile went critical, supporting a self-supporting chain reaction for 28 minutes. In an historic telephone call afterwards Arthur Compton informed the managing committee that "the Italian navigator has just landed in the new world," and that the natives were friendly.

Fermi continued to work on the project and was in fact present in July 1945 when the first test bomb was exploded in the New Mexico desert. He is reported to have dropped scraps of paper as the blast reached him and, from their displacement, to have calculated the force as corresponding to 10,000 tons of TNT.

After the war Fermi accepted an appointment as professor of physics at the University of Chicago where he remained until his untimely death from cancer. His name has been commemorated in physics in various ways. Element 100, *fermium*, and the unit of length of 10^{-13} centimeter, the *fermi*, were named for him, as was the National Accelerator Laboratory, Fermilab, at Batavia, near Chicago.

Ferrel, William (1817–1891) American meteorologist

Born in Fulton County, Pennsylvania, Ferrel moved with his family to farm in West Virginia in 1829. Receiving only the most rudimentary education, his early scientific knowledge was entirely self acquired. Despite this he developed an interest in mathematical physics and, after graduating from Bethany College in West Virginia in 1844, began to study the *Principia* of Isaac Newton and the *Mécanique céleste* (Celestial Mechanics) of Pierre Simon de Laplace. He earned his living as a school teacher from 1844 until 1857 when, having established his scientific reputation, he was appointed to the staff of the American Ephemeris and Nautical Almanac. He worked there until 1867 when he joined the US Coast and Geodetic Survey.

In 1856 he published his most significant work, *Essay on the Winds and Currents of the Oceans*. He showed that all atmospheric motion, as well as ocean currents, are deflected by the Earth's rotation. He went on in 1858 to formulate his law, which states that if a mass of air is moving in any direction there is a force arising from the Earth's rotation that always deflects it to the right in the northern hemisphere and to the left in the southern hemisphere. The air tends to move in a circle whose radius depends upon its velocity and distance from the equator. Ferrel went on to show how this law could be used to explain storms and the pattern of winds and currents. He was in some ways anticipated by Gustave-Gaspard Coriolis whose name is much better known.

Ferrel also did fundamental work on the solar system. He was able to correct Laplace and show that the tidal action of the Sun and Moon on the Earth is slowly retarding the Earth's rotation. In 1864 he provided the first mathematical treatment of tidal friction. His other works included his three-volume *Meteorological Researches* (1877–82). In 1880 he invented a machine to predict tidal maxima and minima.

Feynman, Richard Phillips (1918– 1988) American theoretical physicist

The father of Feynman had been brought

with his immigrant parents from Minsk, Byelorussia, in 1895. Feynman himself was born in New York and educated at the Massachusetts Institute of Technology and at Princeton, where he completed his PhD in 1942 under the supervision of John Wheeler. In 1943 Feynman moved to Los Alamos to work on the Manhattan Project in the theoretical division under Hans Bethe. He was soon recognized to be, in the words of Robert Oppenheimer, "the most brilliant young physicist here." Feynman's own writings about the period deal less with the bomb than with his wife, Arline who was dying of TB. He had married her in 1942 against much family opposition. She moved into a sanatorium in nearby Albuquerque and died in June 1945, a month before the first atomic bomb was tested.

In 1945 Feynman moved to Cornell as professor of physics, a post he held until 1950 when he was appointed to a similar position at the California Institute of Technology, where he remained for the rest of his career. While at Cornell he began to consider anew some of the outstanding problems in quantum electrodynamics (QED) – an area of physics dealing with the interactions between electrons and photons. The electron was seen as a point charge. As the strength of a charged body diminishes with distance in accordance with the inverse square law, it will vary as $1/r^2$. But what about the strength of the charge at the electron itself where $r = 0$? At this point the charge (and for a point, density) of the electron must be infinite. To handle this and other similar absurdities physicists developed a number of artificial mathematical techniques which would allow them to 'renormalize' their equations so as to remove the infinite terms. Yet the charge on the electron is finite and can be measured accurately. Theoretical calculations, it was felt, should reach the same value without requiring artificial manipulation.

Freeman Dyson has described Feynman at this time as claiming that "he couldn't understand the official version of quantum mechanics," and that he had to "reinvent quantum mechanics" in a form he could understand. Feynman first presented his new approach in a paper, turned down by the *Physical Review*, entitled *Space-Time Approach to Non-Relativistic Quantum Mechanics* (1948) in which he introduced the notion of path integrals, also referred to as "sum over histories."

In Feynman's approach, the probability of an event that can happen in a number of different ways, such as finding an electron at a certain place, was the sum of the probabilities of all the possible ways the event

could happen. When all the probabilities were added, Feynman noted, the result was Schrödinger's wave function.

In a 1949 paper, *Space-Time Approach to Quantum Electrodynamics*, Feynman showed how to calculate these path integrals using simple sketches which have since become widely known as *Feynman diagrams*. It was for work in this field that Feynman shared the 1965 Nobel Physics prize with Julian SCHWINGER and Sin-Itiro TOMONAGA. His first reaction had been to decline what he terms "Alfred Nobel's other mistake" on the grounds that he would thereafter become a celebrity and not just someone who wanted to talk about physics. Warned that a refusal would mark him in the media as an even bigger celebrity, Feynman agreed to accept the award.

Feynman also worked on problems connected with superconductivity and with particle physics. In 1955 he devized a new model to represent the structure of liquid helium. During a visit to Stanford in 1968 Feynman began to work on the strong nuclear interaction. He attributed to the proton a set of constituents he named 'partons', which were pointlike and did not interact with each other. Their value lay in their ability to explain the inelastic scattering results emerging from the Stanford Linear Accelerator (SLAC).

With the publication in 1963 of the *Feynman Lectures in Physics*, Feynman began to be known outside the small community of theoretical physicists. However, he gained international celebrity in the 1980s following a number of TV programs and the publication of *Surely You're Joking Mr Feynman* (1985). The picture of a man of rare seriousness and honesty, with little time for honors, institutions, and formality, yet who clearly enjoyed the life of the flesh as well as the mind, had rarely been presented with such clarity. Despite his reluctance to accept the Nobel award, Feynman seems to have enjoyed his fame, and even to accentuate his unconventional character.

When he was asked to serve in 1986 on the presidential commission to investigate the explosion of the *Challenger* space shuttle, he assumed that he was being asked to contribute to a genuine scientific investigation. Pointed in the right direction by sympathetic colleagues, Feynman soon realized that the immediate cause of the explosion had been the O-ring seals used in the booster rocket. On the morning of the shuttle's launch the temperature was below freezing and the seals failed to retain their elasticity at low temperatures. Feynman also found out that the NASA officials had been warned about this potential failure.

Feynman demonstrated the point, unannounced, at a televised meeting of the commission. He placed the O-rings in a glass of iced water for a few minutes and showed that, for several seconds after their removal, the seals had lost their resilience.

Feynman wrote up his findings as a separate appendix. He was aware that, while the commission would not actually suppress any evidence, much that was critical of NASA could be scattered throughout the report and consequently picked up by only the most careful of readers. Before the commission agreed to publish his report in a form acceptable to Feynman, he first found it necessary to threaten to resign and issue the report elsewhere. Feynman found his Washington experiences genuinely distressing. Much of his life had been spent trying to understand various natural phenomena. The work had been hard, demanding many hours of intense intellectual concentration. He went to Washington intending to put the same effort into the service of the commission. Yet he found himself working with people who, though not crooks, liars, or lazy, were only marginally interested in the truth. It was more important for them to find a story acceptable to a community consisting of the Washington establishment, NASA, and "the American people," rather than to set out to establish what happened.

By this time, however, Feynman was a seriously ill man. In 1978 a malignant growth had been removed from his abdomen. A second cancer, involving bone marrow, was diagnosed in 1986. The abdominal cancer returned in late 1987 and soon after Feynman died from renal failure.

Fibiger, Johannes Andreas Grib
(1867–1928) *Danish physician*

Fibiger, born the son of a physician at Silkeborg in Denmark, was educated at the University of Copenhagen, completing his medical studies in 1890. After some hospital work and further study in Berlin under Robert Koch and Emil von Behring, Fibiger joined the Institute of Pathological Anatomy at the University of Copenhagen in 1897, serving there as its director from 1900.

It was realized that cancers could be chemically induced by factors in the environment but all attempts to induce such cancers artificially had failed. Fibiger thought he could change this when, in 1907, he observed extensive papillomatous tumors virtually filling the stomachs of three wild rats. Microscopic examination showed the presence in the stomachs of formations similar to nematode worms, and Fibiger naturally concluded that these parasites were the cause of the tumors. A search of a further 1200 wild rats, however, produced no additional cases of cancer. This suggested to him that the nematodes were transmitted by an intermediate host, and a report published in 1878 confirmed that such nematodes had been found as parasites of a common kind of cockroach. Before long Fibiger found rats from a sugar refinery that fed regularly on the cockroaches there: examination of 61 of these rats showed that 40 had nematodes in their stomachs and 7 of these 40 had the earlier identified tumor.

By 1913 Fibiger was able to claim that he could induce such malignancies in rats by feeding them with cockroaches infested with nematode larvae, noting a proportional relationship between the number of parasites and the degree of anatomic change in the stomach. It was for this work, described somewhat extravagantly by the Nobel Committee as the "greatest contribution to experimental medicine in our generation," that Fibiger was awarded the 1926 Nobel Prize for physiology or medicine.

Although no one disputed that Fibiger had induced cancer it was never completely accepted that such growths were caused by the nematodes. In any case Fibiger's work had little impact on experimental cancer research: simpler methods of carcinogenesis were almost universally preferred.

Fibonacci, Leonardo (c. 1170–c. 1250)
Italian mathematician

Fibonacci lived in Pisa and is often referred to as Leonardo of Pisa. Although he was probably the most outstanding mathematician of the Middle Ages virtually nothing is known of his life. The modern system of numerals, which originated in India and had first been introduced to the West by al-Khwarizmi, first became widely used in Europe owing to Fibonacci's popularization of it. His father served as a consul in North Africa and it is kown that Fibonacci studied with an Arabian mathematician in his youth, from whom he probably learned the decimal system of notation.

Fibonacci's main work was his *Liber abaci* (1202; Book of the Abacus) in which he expounded the virtues of the new system of numerals and showed how they could be used to simplify highly complex calculations. Fibonacci also worked extensively on the theory of proportion and on techniques for determining the roots of equations, and included a treatment of these subjects in the *Liber abaci*. In addition it contains contributions to geometry and Fibonacci later published his *Practica geometriae* (1220; Practice of Geometry), a shorter work that was devoted entirely to the subject.

Fibonacci was fortunate in being able to gain the patronage of the Holy Roman Emperor, Frederick II, and a later work, the *Liber quadratorum* (1225; Book of Square Numbers) was dedicated to his patron. This book, whch is generally considered Fibonacci's greatest achievement, deals with second order Diophantine equations. It contains the most advanced contributions to number theory since the work of Diophantus, which were not to be equaled until the work of Fermat. He discovered the *Fibonacci sequence* of integers in whch each number is equal to the sum of the preceding two (1, 1, 2, 3, 5, 8, ...).

Finsen, Niels Ryberg (1860–1904)
Danish physician

Finsen, the son of a leading civil servant, was born at Thorshavn on the Faeroe Islands, which are part of Denmark; he was educated in Reykjavik and at the University of Copenhagen, where he qualified as a physician in 1890. After teaching anatomy for some time Finsen founded (1895) the Institute of Phototherapy, which he directed until his early death at the age of 43.

In the 1890s, following up some earlier work suggesting that light had the ability to kill bacteria, Finsen began a systematic appraisal of its therapeutic effects. Arguing that it was light, acting slowly and weakly, rather than heat that was effective, he devised various filters and lenses to separate and concentrate the different components of sunlight. He found that it was the short ultraviolet rays, either natural or artificial, that turned out to have the greatest bactericidal power.

Finsen found phototherapy to be of most use against lupus vulgaris, a skin infection produced by the tubercle bacillus. He claimed that on exposure to ultraviolet rays the skin regained its normal color and the ulcerations began to heal. For this Finsen received the third Nobel Prize for physiology or medicine in 1903.

It was, however, an avenue that few physicians were willing to explore. The use of ultraviolet radiation was mainly restricted to the treatment of lupus vulgaris and even this was superseded by x-rays and, more importantly, by such drugs as cortisone when they became available in the 1950s.

Fischer, Edmond H. (1920–   )
American biochemist

Born in Shanghai, China, Fischer was educated at the University of Geneva, where, after graduation, he worked as an assistant in the organic chemistry laboratories (1946–47). After spending two years as a research fellow with the Swiss National Foundation (1948–50) he moved to the University of Washington, Seattle, as a Rockefeller Foundation research fellow (1950–53). After a brief spell at the California Institute of Technology in 1953, he was appointed assistant professor of biochemistry at the University of Washington, subsequently becoming associate professor (1956–61) and professor (1961–90).

Fischer's most acclaimed work was done at Seattle in the 1950s and 1960s in collaboration with the biochemist Edwin Krebs. In 1955–56 the scientists discovered how the enzyme (glycogen phosphorylase) that catalyzes the release of glucose from glycogen in the body is "switched on." The enzyme receives a phosphate group from ATP (adenosine triphosphate – the body's major energy carrier) in a transfer reaction catalyzed by a second enzyme, which Fischer and Krebs termed a "protein kinase." They went on to show that glycogen phosphorylase is then switched off by removal of the phosphate group by a further enzyme (called a protein phosphatase). The addition and removal of the phosphate group reversibly changes the shape of the enzyme molecule, thereby switching it between the inactive and active forms.

These findings opened the way to a major new field of research suggesting how enzymes might function in various physiological processes, such as hormone regulatory mechanisms, gene expression, and fertilization of the egg. Their work also had implications for the understanding of certain diseases; for instance, abnormally phosphorylated proteins have been identified in muscular dystrophy and diabetes, while protein kinases may play a significant role in certain cancers and in airway constriction in asthma.

In recognition of his contributions to our understanding of enzymes Fischer was awarded the 1992 Nobel Prize for physiology or medicine, which he shared with his long-time coworker, Krebs.

Fischer, Emil Hermann (1852–1919)
German organic chemist and biochemist

The son of a successful businessman from Euskirchen, now in Germany, Fischer joined his father's firm on leaving school (1869) but left in 1871 to study chemistry with August Kekulé at Bonn. He was not happy with the chemistry instruction there and came close to abandoning chemistry for physics. In 1872, however, he moved to Strasbourg to study with Adolf von Baeyer. Here, he gained his doctorate in 1874 for work on phthaleins. The same year he made the vital discovery of phenylhydrazine, a compound that was later to prove the vital key for unlocking the structures of the sugars.

Fischer became Baeyer's assistant and together they moved to Munich (1875). At Munich, working with his cousin, Otto Fischer, he proved that the natural rosaniline dyes are derivatives of triphenylmethane. In 1879 Fischer became assistant professor of analytical chemistry and soon after became financially independent. He was then professor at Erlangen (1882), Würzburg (1885), and Berlin (1892).

Fischer has some claim to be called the father of biochemistry. He carried out extremely comprehensive work in three main fields: purines, sugars, and peptides, the last two effectively founding biochemistry on a firm basis of organic chemistry. The work on purines, begun in 1882, resulted in the synthesis of many important compounds, including the alkaloids caffeine and theobromine, and purine itself (1898). Fischer's early structures were incorrect but from 1897 the correct structures were used.

In 1884 Fischer discovered that phenylhydrazine produces well-defined crystalline compounds with sugars, thus affording a reliable means of identification. In 1887 he synthesized first fructose (from acrolein dibromide) and later mannose and glucose. By 1891 he was able to deduce the configurations of the 16 possible aldohexoses, which he represented in the form of the famous Fischer projection formulae.

In 1899 Fischer turned to amino acids and peptides and devised a peptide synthesis that eventually produced a polypeptide containing 18 amino acids (1907). Fischer's other work included the first synthesis of a nucleotide (1914), the 'lock-and-key' hypothesis of enzyme action, work on tannins, and attempts to prepare very high-molecular-weight compounds. He was awarded the 1902 Nobel Prize for chemistry for his work on purines and sugars.

Fischer, Ernst Otto (1918–1994)
German inorganic chemist

Fischer, the son of a physics professor, was educated in his native city at the Munich Institute of Technology, where he obtained his PhD in 1952. He taught at the University of Munich serving as professor of inorganic chemistry from 1957 to 1964, when he became the director of the Institute for Inor-

ganic Chemistry at the Institute of Technology.

Fischer is noted for his work on inorganic complexes. In 1951 two chemists, T. Kealy and P. Pauson, were attempting to join two five-carbon (cyclopentadiene) rings together and discovered the compound $C_5H_5FeC_5H_5$, which they proposed had an iron atom joined to a carbon atom on each ring.

Fischer, on reflection, considered such a structure inadequate for he was unable to see how it could provide sufficient stability with its carbon–iron–carbon bonds. The British chemist Geoffrey WILKINSON suggested a more novel structure in which the iron atom was sandwiched between two parallel rings and thus formed bonds with the electrons in the rings, rather than with individual carbon atoms. Compounds of this type are called 'sandwich compounds'.

By careful x-ray analysis Fischer confirmed the proposed structure of ferrocene, as the compound was called, and for this work shared the Nobel Prize for chemistry with Wilkinson in 1973. Fischer went on to do further work on transition-metal complexes with organic compounds and was one of the leading workers in the field of organometallic chemistry.

Fischer, Hans (1881–1945) *German organic chemist*

Fischer, the son of a chemicals industrialist from Höchst-am-Main in Germany, gained his doctorate in chemistry at the University of Marburg in 1904. He also studied medicine at the University of Munich, gaining his MD in 1908. He was assistant to Emil Fischer before occupying chairs of medical chemistry at Innsbruck (1916) and Vienna (1918). In 1921 he succeeded Heinrich Wieland as professor at the Technical Institute in Munich.

Fischer's life work was the study of the immensely important biological molecules hemoglobin, chlorophyll, and the bile pigments, especially bilirubin. He showed that hemin – the nonprotein, iron-containing portion of the hemoglobin molecule – consists of a system of four pyrrole rings, linked by bridges, with iron in the center. He synthesized hemin in 1929 and extensively investigated similar molecules – the porphyrins. He was awarded the Nobel Prize for chemistry for this work in 1930. He then turned to the chlorophylls and showed that they are substituted porphins with magnesium rather than iron in the center. The bile acids were shown by Fischer to be degraded porphins, and he synthesized bilirubin in 1944. Fischer took his own life at the end of World War II, after his laboratories had been destroyed in the bombing of Munich.

Fisher, Sir Ronald Aylmer (1890–1962) *British statistician and geneticist*

Fisher, a Londoner by birth, studied mathematics and physics at Cambridge University, graduating in 1912. In the years before joining Rothamsted Experimental Station in 1919 he undertook a variety of jobs, including farm work in Canada, employment with an investment company, and teaching in various private schools. In this period he also produced two important papers marking his interest in both statistics and genetics. The first, published in 1915, described a solution for the exact distribution of the correlation coefficient, a problem that had been perplexing other statisticians. The second paper was *The Correlation between Relatives on the Supposition of Mendelian Inheritance* (1918). This demonstrated that the inheritance of continuous variation, which had been thought of as non-Mendelian, is in fact governed by many additive genes, each of small effect and each inherited in a Mendelian manner. Thus continuous variation may be analyzed following Mendelian rules. This work later led to the development of the science of biometric genetics. At Rothamsted, Fisher was appointed to sort out the accumulation of over 60 years' data on field trials. He modified the significance test, enabling more confident conclusions to be drawn from small samples of data, and developed the analysis of variance technique. He emphasized the need for random rather than systematic experimental design so that error due to environmental variation could be analyzed quantitatively. His book *Statistical Methods for Research Workers* (1925) is one of the most influential works in statistics.

Fisher's major researches in genetics at Rothamsted were brought together in *The Genetical Theory of Natural Selection* (1930). In this book he argued that Mendelism, far from contradicting Darwinism as some people believed, actually provides the missing link in the theory of evolution by natural selection by showing that inheritance is particulate rather than blending. (In 1936 Fisher published a paper arguing that probabilistically Mendel's famous results were "too good to be true.") The book also summarizes his views on eugenics and on genes controlling dominant characteristics. He believed that dominance develops gradually by selection, showing selection rather than mutation to be the driving force in evolution.

The Genetical Theory of Natural Selection led to Fisher's appointment as Galton Professor of Genetics at University College, London, in 1933. Here he did important work clarifying the genetics of the Rhesus blood groups. He accepted the chair of genetics at Cambridge University in 1943, remaining there until 1959 although he retired officially in 1957. He spent the last three years of his life working for the Commonwealth Scientific and Industrial Research Organization (CSIRO) in Adelaide. Fisher was knighted in 1952.

Fitch, Val Logsdon (1923–   ) *American physicist*

Born in Merriman, Nebraska, Fitch was educated at McGill and Columbia universities and obtained his PhD from Columbia in 1954. He then joined the Princeton staff, being appointed professor of physics there in 1960.

Working with Leo James Rainwater, Fitch was the first to observe radiation from muonic atoms; i.e., from species in which a muon is orbiting a nucleus rather than an electron. This work indicated that the sizes of atomic nuclei were smaller than had been supposed. He went on to study kaons and in 1964 collaborated with James CRONIN, James Christenson, and René Turley in an experiment that disproved CP conservation. In 1980 Fitch and Cronin shared the Nobel Prize for physics for this fundamental work.

Fittig, Rudolph (1835–1910) *German organic chemist*

Fittig was born in Hamburg and gained his doctorate at Göttingen in 1858, becoming a professor at Tübingen (1870) and at Strasbourg (1876–1902). He was a prolific experimentalist with many discoveries and syntheses to his credit, including pinacol, diphenyl, mesitylene, cymene, coumarone, and phenanthrene in coal tar. He also did extensive work on lactones and unsaturated acids. His name is remembered in the *Wurtz–Fittig reaction*, a variation of the Wurtz reaction for synthesizing alkylaryl hydrocarbons. An example is the reaction to form methylbenzene (toluene):

$$CH_3Cl + C_6H_5Cl + 2Na \rightarrow C_2H_5CH_3 + NaCl$$

Fitzgerald, George Francis (1851–1901) *Irish physicist. See* LORENTZ, HENDRIK.

Fizeau, Armand Hippolyte Louis (1819–1896) *French physicist*

Fizeau, a Parisian by birth, started by studying medicine but his interest turned to optics before he finished the course. In collaboration with Léon Foucault he first tried to improve the newly developed process of photography and, in 1845, they took the first clear pictures of the Sun.

In 1849 he obtained a value for the speed of light in air, using an ingenious toothedwheel apparatus. Light was directed through a gap between two teeth and reflected back between the teeth from a distant mirror. The wheel was rotated, the rate of rotation being changed until the reflected flashes were blocked by the tooth of the wheel. The speed of light could then be calculated from the rate of rotation of the wheel. Fizeau's experiment was performed using a path of 8 kilometers (5 mi) between Suresnes and Montmartre.

The next year both he and Foucault simultaneously proved that light traveled faster in air than in water, thus giving experimental support to the wave theory of light. Fizeau is also known for analyzing the Doppler effect for light waves. The change in wavelength with relative speed is sometimes called the *Doppler–Fizeau shift*.

Fizeau was elected a member of the Paris Academy in 1860 and was awarded the Royal Society's Rumford medal in 1875.

Flamsteed, John (1646–1719) *English astronomer*

Flamsteed was born in Denby. Because of ill health, which was to dog his career, he was forced to leave school early and was therefore largely self educated. He started his scientific career under the patronage of William Brouncker, the first president of the Royal Society, having impressed him by computing an almanac of celestial events for 1670.

A major problem of the time – one tackled at some time by all major astronomers of the 17th century – was the determination of longitude at sea. A suggestion had been made that the motion of the Moon against the stellar background could be used to determine standard time. Flamsteed, asked by Brouncker to comment on this proposal, pointed out that the scheme was impractical because of the inaccuracy of contemporary tables. Charles II subsequently commanded that accurate tables should be constructed, appointing Flamsteed as first Astronomer Royal with this responsibility in 1675, and building the Royal Greenwich Observatory for him, which was opened in 1676. The limited nature of the royal patronage is indicated by the fact that Flamsteed was paid a salary of £100 a year but was expected to provide his own instruments and staff. He eventually

managed to put together two small telescopes and then began his decades of observation, made more difficult by his lack of staff and the crippling headaches from which he suffered. In order to make ends meet he was forced to become a clergyman at Burstow in Surrey from 1684 until his death.

The results of his labors were eventually published posthumously in 1725 as the *Historia coelestis Britannica* (British Celestial Record). It contains the position of over 3000 stars calculated to an accuracy of ten seconds of arc. It was the first great modern comprehensive telescopic catalog and established Greenwich as one of the leading observatories of the world. The publication of the work was not without its difficulties. It involved Flamsteed in a long and bitter dispute with Newton. Flamsteed was reluctant to rush into print with his catalog, claiming, it seemed to Newton, far too much time for the checking of his numerous observations. The dispute lasted from Newton's assumption of the presidency of the Royal Society in 1703 until Flamsteed's death. It involved the virtual seizure of Flamsteed's papers by Newton, the editing and partial publication by Edmond Halley, and their total rejection by Flamsteed who even went so far as to acquire 300 of the 400 printed copies of his own work and burn them. He managed, however, to revise the first volume to his satisfaction before his death in 1719.

Fleischmann, Martin (1927–   ) *British chemist*

Born in Karlsbad, Czechoslovakia, Fleischmann and his family fled to Britain in 1939. He was educated at Imperial College, London where he gained his PhD in 1951. He taught chemistry at the University of Durham (1952–57) and at Newcastle University (1957–67). In 1967 he was appointed professor of electrochemistry at the University of Southampton.

By 1988 Fleischmann had an international reputation as a productive and innovative electrochemist. Between 1985 and 1988 he coauthored 29 papers with his former student, the American chemist **Stanley Pons** (1943–   ). Quite unexpectedly, in March 1989, they announced that they had achieved nuclear fusion by an electrolytic method under laboratory conditions at room temperature.

Nuclear fusion, the fusion of two light atomic nuclei to produce a heavier nucleus, is a process accompanied by large amounts of released energy. For fusion to occur the nuclei have to be brought close together, and this involves overcoming a high energy barrier caused by the mutual repulsion of the nuclei.

In practical cases this is achieved by high temperatures, as in the Sun or in thermonuclear weapons. Experimental thermonuclear reactors such as the tokomak also use high temperatures (about 300 million degrees) to initiate fusion. There is, however, considerable interest in methods of initiating fusion at low temperatures – so-called 'cold fusion'. One approach to this has been *inertial confinement*, in which a sample of material is compressed by intense laser beams or particle beams.

Fleischmann and Pons also thought that pressure might be a way of initiating cold fusion. Palladium metal has a high affinity for hydrogen and, under the right conditions, can absorb large quantities of it. They electrolyzed water containing the deuterium isotope using a palladium cathode and reasoned that the palladium might absorb so much deuterium that the effective deuterium pressure within the electrode would be high enough to cause nuclear fusion. If this occurred, there would be a large increase in temperature, over and above that produced by the heating effect of the current. Fleischmann and Pons reported just such an effect.

Fleischmann was reluctant to reveal too many details of their work lest it prejudice their patent application. He did, however, collaborate with Harwell, the British Atomic Energy Research Establishment, who were best suited to replicate cold fusion. They found no evidence of fusion, no excess heat. Whereas positive results had been obtained by several leading institutions, they were subsequently withdrawn when errors were detected. Despite such setbacks Fleischmann has remained convinced of the essential soundness of his work with Pons.

Since 1990 Fleischmann's work has been mainly supported by Minora Toyoda, a Japanese businessman; he is currently based in Sophia Antipolis, a research center established by Toyoda outside Nice, France, concerned with the development of future technology.

Fleming, Sir Alexander (1881–1955)
British bacteriologist

Fleming was born at Lochfield in Scotland. After his early education at Kilmarnock Academy and the London Polytechnic Institute, he began his career at the age of 16 as a shipping clerk in a London office. With encouragement from his brother, who was a doctor, he became a medical student at St.

Mary's Hospital Medical School in 1902 and graduated from the University of London in 1908. He worked at St. Mary's all his life apart from 1914–18, when he served in the Royal Army Medical Corps. During this time he became interested in the control of wound infections and was a vigorous supporter of the physiological treatment of wounds rather than treatment using harsh chemicals, such as carbolic acid. In the 1920s he studied various body secretions and their effects on bacteria. Thus he discovered lysozyme, a bacteriolytic enzyme that is present in serum, saliva, and tears, publishing his findings in 1922.

In 1928 Fleming was appointed professor of bacteriology and in the same year he made his most important discovery. After accidentally leaving a dish of staphylococcus bacteria uncovered, Fleming noticed certain clear areas in the culture. He found these areas were due to contamination by a mold he identified as *Penicillium notatum*, which produced a substance that killed the bacteria. Fleming named this substance 'penicillin' and tested the bactericidal effect of the mold on various different bacteria, observing that it killed some but not others. He appreciated the potential of his discovery but was unable to isolate and identify the compound. It was not until World War II, with the urgent need for new antibacterial drugs, that penicillin – the first antibiotic – was finally isolated by Howard FLOREY and Ernst CHAIN.

Fleming was awarded the 1945 Nobel Prize for physiology or medicine jointly with Florey and Chain for his discovery, which initiated a whole new range of life-saving antibiotics. He received a knighthood in 1944 and many other honors.

Fleming, Sir John Ambrose (1849–1945) *British physicist and electrical engineer*

Fleming, who was born at Lancaster, studied for a short time at University College, London, but left before graduating. However, he continued his work for a science degree in his leisure hours while employed first in a shipwright's drawing office and later as a stockbroker's clerk. Between 1871 and 1880 he had alternate periods of school science teaching and further study, including working under James Clerk Maxwell from 1877 at the new Cavendish Laboratory in Cambridge. In 1881 he was appointed professor of mathematics and physics at University College, Nottingham. From 1882 to 1885 he worked as consultant to the Edison Electric Light Company in London. He was then appointed professor of electrical technology at University College, London, a post he held for 41 years.

At University College Fleming gave special courses and experimented on wireless telegraphy, cooperating a great deal with Guglielmo Marconi. One of Fleming's outstandingly important inventions was the thermionic vacuum tube, a rectifying device based on an effect discovered by Thomas Edison. Fleming's diode consisted of a glass bulb containing two electrodes. One, a metal filament, was heated to incandescence by an electric current, so that it emitted electrons by thermionic emission. The second electrode (the anode) could collect electrons if held at a positive potential with respect to the filament (the cathode) and a current would flow. Current could not flow in the opposite direction – hence the name 'valve' for such devices. Lee de Forest developed the device into the triode for amplifying current.

Other scientific contributions by Fleming included investigations into the property of materials, transformer design, electrical measurements, and photometry. He was an outstanding teacher and highly successful as a popular lecturer. *Fleming's left hand rule* and *right hand rule* are mnemonics for relating the direction of motion, magnetic field, and electric current in electric motors and generators respectively.

Fleming, Williamina (1857–1911)
Scottish–American astronomer

Williamina Paton, as she was born, came from Dundee and worked for several years as a schoolteacher. In 1877 she married James Fleming and emigrated with him to Boston, Massachusetts, in 1878. Her marriage broke up and, forced to support her young son, she worked for Edward Pickering, director of the Harvard College Observatory, as a maid. As it was his policy to employ young women at the observatory as computers, Pickering, who quickly recognized her intelligence, offered her temporary employment as a copyist and computer in 1879. She was given a permanent post in 1881. She remained at the observatory for the rest of her life, serving as curator of astronomical photographs from 1899 until her death.

She worked with Pickering on the basic classification of stars into spectral types and was thus involved in the introduction of the original 17 classes arranged alphabetically from A to Q in terms of the intensity of the hydrogen spectral lines. This system was later modified and improved by her colleagues Annie Cannon and Antonia Maury. Fleming was largely responsible for the classification of over 10,000 stars, published in 1890 in the *Draper Catalogue of Stellar Spectra*. In the course of her work she discovered 10 novae and over 200 variable stars, and estimated that by 1910 she had examined nearly 200,000 photographic plates.

Flemming, Walther (1843–1905)
German cytologist

Flemming was born at Sachsenberg, now in Germany, and graduated in medicine from the University of Rostock in 1868. However, after a short period working in a hospital, he turned to physiology and became assistant to Willy Kuhne at the Institute of Physiology in Amsterdam. After serving as a physician in the Franco-Prussian War he held professional posts at Prague (1873) and Kiel (1876).

By making use of the newly synthesized aniline dyes Flemming was able to discern the threadlike structures in the cell nucleus, which Heinrich Waldeyer was later to term chromosomes. The new staining techniques made it possible for Flemming to follow in far greater detail the process of cell division, which he named 'mitosis' from the Greek for thread. Most importantly, Flemming detailed the fundamental process of mitosis, that is, the splitting of the chromosomes along their lengths into two identical halves. These results were published in the seminal book *Zell-substanz, Kern und Zelltheilung* (1882; Cytoplasm, Nucleus and Cell Division). It was another 20 years before the significance of Flemming's work was truly realized with the rediscovery of Gregor Mendel's rules of heredity.

Flerov, Georgii Nikolaevich (1913–)
Russian nuclear physicist

Born at Rostov-on-Don, now in Russia, and educated at the Leningrad Industrial Institute of Science, Flerov started his career at the Leningrad Institute of Physics and Technology in 1938. He later became chief of the laboratory of multicharged ions at the Kurchatov Institute of Atomic Energy, Moscow.

Throughout his life, Flerov has been involved in the search for new elements and isotopes through synthesis and discovery. In many ways his work parallels that of Glenn Theodore Seaborg and his research team in America.

Flerov and his coworkers synthesized and analyzed isotopes of elements 102, 103, 104, 105, 106, and 107 (members of the actinide group and transactinides) by bombarding nuclei of heavy elements with heavy ions in a cyclotron. In particular, they have a claim to the first discovery or identification of transactinide elements 104 (1964) and 107 (1968). The correct attribution of these discoveries is still in dispute. Besides his work on the transuranic elements, Flerov has also been involved in the search, both by synthesis and discovery in nature (possibly in cosmic rays), of the postulated superheavy elements. Many theorists believe that although elements beyond the actinides in the periodic table would be highly unstable, there may be 'islands of stability' at higher atomic numbers, if they can only be reached.

In 1960 Flerov became director of the nuclear radiation laboratories of the Joint Institute for Nuclear Research, Dubna, near Moscow.

Florey, Howard Walter, Baron Florey of Adelaide (1898–1968) *Australian experimental pathologist*

Florey was born and educated in Adelaide and graduated in medicine from the university there in 1921. Early in 1922 he arrived in Oxford, on a Rhodes scholarship and studied physiology for two years under Charles Sherrington. He then moved to Cambridge University where he studied the various roles and behavior of cells and their constituents for his PhD degree.

In 1931 he was appointed professor of pathology at Sheffield University and for four years studied mucus secretions and the role of the cell in inflammation. He was especially interested in the chemical action of lysozyme (an enzyme discovered in 1921 by Alexander FLEMING), which is an antibacterial agent that catalyzes the destruction of the cell walls of certain bacteria.

In 1935 Florey became head of the Sir William Dunn School of Pathology at Oxford. Here, along with the biochemist Ernst CHAIN, he took up Fleming's neglected studies on *Penicillium* mold and in 1939 they succeeded in extracting an impure form of the highly reactive compound penicillin. Florey's work on penicillin was a natural extension of his earlier antibacterial work, inspired by the necessity for efficient antibiotics in wartime. Work continued over the next few years on the purification of the drug. The main problem was that vast quantities of mold needed to be grown for just a few milligrams of penicillin. In wartime Britain the necessary financial backing for these innovative biochemical engineering developments could not be obtained, and permission was given to use companies in America for the manufacture of the drug. The considerable problems of large-scale production were overcome and from 1943 onward sufficient penicillin was available to treat war casualties as well as cases of pneumonia, meningitis, syphilis, and diphtheria.

Florey is important as a scientist who took Fleming's discovery and made it into a workable treatment for disease – 15 years after the original discovery. He shared the Nobel Prize for physiology or medicine with Chain and Fleming in 1945. He had been knighted in 1944, and in 1965 he was raised to the British peerage.

Flory, Paul John (1910–1985) *American polymer chemist*

Flory was born at Sterling, Illinois, and educated at Ohio State University, where he obtained his PhD in 1934. His career was divided between industry and university. He worked with Du Pont from 1934 until 1938 on synthetic polymers and then spent the next two years at the University of Cincinnati. After working for Standard Oil from 1940 until 1943, Flory served as Director of Fundamental Research for the Goodyear Tire Company in Akron, Ohio, until 1948. He was then appointed to the chair of chemistry at Cornell. He left Cornell in 1957 to become director of research of the Mellon Institute in Pittsburgh and, finally, in 1961, accepted the chair of chemistry at Stanford University, California.

Flory was one of the people who, in the 1930s, began working on the properties of polymers. A particular problem at the time was that polymer molecules do not have a definite size and structure; a given polymeric material consists of a large number of macromolecules with different chain lengths. Flory approached this problem using statistical methods, obtaining expressions for the distribution of chain lengths.

In further work he developed a theory of nonlinear polymers, which involve cross linkages between molecular chains. He showed how such extended structures can form from a solution of linear polymers. A particular innovation was the concept of *Flory temperature* – a temperature for a given solution at which meaningful measurements can be made of the properties of the polymer.

In later work Flory considered the elasticity of rubbers and similar polymeric materials. He published two authoritative books: *Principles of Polymer Chemistry* (1953) and *Statistical Mechanics of Chain Molecules* (1969). For his major contribution in the field Flory was awarded the Nobel Prize for chemistry in 1974.

Flourens, Jean Pierre Marie (1794–1867) *French physician and anatomist*

Flourens, who was born at Maureilhan in France, studied medicine at the University of Montpellier, graduating in 1813. Moving to Paris he was fortunate enough to be taken in hand by the powerful Georges Cuvier, serving as his deputy at the Collège de France from 1828. After Cuvier's death in 1832, Flourens succeeded him as professor of anatomy and secretary of the Académie des Sciences.

In 1824 Flourens published his highly influential *Recherches expérimentales sur les propriétés et les fonctions du système nerveux dans les animaux vertébrés* (Experimental Researches on the Properties and Functions of the Nervous System in Vertebrates) in which he demonstrated the main roles of different parts of the central nervous system. Extending the work of the Italian anatomist Luigi Rolando on the nervous system, Flourens removed various parts of the brain and carefully observed the resulting changes. Thus he found that removal of the cerebral hemispheres of a pigeon destroyed the sense of perception. Removal of the cerebellum destroyed coordination and equilibrium and excision of the medulla oblongata caused respiration to cease. He also exposed the spinal cord of a dog from head to tail and found that while stimulation lower down would produce movement there came a point higher up where no muscular reaction could be elicited. Flourens is also known for important work on the semicircular canals in the ear, demonstrating their function in balance.

Although Flourens assigned different roles to different anatomical parts of the brain he was not prepared to go further and localize different roles and powers within each part. It was not until 1870 that Gustav Fritsch and Eduard Hitzig were able to break this unitary picture and establish cerebral localization experimentally.

Flourens is also remembered for his attack on Darwin in his *Examen du livre de M. Darwin* (1864; Examination of Mr. Darwin's Book) in which he poured scorn on Darwin's "childish and out of date personifications."

Fock, Vladimir Alexandrovich

(1898–   ) *Soviet theoretical physicist. See* SCHRÖDINGER, ERWIN.

Folkers, Karl August (1906–   )
American organic chemist

Folkers was born in Decatur, Illinois, graduated in chemistry from the University of Illinois in 1928, and gained his PhD from the University of Wisconsin in 1931. After postdoctoral work at Yale he joined the pharmaceutical manufacturers Merck and Company in 1934, becoming director of organic and biochemical research in 1945. He was president of the Stanford Research Institute from 1963 to 1968, and then director of the Institute for Biomedical Research at the University of Texas.

In 1948 Folkers' team isolated the antipernicious anemia factor, vitamin B_{12} (cyanocobalamin) and they played a major role in the lengthy process of determining the structure of this molecule. Folkers has been involved in many investigations of biologically active compounds, especially antibiotics, and the structure of streptomycin was largely determined by his group in 1948.

Forest, Lee de *See* DE FOREST, LEE.

Forrester, Jay (1918–   ) *American computer engineer*

Forrester, born on a cattle ranch in Nebraska, attended a small country school before studying electrical engineering at the University of Nebraska. He went on to do graduate work at MIT on servomechanisms.

This led him, in 1945, to begin work on the design of a flight simulator for the US Navy. He soon discovered that, without high-speed servomechanisms, realistic systems could not be developed. At this point he was directed, in 1946, toward the possibility that digital computers could be used. Forrester set up a laboratory to tackle what became known as the 'Whirlwind Project'. The Whirlwind, the largest computer of the time, became operational in the early 1950s. Problems, however, soon emerged. With several thousand vacuum tubes, each with a life of about 500 hours, regular breakdowns occurred.

Forrester's first advance was to increase the life of the tubes using new materials and a checking system. However, the main problem was with the machine's memory, which consisted of electrostatic storage tubes. These were expensive and unreliable, with each tube lasting no more than 1 month and costing $1000 to replace. Consequently, Forrester began to think about magnetic systems of data storage. He used magnetic ferrite rings on a grid of wires in a three-dimensional array. Each ring could be magnetized in one of two directions to represent the binary digits 1 or 0. The method was first employed in 1953, and gave an access time twice as fast as that using storage tubes.

The improvements were opportune. Following the political crises of the early coldwar years, the SAGE (Semi Automatic Ground Environment) project was initiated by the US Navy under the supervision of Forrester. Very reliable and very fast computers were needed to analyze air traffic, identify any likely threat, and guide interceptors to hostile planes or missiles. SAGE proved remarkably effective, coming into full operation in 1958 and remaining active until 1984.

Forrester left the project in 1956, moving to the MIT Sloan Management School as professor of management with the aim of developing computer systems capable of simulating economic and social systems. He has explained his approach in a number of works, including *Industrial Dynamics* (1961), *Principles of Systems* (1968), and *World Dynamics* (1971).

Forssmann, Werner Theodor Otto
(1904–1979) *German surgeon and urologist*

Forssmann was educated at the university in his native city of Berlin where he qualified as a physician in 1929. He then worked in the 1930s as a surgeon in various German hospitals. After the war he practiced as a urologist at Bad Kreuznach from 1950 until 1958 when he moved to Düsseldorf as head of surgery at the Evangelical Hospital.

In 1929 Forssmann introduced the procedure of cardiac catheterization into medicine. He was struck by the danger inherent in the direct injection of drugs into the heart frequently demanded in an emergency. The alternative that he proposed sounded no less alarming – introducing a catheter through the venous system from a vein in the elbow directly into the right atrium of the heart. Drugs could then be introduced through this.

After practice on cadavers and an unsuccessful attempt on himself made with the aid of a nervous colleague, Forssmann decided to do the whole thing himself. He consequently introduced a 65-centimeter (25.6-in) catheter for its entire length, walked up several flights of stairs to the x-ray department and calmly confirmed that the tip of the catheter had in fact reached his heart. There had been no pain or discomfort.

Unfortunately further development was inhibited by criticism from the medical profession, which assumed the method must be dangerous. Consequently it was left to André COURNAND and Dickinson RICHARDS to develop the technique into a routine clinical tool in the 1940s; for this work they shared the Nobel Prize for physiology or medicine with Forssmann in 1956.

Foucault, Jean Bernard Léon (1819–1868) *French physicist*

Foucault, the son of a Parisian bookseller, originally intended to study medicine, but transferred his interest to physical science. In 1855 he became a physicist at the Paris Observatory.

His main work was on measurements of the speed of light. He helped Armand Fizeau in his toothed-wheel experiment and, in 1850, took over D. F. J. Arago's experiments on comparing the speed of light in air with that in water. The experiment was important for distinguishing between the wave and particle theories of light: the wave theory predicted that light should travel faster in air than in water; the particle theory predicted the opposite. In 1850, Foucault showed that the wave-theory prediction was correct. In 1862 he obtained the first accurate value for the speed of light using a rotating-mirror apparatus.

Foucault also worked on other topics. Thus he noted (1849) that a bright yellow line in the spectrum of sodium corresponded to a dark line in the Fraunhofer spectrum of the sun, although he failed to follow this up.

His most famous experiments began in 1850 and involved pendulums. While trying to construct an accurate timing device for his work on light, he noticed that a pendulum remained swinging in the same plane when he rotated the apparatus. He then used a pendulum to demonstrate the rotation of the Earth. Over a long period of time the plane in which a pendulum is swinging will appear to rotate. In fact the pendulum swings in a fixed plane relative to the fixed stars, and the Earth rotates 'underneath' it.

At the Earth's poles, the plane of the pendulum will make one full rotation every 24 hours; this period increases as the equator is approached. Foucault derived an equation relating the time of rotation to the latitude. He also gave public exhibitions of the effect, including one in which he suspended an iron ball of 28 kilograms (62 lbs) by steel wire 67 meters (222 ft) long from the dome of the Panthéon in Paris. Foucault also invented the gyroscope.

Fourier, Baron (Jean Baptiste) Joseph (1768–1830) *French mathematician*

Fourier, the son of a tailor from Auxerre in France, was educated at the local military school and later at the Ecole Normale in Paris. He held posts at both the Ecole Normale and the Ecole Polytechnique where he was a very effective and influential teacher. In 1798 he accompanied Napoleon on the invasion of Egypt and later contributed to and oversaw the publication of the *Description de l'Egypte* (1808–25), a massive compilation of the cultural and scientific materials brought back from the expedition.

Fourier's most important mathematical work is contained in his *Théorie analytique de la chaleur* (1822; The Analytical Theory of Heat), a pioneering analysis of the conduction of heat in solid bodies in terms of infinite trigonometric series, now known as *Fourier series*. Fourier was led to consider these series when attempting to solve certain boundary-value problems in physics and his interest was always in the physical applications of mathematics rather than in its development for its own sake. His work continues to be extremely important in many areas of mathematical physics, but it has also been developed and generalized to yield a whole new branch of mathematical analysis, namely, the theory of harmonic analysis.

Fowler, Alfred (1868–1940) *British astrophysicist*

Although born into a poor family in Bradford, Fowler gained a scholarship and in 1882 went to the Normal School of Science (later to become the Royal College of Science and now part of Imperial College, London). After graduating with a diploma in mechanics, he became assistant to Norman Lockyer at the Solar Physics Observatory in South Kensington, London. He remained there after Lockyer's retirement in 1901, being made professor of astrophysics in 1915. Finally, from 1923 to 1934 he served as Yarrow Research Professor of the Royal Society. Fowler was one of the leading figures behind the founding of the International Astronomical Union in 1919, serving as its first general secretary until 1925.

Not surprisingly Fowler worked very much in the Lockyer tradition of solar and stellar spectroscopy. He became particularly skilled in identifying difficult spectra, using his experience in producing different spectra in the laboratory. He thus detected magnesium hydride in sunspots and carbon monoxide in the tails of comets, and showed that the band spectra of cool M-type stars were due to titanium oxide. In addition, following the announcement in 1913 of the Bohr theory of the atom, Fowler was outstanding in analyzing the structure of atoms from their special characteristics.

Fowler, William Alfred (1911–1995) *American physicist*

Fowler was born in Pittsburgh, Pennsylvania, graduated in 1933 from Ohio State University, and obtained his PhD in 1936 from the California Institute of Technology. He was immediately appointed to the staff, serving as professor of physics there from 1946 to 1970; he was Institute Professor from 1970 and professor emeritus from 1982.

Fowler worked mainly in nuclear physics, especially on the nuclear reactions that occur in stars and by which energy is produced and the elements synthesized, on nuclear forces, and on nuclear spectroscopy. In 1957 Margaret and Geoffrey BURBIDGE, Fred HOYLE, and Fowler published a key paper dealing with the problem of the creation of the chemical elements in the interiors of stars. They were aware that the hot big bang proposed by George Gamow could produce nothing heavier than helium. Clearly the elements were produced later. They therefore had to identify nuclear reactions that could occur at the immense temperatures of stellar cores; the type of process changed, and hence changed the elements being produced, as the temperature increased and conditions altered inside the stars. A later and fuller version was published by Fowler and Hoyle in their *Nucleosynthesis in Massive Stars and Supernovae* (1965).

Fowler subsequently worked on such fundamental questions as the amount of helium and deuterium in the universe, the answers to such questions having profound implications for knowledge of the age and future development of the universe.

For his work on nuclear astrophysics, Fowler shared the 1983 Nobel Prize for physics with Subrahmanyan CHANDRASEKHAR.

Fox, Harold Munro (1889–1967) *British zoologist*

Fox (originally Fuchs), the son of an officer in the Prussian army, was born in London and educated at Cambridge University; after war service, he served as a fellow from 1920 to 1928. He then moved to Birmingham as professor of zoology, a post he held until 1941 when he accepted a similar chair at Bedford College, London, where he remained until his retirement in 1954.

Fox, a zoologist of wide interests, is best known for his work on invertebrate blood pigments. In 1871 Ray Lankester had noted that the red blood of the water flea *Daphnia*, a crustacean, was due to the presence of the pigment hemoglobin. Other crustaceans, such as lobsters, were blue-blooded with the pigment hemocyanin in their blood.

It had been observed that the transparent *Daphnia* could become redder or paler by synthesizing or breaking down blood hemoglobin. This was done at a rate far in excess of that noted in any other creature. Fox showed by laboratory experiments in the 1940s that the response was controlled by the level of dissolved oxygen in the water. If this were low, hemoglobin, with its affinity for oxygen, was synthesized; if high, *Daphnia* lose their hemoglobin and become colorless.

Earlier, in 1923, Fox had repeated the controversial experiments of Paul Kammerer on the supposed elongations produced in the siphons of the sea squirt *Ciona intestinalis*. He reported that in none of the operated animals was there any further growth of the siphons once the original length had been attained, and went on to suggest that Kammerer's results could have been produced by keeping the animals in a highly nutritious solution, an explanation Kammerer was quick to dismiss.

Fraenkel-Conrat, Heinz L. (1910–   )
German–American biochemist

Fraenkel-Conrat, son of the noted gynecologist Ludwig Fraenkel, was born in Breslau (which was then in Germany and is now Wrocław in Poland). He left Germany for Britain after graduating MD from the University of Breslau in 1934. Having gained his PhD for work on ergot alkaloids and thiamine from the University of Edinburgh in 1936, he moved on to America, where he settled and became an American citizen in 1941. He joined the faculty of the University of California at Berkeley in 1951, becoming professor of virology in 1955 and professor emeritus in 1981.

Fraenkel-Conrat, working with the tobacco mosaic virus (TMV), an RNA virus, provided evidence that RNA, like DNA, can act as the genetic material. This he did by separating the RNA and protein portions of the virus, and then reassembling them to make a fully infective virus. Moreover Fraenkel-Conrat demonstrated that, while the isolated protein was quite dead, the isolated RNA showed slight signs of infectivity. This work was reported in a paper by Fraenkel-Conrat and Robley C. Williams *Reconstitution of Tobacco Mosaic Virus from Its Inactive Protein and Nucleic Acid Components* (1955). In later work with Wendell Stanley the complete amino-acid sequence, consisting of 158 amino acids, of the TMV protein was established.

Fraenkel-Conrat, in collaboration with R. R. Wagner, edited one of the basic texts of modern virology, *Comprehensive Virology* (19 vols.; 1974–84).

Francis, Thomas Jr. (1900–1969)
American virologist

Francis, the son of a methodist clergyman from Gas City, Indiana, was educated at Allegheny College and Yale where he obtained his MD in 1925. He worked with the Rockefeller Institute from 1925 to 1938 and, after serving as professor and chairman of bacteriology at the New York University College of Medicine, moved to the University of Michigan in 1941 as professor of epidemiology, a post he retained until his death.

Francis became known to a wide public when, in 1954, he reported on the Salk polio vaccine trial. Before this however he had worked for over 20 years on the epidemiology of the influenza virus. The first such virus, the A-type, had been detected by Christopher Andrewes and his colleagues in 1933. In the following year Francis found a further strain of the A-type, the PR 8, present in the Puerto Rican epidemic of 1934. In 1940 he went on to detect a completely distinct type, B, with no immunological relationship to the A-type.

The US Army, fearful of a repeat of the 1918 flu epidemic, set up in 1941 a commission to develop a vaccine and asked Francis to be its chairman. By 1942 he was ready to vaccinate 8000 soldiers with his vaccine but, perversely, flu was scarce that year. It was not until 1943 that he was able to report that those vaccinated were 70% less likely to be hospitalized compared with the control group. This encouraged the army to vaccinate some 1,250,000 troops in 1947 but this time it disconcertingly seemed to offer no protection at all.

It soon became clear to Francis why the vaccine had failed – the arrival of a new strain of A-type virus, known as A^1. Francis was thus able to present the dilemma facing flu epidemiologists, namely that while it was certainly possible to develop a vaccine against flu it was more than likely that it would end up as a vaccine against yesterday's flu.

Franck, James (1882–1964) *German–American physicist*

Franck, the son of a banker from Hamburg, was educated at Heidelberg and Berlin where he obtained his doctorate in 1906. After distinguished war service, in which he won two iron crosses, he was appointed to the chair of experimental physics at Göttingen. Although exempt from the 1933 Nazi law that excluded Jews from public office because of his military service, he insisted on publicly resigning. After spending a year in Copenhagen, he emigrated to America in 1935 where he served as professor of physical chemistry at the University of Chicago from 1938 to 1949.

In collaboration with Gustav HERTZ he produced experimental evidence of the quantized nature of energy transfer, work that won them the 1925 Nobel Prize for physics. Their experiment, conducted in 1914, consisted of bombarding mercury atoms with electrons. Most of the electrons simply bounced off losing no energy in the process. When the velocity of electrons was increased it was found that on collision with mercury atoms they lost precisely 4.9 electronvolts (eV) of energy. If an electron possessed less energy than 4.9 eV it lost none at all on collision; if it had more than 4.9 eV it made no difference – only 4.9 eV was absorbed by the mercury atoms. Franck and Hertz had thus succeeded in showing that energy can only be absorbed in quite definite and precise amounts. For mercury the minimum amount was 4.9 eV. Their results were quickly confirmed and shown to hold for other atoms.

In America Franck worked mainly on the physical chemistry involved in photosynthesis although he is better known as the author of the *Franck report* published in 1946. This report, actually produced by a number of distinguished scientists of whom Leo Szilard was probably the most important, was sent to the Secretary of State for War in June 1945. It argued that it was not necessary to drop the recently produced atomic bomb on Japan as its explosion on a barren island would be sufficient to force the Japanese into submission.

Frank, Ilya Mikhailovich (1908–1990)
Russian physicist. See CHERENKOV, PAVEL ALEKSEYEVICH.

Frankland, Sir Edward (1825–1899)
British organic chemist

Born at Churchtown near Lancaster, Frankland was first apprenticed to a pharmacist in Lancaster; he was later encouraged to go to London to study chemistry under Lyon Playfair at the Royal College of Engineers (1845). He became Playfair's assistant in 1847 and studied extensively in Europe with Robert Bunsen and Justus von Liebig. He succeeded Playfair as professor of chemistry in 1850, holding the same position at Owens College, Manchester, (1851–57) and in London at St. Bartholomew's Hospital (1857), the Royal Institution (1863), and the Royal School of Mines (1865), later the Royal College of Science.

Frankland is generally credited as the originator of the theory of valence – this being the number of chemical bonds that a given atom or group can make with other atoms or groups in forming a compound. In 1852 he noticed that coordination with an alkyl group could change the combining power of a metal. He showed that the concept of valence could reconcile the radical and type theories and in 1866 he elaborated the concept of a maximum valence for each element.

In 1864, working with B. F. Duppa, Frankland pointed out that the carboxyl group (–COOH, which he called 'oxatyl') is a constant feature of the series of organic acids. He was also interested in applied chemistry: he investigated the luminosity of flames and his later work was in the field of coalgas supply and water purification. He was knighted in 1897.

Franklin, Benjamin (1706–1790)
American scientist, statesman, diplomat, printer, and inventor

Franklin's father left England in 1682 and the following year settled in Boston, Massachusetts, where he worked as a candle maker and soap boiler. Although originally intended for the clergy, Franklin, who was born in Boston, was forced to leave school at the age of ten for financial reasons; after helping his father for some time he was apprenticed to his brother, a printer, in 1718.

He continued his trade as a printer in London (1724–26), and thereafter in Philadelphia where he published, from 1729, the *Pennsylvania Gazette* and, from 1733, the hugely successful *Poor Richard's Almanac*. Shortly afterward Franklin began his life in public affairs serving as clerk of the State Assembly (1736–51) and as deputy postmaster representing the colonies (1753–74), during which he saw further service in London (1757–62; 1764–75). On his return to America Franklin played an active role in the revolution and was one of the five who drafted the Declaration of Independence in 1776. He was sent to France in 1776 to seek military and financial aid for the colonies and largely through his own popularity succeeded in achieving an alliance in 1778. Returning to America in 1785, he performed his last public duty as a member of the Constitution Convention in 1787 before retiring from public life in 1788.

Despite such an active political and public life Franklin also made important contributions to 18th-century physical theory in the period 1743–52. By conversation with scholars in London, reading, and correspondence with friends, his interest in the newly discovered phenomena of electricity had been aroused.

Franklin would have known of the work

of Stephen Gray and Charles Dufay and the basic distinction established between electrics (such as glass and amber), which could be electrified by rubbing, and non-electrics (such as metals), which resisted such treatment. Electrics were further divided into vitreous substances, such as glass, and resinous substances, such as amber. Dufay had concluded that there were two distinct electric fluids – the vitreous and the resinous – in his two-fluid theory.

Franklin agreed with Dufay that electricity was a fluid. More significant properties of electricity emerged out of Franklin's experiments from 1747 onward. From these experiments, including those on the Leyden jar, Franklin devised his one-fluid theory of electricity. He also introduced the terminology of 'positive' and 'negative' into the science.

Practical gains emerged from Franklin's discovery that lightning is an electric charge. He knew that the electric fluid was attracted by points but wondered if lightning would also be attracted. In 1752 he performed his famous, yet hazardous, experiment with a kite during a thunderstorm and established the identity of lightning with electricity. Following this he suggested the use of lightning rods on tall buildings to conduct electricity away from the building and direct to ground.

Franklin also published works on the problems of light, heat, and dynamics. Outside of physics Franklin's most important scientific work was in oceanography with his study of the Gulf Stream. He measured its temperature at different places and depths, estimated the current's velocity, and analyzed its effects on the weather. From reports supplied to him by Nantucket sea captains he also constructed the first printed chart of the Gulf Stream. Franklin is also remembered for his large number of inventions that included (in addition to his lightning rod) bifocal spectacles, the rocking chair, and an efficient stove.

Franklin, Rosalind (1920–1958) *British x-ray crystallographer*

Franklin was a Londoner by birth. After graduating from Cambridge University, she joined the staff of the British Coal Utilisation Research Association in 1942, moving in 1947 to the Laboratoire Centrale des Services Chimique de L'Etat in Paris. She returned to England in 1950 and held research appointments at London University, initially at King's College from 1951 to 1953 and thereafter at Birkbeck College until

her untimely death from cancer at the age of 37.

Franklin played a major part in the discovery of the structure of DNA by James WATSON and Francis CRICK. With the unflattering and distorted picture presented by Watson in his *The Double Helix* (1968) her role in this has become somewhat controversial. At King's, she had been recruited to work on biological molecules and her director, John Randall, had specifically instructed her to work on the structure of DNA. When she later learned that Maurice WILKINS, a colleague at King's, also intended to work on DNA, she felt unable to cooperate with him. Nor did she feel much respect for the early attempts of Watson and Crick in Cambridge to establish the structure.

The causes of friction were various ranging from simple personality clashes to, it has been said, male hostility to the invasion of their private club by a woman. Despite this unsatisfactory background Franklin did obtain results without which the structure established by Watson and Crick would have been at the least delayed. The most important of these was her x-ray photograph of hydrated DNA, the so-called B form, the most revealing such photograph then available. Watson first saw it in 1952 at a seminar given by Franklin, and recognized that it clearly indicated a helix. Franklin also appreciated, unlike Watson and Crick, that in the DNA molecule the phosphate groups lie on the outside rather than inside the helix.

Despite such insights it was Watson and Crick who first realized that DNA has a double helix. By March 1953 Franklin had overcome her earlier opposition to helical structures and was in fact producing a draft paper on 17 March 1953, in which she proposed a double-chain helical structure for DNA. It did not, however, contain the crucial idea of base pairing, nor did she realize that the two chains must run in opposite directions. She first heard of the Watson–Crick model on the following day.

Fraunhofer, Josef von (1787–1826) *German physicist and optician*

Fraunhofer, whose family was in the optical trade, was born in Straubing (now in Germany); he was apprenticed to an optician in Munich after his parents died. He subsequently moved to the Utzschneider optical institute near Munich.

His great ambition was to perfect the achromatic lens, which John DOLLOND had developed a century earlier, and his scientific discoveries came as by-products of this work. The major difficulty was to measure the refractive indices of the different types of glass used in these lenses. In 1814, while testing prisms in order to determine these constants, he observed that the Sun's spectrum was covered with fine dark lines. He also noticed that these *Fraunhofer lines* occurred in the spectra of bright stars, but that their positions were different. The lines had been observed earlier by William Wollaston, but Fraunhofer studied them in detail, measuring the positions of 576 of them and giving the main ones letters A–G. He also found the lines to be present in spectra produced by reflection from a grating (1821–22), thus proving them to be a characteristic of the light, not the glass of the prism.

Fraunhofer had in his grasp the key to finding the composition of the stars, but this step was taken half a century later by Gustav Kirchhoff, who showed that lines in the solar spectrum resulted from characteristic absorption by elements in the atmosphere of the Sun.

Frege, (Friedrich Ludwig) Gottlob
(1848–1925) *German philosopher and mathematician*

Born at Wismar (now in Germany), Frege studied at the universities of Jena and Göttingen, where he obtained his PhD in 1873. He then returned to Jena as a lecturer, where he remained for the rest of his working life, rising to the position of professor in 1896. In a series of seminal works Frege laid the foundations of modern mathematical logic, transforming logic with an understanding of and notation for the problem of multiple generality – propositions containing predicates, quantifiers, and variables – and showing how the basic concepts and operations of mathematics could be formalized. He also revolutionized modern philosophy through his influence on the philosophy of language. However Frege's work was almost completely ignored, misunderstood, or treated with hostility by his contemporaries – notable exceptions were Bertrand Russell and Giuseppe Peano.

In his first major work, *Begriffsschrift* (Concept Writing, 1879), he provided a new formalism containing an adequate symbolism and an axiomatic base for the rigorous derivation of both propositional and predicate logic. While a few workers, such as the American C.S. Pierce, had been moving in this direction, their work was completely overshadowed by the comprehensive nature of Frege's work.

In *Die Grundlagen der Arithmetik* (1884; The Foundations of Arithmetic) Frege gave a formal definition of cardinal number and showed how basic properties of numbers could be logically derived from it. In *Grundgesetze der Arithmetik* (1893 and 1903; Basic Laws of Arithmetic) he went further in attempting to derive arithmetic from formal logic. The *Grundgesetze* is still regarded as a massive achievement, but his main aim was doomed to failure. On the eve of the publication of the second volume Russell wrote to Frege pointing out a contradiction – Russell's paradox – that could be derived from his system. This, as Frege acknowledged, vitiated his whole project.

Fresnel, Augustin Jean (1788–1827)
French physicist

Fresnel was born in Broglie, France, and grew up in the time of the French Revolution; by the time he was 26, Napoleon had been exiled and Louis XVIII was on the throne. At this time Fresnel was a qualified engineer but, when Napoleon returned from Elba, Fresnel supported the royalists and lost his job as a result.

Fresnel started studying optics in 1814 and was one of the major supporters of the wave theory of light. He worked on interference, at first being unaware of the work of Thomas Young, and produced a number of devices for giving interference effects. *Fresnel's biprism* is a single prism formed of two identical narrow-angled prisms base-to-base. Placed in front of a single source it splits the beam into two parts, which can produce interference fringes. Initially, Fresnel believed that light was a longitudinal wave motion, but he later decided that it must be transverse to account for the phenomenon of polarization.

Another important part of Fresnel's work was his development of optical systems for lighthouses. He invented the *Fresnel lens* – a lens with a stepped surface – to replace the heavy metal mirrors that were in use at the time.

Fresnel became a member of the French Academy of Sciences in 1823 and four years later, shortly before he died, the Royal Society awarded him the Rumford medal.

Freud, Sigmund (1856–1939) *Austrian psychoanalyst*

The son of a wool merchant from Freiberg (now Příbor in the Czech Republic), Freud graduated from the University of Vienna with an MD in 1881 having also spent much time in the study of physiology. He worked at the Vienna General Hospital until 1885 and, after a further period of study in Paris under the neurologist Jean-Martin Charcot, set up in private practice in Vienna in the same year. He took the post of part-time head of the neurological outpatients clinic at the Children's Hospital and also held the position of *Privatdozent* in neuropathology at the University of Vienna.

Before Freud worked out the basic principles of psychoanalysis in the 1890s he had produced a substantial body of research in more orthodox fields. In addition to early work on comparative neuroanatomy, he discovered the euphoric effects of cocaine in 1884 and produced two sizable monographs – one on aphasia (1891) and the other on paralysis in children (1893).

By this time he had developed a more ambitious research program, clearly stated in his unpublished *Project for a Scientific Psychology* (1895). In this unfinished work he aimed to explain "the theory of mental functioning" in terms of quantitative physical concepts that would apply to both normal and abnormal psychology. To this end he went into considerable detail, even supposing the existence of three types of neurones with different physiological properties.

Freud however drew back from such a neurological approach. In 1893 he collaborated with Josef Breuer on *The Psychical Mechanism of Hysterical Phenomena*, later expanded into *Studien über Hysterie* (1895; Studies in Hysteria, 1955), a work that marked the beginning of psychoanalysis. During the period 1892–95 Freud evolved his psychoanalytical method using the technique of free association. Following this he developed his theory that neuroses were rooted in suppressed sexual desires.

Freud's major work, *Die Traumdeutung* (1899; The Interpretation of Dreams, 1953), is regarded as his most original. In this he analyzed dreams in terms of unconscious desires and experiences. His other works included *Zur Psychopathologie des Alltagslebens* (1904; Psychopathology of Everyday Life, 1960), *Totem und Tabu* (1913; Totem and Taboo, 1955), *Jenseits des Lustprinzips* (1920; Beyond the Pleasure Principle, 1955), and *Das Ich und das Es* (1923; The Ego and the Id, 1961).

In 1902 Freud established a circle of colleagues who met to discuss psychoanalytical matters once a week at his house. The group's original members were Alfred Adler, Max Kahane, Rudolf Reitler, and Wilhelm Stekel. This grew, and later became the Vienna Psycho-Analytical Society (1908), and finally, the International Psycho-Analytical Association (1910). Freud, now becoming famous in Europe, made a tour of America in 1909 where he was well received. By 1911 the International Psycho-Analytical Association had begun to break up through differences of opinion, Carl Jung and Alfred Adler being among the most significant to leave. However, by the 1920s Freud had become one of the most famous thinkers of the century.

In 1923 Freud was diagnosed as having cancer of the jaw. During the next 16 years he was to suffer more than 30 operations and be compelled to live with a prosthesis which, by substituting for his excised jaw and palette, allowed him to eat, drink, smoke, and talk.

In 1938 he was forced to leave Vienna by the Nazis for exile in London. He continued to see patients and to work on his last book, *Der Mann Moses und die monotheistische Religion* (1939; Moses and Monotheism, 1960), but within a matter of months it was clear to him that he could continue to work no more. It was then that he reminded his doctor: "My dear Schur ... you promised you would help me when I could no longer carry on." Schur honored his pledge with morphine ensuring a peaceful death.

Freundlich, Herbert Max Finlay
(1880–1941) *German–American physical chemist*

Freundlich was born at Charlottenburg, now a district of Berlin, Germany. He studied physical chemistry at Munich and at Leipzig where he became assistant to Wilhelm Ostwald. From 1911 to 1917 he was professor at the Institute of Technology in Brunswick. He was professor at the Kaiser Wilhelm Institute, Berlin-Dahlem, from 1917 to 1934 when he left Germany because of the Nazi regime. He traveled first to Britain and worked at University College, London, and from 1938 to his death was professor of colloid chemistry at the University of Minnesota.

Freundlich's life work was in colloid chemistry. He showed how colloid stability was changed by the addition of electrolytes and he is well known for the *Freundlich adsorption isotherm*, a theoretical formula for the amount of adsorption on a surface at constant temperature.

Friedel, Charles (1832–1899) *French chemist*

After studying in his native city of Strasbourg with Louis Pasteur and at the Sorbonne with Charles Adolphe Wurtz, Friedel became curator of the mineral collections at the mining school in Paris (1856). Although his most important work was in organic chemistry, he also did much work on the synthesis of minerals. In 1862 he discovered secondary propyl alcohol, thus verifying Hermann Kolbe's prediction of its existence. His most notable work was that carried out with the American chemist **James Crafts** (1839–1917) on the alkylation and acylation of aromatic hydrocarbons – the *Friedel-Crafts reaction* (1877). This was a method of synthesizing hydrocarbons or ketones from aromatic hydrocarbons using aluminum chloride as a catalyst. Friedel and Crafts also did much work on the synthesis of organosilicon compounds. Friedel was professor of mineralogy at the mining school in Paris (1876–84) and professor of organic chemistry at the Sorbonne (1884–99).

Friedman, Herbert (1916–) *American physicist and astronomer*

Born in New York City, Friedman graduated from Brooklyn College in 1936 and obtained his PhD in 1940 from Johns Hopkins University, Baltimore. Shortly afterwards he joined the US Naval Research Laboratory in Washington where he has spent his whole career, being appointed in 1958 as superintendent of the atmosphere and astrophysics division and in 1963 superintendent of the space science division. Also in 1963 he became chief scientist at the E.O. Hulbert Center for Space Research. In addition he has served as adjunct professor at the universities of Maryland and Pennsylvania.

Friedman has been a pioneer in both rocket astronomy and in the study of the x-ray sky. The two went hand in hand in the early days of x-ray astronomy for without rockets it would have been impossible to detect any significant x-ray activity in space since x-rays are absorbed by the Earth's atmosphere. Solar x-rays were detected as early as 1948 by T.R. Burnright and were systematically investigated from 1949 by Friedman and his colleagues, who observed x-ray activity throughout a full solar cycle of 11 years. Friedman also studied ultraviolet radiation from the Sun and in 1960 produced the first x-ray and ultraviolet photographs of the Sun.

X-ray astronomy really came of age in 1962 when nonsolar x-ray activity was first discovered by Bruno Rossi. The x-rays came from a source in Scorpio, since named Sco X–1. A second source was discovered in 1963 in Taurus and named Tau X–1. Friedman made the first attempt to locate accurately an x-ray source two years later: when the Moon passed in front of the Crab nebula, a luminous supernova remnant in Taurus, the x-ray activity of Tau X–1 was found to fade out gradually. Tau X–1 was therefore identified with the Crab nebula and seemed to be a source about a light-year across lying in the center of the nebula.

Since then satellites carrying x-ray equipment have been launched, including Uhuru in 1970 and the Einstein Observatory in 1978. These have enormously extended the scope of x-ray astronomy and shown its value in the search for neutron stars and black holes.

Friedman, Jerome Isaac (1930–) *American physicist*

Chicago-born Friedman was educated at the university in his native city and gained his PhD there in 1956. After spending three years in California at Stanford, Friedman moved to the Massachusetts Institute of Technology in 1961, and was later appointed to a chair of physics in 1967.

Working with his MIT colleague **Henry Kendall** (1926–) and with **Richard Taylor** (1929–) from Stanford, Friedman began to study the internal structure of the proton. They worked with the 3-kilometer linear accelerator recently opened at Stanford (SLAC). Electrons were accelerated to an energy of 20,000 million electronvolts and directed against a target of liquid hydrogen. In a manner reminiscent of the 1911 experiments of Ernest Rutherford, they analyzed the angles and energies of the electrons and protons of the hydrogen nuclei as they scattered after collision. Similar experiments had been performed by Robert Hofstadter in the 1950s and he had found protons not to be mere points, but fuzzy blobs spread out over an area of about 10^{-15} meter. In 1967, however, higher energies were available to Friedman and his colleagues, which led them to hope that they might see into the proton with a little more precision.

In cases of elastic scattering, where beam and target particles retain their identity, the deflections were minor and occurred as expected. When, however, the scattering was inelastic and the protons were struck with sufficient energy to produce new particles, such as pions, the electrons were deflected through much wider angles than expected.

These latter scattering results proved difficult to explain. A possible answer was proposed by Richard Feynmann in 1968 on a visit to SLAC. Protons, he suggested, could be composed of a number of pointlike particles, which he called "partons." From such charged points, electrons could be scattered through large angles. Further, it followed from the angular distribution of the scattered electrons that the partons must have a spin of one half.

As these were the properties calculated for the hypothetical quarks proposed by Murray Gell-Mann, the SLAC experiment was soon taken to be the first experimental evidence for the existence of quarks. It was for this work that Friedman shared the 1990 Nobel Prize for physics with his collaborators Kendall and Taylor.

Friedmann, Aleksandr Alexandrovich (1888–1925) *Russian astronomer*

Born the son of a composer in St. Petersburg, Russia, Friedmann was educated at the university there. He began his scientific career in 1913 at the Pavlovsk Observatory in St. Petersburg and, after war service, was appointed professor of theoretical mechanics at Perm University in 1918. In 1920 he returned to the St. Petersburg Observatory where he became director shortly before his death from typhoid at the age of 37.

Friedmann established an early reputation for his work on atmospheric and meteorological physics. He is, however, better known for his 1922 paper on the expanding universe. This arose from work of Einstein in 1917 in which he attempted to apply his equations of general relativity to cosmology. Friedmann developed a theoretical model of the universe using Einstein's theory, in which the average mass density is constant and space has a constant curvature. Different cosmological models are possible depending on whether the curvature is zero, negative, or positive. Such models are called *Friedmann universes*.

Frisch, Karl von (1886–1982) *Austrian zoologist, entomologist, and ethologist*

Frisch was born in Vienna, Austria, and educated at home and at convent school. He began his academic career by studying medicine at the University of Vienna, but gave this up to study zoology at the Zoological Institute in Munich, an internationally recognized center for research in experimental zoology. He also studied marine biology at the Trieste Biological Institute for Marine Research, taking his PhD for work on the color adaptation and light perception of minnows (1910). Frisch taught at the Munich Zoological Institute and in 1919 became assistant professor of zoology. He then held academic posts at the universities of Rostock and Breslau before returning to Munich in 1925 as director of the Zoological Institute where he continued to work until the end of World War II. In 1946 he assumed the chair of zoology at Graz but returned to Munich where he remained until his retirement in 1958.

Interested in animals from childhood, Frisch devoted 40 years to an intense study of the senses, communication, and social organization of honey (or hive) bees. By means of ingenious experiments he showed that bees can find their way back to the hive, even when the sun is obscured by cloud, by using polarized or ultraviolet light, and that they are able to communicate discovery of a new food source by means of a special "dance." The bee performs its dance on the vertical surface of the comb. Depending on the distance of the food supply, the bee may perform either the round dance – food within about 80 feet (24 m) – or the tail-wagging dance – food beyond about 325 feet (99 m). At intermediate distances various transitional dance forms between these are seen. In the tail-wagging dance the bee makes a straight run over a short distance, wagging its abdomen rapidly, and then makes a semicircle back to the starting point. This movement is repeated, making a semicircle in the opposite direction. The dance gives information on the direction of the food supply because the angle that the straight run makes with the vertical surface of the comb is the same as the angle between the direction of the food and the Sun at the hive or nest.

Frisch also showed that the bees are unable to distinguish between certain shapes, that they have a limited range of color perception, but can see light of shorter wavelength than man. They do not, for example, distinguish red but can see ultraviolet, which is reflected by many flowers. Red poppies are seen as wholly ultraviolet, while many yellow flowers are seen either as yellow or in varying shades of ultraviolet. Frisch's discoveries have proved of practical benefit to beekeepers in that if hives are painted certain colors – a yellow hive next to a blue one for example – this aids the bees' homing. His major contribution to ethology was recognized in 1973 when he was awarded the Nobel Prize for physiology or medicine, jointly with Konrad LORENZ and Niko TINBERGEN. His books include *The Dancing Bees* (1927, trans. 1954) and *Animal Architecture* (1974).

Frisch, Otto Robert (1904–1979) *Austrian–British physicist*

Frisch, the son of a Viennese printer and publisher, was educated at the University of Vienna where he obtained his doctorate in 1926. He was employed in Berlin (1927–30) at the German national physical laboratory, the Physikalisch Technische Reichsanstalt, and moved to the University of Hamburg in 1930. However, with the introduction of Hitler's racial laws, he was sacked in 1933 and consequently traveled via Copenhagen to England. After working at the universities of Birmingham and Liverpool (1939–43) he moved to America and spent the period

1943–45 at Los Alamos, working on the development of the atom bomb. With the end of the war Frisch worked briefly at the Atomic Energy Research Establishment at Harwell, leaving in 1947 to take up the Jackson Chair of Physics at Cambridge, a post he held until his retirement in 1972.

In 1939 Frisch, with his aunt, Lise MEITNER, was closely involved in the crucial discovery of nuclear fission. He spent Christmas in Sweden visiting Meitner, who reported to him some strange results obtained by her former colleague Otto HAHN. Hahn found that when uranium was bombarded with neutrons, one of its decay products was the much lighter element barium. Frisch said that his first reaction was that Hahn had made a mistake, but Meitner was more inclined to trust Hahn's qualities as a good chemist. After some thought and calculation they concluded that this must in fact be what was later called nuclear fission. Frisch rushed back to Copenhagen to inform Niels Bohr who was able to confirm Hahn's experiments. But in all this excitement the most important point had been missed – the mechanism of the neutron chain reaction. However the thought did occur independently to many others.

Frisch did further work on fission while at Birmingham, collaborating with Rudolph Peierls in confirming Bohr's suggestion that a chain reaction would be more likely to result with uranium–235 rather than with the more common isotope, uranium–238. After much work Frisch came to the basic and frightening conclusion that an "explosive chain reaction" could be produced with a pound or two of uranium–235 rather than the tons of it which he first thought would be necessary. Frisch and Peierls were therefore probably the first two people in the world to be aware not just of the possibility of a nuclear bomb but of its practicality. They immediately wrote a report that was sent to Henry Tizard, a scientific adviser to the British government, which Frisch claimed was decisive in getting the British Government to take the atomic bomb seriously.

In 1979 Frisch produced his fascinating and witty memoirs, *What Little I Remember*.

Fritsch, Felix Eugen (1879–1954)
British algologist

Fritsch, the son of a London headmaster, was educated at the University of London and at Munich, where he obtained his DPhil in 1899. He taught at University College, London, from 1902 until 1911, when he moved to Queen Mary College, London,

where he served as professor of botany from 1924 until his retirement in 1948.

Before Fritsch there was no comprehensive work on algae. He remedied this with his classic work *The Structure and Reproduction of the Algae* (2 vols. 1935–45). He was also instrumental in the foundation of the Freshwater Biological Association in 1929.

Fritsch, Gustav Theodor (1838–1927)
German ethnographer, anatomist, and neurologist. See HITZIG, EDUARD.

Fuchs, Leonhard (1501–1566) *German botanist and physician*

Fuchs was born in Wemding, now in Germany, and was professor of medicine at Tübingen University from 1535 until his death, his main interest being the medicinal properties of plants. He is remembered for his herbal manual *De historia stirpium* (1542), in which about four hundred native and a hundred foreign plants are arranged alphabetically, with original descriptions of the form, habitat, and best season for collection of each plant. The herbal is notable for its glossary of botanical terms, accurate woodcut illustrations, and detailed descriptions.

A genus of ornamental shrubs, *Fuchsia*, is named for him.

Fukui, Kenichi (1918–1998) *Japanese theoretical and physical chemist*

Born in Nara, Japan, Fukui was a lecturer in chemistry at Kyoto Imperial University, becoming professor of physical chemistry from 1951 to 1982. He is noted for his theoretical work on the change in molecular orbitals during reaction, especially reactions of methyl radicals. He also investigated the reaction of molecular nitrogen with transition-metal complexes – a topic potentially important for the fixation of nitrogen.

For his work on frontier orbital theory, Fukui shared the 1981 Nobel Prize for chemistry with Roald HOFFMANN.

Funk, Casimir (1884–1967) *Polish-American biochemist*

Funk, born the son of a dermatologist in the Polish capital of Warsaw, obtained his doctorate from the University of Bern in 1904. He worked at the Pasteur Institute in Paris, the University of Berlin, and the Lister Institute in London, before emigrating to America in 1915. Although he became naturalized in 1920, Funk returned to Poland in 1923 as director of the Warsaw Institute of Hygiene, but finding the political conditions unattractive moved to Paris in

1927, where he acted as a consultant to a drug company and founded a private research institute, the Casa Biochemica. In 1939 Funk returned to America, where he served as consultant to the US Vitamin Corporation and as president of the Funk Foundation for medical research.

It was while working at the Lister Institute in 1912 that Funk first clearly formulated his crucial idea that certain diseases are caused by food deficiencies. He was working on the antiberiberi factor, which he succeeded in extracting from rice husks. He went on to postulate that there were comparable ingredients whose absence from a regular diet would produce scurvy, rickets, and pellagra.

Noting that the antiberiberi factor contained an amine ($-NH_2$) group, Funk proposed to call such ingredients 'vital amines', or 'vitamines'. When it became clear that the amine group was not present in all 'vitamines' the term *vitamin* came to be preferred.

Furchgott, Robert F. (1916–)
American pharmacologist

Furchgott was born in Charleston, South Carolina, and graduated with a BS in chemistry from the University of North Carolina in 1937. Three years later he gained his PhD in biochemistry at Northwestern University. From 1956 to 1988 he worked in the department of pharmacology at the State University of New York, and since 1988 has been Distinguished Professor, State University of New York Health Science Center. In 1998 he shared the Nobel Prize for physiology or medicine with Louis IGNARRO and Ferid MURAD for their discovery that molecules of the gas nitrogen monoxide (nitric oxide, NO) can transmit signals in the cardiovascular system.

Nitrogen monoxide, produced by one cell, acts by penetrating membranes and regulating the function of another cell. Nerves and hormones are well known as signal carriers, but this discovery was a totally new signaling principle in a biological system.

Furchgott began by researching the actions of drugs on blood vessels, but often observed contradictory results. Sometimes a drug acted to contract a vessel, but at other times it dilated the vessel. In 1980 he discovered that the neurotransmitter acetylcholine did not act to dilate blood vessels if the endothelium (surface cells) of the receiving cell were damaged. He deduced that the cells of the endothelium produce another hitherto unknown signal substance that makes the smooth muscle cells of the vascular system relax. He called the substance endothelium-derived relaxing factor (EDRF), and other pharmacologists (including Ignarro) set out to find it.

G

Gabor, Dennis (1900–1979)
Hungarian–British physicist

Gabor, the son of a businessman, was born in the Hungarian capital of Budapest; he was educated at the technological university there and in Berlin, where he obtained a doctorate in engineering in 1927. He worked initially as a research engineer for Siemens and Halske from 1927 until 1933 when, with the rise of Hitler, he decided to leave Germany and took a post with the British Thomson–Houston Company, Rugby. In 1948 he joined the staff of Imperial College, London, later serving as professor of applied electron physics from 1958 until his retirement in 1967.

Gabor is credited with the invention of the technique of holography – a method of photographically recording and reproducing three-dimensional images. The modern technique uses lasers to form such images, but the invention came out of work by Gabor on improving the resolution of the electron microscope – work done in 1948, twelve years before the introduction of the laser.

The electron microscope has theoretically much higher resolution than the optical microscope because of the shorter wavelength of electrons (resolution is limited by diffraction effects). One method of improving the resolution of the electron microscope is to improve the electron lenses used to deflect and focus the beam of electrons. Gabor was interested in increasing the resolution to the point at which atoms in a lattice could be 'seen'. Rather than work on the electron optics of the system he had the idea of extracting more information from the electron micrographs produced by existing instruments, and to do this he proposed forming a diffraction pattern between the incident beam of electrons and a background beam that was coherent with it (i.e., one with the same wavelength and phase). The principle was that the image produced would have information on the phase of the electrons as well as the intensity and that it would be possible to reconstruct a true image from the resulting electron micrograph.

Gabor began experiments with light to investigate the technique (which he named holography from the Greek *holos* meaning whole – the record contained the whole information about the specimen). He used a mercury lamp and pinhole to form the first, imperfect, holograms. Subsequently, in 1961, E. Leith and J. Upatnieks produced holograms using laser light. The technique is to illuminate a specimen with light from a laser and form an interference pattern between light reflected from the specimen and direct light from the source, the pattern being recorded on a photographic plate. If the photographic record is then illuminated with the laser light, a three-dimensional image of the specimen is generated.

Gabor received the Nobel Prize for physics for his work in 1971.

Gadolin, Johan (1760–1852) *Finnish chemist*

Gadolin was born the son of an astronomer and physicist in Åbo, now Turku in Finland. He studied under Torbern Bergman at Uppsala and taught at Åbo from 1785, becoming professor of chemistry from 1797 until 1822.

In 1794 Gadolin examined a black mineral from Ytterby, a quarry in Sweden. The rocks from this quarry were found to contain a dozen or so new elements. Gadolin isolated the first lanthanoid element from it in the form of its oxide and named it yttria. The element was named gadolinium after him in 1886 by Lecoq de Boisbaudran. Gadolin also worked on specific heat and published a set of standard tables.

Gajdusek, Daniel Carleton (1923–)
American virologist

Gajdusek was born at Yonkers in New York and educated at the University of Rochester and at Harvard, where he obtained his MD in 1946. He specialized in pediatrics, working at Harvard, the Pasteur Institute in Teheran, and the Walter and Eliza Hall Institute for Medical Research in Melbourne, before joining the National Institute of Health in Bethesda, Maryland, in 1958. Since 1970 he has been with the National Institute of Neurological Diseases.

In 1963 he made an intriguing discovery that could well have profound consequences for the control of a number of serious but little-understood diseases. In the 1950s he began studying the Fore people of New Guinea, a supposedly cannibalistic tribe who suffered from a very localized neurological complaint they called 'kuru'. With the aid of the district medical officer, who first drew his attention to the disease, Gajdusek spent much of the next ten years among the Fore looking for the cause of kuru. He suspected the disease was transmitted by the Fore custom of ritually eating parts of the brain of their deceased relatives so he collected samples from the brains of several kuru victims.

Failing to detect any obvious signs of an organism in the brain tissue he injected filtered extracts into the brains of chimpanzees and waited. After about 12 months the disease at last appeared. This was the first of what were known as 'slow virus infections' to be observed in humans. By 1968 Gajdusek and his colleagues had shown that kuru was not unique and that the rare neurological complaint Creutzfeldt-Jakob disease, a presenile dementia, is transmitted after a comparable delay.

For his work on kuru Gajdusek shared the 1976 Nobel Prize for physiology or medicine with Baruch Blumberg. The prize itself he used to set up a trust for the education of the Fore people. Gajdusek, who is unmarried, has also adopted 16 boys while on his expeditions to the Pacific, and is bringing them up in America.

Galen (c. 130–c. 200) Greek physician

Galen was educated as a doctor supposedly because his father had a dream in which Asklepios, the god of medicine, appeared to him. After an initial period of training in his native city of Pergamum (now Bergama in Turkey), Galen spent the years 148–57 traveling and studying at Corinth, Smyrna, and Alexandria. He then returned home and took the post of surgeon to the Pergamum gladiators. Eventually Galen left for Rome where he made a considerable reputation for himself serving the emperors Marcus Aurelius and Commodus.

In addition to his imperial duties Galen wrote extensively and more than 130 of his texts have survived. Even though some are undoubtedly spurious, there still remains an impressive opus on virtually every aspect of the medicine of his times.

It is this opus that acquired an unprecedented authority, which persisted, unopposed, for another 1500 years. It was not until William HARVEY proposed his new theory of the circulation of the blood (1628) that anatomists were presented with a viable alternative to the traditional system of Galen.

Galen made few advances in pathology believing as he did in Hippocrates' humoral theory – that disease is caused by an imbal-

ance of the four body humors; phlegm, black bile, yellow bile, and blood. It was as an anatomist that Galen's true originality lay. He stressed the importance of dissecting personally and frequently, and combined his anatomical studies with a number of neat and conclusive experiments. Thus he clearly demonstrated the falsity of Erasistratus's view that the arteries carry air not blood by placing ligatures both above and below the point of incision and noting the absence of any air escaping before the discharge of blood. Also, by similar experiments he was able to show that urine passes from the kidneys to the bladder irreversibly down the ureters.

Galen however was less successful in describing the complete system and operation of the body. He thought that blood was made in the liver from the food brought by the portal vein from the stomach. This was then transported by the venous system to nourish all parts of the body. Some of the blood however passed along the vena cava to the right side of the heart where it passed to the left side by some supposed perforations in the dividing wall or septum. Belief in such perforations persisted well into the 16th century. In the left ventricle the blood was mixed wth air brought from the lungs and distributed round the body via the arterial system carrying the vital spirit or innate heat. Some of this blood was carried by the arteries to the head where in the *rete mirabile* (a vascular network not actually found in man) it was mixed with animal spirit and distributed to the senses and muscles by the supposedly hollow nerves. It was this spirit or pneuma that produced consciousness.

Thus instead of a single basic circulation Galen has a tripartite system in which the liver, heart, and brain each inject into the body three different spirits – natural, vital, and animal, which travel through the body via the venous, arterial, and nervous channels respectively. Although such a scheme is now recognized as totally misguided it possessed sufficient plausibility and experimental support to persist into the 17th century.

Galileo (1564–1642) Italian astronomer and physicist

Galileo, whose full name was Galileo Galilei, made major contributions to most branches of physics (especially mechanics), invented and so deployed the telescope to change our view of the nature of the universe completely, and became engaged in a highly dramatic confrontation with the Church.

Born in Pisa, Italy, Galileo was the son of a scholar and musician of some distinction. He entered the University of Pisa in 1581 to study medicine – a subject in which he showed little interest – and failed to complete the course, developing instead a passion for mathematics. He is thought to have made his first important observation in 1583, two years before he left the university. While in Pisa cathedral he noticed that the lamps swinging in the wind took the same time for their swing whatever its amplitude. He timed the swing against his pulse. In 1586 he invented a hydrostatic balance for the determination of relative densities. In 1589 he was appointed to the chair of mathematics at Pisa and later moved to the chair in Padua, in 1592.

It was while in Padua in 1610 that he designed and constructed a simple refracting telescope. He may not have been the first to do so, and there are many other claimants, but he was certainly the first to use the instrument constructively. His initial reaction was sheer amazement at the number of stars in the sky, "So numerous as to be almost beyond belief" he asserted. Merely looking at the Moon immediately revealed that it is not the smooth unchangeable object of Aristotelian theory. He also discovered sunspots. His most exciting moment came in January 1610, when he observed Jupiter for the first time telescopically. To his astonishment he found that the planet has four satellites. Contrary to received opinion as to what was possible, these were new bodies, unmentioned in Aristotle, and certainly not circling the Earth. He published his observations immediately, in 1610, in *Sidereus nuncius* (Starry Messenger), dedicating them to his patron and former pupil Cosimo II of Tuscany, in whose honor he named the satellites *Sidera Medicea* (Medici Stars). Within weeks he had received an invitation to a well-paid research chair in Pisa and returned there at the end of 1610.

In a series of works he was also tackling the problem of motion. His mature views were expressed in his *Discorsi ... a due nuove scienze...* (1638; Discourse on Two New Sciences). In a series of brilliant experiments rolling balls down inclined planes (and not, as is commonly thought, by dropping weights from the leaning tower of Pisa) he showed that the speed with which bodies fall is independent of their weight and correctly formulated the law $s = \frac{1}{2}at^2$ (where s is speed, a acceleration, and t time). He lacked the concept of inertia and could only accept circular motion as being natural since, for Galileo, a body without any force acting on it would move in perfect circular motion. This was one aspect of his medieval

heritage from which he was unable to break away.

After his return to Pisa, Galileo was beginning to meet opposition. Some of this was merely personal; in his criticism of others he wrote with a wit and savagery that many found wounding and impossible to forgive. He also found himself in dispute with many over his numerous discoveries. In these he was never inclined to take a charitable view over the claims of others, and there were many waiting for a chance to humiliate him on his return from the safety of Padua (then part of the independent Venetian republic). Their chance was his open support for the Copernican system. That the Earth moves round the Sun was so contrary to Scripture for many churchmen that those who enthusiastically campaigned for such a view were seen as heretics if not atheists. Galileo made no secret of his views in his writings, talk, and lectures. He openly ridiculed the Aristotelian scholars and supporters of the Ptolemaic (geocentric) system, many of whom were, or were to become, high officers of the Church. To stop the squabbling, Pope Paul V, on the advice of Cardinal Bellarmine, placed Copernicus on the Index (a list of books banned by the Catholic Church) in 1616, summoned Galileo to Rome, and informed him that he could no longer support Copernicus publicly. At this point Galileo had no choice; continued support for Copernicus would be to call the authority of the pope into question and to send him to the stake as it had sent Giordano Bruno in 1600.

In 1623 an old friend of Galileo's, Cardinal Barberini, was elected pope as Urban VIII. Galileo wasted no time in dedicating his new book *Il saggiatore* (1623; The Assayer) to him. It was a work that was savagely critical of Aristotle's account of comets. Although Urban was not prepared to go back on the decision of 1616 publicly, Galileo seems to have thought that he would be safe unless he supported Copernicus specifically. One thing that should have made him more prudent was the death of his patron, Cosimo, and the succession of a powerless minor to the duchy of Tuscany.

Galileo thought he could avoid the problem by writing a dialogue between a (Ptolemaic-) Aristotelian and a Copernican without ostensibly committing himself to either side, and the Church gave him permission to do so. Thus he wrote the *Dialogue Concerning the Two Chief World Systems* (1632). However, the form of the dialogue fooled no one. The Aristotelian, Simplicius, is no match for the brilliance of the Copernican, Salviati. It was even suggested to the pope that the bumbling Simplicius was a portrait of Urban himself. Galileo was once more summoned to Rome, threatened with torture, and forced to renounce Copernicus in the most abject terms. There is a tradition that after his renunciation he whispered, "Eppur si muove" ("Yet it moves"), but this is unlikely. Galileo was truly frightened, and it must be remembered that he was nearly 70 years old and facing a powerful body, which might have tortured and burned him at the stake. In the end he was treated reasonably well. He was allowed to return to his villa at Arcetri in isolation. Later, after he became blind and after the death of his daughter, his disciples Vincenzo Viviani and Evangelista Toricelli were allowed to stay with him.

Galle, Johann Gottfried (1812–1910)
German astronomer

Born at Pabsthaus, in Germany, Galle was chief assistant to Johann Encke at the Berlin Observatory at a crucial moment in the history of planetary astronomy. Urbain Leverrier had worked out what he considered to be the position of an as yet undiscovered planet. Having had some contact with Galle, Leverrier wrote to him on 18 September 1846, asking him to try to check his prediction. Galle started observing on 23 September. He was favored by having an unpublished copy of a new star chart covering the right part of the sky and, aided by Louis D'Arrest, he found a star that was not on the chart. A wait of 24 hours showed that it had moved against the background of the fixed stars and so was a planet – it was the planet Neptune.

Galle also made an important contribution to determine the mean distance of the Sun from the Earth (the astronomical unit or AU). Conventional means of determining the AU had leaned heavily on the two transits of Venus in each century. In practice it turned out to be difficult to measure accurately the moment of first contact. Galle proposed instead, in 1872, that measuring the parallax of the planetoids would give a more reliable figure. (**Harold Spencer Jones** (1890–1960) followed this procedure in 1931 when the planetoid Eros came within 16 million miles of the Earth. He was able to calculate the AU to within 10,000 miles.) In 1851 Galle became director of the Breslau Observatory. He lived long enough to receive the congratulations of the astronomical world on the 50th anniversary of the discovery of Neptune in 1896.

Gallo, Robert Charles (1937–   )
American physician

The son of a metallurgist, Gallo was born at Waterbury in Connecticut and educated at Providence College, Rhode Island, and Jefferson Medical College, Philadelphia, where he received his MD in 1963. He served his internship at the University of Chicago. In 1965, Gallo joined the staff of the National Cancer Institute at the National Institute of Health, Bethesda, Maryland, and since 1972 he has been head of the Institute's Tumor Cell Biology Laboratory.

Gallo is noted as one of the people who first identified the virus responsible for AIDS. The discovery came out of work in his laboratory on leukemia. The first success by Gallo's team was the identification in 1976 of interleukin-2, a factor that stimulates growth in the lymphocytes known as T-cells. This was followed in 1979 by the crucial discovery of the first human retrovirus, HTLV-1 (human T-cell lymphotropic/leukemia virus). Retroviruses were first described in 1970 by Temin and Baltimore and, unlike other viruses, their genetic material is encoded in DNA rather than RNA. HTLV-1 and another virus discovered by Gallo in 1982, HTLV-2, both cause rare forms of leukemia.

In the early 1980s concern was growing about the emergence and spread of AIDS, a disease characterized by suppression of the patient's immune system. Gallo was aware that HTL viruses acted by attacking the immune system of leukemia patients. He made the bold conjecture that AIDS was caused by yet another retrovirus recently discovered in his laboratory, namely, HTLV-3. Similar conclusions were reached by Luc Montagnier at the Pasteur Institute in Paris, who had succeeded in isolating a retrovirus from an AIDS patient. He named the virus LAV (lymphadenopathy associated virus) and sent Gallo a sample in September 1983.

Gallo began work on finding a test for the AIDS virus. At first the virus proved impossible to grow in sufficient quantities, until Mika Popovich in Gallo's laboratory found a particular strain of T-cell (HUT-78 H9) in which the virus replicated without killing the cell. It was consequently a relatively simple matter, once large amounts of virus were available, to test for antibodies in AIDS sufferers' blood.

In April 1984, before Gallo had published his results, the US Department of Health announced that he had found the cause of AIDS, HTLV-3, and took out patents on Gallo's blood test for AIDS antibodies. Gallo published his results in May 1984. He pointed out that he had identified the virus in 48 out of 167 cases from a risk group and that no evidence of its presence was found in the blood of "115 healthy heterosexuals."

The award in May 1985 of an exclusive patent for Gallo's test provoked a strong response from the Pasteur Institute. They argued that Gallo's blood test was based upon a virus substantially identical to the LAV strain first isolated by Montagnier. The Institute sued the American Government, and heads of state became involved in the dispute. The issue was finally resolved in 1986 at a meeting in Frankfurt between Gallo and Montagnier. An agreed chronology about the discovery was established and it was also decided that 80% of royalties from the test should go to a new AIDS research foundation. The names of both Gallo and Montagnier would appear on the patent. The issue of the name of the AIDS virus was resolved in 1986 when the International Committee on the Taxonomy of Viruses diplomatically ignored both LAV and HTLV-3 and proposed the name HIV (human immunodeficiency virus).

Gallo's work made him the most cited scientist of the decade with the 418 papers he published between 1981 and 1990 gaining 36,789 citations. He has published a full and popular account of his work in *Virus Hunting: AIDS, Cancer and the Human Retrovirus* (1991).

Galois, Evariste (1811–1832) *French mathematician*

Galois was born at Bourg-la-Reine, near Paris, during the rule of Napoleon. He entered the Collège Royale de Louis-le-Grand in Paris in 1823 and it was here that his precocious mathematical genius first emerged. He published several papers while still a student and at the age of about 16 embarked upon his noted work on algebraic equations. But his career was marred by lack of advancement, associated with political bitterness. Twice, in 1827 and 1829, he was rejected by the Paris Ecole Polytechnique, and three papers submitted to the Academy of Sciences were rejected or lost. In 1830 he entered the Ecole Normale Supérieure to train as a teacher. That year revolution in Paris caused the abdication of Charles X, who was succeeded by Louis Philippe. Galois – fiercely republican – was expelled for writing an antiroyalist newspaper letter. In 1831 he was arrested twice: once for a speech against the king and the second time for wearing an illegal uniform and carrying arms – for this he received six-months' imprisonment. In the spring of 1832 he died in a duel; the details are uncertain but it may have been provoked by political opponents.

Galois seems to have anticipated that he was to die, for the night before was spent desperately recording his mathematical ideas in a letter to his former schoolmaster, Auguste Chevalier. Here he outlined his work on elliptic integrals and set out a theory of the roots (solutions) of equations, in which he considered the properties of permutations of the roots. Admissible permutations – ones in which the roots obey the same relations after permutation – form what is now known as a *Galois group*, having properties that throw light on the solvability of the equations. The manuscripts were published in 1846 and his work recognized. With the equally tragic Norwegian, Niels Henrik Abel, he is regarded as the founder of modern group theory.

Galton, Sir Francis (1822–1911) *British anthropologist and explorer*

Even though Galton's exceptional intelligence was apparent at an early age, his higher education was unremarkable. Born in the English Midlands city of Birmingham, he studied mathematics at Cambridge University and studied medicine in London but abandoned his studies on inheriting his father's fortune, which enabled him to indulge his passion for travel. Following consultations with the Royal Geographical Society, Galton set out to cover various uncharted regions of Africa, and became known as an intrepid explorer. He collected much valuable information and was elected first a fellow of the Royal Geographical Society and three years later, in 1856, a fellow of the Royal Society.

Galton made important contributions to the science of meteorology, identifying and naming anticyclones and developing the present techniques of weather mapping. This work was published as *Meteorographica* (1863; Weather Mapping). He was also instrumental in establishing the Meteorological Office and the National Physical Laboratory, but he is remembered chiefly for his researches on human heredity, which were stimulated by the publication of *The Origin of Species* by his cousin, Charles Darwin. This led Galton to speculate that the human race could be improved by controlled breeding and he later gave the name *eugenics* to the study of means by which this might be achieved.

Galton studied the histories of notable families to determine whether intelligence is inherited, and concluded that it is. This aroused much controversy amongst those who believed environment is all important. Galton was the first to use identical twins to try to assess environmental influences.

His work was characterized by its quantitative approach and he was also the first to stress the importance to biology of statistical analysis, introducing regression and correlation into statistics.

At a time when most scientists believed in blending inheritance, Galton deviated from contemporary thought and, in a letter to Darwin, outlined a theory of particulate inheritance, which anticipated Gregor Mendel's work, then still undiscovered. Galton also discussed a concept similar to the phenotypes and genotypes of Wilhelm Johannsen, under the terms patent and latent characteristics.

Galton was knighted in 1909. In his will he left a large sum of money to endow a chair of eugenics at University College, London, which was first held by Karl Pearson, an energetic advocate of Galton's ideas on eugenics.

Galvani, Luigi (1737–1798) Italian anatomist and physiologist

Galvani studied medicine at the university in his native city of Bologna, gaining his MD in 1762 for his thesis on the structure and development of bones. He stayed at Bologna to teach anatomy and in the late 1770s began his experiments in electrophysiology. He observed that the muscles of a dissected frog twitched when touched by a spark from an electric machine or condenser, such as a Leyden jar. Similar responses could be obtained when such muscles were laid out on metal during a thunderstorm, or even by simple contact with two different metals, without the deliberate application of an electric current. Galvani concluded that the source of the electricity therefore lay in the living tissue, and did not derive from outside. His finding was later disproved by Alessandro Volta. However Galvani is celebrated for his discovery of Galvanic electricity (the metallic arc), as well as for applications of his principle to the galvanization of iron and steel and the invention of the galvanometer, named in Galvani's honor by André Ampère. Galvani's animal electricity theory was published as *De viribus electricitatis in motu musculari commentarius* (1791; Commentary on the Effect of Electricity on Muscular Motion).

Gamble, Josias Christopher

(1776–1848) *British industrial chemist. See* MUSPRATT, JAMES.

Gamow, George (1904–1968) Ukrainian–American physicist

Gamow was born the son of a teacher at Odessa, now in Ukraine. He was educated at the University of Leningrad where he obtained his doctorate in 1928 and later served as professor of physics (1931–34). Before his move to America in 1934 he spent long periods at Göttingen, Copenhagen, and Cambridge, England, the major centers of the revolution then taking place in physics. In America he spent his career as professor of physics at George Washington University (1934–55) and then at the University of Colorado (1956–68).

Gamow made many contributions to nuclear and atomic physics, but is mainly noted for his work on interesting problems in cosmology and molecular biology.

In cosmology he revised and extended the big-bang theory of the creation of the universe (first formulated by Georges Lemaître). This postulates that the universe expanded from a single point in space and time. It was first announced in Gamow's famous 'alpha beta gamma' paper in 1948, which he wrote in collaboration with **Ralph Alpher** (1921–) and Hans Bethe. A fuller account was later published by Gamow in his *Creation of the Universe* (1952). Gamow dated the expansion to about 17 billion years ago, probably the result of an earlier contraction. The difficulty with any such theory was in accounting for the formation of the chemical elements. He supposed the primeval atom to consist of 'Ylem', an old word used by Gamow to refer to a mixture of protons, electrons, and neutrons. Using the conditions of temperature and density prevailing in the first half hour of the universe's history he tried to work out ways in which the elements could be formed by nuclear aggregation. There was no difficulty in showing that ^{1}H, ^{2}H, ^{3}H, ^{3}He, and ^{4}He would be formed but at that point he could see no way to advance the chain further, for there is no stable element with an atomic weight of 5. Add either a proton or a neutron to the nucleus of ^{4}He and either ^{5}Li or ^{5}He will be formed, both of which are unstable and decay in less than 10^{-20} sec back to the original ^{4}He.

The only solution was to suppose that more than one particle collided with the ^{4}He nucleus simultaneously but, as Gamow realized, the universe by this time would be insufficiently dense and hot enough to permit such collisions to occur with the required frequency. He was therefore forced to conclude in 1956 that most of the heavy elements have been formed later in the hot interior of stars. One prediction that did emerge from his work and was to have important consequences for cosmology was his claim that the original explosion would produce a uniform radiation background;

the discovery of such radiation in 1964 by Arno PENZIAS and Robert WILSON did more than anything else to stimulate interest once more in Gamow's theory.

Gamow later moved from showing how the universe began to the no less interesting question of how life began. He was quick to see the significance of the DNA model proposed by James Watson and Francis Crick in 1953. The problem was to show how the sequences of the four nucleic acid bases that constitute the DNA chain could control the construction of proteins, which may be made from 20 or more amino acids. Gamow had the insight to see that the bases must contain a code for the construction of amino acids. But the question of how this worked still remained. It could not be one base to one amino acid for then there would be only four amino acids. Nor would two bases be sufficient for they could produce only $4 \times 4 = 16$ amino acids. It would therefore need a sequence of three bases to produce one amino acid, a language with a capacity of $4 \times 4 \times 4 = 64$ words, which was more than adequate for the construction of all proteins. Gamow also produced convincing arguments to show that the code is not overlapping.

The work on DNA allowed Gamow to indulge his passion for science fantasy. He founded the RNA tie club for which he actually designed a tie. It was restricted to 20 members, one for each amino acid. Each member took the name of one of the acids – Gamow was 'phe' (the usual abbreviation for phenylalanine) while Crick was 'tyr' (tyrosine). Meetings were held, information was exchanged, and considerable progress was made.

Gamow was also known as one of the most successful popular science writers of his day. He wrote many books, most of which are still in print, which convey much of the excitement of the revolution in physics that he lived through.

Gaskell, Walter Holbrook (1847–1914)
British physiologist

Gaskell, a lawyer's son, was born at Naples in Italy and graduated in mathematics from Cambridge University in 1869. He then studied medicine at University College Hospital, London, but returned to Cambridge to serve as lecturer in physiology from 1883 until his death. His first studies investigated whether the heartbeat is under external nervous control or is an inherent property of the cardiac musculature (myogenic). Skillful work with tortoises and crocodiles showed that the heart's rhythm is indeed myogenic.

Gaskell also greatly increased knowledge of the structure of the autonomic (involuntary) nervous system. In 1886 he noted three major 'outflows' of nerves from the spinal cord and lower part of the brain: the cervico-cranial, thoracic, and sacral. On leaving the central nervous system each nerve passes through a ganglion, or relay station, sited alongside the spine. Gaskell discovered two key properties of the system. He first noted that the nerves of all three groups are enclosed in a white sheath of myelin before entering their adjacent ganglion; on leaving the ganglion however the nerves of the thoracic outflow have lost their sheath in contrast to the still myelinated nerves of the other two outflows. He had thus succeeded in finding a simple anatomical distinction between the myelinated nerves, sacral and cervico-cranial, of the parasympathetic system, and the unmyelinated nerves, thoracic, of the sympathetic nervous system.

He also noted that most parts of the body receive nerves of both types and that their actions seem to be antagonistic. That is, while the myelinated nerves of the parasympathetic system inhibited the action of involuntary muscle, those of the sympathetic system seemed to increase its activity. Although much of Gaskell's work was done on reptiles he realized it had wider implications and boldly predicted that it would apply also to mammals, a prediction soon confirmed. His work was published posthumously in *The Involuntary Nervous System* (1916).

Much of Gaskell's later life was spent studying mammalian evolution. He tried to show how mammals could have evolved from arthropods rather than echinoderms (the orthodox view). His ideas were published in *The Origin of the Vertebrates* (1908), which contains the results of 20 years' work, but his theories have been largely ignored.

Gassendi, Pierre (1592–1655) *French physicist and philosopher*

Gassendi was born at Champtercier in France. After being educated in Aix and Paris, he gained a doctorate in theology from Avignon in 1616, was ordained in 1617, and in the same year was appointed to the chair of philosophy at Aix. In 1624 Gassendi moved to Digne where he served as provost of the cathedral until 1645 when he was elected to the professorship of mathematics at the Collège Royale in Paris, resigning because of illness in 1648.

As a practicing astronomer Gassendi made a large number of observations of comets, eclipses, and such celestial phenomena as the aurora borealis – a term he introduced himself. His most significant observation was of the 1631 transit of Mercury, the first transit to be observed, which he recorded in his *Mercurius in sole visus* (1632; Mercury in the Face of the Sun) as support for the new astronomy of Johannes Kepler.

In physics Gassendi attempted to measure the speed of sound and obtained the (too high) figure of 1473 feet per second. He also, in 1640, performed the much contemplated experiment of releasing a ball from the mast of a moving ship; as he expected, it fell to the foot of the mast in a straight line.

Gassendi's importance to science rests with his role as a propagandist and philosopher rather than as an experimentalist. Even though the Paris parliament declared in 1624 that on penalty of death "no person should either hold or teach any doctrine opposed to Aristotle," Gassendi published in the same year his *Excertitationes...adversus Aristoteleos* (Dissertations...against Aristotle), the first of his many works attacking both medieval Scholasticism and Aristotelianism. Nor did Gassendi find much attraction in the then emerging system of René Descartes. Instead he sought in his influential *Animadversiones in decimum librum Diogenes Laertii* (1649; Observations on the Tenth Book of Diogenes Laertius) to revive the classical atomism of Epicurus, suitably modified to ensure its compatibility with 17th-century Christianity. Unlike Epicurus he insisted that the atoms were created by God who also bestowed on man an immaterial soul; against Descartes he admitted the existence of the void within which his atoms could interact.

Gassendi's works were well known in England and exercised considerable influence on such leading scientists as Robert Boyle.

Gasser, Herbert Spencer (1888–1963)
American physiologist

Gasser, the son of a country doctor from Platteville, Wisconsin, was educated at the University of Wisconsin and at Johns Hopkins University. Having qualified as a physician in 1915, he moved to Washington University, St. Louis, to take up an appointment as professor of pharmacology. Here he joined his old teacher, Joseph ERLANGER, in a famous collaboration that resulted in their sharing the 1944 Nobel Prize for physiology or medicine for work on the differentiated function of nerve fibers. In 1931 Gasser was appointed to the chair of physi-

ology at Cornell Medical School. Finally, in 1935, he was made director of the Rockefeller Institute in New York, a post he retained until his retirement in 1953.

Gauss, Karl Friedrich (1777–1855)
German mathematician

Gauss came of a peasant background in Brunswick, Germany, and his extraordinary talent for mathematics showed itself at a very early age. By the age of three, he had discovered for himself enough arithmetic to be able to correct his father's calculations when he heard him working out the wages for his laborers. Gauss retained a staggering ability for mental calculation and memorizing throughout his life. At the age of ten he astonished his schoolteacher by discovering for himself the formula for the sum of an arithmetical progression. As a result of such precocity the young Gauss obtained the generous patronage of the duke of Brunwick. The duke paid for Gauss to attend the Caroline College in Brunswick and the University of Göttingen, and continued to support him until his death in 1806. Gauss then accepted an offer of the directorship of the observatory at Göttingen. This post probably suited him better than a more usual university appointment since he had little enthusiasm for teaching. Working at the observatory no doubt also stimulated his interest in applied mathematics and astronomy.

Gauss's life was uneventful. He remained director of the observatory for the rest of his life and indeed only rarely left Göttingen. Apart from mathematics he had a very keen interest in languages and at one stage hesitated between a career in mathematics and one in philology. His linguistic ability was evidently very great for he was able to teach himself fluent Russian in under two years. He also had a lively interest in world affairs, although in politics as in literature his views were somewhat conservative.

Gauss's contributions to mathematics were profound and they have affected almost every area of mathematics and mathematical physics. In addition to being a brilliant and original theoretician he was a practical experimentalist and a very accurate observer. His influence was naturally very great, but it would have been very much greater had he published all his discoveries. Many of his major results had to be rediscovered by some of the best mathematicians of the 19th century, although the extent to which this was the case was only revealed after Gauss's death. To give two of many examples – Janos Bolyai and Nikolai Lobachevsky are both known as the creators of non-Euclidean geometry, but their work had been anticipated by Gauss 30 years earlier. Cauchy's great pioneering work in complex analysis is justly famous, yet Gauss had proved but not published the fundamental Cauchy theorem years before Cauchy reached it. The reason for Gauss's extreme reluctance to publish seems to have been the very high standard he set himself and he was unwilling to publish any work in a field unless he could present a complete and finished treatment of it.

Gauss received his doctorate in 1799 from the University of Helmstedt for a proof of the fundamental theorem of algebra, i.e., the theorem that every equation of degree n with complex coefficients has at least one root that is a complex number. This was the first genuine proof to be given; all the supposed previous proofs had contained errors, and it is this standard of rigor that really marks Gauss's work out from that of his predecessors. (Mathematicians of the 18th century and earlier had often possessed an intuitive ability to conjecture mathematical theorems that were in fact true, but their ideas of rigorous mathematical proof fell short of modern standards.)

Gauss's first publication is generally accepted as his finest single achievement. This is the *Disquisitiones Arithmeticae* (Examinations of Arithmetic) of 1801. Appropriately it was dedicated to Gauss's patron the duke of Brunswick. The *Disquisitiones* is devoted to the area of mathematics that Gauss always considered to be the most beautiful, namely the theory of numbers. Gauss's prodigious ability for mental calculation enabled him to arrive at many of his theorems by generalizing from large numbers of examples. Among many other striking results Gauss was able to prove in the *Disquisitiones* the impossibility of constructing a regular heptagon with straight edge and compass – a problem that had baffled geometers since antiquity.

Gauss's interest was not confined to pure mathematics and he made contributions to many areas of applied mathematics and mathematical physics. Thus he discovered the *Gaussian error curve* and also the method of least squares, which he used in his work on geodesy. In his work on electromagnetism he collaborated with Wilhelm Weber on studies that led to the invention of the electric telegraph. The invention of the bifilar magnetometer for his own experimental work was another practical consequence of Gauss's interest in electromagnetism. His interest in mathematical astronomy resulted in many valuable innovations; he obtained a formula for calculating parallax in 1799 and in 1808 he published

a work on planetary motion. When in 1801 the asteroid Ceres was first observed and then 'lost' by Giuseppe Piazzi, Gauss was able to predict correctly where it would reappear. He also made improvements in the design of the astronomical instruments in use at his observatory.

Gauss's work transformed mathematics and he is generally considered to be, with Newton and Archimedes, one of the greatest mathematicians of all time. The cgs unit of magnetic flux density is named in his honor.

Gay-Lussac, Joseph-Louis (1778–1850)
French chemist and physicist

Gay-Lussac was the son of a judge who was later imprisoned during the French Revolution. Born at St. Léonard in France, he entered the recently founded Ecole Polytechnique in 1797 and graduated in 1800. His career was thereafter one of steady promotion. Originally studying engineering, in 1801 he attracted the attention of the chemist Claude-Louis Berthollet who made him his assistant at Arcueil, near Paris. The science of chemistry was then in its infancy. Few chemists were actively engaged in research, and the equipment used was primitive. Chemical symbols had just been introduced, and no chemical formulae were known with certainty. During his career Gay-Lussac contributed to the advancement of all branches of chemistry by his discoveries, and greatly improved and developed experimental techniques.

In 1802, following the researches of the chemist Jacques Charles, Gay-Lussac formulated the law now alternatively attributed to himself and Charles – that gases expand equally with the same change of temperature, provided the pressure remains constant. By using superior experimental techniques, Gay-Lussac largely eliminated the errors of his predecessors in this field, in particular by developing a method of drying the gases. He measured the coefficient of expansion of gases between 0°C and 100°C, thus forming the basis for the idea of the absolute zero of temperature. His law was received with satisfaction as complementary to Boyle's law. It was later shown that Gay-Lussac's and Boyle's laws applied exactly only to a hypothetical 'ideal gas'; real gases obey the law approximately.

Gay-Lussac made his first daring balloon ascent in 1804 with Jean Biot, during which they made scientific observations and established that there was no change in either the composition of the air or in the Earth's magnetic force at the heights they reached.

Gay-Lussac made a second ascent alone, reaching a height of 23,018 feet.

In 1805, by exploding together given volumes of hydrogen and oxygen, Gay-Lussac discovered that one volume of oxygen combined with two volumes of hydrogen to form water. In 1808, after researches using other gases, he formulated his famous law of combining volumes – that when gases combine their relative volumes bear a simple numerical relation to each other (e.g., 1:1, 2:1) and to the volumes of their gaseous product, provided pressure and temperature remain constant. The English chemist John DALTON was immediately interested in Gay-Lussac's discovery, but when, on investigation, the law appeared to conflict with his own theory of the indivisibility of atoms, Dalton rejected the law and sought to discredit Gay-Lussac's experimental methods. The reason for the apparent conflict was that the difference between an atom and a molecule was not clearly understood, and it was left to the Italian chemist Amedeo Avogadro to formulate a theory reconciling the two laws, thus laying the basis of modern molecular theory.

From 1808 Gay-Lussac worked with the chemist Louis Thenard. Following Humphry Davy's isolation of minute amounts of sodium and potassium, the two chemists in 1808 prepared these metals in reasonable quantities. It was during his experiments with potassium as a reagent that Gay-Lussac blew up his laboratory, temporarily blinding himself. In collaboration with Thenard he isolated and named the element boron. Simultaneously with Davy, Gay-Lussac investigated in 1813 a substance first isolated by Bernard Courtois and established that it was an element similar to chlorine. He named it iodine from the Greek 'iode' meaning violet. In 1815 he prepared cyanogen and described it as a compound radical. He proved that prussic acid (hydrogen cyanide) was made up of this radical and hydrogen, completing the overthrow of Lavoisier's theory that all acids must contain oxygen. His recognition of compound radicals laid the basis of modern organic chemistry.

Gay-Lussac also investigated fermentation, the phenomenon of supercooling, the growth of alum crystals in solution, the compounds of sulfur, and the various stages of oxidation of nitrogen. With the young student Justus von Liebig he investigated the fulminates. In his later years he improved on experimental techniques, and laid the basis of modern volumetric analysis.

In 1827 he devised the *Gay-Lussac tower*. Oxides of nitrogen arising from the preparation of sulfuric acid by the lead-chamber process, which formerly escaped into the atmosphere, are absorbed by passing them up a chimney packed with coke, over which concentrated sulfuric acid is trickled. This tower and its modifications are used in many chemically-based industries today.

Gay-Lussac was a chemist of brilliance and determination. Although said to be cold and reserved as a man, as a researcher he was bold and energetic. Shortly before his death he expressed regret at the experiments that he would never be able to perform.

Geber (*c.* 14th century) *Spanish alchemist*

The name Geber, the Latinized form of Jabir, was adopted by an anonymous medieval writer, probably because of the reputation of the great Arabian alchemist, Jabir ibn Hayyan, who is also known better as Geber.

Four of Geber's works are known, the longest being the *Summi perfectionis magisterii*, which was translated into English as *The Sum of Perfection* or *The Perfect Magistery*. The other works are *De investigatione perfectionis* (The Investigation of Perfection), *De inventione veritatis* (The Invention of Verity), and *Liber fornacum* (Book of Furnaces). The four manuscripts were translated into English in 1678.

Geber's major contribution was to spread Arabian alchemical theories through Europe where they had considerable influence.

Geber (Jabir ibn Hayyan) (*c.* 721– *c.* 815) *Arabian alchemist*

Geber seems to have spent his life among the political uncertainties of the decline of the Umayyad dynasty. His father was executed for his part in a plot to oust the caliph and Geber, who was born in Tus (now in Iran), was sent to southern Arabia. He became a courtier to Harun al-Rashid (of *Arabian Nights* fame) but fell out of favor in 803 and left Baghdad for Kufah, where he probably remained for the rest of his life. He was a Sufi as well as being connected with the Isma'ilite sect.

A large number of works carry his name, which is now usually taken to refer to a corpus as a whole without implying actual authorship by one individual. The most important works are *The 112 Books*, *The 70 Books*, *The 10 Books of Rectification*, and *The Books of the Balances*. Geber believed that everything is composed of a combination of earth, water, fire, and air. These elements combined to form mercury and sulfur from which he believed all metals are formed, a view that continued until Robert Boyle. He further held that if the right proportions of each were combined they would produce gold. Geber's theory was of considerable influence on alchemy and the early development of chemistry.

Geber is regarded as the father of Arabian chemistry. In the 14th century his name was adopted by an anonymous Spanish alchemist to add authority to his work.

Geer, Charles de See DE GEER, CHARLES.

Geer, Gerard Jacob de (1858–1943)
Swedish geologist

Geer came from a noble Swedish family in Stockholm and both his father and brother served as prime minister of Sweden. He graduated from Uppsala University in 1879 and worked initially with the Geological Survey on the problem of raised beaches before taking up an appointment as professor of geology at Uppsala in 1897. In 1924 he became the first director of the Stockholm Geochronological Institute.

Geer originated the varve-counting method for dating the geological past in years, a system that gave unprecedented accuracy in age determinations. In 1878 he had begun a study of the Quaternary Period in Sweden and soon became aware of the layered deposits, known as varves, laid down in glacial lakes. Seasonal differences in the material deposited enabled individual years to be identified, the summer layer consisting of light-colored coarse-grained material and the winter layer of dark-colored fine material, and Geer noticed the analogy of the varves to tree rings.

He tried to see if the sequence of varves from one region would correlate in any way with those of other areas and found that this could be done for most parts of Sweden. However, this would only allow him to say that two samples came from the same time without being able to say whether that time was a century or a millenium in the past. He was able eventually to establish a base year at 6839 BC from which point individual years could be counted in either direction.

Geer's work was a major breakthrough although it was soon to be overshadowed by radioactive dating and was limited to certain glaciated areas. In his later years, Geer tried to apply his techniques and to establish correlations with other areas of the world, but with varying success.

Geiger, Hans Wilhelm (1882–1945)
German physicist

Geiger was born at Neustadt in Germany and studied physics at the universities of Munich and Erlangen, obtaining his doctorate (1906) for work on electrical discharges in gases. He then took up a position in England at the University of Manchester, where he worked with Ernest Rutherford from 1907 to 1912. In 1912 he returned to Germany, from then until his death holding a series of important university positions, including that of director of the German physical laboratory, the Physikalisch Technische Reichsanstalt, in Berlin (1912), and professor of physics at Kiel University (1925).

Geiger, a pioneer in nuclear physics, developed a variety of instruments and techniques used for detecting and counting individual charged particles. In 1908 Rutherford and Geiger, investigating the charge and nature of alpha particles, devised an instrument to detect and count these particles. The instrument consisted of a tube containing gas with a wire at high voltage along the axis. A particle passing through the gas caused ionization, and initiated a brief discharge in the gas, and the resulting pulse of current could be detected on a meter. This was the prototype, which Geiger subsequently improved and made more sensitive; in 1928 he produced, with W. Müller, a design of counter that is now widely used (and known as the *Geiger–Muller counter*). With their primitive counter Rutherford and Geiger established that alpha particles are doubly charged helium atoms.

Other important work of Geiger was his investigation with E. Marsden in 1909, of the scattering of alpha particles by gold leaf; this led Rutherford to propose a nuclear theory for the atom.

Geller, Margaret Joan (1947–   )
American astronomer

The daughter of a crystallographer from Ithaca, New York State, Geller was encouraged as a small child to study science and mathematics. She was educated at the University of California, Berkeley, and at Princeton where she obtained her PhD in 1975. After a period at the Institute of Astronomy, Cambridge, England, Geller moved to Harvard in 1980 and was appointed professor of astronomy in 1988. She is also a staff member of the Smithsonian Astrophysical Observatory.

Since the early 1980s Geller and her coworkers have been carrying out for the Center for Astrophysics (CfA) a red-shift survey of some 15,000 galaxies. The intention is to map all galaxies above a certain brightness, out to about 650 million light years, in a particular sector of the heavens.

They were aware that to some observers the sky lacked the uniformity predicted by the big-bang theory. In 1981, for example, a 100-million-light-year gap had been discovered in the constellation Bootes. Geller considered the possibility that this was a local phenomenon, and that the predicted homogeneity would become more apparent on a much larger scale. Further investigations were expected to show a uniform distribution of galaxies.

But when they came to plot the distribution of galaxies they saw neither a uniform spread, nor a random scattering of galaxies, but large-scale clusters grouped into enormous structures. The largest of these, dubbed the *Great Wall*, stretches for more than 500 million light-years. It was difficult to see how anything as massive could have been formed within the context of current cosmological theory; when Geller reported the initial results of the CfA survey in 1989 she noted, "Something fundamental is missing in our models."

Gell-Mann, Murray (1929–) *American theoretical physicist*

Gell-Mann was born in New York City, the son of Austrian immigrants. Having entered Yale at the age of fifteen, he went on to the Massachusetts Institute of Technology, where he completed his PhD in 1951. After spending a year at the Institute for Advanced Study, Princeton, and four years at the University of Chicago, Gell-Mann was appointed professor of physics in 1955 at the California Institute of Technology. In 1967 he was elected R. A. Millikan Professor of Theoretical Physics, a post he held until his retirement in 1993.

Gell-Mann has been mainly concerned with the study of elementary particles. In the early 1950s physicists were puzzled by the 'strange' behavior of some apparently strongly interacting mesons. The kaons, as they were called, should have a lifetime of only 10^{-23} second; they actually survived for some 10^{-10} second. Gell-Mann suspected that some unknown property was conserved and that this explained the rapid decay of the kaons via the strong force. He named the new property 'strangeness' (*S*) and assigned the kaons a value $S = +1$. *S* was later defined as $2Q - B$, or twice the charge minus the baryon number. Thus the proton with a charge of $+\frac{1}{2}$ and a baryon number of $+1$, will take the value $S = 0$, and this value will be conserved in all strong interactions. Similar ideas were proposed in 1954 by K. Nishijima in Japan.

New problems emerged. Physicists had become particularly worried by the discovery of large numbers of supposedly elementary particles. In the late 1950s it was possible to list and classify some thirty subatomic particles. Within five years another 70 'elementary' particles had been discovered. The theorist's first priority was to bring some kind of order to this unwelcome abundance. In 1964, using group theory, and a number of conservation principles, Gell-Mann demonstrated that hadrons – i.e., particles such as baryons and mesons that interact strongly – could be classified into multiplets of 1, 8, 10, or 27 members. One such multiplet constructed with the group SU(3), or symmetry unity theory of dimension 3, yielded the octet. A similar proposal was made at the same time by the Israeli physicist Y. Ne'eman. The new synthesis was described in *The Eightfold Way* (1964), a work edited by Gell-Mann and Ne'eman. That there was more to their theory than arbitrary classifications was soon shown when the Ω^- (omega minus) particle, whose existence was previously unsuspected, was discovered in 1964 at Brookhaven with precisely the properties demanded for it by the SU(3) theory. The name itself alludes to the Buddhist path to enlightenment and to the eight quantum numbers required by the theory.

Following the discovery of the Ω^- Gell-Mann began to consider why the theory should be so successful in explaining hadron behavior. In his 1964 paper *A Schematic Model of Baryons and Mesons*, he proposed the existence of a more fundamental level of reality, that hadrons were composite, built out of more basic entities he proposed to call 'quarks'. The name itself was taken from a phrase in James Joyce's *Finnegans Wake* – "three quarks for muster mark." In Gell-Mann's original formulation he worked with three quarks, up (u), down (d), and strange (s), and three antiquarks ($\bar{u},\bar{d},\bar{s}$). As their most distinctive feature Gell-Mann assigned them fractional units of charge: s and d with a charge of $-\frac{1}{3}$, and u with $+\frac{2}{3}$. It was a simple matter to show that all baryons could be constructed with three quarks, and all mesons from a quark and an antiquark. Similar views were expressed in 1964 by G. Zweig.

The original model soon required some refashioning. A fourth quark property, 'charm', was proposed by Sheldon GLASHOW in 1970 and detected in 1974. This required extending the hadron classification scheme from a SU(3) group to a SU(4) group. Two further quarks have been added the t and b quarks, known variously as top and bottom, or 'beauty' and 'truth'. The fifth b quark was identified by L. Lederman in 1977. The t quark, though occasionally glimpsed by optimistic experimentalists, has yet to be firmly identified. A further complication of quark theory emerged with NAMBU's proposal in 1965 that they came with three varieties of 'color'.

In the 1980s Gell-Mann turned to the study of complexity. He was a cofounder in 1984 of the Santa Fe Institute which works on adaptive complex systems. Reportedly fluent in fifteen languages himself, Gell-Mann has also worked in the field of historical linguistics.

For his numerous contributions to the study of elementary particles Gell-Mann was awarded the 1969 Nobel Prize for physics.

Gennes, Pierre Gilles de (1932–)
French physicist

Parisian-born Gennes was educated at the Ecole Normale in his native city, completing his PhD there in 1955. He was appointed professor of solid-state physics at the University of Paris in 1961; since 1971 he has served as professor of physics at the Collège de France and from 1976 as director of the College of Physics and Chemistry, Paris.

Some areas of science have long been thought to be too unstructured and messy to be conducive to traditional physical analysis. Two such areas, liquid crystals and polymers, were consequently largely ignored by physicists. Gennes, however, saw that they behave in many ways just like other better understood physical processes.

Liquid crystals consist of rodlike molecules in a liquid state. They undergo, like magnets and superconductors, phase changes. Thus in what is known as the smetic A phase, the molecules are oriented with their axes perpendicular to the layers; at lower temperatures they adopt the C phase with a parallel orientation. Using concepts derived from the study of phase changes in other fields Gennes was able to throw light on changes in liquid crystals. The results of his work were described in his *The Physics of Liquid Crystals* (1974). Gennes adopted a similar approach to his study of polymers which he described fully in his *Scaling Concepts of Polymer Physics* (1979).

For his work in these fields Gennes was awarded the 1991 Nobel Prize for physics.

Geoffroy Saint-Hilaire, Etienne
(1772–1844) *French biologist*

The youngest of fourteen children in a poor family from Etampes in France, Geoffroy was supported by the local clergy, who recognized his precocious intelligence. He took a scholarship to the Collège de Navarre, Paris, and was soon appointed as a demonstrator at the Jardin des Plantes, a precursor of the Muséum National d'Histoire Naturelle, as his predecessor, Bernard Lacépède, fled the Revolution. In 1793 Geoffroy became professor of vertebrate zoology at the museum; the comparable chair of invertebrate zoology was held by Lamarck.

In 1798 Geoffroy accompanied Napoleon on his conquest of Egypt and contributed to the celebrated 24 volumes of the *Description de l'Egypte* (1809–28; Description of Egypt). He traveled as far down the Nile as Aswan and while in Egypt he examined a number of mummified cats taken from ancient tombs. They were, he noted, identical to the animals of his day. Did this mean that species were fixed? If they were fixed why were there so many similarities between different forms? Why, for example, despite differences in external form, do the skeletons of bats, whales, and dogs resemble each other so closely?

Geoffroy derived his answer from German *Naturphilosophie* (nature philosophy), which claimed to see beneath an apparent diversity of form, mere variations on a single plan. There was a vertebrate type which could be identified in all vertebrates. Thus he demonstrated in 1807 that pectoral fins in fish and the bones of the front limbs of other vertebrates were morphologically and functionally similar.

But Cuvier had identified in the operculum, a bony flap covering gill slits in fishes, an apparently unique structure. It took Geoffroy a decade's investigation before he could explain it away as equivalent to the auditory bones in mammals. He was thus able in his *Philosophie anatomique* (1818; Anatomical Philosophy) to announce the principle of anatomical connection claiming that the same anatomical structural plan could be identified in all vertebrates.

By 1830 Geoffroy had begun to argue that there was a universal "unity of composition," quoting in evidence work claiming to have detected a unity in crustacea, fish, and mollusks. Such views brought a savage onslaught from Cuvier who insisted that there were distinct forms in nature, and that parts were formed to meet functional needs.

But, once having accepted a unity of composition, it becomes possible to see how one species can be transformed into another. If birds and reptiles are built to the same plan, then "an accident that befell one of the reptiles…could develop in every part of the body the conditions of the ornithological type." Geoffroy was thus moving late in his career to some form of evolutionary theory. A stroke in 1840 which left him blind and paralyzed brought such work to an end.

Geoffroy was succeeded at the museum in 1841 by his son, Isidore (1805–61), also a distinguished biologist and best known for his three-volume work on teratology, *Histoire...des anomalies de l'organisation chez l'homme et les animaux* (1833–37; Account...of Irregularities in the Structure of Man and the Animals).

Gerhardt, Charles Frédéric
(1816–1856) *French chemist*

Gerhardt was the son of an Alsatian chemical manufacturer from Strasbourg. He was educated at the universities of Karlsruhe, Leipzig, and Giessen where he studied under Justus von Liebig. From 1838 he worked in Paris as assistant to Jean Dumas before becoming professor of chemistry at Montpellier (1844). He returned to Paris in 1848 and worked with Auguste Laurent in their private laboratory until he was appointed to the chair at Strasbourg in 1855. He published two original works: *Précis de chimie organique* (1844–45; Summary of Organic Chemistry) and his *Introduction à l'étude de la chimie par le système unitaire* (1848; Introduction to the Study of Chemistry by Means of the Unified System).

Gerhardt is best known for his attempts to rationalize organic chemistry. Like most chemists he was aware that the dualistic system of Jöns BERZELIUS was unsatisfactory and tried to create an alternative. He adopted what became known as 'type theory' in which he saw all organic compounds with reference to four 'types' – hydrogen, hydrogen chloride, ammonia, and water. Organic compounds were referred to these types by replacing a hydrogen atom in one of these compounds by a radical (i.e., by a group of atoms).

Germain, Sophie Marie (1776–1831)
French mathematician

The daughter of a prosperous Parisian merchant, Germain showed an early interest in mathematics and from the age of thirteen read whatever texts she could obtain. Although the main higher education institutions were closed to her, she managed to acquire the lecture notes of the mathematician J. L. Lagrange, which he had delivered at the newly founded Ecole Polytechnique.

She also began to correspond with prominent mathematicians using the pseudonym Le Blanc and allowing them to assume that she was a man. She had been working on number theory and had begun to tackle the celebrated last theorem of Fermat: that there are no integers x,y,z,n, where $n>2$ such that

$$x^n + y^n = z^n$$

Germain made a major contribution to showing that the equation does not hold for the case in which n is equal to 5. She informed Gauss of the result but, typically, he failed to reply.

In 1809 Germain began to work on the theory behind the appearance of curious patterns formed by sand placed on vibrating plates. The phenomenon had first been described by E. F. CHLADNI who had demonstrated them to Napoleon in 1808. The emperor had been so intrigued that he had offered a one-kilogram gold medal to the first person to explain what are now known as *Chladni's figures*.

Germain submitted a solution in 1811 based on Euler's theory of elasticity. She was the only entrant but her work contained a number of errors. It did, however, provoke Lagrange to produce a corrected equation to derive the patterns theoretically. The competition was extended, and after two further attempts, Germain was finally awarded the prize in 1815. She published her work privately in 1821 as *Recherches sur la théorie des surfaces élastiques* (Researches on the Theory of Elastic Surfaces).

Sophie Germain developed breast cancer in 1829 and died two years later.

Germer, Lester Halbert (1896–1971)
American physicist. See DAVISSON, CLINTON JOSEPH.

Giaever, Ivar (1929–   ) *Norwegian–American physicist*

Born in Bergen, Norway, Giaever studied electrical engineering at the Norwegian Institute of Technology. He did service with the Norwegian Army (1952–53) and worked as a patent examiner in the Norwegian Patent Office (1953–54). In 1954 he emigrated to Canada to take up the post of mechanical engineer with the Canadian General Electric Company, transferring to General Electric's Research and Development Center in Schenectady, New York, in 1956. He gained his doctorate in 1964 from the New York Rensselear Polytechnical Institute, where he became professor of physics in 1988.

At General Electric, Giaever worked on tunneling effects in superconductors, a phenomenon explored by Leo ESAKI. In 1960 he performed experiments with metals separated by a thin insulating film through which electrons tunneled, and found that if one of the metals was in the superconducting state, the current–voltage characteristics of such junctions were highly nonlinear and revealed much about the superconducting state. This laid the foundation for Brian JOSEPHSON's important discovery of the Josephson effect.

Giaever, Josephson, and Esaki shared the 1973 Nobel Prize for physics for their various contributions to knowledge of the phenomenon of tunneling and superconductivity. Their work has had important application in microelectronics and in the precise measurement of electromotive force.

Subsequently, Giaever has also published work in the field of visual observation of the antibody-antigen reaction.

Giauque, William Francis (1895–1982)
Canadian–American physical chemist

Born at Niagara Falls in Canada, Giauque spent his whole academic life at the University of California. He began as a student, obtaining his PhD in 1922, and was immediately appointed to the staff at Berkeley, becoming professor of chemistry in 1934.

Giauque was one of the pioneer workers in low-temperature phenomena. His early work in the 1920s concerned the experimental measurement of entropies at very low temperature – work that depended on the use of the third law of thermodynamics introduced in 1906 by Walther Nernst (the Nernst heat theorem). At the same time, Giauque used statistics to calculate the absolute entropies using the energy levels of molecules obtained from spectroscopy. This method, developed by Josiah Willard GIBBS and others, is known as statistical mechanics. Giauque's work provided support for the validity of both statistical thermodynamics and the third law.

Moreover, it led him to a method of attaining very low temperatures, close to absolute zero. The lowest temperature achieved at that time was 0.8 K, reached by Heike KAMERLINGH-ONNES in 1910 by pumping away the vapor of liquid helium and causing it to evaporate under reduced pressure. Giauque, and independently Peter Debye, proposed in 1925 a completely different method known as adiabatic demagnetization.

The basic idea is to take a paramagnetic substance surrounded by a coil of wire in a gas-filled container. The sample can be cooled by surrounding the container by liquid helium and magnetized by a current through the coil. It is thus possible to produce a magnetized specimen at liquid-helium temperature, and then to isolate it in a vacuum by removing the gas from the container. In the magnetized specimen the 'molecular magnets' are all aligned. If the magnetic field on the specimen is reduced to zero the sample is demagnetized, and in this process the molecular magnets become random again. The entropy increases and work is done against the decreasing external field, causing a decrease in the temperature of the specimen.

There were considerable problems in putting this theory into practice, not least in measuring the temperatures produced. In 1933 Giauque had a working apparatus that improved on Kamerlingh-Onnes's in achieving a temperature of 0.1 K. Giauque received the 1949 Nobel Prize for chemistry for his work on low-temperature phenomena.

He also worked on isotopes, showing in 1929 (with H. L. Johnson) that oxygen was a mixture of ^{16}O, ^{17}O, and ^{18}O.

Gibbs, Josiah Willard (1839–1903)
American mathematician and theoretical physicist

Gibbs came from an academic family in New Haven, Connecticut. He entered Yale in 1854, graduated in 1858, and in 1863 received a PhD for research on the design of gears. The same year he traveled to Europe, returning in 1869 to Yale where he remained until his death. In 1871 he was appointed professor of mathematical physics.

His initial work on the theory of James Watt's steam-engine governor led him into a study of the thermodynamics of chemical systems. In a series of long papers published between 1873 and 1876 he developed, and indeed virtually completed, the theory of chemical thermodynamics. Gibbs's most famous paper, *On the Equilibrium of Heterogeneous Substances* (1876), contains the celebrated *Gibbs phase rule*, describing the equilibrium of heterogeneous systems. His name is also associated with the *Gibbs free energy* – a function that determines the conditions in which a chemical reaction will occur – and with several other equations in thermodynamics.

Gibbs was also active in mathematics and physics. He worked on the theory of William Hamilton's quaternions and introduced the simpler, widely used, vector notation. Between 1882 and 1889 he published a series of papers on the electromagnetic theory of light. He also made important contributions to statistical mechanics, introducing the fundamental concept of *Gibbsian ensembles* – collections of large numbers of macroscopic systems with the same thermodynamic properties, used in relating thermodynamic properties to statistical properties.

Gibbs, who never married, lived a quiet retiring life at Yale; he was a poor teacher but a brilliant and productive theorist. His work, carried out far from the European mainstream of science, was largely published in the obscure *Transactions of the Connecticut Academy of Sciences.* However, James Clerk Maxwell understood the importance of his ideas as early as 1875 and in later life Gibbs was widely recognized. Many regard him as the greatest native-born American scientist.

Gilbert, Walter (1932–   ) *American molecular biologist*

Born in Boston, Massachusetts, Gilbert was educated at Harvard and at Cambridge University, England, where he obtained his PhD in physics in 1957. He returned to America to take up an appointment in theoretical physics at Harvard. He changed to molecular biology in 1960 under the influence of James Watson and in 1968 became professor of molecular biology at Harvard. He was elected chairman of the department of cellular and developmental biology in 1987.

In 1961 Jacques MONOD and François JACOB proposed a theoretical answer to one of the most pressing problems of molecular biology, that of genetic control. If the common bacteria *Escherichia coli* is grown in the presence of milk sugar (lactose) it will produce an enzyme, beta-galactosidase, to split it into its component sugars. However, if grown in the absence of lactose, the enzyme will not be produced. There must therefore presumably be a mechanism whereby the gene controlling the production of the enzyme can be switched on and off. Monod and Jacob proposed a detailed account of such a mechanism, part of which involves the existence of a repressor molecule, which could bind itself to the gene and switch it off in the absence of lactose. The lac repressor, as it was called, would be inactivated, thus switching the gene on, by an inducer molecule produced by the lactose itself.

Plausible and powerful though the Monod–Jacob model appeared, it was still only a model until the basic confirmation provided by the isolation and identification of the lac repressor was achieved. Gilbert began such a search in 1965. This was a formidable task as the repressor was known to exist in small quantities only; nor was its chemical nature known. Gilbert himself likened the task to isolating the neutrino.

By 1966, in collaboration with Benno Muller-Hill, Gilbert had devised an ingenious experimental procedure, known as equilibrium dialysis. They used a specially active inducer, isopropyl thiogalactoside (IPTG), discovered by Melvin Calvin. Cells of *E. coli* were ground up and placed in a bag with a cellular membrane, allowing the passage of water and IPTG molecules but excluding such larger molecules as proteins. The bag was then placed in water containing radioactive IPTG.

As IPTG can pass through the bag an equal concentration of the inducer should be achieved. But if IPTG should bind itself to the lac repressor inside the bag then it will be too large to pass freely through the bag membrane. Consequently the concentration of the IPTG bound to the repressor should start to build up inside the bag and, being radioactive, should be readily detectable. Eventually they were able to report a concentration of IPTG 4% greater inside the bag than out. This was enough to encourage Gilbert and Muller-Hill to proceed to the next stage of fractionating, purifying, and isolating the repressor. This proved more difficult than they had expected but in late 1966 they were able to report the existence of a large protein molecule, the lac repressor. The following year their Harvard colleague M. Ptashne obtained a similar result with the lambda phage repressor.

Gilbert has also developed techniques for determining the sequence of bases in DNA, which though similar to Frederick Sanger's method differs in that it can be applied to single as well as double-stranded DNA. It was for this work that he shared the 1980 Nobel Prize for chemistry with SANGER and Paul BERG.

Gilbert, William (1544–1603) *English physicist and physician*

Gilbert, who was born at Colchester, was educated at Cambridge, where he took his degree in 1569 and later became a fellow. He moved to London in 1573, became a member of the Royal College of Physicians, and served as physician to Queen Elizabeth I and briefly to James I. In 1600 he published the first great English scientific work *De magnete, magnetisque corporibus, et de magno magnete tellure* (On the Magnet, Magnetic Bodies, and the Great Magnet Earth) in which he presented his investigations into magnetic bodies and electrical attractions. It is a remarkably modern work – rigorously experimental, emphasizing observation, and rejecting as unproved many popular beliefs about magnetism, such as the supposed ability of diamond to magnetize iron. He showed that a compass needle was subject to magnetic dip (pointing downward) and, reasoning from experiments with a spherical lodestone, explained this by concluding that the Earth acts as a bar magnet. He also introduced the term *magnetic pole*. The book was widely available on the Continent, there being five editions in Germany and Holland alone before 1628, and was very influential in the creation of the new mechanical view of science.

Gill, Sir David (1843–1914) *Scottish astronomer*

Born in Aberdeen, Gill was educated at Marischal College and Aberdeen University. He was in charge of the Earl of Crawford's private observatory at Dunecht before becoming royal astronomer at the Cape of Good Hope, where he remained until 1907. He was knighted in 1900.

Gill spent much time and thought on improving the accuracy of the astronomical unit (AU – the mean distance between the Earth and the Sun, one of the basic measurements of astronomy), then determined from measurements of the distances of Venus and Mars. In 1874 he went to Mauritius to observe the transit of Venus. The difficulty is that Venus, on magnification, presents a disk whose edges are not absolutely sharp, thus making it difficult to estimate the moment of first contact. In 1877 Gill went to Ascension Island to measure the distance of Mars using the distance from Greenwich as a base line. Although he obtained reasonable results he realized (as had Johann Galle) that a more accurate figure could be obtained if the planetoids were used instead for they came closer to the Earth and on magnification presented a starlike appearance. (This idea was taken up with great success later by Harold Spencer Jones.) In 1897, with the cooperation of astronomers in Leipzig and New Haven, Gill made a very accurate determination of the solar parallax.

His other main research was extending Friedrich Argelander's catalog to the southern skies. This began in 1882 when he photographed a comet and was impressed with the clarity of the stars visible in the background. Consequently he started photographing the southern skies, collaborating with the Dutch astronomer Jacobus Kapteyn. In 1904 the *Cape Photographic Dorchmusterung* was published cataloging over 450,000 stars to within 19° of the southern celestial pole.

Gilman, Alfred Goodman (1941–)
American pharmacologist

The son of Alfred Gilman Snr, a noted phar-

macologist, Gilman received his PhD from Case Western Reserve University, Cleveland, Ohio, in 1969. After working at the University of Virginia Medical School from 1971 until 1981, Gilman moved to the University of Texas Southwestern Medical Centre, Dallas, where he became professor of pharmacology.

Gilman's work has been on the processes by which hormones, neurotransmitters, and other stimuli – the so-called 'first messengers' – influence cellular activity. It had been shown by Earl Sutherland in 1971 that hormones do not actually enter cells. They seem to bind to receptor sites on the cell's surface and then produce a "second messenger," cAMP (cyclic adenosine monophosphate), which initiates the appropriate cellular response.

It was further shown by Martin Rodbell that other factors, namely, an amplifier and a transducer, were required in the process. Rodbell identified the enzyme adenylate cyclase (AC) as the amplifier and demonstrated that transducers would only work in the presence of the energy-rich molecule guanine triphosphate (GTP).

Gilman set out to elucidate the process further. He established in the late 1970s that the transducers were in fact proteins. They were initially named 'guanine nucleotide binding proteins', a term quickly shortened to G proteins. Gilman went on to outline the main steps in cellular signaling as:

1. A hormone, neurotransmitter, etc., binds to a cell receptor.
2. The receptor binds to and activates a G protein.
3. The activated G protein binds to GTP.
4. The activated GTP stimulates AC to produce cAMP.
5. cAMP produces an appropriate cellular response.

G proteins have been shown to play a number of important physiological roles. In cholera, for example, a toxin is produced that freezes G proteins into their GTP-bound activated state, producing in the body a massive fluid loss with consequent dehydration. G proteins are also thought to be involved in some aspects of diabetes and some types of cancer.

Gilman shared the 1994 Nobel Prize for physiology or medicine with Martin ROD-BELL for their work on G proteins.

Glaser, Donald Arthur (1926–)
American physicist

Glaser was born in Cleveland, Ohio, and took his degree in physics and mathematics at the Case Institute of Technology there.

After graduating in 1946, he went on to gain his doctorate for cosmic-ray research from the California Institute of Technology in 1950. From 1949 to 1959, Glaser worked in the physics department of the University of Michigan, becoming professor in 1957. In 1959 he moved to the University of California at Berkeley as a professor of physics and subsequently (1964) as a professor of physics and biology.

While at the University of Michigan, Glaser became interested in techniques for the visualization and recording of elementary particles. The Wilson cloud chamber, using supersaturated vapor, had been in use since the 1920s, but was unsuited to the detection of the highly energetic particles emerging from the new accelerators of the 1950s.

Glaser considered other unstable systems that could be used, and experimented with superheated liquids, in which ionizing particles would leave a trail of vapor bubbles. In 1952 he produced the first radiation-sensitive bubble chamber, in which he used diethyl ether under pressure and controlled temperature. A sudden brief reduction in pressure was used and trails of bubbles forming along the tracks of particles could be captured by high-speed photography before the bulk of the liquid boiled. For this invention, and its subsequent development into a useful research tool, Glaser received the 1960 Nobel Prize for physics.

The bubble chamber, using liquid hydrogen at low temperature, is now a basic component of almost all high-energy physics experiments, and has been the instrument of detection of many strange new particles and phenomena. Present-day bubble chambers are much bigger (and more expensive) than Glaser's original, which was only three cubic centimeters in volume. More recently, at the University of California at Berkeley, Glaser's interest has turned to methods of applying physics to molecular biology.

Glashow, Sheldon Lee (1932–   )
American physicist

Glashow was born in New York City and graduated from the Bronx High School there in 1950. He went on to Cornell University, where he gained his bachelor's degree in 1954. His MA (1955) and PhD in physics (1959) were gained at Harvard University, and his postdoctoral research took him to the Bohr Institute, the European Organization for Nuclear Research (CERN) in Geneva, and the California Institute of Technology. After a year at Stanford he joined the faculty of the University of California at Berkeley (1961–66). In 1967 he re-turned to Harvard as a professor of physics, and has remained there since.

The award of the 1979 Nobel Prize, shared with Abdus SALAM and Steven WEINBERG, was for the explanation of the forces that bind together elementary particles of matter. The citation was "for their contribution to the theory of the unified weak and electromagnetic interaction between elementary particles, including *inter alia* the prediction of the weak neutral current."

The Weinberg–Salam theory was a major step in unifying two of the four fundamental forces of physics: the electromagnetic interaction and the weak interaction. The theory was originally applied only to the class of particles known as leptons (electrons and neutrinos). Glashow extended the theory to other elementary particles (including the baryons and mesons) by introducing a new property that he called 'charm'. The quark theory of Murray GELL-MANN could be extended by the introduction of a fourth quark – the 'charmed quark' – and combinations of the four types of quark could lead to a group of particles with symmetry SU4. The idea of charm can be used to explain the properties of the J/psi particle, discovered in 1974 by Burton RICHTER and Samuel TING.

Other extensions of the quark theory have since been made involving 'colored quarks' – the theory is known as *quantum chromodynamics*.

Glisson, Francis (1597–1677) *English physician*

Born at Rampisham in southwest England, Glisson was educated at Cambridge University where he obtained his MD in 1634. He was appointed professor of physics at Cambridge in 1636 and retained the post until his death. However most of his time was spent in private practice in London, so an assistant was employed to fulfill his Cambridge teaching obligations.

Glisson was a member of the group that, beginning in 1645, met regularly in London and out of which the Royal Society was later to emerge. From this 'Invisible College' as it was later known, came one of the earliest examples of cooperative research. A committee of nine was set up in 1645 to investigate rickets but, as Glisson's contribution far exceeded that of any other contributor, it was agreed that he should publish the report *De rachitide* (1650; On Rickets) under his own name. Although the nature of rickets could only begin to be comprehended with the discovery of vitamins by Casimir FUNK in 1912, Glisson must be credited for his clear description of the disease.

He was more original and influential in his account of irritability, first formulated in his work on the liver, *Anatomia hepatis* (1654; Anatomy of the Liver). He argued that muscular irritability, that is their tendency to respond to stimuli, was independent of any external input, nervous or otherwise. This was a considerable improvement over the orthodox position adopted by the followers of René Descartes who believed that muscle could only respond by being pumped up like a tire, with a subtle nervous spirit rather than air. Glisson later reported a simple experiment where he placed his arm in a tube filled with water and noted that when his muscles contracted the level of water actually fell. This showed quite clearly, he claimed, that there had been no flow of anything into the limb.

It was this idea of irritability which, picked up by Albrecht von Haller in the following century, was to find a permanent place in physiology.

Gmelin, Leopold (1788–1853) *German chemist*

Gmelin, whose father and grandfather were botanists, was born at Göttingen (in Germany) and studied at the universities of Tübingen, Göttingen, and Vienna. In 1817 he was appointed to the first chair of chemistry at Heidelberg, where he remained until 1851. In 1817 he published the first edition of what was to become the major chemical textbook of the first half of the 19th century, *Handbuch der Chemie* (Handbook of Chemistry), in three volumes. By 1843 the book was in its fourth edition and had been expanded to nine volumes. In this edition Gmelin adopted the atomic theory and devoted much more space to the growing discipline of organic chemistry. The terms *ester* and *ketone* were introduced by him. His book was translated into English in 1848.

He also worked on the chemistry of digestion, discovering several of the constituents of bile, and introduced *Gmelin's test* for bile pigments. In 1822 he discovered potassium ferrocyanide.

Gödel, Kurt (1906–1978) *Austrian–American mathematician*

Born in Brünn (now Brno in the Czech Republic), Gödel initially studied physics at the University of Vienna, but his interest soon turned to mathematics and mathematical logic. He obtained his PhD in 1930 and the same year joined the faculty at Vienna. He became a member of the Institute for Advanced Study, Princeton, in 1938 and in 1940 emigrated to America. He was a professor at the Institute from 1953 to 1976, and received many scientific honors and awards including the National Medal of Science in 1975. He became a naturalized American citizen in 1948.

In 1930 Gödel published his doctoral dissertation, the proof that first-order logic is complete – that is to say that every sentence of the language of first-order logic is provable or its negation is provable. The completeness of logical systems was then a concept of central importance owing to the various attempts that had been made to reveal a logical axiomatic basis for mathematics. Completeness can be thought of as ensuring that all logically valid statements that a formal (logical) system can produce can be proved from the axioms of the system, and that every invalid statement is disprovable.

In 1931 Gödel presented his famous incompleteness proof for arithmetic. He showed that in any consistent formal system complicated enough to describe simple arithmetic there are propositions or statements that can neither be proved nor disproved on the basis of the axioms of the system – intuitively speaking, there are logical truths that cannot be proved within the system. Moreover, as a corollary Gödel showed (what is known as his second incompleteness theorem) that the *consistency* of any formal system including arithmetic cannot be proved by methods formalizable within that system; consistency can only be proved by using a stronger system – whose own consistency has to be assumed. This latter result showed the impossibility of carrying out Hilbert's program, at least in its original form.

Gödel's second great result concerned two important postulates of set theory, whose consistency mathematicians had been trying to prove since the turn of the century. Between 1938 and 1940 he showed that if the axioms of (restricted) set theory are consistent then they remain so upon the addition of the axiom of choice and the continuum hypothesis, and that these postulates cannot, therefore, be disproved by restricted set theory. (In 1963 Paul Cohen showed that they were independent of set theory.)

Gödel has also worked on the construction of alternative universes that are models of the general theory of relativity, and has produced a rotating-universe model.

Gödel apparently suffered from depression throughout much of his life. In 1936–37 he spent some time in an Austrian sanatorium being treated for the condition.

He was also something of a hypochondriac. He retired from the institute in 1976 and when, soon after, his wife underwent major surgery, he seems to have stopped eating. Apparently he was convinced that he was being poisoned. In late 1977 he was admitted to hospital dehydrated and undernourished. He refused to eat and two weeks later died from "malnutrition and inanition caused by personality disturbance."

Goeppert-Mayer, Maria (1906–1972)
German–American physicist

Maria Goeppert was born at Kattowitz in Poland and educated at the University of Göttingen where she obtained her PhD in 1930. (She changed her name on marrying the physical chemist, Joseph Mayer.) Emigrating to America in 1931 she was employed at Johns Hopkins University, Baltimore (1931–39), Columbia University, New York (1939–46), and the Argonne National Laboratory (1946–60). Finally, in 1960 she took a post at the University of California, San Diego, at La Jolla.

In 1963 she was awarded the Nobel Prize for physics together with the German physicist **Johannes Jensen** (1907–73) and Eugene P. WIGNER for their work on nuclear shell theory. The shell theory of the nucleus is analogous to the shell model of the atom. The theory could help explain why some nuclei were particularly stable and possessed an unusual number of stable isotopes. In particular, in 1948, she argued that the so called 'magic numbers' – 2, 8, 20, 50, 82, and 126 – which are the numbers of either protons or neutrons in particularly stable nuclei, can be explained in this way. She supposed that the protons and neutrons are arranged in the nucleus in a series of nucleon shells. The magic numbers thus describe those nuclei in which certain key shells are complete. In this way helium (with 2 protons and 2 neutrons), oxygen (8 of each), calcium (20 of each), and the ten stable isotopes of tin with 50 protons all fit neatly into this pattern. Also significant was the fact that, in general, the more complex a nucleus becomes the less likely it is to be stable (although there are two complex stable nuclei, lead 208 and bismuth 209, both of which have the magic number of 126 neutrons).

Gold, Thomas (1920–   ) *Austrian–American astronomer*

Born in Vienna, Gold became a refugee from the Austrian Anschluss and gained his BA in 1942 from Cambridge University, England. He lectured there in physics from 1948 to 1952 before he joined the Royal Greenwich Observatory as chief assistant to the Astronomer Royal. He moved to America in 1956, becoming director of the Center for Radiophysics and Space Research at Cornell from 1959 to 1981, and professor of astronomy from 1971 to 1986.

Gold is best known for his contribution to cosmology, the study of the origin, evolution, and large-scale structure of the universe. In the 1940s the prevailing cosmological model was the big-bang theory originally proposed by Georges Lemaître. Since this theory postulated a 'beginning of time' when the incredibly compact universe exploded into being, it was regarded with suspicion and alarm by many astronomers. In 1948 Gold published with Hermann Bondi *The Steady-State Theory of the Expanding Universe.* At the heart of this paper was the adoption of what became known as the 'perfect cosmological principle'. This was an extension of the cosmological principle, which states that the universe looks basically the same from whichever point one observes it; Gold and Bondi added to this that the time of observation was as irrelevant as the place. Thus the universe, on a large scale, is unchanging in time and space. It had no beginning, will never end, and a constant density of matter throughout space will always be maintained.

This theory needed to be reconciled with the work of Edwin HUBBLE, which Gold and Bondi accepted and which showed that the galaxies are receding and the universe is expanding. To maintain the steady state of their universe, Gold and Bondi had to introduce an original and startling proposition, namely, that there must be continuous creation of new matter from nothing. They calculated the amount needed as about one hydrogen atom per cubic kilometer of space every ten years, an amount too small to be detected. Although this proposition conflicted with such deep physical assumptions as the conservation of matter and the laws of thermodynamics they found that it was compatible with all astronomical data.

Consequently the steady-state theory proved attractive to a number of cosmologists and crucial evidence only emerged against it in the 1960s. Then Arno Penzias and Robert Wilson discovered the background microwave radiation in 1965 and Maarten Schmidt produced a survey of the distribution of quasars that seemed to support the evolving universe of the big-bang theory.

In 1968 news of a new type of star, a pulsar, was published by Jocelyn BELL and Antony HEWISH. The distinguishing features of the pulsar were its high-frequency radio signals that had a periodicity of the order of a second or less. Gold quickly proposed a structure capable of producing such an effect: rapidly rotating neutron stars. The same theory was proposed independently by Franco Pacini. Neutron stars are extraordinarily dense stars that have undergone such extreme gravitational collapse following exhaustion of their nuclear fuel that their constituent protons and electrons have combined to form neutrons. These stars would be small and dense enough to rotate with a period equivalent to that of the radio pulses. It had also been shown that they would radiate energy in a narrow beam. If the Earth happened to be in the direction of the beam it would be picked up as a source of pulses, much as the beam of a lighthouse is observed as a series of flashes. The theory of Gold and Pacini was eventually accepted once pulsars rotating even faster than the original one were detected in the Crab and Vela nebulae.

Gold was able to make a prediction that has since been confirmed. He argued that pulsars should be slowing down by a small but measurable amount, because of the loss of energy. Following careful observation of the pulsar in the Crab nebula it was found to be slowing down and its period increasing by 3.46×10^{-10} seconds per day.

Goldberger, Joseph (1874–1920)
American physician

Goldberger, the son of Jewish immigrants, was brought to America at the age of six. He was educated at the College of the City of New York and at Bellevie Hospital Medical School. After a brief period in private practice Goldberger joined the US Public Health Service in 1899, remaining there for the rest of his life.

Goldberger worked as a field officer for many years, making contributions to the understanding and control of such diseases as yellow fever, typhus, and dengue. He is, however, mainly remembered for his authoritative investigation of the nature, causation, and treatment of pellagra. This disease, which became widely known in America after the Civil War, is typified by chronic diarrhea, roughening of the skin, a sore tongue, and involvement of the nervous system. Death from secondary infection or general emaciation was not uncommon.

When Goldberger began his work in 1913 it was thought that the disease was caused by an unknown toxin produced by bacterial fermentation during storage of grain. But stimulated by the work of Frederick Gowland Hopkins and Casimir Funk, Goldberger

directed his attention to deficiency diseases. He began a classic investigation into the connection between pellagra and diet in various asylums and orphanages of the southern states. He was immediately struck by the fact that the staff of such institutions – with a diet containing milk, eggs, cheese, and meat – remained free of the disease while the inmates, subsisting virtually on cereals alone, frequently suffered from epidemics of pellagra.

It was a relatively simple matter to show that the disease could be eliminated by supplementing the inmates' diet with milk. He was further able to trade the offer of a pardon with 11 inmates of a Mississippi prison for their adoption of a diet of corn, rice, sugar, pork fat, potatoes, and turnips. Within a few months 7 of the 11 were showing early symptoms of pellagra. Attempts to transmit the disease by contact with the clothes, excreta, and vomit of the patients ended in failure. Whatever such a factor might be, he was able to show by 1920 that sufficient of it was contained in a daily dose of 15–30 grams of yeast, and by this means alone Goldberger was able to prevent the 10,000 deaths a year attributable to pellagra in the USA.

The active ingredient involved was shown in 1937 by **Conrad Elvehjem** (1901–1962) to be nicotinic acid (niacin), part of the vitamin B complex.

Goldhaber, Maurice (1911–)
Austrian–American physicist

Goldhaber, who was born at Lemberg (now Lvov in Ukraine), was educated at the universities of Berlin and Cambridge, where he obtained his PhD in 1936. He emigrated to America in 1938 where he first taught at the University of Illinois, becoming professor there in 1945. He moved to the Brookhaven National Laboratory in 1950, serving as its director from 1961 until 1973.

In 1934, while at the Cavendish Laboratory of Cambridge University, Goldhaber codiscovered the nuclear photoelectric effect with James Chadwick. This is the disintegration of a nucleus by high-energy x-rays or gamma rays. From this it was later established that the neutron is slightly heavier than the proton. Following Enrico Fermi's discovery of slow neutrons, Chadwick and Goldhaber also discovered (1934–35) the neutron disintegration reactions for lithium, boron, and nitrogen. The nitrogen reaction is the major source of radioactive carbon–14 on Earth.

At the University of Illinois (1938) Goldhaber and his wife, Gertrude Scharff-Goldhaber, demonstrated that electrons and beta particles are the same. In 1940 he discovered that beryllium is a good moderator, i.e., it slows down fast neutrons so that they more readily split uranium atoms.

He has also proposed a cosmological theory in which an initial 'universon' broke up into a 'cosmon' (matter) and an 'anticosmon' (antimatter), with the anticosmon forming a second universe made of antimatter.

Goldschmidt, Victor Moritz (1888–1947) Swiss–Norwegian chemist

Goldschmidt, the son of H. J. Goldschmidt, a physical chemist, was born at Zurich in Switzerland. He attended Christiania (now Oslo) University where he obtained his PhD in 1911, remaining in Norway as director of the Mineralogical Institute until 1929 when he moved to the University of Göttingen in Germany. Being a Jew he returned to Norway in 1935, following the rise of anti-Semitism and the Nazi party. He was later sent to a concentration camp but was released by the Norwegian authorities on the grounds of ill health and escaped to England (1942). His time in England was spent first at the Macaulay Institute for Soil Research near Aberdeen, and later at the Rothamsted Experimental Station, Harpenden. He returned to Oslo after the war.

Goldschmidt is acknowledged as the founder of modern geochemistry. Following the work of Max von Laue and W. H. and W. L. Bragg, he laid the foundation for his work by working out the crystal structure of over 200 compounds. His interest was directed to more practical work when, as a result of the naval blockade in the war, he was called upon to investigate Norway's mineral resources.

By the mid-1920s the atomic radii of elements in various stages of ionization had been established. Using this information, together with his detailed knowledge of crystal structure, Goldschmidt began predicting in which minerals and rocks various elements could or could not be found. His results were published over the years in his eight-volume *Geochemische Verteilungsgesetze der Elemente* (1923–38; The Geochemical Laws of the Distribution of the Elements). His book *Geochemistry* was published posthumously in 1954.

Goldstein, Eugen (1850–1930) German physicist

Goldstein, who was born at Gleiwitz (now Gliwice in Poland), studied for a year at the University of Breslau (1869–70) then worked with Hermann von Helmholtz at the University of Berlin. He was appointed physicist at the Berlin Observatory in 1878, took his doctorate in 1881, and later established his own laboratory. In 1927 he became head of the astrophysical section of the Potsdam Observatory.

Goldstein's best-remembered scientific work is his studies of electrical discharges in gases at low pressures. He gave the name 'cathode rays' to the invisible emanations coming from the cathode of an evacuated discharge tube, showed that the rays could cast sharp shadows, and demonstrated that they were emitted perpendicular to the cathode surface. He later showed that they could be deflected by magnetic fields.

Goldstein, Joseph Leonard (1940–) American medical geneticist

Goldstein attended Washington and Lee Universty, Virginia, and the University of Texas Southwestern Medical School, where he gained his MD in 1966. For two years he worked at Massachusetts General Hospital, Boston. In 1968 he joined the National Institutes of Health as a clinical associate (1968–70). After a stint of research at the University of Washington, Seattle (1970–72), he joined the University of Texas Health Science Center in Dallas. In 1977 Goldstein was appointed professor of medicine and chairman of the Department of Molecular Genetics, and in 1985 he was made regental professor.

Goldstein's work has centered on the metabolism of cholesterol, fats, and other lipids in the body; much of it has been done in collaboration with his fellow biochemist and geneticist, **Michael Brown** (1941–), whom Goldstein met when both were interns at Massachusetts General Hospital in 1966. Starting in the early 1970s, the pair began by studying how cells obtain their cholesterol from blood. Most of the blood's cholesterol is present in the form of low-density lipoproteins (LDLs) – minute particles comprising proteins, cholesterol, and other lipids. Working with cultures of skin cells, Goldstein and Brown discovered receptors on the cell surface that recognize the LDLs and bind them to the cell membrane. The LDL is subsequently enfolded by the cell membrane and taken into the cell, where its contents are metabolized (cholesterol, for instance, is a vital component of cell membranes).

They went on to show that there is a deficiency of LDL membrane receptors in individuals suffering from the inherited disorder knwon as familial hypercholesterolemia. Such persons have abnormally high levels of cholesterol in their blood and run a much greater risk of developing atherosclerosis – the narrowing of the arteries due to a build-up of fatty plaques on their inner surface. This in turn makes them much more prone to heart attacks and strokes. Goldstein and Brown were able to show that in this disorder the gene encoding the LDL receptors is defective, hence the number of such receptors is small and the sufferer's body cells are unable to remove LDLs from the bloodstream. The consequent high blood-cholesterol levels prompt scavenger white cells to remove the cholesterol, turning them into the plaque-forming cells thought to be responsible for atherosclerosis.

The work of the Goldstein and Brown has covered many other aspects of cholesterol metabolism, particularly how the cholesterol absorbed from the gut into the bloodstream is processed and repackaged by the liver, with the formation of high-density, very-low-density, and intermediate-density lipoproteins. They have not only revealed fundamental features of cellular metabolism but have shown ways in which people with elevated blood cholesterol may be treated, for instance by increasing the number of LDL receptors on their cells. This, in turn, may reduce their risk of heart attacks and strokes.

For his work on familial hypercholesterolemia and LDl receptors, Goldstein was awarded the 1985 Nobel Prize for physiology or medcine, which he shared with his longtime colleague, Brown.

Golgi, Camillo (1843–1926) Italian cytologist and histologist

Born at Corteno near Brescia (now in Italy), Golgi studied medicine at Pavia University and thereafter mainly concerned himself with research on cells and tissues. In 1873, while serving as physician at the home for incurables, Abbiategrasso, he devised a method of staining cells by means of silver salts. This allowed the fine processes of nerve cells to be distinguished in greater detail than before and enabled Golgi to confirm Wilhelm von Waldeyer's view that nerve cells do not touch but are separated by gaps called synapses. Golgi also found a specialized type of nerve cell, later called the *Golgi cell*, which, by means of fingerlike projections (dendrites), serves to connect many other nerve cells. This discovery led to the formulation (by Waldeyer) and establishment (by Santiago RAMÓN Y CAJAL) of the neuron theory – a theory that Golgi was nevertheless strongly opposed to.

Golgi was also the first to draw attention to the *Golgi bodies*: flattened cavities parallel to the cell's nuclear membrane whose function appears to be packaging and exporting various materials from the cell. Apart from work on the sense organs, muscles, and glands, Golgi studied varying forms of malaria. He found that different species of the protozoan parasite *Plasmodium* are responsible for the two types of intermittent fever – the tertian and quartan. He also established that the onset of fever coincides with the release into the blood of the parasitic spores from the red blood cells.

Golgi served as professor of histology (1876) and then of general pathology (1881) at Pavia University. In 1906 he shared with Ramón y Cajal the Nobel Prize for physiology or medicine for his work on the structure of the human nervous system.

Good, Robert Alan (1922–) American pathologist and immunologist

Good was the son of a high-school principal who died of cancer when Good was five. Born in Crosby, Minnesota, he was educated at the University of Minnesota where he simultaneously obtained an MD and PhD in 1947. After this triumph he joined the Minnesota staff and served as professor of pediatrics from 1954 until 1973 when he moved to New York as director of the Sloan-Kettering Institute for Cancer Research. In 1982 Good moved to the University of Oklahoma as professor of microbiology, a post held until 1985, when he was appointed to a similar position in the University of South Florida, Tampa.

One of the great achievements of modern immunology has been the demonstration that the immunological system is not a simple unity but rather a complex interrelationship of a number of different units. The unraveling of this particular tangle was not the work of any one man or, indeed, any one group; Good's contribution was, however, as great as any other.

In the 1940s he showed a link between plasma cells, cells found in lymphoid tissue, and antibodies. Later he noted a simple tendency to recurrent infection among his patients suffering from myeloma (a tumor of bone-marrow cells) despite an abundance of plasma cells. This suggested to Good that there must be more to the immune system than simply the ability to make antibodies. This was reinforced when examining patients with agammaglobulinemia, who had no plasma cells at all, yet who were immunologically active enough to reject foreign skin grafts.

In the mid 1950s Good realized that there are two parts to the immune system: one dealing with defenses against typical bacterial infections; the other more concerned with clearing up 'foreign' or unusual cells.

By 1961, independently of Jacques Miller, Good was beginning to suspect that the thymus gland was deeply implicated in providing the latter type of immunity.

Work on chickens' defense mechanisms against bacterial infection had demonstrated that if the bursa (a gland found in the chicken's alimentary canal) was removed, the creature lost the ability to make antibodies in any real quantity. They were in fact just like Good's agammaglobulinemic patients.

Good therefore postulated that there must be two types of immunity – one related to the thymus and the other related to the human equivalent of the chicken bursa producing antibodies. The details of the two systems and their evolution and interrelationship called for major, and as yet far from complete, research programs by immunologists.

Since then Good has become a leading proponent of the view that cancer is somehow the result of an immunological defect, a failure of the system to recognize and destroy the cancerous cell before it has begun to proliferate.

Goodall, Jane (1934–) British primatologist

In 1957 Goodall, a Londoner, approached Louis Leakey for a job of some kind as she "wanted to get closer to animals." Leakey employed her, initially as a secretary, and took her with him to Olduvai. He told her that he had long been searching for someone sufficiently interested in animals to be prepared "to forego the amenities of civilization for long periods of time without difficulty." More precisely he wanted someone to observe the 160 chimps of the Gombe Stream Reserve on the eastern shores of Lake Tanganyika at close quarters over several years. After some initial training at the Royal Free Hospital and the London Zoo, Goodall was installed at Gombe in 1970. She has remained there ever since; under her direction it has become a world-famous and much-respected research center.

In her first full account of her work, *In the Shadow of Man* (1971), Goodall presented what now seems to be a somewhat idealized picture of chimpanzee society. They were seen as mainly vegetarian, living in a relatively peaceful community and spending the bulk of their lives socializing with each other. They were also shown as toolmakers and users, adept at fashioning blades of grass into probes to be inserted into mounds to extract termites.

Her later work, however, presented in *Through a Window* (1990), revealed a darker side of chimpanzee society. The Gombe Reserve was home for three communities of about 50 chimpanzees each. Males will routinely attack and attempt to kill adult females of another group. In 1974, Goodall witnessed the outbreak of war within a single community. At that time the band split into two groups, which she called the Kahama and the Kasakela. Over a period of four years, Goodall noted that the Kasakela systematically and deliberately killed the entire Kahama group, males, females, and infants, presumably to take over their territory. It took several years for Goodall to come to terms with this picture. Goodall also rejected her earlier account of vegetarian chimpanzee bands. She found that they hunted monkeys, baboon infants, bushpig, bushbuck, and other small mammals. Hunting is undertaken by males and always in groups. Cannibalism took place on a number of occasions and the meat, as at other times, shared within the group.

Because of her prolonged observation Goodall has been able to document the social development of the individual in the community as well as the histories of a number of families. Males establish a dominance hierarchy and protect the group, while females remain with their mothers until they reach sexual maturity at about the age of ten. Young males leave a few years earlier to establish their place in the male hierarchy. Sibling and maternal ties, however, remain strong.

In more recent years Goodall has campaigned vigorously for the conservation of chimpanzees in the wild and for a less barbarous confinement of the many held in research institutions and zoos. To this end she has set up the Jane Goodall Institute for Research Education and Conservation with centers in America, Canada, and Britain. She has reported on her life's work at Gombe in a number of popular and often moving books, most recently in *The Chimpanzee* (1992).

Goodpasture, Ernest William
(1886–1960) *American pathologist*

Goodpasture, the son of a lawyer, was born in Montgomery County, Tennessee. He was educated at Vanderbilt University, Nashville, and at Johns Hopkins University, where he gained his MD in 1912. After working as a pathologist for some years at Johns Hopkins and at Harvard, Goodpasture returned to Vanderbilt in 1924 as professor of pathology, a post he retained until his retirement in 1955.

In 1931 Goodpasture devised a method of

virus culture that provided an enormous stimulation to virology. Before this, as viruses will grow only in living tissue, they could be studied experimentally either in a living host, or, after the work of Alexis Carrel in 1911, *in vitro* in a tissue culture. The first method was expensive and difficult to control while the second, before the advent of antibiotics, was susceptible to contamination by bacteria.

Goodpasture, in collaboration with Alice Woodruff, avoided such difficulties by providing a cheap living environment for viral growth – a fertile egg. Their first success was with fowl pox but within a year they had also grown both cowpox and coldsore viruses. Goodpasture went on in 1933 to show that attenuated cowpox vaccine could be produced in a purer and cheaper form in eggs than by the customary method of production in calf lymph.

Within a few years Goodpasture's technique had made possible the production of vaccines against yellow fever by Max Theiler and influenza by Thomas Francis. Thereafter eggs became as standard a part of the virologist's laboratory as the test tube.

Goodricke, John (1764–1786) *Dutch–British astronomer*

Born at Groningen in the Netherlands, Goodricke was a deaf mute who, although he died when he was 21, had already done work of such importance as to receive the Copley medal of the Royal Society three years before he died. Variable stars had been discovered by Fabricius nearly 200 years before but Goodricke was the first scientist to offer a plausible explanation. Noticing the rapid variation in magnitude of Algol he proposed, in 1782, that it was being regularly eclipsed by a dark companion that passed between it and the Earth. His suggestion was confirmed a century later.

Gordan, Paul Albert (1837–1912) *German mathematician*

Gordan studied in his native Breslau, at Königsberg, and at Berlin before becoming professor of mathematics at the University of Erlangen. For most of his mathematical career his research was concentrated on a single field, the study of indeterminates. The central problem in the field, which Gordan eventually solved, was to prove the existence of a finite basis for binary forms of any given degree. His result was subsequently refined and extended by many workers including Gordan himself. Gordan's proof was long and complicated and the result was re-proved in 1888 by David Hilbert using newer and far simpler methods. In collaboration with Rudolf Clebsch, Gordan also wrote a book on Abelian functions that included the central theorem now known as the *Clebsch–Gordan theorem*. This work was influential in giving a new direction to algebraic geometry.

Gorer, Peter Alfred (1907–1961) *British immunologist*

Gorer, the son of a wealthy Londoner who died on the *Lusitania*, was educated at Guy's Hospital, London, graduating in 1929. Ater studying genetics under J. B. S. Haldane at University College, London from 1933 to 1934 Gorer worked at the Lister Institute until 1940 when he returned to Guy's as morbid histologist and hemotologist. In 1948 he became reader in experimental pathology.

As early as 1936 Gorer tried to see if red cells of mice could be divided into antigenic groups similar to the blood groups of humans. Using his own blood serum he distinguished three kinds of mouse red cell on the basis of their ability to agglutinate his serum. He further found that such a property was inherited by the mice in a Mendelian dominant manner. Such work was supported by comparable results obtained in 1937 with the transplantation of a spontaneously appearing tumor among the various distinguished genetic strains of mice.

Gorer had in fact discovered the histocompatibility antigens and established their control at the genetic level, an outstanding result little appreciated in his lifetime but later to be recognized as of fundamental importance in immunology, genetics, and transplantation surgery. One who did recognize the significance of Gorer's work was George Snell who worked with him in 1948. For his later work Snell was to receive the 1980 Nobel Prize for physiology or medicine, a prize Gorer would have undoubtedly shared with him if he had not died some 19 years before from lung cancer.

Goudsmit, Samuel Abraham (1902–1978) *Dutch–American physicist*

Born in The Hague in the Netherlands, Goudsmit was educated at the universities of Amsterdam and Leiden, where he obtained his PhD in 1927. He emigrated to America shortly afterward, serving as professor of physics at the University of Michigan (1932–46) and North Western (1946–48). He then moved to the Brookhaven National Laboratory on Long Island, New York, where he remained until his retirement in 1970.

In 1925 Goudsmit, in collaboration with the Dutch–American physicist **George Uhlenbeck** (1900–1988), put forward the proposal of electron spin. They suggested that electrons rotate about an axis and, as they are charged, set up a magnetic field. This model was successful in clearing up a number of anomalies that were becoming apparent in the fine structure of atomic spectra. A theory of spin was later given by Paul Dirac.

During World War II Goudsmit worked on radar and then became head of a top secret mission codenamed *Alsos* in 1944. The mission was for Goudsmit to follow the front-line Allied troops in Europe, and even in some cases to precede them, looking for any evidence of German progress in the manufacture of an atomic bomb. He found that the German scientists had, in fact, made little progress and it was clear that Hitler would not be presented with such a weapon before the end of the war. For this war service Goudsmit was awarded the Medal of Freedom from the US Department of Defense and he published his account of the mission in his book *Alsos* (1947).

Gould, Benjamin Apthorp

(1824–1896) *American astronomer*

Gould, the son of a merchant and teacher from Boston, Massachusetts, graduated from Harvard in 1844. Having studied for a year at Berlin, he obtained his PhD from Göttingen University in 1848 under the great Karl Friedrich Gauss. On his return to America he served as head of the longitude department of the US Coast Survey from 1852 to 1867, pioneering the use of the telegraph in measuring longitude. At the same time Gould founded the *Astronomical Journal* in 1849 and edited it until 1861 when its publication was halted by the Civil War. He was also connected with the Dudley Observatory, Albany, from 1855 and served as its director briefly in 1858 before being forced to get out of town in the following year. After his traumatic expulsion from Albany he handled his father's business for some time. He set up a private observatory in Cambridge, financed by his wife, and in 1862 produced a star catalog that brought together measurements made at various observatories. He left for Argentina in 1870.

The 15 years spent in Cordoba were by far the most productive of Gould's career. He established the Argentine National Observatory there and began the first major survey of the southern skies. The Observatory's first survey of naked-eye stars, i.e.,

down to 7th magnitude, was published as the *Uranometria Argentina* (1879; Argentinian Survey of the Heavens). This was followed by the fuller recording, published in 1884, of 73,160 stars from 23°S to 80°S and in 1886 by the publication of the *Catàlago General* (General Catalogue) containing the more accurate recording of 32,448 stellar coordinates. This important work was continued by Gould's successor, Juan Thomé. An extended band of young stars, cloud, and dust that forms a spur off one of the spiral arms of our Galaxy and was revealed by the southern surveys was subsequently named *Gould's Belt*.

In 1885 Gould returned to Massachusetts where he restarted the *Astronomical Journal* in 1886 and worked on the 1000 photographic plates of star clusters he brought back with him from Cordoba.

Gould, Stephen Jay (1941–)

American biologist

The grandson of a Hungarian immigrant and the son of a court stenographer, Gould is reported to have developed his interest in biology as a five-year old when he first saw *Tyrannosaurus rex* at the American Museum of Natural History. Born in New York City, he was educated at Antioch University, Pennsylvania, and at Columbia, where he completed his PhD in 1967. He immediately moved to Harvard where he has served as professor of geology and curator of the Harvard Museum of Comparative Zoology since 1973.

Gould is widely known for eight volumes of essays on natural history published since 1978. The articles are usually about some aspect of evolution and are rooted firmly in history, carry a detailed argument, and are relevant to some contemporary issue. He has also published a number of influential monographs. In *Ontogeny and Phylogeny* (1977) he examined the notion of recapitulation – the view that individual development (ontogeny) is a rerun of evolutionary history (phylogeny). *The Mismeasure of Man* (1984) sought to demonstrate that attempts to measure man's intelligence were often designed to serve political rather than scientific ends. In a further monograph, *Wonderful Life* (1990) Gould has surveyed the fossils of the Burgess Shale, first described by C. D. Walcott. He used the fossils to illustrate a familiar theme of his work that evolution is not "a ladder of predictable progress," it is rather "a copiously branching bush, continually pruned by the grim reaper of extinction."

In the fields of paleontology and ecology Gould has worked for many years on the

West Indian land snail, Cerion. As an evolutionary theorist he is best known for proposing in 1972, along with Nils Eldredge, the punctuated equilibrium hypothesis, which views evolution as episodic rather than continuous. Relatively short periods of branching speciation, they argued, are followed by much longer periods of stasis.

In 1981 Gould was very much in the news as one of the biologists called as an expert witness in the so-called Scopes II trial in Arkansas. Fundamentalists had claimed as equal a right to teach creationism in the Arkansas public schools as biology teachers had long claimed for Darwinism. Judge William Overton ruled in 1985 that creationism was a religious doctrine and it would therefore be a violation of the constitution if it were to be taught in public schools.

Graaff, Robert Jemison van de See
VAN DE GRAAFF, ROBERT JEMISON.

Graebe, Karl (1841–1927) German
chemist. See PERKIN, SIR WILLIAM HENRY.

Graham, Thomas (1805–1869) Scottish
chemist

Graham was the son of a prosperous Glaswegian manufacturer. He entered Glasgow University at the age of 14 and attended the classes of the chemist Thomas Thomson. Graham's father was determined that he should enter the ministry and on Graham's persistence with his scientific studies his father withdrew his financial support. To continue in chemistry Graham made his living through teaching and writing. In 1829 he became a lecturer at the Mechanics Institution and in 1830 he was elected to the chair of chemistry at Glasgow University. In 1837 he was appointed professor in the recently founded University College, London. He was the first president of the Chemical Society of London, and of the Cavendish Society, which he founded. In 1854 he was made master of the mint.

In 1829 Graham published a paper on the diffusion of gases. Observations on this subject had been made by Joseph Priestley and Johann Döbereiner, but it was Graham who formulated the law of diffusion. He compared the rates at which various gases diffused through porous pots, and also the rate of effusion through a small aperture, and concluded that the rate of diffusion (or effusion) of a gas at constant pressure and temperature is inversely proportional to the square root of its density.

In 1860 Graham examined liquids. He noticed that a colored solution of sugar placed at the bottom of a glass of water gradually extends its color upwards. He called this spontaneous process *diffusion*. He also noticed that substances such as glue, gelatin, albumen, and starch diffuse very slowly. He classified substances into two types: colloids (from Greek *kolla*, glue), which diffuse only slowly, and crystalloids, which diffuse quickly. He also found that substances of the two types differ markedly in their ability to pass through a membrane, such as parchment, and he developed the method of dialysis to separate them. Graham is regarded as the father of modern colloid science, and many terms that he invented, such as sol, gel, peptization, and syneresis, are still in use. Other work done by Graham includes research into phosphorous acids, the water of crystallization in hydrated salts, and the absorption of hydrogen by palladium. Graham was an excellent and successful teacher.

Gram, Hans Christian Joachim
(1853–1938) *Danish bacteriologist*

Gram graduated in medicine from the university in his native city of Copenhagen in 1878 and from 1883 to 1885 traveled in Europe, studying pharmacology and bacteriology. While in Berlin (1884) he discovered the method of staining bacteria with which his name has become associated. He followed the method of Paul Ehrlich, using aniline-water and gentian violet solution. After further treatment with Lugol's solution (iodine in aqueous potassium iodide) and ethanol he found that some bacteria (such as pneumococcus) retained the stain (*Gram positive*) while others did not (*Gram negative*). This discovery is of great use in the identification and classification of bacteria. It is also useful in deciding the treatment of bacterial diseases, since penicillin is active only against Gram-positive bacteria; the cell walls of Gram-negative bacteria will not take up either penicillin or Gram's stain.

In 1891 Gram became professor of pharmacology at the University of Copenhagen, where he showed a keen interest in the clinical education of the students. During this time he had a large medical practice in the city. He was chairman of the Pharmacopoeia Commission from 1901 to 1921 and director of the medical department of Frederick's Hospital, Copenhagen, until he retired in 1923.

Granit, Ragnar Arthur (1900–1991)
Finnish neurophysiologist

Born in the Finnish capital of Helsinki, Granit qualified as a physician from the university there in 1927. He taught at the university from 1927 until 1940, serving as professor of physiology from 1935. In 1940 he moved to the Karolinska Institute, Stockholm, becoming professor of neurophysiology at the newly founded Medical Nobel Institute in 1946.

In a long career Granit has been a prolific writer on all aspects of the neurophysiology of vision. He demonstrated that light not only stimulates but can also inhibit impulses along the optic nerve. By attaching microelectrodes to individual cells in the retina he showed that color vision does not simply depend on three different types of receptor (cone) cells sensitive to different parts of the spectrum. Rather, some of the eye's nerve fibers are sensitive to the whole spectrum while others respond to a much narrower band and so are color specific.

Granit described his work in *Sensory Mechanisms of the Retina* (1947) and *The Visual Pathway* (1962); for such research he shared the 1967 Nobel Prize for physiology or medicine with George WALD and Haldan HARTLINE. Granit also did important work on the control of muscle spindles by the gamma fibers.

Green, George (1793–1841) *British mathematician*

Green's father was a prosperous baker from Nottingham. Green worked for his father from the age of nine until his father's death in 1829. His father left him a mill which still stands; it has been restored and was opened to the public in 1979.

Green must have been a largely self-taught mathematician. It is known that he joined the Nottingham Subscription Library in 1823 and that the library had copies of such advanced works as the *Mécanique céleste* (Structure of the Heavens) of Laplace. The translator, John Toplis, was head of the local grammar school and may well have influenced Green. In 1828 Green published *An Essay on the Application of Mathematics to Electricity and Magnetism*. It was made available to 51 subscribers and few seem to have been aware of its appearance. The work only became widely known when Lord Kelvin came across a copy in 1845 and was so impressed that he arranged for it to be reissued in *Crelle's Journal*. The *Essay* introduced into science *Green's theorem*, *Green's function*, and the notion of the electric potential.

Following the death of his father, Green felt free to follow his scientific interests. He was encouraged in this by Sir Edward Bromhead, a local landowner, who offered to arrange Green's admission to Cambridge. At first Green was reluctant, doubting that it would be suitable "for a person of my age and Imperfect Classical attainments." Nevertheless he arrived in Cambridge at the age of 40, finished as fourth wrangler, and was elected to a fellowship of his college in 1839. He died two years later after contracting flu, leaving seven illegitimate children.

Gregor, William (1761–1817) *British mineralogist*

Born in Trewarthenick, Gregor was educated at Cambridge University. Although elected a fellow of his college he decided instead to pursue a career in the Church and became rector of Creed, Cornwall, in 1793.

In 1791 he found a strange black sand in Manaccan (then spelled Menacchan), Cornwall. This contained iron and manganese plus an additional substance that Gregor could not identify. He called it menacchanine and succeeded in extracting its reddish-brown oxide, which, when dissolved in acid, formed a yellow solution. Martin Klaproth isolated the same oxide from a different source in 1795 and demonstrated that it was a new element, naming it titanium.

Gregory, James (1638–1675) *Scottish mathematician and astronomer*

Gregory was one of the many 17th-century mathematicians who made important contributions to the development of the calculus, although some of his best work remained virtually unknown until long after his death.

Born at Drumoak, Scotland, he studied mathematics at the University of Padua in about 1665 and produced *Vera circuli et hyperbolae quadratura* (1667; The True Areas of Circles and Hyperbolas). He was particularly interested in expressing functions as series, and he sketched the beginnings of a general theory. It was Gregory who first found series expressions for the trigonometric functions. He introduced the terms 'convergent' and 'divergent' for series, and was one of the first mathematicians to begin to grasp the difference between the two kinds. Gregory also gave the first proof of the fundamental theorem of calculus.

In addition to his mathematical work Gregory's interests in astronomy led him to do some valuable practical work in optics. He anticipated Newton by recommending a reflecting telescope in his *Optica promota* (1663; The Advance of Optics). He realized that refracting telescopes would always be limited by aberrations of various kinds. His solution was to use a concave mirror that reflected (rather than a lens that refracted) to minimize these effects. He solved the problem of the observer by having a hole in the primary mirror through which the light could pass to the observer. However, he was unable to find anyone skilled enough actually to construct the telescope.

Gregory held chairs in mathematics at the University of St. Andrews (1669–74) and the University of Edinburgh (1674–75). He died at the age of 37 shortly after going blind.

Griffin, Donald Redfield (1915–)
American zoologist

Born in Southampton, New York State, Griffin was educated at Harvard where he obtained his PhD in 1942. He spent the war applying physiological principles to the design of such military equipment as cold-weather clothing and headphones. After the war he worked initially at Cornell but returned to Harvard in 1953 as professor of biology, a position he held until his retirement in 1986.

Bat navigation had been first studied by Lazzaro Spallanzani in 1793 when he noted that blinded bats were as efficient in catching insects on the wing as sighted bats. He also noted that impairment of their hearing produced disorientation. How, Griffin asked in 1938, could ears replace eyes in flight guidance? He was fortunate in that he had a colleague in the physics laboratory, G. W. Pierce, with an interest in high-frequency sound who was willing to use his specialized equipment on bats. In this way they soon found that bats were issuing sounds, in the case of the horseshoe bat, with frequencies between 60 and 120 kilohertz; the limit of human hearing is between 15 and 20 kilohertz.

That the bats were operating by echolocation was demonstrated when either their mouths or ears were covered. In either case they would collide in a dark room with anything in their path, even the room's walls. But, when operating freely, they found that the small brown bat, *Myotis lucifugus*, could detect in the dark and fly through a screen with wires no more than 24 centimeters apart. Only when the wires were reduced to a diameter of less than 0.07 millimeter, about the size of a human hair, did their detection system break down. Griffin went on to explore in greater detail the nature of bat sonar systems, describing his work in his *Listening in the Dark* (New Haven, 1958), and the more popular account *Echoes of Bats and Men* (London, 1960).

Griffin has also worked extensively on the problem of bird navigation. Early work inevitably consisted of homing experiments. But from these no more can be established than the percentage of birds arriving safely, and the time taken. They did, however, establish that the number of returns decreased with distance in a way that suggested that birds navigate by identifying local landmarks. To discover more about the process Griffin taught himself to fly and in the late 1940s spent many hours in a Piper Cub observing the flight paths of gannets and gulls. His observations tended to support the idea that homing from unfamiliar territory was not accurately directed, but succeeded eventually because of exploratory flights.

While this was perhaps a reasonable account of the behavior of gannets and gulls, later work by others showed that in the case of homing pigeons, shearwaters, and starlings there did exist a highly developed ability to select a particular direction. Griffin described his own work and the work of others in his *Bird Migration* (London, 1965).

Griffith, Fred (1881–1941) *British microbiologist*

Griffith, who was born at Hale in southern England, has been described variously as a "virtual recluse" or "quiet and retiring." He worked as a bacteriologist at the Ministry of Health's pathology laboratory in London and was killed working in his laboratory during an air-raid.

Despite the general obscurity of his background Griffith has acquired long after his death a reputation as one of the founding fathers of molecular biology by his discovery in 1928 of bacterial transformation in pneumococci. He had first succeeded in distinguishing two types of pneumococci, the nonvirulent R (rough) of serological type I and the virulent S (smooth) of type III.

He inoculated mice with both live nonvirulent R and heat-killed S pneumococci. Although when either were inoculated separately no infection resulted, together they produced in the mice lethal cases of pneumonia. Further, he recovered from the infected mice living, virulent S pneumococci of type III.

It was this awkward result which later led Oswald Avery and his colleagues in 1944 to carry out the experiments that succeeded in explaining Griffith's results by suggesting that the power to transform bacteria lay with the nucleic acid of the cell rather than its proteins or sugars.

Grignard, François Auguste Victor (1871–1935) *French chemist*

Born at Cherbourg in northern France,

Grignard first studied mathematics at the University of Lyons before he switched to chemistry. He was a lecturer at the universities of Besançon, Nancy, and Lyons before he was appointed professor of chemistry at Nancy in 1910. In 1919 he moved to the chair of chemistry at Lyons.

In 1901 he discovered an important class of organic reagents now known as *Grignard reagents*. For this work he shared the Nobel Prize for chemistry with Paul SABATIER in 1912. He was searching for a catalyst for a methylation reaction he was trying to induce; chemists had earlier tried to use zinc in combination with various organic compounds and found it moderately successful. Grignard used magnesium mixed with organic halides in ether solution and obtained compounds of the type RMgX, where X is a halogen (Cl, Br, I) and R an organic group. These Grignard reagents are very versatile and permit the synthesis of a large number of different classes of compounds, particularly secondary and tertiary alcohols, hydrocarbons, and carboxylic acids.

In 1935 he began the publication of his *Traité de chimie organique* (Treatise on Organic Chemistry), which was continued after his death and is now a massive multivolume work.

Grimaldi, Francesco Maria (1618–1663) *Italian physicist*

Grimaldi was born at Bologna, Italy, and became a Jesuit. In 1648 he became professor of mathematics at his order's college in his native city, where he acted as assistant to Giovanni Riccioli. His discovery of the phenomenon that he named the diffraction of light was reported in his posthumous work *Physico-mathesis de lumine, coloribus, et iride* (1665; Physicomathematical Studies of Light, Colors, and the Rainbow). He showed that when a beam of light passed through two successive narrow apertures, the pattern of light produced was a little bigger than it should have been if the light had traveled in an absolutely straight line. Grimaldi considered that the beam had bent outward very slightly, indicating that light must have a wave nature. The result presented difficulties to all 17th-century corpuscular theories of light.

Grisebach, August Heinrich Rudolph (1814–1879) *German plant taxonomist and phytogeographer*

Grisebach was born in Hanover. His uncle was a professor of botany at Göttingen and Grisebach originally studied there, later moving to Berlin.

His first taxonomic work was on the fam-

ily Gentianaceae and in 1838 he published a substantial work *Genera et Species Gentianearum*. The next year, inspired by the scientific expeditions of Alexander Humboldt, he set out on a trip to the Balkan peninsula, where he studied the vegetation. This was the start of his work on phytogeography, which he continued for several years and which resulted in his major work *Vegetation de Erde* published in 1872. Grisebach also worked on the botany of the Caribbean and South America.

Guericke, Otto von (1602–1686) *German physicist and engineer*

Guericke, who was born in Magdeburg, Germany, trained in law and mathematics before becoming an engineer in the army of Gustavus Adolphus of Sweden. After the Thirty Years' War he returned to Magdeburg as mayor, there carrying out numerous dramatic experiments on vacuums and the power of the atmosphere.

In 1650 Guericke constructed the first air pump by modifying a water pump. He used this device to create a vacuum in various containers and performed a number of novel experiments. Guericke was the first to show that sound would not travel in a vacuum, and furthermore that a vacuum would not support combustion or animal life. In 1654 Guericke gave an impressive demonstration in front of the emperor Ferdinand III, of the force of atmospheric pressure. Two identical copper hemispheres 12 feet (3.66 m) in diameter were joined together. When the air was pumped out, 16 horses could not pull them apart although when the air reentered the hemispheres they fell apart by themselves. He also showed that 20 men could not hold a piston in a cylinder once the air had been evacuated from one end of it. The results of these and other experiments were published in his *Experimenta nova Magdeburgica de vacuo spatio* (1672; New Magdeburg Experiments Concerning Empty Space). In 1663 he built the first electrical friction machine by rotating a sulfur globe against a cloth.

Guettard, Jean Etienne (1715–1786) *French geologist*

Guettard was born at Etampes in France. After a training in medicine and chemistry, he worked under the royal patronage of the duc d'Orléans from 1747 as keeper of his natural-history collection. Following the duc's death (1752) he continued this work under the patronage of his son.

In 1751 he made a crucial observation that upset the neptunism theories of Abraham Werner and his followers. While traveling through the Auvergne region he noticed an abundance of hexagonal basalt rocks and, exploring the region, identified the surrounding mountain peaks as the cones of extinct volcanoes (which would explain the presence of basalt). However, Werner's theory stated that all volcanic activity is recent, only occurring after the land has completely emerged from the oceans. Therefore, according to Wernerian theory, no volcanoes as ancient as the Auvergne ones should exist. Guettard published his findings in 1752 in his memoir, *On Certain Mountains in France which once have been Volcanoes*. He later changed his mind, distinguishing basalt from lava as it was not to be found among the recent volcanoes. He also observed the lack of vitrification found in basalt, then taken to be a sure sign of volcanic origin, and explained its formation by crystallization from an aqueous fluid.

Guettard was the first to map France geologically, publishing in 1780 his *Atlas et description minéralogiques de la France* (Mineralogical Atlas and Description of France). In the preparation of this he discovered (1765) a source of kaolin in Alençon, which made possible the production of the celebrated Sèvres porcelain.

Guillaume, Charles Edouard (1861–1938) *Swiss metrologist*

As a child Guillaume learned a good deal of science from his father, a clockmaker with a considerable scientific knowledge. Born in Fleurier, Switzerland, in 1878 he entered the Zurich Federal Institute of Technology, gaining his doctorate in 1882. In 1883 Guillaume became an assistant at the newly established International Bureau of Weights and Measures at Sèvres, near Paris. He was appointed director in 1915 and held this post until his retirement in 1936.

Guillaume's early work at the Bureau was concerned with thermometry; his treatise of 1889 on this subject became a standard text for metrologists. He was also involved in developing the international standards for the meter, kilogram, and liter. His research on thermal expansion of possible standards materials led him from 1890 to investigate various alloys. After a methodical study of nickel–steel alloys he devised an alloy that showed a very small expansion with temperature rise. Guillaume's new material (*invar*) found immediate practical applications, particularly in clocks, watches, and other precise instruments. He also produced a nickel–chromium–steel alloy, known as *elinvar*, with an elasticity that remains nearly constant over a wide range of temperatures. It became widely used, for example, for the hairsprings of watches.

In 1920 Guillaume received the Nobel Prize for physics for his researches into nickel–steel alloys.

Guillemin, Roger (1924–) *French–American physiologist*

Guillemin was educated at the universities of Dijon (his native city), Lyons, and Montreal, where he gained his PhD in physiology and experimental medicine in 1953. The same year he moved to America to join the staff of the Baylor University Medical School, Houston. In 1970 Guillemin joined the staff of the Salk Institute in La Jolla, California, where he remained until 1989, when he moved to the Whittier Institute for Diabetes and Endocrinology, La Jolla, becoming its director in 1993.

Early in his career Guillemin decided to work on the hypothesis of Geoffrey Harris that the pituitary gland is under the control of hormones produced by the hypothalamus. As the anterior pituitary secretes a number of hormones it was far from clear which to begin with. He eventually decided to search for the hypothalamic factor that controls the release of the adrenocorticotrophic hormone (ACTH) from the pituitary – it is known as the corticotrophic releasing factor (CRF). As it turned out, this was an unfortunate choice for after seven years Guillemin had nothing to show for his not inconsiderable efforts. Guillemin then worked for a further six years fruitlessly searching for thyrotropin releasing factor (TRF), which controls the release of the thyroid-stimulating hormone, exposing him to skepticism from many other workers in the endocrine field.

The main difficulty was that such hormones were present in very small quantities. When Guillemin finally did succeed in 1968 in isolating one milligram of TRF it had come from 5 million sheep's hypothalami. It turned out to be a small, relatively simple tripeptide, easy to synthesize. The development of the radioimmunoassay method for the detection of minute quantities by Rosalyn YALOW was also of considerable help. Other successes quickly followed. Andrew SCHALLY isolated the luteinizing-hormone releasing factor in 1971 and Guillemin in 1972 succeeded with somatostatin, which controls the release of the growth hormone.

In 1977 Guillemin shared the Nobel Prize for physiology or medicine with Schally and Yalow.

Guldberg, Cato Maximilian (1836–1902) *Norwegian chemist*

Guldberg was educated at the university in his native city of Christiania (now Oslo) and started his career teaching at the Royal Military School there in 1860. He was appointed to the chair of applied mathematics at the university in 1869.

Guldberg's main work was on chemical thermodynamics. In 1863 he formulated the law of mass action in collaboration with his brother-in-law, the Norwegian chemist **Peter Waage** (1833–1900). The law states that the rate of a chemical change depends on the concentrations of the reactants. Thus for a reaction: $A + B \rightarrow C$ the rate of reaction is proportional to $[A][B]$, where $[A]$ and $[B]$ are concentrations. Guldberg and Waage also investigated the effects of temperature. They did not gain full credit for their work at the time, partly due to their first publishing the law in Norwegian. However, even when published in French (1867) the law received little attention until it was rediscovered by William Esson and Vernon Harcourt working at Oxford University.

In 1870 Guldberg investigated the way in which the freezing point and vapor pressure of a pure liquid are lowered by a dissolved component. In 1890 he formulated *Guldberg's law*. This relates boiling point and critical temperature (the point above which a gas cannot be liquefied by pressure alone) on the absolute scale. The law was discovered independently by Phillippe-Auguste Guye.

Gullstrand, Allvar (1862–1930) *Swedish ophthalmologist*

Gullstrand, a physician's son from Landskrona, Sweden, was educated at the universities of Uppsala, Vienna, and Stockholm, where he obtained his PhD in 1890. After working briefly at the Karolinska Institute in Stockholm Gullstrand moved to the University of Uppsala, where he served as professor of ophthalmology from 1894 until his retirement in 1927.

In 1911 Gullstrand was awarded the Nobel Prize for physiology or medicine for his work on the dioptrics of the eye. Hermann von Helmholtz had earlier shown that the eye solves the problem of accommodation (how to focus on both near and distant objects) by changing the surface curvature of the lens – the nearer the object, the more convex the lens becomes; the further the object, the more concave the lens. Gullstrand showed that this could in fact account for only two thirds of the accommodation a normal eye could achieve. The remaining third was produced by what

Gullstrand termed the 'intracapsular mechanism' and depended on the fact that the eye was not a homogeneous medium.

Gutenberg, Beno (1889–1960) *German–American geologist*

Gutenberg was educated at the Technical University in his native city of Darmstadt and at the University of Göttingen, where he obtained his PhD in 1911. He then taught at the University of Freiburg becoming professor of geophysics in 1926. He emigrated to America in 1930, taking a post at the California Institute of Technology, and later served as director of the seismological laboratory (1947–58).

In 1913 Gutenberg suggested a structure of the Earth that would explain the data on earthquake waves. It was known that there were two main types of waves: primary (P) waves, which are longitudinal compression waves, and secondary (S) waves, which are transverse shear waves. On the opposite side of the Earth to an earthquake, in an area known as the shadow zone, no S waves are recorded and the P waves, although they do appear, are of smaller amplitudes and occur later than would be expected. Gutenberg proposed that the Earth's core, first identified by Richard Oldham in 1906, is liquid, which would explain the absence of S waves as, being transverse, they cannot be transmitted through liquids. Making detailed calculations he was able to show that the core ends at a depth of about 1800 miles (2900 km) below the Earth's surface where it forms a marked discontinuity, now known as the *Gutenberg discontinuity*, with the overlying mantle. Its existence has been confirmed by later work including precise measurements made after underground nuclear explosions.

In collaboration with Charles Richter, Gutenberg produced a major study, *On Seismic Waves* (1934–39), in which, using large quantities of seismic data, they were able to calculate average velocity distributions for the whole of the Earth.

Guth, Alan Harvey (1947–) *American physicist and cosmologist*

Born in New Brunswick, New Jersey, Guth was educated at Massachusetts Institute of Technology, where he obtained his PhD in 1969. After holding postdoctoral appointments at Princeton, Columbia, Cornell, and Stanford, Guth returned to MIT in 1980, becoming professor of physics in 1986.

Initially Guth worked as a theorist in elementary-particle physics, but, stimulated by the work of Steven Weinberg, he began to consider some of the outstanding problems of cosmology. These included a number of difficulties raised against the standard interpretation of the big-bang account of the origin of the universe. Many had found the apparent isotropy of the universe puzzling while James Peebles and Charles Misner had discovered the flatness and horizon problems. The big-bang was clearly in need of revision.

Consequently Guth in 1980 first proposed the *inflationary universe model*. Guth's theory agrees with the standard model after the first 10^{-30} second. Within the initial brief period, he proposed that the universe had undergone an extraordinarily rapid inflation. During this period the diameter of the universe would have increased by a factor of about 10^{50}. An increase of this size would expand a centimeter to 10^{32} light-years.

Thus as the region from which the present universe emerged was so small, thermal equilibrium could have been achieved before the inflation. An observer today would, therefore, detect an isotropic cosmic-background radiation. He would also detect a flat universe – an observer on a globe that had increased 10^{50} times in diameter would have seen his universe flattened.

Guth has conceded that even if the inflationary model is correct "it will be difficult for anyone to ever discover observable consequences of the conditions existing before the inflationary phase transition." He has also pointed out that the grand unified theories of physics allow that the observed universe could have evolved from nothing. The inflationary model comes close to this by providing a mechanism by which the observable universe could have evolved from an infinitesimal region: "They say that there is no such thing as a free lunch – but the universe is the ultimate free lunch!"

Guyot, Arnold Henry (1807–1884)
Swiss–American geologist and geographer

Intending to enter the Church, Guyot, who was born at Boudevilliers in Switzerland, studied at the universities of Neuchâtel, Strasbourg, and Berlin, where his interests in science began to absorb him. After teaching in Paris (1835–40) he was appointed professor of history and physical geography at Neuchâtel in 1839 where he remained until 1848, when he emigrated to America. He taught first at the Lowell Technological Institute in Boston before he was appointed, in 1854, to the chair of geology and physical geography at Princeton University.

While in Switzerland he had studied the structure and movement of glaciers, spending much time testing the new theories of Louis Agassiz. In America, under the auspices of the Smithsonian Institution, he began to develop, organize, and equip a number of East Coast meteorological stations. He also surveyed and constructed topographical maps of the Appalachian and Catskill mountains. In 1849 he published his influential work *The Earth and Man*.

Guyton de Morveau, Baron Louis Bernard (1737–1816) *French chemist*

Born at Dijon in France, Guyton began his career as a lawyer; as a member of the Burgundy parliament (1755–82), however, he met the great Georges Buffon who encouraged his interest in science. In 1782 he gave up law to devote himself to science and he collaborated with Antoine Lavoisier. During the revolutionary period he reentered politics. He was a founder of and teacher at the Ecole Polytechnique (1795–1805) and in 1800 became master of the mint until his retirement in 1814.

In the period 1776–77 Guyton published his three-volume *Eléments de chimie théorique et pratique* (Rudiments of Theoretical and Practical Chemistry), which was a major attempt to quantify chemical affinities. Guyton was a passionate Newtonian and tried to apply Newtonian laws to chemistry. He tried to do this by floating disks of various metals on mercury and measuring the force necessary to remove them. Thus he obtained figures such as gold needs a force of 446 grains to remove it, lead 397, zinc 204, iron 115, and cobalt 8. He attempted to correlate his figures with the chemical affinities of the elements.

Haber, Fritz (1868–1934)
German physical chemist

Haber, the son of a merchant, was born at Breslau, now Wrocław in Poland. He was educated at Berlin, Heidelberg, Charlottenburg, and Jena, and in 1894 he became an assistant in physical chemistry at the Technical Institute, Karlsruhe, where he remained until 1911, being promoted to a professorship in 1906. He moved to Berlin in 1911 to become director of the Kaiser Wilhelm Institute of Physical Chemistry. Though an intensely patriotic German he was also a Jew and with the rise of anti-Semitism he resigned his post in 1933 and went into exile in England, where he worked at the Cavendish Laboratory, Cambridge. He died in Basel en route to Italy.

Haber is noted for his discovery of the industrial process for synthesizing ammonia from nitrogen and hydrogen. The need at the time was for nitrogen compounds for use as fertilizers – most plants cannot utilize free nitrogen from the air, and need 'fixed' nitrogen. The main source was deposits of nitrate salts in Chile, but these would have a limited life.

Haber, in an attempt to solve this problem, began investigating the reaction:

$$N_2 + 3H_2 \leftrightarrow 2NH_3$$

Under normal conditions the yield is very low. Haber (1907–09) showed that practical yields could be achieved at high temperatures (250°C) and pressures (250 atmospheres) using a catalyst (iron is the catalyst now used). The process was developed industrially by Carl BOSCH around 1913 and is still the main industrial method for the fixation of nitrogen. Haber received the Nobel Prize for chemistry for this work in 1918.

During World War I, Haber turned his efforts to helping Germany's war effort. In particular he directed the use of poisonous gas. After the war he tried, unsuccessfully, to repay the indemnities imposed on Germany by a process for extracting gold from seawater.

Hadamard, Jacques Salomon (1865–1963) *French mathematician*

The son of a Latin teacher, Hadamard was born at Versailles in France and educated at the Ecole Normale Supérieure in Paris. He taught first at the University of Bordeaux from 1893 until 1897, before returning to Paris to the Sorbonne. In 1909 he took up the chair of mathematics at the Collège de France where he remained until his retirement in 1937.

In his long life Hadamard worked in many areas of mathematics, but remains best known for his proof in 1896 of the prime number theorem.

Mathematicians have long been interested in prime numbers. There is no simple formula for determining primes, but it is possible to say something about the distribution of prime numbers. If P_n is the nth prime number, $\pi(n)$ is used to denote the number of primes between 1 and n. Both Gauss and Legendre used the formula

$$\pi(n) = n/\log_e n.$$

This does not work at small values of n but Gauss and Legendre suspected that the ratio of $\log_e n$ to $\pi(n)/n$ would approach 1 as n approaches infinity. They were, however, unable to prove it. Hadamard and, independently, Charles de la Vallée-Poussin produced proofs in 1896 using the Riemann zeta function.

Hadley, George (1685–1768) *English meteorologist*

The younger brother of the inventor John Hadley, George Hadley was born in London and educated at Oxford University. Although called to the bar in 1709, he became more interested in physics and was made responsible for producing the Royal Society of London's meteorological observations.

In 1686 Edmond Halley had offered a partial explanation of the trade winds, pointing out that heated equatorial air will rise and thus cause colder air to move in from the tropics, but could not explain why the winds blew from the northeast in the northern hemisphere and the southeast in the southern.

Hadley put forward the explanation, in his paper *Concerning the Cause of the General Trade Winds* (1735), that the airflow toward the equator was deflected by the Earth's rotation from west to east. This circulation is now known as the *Hadley cell*.

Haeckel, Ernst Heinrich (1834–1919)
German biologist

The son of a government lawyer, Haeckel was born at Potsdam in Germany and educated at the universities of Warburg, Vienna, and Berlin, where he qualified as a physician in 1858. His main interests lay elsewhere and, after a brief period in practice, he moved to Jena to study zoology. In 1862 he was appointed professor of zoology and comparative anatomy at Jena, a position he held until his retirement in 1909.

Haeckel's contributions to zoological science were a mixture of sound research and speculation often with insufficient evidence. An advocate of monism, which postulated a totally materialistic view of life as a unity, he based his evolutionary ideas on the embryological laws expounded by Karl von Baer. Expanding the idea of his mentor, Johannes MÜLLER, Haeckel argued that the embryological stages of an animal were a recapitulation of its evolutionary history, and indeed that there had once been complete animals resembling the embryonic stages of higher animal forms living today. He formulated a scheme of evolution for the whole animal kingdom, from inorganic matter upward. His studies, with Müller, of marine life, particularly the crystalline radiolarians, encouraged him to compare the symmetry of crystals with the simplest animals, and led him to postulate an inanimate origin for animal life. In 1866 Haeckel anticipated later proof of the fact that the key to inheritance factors lies in the cell nucleus, outlining this theme in his *Die Perigenesis der Plastidule* (1876; The Generation of Waves in the Small Vital Particles).

Haeckel also proposed the idea that all multicellular animals derived from a hypothetical two-layered (ectoderm and endoderm) animal, the *Gastraea* – a theory that provoked much discussion. He engaged in much valuable research on marine invertebrates, such as the radiolarians, jellyfish, calcareous sponges, and medusae, and wrote a series of monographs on these groups based largely on specimens brought back by the Challenger Expedition. He was also the first to divide the animal kingdom into unicellular (protozoan) and multicellular (metazoan) animals. An ardent Darwinist, Haeckel made several zoological expeditions and founded the Phyletic Museum at Jena and the Ernst Haeckel Haus, which contains his books, archives, and other effects.

In 1906 the Monist League was formed in Jena with Haeckel as its president. The League held a strong commitment to social Darwinism. Man was seen as part of nature and in no way qualitatively distinct from any other organic form. Human society was as much a creation of natural selection as the bird's wing. To such views Haeckel added a strong anticatholicism, a contempt for politicians, and a forecast of impending

doom. After the chaos of World War I, Haeckel's views were taken up by eugenicists, the Volk movement and, more significantly, the National Socialists.

Hahn, Otto (1879–1968) *German chemist*

Hahn's father, a successful merchant in the German city of Frankfurt, was keen for his son to train as an architect and it was against much family opposition that Hahn was finally allowed to study chemistry at the University of Marburg in 1897. After obtaining his doctorate in 1901 he studied abroad, first with William Ramsay in London and then at McGill University, Canada, with Ernest Rutherford. Hahn returned to Germany in 1907, where he took up an appointment at the University of Berlin, being made professor of chemistry in 1910. Two years later he joined the Kaiser Wilhelm Institute of Chemistry where he served as director from 1928 to 1945.

Hahn had trained as an organic chemist and had really gone to London to learn English in order to prepare himself for an industrial career. Ramsay had however asked him to separate radium from some radioactive material he had recently acquired from Ceylon. In so doing Hahn found a new material, a highly active form of thorium which he named 'radiothorium'. So impressed was Ramsay with this work that he wrote to Emil Fischer in Berlin suggesting that he employ Hahn after he had acquired more experience of radioactivity with Rutherford at McGill.

Hahn was thus diverted into an academic career, most of which was spent in research on radioactivity and much of it in collaboration with Lise MEITNER. With her he discovered a new element, protactinium, in 1917. He went on to define, in 1921, the phenomenon of nuclear isomerism. This arises when nuclei with different radioactive properties turn out to be identical in atomic number and mass.

Hahn's most important work however, was done in the 1930s when, with Meitner and the German chemist **Fritz Strassmann** (1902–), he made one of the most important discoveries of the century, namely nuclear fission. One of the strange features about Hahn's work was that he was repeating experiments already done and formulating hypotheses already rejected as nonsense or due to some contamination of the materials used. Chemists at this time felt that they understood the process of nuclear transformation. After all it was some twenty years since Rutherford had first detected the transformation of nitrogen into oxygen, and a newer form of the same 'alchemy' had been described by Irène and Frédéric JOLIOT-CURIE in 1934. Two basic rules were involved in this understanding. First, that nuclear transmutations always involved the emission of either an alpha particle (helium nucleus) or a beta particle (electron); and secondly, that the change could take place only between elements separated by no more than two places in the periodic table. If more substantial transformations appeared to occur, as in the transformation of uranium into lead, this was explained as the result of a series of such intermediate steps, each one taking place with the emission of the appropriate particle.

Thus when in 1938 Hahn bombarded uranium with slow neutrons and detected some strange new half-lives, he assumed that the uranium had changed into radium, a close neighbor, with some undetected alpha particles. But when he tried to remove the radium all he could find was barium. This Hahn simply could not understand, for barium was far too low in the periodic table to be produced by the transmutation of uranium; and if the transformation *was* taking place it should be accompanied by the emission of a prodigious number of alpha particles, which Hahn could not have failed to detect. The thought that the heavy uranium nucleus could split into two lighter ones was too outrageous for him to consider seriously. He could not dismiss it entirely for he asserted at the time that "we must really state that we are not dealing with radium but with barium." But to suppose the barium arose from what he then called nuclear 'bursting' he felt would be "in contradiction to all previous experience in nuclear physics." He did realize that something of importance was going on and quickly sent off for publication a joint paper with Strassmann even though, as he recalled twenty years later, "After the manuscript had been mailed, the whole thing once more seemed so improbable to me that I wished I could get the documents back out of the mail." Appropriately enough it was his old collaborator Meitner, in exile from the Nazis in Sweden, and her nephew Otto Frisch who made the necessary calculations and announced fission to the world early in 1939. Hahn received the Nobel Prize for chemistry in 1944.

Haken, Wolfgang (1928–) *German-born American mathematician. See* APPEL, KENNETH.

Haldane, John Burdon Sanderson
(1892–1964) *British geneticist*

Haldane, who was born at Oxford, became involved in scientific research at an early age through helping in the laboratory of his father, the physiologist John Scott Haldane. His interest in genetics was first stimulated as early as 1901, when he heard a lecture on Mendel's work, and he later applied this by studying inheritance in his sister's (the writer Naomi Mitchison) 300 guinea pigs. On leaving school he studied first mathematics and then the humanities at Oxford University. He served in World War I with the Black Watch Regiment and was wounded at Loos and in Mesopotamia. Some work on gas masks, following the first German gas attacks, marked the beginning of his physiological studies.

In 1919 Haldane took up a fellowship at Oxford, where he continued research on respiration, investigating how the levels of carbon dioxide in the blood affect the muscles regulating breathing. He was next offered a readership in biochemistry at Cambridge, where he conducted some important work on enzymes. These experiments, and later work on conditions in submarines, aroused considerable public interest because he frequently used himself as a guinea pig.

In 1933 Haldane became professor of genetics at University College, London, a position he exchanged in 1937 for the chair of biometry. While at London he prepared a provisional map of the X sex chromosome and showed the genetic linkage between hemophilia and color blindness. He also produced the first estimate of mutation rates in humans from studies of the pedigrees of hemophiliacs, and described the effect of recurring deleterious mutations on a population. With the outbreak of the Spanish Civil War, Haldane joined the Communist Party and advised the republican government on gas precautions. In the 1950s he left the party as a result of Soviet acceptance and promotion of Trofim Lysenko. In protest at the Anglo-French invasion of Suez, Haldane emigrated to India in 1957, becoming an Indian citizen in 1961. He was director of the laboratory of genetics and biometry at Bhubaneswar from 1962 until his death.

Haldane's books include *Enzymes* (1930), *The Causes of Evolution* (1932), and *The Biochemistry of Genetics* (1954); he also wrote a number of books popularizing science.

Haldane, John Scott (1860–1936)
British physiologist

Haldane, the son of a lawyer, was educated

at the university in his native city of Edinburgh, where he obtained his MD in 1884. He worked first at the University of Dundee but moved to Oxford to assist his uncle, John Burdon-Sanderson, the professor of physiology in 1887. Haldane was made reader in physiology in 1907 but resigned in 1913 to become director of the Mining Research Laboratory, initially sited in Doncaster but transferred to Birmingham in 1921.

From the beginning of his career Haldane sought to apply the results of physiological research to the solution of practical social and industrial problems. He was much concerned with problems of ventilation in mines and in 1896 published an important report, *Causes of Death in Colliery Explosions*. He was struck by the fact that in a serious explosion in 1896 only 4 out of 57 miners died from the blast and its effects, the vast majority succumbing to carbon monoxide poisoning. Haldane recommended the simple and effective safety procedure of taking mice down the pit: with their higher metabolic rate they would show the effects of carbon monoxide poisoning long before it reached levels dangerous to man.

He also worked for the admiralty on the problems faced by their divers at high pressures. It had been known for some time that rapid decompression produced the liberation of nitrogen bubbles into the bloodstream, with crippling and often lethal effects. Haldane showed how such effects could be minimized by pointing out that however long a diver had been exposed to compressed air it was always safe to halve the pressure; that is, it is just as safe to ascend from six to three atmospheres as from two to one. Using his technique over £5,000,000 of gold was recovered from the wreck of the *Lusitania* between 1917 and 1924.

Haldane also investigated the response of the human body to high temperatures. Haldane's main work as a pure physiologist, however, was on the mechanism of respiration. In 1906 he published his most significant paper, in collaboration with John Priestley, which demonstrated the key role of carbon dioxide in the regulation of breathing. They showed that it was not a deficiency in oxygen that triggers the respiratory reflex but an excess of carbon dioxide in the arterial blood, acting on the respiratory center in the midbrain. Their work was published in full in *Respiration* (1935; 2nd edition).

In much of his work Haldane used for an experimental subject his precocious son

J. B. S. Haldane, later to become one of the leading biologists of the 20th century.

Hale, Alan (1947–) *American astronomer*

Alan Hale was raised on the outskirts of Almagerdo, New Mexico. His interest in astronomy developed at school and early in 1970 his father bought him his first telescope – a 4½-inch reflector. After graduating from high school he attended the US Naval Academy, Annapolis, Maryland, where he studied physics. He was then stationed at various naval bases. Throughout this period he continued his astronomical observations, in particular the observation of comets.

In 1983 he left the navy and spent 2½ years working for the Deep Space Network at the Jet Propulsion Laboratory, Pasadena. He then went to New Mexico State University, Las Cruces, where he obtained his PhD in 1992. In 1993 he formed an independent research and education organization.

The organization moved in 1995 to a mountain village of Cloudcraft, New Mexico. It was here on the night of 22–23 July that Alan Hale first observed the comet *Hale-Bopp*. It proved to be perhaps the most prominent comet of the century. The comet was discovered independently by an amateur astronomer, Thomas Bopp.

Hale, George Ellery (1868–1938) *American astrophysicist*

Hale's father, William Hale, was a wealthy manufacturer of elevators in Chicago, Illinois, who stimulated in his son an early interest in designing and making his own instruments. This interest was directed to astronomy by Sherburne W. Burnham, a neighbor and passionate observer of double stars, and increased during his four years at the Massachusetts Institute of Technology, where he studied physics. He built a solar observatory, financed by his father, at Kenwood, Chicago, and after graduating in 1890 became its director. In 1892 he was appointed assistant professor and later professor of astrophysics at the new University of Chicago and from 1895 to 1905 he was director of the university's Yerkes Observatory. From 1904 to 1923 he was director of the newly established Mount Wilson Observatory in California. The last 15 years of his life were spent organizing the equipping and building of the Palomar Observatory in California and in the pursuit of his solar researches in his private observatory in Pasadena.

Hale was undoubtedly one of the key figures in 20th-century astronomy. He saw very clearly and very early that astronomy could only develop if much more powerful telescopes were constructed. Thus with great vision and enormous persistence and energy he spent 40 years acting as midwife to a series of bigger and bigger telescopes. His insight was clearly justified for it was with his telescopes that Harlow Shapley, Edwin Hubble, and many others made their observations.

His first triumph came when he persuaded Charles T. Yerkes, a Chicago trolley-car magnate, to provide $349,000 to build a 40-inch (1-m) refracting telescope for the University of Chicago. This was and still is the largest refractor ever built. It was first used in 1897. He was soon anxious, however, to build a large reflecting telescope. In 1896 his father acquired a 60-inch (1.5-m) mirror but the University of Chicago was unable to fund its mounting. Hale once more started raising money. This time he interested the Carnegie Institution of Washington in financing the Mount Wilson Observatory. The observatory was founded in 1904 and the 60-inch reflector eventually went into use in 1908. In 1918 this superb instrument was surpassed by the 100-inch (2.5-m) Hooker telescope, largely financed by a Los Angeles business man, John D. Hooker. For 30 years this was the world's largest telescope and it revolutionized astronomy.

Hale had resigned from his directorship of Mount Wilson Observatory in 1923 on the grounds of ill health but lost little time in seeking to interest the Rockefeller Foundation in building a reflecting telescope that would be the ultimate in size, 200 inches (5 m) across, for Earth-based instruments. In 1929 it was finally agreed that $6 million would be donated for this purpose to an educational institute, the California Institute of Technology, rather than the Carnegie Institution. Hale became chairman of the group directing the planning, construction, and operation of the instrument that was to become his masterpiece.

Thus there began an epic struggle to complete the 200-inch telescope, which was to take nearly 20 years. The first mirror made from fused quartz proved to be a $600,000 failure. Hale next tried Pyrex and the first experimental 200-inch disk cast proved satisfactory. The actual casting was made in December 1934 when the 65 tons of molten Pyrex began its carefully controlled 10 months' cooling. The mirror managed to survive the flooding of the factory, which necessitated shutting down the temperature control for three days, and its long journey in the spring of 1936 from Corning, New York, to California at a maximum speed of 25 mph. The grinding of the mirror was interrupted by the war and took so long that Hale had been dead for nine years when the instrument was finally commissioned as the Hale telescope in 1948. It was set up at the specially constructed Palomar Observatory, which together with the Mount Wilson Observatory was jointly operated by the California Institute of Technology and the Carnegie Institution. The two observatories were renamed the Hale Observatories in 1969. The Hale telescope was the world's largest telescope until the Soviet 6-meter (236-in) reflector went into operation in 1977 but is still considered by many to be the world's finest.

Hale was not just a highly successful scientific entrepreneur for he made major advances in the field of solar spectroscopy. As early as 1889 he had conceived of his spectroheliograph, an instrument that allowed the Sun to be photographed at a particular wavelength. He also designed an appropriate telescope to which it could be attached. In 1908 Hale made his most significant observation. He found that some of the lines in the spectra of sunspots were double. He realized that this demonstrated the presence of strong magnetic fields in sunspots, being due to the effect discovered by Pieter ZEEMAN in 1896, and was the first indication of an extraterrestrial magnetic field.

Hales, Stephen (1677–1761) *English plant physiologist and chemist*

Born at Bekesbourne in Kent, Hales entered Cambridge University in 1696 to study theology. He was ordained in 1703 and appointed curate at Teddington, near London, in 1708 (or 1709). During his time at Cambridge, he studied science and was influenced by Isaac Newton's ideas, which still dominated scientific thought at the university and probably accounted for Hales's consistent use of the quantitative method in his biological researches.

Hales was elected a fellow of the Royal Society in 1718 but his first work, *Vegetable Staticks*, was not published until 1727. In this book, which included his most important observations on plant physiology, Hales demonstrated that plant leaves absorb air and that a portion of air is used in plant nutrition. In addition, he realized that light is necessary for growth and investigated growth rates by marking plants at regular intervals. He measured the rate of water loss (transpiration) in plants, finding that it occurred through the leaves and was responsible for an upward flow of sap in plants. From additional measurements of sap flow he concluded that there was no circular movement of sap in plants analogous to blood circulation in animals.

Hales also made important contributions to the understanding of blood circulation by measuring such properties as blood pressure, output per minute from the heart, rate of flow and resistance to flow in vessels. The results were published in *Haemastaticks* (1733; Blood Statics).

Other notable discoveries include the development of methods for collecting gases over water, distilling fresh water from sea water, and preserving foodstuffs with sulfur dioxide. He also invented a ventilator for introducing fresh air into prisons, ships, and granaries.

Hall, Asaph (1829–1907) *American astronomer*

Born at Goshen in Connecticut, Hall had to leave school at the age of 13 and support his family as a carpenter, following the death of his father. He educated himself, and his interest in astronomy was strong enough for George Bond to employ him as his assistant at Harvard in 1857. In 1863 Hall became professor of mathematics at the Naval Observatory in Washington. He returned to Harvard as professor of astronomy in 1895.

In 1877 Mars was in opposition to the Sun at a distance of about 30 million miles from the Earth. Hall decided to search for Martian satellites using the 26-inch (66-cm) refractor that the Clark firm had provided for the Naval Observatory. On 11 August he discovered a tiny satellite (the smaller moon) but was then compelled to wait a further six nights for the persistent cloud to clear before he could confirm his sighting and discover a further satellite. Both were very small, having diameters of 17 miles (27 km) and 9 miles (15 km) only. He named the larger 'Phobos' and the smaller 'Deimos' (Fear and Terror), after the sons of Mars. One curious feature of the two satellites was that Jonathan Swift had spoken of Martian satellites in *Gulliver's Travels* (1726). Not only did Swift get their number correct but also spoke accurately of their size and orbital period.

In 1876, by noticing a white spot on the surface of Saturn, Hall was able to work out correctly the rotation period as 10.75 hours, which compares well with today's figure of 10 hours 14 minutes (for its equatorial region).

Hall, Charles Martin (1863–1914) *American chemist*

Hall was born in Thompson, Ohio, and educated at Oberlin College, graduating in 1885. He became interested in the costly process of manufacturing aluminum – until the late 19th century aluminum was a precious metal costing about $5.50 an ounce. Napoleon III would have the majority of his guests served from gold plate; he and the chosen few he wished to impress were served from aluminum plates. Hall was stimulated by a remark of his teacher that anyone who could find a cheap way to make aluminum would win great wealth and fame.

Although the ore itself (bauxite, aluminum oxide) was cheap and plentiful, the metal could only be extracted by electrolysis of the molten ore, and aluminum oxide has a very high melting point. Hall tried various added compounds and, in 1886, found that adding 10–15% of cryolite (sodium aluminum fluoride) reduced the melting point to a little over 1000°C. Hall produced his first sample in the form of buttons, which soon became known as the 'aluminum crown jewels'. The French chemist Paul HÉROULT (1863–1914) discovered the process independently at about the same time and the electrolytic method for extracting aluminium is called the *Hall-Héroult process*. Hall helped to found the Pittsburgh Reduction Company (later the Aluminum Company of America), of which he became vice-president in 1890.

Hall, Edwin Herbert (1855–1938) *American physicist*

Hall was born in Great Falls, Maine, and educated at Johns Hopkins University, Baltimore, where he received his PhD in 1880. After a year in Europe he joined the Harvard faculty and was appointed professor of physics in 1895, a post he held until his retirement in 1921.

While working for his thesis, Hall began to consider a problem first posed by Maxwell concerning the force on a conductor carrying a current in a magnetic field. Does the force act on the conductor or the current? Hall argued that if the current was affected by the magnetic field then there should be "a state of stress...the electricity passing toward one side of the wire." Hall used a thin gold foil and in 1879 detected for the first time an electric potential acting perpendicularly to both the current and the magnetic field. The effect has since been known as the *Hall effect*. A simple interpretation is that the charge carriers moving along the conductor experience a transverse force and tend to drift to one side. The sign of the Hall voltage gives information on whether the charge carriers are positive or negative.

Other so-called galvanomagnetic effects were later discovered by Walter Nernst and others. Hall spent much of his later life attempting to measure the various effects as exactly as possible.

More than a century after its discovery Klaus von KLITZING was awarded the 1985 Nobel Prize for physics for his work on the *Hall effect*.

Haller, Albrecht von (1708–1777) *Swiss physiologist*

Born at Bern in Switzerland, Haller studied under Hermann Boerhaave at Leiden, gaining his MD in 1727. He was later appointed professor of anatomy, botany, and medicine (1736–53) at the newly established University of Göttingen. He then retired to Bern to spend more time on his research and writing.

Between 1757 and 1766 Haller published in eight massive volumes his *Elementa Physiologiae Corporis Humani* (Physiological Elements of the Human Body). The work described the advances in physiology made since the time of William Harvey, enriched with Haller's own experimental researches.

Before Haller, physiology followed the views of René Descartes – that bodily systems are essentially mechanical but require some vital principle to overcome their initial inertness. Haller, anticipated somewhat by Francis Glisson, broke radically with this tradition. When stimulated, muscles contract; such 'irritability', according to Haller, is inherent in the fiber and not caused by external factors.

The implications of this work were not immediately apparent to Haller. It was left to the philosophers of the Enlightenment to hammer home the conclusion that if such an inherent force resided in muscles then there no longer remained a need for the assumption of vital principles to imbue them with activity.

Haller also made important contributions to embryology and was a noted botanist, publishing a major work on the Swiss flora. However, his attempt to construct an alternative classification scheme to that of Linnaeus, based on fruits rather than sexual organs, received little support despite being a more logical system.

Halley, Edmond (1656–1742) *British astronomer and physicist*

Edmond (or Edmund) Halley was the son of a wealthy London merchant. He was educated at St. Paul's School, London, and at Oxford University. He left Oxford without a degree in 1676, but having already published his first scientific paper in the *Philosophical Transactions* of the Royal Society on the theory of planetary orbits. Halley's scientific work and his life covered an enormous range. He started his active scientific career by spending two years on St. Helena mapping the southern skies. In 1679 he published *Catalogus stellarum australium* (Catalog of the Southern Stars) the first catalog of telescopically determined star positions. On his return he traveled extensively in Europe meeting such leading astronomers as Johannes Hevelius and Giovanni Cassini.

Halley now began his enormous contribution to just about all branches of physics and astronomy. He prepared extensive maps showing magnetic variation, winds, and tides. In atmospheric physics he formulated the mathematical law relating height and pressure (1686), making many advances in barometric design. He carried out important studies on evaporation and the salinity of lakes (1687–1694), which allowed him to draw conclusions about the age of the Earth. He used Newtonian mathematical techniques to improve and augment Descartes's work on the optics of the rainbow (1697–1721). He almost incidentally constructed mortality tables, estimated the acreage of England and the size of the atom, improved the design of the diving bell, and published numerous articles on natural history and classical studies.

These were sidelines compared to his work in astronomy and to the help he provided Newton. It is owing to Halley that Newton's *Principia* was published in the complete form we know it today. He pressed Newton to publish it, paid for the cost himself, saw it through the press, and even contributed some Latin verses in honor of the author. In 1695 he proposed the secular acceleration of the Moon, in 1718 he discovered the proper motion of the stars, but above all in his *Astronomiae cometicae synopsis* (1705; A Synopsis of the Astronomy of Comets) he laid the foundations of modern cometary study. His grasp of the geometry of cometary orbits allowed him to identify the comet (now known as Halley's comet) of 1531 with those of 1607 and 1682, and confidently to predict its return in 1758 – long after his death.

He held an equally varied and bewildering set of appointments. From 1696 until 1698 he was deputy controller of the mint at Chester. From 1698 to 1700 he actually commanded a Royal Navy man-of-war, the *Paramour*, making prolonged and eventful ocean voyages. In 1702 and in 1703 he made two diplomatic missions to Vienna. In 1703 he was elected to the Savillian Chair of Geometry at Oxford, and in 1720 he succeeded John Flamsteed as Astronomer Royal. He held this post until his death, making observations of nearly 1500 lunar meriodional transits and the full 18-year period of the Moon.

Hamilton, William Donald (1936–)
British theoretical biologist

Hamilton was educated at the universities of Cambridge and London. He served as a lecturer in genetics at Imperial College, London, from 1964 until 1977 when he moved to America to take up an appointment as professor of evolutionary biology at the University of Michigan. He returned to England in 1984 to serve as a Royal Society Research Professor at Oxford.

In the *Origin of Species* (1859) Darwin raised a "special difficulty," which he at first considered unsurmountable. How could natural selection ever lead to the evolution of neuter or sterile insects? Darwin's answer was that selection may be applied to the family, as well as the individual. In a series of papers, beginning in 1964 with *The Genetical Theory of Social Behaviour*, Hamilton has pursued these implications and opened the way for the emergence of sociobiology. The key concept deployed by Hamilton is that of inclusive fitness, which covers not only an individual's fitness to survive but also the effects of his behavior on the fitness of his kin.

Hamilton, Sir William Rowan (1805–1865) *Irish mathematician*

Hamilton was a child prodigy, and not just in mathematics; he also managed to learn an extraordinary number of languages, some of them very obscure. In 1823 he entered Trinity College in his native city of Dublin, and four years later at the age of 22 was appointed professor of astronomy and Astronomer Royal for Ireland; these posts were given to him in order that he could continue to research unhampered by teaching commitments.

In 1827 he produced his first original work, in the theory of optics, expounded in his paper *A Theory of Systems of Rays*. In 1832 he did further theoretical work on rays, and predicted conical refraction under certain conditions in biaxial crystals. This was soon confirmed experimentally. In dynamics he introduced *Hamilton's equations* – a set of equations (similar to equations of Joseph Lagrange) describing the positions and momenta of a collection of particles. The equations involve the *Hamiltonian function*, which is used extensively in quantum mechanics. *Hamilton's principle* is the principle that the integral with respect to time of the kinetic energy minus the potential energy of a system is a minimum.

One of Hamilton's most famous discoveries was that of *quaternions*. These are a generalization of complex numbers with the property that the commutative law does not hold for them (i.e., $A \times B$ does not equal $B \times A$). Hamilton's discovery of such an algebraic system was important for the development of abstract algebra; for instance, the introduction of matrices. Hamilton spent the last 20 years of his life trying to apply quaternions to problems in applied mathematics, although the more limited theory of vector analysis of Josiah Willard Gibbs was eventually preferred. Toward the end of his life Hamilton drank increasingly, eventually dying of gout.

Harden, Sir Arthur (1865–1940) *British biochemist*

Harden was born in Manchester and educated at Owens College there (where he subsequently taught) and at the University of Erlangen, Germany. He was professor of biochemistry at the Jenner (later Lister) Institute of Preventive Medicine, where he began research into alcoholic fermentation, continuing the work of Eduard Buchner who had discovered that such reactions can take place in the absence of living cells.

Harden demonstrated that the activity of yeast enzymes was lost following dialysis (the separation of large from small molecules by diffusion of the smaller molecules through a semipermeable membrane). He went on to show that the small molecules are necessary for the successful action of the yeast enzyme and that, whereas the activity of the large molecules was lost on boiling, the activity of the small molecules remained after boiling. This suggested that the large molecules were proteins but the small molecules were probably nonprotein. This was the first evidence for the existence of *coenzymes* – nonprotein molecules that are essential for the activity of enzymes. Harden also discovered that yeast enzymes are not broken down and lost with time, but that the gradual loss of activity with time can be reversed by the addition of phosphates. He found that sugar phosphates are formed during fermentation as intermediates – phosphates are now known to play a vital part in biochemical reactions. Knighted in 1936, Harden shared the 1929 Nobel Prize for chemistry with Hans von Euler-Chelpin for his work on alcoholic fermentation and enzymes.

Hardy, Godfrey Harold (1877–1947) *British mathematician*

Born at Cranleigh, Hardy had his mathematical education at Cambridge University and remained there as a fellow of Trinity

College until 1919, when he became Savilian Professor of Geometry at Oxford. From 1931 to 1942 he was back in Cambridge as Sadleirian Professor of Pure Mathematics.

His central field of interest was in analysis and such related areas as convergence and number theory. *Hardy classes* of complex functions are named for him. For 35 years, starting in 1911, Hardy collaborated with J. E. Littlewood and together they wrote nearly a hundred papers. The principal areas they covered were Diophantine approximations, the theory of numbers, inequalities, series and definite integrals, and the Riemann zeta-function.

Although primarily a pure mathematician Hardy made one lasting contribution to applied mathematics; the *Hardy–Weinberg law* was discovered independently by Hardy and the physician Wilhelm Weinberg in 1908 and proved to be fundamental to the science of population genetics. It gives a mathematical description of the genetic equilibrium in a large random-mating population and explains the surprising fact that, unless there are outside changing forces, the proportion of dominant to recessive genes tends *not* to vary from generation to generation. The law offered strong confirmation for the Darwinian theory of natural selection.

Hardy was one of the outstanding British mathematicians of his day, an excellent teacher, and one of the first to introduce modern work on the rigorous presentation of analysis into Britain. His *Course of Pure Mathematics* (1908) was influential on the teaching of mathematics in British universities. One of his achievements was his discovery of the young Indian mathematician Srinivasa Ramanujan. Partly through Hardy's efforts Trinity College made funds available for Ramanujan to go to Cambridge to pursue his mathematical researches under Hardy.

Hardy was a passionate devotee of cricket and an equally passionate enemy of the Christian religion. During World War I he was a staunch supporter of Bertrand Russell when Trinity College set about depriving Russell of his position on account of his pacifist activities. Hardy wrote a lively autobiographical sketch *A Mathematician's Apology* (1940).

Hariot, Thomas (1560–1621) *English mathematician, astronomer, and physicist*

Hariot (or Harriot) is best known as a pioneer figure in the British school of algebra, although his interests and activities were very wide ranging. Born in Oxford, he was an associate of Sir Walter Raleigh, whom he accompanied on a voyage to Virginia (1585–86) in the capacity of navigator and cartographer. He later wrote a book about this journey – *A Briefe and True Report of the New Found Land of Virginia* (1588). Among his many innovations in algebra Hariot introduced a number of greatly simplified notations. His central mathematical achievements were in the theory of equations where he discovered important relationships between the coefficients of equations and their roots. This work was published in his *Artis analyticae praxis ad aequationes algebraicas resolvendas* (1631; The Analytical Arts Applied to Solving Algebraic Equations).

Outside mathematics Hariot's achievements as a practical astronomer were noteworthy. He designed and constructed telescopes and made detailed studies of comets and sunspots. Independently of Galileo he discovered the moons of Jupiter. Hariot also discovered the law governing the refraction of light. He was granted a pension by the earl of Northumberland and was briefly imprisoned along with the earl during the Gunpowder Plot of 1605. Hariot conducted numerous experiments in a variety of fields including optics, ballistics, and meteorology. However he published few of his discoveries and it was only after his death that their extent was realized from his voluminous notes and papers.

Harrison, John (1693–1776) *English horologist*

John Harrison was born at Foulby near Pontefract in Yorkshire, the son of a carpenter, a trade he originally took up himself.

In the early 18th century exploration and colonial expansion was an important concern of European governments. A number of naval disasters caused by navigation errors prompted the British Government to set up a Board of Longitude in 1714. The board offered a prize of £20,000 to anyone who discovered a practical method of measuring longitude accurately. The key to determining the position of a ship out of sight of land was accurate timekeeping. The board's conditions effectively meant the construction of a chronometer that kept time to an accuracy of 3 seconds per day.

Harrison became interested in the problem in 1728 and in 1735 completed his first instrument, H1. He improved his design over a period of many years and in 1762 his perfected chronometer, H4, was found to be in error by only 5 seconds (corresponding to 1.25′ of longitude) after a voyage to Jamaica.

Harrison's chronometers all met the conditions set up by the Board of Longitude but he had problems obtaining the prize money. In 1763 he was given £5000 and it was not until 1773, after the intervention of King George III, that he received the full amount less expenses. His chronometer was used in 1776 by James Cook on his voyage to Australia and New Zealand.

Harrison, Ross Granville (1870–1959)
American biologist and embryologist

Born in Germantown, Philadelphia, Harrison graduated from Johns Hopkins University in 1889 and continued studying experimental embryology for the next ten years at Bryn Mawr College, Johns Hopkins University, and in Germany at the University of Bonn. He had an excellent ear for languages and spoke German fluently. In 1899 he gained his MD degree from the University of Bonn and returned to America to become associate professor of anatomy at Johns Hopkins. From 1907 to 1938 he worked at Yale, first as professor of anatomy and then from 1927 as professor of biology.

Harrison's work in experimental embryology formed a bridge between the morphological studies of the 19th century and the new molecular biology of the 20th century based on cell function and structure. In his most influential work (1910) he demonstrated the outgrowth of nerve fibers from ganglion cells in embryonic tissues by devising techniques so that the event could actually be observed. His early attempts used frog-embryo cells hanging in a nutrient medium from the underside of a special microscope slide. The method was gradually refined to give the important new technique of tissue culture. Although Harrison himself did not pursue tissue culture to any great extent the method has proved immensely useful in testing new drugs and in the production of vaccines.

Harrison founded the influential *Journal of Experimental Zoology* in 1906.

Hartline, Haldan Keffer (1903–1983)
American physiologist. See WALD, GEORGE.

Hartmann, Johannes Franz (1865–1936) *German astronomer*

Hartmann was born the son of a merchant in Erfurt, in Germany. He was educated at the universities of Tübingen, Berlin, and Leipzig where he obtained his PhD in 1891. He worked first at the Leipzig and Potsdam observatories before being appointed in 1909 as professor of astronomy and director of the Göttingen University Observatory.

He remained there until 1921 when he became director of the La Plata Observatory in Argentina, only returning to Göttingen in 1935 a few months before his death.

Hartmann was responsible for the important observation in 1904 that provided the first clear evidence for the existence of interstellar gas. He noted that in the spectrum of the star Delta Orion, a binary system, the calcium lines failed to exhibit any periodic Doppler effect arising from the orbital motion of the stars: when a star moves in its orbit toward the Earth the wavelength of lines in its spectrum are shifted toward the blue, while as it moves away from the Earth its spectral lines are shifted toward the red. That there were what Hartmann described as 'stationary lines' of calcium in the spectrum could only mean that the calcium was not part of the atmosphere of Delta Orion and therefore was not participating in the orbital motion. It must occur somewhere between binary system and observer. The existence of interstellar matter and its significance in the estimation of stellar distances was finally demonstrated by Robert Trumpler in 1930.

Harvey, William (1578–1657) *English physician*

Harvey was born in the English coastal town of Folkestone and educated at King's School, Canterbury, and Cambridge University. In 1599 he made the then customary visit to Italy where he studied medicine at the University of Padua under the anatomist Fabricius ab Aquapendente, obtaining his MD in 1602. He was appointed physician at St. Bartholomew's Hospital, London, in 1609 and in 1618 began working at the court as physician extraordinary to James I. He also served Charles I, accompanying him on his various travels and campaigns throughout the English Civil War. He was rewarded briefly with the office of warden of Merton College, Oxford, in 1645 but with the surrender of Oxford to the Puritans in 1646 Harvey, suffering much from gout, took the opportunity to retire into private life.

In 1628 Harvey published *De motu cordis et sanguinis in animalibus* (On the Motion of the Heart and Blood in Animals). This announced the single most important discovery of the modern period in anatomy and physiology, namely, the circulation of the blood. The orthodox view, going back to Galen, saw blood originating in the liver and from there being distributed throughout the body. There was no circulation for Galen and he believed that the arteries and veins carried different substances. Harvey made a simple calculation that revealed the prodigious amounts of blood that would have to be produced if there was no circulation. Harvey also could not understand why the valves in the veins were placed so that they allowed free movement of blood to the heart but not away from it. It did however make sense if blood was pumped to the limbs through the arteries and returned through the veins.

Harvey then set about demonstrating his supposition. He examined the action of the heart of such cold-blooded creatures as frogs, snakes, and fishes as their slower heart rate allows clearer observations to be made. This enabled him to establish that blood passes from the right to the left side of the heart not through the wall, or septum, which was solid, but via the lungs. It was also clear that blood is pumped from the heart into the arteries, for he observed that they begin to fill at the moment when the heart contracts. Between contractions, the heart fills with blood from the veins. The heart is thus, Harvey declared, nothing more than a pump. To show that blood passes from the arteries to the veins rather than vice versa, Harvey resorted to a number of simple and compelling experiments with ligatures.

Harvey's 72-page masterpiece received considerable but by no means universal support. There was, as he was well aware, one weak link in his argument, namely the precise connection, or anastomoses, between the arterial and venous system. He thus had to accept, without observation, that the hair-thin capillaries of the two systems did in fact link up. Harvey only had a magnifying glass at his disposal and it was left to Marcello Malpighi to observe the implied anastomoses through his microscope in 1661. The importance of Harvey's discovery lay in providing an alternative to the Galenic theory, thus encouraging other scientists to question the authority of ancient texts.

Harvey also worked in embryology. He argued that all life arose from the egg thus denying spontaneous generation. To describe the process of generation he thought he had observed in chickens and deer, Harvey coined the term *epigenesis*. By this he meant the female egg possessed an independent existence and was capable of completing its development through the activity of its own vital principle. It did not join with the semen, nor was it fertilized by it. Harvey believed the semen acted by initiating the self-contained development of the egg through its own touch alone. However with the increasing use of the microscope and the earlier identification of anatomical features within the egg by Malpighi in 1673 the alternative preformationist view began to gain ground.

Harvey became a figure of much influence within the College of Physicians. He served as treasurer in 1628 and although offered the presidency in 1654 felt compelled to decline it on grounds of health.

Hassell, Odd (1897–1981) *Norwegian chemist*

Hassell, who was born in the Norwegian capital of Christiania (now Oslo), was educated at the university there and in Berlin where he obtained his doctorate in 1924. He immediately returned to the University of Oslo and served there as professor of chemistry from 1934 until his retirement in 1964.

Early in his career, following studies on how organic dyes photosensitize silver halides, Hassell discovered adsorption indicators. In 1943 he published an important conformational analysis of cyclohexane but, as he refused to use the language of the German conquerors and published it in Norwegian, its influence was considerably reduced. The molecule exists in two main forms, the so-called boat and chair conformations; Hassell was able to show the chair form to be the most stable. It was for his work on conformation that he shared the 1969 Nobel Prize for chemistry with Derek Barton.

Hatchett, Charles (1765–1847) *British chemist. See* MARIGNAC, JEAN CHARLES GALISSARD DE.

Hauksbee, Francis (*c.* 1670–*c.* 1713) *English physicist*

Hauksbee, a student of Robert Boyle, conducted numerous experiments on a wide range of topics. They are fully described in his *Physico-Mechanical Experiments* (1709). He worked as demonstrator at the Royal Society and became a fellow in 1705. Under the supervision of Newton he conducted a series of experiments on capillary action (the movement of water through pores, caused by surface tension) using tubes and glass plates. He also made improvements to the air pump and made a thorough investigation of static electricity, showing that friction could produce luminous effects in a vacuum.

Hauptman, Herb Aaron (1917–   ) *American mathematical physicist*

Born in New York, Hauptman graduated from Columbia in 1939. After two years spent with the US Census he was drafted into the US Air Force where he spent much of the war as a radar instructor. In 1947 he joined the staff of the Naval Research Laboratory, Washington DC. At the same time he pursued his doctorate (awarded 1952) at the University of Maryland. In 1970 Hauptman moved to the Medical Foundation, Buffalo, as its research director, becoming president in 1988.

In collaboration with his Washington colleague Jerome KARLE, Hauptman has made a significant advance in the use of x-ray crystallography. The classic x-ray photograph of a crystal has a diffraction pattern of dots and it was the task of the crystallographer to find a molecular structure that would give this pattern. A likely structure would be assumed and tested against the x-ray data. The method worked reasonably well when restricted to simple structures.

Further progress was made when crystallographers worked out how to apply Fourier analysis to the scattered x-rays. The difficulty was that, although the amplitudes of the waves could be deduced, their phase could not be determined in this way. In 1953, Hauptman and Karle showed mathematically how the phase problem could be overcome. Their method, known as the *direct method*, was mainly statistical and allowed structures to be determined much more quickly. Whereas previously a 15-atom molecule might require many months' work, the structure of larger molecules, following the work of Hauptman and Karle, could be worked out in a matter of days.

For his work in this area Hauptman shared the 1985 Nobel Prize for chemistry with Karle.

Haüy, René Just (1743–1822) *French mineralogist*

Haüy, whose father was a poor clothworker, was born in St. Just in France. His interest in church music attracted the attention of the prior of the abbey, who soon recognized Haüy's intelligence and arranged for him to receive a sound education. While in Paris, his interest in mineralogy was awakened by the lectures of Louis Daubenton. He became professor of mineralogy at the Natural History Museum in Paris in 1802. His *Traité de mineralogie* (Treatise on Mineralogy) was published in five volumes in 1801 and *Traité de cristallographie* (Treatise on Crystallography) in three volumes in 1822.

Haüy is regarded as the founder of the science of crystallography through his discovery of the geometrical law of crystallization. In 1781 he accidentally dropped some calcite crystals onto the floor, one of which broke, and found, to his surprise, that the broken pieces were rhombohedral in form. Deliberately breaking other and diverse forms of calcite, he found that it always revealed the same form whatever its source. He concluded that all the molecules of calcite have the same form and it is only how they are joined together that produces different gross structures. Following on from this he suggested that other minerals should show different basic forms. He thought that there were, in fact, six different primitive forms from which all crystals could be derived by being linked in different ways. Using his theory he was able to predict in many cases the correct angles of the crystal face. The work aroused much controversy and was attacked by Eilhard Mitscherlich in 1819 when he discovered isomorphism in which two substances of different composition can have the same crystalline form. Haüy rejected Mitscherlich's arguments.

Haüy also conducted work in pyroelectricity. The mineral *haüyne* was named for him.

Hawking, Stephen William (1942–)
British theoretical physicist and cosmologist

Hawking, who was born in Oxford, graduated from the university there and obtained his PhD from Cambridge University. After holding various Cambridge posts, he became professor of gravitational physics in 1977 and, in 1979, was appointed Lucasian Professor of Mathematics.

Hawking has worked mainly in the field of cosmology, in particular the theory of black holes. In 1965 Roger PENROSE had shown that a star collapsing to form a black hole would ultimately form a singularity – a point at which the density of matter is infinite and at which there is an infinite curvature of space–time. Hawking realized that by reversing the time in Penrose's theory he could show that the big bang originating the Universe must also have come from a singularity. Similarly, if the Universe were to stop expanding and start contracting it would eventually end at a singularity – the so-called 'big-crunch'. Penrose and Hawking published these results in 1970. The results of Hawking's work using general relativity were summarized in a book with George Ellis, *The Large Scale Structure of Spacetime* (1973).

In fact, at a singularity, with infinite curvature of space–time, the general theory of relativity breaks down and consequently it cannot be applied to the origin of the Universe. This led Hawking to the application of quantum theory to the gravitational interaction. Of the four fundamental interactions, the strong, weak, electromagnetic, and gravitational interactions, the gravitational interaction is the only one not described by quantum theory. The others occur at distances comparable to the sizes of atomic particles and quantum effects are important. Gravitational interactions between masses over long distances are important in cosmology and can be described by the nonquantum theory of relativity. However, at the vanishingly small distances necessarily occurring just after the big bang (or just before a total collapse), quantum effects would be important. Hawking and others turned their attention to quantum gravity.

So far, the general application of quantum mechanics to gravitational interactions has had limited success. One notable discovery has been Hawking's theory showing that black holes are not in fact 'black' – they effectively emit energy as if they were a hot body.

The basis of the mechanism behind 'hot' black holes is the Heisenberg uncertainty principle. According to this free space cannot be empty because a point in space would then have zero energy at a fixed time and this would contradict the principle. In space, pairs of virtual particles and antiparticles are constantly forming and annihilating. One member of the pair has a positive energy and the other has a negative energy. Under normal conditions a virtual particle does not exist in isolation and is not detected. However, Hawking has shown that in the vicinity of a black hole it is possible for the particles to separate. The negative-energy particle can fall into a black hole and its partner may escape to infinity, appearing as emitted energy.

The theory resolves a problem concerning the thermodynamics of black holes. If matter of high entropy falls into a black hole then there has been a net entropy loss unless the black hole itself gains entropy. One interpretation of the entropy of a black hole is its area, which increases whenever matter falls into the hole. However, if a black hole has an entropy it must also have a temperature. Hawking showed that the emission of energy from a black hole was distributed as if it were radiated from a black body at the appropriate temperature.

A black hole produced by a collapsing star would have a temperature within a few millionths of a degree above absolute zero. Hawking has speculated on the existence of 'mini black holes' weighing a billion tons but having a size no bigger than a proton (about 10^{-15} meter). These could be produced during the early stages of the big bang and are consequently known as 'primordial black holes'. Because of their small size they would radiate gigawatts of energy in the X-ray and gamma-ray regions of the electromagnetic spectrum. So far there is no experimental evidence for their existence.

Hawking has innovatively applied quantum gravity to the question of the origin of the Universe, making various modifications to the inflationary theory first proposed by Alan Guth. He has also put forward an original proposal for the origin and evolution of the Universe applying the 'sum over histories' formalism of quantum mechanics of Richard Feynmann. Hawking's model of the Universe is conceptually difficult. It involves an Euclidean space–time in which time is an imaginary quantity (in the mathematical sense). There are no singularities at which the laws of physics break down; space–time is finite but closed, having no boundaries, and no beginning or end.

Hawking is generally regarded as one of the foremost theoretical physicists of this century despite a severe physical handicap. In the early 1960s he developed motor neurone disease and for the past twenty years he has been confined to a wheelchair. Most of his communication is through a computer speech synthesizer. Of this, Hawking has said that he "was fortunate in that I chose theoretical physics, because that is all in the mind." In 1988 Hawking published a popular account of cosmology, *A Brief History of Time*. The book and its author captured the public imagination and made Hawking an international celebrity, even to noncosmologists. In it he looks forward to a time when a complete theory could be found understandable to everyone. "If we find the answer to that, it would be the ultimate triumph of human reason – for then we would know the mind of God."

Haworth, Sir (Walter) Norman
(1883–1950) *British chemist*

Haworth, who was born in Chorley, began work in a linoleum factory managed by his father. This required some knowledge of dyes, which led Haworth to chemistry. Despite his family's objections he persisted in private study until he was sufficiently qualified to gain admission to Manchester University in 1903, where he studied under and later worked with William Perkin, Jr. on terpenes. Haworth did his postgraduate studies at Göttingen where, in 1910, he gained his PhD. In 1912 he joined the staff of St. Andrews University and worked with Thomas Purdie and James Irvine on carbohydrates. He remained there until 1920 when, after five years at the University of Durham, he was appointed Mason Professor of Chemistry at Birmingham, where he remained until his retirement in 1948.

Emil Fischer had dominated late 19th-century organic chemistry and, beginning in 1887, had synthesized a number of sugars taking them to be open-chain structures, most of which were built on a framework of six carbon atoms. Haworth however succeeded in showing that the carbon atoms in sugars are linked by oxygen into rings: either there are five carbon atoms and one oxygen atom, giving a pyranose ring, or there are four carbon atoms and one oxygen atom, giving a furanose ring. When the appropriate oxygen and hydrogen atoms are added to these rings the result is a sugar. He went on to represent the carbohydrate ring by a perspective formula, today known as a *Haworth formula*.

With **Edmund Hirst** (1898–1975) he went on to establish the point of closure of the ring using the technique of converting the sugar into its methyl ester. He later investigated the chain structure of various polysaccharides. In 1929 he published his views in *The Constitution of the Sugars*.

In 1933 Haworth and his colleagues achieved a further triumph. Albert SZENT-GYÖRGYI had earlier isolated a substance from the adrenal cortex and from orange juice which he named hexuranic acid. It was in fact vitamin C and Haworth, again in collaboration with Hirst, succeeded in synthesizing it. He called it ascorbic acid.

For this work, the first synthesis of a vitamin, Haworth shared the 1937 Nobel Prize for chemistry with Paul KARRER.

Hays, James Douglas (1933–)
American geologist

Hays was born in Johnstown, New York, and educated at Harvard, Ohio State, and Columbia universities, obtaining his PhD from the last in 1964. He joined Columbia's Lamont–Doherty Geological Observatory, New York, in 1967 as director of the deep-sea sediments core laboratory and in 1975 was appointed professor of geology.

In 1971 Hays reported that from his study of 28 deep-sea piston cores from high and low latitudes it was shown that during the last 2.5 million years eight species of radiolaria had become extinct. Prior to extinction these species were widely distributed and their sudden extinction, in six out of eight cases, was in close proximity to a magnetic reversal, a change in the Earth's magnetic polarity. Hays concluded that the magnetic reversals influenced the radiolarians' extinction.

Heaviside, Oliver (1850–1925) *British electronic engineer and physicist*

Heaviside, a Londoner, was a nephew of Charles Wheatstone. Being very deaf, he was hampered in school, and was largely self-taught. He was interested in the transmission of electrical signals and used Maxwell's equations to develop a practical theory of cable telegraphy, introducing the concepts of self inductance, impedance, and conductance. However, his early results were not recognized, possibly because the papers were written using his own notation.

After radio waves had been transmitted across the Atlantic in 1901, he suggested (1902) the existence of a charged atmospheric layer that reflected the waves. The same year Arthur Kennelly independently suggested the same explanation. The *Heaviside layer* (which is sometimes called the Kennelly–Heaviside layer) was detected experimentally in 1924 by Edward Appleton.

Later in life his fame grew and he was awarded an honorary doctorate at Göttingen and was elected a fellow of the Royal Society in 1891.

Heezen, Bruce Charles (1924–1977) *American oceanographer*

Born in Vinton, Iowa, Heezen was educated at Iowa State University, graduating in 1948, and at Columbia, New York, where he received his PhD in 1957. He worked at the Lamont Geological Observatory at Columbia from 1948.

Heezen's work has contributed significantly to knowledge of the ocean floor and the processes that operate within the oceans. In 1952 he produced convincing evidence for the existence of turbidity currents; i.e., currents caused by a mass of water full of suspended sediment. Their existence had been suggested by Reginald Daly in 1936 and proposed as the cause of submarine canyons. Heezen used precise records available from the 1929 Grand Bank earthquake to study these currents. As the area off the Grand Bank was rich with communication cables, exact records of the disturbance caused by the earthquake had been obtained. He was able to reconstruct the movement down the bank of about 25 cubic miles (100 cubic km) of sediment moving with speeds approaching 50 miles per hour (85 km per hour).

In 1957, in collaboration with William Ewing and Marie Tharp, the existence of the worldwide ocean rift was demonstrated and its connection with seismic activity postulated. In 1960 Heezen argued for an expanding Earth in which new material is emerging from the rift, increasing the oceans' width and pushing the continents further apart. Such a view, based on the grounds that the gravitational constant decreases slowly with time, had been suggested earlier by Paul DIRAC, but received little support in the early 1960s, particularly when a more plausible mechanism was suggested by Harry H. HESS in 1962.

Heidelberger, Michael (1888–1991)
American immunologist. See AVERY, OSWALD THEODORE.

Heisenberg, Werner Karl (1901–1976)
German physicist

Heisenberg, whose father was the professor of Greek at the University of Munich, was born in Würzburg, Germany. He was educated at the universities of Munich and Göttingen, where in 1923 he obtained his doctorate. After spending the period 1924–26 in Copenhagen working with Niels Bohr, he returned to Germany to take up the professorship of theoretical physics at the University of Leipzig. After the war, Heisenberg returned to Göttingen, where he reestablished the Kaiser Wilhelm Institute for Physics. This was renamed the Max Planck Institute and in 1958 it moved to Munich with Heisenberg as its director, a post he occupied until 1970 when he resigned on the grounds of ill health.

In 1925 Heisenberg formulated a version of quantum theory that became known as matrix mechanics. It was for this work, which was later shown to be formally equivalent to the wave mechanics of Erwin SCHRÖDINGER, that Heisenberg was awarded the 1932 Nobel Prize for physics. Heisenberg began in a very radical way, much influenced by Ernst MACH. Considering the various bizarre results emerging in quantum theory, such as the apparent wave–particle duality of the electron, his first answer was that it is simply a mistake to think of the atom in visual terms at all. What we really know of the atom is what we can observe of it, namely, the light it emits, its frequency, and its intensity. The need therefore was to be able to write a set of equations that would permit the correct prediction of such atomic phenomena. Heisenberg succeeded in establishing a mathematical formalism that permitted accurate predictions to be made. The method was also developed by Max BORN and Pascual Jordan. As they used the then relatively unfamiliar matrix mathematics to develop this system, it is not surprising that physicists preferred the more usual language of wave equations used in the equivalent system of Schrödinger.

In 1927 Heisenberg went on to explore a deeper level of physical understanding when he formulated his fundamental *uncertainty principle*: that it is impossible to determine exactly both the position and momentum of such particles as the electron. He demonstrated this by simple thought experiments of the following type: if we try to locate the exact position of an electron we must use rays with very short wavelengths such as gamma rays. But by so illuminating it the electron's momentum will be changed by its interaction with the energetic gamma rays. Alternatively a lower-energy wave can be used that will not disturb the momentum of the electron so much but, as lower energy implies longer wavelength, such radiation will lack the precision to provide the exact location of the electron. There seems to be no way out of such an impasse and Heisenberg went on to express the limits of the uncertainty mathematically:

$$\Delta x . \Delta p \geq h/4\pi$$

where Δx is the uncertainty in ascertaining the position in a given direction, Δp is the uncertainty in ascertaining the momentum in that direction, and h is the Planck constant. What the equation tells us is that the product of the uncertainties must always be about as great as the Planck constant and can never disappear completely. Further, any attempt made to reduce one element of uncertainty to the minimum can only be done at the expense of increasing the other. The consequence of this failure to know the *exact* position and momentum is an inability to predict accurately the future position of an electron. Thus, like Max Born, Heisenberg had found it necessary to introduce a basic indeterminacy into physics.

After his great achievements in quantum theory in the 1920s Heisenberg later turned his attention to the theory of elementary particles. Thus in 1932, shortly after the discovery of the neutron by James CHADWICK, Heisenberg proposed that the nucleus consists of both neutrons and protons. He went further, arguing that they were in fact two states of the same basic entity – the *nucleon*. As the strong nuclear force does not distinguish between them he proposed that they were *isotopes* with nearly the same mass, distinguished instead by a property he called *isotopic spin*. He later attempted the ambitious task of constructing a unified field theory of elementary particles. Although he published a monograph on the topic in 1966 it generated little support.

Unlike many other German scientists Heisenberg remained in Germany throughout World War II and the whole Nazi era. He was certainly no Nazi himself but he thought it essential to remain in Germany to preserve traditional scientific values for the next generation. At one time he came under attack from the Nazis for his refusal to compromise his support for the physics of Einstein in any way. Thus when, in 1935, he wished to move to the University of Munich to succeed Arnold Sommerfeld he was violently attacked by the party press and, eventually, the post went to the little-known W. Müller.

With the outbreak of war in 1939 Heisenberg was soon called upon to come to Berlin to direct the program to construct an atom bomb. His exact role in the program has become a matter of controversy. He has claimed that he never had any real intention of making such a bomb, let alone giving it to Hitler. As long as he played a key role he was, he later claimed, in a position to sabotage the program if it ever looked like being a success. He even went so far as to convey such thoughts to Niels Bohr in 1941 when he met him in Copenhagen, hinting that the Allies' physicists should pursue a similar policy. Bohr later reported that if such comments had been made to him they were done so too cryptically for him to grasp; he was rather under the impression that Heisenberg was trying to find out the progress made by the Allies.

New information on the role of Heisenberg and other senior German scientists was released in 1992. The Allies had gathered the scientists in a bugged house, Farm Hall, near Cambridge and recorded their conversation for six months. When the possibility of microphones was put to Heisenberg, he casually dismissed the suggestion: "Microphones installed? (Laughing) Oh no, they're not as cute as all that ... they're a bit old fashioned in that respect."

Heisenberg learned of the Hiroshima bomb on 6 August 1945. His first reaction was of disbelief. He insisted that the announcement could refer only to high explosives. During further discussion he declared: "I never thought we would make a bomb." He felt that as a bomb could not have been completed before the war's end, he lacked the urgency to argue the case strongly enough before the military and politicians. He was also arrogant enough to believe that the Allies would do no better. The question of having to make a moral choice, of deliberately sabotaging a German nuclear program, simply never arose.

Helmholtz, Hermann Ludwig Ferdinand von (1821–1894) *German physiologist and theoretical physicist*

Born in Potsdam, Germany, Helmholtz studied medicine at the Friedrich Wilhelm Institute in Berlin and obtained his MD in 1842. He returned to Potsdam to become an army surgeon, but returned to civilian life in 1848 and was appointed assistant at the Anatomical Museum in Berlin. He then held a succession of chairs at Königsberg (1849–55), Bonn (1855–58), Heidelberg (1858–71), and Berlin (1871–77) and later became director of the Physico-Technical Institute at Berlin Charlottenburg.

Helmholtz made major contributions to two areas of science: physiology and physics. In physiology he invented (1851) the ophthalmoscope for inspecting the interior of the eye and the ophthalmometer for measuring the eye's curvature. He investigated accommodation, color vision, and color blindness. His book *Handbuch der physiologische Optik* (Handbook of Physiological Optics) was published in 1867. Helmholtz also worked on hearing, showing how the cochlea in the inner ear resonates for different frequencies and analyzes complex sounds into harmonic components. In 1863 he published *Die Lehre von den Tönemfindungen als physiologische Grundlage für die Theorie der Musik* (The Sensation of Tone as a Physiological Basis for the Theory of Music). Another achievement was his measurement of the speed of nerve impulses (1850).

One of Helmholtz's interests had been muscle action and animal heat and this, inspired by his distaste for vitalism, led him to his best-known discovery – the law of conservation of energy. This was developed independently of the work of James Joule and Julius von Mayer and published as *Über die Erhaltung der Kraft* (1847; On the Conservation of Force). He showed that the total energy of a collection of interacting particles is constant, and later applied this idea to other systems.

Helmholtz also worked in thermodynamics, where he introduced the concept of free energy (energy available to perform work). In electrodynamics he attempted to produce a general unified theory. Heinrich Hertz, who discovered radio waves in 1888, was Helmholtz's pupil.

Helmont, Jan Baptista van (1579–1644) *Flemish chemist and physician*

Van Helmont, who came from a noble Brussels family, was educated at the Catholic University of Louvain in medicine, mysticism, and chemistry, but declined a degree from them. Rejecting all offers of employment he devoted himself to private research at his home. In 1621 he was involved in a controversy with the Church over the belief that it was possible to heal a wound caused by a weapon by treating the weapon rather than the wound. Van Helmont did not reject this common belief but insisted that it was a natural phenomenon containing no supernatural elements. He was arrested, eventually allowed to remain under house arrest, and forbidden to publish without the prior consent of the Church. He wrote extensively and after his death his collected papers were published by his son as the *Ortus medicinae* (1648; Origin of Medicine).

Van Helmont rejected the works of the ancients, although he did believe in the philosopher's stone. He carried out careful observations and measurements, which led him to discover the elementary nature of water. He regarded water as the chief constituent of matter. He pointed out that fish were nourished by water and that substantial bodies could be reduced to water by dissolving them in acid. To demonstrate his theory he performed a famous experiment in which he grew a willow tree over a period of five years in a measured quantity of earth. The tree increased its weight by 164 pounds despite the fact that only water was added to it. The soil had decreased by only a few ounces.

Van Helmont also introduced the term 'gas' into the language, deriving it from the Greek for chaos. When a substance is burned it is reduced to its formative agent and its gas and van Helmont believed that when 62 pounds of wood is burned to an ash weighing 1 pound, 61 pounds have escaped as water or gas. Different substances give off different gases when consumed and van Helmont identified four gases, which he named gas carbonum, two kinds of gas sylvester, and gas pingue. These we would now call carbon dioxide, carbon monoxide, nitrous oxide, and methane.

Hench, Philip Showalter (1896–1965)
American biochemist

Born in Pittsburgh, Pennsylvania, Hench was educated at Lafayette College and the University of Pittsburgh, where he obtained his MD in 1920. He spent most of his career working at the Mayo Clinic, becoming head of the section for rheumatic diseases in 1926. Hench was also connected with the Mayo Foundation and the University of Minnesota, where he became professor of medicine in 1947.

For many years Hench had been seeking a method of treating the crippling and painful complaint of rheumatoid arthritis. He suspected that it was not a conventional microbial infection since, among other features, it was relieved by pregnancy and jaundice. Hench therefore felt it was more likely to result from a biochemical disturbance that is transiently corrected by some incidental biological change. The search, he argued, must concentrate on something patients with jaundice had in common with pregnant women. At length he was led to suppose that the antirheumatic substance might be an adrenal hormone, since temporary remissions are often induced by procedures that stimulate the adrenal cortex. Thus in 1948 he was ready to try the newly prepared 'compound E', later known as cortisone, of Edward KENDALL on 14 patients. All showed remarkable improvement, which was reversed on withdrawing the drug.

For this development of the first steroid drug Hench shared the 1950 Nobel Prize for physiology or medicine with Kendall and Tadeus REICHSTEIN.

Henderson, Thomas (1798–1844)
British astronomer

Born in Dundee, Henderson began work as an attorney's clerk who made a reputation as an amateur astronomer. In 1831 he accepted an appointment as director of a new observatory at the Cape of Good Hope in South Africa. While observing Alpha Centauri he found that it had a considerable proper motion. He realized that this probably meant that the star was comparatively close and a good candidate for the measurement of parallax – the apparent change in position of a (celestial) body when viewed from spatially separate points, or from one point on a moving Earth. All major observational astronomers had tried to detect this small angular measurement and failed. Henderson at last succeeded in 1832 and found that Alpha Centauri had a parallax of just less than one second of arc. The crucial importance of this was that once parallax was known, the distance of the stars could be measured successfully for the first time. Alpha Centauri turned out to be over four light years away. Unfortunately (for Henderson), he delayed publication of his result until it had been thoroughly checked and rechecked. By this time Friedrich BESSEL had already observed and published, in 1839, the parallax of 61 Cygni.

In 1834 Henderson became the first Astronomer Royal of Scotland.

Henry, Joseph (1797–1878) *American physicist*

One of the first great American scientists, Henry came from a poor background in Albany, New York, and had to work his way through college. He was educated at the Albany Academy, New York, where he first studied medicine, changing to engineering in 1825. A year later he was appointed a professor of mathematics and physics at Albany. In 1832 he became professor of natural philosophy at Princeton (then the College of New Jersey) where he taught physics, chemistry, mathematics, and geological sciences, and later astronomy and architecture.

Henry is noted for his work on electricity. In 1829 he developed a greatly improved form of the electromagnet by insulating the wire that was to be wrapped around the iron core, thus allowing many more coils, closer together, and greatly increasing the magnet's power. Through this work he discovered, in 1830, the principle of electromagnetic induction. Soon after, and quite independently, Michael FARADAY made the same observation and published first. Faraday is thus credited with the discovery but Henry has the unit of inductance (the *henry*) named for him. However, Henry did publish in 1832 – prior to Faraday and Heinrich Lenz – his discovery of self-induction (in which the magnetic field from a changing electric current induces an electromotive force opposing the current). Earlier (in 1829) he had invented and constructed the first practical electric motor. In 1835 he developed the electric relay in order to overcome the problem of resistance that built up in long wires. This device had an immediate social impact for it was the key step in the invention of the long-distance telegraph, which played a large part in the opening up of the North American continent. In 1846, he became the first secretary of the Smithsonian Institution, which he formed into an extremely efficient body for liaison between scientists and government support of their research. He also did work on solar radiation and on sunspots.

Henry, William (1774–1836) *British physician and chemist*

Henry's father, Thomas Henry, was a manufacturing chemist in Manchester and an analytical chemist of some repute. Initially qualifying as a physician from Edinburgh University, Henry practiced for five years in the Manchester Infirmary. Later he took over the running of the chemical works established by his father.

In 1801 he formulated the law now known as *Henry's law*, which states that the solubility of a gas in water at a given temperature is proportional to its pressure. His close friend John Dalton was encouraged by this finding, seeing it as a confirmation of his own theory of mixed gases, and the two men discussed the methods of experimentation in detail.

Hensen, Viktor (1835–1924) *German physiologist and oceanographer*

Hensen was born in Schleswig, Germany, and studied science and medicine at the universities of Würzburg, Berlin, and Kiel, graduating from the latter in 1858. He remained at Kiel to work in the physiology department and later served as professor of physiology (1871–1911).

Hensen worked on comparative studies of vision and hearing but also discovered, independently of Claude Bernard, the compound glycogen. He is better remembered however for his work on plankton. He introduced the term plankton in 1887 to describe the minute drifting animals and plants in the oceans. Moreover he advanced beyond the descriptive stage and introduced numerical methods into marine biology, notably in constructing the *Hensen net*, a simple loop net designed to filter a square meter of water. This enabled the number of plankton in a known area of water to be counted. Hensen tested his equipment in the North Sea and the Baltic in 1885.

Satisfied with his techniques he made a more ambitious trip in 1889 covering more than 15,000 miles of the Atlantic. One of his more surprising results was the greater concentration of plankton in temperate than in tropical waters.

Heracleides of Pontus (*c*. 390 BC– *c*. 322 BC) *Greek astronomer*

Heracleides, who was born in Heraclea, now in Turkey, was an associate and possibly a pupil of Plato. Although none of his writings have survived, two views that were unusual for the time have been attributed to him. The philosopher Simplicius of Cilicia, a usually reliable source, reports that "Heracleides supposed that the Earth is in the center and rotates while the heaven is at rest." If this is accurate he must have been the first to state that the Earth rotates, a view that found as little support in antiquity as it did in the medieval period. The second doctrine attributed to him is that Mercury and Venus move around the Sun, which moves around the Earth – a view adopted later by Tycho Brahe in the 16th century.

Heraclitus of Ephesus (*c*. 500 BC) *Greek natural philosopher*

Virtually nothing is known of the life of Heraclitus and of his book *On Nature* only a few rather obscure fragments survive. His doctrines contrast with those of his near contemporary Parmenides for whom, on purely logical grounds, change of any kind was totally impossible. For Heraclitus, everything is continually in a state of change, hence his characteristic aphorism: "We cannot step twice into the same river," and his selection of fire as the fundamental form of matter. The mechanism behind such unremitting change was the constant tension or 'strife' between contraries or opposites.

Herelle, Felix d' *See* D'HERELLE, FELIX.

Hermite, Charles (1822–1901) *French mathematician*

Hermite was born in Dieuze, France. His mathematical career was almost thwarted in his student days, since he was incapable of passing exams. Fortunately his talent had already been recognized and his examiners eventually let him scrape through. Hermite obtained a post at the Sorbonne where he was an influential teacher.

Hermite began his mathematical career with pioneering work on the theory of Abelian and transcendental functions, and he later used the theory of elliptic functions to give a solution of the general equations of the fifth degree – the quintic. One long-standing problem solved was proving that the number 'e' is transcendental (i.e., not a solution of a polynomial equation). He also introduced the techniques of analysis into number theory. His most famous work is in algebra, in the theory of *Hermite polynomials*. Although Hermite himself had little interest in applied mathematics this work turned out to be of great use in quantum mechanics.

Hero of Alexandria (*c.* AD 62) *Greek mathematician and inventor*

Hero produced several written works on geometry, giving formulae for the areas and volumes of polygons and conics. His formula for the area of a triangle was contained in *Metrica* (Measurement), a work that was lost until 1896. This book also describes a method for finding the square root of a number, a method now used in computers, but known to the Babylonians in 2000 BC. In another of Hero's books, *Pneumatica* (Pneumatics), he wrote on siphons, a coin-operated machine, and the aeolipile – a prototype steam-powered engine that he had built. The engine consisted of a globe with two nozzles positioned so that steam jets from the inside made it turn on its axis. Hero also wrote on land-surveying and he designed war engines based on the ideas of Ctesibius. Yet another of his works, *Mechanica* (Mechanics), was quoted by Pappus of Alexandria.

Herophilus of Chalcedon (*c.* 300 BC) *Greek anatomist and physician*

Herophilus, a pupil of Praxagoras of Cos, was one of the founders of the Alexandrian medical school set up at the end of the 4th century BC under the patronage of Ptolemy I Soter. Although none of his works have survived, Galen lists some eight titles of which the *Anatomica* (Anatomy) was probably the most significant.

Herophilus is widely, even notoriously, remembered as the result of a passage in Celsus reporting that, with Erasistratus, he practiced vivisection on criminals. The passage has been regarded as suspect by many scholars on the grounds that no such reference occurs in any extant, earlier Greek text. It is however certain that from the results attributed to him he must have undertaken both human and animal dissection. For example, he described a passage from the stomach to the intestines as being '12 finger widths' (*dodekadaktylon*) or in its Latin form, the duodenum; he also named the retina and the prostate and did much work on the brain.

It has been claimed that Herophilus was the first to distinguish between sensory and motor nerves. Nerves, or neura, for Herophilus were simply channels that carried the pneuma or vital air to different parts of the body. Thus while he probably identified sensory nerves it is unlikely that he was able to distinguish between motor nerves and tendons.

Herophilus was reported to have advanced Praxagoras's work on the pulse by counting its frequency against a water clock. Also, according to Galen, he made the important observation that the arteries carried blood as well as pneuma.

Héroult, Paul Louis Toussaint (1863–1914) *French chemist. See* HALL, CHARLES.

Herschbach, Dudley Robert (1932–) *American chemist*

Herschbach, who was born in San José, California, was educated at the University of Stanford and at Harvard University, where he gained his PhD in 1958. After teaching at the University of California, Berkeley for four years, he returned to Harvard in 1963 as professor of chemistry.

Herschbach has worked on the details of chemical reactions; for example, a simple reaction in which potassium atoms and iodomethane molecules form potassium iodide and methyl radicals as products, that is:

$$K + CH_3I \rightarrow KI + CH_3\cdot$$

He decided to use molecular beams to examine the nature of the reaction. The reagent molecules were formed into two collimated beams at a sufficiently low pressure to make collisions within the beams a negligible event. The beams were allowed to collide and the direction and velocity of the product molecules measured.

Herschbach was able to draw some conclusions about the reaction. He demonstrated, for example, that the reagents would only react if the incoming potassium atoms struck the iodomethane molecules at the iodide end. As techniques were refined and extended Herschbach demonstrated that the study of molecular beams could throw considerable light on reaction dynamics. For his work in this field he shared the 1989 Nobel Prize for chemistry with the American chemist **Yuan Lee** (1936–) and John POLANYI.

Herschel, Caroline Lucretia (1750–1848) *German–British astronomer. See* HERSCHEL, SIR (FREDERICK) WILLIAM.

Herschel, Sir (Frederick) William
(1738–1822) *German–British astronomer*

Herschel, who was born in Hannover, started life in the same occupation as his father – an oboist with the band of the Hannoverian footguards. He moved permanently to England in 1757, where he worked as a freelance itinerant musician until in 1767 he was appointed as organist of a church in Bath. His sister Caroline Herschel joined him in Bath in 1772. He was led by his interest in musical theory to a study of mathematics and ultimately astronomy. Herschel made his own telescopes and his early observations were significant enough to be drawn to the attention of George III in 1782. The king, who had a passionate interest in astronomy and clockwork, was sufficiently impressed with Herschel to employ him as his private astronomer at an initial salary of £200 a year and to finance the construction of very large telescopes. At first Herschel settled at Datchet, near Windsor, but in 1786 he moved to Slough where he remained for the rest of his life.

Herschel's contributions to astronomy were enormous. He was fortunate to live at a time when prolonged viewing with a large reflector could not but be fruitful

and he took full advantage of his fortune. He made his early reputation by his discovery in 1781 of the first new planet since ancient times. He wished to name it after his patron as 'Georgium Sidus' (George's Star) but Johann Bode's suggestion of 'Uranus' was adopted. Herschel's work is notable for the unbelievable comprehensiveness with which he extended the observations of others. Thus he extended Charles Messier's catalog of just over 100 nebulae by a series of publications listing over 2000 nebulae. He not only began the study of double stars but cataloged 800 of them. He also discovered two satellites of Uranus – Titania and Oberon (1787) – and two of Saturn; Mimas and Enceladus (1789–90). He built a large number of telescopes of various sizes culminating in his enormous 40-foot (12-m) reflector. This cost George III £4000 plus £200 a year for its upkeep. The eyepiece was attached to the open end, thus eliminating the loss of light caused by the secondary mirror used in the Newtonian and Gregorian reflectors. The disadvantage was the danger of climbing up to the open end of the 40-foot instrument in the dark. One eminent astronomer, Giuseppe Piazzi, failing to master this skill, fell and broke his arm. It was finally dismantled in 1839 while William's son John conducted his family in a special requiem he had composed for the occasion.

Herschel produced not only observational work but theoretical contributions on the structure of the universe. He established the motion of the Sun in the direction of Hercules and tried to calculate its speed (1806). But, above all, he was the first to begin to see the structure of our Galaxy. Conducting a large number of star counts he established that stars are much more numerous in the Milky Way and the plane of the celestial equator, becoming progressively fewer towards the celestial poles. He explained this by supposing that the Galaxy is shaped like a grindstone. If we look through its short axis we see few stars and much dark space; through its long axis we see a stellar multitude. Herschel was supported in his astronomical life by his sister Caroline. His son John also became an astronomer of note.

Herschel was supported in both his domestic and astronomical life by his sister **Caroline Lucretia Herschel** (1750–1848). She began as his assistant but eventually undertook her own original research. She observed her first comet in 1786 and went on to detect a further seven. She also discovered a number of nebulae. After her brother's death she returned to Hannover where she prepared a catalogue of some 2500 nebulae and star clusters.

Herschel's son, **Sir John Frederick William Herschel** (1792–1871), also became an astronomer of note. He spent the period 1934–38 in South Africa, where he cataloged nearly 2000 nebulae and an equal number of double stars, publishing the results of his surveys in 1847.

Herschel, Sir John Frederick William
(1792–1871) *British astronomer. See* HER-SCHEL, SIR (FREDERICK) WILLIAM.

Hershey, Alfred Day (1908–   )
American biologist

Hershey was born in Owosso, Michigan, and graduated from Michigan State College in 1930, remaining there to do his PhD thesis on the chemistry of *Brucella* bacteria. Having received his doctorate in 1934, he taught at Washington University, St. Louis, until 1950, when he moved to the Genetics Research Unit of the Carnegie Institute, Washington. In 1962 he became director of the unit, a position he retained until his retirement in 1974.

Hershey, along with Salvador LURIA and Max DELBRÜCK, was one of the founders in the early 1940s of the so-called 'phage group'. In 1945, independently of Luria, he demonstrated that spontaneous mutations must occur in bacterial viruses (phage). In the following year he established, at the same time as Delbrück, that genetic recombination takes place between phages present in the same cell.

Hershey is best known, however, for the experiment conducted with Martha Chase and reported in their 1952 paper, *Independent Functions of Viral Proteins and Nucleic Acid in Growth of Bacteriophage*. At the time it was still uncertain whether genes were composed of protein, nucleic acid, or some complex mixture of the two. They utilized the fact that DNA contains phosphorus but no sulfur, while phage protein has some sulfur in its structure but no phosphorus. Phage with a protein coat labeled with radioactive sulfur and DNA with radioactive phosphorus was allowed to infect bacteria. After infection the bacteria were spun in a blender. The labeled protein was stripped off the bacteria while the radioactive DNA remained inside the bacterial cell. When allowed to incubate, the bacteria proved capable of producing a new phage crop. The experiment would seem to show that DNA was more involved than protein in the process of replication.

For his fundamental contributions to molecular biology, Hershey received the 1958 Albert Lasker Award and the 1965 Kimber Genetics Award. However, it was not until 1969 that Hershey, together with Delbrück and Luria, was awarded the Nobel Prize for physiology or medicine.

Hertz, Gustav (1887–1975) *German physicist*

A nephew of the distinguished physicist Heinrich Hertz, Gustav Hertz was born in Hamburg and educated at the universities of Munich and Berlin. He taught in Berlin and Halle before his appointment in 1928 to the professorship of experimental physics at the Technical University, Berlin. Hertz, as a Jew, was dismissed from his post in 1935. He worked for the Siemens company from 1935 until 1945, somehow managing to survive World War II, when he was captured by the Russians. He reemerged in 1955 to become director of the Physics Institute in Leipzig, then in East Germany.

In 1925 Hertz was awarded the Nobel Prize for physics for his work with James FRANCK on the quantized nature of energy transfer.

Hertz, Heinrich Rudolf (1857–1894) *German physicist*

Hertz came from a prosperous and cultured Hamburg family. In 1875 he went to Frankfurt to gain practical experience in engineering and after a year of military service (1876–77) spent a year at the University of Munich. He had decided on an academic and scientific career rather than one in engineering, and in 1878 chose to continue his studies at the University of Berlin under Hermann von Helmholtz. Hertz obtained his PhD in 1880 and continued as Helmholtz's assistant for a further three years. He then went to work at the University of Kiel. In 1885 he was appointed professor of physics at Karlsruhe Technical College and in 1889 became professor of physics at the University of Bonn. His tragic early death from blood poisoning occurred after several years of poor health and cut short a brilliant career.

Hertz's early work at Berlin was diverse but included several pieces of research into electrical phenomena and equipment. With no laboratory facilities at Kiel he had considered more theoretical aspects of physics and had become more interested in the recent work of James Clerk Maxwell on electromagnetic theory. Helmholtz had suggested an experimental investigation of the theory to Hertz in 1879 but it was not until 1885 in Karlsruhe that Hertz found the equipment needed for what became his most famous experiments. In 1888 he succeeded in producing electromagnetic waves using an electric circuit; the circuit contained a metal rod that had a small gap at its midpoint, and when sparks crossed this gap violent oscillations of high frequency were set up in the rod. Hertz proved that these waves were transmitted through air by detecting them with another similar circuit some distance away. He also showed that like light waves they were reflected and refracted and, most important, that they traveled at the same speed as light but had a much longer wavelength. These waves, originally called *Hertzian waves* but now known as radio waves, conclusively confirmed Maxwell's prediction on the existence of electromagnetic waves, both in the form of light and radio waves.

Once at Bonn Hertz continued his analysis of Maxwell's theory, publishing two papers in 1890. His experimental and theoretical work put the field of electrodynamics on a much firmer footing. It should also be noted that in 1887 he inadvertently discovered the photoelectric effect whereby ultraviolet radiation releases electrons from the surface of a metal. Although realizing its significance he left others to investigate and explain it.

Hertz's results produced enormous activity among scientists but he died before seeing Guglielmo Marconi make his discovery of radio waves a practical means of communication. In his honor the unit of frequency is now called the hertz.

Hertzsprung, Ejnar (1873–1967) *Danish astronomer*

Hertzsprung was born in Frederiksberg, Denmark, the son of a senior civil servant who had a deep interest in mathematics and astronomy but who was anxious to see that his son received a more practical education. Consequently Hertzsprung was trained as a chemical engineer at the Copenhagen Polytechnic, graduating in 1898. He worked as a chemist in St. Petersburg and then studied photochemistry under Wilhelm Ostwald in Leipzig before returning to Denmark in 1902. His first professional appointment as an astronomer was in 1909 at the Potsdam Observatory. The bulk of his career, from 1919 to 1944, was spent at the University of Leiden where from 1935 he served as director of the observatory. After his retirement in 1944 he returned to Denmark where he continued his studies for a further 20 years.

Hertzsprung's name is linked with that of Henry RUSSELL as independent innovators of the *Hertzsprung–Russell* (H–R) diagram. In the late 19th and early 20th centuries,

techniques used in photographic spectroscopy were being greatly improved. With his background in photochemistry, Hertzsprung was able to devise methods by which he could determine the intrinsic brightness, i.e., luminosity, of stars. He showed that the luminosity of most of the stars he studied decreased as their color changed from white through yellow to red, i.e., as their temperature decreased. He also found that a few stars were very much brighter than those of the same color. Hertzsprung thus discovered the two main groupings of stars: the highly luminous giant and supergiant stars and the more numerous but fainter dwarf or main-sequence stars. Hertzsprung published his results, although not in diagrammatic form, in 1905 and 1907 in an obscure photographic journal. His work therefore did not become generally known and credit initially went to Russell who published the eponymous diagram in 1913. It would be difficult to exaggerate the importance or usefulness of the H–R diagram, which has been the starting point for discussions of stellar evolution ever since.

Much of Hertzsprung's work concerned open clusters of stars. In 1911 he published the first color-magnitude diagrams of the Pleiades and Hyades clusters, showing how the color of member stars varied with observed brightness. He also measured the proper motions of stars, i.e., their angular motions in a direction perpendicular to the observer's line of sight, and used the results to establish membership of clusters.

One other major achievement of Hertzsprung was the development of a method for the determination of stellar and galactic distances. In the 19th century Friedrich Bessel and Friedrich Georg Struve had been the first to use measurements of annual parallax to calculate stellar distances but this was only accurate up to distances of about a hundred light-years. In 1913, when Hertzsprung announced his results, astronomers had made little progress in measuring distances. The work of Henrietta Leavitt in 1912 had shown that the period of light variation of a group of stars known as Cepheid variables was related to their observed mean brightness. These Cepheids lay in the Magellanic Clouds. Hertzsprung assumed that at the great distance of the Clouds all member stars could be considered to have approximately the same distance. Since observed and intrinsic brightness of a star are directly linked by its distance, the periods of light variation of Cepheids in the Clouds were thus also related to their intrinsic brightness. By extrapolation, Cepheids could thus be an invaluable means of measuring the distance of any group of stars containing a Cepheid by observing the period and apparent brightness of the Cepheid.

The work of establishing the period-luminosity relation on a numerical basis was begun by Hertzsprung and continued by Harlow Shapley. Hertzsprung determined the distances of several nearby Cepheids from measurements of their proper motions. Using his results and Leavitt's values for the periods and apparent brightness of Cepheids in the Small Magellanic Cloud (SMC) he was then able to calculate the distance to the SMC. Although smaller than today's value this was the first measurement of an extragalactic distance.

Herzberg, Gerhard (1904–) Canadian spectroscopist

Born in Hamburg, Herzberg was educated at the Universities of Göttingen and Berlin. He taught at the Darmstadt Institute of Technology from 1930 until 1935 when, with the rise to power of the Nazis, he emigrated to Canada where he was research professor of physics at the University of Saskatchewan from 1935 until 1945. He returned to Canada in 1948 after spending three years as professor of spectroscopy at the Yerkes Observatory, Wisconsin. From 1949 until his retirement in 1969 he was director of the division of pure physics for the National Research Council in Ottawa.

Herzberg is noted for his extensive work on the technique and interpretation of the spectra of molecules. He has elucidated the properties of many molecules, ions, and radicals and also contributed to the use of spectroscopy in astronomy (e.g., in detecting hydrogen in space). His work includes the first measurements of the Lamb shifts (important in quantum electrodynamics) in deuterium, helium, and the positive lithium ion.

Herzberg has written a number of books, notably the two classic surveys *Atomic Spectra and Atomic Structure* (1937) and *Molecular Spectra and Molecular Structure* (4 vols. 1939–79). He received the Nobel Prize for chemistry in 1971 for his "contributions to the knowledge of electronic structure and geometry of molecules, particularly free radicals."

Hess, Germain Henri (1802–1850) Swiss–Russian chemist

Hess, who was born at Geneva in Switzerland, was taken to Russia as a child by his parents. He studied medicine at the University of Dorpat (1822–25) and started his career by practicing medicine in Irkutsk. In 1830 he moved to St. Petersburg, becoming professor of chemistry at the Technological Institute of the university. While there he wrote a chemistry textbook in Russian, which became a standard work.

Hess worked on minerals and on sugars, but his main work was on the theory of heat. By carefully measuring the heat given off in various chemical changes, he was able to conclude in 1840 that in any chemical reaction, regardless of how many stages there are, the amount of heat developed in the overall reaction is constant. *Hess's law*, also called the law of constant heat summation, is in fact a special case of the law of conservation of energy.

Hess, Harry Hammond (1906–1969) American geologist

Hess was born in New York City and educated at Yale, graduating in 1927, and Princeton where he gained his PhD in 1932. He worked first as a field geologist in Northern Rhodesia (now Zambia) in the period 1928–29. After a year at Rutgers in 1932 he moved to Princeton in 1934, becoming professor of geology in 1948.

Hess was a key figure in the postwar revolution in the Earth sciences. He was the first to draw up theories using the considerable discoveries on the nature of the ocean floor that were made in the postwar period. Hess himself discovered about 160 flat-topped summits on the ocean bed, which he named 'guyots' for an earlier Princeton geologist, Arnold Guyot. As they failed to produce atolls he dated them to the Precambrian, 600 million years ago, before the appearance of corals. But in 1956 Cretaceous fossils, from only 100 million years ago, were found in Pacific guyots. The whole of the ocean floor was discovered to be surprisingly young, dating only as far back as the Mesozoic, while the continental rocks were much older.

In 1962 Hess published his important paper, *History of Ocean Basins*. The ocean floors were young, he argued, as they were constantly being renewed by magma flowing from the mantle up through the oceanic rifts, discovered by William Morris Ewing, and spreading out laterally. This became known as the sea-floor spreading hypothesis and was a development of the convection-currents theory proposed by Arthur Holmes in 1929. The hypothesis has been modified since its proposal, notably through the work of Drummond Hoyle Matthews and Frederick Vine on magnetic anomalies, but remains largely accepted.

Hess, Victor Francis (1883–1964)
Austrian–American physicist

Hess, the son of a forester, was born at Waldstein in Austria and educated at the University of Graz where he obtained his doctorate in 1906. He worked at the Institute for Radium Research, Vienna, from 1910 to 1920 and then took up an appointment at the University of Graz where he became professor in 1925. In 1931 he set up a cosmic-ray observatory near Innsbruck but in 1938 he was dismissed from all his official positions as he was a Roman Catholic. Leaving Nazi Austria, he emigrated to America where he served as professor of physics at Fordham University, New York, from 1938 to 1956.

In 1911–12 Hess made the fundamental discovery of cosmic rays, as they were later called by Robert MILLIKAN in 1925. For this work he shared the Nobel Prize for physics with Carl ANDERSON in 1936. The work stemmed from an attempt to explain why gases are always slightly ionized; thus a gold-leaf electroscope, however well insulated it might be, will discharge itself over a period of time. Radiation was clearly coming from somewhere and the most likely source was the Earth itself. To test this, attempts were made to see if the rate of discharge decreased with altitude. But both T. Wulf, who took an electroscope to the top of the Eiffel Tower in 1910, and A. Gockel, who took one up in a balloon in 1912, failed to obtain any clear results.

However when Hess ascended in a balloon to a height of 16,000 feet (4880 m) he found that although the electroscope's rate of discharge decreased initially up to about 2000 feet (610 m), thereafter it increased considerably, being four times faster at 16,000 feet than at sea level. He concluded that his results were best explained by the assumption that a radiation of very great penetrating power enters our atmosphere from above.

He was able to eliminate the Sun as the sole cause for he found that the effect was produced both by day and at night. Further, in 1912, he made a balloon ascent during a total eclipse of the Sun and found that during the period when the Sun was completely obscured there was no significant effect on the rate of discharge. Hess however failed to convince everyone that cosmic rays came from outside the Earth's atmosphere as it could still be argued that the source of the radiation was such atmospheric disturbances as thunderstorms. It was left to Millikan in 1925 finally to refute this objection.

Hess, Walter Rudolf (1881–1973) *Swiss neurophysiologist*

The son of a physics teacher from Frauenfel in Switzerland, Hess was educated at the universities of Lausanne, Bern, Berlin, Kiel, and Zurich where he obtained his MD in 1906. Although he actually began as an ophthalmologist, building up a prosperous practice, he decided in 1912 to abandon it for a career in physiology. After junior posts in Zurich and Bonn he was appointed in 1917 to the directorship of the physiology department at the University of Zurich, where he remained until his retirement in 1951.

In the early 1920s Hess began an important investigation of the interbrain and hypothalamus. To do this he inserted fine electrodes into the brains of cats, and used these to stimulate specific groups of cells. His most startling discovery was that when electrodes in the posterior interbrain were switched on this would instantaneously turn a friendly cat into an aggressive spitting creature – a transformation instantly reversed by a further press of the switch. Other areas found by Hess would induce flight, sleep, or defecation.

Less dramatic perhaps but no less significant were the two main areas identified by Hess in the hypothalamus. Stimulation of the posterior region prepared the animal for action but stimulation of the anterior region tended to cause relaxation. Hess had discovered the control center for the sympathetic and parasympathetic systems.

Hess's work was enormously influential and led to a detailed mapping of the interbrain and hypothalamus by many different workers in various centers over a number of years. For his discovery of "the functional organization of the interbrain" Hess was awarded the 1949 Nobel Prize for physiology or medicine, sharing it with Antonio EGAS MONIZ.

Hevelius, Johannes (1611–1687)
German astronomer

Hevelius was the son of a prosperous brewer from Danzig (now Gdańsk in Poland). He followed his father in the family business as well as devoting himself to civic duties. After studying in Leiden, he established his own observatory on the rooftops of several houses overlooking the Vistula, an observatory which soon gained him an international reputation.

He published several major works of observational astronomy. Four years' telescopic study of the Moon, using telescopes of long focal power, led to his *Selenographia* (1647; Pictures of the Moon). Making his own engravings of the Moon's surface he assigned names to the lunar mountains, craters, and plains taken from the Earth placing, with what the writer Sir Thomas Browne called witty congruity, "...the Mediterranean Sea, Mauritania, Sicily, and Asia Minor in the Moon." This system of naming, apart from the Alps, did not survive long, Giovanni Riccioli's alternative system of scientific eponomy being preferred. Hevelius's star catalog *Prodromus astronomiae* (Guide to Astronomy) was published posthumously in 1690.

Hevelius is today best remembered for his 'aerial' telescopes of enormous focal length and his rejection of telescopic sights for stellar observation and positional measurement. He was widely criticized for the latter eccentricity and in 1679 was paid a famous visit by Edmond Halley who had been instructed by Robert Hooke and John Flamsteed to persuade him of the advantages of the new telescopic sights. Hevelius claimed he could do as well with his quadrant and alidade. Halley tested him thoroughly, finding to his surprise that Hevelius could measure both consistently and accurately. He is therefore the last astronomer to do major observational work without a telescope.

Hevesy, George Charles von (1885–1966) *Hungarian–Swedish chemist*

Hevesy came from a family of wealthy industrialists in Budapest, the Hungarian capital. He was educated in Budapest and at the University of Freiburg where he obtained his doctorate in 1908. He then worked in Zurich, Karlsruhe, Manchester, and Copenhagen, before his appointment to the chair of physical chemistry in 1926 at Freiburg. In 1935 he left Germany for Denmark, fleeing from the Nazis who caught up with him once more in 1942, when he sought refuge in Sweden at the University of Stockholm.

In 1923 Hevesy discovered the new element hafnium in collaboration with Dirk Coster. His most important work, however, began in 1911 in the Manchester laboratory of Ernest Rutherford, where he worked on the separation of 'radium D' from a sample of lead. In fact radium D was a radioactive isotope of lead (lead–210) and could not be separated by chemical means. Hevesy was quick to see the significance of this and began exploring the use of radioactive isotopes as tracers. In 1913, with Friedrich Adolph Paneth, he used radioactive salts of lead and bismuth to determine their solubilities. In 1923 Hevesy made the first application of a radioactive tracer – Pb–212 – to a biological system. The Pb–212 was used to label a lead salt that plants took up in solution. At various time intervals plants were burned and the amount of lead taken up could be determined by simple measurements of the amount of radioactivity present. The drawback of this technique was the high toxicity of lead to most biological systems and it was only with the discovery of artificial radioactivity by Irène and Frédéric JOLIOT-CURIE in 1934 that Hevesy's radioactive tracers developed into one of the most widely used and powerful techniques for the investigation of living and of complex systems. For his work in the development of radioactive tracers Hevesy was awarded the 1943 Nobel Prize for chemistry.

Hewish, Antony (1924–) *British radio astronomer*

Hewish was born at Fowey in Cornwall, and studied at Cambridge University. He obtained his BA in 1948 and his PhD in 1952 after wartime work with the Royal Aircraft Establishment, Farnborough. He lectured in physics at Cambridge until in 1969 he was made reader and in 1971 professor of radio astronomy, becoming professor emeritus in 1989. In 1974 he was awarded the Nobel Prize for physics jointly with Martin RYLE.

One of Hewish's research projects was the study of radio scintillation using the 4.5-acre telescope, which consisted of a regular array of 2048 dipoles operating at a wavelength of 3.7 meters. Radio scintillation is a phenomenon, similar to the twinkling of visible stars, arising from random deflections of radio waves by ionized gas. The three types of scintillation are caused by ionized gas in the interstellar medium, in the interplanetary medium, and in the Earth's atmosphere. All three types were discovered at Cambridge and Hewish was involved in their investigation. In 1967 a research student, Jocelyn Bell (later BELL BURNELL), noticed a rapidly fluctuating but unusually regular radio signal that turned out to have a periodicity of 1.337,301,13 seconds. She had discovered the first pulsar.

To determine the nature of the signal, Hewish's first job was to eliminate such man-made sources as satellites, radar echoes, and the like. Measurements indicated that it must be well beyond the solar system. It seemed possible that it had been transmitted by an alien intelligence and the LGM (Little Green Men) hypothesis, as it became known, was seriously considered at Cambridge, but with the rapid discovery of three more pulsars it was soon dropped.

Hewish did however manage to establish some of the main properties of the pulsar from a careful analysis of its radio signal. Apart from its striking regularity (it was later shown to be slowing down very slightly) it was extremely small, no more than a few thousand kilometers, and was situated in our Galaxy.

By the end of February 1968 Hewish was ready to publish. His account received wide publicity in the popular press and stimulated much thought among astronomers as to the possible mechanism. The proposal made by Thomas GOLD and others that pulsars were rapidly rotating neutron stars has since won acceptance.

Heymans, Corneille Jean François
(1892–1968) *Belgian physiologist and pharmacologist*

Heymans was educated at the university in his native city of Ghent, where his father was professor of pharmacology, obtaining his MD in 1920. He began as a pharmacology lecturer there in 1923 and in 1930 succeeded his father, holding the chair until his retirement in 1963.

In 1924 Heymans began a series of important cross-circulation experiments. The relationship between respiration and blood pressure had been known for some time – high arterial pressure (hypertension) inhibited respiration while low arterial pressure (hypotension) stimulated it – but the mechanism of such a response was far from clear. Heymans's basic experiment consisted of separating the head of a dog from its body in such a way that its only remaining contact with the body was the nervous supply to the heart. The body of the dog could be made to respire artificially while its head could be linked up to the blood supply of a second dog. Even in such circumstances, hypotension produced an increase in the rate of respiration while hypertension inhibited it. This suggested to Heymans that the process was due not to direct action of the blood pressure on the respiratory center but to nervous control.

Heymans went on to show the important role played in the regulation of heart rate and blood pressure by the carotid sinus, an enlargement of the carotid artery in the neck. By severing the sinus from its own blood supply while maintaining its nervous connection and linking it up to the blood supply of another animal he was able to show that changes of pressure initiated nervous reflexes that automatically reversed the process. The sinus was in fact a sensitive pressure receptor. He also demonstrated that a nearby glandlike structure, the glomus caroticum, was a chemorecep-

tor, responding to changes in the oxygen/carbon dioxide ratio in the blood.

For his work on the regulation of respiration Heymans was awarded the 1938 Nobel Prize for physiology or medicine.

Heyrovský, Jaroslav (1890–1967) *Czech physical chemist*

Heyrovský, the son of an academic lawyer, was educated at Charles University in his native Prague and at University College, London. He joined the staff of Charles University in 1919 where he served as professor of physics from 1919 until 1954. From 1950 he was also head of the Central Polarographic Institute, which, since 1964, has borne his name.

Heyrovský is best known for his discovery and development of polarography, which he described in 1922. This is one of the most versatile of all analytical techniques. It depends on the fact that in electrolysis the ions are discharged at an electrode and, if the electrode is small, the current may be limited by the rate of movement of ions to the electrode surface. In polarography the cathode is a small drop of mercury (constantly forming and dropping to keep the surface clean). The voltage is increased slowly and the current plotted against voltage. The current increases in steps, each corresponding to a particular type of positive ion in the solution. The height of the steps indicates the concentration of the ion. For his work, Heyrovský was awarded the Nobel Prize for chemistry in 1959.

Higgins, William (1763–1825) *Irish chemist*

Born at Colooney in Ireland, Higgins worked in London as a young man with his uncle, Bryan Higgins, the chemist. He studied at Oxford University from 1786 and on his return to Ireland became, in 1791, chemist to the Apothecaries Company of Ireland. He moved to Dublin in 1795 to become chemist and librarian to the Royal Dublin Society, this post being made into a professorship in 1800. From 1795 to 1822 he was chemist to the Irish Linen Board.

Higgins is remembered for his contributions to the new atomic theory and for his claim to have anticipated John DALTON. His claim is based on his work *A Comparative View of the Phlogistic and Antiphlogistic Theories with Inductions* (1789), which was written as a reply to Richard Kirwan's work.

He introduced a clearer symbolism system than that of Dalton but did not follow up his work on atomism until he published a strong attack on Dalton's work in his eight-volume work *Experiments and Observations on the Atomic Theory and Electrical Phenomena* (1814).

Higgins spent the intervening years between these publications trying to introduce new chemical technology into Ireland. In 1799 he published an *Essay on the Theory and Practice of Bleaching*, a work written specifically for the bleachers themselves.

Higgs, Peter Ware (1929–) British *theoretical physicist*

Higgs was born at Bristol and educated at Kings College, London, where he completed his PhD in 1955. He worked initially at the University of London but moved to Edinburgh University in 1960 and was elected professor of theoretical physics there in 1980.

Along with many other physicists in the 1960s, Higgs worked on proposals to unify the weak and the electromagnetic forces into a single electroweak theory. At very high temperatures the two forces and their carriers, photons for the electromagnetic force and the W and Z bosons for the weak force, would be indistinguishable. But, at lower temperatures, the symmetry breaks down and massless photons are obviously distinct from the massive W and Z bosons. In 1964, Higgs worked out a mechanism for the breakdown in symmetry, since known as the *Higgs field*, which would endow the bosons with mass. At the same time, he noted, the mechanism would also produce another massive particle, the *Higgs boson*.

The existence of this particle, it has been claimed, will be the ultimate test of the correctness of the electroweak theory, and of the standard model of particle physics itself. Yet no sign of the particle has so far been detected. The failure is normally explained away by pointing out that the Higgs boson probably has a mass in excess of 1 TeV (10^9 electron volts), well beyond the capacity of any current accelerator. It will therefore be the first task of the Superconducting Proton Synchotron, with an expected capacity of 20 TeV, if ever completed, to search for the Higgs boson.

Hilbert, David (1862–1943) German *mathematician*

Hilbert studied at the university in his native city of Königsberg (now Kaliningrad in Russia) and at Heidelberg; he also spent brief periods in Paris and Leipzig. He took his PhD in 1885, the next year became *Privatdozent* at Königsberg, and by 1892 had become professor there. In 1895 he moved to Göttingen to take up the chair that he occupied until his official retirement in 1930.

Hilbert's mathematical work was very wide ranging and during his long life there were few fields to which he did not make some contribution and many he completely transformed. His attention was first turned to the newly created theory of invariants and in the period 1885–88 he virtually completed the subject by solving all the central problems. However his work on invariants was very fruitful as he created entirely new methods for tackling problems, in the context of a much wider general theory. The fruit of this work consisted of many new and fundamental theorems in algebra and in particular in the theory of polynomial rings. Much of his work on invariants turned out later to have important application in the new subject of homological algebra.

Hilbert now turned to algebraic number theory where he did what is probably his finest research. Hilbert and Minkowski had been asked to prepare a report surveying the current state of number theory but Minkowski soon dropped out leaving Hilbert to produce not only a masterly account but also a substantial body of original and fundamental new discoveries. The work was presented in the *Zahlbericht* (1897; Report on Numbers) with an elegance and lucidity of exposition that has rarely been equaled.

Hilbert then moved to another area of mathematics and wrote the *Grundlagen der Geometrie* (1899; Foundations of Geometry), giving an account of geometry as it had developed through the 19th century. Here his interest lay chiefly in expounding and illuminating the work of others in a systematic way rather than in making new developments of the subject. He devised an abstract axiomatic system that could admit many different geometries – Euclidean and non-Euclidean – as models and by this means go much further than had previously been done in obtaining consistency and independence proofs for various sets of geometrical axioms. Apart from its importance for pure geometry his work led to the development of a number of new algebraic concepts and was particularly important to Hilbert himself because his experience with the axiomatic method and his interest in consistency proofs shaped his approach to mathematical logic and the foundations of mathematics.

In mathematical logic and the philosophy of mathematics Hilbert is a key figure, being one of the major proponents of the formalist view, which he expounded with much greater precision than had his 19th-century precursors. This philosophical view of mathematics had a formative impact on the development of mathematical logic because of the central role it gave to the formalization of mathematics into axiomatic systems and the study of their properties by metamathematical means. Hilbert aimed at formalizing as much of mathematics as possible and finding consistency proofs for the resulting formal systems. It was soon shown by Kurt Gödel that *Hilbert's program*, as this proposal is called, could not be carried out, at least in its original form, but it is none the less true that Gödel's own revolutionary metamathematical work would have been inconceivable without Hilbert. Hilbert's contribution to mathematical logic was important, especially to the development of proof theory, as further developed by such mathematicians as Gerhard Gentzen.

Hilbert also made notable contributions to analysis, to the calculus of variations, and to mathematical physics. His work on operators and on *Hilbert space* (a type of infinite-dimensional space) was of crucial importance to quantum mechanics. His considerable influence on mathematical physics was also exerted through his colleagues at Göttingen, who included Minkowski, Hermann Weyl, Erwin Schrödinger, and Werner Heisenberg.

In 1900 Hilbert presented a list of 23 outstanding unsolved mathematical problems to the International Congress of Mathematicians in Paris. A number of these problems still remain unsolved and the mathematics that has been created in solving the others has fully vindicated his deep insight into his subject. Hilbert was an excellent teacher and during his time at Göttingen continued the tradition begun in the 19th century and built the university into an outstanding center of mathematical research, which it remained until the dispersal of the intellectual community by the Nazis in 1933. Hilbert is generally considered one of the greatest mathematicians of the 20th century and indeed of all time.

Hill, Archibald Vivian (1886–1977)
British physiologist and biochemist

Born at Bristol, Hill was professor of physiology at Manchester University (1920–23) and then Jodrell Professor at University College, London, from 1923 to 1925 (and honorary professor from 1926 to 1951). He was Foulerton Research Professor of the Royal Society (1926–51), of which he was also for some years both secretary and foreign secretary. From 1940 until 1946 he was the Independent Conservative member of Parliament for Cambridge University and a member of the War Cabinet Scientific Advisory Committee.

Hill's major research was directed toward accurately recording the minute quantities of heat produced during muscle action. For this he used thermocouples, which recorded the smallest variations in heat generated after the muscle had completed its movement. He was able to show that oxygen was only consumed *after* muscular contraction, and not during it, indicating that molecular oxygen is required only for muscle recovery. In 1922 he shared the Nobel Prize for physiology or medicine (with Otto MEYERHOF) for this work on the physiology of muscular contraction.

Hillier, James (1915–) *Canadian–American physicist*

Born in Brantford, Ontario, Hillier was educated at the University of Toronto, where he gained successively his BA (1937), MA (1938), and PhD in physics (1941). He went to live and work in America in 1940 and became a naturalized citizen in 1945. From 1940 to 1953 he worked for the Radio Corporation of America (RCA) Laboratories as a research physicist, primarily on the development of the electron microscope.

Many efforts were being made around the world to develop a commercial electron microscope that could offer higher resolution than optical microscopes. It had been known since the 1920s that a shaped magnetic field could act as a 'lens' for electrons, and in the 1930s the first electron micrographs had been taken. Hillier and his colleagues at RCA designed and built the first successful high-resolution electron microscope in America in 1940; they had in fact been anticipated by Ernst Ruska and Max Knoll who had produced a similar machine for the Siemens and Halske Company in Germany in 1938. The outbreak of World War II prevented commercial development and exploitation of the German machine.

Hillier made many instrumental advances to the electron microscope. By 1946, he had achieved resolutions (magnifications) approaching close to the theoretical limits. He also involved himself in the development of techniques for the preparation of viral and bacteriological samples for examination.

Hillier's career at RCA continued with only a short break to his present position of executive vice-president for research engineering. He is now principally concerned with research management, and has served on various American governmental, research, and engineering committees.

Hinshelwood, Sir Cyril Norman
(1897–1967) *British chemist*

Hinshelwood, a Londoner, was educated at Oxford University, where he was elected to a fellowship in 1920 and obtained his doctorate in 1924. In 1937 he became Dr. Lee's Professor of Chemistry at Oxford. He retired in 1964 when he moved to Imperial College, London, as a senior research fellow.

Hinshelwood worked mainly in the field of chemical reaction kinetics. He produced a major text on the subject, *The Kinetics of Chemical Change in Gaseous Systems* (1926) and, in 1956, shared the Nobel Prize for chemistry with Nicolay SEMENOV for his work. He later applied his work to a relatively new field in his book, *The Chemical Kinetics of the Bacterial Cell* (1954).

In some papers published earlier, in 1950, Hinshelwood came very close to the true meaning of DNA, established by Jim Watson and Francis Crick three years later. He declared that in the synthesis of protein the nucleic acid guides the order in which the various amino acids are laid down. Little attention was paid to Hinshelwood's proposal at the time although Crick later declared it to be the first serious suggestion of how DNA might work.

Hinshelwood was a linguist and classical scholar as well as a scientist; he had the unique distinction of serving as president of both the Royal Society (1955–60) and the Classical Association. He was knighted in 1948.

Hipparchus (c. 170 BC–c. 120 BC) *Greek astronomer and geographer*

Born at Nicaea, which is now in Turkey, Hipparchus (hi-**par**-kus) worked in Rhodes, where he built an observatory, and in Alexandria. None of his works has survived but many of them were recorded by Ptolemy. In 134 BC he observed a new star in the constellation of Scorpio. This led him to construct a catalog of about 850 stars. By comparing the position of the stars of his day with those given 150 years earlier he found that Spica, which was then 6° from the autumn equinox, had previously been 8°. He used this observation to deduce not the movement of Spica but the east to west precession (motion) of the equinoctial point. He calculated the rate of the precession as about 45 seconds of arc a year – a value close to the 50.27 seconds now accepted. He also introduced the practice of dividing the stars into different classes of magnitude based on their apparent brightness. The brightest stars he classed as first magnitude and those just visible to the naked eye he classed as sixth magnitude.

As a theorist Hipparchus worked on the orbits of the Sun and Moon. He established more accurate lengths of both the year and the month and was able to produce more accurate eclipse predictions. One of his lasting achievements was the construction of a table of chords, which virtually began the discipline of trigonometry. The concept of a sine had not yet been developed. Instead, Hipparchus calculated the ratio of the chord to the diameter of its own circle, which was divided into 120 parts. Thus if a chord produced by an angle of 60° is half the length of the radius, it would have, for Hipparchus, 60 parts. He much improved the geography of Eratosthenes, fixing the parallels astronomically.

Hippocrates of Cos (c. 460 BC–c. 370 BC) *Greek physician*

Very little is known of the life of Hippocrates except that he was born on the Greek island of Cos. The main source, Soranus, dates from the second century AD and was clearly telling a traditional tale rather than writing a biography. Hippocrates is reported to have studied under his father Heraclides, also a physician, and with the atomist Democritus, and the sophist Gorgias. He then seems to have spent most of his life traveling around the Greek world curing the great of obscure diseases and ridding grateful cities of plagues and pestilence.

After the fantasy of his life there is the reality of the *Corpus Hippocraticum* (The Hippocratic Collection). This consists of some 70 works though whether any were actually written by Hippocrates himself will probably always remain a matter of speculation. What is clear, on stylistic and paleographic grounds, is that the corpus was produced by many hands in the second half of the fifth century and the first part of the fourth. Nor do the works represent a single 'Hippocratic' point of view but, it has been suggested, probably formed the library of a physician and acquired the name of its first owner or collector.

Of more importance is the character of these remarkable works. They are surprisingly free of any attempt to explain disease in theological, astrological, diabolic, or any other spiritual terms. Diseases in the *Corpus* are natural events, which arise in a normal manner from the food one has eaten or some such factor as the weather. The cause of the disease is for the Hippocratic basically a malfunction of the veins leading to the brain which, though no doubt false, is the same kind of rational, material, and verifiable claim that could be found in any late 20th-century neurological textbook.

Such rationality was not to rule for many years for in the fourth century BC new cults entered Greece and with them the dream, the charm, and other such superstitions entered medicine. More successful in the length of its survival was the actual theory of disease contained in the *Corpus*. This was the view, first formulated by Alcmaeon in the fifth century BC, that health consists of an *isonomia* or equal rule of the bodily elements rather than a *monarchia* or domination by a single element. By the time of Hippocrates it was accepted that there were just four elements, earth, air, fire, and water with their corresponding qualities, coldness, dryness, heat, and wetness. If present in the human body in the right amounts in the right places health resulted, but if equilibrium was destroyed then so too was health.

A new terminology developed to describe such pathological conditions, a terminology still apparent in most western languages. Thus an excess of earth, the cold/dry element, produced an excess of black bile, or in Greek melancholic, in the body; too much water, the cold/moist element, made one phlegmatic.

One striking contrast between Hippocratic and later medicine is the curious yet impressive reluctance of the former to attempt cures for various disorders: the emphasis is rather on prognosis. For example, the *Epidemics* describes the course, but not treatment, of various complaints. At least knowing the expected course and outcome of an illness helped the practitioner to inform his patient what to expect, information that could be useful and reassuring. Further, if it is known which conditions lead to a disease such conditions could sometimes be avoided.

The works *Regimen in Acute Diseases* and *Regimen in Health*, which deal specifically with therapy, tend to restrict themselves to diet, exercise, bathing, and emetics. Thus the Hippocratic doctor may not have cured many of his patients but he was certainly less likely than his 18th-century counterpart to actually kill them.

Hirst, Sir Edmund Langley (1898–1975) *British chemist. See* HAWORTH, SIR WALTER NORMAN.

Hisinger, Wilhelm (1766–1852) *Swedish mineralogist. See* BERZELIUS, JÖNS JACOB.

Hitchings, George Herbert (1905–1998) *American pharmacologist*

Hitchings, the son of a naval architect, was born in Hoquiam, Washington, and educated at the University of Washington and at Harvard where he obtained his PhD in 1933 and where he taught until 1939. He then moved briefly to the Western Reserve University until in 1942 he joined the Wellcome Research Laboratories where he spent the rest of his career, serving as vice president in charge of research from 1966 until his retirement in 1975.

Hitchings was one of the most productive of modern chemical pharmacologists. He began in 1942 with the study of purines and pyrimidines on the grounds that, as important ingredients in cell metabolism, their manipulation could lead to the control of important diseases at the cellular level. This insight led to the synthesis in 1951 of the purine analog, 6-mercaptopurine (6MP), which, as it inhibited DNA synthesis and thus cellular proliferation, proved valuable in the treatment of cancer, particularly leukemia.

In 1959 6MP was found to inhibit the ability of rabbits to produce antibodies against foreign proteins. A less toxic form, azathioprine or Imuran, was quickly developed by Hitchings and used in 1960 by the surgeon Roy Calne to control rejection of transplanted kidneys.

One further drug was developed from work on 6MP when it was realized that it was broken down in the body by the enzyme xanthine oxydase, the same enzyme that converts purines into uric acid. As gout is caused by an excess of uric acid Hitchings developed allopurinol, which blocks uric acid production by competing for xanthine oxydase.

Other drugs developed by Hitchings include the malarial prophylactic pyrimethamine, or Daraprim, and the antibacterial, trimethoprim. He was awarded the 1988 Nobel Prize for physiology or medicine for his work.

Hitzig, Eduard (1838–1907) *German psychiatrist*

Hitzig, the son of a Berlin architect, was educated at the university there and obtained his MD in 1862. He was later appointed, in 1875, director of the Berghölzi asylum and professor of psychiatry at the University of Zurich. In 1885 Hitzig moved to similar posts at the University of Halle, posts he retained until his retirement in 1903.

In 1870, in collaboration with the German anatomist **Gustav Fritsch** (1838–1927), Hitzig published a fundamental paper, *On the Excitability of the Cerebrum*, which provided the first experimental evidence for cerebral localization. Following the important work of Pierre Flourens in 1824 it was widely accepted that, despite the discoveries of Paul Broca and John Neethlings Jackson, the cerebral hemispheres constituted a unity, the seat of intelligence, sensation, and volition and not the source of movement.

This was shown to be false when Hitzig and Fritsch electrically stimulated the cerebral cortex of a dog and elicited distinct muscular contractions. They identified five localized centers, which produced various movements on the side of the dog opposite to the side of the brain stimulated. Their work was soon confirmed by David Ferrier and opened up a vast research program, still, a century later, unfinished.

Hitzig himself continued with this work and in 1874 tried to define what soon became known as the motor area of the dog and the monkey. He also tried to identify, though less successfully, the site of intelligence, in the sense of abstract ideas, in the frontal lobes.

Hjelm, Peter Jacob (1746–1813)
Swedish chemist and metallurgist. See SCHEELE, KARL WILHELM.

Hoagland, Mahlon Bush (1921–)
American biochemist

Hoagland was born in Boston, Massachusetts, the son of Hudson Hoagland, a distinguished neurophysiologist. Having obtained his MD from Harvard in 1948, he joined the Huntington Laboratories of the Massachusetts General Hospital. He then served in the Harvard Medical School from 1960 until 1967 when he became professor of biochemistry at Dartmouth. From 1970 to 1985 he was scientific director of the Worcester Institute for Experimental Biology, founded by his father and Gregory Pincus in 1944.

In early 1955 Francis Crick published his 'adaptor' hypothesis to explain protein synthesis by the cell. Unaware of this work, Hoagland, in collaboration with Paul Zamecnik and Mary Stephenson, provided the experimental confirmation in 1956. It had earlier been shown by George Palade that protein synthesis occurred outside the nucleus in the ribosomes. Hoagland and Zamecnik discovered that before the amino acids reach the ribosomes to be synthesized into protein, they are first activated by forming a bond with the energy-rich adenosine triphosphate (ATP).

What happened in the ribosome was unveiled by forming a cell-free mixture of ATP, the radioactively labeled amino acid leucine, enzymes, and some of the small soluble RNA molecules found in the cytoplasm. At this point they discovered the crucial step, predicted by Crick, in between the activation of the amino acid and its appearance in the protein; the amino acid became tightly bound to the soluble RNA. Shortly afterward the labeled leucine was no longer bound to the RNA but present in the protein. The discovery of transfer RNA (or tRNA as it soon became known) was also made independently by Paul BERG and Robert HOLLEY.

In his autobiography *Toward the Habit of Truth* (1990), Hoagland described his work as a molecular biologist and sketched the history of the Worcester Institute.

Hodgkin, Sir Alan Lloyd (1914–)
British physiologist

Born at Banbury near Oxford, Hodgkin graduated from Cambridge University and became a fellow in 1936. He spent World War II working on radar for the Air Ministry. He then worked at the physiological laboratory at Cambridge, where he served as Foulerton Research Professor from 1952 to 1969 and as professor of biophysics from 1970 until 1981. He also served from 1978 to 1984 as master of Trinity College, Cambridge; he was knighted in 1972.

In 1951, with Andrew HUXLEY and Bernard Katz, he worked out the sodium theory to explain the difference in action and resting potentials in nerve fibers. Using the single nerve fiber (giant axon) of a squid, they were able to demonstrate that there is an exchange of sodium and potassium ions between the cell and its surroundings during a nervous impulse, which enables the nerve fiber to carry a further impulse. Hodgkin also showed that the nerve fiber's potential for electrical conduction was greater during the actual passage of an impulse than when the fiber is resting. For their work on the 'sodium pump' mechanism and the chemical basis of nerve transmission Hodgkin, Huxley, and John ECCLES shared the Nobel Prize for physiology or medicine in 1963. He is the author of *Conduction of the Nervous Impulse* (1964). In 1992 he published his autobiography *Chance and Design: Reminiscences of Science in Peace and War*.

Hodgkin, Dorothy Crowfoot
(1910–1994) *British chemist*

Born Dorothy Crowfoot in Cairo, Egypt, she was educated at Somerville College, Oxford. After a brief period as a postgraduate student at Cambridge University, she returned to Oxford in 1934 and spent her entire academic career there. She served as Wolfson

Research Professor of the Royal Society from 1960 until 1977.

Hodgkin had the good fortune to fall under the influence of the inspiring and scientifically imaginative physicist J.D. BERNAL at Cambridge. Bernal was keen to use the technique of x-ray diffraction analysis, introduced by Max VON LAUE in 1912, to investigate important complex organic molecules. He gathered around him a group of enthusiastic scientists to work out the appropriate techniques. Of the Bernal group, Hodgkin was probably the most talented; she also possessed a greater single mindedness than Bernal himself and, despite the demands of three young children and a busy political life, it was her persistence and talent that produced some of the first great successes of x-ray analysis.

Her first major result came in 1949 when, with Charles Bunn, she published the three-dimensional structure of penicillin. This was followed by the structure of vitamin B_{12} (by 1956) and, in 1969, that of insulin. For her work on vitamin B_{12} she was awarded the Nobel Prize for chemistry in 1964.

Hoff, Marcian Edward (1937–   )
American computer engineer

Hoff gained his doctorate in 1962 at Stanford, where he worked for a further six years as a research associate. In 1968 he was invited by Robert Noyce to join his newly formed semiconductor firm, Intel.

Noyce had earlier shown how to assemble a large number of transistors into an integrated circuit (IC). Shortly after joining Intel, Hoff was asked to help some Japanese engineers design a number of IC chips to be used in desktop calculators.

Hoff proposed a calculator that could perform simple hardware instructions but could store complex sequences of these instructions in read-only memory (ROM) on a chip. The result of his idea was the first microprocessor – the Intel 4004 – released in 1971. Despite initial debate about its use and marketability, it became the forerunner of a whole range of advanced microprocessors, leading to a new generation of computers.

Hoff left Intel in 1982 to move to the computer company Atari to investigate new products. When Atari was sold in 1984 Hoff set up as an independent consultant.

Hoffmann, Roald (1937–   ) *Polish-born American chemist*

Born in Zloczow, Poland (now Zolochez in Ukraine), Hoffmann was moved at the age of four with his family to a labor camp. His father was executed for trying to escape, but Hoffmann and his mother were smuggled out in 1943 and spent the rest of World War II hiding in the attic of a schoolhouse. Hoffmann has noted that only 80 of the 12,000 Jews of Zloczow survived the war. Following the liberation in mid-1944, Hoffmann's mother returned to Poland and emigrated with her son to America in 1949; he became a naturalized citizen in 1955.

Hoffmann was educated at Columbia and at Harvard, where he obtained his PhD in 1962. He moved to Cornell in 1965 and was appointed professor of chemistry in 1974.

In the mid-1960s Hoffmann began a research collaboration with R. B. WOODWARD on molecular orbital theory. Their work led to the formulation in 1965 of what are now known as the *Woodward-Hoffmann rules*. These laid down general conditions under which certain organic reactions can occur. The rules apply to pericyclic reactions. In reactions of this kind bond breaking and formation occur simultaneously without the presence of intermediates, i.e., they are said to be 'concerted' reactions. The reactions also involve cyclic structures. Woodward and Hoffmann published their work in their *Conservation of Orbital Symmetry* (1969). Hoffmann's collaboration with Woodward won him a share of the 1981 Nobel Prize for chemistry with K. FUKUI; Woodward's death in 1979, however, robbed him of his second Nobel Prize.

Hoffmann has also published two volumes of verse, *The Metamict State*, and *Gaps and Verges*. He has also written and presented a number of television programmes, *The World of Chemistry* and *The Molecular World*, in which he has attempted to introduce chemistry to a wider audience. A similar approach can be seen in his *The Same and Not the Same* (1995), in which he tries to describe for a popular audience how the world behaves at the molecular level.

Hofmeister, Wilhelm Friedrich Benedict (1824–1877) *German botanist*

Hofmeister's father, a music and book publisher from Leipzig, was also a keen amateur botanist and encouraged his son's interest in botany. Wilhelm left school at 15 and served a two-year apprenticeship in a music shop before entering his father's business in 1841. He soon began to study botany seriously in his spare time and was greatly influenced by the views of Matthias Schleiden, who believed that botany could advance rapidly if researchers concentrated on studying cell structure and life histories.

Using procedures recommended by Schleiden, Hofmeister's first work was to disprove Schleiden's theory that the plant embryo develops from the tip of the pollen tube. He believed that a preexisting cell in the embryo sac gave rise to the embryo and his paper *The Genesis of the Embryo in Phanerogams* (1849) gained him an honorary doctorate from Rostock University.

Hofmeister's major discovery, however, was to demonstrate the alternation of generations between sporophyte and gametophyte in the lower plants. The work, published in 1851 as *Vergleichende Untersuchungen* (Comparative Investigations), showed the homologies between the higher seed-bearing plants (phanerogams) and the mosses and ferns (cryptogams) and demonstrated the true position of the gymnosperms between the angiosperms and the cryptogams. In 1863 Hofmeister was appointed professor at Heidelberg University and director of the botanic gardens there, and in 1872 moved to Tübingen University to succeed Hugo von Mohl.

Hofstadter, Robert (1915–1990)
American physicist

A New Yorker by birth, Hofstadter graduated from the College of the City of New York in 1935 and gained his MA and PhD at Princeton University in 1938. From 1939 he held a fellowship at the University of Pennsylvania, and in 1941 returned to the College of the City of New York as an instructor in physics. From 1943 to 1946 Hofstadter worked at the Norden Laboratory Corporation, and from there took on an assistant professorship in physics at Princeton University. In 1950 he moved to Standford University as an associate professor and was made full professor in 1954.

His early research was in the fields of infrared spectroscopy, the hydrogen bond, and photoconductivity. One of his first notable achievements, in 1948, was the invention of a scintillation counter using sodium iodide activated with thallium. He is noted for his studies of the atomic nucleus, for which he received the 1961 Nobel Prize for physics (shared with Rudolph Mössbauer).

At Stanford, Hofstadter used the linear accelerator to study the scattering effects of high electrons fired at atomic nuclei. In many ways these experiments were similar in concept to Rutherford's original scattering experiments. He found that the distribution of charge density in the nucleus was constant in the core, and then decreased sharply at a peripheral region. The radial distribution of charge was found to vary in a mathematical relationship that depended upon the nuclear mass. Further, Hofstadter was able to show that nucleons (protons and neutrons) were not simply point particles, but had definite size and form. Both

appeared to be composed of charged mesonic clouds (or shells) with the charges adding together in the proton, but canceling each other out in the neutral neutron. This led him to predict the existence of the rho-meson and omega-meson, which were later detected.

Hofstadter served as director of the high-energy physics laboratory at Stanford from 1967 to 1974.

Holley, Robert William (1922–1993)
American biochemist

Holley was born in Urbana, Illinois. After graduating in chemistry from Illinois University in 1942, he joined the team at Cornell Medical School that achieved the first artificial synthesis of penicillin. He remained at Cornell to receive his PhD in organic chemistry in 1947.

Two years (1955–56) spent at the California Institute of Technology marked the beginning of Holley's important research on the nucleic acids. He decided that to work out the structure of a nucleic acid he first needed a very pure specimen of the molecule. Back again at Cornell, his research team spent three years isolating one gram of alanine transfer RNA (alanine tRNA) from some 90 kilograms of yeast. In March 1965 he was able to announce that they had worked out the complete sequence of 77 nucleotides in alanine tRNA. For this work Holley received the 1968 Nobel Prize for physiology or medicine, an award he shared with Marshall Nirenberg and Har Gobind Khorana.

Holmes, Arthur (1890–1965) *British*
geologist

Holmes came from a farming background in Hebburn-on-Tyne in the northeast of England. He graduated from Imperial College, London, in 1910, and went on to work with Lord Rayleigh on radioactivity. After an expedition to Mozambique in 1911 he taught at Imperial College until 1920 when he went to Burma as an oil geologist. In 1925 he returned to England to become professor of geology at Durham University, where he remained until 1943 when he moved to Edinburgh University.

Holmes conducted major work on the use of radioactive techniques to determine the age of rocks, leading to his proposal of the first quantitative geological time scale in 1913 and to his estimate of the age of the Earth being about 1600 million years. He continued to revise this estimate throughout his life, producing a figure in 1959 some three times larger.

Holmes also made a major contribution

to the theory of continental drift proposed by Alfred WEGENER in 1915. One of the early difficulties the theory faced was that geologists could not envisage a force capable of moving the continents in the way described by Wegener. In 1929 Holmes proposed the existence of convection currents in the Earth's mantle. Rocks in the Earth's interior are, according to Holmes, heated by radioactivity, causing them to rise and spread out and, when cold and dense, to sink back to the interior. It was only after World War II that hard evidence for such a view could be produced.

In 1944 Holmes published his *Principles of Physical Geology*, a major work on the subject. A substantially revised edition of this book was published in 1965, shortly before Holmes's death.

Hood, Leroy Edward (1938–)
American biologist

Born in Missoula, Montana, Hood was educated at the California Institute of Technology, where he obtained his PhD in biochemistry in 1964, and at Johns Hopkins Medical School, Baltimore, where he qualified as an MD in 1964. He immediately joined the staff of the National Institute of Health, Bethesda, working in the area of immunology. In 1970 Hood returned to the California Institute of Technology and was appointed professor of biology in 1975.

In May 1985 at a meeting in Santa Cruz, California, plans were laid to map the human genome (the Human Genome Project). As the genome consists of 3 billion base pairs of DNA, the ability to sequence the genes rapidly would be a crucial factor.

Fortunately an automatic sequencer was almost at hand in 1985, developed by Hood and his colleague Lloyd Smith. The sequencer operates with fluorescent dyes. Each of the four DNA bases – adenine (A), cytosine (C), guanine (G), and thymine (T) – can be tagged with a different dye. Unsequenced dye-tagged DNA fragments are analyzed by gel electrophoresis, in which they migrate at different rates. The dyes are excited by an argon laser and the light emitted is turned into a digital signal by photomultiplier tubes. The digital signals can be analyzed by a computer and identified as A, T, C, or G.

Hood's automatic sequencer enabled work that once took a week or more to be carried out overnight. Later commercial models of the device can read 12,000 base pairs a day, and operate more accurately than any manual sequencing.

In 1992 Bill Gates of Microsoft presented the University of Washington Medical School, Seattle, with $12 million to establish a department of molecular biotechnology. Hood was persuaded to move to Seattle to head the new department, to work on a faster DNA sequencer, and to analyze the genes controlling the human immune response. That same year Hood, in collaboration with Ronald Cape, a former head of the biotechnology firm Cetus, founded Darwin Molecular in Seattle. Their aim is to develop new drugs utilizing processes comparable to natural selection.

Hooke, Robert (1635–1703) *English physicist*

Hooke, whose father was a clergyman from Freshwater on the Isle of Wight, was educated at Oxford University. While at Oxford he acted as assistant to Robert Boyle, constructing the air pump for him. In 1662 Boyle arranged for Hooke to become first curator of experiments to the Royal Society. There he agreed to "furnish the Society every day they meet with three or four considerable experiments." Even though the society only met once a week the pressure on Hooke was still great and may explain why he never fully developed any of his ideas into a comprehensive treatise. He was also something of an invalid.

Hooke made numerous discoveries, perhaps the best known being his law of elasticity, which states that, within the elastic limit, the strain (fractional change in size) of an elastic material is directly proportional to the stress (force per unit area) producing that strain. He was the first to show that thermal expansion is a general property of matter. He also designed a balance spring for use in watches, built the first Gregorian (reflecting) telescope, and invented a number of scientific instruments including the compound microscope and the wheel barometer.

In 1665 he published his main work *Micrographia* (Micrography), which was an account – fully and beautifully illustrated – of the investigations he had made with his improved version of the microscope. It also contained theories of color, and of light, which he suggested was wavelike. This led to one of the major controversies – over the nature of light and the priority of theories – that he had with Isaac Newton. The other conflict was over the discovery of universal gravitation and the inverse square law. It is true that Hooke had revealed, in a letter to Newton in 1680, that he had an intuitive understanding of the form the inverse square law must take. Newton's reply to Hooke's charge of plagiarism was to distinguish between Hooke's general intuition that may have been well founded, and his own careful mathematical treatment of the law and detailed working out of its main consequences.

Hooke was also a capable architect, having written on the theory of the arch and designed parts of London after the great fire of 1666.

Hooker, Sir Joseph Dalton (1817–1911) *British plant taxonomist and explorer*

Hooker was born at Halesworth in Suffolk and studied medicine at Glasgow University, where his father **William Hooker** (1785–1865) was professor of botany. After graduating in 1839, he joined the Antarctic expedition on HMS *Erebus* (1839–43), nominally as assistant surgeon but primarily as naturalist. Between 1844 and 1860, using collections made on the expedition, Hooker produced a six-volume flora of the Antarctic Islands, New Zealand, and Tasmania.

When he returned from the Antarctic expedition Hooker was congratulated on his work by Charles Darwin, who had been following his progress, and in 1844 Darwin confided to Hooker his theory of evolution by natural selection. This communication later proved important in establishing Darwin's precedence when his theory – together with Alfred Russel Wallace's essentially identical conclusions – was presented by Hooker and George Lyell at the famous Linnaean Society meeting of July 1858.

Following his unsuccessful application in 1845 for the botany chair at Edinburgh University, Hooker was employed to identify fossils for a geological survey, but he took time out between 1847 and 1850 to explore the Indian subcontinent. He visited Sikkim and Assam, Nepal, and Bengal, introducing the brilliant Sikkim rhododendrons into cultivation through the botanical gardens at Kew. Later (1872–97) he produced a seven-volume flora of British India.

In 1855 Hooker was appointed assistant director at Kew Gardens and in 1865 succeeded his father as director. In his 20 years as head of the institute he founded the Jodrell Laboratory and Marianne North Gallery, extended the herbarium, and developed the rock garden. His efforts established Kew as an international center for botanical research and in 1872 he successfully fought a move from the commissioner of works to relegate the gardens to a pleasure park. With George Bentham he produced a world flora, *Genera Plantarum* (1862–83; Genera of Plants) – a major work describing 7569 genera and 97,000 species.

The Kew herbarium is still arranged according to this classification.

Hooker retired from the directorship of Kew in 1885 owing to ill health but continued working until his death.

Hooker, William Jackson (1785–1865)
British botanist. See HOOKER, SIR JOSEPH DALTON.

Hope, Thomas Charles (1766–1844)
British chemist

Hope's father, John Hope, was a professor of botany at Edinburgh University and founder of the new Edinburgh botanic gardens. Thomas, who was born in Edinburgh, studied medicine there and became professor of chemistry at Glasgow in 1787. He returned to Edinburgh in 1795 as joint professor of chemistry with Joseph Black, succeeding Black on his death in 1799. He remained as chemistry professor until 1843.

In 1787 Hope isolated the new element strontium and named it after the town of Strontian in Scotland where it was discovered. At first it was thought to be barium carbonate and was only established as a new metal in 1791. Martin Klaproth made the same discovery independently but a little later.

Hope was also the first to show the expansion of water on freezing and demonstrated that water attains a maximum density a few degrees above its freezing point (actually 3.98°C). He published his results in his paper *Experiment on the Contraction of Water by Heat* (1805).

Hopkins, Sir Frederick Gowland (1861–1947) *British biochemist*

Hopkins was the son of a bookseller and publisher and a distant cousin of the poet Gerard Manley Hopkins. He was born at Eastbourne and, after attending the City of London School, was apprenticed as a chemist in a commercial laboratory, where for three years he performed routine analyses. An inheritance in 1881 allowed him to study chemistry at the Royal School of Mines and at University College, London. His work there brought him to the attention of Thomas Stevenson, who offered Hopkins the post of assistant in his laboratory at Guy's Hospital. Feeling the need of more formal qualifications he began to work for a medical degree at Guy's in 1889, finally qualifying in 1894. In 1898 Hopkins moved to Cambridge, where he remained for the rest of his long life and not only served as professor of biochemistry (1914–43) but also established one of the great research institutions of the century.

In 1901 Hopkins made a major contribution to protein chemistry when he discovered a new amino acid, tryptophan. He went on to show its essential role in the diet, since mice fed on the protein zein, lacking tryptophan, died within a fortnight; the same diet with the amino acid added was life-supporting. This work initiated vast research programs in biochemical laboratories.

In 1906–07 Hopkins performed a classic series of experiments by which he became convinced that mice could not survive upon a mixture of basic foodstuffs alone. This ran against the prevailing orthodoxy, which supposed that as long as an animal received sufficient calories it would thrive. He began by feeding fat, starch, casein (or milk protein), and essential salts to mice, noting that they eventually ceased to grow. Addition of a small amount of milk, however, was sufficient to restart growth. It took several years of careful experiments before, in 1912, Hopkins was prepared to announce publicly that there was an unknown constituent of normal diets that was not represented in a synthetic diet of protein, pure carbohydrate, fats, and salts. Hopkins had in fact discovered what were soon to be called vitamins, and for this work he shared the 1929 Nobel Prize for physiology or medicine with Christiaan EIJKMAN.

At the same time Hopkins was working with Walter Fletcher on the chemistry of muscle contraction. In 1907 they provided the first clear proof that muscle contraction and the production of lactic acid are, as had long been suspected, causally connected. This discovery formed the basis for much of the later work done in this field. Hopkins later isolated the tripeptide glutathione, which is important as a hydrogen acceptor in a number of biochemical reactions.

In England Hopkins did more than anyone else to establish biochemistry as it is now practiced. He had to fight on many fronts to establish the discipline, since many claimed that the chemistry of life involved complex substances that defied ordinary chemical analysis. Instead he was able to demonstrate that it was a chemistry of simple substances undergoing complex reactions. Hopkins was knighted in 1925.

Hopper, Grace (1906–1992) *American mathematician and computer scientist*

Hopper, born Grace Murray, was educated at Vassar and at Yale, where she gained her PhD in 1934. She taught at Vassar until 1944, when she enlisted in the US Naval Reserve and was immediately assigned to Harvard to work with Howard Aiken on the Mark I computer, the ASCC (Automatic Sequence Controlled Calculator), for which she wrote the manual. Although she hoped to remain in the Navy after the war, her age prevented this and she had to be satisfied with the Naval reserve as a second choice. Consequently she remained at Harvard working on the Mark II and the Mark III computers.

In 1949 Hopper moved to Philadelphia to work with J. P. ECKHART and John MAUCHLY on the development of BINAC and remained with the company, despite several changes of ownership, until 1967. During this period she made a number of basic contributions to computer programming. In 1952 she devised the first compiler, a program that translated a high-level language into machine code, named A-O. She went on to produce a data-processing compiler known as Flow-matic.

It was apparent by this time to Hopper and other programmers that the business world lacked an agreed and adequate computer language. Hopper lobbied for a combined effort from the large computer companies and consequently a committee was established in 1959 under the guidance of the Defense Department to develop a common business language. Although she did not serve on the committee, the language developed by them, COBOL (Common Business Oriented Language), was derived in many respects from Flow-matic. For this reason Hopper has often been referred to as 'the mother of COBOL'.

Although Hopper was forced through age to resign from the US Naval reserve in 1966 she was recalled a year later to work on their payroll program. She remained in the Naval reserve until 1986, having by then been promoted to the rank of rear admiral in 1985.

Horrocks, Jeremiah (1619–1641) *English astronomer*

Little is known about the early life of Horrocks (or Horrox) other than that he was born into a Puritan family in Toxteth, Liverpool, and was admitted to Cambridge in 1632. Even though he died 'in his twenty second year' he had made major contributions to astronomy and several original observations.

Horrocks noted that as the orbits of Venus and Mercury fall between the earth and the Sun, it would seem possible that at certain times the inner planets would appear to an observer on the Earth to cross the face of the Sun. The events, known as transits, are so rare that they are unlikely to be seen by chance. Only five transits of

Venus have been observed, those of 1639, 1761, 1769, 1874, and 1882; the next is due in 2004.

At Cambridge, Horrocks had mastered the new astronomy of Kepler. From Kepler's recently published *Rudolphine Tables* (1627), he worked out that a transit of Venus was due on 24 November 1639 at 3 p.m. At this time he was probably working as a curate at Hoole near Preston in Lancashire. He prepared for the transit by directing the solar image on to a large sheet of paper in a darkened room. However, a late November afternoon in Lancashire is not the best time to observe the Sun. For Horrocks there was another problem. The predicted day was a Sunday which meant that the puritan curate could well find himself in church at the crucial moment.

Horrocks was successful in observng the transit, however, and left an account of the day in his *Venus in Sole Visa* (Venus in the Face of the Sun), published posthumously in 1662. The day was cloudy but at 3.15, "as if by divine interposition" the clouds dispersed. He noted a spot of unusual magnitude on the solar disc and began to trace its path; but, he added, "she was not visible to me longer than half an hour, on account of the Sun quickly setting."

With the aid of his observations Horrocks could establish the apparent diameter of Venus as 1′ 12″ compared with the Sun's diameter of 30′, a figure much smaller than the 11′ assigned by Kepler. Horrocks also attempted to determine the solar parallax, and derived, although with little confidence, a figure of 15″, compared with a modern value of 8″.8.

Before his death Horrocks was working on an *Astronomia Kepleriana* (Astronomy of Kepler), and essays on comets, tides, and the Moon. Unfortunately none of this was published until long after his death. Much of his work had been lost in the chaos of the Civil War. Other material sent to a London bookseller was burnt in the Great Fire of 1666. The remainder of his papers were published by John Wallis as *Opera posthuma* (1678; Posthumous Works).

Hounsfield, Sir Godfrey Newbold
(1919–) *British engineer*

Hounsfield was born at Newark in Nottinghamshire and educated in that county before going on to the City and Guilds College, London, and the Faraday House College of Electrical Engineering in London. Having spent the years of World War II in the RAF, he worked for Electrical and Musical Industries (EMI) from 1951 and led the design effort for Britain's first large solid-state computer. Later he worked on problems of pattern recognition. Although he had no formal university education he was granted an honorary doctorate in medicine by the City University, London (1975).

Hounsfield was awarded the 1979 Nobel Prize for medicine, together with the South-African-born physicist Allan CORMACK, for his pioneering work on the application of computer techniques to x-ray examination of the human body. He was knighted in 1981. Working at the Central Research Laboratories of EMI he developed the first commercially successful machines to use computer-assisted tomography, also known as computerized axial tomography (CAT). In CAT, a high-resolution x-ray picture of an imaginary slice through the body (or head) is built up from information taken from detectors rotating around the patient. These 'scanners' allow delineation of very small changes in tissue density. Introduced in 1973, early machines were used to overcome obstacles in the diagnosis of diseases of the brain, but the technique has now been extended to the whole body. Although Cormack worked on essentially the same problems of CAT, the two men did not collaborate, or even meet.

Houssay, Bernardo Alberto (1887–1971) *Argentinian physiologist*

Born in the Argentinian capital, Houssay was the founder and director of the Buenos Aires Institute of Biology and Experimental Medicine. He was also professor of physiology at Buenos Aires from 1910 until 1965, apart from the years 1943–55 when he was relieved of his post by the regime of Juan Perón.

Houssay's work centered upon the role of the pituitary gland in regulating the amount of sugar in the blood, as well as its effects in aggravating or inducing diabetes. Working initially with dogs, he found that diabetic sufferers could have their condition eased by extraction of the pituitary gland, since its hormonal effect is to increase the amount of sugar in the blood and thus counter the influence of insulin. Deliberate injection of pituitary extracts actually increases the severity of diabetes or may induce it when the condition did not previously exist. He was also able to isolate at least one of the pituitary's hormones that had the reverse effect to insulin. Houssay's work on hormones led to his award, in 1947, of the Nobel Prize for physiology or medicine, which he shared with Carl and Gerty Cori. He was the author of *Human Physiology* (1951).

Hoyle, Sir Fred (1915–) *British astronomer*

The son of a textile merchant from Bingley in Yorkshire, England, Hoyle was educated at Cambridge. After graduating in 1936 he remained at Cambridge as a graduate student before being elected to a fellowship at St. John's College in 1939. Hoyle spent World War II working on the development of radar at the Admiralty. After the war he returned to Cambridge and was appointed Plumian Professor of Astronomy in 1958.

Hoyle first came to prominence in 1948 with his formulation of the 'steady-state theory' of the universe. He was aware that cosmology at the time was inadequate in that it required a smaller age for the universe than geologists had attributed to the Earth. Hoyle's ideas about the steady-state theory were provoked one night in 1946, when he went to see a ghost film with **Hermann Bondi** (1919–) and Thomas Gold. The film was in four parts but linked the sections together to create a circular plot in which the end of the film became its beginning. Hoyle later noted that it showed him that unchanging situations need not be static. The universe could perhaps be both unchanging and dynamic.

Hoyle worked out some of the detailed implications of this view in his 1948 paper *A New Model for the Expanding Universe*. Matter, he argued, was created continually. It arose from a field generated by the matter that already exists – that is, in the manner of the film, "Matter chases its own tail." Created matter is spread throughout the whole of space and, according to the theory, is being produced at a rate of about one atom per year in a volume equal to that of a large building. It is this creation that drives the expansion of the universe. Matter is distributed evenly through space and therefore new clusters of galaxies are forming as other galaxies are receding into the distance.

Although Hoyle's work was initially treated sympathetically, the steady-state theory failed to cope with new evidence emerging in the 1960s from radio astronomy. Counts of radio sources by Martin Ryle in the 1960s and, in particular, the discovery by Robert WILSON and Arno PENZIAS of the cosmic background radiation in 1964, convinced most scientists that the universe had begun with a big bang. Hoyle defended his theory strongly, objecting to the accuracy of the radio counts by arguing that they were so constructed as to allow every error to count against the theory. "Properly analyzed," Hoyle wrote in 1980, "the disproof of the theory claimed in the 1950s and early 1960s fails completely." He has

also suggested that there could be alternative explanations for the background radiation.

Hoyle subsequently felt that he was not committed to the details of any cosmological orthodoxy, such as either the big bang or the steady-state theory of 1948. He spent much time exploring the implications of both theories and, in collaboration with Jayant Narlikar, developing a new theory of gravity. In 1964 they proposed, following some early arguments of Ernst Mach, that the inertia of any piece of matter derives from the rest of the matter in the universe. They also predicted that the gravitational constant changes over time.

Hoyle also worked in the 1950s on the formation of the elements. It was widely believed that carbon could be formed, along with many other elements, in the interior of stars. One reaction proposed required three helium nuclei to fuse into a carbon atom as in:

$$^4\text{He} + {}^4\text{He} + {}^4\text{He} \rightarrow {}^{12}\text{C}$$

Hoyle realized that the reaction would take place too infrequently to account for the abundance of carbon in the universe. Another possibility was a two-stage reaction:

$$^4\text{He} + {}^4\text{He} \rightarrow {}^8\text{Be}$$

$$^8\text{Be} + {}^4\text{He} \rightarrow {}^{12}\text{C}$$

In this, two helium nuclei first form a beryllium nucleus which fuses in turn with another helium nucleus to form carbon. As the Be has a longer life-time than the collision time of two ^{4}He nuclei, the reaction should make the production of carbon more likely. Something more was needed and in 1954 Hoyle predicted that there must be a resonance channel easing the two reaction steps. Hoyle's prediction was confirmed when it was shown experimentally that there was an energy level of 7.65 million electronvolts (MeV) in the ^{12}C nucleus, just above the energy of the Be + ^{4}He structure of 7.366 MeV.

Further work on the formation of the elements was carried out by Hoyle in collaboration with William Fowler and Geoffrey and Margaret Burbidge. In 1957 their work resulted in a paper, commonly referred to as B^{2}FH, that is one of the most authoritative and comprehensive works of modern science. It describes precisely how all the naturally occurring elements other than hydrogen and helium are formed in the interior of stars.

Hoyle spent much of the early 1960s working in the U.S. at the Hale Observatories and at Princeton. In 1967 he was appointed director of the newly formed Institute of Theoretical Astronomy at Cambridge. It was not a happy time. There were bitter disputes with Martin Ryle and the radio astronomers, demands for apologies, and threats of legal action. Hoyle had problems with his requests for funds from the research councils. In 1973 he resigned and since then has held no permanent post.

He has, however, continued to publish on a wide variety of topics. Much of this later work, often in collaboration with Chandra Wickramsingh of Cardiff University, stems from his claim that the blind operation of physicochemical laws would have been insufficient to shuffle an assortment of amino acids into an enzyme. The odds against this happening by chance were 1 in $10^{40,000}$, as were the chances that an atom with the properties of carbon could be produced by nature. Such considerations led Hoyle to attack the notion of evolution by natural selection.

Hoyle began his campaign with a frontal attack; he asserted that the fossil of *Archaeopteryx* was a fake. Probably the most famous of all fossils, *Archaeopteryx* had been bought by the British Museum in 1862 for £700 and supposedly links reptiles with birds. Hoyle published a paper in 1985 claiming that the skeleton was genuine and of a reptile, but that the feathers had been glued on. Hoyle went on to publish a book on the issue, *Archaeopteryx, the Story of a Fake* (1987) in which he identified Richard Owen as the culprit. Tests of the fossil by the British Museum have failed to detect any glue or cement.

But if enzymes, let alone organisms could not have evolved on Earth, where did they originate? In *Lifecloud* (1978), *Diseases from Space* (1979), and *Space Travellers* (1981), Hoyle argued that life must have come from space. Hoyle was partly led to this view by a longstanding interest in interstellar grains. They had long been thought to be made of ice, but, as they failed to reveal the appropriate infrared absorption bands, this view had to be ruled out. Hoyle pursued the matter and struggled for twenty years to find a particle with the observed spectral properties of the interstellar grains. In 1980 he decided to compare the grains with bacteria and found, to his great surprise, agreement so close that he was forced to conclude that "hitherto unidentified components of dust clouds were in fact bacterial cells."

Hoyle's new theory allowed him to explain not only the origin of life on Earth but also much about the spread of disease. The abrupt appearance of a new disease, such as syphilis in the 15th century, can be seen as a bacterial seeding from a passing comet. Other epidemiological problems can also be solved in this way. How, for example, Hoyle asks, did a group of Amerindians in Suriname, isolated from all alien contact until recently, become infected with the polio virus? Because, Hoyle believes, both forest and city dwellers were infected with pathogens rained on them from above.

Hoyle's numerous other publications cover such areas as the history of astronomy in his *Copernicus* (1973), an important textbook, *Astronomy and Cosmology* (1975), archeo-astronomy in *From Stonehenge to Modern Cosmology* (1972), and a first volume of autobiography in his *The Small World of Fred Hoyle* (1986). He has also written fourteen science-fiction novels, the first being *The Black Cloud* (1957). In 1994 Hoyle published his long-awaited autobiography, *Home is Where the Wind Blows: Chapters from a Cosmologist's Life*.

Hubble, Edwin Powell (1889–1953)
American astronomer and cosmologist

Hubble, who was born in Marshfield, Missouri, was the son of a lawyer. He was educated at the University of Chicago where he was influenced by the astronomer George Hale and, as a good athlete, was once offered the role of 'Great White Hope' in a match against the world heavyweight champion, Jack Johnson. Instead he went to England, accepting a Rhodes scholarship to Oxford University where, between 1910 and 1913, he studied jurisprudence, represented Oxford in athletics, and fought the French boxer, Georges Carpentier. On his return to America he practiced law briefly before returning in 1914 to the study of astronomy at the Yerkes Observatory of the University of Chicago. He obtained his PhD in 1917. After being wounded in France in World War I he took up an appointment in 1919 at the Mount Wilson Observatory in California where Hale was director and where he spent the rest of his career.

Hubble's early work involved studies of faint nebulae, which in the telescopes of the day appeared as fuzzy extended images. He considered that while some were members of our Galaxy and were clouds of luminous gas and dust, others, known as spiral nebulae, probably lay beyond the Galaxy. After the powerful 100-inch (2.5-m) telescope went into operation at Mount Wilson he produced some of the most dramatic and significant astronomy of the 20th century. In 1923 he succeeded in resolving the outer region of the Andromeda nebula into "dense swarms of images which in no way differ from those of ordinary stars." To his delight he found that several of them were Cepheids, which allowed him to use Harlow Shapley's calibration of the period-luminosity curve to determine their distance as the unexpectedly large 900,000 light-years. Although this conflicted sharply with the results of Adriaan van Maanen, Hubble continued with his observations. Between 1925 and 1929 he published three major papers showing that the spiral nebulae were at enormous distances, well outside our own Galaxy, and were in fact isolated systems of stars, now called spiral galaxies. This was in agreement with the work of Heber Curtis. In 1935 van Maanen reexamined his data and, appreciating their unsatisfactory nature, withdrew the final objection to Hubble's results.

In 1929 Hubble went on to make his most significant discovery and announced what came to be known as *Hubble's law*. Using his own determination of the distance of 18 galaxies and the measurements of radial velocities from galactic red shifts carried out by Vesto Slipher and Milton Humason, he saw that the recessional velocity of the galaxies increased proportionately with their distance from us, i.e., $v = Hd$, where v is the velocity, d the distance, and H is known as *Hubble's constant*. Further measurements made by Hubble in the 1930s seemed to confirm his earlier insight. It was this work that demonstrated to astronomers that the idea of an expanding universe, proposed earlier in the 1920s by Alexander Friedmann and Georges Lemaître, was indeed correct. The expansion of the universe is now fundamental to every cosmological model.

Hubble's law was soon seen as containing the key to the size, age, and future of the universe. Hubble's constant can be found from the mean value of v/d. Hubble himself gave it a value approximately ten times its presently accepted figure. The constant permits a calculation of the observable size of the universe to be made. The limiting value of recession must be the speed of light (c). If we divide this by H we get a 'knowable' universe with a radius of about 18 billion light-years. Beyond that no signal transmitted could ever reach us, for to do so it would need to exceed the speed of light.

It is also possible to calculate the time that must have elapsed since the original highly compact state of the universe, i.e., the age of the universe. Hubble's own estimate was 2 billion years but with revisions of his constant, cosmologists now, none too precisely, assign a value of between 12 and 20 billion years.

Hubble also made a major contribution to the study of galactic evolution by producing the first significant classification of galaxies. William Herschel had simply classified them as bright or faint, large or small, while his son John Herschel introduced five categories in terms of size, brightness, roundness, condensation, and resolvability, each with five subdivisions. Hubble published his scheme in 1926. It involved dividing galaxies into two classes, elliptical and spiral. Ellipticals could be subdivided on the basis of their degree of ellipticity, ranging from the circular form (E0) to the elongated (E7). Spirals could be either barred or normal spirals which were subdivided in terms of their degree of openness. Although anomalous objects were later discovered that failed to fit it, Hubble's scheme is still used as the basis for galactic classification.

Hubel, David Hunter (1926–)
Canadian–American neurophysiologist

Born in Windsor, Ontario, Hubel was educated at McGill University and then worked at the Montreal Neurological Institute. He moved to America in 1954 and after working at Johns Hopkins joined the Harvard Medical School in 1959 where he was appointed professor of neurobiology from 1968 to 1982.

Beginning in the 1960s, Hubel, in collaboration with the Swedish neurophysiologist **Torsten Wiesel** (1924–), published a number of remarkable papers that explained for the first time the mechanism of visual perception at the cortical level.

Their work was made possible by a number of technical advances. From the early 1950s onward it became possible to use microelectrodes to monitor the activity of a single neuron. Further, the work of Louis Sokoloff allowed workers to identify precise areas of neural activity. Using this latter technique it was thus possible to identify the region known as the striate cortex, located at the back of the cortex in the occipital lobes, as one of the key centers of activity during the visual process.

The cells of the striate cortex seemed to be arranged into columns, or 'hypercolumns' as they were soon described, that run the length of the cortex (3–4 millimeters) from the outer surface to the underlying white matter. Such hypercolumns were further clearly divided into distinct layers. Hubel and Weisel went on to probe the structure, function, and contents of such columns in great detail.

Above all they succeeded in establishing two crucial points. First that the retinal image was mapped in some way on to the striate cortex. That is, to each point on the retina there corresponded a group of cells in the striate cortex that would respond to a stimulation of that point and of no other.

Furthermore, the response could be evoked only by a relatively precise stimulus. Thus there were cells that would respond to a spot of light but not to a line. Cells that responded to lines would do so only to those lines with a specific tilt and if the angle of tilt was changed by as little as $10°$, in either direction, the cells' ability to react would be diminished or even abolished.

As a result of such work the visual cortex has become the best known of all cortical regions. Hubel and Wiesel shared the 1981 Nobel Prize for physiology or medicine with Roger SPERRY.

Huber, Robert (1937–) *German chemist. See* DIESENHOFER, JOHANN.

Huchra, John (1948–) *American astronomer*

Huchra, who was born in Jersey City, New Jersey, was educated at the Massachusetts Institute of Technology and the California Institute of Technology, where he obtained his PhD in 1976. He then moved to Harvard serving as professor of astronomy, and as a staff member at the Smithsonian Astrophysical Observatory.

In the early 1980s Huchra worked on the Tully-Fisher relation, which links the intrinsic luminosity of a spiral galaxy with the rotational velocity of its stars. He found that with regard to galaxies in the Coma cluster there was a departure of up to 20% from the supposed correlation. Huchra went on in 1982 with a number of colleagues to apply the relation to the Local Group of galaxies to see if the peculiar motion tentatively identified by Vera Rubin could be detected. The peculiar velocities of several hundred galaxies in the region of the Virgo cluster were measured. They found that velocities in the direction of Virgo steadily increased, while decreasing on the other side. The result has been interpreted by some as evidence for the existence of The Great Attractor, a proposed massive concentration of galaxies lying beyond the Hydra-Centaurus supercluster.

In 1986 in collaboration with Margaret Geller, Huchra began a galactic survey for the Smithsonian Center for Astrophysics (CfA). They used a 1.5-meter telescope located on Mount Hopkins, Tucson, Arizona and sought to measure the red shifts of galaxies below a magnitude of 15.5 and falling within a wedge of sky 6° wide, 120° long, and out to a distance of about 300 million light years. By 1989 they had mapped the positions of 10,000 galaxies.

To their surprise, instead of producing a uniform distribution their maps revealed large voids within which huge clusters of galaxies were distributed. The largest structure they observed, dubbed The Great Wall, stretched 500 million light years without its edge being found.

Hückel, Erich Armand Arthur Joseph (1896–1980) *German chemist*

Born the son of a physician in Berlin, Hückel was educated at the University of Göttingen, gaining his PhD in 1921. He worked at a number of institutions, including the Zurich Technische Hochschule and in Copenhagen, Leipzig, and Stuttgart, before taking the chair of theoretical physics at Marburg in 1937.

Initially Hückel worked with Debye on electrolyte solutions. From 1930, however, he turned his attention to organic compounds. Since Friedrich Kekulé had discovered the structure of benzene (C_6H_6) in 1865, it had continued to puzzle chemists. Kekulé had shown that the six carbon atoms of benzene were formed into a ring joined by alternating single and double bonds. Organic chemists call such molecules as benzene 'aromatic' thereby indicating, among other things, the molecule's great stability. Yet, double bonds normally make a molecule reactive. How, then, it was asked, can certain molecules like benzene with double bonds be so stable?

In the 1930s Hückel developed an answer to this problem based upon molecular orbital theory. Molecular orbitals are formed from overlapping atomic orbitals. Hückel proposed that the electrons of the pi-orbitals were delocalized and spread diffusely above and below the plane of the carbon ring. As this configuration was energetically more stable than placing electrons in isolated double bonds, benzene's stability followed directly from the model.

Hückel went on to generalize his model to cover other cyclic molecules containing alternating double and single bonds. Aromatic molecules were planar compounds which had precisely $4n + 2$ pi-electrons, where $n = 0, 1, 2, 3....$ This is known as the *Hückel rule*. Benzene represents the case where $n = 1$; and $n = 2$ and $n = 3$ represent the 10 and 14 member aromatic rings of naphthalene and anthracene. For $n = 0$, the predicted aromaticity of a 3 member ring was confirmed in 1962 with the discovery of the cyclopropenyl cation.

Huffman, Donald Ray (1935–) *American physicist*

Born at Fort Worth in Texas, Huffman was educated at Texas Agricultural and Mechanical College, at Rice University, Houston, and at the University of California, Riverside, where he completed his PhD in 1966. After spending a postdoctoral year at the University of Frankfurt, Huffman moved to the University of Arizona, Tucson, in 1967 and was later appointed professor of physics in 1975.

In 1985 in the laboratory of Richard Smalley a new form of carbon had been discovered: C_{60}, known as *buckminsterfullerene*. The C_{60} was produced by vaporizing a graphite target with a pulsed laser beam. The sooty carbon produced in this manner certainly contained a detectable amount of C_{60}, but all efforts to extract the substance from the residue in amounts sufficient to carry out a detailed spectroscopic study failed.

Huffman, in collaboration with Wolfgang Kratschmer of the Max Planck Institute for Physical Chemistry, Heidelberg, was involved in the discovery of the new forms of carbon known as *fullerenes*. For many years they had been interested in the nature of interstellar dust, which they believed to be mainly carbon. The interstellar matter has a characteristic broad absorption spectrum and Huffman and Kratschmer were experimenting with various forms of finely divided carbon produced in electric arcs. During this work, around 1982, they found a form of carbon with a peculiar double hump, which they called "the camel."

When, in 1985, they heard of the discovery of C_{60}, buckminsterfullerene, they suspected that this might be the cause of their camel spectrum. Huffman and Kratschmer reproduced their earlier experimental conditions, in which they had formed a carbon powder by striking an arc between graphite electrodes in a low pressure of helium.

They treated the resulting soot with benzene, from which they crystallized a light-yellow solid, which they named *fullerite*. It was later found to contain about 75% of C_{60} together with 25% of another fullerene, C_{70}. The method has allowed the production of fullerenes in large quantities.

Huggins, Charles Brenton (1901–)
Canadian–American surgeon

Huggins, who was born at Halifax in Nova Scotia, was educated at Acadia University and at the Harvard Medical School, where he obtained his MD in 1924. After graduate training at the University of Michigan he moved to the University of Chicago in 1927 where he has served as professor of surgery since 1936 and director of the May Laboratory of Cancer Research from 1951 until 1969.

In 1939 Huggins made a very simple inference that led to the development of new forms of cancer therapy. Noting that the prostate gland was under the control of androgens (male sex hormones) he concluded that cancer of the prostate might be treated by preventing the production of androgens. Admittedly his proposed treatment of orchiectomy (castration) might appear somewhat severe but it did lead to remissions in some cases and an alleviation of the condition in others.

Huggins soon appreciated however that the same results could probably be achieved by the less drastic procedure of the administration of female sex hormones to neutralize the effect of androgens produced by the testicles. Consequently in 1941 he began to inject his patients with the hormones stilbestrol and hexestrol. He was able to report later that of the first 20 patients so treated 4 were still alive after 12 years. Later workers, inspired by Huggins's work, treated women suffering from cancer of the breast with the male hormone testosterone and claimed improvement in some 20% of the cases.

It was for this work that Huggins shared the 1966 Nobel Prize for physiology or medicine with Peyton Rous.

Huggins, Sir William (1824–1910)
British astronomer and astrophysicist

Huggins, the son of a London silkmercer, attended school for a short period before being educated privately. After a few years in business he retired to devote himself exclusively to the study of science. His first interest was in microscopy but he became absorbed in the work of Gustav Kirchhoff and Robert Bunsen on spectroscopy and the solar spectrum and decided that he would try to do the same with the stars. He equipped himself with the best of instruments including a superb 8-inch (20-cm) glass from Alvan Clark. He spent some time making maps of the terrestrial elements before moving to the stars, collaborating with William Miller, professor of chemistry at King's College, London. He then began the first major intensive spectral investigation of the stars, which lasted until he was 84 years old, when he found that he could no longer see clearly enough. In later life he was also helped by his wife, Margaret, whom he married in 1875.

Huggins's first observations, published in 1863, showed the stars to be composed of known elements occurring on the Earth and in the Sun. His next great discovery came when he obtained the spectra of those nebula that earlier astronomers had failed to resolve into stars. His excitement is apparent in his report: "I looked into the spectroscope. No spectrum such as I expected! A single bright line only! ... The riddle of the nebula was solved ... Not an aggregation of stars, but a luminous gas." He quickly examined the spectra of over 50 nebulae and found that a third were gaseous. In the same year he obtained the spectra of a comet and found that it contained hydrocarbons. In 1866 he showed that a nova was rich in hydrogen. He also discovered previously unidentified bright emission lines in the spectra of certain nebulae and attributed them to a new element 'nebulium'. The true explanation for these forbidden lines was not provided until the next century, by Ira Bowen.

In 1868 Huggins successfully employed a use of spectroscopy that has had a more profound impact on cosmology than anything else. It had been shown by Christian Doppler and Armand Fizeau that the light waves of an object leaving an observer would have a lower frequency, and the frequency of an object approaching an observer should increase. In spectral terms this means that the spectra of the former object should be shifted toward the red and the latter toward the blue. In 1868 Huggins examined the spectrum of Sirius and found a noticeable red shift. As the degree of the shift is proportional to the velocity, Huggins was able to calculate that the speed of recession of Sirius was about 25 miles (40 km) per second. He quickly determined the velocity of many other stars. He and Lady Huggins published their spectral work in its entirety as the *Atlas of Representative Stellar Spectra* in 1899. Huggins had tried to photograph Sirius but was only successful in 1876 by which time the gelatine dry plate had been developed.

Huggins was knighted in 1897, and was president of the Royal Society from 1900 to 1905.

Hulse, Russell Alan (1950–) *American astrophysicist*

Hulse was born in New York City. He was interested in science from an early age. In 1963 he entered the Bronx High School of Science and in 1966 went to Cooper Union college in lower Manhattan. In 1974 Hulse was working as a graduate student at the University of Massachusetts, Amherst, under the supervision of Joseph TAYLOR. It was arranged that he would spend the summer in Puerto Rico using the Arecibo Radio Telescope to search for pulsars, a type of

star first observed by Jocelyn Bell Burnell in 1967. Among several pulsars detected by Hulse one particular example, named 1913+16 in the constellation Aquila, proved to be of special significance.

Hulse initially found that the pulsar had a short period of 0.059 seconds. More detailed examination, however, revealed that the pulse rate was not constant but varied by some 5 microseconds from day to day. At first Hulse suspected a computer fault. But despite writing a new program, the variability remained. Eventually Hulse spotted that the variation was cyclical repeating itself every 7.75 hours.

Such phenomena, Hulse argued, would arise naturally if the pulsar was a binary, orbiting an undetected companion star. This would produce a Doppler effect. That is, when the pulsar travels in its orbit towards the Earth the pulses would be crowded together, giving a greater than average pulse rate; when, however, it traveled away from the Earth the pulses would be more spread out and yield a lower than average frequency.

In collaboration with Taylor, Hulse went on to establish some of the basic properties of the pulsar. It appeared to have a mass equivalent to 2.8 solar masses, was thought to be a neutron star with a diameter no more than 20–30 kilometers, and to have an approaching velocity of 300 kps (kilometers per second) and a receding velocity of 75 kps. For his work in this field Hulse shared the 1993 Nobel Prize for physics with Joseph Taylor.

After completing his work on the pulsar 1913+16 in 1977 Hulse moved to Princeton, abandoned astronomy, and began to work at the Plasma Physics Laboratory.

Hulst, Hendrik Christoffell van de
See VAN DE HULST, HENDRIK CHRISTOFFELL.

Humason, Milton La Salle (1891–1972) *American astronomer*

Born in Dodge Center, Minnesota, Humason had no formal university training – in fact he began work as a donkey driver moving supplies to the Mount Wilson Observatory in southern California. Here he quickly developed an interest in astronomy and its techniques, an interest that was stimulated by the staff of the observatory. He was taken on as janitor and by 1919 he was competent enough to be appointed assistant astronomer on the staff of the Mount Wilson Observatory and, after 1948, of the Palomar Observatory, where he spent the rest of his career.

In the 1920s Edwin Hubble formulated

his law that the distance of the galaxies was proportional to their recessional velocity. This work was based on the careful, painstaking, and difficult measurements of galactic red shifts made by Humason and also by Vesto Slipher. Humason developed extraordinary skill in this field. By 1936, using long photographic exposures of a day or more, he was able to measure a recessional velocity of 40,000 kilometers per second, which took him to the limits of the 100-inch (2.5-m) reflecting telescope at Mount Wilson.

With the opening of the Palomar Observatory he was able to use the 200-inch (5-m) Hale reflector and by the late 1950s was obtaining velocities of over 100,000 km per second; this corresponded to a distance, according to Hubble's law, of about six billion light-years.

Hume-Rothery, William (1899–1968)
British metallurgist

The son of a lawyer, Hume-Rothery was born at Worcester Park in Surrey. He originally intended to pursue a military career and consequently entered the Royal Military Academy, Woolwich, on leaving school. An attack of meningitis which left him totally deaf forced him to leave the army and he turned instead to chemistry. Although refused entry to his father's college, Trinity College, Cambridge, because of his deafness, he was more graciously received by Magdalen College, Oxford. After obtaining his PhD from the Royal School of Mines in 1925, Hume-Rothery returned to Oxford where he remained for the rest of his life, being appointed in 1958 to the university's first chair of metallurgy.

With 178 published papers to his credit Hume-Rothery illuminated many areas of metallurgy. His best-known work was concerned with alloys that are solid solutions, in which atoms of the constituent metals share a common lattice. The *Hume-Rothery rules* give the conditions that have to be satisfied for metallic solid solutions to form. The first concerns the atomic size factor and claims that if the atomic diameter of the solvent differs in size from that of the solute by more than 14%, the chances of solubility are small. Secondly, the more electronegative is one component and the more electropositive the other, the more they are likely to form compounds rather than solutions. And, finally, a metal of lower valency is more likely to dissolve one of higher valency than vice versa. Much of his work in this field was published in his book *The Structure of Metals and Alloys* (1936).

Hutchinson, George Evelyn
(1903–1991) *American biologist*

Hutchinson was born in Cambridge, and graduated from the university there in 1924. He was senior lecturer at the University of Witwatersrand (1926–28) before emigrating to America where he served as Sterling Professor of Zoology at Yale from 1945 until 1971. He received American citizenship in 1941.

Hutchinson's most important work was concerned with aquatic ecosystems and the physical, chemical, meteorological, and biological conditions of lakes. He made particular studies of the classification and distribution of aquatic bugs (Hemiptera), and investigated water mixing and movement in stratified lakes, proving the circulation of phosphorus. He also studied lake sediments and investigated certain aspects of evolution. His work took him to many different regions, including the lakes of western Transvaal, Tibet, and northeastern North America. Hutchinson published much of his life's work in his *A Treatise on Limnology* (3 vols., 1957–75); a fourth volume was completed shortly before his death and published in 1993.

Hutchinson, John (1884–1972) *British botanist*

Hutchinson, who was educated at the village school in Wark-on-Tyne where he was born, began work in 1900 under his father, the head gardener on a large estate. In 1904 he was appointed to a junior post at the Royal Botanic Gardens, Kew, where he remained for the rest of his career. Starting as an assistant in the herbarium he was in charge of the Africa section from 1919 until 1936 when he became keeper of the Museum of Economic Botany, a post he occupied until his retirement in 1948.

Hutchinson's most significant work was his *Families of Flowering Plants* (2 vols. 1926–34; 2nd edition 1959), which contains details of 342 dicotyledon and 168 monocotyledon families. Hutchinson drew most of the illustrations for this work himself. In it he concentrated on the different plant families that various workers had considered the most primitive. He concluded that bisexual flowers with free petals, sepals, etc., as seen in the magnolia and buttercup families, are more ancient than the generally unisexual catkinlike flowers found in the nettle and beech families, which lack these parts. This conclusion supported the classification of George Bentham and Joseph Hooker and added weight to arguments against the system of Adolf Engler. Furthermore Hutchinson stated that families with apparently more simple flowers are in fact more advanced, and have evolved by reduction from more complex structures; that is, the families show retrograde evolution. In this, the now generally accepted view, Hutchinson was developing the earlier ideas of the German botanist, Alexander Braun.

An enormously prolific and industrious worker Hutchinson also published, with John Dalziel, the standard work, *Flora of West Tropical Africa* (1927–36) and at the time of his death was engaged in a revision of the *Genera Plantarum* (Genera of Plants) of Bentham and Hooker.

Hutton, James (1726–1797) *British geologist*

Hutton was born in Edinburgh, the son of a merchant who became the city treasurer. He was educated at Edinburgh University, which he left in 1743 to be apprenticed to a lawyer. This did not retain his interest long for, in 1744, he returned to the university to read medicine. He studied in Paris for two years and finally gained his MD from Leiden in 1749. He next devoted several years to agriculture and industry, farming in Berwickshire and commercially producing sal ammoniac. In 1768 he returned to Edinburgh, financially independent, and devoted himself to scientific studies, especially of geology, for the rest of his life.

Hutton's uniformitarian theories were first published as a paper in 1788 and later extended into a two-volume work, *Theory of the Earth* (1795). This work proved difficult to read and it only reached a wide audience when his friend John Playfair edited and summarized it as *Illustrations of the Huttonian Theory* (1802). It marked a turning point in geology. The prevailing theory of the day, the neptunism of Abraham Werner, was that rocks had been laid down as mineral deposits in the oceans. However, Hutton maintained that water could not be the only answer for it was mainly erosive. The water could not account for the nonconformities caused by the foldings and intrusions characteristic of the Earth's strata. Hutton showed that the geological processes that had formed the Earth's features could be observed continuing at the present day. The heat of the Earth was the productive power, according to Hutton, that caused sedimentary rocks to fuse into the granites and flints, which could be produced in no other way. It could also produce the upheaval of strata, their folding and twisting, and the creation of mountains.

A long time scale is essential to Hutton's theory of uniformitarianism as the forces of erosion and combustion work, in general, only slowly, as demonstrated by the presence of visible Roman roads. He concluded that on the face of the Earth "we find no vestige of a beginning – no prospect of an end."

Hutton's work was accepted with little delay by most geologists, including the leading Edinburgh neptunist, Robert Jameson. In the 19th century Charles Lyell expanded the theories of uniformitarianism and these were to influence Charles Darwin in his theory of evolution.

Huxley, Sir Andrew Fielding (1917–) *British physiologist*

Huxley, a grandson of T. H. Huxley, was born in London and graduated in 1938 from Cambridge University, receiving his MA there three years later. He is best known for his collaboration with Alan Hodgkin in elucidating the 'sodium pump' mechanism by which nerve impulses are transmitted, for which they were awarded, with John Eccles, the Nobel Prize for physiology or medicine (1963). He has also done important work on muscular contraction theory and has been involved in the development of the interference microscope and ultramicrotome. Huxley was reader in experimental biophysics at Cambridge (1959–60), and from 1960 to 1969 was Jodrell Professor of Physiology at University College, London. In 1969 he was elected research professor becoming emeritus professor in 1983. In 1980 he succeeded Alexander Todd as president of the Royal Society, a position he held until 1985. He also served as master of Trinity College, Cambridge, from 1984 to 1990 and was knighted in 1974.

Huxley, Hugh Esmor (1924–) *British molecular biologist*

Huxley (no relation to T. H. Huxley or any of his descendants) was born at Birkenhead near Liverpool. He studied physics at Cambridge University where he obtained his PhD in 1952 after wartime research on the development of radar. Like many other physicists after the war Huxley was interested in applying physics to biological problems. After two years in America at the Massachusetts Institute of Technology and the period 1956–61 at the biophysics unit of the University of London, he returned to Cambridge to join the staff of the Medical Research Council's molecular biology laboratory, where he remained until 1987. In 1988 he became director and professor of biology at Brandeis University, Boston. He also served from 1988 to 1994 as director of the Rosenstiel Basic Medical Sciences Research Centre.

In 1953, in collaboration with Jean Hanson, Huxley proposed the sliding-filament theory of muscle contraction. This was based on his earlier study of myofibrils, the contractile apparatus of muscle, with the electron microscope. He found that myofibrils are made of two kinds of filament, one type about twice the width of the other. Each filament is aligned with other filaments of the same kind to form a band across the myofibril, and the bands of thick and thin filaments overlap for part of their length. The bands are also linked by an elaborate system of crossbridges. When the muscle changes length the two sets of filaments slide past each other. Further, the two sorts of filaments can be identified with the two chief proteins of muscle, myosin in the thick filament and actin in the thin. This made possible an elegant solution to how muscles contract at the molecular level.

In the areas where both kinds of protein are in contact, Huxley suggested that one, most probably myosin, serves as an enzyme, splitting a phosphate from ATP and so releasing the energy required for contraction. He concluded that the evidence of the combination of actin and myosin is seen in the bridges between the two kinds of filaments.

The theory has since been much enlarged and taken to deeper levels of molecular understanding. Despite this, the basic insight of Huxley and Hanson has remained intact.

Huxley, Sir Julian Sorell (1887–1975)
British biologist

A grandson of T. H. Huxley, Julian Huxley was born in London and graduated in zoology from Oxford University in 1909. He did research on sponges (Porifera) at the Naples Zoological Station (1909–10) before taking up the post of lecturer in biology at Oxford (1910–12). From 1912 until 1916 he worked at the Rice Institute, Houston, Texas, where he met the famous American geneticist Hermann Muller. Before returning to Oxford to take up the post of senior demonstrator in zoology (1919–25) he saw war service in Italy. He was next appointed professor of zoology at King's College, London (1925–27), resigning from this post to devote more time to writing and research.

Huxley was a keen ornithologist and published, in 1914, a classic paper on the courtship of the great crested grebe. In the 1930s he was involved in the production of natural-history films, the most notable of which was the highly praised *Private Life of the Gannet* (1934), which he produced with

the help of R. M. Lockley. One of the leading popularizers of science of modern times (especially the years before and just after World War II), Huxley spent much of his life explaining advances in natural science to the layman and in advocating the application of science to the benefit of mankind. To many he is best remembered as a most capable and lucid educationalist, but Huxley was also eminent in many other fields.

In 1946 he was appointed the first director-general of UNESCO, a post he held for two years. As an administrator, he also did much to transform the Zoological Society's collections at Regent's Park (London Zoo). Viewing man as "the sole agent of further evolutionary advance on this planet," he caused considerable controversy by advocating the deliberate physical and mental improvement of the human race through eugenics. Huxley's biological research was also extensive, carrying out work on animal hormones, physiology, ecology, and animal (especially bird) behavior as it relates to evolution. He was president of the Institute of Animal Behaviour and the originator of the term 'ethology', now in general use to define the science of animal behavior. He also introduced several other scientific terms, such as cline and clade.

Huxley's publications are extensive and include *Evolution: the Modern Synthesis* (1942, 1963). He was knighted in 1958.

Huxley, Thomas Henry (1825–1895)
British biologist

Huxley, the seventh child of a school teacher, was born in Ealing and received only two years' schooling. From the age of 10 he educated himself, doing sufficiently well to be admitted to Charing Cross Hospital to study medicine. He graduated in 1845 and the following year was employed as surgeon on HMS *Rattlesnake*, which was due to survey the Torres Strait between Australia and Papua. During the voyage Huxley studied the marine life of tropical waters and wrote an important paper on the medusae (jellyfish) and related species, naming a new phylum, the Coelenterata, into which these were placed. Recognizing the value of this work, the Royal Society elected Huxley a member in 1851. In 1854 he became lecturer in natural history at the Royal School of Mines (later the Royal College of Science) and while there gave a lecture entitled "The Theory of the Vertebrate Skull," which disproved the idea that the skull originates from the vertebrae.

Huxley is best remembered as the main advocate of Charles Darwin's theory of evolution, and in 1860 – the year following the publication of *The Origin of Species* – he took part in the famous debate with the bishop of Oxford, Samuel Wilberforce, at the Oxford meeting of the British Association for the Advancement of Science. During the discussion Wilberforce asked whether Huxley traced his ancestry to the apes on his mother's or father's side of the family. Huxley answered witheringly that given the choice of a miserable ape and a man who could make such a remark at a serious scientific gathering, he would select the ape. The meeting resulted in a triumph for science, and after it Huxley continued to gain the better of many other distinguished theologians in long academic wrangles. He introduced the term *agnosticism* to describe his own view that since knowledge rested on scientific evidence and reasoning (and not blind faith) knowledge of the nature and certainty about the very existence of God was impossible.

Huxley worked hard to better educational standards for the working classes and spoke out against the traditional method of learning by rote. He opened Josiah Mason College (later Birmingham University), Owens College Medical School (later part of Manchester University), and Johns Hopkins University, Baltimore. Huxley was the grandfather of the author Aldous Huxley, the Nobel Prize winner Andrew Huxley, and the biologist Sir Julian Huxley.

Huygens, Christiaan (1629–1695)
Dutch physicist and astronomer

Huygens, whose father was the famous Renaissance poet Constantin Huygens, was born in The Hague and studied at the University of Leiden and the College of Breda. He worked in Paris as one of the founding members of the French Academy of Sciences from 1666 to 1681 when, as a Protestant, he found the growing religious intolerance threatening, and returned to The Hague. His first work was in mathematics, but his greatest achievements were in physical optics and dynamics, and his importance to 17th-century science is second only to that of Newton.

Huygens's first great success was the invention of the pendulum clock. Galileo had noted in 1581 that a pendulum would keep the same time whatever its amplitude. Many, including Galileo himself, had tried unsuccessfully to use this insight to construct a more reliable clock. Huygens showed that a pendulum that moves in the arc of a circle does not move with an exactly equal swing. To produce an isochronous (equal-timed) swing it would need to move in a curve called a cycloid. It should be emphasized that Huygens worked this out largely from first principles. He also showed how the pendulum could be constructed so to move in a cycloidal path and how to make the connection to the escapement. The first clock was made to his design by Salomon Coster in 1657 and was described in Huygens's book *Horologium* (1658; The Clock). The pendulum became one of the basic tools of 17th-century scientific investigation.

Huygens also made major contributions to astronomy as a designer of improved telescopes and as an observer of Saturn. He discovered Titan, Saturn's largest satellite, in 1655 and after prolonged observation was able to describe Saturn's rings correctly.

In 1673 Huygens published *Horologium oscillatorium* (The Clock Pendulum), a brilliant mathematical analysis of dynamics, including discussions of the relationship between the length of a pendulum and its period of oscillation, and the laws of centrifugal force. It also included an early formulation of Newton's first law of motion: that without some external force, such as gravity, a body once set in motion would continue in a straight line. His views on gravity were worked out in *Discours de la cause de la pesanteur* (1690; Discourse on the Cause of Gravity). As a Cartesian (a follower of René Descartes) he could not accept Newtonian action at a distance or, in fact, any talk of forces. Instead he would only accept a mechanical explanation, which meant a return to some kind of vortex theory. That is, bodies can only be heavy not because they are attracted by another body but because they are pushed by other bodies.

Huygens's greatest achievement was his development of the wave theory of light, described fully in his *Traité de la lumière* (1690; Treatise on Light). He assumed that space was pervaded by ether formed of particles, the disturbance of which constituted the radiation of light with the disturbance of one particle being passed on to its neighbor and so on. The disturbances can be considered as waves spreading in a regular spherical form from the point of origin – the particles disturbed in phase constituting a wave front. Each point on a wave front may be regarded as a source of new secondary wavelets and a surface tangent joining such wavelets (i.e., the envelope of the secondary wavelets) can be considered as a new wave front. This method of treating light waves is known as the *Huygens construction*. Using it, Huygens dealt with reflection and refraction and predicted – as Newtonian theory did not – that light should travel more slowly in a denser medium. But as Huygens considered the waves to be longitudinal, the theory could not explain polarization.

Newton's *Opticks* (1704) presented a corpuscular (particle) theory of light, and the wave theory lay dormant until it was taken up by Thomas Young and his contemporaries.

Hypatia (c. 370–415) Greek
mathematician

Hypatia, who was born in Alexandria, Egypt, was the daughter of Theon of Alexandria, the author of a well-known commentary of Ptolemy. In 400 she was reported to be head of the Neoplatonic school in Alexandria. None of her work has survived, although some information about her comes from the letters of her pupil Synesius of Cyrene. To her have been attributed commentaries on Ptolemy's *Almagest*, Diophantus's *Arithmetic*, and Apollonius's *Conics*. She also designed several scientific instruments including an astrolabe, a hydrometer, and a still.

Learning and science came to a violent conclusion in Alexandria and in the West, as did Hypatia. In conflict with Cyril, bishop of Alexandria, through her friendship with Orestes, the Roman prefect of the city, she was killed by a Christian mob. The circumstances of her death in March 415 have been described by the fifth-century historian Socrates Scholasticus:

"All men did both reverence and had her in admiration for the singular modesty of her mind. Wherefore she had great spite and envy owed unto her, and because she conferred oft, and had great familiarity with Orestes, the people charged her that she was the cause why the bishop and Orestes were not become friends. To be short, certain heady and rash cockbrains whose guide and captain was Peter, a reader of that Church, watched this woman coming home from some place or other, they pull her out of her chariot: they hail her into the Church called Caesarium: they stripped her stark naked they raze the skin and rend the flesh of her body with sharp shells, until the breath departed out of her body: they quarter her body: they bring her quarters unto a place called Cinaron and burn them to ashes."

The manner of her death and reports of her intellect and beauty have made her a romantic figure. For many centuries, with the possible exception of the alchemist Marie the Jewess, she was regarded as the only woman scientist of the Ancient World.

Ignarro, Louis J. (1941–) *American pharmacologist*

Ignarro, who was born in Brooklyn, New York, graduated with a BA in pharmacy from Columbia University in 1962 and four years later gained his PhD in pharmacology at the University of Minnesota. From 1979 to 1985 he worked in the department of pharmacology at Tulane University School of Medicine, New Orleans. Since 1985 he has been at the UCLA School of Medicine, Los Angeles, California. In 1998 he shared the Nobel Prize for physiology or medicine with Robert FURCHGOTT and Ferid MURAD for their discovery that molecules of the gas nitrogen monoxide (nitric oxide, NO) can transmit signals in the cardiovascular system. The hitherto unknown substance endothelium-derived relaxing factor (EDRF) had been discovered by Furchgott in 1980. Ignarro made a series of brilliant analyses to determine the chemical nature of EDRF and in 1986 concluded, independently of and together with Furchgott, that the mystery substance was indeed nitrogen monoxide.

I-Hsing (c. 681–c. 727) *Chinese mathematician and astronomer*

I-Hsing was a Buddhist monk around whom many legends have grown. Only a small portion of his work has survived so it is difficult to appreciate it in detail. There is, however, no reason to doubt his involvement in two major astronomical achievements. During the period 723–26, in collaboration with the Astronomer Royal, Nankung Yueh, expeditions were organized to measure, astronomically, the length of a meridional line. Over a distance of 1553 miles (2500 km) along this line, simultaneous measurements of the Sun's solstitial shadow were made at nine stations. The estimated length of a degree, on the basis of their measurements, was far too large and it must be supposed that some systematic error in the method of observation was taking place. However, when it is appreciated that research expeditions to determine the length of a meridional degree were not organized in Europe until the 17th century, the amazing nature of I-Hsing's work can be appreciated. He also probably anticipated Su Sung in the use of an escapement in an astronomical clock. It was described in a

13th-century encyclopedia: "Water, flowing into scoops, turned a wheel automatically, rotating it one complete revolution in one day and one night." This turned various rings representing the motion of the celestial bodies. It was soon reported to be corroded, relegated to a museum, and to have fallen into disuse.

Ingenhousz, Jan (1730–1799) *Dutch plant physiologist and physician*

Ingenhousz, who was born at Breda in the Netherlands, studied medicine, chemistry, and physics at the universities of Louvain and Leiden, receiving his MD from Louvain in 1752. In 1765 he visited London and became expert at administering smallpox inoculations using Edward Jenner's method. News of his expertise spread and he was invited to Vienna in 1768 by the Empress Maria Theresa to inoculate her family and to become court physician.

In 1779, Ingenhousz returned to England and published his work on gaseous exchange in plants. His experiments demonstrated that plants absorb carbon dioxide and give off oxygen (in his words, "purify the air") only in the light, and that the reverse process occurs in the dark. The light process later became known as photosynthesis. Ingenhousz also conducted research on soils and on plant nutrition, improved apparatus for generating static electricity, and studied heat conduction in metals.

Ingold, Sir Christopher Kelk (1893–1970) *British chemist*

Ingold, a Londoner, was educated at the University of Southampton and at Imperial College, London. After serving as professor of organic chemistry at the University of Leeds from 1924 until 1930, he moved to the chair of chemistry at University College, London, where he remained until his retirement in 1961.

With over 400 papers to his credit and as the author of the classic text, *Structure and Mechanism in Organic Chemistry* (1953), Ingold was one of the leading figures in British chemistry. The basic aim running through all his work was to understand the mechanism of organic reactions, particularly the kinetics of elimination and substitution reactions. In 1926 he introduced the idea of mesomerism, fully explained in his paper

Principles of an Electronic Theory of Organic Reactions (1934). This was similar to the concept of resonance proposed by Linus Pauling in the early 1930s. The basic idea was that if a molecule could exist in two electronic structures then its normal state was neither one nor the other but some 'hybrid' form. This theory was substantiated by measuring bond lengths in appropriate molecules.

Ingram, Vernon Martin (1924–)
German–British–American biochemist

Ingram, born Immerwahr in Breslau (now Wrocław in Poland), was brought to Britain as a refugee from Nazi Germany as a child. He was educated at Birkbeck College, London, where he obtained his PhD in 1949. After working briefly at Rockefeller and Yale he returned to England and joined the staff of the Medical Research Council's molecular biology unit at the Cavendish Laboratory, Cambridge, in 1952. In 1958 however he moved to the Massachusetts Institute of Technology where he has served as professor of biochemistry since 1961 and as John and Dorothy Wilson Professor of Biology since 1988.

By the mid 1950s it was clear to Francis Crick that it should be possible, and was indeed essential, for molecular biology to be able to show that mutant genes produced changes in the amino acid sequences of proteins. Although such a claim was central to the supposed revolution in molecular biology, there was, as Crick realized in 1955, no direct evidence that proteins are in fact coded by genes.

Consequently Crick and Ingram attempted to reveal such a change in the lysozyme of fowl eggs. However, although they succeeded in distinguishing differences between lysozymes from such different birds as duck and pheasant, they failed to find any difference in lysozymes between two hens of the same species. At this point however Max Perutz gave Ingram some sickle-cell hemoglobin (hemoglobin S) to work with. (Hemoglobin S, possessed by sufferers of a crippling anemia, had been distinguished from normal hemoglobin A by Linus Pauling and his student Harvey Itano in 1949.) Ingram split the hemoglobin into smaller units by using the enzyme trypsin to break the peptide bonds. He then separated these units by electrophoresis and paper chromatography. This allowed him to show that hemoglobin S differs from normal hemoglobin at just one site where the amino acid valine replaces the glutamic acid of the A form. Although it came as a surprise that the alteration of one amino

acid in over 500 could produce such major effects, it also dramatically established that molecular biology was not just an abstract and remote branch of structural chemistry.

Ingram went on to show that this and other point mutations of hemoglobin could be used to trace the evolutionary history of vertebrates, work reported in his *The Hemoglobins in Genetics and Evolution* (1963).

Ipatieff, Vladimir Nikolayevich
(1867–1952) *Russian–American chemist*

Ipatieff, a Muscovite by birth, became an officer in the Imperial Russian Army in 1887 and was educated at the Mikhail Artillery Academy (1889–92) in St. Petersburg. After further study in Germany and France he returned to the academy in 1898 and became professor of chemistry until 1906.

While in Munich (1897) Ipatieff achieved the synthesis of isoprene, the basic unit of the rubber molecule. On his return to Russia he carried out important work on high-pressure catalytic reactions. The first breakthrough in organic catalysis had been due to Paul Sabatier who had demonstrated the use of finely ground nickel to catalyze hydrogenation of unsaturated hydrocarbons (1897). Ipatieff greatly extended this work. He showed how it could be applied to liquids and demonstrated that the process became much more powerful and adaptable at high pressures. To this end he designed the so-called *Ipatieff bomb* – an autoclave that permitted the heating of substances under pressure to above their boiling point. Thus before World War I Ipatieff had synthesized isooctane, and had polymerized ethylene.

During World War I and after the revolutionary years in Russia Ipatieff held a number of important advisory posts, in addition to continuing with his own research, despite his anti-Communist feelings. In 1930, worried for his own safety, he traveled to America. Despite being 64 when he arrived in America Ipatieff still had much to offer, publishing over 150 papers in this last phase of his career. He was appointed professor of chemistry at Northwestern University, Illinois, (1931–35) and also acted as a consultant to the Universal Oil Products Company of Chicago who, in 1938, established at Northwestern University the Ipatieff High Pressure Laboratory, which he directed. With the growth of the petrochemical industry after 1918, Ipatieff's techniques became widely used. Working in America he showed how low-octane gasolines could be converted to high-octane gasoline by 'cracking' hydrocarbons at high temperatures.

Isaacs, Alick (1921–1967) *British virologist and biologist*

Isaacs, who was born in Glasgow, graduated in medicine from the university there in 1944. After three years' work in the department of bacteriology he moved to Sheffield University for a year and then spent two years in Australia at the Hall Institute for Medical Research, Melbourne. During this time he studied influenza, in particular the genetic variation of the various strains of the virus and also the response of the body to attack by the virus. He continued with this work from 1950 at the National Institute for Medical Research in London, where he was director of the World Influenza Centre.

In 1957, together with the Swiss virologist Jean Lindenmann, Isaacs reported that a specific low-molecular-weight protein, which interfered with the multiplication of viruses, was produced by animal cells when under viral attack. This was interferon, which he studied closely for the rest of his life, investigating problems associated with its production and isolation, its mechanism of action, and its chemical and physical properties.

In the early 1960s his health began to deteriorate but he continued work as head of the Laboratory for Research on Interferon at the National Institute.

Ivanovsky, Dmitri Iosifovich (1864–1920) *Russian botanist*

Ivanovsky was born in Gdov, Russia, and studied natural sciences at St. Petersburg University, graduating in 1888. He obtained his master's degree in botany in 1895 and worked (1896–1901) as an instructor in plant anatomy and physiology at the Technological Institute, St. Petersburg. In 1908 he was appointed professor at the University of Warsaw.

In 1892, following his investigations of tobacco mosaic disease in the Crimea, he demonstrated that a filtrate of the sap from infected tobacco plants had the ability to transmit the disease to healthy plants. Ivanovsky showed that minute crystalline particles were present in the filtrate and asserted that they were somehow linked to the disease. However, he wrongly attributed the cause of the disease to minute bacteria. Ivanovsky's work was confirmed in a publication by the Dutch bacteriologist Martinus Beijerinck in 1898. It was Beijerinck who stated that such infective agents are not bacterial and coined the term *virus*. This, together with the work of the French bacteriologist Charles Chamberland on rabies, was one of the earliest pieces of evidence for the existence of viruses although it was not until 1935 that Wendell Stanley confirmed this.

Jackson, Charles Thomas (1805–1880)
American chemist

Born in Plymouth, Massachusetts, Jackson studied medicine at Harvard and continued his education at the Sorbonne in Paris, working on chemistry and geology. He returned to America and set up a practice in Boston. Jackson's professional career consisted of a series of spectacular claims to the work of others. These started on his homeward voyage and were to persist until he finally became insane in 1873.

While sailing from France to America in 1832 Jackson befriended a fellow American, the portrait painter Samuel Morse, with whom he discussed the possibilities of electric telegraphy. When Morse exhibited his telegraph to Congress in 1837 he found that he had to establish a right to his own invention against Jackson's claim that Morse had stolen it from him. It took Morse seven years to prove the validity of his claim.

In July 1844 Jackson recommended to William Morton, a young dentist lodging with him, that he should try treating his patients using ether, which was commonly used by medical students as a joke. Morton took up his suggestion and found it promising. He experimented on himself, gave up his practice to work on dosages and systems of inhalation, and introduced the anesthetic to the medical profession. Nothing was heard from Jackson until it was clear that money and fame were going to be awarded to someone. When Morton went to Congress to ask for compensation for yielding his patent to the US government he found some senators who took him for a thief. When he went to Paris in 1847 to lecture on his discovery he found that Jackson had already lodged a sealed envelope with the Académie claiming a priority going back to 1842. Committees were set up by governments, states, academies, and professional bodies but Jackson managed to so confuse the issue that when Morton collapsed and died in 1868 he was still fighting his claim and still penniless.

Jackson became obsessive about the discovery, ignored his other work, took to drink, and spent the last seven years of his life in a lunatic asylum. He even wrote a book on the subject, *A Manual of Etherisation* (1861). Curiously, both Morton and Jackson have monuments in the same cemetery, both proudly proclaiming their triumph in alleviating the misery of mankind.

Jackson, John Hughlings (1835–1911)
British neurologist

Jackson was born at Green Hammerton in England and educated at York Hospital and St. Bartholomew's Hospital, London. He received his MD from St. Andrews University in 1860. He served on the staff of the London Hospital as assistant physician (1863) and physician (1874–94) and in 1862 began his long association with the National Hospital for the Paralysed and Epileptic, London. Here he specialized in neurology and ultimately exercised a profound influence on the development of clinical neurology. Through his work with epileptics, he described the condition, now called *Jacksonian seizure* or *Jacksonian epilepsy*, in which part of the leg, arm, or face undergoes spasmodic contraction due to local disease of the cerebral cortex in the brain.

Jackson's work supported the findings of Paul Broca and others – that different bodily functions are controlled by different regions of the cerebral cortex. Jackson also described a local paralysis of the tongue and throat caused by disease of the corresponding cranial nerves. This is now known as *Jackson's syndrome*.

Jacob, François (1920–) *French biologist*

Born at Nancy in France, Jacob served with the Free French forces during World War II. Although badly wounded, he resumed his medical studies in 1945, obtaining his MD from the University of Paris in 1947. In 1950 he became André Lwoff's assistant at the Pasteur Institute, Paris, and, with Elie Wollman, began working on the bacteria, discovered by Lwoff, that carry a nonvirulent virus incorporated in their genetic material. In 1961 they introduced the term 'episomes' for genetic elements that become established in bacterial cells. Jacob and Wollman also studied conjugation in bacteria, the process by which genetic material is transferred from one cell to another. They found that the genes of the donor cell enter the recipient cell in a specific order and by interrupting the process, the position of given genes on the chromosome could be determined.

In 1958 Jacob began collaborating with Jacques MONOD and Arthur Pardee on the control of bacterial enzyme production, research that culminated in a greatly increased understanding of the regulation of gene activity. In 1960 Jacob and Monod proposed the existence of the operon, consisting of an operator gene and structural genes that code for the enzymes needed in a given biosynthetic pathway. When the enzymes are not required another gene outside the operon, the regulator gene, produces a protein that binds with the operator and renders the operon ineffective. Jacob and Monod received the 1965 Nobel Prize for physiology or medicine for this research, sharing the award with Lwoff.

Since 1964, Jacob has occupied the chair of cellular genetics at the Collège de France; the chair was created in his honor. He became a foreign member of the Royal Society in 1973 and a member of the Academy of Sciences, Paris, in 1977. He has also written on some of the wider implications of biology in *The Possible and the Actual* (1981) and has published an autobiography, *The Statue Within* (1987).

Jacobi, Karl Gustav Jacob (1804–1851) *German mathematician*

Jacobi was born at Potsdam, in Germany. After studying in Berlin, he became a lecturer at Königsberg where he managed to attract the favorable attention of Karl Friedrich Gauss. He was a superb teacher and had an astonishing manipulative skill with formulae. He made a brief but disastrous foray into politics that resulted in his losing a pension he had been granted by the king of Prussia.

Jacobi's most important contributions to mathematics were in the field of elliptic functions. Niels Hendrik Abel had partially anticipated some of Jacobi's work, but the two were equally important in the creation of this subject. Jacobi also worked on Abelian functions and discovered the hyperelliptic functions. He applied his work in elliptic functions to number theory.

Jacobi worked in many other areas of mathematics as well as the theory of functions. He was a pioneer in the study of determinants and a certain type of determinant arising in connection with partial differential equations is known as the *Jacobian* in his honor. This work was the result of his interest in dynamics, in which field he continued and developed the work of William Hamilton, and produced results that are important in quantum mechanics.

Jansky, Karl Guthe (1905–1950) *American radio engineer*

Born in Norman, Oklahoma, Jansky was educated at the University of Wisconsin and started his career with the Bell Telephone Laboratories in 1928. He was given the task of investigating factors that could interfere with radio waves used for long-distance communication. He designed a linear directional antenna, which, mounted on wheels from a Model T Ford, could scan the sky. He identified all the sources of interference, such as thunderstorms, except for one weak emission. This he found to be unconnected with the Sun and in 1931 he discovered that the radio interference came from the stars.

Jansky published his findings in the *Proceedings of the Institute of Radio Engineers* in December 1932, the date that marks precisely the beginnings of radio astronomy. In his paper Jansky made two astute comments: he suggested that the radio emission was somehow connected with the Milky Way and that it originated not from the stars but from interstellar ionized gas. He did not pursue his suggestions and it was left to Grote Reber, the amateur astronomer, to keep the subject alive until it developed into a major research field after 1945.

The unit of radio-wave emission strength was named the *jansky* in his honor.

Janssen, Pierre Jules César (1824–1907) *French astronomer*

Janssen studied mathematics and physics at Paris university before becoming professor of general science at the school of architecture. In 1857 he went to Peru to determine the magnetic equator. He observed the transits of Venus of 1874 and 1882 in Japan and Algeria and went on all the major eclipse expeditions. So keen was he to witness the 1870 eclipse in Algeria that he had to escape from the siege of Paris by balloon. While in India in 1868, observing the solar eclipse spectroscopically, he noticed the hydrogen lines visible in the solar prominences and wondered if they could still be detected after the eclipse. The next day he found them still visible. This meant that while photography and observation would still depend on eclipse work the spectroscope could be used almost anywhere anytime. Janssen made one further important discovery on the same trip; he discovered lines in the solar spectrum that he could not identify. He sent his results to Norman Lockyer who suggested that they were produced by some element found only on the Sun, which Lockyer named *helium*. In 1895

William Ramsay discovered a substance on Earth that matched exactly with Janssen's spectral lines.

In later life Janssen arranged for an observatory to be built on Mont Blanc to avoid as much atmospheric interference as possible. Using data from observations made there, he showed that absorption lines in the solar spectrum are caused by elements in the Earth's atmosphere.

Janssen, Zacharias (1580–c. 1638)
Dutch instrument maker. See LIPPERSHEY, HANS.

Jeffreys, Sir Alec John (1950–   )
British geneticist

Jeffreys was born at Luton in Bedforshire and educated at Oxford, where he completed his PhD in 1975. After spending two years at the University of Amsterdam as a research fellow he joined the genetics department of the University of Leicester. He was appointed professor of genetics in 1987 and knighted in 1994.

Jeffreys is noted as the discoverer of the technique known as 'genetic (or DNA) fingerprinting'. In 1984 he was working on the gene that codes for the protein, myoglobin. Part of the gene consisted of short sequences repeated a number of times. The number of repeats was found to vary between individuals and became known as VNTRs ('variable number tandem repeats'). Initially Jeffreys saw the VNTRs as no more than useful gene markers of the myoglobin gene. Later he came to the conclusion that they were unique to the individual – they could act like a fingerprint.

The marker sequences can be identified by cleaving the DNA with restriction enzymes and using a gene probe – a single-strand fragment of DNA or RNA with a base sequence complementary to that of the marker. If the bases are labeled with a radioactive tracer, they can be identified on separation by electrophoresis.

Very small samples of DNA can be used, obtained, for example, from blood, semen, saliva, etc., and the technique has been exploited in forensic science and in the investigation of paternity and other family relationships.

Jeffreys, Sir Harold (1891–1989) *British astronomer and geophysicist*

Jeffreys was born in Birtley in the northeast of England and educated in Newcastle upon Tyne and at Cambridge University. After graduating in 1913 he was made a fellow of his college. He was reader in geophysics from 1931 to 1946 before being elected to the Plumian Professorship of Astronomy and Experimental Philosophy where he remained until his retirement in 1958.

In 1924 Jeffreys produced one of the fundamental works in geophysics of the first half of the 20th century, *The Earth: Its Origin, History, and Physical Constitution*. In this he argued forcibly against Alfred Wegener's proposed theory of continental drift. He demonstrated that the forces proposed by Wegener were inadequate. This did much to inhibit interest and research into drift theory for a while but much new evidence in its favor has since been uncovered.

Jeffreys was also joint author, with Keith Bullen, of the *Seismological Tables* (1935). These, more frequently known as the *JB Tables*, were revised in 1940 and are the present standard tables of travel times of earthquake waves. They allow observers to determine from the elapsed time between the arrival of the primary (P) waves and the secondary (S) waves the distance between the observer and the earthquake.

Jeffreys's work in astronomy included studies on the origins of the universe. He developed James Jeans's theory of tidal evolution. He also devised models for the planetary structure of Jupiter, Saturn, Uranus, and Neptune.

He was knighted in 1953.

Jenner, Edward (1749–1823) *British physician*

Jenner, born a vicar's son at Berkeley in Gloucestershire, was apprenticed to the London surgeon John Hunter from 1770 to 1772. He then returned to country practice and established a reputation as a field naturalist. In 1787 Jenner observed that the newly hatched cuckoo, rather than the adult cuckoo, was responsible for removing the other eggs from the nest. He was elected a fellow of the Royal Society in 1789 partly on the basis of this work. Jenner's lasting contribution to science however is his investigations into the disease smallpox.

In 17th-century London some 10% of all deaths were due to smallpox. In response to this the practice of variolation – inoculation with material taken from fresh smallpox sores – was widely adopted. This was first described in England in 1713. However variolation suffered from two major defects for, if too virulent a dose was given, a lethal case of smallpox would develop and, secondly, the subject inoculated, unless isolated, was only too likely to start an epidemic among those in contact with him.

Jenner had heard reports that milkmaids once infected with cowpox developed a lifelong immunity to smallpox. On 14 May 1796, he made the crucial experiment and took an eight-year-old boy and injected him with cowpox. He followed this on 1 July with injections taken from smallpox pustules, repeating the procedure several months later. On both occasions the boy did not develop smallpox and the same happy result was later observed with other experimental subjects. Jenner's conclusion that cowpox infection protects people from smallpox infection was first published in *An Inquiry into the Causes and Effects of the Variolae Vaccinae* (1798).

General acceptance of Jenner's work was almost immediate. In 1802 he was awarded £10,000 by a grateful House of Commons and in 1804 he was honored by Napoleon who made vaccination compulsory in the French army. Variolation was made illegal in England in 1840 and in 1853 further legislation made the vaccination of infants compulsory. As a consequence of this deaths from smallpox, running at a rate of 40 per 10,000 at the beginning of the 19th century, fell to 1 in 10,000 by the end.

Jensen, Johannes Hans Daniel

(1907–1973) *German physicist. See* GOEPPERT-MEYER, MARIA.

Jerne, Niels Kaj (1911–1994) *Danish immunologist*

London-born Jerne was educated at the University of Copenhagen, where he gained his doctorate in medicine in 1951 while working as a researcher at the Danish State Serum Institute (1943–54). After a period of research at the California Institute of Technology (1954–55), he was appointed chief medical officer with the World Health Organization in Geneva (1956–62) and also professor of biophysics at the University of Geneva (1960–62). He returned to America in 1962 to become head of the department of microbiology at the University of Pittsburgh. Subsequently he served for three years (1966–69) as director of the Paul Ehrlich Institute, Frankfurt, before leaving to found the Basel Institute for Immunology, where he served as director until 1980.

Jerne is noted for his theories concerning the diversity and production of antibodies. In 1955 he proposed the *clonal selection theory* of antibody formation to account for how the body's white blood cells (lymphocytes) are able, potentially, to manufacture such a huge range of different antibodies. He refuted the idea that antibodies are formed from scratch as and when required. Instead, Jerne proposed that different cells, each capable of producing a particular antibody, are present in the body from birth. When an agent such as a virus or bacteria enters the body, its chemical components (antigens) activate the relevant lymphocytes and cause them to divide repeatedly, thereby producing a clone of cells and enhancing manufacture of the appropriate antibody. The theory has since been shown to be correct.

The immense diversity of antibodies presents the problem of how the genome accommodates all the genetic information. Jerne was one of the first to advance the notion that some form of somatic mutation may be involved, an idea that was to lead to the theory of so-called 'jumping genes' and its demonstration in mouse cells by Jerne's colleague, Susumu Tonegawa.

Jerne also constructed a model of immune-system self-regulation based on the interactions of antibodies. Although a valuable contribution, the model does not anticipate the great complexity of control mechanisms revealed by recent discoveries of numerous chemical modulators of the immune system.

For his work, which helped to inspire a whole generation of immunologists, Jerne received the 1984 Nobel Prize for physiology or medicine. The prize was shared with César MILSTEIN and Georges KÖHLER, another colleague of Jerne's working at Basel.

Johannsen, Wilhelm Ludwig

(1857–1927) *Danish botanist and geneticist*

Johannsen was born in the Danish capital Copenhagen. On leaving school in 1872 he became apprenticed to a pharmacist as his father could not afford university fees. From his work in Danish and German pharmacies, Johannsen taught himself chemistry and developed an interest in botany. In 1881 he began work under Johan Kjeldahl in the chemistry department of the Carlsberg laboratories, investigating dormancy in seeds, tubers, and buds.

In 1892 Johannsen became lecturer at the Copenhagen Agricultural College. On reading Francis Galton's *Theory of Heredity* he was impressed by experiments demonstrating that selection is ineffective if applied to the progeny of self-fertilizing plants. Johannsen repeated this work using the Princess bean, but found that selection did work on the offspring of a mixed population of self-fertilizing beans. It was only when plants were derived from a single parent that selection had no effect. He called the descendants of a single parent a 'pure line' and argued that individuals in a pure line are genetically identical: any variation among them is due to environmental effects, which are not heritable. In 1905 he coined the terms *genotype* to describe the genetic constitution of an individual, and *phenotype*, to describe the visible result of the interaction between genotype and environment.

Johannsen explained his ideas in *On Heredity and Variation* (1896), which he revised and lengthened with the rediscovery of Gregor Mendel's laws and reissued as *Elements of Heredity* in 1905. The enlarged German edition of this work became available in 1909 and proved the most influential book on genetics in Europe. In the same year Johannsen proposed the term *genes* to describe Mendel's factors of inheritance. Johannsen's research, with its emphasis on the quantitative variation of characters in populations and the application of statistical methods, played a major role in the development of modern genetics from 19th-century ideas.

In 1905 Johannsen became professor of plant physiology at Copenhagen University and was made rector of the University in 1917. He spent his later years writing on the history of science.

Johanson, Donald Carl (1943–)
American paleoanthropologist

Johanson, who was born in Chicago, gained his BA in anthropology from the University of Illinois in 1966; he received an MA from the University of Chicago in 1970 and a PhD in 1972. Two years later he was appointed professor of anthropology at Case Western Reserve University, Cleveland, and was also made associate curator of anthropology at Cleveland Museum of Natural History. He was later given the position of curator of physical anthropology and director of scientific research at the Museum. In 1981 he moved to California as director of the newly founded Institute of Human Origins at Berkeley, and later became professor of anthropology at Stanford University (1983–89).

In 1973, Johanson led his first expedition to Hadar about 100 miles northeast of Addis Ababa. Here he found a hominid knee joint. The following year he discovered further remains of a new species of fossil primate that challenged the existing theories of the evolution of modern man (*Homo sapiens*) and other hominids. The remains were reconstructed to form, remarkably, a 40% complete skeleton, revealing a female hominid about three and a half feet tall with a bipedal stance and a relatively small brain. The fossil proved to be some 3 million years old, making it the oldest known fossil member of the human tribe. Johan-

son named it *Australopithecus afarensis*, after the Afar triangle of NE Ethiopia where the find was made. The skeleton is popularly called Lucy, prompted by the Beatles' song 'Lucy in the sky with diamonds', which was playing in the camp site of Johanson's team on the evening following their momentous discovery.

During the 1975 season Johanson's team made another dramatic find. Scattered in a single hillside were more than 350 fossil pieces from a group of thirteen men, women, and children, all dating from the same time as Lucy. The 'first family', as it was later called, was Johanson's last major find at Hadar. Following the 1976 expedition a series of military coups, civil wars, and famines closed Ethiopia to scientific expeditions.

Johanson's analysis of the Lucy skeleton showed it to belong to an upright chimpanzee-like creature with an ape-like face, a slightly bow-legged gait, and curved toe and finger bones. According to Johanson, Lucy demonstrated that bipedalism preceded enlarged brain capacity, rather than vice versa, and marked a crucial step towards the evolution of all other antecedents of modern humans, as well as the later australopithecines identified by Raymond Dart.

The findings of Johanson's team were published in 1979, and sparked controversy among other workers in the field, notably Richard Leakey. He maintained that the genus *Homo* could be traced back to an age comparable with the Lucy skeleton, and was descended not from an australopithecine ancestor, such as Lucy, but from some earlier, hypothetical, hominid, perhaps some 4–5 million years old.

Although the precise relationship of *A. afarensis* to the early human ancestors remains in doubt, the significance of Johanson's discovery is unquestioned. His account of the discovery of Lucy was published as *Lucy: The Beginnings of Humankind* (with Maitland A. Edey; 1981). Johanson and Edey have also written *Blueprints: Solving the Mystery of Evolution* (1989).

Joliot-Curie, Frédéric (1900–1958)
French physicist

Frédéric Joliot, the son of a prosperous Paris tradesman, was educated at the School of Industrial Physics and Chemistry. In 1923 he began his research career at the Radium Institute under Marie Curie, where he obtained his doctorate in 1930. He was appointed to a new chair of nuclear chemistry at the Collège de France in 1937 and, after World War II in which he played an important part in the French Resistance, was head of the new Commissariat à l'Energie Atomique (1946–50. In 1956 he became head of the Radium Institute.

In 1926 Joliot married the daughter of Marie Curie, Irène, and changed his name to Joliot-Curie. In 1931 they began research that was to win them the Nobel Prize for chemistry in 1935 for their fundamental discovery of artificial radioactivity (1934). His description of the crucial experiment is as follows: "We bombarded aluminum with alpha rays [the heavy nucleus of a helium atom, made of two protons and two neutrons] ... then after a certain period of irradiation, we removed the source of alpha rays. We now observed that the sheet of aluminum continued to emit positive electrons over a period of several minutes." What had happened was that the stable aluminum atom had absorbed an alpha-particle and transmuted into an (until then) unknown isotope of silicon, which was radioactive with a half-life of about 3.5 minutes. The significance of this was that it produced the first clear chemical evidence for transmutation and opened the door to a virtually new discipline. Soon large numbers of radioisotopes were created, and they became an indispensable tool in various branches of science. Dramatic confirmation of the Joliot-Curies' discovery was provided when Frédéric realized that the cyclotron at the laboratory of Ernest Lawrence in California would have been producing artificial elements unwittingly. He cabled them to switch off their cyclotron and listen. To their surprise the Geiger counter continued clicking away, registering for the first time the radioactivity of nitrogen–13.

In 1939 Joliot-Curie was quick to see the significance of the discovery of nuclear fission by Otto HAHN. He confirmed Hahn's work and saw the likelihood of a chain reaction. He further realized that the chain reaction could only be produced in the presence of a moderator to slow the neutrons down. A good moderator was the heavy water that was produced on a large scale only in Norway at Telemark. With considerable foresight Joliot-Curie managed to persuade the French government to obtain this entire stock of heavy water, 185 kilograms in all, and to arrange for its shipment to England out of the reach of the advancing German army.

Joliot-Curie, Irène (1897–1956) *French physicist*

Irène Curie was born in Paris, the daughter of Pierre and Marie Curie, the discoverers of radium. She received little formal schooling, attending instead informal classes where she was taught physics by her mother, mathematics by Paul Langevin, and chemistry by Jean Baptiste Perrin. She later attended the Sorbonne although she first served as a radiologist at the front during World War I. In 1921 she began work at her mother's Radium Institute with which she maintained her connection for the rest of her life, becoming its director in 1946. She was also, from 1937, a professor at the Sorbonne.

In 1926 Irène Curie married Frédéric Joliot and took the name Joliot-Curie. As in so many other things she followed her mother in being awarded the Nobel Prize for distinguished work done in collaboration with her husband. Thus in 1935 the Joliot-Curies won the chemistry prize for their discovery in 1934 of artificial radioactivity.

Irène later almost anticipated Otto Hahn's discovery of nuclear fission but like many other physicists at that time found it too difficult to accept the simple hypothesis that heavy elements like uranium could split into lighter elements when bombarded with neutrons. Instead she tried to find heavier elements produced by the decay of uranium.

Like her mother, Irène Joliot-Curie produced a further generation of scientists. Her daughter, Hélène, married the son of Marie Curie's old companion, Paul Langevin, and, together with her brother, Paul, became a distinguished physicist.

Joly, John (1857–1933) *Irish geologist and physicist*

Joly was born the son of a clergyman from Hollywood, now in the Republic of Ireland. He entered Trinity College, Dublin, in 1876 where he studied literature and engineering. He taught in the engineering school from 1883 and was appointed professor of geology and mineralogy in 1897, a post he held until his death.

Joly's major geological work was in the field of geochronology. He first tried to estimate the age of the Earth by using Edmond Halley's method of measuring the degree of salinity of the oceans, and then by examining the radioactive decay in rocks. In 1898 he assigned an age of 80–90 million years to the Earth, later revising this figure to 100 million years. He published *Radioactivity and Geology* in 1909 in which he demonstrated that the rate of radioactive decay has been more or less constant through time.

Joly also carried out important work on radium extraction (1914) and pioneered its use for the treatment of cancer. His inventions in physics included a constant-volume gas thermometer, a photometer, and a differential steam calorimeter for measuring the specific heat capacity of gases at constant volume.

Jones, Sir Harold Spencer See GALLE, JOHANN GOTTFRIED.

Jordan, (Marie-Ennemond) Camille
(1838–1922) *French mathematician*

Born at Lyons, Jordan studied in Paris at the Ecole Polytechnique, where he trained as an engineer. Later he taught at both the Ecole Polytechnique and the Collège de France until his retirement in 1912. His interests lay chiefly in pure mathematics, although he made contributions to a wide range of mathematical subjects.

Jordan's most important and enduring work was in group theory and analysis. He was especially interested in groups of permutations and grasped the intimate connection of this subject with questions about the solvability of polynomial equations. This basic insight was one of the fundamental achievements of the seminal work of Evariste Galois, and Jordan was the first mathematician to draw attention to Galois's work, which had until then been almost entirely ignored. Jordan played a major role in starting the systematic investigation of the areas of research opened up by Galois. He also introduced the idea of an *infinite* group.

Jordan also passed on his interest in group theory to two of his most outstanding pupils, Felix Klein and Sophus Lie, both of whom were to develop the subject in novel and important ways.

Jordan, Ernst Pascual (1902–1980)
German theoretical physicist and mathematician

Jordan was educated at the Institute of Technology in his native city of Hannover and at the University of Göttingen, where he obtained his doctorate in 1924. He left Göttingen in 1929 for the University of Rostock and after being appointed professor of physics there in 1935, later held chairs of theoretical physics at Berlin from 1944 to 1952 and at Hamburg from 1951 until his retirement in 1970.

Jordan was one of the founders of the modern quantum theory. In 1925 he collaborated with Max Born and in 1926 with Werner Heisenberg in the formulation of quantum mechanics. He also did early work on quantum electrodynamics. He developed a new theory of gravitation at the same time as Carl Brans and Robert Dicke.

Josephson, Brian David (1940–)
British physicist

Josephson was born in Cardiff and educated at Cambridge University, where he obtained his PhD in 1964. He remained at Cambridge and in 1974 was appointed to a professorship of physics.

His name is associated with the *Josephson effects* described in 1962 while he was still a graduate student. The work came out of theoretical speculations on electrons in semiconductors involving the exchange of electrons between two superconducting regions separated by a thin insulating layer (a *Josephson junction*). He showed theoretically that a current can flow across the junction in the absence of an applied voltage. Furthermore, a small direct voltage across the junction produces an alternating current with a frequency that is inversely proportional to the voltage. The effects have been verified experimentally, thus supporting the BCS theory of superconductivity of John BARDEEN and his colleagues. They have been used in making accurate physical measurements and in measuring weak magnetic fields. Josephson junctions can also be used as very fast switching devices in computers. For this work Josephson shared the 1973 Nobel Prize for physics with Leo ESAKI and Ivar GIAEVER.

Later, Josephson turned his attention to the study of the mind and has argued strongly for a connection between parapsychology and quantum mechanics.

Joule, James Prescott (1818–1889)
British physicist

Joule, the son of a brewer from Salford, received little formal education, was never appointed to an academic post, and remained a brewer all his life. He began work in a private laboratory that his father built near to the brewery.

His first major research was concerned with determining the quantity of heat produced by an electric current and, in 1840, Joule discovered a simple law connecting the current and resistance with the heat generated. For the next few years he carried out a series of experiments in which he investigated the conversion of electrical and mechanical work into heat. In 1849 he read his paper *On the Mechanical Equivalent of Heat* to the Royal Society. Joule's work (unlike that of Julius Mayer) was instantly recognized.

In 1848 Joule published a paper on the kinetic theory of gases, in which he estimated the speed of gas molecules. From 1852 he worked with William Thomson (later Lord Kelvin) on experiments on thermodynamics. Their best known result is the *Joule–Kelvin effect* – the effect in which an expanding gas, under certain conditions, is cooled by the expansion.

Jung, Carl Gustav (1875–1961) *Swiss psychologist and psychiatrist*

Born the son of a pastor in Kesswil, Switzerland, Jung (yuung) studied medicine at the universities of Basel (1895–1900) and Zurich, where he obtained his MD in 1902. From 1902 until 1909 he worked under the direction of Eugen Bleuler at the Burghölzi Psychiatric Clinic, Zurich, while at the same time lecturing in psychiatry at the University of Zurich (1905–13). In 1907 Jung met Sigmund Freud, whose chief collaborator he became. Following the formation of the International Psycho-Analytical Association (1910) he served as its first president from 1911 until his break with Freud in 1912.

Jung continued to practice in Zurich and to develop his own system of analytical psychology. He became professor of psychology at the Federal Institute of Technology in Zurich (1933–41) and was appointed professor of medical psychology at the University of Basel in 1943 but was forced to resign almost immediately for health reasons. He continued however to write, hold regular seminars, and treat patients until he was well over 80.

Like Alfred Adler, who had broken away from Freudian orthodoxy earlier, Jung minimized the sexual cause of neuroses but, unlike Adler, he continued to emphasize the role of the unconscious. His final break with Freud followed publication of his *Wandlungen und Symbole de Libido* (1912) translated into English in 1916 as *Psychology of the Unconscious*. To the 'personal' unconscious of the Freudian he added the 'collective unconscious' stocked with a number of 'congenital conditions of intuition' or archetypes. In search of such archetypes Jung spent long periods with the Pueblo of Arizona, and visited Kenya, North Africa, and India, and also sought for them in dreams, folklore, and the literature of alchemy.

Jung also emphasized the importance of personality and in his *Psychologische Typen* (1921; Psychological Types) introduced the distinction he made between introverts and extroverts.

Jussieu, Antoine-Laurent de (1748–1836) *French plant taxonomist*

Jussieu was born into a family of eminent botanists from Lyons in France. His uncles Antoine, Bernard, and Joseph de Jussieu all made important contributions to botany and his son, Adrien, subsequently continued the family tradition.

After graduating from the Jardin du Roi in 1770, Jussieu continued to work there, becoming subdemonstrator of botany in 1778. In his first publication in 1773, which reexamined the taxonomy of the Ranunculaceae, he advanced the idea of relative values of characters; the following year he applied this principle to other plant families.

Jussieu is remembered for introducing a natural classification system that distinguishes relationships between plants by considering a large number of characters, unlike the artificial Linnean system, which relies on only a few. In producing the famous *Genera Plantarum* (1789; Genera of Plants) Jussieu had access to a number of collections, including Linnaeus's herbarium and some of Joseph Banks's Australian specimens. He was also able to include many tropical angiosperm families thanks to the collection made by Philibert Commesson. From all this material he distinguished 15 classes and 100 families, and the value of his work can be seen in the fact that 76 of his 100 families remain in botanical nomenclature today. Both Georges Cuvier and Augustin de Candolle built on Jussieu's system.

Jussieu was in charge of the hospital of Paris during the French Revolution and was professor of botany at the National Natural History Museum (formerly the Jardin du Roi) from 1793 to 1826.

Kaluza, Theodor Franz Eduard (1885–1954) *German mathematical physicist*

The son of a phonetician, Kaluza was born at Ratibor in Germany and educated at the University of Königsberg where he served (1902–29) as a privatdocent (a largely unpaid teaching assistant). On Einstein's recommendation he was appointed in 1929 to a professorship in physics at the University of Kiel. He remained there until 1935, when he moved to a similar appointment at Göttingen University.

In Einstein's theory of general relativity, space and time are joined together into a four-dimensional space–time. In 1921, Kaluza decided to supplement Einstein's model with a fifth spatial dimension. Within this model it proved possible to derive Einstein's four-dimensional gravitational equations as well as the equations for the electromagnetic field. Thus in a world of five dimensions, gravity and electromagnetism were not distinct forces.

There were, however, two major defects in Kaluza's theory. Firstly, he could give no indication of the nature of this fifth dimension. Moreover, his theory assumed that bodies behave classically and quantummechanical effects were not considered. An attempt to remedy these defects was made in 1926 by Oskar Klein. This revised form, known as the *Kaluza–Klein theory*, has proved to be of considerable interest to string theorists such as Ed WITTEN.

Kamerlingh-Onnes, Heike (1853–1926) *Dutch physicist*

Born at Groningen in the Netherlands, Kamerlingh-Onnes was educated at the university there, obtaining his doctorate in 1879. In 1882 he was appointed professor of physics at Leiden, where he remained for the rest of his career. There he started the study of low-temperature physics, at first in order to gather experimental evidence for the atomic theory of matter. However, his interest turned to the problems involved in reaching extremely low temperatures and, in 1908, he became the first to succeed in liquefying helium. Matter at low temperatures – only a few degrees above absolute zero – has such strange properties that a completely new field of cryogenic physics was opened up. The first of these properties to be studied was superconduc-

tivity, which Kamerlingh-Onnes discovered in 1911. This phenomenon involves the total loss of resistance by certain metals at low temperatures.

Kamerlingh-Onnes was elected to the Royal Academy of Sciences in Amsterdam for this research and, in 1913, was awarded the Nobel Prize for physics.

Kammerer, Paul (1880–1926) *Austrian zoologist*

Kammerer, the son of a prosperous factory owner, was educated at the university in his native city of Vienna, where he obtained his PhD. He then joined the staff of the university's recently opened Institute of Experimental Biology, where he worked until the end of 1922 and soon established a reputation as a skilled experimentalist. Much of his work appeared to support the unorthodox doctrine of the inheritance of acquired characteristics associated with Jean Lamarck. The most famous of Kammerer's experiments concerned the breeding behavior of *Alytes obstetricans*, the midwife toad. Unlike most other toads this species mates on land; the male consequently lacks the nuptial pads, blackish swellings on the hand, possessed by water-breeding males in the mating season to enable them to grasp the female during copulation.

Kammerer undertook the experiment of inducing several generations of *Alytes* to copulate in water to see what changes resulted. This involved overcoming the difficult task of rearing the eggs in water and ensuring the developing tadpoles were kept free of fungal infection. After almost ten years following this line he noted that in the F_3 generation (the great grandchildren of the original parents) grayish-black swellings, resembling rudimentary nuptial pads, could be seen on the upper, outer, and palmar sides of the first finger.

In 1923 Kammerer visited Britain in the hope of resolving a controversy that had arisen between himself and the leading Cambridge geneticist William Bateson. As virtually all his animals had been destroyed in the war, he brought with him as evidence one preserved specimen and slides of the nuptial pads from the F_5 generation made some ten years earlier. His lectures at Cambridge and to the Linnean Society were successful and none of the eminent biologists who examined Kammerer's specimen noticed anything suspect.

However when, early in 1926, G. Noble of the American Museum of Natural History came to examine the specimen in Vienna he found no nuptial pads, only blackened areas caused by the injection of ink. Despite the support of the institute's director, Hans Przibram, several possible explanations of the obvious fraud, and a still-open invitation from Moscow to establish an experimental institute there, Kammerer shot himself some six months after Noble's visit.

Kammerer had in fact carried out a whole series of experiments of which the work with *Alytes* was but a part, and for him not the most important part. In 1909 he claimed to have induced inherited color adaptation in salamander, and by cutting the siphons of the sea squirt *Ciona intestinalis*, to have induced hereditary elongations. The few people who attempted to repeat Kammerer's results were unsuccessful although in certain cases Kammerer was able to claim, with some justification, that his protocols had not been scrupulously followed.

Kamp, Peter van de *See* VAN DE KAMP, PETER.

Kapitza, Pyotr Leonidovich
(1894–1984) *Russian physicist*

Pyotr (or Peter) Kapitza was born in Kronstadt, Russia, and educated (1918–21) at the Polytechnic Institute and the Physical and Technical Institute in Petrograd (now St. Petersburg). He lectured at the Polytechnic Institute from 1919 to 1921. From 1921 to 1924 he was involved in magnetic research at the Cavendish Laboratory of Cambridge University under Ernest Rutherford and gained his PhD there in 1923. He was made director of the Royal Society Mond Laboratory at Cambridge in 1930. In 1934 he paid a visit to his homeland but was detained by the Soviet authorities. The next year Kapitza was made director of a newly founded research institute in Moscow – the Institute for Physical Problems – and was able to continue the line of his Cambridge research through the purchase of his original equipment. He worked there until 1946 when, apparently, he fell into disfavor with Stalin for declining to work on nuclear weapons. He was held under house arrest until 1955, when he was able to resume his work at the Institute. Kapitza had shown similar courage earlier in 1938 when he had intervened on behalf of his colleague Lev Landau who had been arrested as a supposed German spy. Without Landau, Kapitza insisted,

he would be unable to complete work considered to be important by the authorities. Soon after, Landau was released.

Kapitza's most significant work in low-temperature physics was on the viscosity of the form of liquid helium known as He–II. This he (and, independently, J. F. Allen and A. D. Misener) found to exist in a 'superfluid' state – escaping from tightly sealed vessels and exhibiting unusual flow behavior. Kapitza found that He–II is in a macroscopic quantum state with perfect atomic order. In a series of experiments, he found also that a novel form of internal convection occurs in this form of helium.

Besides work on the unusual properties of helium, Kapitza also devised a liquefaction technique for the gas, which is the basis of present-day helium liquefiers, and was able to produce large quantities of liquid hydrogen, helium, and oxygen. The availability of liquid helium has led to the production of electric superconductors and enabled much other work at extremely low temperatures to proceed. Kapitza also created very high magnetic fields for his experiments, and his record of 500 kilogauss in 1924 was not surpassed until 1956. Kapitza's low-temperature work was honored after almost forty years by the award of the 1978 Nobel Prize for physics.

From 1955, Kapitza headed the Soviet Committee for Interplanetary Flight and played an important part in the preparations for the first Soviet satellite launchings. In his career, Kapitza collected many awards from scientific institutions of both East and West, including the Order of Lenin on six occasions. In 1965 he was finally allowed to travel outside the Soviet Union. He first visited Copenhagen and in 1966 he spent some time in Cambridge, England, with his colleagues of the 1930s, John Cockroft and Paul Dirac.

Kapteyn, Jacobus Cornelius (1851–1922) *Dutch astronomer*

Born at Barneveld in the Netherlands, Kapteyn studied at Utrecht University and became professor of astronomy at the University of Groningen in 1878. He was a very careful stellar observer and using David Gill's photographs of the southern hemisphere skies, he published in 1904 a catalog of over 450,000 stars within 19 degrees of the south celestial pole. He repeated William Herschel's count of the stars by sampling various parts of the heavens and supported Herschel's view that the Galaxy was lens-shaped with the Sun near the center; but his estimate of its size was different from Herschel's – 55,000 light-years long and 11,000 light-years thick. He pioneered new methods for investigating the distribution of stars in space.

Kapteyn also discovered the star, now called *Kapteyn's star*, with the second greatest proper motion – 8.73 seconds annual motion compared to the 10".3 of Barnard's star. He found this as part of a wider study of the general distribution of the motions of stars in the sky. To his surprise he found, in 1904, that they could be divided into two clear streams: about 3/5 of all stars seem to be heading in one direction and the other 2/5 in the opposite direction. The first stream is directed toward Orion and the second to Scutum, and a line joining them would be parallel to the Milky Way. Kapteyn was unable to explain this phenomenon; it was left to his pupil Jan Oort to point out that this is a straightforward consequence of galactic rotation.

Karle, Isabella Helen (1921–) *American crystallographer*

Karle was born Isabella Lugoski in Detroit, Michigan, the daughter of Polish immigrants; her father was a house painter and her mother a seamstress. She first heard English spoken only when she began school. She was educated at the University of Michigan, where she obtained her PhD in 1943. Here she met Jerome Karle, a physicist who would win the 1985 Nobel Prize for chemistry for work in x-ray crystallography. They married in 1942 and worked together during the war on the Manhattan Project in Chicago. After the war they moved in 1946 to the Naval Research Laboratory in Washington D.C.

With over 200 papers to her credit Karle has made a number of major contributions to the development of x-ray crystallography. In the 1950s, Jerome Karle and Herb Hauptman had developed new and powerful techniques to enable the phase of diffracted x-rays to be calculated directly. Isabella Karle was one of the first to deploy the new method successfully, and thereby to draw the attention of other workers to its potential.

In her first major success in 1969 she established the structure of venom extracted from South American frogs. This was followed in 1975 with the structure of valinomycin, a polypeptide that transports potassium ions across biological membranes. At the time it was the largest molecule to be worked out directly. In 1979 the structure of another peptide, antamanide, was solved. She has also determined the structure of the natural opiate, enkephalin.

Karle, Jerome (1918–) *American physicist*

Born in Brooklyn, New York, Karle was educated at the City College there and at the University of Michigan, where he obtained his PhD in 1943. After working on the Manhattan Project in Chicago, Karle moved in 1946 to the Naval Research Laboratory, Washington D.C., becoming chief scientist in the lab for the structure of matter in 1968.

While in Washington Karle began an important collaboration with Herb Hauptman exploring new ways to determine the structure of crystals using x-ray diffraction techniques. Before their work, the structure of anything but the simplest molecule was usually worked out with the so-called 'heavy-atom' technique. This involved substituting a heavy atom, such as mercury, in a definite position in the structure. The changes produced in the intensities of the diffraction patterns allowed the phases to be inferred. The method, however, is limited and time consuming.

In 1953 Karle and Hauptman published a monograph, *The Phases and Magnitudes of the Structure Factors*, in which they demonstrated how phase structures could be inferred directly from diffraction patterns. For their work in this field, Hauptman and Karle shared the 1985 Nobel Prize for chemistry.

In 1942 Karle had married Isabella Lugoski, also a crystallographer. She was one of the earliest workers to apply the new direct method to a number of important molecules.

Karrer, Paul (1889–1971) *Swiss chemist*

Karrer, the son of a Moscow dentist, was educated at the University of Zurich where he obtained his PhD. After working in Frankfurt he returned to the University of Zurich in 1918, where he served as professor of chemistry until his retirement in 1959.

He began his research career working on the chemistry of plant pigments. Although Karrer tackled a wide variety of such pigments his most significant result was his determination, by 1930, of the structure of carotene, the yellow pigment found in such vegetables as carrots. By 1931 he had also worked out the structure of vitamin A and synthesized it. The similarity between the two molecules did not escape Karrer's attention and it was later shown that vitamin A is derived from the breakdown of carotene in the liver. Karrer went on to synthesize vitamin B_2 (riboflavin) in 1935 and vitamin E (tocopherol) in 1938.

In 1937 Karrer was awarded, along with

Norman HAWORTH, the Nobel Prize for chemistry for his work on the "constitution of carotenoids, flavins, and vitamins A and B." Karrer was the author of a respected textbook, *Lehrbuch der organischen Chemie* (1927; Textbook of Organic Chemistry).

Kastler, Alfred (1902–1984) *French physicist*

Kastler, who was born in Gebweiler (now Guebwiller in France), was educated at the Ecole Normale Supérieure. He then taught at the University of Bordeaux where he became professor of physics in 1938. He moved to the University of Paris in 1941 where he remained until his retirement in 1972.

He worked on double-resonance techniques of spectroscopy, using absorption by both optical and radiofrequency radiation to study energy levels in atoms. He also introduced the technique known as 'optical pumping' – a method of exciting atoms to a different energy state. In practical terms Kastler's work led to new frequency standards and new methods for the measurement of weak magnetic fields. Kastler received the 1966 Nobel Prize for physics for his work on double resonance.

Katz, Bernard (1911–) *German–British neurophysiologist*

Born at Leipzig in Germany, Katz received his MD from the university there in 1934 and his PhD, under Archibald Hill, from the University of London in 1938. He spent the war in Australia first working with John Eccles and later in the Royal Australian Air Force as a radar operator. Katz returned to London in 1946 to University College and in 1952 became professor of biophysics, a post he retained until he retired in 1978.

In 1936 Henry Dale demonstrated that peripheral nerves act by releasing the chemical acetylcholine in response to a nerve impulse. To find how this secretion takes place Katz, working in collaboration with the British biophysicist, Paul Fatt, inserted a micropipette at a neuromuscular junction to record the 'end-plate potential' or EPP. He noted a random deflection on the oscilloscope with an amplitude of about 0.5 millivolt even in the absence of all stimulation. At first he assumed such a reading to be interference arising from the machine but the application of curare, an acetylcholine antagonist, by abolishing the apparently random EPPs, showed the activity in the nerves is real.

Consequently Katz proposed his quantum hypothesis. He suggested that nerve endings secrete small amounts of acetylcholine in a random manner in specific amounts (or quanta). When a nerve is stimulated it does not begin secreting but instead enormously increases the number of quanta of acetylcholine released. Katz was able to produce a good deal of evidence for this hypothesis, which he later presented in his important work *Nerve, Muscle and Synapse* (1966).

It was mainly for this work that Katz shared the 1970 Nobel Prize for physiology or medicine with Julius AXELROD and Ulf VON EULER.

Keenan, Philip Childs (1908–) *American astronomer*

Keenan, who was born in Bellevue, Pennsylvania, graduated in 1929 from the University of Arizona and obtained his PhD from the University of Chicago in 1932. He worked initially at Chicago's Yerkes Observatory from 1929 until 1942 when he joined the Bureau of Ordnance. With the return of peace, Keenan was appointed to the staff of the Perkins Observatory of Ohio State University, becoming professor of astronomy in 1956.

Keenan is best known for his work with William Morgan and Edith Kellman on their *Atlas of Stellar Spectra with an Outline of Spectral Classification* (1943). It was this work that formed the basis for the MKK system of classifying stars by their luminosity in addition to their spectral type.

Keilin, David (1887–1963) *British biologist and entomologist*

Keilin was born in Russia in Moscow and educated at Cambridge University. He was subsequently professor of biology at Cambridge from 1931 until 1952 and also director of the Cambridge Moltena Institute. His most important research was the discovery of the respiratory pigment cytochrome, which, he demonstrated, is present in animal, yeast, and higher plant cells. He also studied the biochemistry of the Diptera (true flies), and investigated the respiratory systems and adaptations of certain dipterous larvae and pupae.

Keith, Sir Arthur (1866–1955) *British anatomist*

Keith, the son of a farmer from Old Machan in Scotland, was educated at the University of Aberdeen, where he qualified as a doctor in 1888. He served as a medical officer in Siam (now Thailand) from 1889 until 1892, when his interest in the comparative anatomy of the primates was first aroused. On his return to Europe he studied anatomy in Leipzig and London before being appointed (1895) demonstrator in anatomy at the London Hospital. In 1908 Keith moved to the Royal College of Surgeons, where he served as curator of the Hunterian Museum until his retirement in 1933.

On 18 December 1912, Arthur Woodward and Charles Dawson announced to the Geological Society the discovery at Piltdown in Sussex of a remarkable skull, which apparently combined the mandible of an ape with the cranium of a human. Here at last, it was felt, was solid evidence for the antiquity of humans. Although some at the meeting were skeptical of the find, suggesting that the skull and jaw must have come from two different individuals, Keith was not among them. It thus appeared that a human with a cranial capacity of 1500 cubic centimeters (as estimated by Keith) and with the jaw of an ape had coexisted with the mastodon. Keith, in the first edition of his *Antiquity of Man* (1915), dated Piltdown man to the beginning of the Pliocene, which was then assumed to be about a million years ago. With the change in geological fashion Keith was forced to halve the date of Piltdown man in the second edition of his book (1925).

In 1915 Keith estimated the actual separation of humans from the apes to have taken place in the lower Miocene, then considered to be some 2–4 million years ago. This meant that Keith was unable to accommodate the discovery of the famous Taung skull by Raymond Dart in 1924, and consequently he denied that Dart's *Australopithecus* was either human or a link between apes and humans, considering it to be a pure ape having affinities with two living apes, the gorilla and the chimpanzee.

Keith lived long enough to witness the exposure of Piltdown man by Kenneth Oakley in 1949, using modern fluorine dating techniques. These showed the fossil to date back only as far as the Pleistocene, while later work (1953) revealed its fraudulent nature by assigning markedly different dates to the skull and jaw. When Oakley made a special journey to the 87-year-old Keith to inform him of his results, Keith commented "I think you are probably right, but it will take me some time to adjust myself to the new view."

Kekulé von Stradonitz, Friedrich August (1829–1896) *German chemist*

Kekulé was born in Darmstadt. As a youth he showed considerable skill in drawing and was consequently encouraged to be an architect. Although he began as a student of architecture at Giessen he soon switched,

despite family opposition, to the study of chemistry, which he continued abroad. He first went to Paris in the period 1851–52 where he studied under Jean Dumas and Charles Gerhardt who influenced him greatly. He worked in Switzerland for a while before taking a post in England in 1854–55 as a laboratory assistant at St. Bartholomew's Hospital, London. While in London he met and was influenced by Alexander Williamson and William Odling. He accepted an unsalaried post at the University of Heidelberg before his appointment to the chair of chemistry at Ghent in 1858. He then moved to the chemistry chair at the University of Bonn in 1867, where he remained for the rest of his life.

Kekulé's main work was done on the structure of the carbon atom and its compounds. It has often been claimed that he had changed his career from the architecture of buildings to the architecture of molecules. Certainly, after Kekulé it was much easier to visualize the form of atoms and their combinations. In 1852 Edward FRANKLAND had pointed out that each kind of atom can combine with only so many other atoms. Thus hydrogen can combine with only one other atom at a time, oxygen could combine with two, nitrogen with three, and carbon with four. Such combining power soon became known as the valency (valence) of an atom. Each atom would be either uni-, bi-, tri-, quadrivalent, or some higher figure.

In 1858 both Kekulé and Archibald Couper saw how to use this insight of Frankland to revolutionize organic chemistry. They both assumed that carbon was quadrivalent and that one of the four bonds of the carbon atom could be used to join with another carbon atom. He published his results in 1858 in his paper *The Constitution and the Metamorphoses of Chemical Compounds and the Chemical Nature of Carbon* and in the first volume of his *Lehrbuch der organische Chemie* (1859; Textbook of Organic Chemistry).

The diagrams of carbon compounds used today come not from Kekulé but from Alexander Crum Brown in 1865. Kekulé's own notation, known as 'Kekulé sausages', in which atoms were represented by a cumbersome system of circles, was soon dropped. The gains from such representations were immediate. It can be seen why two molecules could have the same number of atoms of each element and yet differ in properties. Thus C_2H_6O represents both ethanol and dimethyl ether. If the rules of valence are observed these are the only two ways in which two carbon, six hydrogen, and one oxygen atom can be combined and indeed these are the only two compounds of the formula ever observed.

While Kekulé had dramatic success demonstrating how organic compounds could be constructed from carbon chains, one set of compounds, the aromatics, resisted all such treatment. Benzene, discovered by Michael Faraday in 1825, had the formula C_6H_6, which, on the assumption of a quadrivalent carbon atom, just could not be represented as any kind of chain. The best that could be done with alternating single and double carbon bonds would still violate the valence rules, for at the end of the chain the carbon atoms will both have an unfilled bond. Kekulé has left a description of how the solution of the puzzle came to him. In 1890 he recalled that while working on his textbook in 1865, "I dozed off. Again the atoms danced before my eyes. This time the smaller groups remained in the background. My inner eye ... now distinguished bigger forms of manifold configurations. Long rows, more densely joined; everything in motion, contorting and turning like snakes. And behold what was that? One of the snakes took hold of its own tail and whirled derisively before my eyes. I woke up as though I had been struck by lightning; again I spent the rest of the night working out the consequences."

The snake with its tail in its mouth is in fact an ancient alchemical symbol and is named Ouroboros but, to Kekulé, it meant a more prosaic image, that of a ring. For if the two ends of the benzene chain are joined to each other then benzene will have been shown to have a ring structure in which the valence rules have all been observed. Again the rewards in understanding were immediate. It was now obvious why substitution for one of benzene's hydrogen atoms always produced the same compound. The mono-substituted derivative C_6H_5X was completely symmetrical whichever H atom it replaced. Each of the hydrogen atoms were replaced by NH_2 and in each case the same compound, aniline C_6H_5.NH_2, was obtained.

Such was the revolution in organic chemistry initiated by Kekulé. Together with new methods introduced by Stanislao CANNIZZARO at Karlsruhe in 1860 for the determination of atomic weight, a new age of chemistry was about to dawn in which the conflicts and uncertainties of the first half of the 19th century would be replaced by a unified chemical theory, notation, and practice. After this it comes as something of a shock to discover that Kekulé had no firm belief in the existence of atoms. Whether they exist he argued in 1867 "has but little significance from a chemical point of view;

its discussion belongs rather to metaphysics. In chemistry we have only to decide whether the assumption of atoms is an hypothesis adapted to the explanation of chemical phenomena."

Kellner, Karl (1851–1905) *Austrian chemical engineer. See* CASTNER, HAMILTON YOUNG.

Kelvin, William Thomson, Baron Kelvin of Largs (1824–1907) *British theoretical and experimental physicist*

Born in Belfast, Northern Ireland, William Thomson was an extremely precocious child intellectually and matriculated at Glasgow University at the astonishingly early age of 10. He went on to Cambridge, after which he returned to Glasgow to become professor of natural philosophy. He was to occupy this chair for 53 years. It was in Glasgow that he organized and ran one of Britain's first adequately equipped physical laboratories. In 1892 in recognition of his contributions to science he was raised to the British peerage as Baron Kelvin of Largs. He was also a devout member of the Scottish Free Church.

Kelvin's work on electromagnetism was also important. Together with Faraday he was responsible for the introduction of the concept of an electromagnetic field. Kelvin was of a much more mathematical turn of mind than Faraday, but it was left to Maxwell to weld the ideas of Faraday and Kelvin together into a powerful, elegant, and succinct mathematical theory. But Maxwell's work would have been greatly hampered without some of the penetrating suggestions made by Kelvin. Particularly important is a fundamental paper of 1847 in which Kelvin drew an analogy between an electrostatic field and an incompressible elastic solid. Kelvin made many other innovations including the introduction of the use of vectors to represent magnetic induction and magnetic force. He also put his knowledge of electromagnetism to use in many practical inventions of which the transatlantic electric telegraph cable and the mirror galvanometer were among the most important.

Kelvin's other great area of work was thermodynamics. He was one of the first to understand and appreciate the importance of James Joule's seminal work in the field. In his 1852 paper on the *Dissipation of Mechanical Energy* Kelvin set out the fundamentally important law of conservation of energy that was to be so important in the physics of the second half of the 19th century. In his work on thermodynamics

Kelvin assimilated and developed the work of the great pioneers of the subject, Nicolas Carnot and James Joule. He also collaborated with Joule in experimental work. One of the important results of Kelvin's work was his introduction of the concept of *absolute zero* and his recognition of the theoretical importance of the absolute scale of temperature, which is named in his honor. Kelvin was able to calculate the value of absolute zero from theoretical considerations. One of the first formulations of the second law of thermodynamics was given by Kelvin. With Joule he first demonstrated the *Joule–Kelvin effect*. He also made important contributions to the theory of elasticity and some basic contributions to hydrodynamics in which he collaborated with George Stokes. The unit of thermodynamic temperature, the *kelvin*, is named after him.

Kemeny, John George (1926–1992)
Hungarian–American mathematician

Kemeny was born in Budapest, Hungary. In 1938 his father was so alarmed by the Nazi annexation of Austria that he moved to the United States. The family followed in 1940 and Kemeny entered Princeton in 1943 to study mathematics. A year later he was drafted onto the Manhattan Project and sent to Los Alamos where he operated an IBM calculator. He returned to Princeton in 1946, completed his PhD in 1949, and moved to Dartmouth in 1953, serving as professor of mathematics (1956–68), as president of the college from (1970–81), and once more, from 1981 until his retirement in 1990, as professor of mathematics.

Between 1963 and 1964 Kemeny, working with a Dartmouth colleague, Thomas Kurtz, developed BASIC (Beginner's All Purpose Symbolic Instruction Code), probably the best known of all computer languages. Previously the large computers could only be approached through specialized computer programmers. BASIC was conceived initially as something for Dartmouth students to use on Dartmouth computers. With a few simple self-evident commands and an equally simple syntax and vocabulary, it proved remarkably easy to use.

Because it was meant to be freely available to students, the software was placed in the public domain. Subsequently it became the most widely used computer language of the 1970s and 1980s.

Kemeny himself became something of a public figure. It was during his presidency that Dartmouth became coeducational and he did much to open up the college to minorities. He also campaigned against the Vietnam War. Kemeny was one of the main campaigners for the not altogether successful 'new math' introduced into America in the 1970s. In 1979 he was invited by President Carter to chair the committee set up to investigate the nuclear accident at Three Mile Island.

Kendall, Edward Calvin (1886–1972)
American biochemist

Kendall, a dentist's son from South Norwalk, Connecticut, studied chemistry at Columbia University where he obtained his PhD in 1910. After working briefly at St. Luke's Hospital in New York from 1911 to 1914, Kendall moved to the Mayo Foundation in Rochester, Minnesota, where from 1921 to 1951 he served as professor of physiological chemistry.

In 1914 Kendall achieved an early success by isolating the active constituent of the thyroid gland. The importance of hormones in the physiology of the body had become apparent through the work of William Bayliss and Ernest Starling on the pancreas. Kendall was able to demonstrate the presence of a physiologically active compound of the amino acid tyrosine and iodine, which he named thyroxin.

Kendall was led from this to investigate the more complex activity of the adrenal gland. This gland secretes a large number of steroids, many of which he succeeded in isolating. Four compounds, labeled A, B, E, and F, seemed to possess significant physiological activity. They were shown to affect the metabolism of proteins and carbohydrates and in their absence animals seemed to lose the ability to deal with toxic substances. It was therefore hoped that some of these compounds might turn out to be therapeutically useful. After much effort sufficient compound A was obtained but, to Kendall's surprise and disappointment, it was shown to have little effect on Addison's disease, a complaint caused by a deficient secretion from the adrenal cortex. Kendall was more successful with his compound E – later known as cortisone to avoid confusion with vitamin E – when in 1947 a practical method for its production was established. Clinical trials showed it to be effective against rheumatoid arthritis. It was for this work that Kendall shared the 1950 Nobel Prize for physiology or medicine with Tadeus REICHSTEIN and Philip HENCH.

Kendall, Henry Way (1926–) *American physicist. See* FRIEDMAN, JEROME ISAAC.

Kendrew, Sir John Cowdery (1917–1997) *British biochemist*

Kendrew, who was born at Oxford, graduated in natural science from Cambridge University in 1939. He spent the war years working for the Ministry of Aircraft Production, becoming an honorary wing commander in 1944. In 1946 he joined Max PERUTZ at Cambridge and, like Perutz, used x-ray diffraction techniques to study the crystalline structure of proteins, particularly that of the muscle protein myoglobin. X-ray diffraction, or crystallography, involves placing a crystal in front of a photographic plate and rotating the crystal in a beam of x-rays. The pattern of dots that is formed on the plate by the x-rays can be analyzed to find the positions of the atoms in the crystal. The technique had been used successfully to show the structures of small molecules but Kendrew's progress with the much larger myoglobin structure was slow, especially since diffraction patterns yield no information on the phases of the directed x-rays. However, in 1953 Perutz made a breakthrough by incorporating atoms of heavy elements into the protein crystals. Kendrew modified this new method and applied it successfully in his myoglobin studies, so that four years later he had built up a rough model of the three-dimensional structure of myoglobin. By 1959 he had greatly clarified the structure and could pinpoint most of the atoms.

Kendrew and Perutz received the 1962 Nobel Prize for chemistry for their work on protein structure. Kendrew was knighted in 1974 and served as director general of the European Molecular Biology Laboratory in Heidelberg from 1975 to 1982.

Kepler, Johannes (1571–1630) *German astronomer*

The grandfather of Kepler had been the local burgomaster but his father seems to have been a humble soldier away on military service for most of Kepler's early youth. His mother was described by Kepler as "quarrelsome, of a bad disposition." She was later to be accused of witchcraft. Kepler was born at Würtenburg, in Germany, and was originally intended for the Church; he graduated from the University of Tübingen in 1591 and went on to study in the theological faculty.

In 1594 he was offered a teaching post in mathematics in the seminary at Gratz in Styria. It was from his teacher, Mästlin, who was one of the earliest scholars fully to comprehend and accept the work of Nicolaus Copernicus, that the young Kepler acquired his early Copernicanism. In addition to his teaching at Gratz and such usual duties as mathematicians were expected to do in those days Kepler published his first book – *Mysterium cosmographicum* (1596; Mystery of Cosmography). The book expresses very clearly the belief in a mathematical harmony underlying the universe, a harmony he was to spend the rest of his life searching for. In this work he tried to show that the universe was structured on the model of Plato's five regular solids. Although the work verges on the cranky and obsessive it shows that Kepler was already searching for some more general mathematical relationship than could be found in Copernicus.

He married in 1597 shortly before he was forced to leave Gratz when, in 1598, all Lutheran teachers and preachers were ordered to leave the city immediately. Fortunately for Kepler, he had an invitation to work with Tycho Brahe who had recently become the Imperial Mathematician in Prague. Tycho was the greatest observational astronomer of the century and he had with him the results of his last 20 years' observations. Kepler joined him in 1600 and although their relationship was not an easy one it was certainly profitable. Tycho assigned him the task of working out the orbit of Mars. Somewhat rashly Kepler boasted he would solve it in a week – it took him eight years of unremitting effort. Not only did Kepler lack the computing assistance now taken for granted but he was also working before the invention of logarithms. It was during this period that he discovered his first two laws and thus, with Galileo, began to offer an alternative physics to that of Aristotle. The first law asserts that planets describe elliptic orbits with the Sun at one focus while the second law asserts that the line joining the Sun to a planet sweeps out equal areas in equal times. The laws were published in his magnum opus *Astronomia nova* (1610; New Astronomy).

Tycho had died in 1601 leaving Kepler with his post, his observations, and a strong obligation to complete and publish his tables under the patronage of their master, the emperor Rudolph II. This obligation was to prove even more onerous and time consuming than the orbit of Mars. It involved dealing with Tycho's predatory kin, attempting, vainly, to extract money from the emperor to pay for the work, which he ended up financing himself, and trying to find a suitable printer. All this, it must be realized, was done against the background of the Thirty Years' War, marauding soldiery, and numerous epidemics. His work, the *Tabulae Rudolphinae* (Rudolphine Tables), was not completed until 1627 but remained the standard work for the best part of a century.

While serving the emperor in Prague, Kepler had also produced a major work *Optics* (1604), which included a good approximation of Snell's law, improved refraction tables, and discussion of the pinhole camera. In the same year he observed only the second new star visible to the naked eye since antiquity. He showed, as Tycho had done with the new star of 1572, that it exhibited no parallax and must therefore be situated far beyond the solar system. He studied and wrote upon the bright comet of 1607 – later to be called Halley's comet – and those of 1618 in his *Three Tracts on Comets* (1619). His final work in Prague, the *Dioptrics* (1611), has been called the first work of geometrical optics.

In 1611 Kepler's wife and son died, civil war broke out in Prague, and Rudolph was forced to abdicate. Kepler moved to Linz in the following year to take up a post as a mathematics teacher and surveyor. Here he stayed for 14 years. He married again in 1613. While in Linz he produced a work that, starting from the simple problem of measuring the volume of his wine cask, moved on to more general problems of mensuration – *Nova stereometria* (1615; New Measurements of Volume). One further crisis he had to face was his mother's trial for witchcraft in Würtemburg. The trial dragged on for three years before she was finally freed. His greatest work of this period *Harmonices mundi* (1619; Harmonics of the World) returns to the search for the underlying mathematical harmony expressed in his first work of 1596. It is here that he stated his third law: the squares of the periods of any two planets are proportional to the cubes of their mean distance from the Sun. After the completion of the Rudolphine tables Kepler took service under a new patron, the Imperial General Wallenstein. He settled at Sagan in Silesia. In return for the horoscopes Wallenstein expected from him, Kepler was provided with a press, a generous salary, and the peace to publish his ephemerides and to prepare his work of science fiction – *A Dream, or Astronomy of the Moon* (1634). He left Sagan in 1630, during one of Wallenstein's temporary military setbacks, to see the emperor in Ratisbon hoping for a payment of the 12,000 florins still owed him. He died there of a fever a few days later.

As a scientist Kepler is of immense importance. Copernicus was in many ways a traditional thinker, still passionately committed to circles. Kepler broke away from this mode of thought and in so doing posed questions of planetary motion that it took a Newton to answer.

Kerr, John (1824–1907) *British physicist*

Born at Ardrossan in Scotland, Kerr studied at Glasgow University and carried out research work under Lord Kelvin. He taught mathematics at a training college in Glasgow. He is remembered for his work on polarized light, in which he discovered that certain substances placed in a strong electric field exhibit birefringence (the *Kerr effect*). Kerr also described the behavior of polarized light when reflected from the polished pole of an electromagnet (the *Faraday effect*).

Kettlewell, Henry Bernard Davis (1907–1979) *British geneticist and lepidopterist*

Kettlewell was educated at Cambridge University and St. Bartholomew's Hospital, London, where he gained his medical qualification in 1933. He practiced in Cranleigh and then worked as an anesthetist in Surrey. After the war he worked in South Africa at the International Locust Control Centre in Cape Town before returning to Britain in 1952 as research fellow in genetics at Oxford, a post he continued to hold until his retirement in 1974.

Kettlewell is best known for his work on the occurrence of melanism – black pigmentation in the epidermis of animals. In 1953 he set out to explain why, in the mid-19th century, certain moth species had a light coloration, which camouflaged them on such backgrounds as light tree trunks where they sat motionless during the day. However by the 1950s, of 760 species of larger moths in Britain 70 had changed their light color and markings for dark or even totally black coloration.

Kettlewell suspected that the success of the melanic form was linked with the industrial revolution and the consequent darkening of the trees by the vast amounts of smoke produced by the 19th-century factories. To test his hypothesis he released large numbers of the dark and light forms of the peppered moth, *Biston betularia*, in the polluted woods around Birmingham and in a distant unpolluted forest. As many of the released moths as possible were recaptured and when the results were analyzed it was found that the light form had a clear advantage over the dark in the unpolluted forest but in the polluted Birmingham woods the result was just the opposite. From this Kettlewell concluded that if the environment of a moth changes so that it is conspicuous by day, then the species is ruthlessly hunted by predators until it mutates to a form better suited to its new environment. His work was seen as a convincing and dramatic confirmation of the Darwinian hypothesis of evolution through natural selection.

Khorana, Har Gobind (1922–1993)
Indian–American chemist

Khorana, who was born at Raipur (now in Pakistan), gained his BSc (1943) and MSc (1945) from the University of Punjab. He then traveled to Liverpool University to work for his doctorate. On receiving his PhD in 1948, he did two years postdoctoral research in Switzerland before taking up a Nuffield Fellowship at Cambridge University. There he worked with Alexander Todd, who fired his interest in nucleic acid research – the field in which Khorana later made his name.

Shortly after Khorana joined Wisconsin University in 1960 he became interested in unraveling the genetic code. He synthesized each of the 64 nucleotide triplets that make up the code, and for this work received the Nobel Prize for physiology or medicine in 1968, sharing the award with Marshall NIRENBERG and Robert HOLLEY.

Khorana's next major achievement came in 1970, when he announced the synthesis of the first artificial gene. The same year he moved to the Massachusetts Institute of Technology, where, by 1976, his team had made a second gene, which (unlike the first) was capable of functioning in a living cell. Such work has far-reaching possibilities, bringing scientists a step nearer to understanding gene action. The future could see artificial genes being used to make valuable proteins (e.g., insulin) and perhaps to cure human hereditary diseases.

Kilby, Jack St. Clair (1923–) *American electronics engineer*

The son of an electrical engineer from Jefferson City, Missouri, Kilby failed his entrance to the Massachusetts Institute of Technology. He was drafted into the army, spending most of his time attempting to reduce the size of radio sets for jungle-warfare units. After demobilization, he was admitted to the University of Illinois. After graduating in 1947 he began work for Centralab, Milwaukee, Wisconsin, producing parts for television sets and hearing aids.

In 1952 Centralab decided to use the transistors recently developed by William Shockley and Kilby was sent to Bell Laboratories at Murray Hill, New Jersey, to learn about the new device. In 1958 he moved to Texas Instruments, Dallas, the firm that had had the foresight in 1954 to switch from germanium to silicon transistors. Engineers at TI, and elsewhere, had come up against the difficulty of fitting on a transistor the number of parts and connections demanded by their designs. It was here in July 1958, while the rest of the laboratory was on holiday, that Kilby came up with what was later termed 'the Monolithic Idea'.

His basic intuition was that silicon alone could fill most electronic demands. Undoped, it was a resistor; as a p–n junction, a capacitor. It should be possible to build a whole circuit out of a single piece of material by using different doping levels; no connections would be called for. He built a test circuit and it worked. It was, in fact, the first integrated circuit. Kilby was awarded patent rights in 1967, having first fought off a challenge from Robert Noyce. On appeal the decision was reversed and, in 1968, the patent was awarded to Noyce.

Kilby also worked for Texas Instruments on the development of what was the first pocket calculator, the Pocketronic. It was launched on April 14 1971, weighed 2.5 pounds, cost £150, and could only perform the four main arithmetical functions. By this time Kilby had left TI in 1970 to work in Dallas as a self-employed inventor. He also served as a distinguished professor of electrical engineering at the University of Texas from 1978 to 1985.

King, Charles Glen (1896–1986)
American biochemist. See SZENT-GYÖRGYI, ALBERT VON.

Kinsey, Alfred Charles (1894–1956)
American zoologist

Kinsey was born in Hoboken, New Jersey, and educated at Bowdoin College and Harvard. He was professor of zoology (from 1920) and director of the Institute for Sex Research, Indiana University, which he helped found, from 1942 until his death.

Kinsey's researches on human sexual behavior, published as *Sexual Behavior in the Human Male* (1948) and *Sexual Behavior in the Human Female* (1953), have attracted much interest and some controversy. His work demonstrated that there was considerable variation in behavior in all social classes and helped to dispose of certain erroneous ideas, for example with regard to juvenile sexual activity and homosexuality. Even though based on many (about 18,500) carefully conducted personal interviews, Kinsey's findings have been criticized for sampling limitations and the general unreliability of personal communication in this sphere of human activity.

Kirchhoff, Gustav Robert (1824–1887)
German physicist

Kirchhoff studied in his native city of Königsberg (now Kaliningrad in Russia), graduating in 1847. Three years later he was appointed a professor at Breslau. He moved to Heidelberg, where Robert Bunsen was professor of chemistry, in 1854.

Kirchhoff was one of the foremost physicists of the 19th century and is remembered as one of the founders of the science of spectroscopy. He is also known for *Kirchhoff's laws*, formulated in 1845 while he was still a student, which refer to the currents and electromotive forces in electrical networks.

In 1859 he published an explanation of the dark lines in the solar spectrum discovered by Josef von FRAUNHOFER, in which he suggested that they are due to absorption of certain wavelengths by substances in the Sun's atmosphere. He later formulated *Kirchhoff's law of radiation*, which concerns the emission and absorption of radiation by a hot body. It states that the rate of emission of energy by a body is equal to the rate at which the body absorbs energy (both emission and absorption being in a given direction at a given wavelength). Kirchhoff gave a final proof of this in 1861.

In about 1860 Bunsen was analyzing the colors given off by heating chemicals to incandescence, using colored glass to distinguish between similar shades. Kirchhoff joined this research when he suggested that the observation of spectral lines, by dispersing the light with a prism, would be a more precise way of testing the color of the light. Kirchhoff and Bunsen found that each substance emitted light that had its own unique pattern of spectral lines – a discovery that began the spectroscopic method of chemical analysis. In 1860, a few months after publishing these results, they discovered a new metal, which they called cesium, and the next year found rubidium. Kirchhoff and Bunsen also constructed improved forms of the spectroscope for such work and Kirchhoff showed that, if a gas emitted certain wavelengths of light then it would absorb those wavelengths from light passing through it.

Kirchhoff was crippled by an accident in mid-life but remained in good spirits and, when his health forced him to stop experimental work in 1875, he was offered the chair of theoretical physics in Berlin. He remained there until his death 12 years later.

Kirkwood, Daniel (1814–1895)
American astronomer

Born in Harford County, Maryland, Kirkwood became professor of mathematics at the University of Delaware in 1851, moving to the University of Indiana in 1856. In 1857 he noted that the asteroids (planetoids) are not evenly distributed in between the orbits of Mars and Jupiter but that there are areas in which no – or very few – asteroids orbit. He showed that these gaps in the asteroid belt – since known as *Kirkwood gaps* – occur where the period of revolution of an asteroid would have been an exact simple fraction of the Jovian period. Kirkwood explained that any asteroids in these areas would eventually be forced into other orbits by perturbations caused by Jupiter. Similarly he was able to explain gaps in the rings of Saturn (the Cassini division) as being caused by the satellite Mimas. Kirkwood published his findings in *The Asteroids* (1887).

Kistiakowsky, George Bogdan
(1900–1982) *Russian–American chemist*

Kistiakowsky came from a family of academics in Kiev, now in Ukraine. He began his education in his native city but, after fighting against the Bolsheviks, completed it in Berlin. He moved to America in 1926 working first at Princeton before moving to Harvard where he was appointed professor of chemistry in 1937, a post he retained until his retirement in 1971.

His most important work during World War II was as head of the Explosives Division at Los Alamos (1944–45). On being told of the project his initial reaction had been: "Dr Oppenheimer is mad to think this thing will make a bomb." The basic device, proposed by Seth Neddermeyer, consisted of a thin hollow sphere of uranium that would become critical only when 'squeezed' together. In theory this was achieved by surrounding the subcritical uranium with conventional explosives whose detonation would compress the radioactive material into a critical mass. To work the process must take place in less than a millionth of a second and with great precision and accuracy. Right to the very end there was considerable doubt as to whether Kistiakowsky could solve the technical problems involved.

After the war Kistiakowsky, very much a figure of the scientific establishment, spent much time advising numerous governmental bodies. From 1959 until 1961 he served as special assistant for science and technology to President Eisenhower, later writing an account of this period in *A Scientist at the White House* (1976). Toward the end of his life he spoke out about the dangers of nuclear weapons.

Kitasato, Baron Shibasaburo (1852–1931) *Japanese bacteriologist*

Born in Oguni, Japan, Kitasato graduated from the medical school of the University of Tokyo in 1883 and then went to Berlin to study under Robert Koch. A close and long-lasting friendship developed between the two men.

While in Berlin Kitasato worked with Emil von BEHRING and in 1890 they announced the discovery of antitoxins of diphtheria and tetanus. They showed that if nonimmune animals were injected with increasing sublethal doses of tetanus toxin, the animals became resistant to the disease. Their paper laid the basis for all future treatment with antitoxins and founded a new field in science, that of serology. Kitasato returned to Japan and became director of the Institute of Infectious Diseases in 1892. Two years later there was an outbreak of bubonic plague in Hong Kong and he succeeded in isolating the plague bacillus, *Pasteurella pestis*. In 1898 he isolated the microorganism that causes dysentery.

He founded the Kitasato Institute for Medical Research in 1914 and became dean of the medical school, Keio University, Tokyo. In 1924 he was created a baron. In 1908 Koch visited Japan and Kitasato secretly obtained clippings of the visitor's hair and fingernails. When Koch died in May 1910, Kitasato built a small shrine for the relics in front of his laboratory; when Kitasato died, his remains were placed in the same shrine, next to those of his respected master.

Kjeldahl, Johan Gustav Christoffer Thorsager (1849–1900) *Danish chemist*

Kjeldahl, the son of a physician, was born at Jagerpris in Denmark and educated at the Roskilde Gymnasium and the Technical University of Denmark, Copenhagen. After working briefly at the Royal Veterinary and Agricultural University he joined the laboratory set up by the brewer Carl Jacobsen in 1876 to introduce scientific methods into his Carlsberg brewery founded the previous year. Kjeldahl directed the chemistry department of the laboratory from 1876 until his fatal heart attack in 1900.

Kjeldahl is still widely known to chemists for the method named for him, first described in 1883, for the estimation of the nitrogen content of compounds. It was much quicker, more accurate, and capable of being operated on a larger scale than the earlier combustion-tube method dating back to Jean Dumas. It utilized the fact that the nitrogen in a nitrogenous organic compound heated with concentrated sulfuric acid will be converted into ammonium sulfate. The ammonia can then be released by introducing an alkaline solution, and then distilled into a standard acid, its amount being determined by titration.

His name is also remembered with the *Kjeldahl flask*, the round-bottomed long-necked flask used by him in the operation of his method.

Klaproth, Martin Heinrich (1743–1817) *German chemist*

Born in Wernigerode, Germany, Klaproth was apprenticed as an apothecary. After working in Hannover and Danzig he moved to Berlin where he set up his own business. In 1792 he became lecturer in chemistry at the Berlin Artillery School and in 1810 he became the first professor of chemistry at the University of Berlin.

His main fame as a chemist rests on his discovery of several new elements. In 1789 he discovered zirconium, named from zircon, the mineral from which it was isolated. In the same year he extracted uranium from pitchblende and named it for the newly discovered planet, Uranus. He also rediscovered titanium in 1795, about four years after its original discovery, and discovered chromium in 1798. Klaproth used the Latin *tellus* (earth) in his naming of tellurium (1798), which had been discovered by the Austrian geologist **Franz Joseph Muller** (1740–1825) in 1782. In 1803 he discovered cerium oxide, named for the newly discovered asteroid, Ceres.

Klein, (Christian) Felix (1849–1925) *German mathematician*

Klein, one of the great formative influences on the development of modern geometry, was born in Düsseldorf, Germany, and studied at Bonn, Göttingen, and Berlin. He worked with Sophus Lie – a collaboration that was particularly fruitful for both of them and led to the theory of groups of geometrical transformations. This work was later to play a crucial role in Klein's own ideas on geometry.

Klein took up the chair in mathematics at the University of Erlangen in 1872 and his inaugural lecture was the occasion of his formulation of his famous *Erlangen Programm*, a suggestion of a way in which the study of geometry could be both unified and generalized. Throughout the 19th century, with the work of such mathematicians as Karl Friedrich Gauss, János Bolyai, Nikolai Lobachevsky, and Bernhard Riemann, the idea of what a 'geometry' could be had been taken increasingly beyond the conception Euclid had of it and Klein's ideas helped show how these diverse geometries could all be seen as particular cases of one general concept. Klein's central idea was to think of a geometry as the theory of the invariants of a particular group of transformations. His *Erlangen Programm* was justly influential in guiding the further development of the subject. In particular Klein's ideas led to an even closer connection between geometry and algebra.

Klein also worked on projective geometry, which he generalized beyond three dimensions, and on the wider application of group theory, for example, to the rotational symmetries of regular solids. His name is remembered in topology for the *Klein bottle*, a one-sided closed surface, not constructible in three-dimensional Euclidean space. In 1886 Klein took up a chair at Göttingen and was influential in building Göttingen up into a great center for mathematics.

Klitzing, Klaus von (1943–) *German physicist*

Von Klitzing was born at Poznan but when the town was restored to Poland after 1945 his family moved to West Germany. He was educated at the universities of Brunswick and Würzburg, where he received his PhD in 1972 and where he remained as a teaching fellow until 1980. After Klitzing served as professor of physics at the Technical University, Munich, from 1980 to 1984, he was appointed director of solid-state research at the Max Planck Institute, Stuttgart.

In 1980 von Klitzing began work on the Hall effect, first described by Edwin Hall in 1879. Hall noted that when a current flows in a conductor placed in a magnetic field perpendicular to the sample's surface, a potential difference (the *Hall voltage*) is produced acting at right angles to both the current and field directions. It is possible to measure a *Hall resistance*, defined in the normal way by dividing the Hall voltage by the current it produces.

Von Klitzing set out to make extremely precise measurements of the Hall resistance working with a two-dimensional electron gas. This can be formed by using a special kind of transistor in which electrons can be drawn into a layer between an insulator and a semiconductor. When the layer is thin enough, of the order of 1 nanometer (10^{-9} meter), and the temperature is as low as 1.5 K, the electrons are forced into a two-dimensional plane parallel to the surface of the semiconductor.

Under normal conditions the Hall resistance increases directly with the strength of the magnetic field. In contrast von Klitzing found that under his experimental conditions the resistance became quantized, varying in a series of steps as the magnetic field was changed. Von Klitzing went on to establish that the Hall resistance at each step was a function of Planck's constant h, the fundamental constant of quantum theory, and could be used to measure h very accurately. For his discovery of the *quantized Hall effect* von Klitzing was awarded the 1985 Nobel Prize for physics.

Klug, Sir Aaron (1926–) *South African biophysicist*

Klug was born in Lithuania of South African parents, and moved to South Africa at the age of three. He studied medicine for a year at Witwatersrand University, Johannesburg, and then changed to study science. He moved to Cape Town in 1947 where he took a master's degree in crystallography. In 1949 Klug moved to England, where he worked at the Cavendish Laboratory, Cambridge. In 1954 he went to Birkbeck College, London, and was director of the Virus Structure Research Group there from 1958 to 1962, when he returned to Cambridge.

Klug originally developed a technique of improving results of electron microscopy by illuminating the micrograph with laser light. For micrographs of regular structures, a diffraction pattern is produced, from which extra information on the specimen can be obtained. At Birkbeck, Klug worked with J.D. Bernal on the polio virus. With Donald Caspar he went on to study small viruses. These are either rod-shaped or spherical, and consist of nucleic acids covered by a protein coat. Klug and Caspar developed a theory of how the coat could be formed by an arrangement of smallish quasiequivalent protein molecules.

At Cambridge, Klug worked on helical viruses showing how the protein units form. He went on to investigate the structure and action of transfer DNA in animal cells. More recently he has worked on chromatin in cells. Klug received the 1982 Nobel Prize for chemistry for his work in molecular biology.

Knuth, Donald Ervin (1938–) *American computer programmer*

Knuth showed an early interest in words and numbers. While in the 8th grade he entered a competition to find as many words as possible from the letters in the phrase "Ziegler's Giant Bar" and came up with 4500 – some 2000 more than the judges had compiled. At first he considered devoting himself to music but opted for mathematics and physics, which he studied at Case Institute for Technology, Cleveland, Ohio, and at the California Institute of Technology, where he gained his PhD in 1963. He remained at Cal Tech until 1968, when he moved to Stanford as professor of computer science. He resigned in 1992 to concentrate on writing.

In the 1960s Knuth began compiling what is now widely recognized as the fundamental work on computer science, *The Art of Computer Programming*. It is planned for seven volumes – the first three have already appeared: *Fundamental Algorithms* (1968), *Seminumerical Algorithms* (1969), and *Sorting and Searching* (1973).

Having completed the first three volumes, Knuth spent several years exploring typography. He had long been interested in printing and it occurred to him in 1977 that "printing was a computer science problem." The result was the much-studied book *Tex and Metafont* (1979) and the five-volume *Computers and Typesetting* (1986). Metafont allows the user to construct a custom-designed typesetting font. Tex (which Knuth prints as T_EX, and which is pronounced 'tek') is an automatic typesetting and page makeup program. It is widely available and popular with academic users.

Knuth has said that he intends to return to music once he has completed all seven volumes of his computer book – his house is built around a two-storey pipe organ that he designed himself. He has also written a remarkable science-fiction novel, *Surreal Numbers: How Two Ex-Students Turned On to Pure Mathematics and Found Total Happiness* (1974), based on a number system invented by the mathematician John Conway.

Koch, (Heinrich Hermann) Robert

(1843–1910) *German bacteriologist*

Born the son of a mining official in Klausthal, Germany, Koch studied medicine at the University of Göttingen where he was a pupil of Jacob Henle. After graduating in 1866 and serving in the Franco-Prussian War, Koch was appointed district medical officer in Wollstein. Here, working alone with only the most modest of resources, Koch began the research that was to make him, with Pasteur, one of the two founders of the new science of bacteriology.

Koch saw more clearly than anyone before what was involved in bacteriological research and achieved his first success with anthrax. Whereas Casimir Davaine had succeeded in transmitting anthrax from one cow to another by the injection of blood, Koch saw that the emerging germ theory required something more specific. It needed to be the germ that was injected rather than a fluid that could only be presumed to contain the organism. He thus spent three years devising techniques to isolate the anthrax bacillus from the blood of infected cattle and then to produce pure cultures of the germ.

By 1876 Koch was ready to publish the life history of the anthrax bacillus. He had found that while the bacillus in its normal state is somewhat sensitive and unable to survive long outside the body of its host, it forms resting spores, which are particularly hardy. Such spores, persisting in deserted ground, are responsible for the apparently spontaneous outbreaks of anthrax in healthy and isolated herds. Koch followed this with work on septicemia, during which he developed techniques for obtaining pure cultures.

With these triumphs behind him Koch at last achieved official recognition, being appointed to the Imperial Health Office in Berlin in 1880. In this office Koch, with the aid of his assistants Friedrich Löffler and Georg Gaffky, began one of the great periods of medical discovery. Much of this was based upon techniques of staining and culture growth developed by Koch in the obscurity of Wollstein. He developed culture media suitable for bacterial growth, proceeding from liquid media to boiled potato, to the still commonly used agar plates. Agar plates together with the new stains derived from aniline dyes constituted the heart of Koch's technique.

With them he made, in 1882, his most famous discovery – the bacillus responsible for tuberculosis (TB). In the second half of the 19th century TB, responsible for one in seven of all European deaths, was the most feared of all diseases. The difficulties Koch faced were formidable. The bacillus was only about a third of the size of the anthrax bacillus, grew much more slowly, and in general was more difficult to detect. With great patience Koch managed to culture the thin rod-shaped bacilli, which he used to inoculate four guinea pigs. All four developed TB while two uninoculated controls remained uninfected.

The fame won by Koch for this work brought him into open competition with Pasteur, a competition fanned by Franco-German nationalism in the aftermath of the 1870 war. In 1883 both sides met in Egypt to study cholera. The French, under Emile Roux, seem to have mistakenly confused platelets in the blood with the vibrio responsible for cholera. Koch, noting microorganisms in the small intestines of the victims, took them to be the cause of the disease, an assumption confirmed when he observed the same comma-shaped rods in the intestines of Indian victims. At this point Koch was forced to violate his own rules because, although he failed to infect experimental animals with pure strains of the vibrio, he nonetheless declared the organism to be the cause.

In 1885 Koch was appointed professor of hygiene at the University of Berlin and in 1891 became head of the newly formed Institute of Infectious Diseases. The pressure on Koch to 'earn' this latter appointment led him to announce in 1890 the discovery of a substance he claimed could prevent the growth of tubercle bacilli in the body. The new drug, a sterile liquid containing dead tubercle bacilli, which he named tuberculin, was consequently in huge demand. However it had little effect in most cases and probably exacerbated some. It later proved useful however in testing whether patients have experienced tuberculosis infection, by noting their local reaction to an injection of tuberculin.

Koch resigned the directorship of the Institute in 1904 to become one of the first of the emerging breed of international experts. Indulging his passion for travel, Koch spent his last years advising South Africa on rinderpest, India on bubonic plague, Java on malaria, and East Africa on sleeping sickness.

In 1905 Koch was awarded the Nobel Prize for physiology or medicine for "his discoveries in regard to tuberculosis." Perhaps as important as this, or any of his other specific discoveries, was his formulation of the so-called *Koch's postulates*. To establish that an organism is the cause of a disease we must, Koch declared, first find it in all cases of the disease examined; secondly it must be prepared and maintained in a pure culture; and finally it must, though several generations away from the original germ, still be capable of producing the original infection. Such postulates, first formulated fully in 1890, rigorously followed, established clinical bacteriology as a scientific practice.

Kocher, Emil Theodor (1841–1917)
Swiss surgeon

Kocher, an engineer's son from Bern in Switzerland, graduated in medicine from the university there in 1865. He later studied surgery in Berlin, Paris, and in London under Joseph Lister, and in Vienna under Theodor Billroth. Kocher served as professor of clinical surgery at the University of Bern from 1872 until his retirement in 1911 although he continued as head of the University surgical clinic until his death.

Using the antiseptic techniques developed by Lister, Kocher, following the initiative of Billroth, played an important role in developing the operation of thyroidectomy for the treatment of goiter, a not uncommon complaint in Switzerland. By 1914 Kocher was able to report a mortality of only 4.5% from over 2000 operations.

Earlier however, Kocher discovered that while technically successful the operation was responsible for the unnecessary ruin of many lives. In 1883, he found to his horror that something like a third of his patients who had undergone thyroidectomy were suffering from what was politely termed operative myxedema; they had in fact been turned into cretins once the source of the thyroid hormone (thyroxine) had been removed. Kocher showed that such tragedies could be prevented by not removing the whole of the thyroid, for even a small portion possesses sufficient physiological activity to prevent such appalling consequences.

For this work Kocher was awarded the 1909 Nobel Prize for physiology or medicine.

Köhler, Georges J. F. (1946–1995)
German immunologist

Born at Munich in Germany, Köhler was educated at the University of Freiburg, receiving his doctorate in 1974. He then worked in Cambridge at the Medical Research Council Laboratory of Molecular Biology (1974–76) and at the Basel Institute for Immunology (1977–84). In 1985 he was appointed director of the Max Planck Institute for Immunology in Freiburg.

In 1975, Köhler's work at the MRC Laboratory in Cambridge with the molecular biologist César MILSTEIN, yielded the first monoclonal antibody, i.e., antibody of one specific type manufactured by a culture of genetically identical cells, representing a single clone. This proved to be one of the major scientific breakthroughs of the decade, as anticipated by Köhler and Milstein in their letter to *Nature* briefly describing their achievement, published on August 7 1975: "Such cells can be grown *in vitro* in massive cultures to provide specific antibody. Such cultures could be valuable for medical and industrial use."

The technique of Köhler and Milstein involved fusing a white blood cell (lymphocyte), which manufactures antibody but has a short lifespan, with a cancer cell, which ensures continuous production of the antibody. Specifically, lymphocytes were obtained from the spleen of a mouse that had previously been injected with sheep red blood cells (the antigen) to stimulate antibody production in the mouse cells. The lymphocytes were then mixed with cells from a bone-marrow tumor culture to create a hybridoma – an antibody-secreting cell line.

Köhler and Milstein later adapted their technique to produce a range of hybridoma cultures, each manufacturing pure antibody to specific known antigen.

Monoclonal antibodies have revolutionized biological and medical diagnostic tests and assays and have found applications in various therapeutic techniques. Their great advantage is that they can be tailor-made to target a particular type of cell or subcellular component, and used as a vehicle for precision delivery of powerful drugs.

For their achievement, Köhler and Milstein shared the 1984 Nobel Prize for physiology or medicine with Niels JERNE.

Kohlrausch, Friedrich Wilhelm Georg (1840–1910) German physicist

Kohlrausch was born at Rinteln, the son of R. H. A. Kohlrausch, a famous physicist who served as professor at the University of Erlangen. Friedrich studied at Erlangen and then at Göttingen, where he gained his PhD in 1863. He held a series of professorial appointments at Göttingen, Frankfurt, Darmstadt, Würzburg, Strasbourg, and Berlin and was elected to the Academy of Sciences in Berlin in 1895.

Kohlrausch is remembered for his work on the electrical conductivity of solutions. He was able to measure the electrical resistance of electrolytes (substances that, by transferring ions, conduct electricity in solutions) by introducing an alternating current to prevent polarization of the electrodes. In this way he recorded the conductivity of electrolytes at various solute concentrations and discovered that conductivity increases with increased dilution. This finding led to the formulation of *Kohlrausch's law* of the independent migration of ions.

Kohn, Walter (1923–) Austrian–American theoretical chemist

Kohn was born in Vienna. From 1950 to 1960, he was professor at the Carnegie Institute of Technology in Pittsburgh, USA. He then joined the University of California in San Diego, remaining there until 1979 when he became director of the Institute of Theoretical Physics in Santa Barbara. He gave up that appointment in 1984, although he is still active at the Institute. In 1998 Kohn shared the Nobel Prize for chemistry with John POPLE. Kohn received his award for his development of density-functional theory

in quantum chemistry, for which he used powerful computer techniques.

Quantum chemistry – the solving of chemical problems using quantum mechanics – began to expand in the 1960s when computers became available to do the calculations. Kohn had already shown in 1964 that, for a system described by quantum mechanics, the total energy can be calculated if the electron density (distribution of electrons) is known. His later work concerned the simplification of the mathematics needed to describe the bonding in atoms and in mapping chemical reactions. He demonstrated that it is not necessary to be able to describe the motion of each individual electron in a molecule; it is sufficient to know the average number of electrons located at a particular point in space. The resulting *density-functional theory* is simpler to analyze using a computer, and can be employed for very large biologically important molecules.

Kolbe, Adolph Wilhelm Hermann (1818–1884) German chemist

Kolbe, the son of a clergyman from Göttingen, in Germany, was the eldest of 15 children. He studied under Friedrich Wöhler at Göttingen and then, in 1842, went to Marburg as Robert Bunsen's assistant and learned his method of gas analysis. In 1845 he went to London to work as Lyon Playfair's assistant on the analysis of mine gases for a commission set up to investigate recent explosions in coal mines. He was professor of chemistry at Marburg from 1851 until he moved to Leipzig to succeed Justus von Liebig in 1865.

Kolbe made a number of advances in organic chemistry. He was the first to synthesize acetic acid from inorganic materials (following Wöhler's synthesis of urea). The *Kolbe method* is a technique for making hydrocarbons by electrolysis of solutions of salts of fatty acids. He also produced a *Textbook of Organic Chemistry* (1854–60), which collected together all the methods of preparing organic compounds and in 1854 he edited Liebig and Wöhler's *Dictionary of Chemistry*.

Kölliker, Rudolph Albert von (1817–1905) Swiss histologist and embryologist

Born in Zurich, Switzerland, Kölliker qualified in medicine at Heidelberg in 1842 and later held professorships at Zurich and Würzburg. Celebrated for his microscopic work on tissues, he provided much evidence to show that cells cannot arise freely, but only from existing cells. He was the first to isolate the cells of smooth muscle (1848), as expounded in *Handbuch der Gewebelehre des Menschen* (1852; Manual of Human Histology): probably the best early text on the subject. He showed that nerve fibers are elongated parts of cells, thus anticipating the neuron theory, and demonstrated the cellular nature of eggs and sperm, showing for example that sperm are formed from the tubular walls of the testis, just as pollen grains are formed from cells of the anthers. Again anticipating modern discoveries, Kölliker believed the cell nucleus carried the key to heredity. His pioneering studies of cellular embryology mark him as one of the founders of the science. His book *Entwicklungsgeschichte des Menschen und der höheren Tiere* (1861; Embryology of Man and Higher Animals) became a classic text in embryology.

Kolmogorov, Andrei Nikolaievich
(1903–1987) *Russian mathematician*

Kolmogorov was born at Tambov in Russia and educated at Moscow State University, graduating in 1925. He became a research associate at the university, later a professor (1931), and in 1933 was appointed director of the Institute of Mathematics there. He made distinguished contributions to a wide variety of mathematical topics. He is best known for his work on the theoretical foundations of probability, but also made lasting contributions to such diverse subjects as Fourier analysis, automata theory, and intuitionism.

In 1933 Kolmogorov published his major treatise on probability, translated into English in 1950 as *The Foundations of the Theory of Probability*. The book is a landmark in the development of the theory, for in it he presented the first fully axiomatic treatment of the subject. It also contains the first full realization of the basic and underivable nature of the so-called 'additivity assumption' about probability, first put forward by Jakob I Bernoulli. This claims simply that if an event can be realized in any one of an infinite number of mutually exclusive ways, the probability of the event is simply the sum of the probabilities of each of these ways. This assumption is fundamental to the whole measure-theoretic study of probability.

Kolmogorov's interest in Luitzen BROUWER's intuitionism led him to prove that intuitionistic arithmetic, as formalized by Brouwer's disciple Arend Heyting, is consistent if and only if classical arithmetic is. In 1936 Kolmogorov settled a key problem in Fourier analysis when he constructed a function that is (Lebesgue) integrable, but whose Fourier series diverges at every point. In 1939, the same year in which he was elected an academician of the Soviet Academy of Sciences, he published a paper on the extrapolation of time series. This was later taken much further by Norbert Wiener and became known as 'single-series prediction'.

Köppen, Wladimir Peter (1846–1940)
Russian–German climatologist

Köppen was educated at the university in his native city of St. Petersburg and then at Heidelberg and Leipzig. Although he began his career in 1872 with the Russian meteorological service, he moved to Germany shortly afterward where, in 1875, he was appointed director of the meteorological research department of the German Naval Observatory at Hamburg, a post he retained until the end of World War I when he was succeeded by his son-in-law Alfred Wegener.

Köppen is mainly remembered today for the mathematical system of climatic classification he first formulated in 1900 and subsequently modified several times before 1936. He began by distinguishing between five broad climatic types – tropical rainy, dry, warm temperate, cold forest, and polar – symbolized by the letters A to E respectively. He further defined three patterns of precipitation: a climate with no dry period (f), with a dry summer period (s), and with a dry winter period (w). Four geographical zones were also introduced – steppe (S), desert (W), tundra (T), and perpetual frost (F). With such a technique some 60 climatic types are theoretically possible although Köppen argued that only 11 are in fact realized. Köppen further modified his scheme by introducing six temperature categories, which enabled him to make fine adjustments to his initial 11 classes. Though by no means the only such classification in existence, Köppen's system is still widely and conveniently used on climatic maps.

In his long career Köppen produced a number of substantial volumes, including a joint work with Wegener, *Die Klimate der geologischen Vorzeit* (1924; The Climate of Geological Prehistory), one of the founding texts of paleoclimatology. He also coedited, with Rudolph Geiger, a five-volume *Handbuch der Klimatologie* (Handbook of Climatology), begun in 1927 and nearing completion on his death in 1940.

Kornberg, Arthur (1918–) *American biochemist*

Kornberg was born in Brooklyn, New York, and graduated from the City College of New York in biology and chemistry in 1937.

He then studied medicine at Rochester University, gaining his MD in 1941. He joined the National Institutes of Health, Bethesda, where from 1942 to 1953 he directed research on enzymes. During this period he helped elucidate the reactions leading to the formation of two important coenzymes, flavin adenine dinucleotide (FAD) and diphosphopyridine nucleotide (DPN; later renamed nicotinamide adenine dinucleotide – NAD).

From 1953 to 1959 Kornberg was professor of microbiology at Washington University. In 1956, while investigating the synthesis of coenzymes, he discovered an enzyme that catalyzes the formation of polynucleotides from nucleoside triphosphates. This enzyme, which he named DNA polymerase, can be used to synthesize short DNA molecules in a test tube, given the appropriate triphosphate bases and a DNA template. For the discovery and isolation of this enzyme, Kornberg was awarded the 1959 Nobel Prize for physiology or medicine, sharing the award with Severo OCHOA, who discovered the enzyme catalyzing the formation of RNA.

Kornberg was chairman of the biochemistry department at Stanford University from 1959 and his work there has contributed to the understanding of the synthesis of phospholipids and many reactions of the tricarboxylic acid, or Krebs, cycle.

Kossel, Albrecht (1853–1927) *German biochemist*

Born in Rostock, Germany, Kossel was professor of physiology at the universities of Marburg and Heidelberg (1895–1923). He had first studied medicine, but turned his attention to biochemistry under the influence of Felix Hoppe-Seyler, whose assistant he was at Strasbourg (1877–81). Kossel was also for a time a colleague of Emil Du Bois-Reymond. While with Hoppe-Seyler, Kossel continued the latter's investigations of the cell substance called nuclein, demonstrating that it contained both protein and nonprotein (nucleic acid) parts. He was further able to show that the nucleic acids, when broken down, produced nitrogen-bearing compounds (purines and pyrimidines) as well as carbohydrates. Kossel also studied the proteins in spermatozoa, being the first to isolate the amino acid histidine. He was awarded the Nobel Prize for physiology or medicine in 1910 for his work on cells and proteins.

Kosterlitz, Hans Walter (1903–1996) *German–British psychopharmacologist*

Kosterlitz was educated at the universities of Heidelberg, Freiburg, and Berlin where he obtained his MD in 1929. He remained there as an assistant until 1933 when, with the rise of the Nazis, he sought safety in Britain. He joined the staff of Aberdeen University in 1934 where he later served as professor of pharmacology and chemistry from 1968 until 1973 when he became director of the university's drug addiction research unit.

For many years Kosterlitz had been working on the effects of morphine on mammalian physiology when in 1975, in collaboration with J. Hughes, he made his most dramatic discovery. They were investigating the effect of morphine in inhibiting electrically induced contractions in the guinea-pig intestine and, to their surprise, discovered that the same effect could be produced by extracts of brain tissue. When it turned out that the effect of the extract could be inhibited by naloxone, a morphia antagonist, it seemed likely to them that they had in fact stumbled on the endogenous opiates, discussed earlier by Solomon Snyder, and named by them enkephalins.

They quickly succeeded in isolating two such enkephalins from pigs' brains and found them to be almost identical peptides consisting of five amino acids differing at one site only and consequently known as methionine and leucine enkephalins. When it was further shown that they possessed analgesic properties hopes were raised once more of the possibility of developing a nonaddictive yet powerful pain killer.

Kovalevski, Aleksandr Onufrievich (1840–1901) *Russian zoologist and embryologist*

Kovalevski, who was born at Shustyanka, near Dvinsk (now Daugavpils in Latvia), took a science doctorate at the University of St. Petersburg, where he later taught and became professor (1891–93). He also taught at the universities of Kazan (1868–69), Kiev (1869–74), and Odessa (1874–90) and in 1890 he was elected to the Russian Academy of Sciences.

One of Kovalevski's most notable contributions to zoological science and the fuller understanding of evolution lay in his demonstration that all multicellular animals display a common pattern of physiological development. His research into the embryology of primitive chordates, such as *Amphioxus* (the lancelet), *Balanoglossus* (the acorn worm), and the sea squirts, particularly his demonstration of the links between them and the craniates, provided the basis for later studies of the evolutionary history of the vertebrates and led to Haeckel's theory that all multicellular animals are derived from a hypothetical ancestor with two cell layers. Kovalevski's most important publications are *Development of Amphioxus lanceolatus* (1865) and *Anatomy and Development of Phoronis* (1887).

Kovalevsky, Sonya (1850–1891)
Russian mathematician

The daughter of a wealthy artillery general, Kovalevsky was born in Moscow and brought up in the traditional manner on a large country estate, being educated only by an English governess. Her introduction to mathematics was unusual. One of the children's rooms of the family's large country house had temporarily been papered with Ostragradsky's lecture notes on calculus. Kovalevsky studied the notes as a child, and this gave her a grounding in the subject.

In 1867 the family moved to St. Petersburg and Kovalevsky managed to receive some more formal teaching at the Naval Academy. But the only socially acceptable way to continue her education was as a married woman. Consequently, in 1868 she entered into a marriage of convenience with Vladimir Kovalevsky, a young paleontologist and a translator of Darwin. They moved to Heidelberg in 1869 and two years later to Berlin. Although she could not be admitted to public lectures, Kovalevsky received private classes from Karl Weierstrass, who was so impressed with her work that he persuaded the Göttingen authorities to award her a doctorate in 1874 for a thesis on partial differential equations.

Despite this she remained unemployable as a female professional mathematician. In 1878 the Kovalevskys returned to Russia and speculated unwisely in property. Depressed by mounting debts Vladimir committed suicide in 1883. By this time Weierstrass had arranged for Kovalevsky to be appointed to a lectureship in mathematics at the University of Stockholm. She died from pneumonia in 1891.

Kovalevsky is best known for her work in partial differential equations in which she extended some earlier results of Cauchy. She also won the Borodin prize of the French Académie des Sciences in 1888 for her memoir *On the Rotation of a Solid Body about a Fixed Point.*

Kramer, Paul Jackson (1904–)
American plant physiologist

Kramer was born in Brookville, Indiana, and graduated in botany from the University of Miami, obtaining his PhD from Ohio State University in 1931. He immediately joined the faculty of Duke University, South Carolina, and spent his entire career there serving as professor of botany from 1945 until his retirement in 1974.

Kramer worked on problems of the absorption of water by plants, surveying the subject in his *Plant and Soil Water Relationships* (1949). He demonstrated that two different mechanisms are involved in water uptake by roots, depending on whether the plants are transpiring quickly or slowly. He also showed the importance of taking plant water stress into account when making correlations between soil moisture and plant growth. In studies using radioactively labeled elements he found that the region of maximum absorption in roots is not the tip but the area several centimeters behind the tip where the xylem conducting vessels are fully formed. Other researches led Kramer to the conclusion that substantial amounts of minerals enter plant roots passively in the transpiration stream.

Kramer also worked on the physiology of trees, publishing with Theodore Kozlowski *The Physiology of Woody Plants* (1979), an update of an earlier 1960 joint work.

Krebs, Edwin Gerhard (1918–)
American biochemist

Born in Lansing, Iowa, Krebs was educated at the University of Illinois and Washington University, Seattle, gaining his MD in 1943. For the following two years he worked as an intern and assistant resident at Barnes Hospital, St. Louis, and in 1946 returned to Washington University as a National Institutes of Health research fellow. In 1968, by now professor of biochemistry, Krebs moved to a similar position at the University of California, Davis. In 1977 he again returned to Seattle as professor of pharmacology in the school of medicine. In the same year he joined the Howard Hughes Medical Institute as investigator, becoming senior investigator in 1980 and emeritus professor in 1991.

Krebs is perhaps best known for his work on the regulation of enzyme activity, which he did at Seattle in conjunction with the biochemist, Edmond FISCHER. For this, he and Fischer shared the 1992 Nobel Prize for physiology or medicine.

Krebs, Sir Hans Adolf (1900–1981)
German–British biochemist

Krebs, the son of an ear, nose, and throat specialist, was born in Hildesheim, Germany, was educated at the universities of Göttingen, Freiburg, Munich, Berlin, and Hamburg, obtaining his MD in 1925. He taught at the Kaiser Wilhelm Institute,

Berlin, and the University of Freiburg but in 1933, with the growth of the Nazi movement, decided to leave Germany. Consequently he moved to England, where from 1935 to 1954 he served as professor of biochemistry at Sheffield University; after 1945 he was appointed director of the Medical Research Council's Cell Metabolism Unit at Sheffield. In 1954 Krebs moved to Oxford to take the Whitley Chair of Biochemistry, a post he held until his retirement in 1967.

Krebs is best known for his discovery of the *Krebs cycle* (or tricarboxylic acid cycle) in 1937. This is a continuation of the work of Carl and Gerty CORI, who had shown how carbohydrates, such as glycogen, are broken down in the body to lactic acid; Krebs completed the process by working out how the lactic acid is metabolized to carbon dioxide and water. When he began this work little was known apart from the fact that the process involved the consumption of oxygen, which could be increased, according to Albert SZENT-GYÖRGYI, by the four-carbon compounds succinic acid, fumaric acid, malic acid, and oxaloacetic acid. Krebs himself showed in 1937 that the six-carbon citric acid is also involved in the cycle.

By studying the process in pigeon breast muscle Krebs was able to piece together the clues already collected into a coherent scheme. The three-carbon lactic acid is first broken down to a two-carbon molecule unfamiliar to Krebs; it was in fact later identified by Fritz LIPMANN as coenzyme A. This then combines with the four-carbon oxaloacetic acid to form the six-carbon citric acid. The citric acid then undergoes a cycle of reactions to be converted to oxaloacetic acid once more. During this cycle two molecules of carbon dioxide are given up and hydrogen atoms are released; the hydrogen is then oxidized in the electron transport chain with the production of energy. Much of the detail of this aspect of the cycle was later filled in by Lipmann, with whom Krebs shared the 1953 Nobel Prize for physiology or medicine.

Krebs fully appreciated the significance of the cycle, pointing out the important fact that it is the common terminal pathway for the chemical breakdown of *all* foodstuffs.

In 1932, with K. Henselheit, Krebs was responsible for the introduction of another cycle. This was the urea cycle, whereby amino acids (the constituents of proteins) eliminate their nitrogen in the form of urea, which is excreted in urine. This left the remainder of the amino acid to give up its potential energy and participate in a variety of metabolic pathways.

Krogh, Schack August Steenberg
(1874–1949) *Danish physiologist*

Krogh, the son of a brewer from Grenaa in Denmark, was educated at the Aarhus gymnasium and the University of Copenhagen, where he obtained his PhD in 1903. He spent his whole career at the university, serving as professor of animal physiology from 1916 until his retirement in 1945.

Krogh first worked on problems of respiration. He argued, against his teacher Christian Bohr, that the absorption of oxygen in the lungs and the elimination of carbon dioxide took place by diffusion alone. He made precise measurements to show that the oxygen pressure was always higher in the air sacs than in the blood and, consequently, there was no need to assume any kind of nervous control.

It was, however, with his studies of the capillary system that Krogh achieved his most dramatic success. The simplest explanation of its action was to assume it was under the direct hydraulic control of the heart and arteries: the stronger the heart beat, the greater the amount of blood flowing through the capillaries. Krogh had little difficulty in showing the inadequacy of such a scheme by demonstrating that even among a group of capillaries fed by the same arteriole some were so narrow that they almost prevented the passage of red cells while others were quite dilated, allowing the free passage of the blood. Not content with this descriptive account Krogh went on to make a more quantitative demonstration. Working with frogs, which he injected with Indian ink shortly before killing, he showed that in sample areas of resting muscle the number of visible (stained) capillaries was about 5 per square millimeter; in stimulated muscle, however, the number was increased to 190 per square millimeter. From this he concluded that there must be a physiological mechanism to control the action of the capillaries in response to the needs of the body. It was for this work, fully described in *The Anatomy and Physiology of Capillaries* (1922), that Krogh was awarded the 1920 Nobel Prize for physiology or medicine.

Kronecker, Leopold (1823–1891)
German mathematician

Born in Liegnitz, now Legnica in Poland, Kronecker studied mathematics at Berlin but he did not become a professional mathematician until relatively late in life. He worked, highly successfully, as a businessman until he had made enough money to abandon commerce and devote himself fully to mathematics. He taught at Berlin from 1861, and, in 1883, was appointed professor. Outside mathematics Kronecker's interests were wide. He was a highly cultured man who used his wealth to patronize the arts. He also had a deep interest in philosophy and Christian theology, although he was not converted to Christianity until shortly before his death.

Kronecker's mathematical work was almost entirely in the fields of number theory and higher algebra, although he also made some contributions to the theory of elliptic functions. His work on algebraic numbers was inspired by his constructivist outlook, which involved a distrust of nonconstructive proofs in mathematics and a suspicion of the infinite and all kinds of number other than the natural numbers. This attitude led him to rewrite large areas of algebraic number theory in order to avoid reference to such suspect entities as imaginary or irrational numbers. Kronecker's constructivism is summed up in a famous remark he made during an after-dinner speech: "God made the integers, all else is the work of man." His suspicion of nonconstructive methods led Kronecker into fierce controversy with two of the leading mathematicians of his day, Karl Weierstrass and Georg Cantor. His outlook anticipates to a considerable extent the views of the Dutch mathematician L. E. J. BROUWER.

Kronecker was also one of the first to understand thoroughly and use Evariste Galois's work in the theory of equations. The *Kronecker delta function* is named for him.

Kroto, Harold Walter (1939–   ) *British chemist*

Born at Bolton in Lancashire, Kroto was educated at the University of Sheffield where he completed his PhD in 1964. After a postdoctoral fellowship with the National Research Council of Canada, and two years with Bell Laboratories, New Jersey, Kroto moved to the University of Sussex (1967) where he was appointed professor of chemistry in 1985.

Along with his Sussex colleague David Walton, Kroto had a long-standing interest in molecules containing carbon chains linked by alternate triple and single bonds. Such chains with five, seven, and nine carbon atoms had been identified by radioastronomers in space. In 1984 Kroto heard that the American chemist Richard Smalley had developed new techniques involving laser bombardment for the production of clusters of atoms. He suspected they might be suitable to produce the chains of carbon

atoms which interested him. Consequently in 1985 he visited Smalley in Houston.

Kroto persuaded Smalley to direct his laser beam at a graphite target. Clusters of carbon atoms were indeed produced but, more interesting than the small chains he was looking for, Kroto found a mass-spectrum signal for a molecule of exactly 60 carbon atoms. The first suggestion was that it had a sandwichlike graphite structure. However, such a planar fragment would have reactive carbon atoms at the edges, whereas C_{60} appeared to be stable. An alternative structure with the necessary lack of reactivity would be a spherical one in which the 60 carbon atoms are positioned at the vertices of a polyhedron. In Kroto and Smalley's model, which was later shown to be correct, the faces of the polyhedron are pentagons or hexagons arranged like the panels on a modern soccer ball. The framework also resembles the structure of the geodesic dome designed by the architect Buckminster Fuller. Kroto called C_{60} *buckminsterfullerene*, a name subsequently shortened to *fullerene*. Carbon molecules with this type of structure are informally called 'bucky balls'.

Before the structure could be put beyond doubt sufficient C_{60} would have to be prepared for detailed spectroscopic analysis. This, however, proved unexpectedly difficult. On his return to Sussex Kroto began to work on the problem. Unfortunately funding was unavailable, even for relatively cheap experiments with graphite electrodes. It was consequently left to Kratschmer and Huffman to announce in 1990 that they had synthesized a new form of carbon. When he read a full description of the synthesis Kroto learned that he had been pursuing the same method two years earlier when he had been forced to abandon the project through lack of funds. For his contribution to the discovery of C_{60} Kroto shared the 1996 Nobel Prize for chemistry with Richard SMALLEY and Robert CURL.

Kuhn, Richard (1900–1967) *Austrian– German chemist*

Kuhn was educated at the university in his native city of Vienna and then at Munich, where he obtained his PhD in 1922. He worked at the Federal Institute of Technology in Zurich from 1926 to 1929, when he moved to the University of Heidelberg to serve as professor of chemistry and, from 1950, as professor of biochemistry.

Like Paul KARRER, Kuhn worked mainly on the chemistry of plant pigments and vitamins, repeating many of Karrer's results. In particular Kuhn, independently of

Karrer, worked out the structures of vitamins A and B_2, and, in 1938, he also synthesized vitamin B_6.

For his work on carotenoids and vitamins Kuhn was awarded the Nobel Prize for chemistry in 1938, the year following the same award to Karrer. Hitler however objected to the award and Kuhn was forced to wait until the end of World War II before he was allowed to receive the prize.

Kühne, Wilhelm Friedrich (1837–1900) *German physiologist*

Willy Kühne, the son of a wealthy Hamburg merchant, was educated at the University of Göttingen where he obtained his PhD on induced diabetes in frogs in 1856. He studied further in Jena, Berlin, Paris (under Claude Bernard), and Vienna before joining Rudolf Virchow's Berlin institute in 1861. Kühne later held chairs of physiology, first at Amsterdam from 1868 and from 1871 until his retirement in 1899 at Heidelberg.

Kühne worked with Russell Chittenden on problems of digestion, and he isolated trypsin from pancreatic juice. In 1859, working with the sartorius muscle, he demonstrated that nerve fibers can conduct impulses both ways, and also showed that chemical and electrical stimuli can be used to excite muscle fibers directly.

He also, in the late 1870s, coined the term *rhodopsin* for the substance, also known as visual purple, first discovered in the retinal rods by Franz Boll in 1876. It was soon realized that the pigment was bleached out of the retina by light and resynthesized in the dark. Kühne realized that this could be used to photograph the eye, to take what he termed an 'optogram' by the process of 'optography'. To achieve this he placed a rabbit facing a barred window after having its head covered with cloth to allow the rhodopsin to accumulate. After three minutes it was decapitated and the retina removed and fixed in alum, clearly revealing a picture of a barred window.

Later investigations of rhodopsin by such scholars as George Wald revealed much about the mechanism of vision.

Kuiper, Gerard Peter (1905–1973) *Dutch–American astronomer*

Born at Harenkarspel in the Netherlands, Kuiper studied at the University of Leiden, where he obtained his BSc in 1927 and his PhD in 1933. He immediately emigrated to America where he took up an appointment at the Lick Observatory in California and then lectured (1935–36) at Harvard. In 1936 he joined the Yerkes Observatory and in 1939 moved to the McDonald Observatory in Texas, both run by the University of Chicago. He served as their director (1947–49, 1957–60) and was also professor of astronomy (1943–60). From 1960 to 1973 he was head of the Lunar and Planetary Laboratory of the University of Arizona.

Kuiper's main research work was on the solar system. He discovered two new satellites: Miranda, the fifth Uranian satellite in 1948 and Nereid, the second Neptunian satellite in 1949. He also investigated planetary atmospheres and succeeded in detecting carbon dioxide in the Martian atmosphere in 1948. Four years earlier he had found evidence of methane in the atmosphere of Saturn's largest satellite, Titan.

In 1950 he produced some intriguing data on Pluto. Based on observations made with the 200-inch (5-m) reflector at the Palomar Observatory he estimated the diameter of Pluto as 0.23 seconds of arc, which was equivalent to about 3600 miles (5800 km) or half the Earth's diameter. But as its mass was supposed to be roughly the same as that of the Earth it implied the unlikely conclusion that Pluto had a density of about ten times that of the Earth. Recent measurements, however, reveal that Pluto's mass is only 0.2% and its diameter roughly a quarter of Earth's. Kuiper also speculated on the origin of the planets and proposed in 1949 his theory that each planet evolved from its own gaseous cloud that was not initially part of the Sun. This is not generally accepted.

With the advent of the space age, Kuiper became closely involved with several space missions, including the Ranger program, 1961–65, in which the first close-up photographs of the Moon were obtained, and the Mariner 10 flight to Venus and Mercury, which was launched in 1973 shortly before his death.

Kurchatov, Igor Vasilievich (1903–1960) *Russian physicist*

Kurchatov, born the son of a surveyor at Sim in Russia, was educated at the University of the Crimea, from which he graduated in 1923. Shortly afterwards he was appointed to the Leningrad Physico-Technical Institute where, in 1938, he became director of the nuclear physics laboratory. At some time during the war he moved to Moscow to take control of his country's military and industrial atomic research.

Under Kurchatov's direction the Soviet atomic program was remarkably successful. The Soviet Union exploded its first atomic bomb in 1949, its first hydrogen bomb in 1952, and constructed a nuclear power station in 1954. Before 1978, element-104 was known in the Soviet Union as *kurchatovium*. (The American claimants to the discovery named it *rutherfordium*, which is now the accepted name.)

Kusch, Polykarp (1911–1993) *American physicist*

Although born in Blankenburg, Germany, Kusch spent all but the first year of his life as a resident of the United States, becoming a naturalized citizen in 1922. His early education was in the Midwest of the United States, and his undergraduate studies were at the Case Institute of Technology, Cleveland, Ohio. Starting in chemistry, he made an early switch to physics, and gained his BS in 1931. He followed this with work as a research assistant at the University of Illinois on problems of optical molecular spectroscopy, gaining his MS there in 1933 and his PhD in 1936. This was followed by a short period at the University of Minnesota researching mass spectroscopy (1936–37). From 1937 to 1972 he was associated with the physics department of Columbia University, New York City, apart from interruptions in World War II, when he was engaged in research on the military applications of vacuum tubes and microwave generators at Westinghouse Electric Corporation (1941–42) and Bell Telephone Laboratories (1944–46).

At Columbia, Kusch began work under Isidor Rabi on the first radiofrequency spectroscopy experiments using atomic and molecular beams. His research was principally on the fine details of the interactions of the constituent particles of atoms and molecules with each other and with an externally applied magnetic field. In particular, Kusch made accurate determinations of the magnetic moment of the electron as deduced from the hyperfine structure of the energy levels in certain elements, and in 1947 found a discrepancy of about 0.1% between the observed value and that predicted by theory. Although minute, this anomaly was of great significance to theories of the interactions of electrons and electromagnetic radiation (now known as quantum electrodynamics). It was for his precise work in measuring the electron's magnetic moment that he received the 1955 Nobel Prize for physics, sharing it with Willis LAMB, who performed independent but related experiments at Columbia University on the hyperfine structure of the hydrogen atom.

Kusch's career at Columbia University took him to associate professorship (1946), professorship (1949), and executive director of the Columbia Radiation Laboratory (1952–60), vice president and dean of the faculty (1969–70), and executive vice president and provost (1970–71). In 1972 he left to become professor of physics, and then Eugene McDermott Professor, at the University of Texas at Dallas.

Lack, David Lambert (1910–1973)
British ornithologist

Lack, the son of a well-known and prosperous London surgeon, was educated at Cambridge University. From 1933 to 1940 he taught at Dartington Hall, a progressive private school, except for a year's leave in 1938 spent studying the birds of the Galapagos. During World War II he served with the Army Operational Research Group, helping to develop radar. This experience was later applied when he used radar in his studies of bird migration. In 1945 he finally became a professional ornithologist and served as director of the Edward Grey Institute of Field Ornithology, Oxford, until his death.

Lack's first substantial work, the widely read *Life of the Robin* (1943), was followed by the publication of his Galapagos material in *Darwin's Finches* (1947), a fascinating account of the 14 specialized species of finch that have evolved from an original invading flock of ordinary seed-eating finches. Such fieldwork inevitably led Lack to the consideration of more theoretical questions.

In particular, he studied the factors controlling numbers in natural populations and concluded that such factors act more severely when numbers are high than when they are low. The irregularities of population fluctuation suggested to Lack that the control mechanisms must be very complex. His data and theories are discussed in such works as *Natural Regulation of Animal Numbers* (1954) and *Population Studies of Birds* (1966).

Such data was variously interpreted, for instance by Richard Dawkins, who claimed that it supported the theory of the 'selfish gene'; Lack himself was more inclined to use the data to support the idea of group selection.

Laënnec, René Théophile Hyacinthe (1781–1826) *French physician*

Laënnec was born in Quimper, Brittany, the son of an unsuccessful lawyer. After his mother's death he was brought up mainly by his uncle G. F. Laënnec, professor of medicine at the University of Nantes. He was a pupil of Jean Corvisart at the Charité in Paris, qualifying as a doctor in 1804. He worked at a number of hospitals before becoming in 1814 physician-in-chief at the Hôpital Necker, where he remained until 1822. Then he was appointed professor of medicine at the Collège de France. In 1826 he was forced to retire to Brittany where he died of consumption.

In 1819 Laënnec published one of the classic texts of modern medicine, *De l'auscultation médiate* (On Mediate Auscultation). It advanced the work of Leopold Auenbrugger in describing sounds detected within the body and the various diseases and anatomical defects they were related to. The work is, however, best known for its description of the situation leading to his invention of the stethoscope.

In 1816 he was consulted by a young woman with heart trouble whose age and sex inhibited him from examining her by his usual method, namely, placing his ear on her breasts. Instead, Laënnec tightly rolled a sheaf of paper and placed one end over the heart and the other to his ear. He was surprised and pleased to find that the heartbeat could be heard far more clearly and distinctly than before. The work became widely known and was translated into English in 1821 and only two years later was published in America, where it was vigorously promoted by Austin Flint. The stethoscope itself, in improved flexible versions, rapidly became a standard part of the physician's equipment.

Lagrange, Comte Joseph Louis (1736–1813) *Italian–French mathematician and theoretical physicist*

Lagrange was born at Turin in Italy of French ancestry. At school he was at first more interested in the classics until he read an essay by the astronomer Edmond Halley on the calculus, which converted him to mathematics. By the age of 18 he was teaching at the Artillery School in Turin, eventually becoming professor of mathematics there. He also began a discussion group, which evolved to form the Turin Academy of Sciences in 1758.

By 1760 Lagrange's reputation as one of Europe's greatest mathematicians was established; he received a prize from the Paris Academy of Sciences in 1764 for an essay on the libration of the Moon. On the invitation of Frederick the Great he succeeded Leonhard Euler as mathematical director of the Berlin Academy in 1766, serving there until 1787 when, following Frederick's death, he moved to Paris and a post in the Academy of Sciences.

Lagrange produced his greatest work, *Mécanique analytique* (1788; Analytical Mechanics), in Paris. This summarized the research in mechanics since Isaac Newton, based on Lagrange's own calculus of variations, and finally placed the mechanical theory of solids and fluids on a rigorous and analytical foundation. The book broke away from Euclidean tradition, and Lagrange commented in it that "one cannot find any diagrams in this work."

Lagrange also made many contributions to astronomy and number theory. His work on the theory of equations helped Niels Abel in his later development of group theory. In astronomy he found a special solution to the three-body problem showing that asteroids will tend to oscillate around a certain point now called the *Lagrangian point*. Much of the credit for the revolutionary introduction of the metric system is also due to him.

Despite Lagrange's being technically a foreigner and also a friend of aristocrats he was regarded with respect during the French Revolution, which broke out in 1789, and was made president of the commission for metrication in 1793. He founded the mathematics department in the Ecole Normale in 1795 and later in the Ecole Polytechnique in 1797. Napoleon honored him, making him a count and a senator.

Lamarck, Jean Baptiste Pierre Antoine de Monet, Chevalier de
(1744–1829) *French biologist*

Lamarck was born at Bazantin in France. Although his parents had intended him to enter the Church, when his father died in 1759 Lamarck left his Jesuit school and joined the army, where he was honored for his bravery in the Seven Years' War. He became interested in botany during his postings to camps in the Mediterranean and eastern France and completed his *Flore française* (Flowers of France) in 1778, having left the army some ten years earlier because of poor health.

To simplify the identification of plants, Lamarck presented the flora as a dichotomous key (a systematic list of characteristics in which there are two choices at each step in the classification). This system, which was far easier to use than other classifications of the time, impressed Georges de Buffon, who arranged for it to be published and also ensured that Lamarck was elected to the French Academy of Sciences.

Lamarck was employed as botanist at the Jardin du Roi until the institute was reorganized during the French Revolution. In the newly named Muséum National d'Histoire Naturelle Lamarck was placed in charge of animals without backbones – a group he later named 'invertebrates'. He differentiated the arachnids, insects, crustaceans, and echinoderms and wrote a seven-volume *Natural History of Invertebrates* (1815–22).

Lamarck was also interested in meteorology, geology, chemistry, and paleontology and it is thought that his observations in these fields contributed to the formulation of his evolutionary theory, which he first put forward in *Zoological Philosophy* (1809). Until the late 1790s, he had believed that species remained unchanged, but fossil evidence, and his nonbelief in extinction, combined to change his mind. He saw evolution as a natural tendency to greater complexity and put forward four laws to explain how such complexity is brought about. The second law states that "the production of a new organ in an animal body results from a new need that continues to make itself felt," and the fourth law, for which he is best remembered, states that such acquired characteristics are inherited. A much-quoted example of this view is the neck of the giraffe, which, through stretching for the uppermost leaves, becomes gradually elongated, and this adaptation is passed on to its offspring.

Today Lamarckism has largely been rejected in favor of Darwin's theory of evolution by natural selection, especially in the light of knowledge gained about genetic mutation as a source of the variation on which Darwin's theory is based. However, there have been strong advocates of Lamarck's theory, notably Luther Burbank, Paul Kammerer, and Trofim LYSENKO. Some support for Lamarck's views comes with the interesting work of the immunologists Edward Steele and R. M. Gorczynski who claim to have shown that acquired immunological tolerance is inherited in mice.

Lamb, Sir Horace (1849–1934) *British mathematician and geophysicist*

Born at Stockport, Lamb studied at Cambridge University. His earliest interest had been in classics, but soon after arriving in Cambridge he discovered his true vocation lay in mathematics. Among his teachers were George Stokes and the great mathematical physicist James Clerk Maxwell. Lamb's own interest in mathematics was very much shaped by contact with the ideas of these two men, and was almost entirely in applied mathematics. In 1875 he went to Australia to become the first professor of mathematics at the newly founded University of Adelaide. In 1885 he returned to England to take up the chair of mathematics at Manchester University, and held this post until his retirement in 1920. He was knighted in 1931.

Among the great variety of fields of applied mathematics to which Lamb made important contributions are electricity and magnetism, elasticity, acoustics, vibrations and wave motion, statics and dynamics, seismology, and the theory of tides and terrestrial magnetism. However, it is for his work in fluid mechanics that Lamb is most celebrated. He wrote a book on the subject, *Hydrodynamics* (1895), which immediately became a classic and by 1932 had gone through six editions. Lamb's work in geophysics was also important. He wrote a paper in 1904 on the propagation of waves over the surface of an elastic solid, in which he virtually laid the whole theoretical foundations for modern mathematical seismology.

Lamb, Hubert Horace (1913–   ) *British climatologist*

Lamb graduated in 1935 and, after working at the Meteorological Office, London, where he led the climatic variation research, he started the Climate Research Unit at the University of East Anglia, Norwich. He eventually became honorary professor in the School of Environmental Science at that university.

His main aim has been to build up a detailed picture of the climates of the past and to acquire sufficient understanding of them to be able to see how climate might develop. By examining such records as ships' logs he has been able to reconstruct much of the climate of the last two to three hundred years; for earlier periods he has used such evidence as the fluctuations in tree-ring width. The results of his researches were published in his two-volume *Climate: Present, Past and Future* (1972, 1977).

To understand such major climatic changes as the 'Little Ice Age' (1550–1850) or the unusually warm weather of the 1900–50 period Lamb has searched for possible physical mechanisms. To investigate the effects of volcanic dust, for example, he introduced the Dust Veil Index, which measures the amount of dust released each year on a scale that assigns the arbitrary value 1000 to the great Krakatoa eruption of 1883. As the present cooling has begun in a period with a low index it cannot, Lamb has argued, be the crucial factor.

Lamb, Willis Eugene, Jr. (1913–   ) *American physicist*

Born in Los Angeles, Lamb was a student at the University of California, Berkeley, graduating in chemistry in 1934 and gaining his PhD in physics in 1938. His thesis research, on the electromagnetic properties of nuclear systems, was directed by J. Robert Oppenheimer. In 1938 he became an instructor in physics at Columbia University, New York, becoming a professor in 1948, and from 1943 to 1951 he was also associated with the Columbia Radiation Laboratory. It was at Columbia that he performed the experiments on the fine structure of the hydrogen spectrum that led to his receiving the 1955 Nobel Prize for physics.

Shortly after World War II, Lamb began his work to check the accuracy of the predictions of Paul Dirac as they related to the energy levels and spectral lines of hydrogen. Dirac's quantum mechanical theory predicted that the hydrogen atom had two possible energy states with equal energies. Lamb's accurate work using radiofrequency resonance techniques, reported in 1947, revealed that there was a minute difference in these energy levels. Small as it was, this *Lamb shift* necessitated a revision of the theory of the interaction of the electron with electromagnetic radiation. For this work Lamb was awarded the Nobel Prize for physics, which he shared with another leader of research at Columbia, Polykarp Kusch, with whom he had performed wartime research in developing microwave radar.

In 1951 Lamb was made a professor of physics at Stanford. There he devised microwave techniques for examining the hyperfine structure of the spectral lines of helium. In 1956 he took a professorship in England at Oxford University, and in 1962 returned to America to a professorship at Yale. Since 1974 he has been professor of physical and optical sciences at the University of Arizona's department of physics.

His publications include *Laser Physics* (1974), written in collaboration with M. Sargent and M. O. Scully.

Lambert, Johann Heinrich

(1728–1777) *German mathematician, physicist, astronomer, and philosopher*

Lambert, the son of a poor tailor from Mulhouse (now in France), was largely self-educated. He spent the early part of his life in various occupations, including teaching and bookkeeping, and followed his scientific interests in his spare time. In 1764 he moved to Berlin where he attracted the notice of Frederick the Great and became a member of the Berlin Academy.

Lambert contributed to numerous branches of science and learning generally. His main mathematical achievement was to prove that 'π' is irrational. He did this by use of continued fractions and published the proof in 1768. He also studied the hyperbolic functions and introduced their use into trigonometry. Lambert did some remarkable work in non-Euclidean geometry, but this remained totally unknown until the end of the 19th century when it was published.

In addition to mathematics Lambert was an astronomer of note. The suggestion that there might be further galaxies beyond our own was first made by him and this was subsequently confirmed observationally by William Herschel. Lambert was the first to invent an accurate way of measuring light intensities and the *lambert*, a measurement of light intensity, was named for him.

In his philosophical ideas Lambert largely developed the ideas of the great German rationalist philosopher Gottfried Leibniz and his chief philosophical work, *Neues Organon* (New Organon), was published in 1764.

Lamont, Johann von (1805–1879)
Scottish–German astronomer

Lamont, whose father worked in the customs service, came from an old but impoverished family in Braemar, Scotland. After his father's death in 1816 the young Lamont was sent to the Scottish Benedictine monastery at Ratisbon and given a rigorous mathematical training from the abbot. He was admitted to the Munich Academy of Science in 1827 and became assistant astronomer at the Bogenhausen Observatory in 1828 and director in 1835. In 1852 he became professor of astronomy at Munich University.

Lamont published a major catalog in six volumes (1866–74) of 34,674 small stars but his most important work was on terrestrial magnetism. He began keeping local records in 1836 and performed magnetic surveys of Bavaria, France, Spain, Denmark, and North Germany. He announced the important discovery of the Earth's (approximately) ten-year magnetic cycle in 1850, only a few years after Heinrich Schwabe had announced a similar cycle for sunspots. It was not long before scientists began to speculate on a possible connection.

Land, Edwin Herbert (1909–1991)
American inventor

Born in Bridgeport, Connecticut, Land began his education at Harvard but left to develop a number of commercial ideas.

His first success was a method of producing a relatively cheap filter that would transmit polarized light. The material, sold under the tradename Polaroid, was a plastic containing aligned crystals, which restrict the light vibrations to one plane. Land set up the Polaroid Corporation in 1937 in Cambridge, Massachusetts. With the onset of World War II there was an increased demand for polarizing filters for sunglasses, binoculars, and other optical instruments, and Land's company flourished.

Following the end of the war Land sought new areas to exploit. He chose photography and concentrated on designing an instant camera. Chemicals to develop the film were contained in a lead pod pierced as it was squeezed through a pair of rollers. Early instant cameras required a wait of a minute or more before peeling away the protective plastic. Land's SX70 camera, launched in 1972, ejected the print instantly for the image to develop within seconds.

Land also tried to develop a new theory of color vision that began by rejecting the old trichromatic theory linked with Newton and Young. How, he asked, does the eye cope with an excess of red in a room lit by an incandescent tungsten light? Familiar objects like green apples and yellow lemons do not appear to redden in this artificial light, despite the fact that it does not have the same spectral distribution as sunlight. How do objects retain their 'color identity' under a great variety of lighting conditions? It cannot simply be the responses of the retinal photoreceptors to radiant energy; also involved are high-level brain processes. Thus for Land, vision was a retina-and-cortex system, which he called a *retinex system*.

Landau, Lev Davidovich (1908–1968)
Azerbaijani theoretical physicist

Landau, whose father was a petroleum engineer and whose mother was a physician, was born in Baku, the capital of Azerbaijan. He studied at the university in his native city (1922–24) and at Leningrad (now St. Petersburg) (1924–27), graduating in 1927. In 1929 he visited various scientific centers in Europe, including Copenhagen where he developed a long-lasting friendship and working relationship with Niels Bohr. He returned to the Soviet Union and in 1932 went from Leningrad to Kharkov to head the theoretical physics groups at two of the institutes there. He was appointed professor of physics at Kharkov University in 1935. In 1937, at the request of Pyotr

Kapitza, he moved to Moscow as director of theoretical physics at the Institute of Physical Problems and in 1943 became professor of physics at the Moscow State University.

Landau was one of the major theoretical physicists of his day, making numerous contributions to many branches of physics. These included quantum mechanics, atomic and nuclear physics, astrophysics, thermodynamics, particle physics, quantum electrodynamics, and low-temperature physics. In Moscow he collaborated with E. M. Lifshitz on a highly successful series of monographs on theoretical physics, published in 1938. In 1962 he was awarded the Nobel Prize for physics for his work on condensed matter (i.e., matter in the solid or liquid state), especially liquid helium. Liquid helium has such unusual properties when its temperature falls below 2.2 kelvin that physicists describe it as helium II, as opposed to helium I above 2.2 K. To explain the strange superfluidity and superconductivity of helium II, Landau introduced the idea of a 'phonon', a quantum of thermal energy, and a 'roton', an elementary quantum of vortex motion. The existence of such entities has since been confirmed experimentally.

Under Landau a vigorous school of theoretical physics was created in Moscow. Tragically he was involved in a serious motor accident in 1962 and although strenuous efforts were made to keep him alive his physical powers never returned to normal and he died six years later.

Landsteiner, Karl (1868–1943)
Austrian–American pathologist

Landsteiner, the son of a prominent Viennese journalist, was educated at the University of Vienna, where he obtained his MD in 1891. After studying chemistry in Germany under Emil Fischer and in Switzerland under the German chemist Arthur Hantzsch, Landsteiner returned to the University of Vienna to work as a pathologist, serving as professor of pathology from 1911 to 1919. He then spent a couple of years in Holland before moving to America, where he took up an appointment with the Rockefeller Institute, New York, in 1922, remaining there until his death.

In 1902 Landsteiner announced one of the major medical discoveries of the century, that of the ABO blood group system. It was already known that the proteins in any animal or plant species were specific to that species and differed from those of other species, but Landsteiner went on to suggest that individuals within a species showed similar though small differences in their proteins. He knew that if serum (blood from which the cells and clotting factors have been removed) of one species is mixed with the erythrocytes (red cells) of another species the resulting mixture will agglutinate (clump together); he therefore decided to see what would happen when serum and erythrocytes from different humans were combined. In many cases there was no agglutination – it was as if the blood cells were mixed with their own serum – but in others he noted that agglutination occurred with just as strong an interaction as that between serum and cells of different species. The pattern of agglutination was such that Landsteiner proposed the existence of four distinct human blood groups, which he named A, B, AB, and O, based on the presence or absence in the blood of one or both of two antigens (substances against which antibodies react), which he named A and B. On this supposition individuals of blood group A (i.e., with antigen A) possess in their serum an antibody to antigen B, while group B individuals possess an antibody against antigen A; type AB individuals possess both antigens A and B (and therefore neither anti-A nor anti-B antibody), while type O individuals possess neither antigen and both antibodies.

Not only did Landsteiner's work at last permit successful blood transfusions and save many thousands of lives, it also raised profound questions about the nature of the immunological system – questions still being vigorously pursued. The ABO grouping was the first of many different groups to be discovered; Landsteiner himself, in 1927, discovered the second and third systems, the MN and the P. For his work on blood groups Landsteiner was awarded the 1930 Nobel Prize for physiology or medicine.

He also produced major results outside the field of serology, making (in 1908) one of the earliest breakthroughs in the conquest of polio. By taking pieces of the spinal cord of a polio victim and soaking them in liquid, he produced a mixture capable of infecting monkeys. Further work led him to conclude that a virus caused the disease. Landsteiner's approach permitted laboratory investigation and experimentation, which is the initial step in gaining understanding and control of any infective organism.

In the field of immunology Landsteiner demonstrated the specificity of antibodies by introducing the concept of the hapten. Haptens are small organic molecules that can stimulate antibody production only when combined with a protein molecule. Landsteiner combined haptens of known structures with such proteins as albumin and showed that small changes in the hapten would radically affect the production of antibodies.

Landsteiner was fortunate to be able to continue with creative scientific work virtually to the end of his life: he in fact suffered his fatal heart attack while working at his laboratory bench with a pipette in his hand. He was over 70 when, in 1940, he announced the discovery of the rhesus (Rh) factor, then responsible for the consequent serious illness or death of 1 in 200 white babies. The factor was so named as it was first detected in the blood of rhesus monkeys.

Landsteiner's work has continued to be the foundation for studies in many other related fields including that, for example, of the American biochemist **William Boyd** (1903–). In his *Genetics and the Races of Man* (1950) Boyd demonstrated that analysis of blood samples allowed us to distinguish 13 races, namely, early European, northern and eastern European, Lapp, Mediterranean, African, Asian, Deavidian, Amerind, Indonesian, Melanesian, Polynesian and Australian aborigine.

Langevin, Paul (1872–1946) *French physicist*

Langevin, a native Parisian, studied at the Cavendish Laboratory in Cambridge under J. J. Thomson and at the Sorbonne, where he obtained his PhD under Pierre Curie in 1902. He became physics professor at the Collège de France in 1904 and at the Sorbonne in 1909.

Langevin worked on the application of ultrasonic vibrations, which, following Pierre Curie's discovery of piezoelectricity, could be generated by applying a rapidly changing electric potential to a crystal, making it vibrate and produce sound waves in the ultrasonic region. Because ultrasonic wavelengths are shorter than those in the audible range, they are better reflected and Langevin saw that this might be put to military use in World War I. His development of echo location to detect submarines in fact came too late to be used in the war, but this work was the grounding for the later sonar.

Langevin also studied paramagnetism and gave a modern explanation of it incorporating electron theory. In this way he was able to deduce a formula correlating paramagnetism with absolute temperature, which gave a theoretical explanation of the experimental observation that paramagnetic moment changes inversely with temperature. The formula also enabled Langevin to predict the occurrence of para-

magetic saturation – a prediction later confirmed experimentally by Heike Kamerlingh-Onnes.

Langevin also studied the properties of ionized gases, and Brownian movement in gases. He publicized in France Einstein's views on the equivalence of energy and mass.

Langley, John Newport (1852–1925) *British physiologist*

Langley, the son of a schoolmaster, was born in Newbury and educated at Exeter Grammar School and Cambridge University. Although he originally intended to join the Indian Civil Service, Langley fell under the influence of Michael Foster, professor of physiology at Cambridge, and turned to physiology instead. He was appointed lecturer in histology in 1884 and in 1903 he succeeded Foster as professor of physiology, a post he retained until his death.

Langley began his research career in 1875, when Foster asked him to observe the physiological effects of jaborandi juice, an alkaloid derived from an American shrub. Foster was particularly interested in its effects on the heart but Langley was more impressed by its power to evoke copious secretion, a process he spent the next 15 years studying.

His most significant work, however, was done on the autonomic nervous system, a term he himself coined in 1898. In collaboration with William Dickinson, Langley began (in 1889) to explore the sympathetic nervous system in some detail. This was made possible by the discovery that nicotine would selectively block nerve impulses at the sympathetic ganglia, enabling Langley to distinguish those nerves that actually ended at the ganglia from those that merely passed through them. Langley was thus able to show that only one ganglion lay along the sympathetic nerve on its path from the spinal cord to its goal.

In 1901 Langley followed this by exploring the problem of how nerves communicate with the muscle cells with which they form junctions. Basically the sympathetic system increases heartbeat, raises blood pressure, and contracts smooth muscle, i.e., it prepares an animal for action. Langley noted that when an extract from the adrenal gland was injected into an animal, these responses were produced. It was left to the British physician Thomas Elliott, a pupil of Langley, to propose that it was the adrenal extract, later termed adrenaline (epinephrine), that was released from sympathetic nerves to stimulate muscle.

Langley later published the details of his work in his *Autonomic Nervous System* (1921).

Langmuir, Irving (1881–1957) *American chemist*

Langmuir, who was born in Brooklyn, New York, studied metallurgical engineering at the Columbia School of Mines, New York. He then went on to do postgraduate work under Walther Nernst at Göttingen, where he obtained his PhD in 1906. On his return to America he taught for a short time at the Stevens Institute of Technology, New Jersey, before joining the research laboratory of the General Electric Company (GEC), Schenectady, New York, (1909) where he remained until his retirement in 1950.

Langmuir was an extremely original and productive industrial physical chemist. In 1913 he achieved a major breakthrough in the design of electric light bulbs. The vacuum tubes (tungsten bulbs) then in use contained an incandescent tungsten wire that tended to break and also deposited a black film inside the bulb. Most research to rectify this was concentrating on improving the quality of the vacuum in the bulb. Langmuir saw that the same effect could be obtained more cheaply and efficiently by filling the bulb with an inert gas. After much experimentation he found that a mixture of nitrogen and argon did not attack the tungsten filament and eliminated the oxidation on the bulb.

In 1919 Langmuir tried to develop the theory of the electron structure of the atom published by Gilbert LEWIS in 1916. Lewis had only dealt with the first two rows of the periodic table and Langmuir tried to extend it. He proposed that electrons tend to surround the nucleus in successive layers of 2, 8, 8, 18, 18, and 32 electrons respectively. Then using similar arguments to those of Lewis he went on to try and explain the basic facts of chemical combination. It was not until after the development of quantum theory in the 1920s that a definitive account could be provided by Linus PAULING.

Langmuir also developed a vacuum pump, constructed a hydrogen blowtorch (1927) for welding metals at high temperatures, and worked on the production of artificial rain with Vincent Schaefer in 1947. In his research career he conducted a prolonged investigation into the chemistry of surfaces, tackling such problems as how and why certain substances spread on water and how gases interact with metal surfaces. Langmuir introduced the idea of adsorption of a single layer of atoms (a monolayer) on a surface and the theory that surface reactions (as in heterogeneous catalysis) take place between adsorbed molecules or atoms. The *Langmuir isotherm* is an expression relating the amount of adsorption on a surface with the gas pressure (at constant temperature). He was awarded the Nobel Prize for chemistry in 1932 for his research into surface reactions.

Laplace, Marquis Pierre Simon de (1749–1827) *French mathematician, astronomer, and physicist*

Laplace, born the son of a small estate owner in Beaumont-en-Auge, France, was educated at the University of Caen. Jean D'Alembert, impressed by a letter on mechanics sent to him by Laplace, arranged for him to become professor of mathematics in the Ecole Militaire in Paris. He became a full member of the French Academy of Sciences in 1785. Laplace prospered during the reign of Napoleon who had a genuine interest in mathematics, taking pleasure in rewarding the eminent mathematicians of his day. Laplace served briefly as Napoleon's minister of the interior in 1799 and much longer as one of his senators. He was also made a count by the emperor. Laplace was clearly one of nature's survivors, for with the Bourbon restoration in 1814 he found no embarrassment in signing the decree banishing his patron. He was made a marquis by Louis XVIII.

Laplace's greatest work was the *Traité de mécanique céleste* (Celestial Mechanics) published in five volumes between 1799 and 1825. Although Newton had derived the laws that govern the movements of the heavenly bodies it was clear to him that there were certain irregularities or perturbations in the movements of the planets that would lead to the end of the universe if not corrected. Newton was willing to accept God's intervention in the system to prevent its collapse. What Laplace showed was that while it was true that there were irregularities in the system they were periodic and not cumulative. The system was basically stable. When Napoleon pointed out to him that he had not mentioned God in his book Laplace proudly retorted that he had no need of that hypothesis. A popular account, *Exposition du système du monde* (Exposition of the System of the World), was published in 1796. It is in this work that he proposed the nebular hypothesis. Here he argued that the solar system had evolved from a rotating mass of gas that had condensed to form the Sun. From this had been thrown off the planets which in turn threw off their various satellites. The theory had in fact been proposed earlier by

Immanuel Kant (in 1755) and was soon to run into trouble with the discovery of retrograde orbits in the system. However, a new form of the nebular hypothesis has been introduced into astronomy by Carl von Weizsäcker.

Laplace's second great achievement was the establishment of probability theory on a rigorous basis in his *Théorie analytique des probabilités* (1812; Analytic Theory of Probabilities) and *Essai philosophique sur les probabilités* (1814; Philosophical Essay on Probabilities). His third great achievement was his development of the concept of a 'potential' and its description by the *Laplace equation*:

$$\Delta^2 u = \partial^2 u/\partial x^2 + \partial^2 u/\partial y^2 + \partial^2 u/\partial z^2 = 0$$

For Laplace *u* was a 'velocity potential' but it was soon seen to have an enormous number of applications in all kinds of areas and became an essential means of dealing with motion in any field be it electromagnetic, gravitational, or hydrodynamic.

Although Laplace has the reputation among mathematicians of being both a careerist and a plagiarizer he did much to help others and to encourage the growth of French science. His home at Arcueil, Paris, was the center for the greatest concentration of scientific talent of his or any other time. He died there uttering what sound like some well-prepared last words: "What we know is very slight; what we don't know is immense."

Lapworth, Charles (1842–1920) *British geologist*

Lapworth was born at Faringdon in Oxfordshire. In 1864 he became a schoolmaster in Scotland where his interest in geology developed. There he studied the Lower Paleozoic rocks, publishing his results between 1878 and 1882. He used graptolites, the fossil skeletons of colonial animals found in the Lower Paleozoic, to determine the stratigraphy of Scotland and later published a series of monographs on the fossils (1901–18).

In 1879 Lapworth introduced the Ordovician system of geological strata. There had been a bitter dispute between Adam Sedgwick, who considered this complex series of strata to be Upper Cambrian and Robert Murchison, who considered it to be Lower Silurian. Lapworth's suggestion that it was in fact a separate system, which he named Ordovician after a Welsh tribe, settled the dispute.

Lapworth was appointed to the chair of geology at Birmingham University in 1881. His son, Arthur, was a chemist of some distinction.

Larmor, Sir Joseph (1857–1942) *Irish physicist*

Born at Magheragall in Ireland, Larmor gained his BA and MA from Queen's University, Belfast; he entered Cambridge University in 1877, gaining a fellowship in 1880. He then became professor of natural philosophy at Queen's College, Galway. In 1885 he returned to Cambridge as a university lecturer in mathematics and in 1903 became Lucasian Professor of Mathematics. He retired from this post in 1932. Apart from his scientific work Larmor served as member of parliament for Cambridge University from 1911 to 1922.

Larmor's central interests were in applied mathematics and physics, specifically in electromagnetic theory, optics, mechanics, and the dynamics of the Earth. Like the work of his contemporary, Hendrik Lorentz, Larmor's work belongs to the final phase of classical physics that paved the way for the revolutions of relativity and quantum theory. An example of Larmor's basic scientific conservatism was his support of the concept of the ether as the wave-bearing medium thought to pervade all space and his work, published in 1900 as *Aether and Matter*, on the motion of matter through the ether. He believed that matter could only interact with the ether through the effects of electrically charged particles that formed part of the ether.

Larmor made two particularly important contributions to electrodynamics. He was the first to predict in 1897 the *Larmor precession*. This is the wobbling motion of the orbital plane of an electron moving in an atom when subjected to a magnetic field. The axis at right angles to the plane of the orbit sweeps out a conical area. Larmor also derived a nonrelativisitic formula that expresses the power radiated by an accelerated electron as being proportional to the square of the product of charge and acceleration.

Lartet, Edouard Armand Isidore Hippolyte (1801–1871) *French paleontologist*

After studying law at Toulouse, Lartet – the son of a wealthy landowner – spent the earlier part of his life managing the family estates at St. Guiraud. His interest in paleontology was aroused in the early 1830s when he was shown a locally discovered mastodon tooth. Beginning with his discovery in 1836 of *Pliopithecus*, the ancestor of the gibbon, he made a number of significant fossil discoveries. In 1856 he found remains of *Dryopithecus*, the fossil ancestor of the other apes, and in 1868, at Cro-Magnon in the Dordogne, he came across several adult human skeletons, later to be named Cro-Magnon man, that were found to belong neither to Neanderthal nor to modern man. These are the earliest known fossils of humans in Europe. They have modern teeth and jaw bones and a brain capacity averaging about 1300 cubic centimeters.

Lartet's most important work, however, helped to solve one of the major problems of 19th-century science, namely the antiquity of humans. Early proposals that human history could be pushed back into glacial times lacked conclusive proof: attempts to link human remains with the bones of extinct animals were always open to the objection that they were accidental assemblies that had come together at some historic time. Nor was the argument that some of the animal bones had been worked by humans any more persuasive, since the working of ancient bones could have taken place at any time.

In the early 1860s Lartet began a careful study of the caves of the Dordogne and the Pyrenees in collaboration with the British banker Henry Christy. In a cave at La Madelaine in 1863 he found a piece of ivory with a woolly mammoth clearly engraved upon it. Excluding forgery, there seemed no other explanation than that an animal of the ice age and a human witness had coexisted.

Lartet went on to propose a sequence for the Paleolithic based on the presence of animals, but scholars preferred alternative classifications based on tools. The results of his researches were published posthumously in *Reliquiae Aquitanicae* (1875; *Aquitanian Remains*), a work that did much to establish the prime importance of the archeological sites of southern France. In 1869 Lartet was appointed professor of paleontology at the museum of the Jardin des Plantes – a post he held until his death.

Lassell, William (1799–1880) *British astronomer*

Lassell, who was born at Bolton in Lancashire, was a brewer by profession who became interested in astronomy. He built an observatory for himself at Starfield near Liverpool and developed an interest in techniques for building very large reflectors, which he used himself. In 1844 he began building a 24-inch (61-cm) reflector with which – just 17 days after the discovery of Neptune in 1846 – he discovered Neptune's largest satellite, Triton. He also discovered Hyperion (a satellite of Saturn) and the crepe ring of Saturn independently of William BOND. In 1851 he discovered two satellites of Uranus – Ariel and Umbriel –

from observations made in Malta (where the atmosphere was clearer than in industrial England). In Malta in 1861 he built a 48-inch (122-cm) reflector and observed and cataloged hundreds of new nebulae.

Laue, Max von *See* VON LAUE, MAX THEODOR FELIX.

Laughlin, Robert B. (1950–)
American physicst

Laughlin was born in Visalia, California, and gained his PhD in physics in 1979 from the Massachusetts Institute of Technology. In 1989 he became professor of physics at Stanford University, where he did research on the fractional quantum Hall effect. For this work he shared the 1998 Nobel Prize for physics with Horst STÖRMER and Daniel TSUI, for explaining their discovery of a new form of quantum fluid with fractionally charged excitations.

Laughlin showed how electrons in a powerful magnetic field can condense to form a so-called 'quantum fluid' similar to those that occur in liquid helium and in superconductors. The theory derives ultimately from the Hall effect (the production of a voltage in a current-carrying conductor or semiconductor at right angles to a magnetic field), discovered in 1879 by the American physicist Edwin HALL. It occurs because electrons – the charge carriers – are deflected laterally in the magnetic field. A century later the German physicist Klaus von KLITZING discovered that in a powerful magnetic field at extremely low temperatures the Hall resistance of a semiconductor is quantized in integral 'steps'.

Using even stronger magnetic fields and lower temperatures, Störmer and Tsui discovered more steps, called the *fractional quantum Hall effect*. A year later Laughlin theorized that the low temperature and powerful magnetic field forced the electrons to form a new type of quantum fluid. The addition of a single electron to this superfluid produced a number of fractionally charged quasiparticles, with the correct charges to account for the results of Störmer and Tsui.

Laurent, Auguste (1807–1853) *French chemist*

The son of a mining engineer, Laurent was born at La Folie in France. He was educated at the mining school in Paris and worked for some time as a mining engineer before becoming an assistant to Jean Dumas in Paris. He was appointed professor of chemistry at Bordeaux in 1838. He returned to Paris in 1846 but he found it difficult to find employment, largely, it is thought, because of his unpopular chemical views. He worked for a short time as an assayer in the Mint in 1848 and later at Sèvres. Laurent worked closely with Charles Gerhardt, so that it is not always possible to separate their ideas very precisely. His collected papers were published posthumously in his *Methode de Chimie* (1854; Method of Chemistry).

Dumas had formulated his theory of substitution in 1834. According to this theory hydrogen can be actually removed from certain substances and replaced by other substances. Laurent used this to demolish Berzelius's electrochemical theory, pointing out that in the synthesis of trichloroacetic acid the electronegative chlorine replaces the electropositive hydrogen. Laurent's powerful arguments against the orthodox chemistry won him little support and less popularity.

With Gerhardt, he introduced type theory, in which organic compounds are recognized as having common structural features by which they can be assigned to various types. Thus alcohol, water, ammonia, ether, and numerous other types were distinguished. Type theory, soon to be superseded by the chemistry of Stanislao CANNIZZARO and August KEKULÉ, was valuable in that it provided a tolerable basis of classification and some understanding of the chemistry of organic compounds.

It was Laurent who saw that chemists must distinguish clearly between atoms, molecules, and equivalents. He regarded the molecules of hydrogen, oxygen, and others as consisting of two atoms, forming what he called an 'homogeneous compound', which, by double decomposition, could form 'heterogeneous compounds'. This provided a sound base for the accurate determination of atomic weights. Unfortunately, Laurent did not have the funds, facilities, or time to provide the necessary experimental support for his theories, and without the essential laboratory work his views were ignored.

Laveran, Charles Louis Alphonse

(1845–1922) *French physician and parasitologist*

The son of a military surgeon, Lavaran was born in Paris and studied medicine at the University of Strasbourg, obtaining his MD in 1867. Like his father, he joined the Army Medical Service and served in Algeria (1878–83).

In 1880 Laveran made one of the most important discoveries of 19th-century medicine, namely, the causative agent of malaria. In Algeria he frequently performed autopsies on malaria victims who, he noted, had numerous pigmented bodies in their blood. Although some of these bodies were in the red blood cells he also noted other free bodies, at the edge of which he observed moveable filaments or flagella. The extremely rapid and varied movements of these flagella indicated to Laveran that they must be parasites. He found such parasites in 148 out of 192 cases and thus assumed them to be the cause of malaria. He called the parasite *Oscillaria malariae* but the Italian name *Plasmodium* later won favor.

Laveran also speculated that mosquitoes might play a part in transmitting malaria but he failed to follow up this insight. In 1883 he returned to France to become professor of military hygiene and parasitology at the Val-de-Grace School of Military Medicine and in 1897 moved to the Pasteur Institute where he remained until his death. Here he published important works on leishmaniasis and trypanosomiasis.

In 1884 Laveran published *Traité des fièvres palustres* (Treatise on marsh Fevers), which later won him the 1907 Nobel Prize for physiology or medicine for showing the role played by protozoa in causing disease. With the prize money he founded a laboratory of tropical medicine at the Pasteur Institute.

Lavoisier, Antoine Laurent (1743–1794) *French chemist*

Lavoisier is regarded as the founder of modern chemistry. Born in Paris, he studied both law and science, but after graduating concentrated his attention on science. He invested his money in a private tax-collecting company, the Ferme Générale, and thereby became rich enough to build a large and well-equipped laboratory. He then proceeded to study combustion.

During the 18th century combustible matter was thought to contain a substance called phlogiston, which was released when combustion took place. This theory, which was developed by Georg Stahl, had one obvious flaw; substances frequently increase in weight as a result of combustion. Lavoisier performed a number of experiments in which he burned phosphorus, lead, and other elements in closed containers; he noted that the weight of the container and its contents did not increase though that of the solid did. In 1772 he recorded his observations that phosphorus and sulfur burn with a gain in weight caused by their combination with air. In 1774 he discovered that when a calx (oxide) was heated with charcoal (carbon) the gas produced was the 'fixed air' found by Joseph Black. This suggested that the element was combining with air. Soon after this, Lavoisier was visited by Joseph PRIESTLEY in Paris. Priestley had recently discovered that mercury(II) oxide gives off a gas when heated, leaving behind mercury. Priestley called the gas 'dephlogisticated air'. Lavoisier repeated Priestley's experiments and, by 1778, had convinced himself of the existence in the air of a gas that combines with substances during combustion and is the same gas as that given off by heating mercury(II) oxide. Lavoisier named the gas 'oxigine' from the Greek 'acid producing' – he held the erroneous belief that all acids contain oxygen. He further recognized the existence of a second, inert, gas in the air – 'azote' (named from the Greek 'no life' and later renamed nitrogen). In 1783 he explained the formation of water from hydrogen and oxygen, work that led to a controversy involving Henry Cavendish. Lavoisier then went on to study respiration and deduced that oxygen is essential to animal life.

In 1783 he collaborated with Claude BERTHOLLET, Antoine François de Fourcroy and L. B. Guyton de Morveau in publishing *Méthode de nomenclature chimique* (System of Chemical Nomanclature), which proposed new names for the elements. In 1789 he published *Traité élémentaire de chimie* (Elementary Treatise on Chemistry) – an influential work summarizing his ideas and stating the law of conservation of mass. The book also contained a list of the known elements, although this included light and heat (caloric).

In 1771 Lavoisier married the attractive and talented fourteen-year-old Marie Anne Pierrette Paulze (1758–1836), the daughter of a wealthy tax-farmer. **Marie Lavoisier** had studied under the painter David and had learned English and Latin. Her skills as a draftswoman are evident in the thirteen pages of copperplate illustrations accompanying her husband's *Traité* and signed "Paulze Lavoisier sculpsit". She translated a number of important texts including Richard Kirwan's *Essay on Phlogiston* (1784). It is also clear that Madame Lavoisier actually worked with her husband in his laboratory and there is a celebrated painting by David dating from about 1788 showing them so occupied. The nature of the collaboration, however, remains unclear. Her last service for her husband was to collect and publish his *Mémoires de chemie* (1803, 2 vols; Memoirs of Chemistry).

Lavoisier became, in 1775, director of the government powder mills and as such considerably improved the production of gun-

powder. He also made contributions to agriculture and demonstrated the advantages of scientific farming on a model farm at Fréchines. He was a member of the commission, appointed in 1790, that eventually led to the adoption of the metric system in France.

Tragically Lavoisier's involvement with the tax-gathering company was to prove his downfall. In the 1790s France was in the middle of a protracted revolution and, in 1794, Paris was ruled by a radical group of republicans – the Jacobins – who ruthlessly executed thousands of alleged opponents of the revolution. Among these were included the tax gatherers and Lavoisier, despite his work for the state, was tried as a farmer of taxes, found guilty, and guillotined in Paris.

Lavoisier, Marie Anne Pierrette

(1758–1836) *French chemist. See* LAVOISIER, ANTOINE.

Lawes, Sir John Bennet (1814–1900)
British agricultural chemist

Lawes was the only son of the lord of the manor of Harpenden in Hertfordshire and inherited his father's estates in 1822. He was educated at Eton and Oxford University, but he left without taking a degree. He developed an interest in science, particularly chemistry, and at the age of 20 he constructed a laboratory for himself at his home.

He turned his attention to the problems of agricultural chemistry when a neighbor pointed out to him that on some local farms bone meal increased turnip production, while on others it seemed to have no effect. This started him on his life's work, the chemistry of fertilizers.

After experimentation, Lawes showed that it was necessary to make the phosphate in the bones more readily soluble in the soil for absorption by plants. This he achieved by adding sulfuric acid to the crushed bones. Lawes took out a patent on these 'superphosphates' in 1842, opening his first factory for their production in 1843. By the 1870s he was producing 40,000 tons of superphosphates a year using phosphate rock rather than bones.

Also in 1843, Lawes was joined by Henry Gilbert, beginning a lifelong collaboration, and he started the Rothamsted Experimental Station, the first agricultural research station in the world. Experiments were conducted on different fertilizers; crops which were normally grown in rotation were grown here year after year on the same plot using a variety of manures and fertilizers. Animal feed was also examined and varied to find the most economical and efficient. Well over 100 papers were produced by Lawes and Gilbert on their Rothamsted work.

Lawes established the Lawes Agricultural Trust in 1889 to safeguard the continuation of research following his death. He was created a baronet in 1882.

Lawrence, Ernest Orlando (1901–1958) *American physicist*

Lawrence was the son of a superintendent of public schools in Canton, South Dakota. He was educated at the universities of South Dakota, Minnesota, Chicago, and Yale (where he obtained his PhD in 1925). He taught at Yale before moving in 1928 to the University of California at Berkeley. He was appointed professor there in 1930 and director of the radiation laboratory in 1936.

Lawrence was awarded the 1939 Nobel Prize for physics for his invention of the cyclotron. In the 1920s, experiments on bombardment of nuclei relied on low-energy linear accelerators. Lawrence, in 1930, began experiments to construct a cyclic accelerator. In this device charged particles move in spiral paths under the influence of a vertical magnetic field. The particles move inside two hollow D-shaped metal pieces arranged with a small gap between them. A high-frequency electric field applied between the 'dees' gives a 'kick' to the particle each time it crosses the gap. By early 1931 the first model (4 inches (10.2 cm) in diameter) produced energies of 13,000 electronvolts.

Subsequently, Lawrence, and other workers, developed larger machines capable of achieving much higher energies for nuclear research. Lawrence also played an important part in the development of the atomic bomb. He was responsible for developing the radiation laboratory (now named for him) into one of the world's leading centers for high-energy physics. Element 103, *lawrencium*, is named in his honor.

Leakey, Louis Seymour Bazett (1903–1972) *British anthropologist and archaeologist*

Leakey was born at Kabete in Kenya and educated at Cambridge University, where he studied French and Kikuyu. He held various academic posts at British and American universities, and was curator of the Coryndon Memorial Museum at Nairobi (1945–61). Apart from anthropological studies, notably of the Kikuyu people, Leakey is best known for his excavations of fossils of early humans, notably in Tanzania's Olduvai Gorge. Here, in 1959, jaw, skull, and huge

teeth fragments of a species that Leadky called *Zinjanthropus* (*Australopithecus*) were uncovered by his wife Mary. The following year his son Jonathan discovered remains of the larger-brained *Homo habilis*. Both have been estimated at between 1,750,000 and 2,000,000 years old, but Leakey considered that only *H. habilis* was the true ancestor of modern humans, *Zinjanthropus* having died out: a view not shared by other researchers. Leakey also found, in western Kenya, remains of the earliest known hominid *Proconsul africanus*. Leakey's work has not only provided evidence for the greater age of humans but suggests that Africa, and not, as was previously thought, Asia, may have been the original center of human evolution.

Much of Leakey's work was carried out in close collaboration with his wife, **Mary Leakey**. She accompanied him on all his major field trips and worked alongside him as excavator, paleontologist, and author. She continued independent field work after her husband's death in 1972. In 1976, working in northern Tanzania in the Laetoli beds near Lake Eyasi, she made what she described as "the most remarkable find" of her whole career. Still preserved in the volcanic ash she discerned footprints of hominids, clear evidence that human ancestors had already adopted an upright posture some 3.75 million years ago. An account of her own researches was included in her autobiography *Disclosing the Past* (1984).

Leakey, Mary (1913–1996) *British paleoanthropologist. See* LEAKEY, LOUIS SEYMOUR BAZETT.

Leakey, Richard Erskine (1944–) *Kenyan anthropologist*

Richard Leakey was born at Nairobi in Kenya, the son of the famous scholars Louis and Mary Leakey. Having left school at sixteen, he first worked as a hunter and animal collector before turning in 1964 to the search for fossil humans. His parents had spent much of their lives exploring the Rift Valley and working at Olduvai in Northern Tanzania.

In contrast Leakey undertook his first field trip to the Omo valley in Ethiopia. In 1965 he shifted his interest to Lake Turkana in northern Kenya, concentrating his work in the Koobi Fora area. At the same time he was appointed to the directorship of the Kenya National Museum, Nairobi.

In 1972 he made his first major find at Koobi Fora. This was a skull with a brain capacity of about 800 cc, given the number 1470. Leakey identified 1470 as *Homo* rather than an australopithecine precursor, and took it to be *Homo habilis*. The age of the skull, however, was in dispute varying from 1.8 to 2.4 million years; the former age was eventually accepted.

In 1975 a second skull was found, this time *Homo erectus*, a more advanced form than 1470. By this time Leakey was finding that the demands of administration, producing TV series, and writing popular accounts of his work were limiting his research activities. Moreover, he suffered the onset of kidney failure in 1979. The donation of a kidney by his brother Philip restored Leakey to what he termed in his autobiography *One Life* (1983), the beginning of his "second life." Much of this second life has been devoted to conservation and Leakey has been a leading figure in the fight to preserve the African elephant by banning the trade in ivory. In 1990 he was appointed director and executive chairman of the Kenyan Wildlife Service.

However, during his fight against ivory smugglers, Leakey made many enemies. His determination, outspokenness, and ruthlessness alienated him from many leading Kenyan politicians and administrators. Consequently, in 1994, he resigned his post with the Kenyan Wildlife Service and decided to enter politics, despite an airplane crash in 1993 that led to the amputation of both legs. In 1995 Leakey formed a new political party, Safina (Noah's Ark), and announced his intention to challenge the ruling KANU (Kenya African National Union) in the next elections.

Throughout his career Leakey has described the development of humans in terms similar to those adopted by his father. He has rejected the claims of Don Johanson that 'Lucy', *Australopithecus afarensis*, is a joint ancestor of *Homo* as well as the australopithecines first described by Raymond Dart. Leakey has continued to claim that it is too simple to present the human evolutionary tree as having only two branches; rather, there were at least three, and it was more than likely that future discoveries would add to the number. Human evolution, for Leakey, seems more like a bush than a tree.

Leavitt, Henrietta Swan (1868–1921)
American astronomer

Henrietta Leavitt was born the daughter of a Congregational minister in Lancaster, Massachusetts. Her interest in astronomy was aroused while she was at Radcliffe College (then the Society for the Collegiate Instruction of Women), from which she graduated in 1892. In 1895 she became a volunteer research assistant at the Harvard College Observatory, receiving a permanent post in 1902. She was soon head of the department of photographic photometry. Like her colleague Annie Cannon, she was extremely deaf.

Leavitt's work involved the determination of the photographic magnitudes of stars, i.e., their brightness as recorded on a photographic plate. The photographic magnitude of a star differs somewhat from its visual magnitude since a photographic emulsion is more sensitive to blue light than the eye. The accurate measurement of visual magnitudes had been part of the program of the Harvard College Observatory since the 1870s. In 1907 the director of the observatory, Edward Pickering, announced plans to redetermine stellar magnitudes by photographic techniques. The photographic magnitudes of a group of stars near the north celestial pole were to act as standards of reference for other stars. Leavitt was selected to measure these magnitudes, known as the 'north polar sequence', and the results were published in 1917 in the *Annals of Harvard College Observatory* (vol. 71 no. 3). She also spent many years measuring secondary stellar magnitudes, based on the north polar sequence, which was adopted as an international standard until superseded by photometric measurements of magnitude.

Leavitt also did much work on variable stars, discovering about 2400 – roughly one half of those known in her time. She is best known, however, for her studies of Cepheid variables. At Harvard Observatory's field station at Arequipo, Peru, a series of photographic plates had been taken of the Magellanic Clouds (now known to be small neighboring galaxies). From her analysis of the plates, Leavitt detected nearly 1800 variable stars, some of which belonged to a class known as Cepheid variables. The variation in brightness of Cepheids is extremely regular and in 1908 Leavitt noted that the brighter Cepheids had the longer periods. By 1912 she was able to show that the apparent magnitude, i.e., observed brightness, of Cepheids decreased linearly with the logarithm of the period.

It was this seemingly simple discovery that led to an invaluable means for determining very great distances; previous to this only distances out to a hundred light-years could be estimated. Leavitt's work on the light variation of Cepheids was extended first by Ejnar Hertzsprung and Harlow Shapley and then by Walter Baade to give the period–luminosity relation of Cepheids. Using this relation the luminosity, or intrinsic brightness, of a Cepheid can be determined directly from a measure of its period and this in turn allows the distance – of the Cepheid and its surroundings – to be calculated. Distances of galaxies up to ten million light-years away can be determined this way.

Le Bel, Joseph Achille (1847–1930)
French chemist

Born in Pechelbron, France, Le Bel came from a family with oil interests. He was a student at the Ecole Polytechnique and for a short while was assistant to Charles Würtz at the Ecole de Médecine. He sold his share of the family oil interests and devoted himself to independent scientific research.

He is best known for his account of the asymmetric carbon atom, although his achievement was overshadowed by the almost simultaneous account given by Jacobus van't Hoff. Le Bel's account was published in November 1874, two months after that of van't Hoff. Their work is virtually identical; what difference there is arises from a difference of origin. Le Bel wished to explain the molecular asymmetry of Louis Pasteur while van't Hoff was more concerned with understanding the quadrivalent carbon atom recently introduced by August Kekulé.

Lebesgue, Henri Léon (1875–1941)
French mathematician

Lebesgue, who was born at Beauvais in northern France, studied at the Ecole Normale Supérieure. He obtained posts at Rennes (1902) and Poitiers (1906) universities, at the Sorbonne (1910), and at the Collège de France (1921).

Lebesgue's extremely important contributions to measure theory and the theory of integration were stimulated by the earlier work of Emille Borel and by Camille Jordan's famous *Cours d'Analyse* (Lessons in Analysis). The importance of Lebesgue's work resides in the fact that he was the first mathematician to develop integration in a measure-theoretic context. This allowed natural generalizations of both concepts to be made. Lebesgue's definition of integral is considered, in many respects, smoother and more useful than those that came before.

Lebesgue also worked on the theory of point sets, the calculus of variations, and dimension theory. He wrote a very large number of books and papers and had interests in the pedagogy and history of mathematics.

Le Chatelier, Henri Louis (1850–1936)
French chemist

Le Chatelier was born in Paris, the son of the inspector-general of mines for France. He himself began studying mining engineering, before becoming professor of chemistry at the School of Mines in 1877. He later became professor of mineral chemistry at the Collège de France and finally took the chemistry chair at the Sorbonne in 1907.

He was particularly interested in metallurgy, cements, ceramics, and glass, and his studies of flames led him to study heat and its measurement.

He made a number of contributions to thermometry, the most important of which was his first successful design of a platinum and rhodium thermocouple for measuring high temperatures (1887). This was based on the principle shown by Thomas SEEBECK in 1826 that if a circuit is made from two different metals and heated, a current will flow, and that the current is proportional to the temperature difference between the junctions. It was quickly appreciated that the Seebeck effect could be used in a variety of measuring devices; if one junction was placed on the object to be measured and the other kept at a known constant temperature then the first temperature could be calculated by measuring the current. By using platinum and platinum–rhodium alloy rods, Le Chatelier succeeded where many others had failed.

His most important discovery, *Le Chatelier's principle*, was made in 1884. This simply states that any change made in a system of equilibrium results in a shift of the equilibrium in the direction that minimizes the change. In his original 1884 version he referred only to pressure but soon generalized the principle to cover any kind of external constraint. Le Chatelier published his principle in 1888 as the *Loi de stabilité de l'equilibre chimique* (Law of Stability of Chemical Equilibrium). The principle is important in studies of chemical equilibrium for predicting the effects of pressure and temperature on an equilibrium reaction.

Le Chatelier's principle fitted in well with the law of mass action recently formulated by Cato Guldberg and Peter Waage and the new chemical thermodynamics of Josiah Willard Gibbs, whose work Le Chatelier was responsible for introducing to France. The principle was soon shown to have industrial implications, for Fritz Haber successfully utilized it in his process for the production of ammonia.

Leclanché, Georges (1839–1882)
French engineer and inventor

Leclanché, who was born in Paris, is best known for his invention of the electrical battery, now known as the dry cell. This he developed in 1866, six years after completing his formal technical education and starting work as an engineer. The cell, which uses ammonium chloride as the electrolyte and zinc and carbon as the electrodes, was used extensively in the telegraph system from 1868 onward.

Lecoq de Boisbaudran, Paul-Emile
(1838–1912) *French chemist*

Lecoq de Boisbaudran came from a wealthy family of distillers from Cognac in southwestern France. Of independent means and excited by the new spectroscopy of Gustav Kirchhoff, he built his own laboratory. In 1859, using spectroscopic techniques, he began searching for new minerals and elements.

In 1874, while examining a sample of zinc ore from the Pyrenees, Lecoq de Boisbaudran noticed some new spectral lines and discovered a new element, which he named *gallium* after the old name of his country. On hearing of the new element in 1875 Dmitri MENDELEEV claimed this to be his long-predicted eka-aluminum, thus providing the first dramatic confirmation of his periodic table.

Lecoq de Boisbaudran later discovered two more elements: samarium (1879) and dysprosium (1886).

Lederberg, Joshua (1925–   ) *American geneticist*

Lederberg was born in Montclair, New Jersey, and educated at Columbia and Yale where he gained his PhD in 1948. He later held chairs of genetics at the University of Wisconsin, where he had taught since 1947, and at Stanford from 1959 until his appointment as president of Rockefeller University in 1978, a post he held until 1990.

When Lederberg began work as a graduate student it was widely believed that bacteria had no genes, nuclei, or sex. However, as a result of experiments undertaken with his supervisor Edward TATUM he was able to show in 1946 that bacteria do possess genetic and behavior systems with nuclei, genes, and in certain cases even true sexual mechanisms.

The technique used to demonstrate recombination and hence sexuality was a spin-off from those developed by Tatum and George BEADLE in their work on the fungus *Neurospora*. Two distinct mutants of the K 12 strain of the *Escherichia coli* bacillus were used; the first (A) was incapable of synthesizing the essential ingredients methionine and biotin (M^-B^-) while the second (B) was incapable of producing proline and threonine (P^-T^-). As long as they were grown in a medium rich in the essential ingredients both the A and B mutants could flourish. If, however, they were grown in a medium totally deficient in all four essential ingredients then, assuming reproduction by fission without genetic interaction, both mutants should fail to develop.

In such a context Lederberg in fact found that about one in every ten million bacteria did yield visible colonies. That is, from plaque containing only the A-type $M^-B^-P^+T^+$ and the B-type $M^+B^+P^-T^-$ a normal form, $M^+B^+P^+T^+$, had emerged, which could only have arisen from a sexual mating process. Lederberg went on to show that the process of 'conjugation', as he called it, was common and could be used to map bacterial genes.

Lederberg, working with Norton Zinder in 1952, made the equally significant discovery of bacterial transduction. Here they took two strains of *Salmonella typhimurium* lacking in the ability to synthesize different but essential amino acids. They were placed on either side of a U-tube separated by a fine filter positioned in the bend. The nutrient broth, which alone could pass through the filter, lacked the relevant amino acids. Yet despite the isolation of the two *Salmonella* strains, recombinant bacteria appeared and multiplied. Something must therefore have carried genetic information through the barrier. But it could not be the bacteria themselves as the filter was too small nor, they showed, was it DNA for the process continued in the presence of an enzyme which destroyed free DNA. They finally established that it must be a bacteriophage (a bacteria-infecting virus). It was this experiment that gave the first hint that genes could be deliberately inserted in cells – the start of genetic engineering.

For his discoveries concerning genetic recombination and the organization of the genetic apparatus of bacteria Lederberg shared the 1958 Nobel Prize for physiology or medicine with Tatum and Beadle.

Lederman, Leon Max (1922–   )
American physicist

The son of Russian immigrants, Lederman was born in New York and educated at City College there. After three years with the US Signal Corps during the war, he went to Columbia where he gained his PhD in 1951. He was appointed professor of physics in 1958 and remained at Columbia until 1979, when he accepted the directorship of the Fermi National Accelerator Laboratory, Batavia, Illinois, a post he held until his retirement in 1989.

In 1959 T. D. Lee asked his Columbia colleagues Lederman, **Melvin Schwartz** (1932–), and **Jack Steinberger** (1921–) if it was possible to study the weak fundamental interaction at high energies. While well understood at low energies, Lee noted, theories of weak interactions at high energies led to absurdities. Yet it was difficult to explore the interaction experimentally, for at high energies other forces tended to obscure all other reactions.

Lederman and his coworkers began to investigate decay processes that lead to neutrinos. These proceed by a weak interaction, and there are two processes in which they can occur. In one, pions decay to give muons and neutrinos. The other, beta decay, is decay of a neutron to give a proton, an electron, and a neutrino.

In what has become known as the *two-neutrino experiment*, the team investigated the question of whether the two types of neutrino were identical – whether the muon neutrino was the same particle as the electron neutrino. The experiment was difficult since neutrinos have a very low probability of interacting with matter. It required an intense beam of high-energy neutrinos and a large detector to have any chance of yielding a measurable number of events.

Using the Alternating Gradient Synchrotron at Brookhaven, a beam of 10^{11} protons per second were directed with an energy of 30 billion electronvolts (30 GeV) at a beryllium target. This produced a large number of pions, which rapidly decay into muons and neutrinos. The muons were filtered out by a steel barrier 44-feet thick built from the plates of an old battleship. The neutrinos passed through untouched into a ten-ton aluminum detector. The experiment ran for ten days and diverted 10^{14} high-energy neutrinos through the detector. If there was only one type of neutrino it should react in the experiment with neutrons to produce an equal number of muons and electrons; if, however, the experiment produced a unique muon-linked neutrino, only muons should be created. Fifty-one neutrino collisions were recorded by the detector; all produced muons and none an electron.

For this work Lederman and his Columbia colleagues Schwartz and Steinberger shared the 1988 Nobel Prize for physics.

In 1977 Lederman led another team that made a second fundamental discovery. Working with the Fermilab accelerator they discovered a new particle nine times heavier than the proton. It was named the *upsilon particle* and provided the first evidence of the fifth quark – the so-called 'bottom quark'. Lederman has given a popular account of particle physics in his 1992 book *The God Particle* (the title refers to the Higgs boson).

Lederman was a key figure in the campaign to build a superconducting super collider (SSC), the giant accelerator which would supposedly finally detect the Higgs boson. To further the project Lederman made a ten-minute video for President Reagan to explain what they hoped to achieve. On the strength of the video, Reagan agreed to back the SSC. A later administration, however, decided in 1993 that the planned expenditure of $8 billion could not be supported and canceled the project.

Lee, David Morris (1931–) *American physicist*

Lee was born in Rye, a small town just outside New York City. He originally studied physics at Harvard, graduating in 1952. After a period spent in the army, he joined the university of Connecticut in 1954, and in 1955 enrolled at Yale to work for a PhD in the low-temperature research group.

Superfluidity in the helium isotope, helium-4, had first been detected by Pyotr KAPITZA in 1938 at a temperature of about two degrees above absolute zero (2.17 K). Helium-4 has a nucleus containing two protons and two neutrons and has two orbiting electrons. This means that it has an integral spin and belongs to the class of particles known as bosons. It was recognized that helium-3, with a nucleus consisting of one neutron and two protons, would have a spin of $+\frac{1}{2}$ and therefore must be a fermion. As only bosons could occupy the same quantum state, only bosons, it was thought, could ever become superfluids. However, theoretical considerations proposed by John BARDEEN and his colleagues suggested that under certain conditions fermions could behave like bosons and that helium-3 could possibly display superfluidity.

In 1971, Lee's graduate student Douglas OSHEROFF stumbled on precisely the conditions that would lead to superfluidity. Further work by Lee and his colleagues established that there are three distinct superfluid phases of helium-3 at 0.0027 K, 0.0021 K and 0.0018 K.

For this work, Lee was awarded the 1996 Nobel prize for physics with Douglas Osheroff and Robert RICHARDSON.

Lee, Tsung-Dao (1926–) Chinese–American physicist

Lee was born in Shanghai, China. His early studies at the National Chekiang University in Guizhou province, southern China, were interrupted by the Japanese invasion during World War II. He fled to Kunming, Yunnan, where from 1945 to 1946 he studied at the National Southwest Associated University. In 1946 he received a Chinese government scholarship, which enabled him to study at the University of Chicago in America. In 1950 he gained his PhD there for his astrophysics work on the composition of certain types of stars. In the years 1950–51 he worked as a research associate in astronomy at the Yerkes Astronomical Observatory, Wisconsin, and taught physics at the University of California at Berkeley. The next two years he spent at the Princeton Institute of Advanced Study, leaving to take up an assistant professorship in physics at Columbia University. He was made full professor in 1956.

While at Berkeley and Princeton, Lee worked with a fellow countryman he had known briefly in Kunming – Chen Ning YANG. These two maintained contact while Lee was at Columbia, working on problems of elementary particle physics. In a great insight, the two men challenged one of the fundamental concepts of that time – the conservation of parity. Put simply, it had been assumed that the laws of nature are unchanged in mirror-image transformations. Lee and Yang realized that this assumption had never been explicitly tested, and that it might not be valid in the case of the so-called 'weak' interactions between particles. They published a controversial paper in 1956, and within months experiments had been performed (by another Chinese, Chien Shiung Wu) which showed that the 'law' of parity is indeed violated in such interactions. In 1957, only a year later, Lee and Yang were jointly honored with the Nobel Prize for physics.

Lee went on to consider some of the implications of this discovery, particularly as it affected ideas about the neutrino. He has also made contributions in the fields of statistical mechanics, nuclear physics, field theory, and turbulence. With the exception of a three-year break (1960–63) at the Princeton Institute of Advanced Study, he has continued his work at the physics department of the University of Columbia.

Lee, Yuan Tseh (1936–) American chemist. See HERSBACH, DUDLEY ROBERT.

Leeuwenhoek, Anton van (1632–1723) Dutch microscopist

Born the son of a basket maker at Delft in the Netherlands, Leeuwenhoek received little formal education and was apprenticed to a linendraper at the age of 16. In about 1654 he set up in business in Delft as a draper. He also served from 1660 as chamberlain of the town's law courts.

In 1673 Henry Oldenburg, secretary of the Royal Society, received a letter from a Dutch correspondent informing him that "a certain most ingenious person here Leeuwenhoek has devised microscopes which far surpass those manufactured by others." A letter from Leeuwenhoek describing his observations of bees, mold, and lice was enclosed. It was published in the *Philosophical Transactions* of the Royal Society in 1673. It was the first of 165 letters reporting Leeuwenhoek's observations which would appear in the Transactions between 1672 and his death in 1723. Leeuwenhoek wrote no books and, lacking Latin, reported his work in Dutch, which was then translated into English or Latin for publication.

Among the highlights of the *Letters* are his 1674 observations of his 'little animalcules' (protozoa) discovered in rainwater that had stood for a few days. They were, he estimated, some 10,000 times smaller than water fleas. He also gave some idea of the profusion of nature by calculating that "there were upwards of 1 million living creatures in one drop of pepper-water." He was sufficiently detached to examine with his microscope his own faeces and note that "when of ordinary thickness" no animalcules were observed but whenever "the stuff was a bit looser than ordinary I have seen animalcules therein."

Leeuwenhoek also announced in 1679 his discovery of human spermatazoa. In 1677 a Mr Ham brought him "the spontaneously discharged semen of a man who had lain with an unclean woman and was suffering from gonorrhea." He observed little animals within, "animalcula in semine masculino" (animalcules in human semen), and noted they had tails and lived for a few hours only. He went on to examine the sperm of birds, frogs, insects, cattle, and several other species. A further important biological observation was Leeuwenhoek's 1684 description of red blood cells, which he estimated to be 25,000 times smaller than a fine sand grain.

Leeuwenhoek's instruments were all simple microscopes with a single small lens clamped between two metal plates. The object was placed on a fine pin and its distance from the plates adjusted by turning a screw. On his death he left 247 completed microscopes and 172 mounted lenses. They were auctioned and dispersed in 1747. A further 26 mounted in silver were bequeathed to the Royal Society but disappeared without trace in the mid-nineteenth century. Nine of Leeuwenhoek's original microscopes have survived, with a highest magnification of 266 and resolution of 2 micrometers.

Towards the end of his life Leeuwenhoek became something of a European celebrity. Monarchs such as Peter the Great and Queen Mary traveled to Delft to be shown the 'little animalcules' by Leeuwenhoek himself.

Lehmann, Inge (1888–1993) *Danish seismologist*

It was Lehmann who, in 1936, first put forward the view that the Earth's core consisted of two parts – an inner and an outer, separated by a discontinuity. For many years it had been thought that the Earth consisted merely of a core, mantle, and crust that were separated by the discontinuities discovered by Beno Gutenberg and Andrija Mohorovičić. This was partly based on the realization that the primary (P) waves of an earthquake are not detected in a shadow zone between 105° and 145° from the epicenter. The reason for this was their diffraction by the Earth's core.

Lehmann found that P-waves increased their velocity quite sharply within the core. She reasoned from this that there is an outer core and an inner core separated by a further discontinuity about 700 miles (1200 km) from the center of the Earth and sufficient to bend some of the P-waves into the shadow zone.

Lehn, Jean Marie Pierre (1939–) *French chemist*

Born at Rosheim in France, Lehn was educated at Strasbourg where he obtained his PhD in 1963, and at Harvard. After working in Strasbourg from 1966 to 1970, Lehn returned to Harvard as professor of chemistry. In 1979 he took up the chair of chemistry at the Collège de France, Paris.

In 1963 Charles PEDERSEN had discovered the first of the crown ethers. While Pedersen had worked with two-dimensional rings, Lehn sought to extend his work into three dimensions. If two nitrogen atoms replaced the oxygen atoms of the original crown ether, Lehn found, two crowns could be made to combine into a cage-like structure; a 'cryptand' in Lehn's terminology. He found that cryptands were capable of binding metal cations more selectively than the crown ethers. Lehn went on to develop cryptands that would bind selectively with other molecules, including important biologically active molecules as the neurotransmitter, acetylcholine. The molecules found in this way are known as 'supramolecules' and their discovery has opened up an important new field known as 'host–guest chemistry'.

For his work in this new field Lehn shared the 1987 Nobel Prize for chemistry with Pedersen and Donald CRAM.

Leibniz, Gottfried Wilhelm (1646–1716) *German mathematician, philosopher, historian, and physicist*

Born the son of a Lutheran professor of moral philosophy in Leipzig, Germany, Leibniz was educated at the universities of Leipzig, Jena, and Altdorf where he gained his doctorate in 1666. In 1667 he entered the service of the elector of Mainz for whom he spent the period 1673–76 on a diplomatic mission to Paris. Through meeting with such scholars as Christian Huygens in Paris and with members of the Royal Society, including Robert Boyle, during two trips to London in 1673 and 1676, Leibniz was introduced to the outstanding problems challenging the mathematicians and physicists of Europe. On leaving Paris he joined the staff of John Frederick the duke of Brunswick-Lüneburg, also Elector of Hannover, where he was given the commission to write the history of the House of Brunswick and the position of librarian. For the remaining 40 years of his life Leibniz dissipated his prodigious talents under three electors, including the future George I of Great Britain and Ireland, constructing genealogies of the numerous Brunswick progeny, both legitimate and, even more numerous, illegitimate. He also undertook a variety of administrative and diplomatic duties of which his attempt to unite the Protestant and Catholic churches in 1683 and the founding of the Berlin Academy of Sciences in 1700 are the most noteworthy. It was also to his Brunswick years that most of his philosophical writings belong although many of them remained unpublished until well after his death.

Leibniz's greatest achievement was undoubtedly his discovery of the differential and integral calculus, work which was to involve him in a bitter priority dispute with Isaac Newton. Newton's ideas on the calculus were developed first, as early as 1665, but remained unpublished until 1687; Leibniz, however, began work on problems of the calculus during his Paris years and published his results in 1684 in *Nova methodus pro maximis et minimis* (New Method for the Greatest and the Least). It was later suggested in 1699 that Leibniz's original inspiration may well have come from conversations in London in 1673 and in 1676 as well as letters of Newton to Henry Oldenburg shown to Leibniz. From this point the dispute became open to all and was conducted with considerable ferocity and not a little dishonesty. In fact, as became clear later on, the discoveries were made independently; the final triumph lay with Leibniz because it was his notation of differentiation and integration, rather than the fluxions of Newton, that have survived in modern textbooks.

In physics, Leibniz's metaphysical principles also led him to deny Newtonian gravity acting at a distance on the grounds that: "A body is never moved naturally, except by another body which touches it and pushes it; after that it continues until it is prevented by another body which touches it. Any other kind of operation on bodies is either miraculous or imaginary." He also rejected Newtonian concepts of absolute space and time, arguing more plausibly that space was simply "the order of bodies among themselves" while time was their order of succession. Leibniz also, with Huygens, developed the concept of kinetic energy.

As well as his contributions to metaphysics and philosophy, Leibniz established the foundations of symbolic logic, probability theory, and combinatorial analysis, and was led to design a practical calculating machine. It was actually built and shown to the Royal Society in 1794.

Leishman, Sir William Boog (1865–1926) *British bacteriologist*

Leishman was born in Glasgow, the son of the regius professor of medicine at the university there. He himself was educated at the university, where he obtained his MD in 1886. He immediately joined the Army Medical Service and began his career in India, where he served from 1890 to 1897. On his return to England he took up an appointment at the Army Medical School at Netley as an assistant to Almroth Wright, succeeding him in 1903 as professor of pathology when the school moved to Millbank. In 1913 Leishman transferred to the War Office, where he served in various advisory positions before being appointed director of pathology (1919) and director general of Army Medical Services (1923), a post he held until his death.

Leishman's first major success was his discovery in 1900 of the protozoan parasite (*Leishmania*) responsible for the disease

known variously as kala-azar and dumdum fever. As he delayed publication until 1903 he was forced to share his discovery with C. Donovan, who independently repeated his work (the form of the parasite found in humans became known as the *Leishman–Donovan body*). The disease caused by the parasite is now known as *leishmaniasis*.

In 1900 he went on to develop the widely used *Leishman's stain*. This is a compound of methylene blue and eosin that soon became adopted as the standard stain for the detection of such protozoan parasites as *Plasmodium* (malaria parasite) in the blood.

Leishman also made major contributions to the development of various vaccines, particularly those used against typhoid. By 1896 Wright had developed a safe vaccine of killed typhoid bacilli, which he persuaded the Army to test during the Boer War (1899–1902). The extent of the protection provided by the vaccine became a matter of violent controversy between Wright and the English statistician Karl Pearson; the Army Council therefore invited Leishman in 1904 to resolve the dispute. By 1909 Leishman was able to report that those inoculated in India carried a significantly smaller risk of dying from enteric complaints (5 died out of 10,378 vaccinated, compared with 46 out of the 8936 not vaccinated).

It was mainly as a result of this work, together with improvements introduced by Leishman in the actual quality of the vaccine, that a policy of mass vaccination was adopted in 1914. Consequently only 1191 deaths due to typhoid were reported by the British Army throughout the whole of World War I.

Leishman was knighted in 1909.

Leloir, Luis Frederico (1906–1987) *Argentinian biochemist*

Born in Paris, Leloir was educated at Buenos Aires University, obtaining his MD there in 1932. He spent a year in Cambridge, England, studying under Gowland Hopkins, returning to Argentina to work at the Institute of Physiology until 1944, when – in conflict with the president, Juan Peron – he went into exile in America. In 1945 Leloir returned to Argentina, where he worked at the Institute of Biology and Experimental Medicine, set up in Buenos Aires by Bernard Hussey with private funding.

Despite working well away from the main biochemical research centers and using equipment that would have been thrown out of more fashionable laboratories, Leloir and his colleagues managed to surprise the biochemical world and make one of the major discoveries of the postwar years. In the 1930s Carl and Gerty Cori had demonstrated a process by which glycogen is synthesized and broken down. It was assumed that because there were enzymes capable, in vitro, of both breaking down glycogen into lactic acid and reversing the whole process, that this is what actually happened in the body.

It was therefore a matter of some surprise when Leloir and his colleagues announced in 1957 an alternative mechanism for the synthesis of glycogen. They discovered a new coenzyme, uridine triphosphate (UTP), analogous to adenosine triphosphate (ATP), which combined with glucose-1-phosphate to form a new sugar nucleotide, uridinediphosphate glucose (UDPG). In the presence of a specific enzyme and a primer UDPG will yield uridine diphosphate (UDP) and transfer the glucose to the growing glycogen chain. In the presence of ATP, UDP is converted back into UTP and the reaction can continue.

It was soon made clear that this is the actual process of glycogen synthesis taking place in the body; the Cori process is, in contrast, mainly concerned with the degradation of glycogen. It was for this work that Leloir was awarded the 1970 Nobel Prize for chemistry, the first Argentinian to be thus honored.

Lemaître, Abbé Georges Edouard
(1894–1966) *Belgian astronomer and cosmologist*

Lemaître was born at Charleroi in Belgium. After serving in World War I, he studied at the University of Louvain in Belgium from where he graduated in 1920. He then attended a seminary at Mailines, becoming ordained as a Roman Catholic priest in 1923. Before taking up an appointment at the University of Louvain in 1925, he spent a year at Cambridge, England, where he worked with Arthur Eddington, and a year in America where he worked at the Harvard College Observatory and the Massachusetts Institute of Technology. He remained at Louvain for the whole of his career, being made professor of astronomy in 1927.

Lemaître was one of the propounders of the big-bang theory of the origin of the universe. Einstein's theory of general relativity, announced in 1916, had led to various cosmological models, including Einstein's own model of a static universe. Lemaître in 1927 (and, independently, Alexander Friedmann in 1922) discovered a family of solutions to Einstein's field equations of relativity that described not a static but an expanding universe. This idea of an expanding universe was demonstrated experimen-

tally in 1929 by Edwin Hubble who was unaware of the work of Lemaître and Friedmann. Lemaître's model of the universe received little notice until Eddington arranged for it to be translated and reprinted in the *Monthly Notices of the Royal Astronomical Society* in 1931. It was not only the idea of an expanding universe which was so important in Lemaître's work, on which others were soon working, but also his attempt to think of the cause and beginning of the expansion.

If matter is everywhere receding, it would seem natural to suppose that in the distant past it was closer together. If we go far enough back, argued Lemaître, we reach the 'primal atom', a time at which the entire universe was in an extremely compact and compressed state. He spoke of some instability being produced by radioactive decay of the primal atom that was sufficient to cause an immense explosion that initiated the expansion.

This big-bang model did not fit too well with the available time scales of the 1930s. Nor did Lemaître provide enough mathematical detail to attract serious cosmologists. Its importance today is due more to the revival and revision it received at the hands of George Gamow in 1946.

Lenard, Philipp Eduard Anton (1862–1947) *German physicist*

Born the son of a wine merchant in Pozsony (now Bratislava in Slovakia), Lenard studied at the universities of Budapest, Vienna, Berlin, and Heidelberg, where he obtained his doctorate. He taught at the universities of Bonn (1893), Breslau (1894), Aachen (1895), and Heidelberg (1896). In 1898 he was appointed professor of experimental physics at Kiel. He returned to Heidelberg in 1907, where he remained until his retirement in 1931.

Lenard's career falls naturally into two distinct periods. Before 1914 he made several major contributions to fundamental physics. In particular he investigated the photoelectric effect. It had been known for some time that light falling on certain metals would cause the emission of electrons. Starting in 1899 Lenard investigated why the effect could only be produced by ultraviolet or shortwave light. In the course of his experiments he established two anomalous results. He found that the speed with which the electron was emitted was a function of the wavelength of the light used – the shorter the wavelength the faster the electron. Increasing the intensity of the light did not affect the speed but did, surprisingly, increase the number of electrons emitted. It was left to Albert EINSTEIN to explain the significance of these results in 1905 by linking them to the new quantum theory of Max Planck.

Lenard also did important work on cathode rays (electrons) for which he received the Nobel Prize for physics in 1905. He demonstrated how they could be induced to leave the evacuated tube in which they were produced, penetrate thin metal sheets, and travel a short distance in the air, which would become conducting. On the basis of this work he proposed a model of the atom in which it is made from 'dynamids', units of positive and negative charge. This was, however, soon superseded by the nuclear atom of Ernest Rutherford.

Lenard also seems to have come close to making two other discoveries. He almost discovered x-rays and felt that if he had not moved to Aachen in 1895 he would have been successful. He did in fact help their discoverer Wilhelm Röntgen with equipment – aid which, he argued, was never duly acknowledged. He also felt that J. J. Thomson had used some of his work without due recognition.

His suspicions of other workers were the first signs that Lenard was developing a somewhat idiosyncratic view of physics. The latter half of his career, from 1919, was spent arguing for the establishment of a new physics, a 'German' physics untainted with Jewish theories. Although Lenard was a German patriot who was deeply affected by Germany's defeat in 1918, he was not simply an anti-Semite. He attacked Einstein as a socialist, a pacifist, and, indeed, as a Jew; however his strongest abuse was directed toward him as a *theoretical* physicist. In 1920 Lenard organized a conference at Bad Neuheim to discuss relativity theory and attacked Einstein for somehow misleading people with a very abstract theory with little experimental support. He was also deeply upset by Einstein's dismissal of theories of the ether.

The only course for him was to develop a non-Jewish physics and to this end he produced a curious four-volume work, *Deutsche Physik* (1936–37; German Physics). Faced with the objection that science is international he replied, "It is false. Science like every other human product is racial and conditioned by blood." The atmosphere produced by Lenard did much to cause the general exodus of scientists from Germany and to destroy creative science there for a generation.

Just why Lenard was transformed from a talented experimentalist into a bigoted and almost pathological crank is not clear. Germany's losing the war followed by the death of his son and the loss of all his savings in the postwar inflation no doubt contributed, but the ultimate source seems to have been his distaste, as an experimentalist, for the increasing mathematical abstraction introduced into physics by such scientists as Einstein.

Lennard-Jones, Sir John Edward
(1894–1954) *British theoretical chemist*

Lennard-Jones was born at Leigh in Lancashire, the son of a retail furnisher, was educated at Manchester University and, after service in the Royal Flying Corps, at Cambridge University, where he obtained his PhD in 1924. He moved to Bristol University in 1925, serving as professor of theoretical physics from 1927 until 1932 when he returned to Cambridge as professor of theoretical chemistry. He resigned in 1952, shortly before his death, to become principal of the University of Keele.

Lennard-Jones began his research career in the early 1920s by attempting to produce a formula from which interatomic forces could be calculated. He later moved into the field of theoretical chemistry, doing much to promote the molecular-orbital theory of Robert MULLIKEN.

Lenz, Heinrich Friedrich Emil (1804–1865) *Russian physicist*

While a student at the university in his native city of Dorpat (now Tartu in Estonia), Lenz accompanied a voyage around the world as a geophysicist. Soon after his return he started teaching at the University of St. Petersburg, where he became professor in 1836.

Lenz worked on electrical conduction and electromagnetism. In 1833 he reported investigations into the way electrical resistance changes with temperature, showing that an increase in temperature increases the resistance (for a metal). He is best-known for *Lenz's law*, which he discovered in 1834 while investigating magnetic induction. It states that the current induced by a change flows so as to oppose the effect producing the change. Lenz's law is a consequence of the, more general, law of conservation of energy.

Leucippus (c. 500 BC–450 BC) *Greek philosopher*

Very little is known about the life of Leucippus; he probably came from Miletus in Asia Minor, although Elea, Italy, and Abdera in Thrace have also been suggested.

Our knowledge of Leucippus comes from the writings of Aristotle and Theophrastus.

He is said to have been the teacher of Democritus and author of the *Great World System* and *On Mind.* He is also credited with being the originator of atomic theory, although it is difficult to distinguish his contributions from those of his pupil Democritus.

Levene, Phoebus Aaron Theodor

(1869–1940) *Russian–American biochemist*

Levene was born in Sagor, Russia, and gained his MD from St. Petersburg in 1891. He then emigrated with his family to America where he attended courses in chemistry at Columbia University, New York. He continued his chemical studies in Germany under Emil Fischer and Albrecht Kossel, who introduced him to the study of nucleic acids. In 1905 he joined the newly formed Rockefeller Institute for Medical Research where he remained for the rest of his career.

It was known that nucleic acid exists in two forms, one found in the thymus of animals and the other in yeast. Kossel had shown that thymus nucleic acid contained the four nitrogen compounds adenine, guanine, cytosine, and thymine, whereas yeast nucleic acid differed by containing uracil instead of thymine. Carbohydrate and phosphorus were also known to be present. Virtually nothing, however, was known about its structure and function. The work of Levene allowed some conclusions to be drawn on these issues.

In 1909 Levene found that the carbohydrate present in yeast nucleic acid is the pentose sugar ribose; it was not, however, until 1929 that he succeeded in identifying the carbohydrate in thymus nucleic acid. It is also a pentose sugar but lacks one oxygen atom of ribose and was therefore called deoxyribose.

These facts enabled Levene to suggest a simple tetranucleotide structure for the inevitably named ribonucleic and deoxyribonucleic acids (RNA and DNA). (A nucleotide is simply one of the four bases plus a sugar and a phosphate group.) According to Levene each of the four bases occurred just once in each DNA and RNA molecule and were joined together by the sugar and phosphate groups. This structure could then be repeated to form a polynucleotide with the bases occurring in the same order throughout.

Levene had succeeded in establishing the nucleic acids as genuine molecules existing independently of the proteins but the price he paid for this clarification was to impose on them an absurdly simple and repetitive structure. Consequently, when the search for biological individuality reached the molecular level, the far more complex and varied structure of the proteins was favored over the 'monotonous' form of the nucleic acids, and a generation of biochemists mistakenly sought for the structure of the gene among the inexhaustible potential of the amino acids.

When Levene was told, shortly before his death, of the classic work of Oswald Avery, which showed the crucial part played by DNA, he was reported to be skeptical. It took a further 13 years before James Watson and Francis Crick came up with their famous double helical structure and completed the revolution begun by Levene and other biochemists earlier in the century.

Le Verrier, Urbain Jean Joseph

(1811–1877) *French astronomer*

Born the son of a local government official in St. Lô, northern France, Le Verrier was educated at the Ecole Polytechnique and worked afterward on chemical problems with Joseph Gay-Lussac. He became a lecturer in astronomy at the Ecole Polytechnique in 1836 and succeeded Dominique Arago as director of the Paris Observatory in 1854.

Le Verrier worked on celestial mechanics, and in particular considered the problems associated with the motion of Uranus. In 1821 Alexis Bouvard, of the Paris Observatory, had published a set of tables of the motion of Uranus. Within a few years there was a noticeable discrepancy between the predicted and the observed position of Uranus. Assuming the correctness of Bouvard's work there were only two possibilities: either Newton's gravitational theory was not as universal as had been supposed, or there was an undetected body further out than Uranus but exerting a significant gravitational influence over its orbit. After much effort Le Verrier managed to deduce the mass and position that such a body would have to have to cause such disturbances in the orbit. (Le Verrier was unaware – as were most astronomers – that John Couch Adams had made these calculations in the previous year.) He asked Johann GALLE in Berlin to search for the proposed planet. Galle was immediately successful, sighting Neptune on his first night of observation, 23 September 1846. The new planet was named Neptune and Le Verrier immediately became famous. He went into politics for a short time but wisely returned to astronomy in 1851.

Continuing with problems of celestial mechanics, Le Verrier reworked and revised much of the work of Pierre Simon Laplace.

He discovered the advance of the perihelion (the point of the orbit nearest the Sun) of Mercury and was convinced that this anomaly was caused by an undiscovered planet between Mercury and the Sun. So confident was he of its existence that he named it Vulcan, but despite much searching Vulcan still remained undetected. (The discrepancies in the position of Uranus could be seen as an impressive vindication of Newtonian mechanics, but the true explanation of the anomalous motion of Mercury was to play a vital role in confirming Einstein's general theory of relativity.)

Camille Flammarion claimed that Le Verrier had never taken the trouble to look through a telescope at Neptune, being satisfied with his equations and the words of others.

Levi-Montalcini, Rita (1909–   ) *Italian cell biologist*

Levi-Montalcini was educated at the university in her native city of Turin, graduating from medical school just before the outbreak of World War II. Being of Italian-Jewish descent, she found that posts in Italy's academic establishments were closed to her as a result of growing antisemitism. Undaunted, she converted her bedroom into a makeshift laboratory and proceeded with her studies of the development of chick embryos. In this she was joined by her former professor, Giuseppe Levi, a Jew who had been purged from his job by the Fascists. Between 1941 and 1943, Levi-Montalcini lived in a country cottage in the Piedmont region, then in hiding in Florence. After the Allied liberation of Italy in 1944 she worked as a doctor among refugees in Florence and in 1945 she returned to the University of Turin. Two years later she moved to the Washington University, St. Louis, becoming associate professor (1956) and professor (1958–77). She was appointed director of the Institute of Cell Biology of the Italian National Research Council in Rome in 1969, a post she held until her retirement in 1978.

After moving to St. Louis in 1947, Levi-Montalcini continued her work on chick embryos under professor Viktor Hamburger (b. 1900). By the early 1950s she had demonstrated that the number of nerve cells produced in these embryos could be influenced by an agent (later termed *nerve growth factor*) obtained from a mouse tumor-cell culture. In 1952 the Italian embryologist was joined by an American biochemist, Stanley COHEN, who collaborated with her in determining the chemical nature of this growth factor. Cohen went on

to investigate another growth factor, epidermal growth factor, which controls the embryological development of tissues such as eyes and teeth.

The early studies of Levi-Montalcini represent a key advance in the understanding of mechanisms controlling embryological tissue development. Indeed, in the 1980s it was established that the nerve growth factor discovered by Levi-Montalcini influences the growth of nerves in the brain and spinal cord. The value of her work earned her the 1986 Nobel Prize for physiology or medicine, which she shared with Stanley Cohen.

Lewis, Edward B. (1918–   ) *American geneticist*

Lewis was educated at the University of Minnesota, and at the California Institute of Technology gaining his PhD in 1942. In 1946 he joined the Cal Tech faculty, where he served as Professor of Biology from 1956 until his retirement in 1988.

Lewis has worked mainly in the field of developmental biology concentrating on the manner in which genes control the development of the fruit fly *Drosophila melanogaster*. In 1894, William Bateson described a characteristic set of mutations, named by him "homeotic mutations," in which one body structure is replaced by a different structure. For example, an insect leg may be replaced by an insect wing. In the late 1940s, Lewis began to study a group of genes known as the bithorax complex, which control the manner in which Drosophila embryos become segmented as they develop. After decades spent breeding numerous generations of fruit flies Lewis finally published his main results in 1978.

Drosophila is divided into one head, three thoracic, and eight abdominal segments. The development of the head and first thoracic segment are controlled by the antennapedia complex; the remaining segments by the bithorax complex. Lewis found that a minimum of eight genes, clustered on chromosome 3, were involved in the segmentation of the fly's abdomen and thorax. Lewis demonstrated that the production of the second thoracic segment, which is the first to be controlled by the bithorax complex, was controlled by the fewest homeotic genes. Each later segment required the activation of one or more additional genes. The sequence of genes along the chromosome exactly matched the segments of the insect's body.

He also realized that a single mutation could lead to major homeotic transformations even though, for example, hundreds of active genes would be required to create misplaced legs and wings. This could only mean that mutations were also taking place in a master gene of some kind, a gene capable of controlling the activity of many other subordinate genes.

For his work on homeotic genes Lewis shared the 1995 Nobel Prize for physiology or medicine with Eric WIESCHAUS and Christiane NÜSSLEIN-VOLLARD.

Lewis, Gilbert Newton (1875–1946)
American physical chemist

Lewis, born the son of a lawyer in Weymouth, Massachusetts, was educated at the University of Nebraska and at Harvard, where he obtained his PhD in 1899. After a period abroad at Göttingen and Leipzig he returned to teach at Harvard and the Massachusetts Institute of Technology until 1912, when he moved to the University of California at Berkeley to take up an appointment as professor of physical chemistry.

In about 1916 he first introduced the notion of a covalent bond, in which the chemical combination between two atoms derives from the sharing of a pair of electrons, with one electron contributed by each atom. This was part of Lewis's more general octet theory and he published his views in *Valence and the Structure of Atoms and Molecules* (1923). Here he proposed that the electrons in an atom are arranged in concentric cubes and that a neutral atom of each element contains one more electron than a neutral atom of the element preceding it. The cube of eight electrons is reached in the atoms of the rare gases.

These simple ideas enabled Lewis to explain many of the facts of chemical combination. Thus neon and argon with all vertices of the cube occupied are obviously inert, having no space to interact with other atoms. The tendency is for other atoms to attain the same configuration. Thus sodium with one vertex occupied will react readily with the seven occupied vertices of chlorine to produce a combination with all vertices occupied. And so, with considerable success, Lewis went on to explain the basic combinations of the lighter elements.

The theory became widely known as the *Lewis–Langmuir* theory. This was partly due to the failure of Lewis, a shy and reserved man, to publicize his theory and the willingness of Irving LANGMUIR, a brilliant lecturer, to fill the gap.

Lewis also carried out significant work in the field of chemical thermodynamics and published, with Merle Randall, *Thermody-namics and the Free Energy of Chemical Substances* (1923), which did much to introduce the basic ideas of Josiah Willard Gibbs to a generation of students. He is also known for his general theory of acids and bases (1923): a *Lewis acid* is a substance that can donate an electron pair; a *Lewis base* is one that can accept a pair of electrons.

L'Hôpital, Marquis Guillaume François Antoine de (1661–1704)
French mathematician

L'Hôpital, a Parisian by birth, began his career as a cavalry officer. However, he was forced to resign because of his short-sightedness and devoted the rest of his life to mathematical study and research. To this end he invited the German mathematician Jean BERNOULLI to his château in 1691 to teach him the details of his newly-worked-out differential calculus. Shortly afterward L'Hôpital published his *Analyse des infiniment petits pour l'intelligence des lignes courbes* (Analysis of Infinitely Small Quantities for the Understanding of Curved Lines) (1696), the first calculus textbook ever to appear. L'Hôpital's basic assumption was that "...a quantity, which is increased or decreased only by an infinitely smaller quantity, may be considered as remaining the same." It was in this work that he first formulated the rule for finding the limiting value of a fraction with a numerator and denominator simultaneously tending to zero (0/0), since known to mathematicians as *L'Hôpital's rule*.

Bernoulli appeared none too pleased with L'Hôpital's book considering it to be largely his own work, a belief supported by the discovery in 1921 of *Die Differentialrechnung*, a manuscript of Bernoulli, on which L'Hôpital had clearly based his own text.

Libby, Willard Frank (1908–1980)
American chemist

Born in Grand Valley, Colorado, Libby was educated at the University of California at Berkeley where he obtained his PhD in 1933 and began teaching. In 1941, he moved to Columbia, New York, to work on the development of the atom bomb. After World War II he was appointed professor of chemistry at the Institute for Nuclear Studies at the University of Chicago before returning to the University of California (1959) as director of the Institute of Geophysics.

Libby was responsible for considerably improving dating techniques. In 1939 Serge Korff discovered the existence of the radioactive isotope, carbon–14. This is different from the common stable isotope carbon–12 in that it contains an extra two neutrons in its nucleus. It is absorbed by all carbon users, such as animals and plants, during their lifetimes. It was established that the ratio of carbon–12 to carbon–14 in living organisms was constant and that on death the carbon–14 in the organism began to decay into nitrogen at a constant and measurable rate – carbon–14 has a half-life of 5730 years.

In 1947 Libby and his students at the University of Chicago's Institute for Nuclear Studies developed the radiocarbon dating technique using a highly sensitive geiger counter. He tested the process on objects of known age, such as timbers from Egyptian tombs. The test proved the technique to be reliable for the past 5000 years and it was assumed from this to be accurate as far back as radiocarbon could be measured, about 50,000 years. A later improvement extended the range to over 70,000 years.

The radiocarbon dating technique proved of immense value to the earth sciences, archaeology, and anthropology, and for its development Libby was awarded the 1960 Nobel Prize for chemistry. His published works included *Radiocarbon Dating* (1952).

Lie, (Marius) Sophus (1842–1899)
Norwegian mathematician

Born at Nordfjordeid in Norway, Lie was a friend of Felix Klein, whose ideas influenced him. Among Lie's most important work is his founding of the theory of continuous groups, which are now called *Lie groups* in his honor. Another contribution was his discovery of contact transformations. On both these subjects Lie wrote major treatises. In 1886 he became professor of mathematics at Leipzig and in 1898 he returned to Norway to take up a post that had been instituted for him at the University of Kristiania. By now, however, his health was poor and he died in Kristiania the following year. Lie also did notable work on differential geometry and on the study of differential equations.

Liebig, Justus von (1803–1873) *German chemist*

Liebig, who was born in Darmstadt, Germany, was the son of a dealer in drugs, dyes, and associated chemicals. Aided by his father he developed an early interest in chemistry and was apprenticed to an apothecary. He studied chemistry at Bonn and Erlangen, after which the grand duke of his native Hesse was persuaded to finance Liebig to pursue his chemical studies overseas. Consequently he went to Paris, where he worked in the laboratory of Joseph Gay-Lussac. While there he came

into contact with Alexander von Humboldt, who exercised his patronage to have Liebig appointed to the chair of chemistry at Giessen in 1825, when he was still only 21. He remained there until 1852, when he moved to the University of Munich.

Liebig did much to establish chemistry as a discipline. At Giessen he set up one of the first laboratories for student instruction through which most of the great chemists of the 19th century passed. He also started the first scholarly chemical periodical. In 1832 he took over the *Annalen der Pharmacie* (Annals of Pharmacy) and renamed it in 1840 the *Annalen der Chemie* (Annals of Chemistry; the periodical still exists). He was constantly looking for ways to spread chemistry into new areas, to assert its dominance in previously autonomous disciplines. Thus in a series of works after 1840, when he moved from pure to applied organic chemistry, he tried to show that such studies as agriculture, physiology, and pathology were only intelligible when based on sound chemical principles. His *Chemistry in its Applications to Agriculture and Physiology* (1840) was one of the great books of the century. By 1848 it had gone through 17 editions and appeared in 8 languages. It was followed two years later by his *Organic Chemistry in its Application to Pathology and Physiology*.

Liebig's first significant discovery was made with the aid of Friedrich Wöhler, his lifelong collaborator and friend. While working in the laboratory of Gay-Lussac, Liebig had prepared silver fulminate; Wöhler working in Sweden in the laboratory of Berzelius had prepared silver cyanate. To their surprise these two different chemicals appeared to have the same formula. They had unwittingly discovered what Berzelius was to call *isomerism*, that is, the condition in which two different chemical compounds have the same molecular formula.

They decided to work together on the growing crisis in organic chemistry: how to deal with the sheer size and complexity of the molecules. (Molecules of inorganic compounds tend to be relatively small and straightforward and thus presented fewer problems.) Together they developed a method of analyzing the amounts of carbon and hydrogen present in organic compounds.

Liebig and Wöhler came up with a theory of compound radicals. In 1832 they introduced the benzoyl radical, arguing for the existence of a family of chemicals all made from the same radical with the addition of one or more atoms to differentiate them. Thus to the benzoyl radical, C_6H_5CO, can be added OH to make benzoic acid, H to make oil of bitter almonds (benzaldehyde), Cl for benzoyl chloride, Br for benzoyl bromide, and so on. Unfortunately it was difficult to find another radical as productive and convincing as benzoyl. However, this could not detract from the important fact that they had shown that organic compounds could be dealt with in a rational way.

After organic chemistry Liebig's greatest work was carried out in agricultural science. His first achievement was in rejecting the current humus theory – the belief that plants absorb carbon from humus, the organic part of the soil, and turn it into the minerals they need. He demonstrated the falsity of this by showing that some crops left the soil richer in carbon than they found it, claiming that plants obtain carbon from the air. On burning plants he found various minerals present and argued that these must be obtained from the soil. He also thought that nitrogen was obtained from the ammonia in the soil, which ultimately derived from the rain. Thus plant growth could be stimulated with nitrates, manures, and minerals in which the soil was deficient. He experimented on a plot of land from 1845 until 1849 but had very disappointing results. Fearful of his additives being leached away he was using a fertilizer too insoluble for the plants to absorb. Once this was corrected, he demonstrated the power of minerals and nitrates in increasing crop yield.

During his visit to England he was shocked to observe the sewage of Britain being sent out to sea. He delivered a tremendous tirade against the British for their practice of importing bones from Europe instead of using their sewage as a fertilizer.

In the field of biochemistry Liebig became involved in a famous dispute with Louis Pasteur. As a supporter of Berzelius, he claimed that all chemical changes were brought about by catalysts and that no organisms were involved. In 1869 he argued that there was nothing biological about fermentation. Pasteur, however, managed to demonstrate that vinegar produced by wine souring on contact with air resulted from the action of yeast. In chemical physiology Liebig showed that animal heat could be entirely accounted for by the oxidation of food. Although he misrepresented the role of protein he pioneered attempts to calculate the calorific values of different foods.

Liebig was remarkable for the wide range of his work. There were greater chemists in the 19th century but none who worked with such authority over such an enormous field.

Lin, Chia-Chiao (1916–) *Chinese–American mathematician*

Born in Fujian, China, Lin graduated from the National Tsing Hua University on Taiwan. He then obtained his MA from the University of Toronto in 1941 and his PhD in 1944 from the California Institute of Technology, Pasadena. After teaching briefly at Brown University, Rhode Island (1945–47), he moved to the Massachusetts Institute of Technology. He was appointed professor of applied mathematics in 1953, becoming Institute Professor in 1966.

Lin has worked on problems of hydrodynamics and turbulent flow in general. At a more particular level he has considered and is widely known for his account of how the spiral structure of spiral galaxies is sustained. Lin's account, known as the 'density-wave theory,' is based on work by Bertil Lindblad and was worked out in collaboration with Frank Shu in 1964.

They propose that the spiral structure is a rotating density wave that sweeps through the galaxy. The spiral pattern is always there but the material in the pattern is continuously changing under the influence of gravity. It is further supposed that as the spiral wave moves through a region it compresses the gas there sufficiently to trigger the process of star formation along the lines of compression. Young stars should therefore be found in the arms of a spiral galaxy, as indeed they are. The model has received some additional observational support by predicting that spiral arms must trail and cannot lead as the galaxy rotates. Its universality has, however, been challenged by H. Gerola and P. Seiden who proposed in 1977 an alternative mechanism triggered by supernovae, without needing to to assume the presence of an underlying density wave.

Lindblad, Bertil (1895–1965) *Swedish astronomer*

Lindblad was born in Örebro, Sweden, and educated at the University of Uppsala where he obtained his PhD in 1920. After two years in America at the Lick and Mount Wilson observatories in California he returned to Uppsala. He was appointed in 1927 to the directorship of the Stockholm Observatory while serving at the same time as professor of astronomy at Stockholm University. He was followed by his son, Per Olof, who became director at the observatory in 1967.

It was Lindblad who in 1926 put forward the fundamental idea of the rotation of our Galaxy. This was based partly on the discovery by Jacobus KAPTEYN in 1904 of the two main streams of stars that appear to be moving in opposite directions and also on studies of the motions of stars with high radial velocity. Lindblad realized that these and other phenomena only made sense on the assumption of galactic rotation. Confirmation of Lindblad's conjecture was soon provided by Jan Oort.

Lindblad also studied the structure of the Galaxy and suggested a mechanism by which its spiral structure is sustained.

Linde, Karl von (1842–1934) German engineer

Linde, who was born in Berndorf (now in Austria), studied engineering under Rudolf Clausius in Zurich. He taught in Munich at the Polytechnic as assistant professor of machine design from 1868 before moving into the refrigeration business in the 1870s.

His first breakthrough came in 1876 when he produced an ammonia refrigerator. This was a much more efficient cooler than the compression machine introduced by Jacob Perkins in 1834. By 1908 the Linde Company had sold 2600 machines, of which just over half were bought by breweries. Linde also developed an equally successful domestic version.

Linde was also the first industrialist to use the new developments in low-temperature physics. Oxygen had been first liquefied by Raoul Pictet and Louis Cailletet in 1877. In 1895 Linde set up the first large-scale plant for the manufacture of liquid air using the Joule–Kelvin effect. Within six years he also developed a method for separating liquid oxygen from liquid air on a large scale. New industrial processes needed oxygen, and consequently Linde's process was rapidly taken up.

Lindemann, Carl Louis Ferdinand von (1875–1939) German mathematician

Born at Hannover in Germany, Lindemann is principally known for solving one particular mathematical problem, namely the question of whether or not the number π is transcendental. In his paper *Über die Zahl π* (1882; On the Number π) he showed that it *is* and thus disposed of the ancient problem of squaring the circle, i.e., whether it is possible using only straight edge and compasses to construct a square equal in area to a given circle. Lindemann's result established its impossibility. Lindemann held posts as professor of mathematics at both the universities of Königsberg and Munich. His other mathematical work was chiefly in analysis and geometry.

Linnaeus, Carolus (1707–1778) Swedish botanist

Linnaeus, born Carl Linné, a pastor's son in Råshult, Sweden, began studying medicine at the University of Lund in 1727, transferring to Uppsala University the following year. While at college he investigated the newly proposed theory that plants exhibit sexuality and, by 1730, had begun formulating a taxonomic system based on stamens and pistils. He extended his knowledge of plants on travels through Lapland in 1732, where he discovered a hundred new species, and around Europe from 1733 to 1735.

In 1735 he settled in Holland and published his first major work, *Systema Naturae* (The System of Nature), in which he systematically arranged the animal, plant, and mineral kingdoms. In it, he classified whales and similar creatures as mammals and recognized man's affinity to the apes to the extent of naming the orang-utan *Homo troglodytes*. The flowering plants were divided into classes, depending on the number and arrangement of their stamens, and subdivived into orders, according to the number of their pistils. This system, because it was based simply on sexual characters, only partly showed the natural relationships between plants. It was undoubtedly useful in its time, however, for ordering the many new species that were arriving in Europe from all over the world.

Linnaeus's lasting contribution to taxonomy was his introduction, in 1749, of binomial nomenclature, which he applied in *Species Plantarum* (Species of Plants) (1753) by giving each plant a generic and a specific name. For example, applying the Linnean system, the Texas bluebonnet is named *Lupinus subcarnosus* where *Lupinus* is the generic name and *subcarnosus* the specific name. Until then scientific plant names were polynomial – a short Latin description of the distinguishing features. This combination of name and description was unsatisfactory, being too long for the name and too brief for the description. Linnaeus's innovation, separating the two functions, is the basis of modern nomenclature.

Linnaeus had returned to Sweden in 1738 and practiced there as a physician until he was appointed professor at Uppsala University in 1741. His botanical teaching stimulated many pupils, such as Daniel Solander, Carl Per Thunberg, and Anders Dahl, to travel widely collecting specimens. On Linnaeus's death his collection was bought by the English naturalist Sir James Smith. The London-based Linnean Society, founded by Smith in 1788, purchased the books and herbarium specimens from Smith's widow in 1828.

Lipmann, Fritz Albert (1899–1986)
German–American biochemist

After attending the university in his native city of Königsberg (now Kaliningrad in Russia), Lipmann studied in Berlin, where he obtained his MD in 1922 and his doctorate in 1927. He then worked with Otto Meyerhof in Heidelberg and taught at the Kaiser Wilhelm Institute in Berlin (1927–31), but with the rise of the Nazis decided to abandon Germany and consequently accepted a position with the Carlsberg Foundation in Copenhagen. In 1939 he moved to America, where he worked at the Cornell Medical School (1939–41), Harvard (1941–49), and the Massachusetts General Hospital in Boston (1949–57), before becoming professor of biochemistry at the Rockefeller Institute for Medical Research in New York, a post he occupied until his retirement in 1970.

It was widely known that the breakdown of such carbohydrates as glucose provides energy for the body's cells, but just how the cell obtains the energy released was a mystery. Lipmann's work, recently described by a historian of molecular biology as "the most magnificent achievement of late-classical biochemistry," began in 1937, when he was working on the breakdown of glucose by a particular bacterium. Quite fortuitously he found that a certain oxidation would not proceed without the addition of some phosphate.

This was all he needed to see that the real purpose of metabolism was to deliver energy into the cell. Lipmann sought for the phosphate that delivered the energy and found a molecule, adenosine triphosphate (ATP), which had been identified as the probable source of muscular energy by K. Lohmann in 1929. The molecule consisted of adenosine monophosphate (a nucleotide of the nucleic acid RNA), with the addition of two energy-rich phosphate bonds. When ATP is hydrolyzed to adenosine diphosphate (ADP), some of this energy is released ready for use in the cell.

It was not for this work, however, that Lipmann shared the 1953 Nobel Prize for physiology or medicine with Hans KREBS but for his discovery of coenzyme A and its importance for intermediary metabolism in 1947. While working on the role of phosphate in cell metabolism, Lipmann discovered that a heat-stable factor was acting as a carrier of acetyl (CH_3CO-) groups. It could not be replaced by any other known cofactor. Lipmann eventually isolated and identified what he termed 'cofactor A', or CoA (the A stands for acetylation), showing it to contain pantothenic acid (vitamin B_2). He also realized that the two-carbon compound in the Krebs cycle that joined with

oxaloacetic acid to form citric acid was in fact acetyl CoA. The coenzyme was soon shown to have wider application than the Krebs cycle, when in 1950 Feodor Lynen found that it played a key role in the metabolism of fats.

Lippershey, Hans (*c.* 1570–*c.* 1619)
Dutch spectacle maker

Lippershey was a maker of eyeglasses in Wesel, Germany. According to tradition, an apprentice playing with a couple of lenses suddenly found that a distant weathercock looked much bigger and nearer. Lippershey realized the significance of this and made the first telescope in 1608. He offered his invention to the Estates of Holland for use in warfare and initially an attempt was made by the Estates to keep the invention secret, but it was much too easy to reconstruct. All Galileo needed was a report of the 'Dutch invention' to allow him to make his own. There are many other claimants to Lippershey's invention, including his compatriot Zacharias Janssen.

Lippmann, Gabriel (1845–1921) *French physicist*

Born at Hollerich in Luxembourg, Lippmann was educated at the Ecole Normale in Paris. After conducting research in Germany he became professor of probability and mathematical physics at the Sorbonne in 1883. In 1886 he became director of the laboratories for physical research and professor of physics at the Sorbonne.

In 1873 he invented the *Lippmann capillary electrometer*, an instrument for measuring extremely small voltages. Lippmann is, however, better known for producing the first color photographic plate (1891). His color-photography process involved placing a coat of mercury behind the emulsion on the photographic plate. It is the only direct method of color photography but requires a long exposure time. For this work Lippmann was awarded the Nobel Prize for physics in 1908. Lippmann's other inventions included a galvanometer, a seismograph, and a coelostat.

Lipscomb, William Nunn (1919–)
American inorganic chemist

Born in Cleveland, Ohio, Lipscomb was educated at the University of Kentucky (graduating in 1942) and the California Institute of Technology where he obtained his PhD in 1946. He worked at the University of Minnesota from 1946 to 1959, being appointed professor of chemistry in 1954. In 1959 Lipscomb moved to the chair of chemistry at

Harvard where he remained until his retirement in 1990.

Lipscomb is best known for his work on boranes – hydrides of boron first investigated by Alfred Stock in the early part of the century. Boranes have such typical formulae as B_2H_6, B_4H_{10}, $B_{10}H_{14}$, and $B_{18}H_{22}$, which immediately appear to the chemist as analogous to the comparable hydrocarbon series, CH_4, C_2H_6, C_4H_{10}, etc. However, as boron has only three electrons in its outer shell, it was difficult to see how the covalent electron-pair bonds could work with boron hydrides.

Using low-temperature x-ray diffraction analysis, Lipscomb tackled the problem of investigating the notoriously unstable boranes, producing evidence of some remarkable structures, totally original and completely unsuspected by earlier chemists. The basic concept of a three-center bond was derived from a structure for diborane proposed by H. C. Longuet-Higgins. This differs from the normal covalent bond found in hydrocarbons where adjacent carbon and hydrogen atoms share two electrons. In a three-center bond, a pair of electrons is shared equally by three atoms.

Lipscomb's work on boron hydrides involved new techniques that proved to have a wider application in chemistry and produced results that led to the formulation of more general theories. In particular, Lipscomb produced a theory of chemical effects in nuclear magnetic resonance studies of complex molecules. He also worked on the quantum mechanics of large complex molecules.

His group has also applied low-temperature x-ray diffraction techniques to other substances, including single crystals of such gases as oxygen and nitrogen, other inorganic compounds, and naturally occurring organic compounds. More recently he has turned to determinations of the structures of proteins, enzymes, and other substances of biochemical interest.

Lipscomb received the Nobel Prize for chemistry in 1976.

Lissajous, Jules Antoine (1822–1880)
French physicist

Born at Versailles, Lissajous graduated from the Ecole Normale Supérieure in 1847 and then taught physics at a school in Paris.

He was interested in finding a way of making sound vibrations visible. Chladni had already produced his sand-pattern method but this only determined the nodal lines, where there was no vibration. Lissajous's method was to reflect light off mirrors attached to two tuning forks set at

right angles. The superposition of the vibrations formed dynamic patterns on a screen, which are now called *Lissajous figures*. From the form of these curves he could calculate the relative frequencies of the forks and thus provided a precise way of measuring pitch. He also invented the vibrating microscope, which produced Lissajous figures when vibrating objects, such as violin strings, were viewed through it.

Lister, Joseph, Baron (1827–1912)
British physician

Lister, the son of Joseph Jackson Lister, was born at Upton in England and educated at Quaker schools before entering University College, London, in 1843. University College was, at the time, the only English university open to religious dissenters. After graduating in arts, Lister studied medicine, obtaining his MB in 1852. He then served as assistant to the leading Scottish surgeon James Syme at the Royal Infirmary, Edinburgh, from 1854 until 1860 when he was appointed professor of surgery at Glasgow University. Lister returned to Edinburgh in 1869 as professor of clinical surgery but in 1877 became professor of surgery at King's College, London, serving there until his retirement in 1892.

In 1867 Lister published two short but revolutionary papers, which introduced the principles of antiseptic surgery into medicine. In 1846 he had been present when Robert Liston had first successfully used ether as an anesthetic in England. Yet this, apart from making surgery tolerable for both patient and surgeon, had not greatly advanced the profession. The full potential of anesthesia did not develop because of the high mortality produced by the infection that inevitably followed major surgery. The inevitable consequence was that a surprisingly small amount of surgery was actually attempted, even in the major centers with ready access to anesthetics.

Lister acknowledged the twin sources of his innovations in his 1867 papers. The first and most important were the writings of Louis Pasteur. These revealed the cause of the widespread surgical sepsis to be the germs present in the air. To control them Lister reported that he had been impressed by an account of the effects produced by carbolic acid on sewage in Carlisle. Carbolic acid (phenol, C_6H_5OH) is a weak acid derived from benzene. Although Lister's first attempt to use it as an antiseptic in March 1865 ended in failure he persisted and in August dressed a compound fracture of the leg, that is one in which the skin has been broken, with a piece of lint dipped in liquid carbolic acid. The wound healed well.

This encouraged Lister to introduce the carbolic acid dressings into his regular surgical procedure. By 1870 he claimed that mortality for amputations had dropped from over 40% to 15%. He later analyzed his figures for his Edinburgh period, reporting that from 1871 to 1877 he performed 725 major operations with a mortality of only 5.1%.

Another of Lister's major innovations was his introduction, in 1869, of cat-gut ligatures to replace the traditional silk thread, which was a major source of infection. Lister's experiments showed that cat-gut ligatures were absorbed by the body and if soaked in carbolic acid could be made sterile. He also attempted to maintain an antiseptic atmosphere in the operating theater by introducing a carbolic spray. This, however, made working conditions very unpleasant and the procedure was abandoned.

The Listerian system appears to have been accepted with little dissent and remarkable speed for by 1880 it had become the standard mode of surgical procedure virtually everywhere. Lister, an intensely shy and reserved man, achieved considerable fame and received many honors. In 1897 he became the first physician to be made a peer and sit in the House of Lords.

Littlewood, John Edensor (1885–1977) *British mathematician*

Born at Rochester, Littlewood studied at Cambridge University and in 1907 obtained a lectureship at Manchester. By 1910 he had returned to Cambridge where in 1928 he became Rouse Ball Professor of Mathematics. He retired in 1950 but continued active mathematical research until shortly before his death.

Littlewood is primarily known for his work in analysis, but he made contributions to many other fields, including mathematical astronomy, physics, differential equations, and probability theory. One of the most notable features of his career was his 35-year collaboration with G. H. Hardy. Among their most important joint work was the systematic investigation of problems of the convergence and summability of Fourier series. In 1914 Littlewood proved a famous theorem about the error term in the prime number theorem. In collaboration with R. E. A. C. Paley, Littlewood created and developed a new and specific link between trigonometric series and analytical functions. His work with Mary Cartwright on nonlinear differential equations was also of importance.

Lobachevsky, Nikolai Ivanovich (1793–1856) *Russian mathematician*

Lobachevsky was born at Nizhny Novgorod in Russia. Throughout his life he was associated with the University of Kazan; he was a student there and held various posts, including the chair in mathematics and finally the rectorship. Later he was deprived of his position for political reasons.

Lobachevsky's fame is due to his epoch-making discovery, announced in 1826 and published in 1829, that there could be consistent systems of geometry based on other postulates than those of Euclid. In particular Lobachevsky constructed and studied a type of geometry in which Euclid's parallel postulate is false (the postulate states that through a point not on a certain line only one line can be drawn not meeting the first line). János Bolyai had, at the same time though quite independently, come to a similar result and the same discovery had in fact been made decades earlier by Karl Friedrich Gauss, but he never published his work.

For centuries the status of Euclid's geometry and in particular of his parallel postulate had been a matter of controversy. Attempts had been made to show that it followed from the other axioms and it was widely held that Euclid's geometry described the necessary structure of space. By revealing the coherence of a non-Euclidean geometry Lobachevsky showed that Euclidean geometry has no such privileged position, helped mathematicians to break free from undue reliance on intuition, and paved the way for the systematic study of different kinds of non-Euclidean geometry in the work of Bernhard Riemann and Felix Klein.

Although it was not well received at first the value of Lobachevsky's work was fully appreciated once Riemann began his investigations into the fundamental concepts of geometry. Perhaps his fullest vindication came with the advent of Einstein's theory of relativity when it was demonstrated experimentally that the geometry of space is not described by Euclid's geometry.

Apart from geometry, Lobachevsky also did important work in the theory of infinite series, algebraic equations, integral calculus, and probabilty.

Lockyer, Sir Joseph Norman (1836–1920) *British astronomer*

Lockyer, born the son of a surgeon-apothecary at Rugby in the English Midlands, started his career as a civil servant. He turned to astronomy and taught at the Royal College of Science, becoming director of the solar physics observatory and professor of astronomical physics from 1890 to 1901. He was one of the founders and the first editor of the British periodical *Nature*. He made many eclipse trips and played a leading role in attempts to reorganize the structure of British science. He wrote numerous books on popular science and virtually created the new discipline of astroarchaeology. Lockyer was knighted in 1897.

The spectroscopic work of Robert Bunsen and Gustav Kirchhoff so stimulated Lockyer that he moved from traditional astronomy to spectral studies. He worked mainly on the Sun, publishing *The Chemistry of the Sun* in 1887. He investigated sunspots and solar prominences discovering, with Pierre Janssen in 1868, that they could be observed spectroscopically in daylight without an eclipse. He also successfully identified the spectral line observed by Janssen in the 1868 eclipse as being an unknown element (found, he thought, only in the Sun), which he proposed to name helium (from the Greek for Sun: *helios*). His supposition about the existence of the element was confirmed in 1895 when William Ramsay isolated it from gases in the atmosphere. In 1873 Lockyer published his theory of dissociation to explain the appearance of further unfamiliar spectral lines. William Huggins had found a new bright line in the spectra of nebulae and thought it could be a new substance that he proposed to call 'nebulium'. Lockyer argued instead that it could be an earthly element that had 'dissociated' into simpler substances under conditions of great heat and temperature, producing unrecognizable spectral lines. It was, however, difficult to make much sense of this view until the discovery of the electron some 20 years later and the correct explanation for the new spectral lines was not to be provided until the next century (by Ira Bowen).

In 1894 Lockyer published *The Dawn of Astronomy*, the first classic of what has since been called astroarchaeology, and in 1906 he produced *Stonehenge and Other British Monuments Astronomically Considered*. His aim in these works was to establish (without, of course, the benefit of computer and TV camera) that many ancient buildings were astronomically aligned. He did a good deal of field work, paying regular trips to Egypt and Greece as well as to the standing stones of Britain.

Not the least of his achievements was the creation of a new type of scientific periodical with *Nature* in 1869. It was by no means obvious that *Nature* would survive and it owes much to Lockyer's half century of editorship. The virtues of *Nature* were in fact

the virtues of Lockyer himself – it relished controversy, was tolerant of a wide range of scientific views, and was quick to publish scientific results.

Lodge, Sir Oliver Joseph (1851–1940)
British physicist

Born at Penkhull in England, Lodge entered his father's business in 1865. However, at the age of 22 he resumed a formal education, studying at the Royal College of Science (now part of Imperial College) and at University College, both in London; he was awarded a DSc in 1877. After several teaching posts he was appointed the first professor of physics at University College, Liverpool, in 1881. In 1900 he became the first principal of the new Birmingham University, remaining there until his retirement in 1919. He was knighted in 1902.

Lodge's principal scientific contributions were concerned with the transmission of electromagnetic waves, which led to developments in radio broadcasting. His experiments in the field of electricity started in the late 1870s. In 1887–88 he discovered that electromagnetic waves could be produced by electrical means and transmitted along conducting wires. These results were somewhat overshadowed by the work of Heinrich Hertz who in 1888 succeeded in producing electromagnetic waves, transmitted them through air, and demonstrated their similarities with light waves. In 1894 Lodge made his mark, however, by greatly improving the means of detecting these 'Hertzian' waves (now known as radio waves) by developing the coherer. This was an electrical device whose function was based on a discovery made in 1890 by E. Branley: that electrical discharges in certain metallic powders, caused by radio waves, resulted in a drop in electrical resistance.

Lodge is also remembered for his work on the ether, which had been postulated as the wave-bearing medium filling all space. In 1893 he devised an experiment that helped to discredit the theory. Other scientific work included investigations on lightning, the source of the electromotive force in the voltaic cell, electrolysis, and the application of electricity to the dispersal of fog and smoke. He played a part in establishing the National Physical Laboratory.

From 1900 Lodge increasingly devoted himself to administrative work. He was also interested in the history of science and wrote several scientific memoirs. In his writings he made attempts to reconcile what seemed to him the divergence between science and religion.

After 1910 he became deeply involved in

psychical research. He believed in the possibility of communicating with the dead, a belief sustained by the hope of somehow communicating with his youngest son Raymond, who was killed in World War I.

Loeb, Jacques (1859–1924) German–American physiologist

Loeb was born at Mayen in Germany. After studying medicine at Strasbourg, he settled in America (1891) where he held professorships at Bryn Mawr College, Pennsylvania, and the universities of Chicago and California, before becoming a member of the Rockefeller Institute for Medical Research (1910).

Much of Loeb's major research was concerned with plant and animal tropisms (involuntary movements in response to stimuli such as light, water, and gravity); he postulated that these occur not only in primitive animals but also in higher animals, including man (*Forced Movements, Tropisms, and Animal Conduct*, 1918). He also carried out important work on artificial parthenogenesis, showing that unfertilized frogs' eggs could be induced to divide by altering their environment. Another discovery was that sea-urchin eggs are hatched by the osmotic pressure exerted by various substances dissolved in water.

Loewi, Otto (1873–1961) German–American physiologist

Loewi was born at Frankfurt am Main in Germany and qualified in medicine at the University of Strasbourg before taking up professorships in physiology and pharmacology at Vienna and Graz Universities. For a time he worked under Ernest Starling in London, and in 1940 emigrated to America where he became research professor at the New York University College of Medicine.

Loewi's most important work was concerned with nerve action in vertebrate animals, demonstrating, for example, that chemical reactions are involved in nerve impulses. In 1921 he discovered that certain chemical substances are released when the nerves of a frog's heart are electrically stimulated. Loewi's *vagus material* (thus named because it was obtained by stimulation of the vagus nerve) was subsequently shown by Henry DALE to be acetylcholine. It can be used to stimulate the activity of another heart without the need for nervous activity. Loewi and Dale shared the Nobel Prize for physiology or medicine in 1936 for their work in this field.

Löffler, Friedrich August Johannes (1852–1915) German bacteriologist

Löffler was born at Frankfurt in Germany, the son of an army surgeon. He was educated at the University of Würzburg and the Berlin Institute of Military Medicine, where – after serving in the Franco–Prussian War – he obtained his MD in 1874. After various official positions Löffler worked with Georg Gaffky as an assistant to Robert Koch from 1884 to 1888. He later served as professor of hygiene at the University of Griefswald (1888–1913), after which he succeeded Gaffky as director of the Koch Institute in Berlin, where he remained until his death.

Löffler's major contribution to the new field of bacteriology was the isolation and cultivation in 1884 of the bacillus responsible for diphtheria, which had first been observed by the German physiologist Theodor Klebs in the throats of diphtheria patients (the organism became known as the *Klebs–Löffler bacillus*). The isolation and cultivation of pure cultures involved a number of formidable technical problems; Löffler found it necessary to develop a new medium, thickened serum, as the conventional gelatin used by Koch required temperatures far too low for the diphtheria pathogen.

Earlier (in 1882) Löffler had discovered the organism responsible for glanders (a contagious disease, especially of horses) and in 1898, in collaboration with the pathologist Paul Frosch, he succeeded in demonstrating for the first time that viruses could cause diseases in animals. This was achieved by passing foot-and-mouth disease from one cow to another by inoculation with cell-free filtrates taken from lesions. Löffler's work, together with Dmitri Ivanovsky's demonstration in 1892 that plants were susceptible to viral infections, constituted the start of modern virology.

Lomonosov, Mikhail Vasilievich (1711–1765) Russian scientist and scholar

Lomonosov was the son of a fisherman from Deniskova, now Lomonosov, in Russia. He left for Moscow in 1730 to obtain an education and studied science there until 1735. In 1736 he attended the St. Petersburg Academy of Sciences before traveling to Marburg where he studied under Christian Wolff. Following his return to St. Petersburg in 1741 he was put under arrest (1743) and in prison began work on his *276 Notes on Corpuscular Philosophy and Physics*, in which he outlined his scientific ideas. He became professor of chemistry at St. Petersburg in 1745.

Lomonosov campaigned successfully for a laboratory for teaching and research at St.

Petersburg and this was opened in 1749. On the basis of the results of experiments conducted in the laboratory he set up a glass factory to produce, in particular, colored-glass mosaics. As an administrator he helped to found Moscow University (1755) with Leonhard Euler.

As a chemist Lomonosov was opposed to the phlogiston theory and is reported to have anticipated Antoine Lavoisier on the conservation of mass, Benjamin Rumford on the kinetic theory of heat, and Thomas Young on the wave theory of light.

Lomonosov also made equally important contributions to Russian literature. He wrote the grammar that systematized the Russian literary language and was himself a poet. His work, *Ancient History of Russia*, published posthumously in 1766, was the first work on the history of Russia.

London, Fritz (1900–1954) *German–American physicist*

London was born in Breslau, now Wrocław in Poland, the son of a mathematics professor at Bonn and the elder brother of the well-known physicist, Heinz London. He originally received a classical education at the Universities of Frankfurt, Munich, and Bonn, where in 1921 he was awarded his doctorate for a philosophical thesis. London taught in secondary schools for some years and then began work as a physicist in 1925 at Munich. After appointments in Stuttgart, Zurich, and Berlin he left Germany in 1933 with the rise of Hitler. He worked first in the Clarendon Laboratory in Oxford and from 1935 at the Institut Poincaré, Paris, before moving to America to become professor of theoretical chemistry at Duke University, North Carolina – a post he retained until his death in 1954.

In 1927 London, in collaboration with Walter Heitler, succeeded in providing an account of the covalent bond in the hydrogen molecule using wave mechanics. In the 1930s he collaborated with his brother in gaining a major insight into the nature of superconductivity. This was followed by his own researches, beginning in 1938, into the nature of superfluidity, a phenomenon first described by Pyotr KAPITZA.

London, Heinz (1907–1970) *German–British physicist*

Born at Bonn in Germany, London was the son of a mathematics professor and the younger brother of the distinguished physicist, Fritz London, with whom he collaborated on some of his early work. He was educated at the universities of Bonn, Berlin, Munich, and Breslau, where he obtained his

PhD under Francis Simon in 1933. Abandoning Nazi Germany immediately afterwards, London first joined his brother at the Clarendon Laboratory in Oxford but moved to Bristol in 1936, remaining there until his brief internment as an enemy alien in 1940. On his release he worked on the separation of uranium isotopes for the development of the atomic bomb. With the coming of peace, in 1946 London joined the staff of the Atomic Energy Research Establishment at Harwell where he remained until his death.

In Oxford London continued the work of his thesis in his collaboration with his brother on a number of pressing problems in superconductivity. In particular they explained the discoveries of W. MEISSNER that at the moment a metal becomes superconductive it expels the magnetic field produced by an electric current; if, however, a strong external magnetic field is applied normal resistivity will return.

At Harwell after the war London worked until the 1950s on isotope separation. His attention was also drawn to the problem of superfluidity in liquid helium, which led him to develop his dilution refrigerator. This consisted in mixing the two isotopes of helium, helium-3 and helium-4, at temperatures below 1 K in a dilution of 1:1000. Some of the helium-3 would pass to and fro across the boundary between the isotopes separated by their different densities and reduce the temperature by a small amount with each passage. The machine was first described in 1951 and a working apparatus was built in 1963. The device has reached temperatures as low as 0.005 K.

Long, Crawford Williamson (1815–1878) *American physician*

Long, who was born in Danielsville, Georgia, received his MD from the University of Pennsylvania in 1839. He then practiced in the small Georgian village of Jefferson where he became probably the first physician to perform surgery using ether as an anesthetic. (There is one earlier record of the administration of ether, for a tooth extraction: in January 1842, William Clark gave ether to a patient whose tooth was then removed by Elijah Pope.)

The idea of using ether came to Long after he had engaged in 'ether frolics' – wild parties at which ether was inhaled for exhilarative effect. Long noticed that he developed many bruises during such parties but had no recollection of sustaining any injuries. This suggested to him the possibility of using it more constructively to provide surgical anesthesia. Consequently on 30

March 1842, Long removed a small tumor from the neck of an etherized patient who assured him, when he regained consciousness, that he had not experienced any pain. Long followed this up in July by painlessly amputating the toe of a young etherized boy. However, Long had little chance to use his dramatic discovery in major operations and did not publish details until 1849. By this time William MORTON had already (1846) given a public demonstration of the use of ether as an anesthetic and Long thus received little credit for his discovery.

Lonsdale, Dame Kathleen (1903–1971) British crystallographer

The daughter of a postman, Lonsdale (née Yardley) was born at Newbridge in Ireland and moved to England with her family in 1908. She studied physics at Bedford College, London, graduating in 1922, and spent most of the following 20 years based at the Royal Institution in the research team of William Henry Bragg. In 1946 she moved to University College, London, where she served as professor of chemistry and head of the department of crystallography from 1948 until her retirement in 1968.

Lonsdale was one of the early pioneers of x-ray crystallography, centered on the Royal Institution and the team headed by Bragg and including such scholars as William Astbury, John Bernal, Dorothy Hodgkin, and John Robertson. It was from this group that most of the concepts and techniques of the new discipline emerged in the 1920s and 1930s. Lonsdale herself was responsible for one of the first demonstrations of the power of the new techniques when, in 1929, she published details of the structure of benzene. Working with a large crystal of hexamethylbenzene she established the hexagonal nature of the ring, that it was planar to within 0.1 angstrom ($1 \text{ Å} = 10^{-10}$ m), and that the carbon–carbon bonds were 1.42 Å. This was followed in 1931 by the equally significant structure of the more difficult hexachlorobenzene, the first investigation of an organic compound in which Fourier analysis was used.

Other crystallographic subjects researched by Lonsdale included the magnetic susceptibility of crystals and the structure of synthetic diamonds and, in the 1960s, that of bladder stones. She edited the first three volumes of the *International Tables for X-ray Crystallography* (1952, 1959, 1962) and also produced a survey of the subject in her *Crystals and X-rays* (1948).

As a Quaker and a convinced pacifist Lonsdale refused to register in 1939 for government service or civil defense despite the fact that as a mother of three young children she would have been exempted from any such service. Fined £2 in 1943, she refused to pay and served a month in Holloway prison instead.

When, 285 years after its foundation, the Royal Society finally decided to admit women to its fellowship Lonsdale was the first to be elected (1945) and she became the society's vice-president in 1960. She was appointed a Dame of the British Empire in 1956 and also became, in 1968, the first woman to serve as president of the British Association for the Advancement of Science.

Lorentz, Hendrik Antoon (1853–1928) Dutch theoretical physicist

Lorentz, who was born at Arnhem in the Netherlands, studied at the University of Leiden and received his doctorate in 1875. In 1877, aged only 24, he became professor of theoretical physics at Leiden. This was the Netherlands' first chair in the newly independent field of theoretical physics, and one of the first in Europe, and Lorentz did a great deal in shaping and developing the field. On his retirement in 1912 he was appointed director of the Teyler Laboratory in Haarlem, a museum of science and art with a laboratory where he could continue his research. He still retained contact with the world of advanced physics, giving every week at Leiden his famous 'Monday morning lectures' on current scientific problems.

Lorentz had wide-ranging interests in physics and mathematics, his linguistic abilities allowing him to follow the scientific trends in Europe. His major work, however, was spent in the development of the electromagnetic theory of James Clerk MAXWELL. He brought this to a point where a need for a radical change in the foundations of physics became noticeable and thus provided the inspiration for Einstein's theory of relativity.

Lorentz's early work on this highly complex and confused subject followed from the writings of Hermann von Helmholtz and began in his doctoral thesis. Lorentz refined Maxwell's theory so that for the first time various effects including the reflection and refraction (bending) of light could be fully explained. In a series of articles published between 1892 and 1904 Lorentz put forward his 'electron theory': he proposed that the atoms and molecules of matter contained small rigid bodies that carried either a positive or negative charge. By 1899 he was referring to these charged particles as 'electrons'. It was through the effects of these electrons that many phenomena in science were explained. Lorentz believed that matter and the wave-bearing medium known as the 'ether' were distinct entities and that the interaction between them was mediated by electrons. He saw that the interaction of light waves and matter resulted from the presence of electrons in matter and that if set into vibration these charged particles would produce light waves, as predicted by Maxwell's equations.

In 1895 he described the force, now known as the *Lorentz force*, on charged particles of matter in an electromagnetic field. In 1900 he identified the negatively charged particles that had been found to constitute cathode rays as the negative electrons of his theory. He also used the theory to explain the effect discovered by Pieter ZEEMAN in 1896 whereby the spectral lines of sodium atoms were split by the action of a magnetic field. Lorentz and Zeeman shared the 1902 Nobel Prize for physics for their investigations of the influence of magnetic fields on radiation. However, other phenomena, such as the photoelectric effect, could not be explained and, in fact, were inconsistent with Lorentz's theory; it was these anomalies that inspired the development of the quantum theory.

The other work for which Lorentz is famous is his suggested method of resolving the problems raised by the experiments in the 1880s of Albert MICHELSON and Edward Morley on the motion of the Earth through the ether. Lorentz showed that if it were assumed that moving bodies contracted in the direction of motion, then the observed effects would follow. This solution was derived independently by George Fitzgerald and came to be known as the *Lorentz–Fitzgerald contraction*. Lorentz extended his idea, putting it on a firmer mathematical footing, and in 1904 published in final form what became known as the *Lorentz transformations*. These transformations of the space and time coordinates of an event in one frame of reference to those in another frame again figured largely in Einstein's theory of special relativity (1905), in which Einstein could be said to have reinterpreted Lorentz's ideas.

Lorentz devoted much time to education and the teaching of science and medicine. In later life he was very active in international science conferences, acting as president of the first Solvay Congress for physics in Brussels and continuing as president until his death. He also played a major role in restoring international scientific relations after World War I.

Lorenz, Edward Norton (1917–   )
American meteorologist

Born in West Hartford, Connecticut, Lorenz was educated at Dartmouth College, New Hampshire, at Harvard, and at the Massachusetts Institute of Technology. He joined the MIT faculty in 1946 and served as professor of meteorology from 1962 until 1987.

Lorenz had trained initially as a mathematician, but after serving in the US Army Air Corps as a weather forecaster, he decided to continue as a meteorologist and work on the more theoretical aspects of the subject. Could forecasting, he asked, be significantly improved? If astronomers could predict the return of a comet decades ahead, it should surely be possible, given enough computing power, to forecast the state of the atmosphere for more than a few hours in advance. The pioneer of this method was the mathematician Von Neumann, who planned a program to predict, and even control, the weather. One day in 1961 Lorenz discovered that there were more than a few simple, practical obstacles to overcome.

In order to follow variations in weather conditions Lorenz set up a system in which he fed a set of initial conditions into the computer and allowed it to run on showing graphically the values taken by a single variable, such as temperature, over a long period of time. On one occasion he wished to examine part of one run in greater detail and fed in the initial conditions taken from an earlier run. To his surprise the computer produced a markedly different sequence from the original printout. Eventually Lorenz traced the source of the discrepancy. The initial conditions of the program, stored in the computer memory, had used the number 0.506127, correct to six decimal places; the printout, however, gave just three decimal places, 0.506. Lorenz, like everyone else, had assumed that so small a difference could have no significant effect. In fact, a small difference can, over a long period of time, build up to produce a large effect. Moreover, the way the difference affects the outcome is very sensitive to small changes. Technically, this is termed 'sensitive dependence on initial conditions'. More graphically, it is called the 'butterfly effect', from the idea that a single butterfly flapping its wings in China might, weeks later, 'cause' a hurricane in New York.

The butterfly effect occurs because the weather depends on a number of factors – temperature, humidity, air flow, etc. – and these are to a certain extent interdependent. Thus the way the temperature changes depends on the humidity, but this depends on temperature. Consequently, equations relating these factors are nonlinear – a variable is a function of itself. And it is this nonlinearity that causes the sensitive dependence on initial conditions. The weather is a system that repeats itself, giving periods of dry weather and periods of wet, but it repeats itself in an unpredictable way. There are a number of similar nonlinear systems – for example, population cycles or economic cycles – that depend on nonlinear equations. The study of such systems has come to be known as 'chaos theory.'

Lorenz went on to study behavior of this kind in a more rigorous and abstract manner. He considered some simple nonlinear equations describing fluid flow in a system with three degrees of freedom. He appeared to discover in the process a new kind of 'attractor'. In broad terms an attractor is what the behavior of a system settles down to, or is attracted to. The simplest kind, a fixed-point attractor, is represented by a pendulum subject to friction. The pendulum, no matter how it starts swinging, will always come to rest in the same position. Its final state is predictable.

The *Lorenz attractor*, however, proved to be both chaotic and unpredictable. It was the first example of a 'strange attractor', a term introduced by David Ruelle in 1971. Lorenz discovered the attractor by examining the changing relationships between the three variables described by the equations. At any moment in time the variables will be defined by a point in three dimensional space. The point can be plotted. Lorenz found that the point never followed the same path, nor did the paths it followed ever intersect; instead it displayed a system of complex loops, something in fact like the wings of a butterfly.

Lorenz first published his work in 1963 in a paper entitled *Deterministic Nonperiodic Flow*. Although it received little early attention, it became one of the most cited papers of the 1980s.

Lorenz, Konrad Zacharias (1903–1989) *Austrian ethologist*

Alfred Lorenz, father of Konrad, was a very wealthy Viennese orthopedic surgeon who had developed a new operation for a congenital dislocation of the femur, a common complaint of the period. He was keen for his son to follow him into medicine and consequently, though reluctantly, Lorenz studied medicine at Columbia in New York and at the University of Vienna, where he gained his MD in 1929. He remained at Vienna to complete his PhD in 1933 on the comparative anatomy and evolution of avian wings. Lorenz was appointed lecturer in animal psychology in 1937.

Alfred Lorenz had bought a sizeable estate at Altenberg, a site about twenty miles outside Vienna. It was on this family estate that Lorenz first began his researches on animal behavior. Here he studied a jackdaw colony that had settled on the roof of his father's house. He also began to rear goslings; wild geese had proved to be too difficult to study profitably. Among other tasks Lorenz systematically classified the signals and behavior patterns of his goslings. Before long he had constructed a 'glossary' of their various calls and behavior patterns. They presented a number of problems. What did they mean? How did they originate in the individual? And how could such behavior patterns evolve?

In his bird studies Lorenz made good use of the phenomenon of imprinting, first described by Heinroth in 1911. Goslings, as they hatch tend to take the first object they encounter to be their mother. Lorenz would allow goslings and other birds to imprint themselves upon him and thereby gain easy access to them without actually taming them. It became a common sight at Altenberg to see Lorenz followed by a line of goslings who, if threatened, would scurry to him in alarm. He noted some of the properties of the process and defined it as "a developmental process by which behavior becomes attached to a particular object." No reinforcement is required; mere passive exposure will suffice. It is also irreversible, and is clearly innate.

In 1937 Lorenz began to offer an explanatory system – a new theory of instinct – to account for many aspects of animal behavior. Much complex behavior, he noted, came perfectly formed and required no initial learning period. Nor did it necessarily arise from external stimuli. For example, Lorenz noted starlings in mid-winter hunting nonexistent flies, presumably responding to some internal drive – a form of behavior he described as 'vacuum activities'.

He went on to characterize instincts in terms of four properties: they were clearly innate; they were species-specific; they involved stereotyped behavior; and instincts also involved what Lorenz termed 'action specific energies', which were discharged by the presence of innate releasing mechanisms, also known as 'releasers'.

Thus the sight of a male stickleback's red belly (releaser) in the breeding season induces a stereotyped aggressive response in a rival male. The response is species and action specific. Lorenz likened the process to liquid in a reservoir. Just as water is released by opening a valve, the instinctive behavior innate in the system is discharged when presented with the appropriate releaser. Later ethologists have objected that Lorenz's model underestimates environmental influences.

Lorenz's work at Altenberg was interrupted by the onset of World War II. He served as a physician in the German army and was taken prisoner by the Russians in 1944. He was released in 1948 and on his return to Austria he was invited by the Max Planck Institute to establish a Department of Comparative Ethology at Buldern, Westphalia. The department moved in 1961 to the Institute for Behavioral Physiology, Seewiesen, Bavaria. On his retirement in 1973 Lorenz returned, along with his geese, to Grunau in Austria where he established his own research institute with funds provided by the Austrian Academy.

By this time Lorenz had become world famous. Two books published in the 1950s, *King Solomon's Ring* (1952) and *Man Meets Dog* (1954), were immensely popular and have remained in print. He assumed a more controversial role in 1966 with his *On Aggression*, in which he argued that aggression was not necessarily an evil as it also served a number of evolutionary purposes. Man, he claimed, actually suffered from "an insufficient discharge of his aggressive drive." Equally controversial was *Man's Eight Deadly Sins* (1974), in which he warned against the genetic deterioration of the human race.

For his work on ethology Lorenz shared the 1973 Nobel Prize for physiology or medicine with Niko TINBERGEN and Karl von FRISCH.

Loschmidt, Johann Josef (1821–1895)
Austrian chemist

Born into a peasant family in Carlsbad, Bohemia, Loschmidt was educated by the local clergy, who encouraged him to pursue his studies at the Prague Gymnasium and at the German University in Prague. After graduating in 1843 he struggled with various businesses before ending his commercial career in 1854 as a bankrupt. He turned to academic life and in 1856 was appointed to the Vienna Realschule where he remained until 1868 when he moved to the University of Vienna as professor of physical chemistry.

In 1861 Loschmidt published a brief work, *Chemische Studien* (Chemical Studies), in which he listed 368 formulae. Like most chemists of the time, Loschmidt was seeking for ways to express chemical structure and composition accurately and graphically. In his system, atoms were represented by circles, with a large circle for carbon and a smaller one for hydrogen. Thus four years

before Kekulé announced his own results, Loschmidt represented the benzene molecule by a single large ring (the carbon) with six smaller circles (hydrogen) around the rim. Little attention seems to have been paid to his work at the time.

He is far better known for a paper published in 1865 entitled *Zur Grosse der Loftmolecule* (On the Magnitude of Air Molecules) in which he made the first accurate estimate of the size of molecules. Using the kinetic theory of gases, Loschmidt derived the equation $s = 8el$, where s is the molecular diameter, l is the mean free path (the distance a molecule moves between successive collisions), and e is the condensation coefficient. This latter factor was derived from changes in volume due to evaporation and condensation. Using published data for e and l, he obtained the value 10^{-7} centimeter. In his honor, the number of particles per unit volume of an ideal gas at standard temperature and pressure is known as *Loschmidt's constant* (or *Loschmidt's number*). It has the value 2.686763 $\times 10^{25}$ m^{-3}.

Love, Augustus Edward Hough
(1863–1940) *British mathematician and geophysicist*

Born at Weston-super-Mare in the west of England, Love studied at Cambridge University and was a fellow there from 1886 until 1889. In 1889 he moved to Oxford to take up the Sedleian Chair in Mathematics and remained there for the rest of his career.

Love's most important research was in the theory of deformable media and in theoretical geophysics. He also did important work in the theory of waves and in ballistics. He wrote a major two-volume treatise on elasticity – *A Treatise on the Mathematical Theory of Elasticity* (1892–93) – that went through several subsequent editions. It soon established itself as a classic and is still a standard work of reference. Love's work on geophysics led to a considerable number of practical discoveries. Among his original concepts now much used in geophysics are the so-called *Love numbers* and *Love waves*. Love numbers play a key role in tidal theory. In the formal theory of Love waves, which are surface seismic waves, he was building on and much improving work begun by Siméon-Denis Poisson, Sir George Stokes, and Lord Rayleigh. This was perhaps Love's single most significant piece of mathematical work.

Lovell, Sir (Alfred Charles) Bernard
(1913–   ) *British radio astronomer*

Lovell was born at Oldland Common and received his PhD in 1936 from the University of Bristol; in the same year was appointed as a lecturer in physics at the University of Manchester. In 1945, after war service on the development of radar, he returned to Manchester. He was elected in 1951 to the chair of radio astronomy and the directorship of Jodrell Bank (now the Nuffield Radio Astronomy Laboratories), a post he held until his retirement in 1981. He was knighted in 1961.

Lovell's first research was done in the field of cosmic rays. In the course of his work during World War II he realized that radio waves were a possible tool with which to pursue his studies. Thus in 1945 two trailers of radar equipment that had been used in wartime defense work were parked in a field at Jodrell Bank in Cheshire to begin radio investigation of cosmic rays, meteors, and comets. Lovell soon produced worthwhile results on meteor velocities and other topics and began to feel that a more permanent and ambitious telescope should be built.

Thus Lovell began a heroic ten-year struggle to finance a 250-foot (76-m) steerable radio telescope with a parabolic dish that would be able to receive radio waves as short as 30 centimeters. The main problem was to find sufficient funds to meet the rising costs of the project at times of government cuts. Thus in 1955 the project found itself £250,000 in debt. The Department of Scientific and Industrial Research agreed to find half if Lovell could raise the rest. A public appeal failed to raise more than £65,000 and it required a strong public press campaign to move the Treasury to meet the outstanding costs in 1960, three years after the telescope was first used.

The Jodrell Bank telescope came to public notice when it was used to track the first Sputnik in 1957. It was not just an adjunct to the space program, however, but a major tool for astronomical research of which Lovell has given a full account in his *Out of the Zenith* (1973). He there showed the power of the giant telescope to supplement and advance the discoveries of others. Thus it was the Cambridge radio astronomers under Antony Hewish who discovered pulsars, but they were limited to observing them only for the few minutes each day that the pulsars were on the Cambridge meridian. The steerable Jodrell Bank telescope could observe objects for as long as they were above the horizon and it was no accident that of the 50 pulsars discovered in the northern hemisphere before 1972, 27 were detected at Jodrell Bank. So too with those other mysterious phenomena of the 1960s, quasars. Once more the initial discov-

ery was made elsewhere but Jodrell Bank possessed the instruments to show that some quasars had angular diameters of one second of arc or less, which was surprisingly small for such prodigious sources of energy.

Lovell has written a number of important books recounting the story – political, financial and scientific – of Jodrell Bank. They include *The Story of Jodrell Bank* (1968), *The Jodrell Bank Telescopes* (1985), and his autobiography *Astronomer by Chance* (1996).

Lovelock, James Ephraim (1919–   )
British scientist

A Londoner, Lovelock was educated at the universities of London and Manchester during the early years of World War II. After graduating in 1941 he joined the staff of the National Institute for Medical Research (NIMR) in London, where he worked on a variety of technical war-time problems including the measurement of blood pressure under water, the freezing of viable cells, and the design of an acoustic anemometer.

After twenty years with the NIMR Lovelock began to feel that his creativity was being stifled by the security of his position as a scientific civil servant. Consequently he resigned and took up a short-term appointment with NASA. He was assigned to work on the first lunar Surveyor mission at the Jet Propulsion Laboratory, California.

Lovelock left America in 1964 determined to set up as an 'independent' scientist. He claimed that he did not wish to be just one more consultant serving the needs, whatever they might be, of multinational companies – he wished to work at science without constraints, in the manner of a novelist or painter. In this manner Lovelock was able to make a number of important observations. While at NIMR he had developed a sensitive electron-capture detector. In the summer of 1966 he used it to monitor the supposedly clean Atlantic air blowing onto the west coast of Ireland. He detected chlorofluorocarbons (CFCs). Although unable to pursue the matter further through lack of funding, Lovelock managed to travel to the Antarctic in 1971 where, again, he found atmospheric CFCs. It was partly as a result of this work that Sherry Rowland began to ponder over their role in the atmosphere.

It is, however, as the author of the Gaia hypothesis, first presented in his *Gaia* (London, 1979), and developed further in several sequels, that Lovelock is best known. Gaia has been widely accepted by Greens, conservationists, and New-Age thinkers. Lovelock argued in 1979 that the Earth, including its rocks, oceans, and atmosphere, as well as its flora and fauna, was a living organism "maintained and regulated by life on the surface." He referred to it as 'Gaia' after the Greek Earth goddess – a suggestion made by the novelist William Golding. The hypothesis has been dismissed by scientists as "crudely anthropomorphic" and "pseudoscientific idiocy." However, some see Gaia as a working hypothesis that can be tested and evaluated in the normal manner.

Lowell, Percival (1855–1916) American astronomer

Born in Boston, Massachusetts, Lowell graduated from Harvard in 1876. His first interest was oriental studies but Giovanni SCHIAPARELLI's report in 1877 of the 'canali' (mistranslated as 'canals') of Mars had interested him and he finally decided to devote the rest of his life to astronomy. As he was a member of a famous, aristocratic, and wealthy Boston family, he had no difficulty in financing his own observatory. He built it at a height of 7200 feet (2200 m) in the clear skies of Arizona, giving him good observing conditions, and began his studies of the planets in 1894. He was appointed professor of astronomy at the Massachusetts Institute of Technology in 1902.

Lowell spent 15 years observing Mars with an excellent 24-inch (61-cm) refractor built by Alvan Clark. He had no difficulty in seeing the 'canals' of Schiaparelli, also claiming to see oases and clear signs of vegetation. He soon concluded that Mars was inhabited and wrote a series of books on this topic: Mars (1895), Mars and its Canals (1906), and Mars as the Abode of Life (1908). He was by no means alone among professional astronomers in his, what now appears to be extravagant, claim.

It should be realized that large telescopes do little to improve the visual appearance of the planets because of the constantly shifting terrestrial atmosphere. It was not until the Martian surface was mapped by the Mariner and Viking spacecraft in the 1960s and 1970s that the idea of artificial canals could be definitely dispelled.

Lowell was more successful in his work on a trans-Neptunian planet. Even making full allowances for the disturbing effects of Neptune, the orbit of Uranus still was not free from anomalies. Lowell thought that this could be due to an unknown Planet X still further out in space. He calculated its orbit and position, beginning his search in 1905. He published his negative results in 1914. Fourteen years after his death Clyde TOMBAUGH, observing at the Lowell Observatory in 1930 and using a blink comparator,

discovered the new planet. It was named Pluto since like the god it ruled as prince of outer darkness but also because its first two letters stood appropriately for Percival Lowell.

Lowry, Thomas Martin (1874–1936) English chemist

Lowry was the son of a Wesleyan army chaplain from Bradford in England. He was educated at the Central Technical College (later part of Imperial College), London, where from 1896 to 1913 he served as assistant to Henry Armstrong. From 1904 he was also head of chemistry at Westminster Training College until he moved to Guy's Hospital, London, in 1913 to become head of the chemistry department. In 1920 he was appointed as the first professor of physical chemistry at Cambridge University.

As a physical chemist Lowry was largely concerned with the optical activity of certain compounds. In 1898 he first described the phenomenon of mutarotation. He found that the optically active compound nitro-camphor revealed an alteration of rotatory power over time. Later, in the 1920s, he confirmed experimentally that there is a relationship between the optical rotatory power of compounds and the wavelength of light passing through them. He published an account of this aspect of his work in Optical Rotatory Power (1935).

He is also remembered for his theory of acids and bases which he formulated in 1923 simultaneously with but independently of the Danish chemist **Johannes Bronsted** (1879–1947). They simply defined an acid as any ion or molecule able to produce a proton, while a base is any ion or molecule able to take up a proton.

Lucas, Keith (1879–1916) British neurophysiologist

Lucas, the son of an engineer, was born at Greenwich and graduated from Cambridge University, where he was elected a fellow in 1904. In 1914 he joined the research department of the Royal Aircraft Establishment, Farnborough, and while carrying out his duties died in a midair collision.

In 1905 and 1909 Lucas published two papers that clearly stated the all-or-none law of nervous stimulation: a stimulus can evoke a maximum possible response or nothing. If stimuli of varying strength appear to elicit responses of increasing contraction this is because, Lucas demonstrated, more nerve fibers are responding rather than that the same number of fibers are reacting with greater vigor.

Lucas's work became more widely known

through its later development by his youthful collaborator, Edgar ADRIAN.

Lummer, Otto (1860–1925) German physicist

Born at Jena, in Germany, Lummer became professor at the University of Breslau in 1905. In 1889 he designed, wth Eugen Brodhum, a photometer with an arrangement of prisms, which was an improved version of the grease-spot photometer invented by Robert Bunsen.

Lummer's research was chiefly on radiation energy and temperature. Working with Wilhelm Wien he achieved in practice the black-body radiator, which had been conceived as a theoretical abstraction in the study of radiant heat. In 1899 he did further work with Ernst Pringsheim on the distribution of energy in black-body radiation – work that eventually led to Max Planck's formulation of the quantum theory.

Lummer also built, with Leon Arons, a mercury vapor lamp in 1892.

Lundmark, Knut (1889–1958) Swedish astronomer

Lundmark was born at Norrbotten in Sweden and educated at the University of Uppsala. After working at the Lick and Mount Wilson observatories in California in the 1920s, he served as professor of astronomy at the University of Lund from 1929 to 1955.

He published a series of papers in the 1920s in which he attacked Adriaan van Maanen's claim to have measured significant amounts of internal rotation in some spiral nebulae and supported the claim of Heber Curtis that such nebulae were isolated star systems too far away for such rotation to be detected. He repeated the measurements by the same methods and with the same instruments, concluding that "the nebulae are stationary for me and if I got a rotational effect it is very small compared with that of van Maanen." By 1929 Lundmark's views had been backed by the observations of Edwin Hubble who demonstrated conclusively the great distances of the spiral nebulae, or spiral galaxies as they are now called.

In 1926 Lundmark published a preliminary classification of galaxies, on which Hubble was also working. Hubble, somewhat angrily, accused Lundmark of having 'borrowed' his results. Lundmark replied that he had had no access to Hubble's work and in any case the two schemes were different.

Luria, Salvador Edward (1912–1991) Italian–American biologist

Having studied medicine in his native city of Turin, physics and radiology in Rome, and bacteriophage research techniques in Paris, Luria emigrated to America in 1940. There he met Max Delbrück and became associated with the American Phage Group, a body formed to study virus replication. He served as professor of microbiology at the Massachusetts Institute of Technology from 1950 to 1958, and in 1964 became Sedgwick Professor of Biology there.

Luria was interested in the way bacteria acquire resistance to virus infection and investigated whether this is due to an adaptive response or spontaneous mutation. His development of the fluctuation test, and its subsequent mathematical analysis by DELBRÜCK, showed that resistance is indeed due to spontaneous mutation. The same year (1943) Luria also demonstrated mutation in bacteriophage; he completed his analysis of this phenomenon in 1951. He then worked on lysogeny, transduction, and host-controlled properties of viruses. For his contributions to the genetics of viruses and bacteria Luria shared the 1969 Nobel Prize for physiology or medicine with Delbrück and Alfred HERSHEY.

Lwoff, André Michael (1902–1994) French biologist

Born at Ainy-le-Château in France, Lwoff graduated in natural sciences in 1921 and joined the Pasteur Institute in the same year. He went on to become head of the laboratory in 11929 and from 1938 was head of the microbiology department. Lwoff moved to the Sorbonne in 1958, where he served until 1968 as professor of microbiology.

During the 1920s he demonstrated that vitamins function as coenzymes and also found that certain characters of protozoans are controlled by genes outside the nucleus. His most notable work, however, was his explanation of the phenomenon of lysogeny in bacteria. Lysogenic bacteria contain the DNA of a virus in their own DNA, the virus duplicating along with the bacterial chromosome and being passed on to subsequent generations. The virus, however, is nonvirulent and rarely destroys its host. When Lwoff began his research the prevailing view of lysogeny was that the phage–host association rendered the bacteria resistant to later viral destruction and that this association was perpetuated by the added presence of exogenous bacteriophage on the surface of the host. Further, it was believed that the increase in phage numbers in a lysogenic bacterial culture was due to the presence of some susceptible bacteria. Lwoff showed firstly that exogenous phage were not necessary to the association, and secondly that the increase of phage numbers in cultures is due to a reversal of the phage state from nonvirulent to virulent, which leads to the multiplication of phage particles in the host and subsequent breakdown or lysis of the host with release of these particles. He named the noninfective structure in lysogenic bacteria the prophage, and showed that ultraviolet light is one agent that can induce the prophage to produce infective viral particles.

In recognition of this work, Lwoff received the 1965 Nobel Prize for physiology or medicine, along with François JACOB and Jacques MONOD.

Lyell, Sir Charles (1797–1875) *British geologist*

Lyell was the son of a notable botanist. He was born at Kinnordy in Scotland and educated at Oxford University, where he developed an interest in geology and attended the lectures of William Buckland. While a student at Oxford he made, in 1819, the first of his many geological trips to the Continent and he met Alexander von Humboldt and Georges Cuvier in France in 1823. He studied law and was called to the bar in 1825, but because of strained eyesight he turned increasingly to geological investigation.

During the following years Lyell traveled extensively on the Continent, his studies culminating in the publication of his three-volume masterpiece *The Principles of Geology* (1830–33). This was to be published in 11 editions in his lifetime and established him as a leading authority on geology. He became professor of geology at King's College, London (1831–33), but gave this up to continue his geological studies, traveling throughout Europe and visiting America in 1841 and 1845.

In *Principles* Lyell established the doctrine of uniformitarianism already stated by James HUTTON and John PLAYFAIR and the first volume, published in 1830, was subtitled "Being an Attempt to Explain the Former Changes of the Earth's Surface by Reference to Causes now in Operation." Lyell explicitly rejected the work of Abraham Werner, in which some unique deluge is the chief agent producing the Earth's topography. Uniformitarianism also involved the rejection of the catastrophism theory followed by zoologists such as Cuvier to explain dramatic changes in the flora and fauna of the Earth. Instead Lyell saw the crust of the Earth as being shaped by forces operating over unlimited time.

Lyell contributed considerable knowledge and analysis to geology. In 1833 he introduced the structure of the Tertiary in which it spread from the Cretaceous to the emergence of man and was subdivided on the basis of the ratio of living to extinct species – Eocene, Miocene, Pliocene, and Pleistocene. His other works included *Elements of Geology* (1838) describing European rocks and fossils from the most recent to the oldest then known.

Charles Darwin, in his work *Origin of Species* (1859), drew heavily on Lyell's *Principles*. Lyell did not at first share Darwin's views and it was not until the tenth edition of the *Principles* (1867–68) that he expressed any support for evolutionary theory. Even then in his *The Antiquity of Man* (1863), which was published in four editions before 1873, Lyell denied that the theory could be applied to man.

Lyell was knighted in 1848 and created a baron in 1864. He became president of the British Association in 1864.

Lyman, Theodore (1874–1954) *American physicist*

Lyman came from an old and wealthy Boston family and was educated at Harvard where he obtained his PhD in 1900. After a short spell studying abroad at Göttingen, Germany, and Cambridge, England, he returned to Harvard where he served as Hollis Professor of Physics (1921–25) and director of the Jefferson Physical Laboratory (1910–47).

Lyman was a spectroscopist who first developed a technique of investigating spectra in the ultraviolet region. In 1906 he observed the *Lyman series* of lines in the ultraviolet spectrum of hydrogen (similar to the series discovered by Johann Balmer in the visible region).

Lynen, Feodor (1911–1979) *German chemist*

Lynen was educated at the university in his native city of Munich, where he obtained his doctorate under Heinrich Wieland in 1937. That same year he married Wieland's daughter. He was appointed to the faculty at Munich in 1942, being made professor of chemistry in 1947. In 1954 he became director of the Max Planck Institute for Cell Chemistry, Munich.

In 1950 Lynen showed that coenzyme A (described in 1947 by Fritz Lipmann) plays the central role in the breakdown of fats in the body. Fats are first broken down by the enzyme lipase into a number of free fatty acids. It had been shown in 1904 that these are then degraded two carbon atoms at a time. This is done by coenzyme A combining with the fatty acid and forming, after a number of intermediate steps, acetoacetyl coenzyme A at one end of the chain. This can now react with another molecule of coenzyme A causing a two-carbon fragment of acetyl coenzyme A to split off. The process can now be repeated with the result that a fatty acid chain of n carbon molecules is eventually reduced to half that number of acetyl coenzyme A molecules.

For this work on fatty acid metabolism and on cholesterol Lynen shared the 1964 Nobel Prize for physiology or medicine with Konrad Bloch.

Lysenko, Trofim Denisovich
(1898–1976) *Ukrainian agriculturalist*

A peasant's son from Karlovka (now in Ukraine), Lysenko began work at the Kirovabad Experimental Station in 1925, after completing his studies at the Kiev Agricultural Institute. In 1929 he became a senior specialist in the physiology department at the Institute of Selection and Genetics in Odessa and in the same year he first claimed success using vernalized grain on his father's farm. Vernalization is the cold treatment of soaked grains and it promotes flowering in spring-sown plants that might otherwise take two years to flower. Lysenko was later credited with inventing the method, although it had long been an established agricultural practice.

Lysenko claimed that the effects of vernalization could be inherited and so the treatment need not be repeated each year.

This reversion to a belief in the inheritance of acquired characteristics was the hallmark of his career, and he is remembered for his single-minded application of this belief to Soviet biology. The validity of the chromosome theory of inheritance had been generally accepted in the West, especially since the publication of T. H. Morgan's results. Naturally, many Soviet scientists also followed the Mendel–Morgan theory of heredity, notably Nikolai Vavilov, who was president of the Lenin All-Union Academy of Agricultural Sciences and head of the Institute of Plant Protection. Vavilov was publicly discredited by Lysenko and in 1940 exiled to Siberia, Lysenko taking over his scientific posts. Other dissenting scientists were brought into line at the genetics debate held at the Lenin All-Union Academy of Agricultural Sciences in 1948. At this meeting Lysenko announced that he had the backing of the central committee of the communist party, and a motion was passed directing all textbooks and courses to be changed in accordance with his views. This dictatorial state of affairs continued until 1964, and Lysenko was finally ousted from his powerful position in 1965.

Soviet science suffered immeasurably from Lysenko's refusal to acknowledge "alien foreign bourgeois biology" or the existence of the gene. His theories complemented Stalinist party dogma very conveniently and it is to this rather than any great scientific ability that his rise to prominence may be attributed.

Mach, Ernst (1838–1916) *Austrian physicist*

Mach, who was born at Turas (now in the Czech Republic), had a somewhat unorthodox upbringing and education. His father was a man knowledgable in both the classics and the sciences who retired to farm near Vienna where he educated his son academically, but also emphasized the importance of such practical skills as carpentry and farming. He received his higher education from the University of Vienna obtaining his PhD there in 1860. He was appointed professor of mathematics at Graz in 1864 and in 1867 was appointed to the chair of physics at the University of Prague, moving to Vienna in 1895 where he became professor of the history and theory of the inductive sciences. He was forced to retire in 1901 after being partially paralyzed by a stroke.

Mach made a large number of contributions to science in a variety of fields, but it is as a critic of science and as a philosopher that he exercised such a powerful influence over several generations of scientists. He began his research career in experimental psychology, inspired by the work of such scholars as Gustav Fechner. For several years he investigated various perceptual processes; in the course of this work he discovered the function of the semicircular canals of the ear.

He is however best known to a wider public for his work on shock waves, which eventually led to the *mach number* being introduced (1929) as a measure of speed (it is the ratio of the speed of an object in a fluid to the speed of sound in the fluid). Mach's interest in shock waves was aroused by a claim made by L. Melsen that the savage wounds of those shot in the Franco-Prussian war were not due to the ammunition used by the French but by the impact of compressed air pushed ahead of the bullet. In 1884 Mach began his attempt to photograph the shock and sound waves produced by projectiles. It was not until 1886 that he was successful and able to conclude that Melsen was wrong.

Mach is also known to cosmologists for his controversial statement of the principle of inertia, called *Mach's principle* by Einstein over whom Mach exerted considerable influence. For Newton the inertia of a body was an intrinsic property independent of the presence or absence of any other matter. For Mach the concept of inertia could only acquire quantitative meaning through Newton's laws. But Newton formulated his laws against the background of absolute space and time. This latter point Mach rejected completely, claiming that only relative motion exists.

Thus for Mach, it should make no difference whether we talk of the Earth rotating on its axis relative to the fixed stars or whether we see the Earth as fixed and talk of the stars as moving relative to the Earth. There is however, the significant difference that only in the first case can the concept of inertia be used to understand such phenomena as the flattening of the Earth and Foucault's pendulum. But Mach was a radical thinker and argued that, the inertia is not an intrinsic property of matter but is itself caused by the background of the fixed stars. If these were removed inertia would disappear with them.

Mach's elimination of absolute space was simply part of a more general program in which he hoped to eliminate metaphysics – all those purely 'thought-things' which cannot be pointed to in experience – from science. He began by asserting that the world contains nothing but sensations and their connections; scientific laws describe such connections in the simplest possible way; they provide an "economy of thought." His views influenced the important philosophical movement of logical positivism and also had some impact on scientific practice, influencing Einstein in his theory of relativity.

There is no doubt however that his approach could lead him astray. He never, for example, accepted the existence of atoms. They were rather, "economical ways of symbolizing experience. But we have as little right to expect from them, as from the symbols of algebra, more than we have put into them." Nor did he ever accept the relativity theory of Einstein.

Maclaurin, Colin (1698–1746) *Scottish mathematician*

Maclaurin, who was born at Kilmoden in Scotland, was a child prodigy. He entered Glasgow University at the age of 11 and became professor of mathematics at Marischal College, Aberdeen, at the age of 19.

His chief work was *Geometrica organica;*

sive descriptio linearum curvarum universalis (1720; Organic Geometry, with the Description of the Universal Linear Curves) and in this he proposed several theorems that developed along similar lines to those contained in Isaac Newton's *Principia*. Maclaurin became a friend of Newton and defended Newton's new theory of calculus against the polemics of the Irish philosopher George Berkeley. Maclaurin was one of the first to treat the theory of maxima and minima properly. He also contributed to the theory of the equilibrium of rotating bodies of fluid. The *Maclaurin expansion*, which is a special case of the Taylor series, was named for him.

Maclaurin played an important role in organizing the defense of Edinburgh against the Jacobites in 1745 and when they captured the city he was forced to flee to England.

MacLeod, John James Rickard (1876–1936) *British physiologist*

MacLeod, born the son of a clergyman in Cluny, Scotland, was educated at Aberdeen Grammar School and Aberdeen University, where he gained his MD in 1898. After postgraduate work in Leipzig and hospital work in London, MacLeod moved to America in 1903 as professor of physiology at Western Reserve University, Cleveland, Ohio. In 1918 he accepted a similar post at the University of Toronto but returned to Scotland in 1928 to become professor of physiology at Aberdeen.

Before his move to Toronto, MacLeod worked mainly on problems of carbohydrate metabolism, producing from 1907 a series of papers entitled *Studies in Experimental Glycosuria*. He also produced a standard textbook, *Physiology and Biochemistry in Modern Medicine* (1918), which went through seven editions before his death.

However his most significant work arose from his association at Toronto with the young surgeon Frederick BANTING. In early 1921 Banting asked if he could attempt to extract the pancreatic hormone believed to control the level of sugar in the blood. MacLeod apparently did his best to discourage Banting, pointing out to him that expert physiologists had made no progress with such a task over many years, but eventually offered him use of the laboratory and the help of a young student, Charles BEST, as a research assistant.

MacLeod left shortly afterward for Scotland, returning in September to find that the two researchers had succeeded in extracting a substance that controlled the level of blood sugar in dogs whose pancreases had been removed. Realizing the importance of obtaining as pure an extract as possible, MacLeod arranged for the laboratory's chemist, James Collip, to work on the problem. By January 1922, Collip had been so successful that they were ready to try the new hormone, named insulin by MacLeod, on a human patient.

In 1923 Banting and MacLeod were awarded the Nobel Prize for physiology or medicine for their discovery of insulin. Banting, distressed that his young colleague Best was apparently to receive no recognition, wished to refuse the prize. He finally decided to accept and shared the money with Best. MacLeod, too, was presumably feeling some discomfort at his award for he shared his prize with Collip.

Maiman, Theodore Harold (1927–   ) *American physicist*

Maiman, the son of an electrical engineer, was born in Los Angeles, California, and graduated in engineering physics from the University of Colorado in 1949. He gained his PhD from Stanford University in 1955, following which he joined the Hughes Research Laboratories, Miami.

Maiman was especially interested in the maser, which had been developed independently by Charles TOWNES in America and Nikolai BASOV and Aleksandr PROKHOROV in the USSR in 1955. It was realized that the principles by which the maser produced microwaves at selected well-defined wavelengths could be extended to emissions at the shorter visible wavelengths. In 1960, at the Hughes Research Laboratory, Maiman designed and operated the first instrument to achieve this, now known as the laser (light amplification by stimulated emission of radiation). He used a ruby cylinder with mirror-coated ends as a resonant cavity, and succeeded in converting flashes of white (incoherent) light into a pulsed beam of monochromatic coherent light. Such a beam can travel long distances with little dispersion and can concentrate optical energy on a small spot. The first continuous (as opposed to pulsed) laser was made by Ali Javan and his colleagues at the Bell Telephone Laboratories in 1961. The laser has since been developed in many forms as a research and engineering tool.

Maiman founded his own company, Korad Corporation, in 1962, which became the leading developer and manufacturer of high-power lasers. He founded Maiman Associates in 1968, acting as a consultant on lasers and optics, and cofounded the Laser Video Corporation in 1972. In 1977 he joined

TRW Electronics of California as assistant for advanced technology.

Mallet, Robert (1810–1881) *Irish industrialist and seismologist*

After graduating from Trinity College in his native city of Dublin in 1830, Mallet joined his father's foundry business. He remained there until 1861 when, with the completion of the Irish railroad network, there was such a marked decline in his business that he moved to London as a consultant engineer. Mallet was an engineer of some skill; he constructed several bridges, the Fastnet Lighthouse, and erected the 133-ton roof of St. George's in Dublin.

As a geologist he is mainly remembered for pioneering observational and experimental seismology. In 1857 he spent two months in Naples studying the effects of the recent earthquake. He showed that by noting the direction of cracks in walls and the arrangement of fallen masonry, it was possible to determine the epicenter and the depth of the earthquake. His results were published in *The Great Neapolitan Earthquake of 1857: the First Principles of Observational Cosmology* (1862).

In a series of experiments starting in 1850, Mallet attempted to determine the speed of earthquake waves. He did this by setting off small explosives at different depths in different soils and measuring the time taken for the seismic waves to travel varying distances. James Michel, working in the 18th century, had estimated a speed of 20 miles (32 km) per minute but this could not compare with Mallet's precise measurements.

Malpighi, Marcello (1628–1694) *Italian histologist*

Born at Crevalcore in Italy, Malpighi graduated firstly in philosophy and then medicine from the University of Bologna. He subsequently served as professor of medicine at Pisa, Bologna, and Messina. In later life he became private physician to Pope Innocent XII.

Malpighi may be considered the father of microscopy: he was one of the first to reveal the hitherto hidden world of the detailed structure of animals and plants. Some of his most important investigations were concerned with mammalian blood. In 1660 he provided a clue to the mechanism of respiration by his discovery that blood flowed over the lungs by means of a complex system of minute vessels. He also discovered the fine capillaries or blood vessels in the wing membrane of bats by means of the microscope, and demonstrated their linkage with minute arteries and veins, in this way amplifying the blood circulation theories of William HARVEY and Malpighi's contemporary Olof Rudbeck. He was also able to locate the filtering units of the vertebrate kidney, which became known as *Malpighian bodies* or *corpuscles*, and discovered traces of gill-like structures in chick embryos, although the true nature and significance of his discovery was not recognized until later. Using a chick as his model, he was able to describe the formation of the heart from undifferentiated tissue. Studies of the skin resulted in his description of the layer of epidermis (the *Malpighian layer*) next to the dermis in which active cell division takes place.

Malpighi was also interested in insect physiology, showing that the insect respiratory system was based on the simple diffusion of gases in vessels called tracheae. In the first published treatise to deal exclusively with an invertebrate animal, he described the internal organs and anatomy of the silkworm moth. In the world of plants, Malpighi noted the stomata on the undersides of leaves, appreciated the differences in development between monocotyledons and dicotyledons, and described the annual rings of dicotyledon stems.

In 1669, Malpighi became the first Italian to be named an honorary member of the Royal Society, following which much of his research was published in the *Philosophical Transactions* of the society.

Malus, Etienne Louis (1775–1812) *French military engineer and physicist*

Malus, who was born in Paris, attended the military school in Mezières (1793) and the newly established Ecole Polytechnique (1794–96) where he received his basic scientific education. He was commissioned in 1796 and served as a military engineer in Napoleon's expedition to Egypt and Syria. After his return to France he held various military engineering appointments. He became an examiner in geometry and analysis in 1805 and an examiner in physics in 1806 at the Ecole Polytechnique; these posts brought him into contact with other physicists.

Malus carried out many researches in optics, which was his main scientific interest. He is remembered for his discovery made in 1808 that light rays may be polarized by reflection. He found this while looking through a crystal of Iceland spar at the windows of a house reflecting the rays of the Sun; he noticed that on rotating the crystal the light was extinguished in certain positions. In explaining his observations Malus, a Newtonian and believer in corpuscular theory, argued that light particles have sides or poles and used for the first time the word 'polarization' to describe the phenomenon.

Malus's work in optics gave considerable impetus to investigations into polarization and the optical properties of crystals.

Mandelbrot, Benoit (1924–) Polish-born American mathematician

The son of a Lithuanian Jewish merchant, Mandelbrot was born in the Polish capital Warsaw but moved with his parents to Paris in 1936. In 1939 they found it necessary to flee once more and lived in Tulle in southern France for the duration of World War II. Despite an interrupted and irregular education, Mandelbrot gained acceptance at the École Polytechnique after the war even though, he later claimed, he had never learned the alphabet, nor progressed beyond the five-times table. He gained his PhD from the University of Paris in 1952 and spent several years in short-term appointments at the Institute of Advanced Studies, Princeton, and at the University of Geneva and Lille University. In 1958 he moved to the IBM Research Center, Yorktown Heights, New York, where he remained until 1987, when he was appointed professor of mathematics at Yale.

Mandelbrot studied a number of such seemingly unrelated topics as fluctuations in commodity prices, noise in telephone lines, and linguistics. He also considered the seemingly innocent question, "How long is the coast of Britain?" Encyclopedias gave lengths differing by as much as 20%. Mandelbrot pointed out that it depended on how the measurement was done. From a distant space craft, many inlets would reveal their own inlets. Mandelbrot dealt with this and other matters in his *The Fractal Geometry of Nature* (1982). "Clouds are not spheres," he declared, "mountains are not cones, coastlines are not circles, and bark is not smooth, nor does lightning travel in a straight line." To understand this structured irregularity of nature Mandelbrot introduced the term 'fractal' based on the idea of fractional dimension.

An example of a fractal is the snowflake curve first described by Helge von Koch in 1904. It begins with an equilateral triangle. Each side is divided into three equal parts and the middle section is used as the base of a smaller equilateral triangle, resulting in a six-pointed star. The process can be continued indefinitely and has an infinite perimeter bounding a finite area. It is fractal in the sense that it is self-similar, and

also in the sense that it has fractional dimension.

Mandelbrot saw that shrinking the unit that a side is measured in by a factor of P, increases the number of units along that side by a factor of Q. In the case of the *Koch curve*, shrinking the side by a factor of 3 increases the units by a factor of 4. The fractal dimension A can be defined as:

$$A = \log Q/\log P = \log 4/\log 3 = 1.2618$$

Mandelbrot went on to determine the fractal dimensions of other similar objects.

Mandelbrot is equally well known for his discovery of the *Mandelbrot set*. The set is constructed from the simple mapping $z \rightarrow z^2 + c$, where z and c are complex numbers, with z arbitrarily chosen and c fixed. If a fixed value is assigned to c and $z = 0$, the answer is calculated and fed back into the mapping as a new value for z. The process is repeated, substituting each new output for z. Some values for c when plugged back into the mapping rapidly approach infinity; other values remain within a certain boundary. For example, when $c = 1 + 0i$, the sequence begins 0, 1, 2, 5, 26, 677, 458, 330... and is unbounded. But when $c = -1 + 0i$, the sequence is 0, –1, 0, –1, 0, –1... and is clearly bounded.

The set is constructed by marking a black dot on the complex plane for those points c where the sequence is unbounded, and leaving all other values white. The result, best displayed in color on a computer screen, takes on the distinctive shape described as a warty figure of eight on its side. Yet at higher magnifications borders reveal endless detail and startling images, apparently copies of the original but also displaying small differences.

Mansfield, Peter (1933–) British physicist

Mansfield was born in London and educated at Queen Mary College there, completing his PhD in 1962. After a two-year period at the University of Illinois as a research associate, he took up a position at Nottingham University in 1964; he was professor of physics from 1979 to 1994.

Mansfield began work in the early 1970s on the use of nuclear magnetic resonance (NMR) to investigate conditions in the human body. The NMR technique was investigated in the 1940s by BLOCH and PURCELL. It depends on the fact that the nuclei of certain atoms have a net magnetic moment. In an external magnetic field these nuclei can take up allowed orientations with the field direction, each corresponding to a particular quantized energy state. Electromagnetic radiation in the radiofrequency region of the spectrum can be absorbed at a particular resonance frequency corresponding to a transition from one energy state to a higher one. The nuclei, in reverting to the lower state, emit radiation.

Mansfield and his colleagues used this as a nonintrusive method of producing images of the body by detecting the emitted radiation and forming an image by computer-aided tomography (CAT). The x-ray CAT scanner had been developed earlier by Geoffrey HOUNSFIELD. However, light elements such as hydrogen are relatively transparent to x-rays. NMR, on the other hand, is particularly suitable for detecting hydrogen and magnetic resonance imaging (MRI) is especially useful for showing soft tissues. A prototype MRI scanner had been developed by 1980. Initially, it was designed to take cross-sectional images of the brain, but before long whole-body machines were available.

Manson, Sir Patrick (1844–1922)
British physician

Manson was the son of a local laird and farmer in Oldmeldrum, Scotland. He studied medicine at Aberdeen University, obtaining his MD in 1866. He then became a medical officer, firstly in Formosa (1866–71) and then for a further 13 years in Amoy. Manson completed his 23 years' service in the Far East by running a profitable private practice in Hong Kong until 1889. Back in Britain he set up as a consultant in London, served as medical adviser to the Colonial Office from 1897 to 1912, and was the prime mover in the foundation of the London School of Tropical Medicine in 1899. In 1914 Manson finally retired to Ireland, where he spent his last years fishing on Lough Mask in Galway.

Manson was an original and creative scientist. His greatest achievement was to demonstrate conclusively what had long been suspected, namely, that certain diseases are transmitted by insects. His first success, in 1877, was to link the mosquito *Culex fatigans* with the presence of the parasite *Filaria sanguinis hominis* (FSH) in many of his patients suffering from elephantiasis. Full details of the life cycle of the FSH were published later in 1884. The clinical effects of the parasites, which eventually obstruct the lymphatic system, he published in his monograph, *The Filaria sanguinis hominis, and Certain New Forms of Parasitic Disease* (1883).

With this success behind him Manson was able to throw considerable light on a wide range of further tropical diseases. He thus made numerous suggestions on the mode of transmission of such widespread diseases as sleeping sickness and bilharzia. He also played a crucial role in the working out of the etiology and spread of the biggest killer of all, malaria. It was Manson who suggested to Ronald ROSS in 1894 that mosquitoes carry malaria, who guided Ross throughout his research, and who, in 1900, performed one of the crucial experiments confirming his earlier hypothesis.

Manson used mosquitoes of the species *Anopheles maculipennis*, which were sent him by Giovanni Grassi from Rome, and allowed them to feed on his son Patrick Manson, then a medical student at Guy's Hospital, London. Within 15 days his son had developed malaria and parasites were clearly visible in his blood.

For such work Manson was elected to the Royal Society in 1900 and knighted in 1903. But although Ross was awarded the 1902 Nobel Prize for physiology or medicine for his work on malaria, Manson was surprisingly ignored.

Mantell, Gideon Algernon (1790–1852) *British geologist*

The son of a shoemaker from Lewes in Sussex, Mantell was apprenticed to a local surgeon and set up in practice in Lewes in 1812. As the area around Lewes, the South Downs, is rich in Cretaceous deposits, fossil hunting was something of a local pastime and Mantell began collecting fossils in his schooldays.

His interest grew and in 1822, in the area known as the Tillgate Forest, he made his most important find – a large tooth with a worn smooth surface. It obviously belonged to a large herbivore and initially reminded Mantell of an elephant's tooth. However, mammals were unknown in the Cretaceous while reptiles, which were common, did not masticate food. Baffled by his find, Mantell sent his tooth to the great Baron Cuvier in Paris for identification. But Cuvier's judgment that it was the upper incisor of a rhinoceros Mantell knew to be nonsense. He continued to search for an answer and eventually in the Museum of the Royal College of Surgeons he found a smaller but identical tooth belonging to the South American iguana. The tooth, he concluded, came from a lizard after all, a giant toothed lizard he named *Iguanadon* (iguana tooth).

In 1834 an *Iguanadon* skeleton was discovered in a Maidstone quarry. Mantell bought the remains for £25 to make, as the joke went, "a famous Mantel-piece." Mantell also discovered, in 1832, the first armored dinosaur, *Hylaeosaurus*.

Mantell described his work in his 67

books and memoirs. The best known of these are the once widely read *The Geology of South East England* (1833) and *The Wonders of Geology* (1838). His private life, however, fared less well. He moved to Brighton in 1835 in search of patronage and a more affluent practice. He failed on both accounts and sold his vast collection of fossils to the British Museum in 1838 for £4000. Abandoned by his wife and children, he moved to London in 1839, spending most of his time lecturing and writing on geology. He died from an overdose of opium taken to relieve persistent back pain.

Marconi, Marchese Guglielmo

(1874–1937) *Italian electrical engineer*

Marconi, the second son of a prosperous Italian country gentleman and a wealthy Irishwoman, was born in Bologna, Italy, and educated there and in Leghorn (Livorno). He studied physics under several well-known teachers and had the opportunity of learning about the work carried out on electromagnetic radiation by Heinrich HERTZ, Oliver LODGE, Augusto Righi, and others.

Marconi became interested in using Hertz's 'invisible rays' to signal Morse code and in 1894 began experimenting to this end at his father's estate. Similar work was being done at the time in Russia by Aleksandr Popov. Although he convinced himself of the importance of this new system and was soon able to transmit radio signals over a distance of more than a mile, he received little encouragement to continue his work in Italy and was advised to go to England.

Shortly after arriving in London in February 1896 Marconi secured the interest of government officials from the war office, the admiralty, and the British postal service. The next five years he spent demonstrating and improving the range and performance of his equipment, and overcoming the prevailing skepticism about the usefulness of this form of transmission. In 1897 he helped to form the Wireless Telegraphic and Signal Co. Ltd., which in 1900 became Marconi's Wireless Telegraph Co. Ltd. He achieved the first international wireless (i.e., radio) transmission, between England and France, in March 1899; this aroused considerable public interest and attracted attention in the world's press. In the same year the British fleet's summer naval maneuvers, for which Marconi equipped several ships with his apparatus, helped to convince the admiralty and mercantile ship owners of the value of radio telegraphy at sea.

In December 1901 Marconi succeeded in transmitting radio signals in Morse code for the first time across the Atlantic, a distance of some 2000 miles (3200 km). Already well known, Marconi created a sensation, became world famous overnight, and silenced many of his critics from the scientific world who had believed that because radio waves travel in straight lines they could not follow the curvature of the Earth. This phenomenon was explained by Arthur Kennelly the following year as being due to the presence of a reflecting layer – the ionosphere – in the Earth's atmosphere. Thus by 1901 radio telegraphy had become a practical system of communication, especially for maritime purposes. Marconi spent the rest of his life improving and extending this form of communication, and managing his companies.

Although a good deal of Marconi's work was based on the ideas and discoveries of others he was granted various patents and was responsible for some notable inventions. These included the first of all patents on radio telegraphy based on the use of waves (1896), the elevated antenna (1894), patent 7777, which enabled several stations to operate on different wavelengths without mutual interference (1900), the magnetic detector (1902), the horizontal directional antenna (1915), and the timed-spark system of generating pseudo-continuous waves (1912).

From about 1916, Marconi began to exploit the use of radio waves of short wavelength, which allowed a more efficient transmission of radiant energy. In 1924 the Marconi company obtained a contract to establish short-wave communication between England and the British Commonwealth countries and by 1927 a worldwide network had been formed. In 1932 Marconi installed a short-wave radio telephone system between the Vatican and Castel Gandolfo, the Pope's summer residence.

Despite having little interest in anything outside radio Marconi several times acted in an official capacity for his government: he was sent as a plenipotentiary delegate at the 1919 Paris peace conference. In 1923 he joined the Fascist Party and became a friend of Mussolini. Marconi received several honorary degrees and many awards, which included the Nobel Prize for physics jointly with Karl BRAUN (1909), being made a marquis (marchese) in 1929, and president of the Royal Italian Academy (1930). At his death he was accorded a state funeral by the Italian government. All Post Office wireless telegraph and wireless telephone services in the British Isles observed a two-minute silence at the hour of his funeral.

Marcus, Rudolph Arthur (1923–)
Canadian-born American chemist

Marcus was born in Montreal and educated at McGill University there. After graduating he taught at the Polytechnic Institute, Brooklyn (1951–64) and at the University of Illinois (1968–78). In 1978 he was appointed professor of chemistry at the California Institute of Technology.

In the 1950s Marcus began to work on electron-transfer reactions. The addition, removal, and transfer of electrons is the driving force behind many basic chemical processes including photosynthesis, respiration, and the production of solar energy. Such reactions are, in principle, very simple involving the movement of an electron from one ion to form another ion. The rates of such reactions can, however, vary widely. Marcus was able to explain electron-transfer reaction rates in terms of the way in which the solvent molecules, initially configured to solvate the reactant, reorganize to solvate the products.

Marcus was awarded the 1992 Nobel Prize for chemistry for his work in this field.

Margulis, Lynn (1938–) *American biologist*

Margulis was educated at the university in her native city of Chicago, at Wisconsin, and at Berkeley where she obtained her PhD in 1965. After working briefly at Brandeis she moved to Boston University in 1966 and served there as professor of biology from 1977 to 1988. She became Distinguished Professor of the University of Massachusetts in 1988.

With the success of modern biochemistry, genetics, and cytology it became apparent that there was a fundamental division in nature between cells with nuclei (eukaryotes) and those without (prokaryotes). In terms of metabolism, chemistry, genetics, and structure, higher organisms differ radically from bacteria and blue-green algae, the prokaryotes. She studied the question of how eukaryotes evolve and her answer, in terms of hereditary endosymbiosis, was fully formulated in her *Origin of Eukaryotic Cells* (1970). She argued that eukaryotes are basically colonies of prokaryotes and that such features of cells as mitochondria were once free-living bacteria but have, "over a long period of time, established a hereditary symbiosis with ancestral hosts that ultimately evolved into animal cells." Similarly she proposes that chloroplasts and flagella evolved in the same way.

The actual evolutionary sequence proposed begins with a 'fermenting bacterium' entering into a symbiotic relationship with some oxygen-using bacteria, the first mitochondria. Such a complex might join with "a second group of symbionts, flagellum-like bacteria comparable to modern spirochaetes," which, attached to the host's surface, would greatly increase its motility.

As Margulis points out, the proof for such an imaginative model requires that the cell organelles are separated, cultured independently, and then brought back into symbiotic association again. So far no one has managed to grow an organelle outside the cell. Margulis published (with Karlene Schwartz) "a catalog of the world's living diversity" in *Five Kingdoms* (1982).

Marignac, Jean Charles Galissard de (1817–1894) *Swiss chemist*

Marignac, who was born in Geneva, Switzerland, was educated in Paris at the Ecole Polytechnique and the School of Mines. He worked in Justus von Liebig's laboratory in Giessen for a year and at the Sèvres porcelain factory before his appointment to the chair of chemistry at Geneva (1841). He also became professor of mineralogy in 1845 and held the two posts until his retirement in 1878.

He was known as a careful analyst who carried out many accurate determinations of atomic weights. He was an enthusiastic supporter of Prout's hypothesis that all elements have an atomic weight that is an integral multiple of the hydrogen atom and defended it from the criticism that refined measurements show it to be false (e.g., chlorine has an atomic weight of 35.4) by claiming it to be sufficiently accurate for the practical calculations of chemistry.

Marignac discovered silicotungstic acid in 1862 and was the first to isolate ytterbium (1878). He also codiscovered gadolinium (1880).

Mariotte, Edmé (c. 1620–1684) *French physicist*

Mariotte was born at Dijon in France. A priest, he was prior of Saint-Martin-sous-Beaune and also a founder member of the French Academy of Sciences.

In 1662 Robert Boyle had stated his law that the pressure and volume of a gas are inversely proportional. In 1676 Mariotte formulated the law quite independently, deriving it in a less inductive manner than Boyle. More importantly, he stated that the law holds only if there is no change in temperature, as he realized that a gas expands with an increase in temperature and contracts with a fall. Mariotte also investigated a large number of other topics connected with pressure. He performed some of the earliest experiments on the physiology of plants showing the high pressure of the sap. In France, Boyle's law is naturally referred to as *Mariotte's law*.

Markov, Andrey Andreyevich
(1856–1922) *Russian mathematician*

Born at Ryazan in Russia, Markov studied at the University of St. Petersburg and later held a variety of teaching posts at the same university, eventually becoming a professor in 1893. He was an extremely enthusiastic and effective teacher. His mathematical interests were very wide, ranging over number theory, the theory of continued fractions, and differential equations. It was, however, his work in probability theory that constituted his most profound and enduring contribution to mathematics.

Among Markov's teachers was the eminent Russian mathematician Pafnuti CHEBYSHEV, whose central interest was in probability. One of Markov's first pieces of important research centered on a key theorem of Chebyshev's – 'the central limit theorem'. He was able to show that Chebyshev's supposed proof of this result was erroneous, and to provide his own, correct, proof of a version of the theorem of much greater generality than that attempted by Chebyshev. In 1900 Markov published his important and influential textbook *Probability Calculus*, and by 1906 he had arrived at the fundamentally new concept of a *Markov chain*. A sequence of random variables is a Markov chain if the two probabilities conditioned on different amounts of information about the early part of the sequence are the same. This aspect of Markov's work gave a major impetus to the subject of stochastic processes.

The great importance of Markov's work was that it enabled probability theory to be applied to a very much wider range of physical phenomena than had previously been possible. As a result of his work a whole range of subjects, among them genetics and such statistical phenomena as the behavior of molecules, became amenable to mathematical probabilistic treatment.

Martin, Archer John Porter (1910–)
British chemist

Martin, a Londoner by birth, was educated at Cambridge University, obtaining his PhD in 1936. He worked as a research chemist with the Wool Industries Research Association in Leeds from 1938 to 1946 and with Boots Research Department in Nottingham until 1948 when he joined the Medical Re-

search Council. From 1959 until 1970 Martin was director of Abbotbury Laboratories Ltd.

In 1944 Martin and his colleague **Richard Synge** (1914–1994) developed a chromatographic technique that proved indispensable to later workers investigating protein structures. Without this technique the explosive growth of knowledge in biochemistry and molecular biology would have been dampened by prolonged and tedious analyses of complex molecules.

Column chromatography was first invented by Mikhail TSVET for the analysis of plant pigments in 1906. Martin was trying to isolate vitamin E and developed a new method of separation involving the distribution and separation of molecules between two immiscible solvents flowing in different directions – countercurrent extraction. From this rather cumbersome apparatus evolved the idea of partition chromatography, in which one solvent is stationary and the other moves across it. Martin and Synge tried different substances, such as silica gel and cellulose, to hold the stationary solvent and hit on the idea of using paper. Thus paper chromatography was introduced.

In this process a drop of the mixture to be analyzed is placed at the corner of a piece of absorbent paper the edge of which is dipped into an organic solvent. This will soak into the paper by capillarity taking with it the components of the mixture to be analyzed to different distances depending on their solubility. In the case of a protein, the identity of the various amino acids can be discovered comparing positions of the spots with a reference chart. The basic technique is easy to operate, quick, cheap, works on small amounts, and can separate out closely related substances.

For their work Martin and Synge were awarded the 1952 Nobel Prize for chemistry. Martin tended to treat the value of their contribution somewhat dismissively, pointing out that "All the ideas are simple and had peoples' minds been directed that way the method would have flourished perhaps a century earlier."

Maskelyne, Nevil (1732–1811) *British astronomer*

Maskelyne, who was born in London, was educated at Westminster School and Cambridge University. He became the fifth Astronomer Royal in 1765 and, from 1782, rector of North Runcton in Norfolk.

Maskelyne spent considerable time trying to solve the problem of determining longitude at sea. His preferred method was by means of lunar observation, since, on a trip to St. Helena in 1761, he had successfully used such a method. To popularize his technique he published his *British Mariner's Guide* in 1763 and started publishing in 1767 the *Nautical Almanac* to provide the necessary information. He was a member of the Board of Longitude, which had been set up in 1714 to decide on the award of the £20,000 prize for a solution to the problem. Perhaps his commitment to his lunar method made him blind to the value of the chronometer invented by John HARRISON, which he was asked to judge. He refused to recommend it for the award.

Mather, Kenneth (1911–1990) *British geneticist*

Born at Nantwich in Cheshire, Mather graduated from the University of Manchester in 1931. He then joined the John Innes Horticultural Institution at Merton, Surrey, where the chromosome theory of heredity was then being developed. Here Mather investigated chromosome behavior, especially crossing over, his research being influenced by his association with Cyril Darlington.

Mather gained his PhD in 1933 and then spent a year at the plant breeding institute, Svalöf, Sweden. Experience at Svalöf convinced him that characters that vary continuously through a population are extremely important in breeding work. On his return to England he took up a lectureship at University College, London, under Ronald Fisher, who was developing statistical techniques that could be used to analyze such quantitative variation.

In 1938, after a year with T. H. Morgan in America, Mather returned to John Innes as head of the genetics department. It was already appreciated that quantitative variation is governed by many genes, each of small effect, and Mather termed such complexes 'polygenic systems'. He demonstrated that by applying selection to continuously varying characters one could greatly increase the range of variation beyond that found in the normal population. Continuous variation cannot be analyzed satisfactorily by conventional segregation ratios and Mather thus applied statistics to his results, terming this combination 'biometrical genetics'.

In 1948 Mather became professor of genetics at Birmingham University, where he remained until his appointment as vice-chancellor at Southampton University in 1965. As founder of biometrical genetics he wrote a number of books on the subject, which he greatly developed during his time at Birmingham in collaboration with J. L. Jinks. Mather returned to Birmingham in 1971 as honorary professor of genetics.

Matthews, Drummond Hoyle (1931–1997) *British geologist.* See VINE, FREDERICK.

Matthias, Bernd Teo (1918–1980) *German–American physicist*

Matthias was born in Frankfurt, Germany, and educated at Rome University and at the Federal Institute of Technology, Zurich, where he obtained his PhD in 1943. He moved to America in 1947, became naturalized in 1951, and, after a brief period at the University of Chicago, joined the staff of the Bell Telephone Laboratories. In 1961 he returned to academic life when he was appointed professor of physics at the University of California, San Diego.

Matthias carried out extensive work on superconducting materials. In the early 1950s no existing theory of superconductivity allowed deductions as to which metals were superconductors and at what temperature – their transition point – they became so. Consequently Matthias set out to find such materials by experiment, testing thousands of alloys in the hope that some kind of pattern would emerge. He found that superconductivity depended on the number of outer electrons in the atom; substances with five or seven valence electrons most readily became superconductors and that they had transition points furthest above absolute zero. The crystal structure of the solid was another important factor. As a result of these empirical observations, Matthias and his collaborators were able to make new superconducting materials, including a niobium–germanium alloy with a transition temperature of 23 K. Matthias also did important work on ferroelectric materials.

Matuyama, Motonori (1884–1958) *Japanese geologist*

Matuyama, who was born at Uyeda (now Usa) in Japan, was the son of a Zen abbot. He was educated at the University of Hiroshima and the Imperial University in Kyoto, where he was appointed to a lectureship in 1913. After spending the period 1919–21 at the University of Chicago working with Thomas Chamberlin he was made professor of theoretical geology at the Imperial University.

He conducted a gravity survey of Japan during the period 1927–32, extending this to also cover Korea and Manchuria, and studied marine gravity using the Vening-Meinesz pendulum apparatus in a submarine.

Matuyama made a significant discovery of the Earth's magnetic field and announced this in his paper *On the Direction of Magnetization of Basalt* (1929). From studying the remnant magnetization of some rocks he observed that it had appeared that the Earth's magnetic field had changed, even reversing itself in comparatively short times. The period between the late Pliocene and the mid Pleistocene during which the field appeared to be opposite to present conditions became known as the *Matuyama reversed epoch*. This reversed polarity, particularly as shown by the rocks of the ocean floor, was to prove crucial evidence for the sea-floor spreading hypothesis of Harry H. HESS.

Maunder, Edward Walter (1851–1928)
British astronomer

Maunder, who was born in London, took some courses at King's College there but did not obtain a degree. After working briefly in a bank he became photographic and spectroscopic assistant at the Royal Observatory, Greenwich, in 1873. Maunder's appointment allowed Greenwich to branch out from purely positional work, for Maunder began a careful study of the Sun, mainly of sunspots and related phenomena. After 1891 he was assisted by Annie Russell, a Cambridge-trained mathematician, who must have been one of the first women to be so employed. She became his wife in 1895.

It had been known since 1843 that the intensity of sunspot activity went through an 11-year cycle. In 1893 Maunder, while checking the cycle in the past, came across the surprising fact that between 1645 and 1715 there was virtually no sunspot activity at all. For 32 years not a single sunspot was seen on the Sun and in the whole period fewer sunspots were observed than have occurred in an average year since. He wrote papers on his discovery in 1894 and 1922 but they aroused no interest.

More sophisticated techniques developed in recent years have established that Maunder was undoubtedly correct in the detection of the so-called *Maunder minimum*. Also, the realization that the period of the minimum corresponds to a prolonged cold spell suggests that Maunder's discovery is no mere statistical freak. It may throw light on the Sun's part in long-term climatic change and on possible variations in the processes within the Sun that produce the sunspots.

Maupertuis, Pierre-Louis Moreau de
(1698–1759) *French mathematician, physicist, and astronomer*

Maupertuis, who was born at Saint-Malo in northwest France, joined the army as a youth, leaving in 1723 to teach mathematics at the French Academy of Sciences in Paris. He traveled to England in 1728 where he became an admirer of Isaac Newton's work and was made a member of the Royal Society of London. He was responsible for introducing Newton's theories on gravitation into France on his return.

In 1736 Maupertuis led an expedition to Lapland to verify Newton's hypothesis that the Earth is not perfectly spherical by measuring the length of a degree of longitude. This was successful and as a result Maupertuis was invited by Frederick the Great to join his Academy of Sciences in Berlin.

Maupertuis is best known as being, in 1744, one of the first to formulate the principle of least action, which was published in his *Essai de cosmologie* (1750; Essay on Cosmology). A similar principle had previously been formulated by Leonhard EULER as a result of his mathematical work on the calculus of variations, whereas Maupertuis had been led to formulate his version of the principle through his work in optics. In particular Maupertuis's attention was drawn to the need for such a principle by his interest in the work of Willebrord Snell and Pierre de Fermat. Fermat had shown how to explain Snell's law of refraction, which describes the behavior of a ray of light at the boundary of two media of different densities on the assumption that a ray of light takes the least time possible in traveling from the first medium to the second. However, Fermat's explanation implied that light travels more slowly in a denser medium and Maupertuis set out to devise an explanation of Snell's law that did not have this, to him, objectionable consequence. Maupertuis thought of his principle as the fundamental principle of mechanics, and expected that all other mechanical laws ought to be derivable from it. He attempted to derive from his principle a proof of the existence of God.

Maupertuis was not a mathematician of Euler's stature and his version of the principle was not as precisely formulated mathematically. However, his attempts to apply it to a much wider range of problems made it an influential formative principle in 18th- and 19th-century physical thinking. Joseph Lagrange, in his work on the calculus of variations, dispensed with the teleological and theological trimmings Maupertuis had given the principle and found wide application for it in mechanics. Subsequently the principle became less influential until it was revived and refined by William Hamilton.

Maupertuis, who had a quarrelsome character, became involved in violent controversy over the principle. Samuel König, another scientist at Frederick's court, claimed that it had been formulated earlier by Gottfried Liebniz. Maupertuis found himself on the receiving end of some of Voltaire's most biting satires, and eventually he was hounded out of Berlin.

Maury, Antonia Caetana de Paiva Pereira (1866–1952) *American astronomer*

Maury, who was born at Cold Spring-on-Hudson, New York, came from a family with a distinguished scientific background. She was a cousin of Matthew Maury, the oceanographer, a niece of Henry Draper, the physician and astronomer after whom the Harvard star catalog was named, her sister became a paleontologist, while her father, a clergyman, was also a well-known naturalist. She herself was educated at Vassar, graduating in 1887, and in 1889 became an assistant to Edward Pickering at Harvard College Observatory. There she worked alongside an unusually large collection of women astronomers of whom the most eminent were Annie Cannon and Henrietta Leavitt. Apart from the years 1899–1908, when she lectured at various eastern colleges, she retained her position at Harvard until her retirement in 1935.

Much of her work was on the classification of stellar spectra for the Harvard catalog. At about the same time that Cannon was revising the system of spectral classification of stars, Maury proposed an additional modification that turned out to be of permanent significance. It was important to notice, she argued, not just the absence or presence of a particular spectral line but also its appearance. Stars with normal lines she marked 'a', those with hazy lines 'b', and those with sharp she marked 'c'; intermediate cases were marked 'ab' or 'ac'. This has been described as the first step in using spectroscopic criteria for the luminosities of stars. Maury's spectral classifications, including those of 681 bright northern stars, were published in 1896 in the Harvard *Annals*. Ejnar Hertzsprung was quick to see the significance of her classification system and in 1905 pointed out that c-type and ac-type stars were brighter than a- or b-type stars and were in fact giants.

Maury spent many years studying and detecting spectroscopic binary stars and as early as 1889 had determined the period of Mizar, in Ursa Major. This was the first spectroscopic binary to be discovered, identified by Pickering earlier in the year. The two stars in a spectroscopic binary cannot be resolved visually but as they revolve they will each alternately approach and recede from an observer on the Earth. This causes an alternate lengthening and shortening of the emitted light waves and will produce a periodic doubling of the spectral lines. Maury's particular interest was the binary Beta Lyrae, the investigation of which she continued long after her retirement.

Maury, Matthew Fontaine (1806–1873) *American oceanographer*

Maury, who was born in Fredericksburg, Virginia, graduated from Harpeth Academy in 1825 and joined the US Navy as a midshipman. A leg injury in 1839 ended his sea career but, having made his reputation by his publication in 1836 of his *Treatise on Navigation*, he was chosen in 1842 to be superintendent of the Depot of Charts and Instruments in Washington. This post carried with it the directorship of the US Naval Observatory and Hydrographic Office. Maury largely ignored astronomical work, emphasizing instead the study of oceanography and meteorology, and consequently aroused the opposition of the scientific establishment centered upon Joseph Henry and Alexander Bache.

He resigned his position with the outbreak of the American Civil War (1861) to become a commander in the Confederate Navy. After the war he took on, in 1865, the post of Imperial Commissioner for Immigration to the doomed Emperor Maximilian of Mexico to establish a confederate colony. Following the collapse of the Mexican Empire he spent some time in England writing textbooks before he was permitted to return to America where he became, in 1868, professor of meteorology at the Virginia Military Institute, remaining there until his death.

Maury has often been described as the father of oceanography. He wrote one of the earliest works on the topic, *The Physical Geography of the Sea* (1855), and he demonstrated the rewards to be gained from an increased knowledge of the oceans. From 1847 he began to publish his *Wind and Current* pilot charts of the North Atlantic, which could shorten sailing times dramatically. Claims were made that as much as a month could be saved on the sailing time for the New York–California voyage. This knowledge was acquired by the study of especially prepared logbooks and the collection of data in a systematic way from a growing number of organized observers.

After 1849 Maury had the use of two research vessels and began a study of ocean temperature and a collection of samples of the ocean floor. He was thus able to publish his *Bathymetrical Map of the North Atlantic Basin* (1854) showing a profile of the Atlantic floor between Yucatan and Cape Verde.

Maxwell, James Clerk (1831–1879)
British physicist

Maxwell was born in Edinburgh and studied at the university there (1847–50) and at Cambridge (1850–54), becoming a fellow in 1855. He was professor of natural philosophy at Marishal College, Aberdeen, from 1856 until 1860, when he became professor of natural philosophy and astronomy at King's College, London. He resigned in 1865 and worked on his estate in Scotland researching and writing. From 1871 he was professor of experimental physics at Cambridge.

Maxwell is regarded as one of the great physicists of the 19th century. At the age of 15 he produced a paper on methods of drawing oval curves. In 1857 he published a paper on the rings of Saturn, in which he analyzed the dynamics of the rings and proved that they could not be wholly solid or liquid. His own theory was that they were made up of many particles, and he showed that such a system would be stable.

Maxwell is regarded as one of the founders of the kinetic theory of gases – the calculation of the properties of a gas by assuming that it is composed of a large number of atoms (or molecules) in random motion. Maxwell, around 1860, put forward a statistical treatment of gases in *Illustrations of Dynamical Theory of Gases*. Maxwell and Ludwig Boltzmann obtained a formula for the way in which the speeds of molecules were distributed over the number of molecules – the *Maxwell–Boltzmann distribution law*. The kinetic theory of gases disposed of the idea of heat as a fluid ('caloric').

One interesting notion coming out of his work on the kinetic theory was the statistical interpretation of thermodynamics. A particular point was the idea of *Maxwell's demon* (1871) – a small hypothetical creature that could open or close a shutter between two compartments in a vessel, separating the fast molecules from the slow ones, and thus causing one part of the gas to become hotter and the other colder. The system would appear to violate the second law of thermodynamics. (In fact it does not; the gas decreases in entropy but there is an increase in entropy in the demon, using the idea that entropy is connected with 'information').

Maxwell's greatest work was his series of papers on the mathematical treatment of the lines of force introduced by Michael Faraday to visualize electromagnetic phenomena. He showed the connection between magnetism and electricity and demonstrated that oscillating electric charges would produce waves propagated through the electromagnetic field. He showed that the speed of such waves was similar to the experimentally determined speed of light, and concluded that light (and infrared and ultraviolet radiation) was in fact this electromagnetic wave. Maxwell went on to predict the existence of other forms of electromagnetic radiation with frequencies and wavelengths outside the infrared and ultraviolet regions. Heinrich Hertz first detected radio waves in 1888. Maxwell's theory was developed further by Hendrik Lorentz.

In *Dynamical Theory of the Electric Field* (1864) Maxwell put forward four famous differential equations (known simply as *Maxwell's equations*) describing the propagation of electromagnetic waves. The equations contain the speed of the waves c, a value that is independent of the velocity of the source. This was one of the facts that led EINSTEIN to his special theory of relativity. Maxwell also wrote *Treatise on Electricity and Magnetism* (1873).

Mayer, Julius Robert von (1814–1878)
German physician and physicist

Mayer, the son of an apothecary from Heilbronn in Germany, studied medicine at the University of Tübingen, where he seems to have been a mediocre student. He continued his studies abroad in Vienna and Paris before taking up an appointment in 1840 as a ship's physician on a vessel bound for Java. On his return in 1841 he settled in Heilbronn working as a general practitioner.

When Mayer sailed to Java he was familiar with the views of Antoine Lavoisier that animal heat is produced by slow combustion in the body. Being forced to bleed some of the crew at Surabaya, he found that venous blood was surprisingly bright. Indeed, at first he thought that he had cut an artery by mistake. "This phenomenon riveted my earnest attention," he reported, drawing the correct conclusion that the blood was redder because in the tropics the body does not need to burn as much oxygen to maintain body temperature as it does in temperate regions. The observation led Mayer to speculate about the conversion of food to heat in the body, and also the fact that the body can do work. He came to the view that heat and work are interchangeable – that the same amount of food can be converted to different proportions of heat and work, but the total must be the same.

Moreover, Mayer appreciated that this equivalence should hold universally and tried to apply it to other systems and to make it quantitative. Unfortunately, at the time he was confused about such concepts as force and work and his ideas were presented in an obscure metaphysical style. His first paper on the subject was sent to *Annalen der Physik* (Annals of Physics); the editor, Johann Poggendorf, did not even acknowledge Mayer's letter. The paper was published in 1842 by Justus von Liebig in the journal *Annalen der Chemie und Pharmazie* (Annals of Chemistry and Pharmacy). The paper was almost totally ignored and Mayer published, in 1845, a pamphlet at his own expense – *Organic Motion Related to Digestion* – which fared no better than his paper.

In his arguments Mayer used the specific heat capacities of gases, i.e., the heat required to produce unit temperature rise in unit mass of gas. It was known that the specific heat capacity of a gas maintained at constant volume is slightly smaller than that at constant pressure. This difference in heat, for a given quantity of gas, Mayer interpreted as the work done by a gas expanding at constant pressure. He was able to find the amount of work required to produce unit amount of heat – thus obtaining what was later known as the mechanical equivalent of heat (J). He found a weight of 1 gram falling 365 meters corresponds to heating 1 gram of water 1°C. (This is equivalent to a value of J of 3.56 joules per calorie; the modern conversion factor is 4.18 joules per calorie.)

Mayer clearly anticipated James JOULE and Hermann von HELMHOLTZ in the discovery of the law of conservation of energy. The lack of recognition seems to have affected him strongly, for in the early 1850s he attempted suicide. His work was eventually recognized and he received many honors, including the Rumford medal of the Royal Society (1871).

Maynard Smith, John (1920–   )
British biologist

Maynard Smith was educated at Cambridge University, where he qualified as an engineer in 1941. He spent the next six years designing aircraft before deciding they were "noisy and old-fashioned" and moving to University College, London, to study zoology under J. B. S. Haldane. After obtaining his BSc in zoology in 1951 he remained as a lecturer in zoology until 1965 when he was appointed professor of biology at the University of Sussex. He became emeritus professor in 1985.

Maynard Smith, known to a wide public for his lucid *Theory of Evolution* (1958), has emerged as one of the leading theorists of the postwar years. Much influenced by W. D. Hamilton and Robert MacArthur, and using concepts taken from the theory of games formulated by John von Neumann in the 1940s, he introduced in the 1970s the idea of an evolutionary stable strategy (ESS).

Assuming that two animals are in conflict, then an ESS is one that, if adopted by the majority of the population, prevents the invasion of a mutant strategy. Stable strategies by definition thus tend to be mixed strategies.

Much of Maynard Smith's work on ESS was published in his *Mathematical Ideas in Biology* (1968). He also discussed why sexual modes of reproduction predominate over other means in *The Evolution of Sex* (1978). Maynard Smith has continued to write on evolutionary theory in such works as *Evolutionary Genetics* (1989) and *The Major Transitions of Evolution* (1995).

Mayow, John (1640–1679) *English physiologist and chemist*

Mayow was born at Morvah in Cornwall and educated at Oxford University. He became a doctor of law in 1670 but then turned to medicine.

In 1674 he published his *Tractatus quinque* (Fifth Treatise) in which he came close to discovering the composite nature of the atmosphere. He showed that if a mouse is kept in a closed container over water then the air in the container will diminish in quantity, its properties change, and the water will rise up into the container. The same effect, he realized, could be produced by burning a candle. He further pointed out that combustion and respiration stopped before all the air was used up. He preceded Joseph Priestley and Antoine Lavoisier by about a hundred years with his discoveries relating to respiration and combustion.

Mayr, Ernst Walter (1904–   )
German–American zoologist

Born at Kempten in Germany, Mayr was educated at the universities of Griefswald and Berlin, where he obtained his PhD in 1926. He then served as assistant curator of the museum there before moving to America in 1932. After spending many years at the Museum of Natural History, New York, he moved to Harvard in 1953 to serve as Agassiz Professor of Zoology, in which post he remained until his retirement in 1975.

As a field zoologist Mayr has worked extensively on the birds of the Pacific. Beginning with his *New Guinea Birds* (1941), he published a number of surveys and monographs on the ornithology of the area.

He is, however, better known for such works as *Systematics and the Origin of Species* (1942) and *Animal Species and Evolution* (1963) in which, at the same time as such other scholars as George Simpson and Theodosius Dobzhansky in America and Julian Huxley in Britain, he attempted to establish a neo-Darwinian synthesis. The enterprise has continued to hold together fairly well against the onslaughts of such critics as Motoo Kimura and has so far absorbed, without major upset, the massive inflow of data from the new discipline of molecular biology.

McClintock, Barbara (1902–1992)
American geneticist

The daughter of a physician, McClintock was born in Hartford, Connecticut, and educated at Cornell's College of Agriculture, where she received her PhD in 1927 for work in botany. She remained at Cornell until 1936 supported by various grants from the National Research Council and the Guggenheim Foundation. But there was no future at Cornell for her as, until 1947, only the department of home economics appointed women professors. Fortunately a new genetics department was being set up in the University of Missouri by Craig Stadler, who knew and admired her work, and she was offered a post as assistant professor there, although it was made clear to her that any further advancement would be unlikely. She left in 1941, and in 1944 was elected to the National Academy of Sciences, becoming only the third woman to be so honored. McClintock then joined the Carnegie Institute's Cold Spring Harbor Laboratory, New York, where she remained until her death.

By the 1920s MORGAN and other geneticists, working mainly with the *Drosophila* fruit fly, had established that gene action was connected with chromosomes and thereby established the new discipline of cytogenetics. *Drosophila* chromosomes, however, before the discovery of the giant salivary chromosomes by T. Painter in 1931, were too small to reveal much detail. McClintock chose to work with a variety of maize that possessed much more visible chromosomes. Further, the development of new staining techniques allowed McClintock to identify, distinguish, and number the ten maize chromosomes.

Morgan and his group had also demonstrated the existence of 'linkage groups' in *Drosophila* – groups of genes, such as those for white eyes and maleness, linked together because the genes themselves were sited near each other on a chromosome. In a series of papers published between 1929 and 1931, McClintock established similar linkage groups in maize. Because maize chromosomes were more visible under the microscope than those of *Drosophila*, McClintock was able to identify the chromosomal changes responsible for a change in phenotype and thus confirmed Morgan's work.

McClintock's own Nobel Prize for physiology or medicine, awarded in 1983, was for later work done on the so-called 'jumping genes'. In the 1940s at Cold Spring Harbor, McClintock planted her maize and began to track a family of mutant genes responsible for changes in pigmentation. She was struck by the fact that mutation rates were variable. After several years' careful breeding, McClintock proposed that in addition to the normal genes responsible for pigmentation there were two other genes involved, which she called 'controlling elements'.

One controlling element was found fairly close to the pigmentation gene and operated as a switch, activating and turning off the gene. The second element appeared to be located further away on the same chromosome and was a 'rate gene', controlling the rate at which the pigment gene was switched on and off. She further discovered that the controlling elements could move along the chromosome to a different site and could even move to different chromosomes where they would control different genes. McClintock gave a full description of the process of *transposition*, as it became known, in her 1951 paper, *Chromosome Organization and Genic Expression*. McClintock's work was largely ignored until 1960 when controlling elements were identified in bacteria by MONOD and JACOB.

McCollum, Elmer Verner (1879–1967)
American biochemist

Born in Fort Scott, Kansas, McCollum was educated at the University of Kansas and at Yale, where he obtained his PhD in 1906. He taught at the University of Wisconsin from 1907 until 1917, when he was appointed to the chair of biochemistry at Johns Hopkins University, a post he retained until his retirement in 1944.

McCollum made a number of advances in the study of vitamins. He was the first, in collaboration with M. Davis in 1913, to demonstrate clearly their multiplicity. They found that rats fed with a diet lacking butterfat failed to develop. They assumed, therefore, the existence of a special factor present in butterfat without which the normal growth process could not take place. As it was clearly fat-soluble, it must be distinct from the antiberiberi factor proposed by Casimir FUNK in 1912, which was water-soluble. McCollum named them fat-soluble–A and water-soluble–B, which later became vitamins A and B. In 1920 Mc-Collum was able to extend the alphabet further by naming the antirachitic factor found in cod-liver oil vitamin D (C had already been appropriated to describe the antiscorbutic factor).

McCollum wrote widely on the subject of nutrition, his books including a standard text of the subject, *Newer Knowledge of Nutrition* (1918), which went through many editions, and *A History of Nutrition* (1957).

McKusick, Victor Almon (1921–)
American physician and geneticist

The son of a dairy farmer, McKusick was born in Parkman, Maine, and educated at Tufts University, Medford, Massachusetts. He went on to Johns Hopkins, Baltimore, where he qualified as an MD in 1946 and where he trained as a cardiologist. McKusick has remained at Johns Hopkins and has served as professor of medicine from 1960 and, from 1985, as professor of medical genetics.

The name of McKusick has become identified with a book, an encyclopedic listing of human gene loci, titled *Mendelian Inheritance in Man*, but more commonly referred to as MIM. In 1911 E. B. Wilson identified the first gene locus – the gene for color blindness on the X-chromosome. Over the years other genes were identified and located. By 1966, when the first edition of MIM appeared, 68 genes had been mapped on the X-chromosome. McKusick went on to describe a total number of 1487 human genes. By the eighth edition of MIM, published in 1988, improved techniques in cytogenetics allowed the identification of 4344 gene loci. Two further editions of MIM, in 1990 and 1992, continued to add to the total. A version now exists on the World Wide Web.

McMillan, Edwin Mattison
(1907–1991) *American physicist*

Born in Redonda Beach, California, McMillan was educated at the California Institute of Technology and at Princeton, where he obtained his PhD in 1932. He took up an appointment at the University of California at Berkeley in 1935, being made professor of physics in 1946 and director of the Lawrence Radiation Laboratory in 1958, posts he held until his retirement in 1973.

In 1940 McMillan and Philip Abelson announced the discovery of the first element heavier than uranium. The new element had a mass number 93 and a relative atomic mass of 239. It was named neptunium after the planet Neptune, just as 150 years earlier Martin Klaproth had named uranium after the planet Uranus. McMillan also suspected the existence of element 94 and in the same year was proved right by the discovery of the new element (plutonium) by Glenn SEABORG with whom he was to share the 1951 Nobel Prize for chemistry. The new elements were produced when uranium was bombarded with neutrons and were detected by virtue of their characteristic half-life.

McMillan also made a major advance in the development of Ernest Lawrence's cyclotron, which, in the early 1940s, had run up against a theoretical limit. Lawrence found that as his particles accelerated beyond a certain point their increase in mass, as predicted by Einstein's theory of relativity, was putting them out of phase with the electric impulse they were supposed to receive inside the cyclotron.

In 1945 McMillan proposed a neat solution in the synchrocyclotron (also independently suggested by Vladimir Veksler) in which the fixed frequency of the cyclotron was abandoned. The variable frequency of the synchrocyclotron could thus be adjusted to correspond to the relativistic mass gain of the accelerating particles and once more get into phase with them. In this way accelerators could be built that were forty times more powerful than Lawrence's most advanced cyclotron.

Medawar, Sir Peter Brian (1915–1987)
British immunologist

The son of an Englishwoman and a Lebanese businessman trading in Brazil, Medawar was born in Rio de Janeiro and brought to Britain at the end of World War I. He was educated at Oxford, graduating in zoology in 1937, and remained there to work under Howard Florey. His first researches concerned factors affecting tissue-culture growth but during World War II he turned his attention to medical biology. He subsequently developed a concentrated solution of the blood-clotting protein fibrinogen, which could be used clinically as a biological glue to fix together damaged nerves and keep nerve grafts in position.

The terrible burns of many war casualties led Medawar to study the reasons why skin grafts from donors are rejected. He realized that each individual develops his own immunological system and that the length of time a graft lasts depends on how closely related the recipient and donor are. He found that grafting was successful not only between identical twins but also between nonidentical, or fraternal, twins. It had already been shown in cattle that tissues, notably the red-cell precursors, are exchanged between twin fetuses. This led to the suggestion by Macfarlane BURNET that the immunological system is not developed at conception but is gradually acquired. Thus if an embryo is injected with the tissues of a future donor, the animal after birth should be tolerant to any grafts from that donor.

Medawar tested this hypothesis by injecting mouse embryos, verifying that they do not have the ability to form antibodies against foreign tissue but do acquire immunologic tolerance to it. For this discovery Medawar and Burnet were awarded the 1960 Nobel Prize for physiology or medicine.

Medawar moved from Oxford in 1947 to the chair of zoology at Birmingham, a post he held until 1951 when he was appointed professor of zoology at University College, London. In 1962 he accepted the important post of director of the National Institute for Medical Research. For some years he tried to combine his research work with a heavy administrative load. But in 1969 Medawar suffered his first stroke. Although he continued as director until 1971, the stroke had seriously restricted his mobility and dexterity. Despite this he continued his research work on cancer at the Clinical Research Centre, London. A second stroke in 1980, and a third in 1984, brought Medawar's research career to an end.

He continued to write, however, and in 1986 published his autobiography, *Memoirs of a Thinking Radish*, and collected most of his early essays in *Pluto's Republic* (1982). It was in one of these essays, first published in 1964, that Medawar characterized science in a much quoted phrase as "the art of the soluble."

Meissner, Fritz Walther (1882–1974)
German physicist

In 1933 Meissner, in collaboration with R. Oschenfeld, discovered what has since been known as the *Meissner effect*. He was examining the magnetic properties of materials as they became superconductive, a condition met with as the temperature of the element or compound falls below a critical point, T_c. It was found, quite unexpectedly, that if a solid lead sphere is placed in a magnetic field and the temperature allowed to fall below the T_c of lead, the magnetic field is expelled from the lead sphere, which becomes perfectly diamagnetic. The presence of the Meissner effect is now used as a routine test for superconductivity.

Meitner, Lise (1878–1968) *Austrian– Swedish physicist*

Meitner, the daughter of a lawyer, was born in Vienna and entered the university there in 1901. She studied science under Ludwig Boltzmann and obtained her doctorate in 1906. From Vienna she went to Berlin to attend lectures by Max Planck on theoretical physics. Here she began to study the new phenomenon of radioactivity in collaboration with Otto HAHN, beginning a partnership that was to last thirty years.

At Berlin she met with remarkable difficulties caused by prejudice against women in academic life. She was forced to work in an old carpentry shop and forbidden, by Emil Fischer, to enter laboratories in which males were working. In 1914, at the outbreak of World War I, she became a nurse in the Austrian army, continuing work with Hahn during their periods of leave. In 1918 they announced the discovery of the radioactive element protactinium.

After the war Meitner returned to Berlin as head of the department of radiation physics at the Kaiser Wilhelm Institute. Here she investigated the relationship between the gamma and beta rays emitted by radioactive material. In 1935 she began, with Hahn, work on the transformation of uranium nuclei under neutron bombardment. Confusing results had been obtained earlier by Enrico Fermi.

But by this time she was beginning to fear a different sort of prejudice. Following Hitler's annexation of Austria in 1938 she was no longer safe from persecution and, like many Jewish scientists, left Germany. With the help of Dutch colleagues she found refuge in Sweden, obtaining a post at the Nobel Institute in Stockholm. Hahn, with Fritz Strassman, continued the uranium work and published, in 1939, results showing that nuclei were present that were much lighter than uranium. Shortly afterward Lise Meitner, with Otto FRISCH (her nephew), published an explanation interpreting these results as fission of the uranium nuclei. The nucleus of uranium absorbs a neutron, and the resulting unstable nucleus then breaks into two fragments of roughly equal size. In this induced fission, two or three neutrons are ejected. For this she received a share in the 1966 Enrico Fermi Prize of the Atomic Energy Commission.

Lise Meitner became a Swedish citizen in 1949 and continued work on nuclear physics. In 1960 she retired to Cambridge, England. In 1997 the International Union of Pure and Applied Chemistry approved the name *meitnerium* for element 109.

Melville, Sir Harry Work (1908–   )
British chemist

Melville was educated at the university in his native city of Edinburgh, where he obtained his PhD. After a period (1933–40) at Cambridge University, Melville served as professor of chemistry at the University of Aberdeen (1940–48) and at Birmingham University (1948–56).

At this point in his career Melville moved mainly into science administration. He advised such bodies as the Ministry of Power and the Electricity Authority and from 1956 to 1965 served as secretary of the Department of Scientific and Industrial Research. He finally held the post of head of Queen Mary College, London, from 1967 until his retirement in 1976.

As a chemist, Melville is noted for his work on chain reactions involving free radicals, in which he followed up the ideas of Cyril Hinshelwood and Nikolay Semenov and showed experimentally that they were correct. Later he studied the kinetics of polymerization chain reactions. He wrote *Experimental Methods in Gas Reactions* (1938) with Adalbert Farkas.

Mendel, Gregor Johann (1822–1884)
Austrian plant geneticist

Born in Heinzendorf (now Hynčice in the Czech Republic), Mendel studied at Olmütz University before entering the Augustinian monastery at Brünn (now Brno in the Czech Republic) in 1843. His childhood experience of horticultural work as the son of a peasant farmer had given him an interest in the role of hybrids in evolution, and in 1856 he began plant-breeding experiments. He studied seven characters in pea plants and obtained important .results after much laborious recording of character ratios in the progeny of crosses. From his experiments Mendel concluded that each of the characters he studied was determined by two factors of inheritance (one from each parent) and that each gamete (egg or sperm cell) of the organism contained only one factor of each pair. Furthermore he deduced that assortment into gametes of the factors for one character occurred independently of that for the factors of any other pair. Mendel's results are summarized today

in his law of segregation and law of independent assortment (*Mendel's laws*).

Mendel's work is now recognized as providing the first mathematical basis to genetics but in its day it stimulated little interest. He read a brief account of his research to the Brünn Natural History Society in 1865 and asked members to extend his methods to other species, but none did. In 1866 he published his work in the society's *Verhandlungen* (Proceedings), a journal distributed to 134 scientific institutions, and sent reprints of the paper to hybridization 'experts' of the time. Karl Naegeli, the Swiss botanist, was skeptical of his results and suggested that he continue work on the hawkweeds (*Hieracium*), a genus now known to show reproductive irregularities and with which Mendel was bound to fail.

Mendel's work with peas, and later with *Matthiola*, *Zea*, and *Mirabilis*, had shown that characters do not blend on crossing but retain their identity, thus providing an answer to the weakness in Charles Darwin's theory of natural selection. Mendel read a copy of Darwin's *Origin of Species*, but unfortunately, Darwin never heard of Mendel's work.

Mendel became abbot of the monastery in 1868 and thereafter found less time to devote to his research. It was not until 1900, when Hugo de Vries, Karl Correns, and Erich von Tschermak came across his work, that its true value was realized.

Mendeleev, Dmitri Ivanovich (1834–1907) *Russian chemist*

Mendeleev was the youngest child of a large family living in Tobolsk, Siberia. His father was a local school teacher whose career was ended by blindness and to support the family his mother ran a glass factory. Mendeleev learned some science from a political refugee who had married one of his sisters. His father died in 1847, and soon after his mother's factory was destroyed by fire. She left Tobolsk with Mendeleev, determined that her last son should receive a good education, and placed him at the Pedagogic Institute of St. Petersburg only ten weeks before her death. He later studied in France under Henri Regnault and in Heidelberg with Robert Bunsen and Gustav Kirchhoff.

While abroad Mendeleev attended the famous conference at Karlsruhe in 1860 which did so much to settle the question of atomic weights. He returned to Russia shortly after and in a short time had completed his doctorate, written a textbook, and married. In 1866 he was elected to the chair of chemistry at St. Petersburg University where he remained until his retirement in 1890. His textbook *The Principles of Chemistry* was published between 1868 and 1870.

In 1869 Mendeleev published his classic paper *On the Relation of the Properties to the Atomic Weights of Elements*, which brought order and understanding to this confused subject. His first major proposal was his claim that the only way of classifying the elements is by their atomic weights. Optical, magnetic, and electrical properties vary with the state the body is in at any particular moment; other properties, such as valence, yield conflicting results. When the elements are arranged in order of increasing atomic weight, Mendeleev found that they show a distinct periodicity of their properties. Arranging them in rows of increasing atomc weights produced columns of similar elements.

The table did not at first receive universal acceptance, but its value became apparent during the following 20 years. Through it Mendeleev was able to spot those elements that had been assigned incorrect atomic weights. Thus he suggested that the atomic weights of gold and tellurium must be wrong. There were three missing elements in his table, and he was able to predict their existence, valences, and certain physical properties. The three were eventually discovered – 'eka-aluminum' (gallium, Paul Lecoq de Boisbaudran, 1875), 'eka-boron' (scandium, Per Cleve, 1879), and 'eka-silicon' (germanium, Clemens Winkler, 1885).

Mendeleev became the most famous Russian scientist of his day and received numerous medals and prizes although not, surprisingly, the Nobel Prize (in 1906 it was awarded to Ferdinand Moissan by one vote). Element 101 was named *mendelevium* in his honor.

Mercator, Gerardus (1512–1594) *Dutch cartographer and geographer*

Mercator, originally named Kremer, was born at Rupelmonde, now in Belgium. At the University of Louvain (1530–32) he was a pupil of Gemma Frisius. After learning the basic skills of an instrument maker and engraver, he founded his own studio in Louvain in 1534. Despite accusations of heresy and imprisonment in 1544, he remained in Louvain until 1552, when he moved to Duisburg and opened a cartographic workshop.

Mercator first made his international reputation as a cartographer in 1554 with his map of Europe in which he reduced the size of the Mediterranean from the 62° of Ptolemy to a more realistic, but still excessive, 52°. He produced his world map in 1569 and his edition of Ptolemy in 1578, while his *Atlas*, begun in 1569, was only published by his son after his death. It was intended to be a whole series of publications describing both the creation of the world and its subsequent history. Mercator was the first to use the term 'atlas' for such works, the book having as its frontispiece an illustration of Atlas supporting the world.

The value of Mercator's work lies not just in his skills as an engraver, but also in the introduction of his famous projection in his 1569 map of the world. Navigators wished to be able to sail on what was called a rhumb-line course, or a loxodrome, i.e., to sail between two points on a constant bearing, charting their course with a straight line. On the surface of a globe such lines are curves; to project them onto a plane chart Mercator made the meridians (the lines of longitude) parallel instead of converging at the Poles. This made it straightforward for a navigator to plot his course but it also produced the familiar distortion of the *Mercator projection* – exaggeration of east–west distances and areas in the high latitudes.

The big difference, apart from projection, between Mercator's and classical maps was in the representation of the Americas. He was not the first to use the name America on a map, that distinction belonging to Martin Waldseemüller in 1507, but he was the first to divide the continent into two named parts – *Americae pars septentrionalis* (northern part of America) and *Americae pars meridionalis* (southern part of America).

Merrifield, Robert Bruce (1921–) *American biochemist*

Born in Fort Worth, Texas, Merrifield was educated at the University of California, Los Angeles, where he received his PhD in 1949. He began work immediately at Rockefeller University, New York, and was appointed to the chair of biochemistry in 1966, a post he held until his retirement in 1992.

In the 1950s Merrifield began work on solid-phase peptide synthesis (SPPS). Peptides, like proteins, are composed of chains of amino acids, but have shorter and less complicated chains. Naturally occurring ones possess important physiological properties. The ability to synthesize peptides cheaply and quickly would lead to numerous commercial and medical gains. Yet the synthesis of a polypeptide using traditional methods could take many months.

In peptides the amine end ($-NH_2$) of one amino acid reacts with the carboxyl end ($-COOH$) of another. To prepare a pure product of known structure, amino acids have to be coupled in a specific sequence. To achieve this the amine group on one amino acid and carboxyl group on the other must be blocked, so that the other two ends are the ones reacting. And this must be done as each further amino acid is added. In addition, at each stage the product must be isolated and purified. This will involve crystallizing the products. The synthesis of a hundred-unit peptide would involve ninety-nine such procedures. The need for improvement in the technique was painfully clear to peptide chemists.

Merrifield's innovation was to apply an ion-exchange technique by bonding the amino acids, one at a time, to an insoluble solid support. A polystyrene resin was the original choice. As the solid support was insoluble in the various solvents used, all the intermediate products and impurities could be simply washed away by using the appropriate reagent. Much initial work was required in setting up the right kinds of activating agents, blocking agents, and solvents. In 1964 in eight days Merrifield single-handedly synthesized bradykinin, a nine-amino-acid peptide that dilates blood vessels.

One further aspect of Merrifield's process is that it can be fully automated. To demonstrate the power and potential of his method Merrifield undertook in 1965 the automatic synthesis of insulin. With 51 amino acids and two peptide chains held together by two disulfide bridges, the molecule was a formidable challenge. Although more than 5000 operations were involved in assembling the chains, most of these were carried out automatically in a few days. The linking of the two chains, however, was achieved by more traditional methods. The resulting insulin was active in the standard biological assay.

For his development of the technique Merrifield was awarded the 1984 Nobel Prize for chemistry.

Merrill, Paul Willard (1887–1961)
American astronomer

Merrill was born in Minneapolis, Minnesota, and graduated from Stanford University in 1908. He obtained his PhD in 1913 from the University of California. After teaching at the University of Michigan from 1913 to 1916 and serving briefly with the US Bureau of Standards in Washington, he was appointed to the staff of the Mount Wilson Observatory in 1919, remaining there until his retirement in 1952.

It was in his retirement year that he detected the lines of technetium in the spectra of S-type stars, a class of cool red giant stars. This was surprising for the most stable isotope of technetium has a half-life of about 2.6 million years, which is much shorter than the lifetime of a star. Merrill thought it unlikely that there was an unknown stable isotope of technetium found only on S-type stars and argued rather that it was being produced within the stars by some form of nuclear reaction. The technetium lines are now accepted as strong evidence for one of the nuclear processes by which the heavy elements are thought to be created in the interiors of stars.

Meselson, Matthew Stanley
(1930–   ) *American molecular biologist*

Meselson, who was born in Denver, Colorado, studied liberal arts at the University of Chicago and physical chemistry at the California Institute of Technology, Pasadena. After he obtained his PhD in 1957 he remained at the Institute until 1960 when he moved to Harvard, where he served from 1964 as professor of biology and from 1976 as Thomas Dudley Cabot professor of natural sciences.

In 1957 Meselson, in collaboration with the American biologist **Franklin Stahl** (1910–   ), conducted one of the classic experiments of molecular biology, which clearly revealed the semiconservative nature of DNA replication. It seemed likely that when the double helix of DNA duplicated, each new helix, and hence each daughter cell, would contain one DNA strand from the original helix; in the jargon of the time, replication would be semiconservative. The other possibility was that one daughter molecule would contain both the old strands and the other daughter molecule both the new strands – conservative replication.

Meselson and Stahl grew many generations of the bacterium *Escherichia coli* on a simple culture medium containing ammonium chloride (NH_4Cl), labeled with the heavy isotope of nitrogen, ^{15}N, as the only nitrogen source. They then added normal ^{14}N nitrogen to the medium and removed bacterial cells at intervals, extracting their DNA by ultracentrifugation. The density of the DNA in successive samples could be determined by the method of equilibrium density gradient centrifugation, in which samples of differing density diffuse into discrete bands corresponding to their own effective density. Ultraviolet absorption photographs of these bands allowed the concentration of DNA in each band to be determined. The results showed that (following the introduction of ^{14}N) after one doubling of the *E. coli* bacteria all the DNA molecules contained equal amounts of ^{15}N and ^{14}N, i.e., they were all half labeled. After two generations there were equal amounts of half-labeled DNA molecules and wholly ^{14}N molecules. This effectively demonstrated that replication is semiconservative. The results were published in the Proceedings of the National Academy of Sciences, as *The Replication of DNA in Escherichia coli* (1958).

Meselson has also worked with Sidney Brenner and François Jacob on the mechanism of viral infection. In 1961, working with the virus T4, they showed that on invasion of a host bacterial cell the viral DNA releases messenger RNA, which, when it arrives at the host ribosomes, instructs these to make viral protein rather than bacterial proteins.

Messier, Charles (1730–1817) *French astronomer*

Messier, who was born in Badonviller in France, arrived in Paris in 1751 and was taken on as a clerical assistant by J. Delisle at the Naval Observatory sited in the Collège de Cluny. He quickly learned how to use the Observatory instruments and began a lifetime's obsessive search for comets. Dubbed the 'comet ferret' by Louis XV, Messier is credited with the discovery of 13 comets between 1759 and 1798. The computation of the cometary orbits, however, was left to his more mathematically sophisticated colleagues.

In 1758 he observed what appeared to be a faint comet in Taurus. Further examination revealed it to be a nebula, an immense cloud of gas. Messier thought it sensible to provide a list of such objects "so that astronomers would not confuse these same nebulae with comets just beginning to shine." He published his first list of 45 nebulae in 1774 under the title *Catalogue des nebeleuses et des amas étoiles* (Catalog of Nebulae and Star Clusters). Two supplements published in 1783 and 1784 increased the number of nebulae to 103.

The nebulae listed in the catalogs were given the identifying letter M and a number; for example, the Andromeda nebula is commonly referred to as M31.

Metchnikoff, Elie (1845–1916) *Russian–French zoologist and cytologist*

Metchnikoff was born at Ivanovka near Kharkov (now in Ukraine) and educated at Kharkov University. After holding posts under Rudolf Leuckart at Göttingen and Giessen, and under Karl Siebold at Munich, he taught zoology at Odessa and St. Peters-

burg. From 1873 to 1882 he was professor of zoology and comparative anatomy at Odessa.

He spent the years 1882–86 at Messina in Italy where, working on starfish larvae, he first noticed that certain nondigestive cells enclose and engulf foreign particles introduced into the body. These cells he called phagocytes and, extending his studies, he demonstrated that they also occur in humans – they are the white blood corpuscles. He realized that they are important in the body's defenses against disease, in engulfing bacteria and other foreign bodies in the blood. These advances were outlined in such publications as *Intra-Cellular Digestion* (1882), *The Comparative Pathology of Inflammation* (1892), and *Immunity in Infectious Diseases* (1905). For his work on phagocytosis, Metchnikoff was awarded, in 1908, the Nobel Prize for physiology or medicine jointly with Paul EHRLICH.

In 1886 Metchnikoff was appointed director of the new bacteriological institute at Odessa; two years later he went to the Pasteur Institute in Paris, which he directed from 1895 to 1916, succeeding Pasteur himself.

In 1903 Metchnikoff succeeded, with Emile Roux, in transferring syphilis to apes. He also did research on cholera. His later years were largely concerned with a study of the aging factors in humans and means of inducing longevity – discussed in *The Nature of Man* (1904) and *The Prolongation of Human Life* (1910).

Metius, Jacobus (1580–1628) *Dutch instrument maker*

Metius was born at Alkmaar in the Netherlands; together with Hans Lippershey and Zacharias Janssen, he is credited with the invention of the telescope. His father was a cartographer while his brother, Adriaen, was an astronomer and mathematician who had worked with Tycho Brahe at Hven and had taught the famous mathematician and philosopher René Descartes.

Metius put in a claim for a patent for his 'perspicilla' (telescope) in October 1608, but he was beaten to it by Lippershey who had put in a similar claim just two weeks earlier.

Meton (c. 432 BC) *Greek astronomer*

Nothing is known about the life and personality of Meton. His proposed cycle, called the *Metonic cycle*, which was not accepted by the citizens of Athens, was designed to bring the lunar month and the solar year into some form of acceptable agreement. As the lunar month is about 29½ days and the solar year is 365¼ days there is no way a whole number of months can make up a year. An early solution to the problem was the *octaeteris*, in which three intercalary (inserted) months are added to each eight-year cycle. This would lead to an error of alignment of a day and a half each eight years. Meton's suggestion was an improvement on this. He realized that 235 lunar months and 19 solar years are both 6939 days. To bring the two cycles into phase would need 7 intercalary months spread over the 19 years of the full cycle. This would produce a solar year only 30 minutes too long. The Metonic cycle was eventually adopted by the Greeks and was used until the introduction of the Julian calendar in 46 BC. The Jewish calendar still uses it.

Meyer, Julius Lothar (1830–1895)
German chemist

Meyer was the son of a doctor from Varel in Germany. He qualified in medicine himself in 1854 after studying at Zurich and Würzburg and gained his PhD from the University of Breslau in 1858. At first his interests were physiological but he slowly moved into chemistry. He became professor of chemistry at Karlsruhe in 1868 where he stayed until he moved to the chair at Tübingen (1876–95).

Meyer is best remembered for his early work on the periodic table. He was much impressed by Stanislao CANNIZZARO, expounding his work in his book *Die modernen Theorien der Chemie* (1864; Modern Chemical Theory). In writing his textbook it had occurred to him that the properties of an element seem to depend on its atomic weight. Meyer plotted the values of a certain physical property, atomic volume, against atomic weight. He found clear signs of periodicity, the graph consisting of a series of four sharp peaks. He noticed that elements with similar chemical properties occur at comparable points on the different peaks; e.g., the alkali metals all occur at the tops of the peaks.

Meyer did not publish his table until 1870 so he was preempted by Dmitri MENDELEEV, who had published his periodic table in 1869. Meyer never disputed Mendeleev's priority and later stated that he lacked sufficient courage to have gone on to predict the existence of undiscovered elements.

Meyer, Karl (1899–1990) *American biochemist*

Meyer gained his MD from the university in his native city of Cologne in 1924 and his PhD from Berlin University in 1928. He moved to the University of California,

Berkeley, in 1930, and in 1933 transferred to the College of Physicians and Surgeons at Columbia, where he has spent the rest of his career. He served as professor of biochemistry from 1954 until his retirement in 1967.

Meyer studied the acidic mucopolysaccharides found in connective tissue and isolated two of these, hyaluronic acid and chondroitin sulfate. He also discovered that various bacteria have enzymes – hyaluronidases – that can break down hyaluronic acid. It was later shown that these enzymes are the same as the 'spreading factors' isolated from various sources, such as snake venom and leeches. Meyer and his colleagues found that there are three different types of chondroitin sulfate, and in 1953 he isolated a third mucopolysaccharide, keratosulfate, found in the cornea. This was later also found in cartilage. Meyer also investigated the production and distribution of mucopolysaccharides and was able to show that Marfan's syndrome, an inherited disease of connective tissue, is associated with large amounts of keratosulfate in cartilage.

Meyerhof, Otto Fritz (1884–1951)
German–American biochemist

Meyerhof, who was born at Hannover in Germany, devoted the greater part of his academic life to the study of the biochemistry and metabolism of muscle; he shared the Nobel Prize for physiology or medicine with Archibald HILL in 1922. He held professorships at Kiel and Heidelberg universities, was director of physiology at the Kaiser Wilhelm Institute for Biology, Berlin, and was director of research at the Paris Institute of Biology. In 1940 he emigrated to America, where he joined the medical faculty of the University of Pennsylvania.

Meyerhof demonstrated that the production of lactic acid in muscle tissue, formed as a result of glycogen breakdown, was effected without the consumption of oxygen (i.e., anaerobically). The lactic acid was reconverted to glycogen through oxidation by molecular oxygen, during muscle rest. This line of research was continued by Gustav EMBDEN and Carl and Gerty CORI who worked out in greater detail the steps by which glycogen is converted to lactic acid – the *Embden–Meyerhof pathway*.

Michaelis, Leonor (1875–1949)
German–American chemist

Michaelis was educated at the university in his native city of Berlin and at Freiburg. He worked in the laboratory of the Berlin Municipal Hospital from 1906 to 1922, when he took up the post of professor of biochemistry at the Nagoya Medical School, Japan. In 1926 Michaelis emigrated to America and after spending four years at Johns Hopkins moved to the Rockefeller Institute of Medical Research, where he remained until his retirement in 1940.

In 1913 Michaelis, in collaboration with L. M. Menten, formulated one of the earliest precise and quantitative laws applying to biochemical systems. They were trying to picture the relation between an enzyme and its substrate (the substance it catalyzes) and, in particular, how to predict and understand the reaction rate, that is, how much substrate is acted upon by an enzyme per unit time, and the basic factors that stimulate or inhibit this rate.

The kind of graph obtained when reaction rate is plotted against substrate concentration showed that additional substrate concentration sharply increases the reaction rate until a certain point is reached when the rate appears to become completely indifferent to the addition of any further amounts of substrate.

Michaelis saw this as indicating that the reaction between enzyme and substrate is a very specific one. In the early phase of the curve there was enzyme lacking substrate; as this was increased more and more enzyme came into play, increasing the reaction rate. Eventually, however, there will come a point when all the enzyme is being used and from that point the addition of any amount of substrate can have no effect on the reaction rate. This variation in rate was subsequently described by the *Michaelis–Menten equation.*

Michaelis's insight into the working of the enzyme–substrate complex was quite remarkable as no hard evidence for its existence was to emerge for a good many years, not in fact until Britton Chance was able to produce spectroscopic evidence in 1949.

Michel, Hartmut (1948–) *German chemist*

Michel was born at Lüdwigsburg in Germany and educated at the University of Warburg, where he obtained his PhD in 1977. He moved to the Max Planck Institute for Biochemistry at Martinsried, near Munich, and remained there until 1987, when he moved to Frankfurt to head the biophysics division.

By 1970 chemists had succeeded in uncovering the basic chemistry of photosynthesis but little was known about the process at the molecular level. It was established that the process occurred in the photosynthetic reaction centers first identified by Roderick

Clayton in the late 1960s. These are to be found embedded in the membranes of the photosynthetic vesicles. Within the reaction centers was a complex protein structure. Before further progress could be made, the structure of the proteins would have to be worked out, but first it would be necessary to crystallize the proteins.

Michel first tackled the problem in 1978. While it was relatively easy to crystallize water-soluble proteins, membrane proteins, which react with both fats and water, were only partially soluble in water. Michel used a molecule in which one end was attracted to water (hydrophilic) while the opposite end was water repellent (hydrophobic). By binding the hydrophobic ends of the organic molecules to the hydrophobic ends of the protein membranes the hydrophilic ends alone would lie exposed. The complex structure could then be dissolved in water and crystallized. By 1982 Michel had succeeded in crystallizing the membrane proteins of the bacterium *Rhodopseudomonas viridis.*

For this work Michel shared the 1988 Nobel Prize for chemistry with Johann DIESENHOFER and Robert HUBER.

Michell, John (1724–1793) *English geologist and astronomer*

Michell studied at Cambridge University and became a fellow. In 1762 he was appointed Woodward Professor of Geology but left academic life to take up a post as rector at Thornhill, Yorkshire, in 1764.

Before his departure from Cambridge he published, in 1760, a fundamental paper, *Conjectures Concerning the Cause, and Observations upon the Phenomena of Earthquakes.* After the great Lisbon earthquake (1755) this was a fashionable subject. Michell assigned the cause of earthquakes to the force generated by high-pressure steam, produced when water suddenly met subterranean fires. He appreciated that such a force would generate waves in the Earth's crust and tried to estimate the velocity of these, giving a not unreasonable figure of 1200 miles per hour. Finally, Michell showed various means to determine the point of origin of the earthquake.

In 1790 he constructed a torsion balance to measure gravitational attraction and thus the mean density of the Earth. Michell was unable to use this before his death, but Henry CAVENDISH carried on his work, deriving a value for the density of the Earth in 1798.

Michell also made contributions to astronomy. In 1767 he published a paper on double stars, pointing out with originality and insight that there are far too many of them to result from a random scattering and therefore they must in many cases constitute a genuine binary system. He also devised a method for calculating the distance of the stars.

Michelson, Albert Abraham (1852–1931) *American physicist*

Michelson, who was born at Strelno (now Strzelno in Poland), came to America with his parents when he was two years old. He graduated from the US Naval Academy in 1873 and remained there to teach physics and chemistry. Some five years later he began his work on measuring the speed of light and to this end he traveled to Europe to study optics at the Collège de France, Heidelberg, and Berlin. When he returned to America he left the navy to become professor of physics at the Case School, Cleveland. In 1882 he estimated the speed of light as 186,320 miles per second. This was the most accurate value then available and remained so for another ten years, when Michelson made an even more accurate measurement.

In the course of this work Michelson developed an interferometer, an instrument that can divide a beam of light in two, send the beams in different directions, and then unite them again. If the two beams traveled the same distance at different speeds (or different distances at the same speed) then, on being brought together again, the waves would be out of step and produce interference fringes on a screen. Michelson used the interferometer to test whether light travelng in the same direction as the Earth moves more slowly than light traveling at right angles to the Earth's surface. This was effectively testing the presence of the 'ether' – a substance that was supposed to exist in all space beyond the Earth's atmosphere. Because the ether was thought to be motionless and the Earth moved through it, it followed that light traveling in the same direction as the Earth would be more impeded than light going at right angles to it.

Michelson first conducted this experiment in 1881 in Berlin and got a negative result, that is there were no interference fringes and thus no evidence that the two beams were traveling at different speeds. He repeated the procedure several times under increasingly elaborate conditions until, in 1887, with **Edward Morley** (1838–1923), the experiment was made under near perfect conditions at the Case School. Again the ether could not be detected and physicists had seriously to consider that the ether did not exist. This result questioned much orthodox physical theory, and it remained for Einstein to develop the special theory of relativity to explain the constancy of the speed of light. Michelson was awarded the 1907 Nobel Prize in physics for this work.

Others, however, continued to report that they had found a measurable difference. Thus **Dayton Miller** (1866–1941), professor of physics at the Case School of Applied Science, Cleveland, Ohio took his equipment in 1925 to the 6000-ft summit of Mount Wilson in California. He claimed to have detected a difference of 6 miles per second for light travelling at right angles to the Earth's orbit. It was later established, however, that Miller's results were caused by different temperature conditions.

Michelson also applied interference techniques to astronomical measurements and was able to measure the diameters of various heavenly bodies by contrasting the light emitted from both sides. He also continued to make increasingly more accurate estimates of the speed of light and he suggested that the wavelength of light waves should be used as the length standard rather than the platinum–iridium meter in Paris. This suggestion was taken up in 1960 when light waves from the inert gas krypton became the standard measure.

Miescher, Johann Friedrich (1844–1895) *Swiss biochemist*

Miescher came from a distinguished scientific family from Basel in Switzerland: both his father, also called Johann Friedrich, and his uncle, Wilhelm His, held the chair of anatomy at the University of Basel. Miescher himself studied medicine at Basel but, feeling that his partial deafness (produced by a severe attack of typhus) would be a drawback for a physician, turned to physiological chemistry. He consequently spent the period from 1868 to 1870 learning organic chemistry under Felix Hoppe-Seyler at Tübingen and physiology at Leipzig in the laboratory of Carl Ludwig. In 1871 he was appointed professor of physiology at Basel.

It was while working on pus cells at Tübingen in 1869 that Miescher made his fundamental discovery. It was thought that such cells were made largely of protein, but Miescher noted the presence of something that "cannot belong among any of the protein substances known hitherto." In fact he was able to show that it was not protein at all, being unaffected by the protein-digesting enzyme pepsin. He also showed that the new substance was derived from the nucleus of the cell alone and consequently named it 'nuclein'. Miescher was soon able to show that nuclein could be obtained from many other cells and was unusual in containing phosphorus in addition to the usual ingredients of organic molecules – carbon, oxygen, nitrogen, and hydrogen. It was not until 1871 that Miescher's paper, delayed by Hoppe-Seyler (who wanted to confirm the results), was published. In it he announced the presence of a nonprotein phosphorus-containing molecule in the nuclei of a large number of cells.

Just what precise role the molecule played in the cell was not revealed until the structure of nucleic acid, as it was renamed by Richard Altmann in 1889, was announced by James Watson and Francis Crick in 1953. Miescher continued to work on the nuclein extracted from the sperm of the Rhine salmon for the rest of his short life. He spent much time puzzling on the chemistry of fertilization, even speculating in 1874 that "if one wants to assume that a single substance...is the specific cause of fertilization then one should undoubtedly first of all think of nuclein." Unfortunately Miescher failed to follow up his suggestion, preferring to explore physical models of fertilization. However, his work on nuclein was eagerly taken up by other organic chemists, and by 1893 Albrecht KOSSEL had succeeded in recognizing four nucleic acid bases.

Milankovich, Milutin (1879–1958)
Yugoslavian mathematician

Milankovich was born at Dalj in Croatia and was educated at the Institute of Technology in Vienna, where he obtained his PhD in 1904. He then moved to the University of Belgrade, remaining there for the rest of his career except for the period 1914–18, during which he was a prisoner of war, but was allowed to pursue his researches in the library of the Hungarian Academy of Science in Budapest.

Milankovich was the most talented of the scientists who worked in the tradition of James CROLL in trying to explain the development of the Earth's climate by reference to astronomical events. From 1911 to 1941, when he published his *Canon of Insolation and the Ice Age Problem*, he tried obsessively, in numerous works, to reconstruct the past climate of the Earth and the planets.

Milankovich realized that the key to past climates was the amount of solar radiation received by the Earth, which varies at different latitudes and depends upon three basic factors. One is the degree of ellipticity of the Earth's orbit, which varies over 100,000 years from being nearly circular to

a noticeable ellipticity and which could reduce the amount of insolation by 30%. Secondly, over about 21,000 years a precessional change occurs, which will determine whether the northern or the southern hemisphere receives the most radiation. Finally, the tilt of the Earth's axis to the plane of its orbit changes over about 40,000 years from 21.8° to 24.4°.

Over a period of 30 years Milankovich constructed radiation curves for the last 650,000 years for the summer northern hemisphere from 5°N to 75°N. At first his results looked most impressive for he identified nine climatic minima, which fitted closely the four ice ages identified by Albrecht Penck. However, with the advent of more precise and accurate dating techniques his results are now considered doubtful.

Miller, Dayton Clarence (1866–1941)
American physicist. See MICHELSON, ALBERT ABRAHAM.

Miller, Jacques Francis Albert Pierre
(1931–   ) *French–Australian immunologist*

Miller, who was born at Nice in the south of France, was educated at the University of Sydney, Australia, and at University College, London, where he obtained his PhD in 1960. He then held brief appointments at the Chester Beatty Research Institute in London and the National Cancer Institute in Bethesda, Maryland. Miller returned to Australia in 1966 to serve as head of the experimental pathology department at the Hall Institute of Medical Research, Melbourne.

In 1961 Miller succeeded in solving an ancient medical mystery. The thymus gland is a large organ placed in the chest beneath the breastbone. Surprisingly, until 1961 scientists lacked any clear idea of the role played by such a prominent body. The normal technique in such a situation is to watch for any changes in the behavior of the subject when the organ has been removed. In this case thymectomy seemed to make no discernible difference to the behavior of any experimental animal.

Working within this tradition Miller performed a surgical operation of great skill, the removal of the thymus from one-day-old mice. As the mice weigh no more than a gram and are no bigger than an inch it is not difficult to see why such an operation had been little attempted before. In this case, however, the excision did lead to dramatic and obvious changes. The mice failed to develop properly and usually died within two to three months of the operation. Just what was wrong with them became clear when Miller went on to test their ability to reject skin grafts, a sure sign of a healthy immune system. Miller's mice could tolerate grafts from unrelated mice and sometimes even from rats. This made it quite clear that the thymus was deeply involved in the body's immune system but just what precise role it played was to occupy immunologists for a decade or more.

Much of Miller's work was performed independently, also in 1961, by a team under the direction of Robert Good at Minnesota.

Miller, Stanley Lloyd (1930–)
American chemist

Born at Oakland in California, Miller was educated at the universities of California and Chicago where, in 1954, he was awarded his PhD. Since 1960 he has taught at the University of California, San Diego, being appointed to a professorship in chemistry in 1968.

In 1953 Miller published a famous paper, *A Production of Amino Acids under Possible Primitive Earth Conditions*, in which he reported the results of an experiment carried out while still a graduate student at Chicago under the direction of Harold Urey.

It was thought that the early atmosphere of the Earth could well have been something like that now existing on Jupiter and Saturn, namely one rich in methane (CH_4) and ammonia (NH_3). Miller mixed water vapor with ammonia, methane, and hydrogen in a closed flask and subjected it to a high-voltage electrical discharge. Sensitive analysis with paper chromatography revealed a number of organic molecules. In addition to hydrocyanic acid, formic acid, acetic acid, lactic acid, and urea were two of the simpler amino acids, alanine and glycine.

As it is from the amino acids that the proteins are constructed many scholars saw this as clear evidence for the spontaneous origin of life. It has however been shown that such random processes could not yet have produced a single protein without the assumption of various additional operating principles.

Millikan, Robert Andrews (1868– 1953) *American physicist*

The son of a Congregational minister from Morrison, Illinois, Millikan was educated at Oberlin, where he studied classics, and Columbia University, where he obtained his PhD in 1895. After a year in Europe, studying under Max Planck and Walther Nernst, he took up an appointment in 1896 at the University of Chicago, being promoted to a full professorship in 1910. Millikan moved

to the California Institute of Technology in 1921 as director of the Norman Bridge Laboratory, a position he held until his retirement in 1945.

In 1909 Millikan started on a project that was to win for him the 1923 Nobel Prize for physics – the determination of the electric charge of the electron. His apparatus consisted of two horizontal plates that could be made to take opposite charges. Between the plates he introduced a fine spray of oil drops whose mass could be determined by measuring their fall under the influence of gravity and against the resistance of the air. When the air was ionized by x-rays and the plates charged, then an oil drop that had collected a charge would be either repelled from or attracted to the plates depending on whether it had collected a positive or negative charge. By measuring the change in the rate of fall and knowing the intensity of the electric field Millikan was able to calculate the charges on the oil drops. After taking many careful measurements he was able to come to the important conclusion that the charge was always a simple multiple of the same basic unit, which he found to be $4.774 \pm 0.009 \times 10^{-10}$ electrostatic units, a figure whose accuracy was not improved until 1928. Millikan followed this with a prolonged attempt from 1912 to 1916 to demonstrate the validity of the formula introduced by Albert Einstein in 1905 to describe the photoelectric effect, work that was cited in Einstein's Nobel award.

In 1923 he began a major study of cosmic rays, first identified in 1912 by Victor Hess, which was to occupy him for the rest of his career. His first aim was to show that they did not originate in our atmosphere. To do this he devised an ingenious set of observations made at two lakes in the San Bernadino mountains of southern California. The lakes were many miles apart and differed by 6700 feet (2042 m) in altitude. The difference in altitude would have the same effect on intensity of cosmic rays as six feet of water. He found that the intensity of ionization produced by the incoming cosmic rays in the lower lake was the same as the intensity six feet deeper in the higher lake. This showed, he claimed, that the rays do come in definitely from above and that their origin is entirely outside the layer of atmosphere between the levels of the two lakes.

Millikan then went on to theorize about the nature of the cosmic rays. He argued that they were electromagnetic radiation photons, for if they were charged particles they would be influenced by the Earth's magnetic field and therefore more likely to arrive in higher rather than lower latitudes. Millikan had failed to detect any such effect with latitude. In fact Millikan's theories were soon disproved for Arthur Compton did detect a latitude effect.

Milne, John (1850–1913) *British seismologist*

Milne, who was born at Liverpool, was educated at King's College, London, and at the Royal School of Mines. After fieldwork in Newfoundland and Labrador (1872–74) he was appointed, in 1875, professor of geology and mining at the Imperial College of Engineering, Tokyo.

Milne developed a passion for seismology and became known as 'Earthquake Milne' in Tokyo. He was instrumental in forming the Seismological Society of Japan in 1880. His first priority was to organize the recording, collecting, and distribution of data. He asked the postal authority in each town throughout Japan to return to him a weekly record of the numbers of earthquakes experienced and he also set up over 900 stations for more detailed recording of seismic activity. Milne also invented, in 1880, a seismograph and he spent much time devising simple and hardy seismographs, which could be used by the relatively unskilled in a wide variety of conditions.

Milne returned to England in 1894 and made his home at Shide, on the Isle of Wight. This became the center of an international system for the collection and distribution of seismological data. His publications included *Earthquakes* (1883) and *Seismology* (1898).

Milstein, César (1927–) *British molecular biologist*

Milstein was born at Bahia Blanca in Argentina and attended the University of Buenos Aires, receiving his degree in 1952 and his doctorate in 1957. Three years later he was granted a PhD by Cambridge University. Milstein returned to his native Argentina in 1961 to head the Molecular Biology Division of the Instituto Nacional de Microbiología in Buenos Aires. In 1963 he joined the staff of the Medical Research Council's Laboratory of Molecular Biology in Cambridge and in 1983 he was appointed head of the Division of Protein and Nucleic Acid Chemistry, a post in which he remained until his retirement in 1994.

Milstein is best known for producing the first monoclonal antibodies, using a technique developed at the MRC's Laboratory in collaboration with the German immunologist, George KÖHLER, and first reported by them in 1975. The pair went on to show how it was possible to manufacture quantities of antibody of any desired specificity employing cultures of so-called 'hybridoma' cells. Monoclonal antibodies have found wide-ranging application in biology, medicine, and industry, especially for diagnostic tests and assays. For his part in developing this revolutionary technology, Milstein was awarded the 1984 Nobel Prize for physiology or medicine, which he shared with Köhler and Niels JERNE.

Minkowski, Hermann (1864–1909) *Russian–German mathematician*

Minkowski was born at Alexotas in Russia to parents of German origin. In 1872 the family returned to Germany, settling in Königsberg (now Kaliningrad). Minkowski studied alongside David Hilbert at the University of Königsberg, under Adolf Hurwitz, and gained his PhD in 1885. He taught at Bonn (1885–94) and Königsberg (1894–96) and then worked with Hurwitz at the Zurich Federal Institute of Technology (1896–1902). At Hilbert's instigation a new chair of mathematics was created for Minkowski at the University of Göttingen and he worked there (1902–09) until his death.

In 1883, when still 18, Minkowski was awarded the Grand Prix des Sciences Mathématiques of the Paris Academy of Sciences. The award was shared with Henry J. Smith for their work on the theory of quadratic forms. Minkowski remained occupied with the arithmetic of quadratic forms for the rest of his life. In 1896 he gave a detailed account of his 'geometry of numbers' in which he developed geometrical methods for the treatment of certain problems in number theory.

During his short period at Göttingen Minkowski worked closely with David Hilbert and decisively influenced Hilbert's interest in mathematical physics. Minkowski's most celebrated work was in developing the mathematics that played a crucial role in Einstein's formulation of the theory of relativity. EINSTEIN knew when he published the special theory of relativity in 1905 that the universe could not be adequately described using normal, or Euclidean, three-dimensional geometry. Minkowski's seminal idea was to view space and time as forming together a single four-dimensional continuum or manifold, known as space–time, rather than two distinct entities. In normal three-dimensional geometry, any point in space can be identified by three coordinates. The analog of this point in three-dimensional space is an event localized both in space and time in four-dimensional space–time.

Minkowski put forward his concept of space–time, or *Minkowski space* as it is sometimes called, in 1907 in his book *Space and Time*. Einstein himself was very forthright about the extent to which the theory of relativity depended on Minkowski's innovatory work. Space–time was a useful and elegant format for special relativity, and was essential for general relativity, published in 1916, in which space–time is allowed to be curved. It is the curvature of space–time that accounts for the phenomenon of gravitation.

Minot, George Richards (1885–1950)
American physician. See WHIPPLE, GEORGE.

Minsky, Marvin Lee (1927–)
American computer scientist

The son of a surgeon, Minsky was born in New York and educated at Harvard and at Princeton, where he obtained his PhD in 1954. He taught at Harvard before moving to the Massachusetts Institute of Technology in 1957 as professor of mathematics, a post he occupied until 1962 when he became professor of electrical engineering. He also served as director of the Artificial Intelligence (AI) Laboratory (1964–73).

In the summer of 1956 Minsky attended a conference on AI at Dartmouth, New Hampshire. Here, it was generally agreed that powerful modern computers would soon be able to simulate all aspects of human learning and intelligence. Much of Minsky's later career has been spent testing this claim.

Under Minsky's direction a number of AI programs have been developed at MIT. One of the earliest, a program to solve problems in calculus, showed that most problems could be solved by a careful application of about 100 rules. The computer actually received a grade A in an MIT calculus exam. Other programs developed such topics as reasoning by analogy, handling information expressed in English, and how to catch a bouncing ball with a robotic arm.

But Minsky soon became aware that AI had a number of problems to overcome. For example, in one project a computer with a robotic arm and a TV camera was programmed to copy an assembly of bricks. Although it could quickly recognize the bricks and their relationships to each other, it found the stacking more difficult. It tried to stack the blocks from the top down, releasing brick after brick in midair. Computers simply do not have an innate knowledge of gravity or, he has pointed out, many

other things we take for granted, such as that chairs painted a different color remain the same chair, or that boxes must be opened before things can be put inside.

He also noted problems with 'perceptrons', designed by Frank ROSENBLATT in 1960 with the supposed ability to respond to and recognize certain patterns with the aid of an array of 400 photocells. In collaboration with Seymour Papert, Minsky published a critical account of this work in *Perceptrons* (1968) showing, in purely formal terms, that the powers of perceptrons were strictly limited. They could not, for example, be relied upon to tell when a figure was connected. A cat's tail protruding from a chair would prevent the perceptron from identifying either the cat or the chair.

In 1974 Minsky introduced the notion of 'frames'. A frame is a package of knowledge stored in the mind, which allows us to understand many things about a certain topic. For example, the 'dog frame' includes what dogs look like, the sorts of things they do, and many other aspects of their nature and behavior. Because we possess numerous such frames we are able to communicate about the world without too much confusion, and to distinguish routinely between the 'bark' of a tree and the 'bark' of a dog. Only when a computer could be stocked with an enormous number of 'frames', some interlocking, others slotted hierarchically in other frames, could it begin to show signs of intelligence.

While speculating about developments in the 1990s Minsky has referred to 'societies of the mind'. A computer capable of recognizing shadows would be unable to process perspective or parallax. Yet, the untutored human mind can normally handle all three. The aim should therefore be to write a program "that allows each expert system to exploit the body of knowledge that lies buried in the others."

Mitchell, Maria (1818–1889) *American astronomer*

Mitchell was born in Nantucket, Massachusetts, the daughter of William Mitchell, who started life as a cooper and became a school teacher and amateur astronomer of some distinction. Her brother, Henry Mitchell, became the leading American hydrographer. She herself was mainly educated by her father, whom she helped in the checking of chronometers for the local whaling fleet and in determining the longitude of Nantucket during the 1831 eclipse. From 1824 to 1842 she worked as librarian at the Nantucket Athenum and in 1849 she became the first woman to be employed full time by the US Nautical Almanac, with whom she computed the ephemerides of Venus. Finally, in 1865 she was appointed professor of astronomy and director of the observatory at the newly founded Vassar College.

Maria Mitchell was clearly fortunate to come from a highly talented family. She was also helped by coming from Nantucket, an area where women were expected to demonstrate an unusual degree of independence while the local men were absent on their long whaling voyages. It was also an area where it was common for the average person to possess a familiarity with mathematics, astronomy, and navigation.

She is mainly remembered today for her discovery, in 1847, of a new comet.

Mitchell, Peter Dennis (1920–1992)
British biochemist

Born at Mitcham in Surrey, Mitchell was educated at Cambridge University, where he obtained his PhD in 1950. He remained at Cambridge, teaching in the department of biochemistry until 1955, when he moved to Edinburgh University as director of the Chemical Biology Unit. In 1964 Mitchell made the unusual decision to set up his own private research institution, the Glynn Research Laboratory, in Bodmin, Cornwall.

It was well known that the cell obtains its energy from the adenosine triphosphate (ATP) molecule; it was also clear that ATP was made by coupling adenosine diphosphate (ADP) to an inorganic phosphate group by the process known to biochemists as oxidative phosphorylation. What was less clear was just how this happened and it was widely assumed that it was controlled by a number of enzymes. Despite considerable effort the proposed enzymes remained surprisingly elusive.

Beginning in 1961 Mitchell proposed a completely different and totally original model, without any obvious precursors and judged to be unorthodox to the point of eccentricity. He suggested a physical mechanism by which an electrochemical gradient is created across the cellular membrane; this, in turn, creates a proton current capable of controlling the phosphorylation.

For his account of such processes Mitchell was awarded the 1978 Nobel Prize for chemistry.

Mitscherlich, Eilhardt (1794–1863)
German chemist

Mitscherlich, who was born at Neuende in Germany, studied oriental languages at Heidelberg and Berlin. He then turned to the study of medicine at Göttingen in 1817, where he became interested in crystallography. For two years he worked with Jöns Berzelius in Stockholm, returning to Berlin in 1821, where he was appointed to the chair of chemistry.

While working on arsenates and phosphates, Mitscherlich realized that substances of a similar composition often have the same crystalline form, and from this he formulated, in 1819, his law of isomorphism. This was in opposition to the orthodox view of René Haüy that each substance has a distinctive crystalline form. Despite Haüy's rejection of the law, Berzelius accepted it and was quick to spot its significance, for if the composition of a substance X is known, and it is also known that X has a similarity of crystalline form with Y, then Y's composition can be derived. Thus knowing the composition of sulfur trioxide as SO_3, and that it has a similar form to 'chromic acid', Berzelius was able to give this compound the composition CrO_3. Using this technique Berzelius produced his revised table of atomic weights in 1826.

Mitscherlich also discovered selenic acid (1827), named benzene, and showed, in 1834, that if benzene reacts with nitric acid it forms nitrobenzene.

Möbius, August Ferdinand (1790–1868)
German mathematician

Möbius worked mainly on analytical geometry, topology, and theoretical astronomy. He was born at Schulpforta in Germany and held a chair in theoretical astronomy at Leipzig, making numerous contributions to the field with publications on planetary occultations ('eclipses') and celestial mechanics. His more purely mathematical work centers on geometry and topology.

Möbius is chiefly famed for his discovery of the *Möbius strip*, a one-sided surface formed by giving a rectangular strip a half-twist and then joining the ends together. He introduced the use of homogeneous coordinates into analytical geometry and did significant work in projective geometry, inventing the *Möbius net*, which became of central importance in the future development of the subject.

Mohorovičić, Andrija (1857–1936)
Croatian geologist

Mohorovičić was born the son of a shipwright in Volosko, Croatia, and educated at the University of Prague. He worked initially as a teacher and at the meteorological station in Bakar before being appointed a professor at the Zagreb Technical School in 1891 and at Zagreb University in 1897.

In 1909 he made his fundamental discovery of the *Mohorovičić discontinuity* (or *Moho*). From data obtained while he was observing a Croatian earthquake in 1909, Mohorovičić noticed that waves penetrating deeper into the Earth arrived sooner than waves traveling along its surface. He deduced from this that the Earth has a layered structure, the crust overlaying a more dense mantle in which earthquake waves could travel more quickly. The abrupt separation between the crust and the mantle Mohorovičić calculated as being about 20 miles (32 km) below the surface of the Earth.

As the crust is much thinner under the ocean beds – in some places only 3 miles thick – a project was set up in the 1960s to drill through the crust to the mantle. Mohole, as it became known, failed, however, largely as a result of the great financial cost involved and the inadequate technological expertise available for such a project.

Mohs, Friedrich (1773–1839) *German mineralogist*

Mohs was born at Gernrode in Saxony and studied at Halle and at the Freiberg Mining Academy under Abraham Werner. In 1812 he became curator of the mineral collection at the Johanneum in Graz. He succeeded Werner at Freiberg in 1818 and in 1826 he was appointed professor of mineralogy at Vienna.

In 1812 Mohs introduced the scale of mineral hardness – *Mohs scale* – named for him. Ten minerals whose hardness is known are ordered on a scale ranging from 1 (talc) to 10 (diamond), the general rule being that a higher number will scratch all lower numbers. The hardness of a mineral is judged by the ease with which its surface is scratched by these minerals whose values are known, and it can be given a numerical value.

Moissan, Ferdinand Frédéric Henri (1852–1907) *French chemist*

Moissan came from a poor background in Paris, France. He was the son of a railroad worker and was apprenticed to a pharmacist before studying chemistry under Edmond Frémy at the Muséum National d'Histoire Naturelle, Paris (1872). From 1880 he worked at the Ecole Supérieure de Pharmacie, being elected to the chair of toxicology in 1886 and the chair of inorganic chemistry in 1889. In the next year he became professor of chemistry at the University of Paris.

Moissan began studying fluorine compounds in 1884 and in 1886 succeeded in isolating fluorine gas by electrolyzing a solution of potassium fluoride in hydrofluoric acid, the whole process being contained in platinum. He received the Nobel Prize for chemistry for this work in 1906.

He also worked on synthetic diamonds. He was impressed by the discovery of tiny diamonds in some meteorites and concluded from this that if the conditions undergone by these in space could be reproduced in the laboratory it would be possible to convert carbon into diamond. He therefore put iron and carbon into a crucible, heated it in an electric furnace, and while white hot cooled it rapidly by plunging it into liquid. In theory, he felt that the cooling should exert sufficient pressure on the carbon to turn it into diamond. He claimed to have succeeded in producing artificial diamonds but there was a suggestion that one of his assistants had smuggled tiny diamonds into the mixture at the beginning of the experiment. Moissan did, however, use his electric furnace for important work in preparing metal nitrides, borides, and carbides, and in extracting a number of less common metallic elements, such as molybdenum, tantalum, and niobium.

Moivre, Abraham De *See* DE MOIVRE, ABRAHAM.

Molina, Mario José (1943–) *Mexican physical chemist*

Molina, the son of a diplomat, studied chemical engineering at the University of Mexico. After further study in Europe at the University of Freiburg and at the Sorbonne, Molina moved to the University of California, Berkeley, where he gained his PhD in 1972. He worked initially as a postdoctoral student at the Irvine campus of the University of California with F. S. Rowland. Following a spell at the Jet Propulsion Laboratory he moved to MIT in 1989 as professor of environmental sciences.

Rowland had become interested in the fate of the chlorofluorocarbons (CFCs) used as the propellant in most aerosol cans, and asked his new colleague if he would be interested in working out what happened to them as they rose into the stratosphere. It would be, Molina later confessed, "a nice, interesting, academic exercise."

He quickly worked out that as CFCs were stable they would eventually accumulate in the upper atmosphere. There, he argued, they would be broken up by ultraviolet light and chlorine atoms would be released. Rowland suggested that Molina should analyze how free chlorine atoms would behave. Molina suspected that a chain reaction would be produced, reducing the amount of ozone in the upper atmosphere. Despite this, Molina still thought the effect would be negligible. It was only when he discovered that the amount of CFCs released each year was about 1 million tonnes that he realized that much of the ozone layer could be destroyed. Molina published his results in a joint paper with ROWLAND in 1974. The National Academy of Sciences issued a report in 1976 confirming the work of Molina and Rowland and in 1978 CFCs used in aerosols were banned in the United States. In 1984 Joe Farman detected a 40% ozone loss over Antarctica.

For his work on CFCs and the ozone layer Molina shared the 1995 Nobel Prize for chemistry with Rowland and Paul CRUTZEN, thus becoming the first Mexican to receive a Nobel Prize for science.

Monge, Gaspard (1746–1818) French mathematician

Monge, who was born at Beaune in France, was trained as a draftsman at Mézières, where he later became professor of mathematics (1768). During the French Revolution he served on the committee that formulated the metric system (1791), became minister of the navy and the colonies (1792–93), and played a vital part in organizing the defense of France against the counterrevolutionary armies. He contributed significantly to the founding of the Ecole Polytechnique in 1795. Monge met Napoleon in 1796 and saw active service in Napoleon's army during the Egyptian campaign (1798–1801).

Monge's major mathematical achievements were the invention of descriptive geometry and the application of the techniques of analysis to the theory of curvature. The latter ultimately led to the revolutionary work of Georg RIEMANN on geometry and curvature.

Following Napoleon's fall from power in 1815, Monge was expelled from the French Academy and deprived of all his honors.

Moniz, Antonio Egas See EGAS MONIZ, ANTONIO.

Monod, Jacques Lucien (1910–1976) French biochemist

Monod was born in Paris, and graduated from the university there in 1931; he became assistant professor of zoology in 1934, having spent the years immediately following his graduation investigating the origin of life. After World War II, in which he served in the Resistance, he joined the Pasteur Institute, becoming head of the cellular biochemistry department in 1953.

In 1958 Monod began working with François JACOB and Arthur Pardee on the regulation of enzyme synthesis in mutant bacteria. This work led to the formulation, by Monod and Jacob, of a theory explaining gene action and particularly how genes are switched on and off as necessary. In 1960 they introduced the term 'operon' for a closely linked group of genes, each of which controls a different step in a given biochemical pathway. The following year they postulated the existence of a molecule, messenger RNA, that carries the genetic information necessary for protein synthesis from the operon to the ribosomes, where proteins are made. For this work Monod and Jacob were awarded the 1965 Nobel Prize for physiology or medicine, which they shared with André LWOFF, who was also working on bacterial genetics.

In 1971 Monod became director of the Pasteur Institute and in the same year published the best-selling book *Chance and Necessity*, in which he argued that life arose by chance and progressed to its present level as a necessary consequence of the pressures exerted by natural selection.

Montagnier, Luc (1932–) French virologist

Montagnier, who was born at Chabris in France, was educated at the universities of Poitiers and Paris. He joined the Viral Oncology Unit of the Pasteur Institute in 1972 and was appointed professor of virology in 1985.

Montagnier's team at the Institute were searching for, among other things, possible links between cancers and retroviruses. The retroviruses had been described in 1970 by Temin and Baltimore and were distinguished from other viruses by having RNA rather than DNA genes. In early 1983 they were presented with a blood sample from a patient showing early signs of AIDS. Reverse transcriptase, an enzyme characteristic of retroviruses, was found in the blood. Montagnier sought to identify the virus. It was not HTLV-1, a retrovirus recently discovered by Robert GALLO, as serum from the AIDS patient did not react with samples of HTLV-1 provided by Gallo. The virus was found in T-4 cells, specialized lymphocytes of the immune system, and was therefore named LAV as an acronym for 'lymphadenopathy associated virus'. Electron micrographs taken of LAV differed from those of HTLV-1.

Montagnier went on to develop a blood test for the presence of LAV. Antibodies to LAV were found in a number of patients with AIDS. As the sensitivity of the test increased, Montagnier was able to identify more and more AIDS patients and by October 1983 he was convinced that LAV was the cause of AIDS. By this time, however, Gallo had isolated a new retrovirus, HTLV-3, which he was equally convinced was the cause of AIDS. It was eventually agreed, despite some considerable initial controversy, that HTLV-3 and LAV were to all intents and purposes the same virus. In 1986 it was officially renamed HIV and the patent for HIV blood tests carried the names of both Gallo and Montagnier.

A further advance was made by Montagnier in late 1985 while examining blood samples from Guinea-Bissau in West Africa. He was puzzled by the fact that some of the samples came from apparently HIV-negative AIDS patients, even though they had been tested with a sensitive new probe. Montagnier resolved the issue by isolating a virus from the samples which differed from electronmicrographs of HIV-1. Montagnier named the virus HIV-2 and demonstrated that antibodies to the new virus were commonly found in blood samples from West African AIDS patients.

Montgolfier, Etienne Jacques de

(1745–1799) *French balloonist. See*
MONTGOLFIER, MICHEL JOSEPH DE.

Montgolfier, Michel Joseph de

(1740–1810) *French balloonist*

Etienne and Michel Montgolfier, the sons of a paper manufacturer from Vidalon-les-Annonay, Lyons, engaged themselves in various enterprises. Michel founded his own paper factory in 1771, while Etienne practiced as an architect until 1782 when called upon to run the family factory at Vidalon. In later life Michel abandoned business and was appointed in 1800 to the faculty of the Conservatoire des Arts et Métiers.

Like many before, the brothers had noticed how pieces of paper thrown into the fire would often rise aloft in a column of hot air. They were interested enough to see whether paper bags filled with hot smoke would rise. Satisfied with their small-scale experiments they became convinced that something much larger was viable. On June 4 1783 they gave the first public demonstration of their work at Annonay. The balloon was made of linen and lined with paper, measured 36 feet across, and weighed 500 pounds. Once inflated over a fire burning chopped straw, the balloon ascended to a height of 6000 feet before coming down ten minutes later, a mile and a half away. News quickly spread throughout France. Called to Versailles they demonstrated their balloon, this time carrying a sheep, a cock,

and a duck, before Louis XVI and Marie Antoinette. The balloon landed two miles away in a wood with the animals none the worse for their journey.

The first manned flight was made by François de Rozier in Paris in October 1783. Of the brothers, only Michel flew in the balloon, making an ascent of 3000 feet with seven other people in 1784.

Moore, Stanford (1913–1982) *American biochemist*

Moore, who was born in Chicago, Illinois, graduated in chemistry from Vanderbilt University in 1935 and received his PhD from the University of Wisconsin in 1938. He then joined the staff of the Rockefeller Institute, spending his entire career there and serving as professor of biochemistry from 1952 onward.

One of the major achievements of modern science has been the determination by Frederick SANGER in 1955 of the complete amino acid sequence of a protein. Sanger's success with the insulin molecule inspired Moore and his Rockefeller colleague, **William Stein** (1911–1980), to tackle the larger molecule of the enzyme ribonuclease. Although their work was lightened by the availability of techniques pioneered by Sanger the labor involved was still immense until eased by their development of the first automatic amino-acid analyzer.

They inserted a small amount of the amino-acid mixture into the top of a five-foot column containing resin. They then washed down the mixture using solutions of varying acidity. The individual amino acids travel down the column at different rates depending on their relative affinity for the solution and for the resin. It is possible to adjust the rates of travel so that the separate amino acids emerge from the bottom of the column at predetermined and well-spaced intervals. The colorless amino acids were then detected with ninhydrin, a reagent that forms a blue color on heating with proteins and amino acids. A continuous plot of the intensity of the blue color gives a series of peaks, each corresponding to a certain amino acid with the area under the peak indicating the amount of each.

By the end of the 1950s Moore and Stein had not only established the sequence of ribonuclease but they were also able to indicate the most likely active site on the single-chained molecule. For this work they shared the 1972 Nobel Prize for chemistry with Christian ANFINSEN.

Morgan, Thomas Hunt (1866–1945)
American geneticist

Born in Lexington, Kentucky, Morgan studied zoology at the State College of Kentucky, graduating in 1886. He received his PhD from Johns Hopkins University in 1890 and from 1891 to 1904 was associate professor of zoology at Bryn Mawr College. He carried out his most important work between 1904 and 1928, while professor of experimental zoology at Columbia University. Here he became involved in the controversy that followed the rediscovery, in 1900, of Gregor Mendel's laws of inheritance.

Many scientists had noted that Mendel's segregation ratios fitted in well with the observed pattern of chromosome movement at meiosis. Morgan, however, continued to regard Mendel's laws with skepticism, especially the law of independent assortment, and with good reason. It was known by then that many more characters are determined genetically than there are chromosomes and therefore each chromosome must control many traits. It was also known that chromosomes are inherited as complete units, so various characters must be linked together on a single chromosome and would be expected to be inherited together.

In 1908 Morgan began breeding experiments with the fruit fly *Drosophila melanogaster*, which has four pairs of chromosomes. Morgan's early results with mutant types substantiated Mendel's law of segregation, but he soon found evidence of linkage through his discovery that mutant white-eyed flies are also always male. He thus formulated the only necessary amendment to Mendel's laws – that the law of independent assortment only applies to genes located on different chromosomes.

Morgan found that linkages could be broken when homologous chromosomes paired at meiosis and exchanged material in a process known as 'crossing over'. Gene linkages are less likely to be broken when the genes are close together on the chromosome, and therefore by recording the frequency of broken linkages, the positions of genes along the chromosome can be mapped. Morgan and his colleagues produced the first chromosome maps in 1911.

For his contributions to genetics, Morgan received the Nobel Prize for physiology or medicine in 1933. A prolific writer, his most influential books – produced with colleagues at Columbia – are *The Mechanism of Mendelian Heredity* (1915) and *The Theory of the Gene* (1926).

Morgan, William Wilson (1906–1994)
American astronomer

Morgan, who was born in Bethesda, Tennessee, studied at the Washington and Lee University and then at the University of Chicago where he obtained his BSc in 1927 and his PhD in 1931. The following year, he took up an appointment at the Yerkes Observatory, where he served as professor from 1947 to 1966 and Sunny Distinguished Professor of Astronomy from 1966 to 1974. He was Director of the Yerkes and McDonald observatories from 1960 to 1963.

The standard system of spectral classification of stars, the Henry Draper system, assigned the majority of stars to one of the classes, O, B, A, F, G, K, or M, which were each subdivided into ten categories numbered from 0 to 9. In this classification our Sun is assigned the number G2. Useful as the Draper system is, Morgan realized that it had its limitations. He pointed out that the system was based only on the surface temperature of stars and commonly produced cases where two stars, like Procyon in Canis Minor and Mirfak in Perseus, fell into the same spectral class, F5 in this case, yet differed in luminosity by a factor of several hundreds.

Consequently, in collaboration with Philip Childs Keenan and Edith Kellman, he introduced the *Yerkes system* or *MKK system* (also known as the Morgan–Keenan classification) in 1943 in *An Atlas of Stellar Spectra with an Outline of Spectral Classification*. The new system was two dimensional, containing in addition to the spectral typing a luminosity index. This was used to classify stars in terms of their intrinsic brightness by means of Roman numerals from I to VI, and ranged from supergiants (I), giants (II and III), subgiants (IV), main-sequence stars (V), to subdwarfs (VI). Procyon thus becomes a F5 IV star while Mirfak is a distinguishable F5 I supergiant.

In the 1940s Walter Baade had shown that hot O and B stars were characteristic members of the spiral arms of a galaxy. Morgan and his colleagues thus began to trace out the structure of our own Galaxy by searching for clouds of hydrogen ionized by O and B stars. By 1953 they claimed to have identified the Perseus, Orion, and Sagittarius arms of the Galaxy, thus providing good evidence for its spiral structure. Morgan also worked on star brightness and discovered so-called 'flash' variables – stars that change their luminosity very quickly.

Morley, Edward Williams (1838–1923)
American chemist and physicist. See MICHELSON, ALBERT ABRAHAM.

Morton, William Thomas Green
(1819–1868) *American dentist*

Morton, who was born the son of a small farmer and village shopkeeper in Charlton City, Massachusetts, is believed to have trained as a dentist at the Baltimore College of Dentistry. After a brief partnership with Horace Wells, Morton set up in practice in Boston.

To alleviate the pain of tooth extraction Morton experimented with such drugs as opium and alcohol, but only succeeded in making his patients violently sick. The chemist Charles Jackson advised Morton to try ether, an old student standby, as a local anesthetic. This was moderately effective and Morton decided to try ether inhalation to produce general anesthesia. He first used ether to extract a tooth on 30 September 1860. His initial successes left Morton confident enough to offer to demonstrate his technique at the Massachusetts General Hospital. He was successful in using it on a patient who was undergoing a tumor operation. His innovation was well received by the leading surgeon John Warren and the use of ether quickly gained acceptance in medical practice. The news soon spread to Europe and in December 1846 Robert Liston, the skilled British surgeon, used ether in a painless and successful leg amputation at University College Hospital, London.

Morton subsequently went to a lot of trouble trying to patent his anesthetic and fight off competitors, notably Jackson, who were claiming priority. His wrangling with Jackson, the government, and the law courts achieved little and Morton died virtually penniless while traveling to New York to answer yet another attack on him from Jackson.

Mosander, Carl Gustav (1797–1858)
Swedish chemist

Born at Kalmar in Sweden, Mosander started his career as a physician and became Jöns Berzelius's assistant after a time in the army. He became curator of minerals at the Royal Academy of Science in Stockholm before succeeding Berzelius as secretary. In 1832 he became professor of chemistry and mineralogy at the Karolinska Institute, Stockholm.

Mosander worked chiefly on the lanthanoid elements. These had been known since the discovery of yttrium by Johan Gadolin in 1794 and cerium by Martin Klaproth in 1803. He began by examining the earth from which cerium had been isolated, ceria. From this he derived in 1839 the oxide of a new element, which he called lanthanum, from the Greek meaning 'to be

hidden'. In 1843 he announced the discovery of three new rare-earth elements – erbium, terbium, and didymium. As it happened, didymium was not elementary, being shown in 1885 by Karl Auer von Welsbach to consist of two elements – praseodymium and neodymium.

Moseley, Henry Gwyn Jeffreys
(1887–1915) *British physicist*

Moseley came from an academic family in Weymouth. He graduated in natural sciences from Oxford University in 1910 and then joined Ernest Rutherford at Manchester University to work on radioactivity, although he soon turned his attention to x-ray spectroscopy. He returned to Oxford in 1913 to continue his work under J. S. E. Townsend.

When x-rays are produced by an element a continuous spectrum is emitted together with a more powerful radiation of a few specific wavelengths characteristic of the element. To investigate the positive charge on atomic nuclei Moseley examined these characteristic spectral lines using crystal diffraction. For a number of elements, he discovered a regular shift in the lines with increasing atomic weight. From this he determined for each element an integer approximately proportional to the square root of the frequency of one of its spectral lines. This integer, now called the atomic number (or proton number), equaled the positive charge on the atomic nuclei. Moseley's work led to major improvements in Dmitri MENDELEEV's periodic table and enabled elements to be classified in a new and more satisfactory manner.

At the outbreak of World War I Moseley enlisted in the army and was commissioned in the Royal Engineers. His death, from a sniper's bullet at Gallipoli, cut short what promised to be a most brilliant career in science.

Mössbauer, Rudolph Ludwig
(1929–) *German physicist*

Born at Munich in Germany, Mössbauer was educated in Munich-Pasing and, after a year in industrial laboratories, studied physics at the Munich Technical University. There he passed his intermediate degree in 1952, and completed his thesis in 1954. From 1955 to 1957 he did postgraduate research at the Max-Planck Institute for Medical Research in Heidelberg, gaining his doctorate from the Technical University in 1958.

From 1953 he had been studying the absorption of gamma rays in matter, in particular the phenomenon of nuclear resonance absorption. Normally, when an atomic nucleus emits a gamma ray, it will recoil, and this recoil action will influence the wavelength of the gamma ray emitted. Mössbauer discovered that, contrary to classical predictions, at a sufficiently low temperature the nucleus can be locked into position in the crystal lattice, and it is the lattice itself that recoils, with negligible effect on the wavelength. The result is that the wavelength can be defined with extremely high precision (about 1 part in 10^{12}). As with emission, so it is with absorption; a crystal of the same material under similar conditions absorbs gamma rays at the same highly specific wavelength – a resonance phenomenon akin to a well-tuned radio receiver and transmitter. If, however, the conditions are slightly different, the small changes in wavelength can be accurately compensated and thus measured using the Doppler effect (by moving the source relative to the receiver).

This phenomenon of recoilless nuclear resonance absorption, now known as the *Mössbauer effect*, has given physicists and chemists a very useful tool through the high precision of measurement it allows. In particular, it allowed the first laboratory testing (and verification in 1960) of the prediction of Einstein's general theory of relativity that the frequency of an electromagnetic radiation (in this case gamma rays) is influenced by gravity. The Mössbauer effect is now commonly employed as a spectroscopic method in chemical and solid-state physics because of its ability to detect differences in the electronic environments surrounding certain nuclei (*Mössbauer spectroscopy*).

In 1960, after finishing his studies at the Technical University, Mössbauer went on to continue his investigations of gamma absorption at the California Institute of Technology, Pasadena, where he was appointed professor of physics the next year. In 1961 he also received the Nobel Prize for physics, sharing the honor with Robert Hofstadter who had advanced knowledge of the nucleus by electron-scattering methods.

Mott, Sir Nevill Francis (1905–1996)
British physicist

Born in Leeds, Mott studied at Cambridge University, gaining his bachelor's degree in 1927 and his master's in 1930. He never pursued a doctorate, but from 1930 until 1933 was a lecturer and fellow of Gonville and Caius College, Cambridge. Subsequently he moved to Bristol University as a professor of theoretical physics. In 1948 he became director of Bristol's physics laboratories, but returned later to Cambridge as Cavendish

Professor of Experimental Physics, where he served from 1954 until his retirement in 1971.

Mott's work in the early 1930s was on the quantum theory of atomic collisions and scattering. With Harrie Massey he wrote the first of several classic texts, *The Theory of Atomic Collisions* (1934). Other influential texts that followed were on *The Theory of Properties of Metals and Alloys* with H. Jones (1936) and *Electronic Processes in Ionic Crystals* with R. W. Gurney (1940). Each marked a significant phase of active research. Mott began to explore also the defects and surface phenomena involved in the photographic process (explaining latent-image formation), and did significant work on dislocations, defects, and the strength of crystals.

By the mid 1950s, Mott was able to turn his attention to problems of disordered materials, liquid metals, impurity bands in semiconductors, and the glassy semiconductors. His models of the solid state became more and more complex, and included an analysis of electronic processes in metal–insulator transitions, often called *Mott transitions*.

In 1977 Mott shared the Nobel Prize for physics with Philip ANDERSON and John VAN VLECK for their "fundamental theoretical investigations of the electronic structure of magnetic and disordered systems." Mott was knighted in 1962. His autobiography, *A Life in Science*, was published in 1986.

Mottelson, Benjamin Roy (1926–   )
American–Danish physicist

Mottelson, who was born in Chicago, Illinois, graduated from Purdue University in 1947 and gained his PhD in theoretical physics at Harvard University in 1950.

From Harvard, Mottelson gained a traveling fellowship to the Institute of Theoretical Physics in Copenhagen (now the Neils Bohr Institute). There he worked with Neils Bohr's son, Aage BOHR, on problems of the atomic nucleus. In particular, they considered models of the nucleus and combined the two principal theories current at the time – one based on independent particles regarded as arranged in shells and the other treating the nucleus as a collective entity exhibiting liquid-drop-like behavior – and advanced a unified theory. They worked out the consequences of the interplay between the individual particles and the collective motions, specified the structure of the rotational and vibrational excitations and the coupling between them, and showed how the collective concepts could be applied to the nuclei of various elements. For their work on nuclear structure Mottelson, Bohr, and James RAINWATER (Bohr's earlier collaborator at Columbia University) shared the 1975 Nobel Prize for physics.

Mottelson held a research position in CERN (the European Center for Nuclear Research) from 1953 until 1957, then returned to Copenhagen to take up a professorship at the Nordic Institute for Theoretical Atomic Physics (NORDITA) adjacent to the Neils Bohr Institute. He took Danish nationality in 1973.

Together with Aage Bohr, he has published *Nuclear Structure* (2 vols. 1969–75).

Moulton, Forest Ray (1872–1952)
American astronomer

Born in Osceola County, Michigan, Moulton was educated in frontier schools, Albion College, and the University of Chicago where he obtained his PhD in 1899. He taught there until 1926, being made full professor in 1912. From 1927 to 1936 he worked in business before returning to science as executive secretary of the American Association for the Advancement of Science from 1936 to 1948.

Moulton is still remembered for his formulation of the planetismal theory of the origin of the planets in collaboration with Thomas Chamberlin in 1904. They suggested that a star had passed close to the Sun and that this resulted in the ejection of filaments of matter from both stars. The filaments cooled into tiny solid fragments, 'planetesimals'. On collision the small particles stuck together (a process known as 'accretion'). Thus over a very long period, grains became pebbles, then boulders, then even larger bodies. For larger bodies, the gravitational force of attraction would accelerate. In this way the protoplanets formed. This formation by accretion is still accepted although the stellar origin of the planetesimals has been largely dropped.

Mueller, Erwin Wilhelm (1911–1977)
German–American physicist

Mueller was born in Berlin and studied engineering at the university there, gaining his PhD in 1935. He worked in Berlin at Siemens and Halske (1935–37) and at Stabilovolt (1937–46). Subsequently he was at the Altenberg Engineering School (1946–47) and the Fritz Haber Institute (1948–52), from where he moved to the Pennsylvania State University. He became a naturalized American in 1962.

He is noted for his fundamental experimental work on solid surfaces. In 1936 he invented the field-emission microscope. In this device a fine metal point is placed a distance away from a phosphorescent screen in a high vacuum with a very high negative voltage applied to the point. Electrons are emitted from the surface under the influence of the electric field (field emission) and these travel to the screen where they produce a magnified image of the surface of the tip. The instrument is used to study reactions at surfaces.

In 1951 he made a further advance using the principle of field ionization. In the field-ion microscope the tip is at a positive potential in a low pressure of inert gas. Atoms of gas adsorbing on the tip are ionized and the positive ions are repelled from the tip and produce the image. The resolution is much better than in the field-emission microscope; in 1956, by cooling the tip in liquid helium, Mueller was able to resolve individual surface atoms for the first time.

As a further refinement Mueller used a field-ion microscope with a mass spectrometer, so that individual atoms on the surface could be seen, desorbed, and identified (the atom-probe field-ion microscope).

Muller, Alex (1927–) *Swiss physicist*

Born at Basel in Switzerland, Muller was educated at the Federal Institute of Technology, Zurich, where he obtained his PhD in 1958. After working for a few years at the Batelle Institute in Geneva, he returned to Zurich (1963) to take up a post at the IBM Research Laboratory at Rüschlikon, where he has remained ever since.

In 1911 KAMERLINGH-ONNES discovered the phenomenon of superconductivity. He found that a current passing through mercury at 4 K, that is four degrees above absolute zero, met with no resistance. To utilize this discovery fully the temperature at which materials became superconductive, the critical temperature (T_c), would have to be raised to some more economically accessible level. Yet 75 years' intensive research had raised the critical temperature no higher than 23.3 K for a niobium–germanium alloy. And to cool the alloy to this point requires bathing it in either expensive liquid helium (bp 4.2 K) or the cheaper but flammable liquid hydrogen (bp 20.3 K).

Muller first began to work on the problem in 1983. He ignored the usual candidates for a high critical temperature and turned instead to look at ceramic metal oxides. This was partly because his laboratory had worked with oxides of this kind for many years and had built up a considerable expertise in them. Also, he suspected, their lattice structure was of the right kind to allow superconductivity. In January 1986 Muller, working with his IBM colleague

Georg BEDNORZ, found that a mixed lanthanum, barium, and copper oxide showed a change to superconducting behavior below 35 K (−238° C). Once the initial advance had been made, other physicists were quick to follow and to confirm and extend Muller's work.

The significance of Muller's discovery was recognized with unusual speed by the Nobel authorities when, in the following year, they awarded the Nobel Prize for physics jointly to Muller and Bednorz.

Müller, Franz Joseph, Baron von Reichenstein (1740–1825) *Austrian geologist*. See KLAPROTH, MARTIN HEINRICH.

Muller, Hermann Joseph (1890–1967) *American geneticist*

Born in New York City, Muller was awarded a scholarship to Columbia University in 1907 and specialized in heredity during his undergraduate studies. On graduation he took up a teaching fellowship in physiology at Cornell Medical School, gaining his master's degree in 1912 for research on the transmission of nerve impulses. During this period he continued working at Columbia in his spare time, contributing to the genetic researches on *Drosophila* fruit flies. He was employed officially at Columbia in 1912 and received his PhD in 1916 for his now classic studies on the crossing over of chromosomes. He was also a coauthor of *The Mechanism of Mendelian Heredity* (1915), a fundamental contribution to classical genetics.

In 1915, at the request of Julian Huxley, Muller moved to the Rice Institute, Houston, Texas, where he began studying mutation. By 1918 he had found evidence that raising the temperature increases mutation rate. In 1920, after a brief spell back at Columbia, he joined the University of Texas as an associate professor, becoming a professor in 1925. In 1926 he found that x-rays induce mutations, a discovery for which he eventually received the 1946 Nobel Prize for physiology or medicine.

In 1933 Muller spent the first of eight years in Europe at the Institute for Brain Research, Berlin. Hitler's rise to power forced him to leave Germany and he moved to the Academy of Sciences, Leningrad, at the invitation of Nikolai Vavilov. Muller believed that in a communist state he would be able to develop his own socialist ideas and apply his research to improve the human condition. However, the advent of Lysenkoism effectively hampered most genetic research in Russia and Muller left, volunteering to serve in the Spanish Civil War. He then worked at the Institute of Animal Genetics, Edinburgh, returning to America in 1940. He held a position at Amherst College, Massachusetts, from 1942 until 1945, when he became professor of zoology at Indiana University, remaining there for the rest of his life.

Muller made important theoretical contributions to genetics. He visualized the gene as the origin of life, because only genes can replicate themselves, and he believed all selection and therefore evolution acted at the level of the gene. He worried about the increasing number of mutations accumulating in human populations, which can survive because of modern medical technology, and proposed a program of eugenics to overcome the problem. He fully realized the harm to human chromosomes that can result from ionizing radiation and campaigned against excessive use of x-rays in medicine, careless handling of nuclear fuels, and testing of atomic bombs.

Muller is seen by many as the most influential geneticist of the 20th century, mainly through his appreciation of genetic mutation as fundamental to future genetic research. He published over 350 works, the most important paper being *Artificial Transmutation of the Gene* (1927).

Müller, Johannes Peter (1801–1858) *German physiologist*

Müller, a shoemaker's son from Koblenz in Germany, graduated in medicine from the University of Bonn in 1822. He worked as a pathologist in Bonn until 1833 when he moved to the University of Berlin as professor of anatomy and physiology, a post he retained until his death.

Müller was the most important figure in 19th-century German physiology. Not only did he number among his pupils such figures as Hermann von Helmholtz, Carl Ludwig, Rudolf Virchow, and Max Schultze but those he did not teach were reached by his influential work, *Handbuch der Physiologie des Menschen* (2 vols., 1834–40; Handbook of Human Physiology).

It was in the field of neurophysiology that Müller made his major contribution to science. In 1831 he neatly and conclusively confirmed the law of Charles Bell and François Magendie, which first clearly distinguished between motor and sensory nerves. Using frogs and dogs, Müller cut through the posterior roots of nerves from a limb as they entered the spinal cord. The limb was insensible but not paralyzed. When however Müller severed the anterior root he found that the limb had become paralyzed but had not lost its sensibility.

He also worked on the cranial nerves and succeeded in showing that the first two branches of the trigeminal nerve are sensory while the third branch, to the jaw, contains motor fibers also. The vagus and the glossopharyngeal were, Müller claimed, mixed nerves.

Müller also formulated, in 1826, the law of specific nervous energies, which claimed that nerves are not merely passive conductors but that each particular type of nerve has its own special qualities. For example, the visual nerves, however they may be stimulated, are only capable of transmitting visual data. More specifically, if such a nerve is stimulated, whether by pressure, electric current, or a flashing light, the result will always be a visual experience.

After the completion of the *Handbuch* in 1840 Müller turned more to problems of anatomy and physiology. He worked with Robert Remak on embryological problems and was the first to describe what later became known as the *Müllerian duct*. This is a tube found in vertebrate embryos, which develops into the oviduct in females; it is found only vestigially in males. He also spent a large amount of time collecting and classifying zoological specimens.

Müller was much given to fits of depression, frequently feeling that his own creativity was exhausted. Consequently when he was found dead in bed, although no autopsy was ever performed, it was widely assumed that he had died by his own hand.

Müller, Paul Hermann (1899–1965)
Swiss chemist

Müller, who was born in Olten, Switzerland, was educated at the University of Basel where he obtained his PhD in 1925. From then until 1961 when he retired Müller worked for the Swiss dye firm of J.R. Geigy as a research chemist.

In 1935 Müller began looking for a potent and persistent insecticide that would nevertheless be harmless to plants and warm-blooded animals. Five years later he took out a patent on a chemical that had first been prepared in 1873. The compound was dichlorodiphenyltrichloroethane which not surprisingly, was soon abbreviated to DDT. It turned out to be cheap and simple to manufacture, requiring only chlorine, ethanol, benzene, and sulfuric acid, all of which were available in bulk from the heavy chemical industry.

It soon proved its effectiveness as an insecticide during World War II. Müller thought it to be toxic only against insects and soon extravagant claims were being made about the elimination of arthropod-borne diseases. Before long, however, the insects appeared to be more resilient than chemists had supposed and DDT more destructive of life and ecosystems than they imagined. Several advanced countries were to ban it.

Müller was awarded the Nobel Prize for physiology or medicine in 1948 for his discovery.

Mulliken, Robert Sanderson (1896–1986) *American physicist and chemist*

Mulliken was born in Newburyport, Massachusetts, the son of an organic chemist. He was educated at the Massachusetts Institute of Technology and at the University of Chicago, where he obtained his PhD in 1921. After working briefly at Washington Square College, New York, he was appointed to the staff of the University of Chicago, where he served as professor of physics from 1931 until he retired in 1961. From 1961 he was Distinguished Service Professor of Physics and Chemistry at Chicago and Distinguished Research Professor of Chemical Physics at Florida State University.

It was Mulliken, in 1922, who first suggested a method of isotope separation by evaporative centrifuging. Most of his research career was concerned with the interpretation of molecular spectra and with the application of quantum theory to the electronic states of molecules.

Mulliken, with Friedrich Hund, developed the molecular-orbital theory of chemical bonding, which is based on the idea that electrons in a molecule move in the field produced by all the nuclei. The atomic orbitals of isolated atoms become molecular orbitals, extending over two or more atoms in the molecule. He showed how the relative energies of these orbitals could be obtained from the spectra of the molecule.

Mulliken's approach to finding molecular orbitals was to combine atomic orbitals (LCAO, or linear combination of atomic orbitals). He showed that energies of bonds could be obtained by the amount of overlap of atomic orbitals.

Another of Mulliken's contributions is the application of electronegativity – the ability of a particular atom in a molecule to draw electrons to itself. He showed that this property was given by the formula $\frac{1}{2}(I + E)$, where I is the ionization potential of the atom and E is its electron affinity.

He also made major contributions to the theory and interpretation of molecular spectra. In 1966 he was awarded the Nobel Prize for chemistry for "his fundamental work concerning chemical bonds and the electronic structure of molecules by the molecular-orbital method."

Mullis, Kary Banks (1944–) *American biochemist*

Born in Lenoir, North Carolina, Mullis was educated at Georgia Institute of Technology and at the University of California, Berkeley, where he completed his PhD in 1973. After postdoctoral periods at the University of Kansas Medical School and at the San Francisco campus of the University of California, Mullis joined the Cetus Corporation of Emeryville, California, in 1979.

One Friday night in April 1983 while driving to his weekend cabin, Mullis has recorded, it suddenly struck him that there was a method of producing unlimited copies of DNA fragments simply and *in vitro* (i.e., outside living cells). Previously, fragments could only be produced in limited numbers, in cells, and with much effort. Mullis named his method the 'polymerase chain reaction' (PCR). The significance of the reaction can be judged by the price of $300 million placed by Cetus on the PCR patent sold to Hoffman-La Roche in 1991.

The first stage of the process is to heat DNA containing the required genetic segment in order to unravel the helix. Primers can then be added to mark out the target sequence. If, then, the enzyme DNA polymerase together with a number of free bases are added, two copies of the target sequence will be produced. These two copies can then be heated, separated, and once more produce two further copies each. The cycle, lasting no more than a few minutes, can be repeated as long as supplies last, doubling the target sequence each time. With geometric growth of this kind, more than 100 billion copies can be made in a few hours.

Relations between Mullis and Cetus quickly soured. He left the corporation in 1986 to work for a plastics manufacturer. But as the importance of his work began to be recognized Mullis found himself in sufficient demand to warrant his setting up as a consultant. One of his clients was Cetus as they fought off challenges to the PCR patent from DuPont and others. Mullis himself claims to be "tired of PCR" and more interested in "artificial intelligence, tunneling microscopes, science fiction, and surfing lessons."

Murad, Ferid (1936–) *American physician and pharmacologist*

Murad was born in Whiting, Indiana, and graduated as an MD from the Western Reserve University School of Medicine, Cleveland, Ohio, in 1965. Three years later he gained his PhD from the department of pharmacology at the same university. He has held many important appointments; since 1988 he has worked at the Northwestern University Medical School, Chicago, Illinois. In 1998 he shared the Nobel Prize for physiology or medicine with Robert FURCHGOTT and Louis IGNARRO for their discovery that molecules of the gas nitrogen monoxide (nitric oxide, NO) can transmit signals in the cardiovascular system.

The hitherto unknown substance endothelium-derived relaxing factor (EDRF) had been discovered by Furchgott in 1980. Murad researched the action of glyceryl trinitrate (nitroglycerin) and related vasodilators, and in 1977 discovered that they release nitrogen monoxide, which relaxes the walls of smooth muscle cells. It thus has the effect of controlling the blood pressure and this is why glyceryl trinitrate is prescribed as a drug to treat the heart condition atherosclerosis (as ironically it once was for Alfred Nobel, who invented the nitroglycerin-containing dynamite). Murad also speculated that hormones and other endogenous factors might act in a similar way, although no evidence of this was forthcoming.

Murphy, William Parry (1892–1987) *American physician. See* WHIPPLE, GEORGE HOYT.

Murray, Joseph Edward (1919–) *American surgeon*

Murray was born in Milford, Massachusetts. Educated at Holy Cross College and at Harvard University, he embarked on a career in medicine, specializing in plastic surgery. He worked at the Peter Bent Brigham Hospital, Boston, becoming chief plastic surgeon (1964–86), held a similar position at the Children's Hospital Medical Center, Boston (1972–85), and served as professor of surgery at Harvard Medical School from 1970 to 1986.

Murray was a pioneer of kidney transplantation. In December 1954 he performed the first operation to implant a donor kidney into the pelvis of the recipient and attach it via the ureter to the bladder. Earlier attempts had placed the transplanted organ outside the body cavity, at sites such as the groin and armpit. The patient in Murray's operation was Richard Herrick, who received a kidney from his identical twin, Ronald.

The use of an organ from an identical sibling overcame the great obstacle of transplant surgery, namely rejection of the transplanted organ by the recipient's immune system. By receiving an organ of virtually identical tissue type, this first patient survived for eight years. For patients receiving organs from less closely related donors, the outlook was much worse.

Murray endeavored to improve the survival of the transplanted organ by suppressing the recipient's immune responses immediately prior to the operation. He conducted trials of the drug azathioprine, which killed cells of the immune system and so reduced the ability of the patient's own defense mechanism to reject the 'foreign' tissue of a transplanted organ. Azathioprine had been developed by the British researcher, Roy Calne (1930–), working in collaboration with Murray at Boston. The drug proved to be an effective and much less hazardous alternative to Murray's initial method of using a massive dose of x-rays to suppress the recipient's immune system. (Azathioprine has now been superseded by cyclosporine, also developed by Calne.)

For his work in developing fundamental techniques in transplantation surgery, Murray was awarded the 1990 Nobel Prize for physiology or medicine, jointly with E. Donnall THOMAS.

Muspratt, James (1793–1886) *Irish industrial chemist*

Muspratt, the son of a cork-cutter, was born and educated in Dublin before being apprenticed to a druggist. He developed an early interest in chemistry but before going into business he led an adventurous life and fought in Spain in the Peninsular War in both the army and the navy. He returned to Dublin in 1814 where, with the help of a small inheritance received in 1818, he manufactured various chemicals in a small way.

Muspratt moved to Liverpool, where he produced sulfuric acid, in 1822 and was quick to see the importance of the abolition in 1823 of the £30 per ton duty on salt. Cheap salt and the Leblanc process meant that a plentiful supply of soda could be produced for the large demands of the soap, glass, and dyeing industries. With this financial incentive Muspratt set up on Merseyside the third soda plant in Britain. Close to both the salt mines of Cheshire and the textile industry of Lancashire, he was ideally situated. The need for expansion drove him into partnership with Josias Gamble and they founded the alkali industry in St. Helens (1828), but two years later he moved to Newton-le-Willows on his own.

(The area close to his original works is still known in the town as 'Vitriol Square'.)

One of the major problems of the Leblanc process was its production of quantities of hydrochloric acid gas as a waste product. This pollution raised protests, such as the letters appearing in a Liverpool paper in 1827 lamenting that the local church could not be seen from a distance of 100 yards (91 m) and was rapidly turning a dark color. The move to St. Helens only delayed the inevitable prosecutions. Muspratt was unwilling to use William Gossage's tower and following litigation (1832–50) he was eventually successfully prosecuted by the neighboring farmers whose land was being destroyed. For this reason he moved his factories to Widnes and Flint in 1850. Following his retirement in 1857 they were run by his sons until in 1890 they became part of the United Alkali Company.

Musschenbroek, Pieter van (1692–1761) *Dutch physicist*

Musschenbroek came from a family of instrument makers in Leiden in the Netherlands. He studied at the University of Leiden, where he gained an MD in 1715 and a PhD in 1719. After holding a chair of medicine at Duisburg (1721–23) and of natural philosophy at Utrecht (1723–40), Musschenbroek returned to Leiden and served as professor of physics until his death.

On 20 April 1746 Musschenbroek reported in a letter to René Reaumur details of a new but dangerous experiment he had carried out. He had suspended, by silk threads, a gun barrel, which received static electricity from a glass globe rapidly turned on its axis and rubbed with the hands. From the other end he suspended a brass wire, which hung into a round glass bottle, partly filled with water. He was in fact trying to 'preserve' electricity by storing it in a nonconductor.

When Musschenbroek held the bottle with one hand while trying to draw sparks from the gun-barrel he received a violent electric shock. He had accidentally made the important discovery of the Leyden jar – an early form of electrical capacitor. It was an event that captured both the popular and the scientific imagination and led to much effort by such scientists of the latter half of the 18th century as Benjamin Franklin to understand the nature and behavior of electricity. The German inventor Georg von Kleist independently discovered the Leyden jar in 1745.

Muybridge, Eadweard James (1830–1904) *American photographer*

Muybridge was born Edward James Muggeridge at Kingston-on-Thames in Surrey. He changed his surname and forename in his early twenties, the latter after the Saxon kings who were crowned at Kingston in the 10th century. Although Muybridge spent much of his life in America, making his first trip there in 1852, he always retained links with his birthplace. Indeed, following a serious stagecoach accident in 1860 he returned to England to recuperate from his injuries.

By 1867 Muybridge was back in America, working as partner to the San Francisco-based photographer, Carleton E. Watson, and he quickly established a reputation as a skilled exponent of landscapes with a series of prints taken in California's Yosemite Valley. In 1868 he was appointed director of photographic surveys for the US Government, and undertook photographic surveys of several remote regions, including the ports and harbors of newly purchased Alaska.

An interest in high-speed photography can be traced to the year 1872, when Muybridge was commissioned by the wealthy Californian racehorse owner, Leland Stanford, to attempt to settle the contentious issue of whether a trotting or galloping horse lifted all four feet clear of the ground at any point during its stride. Muybridge's attempts to capture this on film were of poor quality and less than convincing.

In October 1874 Muybridge's personal life was shattered when he was arrested for the murder of his wife's lover, whom Muybridge suspected was the father of the son born in April that year. Muybridge was held in prison for several months, but after a lengthy trial he was acquitted in February 1875. His wife, who had unsuccessfully sued for divorce, died later that year, leaving Muybridge to support the child.

Following a trip to Central America in 1875, and a dramatic panoramic sequence of pictures taken of San Francisco in 1877, Muybridge returned to his attempts at high-speed photography. He developed a more efficient shutter mechanism for the camera, and by using a battery of 12 cameras he was able to produce 12 sharply defined consecutive images of a galloping horse, all taken within half a second.

It was readily apparent that if such a sequence of pictures were viewed in rapid succession, the motion of the horse or other subject would be reproduced. Muybridge mounted the silhouettes of the horse on a glass disk, which was rotated and projected onto a screen through a device invented by the photographer and called a 'zoopraxiscope'. This was first demonstrated to the public in 1880, in what some would claim to be the first moving picture.

Muybridge's work was by now attracting considerable scientific interest, and in 1884 he began work at the University of Pennsylvania on what was to prove a celebrated series of high-speed studies of movement in both animals and human subjects. His new multilens camera could take 12 pictures on a single photographic plate in as little as one-fifth of a second. The results of this work were published in 11 volumes as *Animal Locomotion: an electro-photographic investigation of consecutive phases of animal movement* (1887). Included in this were his famous sequences of nude human subjects, often performing bizarre actions such as carrying a pan of water and sweeping with a broom.

The technique used by Muybridge could produce only very short sequences of moving pictures in the zoopraxiscope. However, the American inventor Thomas EDISON was impressed by them, and may have found in them inspiration for his own invention, the cine camera and its perforated roll film. Certainly Muybridge and Edison collaborated on an abortive attempt to match sound to Muybridge's picture sequences.

Muybridge returned to Kingston in 1900, and spent his final years there. He bequeathed his zoopraxiscope and other apparatus to the public library in his home town.

Naegeli, Karl Wilhelm von (1817–1891) *Swiss botanist*

Naegeli, the son of a physician from Kilchberg in Switzerland, began medical studies at Zurich but went on to study botany under Alphonse de Candolle at Geneva. After graduating in 1840 he studied philosophy in Berlin but resumed his botanical studies in 1842, when he left for Jena to work with Matthias Schleiden.

In 1842 Naegeli published an essay on pollen formation in which he accurately described cell division, realizing that the wall formed between two daughter cells is not the cause but the result of cell division. He noted the division of the nucleus and recorded the chromosomes as 'transitory cytoblasts'. By 1846 these investigations had convinced him that Schleiden's theory of cells budding off the nuclear surface was incorrect.

Naegeli discovered the antherozoids (male gametes) in ferns and archegonia (female sex organs) in *Ricciocarpus* but did not realize the analogy of these to the pollen and ovary of seed plants. In 1845 he began investigating apical growth, which led to his distinguishing between formative (meristematic) and structural tissues in plants. Naegeli's micellar theory, formulated from studies on starch grains, gave information on cell ultrastructure.

In the taxonomic field, Naegeli made a thorough study of the genus *Hieracium* (hawkweeds), investigating crosses in the group. He had strong views on evolution and inheritance, which led him to reject Mendel's important work on heredity and hybrid ratios.

Nagaoka, Hantaro (1865–1950) *Japanese physicist*

Nagaoka was born in Nagasaki, Japan, and educated at Tokyo University. After graduating in 1887 he worked with a visiting British physicist, C. G. Knott, on magnetism. In 1893 he traveled to Europe, where he continued his education at the universities of Berlin, Munich, and Vienna. He also attended, in 1900, the First International Congress of Physicists in Paris, where he heard Marie Curie lecture on radioactivity, an event that aroused Nagaoka's interest in atomic physics. Nagaoka returned to Japan in 1901 and served as professor of physics at Tokyo University until 1925.

Physicists in 1900 had just begun to consider the structure of the atom. The recent discovery by J. J. Thomson of the negatively charged electron implied that a neutral atom must also contain an opposite positive charge. In 1903 Thomson had suggested that the atom was a sphere of uniform positive electrification, with electrons scattered through it like currants in a bun.

Nagaoka rejected Thomson's model on the ground that opposite charges are impenetrable. He proposed an alternative model in which a positively charged center is surrounded by a number of revolving electrons, in the manner of Saturn and its rings. Nagaoka's model was, in fact, unstable and it was left to Ernest RUTHERFORD and Niels BOHR, a decade later, to present a more viable atomic model.

Nambu, Yoichipo (1921–) *Japanese physicist*

Nambu was educated at the university in his native Tokyo, serving (1945–49) as a research assistant there before being appointed professor of physics at Osaka City University. He moved to America in 1952 and, after a two-year spell at the Institute of Advanced Studies, Princeton, he joined the University of Chicago and was appointed professor of physics in 1958, a position he held until his retirement in 1991.

In 1965 Nambu, in collaboration with M. Y. Han, tackled a major problem arising from the supposed nature of quarks. Baryons, i.e., is particles that interact by the strong force and have half-integer spin, were composed of three quarks. Thus the proton consists of two up and one down quark and consequently has a configuration written uud. But some baryons are composed of three identical quarks. The omega minus (Ω^-) particle, for example, is composed of three strange quarks with an sss configuration. Quarks, however, are fermions and are thus governed by the Pauli exclusion principle – i.e., no two identical particles can be in the same quantum state. As three s quarks will have the same quantum number, and as their spins can be aligned in only two ways, it seemed that at least two of the s quarks of the Ω^- particle occupy the same state.

Nambu proposed that quarks have an

extra quantum number, which can take one of three possible values. The quantum number was arbitrarily referred to as 'color', and the varieties equally arbitrarily as red, green, and blue. In this manner three up (uuu), down (ddd), or strange (sss) quarks could coexist without violating any quantum rules, as long as they had different colors. Nambu's work has been confirmed experimentally and is part of what is known as the standard model.

Nambu went on to consider the problem of quark confinement. How could it be, he asked, that free quarks were never encountered? When baryons decay they do not break down into quarks, but into different baryons and other particles. In response to this problem Nambu introduced string theory into physics in 1970. Particles were seen not as small spheres, but as massless rotating one-dimensional entities about 10^{-13} centimeters long, with an energy proportional to their length. The quarks are located at the string's ends. In the simplest case, a meson, a quark is located at one end and an antiquark at the other.

The quarks that make up a meson cannot be separated by stretching the string because the energy required rapidly increases with length. Nor would cutting the string suffice, for at the breaking point a newly created quark–antiquark pair would be created, yielding not a free quark but a further meson.

Though Nambu's string theory had its attractions as a theory of elementary particles it soon ran into other difficulties. Nonetheless, it has been revised by such theorists as John Schwarz in the form of superstring theory.

Nansen, Fridtjof (1861–1930)
Norwegian explorer and biologist

One of the greatest men in Norway's history, Nansen is best remembered for his explorations of the Arctic, although he made many contributions to science, humanitarianism, and politics. Born at Store-Froen in Norway, he graduated in zoology from the University of Christiania, now Oslo. Nansen was appointed curator of the Bergen Natural History Museum in 1882, later becoming successively professor of zoology (1896) and professor of oceanography (1908) at the Royal Frederick University, Christiania. He helped found the International Commission for the Study of the Sea and was director of its Central Laboratory from 1901.

In 1888–89, after several preliminary expeditions, Nansen was the first to explore and describe the uncharted Greenland ice-cap, trekking from east to west and proving that the island is uniformly covered with an ice sheet. While wintering at Godthaab, Nansen spent some time studying the Eskimos, later publishing his observations as *Eskimoliv* (1891; Eskimo Life). Using a specially constructed ship, *Fram* (Forward), designed to withstand ice-pressure, Nansen then (1893–96) proceeded on his epic expedition to the North Pole. Allowing his ship to freeze in the ice, it drifted northwards (thus proving the existence of a warmer current from Siberia to Spitzbergen). Nansen left the ship and continued northward by sled to 86°14′N − only 200 miles (320 km) from the North Pole and further north than anyone had ever been before. Nansen described his Arctic journey in *Farthest North* (2 vols. 1897). He made further oceanographic expeditions to the northeast Atlantic, Spitzbergen, the Barents and Kara Seas, and to the Azores. In addition to explaining the nature of wind-driven sea currents and the formation of deep- and bottom-water, Nansen did much valuable work in improving and designing oceanographic instruments. In a quite different field his paper on the histology of the central nervous system is considered a classic.

In later life Nansen became a dedicated humanitarian. He assisted in famine relief and aid for refugees after World War I, for which he received the Nobel Peace Prize in 1922. As a politician, he influenced the separation of Norway from Sweden (1905), was a member of the Disarmament Committee (1927), and was Norway's first ambassador to Britain (1906–08).

Napier, John (1550–1617) *Scottish mathematician*

Born in Edinburgh, Napier studied at the University of St. Andrews but left before taking his degree and then traveled extensively throughout Europe. He was a fervent Protestant and wrote a diatribe attacking Catholics and others whose religious views he disapproved of. Napier was also very active in politics and he designed a number of war-engines of various kinds when it was believed that the Spanish were about to invade Scotland.

Napier devoted his spare time to mathematics, in particular to methods of computation. He introduced the concept of logarithms, publishing his work on this in *Mirifici logarithmorum canonis descriptio* (1614; Description of the Marvelous Canon of Logarithms). Napier's tables used natural logarithms, i.e., to base e, and soon after their publication the tables were slightly modified by Henry Briggs to base 10.

Napier's further work on logarithms was published after his death in *Mirifici logarithmorum canonis constructio* (1619; Construction of the Marvelous Canon of Logarithms). Napier did some other mathematical work, in particular in spherical trigonometry and in perfecting the decimal notation.

Nash, John F. (1928–) *American mathematician and economist*

Nash was born at Bluefield, West Virginia. His father was an electrical engineer and his mother was a teacher. He originally studied chemical engineering at Carnegie Tech. in Pittsburg but moved courses, first to chemistry and then, encouraged by the mathematics faculty, to mathematics.

Nash then entered Princeton on a fellowship as a graduate student. At Carnegie he had taken a course on international economics and this had led to a paper on what he called 'The Bargaining Problem'. At Princeton, he developed this further using the ideas of game theory first discussed by VON NEUMANN and Morgenstern. The result was Nash's theory of *non-cooperative games*, which he wrote up for his PhD thesis. The theory, which could be applied to any finite number of players, later found applications in economics.

Nash was not certain that this work would be an acceptable topic for a thesis and, during this period, he also made certain discoveries in pure mathematics concerning manifolds. This work was published later when he was an instructor at the Massachusetts Institute of Technology, a post he took up in 1951. At MIT he also worked on problems in differential geometry, which were relevant to general relativity theory.

At this point Nash seemed set for a brilliant mathematical career but, early in 1959, he began to suffer mental problems. In his own words, it was "the time of my change from scientific rationality of thinking into the delusional thinking characteristic of persons who are psychiatrically diagnosed as 'schizophrenic' or 'paranoid schizophrenic'". He resigned his academic post and spent periods in mental hospitals. After some 25 years Nash appears to have recovered and to have started serious mathematical work again. In 1997 he was awarded the Nobel Prize for economics for the work he had done as a young man many years before on noncooperative game theory.

Nathans, Daniel (1928–) *American molecular biologist*

Born in Wilmington, Delaware, Nathans was educated at the University of Delaware and at Washington University, St. Louis, where he obtained his MD in 1954. After first working at the Presbyterian Hospital and Rockefeller University in New York he moved in 1962 to Johns Hopkins as professor of microbiology.

With the identification of the first restriction enzyme, HIND II extracted from the *Hemophilus influenzae* bacterium by the American biologist Hamilton Smith (1931–) in 1970, it was clear to many microbiologists that at last a technique was available for the mapping of genes. Nathans immediately began working on the tumor-causing SV40 virus and by 1971 was able to show that it could be cleaved into 11 separate and specific fragments. In the following year he determined the order of such fragments, after which the way was clear for a full mapping. This also helped advance the techniques of DNA recombination.

It was for this work that Nathans shared the 1978 Nobel Prize for physiology or medicine with Smith and Werner Arber.

Natta, Giulio (1903–1979) *Italian chemist*

Natta, who was born at Imperia in Italy, was educated at the Milan Polytechnic Institute where he obtained his doctorate in chemical engineering in 1924. He was professor at the University of Pavia (1933–35), the University of Rome (1935–37), and the University of Turin (1937–38). Natta returned to Milan in 1939 as professor of industrial chemistry. In 1963 he became the first Italian to be awarded the Nobel Prize for chemistry, which he shared with Karl ZIEGLER for their development of *Ziegler–Natta catalysts*.

Natta's early work was on x-ray crystallography and on catalysis. In 1938 he began to organize research in Italy for the production of synthetic rubbers – work that led him on to his discoveries in polymer chemistry. Ziegler in 1953 had introduced catalysts for polymerizing ethene (ethylene) to polyethene (polythene) – these catalysts gave straight-chain polymers producing a superior form of polyethene. Natta applied these catalysts (and later improved catalysts) to propene (CH_3CHCH_2) to form polypropene. In 1954 he showed that polymers could be formed with regular structures with respect to the arrangement of the side groups (CH_3–) along the chain. These so-called stereospecific polymers had useful physical properties (strength, heat resistance, etc.). Natta extended the technique to the polymerization of other molecules.

Néel, Louis Eugène Félix (1904–)
French physicist

Néel, who was born at Lyons in France, studied at the Ecole Normale Supérieure, later becoming professor of physics at the University of Strasbourg and subsequently at Grenoble. He became director of the Grenoble Polytechnic Institute in 1954 and director of the Center for Nuclear Studies there in 1956. He retired in 1976.

Most of his work has been concerned with the magnetic properties of solids. About 1930 he suggested that a new form of magnetic behavior might exist – called antiferromagnetism. This is exhibited by such substances as manganese(II) oxide (MnO), in which the magnetic moments of the Mn atoms and O atoms are equal and parallel but in opposite directions. Above a certain temperature (the *Néel temperature*) this behavior stops. More generally, Néel pointed out (1947) that materials could also exist in which the magnetic moments were unequal – the phenomenon is called ferrimagnetism.

Néel has also done considerable work on other magnetic properties, including an explanation of the weak magnetism of certain rocks that has made it possible to study the past history of the Earth's magnetic field. He was awarded the Nobel Prize for physics in 1970.

Ne'eman, Yuval (1925–) *Israeli physicist*

Ne'eman, who was born at Tel Aviv, was educated at the Israel Institute of Technology (Haifa) where he graduated in engineering in 1945. His academic career was interrupted by service in the Israeli army in the post-World War II troubles of Palestine.

In 1948, with the formation of the independent Israeli state, Ne'eman was able to return to his studies, while still serving with the Israeli defense forces. He went to the Ecole de Guerre in Paris and, while serving as a military attaché at the Israeli embassy in London, gained his PhD in physics from the University of London in 1962.

In 1961 Ne'eman and the American Murray GELL-MANN, working independently, developed a mathematical representation for the classification of elementary particles. This was known as the SU(3) theory and it successfully predicted the mass of the omega-minus particle observed for the first time in 1964. The theory was consolidated in a book by the two men with the title *The Eightfold Way* (1964) and later formed the basis of a further significant theoretical development – the 'quark' hypothesis.

From 1961 to 1963 Ne'eman was scientific director of the Saraq Research Establishment of the Israeli Atomic Energy Commission, and from 1963 was head of the physics department and an associate professor at Tel Aviv University. In 1964 he became a full professor and was appointed vicerector of the university.

Neher, Erwin (1944–) *German biophysicist*

Neher was born in Landsberg, Germany. After attending the Technical University of Munich and the University of Wisconsin, he joined the Max Planck Institute of Psychiatry, Munich, in 1970, as a research associate. In 1972 he moved to the Max Planck Institute for Biophysical Chemistry in Göttingen, being appointed research director in 1983. Two periods of research in America took him to Yale University (1975–76) and the California Institute of Technology (1988–89).

Neher is best known for his studies of the minute channels in the membranes of living cells that allow ions to pass in and out of the cell. In the mid-1970s, working in collaboration with Bert SAKMANN, Neher developed the so-called 'patch-clamp technique' to detect the tiny electrical currents produced by the passage of ions through the membrane. Detection posed considerable technical challenges, given that the currents associated with each channel are of the order of 10^{-12} ampere, and the channels have a diameter comparable to the diameter of the ions.

The technique involved applying the tip of a saline-containing micropipette to the cell's membrane and applying suction to form a seal around the patch of membrane. The currents produced by the ions passing through the ion channel was monitored using a special amplifier. The technique had the great advantage of eliminating electrical noise generated by other parts of the membrane, which hitherto had obscured signals from any one channel.

Using their technique, Neher and Sakmann were able to demonstrate that the ion channels are either 'open' or 'shut', i.e., producing an 'all or nothing' signal. Also, each channel is specific to a particular type of ion.

The patch-clamp technique has proved itself to be both sensitive and elegant, and has found application in many fields of basic and applied research. Ion channels are involved in a range of biological processes, such as the generation of nerve impulses, the fertilization of eggs, and the regulation of the heartbeat. The way in which their behavior is altered by disease or drugs can have far-reaching implications. The technique has been applied in analytical devices known as biosensors.

This crucial development in cellular research techniques earned Neher and Sakmann the 1991 Nobel Prize for physiology or medicine.

Neisser, Albert Ludwig Siegmund
(1855–1916) *German bacteriologist*

Neisser was born in Schweidnitz (now Swidnica in Poland), the son of a physician. He was educated at Munsterberg and at Breslau, where he qualified in medicine (1877) and held the professorship of dermatology (from 1882).

In 1879 Neisser discovered the gonococcus, the causative agent of gonorrhea, which was named for him (*Neisseria*). In the same year he also identified the bacillus *Mycobacterium leprae* as the cause of leprosy, but in this he had been anticipated by Armauer Hansen. Neisser also worked on syphilis and collaborated with August von WASSERMAN in 1906 on the development of his diagnostic test.

Nernst, Walther Hermann
(1864–1941) *German physical chemist*

Nernst, who was born at Briesen in Germany, studied at the universities of Zurich, Berlin, Würzburg, and Graz. After working as assistant to Wilhelm Ostwald in Leipzig from 1887 he became professor of chemistry at Göttingen in 1890. In 1904 he became professor of physical chemistry at Berlin and later was appointed director of the Institute for Experimental Physics there (1924–33). In 1933, out of favor with the Nazis, he retired to his country estate.

Nernst's early work was in electrochemistry – a field in which he made a number of contributions. Thus in 1889 he introduced the idea of the solubility product, i.e., the product of the concentrations of the different types of ions in a saturated solution. The product is a constant for sparingly soluble compounds (at constant temperature). Nernst also suggested (1903) the use of buffer solutions – mixed solutions of weak acids (or bases) and their salts, which resist changes in pH.

His main work, in 1906, was in thermodynamics. It came out of attempts to predict the course of chemical reactions from measurements of specific heats and heats of reaction. If heat is absorbed during a reaction, the amount absorbed falls with temperature and would become zero at absolute

zero. Nernst postulated that the *rate* at which this reduction occurred would also become zero at absolute zero of temperature, and, as a consequence, derived the *Nernst heat theorem*, which states that if a reaction occurs between pure crystalline solids at absolute zero, then there is no change in entropy.

The theorem, stated in a slightly different form, is now known as the third law of thermodynamics. It is equivalent to the statement that absolute zero cannot be attained in a finite number of steps. At the time it allowed the calculation of absolute values of entropy (and then equilibrium constants), rather than changes in entropy. It is now known to be a consequence of the quantum statistics of the particles. For his work in thermodynamics, Nernst received the Nobel Prize for chemistry in 1920.

He also made contributions to photochemistry and, in addition, produced one of the standard texts of the period, *Theoretische Chemie* (1893; Theoretical Chemistry), which went through numerous editions and translations.

He managed to make a large fortune by the turn of the century by selling a form of electric light, which though superior to the Edison carbon-filament lamp soon became obsolete with the invention of the tungsten-filament lamp.

Neumann, John von *See* VON NEUMANN, JOHN.

Newcomb, Simon (1835–1909)
American astronomer

The son of an itinerant teacher, Newcomb was born at Wallace in Nova Scotia and had little formal education. He was apprenticed to a herbalist in Nova Scotia but ran away to join his father in the United States. In 1857 he joined the American Nautical Almanac Office, and he graduated from Harvard in 1858. He joined the corps of professors of mathematics in the navy, and became professor of mathematics at the Naval Observatory in Washington in 1861. From 1884 to 1894 he was professor of mathematics and astronomy at Johns Hopkins University. He was also superintendent of the American Nautical Almanac from 1877 to 1897, retiring with the rank of rear admiral. In addition he was the editor of the *American Journal of Mathematics* and the author of over 350 scientific papers and a number of popular works on astronomy.

Newcomb worked for many years on new tables for the planets and the Moon, which were published in 1899. These, together with his organization of the Nautical Almanac, were his major astronomical work. His tables, the result of detailed observations and sophisticated mathematics, were the most accurate ever made and were in constant use until the middle of this century. Also of major importance was his production and promotion of a new, unified, and more accurate system of astronomical constants, which was adopted worldwide in 1896.

He did much to encourage younger scientists. Hearing the young Albert Michelson lecture to the American Association for the Advancement of Science on new methods for accurately determining the speed of light, he went out of his way to raise money for the unknown young scientist to continue with his work.

Newlands, John Alexander Reina
(1837–1898) *British chemist*

Newlands, who was born in London, studied under August von Hofmann at the Royal College of Chemistry. In 1860, being of Italian ancestry, he fought with Giuseppe Garibaldi's army in its invasion of Naples. On his return from Naples he set up as a consultant with his brother in 1864 but, after the failure of his business, worked as an industrial chemist in a sugar refinery.

In various papers published in 1864 and 1865 Newlands stated his law of octaves and came close to discovering the periodic table. He claimed that if the elements were listed in the order of their atomic weights a pattern emerged in which properties seemed to repeat themselves after each group of seven elements. He pointed out the analogy of this with the intervals of the musical scale.

Newlands's claim to see a repeating pattern was met with savage ridicule on its announcement. His classification of the elements, he was told, was as arbitrary as putting them in alphabetical order and his paper was rejected for publication by the Chemical Society. It was not until MENDELEEV's periodic table was announced in 1869 that the significance of Newlands's idea was recognized and he was able to publish his paper *On the Discovery of the Periodic Law* (1884).

Newton, Sir Isaac (1642–1727) *English physicist and mathematician*

Newton's father, the owner of the manor of Woolsthorpe in Lincolnshire, died three months before Newton was born. The family had land but were neither wealthy nor gentry. Left by his mother in the care of his grandmother, the young Newton is reported to have been quiet, unwilling to play with the village boys, and interested in making things. His mother returned to Woolsthorpe in 1656 after the death of her second husband. By this time Newton was at school in Grantham where he stayed until 1658, lodging with a local apothecary. There is no evidence that he was especially gifted at this time, although he was certainly skillful for he made a water clock, sundials (which still survive at Woolsthorpe), and model furniture for his stepsisters. After two years helping his mother to run the family farm, he went to Cambridge University in 1661, where he stayed for nearly 40 years.

Not much is known of Newton's student life. In 1665 he was forced by the plague to leave Cambridge and return to Woolsthorpe. Here, during his so-called *annus mirabilis* (miraculous year), he began to develop the ideas and insights for which he is so famous. Here he first began to think about gravity, and also devoted time to optics, grinding his own lenses and considering the nature of light. During this period he also worked out his mathematical ideas about 'fluxions' (the calculus).

When he returned to Cambridge after the plague had died down he was elected a fellow of his college, Trinity, in 1667, and in 1669 he succeeded Barrow as Lucasian Professor. He served as member of parliament for the university for the periods 1689–90 and 1701–02, although he does not appear to have been politically very active. His public career was pursued through Charles Montague, first earl of Halifax, who was able to introduce Newton into court and society circles. When Montague became chancellor of the exchequer he was able to offer Newton the post of warden of the Mint in 1696. He was made master of the Mint in 1699 and knighted for his services in 1705. From this time he did virtually no new science apart from publishing and revising works already written. He did concern himself with the affairs of the Royal Society, of which he became president in 1703. He resigned his Cambridge post in 1701.

At the Mint, his first task was to supervise 'the great recoinage' – the replacement of the old hammered coins with new pieces with milled edges. It was also Newton's business to pursue the counterfeiters and clippers of his day. As ever, he took his duties seriously and could be found regularly visiting suspects in Newgate and other prisons. Between June 1698 and Christmas 1699 he interviewed 200 witnesses on 123 separate occasions. In the same period 27 counterfeiters were executed. Other major tasks undertaken by Newton included the introduction of a union coinage in 1707 following the union of the Kingdoms of England and Scotland, the issue of new copper coins in 1718, the revaluation of the guinea to 21 shillings in 1717, and a general improvement in the assaying of the currency. The Mint made Newton a wealthy man. In addition to a salary of £600 a year he also received a commission on the amount of silver minted, which brought in on average £1000 a year. At the time of his death Newton had accumulated £30,000 in cash and securities.

Much of Newton's later life was also spent in needless priority disputes. These arose largely through his reluctance to publish his own work. It was not until 1704, when Newton was over 60, that he actually published a mathematical text. Even then his main work on the calculus, *Methodis fluxionum* (Method of Fluxions), composed between 1670 and 1671, was only published posthumously in 1736. At the same time manuscripts of unpublished works were shown to friends and colleagues.

When, therefore, LEIBNIZ published his own work on the differential and integral calculus in 1684, he felt no need to acknowledge any unpublished work of Newton. He had developed his methods and notation largely from his own vast intellectual resources. He had seen some Newtonian manuscripts on a visit to London in 1673, and letters from Newton in 1676 contained further details. None of this, it is now accepted, was sufficient to account for Leibniz's 1684 paper. The dispute began in 1700 when Leibniz objected to the practice of the Newtonians referring to him as the 'second inventor' of the calculus. The dispute dragged on until the 1720s, long outlasting the death of Leibniz in 1716. After a decade of bitter and anonymous dispute Leibniz unaccountably applied to the Royal Society in 1712 to conduct an inquiry into the matter. Newton behaved quite shamelessly. He appointed the committee, decided what evidence it should see, and actually drafted the published report himself. Thereupon, in later stages of the dispute, he would appeal to the report, the *Commercium epistolicum* (1713; On the Exchange of Letters), as an independent justification of his position.

Newton is best known for his work on gravitation and mechanics. The most famous story in the history of science has the unusual distinction of being true, at least according to Conduit, who married Newton's niece Catherine. He reported that "In the year 1665, when he retired to his own estate on account of the plague, he first thought of his system of gravity, which he hit upon by observing an apple fall from a tree." His ideas were not published until 1684 when Edmond Halley asked Newton to find what force would cause a planet to move in an elliptical orbit. Newton replied that he already had the answer. Finding that he had lost his proof, he worked it out again.

His result was that two bodies – such as the Sun and a planet, or the Earth and the Moon – attract each other with a force that depends on the product of their masses and falls off as the square of their distance apart. Thus the force is proportional to m_1m_2/d^2, where m_1 and m_2 are the masses and d is their distance apart. Originally he applied this to point masses but in 1685 he proved that a body acted as if its mass were a point mass of the same magnitude acting at the center of the body (for a symmetrical body).

Newton's original work on gravity, in 1665, had been applied to the motion of the Moon. His insight was that the Moon in its motion 'falls' to the Earth under the same cause as the apple falls. His calculations at this time used an erroneously low value for the Earth's radius and it was possibly this that made him lay aside his calculations until 1684.

Then in 1684 he took up the subject again and began to write his great work *Philosophiae Naturalis Principia Mathematica* (Mathematical Principles of Natural Philosophy) – known as the *Principia*. The first edition was published in 1687. Here he set out his three laws of motion. His first law states that a body at rest or in uniform motion will continue in that state unless a force is applied. His second law gives a definition of force – that it equals the mass of a body multiplied by the acceleration it produces in the body. His third law puts forward the idea that if a body exerts a force (action) on another there is an equal but opposite force (reaction) on the first body.

What Newton did in his work in mechanics was to establish a unified system: one in which a simple set of basic laws explained a range of diverse phenomena – the motion of the Moon and planets, motion of the Earth, and the tides. Newton did not give any explanation of what gravity actually *is*. How it acts, its mechanism, and its cause were matters that Newton claimed we should not frame hypotheses on. That it has a cause Newton was sure of, for the idea that a body may act on another through a vacuum over a long distance "without the mediation of anything else ... is to me so great an absurdity that I believe no man can ever fall into it. Gravity must be caused ... but whether this agent be material or immaterial I have left to the consideration of my reader." Newton did not always obey his own injunction and in the 1713 edition of the *Principia* speculated about the existence of "certain very subtle spirits that pervade all dense bodies," which might explain light, electricity, sensation, and much besides.

Newton's reluctance to provide a gravitational mechanism was seen as a basic weakness of his system by the Cartesians. Whatever the defects of the physics of René Descartes at least he provided mechanisms, in the form of vortices, to explain all movements. To some Newton's gravity seemed a retrograde step in that it was reintroducing into physics the occult, meaningless forces that Descartes had recently eliminated. Nevertheless, Newton's system received great acclaim in England and was to become the model for all succeeding scientific theory.

Newton also worked extensively on light. He began by rejecting the Cartesian account of color. For Descartes white light was natural light; colored light was the modification produced in light by the medium through which it passes. Thus light passing through a prism is spread into a spectrum because the light has been differentially modified by the varying thickness of the prism.

Newton published his own account in 1672 in his first published paper, *New Theory about Light and Colours*. "I procured me a Triangular glass-Prisme to try therewith the celebrated Phenomena of Colours," he began. When he passed a ray of light through a prism he found that it formed an oblong, not a circular image, five times longer than its breadth. He found that, as was well known, light passing through a prism was dispersed and formed a colored spectrum. But when a second prism was taken and colored light rays passed through it, no further change was discernible. Red light remained red, and blue light blue. From this, his famous *experimentum crucis* (cross experiment), he derived two important conclusions: firstly, ordinary white light was composite, a mixture of the various colors of the spectrum; secondly, he concluded, "Light consists of Rays differently Refrangible," and it was this difference in refrangibility that produced the oblong image which had so puzzled Newton.

Newton's views found little favor and over the next few years he was repeatedly called upon to explain and defend his position. By 1676 he had had enough. "I see a man must either resolve to put out nothing new or become a slave to defend it," he wrote to Oldenburg, and published no more on light until 1704.

He had, however, already in 1675 sent a paper to the Royal Society entitled *An Hypothesis Explaining the Properties of Light*. He refused to allow it to be published and it first appeared in 1757, long after Newton's death. The paper contains Newton's analysis of light as "multitudes of unimaginable small and swift corpuscles of various sizes, springing from shining bodies." He dismissed the view that light, like sound, could consist of waves, because light unlike sound could not travel around corners. The paper also contained an account of what have since become known as *Newton's rings*. These consist of a series of concentric colored rings and can be produced by putting a plano-convex lens of large radius of curvature on a flat reflecting surface. They were explained by Newton with some ingenuity and some difficulty in terms of his corpuscular theory of light. Newton's mature views on these and many other matters were presented in his *Opticks* (1704).

Not all of Newton's work on light was of a theoretical kind. He was an extremely talented experimentalist and in the late 1660s he designed and built the first reflecting telescope. This involved grinding and polishing the mirrors himself. The idea of a reflecting telescope had occurred earlier to James GREGORY but his attempts at constructing a model, despite receiving professional help, led nowhere. The advantage of the Newtonian telescope over the refractor of Galileo is that mirrors do not suffer from chromatic aberration.

But above all else Newton was a mathematician of incomparable power. In 1696 Johann BERNOULLI posed a problem to the mathematicians of Europe, allowing them six months to solve it. Newton solved the problem in a single night and published the result anonymously in the *Transactions* of the Royal Society. Bernoulli was not fooled, claiming to recognize the author or, "the lion by his claw." Again in 1716 Leibniz issued another difficult problem, which Newton solved before going to bed after a day's work at the Mint.

Newton communicated the generalized form of the binomial theorem to Henry Oldenbourg in 1676. It was also in that year that he deposited with Oldenbourg his *epistola prior* (first letter) claiming discovery of his method of fluxions in an anagram. The terminology arose from his considering the path of a continuously moving body as a curve made by a continuously moving point. The moving point he called a fluent and its velocity he called a fluxion. This he symbolized by $\dot{x}$ and its acceleration as $\ddot{x}$. This, independently of Leibniz, was Newton's discovery of the calculus, although

Leibniz's notation was the one eventually adopted.

Throughout his life Newton also displayed a deep interest in two other areas: religion and alchemy. At his death over 1000 manuscript pages, running to nearly 1.5 million words, and two completed books were discovered, devoted entirely to religious matters. Newton was a unitarian, a matter kept fairly secret during his life as it would have excluded him from his Lucasian chair and his post at the Mint. Much of his life was spent on deep studies of church history, the Bible, and ancient chronology. His aim was to show that the text of the Bible had been corrupted by later trinitarian editors, and that the history of the early church revealed a similar corruption introduced by Athanasius in the fourth century. The matter was dealt with at length in his *Two Notable Corruptions of Scripture* (1754) and in numerous manuscripts.

Equally extensive were Newton's alchemical manuscripts. In his library were 138 books on alchemy, and his manuscripts on the subject exceed 600,000 words. It is less clear, however, whether Newton was a genuine alchemist committed to dreams of transmutation and the philosopher's stone, or whether he was merely using whatever sources he could find to further his chemical interests. His interests in chemistry were sufficient to lead him to establish a laboratory in Trinity College and for a while in the 1680s, it was reported, "the laboratory fire scarcely went out night or day." He published during his life just one brief work on chemistry, *De natura acidorum* (1710; On the Nature of Acids). There are, however, several passages devoted to chemistry scattered among the *Queries* added by Newton to his *Opticks* (1704).

Newton died in 1727 at the age of 85 after a fairly short illness. He managed to preside over a meeting of the Royal Society a fortnight before his death. Shortly after he was diagnosed as having a stone in the bladder and seems to have spent the last days of his life in great pain. He was buried in Westminster Abbey where a most unattractive monument can still be seen. Many words have been written about his greatness as a scientist; the most apposite remain the often quoted words of Alexander Pope, composed for Newton's tomb but, for some reason, rejected:

Nature and Nature's laws lay hid in night:
God said, let Newton be! and all was light.

Nicholson, Seth Barnes (1891–1963)
American astronomer

Nicholson was the son of a farmer from Springfield, Illinois. He graduated from Drake University, Des Moines, Iowa, in 1912 and in 1915 obtained his PhD from the University of California. From then until his retirement in 1957 he worked at the Mount Wilson Observatory, California.

While still a graduate student at the Lick Observatory, Nicholson discovered the ninth satellite of Jupiter (Sinope) in 1914, working close to the limits of resolution of the Lick telescope and the photographic plates then available. He went on to discover a further three satellites, Jupiter X (Lysithea) and XI (Carme) in 1938 and Jupiter XII (Ananke) in 1951. All four satellites are very small, about 15–20 kilometers (9–12 mi) in diameter.

Nicholson studied the surface features and spectrum of the Sun and also, in collaboration with Edison Petit, worked on planetary and lunar temperatures. Thus they showed in 1927 that the Moon undergoes enormous temperature changes, for in the course of an eclipse its surface temperature dropped from 160°F to −110°F (71°C to −79°C) in about an hour.

Nicol, William (1768–1852) *British geologist and physicist*

Little is known about Nicol's early life except that he was born in Scotland. Primarily a geologist, he lectured in natural philosophy at the University of Edinburgh where James Clerk Maxwell was probably one of his pupils. His first publication came when he was nearly 60.

Nicol is best remembered for his invention, announced in 1828, of the *Nicol prism*. This device, constructed from a crystal of Iceland spar (a natural form of calcium carbonate), made use of the phenomenon of double refraction discovered by Erasmus BARTHOLIN. The crystal was split along its shorter diagonal and the halves cemented together in their original position by a transparent layer of Canada balsam. The ordinary ray was totally reflected at the layer of Canada balsam while the extraordinary ray, striking the cement at a slightly different angle, was transmitted. Nicol prisms made it easy to produce polarized light. For a long time they became the standard instrument in the study of polarization and played a part in the formation of theories of molecular structure.

Nicol also developed new techniques of preparing thin slices of minerals and fossil wood for microscopic examination. These techniques allowed the samples to be viewed through the microscope by transmitted light rather than by reflected light, which only revealed surface features. His lack of publications resulted in some 40 years elapsing before these techniques were incorporated into studies in petrology.

Nicolle, Charles Jules Henri (1866–1936) *French bacteriologist*

Nicolle, the son of a physician, was born at Rouen in France and educated there and in Paris, where he obtained his MD in 1893. He returned to Rouen to join the faculty of the medical school but in 1902 moved to Tunis, where he served as director of the Pasteur Institute until his death.

In 1909 Nicolle revolutionized the study and treatment of typhus. He noticed that typhus patients outside the hospital transmitted the disease to their families, to the doctors who visited them, to the staff admitting them into hospital, to the personnel responsible for taking their clothes and linen, and to hospital laundry staff. But once admitted to the ward the typhus patients did not contaminate any of the other patients, the nurses, or the doctors. Since all newly admitted patients were stripped, washed, and changed, Nicolle concluded that the disease carrier was attached to the patient's skin and clothing and could be removed by washing. The obvious carrier was the louse.

Nicolle lost no time in providing experimental evidence for his reasoning. He transmitted typhus to a monkey by injecting it with blood from an infected chimpanzee. A louse was allowed to feed on the monkey and when transferred to another monkey succeeded in infecting it by its bite alone. It was for this work that Nicolle was awarded the Nobel Prize for physiology or medicine in 1928.

Nicolle actually considered his discovery of 'apyretic typhus' the most important of his achievements. He found guinea pigs to be susceptible to typhus but that some of them, with blood capable of infecting other animals, showed no symptoms of the disease at all. He had in fact discovered the carrier state, which was to have significance for the emerging science of immunology.

Nicolle also attempted to develop vaccines against typhus and other infections. He was mildly successful in using serum from patients recovering from typhus and measles to induce a short-lasting passive immunity on those at risk.

Niepce, Joseph-Nicéphore (1765–1833) *French inventor*

Niepce, who made the first permanent photographic image, came from a wealthy family in Châlon-sur-Saône, eastern France, that fled the French Revolution. He returned to serve with Napoleon Bonaparte's army, but after being dismissed because of ill health, went back to his birthplace (1801) to do scientific research.

With his brother, Niepce built an internal-combustion engine (1807) for boats using carbon and resin for fuel. In 1813 he started the attempt to record images, on paper coated with silver chloride. He produced his first image, a view from his workroom, in 1816, but was only able to fix this partially with nitric acid. In 1822 he produced a photographic copy of an engraving using a glass plate coated with bitumen of Judea. Later (1826) he used a pewter plate to make the first permanent camera photograph. He also devised the first mechanical reproduction process. The main difficulty was the long exposure times needed – over eight hours. Niepce formed a partnership with the Parisian painter, Louis-Jacques-Mandé Daguerre in 1826 to perfect the process of heliography but he died before seeing the final success of his efforts.

Nilson, Lars Fredrick (1840–1899) *Swedish chemist. See* Cleve, Per Teodor.

Nirenberg, Marshall Warren (1927–) *American biochemist*

Nirenberg, who was born in New York City, graduated from the University of Florida in 1948 and gained his PhD in biochemistry from the University of Michigan in 1957. He then joined the National Institutes of Health in Bethesda, Maryland, where he began the work that culminated in the cracking of the genetic code.

When Nirenberg began this research it had already been surmised that different combinations of three nucleotide bases (triplets) each coded for a specific amino acid and that through the operation of this 'genetic code' amino acids are aligned in the right order to make proteins. The big question was; which of the 64 possible combinations of triplets codes for each of the 20 amino acids? Severo Ochoa's discovery of the technique to synthesize RNA artificially enabled Nirenberg to make an RNA molecule consisting entirely of uracil nucleotides. Thus the only triplet possible would be a uracil triplet (UUU of the code). Nirenberg found that the protein made by this RNA molecule consisted entirely of the amino acid phenylalanine, indicating that UUU must code for phenylalanine. With this first important step completed others were quick to unravel the rest of the code.

Nirenberg received the 1968 Nobel Prize for physiology or medicine for this work, sharing the award with Har Gobind KHO-RANA and Robert HOLLEY.

Nobel, Alfred Bernhard (1833–1896)
Swedish chemist, engineer, and inventor

Nobel left Stockholm, where he was born, in 1842 to join his father, an engineer, who had moved to St. Petersburg. He was taught chemistry by his tutors and spoke fluently in English, French, German, Swedish, and Russian. In 1850 he went to Paris to study chemistry and then went on to America for four years, before returning to work in his father's factory in St. Petersburg.

In 1859 Nobel moved back to Sweden and set up a factory there (1864) to make nitroglycerin, a liquid explosive. After an explosion at the factory in 1864 in which his brother, Emil, and four others were killed, the Swedish government would not allow the factory to be rebuilt. Nobel then started to experiment to find a more stable explosive. Discovering that nitroglycerin was easily absorbed by a dry organic packing material, he invented dynamite and the detonating cap. These were patented in 1867 (UK) and 1868 (Unites States). From such work and from oil fields in Russia that he owned, Nobel amassed a vast fortune. He traveled widely and was a committed pacifist. He left the bulk of his money in trust for international awards – the Nobel Prizes for peace, literature, physics, chemistry, and medicine. The Nobel Prize for economics was introduced in his honor in 1969 and financed by the Swedish National Bank.

Noddack, Ida Eva Tacke (1896–1979)
German chemist

Noddack, who was born at Lackhausen in Germany, was educated at the Technical University, Berlin, where she obtained her doctorate in 1921. After her marriage to the chemist Walter Noddack she worked at the same institutions as her husband.

In 1926 she collaborated with her husband and O. Berg in the discovery of rhenium. More intriguing, however, was her interpretation of a famous experiment of Enrico FERMI in which he had bombarded uranium with slow neutrons in the hope of producing artificial elements. Although their results were not particularly clear Noddack, in 1934, argued that "It is conceivable that in the bombardment of heavy nuclei with neutrons, these nuclei break up into several large fragments which are actually isotopes of known elements, not neighbors of the irradiated element." This is, in fact, the hypothesis of nuclear fission which, when it was published five years

later by Otto FRISCH, was immediately seen to be of fundamental importance.

Noddack's contribution seems rather to have passed unnoticed. Fermi was aware of her work as she had sent him a copy, but he remained unconvinced and continued to believe that he had made transuranic elements.

Noddack, Walter (1893–1960) *German chemist*

Noddack was born in Berlin and educated at the university there, obtaining his doctorate in 1920. He worked first at the Physikalische Technische Reichsanstadt, the German national physical laboratory, until 1935, and then held chairs in physical chemistry at Freiburg and Strasbourg until, in 1946, he moved to Bamberg. Noddack taught chemistry at the local Hochschule there before serving (1955–60) as the director of the Bamberg Institute of Geochemistry.

In 1926, in collaboration with his wife Ida Tacke, Noddack discovered the element rhenium. They thought that they had found element 43, which they named 'masurium'. In fact this element was correctly identified in 1937 by Emilio Segrè, who named it technetium.

Noddack is also remembered for arguing for a concept he called *allgegenwartskonzentration* or, literally, omnipresent concentration. This idea, somewhat reminiscent of the early Greek philosopher Anaxagoras, assumed that every mineral actually contained every element. The reason they could not all be detected was, of course, because they existed in too small quantities.

Noguchi, (Seisako) Hideyo (1876–1928) *Japanese bacteriologist*

Noguchi was born at Okinashimamura in Japan. In spite of a humble family background and a physical handicap caused by a childhood accident, he pursued a career in medicine. After considerable perseverance he entered medical school in Tokyo, obtaining his diploma in 1897. Three years later he traveled to America and commenced work at the University of Pennsylvania, studying animal venoms and their antivenins. In 1904, after a year spent in Copenhagen, Noguchi joined the Rockefeller Institute for Medical Research, New York. Here he successfully cultured the spirochete bacterium, *Treponema pallidum*, which causes syphilis. This enabled Noguchi to devise a diagnostic skin test for syphilis using an emulsion of his spirochete culture. He further showed that *T. pallidum* invades the nervous system as the disease progresses. In recognition of his work, Noguchi was awarded the Order of the Rising Sun in his home country in 1915.

Noguchi went on to study the possible causes of other diseases. After investigating Oroya fever in South and Central America, he showed that it was caused by a bacterium, *Bartonella bacilliformis*, which was transmitted to humans by sand flies. Between 1919 and 1922, Noguchi became certain that yellow fever also was caused by a bacterium. However, by 1927 this view had been discredited with the discovery that a virus was responsible.

In the same year, Noguchi went to West Africa and worked doggedly to prove to himself that yellow fever was in fact a virus disease. Within six months he had confirmed this but just before his departure for New York he contracted yellow fever himself and died shortly after.

Nollet, Abbé Jean Antoine (1700–1770) *French physicist*

Born at Pimprez in France, Nollet was one of the great popularizers of the new electrical science in the salons and at the court of 18th-century France. He had collaborated with Charles Dufay in the period 1730–32 and tended to follow him in his electrical theory. Nollet saw electricity as a fluid, subtle enough to penetrate the densest of bodies. In 1746 he first formulated his theory of simultaneous 'affluences and effluences' in which he assumed that bodies have two sets of pores in and out of which electrical effluvia might flow. He was later involved with Benjamin Franklin in a dispute over the nature of electricity.

After the discovery of the Leyden jar (a device for storing electrical charge) by Pieter van Musschenbroek in 1745, Nollet arranged some spectacular demonstrations of its power. He once gave a shock to 180 royal guards and, even more dramatically, joined 700 monks in a circle to a Leyden jar with quite startling results. Nollet also contributed to the theory of sound when he showed in 1743 that sound carried in water (he had taken care to expel the dissolved air from the water first).

Norrish, Ronald George Wreyford (1897–1978) *British chemist*

Norrish was educated at the university in his native Cambridge. Apart from the war years, he spent his whole career there, serving as professor of physical chemistry from 1937 until 1965.

Norrish made his important contributions to chemistry in the fields of photochemistry and chemical kinetics, being introduced to these by Eric Rideal during his PhD work. From 1949 to 1965 he collaborated with his former pupil George Porter in the development of flash photolysis and kinetic spectroscopy for the investigation of very fast reactions. For their work they shared the 1967 Nobel Prize for chemistry with Manfred Eigen.

Norrish also made a significant contribution to chemistry when he showed the need to modify Draper's law. In the mid-19th century John Draper proposed his law that the amount of photochemical change is proportional to the intensity of the light multiplied by the time for which it acts. Norrish was able to show that the rate should be proportional to the square root of the light intensity.

Northrop, John Howard (1891–1987) *American chemist*

The son of biologists, Northrop was born in Yonkers, New York, and educated at Columbia, obtaining his PhD there in 1915. In 1917 he joined the Rockefeller Institute of Medical Research, only leaving on his retirement in 1961.

In the early 1930s Northrop confirmed some earlier results of James Sumner. Between 1930 and 1935 he and his coworkers succeeded in isolating a number of enzymes, including pepsin, trypsin, chymotrypsin, ribonuclease, and deoxyribonuclease, crystallizing them and unequivocally exhibiting their protein nature. This was sufficient finally to convince chemists that Sumner was correct, and Richard Willstätter had been wrong in his assertion that enzymes are nonprotein.

Using Northrop's techniques, Wendell Stanley was able in 1936 to isolate and crystallize the tobacco mosaic virus, and showed it to be composed of nucleoprotein. Subsequently (1938) Northrop isolated a bacteriophage (bacterial virus) and demonstrated that this also consisted of nucleoprotein. For such work on the isolation and crystallization of proteins and viruses, Northrop, Sumner, and Stanley shared the 1946 Nobel Prize for chemistry.

Noyce, Robert Norton (1927–1990) *American physicist*

Noyce was the son of a congregational minister from Denmark, Iowa. He was educated at Grinnell College, Iowa, and at the Massachusetts Institute of Technology, where he obtained his PhD in 1953. After working briefly for Philco, Philadelphia, Noyce moved to Mountain View, California, to work for William Shockley, coinventor of the transistor, at his Semiconductor Laboratory. But Shockley was not an easy man to work for; nor did Noyce trust his commercial judgment. Consequently, Noyce and a number of colleagues, the 'traitorous eight' according to Shockley, decided to set up in business themselves. Financed by the Fairchild Corporation of New York, Noyce and his associates set up Fairchild Semiconductor in the Santa Clara Valley, fifty miles south of San Francisco, a site better known today as 'Silicon Valley'.

The first major success was the integrated circuit, the foundation of the modern electronics industry. Noyce filed his patent in April 1959, some six weeks after a similar patent had been filed by Jack Kilby at Texas Instruments. Although Noyce's design was more advanced, priority seemed to lie with Kilby. Yet in 1968 the Supreme Court awarded all rights to Noyce and Fairchild on the grounds that Kilby's patent application lacked sufficient clarity.

Whereas Kilby's circuit had used the silicon mesa transistor, Noyce opted for a planar model. Unlike the mesa, Noyce's model had no raised parts to attract contaminants and was more easily protected by a layer of silicon dioxide. Parts were no longer connected by wires but by evaporating the aluminum wires onto the insulating surface. As an extra bonus it also proved much easier to mass-produce planar transistors.

At this point Noyce was able to sell back to Fairchild his initial investment of $500 for $250,000. He went on in 1968 to found Intel (Integrated Electronics). It gained an early success with the production of a one-kilobyte RAM chip. Further improvements were quickly made and, with the 1973 launch of a 4K RAM chip, sales soared above $60 million. Intel's success rapidly made Noyce one of Silicon Valley's first multimillionaires; it continued with the production of the 486 chip in 1989 and the 60 MHz Pentium chip in 1993.

Noyes, William Albert (1857–1941)
American chemist

Noyes, born the son of a farmer in Independence, Iowa, was educated at Johns Hopkins University where he obtained his PhD in 1882. After working at the University of

Tennessee (1883–86) and Rose Polytechnic, Terre Haute, Indiana (1886–1903), he held the post of chief chemist at the Bureau of Standards (1903–06). He then moved to the University of Illinois where he served as professor of chemistry until his retirement in 1926.

Noyes is mainly remembered for his careful and accurate determination of certain crucial atomic weights while at the Bureau of Standards. His measurement of the hydrogen-to-oxygen ratio as 1.00787:16 differs only at the fourth decimal place from currently accepted values. He also, in addition to writing a number of textbooks, founded *Chemical Abstracts* in 1907 and was the first editor of *Chemical Reviews* (1924–26).

Nüsslein-Volhard, Christiane
(1942–   ) *German biologist*

Nüsslein-Volhard was educated at the university of Tübingen. After a spell at the European Molecular Biology Laboratory at Heidelberg, she moved in 1981 to the Max Planck Institute for Development, Tübingen, where she has served since 1990 as the director of the department of genetics.

From 1978 to 1981, Nüsslein-Volhard collaborated with Eric WIESCHAUS on identifying the genetic factors responsible for the development of the fruit fly *Drosophila melanogaster*. Large numbers of mutants were bred by feeding adult flies mutagenic chemicals. After examining many thousands of flies they had managed, by 1980 to identify the main development sequence in *Drosophila*.

Nüsslein-Volhard has also succeeded in illuminating the general process of development. It has long been thought that differentiation in early embryos – anterior from posterior, for example, or dorsal from ventral – was caused by varying concentration of substances along the axes of the egg. The theory of morphological gradients, as it is known, has recently been supported by experimental work carried out by Nüsslein-Volhard and her Tübingen colleagues.

Nüsslein-Volhard shared the 1995 Nobel prize for physiology or medicine with Edward LEWIS and Eric Wieschaus for their work on the development of *Drosophila*.

Occhialini, Giuseppe Paolo Stanislao (1907–) *Italian physicist. See* BLACKET, PATRICK MAYNARD STUART; POWELL, CECIL FRANK.

Ochoa, Severo (1905–1993) *Spanish–American biochemist*

Born at Luarca in Spain, Ochoa graduated from Málaga University in 1921 and then proceeded to study medicine at Madrid University, receiving his MD in 1929. Having held research positions in Germany, Spain, and England, he became a research associate in medicine at New York University in 1942, taking American citizenship in 1956. He became a full professor in 1976 and in 1985 was appointed honorary director of the center for molecular biology, University of Madrid.

Ochoa was one of the first to demonstrate the role of high-energy phosphates, e.g., adenosine triphosphate, in the storage and release of the body's energy. While investigating the process of oxidative phosphorylation, in which such triphosphates are formed from diphosphates, he discovered the enzyme polynucleotide phosphorylase. This can catalyze the formation of ribonucleic acid (RNA) from appropriate nucleotides and was later used for the synthesis of artificial RNA. Ochoa was awarded the 1959 Nobel Prize for physiology or medicine for this discovery, sharing the prize with Arthur KORNBERG, who synthesized deoxyribonucleic acid (DNA). Ochoa also isolated two enzymes catalyzing certain reactions of the Krebs cycle.

Odling, William (1829–1921) *British chemist*

Odling, the son of a London surgeon, studied medicine at London University before moving into chemistry. He studied in Paris under Charles Gerhardt and in 1863 was appointed professor of chemistry at St. Bartholomew's Hospital, London. In 1867 he succeeded Michael Faraday as Fullerian Professor at the Royal Institution, London, and in 1872 he moved to Oxford University to take up the Waynflete Chair of Chemistry until his retirement in 1912.

Odling was one of the pioneers of the valence theory first propounded by Edward Frankland in 1852. Although the term 'valence' was not in use in 1854 when Odling first wrote on the topic, he had a clear idea of the concept, which he referred to as replaceable or representative value. Odling, like many of his contemporaries, was skeptical of the existence of atoms, and it was not until the 1890s that his misgivings were overcome. From his work on atomic weights he was led to suggest that the atomic weight of oxygen should be 16, not 8. In 1861 he was able to clear up a troublesome problem over oxygen by suggesting that ozone was triatomic; this was later confirmed by J. Soret in 1866. Odling also studied and classified silicates.

Oersted, Hans Christian (1777–1851) *Danish physicist*

Oersted was born at Rudkjöbing in Denmark and studied at Copenhagen University, where he received a PhD in 1799 for a thesis defending Kantian philosophy. To complete his scientific training he then traveled through Europe visiting the numerous physicists working on aspects of electricity. On his return to Denmark he started giving public lectures, which were so successful that, in 1806, he was offered a professorship at Copenhagen. Here he became well known as a great teacher and did much to raise the level of Danish science to that of the rest of Europe.

It was while lecturing that he actually first observed electromagnetism (although for years he had believed in its existence) by showing that a needle was deflected when brought close to a wire through which a current was flowing. By the summer of 1820 he had confirmed the existence of a circular magnetic field around the wire and published his results. They produced an enormous flurry of new activity in the scientific world, which up to that time had accepted Coulomb's opinion that electricity and magnetism were completely independent forces.

Ohm, Georg Simon (1787–1854) *German physicist*

Ohm, who was born at Erlangen in Germany, seems to have acquired his interest in science from his father, a skilled mechanic. He studied at the University of Erlangen and then taught at the Cologne Polytechnic in 1817. From 1826 to 1833 he taught at the Military Academy in Berlin, moving to the Polytechnic at Nuremburg before finally obtaining a chair in physics at Munich in 1849.

Despite the fact that he published his famous law in 1827 in his *Die galvanische Kette mathematisch bearbeitet* (The Galvanic Circuit Investigated Mathematically) he received no recognition or promotion for more than twenty years. Ohm seems to have been stimulated by the work on heat of Joseph Fourier. The flow of heat between two points depends on the temperature difference and the conductivity of the medium between them. So too, argued Ohm, with electricity. If this line of thought is pursued it soon leads to the general form of *Ohm's law* that the current is proportional to the voltage. Using wires of different sizes he was able to show that the resistance was proportional to the cross-sectional area of the wire and inversely proportional to its length.

Ohm also worked on sound, suggesting in 1843 that the ear analyzes complex sounds into a combination of pure tones. This result was rediscovered by Hermann von HELMHOLTZ in 1860.

The unit of electrical resistance, the *ohm*, was named in his honor.

Olah, George Andrew (1927–)
Hungarian–American chemist

Olah gained his PhD from the Technical University, Budapest, in 1949. He moved to Canada in 1956 following the Hungarian uprising and joined the staff of the Dow Chemical Company in Ontario. In 1964 he moved to America and in 1965 joined the faculty of the Case Western Reserve University, Cleveland, Ohio. In 1977 he moved to the University of Southern California, becoming director of the Loker Hydrocarbon Research Institute in 1991. Olah became a naturalized American citizen in 1970.

In certain chemical reactions involving hydrocarbons, extremely short-lived highly reactive positively charged carbon intermediates are often formed. These have a positive charge on the carbon atom and are known as 'carbonium ions' or 'carbocations'. Because of their short lifetime, little had been established about these intermediates.

Olah, while working at Dow, discovered a way to preserve the intermediates and to allow their properties to be investigated. He found that solutions of a very strong acid, variously described as a 'superacid' or a 'magic acid', would preserve carbocations for months at a time and thus allow their structure to be determined with such techniques as nuclear magnetic resonance spectroscopy (NMR). Olah's superacids were formed by dissolving compounds such as antimony pentafluoride in water at low temperature. The result was an acid some 10^{18} times stronger than sulfuric acid. The stable carbocations formed in this way proved to be quite unusual, with structures quite unlike the more familiar tetrahedral forms. Olah's work quickly found important applications in industry; it has, for example, been widely used in synthesizing high-octane gasoline.

For his work on carbocations Olah was awarded the 1995 Nobel Prize for chemistry.

Olbers, Heinrich (1758–1840) *German astronomer*

Olbers, who was born at Arbegen in Germany, was a physician who practiced medicine at Bremen. He became a good amateur astronomer, and converted part of his house into an observatory. He became interested in searching for a planet in the 'gap' between Mars and Jupiter, and rediscovered the first minor planet (or asteroid) Ceres after it had been lost by its discoverer Giuseppe Piazzi. In 1802 he discovered the second asteroid, Pallas, and in 1807 the fourth, Vesta. He also devised a method of calculating comet orbits, called *Olbers's method*, and discovered five comets. The one named for him was last seen in 1956.

Olbers's modern fame, however, rests on his statement of a very simple problem, the solution of which has had a profound impact on modern cosmology. He asked the naive question: why is the sky dark at night? Olbers assumed that the heavens are infinite and unchanging and that the stars are evenly distributed. The amount of light reaching the Earth from very distant stars is very small – in fact, the illumination decreases with the square of the distance. On the other hand, this is compensated for by the increased number of stars – the average number at a given distance increases with the square of the distance. The result is that the whole sky should be about as bright as our Sun. Olbers's solution to this problem was that the light is absorbed by dust in space, but this is an unsatisfactory explanation since the dust would eventually become incandescent and radiate energy. In the 20th century it became clear that the solution lies in the fact that the universe is not uniform, infinite in time, or unchanging; the red shift of the light from distant galaxies results in a reduction of the energy of the radiation from stars. The paradox had been discussed earlier (1744) by J. P. L. Chesaux.

Oldham, Richard Dixon (1858–1936)
British seismologist and geologist

Oldham's father, Thomas, was professor of geology at Trinity College, Dublin, and director of the Geological Surveys of India and Ireland. Oldham, who was born in Dublin, was educated at the Royal School of Mines; in 1879 he followed his father in joining the Geological Survey of India, rising to the rank of superintendent. He retired in 1903 and became director of the Indian Museum in Calcutta.

Oldham made two fundamental discoveries. He made a detailed study of the Assam earthquake of 1897 and, in 1900, was the first to identify clearly the primary (P) and secondary (S) seismic waves transmitted through the Earth, which had been predicted by the mathematician Siméon Poisson on theoretical grounds. Secondly, in 1906 he provided the first clear evidence that the Earth had a central core. He found that the arrival of the primary, or compressional, waves was delayed at places opposite to the focal point of an earthquake. He deduced from this that the Earth contains a central core that is less dense and rigid than the rocks of the mantle, and through which compressional waves would travel less fast. A detailed analysis of the arrival and distortion of the P and S waves that had traveled through or near to the center of the Earth later provided much insight into the structure of the Earth.

Oliphant, Marcus Laurence Elwin
(1901–   ) *Australian physicist*

Born in Adelaide, Oliphant was educated at the university there and at Cambridge University, England, where he obtained his PhD in 1929. He then worked at the Cavendish Laboratory in Cambridge before being appointed (1937) to the Poynting Professorship of Physics at Birmingham University. Oliphant returned to Australia in 1950 and held research chairs at the Australian National University, Canberra, until his retirement in 1967.

Hydrogen, the simplest of all atoms, normally has a nucleus of a single proton, but in 1932 Harold Urey had discovered a heavier form that he called deuterium, with a nucleus consisting of a proton and a neutron. The enlarged nucleus became known as the deuteron. In 1934 Oliphant and his collaborator Paul Harteck produced an even heavier form of hydrogen by bombarding deuterium with deuterons. This new isotope has a nucleus consisting of one proton and two neutrons (hydrogen–3). They named it 'tritium' and called the nucleus a 'triton'. The isotope is radioactive with a half-life of 12.4 years and for this reason is not found in significant amounts in nature.

During World War II Oliphant did important work on the development of radar. It was in his laboratory that two German refugees, Rudolf Peierls and Otto Frisch, made some of the vital calculations and experiments that revealed the real possibility of an atomic bomb.

Omar Khayyam (c. 1048–c. 1122)
Persian astronomer, mathematician, and poet

Omar Khayyam, who was born at Nishapur (now in Iran), produced a work on algebra that was used as a textbook in Persia until this century. He gave a rule for solving quadratic equations, he could solve special cases of the cubic, and – in a last work – seemed to have some inkling of the binomial theorem. He also worked on the reform of the Persian calendar, which was basically the Egyptian one of 365 days, introducing a sixth epagomenic (extra) day and obtaining an accurate estimate of the tropical year.

Onsager, Lars (1903–1976) *Norwegian–American chemist*

Born at Christiania (now Oslo) in Norway, Onsager was educated at the Norwegian Institute of Technology. He moved to America in 1928 and obtained his PhD at Yale in 1935. He spent virtually his whole career at Yale, serving as J. W. Gibbs Professor of Theoretical Chemistry from 1945 until 1972.

Onsager made two important contributions to chemical theory. In 1926 he showed the need to modify the equation established by Peter DEBYE and Erich Hückel in 1923 which described the behavior of ions in a solution, by taking Brownian motion into consideration.

Onsager's main work, however, was in the foundation of the study of nonequilibrium thermodynamics. Here an attempt is made to apply the normal laws of thermodynamics to systems that are not in equilibrium – where there are temperature, pressure, or potential differences of some kind. For his work in this field Onsager was awarded the Nobel Prize for chemistry in 1968. The study of nonequilibrium thermodynamics was further developed by Ilya PRIGOGINE.

Oort, Jan Hendrik (1900–1992) *Dutch astronomer*

The son of a physician from Franeker in the Netherlands, Oort was educated at the University of Gröningen where he worked under Jacobus Kapteyn and gained his PhD in 1926. After a short period at Yale University in America he was appointed to the staff of the University of Leiden where he was made professor of astronomy in 1935 and from 1945 to 1970 served as director of the Leiden Observatory. He also served as director of the Netherlands Radio Observatory.

Oort's main interest was in the structure and dynamics of our Galaxy. In 1927 he succeeded in confirming the hypothesis of galactic rotation proposed by Bertil Lindblad. He argued that just as the outer planets appear to us to be overtaken and passed by the less distant ones in the solar system, so too with the stars if the Galaxy really rotated. It should then be possible to observe distant stars appearing to lag behind and be overtaken by nearer ones. Extensive observation and statistical analysis of the results would thus not only establish the fact of galactic rotation but also allow something of the structure and mass of the Galaxy to be deduced.

Oort was finally able to calculate, on the basis of the various stellar motions, that the Sun was some 30,000 light-years from the center of the Galaxy and took about 225 million years to complete its orbit. He also showed that stars lying in the outer regions of the galactic disk rotated more slowly than those nearer the center. The Galaxy does not therefore rotate as a uniform whole but exhibits what is known as 'differential rotation'.

Oort was also one of the earliest of the established astronomers to see the potential of the newly emerging discipline of the 1940s, radio astronomy. As one of the few scientists free to do pure research in the war years, he interested Hendrik van de HULST in the work that finally led to the discovery in 1951 of the 21-centimeter radio emission from neutral interstellar hydrogen.

By measuring the distribution of this radiation and thus of the gas clouds Oort and his Leiden colleagues lost little time in tracing the spiral structure of the galactic arms and made substantial improvements to the earlier work of William Morgan. They were also able to make the first investigation of the central region of the Galaxy: the 21-centimeter radio emission passed unabsorbed through the gas clouds that had hidden the center from optical observation. They found a huge concentration of mass there, later identified as mainly stars, and also discovered that much of the gas in the region was moving rapidly outward away from the center.

Oort made major contributions to two other fields of astronomy. In 1950 he proposed that a huge swarm of comets surrounded the solar system at an immense distance and acted as a cometary reservoir. A comet could be perturbed out of this *Oort cloud* by a star and move into an orbit taking it toward the Sun. In 1956, working with Theodore Walraven, he studied the light emitted from the Crab nebula, a supernova remnant. The light was found to be very strongly polarized and must therefore be synchrotron radiation produced by electrons moving at very great speed in a magnetic field.

Oppenheimer, Julius Robert
(1904–1967) *American physicist*

Oppenheimer came from a wealthy New York City family. He was educated at Harvard, at Cambridge, England, and at Göttingen where he obtained his PhD in 1927. From 1929 to 1942 he was at the University of California, and while there accepted the post of director of the Los Alamos laboratory where he worked on the development of the atom bomb. After the war in 1947 he was appointed director of the Institute for Advanced Studies at Princeton, a post he held until his death. He also served (1947–52) as chairman of the important General Advisory Committee of the Atomic Energy Commission.

He is mainly remembered, however, for his work on the Los Alamos project. It has been argued that only Oppenheimer could have made Los Alamos viable for only he could have commanded the allegiance of the world's best talents in physics, who gathered around him in the New Mexico desert. It was also only Oppenheimer who had sufficient independence and authority to persuade the military and General Groves, his superior, to grant sufficient freedom to the scientists to make the project workable.

Freeman Dyson, who saw Oppenheimer in the early 1950s at Princeton with some of his old colleagues, caught in their talk "a glow of pride and nostalgia. For every one of these people the Los Alamos days had been a great experience, a time of hard work and comradeship and deep happiness." But Oppenheimer stayed on after the war when, by all accounts, there was little comradeship, much divisiveness and, ultimately, tragedy for Oppenheimer and some of his friends. In 1948 he was on the cover of *Time* magazine; four years later he was summarily dismissed from his post with the Atomic Energy Commission.

Oppenheimer had actually been under investigation since 1942, first as a matter of routine and then more rigorously when reports critical of his loyalty began to arrive at the office of Colonel Pash, who was responsible for security at Los Alamos. It should be emphasized that at no time has any evidence been published to suggest that Oppenheimer was disloyal to his country. Suspicions were aroused because some of his friends had been members of the Communist party and because he had moved freely in left-wing circles. Both his wife and brother were well-known left-wing sympathizers, if not communists.

Before long the suspicions became more precise: it was felt that a Russian agent had made an approach to Oppenheimer and although he had not responded he was guilty of failing to report the approach to the authorities. Oppenheimer finally admitted that an approach had been made to him but he refused to disclose any names for he felt the man was no longer involved and in any case had merely been a messenger. In a classic dialogue with his inquisitor he kept insisting that, "I feel that I should not give it. I don't mean that I don't hope that if he's still operating that you will find it ... But I would just bet dollars to doughnuts that he isn't still operating."

Finally, at the end of 1943, the Army lost patience and Groves put it clearly to Oppenheimer that he must either provide names or go. He named Haakon Chevalier, a professor of romance languages at the University of California whom he had known since 1938. Chevalier was of course ruined and, although no charges were ever laid against him, it became impossible for him to find academic employment ever again in America. Whether Oppenheimer had behaved honorably by his own judgment is far from clear as there is too much conflicting evidence about the crucial approach. For some, Chevalier was a totally innocent man maligned by a man consumed by ambition; for others Chevalier was a Russian agent who was lucky not to collect a heavy sentence. Where precisely the truth lies must await the release of further documentation.

Oppenheimer was thus free to develop the bomb and at 5.30 a.m. on 16 July 1945 the first bomb was tested. When Oppenheimer saw the huge cloud rising over the desert, he later reported, a passage from the *Bhagavad Gita* came to him: "I am become Death, the shatterer of worlds." A move by senior scientists led by James Franck and Leo Szilard to arrange for a public demonstration of the bomb's power rather than its military use on a Japanese city was referred to Oppenheimer for commment. He was in favor of using it on a Japanese town.

After the war, when he could reasonably have left Government service and devoted himself to theoretical physics, he – for reasons that are not clear – remained as the leading adviser on nuclear weapons, taking responsibility for the development of the hydrogen bomb. Oppenheimer had made many enemies and when accusations were made that he had in fact obstructed the program to build the fusion bomb they were more than willing to work for his downfall. A commission to investigate his loyalty reported in 1954 that "Dr. Oppenheimer did not show the enthusiastic support for the Super (H-bomb) program which might have been expected of the chief adviser of the Government" and rendered its judgment that he was unfit to serve his country. Although Oppenheimer never regained his security clearance, peace of a sort was made with the authorities when in 1963 he received the Fermi award from President Kennedy. Four years later, after bearing his illness with great courage, he died of cancer of the throat.

Osheroff, Douglas (1945–   ) *American physicist*

Osheroff was educated at California College of Technology, Pasadena, and at Cornell, where he gained his PhD in 1973. After working at Bell Labs he moved to Stanford in 1987 as professor of physics.

In 1972, while still a Cornell graduate student of David LEE, Osheroff made a crucial observation that led to the discovery of the supposedly impossible superfluidity of helium-3. He was actually studying magnetism in helium-3 but, because the magnetic equipment was required elsewhere, Osheroff was detailed to test a new refrigeration device. He noted an unexpected blip in the cooling rate when the solid–liquid mixture fell to 2.6 millikelvins (2.6 millionth of a degree above absolute zero). He had in fact observed a phase transition. Further work revealed that the transition was from a normal fluid to a superfluid.

For his work on superfluidity Osheroff shared the 1996 Nobel Prize for physics with David LEE and Robert RICHARDSON.

Ostwald, Friedrich Wilhelm (1853–1932) *German chemist*

Ostwald was born of German parents who had settled at Riga, now in Latvia. He was educated at the University of Dorpat and the Riga Polytechnic, where he was professor of physics from 1881 until he left to take the chair of physical chemistry at

Leipzig in 1887. He retired from his chair in 1906 and spent the rest of his life mainly in literary, philosophical, and editorial work.

Ostwald probably did more than anyone else to establish the new discipline of physical chemistry. He was a great teacher and built up an important research school at Leipzig through which most major chemists passed at some time in their career. He founded in 1887 the *Zeitschrift für physikalische Chemie* (Journal of Physical Chemistry), the first journal in the world devoted to the new discipline, translated the writings of the American physical chemist Josiah Willard Gibbs into German in 1892, and also produced an inspiring two-volume textbook on the subject, *Lehrbuch der allgemeinen Chemie* (1885, 1887; Textbook of General Chemistry).

Ostwald's own research was mainly on catalysts, for which he received the Nobel Prize for chemistry in 1909. He defined catalysis in 1894 as "the acceleration of a chemical reaction, which proceeds slowly, by the presence of a foreign substance." He emphasized that the catalyst for the reaction does not alter the general energy relations or the position of equilibrium. In 1888 he formulated his dilution law, which allows the degree of ionization of a weak electrolyte to be calculated with reasonable accuracy. The *Ostwald process* (patented in 1902) was an industrial process for oxidizing ammonia to nitric acid.

Philosophically Ostwald was a positivist and denied the reality of atoms until well into the 20th century. The chemist, he argued, does not observe atoms but studies the simple and comprehensive laws to which the weight and volume ratios of chemical compounds are subject. He believed that atoms were a hypothetical conception but by 1908 he had been converted to atomism.

Ostwald's son, Wolfgang, also became a chemist of some note.

Oughtred, William (1575–1660) *English mathematician*

Oughtred was born at Eton and educated at the famous school there (where his father taught writing) and at Cambridge University. He was ordained a priest in 1603 and eventually became rector of Albury.

Despite his clerical post he found time to work on mathematics and he produced what was to become a very famous book on mathematics, the *Clavis mathematicae* (1631; The Key to Mathematics). This work dealt with arithmetic and algebra, and it is of historical importance because Oughtred managed to put into it more or less everything that was known at that time in those areas of mathematics. It rapidly became an influential and widely used textbook and held in high regard by mathematicians of the stature of Isaac Newton and John Wallis, himself a pupil of Oughtred. A number of mathematical symbols that are still used were first introduced by Oughtred. Among these were the sign '×' for multiplication, and the 'sin' and 'cos' notation for trigonometrical functions. Oughtred also invented the earliest form of the slide rule in 1622 but only published this discovery in 1632. As a result, he became embroiled in a violent dispute with one of his former students, Richard Delamain, who had made the same invention independently.

Palade, George Emil (1912–)
Romanian–American physiologist and cell biologist

Palade was born at Iasi in Romania. Educated at Bucharest University, where he was professor of physiology during World War II, he emigrated to America in 1946, becoming a naturalized citizen in 1952. He worked at the Rockefeller Institute for Medical Research, New York, becoming professor of cytology there (1958–72). In 1972 he became director of studies in cell biology at Yale University's medical school. In 1990 he was appointed dean of scientific affairs at the University of California at San Diego.

Palade's work has been primarily concerned with studies of the fine structure of animal cells, although he has also investigated the nature of plant chloroplasts. He has shown that minute semisolid structures in cells, known as mitochondria, have an enzymic effect, oxidizing fats and sugars and releasing energy. His discovery of even smaller bodies called microsomes, which function independently of the mitochondria (of which they were previously thought to be part), showed them to be rich in ribonucleic acid (RNA) and therefore the site of protein manufacture. The microsomes were subsequently renamed ribosomes. For his work in cellular biology, Palade received, with Albert CLAUDE and Christian DE DUVE, the Nobel Prize for physiology or medicine (1974).

Pappus of Alexandria (c. 320) *Greek mathematician*

Pappus was the last notable Greek mathematician and is chiefly remembered because his writings contain reports of the work of many earlier Greek mathematicians that would otherwise be lost. His chief work, *Synagogue* (c. 340; Collection), consisted of eight books of which the first and part of the second are now lost. It was intended as a guide to the whole of Greek mathematics and this is what makes it such a significant historical source. Among the mathematicians whose work Pappus expounds are Euclid, Apollonius of Perga, Aristaeus, and Eratosthenes. Pappus did contribute some original work, however, notably in projective geometry.

As with many Greek mathematicians Pappus was as interested in astronomy as in pure mathematics and his other work included comments on Ptolemy's astronomical system contained in the *Almagest*.

Paracelsus, Philippus Aureolus
(1493–1541) *German physician, chemist, and alchemist*

Paracelsus, born Theophrastus Bombastus von Hohenheim in Einsiedeln, Switzerland, was the son of a physician from whom he received his early training in medicine and alchemy. His assumed name stems from his claim to have surpassed the Roman physician Celsus. He traveled with his father to Villach in Austria where he worked as an apprentice in the mines and acquired much of his practical knowledge of mineralogy and metallurgy. He left the mines in 1507, attended various German universities, and may have obtained an MD from Ferrara. After practicing medicine in Sweden, Strasbourg, Basel, Nuremburg, and a host of other places, in 1540 Paracelsus settled in Salzburg where he died in the following year.

Paracelsus was the first to reject totally the authority of antiquity, suggesting its replacement by nature and experiment. To show his seriousness he burned the great medieval compilation of medical knowledge, the *Canon* of Avicenna, before his students. In Basel he was lucky enough to cure the infected limb of an influential publisher Frebenius, for which orthodox physicians had recommended amputation. This led to his appointment as professor of medicine and city physician at Basel.

His contempt for traditional learning and the reason the medical authorities found him so distasteful is best conveyed by his much quoted riposte to them: "Let me tell you this: every little hair on my neck knows more than you and all your scribes, and my shoe-buckles are more learned than your Galen and Avicenna, and my beard has more experience than all your high colleges." The alternative proposed by Paracelsus contained a number of not particularly coherent strands. There was much in his work that belonged to, or at least overlapped with, the occult tradition but there was an eagerness to embrace new sources of knowledge. He would willingly learn his chemistry from the craftsmen in the mines and claimed to gain knowledge from gypsies, magicians, and elderly country folk.

His greatest influence on 16th-century science arose from his chemical philosophy in which he posed the 'tria prima': salt, sulfur, and mercury. These terms were meant to emphasize the principles of solidity, combustibility, and liquidity inherent in any substance. It was by following through the implications of such schemes that later chemists such as Robert Boyle were led to the corpuscular view of matter.

In medicine Paracelsus took the revolutionary step of introducing chemically prepared drugs rather than persisting exclusively with the herbal medicines or 'simples' of antiquity. While he was perhaps not the first to use such new remedies as mercury, sulfur, potassium, and antimony his dramatic use of them, often with supposedly verified cures, brought them sharply before the attention of the public. It is from this work that medicine begins to take on its modern aspect as being concerned with the discovery of specialized drugs providing complete and harmless cures.

Parkes, Alexander (1813–1890) *British chemist and inventor*

Parkes, the son of a Birmingham lock manufacturer, was apprenticed to a brass founder and started his career in charge of the casting department at Elkington. He took out his first patent, which was for electroplating delicate objects such as works of art, in 1841. Eventually Parkes took out over 50 patents in this field; when the prince consort, Prince Albert, visited Elkington, Parkes presented him with a silver-plated spider's web. In metallurgy, Parkes also invented a process for removing silver from lead by extraction with molten zinc (the *Parkes process*).

He also worked on rubber and plastics. In 1846 he discovered the cold vulcanization process, which was important in the manufacture of thin-walled rubber articles. In 1855 he took out a number of patents on a new product initially called xylonite (or parkesine). Aiming to produce a synthetic form of horn, Parkes found that if the recently discovered nitrocellulose was mixed with camphor and alcohol, a hornlike substance was produced. It was not fully developed by Parkes however and it was left to the Hyatt brothers of New Jersey to develop it as celluloid, the first synthetic plastic material.

Pascal, Blaise (1623–1662) *French mathematician, physicist, and religious philosopher*

Pascal was the son of a respected mathematician and a local administrator in Clermont-Ferrand, France. Early in life Pascal displayed evidence that he was an infant prodigy and apparently discovered Euclid's first 23 theorems for himself at the age of 11. While only 17 he published an essay on mathematics that René Descartes refused to acknowledge as being the work of a youth. Pascal produced (1642–44) a calculating device to aid his father in his local administration; this was in effect the first digital calculator.

Pascal conducted important work in experimental physics, in particular in the study of atmospheric pressure. He tested the theories of Evangelista Torricelli (who discovered the principle of the barometer) by using mercury barometers to measure air pressure in Paris and, with the help of his brother-in-law, on the summit of the Puy de Dôme (1646). He found that the height of the column of mercury did indeed fall with increasing altitude. From these studies Pascal invented the hydraulic press and the syringe and formulated his law that pressure applied to a confined liquid is transmitted through the liquid in all directions regardless of the area to which the pressure is applied. He published his work on vacuums in 1647.

Pascal corresponded with a contemporary mathematician, Pierre de Fermat, and together they founded the mathematical theory of probability. Pascal had been converted to Jansenism in 1646 and religion became increasingly dominant in his life, culminating in the religious revelation he experienced on the night of November 23, 1654. Following this he entered the Jansenist retreat at Port-Royal (1655) and devoted himself to religious studies from then on.

Pasteur, Louis (1822–1895) *French chemist and microbiologist*

Pasteur, the son of a tanner, was born at Dôle in France and studied chemistry at the Ecole Normale Supérieure in Paris where he obtained his doctorate for crystallographic studies in 1847. His first appointments were as professor of chemistry firstly at Strasbourg (1849) and then at Lille (1854). In 1857 Pasteur returned to Paris as director of scientific studies at the Ecole Normale but moved to the Sorbonne in 1867 as professor of chemistry. He returned once more to the Ecole Normale in 1874 to direct the physiological chemistry laboratory but spent his last years, from 1888 to 1895, as director of the specially created Pasteur Institute.

Although not a physician, Pasteur was undoubtedly the most important medical scientist working in the 19th century. His work possessed an originality, depth, and precision that was apparent even in his early work, which led to the discovery of molecular asymmetry. Tartaric and racemic acid were known to have the same formula, but their crystalline salts possessed different optical properties in solution: tartrate rotates a ray of polarized light to the right, and was accordingly described as dextrorotatory or d-tartrate, while the racemic salts were optically inactive. How, it was asked, could the same compound have such contrasting properties?

Pasteur, in 1848, examined d-tartrate crystals under a hand lens and noticed that they all possessed an identical asymmetry, which he assumed to be sufficient to twist a ray of light to the right. The racemate however, while also asymmetrical, appeared to contain crystals divided equally between the d-tartrate form and its mirror image. Pasteur painstakingly separated the crystals into two piles and found that, in solution, one pile behaved exactly as d-tartrate while the other rotated polarized light to the left. Racemic acid was therefore, he concluded, an equal mixture of d-tartrate and its mirror image, the levorotatory l-tartrate, each of which was optically active on its own but together neutralized each other.

Such facts would later have profound consequences for structural chemistry and Pasteur, in 1860, suggested that the effect was a result of the internal arrangement of atoms. Thus he asked "Are the atoms of the dextro acid arranged on a right-hand helix, or positioned at the corners of an irregular tetrahedron, or have they some other asymmetric grouping? We cannot answer these questions. But there is no doubt that an asymmetric arrangement exists that has a non superposable image. It is not less certain that the atoms of the levo acid have exactly the inverse asymmetric arrangement." The idea of an asymmetric tetrahedral carbon atom was put forward in 1874 by Jacobus VAN'T HOFF and Joseph LE BEL. In 1857 Pasteur also noted that a mold accidentally growing on a tartrate solution selected just one of the two racemic forms, the d-form. More generally, he realized that only living organisms could distinguish between such asymmetric forms and even went so far as to argue that this ability marks the only sharply defined difference between the chemistry of dead and living matter.

By 1856 Pasteur had also begun to work on fermentation, beginning with the fermentation of milk into lactic acid. He reported the presence of microorganisms, which continued to bud and multiply; if excluded, fermentation failed to occur but they could be transferred from one ferment to produce another in uncontaminated milk. Further, such organisms were quite specific, as the yeast used to produce beer was incapable of producing lactic acid from milk. With these and many other observations and experiments behind him Pasteur was ready to dispute the chemical theory of Justus von Liebig. He declared that all true fermentations are caused by the presence and multiplication of organisms, and are not, as Liebig insisted, purely chemical phenomena. With his germ theory of fermentation Pasteur anticipated much of his later work.

He next turned to the origin of such 'organisms' and 'ferments' and investigated spontaneous generation. In 1862 Pasteur published his famous paper, *Mémoire sur les corpuscles organisés qui existent dans l'atmosphère* (Note on Organized Corpuscles that Exist in the Atmosphere), which finally brought to an end centuries of earlier debate. Pasteur demonstrated that if sterilized fermentable fluid was placed in a swan-neck flask (a flask with a long curved thin neck that allows air to enter but prevents dust and microorganisms entering) then the fluid remained clear. However if the neck of the flask was then broken off, allowing dust to enter, contamination soon resulted.

In 1865 Pasteur was asked to investigate a new disease devastating the silkworms of southern France. Despite his protest that "I have never even seen a silkworm," despite considerable confusion caused by the presence of two quite independent infections, and despite a stroke in 1868, which partially paralyzed his left side, Pasteur still managed to provide a comprehensive analysis of the disease and its prevention.

It was not until 1877 that Pasteur finally turned to human disease and pioneered effective methods of treatment against virulent infections such as anthrax. The breakthrough came in 1880 as a result of an oversight by his assistant, who had inadvertently left a batch of chicken cholera bacilli standing in the laboratory over a long hot summer. On injection into some healthy chickens the culture produced only mild and transient signs of disease. Pasteur then instructed his assistant to prepare a fresh batch of the bacillus and once more inject it into the chickens. They survived unscathed, whereas chickens fresh from the market succumbed rapidly to a similar injection. Pasteur had accidentally discovered an attenuated vaccine for chicken cholera. By May 1882 he had succeeded in deliberately producing a comparable vaccine against anthrax and was ready to test it publicly at Pouilly-le-Fort. Here his success was total with all 24 unvaccinated sheep dying of anthrax while those receiving his vaccine survived.

Events even more dramatic followed in 1885 when Pasteur used a rabies vaccine recently developed by him on a badly bitten nine-year-old boy, Joseph Meister. Against the advice of such colleagues as Emile Roux he began the course of 14 injections using virus attenuated in the spine of rabbits. Meister survived. He committed suicide 55 years later in 1940 when, as a caretaker at the Pasteur Institute, he preferred to die rather than open the tomb of Pasteur to the invading Nazi forces.

Thus nearly a century after Edward JENNER, Pasteur had introduced only the second vaccine effective against a serious human disease. Others would rapidly follow him so that by the turn of the century several would be in use. Shortly after his triumph Pasteur suffered a second stroke in 1887, one which affected his speech. Although he lived a further seven years his long creative period was at an end.

Paul, Wolfgang (1913–1993) German physicist

Paul, who was born at Lorenzkirch in Germany, was educated at the universities of Kiel and Berlin, where he obtained his PhD in 1939. After World War II, he taught physics at Göttingen until 1952, when he was appointed professor of physics at the University of Bonn.

During the 1950s he developed the so-called *Paul trap* as a means of confining and studying electrons. The device consists of three electrodes – two end caps and an encircling ring. The ring is connected to an oscillating potential. The direction of the electric field alternates; for half the time the electron is pushed from the caps to the ring and for the other half it is pulled from the ring and pushed towards the caps.

For his work in this field Paul shared the 1989 Nobel Prize for physics with Hans DEHMELT and Norman RAMSEY.

Pauli, Wolfgang (1900–1958) Austrian–Swiss physicist

Born in the Austrian capital of Vienna, Pauli was the son of a professor of physical chemistry at the university there and the godson of Ernst Mach. He was educated at the University of Munich, where he obtained his PhD in 1922. After further study in Copenhagen with Niels Bohr and at Göttingen with Max Born, Pauli taught at Heidelberg before accepting the professorship of physics at the Federal Institute of Technology, Zurich. Apart from the war years, which he spent working in America at the Institute of Advanced Studies, Princeton, he remained there until his early death in 1958.

Pauli was a physicist much respected by his colleagues for his deep insight into the newly emerging quantum theory. His initial reputation was made in relativity theory with his publication in 1921 of his *Relativitätstheorie* (Theory of Relativity). His name is mainly linked with two substantial achievements. The first, formulated in 1924, is known as the *Pauli exclusion principle*. It follows from this that as an electron can spin in only two ways each quantum orbit can hold no more than two electrons. Once both vacancies are full further electrons can fit only into other orbits. With this principle the distribution of orbital electrons at last became clear, that is, they could be explained and predicted in purely quantum terms.

The early model of the atom by Niels BOHR had been extended by Arnold Sommerfeld in 1915. In the Bohr–Sommerfeld atom, each electron orbiting the nucleus had three quantum numbers: n, l, and m. Pauli introduced a fourth quantum number (s), which could have values of $+1/2$ or $-1/2$ and corresponded to possible values of the 'spin' of the electron. Pauli's exclusion principle stated that no two electrons in an atom could have the same four quantum numbers (n, l, m, and s). The concept of electron spin was verified in 1926 by Samuel GOUDSMIT and George UHLENBEK. The exclusion principle explained many aspects of atomic behavior, including the spectral effects discovered by Pieter Zeeman. It has also been applied to other particles. It was for his introduction of the exclusion principle that Pauli was awarded the 1945 Nobel Prize for physics.

Pauli's second great insight was in resolving a problem in beta decay – a type of radioactivity in which electrons are emitted by the atomic nucleus. It was found that the energies of the electrons covered a continuous range up to a maximum value. The difficulty was in reconciling this with the law of conservation of energy; specifically, what happened to the 'missing' energy when the electrons had lower energies than the maximum? In 1930, in a letter to Lise Meitner, Pauli suggested that an emitted electron was accompanied by a neutral particle that carried the excess energy. Enrico Fermi suggested the name 'neutrino' for this particle, which was first observed in 1953 by Frederick Reines.

Pauling, Linus Carl (1901–1994)
American chemist

Pauling, a pharmacist's son, was born at Portland, Oregon, and graduated in chemical engineering from Oregon State Agricultural College in 1922. Having gained his PhD in physical chemistry from the California Institute of Technology in 1925, he spent two years in Europe working under such famed scientists as Arnold Sommerfeld, Niels Bohr, Erwin Schrödinger, and William Henry Bragg. He was appointed associated professor of chemistry at Cal Tech in 1927 and full professor in 1931.

Pauling worked on a variety of problems in chemistry and biology. His original work in chemistry was on chemical bonding and molecular structure. He applied physical methods, such as x-ray diffraction, electron diffraction, and magnetic effects, to determining the structure of molecules. He also made significant contributions to applying quantum mechanics to the bonding in chemical compounds. In this field he introduced the idea of hybrid atomic orbitals to account for the shapes of molecules. Another of his innovations was the idea of resonance hybrid – a molecule having a structure intermediate between two different conventional structures. Pauling also worked on the partial ionic character of chemical bonds, using the concept of electronegativity. Pauling's ideas on chemical bonding were collected in his influential book *The Nature of the Chemical Bond and the Structure of Molecules and Crystals* (1939).

From about 1934 he began to work on more complex biochemical compounds. He studied the properties of hemoglobin using magnetic measurements. This work led on to extensive studies of the nature and structure of proteins. With Robert B. Corey, he showed that the amino-acid chain in certain proteins can have a helical structure.

He also made a number of original contributions on other biological topics. In 1940, with Max Delbrück, he introduced a theory of antibody–antigen reactions that depended on molecular shapes. In the 1940s he also studied the genetic disease sickle cell anemia. In 1960 he published a theory of anesthesia and memory. He is noted for his originality and intuition in tackling complex problems and his deep understanding of chemistry. In his book *The Double Helix*, describing the race to determine the structure of DNA, James Watson describes the concern caused by the knowledge that Pauling was working on the same problem.

Pauling was awarded the 1954 Nobel Prize for chemistry. By this time, he had been campaigning for some years against the development of nuclear weapons. He had earlier refused to join the Manhattan project, but had overcome his pacifist principles sufficiently to work on conventional weapons: "Hitler had to be stopped," he noted. By the early 1950s, campaigns against nuclear weapons were being interpreted as 'un-American' and Pauling's passport was withdrawn making it impossible to travel to Stockholm for the Nobel ceremonies; his passport was returned at the last moment. Pauling continued with his campaign, publishing a book, *No More War* (1958), and organizing a petition of scientists against nuclear testing. He was awarded the Nobel Peace Prize in 1962.

Pauling later began to campaign on another issue, namely the therapeutic value of high doses of vitamin C. In 1971, in his *Vitamin C and the Common Cold*, Pauling claimed that large vitamin C doses, over 10 grams a day, would also reduce the risk of heart disease. Pauling himself took 18 grams of vitamin C daily, a figure 300 times the recommended dose, for the last 27 years of his life. To pursue the matter further Pauling set up in 1973 the Pauling Institute of Science and Medicine in Palo Alto, California.

Pavlov, Ivan Petrovich (1849–1936)
Russian physiologist

Born at Ryazan in Russia, Pavlov studied medicine and general science at the University of St. Petersburg and the Military Medical Academy. He subsequently carried out research in Breslau (now Wrocław, in Poland) and Leipzig (1883–86). Returning to St. Petersburg, he became professor of physiology at the Medical Academy and director of the physiology department of the Institute of Experimental Medicine.

Pavlov's early research lay in the physiology of mammalian digestion, showing, for example, that the secretion of digestive juices in the stomach is prompted by the sight of food and nerve stimulation via the brain. For this work Pavlov received the Nobel Prize for physiology or medicine (1904). He then went on to study the way that dogs and other animals may be induced to salivate and show signs of anticipation of food by actions, such as the ringing of a bell or even a powerful electric shock, that they have learned to associate with the appearance of food. Pavlov's work on conditional or acquired reflexes, which he believed to be associated with different areas of the brain cortex, has led to a new psychologically-oriented school of physiology and has stimulated ideas as to the probability of many aspects of human behavior being a result of 'conditioning'.

Pavlov openly criticized communism and the Soviet government. In 1922 he requested and was refused permission to move his laboratory abroad. Following the expulsion of priests' sons from the Medical Academy, Pavlov, himself the son of a priest, resigned from the chair of physiology in protest. Despite such actions his work continued to be supported by state funds and Pavlovian psychology remained popular in the Soviet Union.

Peano, Giuseppe (1858–1932) *Italian mathematician and logician*

Peano, who was born at Spinetta near Cuneo, in Italy, studied at the University of Turin and was an assistant there from 1880. He became extraordinary professor of infinitesimal calculus in 1890 and was full professor from 1895 until his death. He was also professor of the military academy in Turin from 1886 to 1901.

Peano began his mathematical career as an analyst and, like Richard Dedekind before him, his interest in philosophical and logical matters was awakened by the lack of rigor in some presentations of the subject. Peano was particularly keen to avoid all illegitimate reliance on intuition in analysis. His discovery in 1890 of a curve that was continuous but filled space went against intuition. A similar discovery was Karl Weierstrass's famous function that was everywhere continuous but nowhere differentiable. As with Weierstrass's function, *Peano's curve* shows that the concept of a continuous function cannot be identified with that of a graph.

His interest in rigorous and logical presentation of mathematics led Peano naturally to an interest in the mathematical development of logic. In this field he was one of the great pioneers along with Georg Boole, Gottlob Frege, and Bertrand Russell. Peano's achievement was twofold. First he devised, in his *Notations de logique mathématique* (1894; Notations in Mathematical Logic), a clear and efficient notation for mathematical logic which, as modified by Bertrand Russell, is still widely used. Secondly, he showed how arithmetic can be derived from a purely logical basis. To do this he formulated, in his *Nova methodo exposita* (1889; New Explanation of Method), nine axioms, four dealing with equality, and the remaining five, listed below, characterizing the numbers series:

1 is a number
The successor of any number is a number
No two numbers have the same successor
1 is not the successor of any number
Any property that belongs to 1 and the successor of any number that also has that property, belongs to all numbers (mathematical induction).

Peano's axioms had been proposed, in a more complicated form, by Dedekind a year earlier.

Peano also did notable work in geometry and on the error terms in numerical calculation. Among his extramathematical interests he was a keen propagandist for a proposed international language, Interlingua, which he had developed from Volapük.

Pearson, Karl (1857–1936) *British biometrician*

Pearson, the son of a London lawyer, studied mathematics at Cambridge University. He then joined University College, London, initially (from 1884) as professor of applied mathematics and mechanics and from 1911 until his retirement in 1933 as Galton Professor of Eugenics.

Pearson's career was spent largely on applying statistics to biology. His interest in this derived ultimately from Francis Galton and was much reinforced by the work of his colleague Walter Weldon. In 1893 Weldon had argued that variation, heredity, and selection are matters of arithmetic; Pearson started in the 1890s to develop the appropriate 'arithmetic' or statistics as it came to be called. Between 1893 and 1906 Pearson published over a hundred papers on statistics in which such now familiar concepts as the standard deviation and the chi-square test for statistical significance were introduced. Later work was published in *Biometrika*, the journal founded by Pearson, Galton, and Weldon in 1901 and edited by Pearson until his death. This he ran with an unashamed partisanship, rejecting outright or correcting without invitation papers expressing views Pearson considered "controversial." It is for this reason that Ronald Fisher, the most creative British statistician of the century, decided after receiving the treatment from Pearson in 1920 to publish elsewhere.

Pearson and Weldon became involved in an important controversy with William BATESON on the nature of evolution and its possible measurement. The biometricians emphasized the importance of continuous variation as the basic material of natural selection and proposed that it be analyzed statistically. Bateson and his supporters, whose views were reinforced by the rediscovery of the works of Gregor Mendel in 1900, attached more importance to discontinuous variation and argued that breeding studies are the best way to illuminate the mechanism of evolution.

The validity of Mendelism eventually became generally accepted. At the same time, however, the immense value of biometrical techniques in analyzing continuously variable characters like height, which are controlled by many genes, was also recognized. Following Weldon's death in 1906, Pearson spent less time trying to prove the biometricians' case and devoted himself instead to developing statistics as an exact science. He prepared and published many volumes of mathematical tables for statisticians. He also devoted much of his time to the study of eugenics, using Galton's data to issue various volumes of the *Studies in National Deterioration* (1906–24). In 1925 he founded and edited until his death the *Annals of Eugenics*.

To many Pearson is best known as the author of *Grammar of Science* (1892), a widely read positivist work on the philosophy of science in which he argued, like his earlier teacher Ernst Mach, that science does not explain but rather summarizes our experience in a convenient language.

Pedersen, Charles (1904–1989)
American chemist

The son of Norwegian parents, Pedersen was born in Pusan, Korea, and moved with his family to America in the 1920s. He became a naturalized American citizen in 1953. Pedersen was educated at the Massachusetts Institute of Technology and, for most of his career up to his retirement in 1969, he worked as a research chemist for DuPont.

While working on synthetic rubber, Pedersen noted that one of his materials had been contaminated. He investigated the impurity and found that it had a ring structure of 12 carbon and 6 oxygen atoms, with a pair of carbon atoms between each oxygen. Such structures are known as cyclic polyethers. Normally, organic solvents such as ether and benzene will not dissolve sodium hydroxide. Yet Pedersen found that caustic soda did dissolve in his new compound, with the sodium ions binding loosely to the oxygen atoms of the ether. To accomplish this the polyether formed a nonplanar ring with a crownlike structure, with the sodium ions sitting neatly in the center. For this reason, Pedersen named what turned out to be a new class of com-

pounds 'crown ethers'. Although he made his first observations in 1964, DuPont delayed publication until 1967.

The implications of Pedersen's work were varied and important. If one crown ether could coordinate sodium ions, it was likely that others of different ring size would be able to bind to other metal ions. Crown ethers could therefore be used as a simple means of gathering specific ions from aqueous solutions.

Other chemists were also quick to see the implications of Pedersen's work and it was with two of these, Jean LEHN and Donald CRAM, that he shared the 1987 Nobel Prize for chemistry.

Peebles, James (1935–) *Canadian astronomer*

Born at Winnipeg in Canada, Peebles was educated at the University of Manitoba and at Princeton, where he took his PhD in 1962. He has remained at Princeton ever since, becoming Einstein Professor of Science in 1984.

Peebles has made a number of contributions to modern cosmology. In 1965, in collaboration with Robert Dicke, he made the important prediction that a background radiation should be detectable as a remnant of the big bang. He also calculated that the amount of helium present in the universe as a consequence of the big bang should be about 25–30%, a figure that agrees with current observations.

In 1979, again in collaboration with Dicke, Peebles drew the attention of cosmologists to the so-called 'flatness problem' and asked how the standard model of the big-bang theory could deal with it. Cosmologists ask if the universe is 'open' or 'closed'. If it is open it will continue to expand forever; if closed, the expansion will cease at some future point and it will begin to contract. To answer the question the value of omega (Ω) must be found.

Omega (Ω) is the ratio of the average density of mass in the universe to the critical mass density. This latter factor is the mass density needed just to halt the universe's expansion. If Ω is less than 1 the universe is open, and if Ω is greater than 1 the universe is closed. If Ω is equal to 1 the universe will be flat, that is, the universe will continue to expand, although at a decreasing rate.

The actual measured value of Ω is close to 1. A bit more matter in the universe and it would have collapsed long ago; a little less matter, and it would have expanded too quickly for galaxies to form. But if Ω is close to 1 now, it must have been close to 1 soon after the big bang. If it had differed significantly, Ω would either be approaching infinity and the universe would have the density of a black hole, or equal to 0 and the universe would be indistinguishable from a vacuum.

The question thus becomes why so early in the history of the universe was Ω so close to 1? Instead of merely laying this down as an arbitrary initial condition, there should be some way to see why, given the big bang, Ω should have this value. As Peebles's problem seemed to have no solution in the standard model of the big bang, it has been left to astronomers such as Alan GUTH to propose alternative foundations based on an inflationary model.

Peebles is also the author of two important books, *Physical Cosmology* (Princeton, 1971) and *The Large Scale Structure of the Universe* (Princeton, 1980), which have between them done much to define the subject of cosmology for a generation of astronomers.

Pelletier, Pierre Joseph (1788–1842)
French chemist

Pelletier was born the son of a pharmacist in Paris, France. He both studied and taught at the Ecole de Pharmacie until his retirement in 1842. His major work was the investigation of drugs, which he began in 1809. By pioneering the use of mild solvents he successfully isolated numerous important biologically active plant products: working with the French pharmacist **Bienaimé Caventou** (1795–1877) he discovered caffeine, strychnine, colchicine, quinine, and veratrine. Their greatest triumph, however, came in 1817, when they discovered chlorophyll – the green pigment in plants that traps light energy necessary for photosynthesis.

Peltier, Jean Charles Athanase
(1785–1845) *French physicist*

Born in the Somme department of France, Peltier was a watchmaker who gave up his profession at the age of 30 to devote himself to experimental physics. In 1821 T. J. Seebeck had shown that if heat is applied to the junction of a loop of two different conductors a current will be generated. In 1834 Peltier demonstrated the converse effect (the *Peltier effect*). He found that when a current is passed through a circuit of two different conductors a thermal effect will be found at the junctions. There is a rise or fall in temperature at the junction depending on the direction of current flow.

Penrose, Sir Roger (1931–) *British mathematician and theoretical physicist*

Penrose, the son of the geneticist Lionel Penrose, was born at Colchester in Essex. He graduated from University College, London, and obtained his PhD in 1957 from Cambridge University. After holding various lecturing and research posts in London, Cambridge, and in America at Princeton, Syracuse, and Texas, Penrose was appointed professor of applied mathematics at Birkbeck College, London, in 1966. In 1973 he was elected Rouse Ball Professor of Mathematics at Oxford.

Penrose has done much to elucidate the fundamental properties of black holes. These result from the total gravitational collapse of large stars that shrink to such a small volume that not even a light signal can escape from them. There is thus a boundary around a black hole inside which all information about the black hole is trapped; this is known as its 'event horizon'. With Stephen HAWKING, Penrose proved a theorem of Einstein's general relativity asserting that at the center of a black hole there must evolve a 'space-time singularity' of zero volume and infinite density where the present laws of physics break down. He went on to propose his hypothesis of 'cosmic censorship', that such singularities cannot be 'naked'; they must possess an event horizon. The effect of this would be to conceal and isolate the singularity with its indifference to the laws of physics.

Despite this Penrose went on in 1969 to describe a mechanism for the extraction of energy from a Kerr black hole, an uncharged rotating body first described by Roy KERR in 1963. Such bodies are surrounded by an ergosphere within which it is impossible for an object to be at rest. If, Penrose demonstrated, a body fell into this area it would split into two particles; one would fall into the hole and the other would escape with more mass-energy than the initial particle. In this way rotational energy of the black hole is transferred to the particle outside the hole.

From the mid-1960s Penrose has been working on the development of a new cosmology based on a complex geometry. Penrose began with 'twistors' – massless objects with both linear and angular momentum in twistor space. From these he attempted to reconstruct the main outlines of modern physics. The matter is pursued not only by Penrose but through a number of 'twistor groups' who communicate through a *Twistor Newsletter*. The fullest account of twistor theory is to be found in *Spinors and Space-Time* (2 vols., 1984–86) by Penrose and W. Windler.

In 1974 Penrose introduced a novel tiling of the affine plane (*Penrose tiling*). Periodic tilings in which a unit figure is endlessly repeated can be constructed from triangles, squares, and hexagons – figures with three-, four-, or six-fold symmetry. The plane cannot be tiled by pentagons, which have a five-fold symmetry; three pentagons fitted together always leave a crack, known to crystallographers as a 'frustration'. It was also known that crystal structures could have two-, three-, four-, or six-fold rotational symmetries only. No crystal, that is, could have a five-fold rotational symmetry.

Penrose's method of tiling the plane involved constructing two rhombuses by dividing the diagonal of a regular parallelogram by a golden section. These could be combined according to simple rules so as to cover the plane, even though there was no simple repeated unit cell. The rhombuses can be assembled in such a way as to have an almost five-fold symmetry. As such they were seen as an interesting oddity, usually discussed in columns devoted to recreational mathematics. However, things changed dramatically in 1984 when Dany Schectman of the National Bureau of Standards and his colleagues found that a rapidly cooled sample of an aluminum–manganese alloy formed crystals that displayed a five-fold symmetry. 'Quasicrystals', as they soon became known, developed rapidly into a major new research field and became the subject of hundreds of research papers.

In addition to continuing his work on twistor theory Penrose also published a widely read book, *The Emperor's New Mind* (1989). The book is an attack on aspects of artificial intelligence. In it he argues that there are aspects of mathematics that cannot be tied to a set of rules. We cannot allow "one universally formal system... equivalent to all the mathematicians' algorithms for judging mathematical truth." Such a system would violate Gödel's theorem. Nor can we accept that algorithms used are so complicated and obscure that their validity can never be known. We do not in fact ascertain mathematical truth solely through the use of algorithms. "We must see the truth of a mathematical argument to be convinced of its validity," Penrose has insisted. Consequently when we *see* the validity of a theorem, in *seeing* it "we reveal the very nonalgorithmic nature of the 'seeing' process itself."

He further developed his arguments in *Shadows of the Mind* (1994), in which he also answered many of the objections raised against the earlier work. Penrose has also published (in collaboration with Stephen Hawking) *The Nature of Space and Time* (1996), in which they develop their own cosmological viewpoints. Thus while Penrose presents his own twistor view of the universe, Hawking concentrates on problems connected with quantum cosmology.

Penzias, Arno Allan (1933–)
American astrophysicist

Penzias, who was born in Munich, Germany, earned his BS at City College, New York, in 1954 after fleeing with his parents as a refugee from the Nazis. He gained his PhD from Columbia University in 1962. In 1961 he joined Bell Laboratories at Holmdel, New Jersey, and was made director of their radio research laboratory in 1976. From 1979 he has been executive director of research in the communications division.

Penzias and his coworker **Robert W. Wilson** (1936–) are credited with one of the most important discoveries of modern astrophysics, the cosmic microwave background radiation. This is considered to be the remnant radiation produced in the 'big bang' in which the universe was created some billions of years ago. As the universe has expanded, the radiation has lost energy: it has effectively 'cooled'. Its existence was originally predicted by George Gamow and Ralph Alpher in 1948, who calculated that the radiation should now be characteristic of a perfectly emitting body (a black body) at a temperature of about 5 kelvin (−268°C). This radiation should lie in the microwave region of the spectrum. Similar calculations were later made by Robert Dicke and P. J. E. Peebles.

The discovery of the remnant radiation was made while Penzias and Wilson were working at the Bell Laboratories. They were using a 20-foot (6-m) directional radio antenna, designed for communication with satellites, and found what appeared to be excessive radio noise in their instrument. They decided to investigate further, thinking that it could be due to radio waves from our own Galaxy. In May 1964 they found that there was a background of microwave radiation that came from all directions uniformly and was not accountable simply as instrumental noise. They calculated its effective temperature as about 3.5 kelvin. An explanation was proposed by Dicke at nearby Princeton University that this was the predicted remnant radiation of the creation of the universe. Subsequent experiments confirmed that it was isotropic and apparently unchanging (on human timescales).

For their discovery Penzias and Wilson were awarded the 1978 Nobel Prize for physics, which they jointly shared with Pyotr L. KAPITZA, who received the award for his (unrelated) developments in low-temperature physics. Penzias and Wilson have continued to collaborate on research into intergalactic hydrogen, galactic radiation, and interstellar abundances of the isotopes. In particular their work has led to the discovery of a large number of interstellar molecules and rare isotopic species.

Perey, Marguerite Catherine (1909–1975) *French nuclear chemist*

Perey, the daughter of an industrialist, was born at Villemomble in France and educated at the Faculté des Sciences de Paris. She began her career in 1929 as an assistant in the Radium Institute in Paris under Marie Curie. In 1940 she moved to the University of Strasbourg, becoming professor of nuclear chemistry in 1949 and director of the Center for Nuclear Research in 1958.

By the 1930s chemists had discovered all the elements of the periodic table below uranium except for those with atomic numbers 43, 61, 85, and 87. Many claims had been made for the discovery of element 87 with it being variously and prematurely named russium, moldavium, and virginium. In 1939 Perey found in the radioactive decay of actinium–227 the emission of alpha-particles as well as the expected beta-particles. As an alpha-particle is basically a helium nucleus with an atomic mass of 4 this implied that Perey had discovered a nuclide of mass number 223. Further investigation showed it to be one of the missing elements, with an atomic number of 87. She originally called it actinium K but in 1945 named it francium (for France).

Perkin, Sir William Henry (1838–1907) *British chemist*

Perkin was born in London, the youngest son of a builder. His interest in chemistry was aroused early by some experiments shown to him by a young friend and he was fortunate to attend the City of London School, which was one of the few London schools where science was taught. Perkin's teacher there, Thomas Hall, was a pupil of Johann Hofmann at the Royal College of Chemistry and Hall pleaded with Perkin's father to allow his son to study chemistry and not to force him into a career in architecture. Hall was successful and Perkin entered the college in 1853.

In 1855 he was made Hofmann's assistant and the following year was given the task of synthesizing quinine (despite much effort, this difficult task was not achieved until 1944, by Robert Burns Woodward and William von Eggers Doering). Perkin started from the coal-tar derivative allyltoluidine,

which has a formula very similar to that of quinine. He thought the conversion could be achieved by removing two hydrogen atoms and adding two of oxygen. Although no quinine was formed by this reaction, it did produce a reddish-brown precipitate. Perkin decided to treat a more simple base in the same manner and tried aniline and potassium dichromate. This time a black precipitate was produced. Addition of alcohol to this precipitate yielded a rich purple color. Perkin soon realized that this coloring matter had the properties of a dye and resisted the action of light very well. He sent some specimens of dyed silk to a dyeing firm in Perth, Scotland, which expressed great interest provided that the cost of the cloth would not be raised unduly. With this behind him, Perkin took out the appropriate patents, borrowed his father's life savings, and in 1857 built a dye factory at Greenford Green, near Harrow, for mass production of the first synthetic dye – mauveine.

Initially there were difficulties. Since aniline was not readily available, it had to be produced at the factory from benzene. There was also the conservatism of the dye industry to overcome.

The significance of Perkin's discovery lay in its being the first *synthetic* dye; before this all dyes were derived from such organic sources as insects, plants, and mollusks. Purple had traditionally come from a Mediterranean shellfish and could be produced only at great cost, so that it was used only by royalty. Apart from the difficulty of supply there was also the problem of the quality of the dyes: vegetable and animal dyes were not particularly fast and tended to fade in the light. The market was ripe for anyone who could provide a dye in bulk that was cheap, fast, and did not fade. Perkin quickly made his fortune and stimulated a rush to find other synthetics. Carl Graebe and C. T. Liebermann soon synthesized alizarin, the coloring ingredient of madder. Magenta and Bismarck brown were among the other new colors that were soon to flood the market.

In 1874 Perkin sold his factory and retired, a wealthy man, at the age of 35, devoting the rest of his life to research in pure science. He became particularly interested in Faraday rotation and produced over 40 papers on this topic.

Perkin was knighted in 1906. His son and namesake was also a chemist.

Perkin, William Henry, Jr. (1860–1929) *British chemist*

Perkin, who was born at Sudbury near London, was the elder son of the famous chemist who discovered the aniline dyes, also called William Henry Perkin. As a child he assisted his father in his private laboratory. He was educated at the City of London School and then in 1877 followed his father to the Royal College of Chemistry. He then went to Germany where he studied at the universities of Würzburg and Munich. On his return to England he worked at Manchester before being appointed professor of chemistry at Heriot-Watt College, Edinburgh, in 1887. In 1892 he returned to Manchester as professor of organic chemistry and in 1912 he became Waynflete Professor of Chemistry at Oxford.

Perkin was a very practical chemist who, in a long career, achieved many syntheses and analyses. His first success came in his student days in Munich. It had been argued by Victor Meyer in 1876 that no ring with fewer than six carbon atoms could exist. Perkin succeeded in 1884 in preparing rings with four carbon atoms.

Of the many molecules he synthesized are the terpenes, limonene (1904), the oxygenated terpineol (1904), and camphoric acid (1903). He worked on many alkaloids, including strychnine and on natural coloring compounds like brazilin. Perkin also worked with William Pope, showing that optical activity can be found in compounds in which the carbon atoms are not necessarily asymmetrical.

He produced three chemical works in collaboration with Frederic Kipping and also did much to stimulate the growth of chemistry at Oxford by campaigning for the new laboratories that were opened there in 1922.

Perl, Martin Lewis (1927–) *American physicist*

Born in New York, Perl first graduated in chemistry in 1948 at the Brooklyn Polytechnic Institute. After working in industry as a chemical engineer for General Electric, Perl became interested in nuclear physics. Consequently he returned to college and in 1955 he was awarded his PhD from Columbia, New York. He immediately moved to the University of Michigan, where he remained until he took up his present position of professor of physics at Stanford, California, in 1963.

In 1972 physicists were aware of four leptons: the electron, the muon, and their corresponding neutrinos. Further, leptons, unlike hadrons such as the proton, are genuinely pointlike elementary particles, which interact by the weak force. In 1972 Stanford opened its new accelerator, SPEAR (Stanford Positron–Electron Asymmetry Ring). While no new lepton had been found since the discovery of the muon in 1936, Perl decided to use the SPEAR facilities to see whether the lepton family could be extended.

Theoretical reasons led him to believe that any new lepton would have a charge of plus or minus 1, have a mass greater than a billion electronvolts (1 GeV), decay in less than a billionth of a second, and respond only to the weak and electromagnetic forces. Like any other particle, the new lepton would have to be identified by detecting its characteristic decay products. The particle had been named the 'tau particle' from the initial letter of the Greek word for third, 'triton'. Perl argued that the tau would decay into either a muon or an electron, plus a neutrino and an antineutrino. In 1974 a sample of 10,000 events yielded twenty-four of the predicted kind. Despite some initial skepticism the existence of a heavy lepton with a mass greater than the proton was quickly confirmed.

Perl's discovery had an important theoretical implication. The four previously known leptons were linked with the four known quarks. The discovery of a new lepton, therefore, suggested the symmetry could only be maintained by the existence of a new quark. The prediction was confirmed in 1977 when Leon Lederman discovered the upsilon particle. For his discovery of the tau particle, Perl shared the 1995 Nobel Prize for physics with Frederick REINES.

Perrin, Jean Baptiste (1870–1942) *French physicist*

Perrin was born in Lille, France, the son of an army officer. He was educated at the Ecole Normale, where he received his doctorate in 1897. He was appointed to the Sorbonne where he was made professor of physical chemistry in 1910. He remained there until 1941, when he went to America to escape the Nazis.

Perrin's early work was in the developing field of cathode rays and x-rays. In 1895 he established the important result that cathode rays are deflected by a magnetic field and thus carry a negative charge. He began to calculate the ratio of charge to mass for these particles but was anticipated by J. J. Thomson. In 1901 he produced a work on physical chemistry, *Les Principes* (Principles).

His most important work however was on Brownian motion and the molecular hypothesis. In 1828 Robert Brown had reported that pollen granules immersed in water moved continuously and erratically. However, it was left to Albert Einstein to provide some quantitative explanations for the motion in 1905. Assuming that the pollen was being moved by water molecules, he showed that the average distance traveled by a particle increased with the square of the elapsed time. Making the necessary corrections for temperature, size of particles, and nature of the liquid involved, Einstein made precise predictions about how far a particle should travel in a given time.

In 1908 Perrin was finally able to confirm Einstein's predictions experimentally. His work was made possible by the development of the ultramicroscope by Richard Zsigmondy and Henry Siedentopf in 1903. He was able to work out from his experimental results and Einstein's formula the size of the water molecule and a precise value for Avogadro's number.

The fundamental importance of this work was that it established atomism as something more than a useful hypothesis. It was mainly as a result of Perrin's work that the most eminent skeptic, Wilhelm Ostwald, at last relented. Perrin was awarded the Nobel Prize for physics in 1926 for his work on Brownian motion and sedimentation.

In 1913 he published *Les Atomes* (Atoms), which collected together not only his own work on molecules but new material from radiochemistry, black-body radiation, and many other fields, to demonstrate the reality of molecules. It was an enormously influential work, going through four editions in its first year and being translated into many languages.

Perutz, Max Ferdinand (1914–)
Austrian–British biochemist

While studying chemistry at the university in his native Vienna, Perutz became interested in x-ray diffraction techniques; after graduation he went to England to work on the x-ray diffraction of proteins with William L. Bragg at the Cavendish Laboratory, Cambridge. A meeting in Prague with the biochemist Felix Haurowitz in 1937 turned his attention to the blood protein hemoglobin and he received his PhD in 1940 for work in this field. Soon after, he was arrested as an alien and interned, first on the Isle of Man and then in Canada with Hermann Bondi and Klaus Fuchs. He was released and allowed to return to Britain in 1941. In the following year he joined the staff of Lord Mountbatten, examining various applications of science for the war effort.

After the war Perutz organized the setting up, in 1946, of the molecular biology laboratory in Cambridge, where he was soon joined by John KENDREW. After seven years' hard work Perutz was still far from his objective of working out the three-dimensional structure of hemoglobin, a molecule containing some 12,000 atoms. Then in 1953 he applied the heavy atom or isomorphous replacement technique to his work whereby heavy metal atoms, e.g., mercury or gold, are incorporated into the molecule under study. This alters the diffraction patterns, making it easier to compute the positions of atoms in the molecule. By 1959 he had shown hemoglobin to be composed of four chains, together making a tetrahedral structure, with four heme groups near the molecule's surface.

For this achievement Perutz received the 1962 Nobel Prize in chemistry, sharing it with Kendrew, who had worked out the structure of the muscle protein, myoglobin, using similar methods. In later work Perutz demonstrated that in oxygenated hemoglobin the four subunits are rearranged. This explained the change in structure noted by Haurowitz in 1938. Perutz also investigated the various mutated forms of hemoglobin characteristic of inherited blood diseases.

While indulging his hobby of mountaineering, Perutz made some notable contributions to the understanding of glaciers, particularly by his demonstration that the rate of flow is faster at the glacier surface than at the base.

Perutz continued as head of the Medical Research Council molecular biology unit at Cambridge until his retirement in 1979. He published a brief account of his early life and his views on science in his *Is Science Necessary?* (1989).

Peters, Sir Rudolph Albert (1889–1982) *British biochemist*

Peters, the son of a London doctor, was educated at Cambridge University and St. Bartholomew's Hospital, London. After teaching briefly in Cambridge, he accepted the Whitley Chair of Biochemistry at Oxford, which he held from 1923 until his retirement in 1954.

Between 1928 and 1935 Peters and his Oxford colleagues succeeded in showing for the first time the precise activity of a vitamin in the body. Working with vitamin B_1, or thiamine – the antiberiberi factor first described by Christiaan Eijkman – they fed pigeons on a diet of polished rice. This was free of thiamine and produced a number of debilitating symptoms in most of the birds. As one of these symptoms was convulsions, Peters suspected that the thiamine deficiency could involve the central nervous system. He consequently began a search of the pigeon's brain for what he termed a 'biochemical lesion'.

The first hint of the role of thiamine was provided by the failure of minced pigeon brain to take up as much oxygen as the brain of a normally fed bird. The lesion was promptly reversed by the addition of thiamine. Further work showed an accumulation of lactic acid in the pigeon brain. As this is one of the intermediate products in the metabolism of carbohydrates into carbon dioxide and water it seemed clear that thiamine must be an essential ingredient in this metabolic pathway.

Peters's work therefore provided the first proof of the action of any vitamin upon an enzyme system *in vitro*.

Petit, Alexis-Thérèse (1791–1820)
French physicist

Petit, who was born at Vesoul in France, entered the Ecole Polytechnique in 1807. He spent a period teaching physics in Paris, and received a doctorate in 1811. He was one of the professors of physics at the Ecole Polytechnique. Petit did some research with his brother-in-law D. F. J. Arago on the variation of refractive index with temperature. However, he is known solely for his work with his colleague **Pierre Dulong** (1785–1836) in which they established the law (*Dulong and Petit's law*) that the specific heat of a solid multiplied by the atomic weight is (approximately) a constant for different solids.

Phillips, William (1948–) *American physicist*

Phillips, who was born in Wilkes-Barre, Pennsylvania, was educated at the Massachusetts Institute of Technology, where he gained his PhD in 1976. He then joined the staff of the National Bureau of Standards and Technology, Maryland.

In the early 1980s Phillips and his colleagues showed how beams of sodium atoms could be cooled down to temperatures of about 0.1 kelvin, just a tenth of a degree above absolute zero. The method involved exposing the sodium atoms to a laser beam tuned to a frequency lower than the resonant frequency of the atoms. Some of the atoms moving toward the laser light, because of an appropriate Doppler shift, will absorb and emit light photons. The process, repeated endlessly, will slow the atoms down. Atoms moving in the direction of the laser beam, however, because the frequency will be shifted lower, are less likely to absorb radiation and their motion is little affected.

Soon after this, Steven CHU developed the technique so that it could be applied to a gas rather than a beam of atoms and isolated and cooled individual atoms to a temperature of 240 microkelvins. Unfortunately, atoms could be contained in Chu's optical laser trap for no more than a second. In 1988 Phillips sought to improve the trap by using a varying magnetic field placed above and below the area in which the laser beams intersected. This reduced the temperature of the confined atoms to 40 microkelvins. With this technique Phillips found that he need only reduce the atom's speed to less than 3.5 meters per second, corresponding to a temperature of 17 millikelvins, for the atoms to be held in the laser trap for several seconds.

For his work in this field Phillips shared the 1997 Nobel Prize for physics with Steven Chu and Claude COHEN-TANNOUDJI.

Piazzi, Giuseppe (1746–1826) *Italian astronomer*

Born at Ponte in Valtellina, Italy, Piazzi was a monk who originally taught philosophy but later in life developed an interest in astronomy. He became professor of mathematics at Palermo, Sicily, setting up an observatory there in 1787. He was a careful observer, publishing a catalog of 7646 stars in 1814. In his work he had found that proper motion was not the rarity assumed by some but the property of most stars and he found that 61 Cygni had a very large proper motion of 5.2″. His most dramatic discovery was that of the minor planet Ceres in 1801. He named it after the goddess of agriculture, once widely worshipped in Sicily. Although Piazzi lost the planet, its position was precisely predicted by Karl Gauss after a staggering feat of calculation based on three observations of Piazzi. Three more similar bodies were quickly found. He had a dispute with William Herschel over their nature. Piazzi proposed that they shoud be called 'planetoids' but Herschel's alternative suggestion of 'asteroid' has proved more acceptable until quite recently.

Picard, Jean (1620–1682) *French astronomer*

Born at La Flèche in northwestern France, Picard succeeded Pierre Gassendi as professor of astronomy at the Collège de France in 1655. He helped to found the Paris Observatory and conducted fundamental researches into the size of the Earth. Using new instruments such as William Gascoigne's micrometer he established an accurate baseline and by a series of 17 triangles between Malvoisin and Amiens calculated one degree to be 69.1 miles (111.2 km). This result proved to be extremely valuable to Newton in his calculations on the attractive force of the Moon.

Picard also determined accurately the position of Tycho Brahe's observatory at Uraniborg (this information was necessary in order to analyze and interpret Tycho's observations). He further noted, but was not able to explain, an annual periodic motion of Polaris (approximately 40″). James BRADLEY later explained this as the aberration of light.

Pickering, Edward Charles (1846–1919) *American astronomer*

Born in Boston, Massachusetts, Pickering graduated from Harvard in 1865. He taught physics at the Massachusetts Institute of Technology before becoming professor of astronomy and director of the observatory at Harvard in 1876, remaining there until his death in 1919.

Pickering made innovations in spectrography. Instead of placing a small prism at the focus to capture the light of a single star, he put a large prism in front of the objective, obtaining at the same time a spectrogram of all the stars in the field sufficiently bright to affect the emulsion. This made possible the massive surveys he wanted to organize and enabled the publication in 1918 of the *Henry Draper Catalogue*, compiled by Annie Cannon, giving the spectral types of 225,300 stars. The other innovation in instruments due to him was the meridian photometer introduced in 1880. In this, images of stars near the meridian would be reflected at the same time as the image of Polaris. The brightness could then be equalized and as the brightness of Polaris was known, that of the meridian stars could easily be calculated. More than a million observations with such instruments permitted the compilation of the Harvard catalog giving the magnitude of some 50,000 stars. He was able to include stars of the southern hemisphere in this catalog, for in 1891 he had established an observatory in Arequipa, Peru, with the help of his brother William Henry Pickering.

One further improvement due to Edward Pickering was his introduction, around 1900, of the alphabetic system of spectral classes.

Pickering, William Henry (1858–1938) *American astronomer*

Pickering, the younger brother of Edward Pickering, was also an astronomer. Born in Boston, Massachusetts, he studied at the Massachusetts Institute of Technology where he worked after graduating in 1879. In 1887 he moved to the Harvard College Observatory where his brother was director. He set up a number of observing stations for Harvard including that at Arequipa, Peru, in 1891 and Mandeville, Jamaica, in 1900. He took charge of the latter in 1911, converting it into his own private observatory following his retirement in 1924.

He also helped Percival Lowell set up his private observatory in Flagstaff, Arizona, and, also like Lowell, concerned himself with the trans-Neptunian planet. In 1919, on the basis of past records, he predicted that a new planet would be found near the constellation of Gemini but photographic surveys failed to confirm his prediction. When the planet Pluto was finally detected in 1930 by Clyde TOMBAUGH, Pickering made a somewhat exaggerated claim to be its discoverer.

He made extensive observations of Mars and claimed, like Lowell, that he saw signs of life on the planet by observing what he took to be oases in 1892. He went further than Lowell however when in 1903 he claimed to observe signs of life on the Moon. By comparing descriptions of the Moon from Giovanni Riccioli's 1651 chart onward, he thought he had detected changes that could have been due to the growth and decay of vegetation.

He was more successful in 1899 when he discovered Phoebe, the ninth satellite of Saturn. This was the first planetary satellite with retrograde motion to be detected, i.e., with orbital motion directed in an opposite sense to that of the planets. His 1905 report of a tenth satellite, which he confidently named Themis, was not substantiated.

Pictet, Raoul Pierre (1846–1929) *Swiss chemist and physicist*

Born in Geneva, Pictet was professor of physics at the university there from 1879 and at the University of Berlin from 1886. He later moved to Paris.

Pictet was first interested in the production of artificial ice and then turned his attention to the study of extremely low temperatures and the liquefaction of gases. On 22 December 1877 he was involved in one of those strange simultaneous discoveries that sometimes occur in science. He announced on that day, by telegram to the French Academy, that he had liquefied oxygen. Just two days later the French physicist Louis Cailletet made a similar announcement.

Both Pictet and Cailletet had recognized that both cooling and compression were necessary to liquefy oxygen but they had achieved this using different techniques. Pictet had used his cascade method, in which he evaporated liquid sulfur dioxide to liquefy carbon dioxide, which in turn was allowed to evaporate and to cool oxygen to below its critical temperature. The oxygen could then be liquefied by pressure. The advantage over Cailletet's method was that it produced the liquid gas in greater quantity and was easier to apply to other gases.

Pincus, Gregory Goodwin (1903–1967) American physiologist

Born in Woodbine, New Jersey, and educated at Cornell and Harvard, Pincus was research director at the Worcester Foundation for Experimental Biology, Shrewsbury, Massachusetts. His most significant work was in reproductive physiology, notably his investigations of human birth control, which led to his developing, with Min Chueh Chang and John Rock, the now famous 'pill'. This form of oral contraception is based upon the use of synthetic hormones that have an inhibitory effect on the female reproductive system, preventing fertilization but still allowing sexual freedom. Pincus discovered that the steroid hormone progesterone, which is found in greater concentrations during pregnancy, is responsible for the prevention of ovulation in pregnancy. With the development, in the fifties, of synthetic hormones, similar in action to progesterone, Pincus saw the possibility of using such synthetics as oral contraceptives. The first clinical trials were conducted in 1954 and proved extremely successful.

In 1963, Pincus became the first chairman of the Oral Advisory Group of the International Planned Parenthood Federation.

Pippard, Sir Alfred Brian (1920–   ) British physicist

Pippard, the son of a professor of engineering, was born at Leeds and educated at Cambridge University. After wartime research on the development of radar, he obtained his PhD from Cambridge in 1947. He remained at the university for the rest of his career, serving as Plummer Professor of Physics from 1960 until 1971 and Cavendish Professor until 1982.

After World War II Pippard began to use microwaves to study superconductors, in particular the conduction in a thin layer at the surface of the material. He introduced the idea of 'coherence' in superconductors – the way in which electrons 'act together' so that an effect at one point influences electrons a certain distance away. Pippard's ideas were explained by the BCS theory of John Bardeen and his colleagues. Pippard has also worked on microwave absorption at metal surfaces as a method of investigating the conduction electrons. His book *Dynamics of Conduction Electrons* (1964) deals with metallic conductivity. His most recent work is *Magnetoresistance in Metals* (1989).

Planck, Max Karl Ernst Ludwig (1858–1947) German physicist

Planck was born at Kiel in Germany, where his father was a professor of civil law at the university. He was educated at the universities of Berlin and Munich where he obtained his doctorate in 1880. He began his teaching career at the University of Kiel moving to Berlin in 1889 and being appointed (1892) professor of theoretical physics, a post he held until his retirement in 1928.

Although Planck's early work was in thermodynamics, in 1900 he published a paper, *Zur Theorie des Gesetzes der Energieverteilung im Normal-Spektrum* (On The Theory of the Law of Energy Distribution in the Continuous Spectrum), which ranks him with Albert Einstein as one of the two founders of 20th-century physics. It is from this paper that quantum theory originated.

A major problem in physics at the end of the 19th century lay in explaining the radiation given off by a hot body. It was known that the intensity of such radiation increased with wavelength up to a maximum value and then fell off with increasing wavelength. It was also known that the radiation was produced by vibrations of the atoms in the body. For a perfect emitter (a so-called black body, which emits and absorbs at all wavelengths) it should have been possible to use thermodynamics to give a theoretical expression for black-body radiation. Various 'radiation laws' were derived. Thus Wilhelm Wien in 1896 derived a law that applied only at short wavelengths. Lord RAYLEIGH and James JEANS produced a law applying at long wavelengths, but predicting that the body should have a massive emission of short-wavelength energy – the so-called 'ultraviolet catastrophe'.

Planck's problem was initially a technical one; he was simply searching for an equation that would allow the emission of radiation of all wavelengths by a hot body to be correctly described. He hit upon the idea of correlating the entropy of the oscillator with its energy. Following his intuition he found himself able to obtain a new radiation formula, which was in close agreement with actual measurements under all conditions.

There was, however, something unusual about the Planck formula. He had found that in seeking a relationship between the energy emitted or absorbed by a body and the frequency of radiation he had to introduce a constant of proportionality, which could only take integral multiples of a certain quantity. Expressed mathematically, $E = nh\nu$, where E is the energy, h is the constant of proportionality, ν is the frequency, and $n = 0, 1, 2, 3, 4$, etc. It follows from this that nature was being selective in the amounts of energy it would allow a body to accept and to emit, allowing only those amounts that were multiples of $h\nu$. The value of h is very small, so that radiation of energy at the macroscopic level where n is very large is likely to *seem* to be emitted continuously.

Planck's introduction of what he called the 'elementary quantum of action' was a revolutionary idea – a radical break with classical physics. Soon other workers began to apply the concept that 'jumps' in energy could occur. Einstein's explanation of the photoelectric effect (1905), Niels BOHR's theory of the hydrogen atom (1913), and Arthur COMPTON's investigations of x-ray scattering (1923) were early successes of the quantum theory. In 1918 Planck was awarded the Nobel Prize for physics. The constant h (6.626196×10^{-34} joule second) is known as the *Planck constant* – the value

"$h = 6.62 \times 10^{-27}$ erg.sec"

is engraved on his tombstone in Göttingen.

By the time of his retirement Planck had become the leading figure in German science and was therefore to play a crucial role in its relations with the Nazis. His attitude was that of prudent cooperation with the overriding aim of retaining the integrity of German science and preventing it from falling into international ridicule. Although he did not publicly protest against the harassment of Jewish scientists, considering such barbarisms a temporary madness, he did, in 1933, raise the issue with Hitler himself. He argued that the racial laws of 1933, barring Jews from government positions, would endanger the preeminence of German science. Hitler is reported to have expressed a willingness to do without science for a few years. Nor did Planck succeed in protecting the institutions of German science for in 1939 the presidency of the academy went to a party member, T. Vahlen, who lost no time in turning it virtually into an organ of the party.

Planck's later years, despite the honors that came his way, were indeed bitter ones. "My sorrow cannot be expressed in words," he lamented at one point. During World War I his elder son Karl died from wounds suffered in action, and his twin daughters, Grete and Emma, died during childbirth in 1917 and 1919 respectively. In World War II he was forced to witness the destruction of his country and of German science and its institutions. His own home, with all his possessions, was totally destroyed by allied bombing in 1944. Worst of all, his one surviving child, Erwin, was executed in 1945 for complicity in the 1944 attempt to assassinate Hitler.

Plaskett, John Stanley (1865–1941)
Canadian astronomer

Plaskett, who was born at Woodstock, Ontario, was initially trained as a mechanic and began work as such for the physics department of the University of Toronto. He eventually graduated from there in physics and mathematics in 1899. When he moved, in 1903, to the Dominion Observatory in Ottawa it was as mechanical superintendent and not as an astronomer. He gradually moved into astronomy, however, and in 1918 became director of the newly established Dominion Astrophysical Observatory at Victoria, British Columbia, for which he had organized the design, construction, and installation of a new 72-inch (1.8-m) reflecting telescope. He retired in 1935.

Plaskett's field of research was spectroscopy, in particular the measurement of radial velocities of celestial bodies, i.e., their velocities along the line of sight, from the shift in their spectral lines. Using the 72-inch reflector and a highly sensitive spectrograph, many spectroscopic binary systems were discovered. In 1922 Plaskett identified an extremely massive star as a binary, now known as *Plaskett's star*. In 1927 Plaskett provided confirmatory evidence for the theory of galactic rotation put forward by Bertil LINDBLAD and Jan Oort.

By 1928 Plaskett, in collaboration with J. A. Pearce, had obtained evidence for the hypothesis formulated by Arthur Eddington in 1926 that interstellar matter was widely distributed throughout the Galaxy; their results showed that interstellar absorption lines, mainly of calcium, took part in the galactic rotation and so the interstellar matter was not confined to separate star clusters. Although this result was first announced by Otto Struve in 1929, Plaskett felt he had priority and was convinced that Struve had obtained his results from him.

Plato (c. 428 BC–347 BC) *Greek philosopher*

Little is known of Plato's early life. He apparently came from an established Athenian family active in politics. With the execution of Socrates in 399 BC he left Athens for some years and visited, among other places, Sicily in about 389 where he made contact with the Pythagoreans and much impressed Dion, the brother-in-law of Dionysius I, the tyrant of Syracuse. On his return to Athens shortly afterward he founded in about 387 the most famous of all institutions of learning, the Academy, which in one form or another remained viable until its closure by the emperor Justinian in AD 529. On the death of Dionysius I in 367 Plato returned to Sicily at the invitation of Dion to try to educate Dionysius II as the new philosopher-king, attempting once more in 361. The visits were disastrous and ended with Plato dismissing Sicily as a place where "happiness was held to consist in filling oneself full twice a day and never sleeping alone at night."

It is virtually impossible to overestimate the impact of Plato on Western thought. His views, preserved and transmitted through the distorting medium of neo-Platonists and Christian fathers alike, came to influence theology, politics, ethics, education, and aesthetics just as much as they have (and still do) metaphysics and logic. Nor were his contributions to the development of science negligible. It was Plato who posed to the astronomers of his day, such as Eudoxus, the question: "By the assumption of what uniform and orderly motions can the apparent motions of the planets be accounted for?" The request that there should be but one explanation applying to the seemingly disparate observed motions of each planet did much to shape the development of Greek astronomy and to add to it a characteristic dimension of model building lacking, for example, in Babylonian astronomy.

He also, in the *Timaeus*, under the influence of the Pythagoreans of Sicily, introduced an alternative form of atomism to that of Democritus. He began with the result of Theaetetus that there can be only five regular solids, the tetrahedron, cube, octahedron, dodecahedron, and icosahedron, and went on to assign to each of the four elements of Empedocles a characteristic shape of one of the regular solids. The cube as the most stable is assigned to the least mobile element, earth; the pyramid is assigned to fire; the octahedron to air; and the icosahedron to water. To the remaining figure, the dodecahedron, most closely approaching the sphere, Plato associated the 'spherical heaven'.

The main significance of Plato's thought for science was thus to establish the vital tradition, originating with the Pythagoreans and finding ready echoes in the work of Galileo and Kepler, of the mathematical analysis of nature. It is said that an inscription over the vestibule of the Academy read: "Let no one enter here who is ignorant of Geometry."

Playfair, John (1748–1819) *Scottish mathematician and geologist*

Born at Benvie in Scotland, Playfair studied at St. Andrews University before becoming minister of Liff and Benvie in 1773. He was made a professor of mathematics at Edinburgh University in 1785 and professor of natural philosophy in 1805.

Playfair was a friend of the geologist James Hutton and in his *Illustrations of the Huttonian Theory of the Earth* (1802) he amplified and explained Hutton's uniformitarian ideas. Hutton's own work had been notoriously hard to follow and Playfair brought uniformitarianism to a considerably larger public. He also pioneered the idea that a river carves out its own valley.

Although he is better known as a geologist Playfair did make contributions of note to mathematics, in particular to geometry. In 1795 he published his *Elements of Geometry* in which he set out an alternative version of Euclid's fifth postulate, which, given the truth of the other postulates, is equivalent to Euclid's original formulation. This postulate is consequently now known as *Playfair's axiom* and asserts that for any line (L) and point (P) not on L there is one and only one line L' through P parallel to L.

Pogson, Norman Robert (1829–1891) *British astronomer*

Pogson, who was born at Nottingham, started his career in 1852 as an assistant at the Radcliffe Observatory in Oxford. While there he discovered four new asteroids: Amphitrite in 1854, Isis in 1856, and Ariadne and Hestia in 1857. He was to discover nine in all, including the first to be discovered on the continent of Asia and consequently called Asia (1891).

In 1860 he was appointed government astronomer at Madras. He remained in India for the rest of his life, conscious of the enormous amount of observational work that could be done there. He constructed star catalogs and a variable star atlas while there.

His most lasting achievement was the introduction of *Pogson's ratio*. It had been realized that the average first-magnitude star is about a hundred times brighter than stars of the sixth magnitude. He therefore proposed that this interval should be represented by five equal magnitudes, that is, one magnitude would equal $\sqrt[5]{100}$, which equals 2.512. This means that stars of increasing magnitude are roughly 2.5 times brighter. The system has survived in the form proposed by Pogson more than a century ago.

Poincaré, (Jules) Henri (1854–1912)
French mathematician and philosopher of science

Poincaré was born at Nancy in eastern France and studied at the Ecole Polytechnique and the School of Mines. At first he had intended to become an engineer, but fortunately his mathematical interests prevailed and he took his doctorate in 1879 and then taught at the University of Caen. He was professor at the University of Paris from 1881 until his death.

As Poincaré is commonly referred to as the great universalist – the last mathematician to command the whole of the subject – an account of his work would have to cover the whole of mathematics. In pure mathematics he worked on probability theory, differential equations, the theory of numbers, and in his *Analysis situs* (1895; Site Analysis) virtually created the subject of topology. He was, however, hostile to the work on the foundations of mathematics carried out by Bertrand Russell and Gottlob Frege. The discovery of contradictions in their systems, disasters to Frege and Russell, was happily welcomed by Poincaré: "I see that their work is not as sterile as I supposed; it breeds contradictions."

He also deployed the powerful weapons of modern mathematics against a number of problems in mathematical physics and cosmology. In 1887 Oscar II of Sweden offered a prize of 2000 krona for a solution to the question of whether or not the solar system is stable. Will the planets continue indefinitely in their present orbits? Or will some bodies move out of the system altogether, or collide catastrophically with each other? Poincaré published his answer in the monograph *Sur les trois corps et les equations de la dynamique* (1889; On the Three Bodies and Equations of Kinetics). The title refers to what is now known as the 'three-body problem': given three point masses with known initial positions and velocities, to work out their positions and velocities at any future time. The three-body problem had resisted all previous attempts to find a general solution. Poincaré also failed to find an analytical general solution, but he was awarded the prize for making significant advances in the ways of finding approximate solutions.

Poincaré also formulated a famous conjecture which, despite considerable effort and many false alarms, remains unsolved. To a topologist an ordinary sphere is a two-dimensional manifold (a 2-sphere) – two-dimensional because, although it looks like a three-dimensional solid, only its surface is significant. A loop placed on its surface can be shrunk to a point, or, in the language of topology, the 2-sphere is 'simply connected'. This is seen as a defining property of a sphere. A torus, on the other hand, is not a sphere because not all loops placed upon it can be shrunk to points.

What about an n-sphere, the surface of an $n+1$-dimensional body? Poincaré's conjecture is that the n-sphere is the only simply connected manifold in higher dimensions, as the 2-sphere is the only simply connected 2-manifold. Stephen Smale proved in 1969 that the conjecture would hold for all dimensions $n @ t4$, and in 1984 Michael Freedman added the case $n = 4$. The case of $n = 3$ remains a conjecture.

Poincaré, in such later books as *Science and Hypothesis* (1905), developed a radical conventionalism. The high-level laws of science, he argued, are conventions, adopted for ease and simplicity and not for 'truth'. What would happen, he asked, if we found a very large triangle defined by light rays with angles unequal to 180°? As Euclidean geometry is so useful in countless other ways we would more likely sacrifice our physics to preserve our geometry and conclude that light rays do not travel in straight lines.

Poisson, Siméon-Denis (1781–1840)
French mathematician and mathematical physicist

Poisson, born the son of a local government administrator at Pithiviers in France, studied at the Ecole Polytechnique, where his teachers included Pierre Simon Laplace and Joseph Lagrange. He himself later held various teaching posts at the Ecole. His important mathematical work was largely in mathematical physics and he also did a considerable amount of experimental work on heat and sound. In thermodynamics he played an important role in making the whole subject amenable to mathematical treatment by showing how to quantify heat precisely. He is also one of the principal founders of the mathematical theory of elasticity.

Poisson is possibly best known for his work on probability, and he was something of a pioneer in applying the techniques of mathematical probability to the social sciences, something that was extremely controversial at the time. The term 'law of large numbers' was introduced by Poisson in his seminal work, *Recherches sur la probabilité des jugements* (1837; Researches on the Probability of Opinions), in which he put forward his discovery of the *Poisson distribution*. This is the distribution that is a special case of the binomial distribution obtained when the probability of success in a given trial is some constant divided by the number of trials.

Although chiefly an applied mathematician Poisson also made some significant contributions to pure mathematics, in particular to complex analysis. It was Poisson who first thought of integrating complex functions along a path in the complex plane.

Polanyi, John Charles (1929–)
Canadian chemist

John Polanyi was the son of the distinguished physical chemist Michael Polanyi. Born in Berlin, Germany, he was educated at Manchester University and at Princeton, where he obtained his PhD in 1952. He moved soon after to Toronto University, being appointed professor of chemistry in 1962.

Beginning in the 1950s Polanyi has sought to throw light on the nature of chemical reactions. What actually happens, he asked, during the reaction $H + Cl_2 \rightarrow HCl + Cl$? The reaction was known to be strongly exothermic; it was not known, however, how this released energy was distributed in the various degrees of freedom of the reaction products. D. HERSCHBACH had begun detailed investigations of reaction mechanics by measuring the velocities and angular distribution of the reaction products using molecular beams. In contrast Polanyi described his own method as one in which "the molecules formed in chemical reaction do the work by signaling to us their state of excitation...through infrared emission."

Initially Polanyi and his coworkers had to work with a detector "only slightly more sensitive than the palms of our hands...a thermocouple." They were soon able to replace this with semiconductor infrared detectors. By analyzing the infrared emission, Polanyi was able to measure how much of the reaction energy was stored as molecular vibration and rotation. In this way he was able to show that in the example cited above two distinct states of the molecule HCl were formed: one with high vibrational and rotational excitation, but low translational energy; and the less common state with low vibrational and rotational energy but high translational energy. Polanyi has continued to work in the field of reaction dynamics and has developed many new

techniques and derived numerous insights into the subject. For his contributions he shared the 1986 Nobel Prize for chemistry with Herschbach and Y. T. LEE.

Polanyi's work in infrared chemical luminescence led to the development of chemical lasers by G. Pimental and J. Kaspar in 1960.

Pons, Jean Louis (1761–1831)
French astronomer

Born at Peyres in France, Pons started his astronomical work in Marseilles before moving to Florence as director of the observatory in 1819. He was an assiduous comet hunter, discovering 37. He is known as the codiscoverer of the *Pons–Winnecke* and the *Pons–Brooks* comets. True fame seems to have missed him, however, for though he did in fact discover the comet with the shortest period of 3.3 years it was named for ENCKE, who first worked out its orbital period.

Pons, Stanley (1943–) *American chemist. See* FLEISCHMANN, MARTIN.

Pontecorvo, Guido (1907–)
Italian–British geneticist

Pontecorvo was born in Pisa, Italy. Having graduated in agricultural sciences from the university in his native city of Pisa in 1928, he spent the following nine years in Florence, supervising the Tuscany cattle-breeding program. Political conditions caused him to leave Italy in 1938, his intention being to continue with similar work in Peru. However he first accepted an invitation to the Institute of Animal Genetics in Edinburgh, where he met the famous American geneticist Hermann Muller, another visitor at the institute. Under Muller's influence Pontecorvo became increasingly interested in pure genetics and together with Muller he devised an elegant method for investigating the genetic differences between species that produce sterile hybrids on crossing.

Pontecorvo remained in Edinburgh working on *Drosophila* species and gained his PhD in 1941. Two factors then prompted him to change from *Drosophila* genetics to fungal genetics, firstly the dire need for penicillin during World War II and secondly his interest in the structure and function of the gene, a topic more easily investigated in the fungi.

Pontecorvo's work on the fungus *Aspergillus nidulans* led to the discovery, with Joseph Roper, of the parasexual cycle in 1950. This cycle gives rise to genetic reassortment by means other than sexual reproduction and its discovery provided a method of genetically analyzing asexual fungi. Pontecorvo also put forward the idea of the gene as a unit of function, a theory substantiated by Seymour Benzer in 1955. Pontecorvo occupied the first chair of genetics at Glasgow University from 1955 until 1961, when he moved to the Imperial Cancer Research Fund. He retired in 1975.

Pople, John A. (1925–) British theoretical chemist

Pople was born in Burnham-on-Sea, Somerset, and gained his PhD in mathematics in 1951 at Cambridge. In 1964 he became professor of chemical physics at Carnego-Mellon University, Pittsburgh, and in 1986 moved to Northwestern University as professor of chemistry. In 1998 he shared the Nobel Prize for chemistry with Walter KOHN. Pople received his award for the development of computational methods in quantum chemistry.

Pople developed the whole quantum-chemical methodology currently used in various areas of chemistry. This makes it possible to study the configurations and properties of molecules and how they interact, using the basic principles of quantum mechanics. Details of a molecule or a reaction are fed to a computer, which outputs a list of properties of the molecule or describes how the reaction will proceed. Pople's main contribution to the process was the development in 1970 of a user-friendly program known as GAUSSIAN-70, now used by theoretical research chemists throughout the world. He continued to refine the methodology, accumulating a well-documented model chemistry, which by the early 1990s was able to incorporate Kohn's density-function theory.

Popov, Aleksandr Stepanovich (1859–1906) Russian physicist and electrical engineer

Popov, the son of a priest from Bogoslavsky in Russia, was educated in a seminary to prepare him for a clerical profession. His interest however turned to physics and mathematics, which he studied at the University of St. Petersburg between 1877 and 1882. While still a student he worked in 1881 at the Electrotekhinik artel, which operated Russia's first electric power stations. He taught for a short time at the university and then in 1883 joined the staff of the Torpedo School at Kronstadt, where naval specialists were trained in all branches of electrical engineering and where he was able to conduct his own research. He subsequently became head of the physics depart-

ment and remained there until 1900. Popov returned to St. Petersburg as professor at the Institute of Electrical Engineering in 1901 and was appointed its director in 1905. Later that year Popov's health was undermined by his refusal to take severe action against the political disturbances among his students and he died shortly after.

In 1888 Heinrich HERTZ had produced and transmitted electromagnetic waves, arousing the interest of many scientists. Popov began experiments on the transmission and reception of the so-called Hertzian waves (radio waves) somewhat earlier than Marconi. He modified the coherer developed by Oliver Lodge for detecting these waves, making the first continuously operating detector. Connecting his coherer to a wire antenna, he was able in 1895 to receive and detect the waves produced by an oscillator circuit. His interests at this time, however, seemed more toward the investigation of atmospheric phenomena such as thunderstorms and lightning; he used his coherer connected to lightning conductors for this purpose. Stimulated by the 1896 patent awarded to MARCONI, Popov again turned his attention to radio transmission and enlisted the help of the Russian navy. In 1897 he was able to transmit from ship to shore over a distance of 3 miles (5 km) and managed to persuade the naval authorities to begin installing radio equipment in its vessels. By the end of 1899 he had increased the distance of his ship to shore transmissions to 30 miles (48 km). He received little encouragement or support from the Russian government and did not commercialize his discoveries.

The Russian claim that Popov invented radio communication is not widely accepted, although he did publish in January 1896 a description of his receiving apparatus that coincides very closely with that described in Marconi's patent claim of June 1896. Popov is credited however with being the first to use an antenna in the transmission and reception of radio waves.

Porter, George, Baron (1920–) British chemist

Born at Stainforth in Yorkshire, Porter was educated at the universities of Leeds and Cambridge, where he obtained his PhD. After working on radar during World War II, he returned to Cambridge until, in 1955, he was appointed professor of chemistry at Sheffield University. From 1966 until 1985 he held one of the leading positions in British science, namely, the directorship of the Royal Institution and the Fullerian Professorship of Chemistry. In 1987 he was appointed professor (from 1990, chairman) of the Centre for Photomolecular Science at Imperial College, London.

In collaboration with his Cambridge teacher, Ronald NORRISH, Porter developed from 1949 onward the new technique of flash photolysis. There were good reasons for thinking that the course of a chemical reaction was partly determined by a number of intermediate species too short-lived to be detected, let alone investigated. Porter therefore set out to study what he called the spectroscopy of transient substances.

The apparatus used involved a long glass or quartz tube containing the gas under investigation. This was subjected to a very brief pulse of intense light from flash tubes, causing photochemical reactions in the gas. The free radicals and excited molecules produced have only a transient existence, but could be detected by a second flash of light, directed along the axis of the reaction tube, used to record photographically an absorption spectrum of the reaction mixture. In this way the spectra of many free radicals could be detected.

In addition, it was possible to direct a continuous beam of light down the reaction tube and focus on one particular absorption line of a species known to be present. The change of this line with time allowed kinetic measurements of the rates of very fast gas reactions to be made.

The methods of flash photolysis have since been extended to liquids and solutions, to gas kinetics, and to the study of complex biological molecules such as hemoglobin and chlorophyll. Porter shared the Nobel Prize for chemistry in 1967 with Norrish and with Manfred EIGEN for "their studies of extremely fast reactions effected by disturbing the equilibrium by means of very short pulses of energy."

In 1990 Porter was raised to the British peerage as Baron Porter of Luddenham.

Porter, Keith Roberts (1912–1977)
Canadian biologist

Porter, who was born at Yarmouth in Nova Scotia, Canada, studied biology at Acadia University and Harvard, receiving his PhD in 1938. After working at the Rockefeller Institute (1939–61) he held chairs of biology, first at Harvard (1961–70) and thereafter at the University of Colorado.

While working with Albert Claude at the Rockefeller Institute, Porter studied the endoplasmic reticulum, a network of membranes within cells. More significant was his study of its equivalent form in muscle fibers, the sarcoplasmic reticulum. Although this had first been discussed by E.

Veratti in 1902, it required the development of the electron microscope to permit Porter to describe, in the 1950s, its pervasive character as a network of extremely fine channels enclosing each myofibril. He went on to propose that it served to coordinate and harmonize the complex response of the contractions of millions of fibers.

The actual mechanism of contraction was initiated by the release of calcium ions into the fluid surrounding the muscle fibers. The source of such ions was shown to be the sarcoplasmic reticulum, to which they were quickly returned and stored by what became known as a 'calcium pump'.

Porter, Rodney Robert (1917–1985)
British biochemist

Porter was educated at the university in his native city of Liverpool and at Cambridge University, where he was a pupil of Frederick Sanger. After working at the National Institute of Medical Research from 1949 to 1960 he moved to the chair of immunology at St. Mary's Hospital, London. Porter remained there until 1967 when he accepted the post of professor of biochemistry at Oxford.

In 1962 Porter proposed a structure for the important antibody gamma globulin (IgG). Ordinary techniques of protein chemistry revealed that the molecule is built up of four polypeptide chains paired so that the molecule consists of two identical halves, each consisting of one long (or heavy) chain and one short (or light) chain.

Further evidence was obtained by splitting the molecule with the enzyme papain. This split IgG into three large fragments, two similar to each other known as F_{ab} (fragment antigen binding) and still capable of combining with antigen, and a crystalline fragment known as F_c (fragment crystalline) without any activity. This immediately suggested to Porter that, because crystals only form easily from identical molecules, the halves of the heavy chain that make up the F_c fragment are probably the same in all molecules. Thus the complexity is mainly in the F_{ab} fragments where the combining sites are found.

Linking such insights with results obtained by Gerald EDELMAN and data derived from electron microscopy allowed Porter to propose the familiar Y-shaped molecule built from four chains joined by disulfide bridges with the variable combining part at the tips of the arms of the Y.

In 1972 Porter shared with Edelman the Nobel Prize for physiology or medicine for their work in determining the structure of an antibody.

Powell, Cecil Frank (1903–1969) *British physicist*

The son of a gunsmith, Powell was born at Tonbridge, Kent, and educated at Cambridge University, where he obtained his PhD in 1927. He spent virtually his entire career at Bristol University where he became Wills Professor of Physics in 1948 and director of the Wills Physics Laboratory in 1964.

Under Powell Bristol became a leading center for the study of nuclear particles by means of photographic emulsions. In this technique an ionizing particle crossing a sensitive plate coated with grains of silver bromide leaves clear tracks of its passage. From the size and path of the track much information about the nature of the particle can be inferred. In 1947 Powell, in collaboration with Giuseppe Occhialini, published a standard work on the subject, *Nuclear Physics in Photographs*. It was this technique that allowed Powell to discover the pimeson (or pion) in 1947 in the plates of cosmic rays. The existence of such a particle had been predicted in 1935 by Hideki Yukawa, and Powell's discovery thus went some way to establish a coherent picture of nuclear phenomena.

For his discovery Powell was awarded the 1950 Nobel Prize for physics.

Poynting, John Henry (1852–1914) *British physicist*

Poynting was born at Monton, near Manchester, and educated at the universities of Manchester and Cambridge (1872–76). He served as professor of physics at Mason Science College (later the University of Birmingham) from 1880 until his death in 1914.

He wrote on electrical phenomena and radiation and is best known for *Poynting's vector*, introduced in his paper *On the Transfer of Energy in the Electromagnetic Field* (1884). In this he showed that the flow of energy at a point can be expressed by a simple formula in terms of the electric and magnetic forces at that point.

In 1891 he determined the mean density of the Earth and made a determination of the gravitational constant in 1893 through the accurate use of torsion balances. His results were published in *The Mean Density of the Earth* (1894) and *The Earth; Its Shape, Size, Weight and Spin* (1913). Poynting was also the first to suggest, in 1903, the existence of the effect of radiation from the Sun that causes smaller particles in orbit about the Sun to spiral close and eventually plunge in. This was developed by the American physicist Howard Robertson and was related to the theory of relativity in 1937, becoming known as the *Poynting–Robertson effect*.

Pratt, John Henry (1809–1871) *British geophysicist*

Pratt was the son of a secretary to the Church Missionary Society; after graduating from Cambridge University in 1833 he went to India as a chaplain with the East India Company. In 1850 he became archdeacon of Calcutta.

An amateur scientist, Pratt became interested in geophysics and in 1854 his most important work was published when he formulated the theory of isostasy. While conducting his triangulation of India the surveyor, George Everest, found a discrepancy in the astrogeodetic and triangulation measurements between two stations – Kaliana and Kalianpur – near the Himalayas. From this Pratt surmised that mountain ranges failed to exert the gravitational pull expected of them and thus distorted measurements made with pendulums. He saw the Himalayas as having a lesser density than the crust below, and generalized that the higher the mountain range, the lower is its density. He compared the raising of mountains to fermenting dough in which the density decreases as the dough rises.

Some of the same ideas were present in a paper submitted just six weeks after Pratt's by George Airy although Airy preferred the image of an iceberg to that of rising dough.

Pratt wrote *Mathematical Principles of Mechanical Philosophy* (1836), a work that was expanded to *On Attractions, Laplace's Functions, and The Figure of the Earth* (1860, 1861, 1865).

Pregl, Fritz (1869–1930) *Austrian chemist*

Pregl, who was born at Laibach (now Ljubljana in Slovenia), was the son of a bank official. He graduated in medicine from Graz (1893) where he became an assistant in physiological chemistry in 1899. In 1910 he became head of the chemistry department at Innsbruck, remaining there until 1913 when he returned to Graz to become director of the Medico-Chemical Institute.

Pregl began research on bile acids in about 1904 but soon found that he could only obtain tiny amounts. This led him to pioneer techniques of microanalysis. Justus von Liebig had needed about 1 gram of a substance before he could make an accurate analysis; through his new techniques Pregl was capable of working with 2.5 milligrams. This was achieved by the careful scaling down of his analytic equipment and the design of a new balance, which was produced in collaboration with the instrument maker W. Kuhlmann of Hamburg. With this he was capable of weighing 20 grams to an accuracy of 0.001 milligram.

The techniques developed by Pregl are of immense importance in organic chemistry and he was awarded the Nobel Prize for chemistry in 1923 for this work.

Prelog, Vladimir (1906–) *Swiss chemist*

Born in Sarajevo (now in Bosnia and Herce-govina), Prelog studied chemistry at the Prague Institute of Technology where he received his doctorate in 1929. He then worked in Prague as an industrial chemist until 1935 when he moved to the University of Zagreb. With the German invasion of Yugoslavia in 1941 Prelog joined the staff of the Federal Institute of Technology in Zurich, serving there as professor of chemistry from 1950 until his retirement in 1976.

Prelog's early work was with the alkaloids. His research resulted in the solution of the configuration of *Cinchona* alkaloids (antimalarial compounds), the correction of the formulas for *Strychnos* alkaloids, and the elucidation of many other indole, steroid, and aromatic alkaloid configurations. He later investigated the metabolites of certain microorganisms and in so doing discovered many new natural substances including the first natural compound found to contain boron, boromycin.

Prelog intensively studied the relationship between conformation and chemical activity in medium-sized (8–11 ring members) ring structures. This brought to light a new type of reaction that can occur in such compounds. Prelog next showed that conformation affects the outcome of syntheses where different-sized atoms or groups are being substituted into a compound. The regular way in which this occurs allowed the configurations of many important compounds to be worked out. Applying such work to the reactions between enzymes, coenzymes, and substrates gave interesting results about the stereospecificity of microorganisms.

With Christopher INGOLD, Prelog introduced the so-called R–S system into organic chemistry, which allowed, for the first time, enantiomers, or mirror images, to be described unambiguously.

For such wide ranging work on the "stereochemistry of organic molecules and reactions" Prelog was awarded the 1975 Nobel Prize for chemistry, which he shared with John CORNFORTH.

Prévost, Pierre (1751–1839) *Swiss physicist*

Born in Geneva, Switzerland, Prévost was professor of physics at Berlin and then at the university in his native city. In 1792 he published his *Sur l'équilibre du feu* (On the Equilibrium of Heat), which did much to clarify the nature of heat.

If, as was widely believed at the time, heat was a fluid, called caloric, which flowed from hot bodies to colder ones, then it was reasonable to suppose that cold was also a fluid, 'frigoric', which flowed from cold bodies to warmer ones. In favor of the existence of frigoric was a body of experimental work that dated back to the 17th century. Thus it was known that if a piece of ice was placed near a thermometer in a room of constant temperature then the temperature of the thermometer would fall. More impressively, if two concave mirrors are arranged so that they face each other and a piece of ice is placed at one focus and a thermometer at the other, then the indicated temperature will fall. Experiments like this readily lent themselves to the interpretation that the fluid frigoric can be emitted and reflected.

Prévost argued in 1791 that there is but a single fluid involved. Snow melting in the hand was a case of heat flowing from the hand to the snow rather than conversely. He introduced the idea of dynamic equilibrium in which all bodies are radiating and absorbing heat. When one body is colder than another it absorbs more than it radiates. Its temperature will rise until it is in equilibrium with its surroundings. At this point, it does not stop radiating heat but absorbs just as much as it loses to remain in equilibrium. The idea is known as the *Prévost theory of exchanges*.

Although Prévost was a supporter of the caloric theory of heat, his views influenced a later generation of physicists who introduced the kinetic theory of heat on a quantitative basis toward the end of the 19th century.

Priestley, Joseph (1733–1804) *British chemist and Presbyterian minister*

Priestley was the greatest British chemist of the 18th century and also one of the century's greatest men. Born in the English city of Leeds, his father was a cloth dresser and a Congregationalist. Priestley was educated at a nonconformist seminary, later becoming a minister at Needham Market in 1755. After a few years in Nantwich in a similar post he went to teach at Warrington Academy in 1761.

On visits to London he met Benjamin Franklin, who aided him in his *History of Electricity* (1767). He moved to Leeds in 1767 and, being near a brewery, "began to make experiments in the fixed air that was continually produced in it." It was around this time that he invented soda water with the ample supply of carbon dioxide ('fixed air') from the brewery. In 1772 he became Lord Shelburne's librarian, which involved only nominal duties and allowed him to do some of his most important work. He left in 1780 to become a minister in Birmingham, where he mixed with such members of the Lunar Society as Erasmus Darwin, James Watt, Josiah Wedgwood, and Matthew Boulton. As a dissenting radical he preached against the discrimination suffered by non-Anglicans and, in reply to Edmund Burke's *Reflections on the French Revolution*, wrote in favor of the principles of the French Revolution. This led a Birmingham mob to break into his home (1791) and burn it, destroying all his books, papers, and instruments. He moved to London for a short while but finding no security there moved to America in 1794 to join his sons who had emigrated there earlier. In Pennsylvania he continued with his scientific and theological work until his death.

Priestley attempted to understand the facts of combustion and respiration. His first insight came from the realization that, since even a small candle uses an enormous amount of pure air, there must be a provision in nature to replace it. After trying various techniques to purify the foul air left after combustion he eventually found that a sprig of mint would revive the air so it could support combustion once more (1771). In the next few years, using a variety of new techniques, he isolated various gases – nitrous oxide, hydrogen chloride, sulfur dioxide – and, in 1774, he produced oxygen. Using a powerful magnifying glass to focus the rays of the Sun, he heated oxides of mercury and lead confined in glass tubes over mercury. He found that they gave off large amounts of a gas in which a candle would burn with an enlarged flame. At first he identified the gas as nitrous oxide but found that, unlike that gas, it was barely soluble in water. He next thought it might simply be ordinary air but on putting mice in it he found that they lived longer than in a similar volume of normal air. Being an ardent believer in the phlogiston theory, he named this gas 'dephlogisticated air'. Antoine LAVOISIER realized the crucial value of this discovery in explaining combustion and named the gas 'oxygine'.

Priestley continued to discover more compounds. He determined the relative densities of various gases by weighing balloons filled with them and also investigated gaseous diffusion, conductivity of heat in gas, and the effect of electrical discharge on gases at low pressure. He also produced numerous substantial theological works.

Prigogine, Ilya (1917–) *Belgian chemist*

Prigogine was born in Moscow and educated at the Free University of Belgium where he served as professor of chemistry from 1947 to 1987. He was appointed director of the Statistical Mechanics and Thermodynamics Center of the University of Texas, Austin in 1967.

In 1955 Prigogine produced a seminal and revolutionary work, *Thermodynamics of Irreversible Processes*. In this book he pointed out a serious limitation in classical thermodynamics of being restricted to reversible processes and equilibrium states. He argued that a true thermodynamic equilibrium is rarely attained; a more common state is met with in the cell, which continuously exchanges with its surroundings, or in the solar system with the steady flow of energy from the Sun preventing the atmosphere of the Earth from reaching thermodynamic equilibrium.

A beginning had been made by Lars ONSAGER to cover nonequilibrium states but this applied only to states not too far away from equilibrium. Prigogine, in a quite radical way, developed machinery to deal with states far from equilibrium. These he called 'dissipative structures'. He went on to suggest that, "On a broader scale, it is difficult to avoid the feeling that such instabilities related to dissipative processes should play an extensive role in biological processes." Such a possibility Prigogine began to explore in his *Membranes, Dissipative Structures and Evolution* (1975).

Prigogine was awarded the 1977 Nobel Prize for chemistry for his work on "nonequilibrium thermodynamics particularly his theory of dissipative structures."

Pringsheim, Nathanael (1823–1894) *German botanist*

Pringsheim, who was born at Wziesko (now in Poland), studied medicine at the universities of Breslau and Leipzig. However, his interest turned to natural science when he moved to the University of Berlin; he gained his PhD in 1848 with a thesis on the growth and thickness of plant cell walls. In 1864 he was appointed professor of botany at the University of Jena but resigned the post in 1868 to conduct private research in a laboratory attached to his home in Berlin.

Pringsheim was one of the leaders in the botanical revival of the 19th century with his contribution to studies of cell development and life history, particularly in the algae and fungi. He was among the first to demonstrate sexual reproduction in algae and observe alternation of generations between the two sexually differentiated motile zoospores and the resting undifferentiated spore that results from their fusion. He further showed that sexual reproduction involves fusion of material of the two sex cells.

From studies (1873) on the complex morphological differentiation in a family of marine algae, the Sphacelariaceae, Pringsheim opposed the Darwinian theory of evolution by natural selection. Like the Swiss botanist, Karl Naegeli, he believed the increase in structural complexity to be a spontaneous morphological phenomenon, conferring no survival value.

Pringsheim's studies of the origin of plant cells contributed evidence for the theory that cells are only produced by the division of existing cells. With Julius von Sachs, Pringsheim also described the plastids, organelles unique to plant cells. In later years he concentrated more on physiology than morphology but his contributions to this field were not acknowledged or developed by other workers.

He was founder of the *Jahrbücher für Wissenschaftliche Botanik* (1858; Annals of Scientific Botany) and the German Botanical Society (1882). He wrote memoirs on *Vaucheria* (1855), *Oedogonium* and *Coleochaete* (1856–58), *Hydrodictyon* (1861), and *Pandorina* (1869).

Prokhorov, Aleksandr Mikhaylovich
(1916–) *Russian physicist*

Prokhorov graduated in 1939 from the faculty of physics of the Leningrad State University, where he later became a doctor of physics, mathematics, and science (1946). During World War II he served in the Russian army.

Subsequently, working at the Physics Institute of the Soviet Academy of Sciences with Nikolai BASOV, Prokhorov performed fundamental work in microwave spectroscopy, which led to the development of the maser in 1955, and later the laser. Basov and Prokhorov, together with the American physicist Charles TOWNES, received the 1964 Nobel Prize for physics for their development of the maser principle, and were pioneers of the new science of quantum radio physics (now referred to by the broader term, quantum electronics).

Proust, Joseph Louis (1754–1826)
French chemist

Proust was born the son of an apothecary at Angers in northwest France. He studied in Paris and became chief apothecary at the Saltpêtrière Hospital. In 1789 he went to Madrid to become director of the Royal Laboratory under the patronage of Charles IV. After the invasion of Spain by Napoleon, the fall of his patron, and the destruction of his laboratory by the invading army, he returned to France in 1808. He lived in poverty for some years before being awarded a pension by Louis XVIII.

In 1799 Proust formulated his law of definite proportions. He pointed out that copper carbonate must always be made from the same fixed proportions of copper, carbon, and oxygen. From this he generalized that all compounds contained elements in certain definite proportions. Proust's law was not immediately accepted by all chemists; in particular, his proposal led to a long and famous controversy with Claude-Louis Berthollet who argued that elements could combine in a whole range of different proportions. It is now clear that Proust was talking about compounds whereas Berthollet was thinking of solutions or mixtures. Berthollet eventually admitted his error.

The strength of Proust's law was seen a few years later when John Dalton published his atomic theory. The law and the theory fitted exactly – Proust's definite proportions being in fact a definite number of atoms joining together to form molecules.

Prout, William (1785–1850) *British chemist and physiologist*

Prout was born at Horton in England and studied medicine at Edinburgh, graduating in 1811. He established himself as a physician in London and became a pioneer of physiological chemistry, in which he lectured. He wrote on the stomach and urinary diseases and on the chemistry of the blood, urine, and kidney stones. In 1818 he prepared urea for the first time and in 1824 he identified hydrochloric acid in stomach secretions. He was also one of the first to divide food components into the groups of fats, carbohydrates, and protein.

Prout's fame also rests on a paper he published anonymously in 1815, *On the Relation between the Specific Gravities of Bodies in Their Gaseous State and the Weight of Their Atoms*. In this he formulated what has since been called *Prout's hypothesis*: the atomic weight of all atoms is an exact multiple of the atomic weight of hydrogen. Determination of atomic weights had made this view plausible. At the time there was considerable interest in the hypothesis as it implied that elements were themselves 'compounds' of hydrogen, and Prout suggested that hydrogen was the *prima materia* (basic substance) of the ancients. However, more accurate determinations of atomic weight, particularly by Jean Stas, showed that many were not whole numbers. Stas described the hypothesis as "only an illusion" although he also remarked that there was "something at the bottom of it." Interest was revived with the publication of Dmitri MENDELEEV's periodic table, although Mendeleev described the idea of a *prima materia* as "a torment of classical thought." The discovery of isotopes in the 20th century resolved the position.

Pruisner, Stanley Ben (1942–)
American biochemist

Pruisner was born in Des Moines, Iowa, and qualified as an MD at the University of Pennsylvania in 1968. In 1972 he began a residency at the University of California School of Medicine, San Francisco, where he was appointed professor of neurology in 1980 and professor of biochemistry in 1988.

Early in his career in 1972, Pruisner, following the death of a patient from Creutzfeldt-Jakob disease (CJD), discovered that virtually nothing was known about the condition. It was thought to be one of a class of diseases known as transmissible spongiform encephalopathies (TSEs), which include scrapie in sheep, the more familiar BSE in cattle, and kuru and CJD in man. Following the work of Carleton GAJDUSEK, it was proposed that CJD and the other TSEs were probably caused by slow viruses and could be transmitted by injecting extracts from diseased brains into healthy animal brains.

Pruisner began to suspect that something unusual was going on when he read reports suggesting that the agent responsible for scrapie could lack both DNA and RNA. Working with infected hamster brains, he established that procedures known to damage nucleic acids failed to lessen the infection whereas steps that denatured proteins did reduce infectivity. In 1982 he introduced the term *prion* (standing for *proteinaceous infectious particle*) to refer to an agent that is distinct from viruses, bacteria, fungi and all other known causes of disease and is responsible for scrapie and other TSEs.

He went on to claim that scrapie prions contained a single protein, PrP (prion protein), which was shown to consist of some 15 amino acids. A gene for PrP was found in the chromosomes of hamsters, mice, humans, and all other examined mammals. Why then did not all mammals suffer from prion diseases? Because, Pruisner argued, PrP could be found in two forms: PrP^c, nor-

mal cellular protein and PrP^{Sc}, the abnormal disease-causing form.

Although it has as yet proved impossible to produce infections with synthesised PrP, and although it is widely held that, at best, prions are only partly responsible for the numerous TSEs, Pruisner was awarded the 1997 Nobel Prize for physiology or medicine for "finding a new biological principle of infection."

Ptolemy (*c.* 2nd century AD) *Egyptian astronomer*

Virtually nothing is known about the life of Ptolemy (full name Claudius Ptolemaeus). He was probably a Hellenized Egyptian working in the library at Alexandria. He produced four major works the *Almagest*, the *Geography*, the *Tetrabiblos* (Four Books), and the *Optics*. The first work – the culmination of five hundred years of Greek astronomical and cosmological thinking – was to dominate science for 13 centuries. Ptolemy naturally relied on his predecessors, especially Hipparchus. A work of such staggering intellectual power and complexity could never be created by one person alone. The basic problem he faced was to try to explain the movements of the heavens on the assumption that the universe is geocentric and all bodies revolve in perfectly circular orbits moving with uniform velocity. As the heavenly bodies move in elliptical orbits with variable velocity around a center other than the Earth, some quite sophisticated geometry is called for to preserve the basic fiction. Ptolemy used three complications of the original scheme: epicycles, eccentrics, and equants. These devices worked reasonably well except that they did not lead to particularly accurate predictions. Nor did they permit Ptolemy to develop a system of the universe as a whole. He could give a reasonable account of the orbit of Mars, and of Venus, and of Mercury, and so on, taken separately, but if they were put together into one scheme then the dimensions and the periods would start to conflict. Whatever its faults the system remained intact for 1300 years until it was overthrown by Copernicus in the 15th century.

In the *Geography* Ptolemy explains fully how lines of latitude and longitude can be mathematically determined. However no longitudes were astronomically determined and only a few latitudes had been so calculated. Positions of places were located on this dubious grid by reducing distances measured on land to degrees. Distances over seas were simply guessed at. As he had put the Canaries 7° east of their true position his whole grid was thrown out of alignment. The *Geography* had almost as great (and as enduring) an influence on the western world-view as the *Almagest*. Columbus might never have sailed without Ptolemy's erroneous view that Asia was closer (westward) than it really is, a view endorsed by the map-makers contemporaneous with Columbus.

The only book of Ptolemy's that is readily available today and still widely read is the *Tetrabiblos*, which is a work on astrology. The work is long and comprehensive and is probably as well argued as the case for astrology can be. It is naturalistic in that he supposes that there might be some form of physical radiation from the heavens that affects mankind. Most of the concepts and arguments of modern astrology can be traced back to this Ptolemaic work.

The final major work of Ptolemy, the *Optics*, in which he sets out and demonstrates various elementary principles, is in many ways the most successful of all his works. Although he understood the principles of reflection reasonably well his understanding of refraction seems to be purely empirical. He gives tables he has worked out for the refraction of a ray of light passing from light into water for various angles of incidence.

His main work was known in Greek as the *Syntaxis*; it was the Arabs who named it the *Almagest* from the Arabic definite article 'al' and their own pronunciation of the Greek word for 'great.' Such was the tribute posterity has paid to Ptolemy.

Purbach, Georg von (1423–1461)
Austrian astronomer and mathematician

Purbach (or Peurbach) took his name from his birthplace in Austria. He had traveled in Italy and studied under Nicholas of Cusa before becoming professor of mathematics and astronomy at the University of Vienna in about 1450. Purbach's main aim as a scholar was to produce an accurate text of Ptolemy's *Almagest*. The most common available text was that of Gerard of Cremona, which was a Latin translation of an Arabic translation and was nearly 300 years old. Purbach began by writing a general introduction to Ptolemy that described accurately and briefly the constructions of the *Almagest*. Unfortunately he died before he could embark on the translation. His place was taken by his pupil, Regiomontanus, who completed a textbook begun by Purbach but failed to produce the edition and translation of Ptolemy so much wanted by Purbach.

One of his most significant works, the fruit of much observational and theoretical work, was a very thorough table of lunar eclipses, which he published in 1459. Purbach wrote a textbook, *Theoricae novae planetarum*, which became an influential exposition of the Ptolemaic theory of the solar system, a theory whose influence lasted until Tycho Brahe finally disproved the existence of the solid spheres postulated by Ptolemy. Such was the accuracy of Purbach's set tables that they were still in use almost two hundred years later. He also compiled a table of sines, using Arabic numerals, and was one of the first to popularize their use instead of chords in trigonometry.

Purcell, Edward Mills (1912–)
American physicist

Purcell was born at Taylorville, Illinois. He gained his BSc degree in electrical engineering at Purdue University, Illinois (1933) and his masters degree and PhD from Harvard (1938), having also spent a year in Germany at the Technische Hochschule, Karlsruhe. At Harvard his career advanced from instructor in physics (1938), to associate professor (1946), full professor (1949), and professor emeritus (1980). During the war years 1941–45 he was a group leader at the Massachusetts Institute of Technology Radiation Laboratories.

Purcell's research has spanned nuclear magnetism, radio astronomy, radar, astrophysics, and biophysics. In the field of nuclear magnetism, he was awarded the 1952 Nobel Prize for physics (shared with Felix BLOCH) for his work in developing the nuclear magnetic resonance (NMR) method of measuring the magnetic fields of the nuclei of atoms. As a result of these experiments, measurements of nuclear magnetic moment could now be performed on solids and liquids, whereas previously they had been confined to molecular beams of gases. Nuclear magnetic resonance is now commonly applied in chemical analysis.

Purcell's major contribution to astronomy was the first detection of microwave emission from neutral hydrogen in interstellar space at the wavelength of 21 centimeters (1420 Hz). The phenomenon had been predicted theoretically by Hendrik van de Hulst and others and was first observed in 1951 by three independent groups of radio astronomers – American, Dutch, and Australian – the American group being the first to report their findings. This, and the subsequent observation of the corresponding absorption line by the Dutch group in 1954, has made possible the mapping of a large part of our own galaxy, and allowed the calculation of the excitation temperature in interstellar space. Purcell was also aware of the possible future implications of his discovery for interstellar communications.

Purkinje, Johannes Evangelista
(1787–1869) *Czech physiologist*

Born at Libochovice (now in the Czech Republic), Purkinje began studying to be a priest but changed to medicine and graduated MD from Charles University, Prague, in 1819. He became professor of physiology and pathology at the University of Breslau in 1823 but returned to Charles University in 1850 to take the chair of physiology, which he held until his death. Purkinje's most celebrated research was concerned with the eye, although he also did valuable work on the brain, muscles, sweat glands, digestion, animal and plant cells, and embryology. He explored various aspects of vision, drawing attention, for example, to the fact that in subdued light blue objects appear brighter to the eye than red objects – the *Purkinje effect*. He located *Purkinje cells* in the middle layer of the brain's cerebellar cortex and was the first to apply the term 'protoplasm' to the living embryonic material contained in the egg. He also discovered, in the inner walls of the ventricles of the heart, the *Purkinje fibers*, which transmit the pacemaker stimulus. His comparative studies of cellular structure in plants and animals were continued by Matthias SCHLIEDEN and Theodor SCHWANN and led to subsequent increased knowledge of the factors involved in inheritance. Purkinje was among the first to use a microtome for preparing thin slices of tissue for microscopic examination, and may have been the first to teach microscopy and microscopical technique as part of his college courses. He also realized that fingerprints can be used as a method of identification.

Pythagoras (c. 580 BC–c. 500 BC) *Greek mathematician and philosopher*

All that is known of the life of Pythagoras with any certainty is that he left his birthplace, Samos, in about 520 BC to settle in Croton (now Crotone) in southern Italy and, as a result of political trouble, made a final move to Metapontum in about 500.

In Croton Pythagoras established his academy and became a cult leader. His community was governed by a large number of rules, some dietary, such as those commanding abstinence from meat and from beans, and others of obscure origin, such as the commands not to let a swallow nest under the roof or not to sit on a quart measure.

The movement was united by the belief that "all is number." While the exact meaning of this may be none too clear, that it led to one of the great periods of mathematics is beyond doubt. Not only were the properties of numbers explored in a totally new way and important theorems discovered, of which the familiar theorem of Pythagoras is the best example, but there also emerged what is arguably the first really deep mathematical truth – the discovery of irrational numbers with the realization of the incommensurability of the square root of 2.

R

Rabi, Isidor Isaac (1898–1988)
Austrian–American physicist

Rabi and his parents emigrated to America from Rymanow in Poland, where he was born, while he was still young. He subsequently grew up in a Yiddish-speaking community in New York, where his father ran a grocery store. He was educated at Cornell, graduating in 1919, and Columbia, where he obtained his PhD in 1927. After two years in Europe he returned to Columbia where he spent his whole career until his retirement in 1967, being appointed professor of physics in 1937 and the first University Professor (a position with no departmental duties) there in 1964.

While in Germany (1927) Rabi had worked under Otto STERN and was impressed with the experiment Stern had performed with Walter Gerlach in which the use of molecular beams led to the discovery of space quantization (1922). Consequently Rabi began a research program at Columbia where he invented the atomic- and molecular-beam magnetic-resonance method of observing atomic spectra, a precise means of determining the magnetic moments of fundamental particles. Using his techniques after World War II, experimentalists were able to measure the magnetic moment of the electron to nine significant figures, thus providing a powerful tool for the testing of theories in quantum electrodynamics. The method had wide applications to the atomic clock, to nuclear magnetic resonance, and to the maser and laser. For this work Rabi was awarded the Nobel Prize for physics in 1944.

During the war Rabi worked on the development of microwave radar. In the postwar years he was a member of the General Advisory Committee of the Atomic Energy Commission, serving as its chairman (1952–56) following the resignation of J. Robert Oppenheimer. As a member of the American delegation to UNESCO he originated the movement that led to the foundation of the international laboratory for high-energy physics in Geneva known as CERN.

Rainwater, (Leo) James (1917–1986)
American physicist

Born in Council, Idaho, and educated at the California Institute of Technology, Rainwater went on to gain his BS, MA, and PhD from Columbia University. At Columbia he progressed through physics assistant (1939–42), to instructor (1946), assistant professor (1947), and associate professor (1949), to become full professor of physics in 1952. In the intervening years of World War II he worked for the Office of Scientific Research and Development and on the Manhattan (atom bomb) project.

Rainwater's principal academic achievement was in explaining the structure and behavior of the atomic nucleus. At the time, two independent models existed, each explaining some of the properties of the atom – the 'shell' model of independent particles, and the 'liquid-drop' model of collective motion. Rainwater, in collaboration with Aage BOHR, showed how these theories could be unified (1950).

Rainwater, Bohr, and Benjamin MOTTELSON (Bohr's principal collaborator in Denmark) are credited with developing a unified theory that reconciled the individual motions of the nuclear particles with the collective behavior of the nucleus. For this the three men shared the 1975 Nobel Prize for physics.

From 1951 until 1953 and again in the period 1956–61, Rainwater was director of the Nevis Cyclotron Laboratory. From 1965 he spent much of his time supervising the conversion of the synchrocyclotron there.

Raman, Sir Chandrasekhara Venkata (1888–1970) *Indian physicist*

Raman was born at Trichinopoly (now Tiruchirappalli) in India and educated at the University of Madras. However, although he revealed considerable talent, he was unable to pursue his education overseas because of ill health. Instead, he chose to enter the civil service where he worked as an auditor for ten years while continuing with his own private research. In 1917 he took up an appointment as professor of physics at the University of Calcutta. In 1933 he moved to Bangalore where he first headed the physics department at the Indian Institute of Science and later, in 1948, became founding director of the Raman Institute.

In 1928 he discovered a spectral effect for which, in 1930, he was awarded the Nobel Prize for physics, thus becoming not only the first Indian but the first Asian to be so honored. The *Raman effect* (as it is now known) occurs when visible radiation is scattered by the molecules in the medium. Not only will the original frequency of the incident light be found but in addition specific new-frequency lines will be detected as a result of the interaction of photons with the molecules. From these new lines in the spectrum (Raman lines) information can be deduced about the molecular structure. The effect is similar to that found by Arthur COMPTON for x-rays and had in fact been predicted by Werner Heisenberg some years earlier.

Ramanujan, Srinivasa Iyengar
(1887–1920) *Indian mathematician*

Ramanujan, the son of a clerk, was born into a poor Brahmin family in Erode near Madras, India. Sometime in 1903, while a student at Kumbakonam High School, he acquired a copy of G.S. Carr's *Synopsis of Elementary Results in Pure Mathematics*. Carr is an unusual work, normally of use as a reference work for a professional mathematician: it consists of about 6000 theorems presented without comment, explanation, or proof. Ramanujan set himself the task of demonstrating all the formulas, a task only a natural-born mathematician would contemplate, let alone pursue. Indifferent to other subjects, Ramanujan failed every exam he entered. For a time he was supported by Ramachandra Rao, a senior civil servant and secretary of the Indian Mathematical Society (IMS). In 1912 he took a clerical position with the Madras Port Trust. At the same time it was suggested that he should seek the advice of a number of British mathematicians about his work and career.

In January 1913 Ramanujan sent a letter to a number of British mathematicians containing a number of formulas. The only one to respond was the Cambridge mathematician G.H. Hardy. Hardy noted that, while some of the formulas were familiar, others "seemed scarcely possible to believe." Some he thought he could, with difficulty, prove himself; others, he had never seen anything like before, and they defeated Hardy completely. Despite this, it was obvious to Hardy that the formulas must be true and could only come from a mathematician of the very highest class. With Hardy's backing, Ramanujan was awarded a scholarship by the University of Madras and invited to visit Cambridge.

There were, however, religious problems facing the devout Ramanujan but these were resolved when the goddess Namagiri appeared in a dream to Ramanujan's mother absolving him from his traditional obligations. By June 1913 Ramanujan was in Cambridge working with Hardy. They collaborated on five important papers. Ramanujan was elected to the Royal Society in 1918, the first Indian to be honored in this way, and was made a fellow of Trinity College, Cambridge, in 1919. By this time his health had begun to fail. He returned to India in 1919 and died soon after from TB.

Part of Ramanujan's mathematical ability came from his ability to do mental calculations extremely quickly. It is said that he was traveling in a cab with Hardy when Hardy observed that the number of the cab in front, 1729, was a dull number. "No," replied Ramanujan, "it is a very interesting number; it is the smallest number expressible as a sum of two cubes in two different ways." ($1729 = 1^3 + 12^3$ and $9^3 + 10^3$.)

Ramón y Cajal, Santiago (1852–1934)
Spanish histologist

The son of a country doctor from Petilla in Spain, Ramón y Cajal embarked on medical studies only after being apprenticed first to a barber and then to a shoemaker. He obtained his license to practice in 1873, and after a year's service in the army in Cuba returned to Madrid and graduated as a doctor of medicine in 1877.

He is remembered for his research into the fine structure of nervous tissue. Before the development of the nerve-specific silver nitrate stain by the Italian cytologist Camillo GOLGI in 1873, it was difficult (in neurohistological preparations) to distinguish true nervous elements from the surrounding supporting tissue (neuroglia). Ramón y Cajal refined Golgi's staining technique and subsequently used it to show the intricacy of the structure and connections of cells in the gray matter of the brain and spinal cord. He also used the stain to elucidate the fine structure of the retina of the eye, and the stain has proved useful in the diagnosis of brain tumors.

In 1906 Ramón y Cajal (together with Golgi) was awarded the Nobel Prize for physiology or medicine for establishing the neuron as the fundamental unit of the nervous system – a finding basic to the present understanding of the nerve impulse. He also advanced the neuron theory, which states that the nervous system is made up of numerous discrete cells and is not a system of fused cells.

Between 1884 and 1922 Ramón y Cajal held professorships successively at the universities of Valencia, Barcelona, and Madrid and in 1900 became director of the newly established Instituto Nacional de Higiene.

In 1920 the Institute Cajal was commissioned by King Alfonso XIII of Spain and here Ramón y Cajal worked until his death.

Ramsay, Sir William (1852–1916)
British chemist

Ramsay came from a scientific background in Glasgow, his father being an engineer and one of his uncles a professor of geology. He studied at Glasgow University (1866–69) and returned there as an assistant in 1872 after postgraduate work in chemistry at Tübingen, where he studied under Robert Bunsen. He was appointed professor of chemistry at University College, Bristol, in 1880 and moved to a similar post at University College, London (1887–1912).

Ramsay's early research was mainly in the field of organic chemistry but in 1892 he came across some work of Lord Rayleigh that dramatically changed the direction of his work. Rayleigh reported that nitrogen obtained from the atmosphere appeared to be denser than nitrogen derived from chemical compounds. Rayleigh's original view of this was that the synthetic nitrogen was probably contaminated with a lighter gas. Ramsay, however, predicted that the atmosphere contained some unknown denser gas. He favored this view for he remembered some experiments performed by Henry Cavendish in 1785 in which he showed that present in the air, after removal of all its oxygen and nitrogen, there remained an unabsorbable 1/20th part of the original. Ramsay experimented with methods of totally removing the oxygen and nitrogen from samples of air and found (1894) that a bubble of gas remained. The gas was identified as a new element spectroscopically by Sir William Crookes. Ramsay and Rayleigh announced the discovery of the element in 1898, naming it argon from the Greek 'inert'.

In the following year Ramsay heard that in America a strange gas had been discovered by heating uranium ores. Ramsay obtained some of the gas from the mineral cleveite and Crookes was able to establish spectroscopically that this was in fact helium, the element whose spectrum had first been observed in a solar eclipse by Pierre Janssen in 1868.

From the positions of argon and helium in the periodic table of elements it appeared that three more gases should exist. In 1898 Ramsay began the search for these, assisted by Morris Travers. They liquefied argon and by its fractional distillation were able to collect three new gases, which they named neon, krypton, and xenon, from the Greek words for 'the new,' 'the hidden,' and

'the strange'. Ramsay completed his work on the inert gases when, in 1904, with R. Whytlaw-Gray he discovered niton (now known as radon), the radioactive member of the series, first isolated by the German physicist **Friedrich Dorn** (1848–1916) in 1900.

In 1903, with Frederick Soddy, Ramsay demonstrated that helium is continually produced during the radioactive decay of radium. The significance of this was not apparent for some time but its explanation by Ernest Rutherford was to lead to the foundation of the new discipline of nuclear physics.

Ramsay was knighted in 1902 and in 1904 was awarded the Nobel Prize for chemistry. His published works included *The Gases of the Atmosphere* (1896) and his two-volume *Modern Chemistry* (1900).

Ramsey, Norman Foster (1915–)
American physicist

Born in Washington DC, Ramsey was educated at Columbia and at Harvard, where he obtained his PhD. He has served as professor of physics at Harvard since 1947.

Ramsey was a student of Isidor Rabi and worked with him on the rotational magnetic moments of molecules, showing how these depend on the mass of the nuclei. During World War II he worked first on radar, and later at the Los Alamos Laboratory. His subsequent work was on both high-energy particle scattering and on low-energy magnetic resonance.

In 1947 he began work on a new, more accurate, molecular-beam resonance technique using two separate radiofrequency fields. This was used to measure nuclear magnetic moments and nuclear quadrupole moments and also to investigate the magnetic interactions within simple molecules. Ramsey used the idea of magnetic shielding to interpret the chemical shifts found in nuclear magnetic resonance spectra.

Ramsey, along with D. Kleppner and H. M. Goldenberg, also developed the hydrogen maser. This used a molecular beam of hydrogen atoms and depended for its action on the hyperfine splitting of energy levels (splitting caused by interaction of electron energy levels with the nuclear magnetic moment). It was a highly accurate device, capable of measuring frequency to an accuracy of 1 part in 10^{12}.

Ramsey has also worked on the thermodynamics and statistical mechanics of systems at low temperatures, pointing out that there is a possibility of certain nuclear spin systems having a negative thermodynamic temperature (i.e., a temperature below absolute zero).

For his work on molecular beams Ramsey was awarded the 1989 Nobel Prize for physics, which he shared with H. DEHMELT and W. PAUL. He is also the author of a standard work on the subject, *Molecular Beams* (Oxford, 1963).

Randall, Sir John Turton (1905–1984)
British physicist

The son of a nurseryman, Randall was born at Newton-le-Willows, then in Lancashire, and educated at the University of Manchester. He began work with General Electric at their Wembley laboratory, originally seeking to develop luminescent powders. He was subsequently appointed in 1937 to a Royal Society Fellowship at Birmingham University to conduct research into luminescence.

But the coming of World War II stopped all such nonmilitary work and Randall, along with his Birmingham colleagues, began work on improving current radar techniques. By 1943, in collaboration with his colleague **Henry Boot** (1917–1983), he had developed the cavity magnetron, one of the most vital inventions of the war.

Radar operates by reflecting radio waves off objects. As only a tiny part of the transmitted radiation is reflected back, and as only a fraction of this could be picked up by the receiving antena, considerable power had to be transmitted. Moreover the precision with which a target's position could be located was a function of the narrowness of the transmitted beam. Early transmitters had operated with wavelengths as long as 15 meters spreading the signal over a 100° sector. The demand was for 'centimetric radar'; i.e., radar using wavelengths of a centimeter or two.

The answer came with Boot and Randall's cavity magnetron, first revealed in November 1939. The device consists of a block of copper with accurately machined cavities through which circulating electrons subject to a magnetic field would generate intense electromagnetic radiation. When tested the magnetron delivered 400 watts on a 9-cm wavelength. The magnetron was passed to the research department of General Electric who increased its power to 10 kW. The new magnetron radar was first used by Bomber Command but soon became available to fighter aircraft and convoy escorts.

With the end of the war in sight Randall was appointed professor of natural philosophy in 1944 at St. Andrews in Scotland. In 1946 he accepted the post of head of a new department of biophysics set up by the Medical Research Council at King's College, London. Under him were Maurice WILKINS and Rosalind FRANKLIN, two scientists intimately connected with the elucidation in 1953 of the structure of DNA.

Randall himself worked on the structure of collagen, an important protein giving the skin its elasticity; it was found to consist of three helices coiled into a superhelix. On his retirement to Edinburgh in 1970 Randall continued to work with an informal research group on problems in biophysics.

Raoult, Francois-Marie (1830–1901)
French chemist

Raoult came from a poor background in Fournes-en-Weppes, France. He obtained his PhD in 1863 from the University of Paris and was 37 years old when he took up his first academic appointment at the University of Grenoble, where he was made professor of chemistry in 1870.

Raoult is noted for his work on the properties of solutions, in particular the effect of a dissolved substance in the lowering of freezing points. In 1882 he showed (*Raoult's law*) that the depression in the freezing point of a given solvent was proportional to the mass of substance dissolved divided by the substance's molecular weight. He later showed a similar effect for the vapor pressure of solutions. Measurement of freezing-point depression became an important technique for determining molecular weights.

Raoult's work was also important in validating Jacobus van't Hoff's theory of solutions. Also of significance in his work was his observation that the depression of the freezing point of water caused by an inorganic salt was double that caused by an organic solute (given the same molecular weight). This was one of the anomalies whose explanation led Sven Arrhenius to formulate his theory of ionic dissociation.

Raunkiaer, Christen (1860–1938)
Danish botanist

Raunkiaer was born in Varde. He graduated in botany in 1885 and was a scientific assistant at the Botanical Garden and Botanical Museum in Copenhagen from 1893 to 1911. From 1912 until 1923 he was professor of botany at the University of Copenhagen.

Raunkiaer is best known for his method of classifying 'life forms' based on the position of the perennating buds of plants and the degree of protection that these give in cold conditions or in drought. In general, the closer these buds are to the ground, the greater the protection. *Raunkiaer's classification* is useful for dividing areas of vegetation into groups and for investigating the occurrence of these groups under different climatic conditions.

Raup, David Malcolm (1933–)
American paleontologist

Born in Boston, Massachusetts, Raup was educated at the University of Chicago and at Harvard, where he obtained his PhD in 1957. After a brief spell at the California Institute of Technology, Raup spent the period from 1957 to 1965 at Johns Hopkins, Baltimore, and from 1966 to 1978 as professor of geology at the University of Rochester, New York. In 1980 Raup returned to the University of Chicago as professor of geophysics.

Much of Raup's work has been devoted to the problem of extinction. In 1983, in collaboration with John Sepkoski, Raup proposed the controversial thesis that extinction rates were cyclical, peaking periodically every 26 million years. The evidence for the hypothesis was derived from a large body of data collected by Sepkoski.

Initially Raup offered no explanation for such periodicity, other than to suggest that an extraterrestrial cause was more likely than a terrestrial one. Physicists were quick to take up the challenge with Richard Muller proposing the existence of a companion star of the sun, later named Nemesis, with a 26-million-year orbit, bringing with it periodic asteroid showers. Raup described the controversy which developed in his *The Nemesis Affair* (New York, 1986).

But, writing later in his *Extinction* (Oxford, 1993), he has noted that most astronomers have rejected the Nemesis and similar hypotheses. As to the 26-million-year periodicity, expert opinion is apparently evenly divided.

Raup has also published, with S. M. Stanley, a widely used textbook, *Principles of Paleontology* (San Francisco, 1978).

Ray, John (1627–1705) English naturalist and taxonomist

Ray, a blacksmith's son from Black Notley, Essex, attended Braintree Grammar School, where he benefited from a trust established to finance needy scholars at Cambridge University. He graduated in 1648 and became a fellow the following year, but his university career ended with the Restoration: as a Puritan, he refused to take the oath required by the Act of Uniformity and he lost his fellowship in 1662.

His activities as a naturalist were funded thereafter by friends from Cambridge, in particular by Francis Willughby, who helped him with the ambitious project of describing all known living things. From 1663 to 1666 Ray and Willughby traveled through Europe, widening their knowledge of the flora and fauna. On their return Ray moved into Willughby's house so that they could collaborate in writing up the work. In 1667 Ray published a catalog of British plants. In the same year he was elected a fellow of the Royal Society.

Willughby died in 1672 but left money in his will to enable Ray to continue their project. Between 1686 and 1704 Ray published *Historia plantarum* (History of Plants), a three-volume encyclopedia of plants describing 18,600 species. In it he emphasized the importance in classification of distinguishing between the monocotyledons and the dicotyledons but more importantly he fixed the species as the basic unit in the taxonomic hierarchy.

Ray also attempted to classify the animal kingdom. In 1693 he published a system based on a number of structural characters, including internal anatomy, which provided a more natural classification than those being produced by his contemporaries.

Ray is also remembered for his theological writings, in which he used the homologies he had perceived in nature as evidence for the necessity of an omniscient creator.

Rayleigh, John William Strutt, third baron (1842–1919) British physicist

Rayleigh, born at Witham in Essex, succeeded to his father's title in 1873. He graduated in mathematics from Cambridge University in 1865 and remained at Cambridge until his marriage, in 1871, to Evelyn Balfour, sister of the statesman Lord Balfour. In the following year poor health, which had also disrupted his schooling as a child, necessitated a break from academic life and recuperation in a warmer climate. During this convalescence, which was spent traveling up the Nile in a houseboat, Rayleigh wrote *The Theory of Sound*, which remains a classic in writings on acoustics.

On his return to England, Rayleigh built a laboratory next to his family home. Apart from the period 1879–84, when he succeeded James Clerk Maxwell as Cavendish Professor of Experimental Physics at Cambridge, Rayleigh carried out most of his work in this private laboratory. Of his early work the best known is his equation to account for the blue color of the sky, which (confirming John Tyndall's theory) concerned light scattering by small particles in the atmosphere. The amount of scattering depends on the wavelength of the light, and this causes the blue color. From this theory came the scattering law, an important concept in studies of wave propagation. Rayleigh also did a vast amount of work on other problems in physics, particularly in optics and acoustics.

While serving as Cavendish Professor, Rayleigh concerned himself with the precise measuring of electrical standards. He invented the *Rayleigh potentiometer* for precise measurement of potential difference. He extended this precision to the determination of the density of gases, and made the seemingly strange observation that nitrogen from air is always slightly denser than nitrogen obtained from a chemical compound. This led to his collaboration with William Ramsay that resulted in the discovery of argon. Rayleigh received the Nobel Prize for physics for this work in 1904; in the same year Ramsay was awarded the chemistry prize.

Réaumur, René Antoine Ferchault de (1683–1757) *French entomologist, physicist, and metallurgist*

Born at La Rochelle in western France, Réaumur traveled to Paris in 1703 and was admitted to the French Academy of Sciences in 1708. He was commissioned by Louis XIV (1710) to compile a report on the industry and arts of France, published as the *Description des arts et métiers* (Description of the Arts and Skilled Trades).

Réaumur made contributions to many branches of science and industry. He developed improved methods for producing iron and steel; the cupola furnace for melting gray iron was first built by him (1720). In 1740 he produced an opaque form of porcelain, still known as *Réaumur porcelain*. Perhaps his greatest individual achievement was the six-volume *Memoires pour servir à l'histoire des insectes* (1734–42; Memoirs Serving as a Natural History of Insects), the first serious and comprehensive entomological work.

Réaumur also devised a thermometer (1731), using a mixture of alcohol and water, with its freezing point of water at 0° and its boiling point at 80° (the *Réaumur temperature scale*). Through his research into digestion he established that this was a chemical rather than a mechanical process and he isolated gastric juice in 1752.

Reber, Grote (1911–   ) *American radio astronomer*

Reber, who was born in Wheaton, Illinois, studied at the Illinois Institute of Technology and became a radio engineer. His work in radio astronomy has taken him to many places including Washington DC in the late 1940s where he was chief of the Experimental Microwave Research Section, Hawaii, in 1951, and Tasmania in 1954 where he joined the Commonwealth Scientific and Industrial Research Organization. From 1957 to 1961 he worked at the National Radio Astronomy Observatory in Virginia and then returned to Tasmania to complete the studies he had started there.

Reber built the first antenna to be used specifically for extraterrestrial radio observations and was largely responsible for the early developments in radio astronomy. For many years he was probably the world's only radio astronomer. His interest was aroused in 1933 by the work of Karl Jansky. In 1937 he built, in his own backyard, a 30-foot (9.4-m) steerable parabolic bowl-shaped radio reflector with an antenna at its focus. Working at a shorter wavelength than Jansky, 60 centimeters instead of 15 meters, he began to spot emission peaks in the Milky Way. These were the intense radio sources in the constellations Cygnus, Taurus, and Cassiopeia. He published his results from 1940 onward and these came to the attention of many astronomers who, although unable to follow him immediately owing to the war, recognized the value of his work. Over the years Reber has constructed several telescopes so that he could map the radio sky at different wavelengths. His Hawaiian instrument operated at 5.5–14 meters while in Tasmania he used radio waves of 144 meters.

It was reading Reber's results that stimulated Jan Oort to pose the problem that led to Hendrik van de Hulst's discovery of the 21-centimeter hydrogen emission.

Redi, Francesco (1626–1697) *Italian biologist, physician, and poet*

Redi, who was born at Arezzo in Italy, studied medicine and philosophy at the University of Pisa, graduating in 1647. He was employed as personal physician to Ferdinand II and Cosimo III, both grand dukes of Tuscany. Intellectually, Redi displayed a variety of talents, being a noted poet, linguist, literary scholar, and student of dialect. On the scientific side, he laid the foundations of helminthology (the study of parasitic worms) and also investigated insect reproduction.

As a biologist he is best known for his experiments to test the theory of spontaneous generation. These were planned to explore the idea, put forward by William Harvey, that flies and similar vermin do not arise spontaneously but develop from eggs too small to be seen. Redi prepared eight flasks of various meats, with half left open to the air and half sealed. Maggots were found only in the unsealed flasks where flies had been able to enter and lay their eggs. That this effect was not due to the presence or absence of fresh air was shown by a second experiment in which half the flasks were covered with fine gauze. Again, no maggots developed in these. This was one of the earliest examples of a biological experiment planned with proper controls. Redi still believed, however, that spontaneous generation occurred in such animals as intestinal worms and gall flies, and it was not until the time of Louis Pasteur that the spontaneous-generation theory was finally discredited.

Regiomontanus (1436–1476) *German astronomer and mathematician*

Regiomontanus, as befitted a Renaissance humanist, changed his name, Johann Müller, for a Latin version of the name of his home town Königsberg (now Kaliningrad in Russia). His father was a miller. He was educated at Leipzig and Vienna where he was a pupil of Georg von Purbach. One of the ambitions of Purbach had been to produce a good text of Ptolemy's *Almagest* based on the original Greek rather than translations from Arabic at third or fourth hand. He had intended to go to Italy in quest of manuscripts of Ptolemy and other ancient scientists with the great Greek scholar Cardinal Bessarion. The death of Purbach in 1461 allowed Regiomontanus to take his place and spend six years in Italy searching for, translating, and editing manuscripts. After his return he settled in Nuremberg where his wealthy benefactor, Bernard Walther, built him an observatory and provided him with instruments. In 1475 he was called to Rome by the pope, Sixtus IV, to help in the reform of the calendar but died of the plague (or, possibly, poison) in 1476.

Regiomontanus was one of the key figures of 15th-century science. In the 1460s he wrote *De triangulis* (On Triangles), a work not printed until 1533 but that was, together with *Tabulae directionum* (1475; Tables of Direction), the main channel for the introduction of modern trigonometry into Europe. In the latter work he broke away from the ancient tradition of chords and instead gave tables of sines for every minute and tangents for every degree.

Regnault, Henri Victor (1800–1878) *French physicist and chemist*

Regnault came from a poor background in Aachen (now in Germany) and started work as a draper's assistant. He entered the Ecole Polytechnique in 1830 and later worked under Justus von Liebig at Giessen. He was successively professor of chemistry at the University of Lyons and the Ecole Polytechnique (1840). He became professor of physics at the Collège de France (1841) and finally director of the Sèvres porcelain factory in 1854.

Regnault's main work was in physics on the properties of gases and in particular the more accurate determination of many physical and chemical effects. Through his meticulous studies he showed, for example, that the law of Pierre Dulong and Alexis Petit was only approximately true when pure samples were taken and temperatures carefully measured. He also worked on the properties of gases – Joseph GAY-LUSSAC had claimed that a gas will increase by 1/266 of its volume for each increase of temperature of 1°C but Regnault showed that the true increase was 1/273. In addition he made accurate measurements of specific and latent heats and reliable determinations of atomic weights. Regnault is credited with the invention of the air thermometer.

In chemistry, Regnault discovered various organic chlorides that have since become important industrially, including vinyl chloride and carbon tetrachloride. He also took samples of air from different parts of the world and demonstrated that wherever it comes from it contains about 21% oxygen.

Reich, Ferdinand (1799–1882) *German mineralogist*

Reich, who was born at Bernburg in Germany, studied at the University of Göttingen and taught at the Freiberg Mining Academy. In 1863 he obtained a yellow precipitate from some local zinc ores. Convinced that it contained a new element he asked his assistant Hieronymus Richter to examine it spectroscopically (he himself was color blind). Richter found a new line in the dark blue region that confirmed Reich's original conviction; the new element was named 'indium' after the bright indigo line characteristic of its spectrum.

Reichstein, Tadeus (1897–1996) *Polish–Swiss biochemist*

Reichstein, the son of an engineer, was born in Wloclawek, Poland, and educated at the Federal Institute of Technology, Zurich, where he obtained his PhD in 1922. After some years in industry, Reichstein returned to work on the staff of the Institute in 1929. In 1938 he moved to the University of Basel, becoming in 1946 head of the Institute of Organic Chemistry, a position he held until his retirement in 1967.

In the 1930s Reichstein began to investigate the chemical role of the adrenal cortex. These are small glands, found on the kidneys, whose removal is invariably fatal. Beginning with a ton of beef adrenals he managed to reduce it to a mere ten grams of biologically active material.

From such samples he had, by 1946, isolated 29 different steroids, six of which he found would prolong the life of an animal with its adrenal gland removed. Of these, aldosterone, corticosterone, and hydrocortisone later proved the most active. Reichstein managed a partial synthesis of desoxycorticosterone, which for many years was the only corticoid that lent itself to large-scale production. At that time it was also the most effective treatment for Addison's disease.

Similar work was being done in America by Edward KENDALL who shared with Reichstein the 1950 Nobel Prize for physiology or medicine together with Philip HENCH.

In 1933 Reichstein succeeded in synthesizing ascorbic acid, vitamin C, at about the same time as Norman Haworth in England. He found a better technique for making the vitamin later that year, and this method is still used in commercial production.

Reines, Frederick (1918–1998)
American physicist

Born at Paterson in New Jersey, Reines was educated at the Stevens Institute of Technology and gained his PhD in theoretical physics at New York University in 1944. From 1944 to 1959 he was a group leader at the Los Alamos Scientific Laboratory, concerned with the physics and effects of nuclear explosions.

He was also concerned with investigations into the neutrino, and with Clyde Cowan performed the first experiments that confirmed its existence in the intense radiations from nuclear reactors. The first tentative observation was in 1953, but more definitive experiments were carried out at the Savannah River nuclear reactors in 1956. Detection of the neutrino is difficult because it can travel very long distances through matter before it interacts. Reines subsequently refined the techniques of detection and measurement.

Reines later turned his attention to looking for the relatively small numbers of natural neutrinos originating in cosmic radiation, and to this end constructed underground detectors looking for signs of interactions in huge vats of perchloroethyl-

ene. In the course of this work he devised a method of distinguishing cosmic-ray neutrinos from the muons they produce in traveling through the atmosphere.

In 1959 Reines was appointed head of the physics department at the Case Institute of Technology, Cleveland and was professor of physics and dean of physical sciences at the University of California at Irvine (1966–87). In 1995 he shared the Nobel Prize for physics with Martin PERL.

Reinhold, Erasmus (1511–1553)
German astronomer and mathematician

Little is known about the life of Reinhold other than that he was born at Saalfeld in Germany and became a student at Wittenberg, where he was appointed professor of astronomy in 1536 and rector of the university in 1549. He died a few years later from bubonic plague.

In 1542 Reinhold published a commentary on the *Theoricae novae planetarum* (New Theories about Planets) of Georg von Purbach, a traditional Ptolemaic text dating from about 1454. He is best known, however, for his *Tabulae Prutenicae* (Prussian Tables, 1551), the first work to provide astronomical tables based upon the new heliocentric system of Copernicus. He referred to Copernicus as "a second Atlas, a second Ptolemy," but went on to complain that the computations in Copernicus did not agree with Copernicus's own observations. Comparison between the two based upon recalculations with a computer have established that the accuracy of Reinhold's calculations systematically exceeds that of Copernicus. Although Reinhold's work did much to extend Copernican views, Reinhold made no reference to heliocentric assumptions in his tables.

Remak, Robert (1815–1865) *Polish–German embryologist and anatomist*

Remak, born the son of a shopkeeper in Posen (now in Poland), obtained his MD from the University of Berlin in 1838. Although he spent most of his career there and despite his considerable scientific achievements Remak was denied appropriate promotion and a teaching position because he was a Jew.

In 1838 Remak finally disposed of the ancient myth, probably dating back to Alcmaeon of Croton, that nerves were hollow tubes. In the long history of medicine they had been authoritatively described by centuries of keen-eyed anatomists as carrying various spirits, fluids, and airs. Even the introduction of the microscope in the 17th century made no difference. It was left to

Remak to point out that the nerve fiber is not hollow, but solid and flat.

In 1844 Remak discovered ganglion cells in the heart, thus showing that it could maintain a rhythmic beat independently of the central nervous system. He further noted that certain fibers of the nervous system, the sympathetic fibers, have a distinctly gray color rather than the more common white. They in fact lack the myelin sheath enclosing other nerve fibers.

In the mid 1840s, in collaboration with Johannes Müller, Remak made a major revision to the orthodox embryology of Karl von Baer. They reduced the four germ layers of von Baer to three by taking the two middle layers as only one. They also at this point introduced the modern terminology of endoderm, mesoderm, and ectoderm.

It was also Remak who, in 1841, first fully described the process of cell division. He went on to insist that the nucleus was a permanent feature of the cell even though it did become less noticeable after cell division. By 1855 Remak was ready to assert the general conclusion implicit in much of the early cell theory: that the production of nuclei or cells is really only division of pre-existing nuclei or cells.

Revelle, Roger (1909–1991) American oceanographer

Born in Seattle, Washington, Revelle was educated at Pomona College, California, and at the University of California, where he obtained his PhD in 1936. At the same time he joined the Scripps Institute of Oceanography, La Jolla, California, serving as director from 1951 until 1964. He then moved to Harvard as director of the Center for Population Studies, a post he held until 1976.

Revelle was responsible for directing much of the work at Scripps that eventually led to the discovery of sea-floor spreading and magnetic reversals. He also turned in the 1950s to what was then the far from fashionable topic of global warming.

The issue had first been raised by Arrhenius in 1895. He had calculated that a doubling of atmospheric carbon dioxide would raise the temperature by about 10°C. This would, in theory, occur because energy from the Sun arrives at the Earth's surface in the form of light and ultraviolet radiation, which are not absorbed by carbon dioxide. The energy is radiated by the Earth as infrared radiation, which is absorbed by carbon dioxide. The atmosphere thus acts in a similar way to the glass in a greenhouse, and the consequent warming is known as the 'greenhouse effect'. Revelle lobbied for real measurements and as a result gas recorders were set up in 1957 at Mauna Loa, Hawaii, and at the South Pole. By 1990 the carbon dioxide concentration had risen to 350 parts per million, an increase of 11%.

Revelle was also largely responsible for the foundation of the San Diego campus of the University of California in 1959, and was appointed to be its first dean of science. He returned to San Diego in 1976 as professor of science and public policy.

Rheticus (1514–1576) Austrian astronomer and mathematician

Rheticus born Georg Joachim von Lauchen in Feldkirch, Austria, but, in the manner of the time, he adopted a professional name from the Latinized form of his birth district, Rhaetia. After traveling in Italy and after attending several German universities, Rheticus was appointed professor of mathematics at Wittenberg in 1536; the chair of astronomy at the time was held by Reinhold. Both were Copernicans and both knew that the doctrine was opposed by the authorities, Protestant and Catholic alike.

Nevertheless the Protestant Rheticus traveled to Catholic Poland in 1539 to see Copernicus. As it happened Copernicus had completed the manuscript of his De revolutionibus (On Revolutions) many years before but, for a number of reasons, was unwilling to publish the work. Rheticus was a man of some charm and consequently persuaded Copernicus to allow a brief summary of his work to appear. The result was the Narratio Prima of Rheticus (Danzig, 1539; Basel, 1541; The First Narrative of Rheticus). It caused no major reactions and consequently Copernicus released the manuscript of the De revolutionibus to Rheticus.

A brief stay of a few weeks was extended to two years as Rheticus first copied the manuscript and then prepared the text for publication. By May 1542 Rheticus was ready to take the manuscript to the Nuremberg printers. When the work finally appeared in 1543 Copernicus failed to acknowledge the help of Rheticus in any way at all.

By this time Rheticus, reportedly because of his homosexuality, was no longer acceptable at Wittenberg and moved accordingly to the Leipzig chair of mathematics in 1542. But in 1550 he was once more forced into flight charged with indulging in 'Italian perversions'. Thereafter Rheticus seems to have practiced medicine and is occasionally met with in the service of some noble house.

During the latter part of his life Rheticus had, with the assistance of several calculators, prepared a massive set of trigonometrical tables. Whereas previous workers had expressed the functions in terms of arcs of circles, Rheticus introduced the modern practice of defining them as ratios between the sides of right triangles. Ten-place tables were computed for all six trigonometric functions for every 10″ of arc. The work was incomplete at his death and Rheticus needed his own disciple to publish his manuscript. It finally appeared in 1596 edited by Valentin Otho as the *Opus palatinum de triangulis* (The Imperial Work on Triangles).

Riccioli, Giovanni Battista (1598–1671) *Italian astronomer*

Born at Ferrara in Italy, Riccioli was a Jesuit priest who spent most of his life at Bologna where he was professor of astronomy. In 1651 he produced his famous work *Almagestum novum* (The New Almagest). It is in this work that the system of naming craters and mountains on the Moon after famous astronomers was introduced. Although the work is not Copernican – Riccioli presents no less than 77 arguments against Copernicus – it is not, despite the title, Ptolemaic either. Riccioli was a follower of Tycho Brahe, naming the largest lunar crater after him. As an observational astronomer he found that Mizar was a double star. He was also a skilled and patient experimenter who attempted to work out the acceleration due to gravity or *g*. He first tested Galileo's claim for the isochronicity of the pendulum and the relationship between the period and the square of the length. To measure the time a falling body takes he needed a pendulum that would beat once a second or 86,400 times per sidereal day. This led to the farce of using a team of Jesuits day after day to count the beats of his pendulum but the magic figure of 86,400 escaped them. Eventually the fathers could no longer tolerate staying up night after night counting pendulum beats and he was left with his pupil Francesco Grimaldi having to accept a less than perfect pendulum. He then performed with Grimaldi the type of experiment Galileo is supposed to have done from the leaning tower of Pisa. He dropped balls of various sizes, shapes, and weights from the 300-foot (92-m) Torre dei Asinelli in Bologna. He succeeded in confirming Galileo's results and establishing a figure for *g* of 30 feet (9.144 m) per second per second, which is close to the value of 9.80665 meters per second per second accepted today.

Richard of Wallingford (c. 1291–1336) *English astronomer and mathematician*

After the death of his father, a blacksmith of Wallingford, Oxfordshire, Richard was adopted by the prior of Wallingford. He was at Oxford University as a student from 1308 to 1314 and taught there from 1317 to 1326 before becoming the abbot of St. Albans. He is thought to have contracted leprosy in early life and there is a manuscript illustration of him in the British Museum that shows him with a spotty or scarred face.

Oxford at this time had gone through a minor renaissance. There were a number of scholars including Richard who were profoundly aware of the limitations imposed by traditional mathematical methods in dealing with virtually any problem of physics. It was Richard who introduced trigonometry into England in its modern form and in a series of manuscripts he produced the basic texts that could have initiated a mathematical revolution. (He was, however, two centuries too soon. The political troubles of the next 200 years and the Black Death were sufficient to smother any premature intellectual birth.) He was not just a theoretical mathematician for he designed and made his own instruments and, above all, he designed a marvelous clock for his abbey. It has been suggested that he introduced the work 'clock' into the English language, from the Latin 'clocca' for bell. His clock, the plans for which survive, probably predated that of Giovanni de Dondi in the use of an escapement. It showed the position of the Sun, the Moon, the stars, the state of the tide – in fact, it seemed, like most of the medieval clocks, to do just about everything except tell the time.

Richards, Dickinson Woodruff (1895–1973) *American physician. See* COURNAND, ANDRÉ FREDERIC.

Richards, Theodore William (1868–1928) *American chemist*

Richards came from an artistic background in Germantown, Pennsylvania: his father was a well-known painter and his mother a writer. He originally had ambitions in astronomy but his poor eyesight and the influence of his professor, Josiah P. Cooke, turned him to chemistry. After obtaining his doctorate from Harvard (1888) he continued his studies in Germany before returning to Harvard to take up a professorship in chemistry (1894).

In his doctoral work Richards made an accurate measurement of the ratio of the atomic weight of oxygen to that of hydrogen. His career continued to be devoted almost exclusively to the more accurate determination of atomic weights. He obtained the atomic weights of approximately 60 elements, improving considerably on those achieved by Jean STAS in the 1860s. His determination of the atomic weight of silver, for example, lowered this from Stas's 107.93 to 107.88. In 1913 his team showed that lead present in uranium had a lower atomic weight than normal specimens of lead, thus supporting the idea that it was formed by radioactive decay. In 1914 Richards was awarded the Nobel Prize for chemistry for his work on atomic weights.

In the latter half of his life he became interested in more theoretical problems. In 1902 he published an article which seemed to anticipate some of the ideas of the heat theorem of Nernst; he also worked on the compressibility of the elements.

Richardson, Lewis Fry (1881–1953)
British meteorologist and physicist

Richardson, the son of a farmer, was born in Newcastle-upon-Tyne and educated at Durham College and Cambridge University, graduating in 1903. In 1913 he became superintendent of the meteorological observatory at Eskdalemuir, Scotland. His work was interrupted by World War I and he resigned from the Meteorological Office in 1920. He was head of the physics department at Westminster Training College, London, until in 1929 he became principal of Paisley Technical College, Scotland, where he remained until his retirement in 1940.

Richardson was the first to try to apply mathematical techniques to weather prediction, publishing his ideas in *Weather Prediction by Numerical Process* (1922). In this he argued that the state of the atmosphere is defined by its temperature, pressure, and velocity. Once these were known, he believed that equations could be used to predict future weather conditions. The main problem with implementing his program was the time taken for computation, and it also suffered from a shortage of information. This was partially resolved with the advent of electronic computers following World War II.

The *Richardson number*, a value involving the gradients of temperature and wind velocity, is named for him.

Richardson also attempted to apply a mathematical framework to the study of the causes of war, publishing his work in *Generalized Foreign Politics* (1939), *Arms and Insecurity* (1949), and *Statistics of Deadly Quarrels* (1950).

Richardson, Sir Owen Willans (1879–1959) *British physicist*

Richardson, the son of a woollen manufacturer from Dewsbury in the north of England, was educated at Cambridge University and at London University, where he became a DSc in 1904. He taught at Princeton in America from 1906 to 1913, when he returned to England to become Wheatstone Professor of Physics at King's College, London, where he remained until his retirement in 1944.

Richardson is noted for his work on the emission of electrons from hot surfaces – the phenomenon first observed by Thomas Edison and used by Edison, John Fleming, Lee de Forest, and others in electron tubes. Richardson proposed an explanation of what he named 'thermionic emission', suggesting that the electrons came from within the solid and were able to escape provided that they had enough kinetic energy to overcome an energy barrier at the surface – the work function of the solid. Thus thermionic emission of electrons is analogous to evaporation from a liquid. The *Richardson law* (1901) relates the electron current to the temperature, and shows that it increases exponentially with increasing emitter temperature.

Richardson published an account of his extensive work on thermionic emission in his book *The Emission of Electricity from Hot Bodies* (1910). His work was important for the development of electron tubes used in electronic devices, and he was awarded the 1928 Nobel Prize for physics for this work. During World War II he worked on radar.

Richardson, Robert Coleman
(1937–) *American physicist*

Richardson was educated at Virginia State University and at Duke University, North Carolina, where he obtained his PhD in 1966. He moved immediately to Cornell and was appointed professor of physics in 1975.

In the early 1970s work with Douglas OSHEROFF and David LEE revealed that, contrary to expectations, helium-3 became a superfluid at a temperature of 0.0027 degrees above absolute zero. Richardson shared the 1996 Nobel Prize for physics with Osheroff and Lee for his work in this field.

Richer, Jean (1630–1696) *French astronomer*

Richer is a rather anonymous figure who is known only through his work with others. In 1671 he went on a scientific mission to Cayenne, where it was intended that he should observe meridian transits of the Sun and also measure the distance of Mars from any nearby stars while Giovanni Cassini performed similar observations in Paris. Apart from the obvious advantage of having two observers making the same measurements with a long base line, there was also the hope that Cayenne, 5° from the equator, would provide better viewing and that, because of its equatorial position, meridian sightings would be subject to less atmospheric refraction than in Paris.

But more important discoveries were to be made. The observations of Mars were made successfully, allowing Cassini to use the parallax obtained to give a distance of the Sun from the Earth of 86 million miles (138 million km). This was not particularly accurate – being 7% out – but at least it was properly determined and could easily be improved. What, however, really surprised Richer was that his pendulum timings were all slightly different from what they would have been in Paris; the pendulum was running slow, even at sea level. Cassini, at first, seems to have doubted the competence of Richer's observations but was eventually convinced. It was this work that provided Newton with the essential information in working out the size and shape of the Earth. If the pendulum slowed down then there must be a smaller gravitational force operating on it. The only way this could reasonably happen was if Cayenne was further from the center of the Earth than Paris; that is, if the Earth bulged at the equator, or to be precise, is an oblate spheroid.

Richet, Charles Robert (1850–1935)
French physiologist

Richet, the son of a distinguished Parisian surgeon, studied medicine at the University of Paris. After graduation in 1877 he worked at the Collège de France before he returned to the University of Paris where he served as professor of physiology from 1887 until his retirement in 1927.

Richet worked on a wide variety of problems, which ranged from heat regulation in mammals to the unsuccessful development of an anti-TB serum. His most important work began, however, with his investigation of how dogs react to the poison of a sea anemone. He found that he could induce a most violent reaction in dogs that had survived an original injection without any distress. If 22 days later he gave them a second injection of the same amount then they immediately became extremely ill and died in 25 minutes. Richet had discovered the important reaction of anaphylaxis, a term he coined in 1902 to mean the opposite of phylaxis or protection.

By 1903 he was able to show that the same effect could be produced by any protein whether toxic or not as long as there was a crucial interval of three to four weeks between injections. His work was to have profound implications for the newly emerging science of immunology and gained for Richet the 1913 Nobel Prize for physiology or medicine.

Richter, Burton (1931–) *American physicist*

Richter was joint winner of the 1976 Nobel Prize for physics. A New Yorker by birth, he studied first at the Massachusetts Institute of Technology, gaining his BS in 1952 and his PhD in physics in 1956. His interest in the physics of elementary particles took him subsequently to Stanford University's high-energy physics laboratory where he became a member of the group building the first pair of electron-storage rings. In this machine, intense beams of particles were made to collide with each other in order to study the validity of quantum electrodynamic theory.

In the 1960s, Richter designed the Stanford Positron Electron Accelerating Ring (SPEAR), which was capable of engineering collisions of much more energetic particles. It was on this machine that, in November 1974, Richter and his collaborators created and detected a new kind of heavy elementary particle, which they labeled psi (ψ). The discovery was announced in a 35-author paper (typical of today's high-energy-research teams) in the journal *Physical Review Letters*. The particle is a hadron with a lifetime about one thousand times greater than could be expected from its observed mass. Its discovery was important as its properties are consistent with the idea that it is formed from a fourth type of quark, thus supporting Sheldon Glashow's concept of 'charm'.

Almost simultaneously, another group led by Samuel TING 2000 miles away at the Brookhaven Laboratory, Long Island, made the same discovery independently in a very diffferent experiment. Richter and Ting met to discuss their findings, and confirmation came quickly from other laboratories when they knew the energy of the new particle and were able to tune their own machines accordingly. Ting called the new particle J; it is now usually referred to as the J/psi in recognition of the simultaneity of its discovery. The discovery led to the finding of many other similar particles as a 'family' and has stimulated new attempts to rationalize the underlying structure of matter. Within only two years, Richter and Ting were to be the recipients of the Nobel Prize for physics.

Richter has been a full professor at Stanford University since 1967, taking a sabbatical year at the European Organization for Nuclear Research (CERN) in Geneva (1975–76). He became director of the Linear Accelerator Center in 1984.

Richter, Charles Francis (1900–1985)
American seismologist

Born in Hamilton, Ohio, Richter was educated at the University of Southern California, Stanford, and the California Institute of Technology, where he obtained his PhD in 1928. He worked for the Carnegie Institute (1927–36) before being appointed to the staff of the California Institute of Technology. He became professor of seismology there in 1952.

Richter developed his scale to measure the strength of earthquakes in 1935. Earlier scales had been developed by de Rossi in the 1880s and by Giuseppe Mercalli in 1902 but both used a descriptive scale defined in terms of damage to buildings and the behavior and response of the population. This restricted their use to the measurement of earthquakes in populated areas and made the scales relative to the type of building techniques and materials used.

Richter's scale is an absolute one, based on the amplitude of the waves produced by the earthquake. He defined the magnitude of an earthquake as the logarithm to the base 10 of the maximum amplitude of the waves, measured in microns. This means that waves whose amplitudes differ by a factor of 100 will differ by 2 points on the Richter scale. With Beno Gutenberg he tried to correlate the points on his scale with the amount of energy released during an earthquake. In 1956 they showed that magnitude 0 corresponds to about 10^{11} ergs (10^4 joules), while magnitude 9 equals 10^{24} ergs (10^{17} joules). A one unit increase will mean about 30 times more energy being released. The strongest earthquake so far recorded had a Richter-scale value of 8.6. In 1954 Richter and Gutenberg produced one of the basic textbooks on seismology, *Seismicity of the Earth.*

Riddle, Oscar (1877–1968) *American biologist*

Born in Cincinnati, Ohio, Riddle was educated at Indiana University and at Chicago, where he obtained his PhD in 1907. After serving on the Chicago faculty from 1904 to 1911, he joined the research staff of the Carnegie Institution at their Station for Experimental Evolution, Cold Spring Harbor, New York, where he remained until his retirement in 1945.

In 1928 it was found that an extract from the anterior pituitary would stimulate milk secretion in rabbits. Riddle and his colleagues soon succeeded in isolating the hormone, which he named prolactin in 1932, and began a prolonged study of its physiological effects. He discovered that it would stimulate the growth of the crop sac in pigeons and inhibit gonadal growth in a number of animals.

His most dramatic and controversial finding, however, was that he could induce maternal behavior in hens by the injection of prolactin. Rats too were shown to adopt such normal maternal behavior as licking and retrieving despite their virgin state.

Riemann, (Georg Friedrich) Bernhard (1826–1866) *German mathematician*

Riemann was born at Breselenz in Germany and, before studying mathematics in earnest, studied theology in preparation for the priesthood at his father's request. Fortunately he was able to persuade his father, a Lutheran pastor, that his real talents lay elsewhere than in theology. He attended the University of Göttingen and his mathematical abilities were such that his doctoral thesis won the rarely given praise of Karl Friedrich Gauss. After gaining his doctorate Riemann worked on the inaugural lecture necessary in order to gain the post of *Privatdozent* at Göttingen and this too gained Gauss's praise. Eventually Riemann succeeded his friend, Lejeune Dirichlet, as professor of mathematics at Göttingen in 1859 but by then his health had begun to decline and he died of tuberculosis while on holiday in Italy.

Riemann's work ranges from pure mathematics to mathematical physics and he made influential contributions to both. His first mathematical work was on the functions of a complex variable. His work in analysis was profoundly important. The *Riemann integral* is a definite integral formally defined in terms of the limit of a summation of elements as the number of elements tends to infinity and their size becomes infinitesimally small.

One of Riemann's most famous pieces of work was in geometry. This was initiated in his inaugural lecture of 1854 that so impressed Gauss, entitled "Concerning the Hypotheses that Underlie Geometry." What Riemann did was to consider the whole question of what a geometry was from a much more general perspective than anyone had previously done. Riemann asked questions, such as how could concepts like curvature and distance be defined, in such a way as to be applicable to geometries that were not Euclidean. János Bolyai and Nikolai Lobachevsky (and, at the time unknown to everyone, Gauss) had developed particular non-Euclidean geometries, but Riemann went further and opened up the possibility of a range of geometries different from Euclid's. This work had far-reaching consequences, not just in pure mathematics but also in the theory of relativity.

Riemann was also interested in applied mathematics and physics and was a coworker of Wilhelm Weber.

Robbins, Frederick Chapman

(1916–   ) *American virologist and pediatrician*

Robbins was born in Auburn, Alabama, the son of plant physiologist William Robbins. He obtained his MD from Harvard Medical School in 1940 and from 1942 to 1946 headed the virus and rickettsial section of the US army's 15th medical general laboratory. Here he worked on the isolation of the parasitic microorganisms causing Q fever, which are also responsible for certain kinds of typhus.

After World War II Robbins became assistant resident at the Children's Hospital, Boston. In 1948 he became a National Research Fellow in virus diseases, working with John ENDERS and Thomas WELLER. By 1952 Robbins and his coworkers had managed to propagate the poliomyelitis virus in tissue cultures. They established that the polio virus can multiply outside nerve tissue and, in fact, exists in the extraneural tissue of the body, only later attacking the lower section of the brain and parts of the spinal cord.

This research enabled the production of polio vaccines, the development of sophisticated diagnostic methods, and the isolation of new viruses. In recognition of this work, Robbins, together with Enders and Weller, received the Nobel Prize for physiology or medicine in 1954.

Robbins was director of the pediatrics and contagious diseases department at Cleveland Metropolitan General Hospital, and professor of pediatrics at the Case Western Reserve University, from 1952 until his retirement in 1980. He is married to Alice Havemeyer Northrop, daughter of the Nobel Prize winner John Northrop.

Roberts, Richard (1943–   ) *British molecular biologist*

Born in Derby, Roberts was educated at the University of Sheffield where he gained his PhD in 1968. He moved soon after to America and, after spending a year at Harvard,

he moved to the Cold Spring Harbor Laboratory, New York, in 1971. He is currently serving as research director at New England Biolabs, Beverly, Massachusetts.

By the late 1970s it had become clear that the cells of some organisms seemed to have far too much DNA. Prokaryotic cells, i.e., cells without a nucleus, such as the bacteria *Escherichia coli*, have a single chromosome consisting of about 3 million DNA bases. A protein of about 300 amino acids will require 900 base pairs. Consequently a prokaryotic cell should be able to produce about 3000 proteins, a figure in reasonable agreement with experience. Eukaryotic cells, however, i.e., cells with a nucleus, as in mammals, have a genome of 3–4 billion base pairs, capable of producing some 3 million proteins, a number far in excess of the 150,000 or so proteins found in mammals. The disparity was solved in 1977 when Roberts, working with adenoviruses, stumbled upon the phenomenon of split genes. While all the DNA of prokaryotic cells was transcribed into messenger RNA (mRNA), which was then used as a template upon which amino acids could be assembled into proteins, something quite different seemed to be happening in the nuclei of eukaryotic cells. Only a part of the DNA, sometimes as little as 10%, was actually transcribed into mRNA. DNA appeared to be composed of several stretches, termed 'introns', serving no known purpose, but which separated the active DNA sequences, soon to be called 'exons'. In the process of transcription the introns were neatly excised and the exons consequently spliced together to form the mature mRNA responsible for the production of protein.

The work of Roberts was independently confirmed by Phillip SHARP, with whom he shared the 1993 Nobel Prize for physiology or medicine.

Robertson, John Monteath (1900–1989) *British x-ray crystallographer*

Robertson was born in Auchterarder, Scotland, and educated at Glasgow University where he obtained his PhD in 1926. From 1928 until 1930 he studied at the University of Michigan and then worked at the Royal Institution throughout the 1930s. After brief periods at the University of Sheffield and with Bomber Command of the Royal Air Force, he returned to Glasgow in 1942 and served as professor of chemistry until his retirement in 1970.

Robertson was one of the key figures who, centered on the Braggs and the Royal Institution, developed x-ray crystallography in the interwar period into one of the basic tools of both the physical and life sciences. He established structures for a large number of molecules, including accurate measurements of bond length in naphthalene, anthracene, and similar hydrocarbons. He also worked on the structure of the important pigment phthalocyanine (1935), durene (1933), pyrene (1941), and copper salts (1951). A notable contribution to the technique was his development of the heavy-atom substitution method, which he used in his investigation of phthalocyanine. This involves substituting a heavy atom into the molecule investigated. The change in intensity of diffracted radiation gives essential information on the phases of scattered waves.

In 1953 Robertson published a full account of his work in his *Organic Crystals and Molecules* in which he demonstrated the growing success in applying the new techniques of x-ray crystallography to complex organic molecules.

Robertson, Sir Robert (1869–1949)
British chemist

Robertson, born the son of a dental surgeon in Cupar, Scotland, was educated at St. Andrews University. After graduating in 1890 he served briefly from 1890 to 1892 in the City Analyst's Office, Glasgow, before entering government service on the staff of the Royal Gunpowder Factory, Waltham Abbey. In 1900 he became chemist in charge, but moved to the Royal Arsenal, Woolwich, in 1907 to serve as superintendent chemist of the research department. In 1921 he became government chemist in charge of the Government Chemical Laboratory in the Strand, London. Robertson remained there until his retirement in 1936 but returned to public service during World War II, which he spent working on explosives at the University of Swansea.

Robertson made a number of advances in the chemistry and technology of explosives. He carried out early work on the decomposition of gun cotton and also improved the process of TNT manufacture. More important was his introduction in 1915 of amatol, a mixture of up to 80% ammonium nitrate to 20% TNT, an explosive more efficient and much cheaper than conventionally produced TNT. It was in fact said of amatol by the director of artillery that it "won the war."

As a pure chemist Robertson was one of the first to see the value of infrared spectroscopy for determining molecular structure. He consequently used it to explore ammonia and arsine (AsH_3).

Robinson, Sir Robert (1886–1975)
British chemist

Robinson's father was a manufacturer of surgical dressings and one of the inventors of cotton wool. Robinson, who was born at Chesterfield in Derbyshire, was educated at the University of Manchester where he obtained a DSc in 1910. From 1912 to 1930 Robinson held chairs in organic chemistry successively at Sydney (1912–15), Liverpool (1915–20), St. Andrews (1921–22), Manchester (1922–28), and University College, London (1928–30). In 1930 he was appointed to the chair of chemistry at Oxford, a post he occupied until his retirement in 1955.

Early in his career, while working with William Perkin Jr. at Manchester, Robinson became interested in the natural dyes brazilin and hematoxylin. Important advances were achieved in understanding the chemistry of these compounds and their derivatives, which eventually led to his syntheses of anthocyanins and flavones, important plant pigments. Robinson also worked on the physiologically active alkaloids and established the structure of morphine (1925) and strychnine (1946). For his "investigations of plant products of biological importance, especially the alkaloids" Robinson was awarded the 1947 Nobel Prize for chemistry.

From 1945 to 1950, Robinson served as president of the Royal Society.

Roche, Edouard Albert (1820–1883)
French mathematician

Roche studied at the university in his native city of Montpellier, obtaining his doctorate there in 1844. After further study in Paris he returned to Montpellier in 1849 and served as professor of pure mathematics from 1852 until his retirement in 1881.

Roche's name is still remembered by astronomers for his proposal in 1850 of the limiting distance since named for him. He calculated that if a satellite and the planet it orbited were of equal density then the satellite could not lie within 2.44 radii, the *Roche limit*, of the larger body without breaking up under the effect of gravity. As the radius of Saturn's outermost ring is 2.3 times that of Saturn it was naturally felt that the rings could well consist of broken-down fragments of a former satellite that had transgressed the forbidden limit. It is now thought, however, that the Roche limit has prevented the fragments from aggregating into a satellite.

Roche later worked on the nebular hypothesis of Pierre Simon de Laplace, submitting it to a rigorous mathematical analysis and concluding in 1873 that a rapidly rotating lens-shaped body was in fact unstable. He also published work on the structure and density of the Earth and produced a generalization of Taylor's theorem, much used in mathematics.

Rodbell, Martin (1925–) *American biochemist*

Rodbell was educated at the University of Washington where he gained his PhD in 1954. He first worked at the National Institute of Health, Bethesda, Maryland. In 1985 he was appointed Scientific Director of the National Institute for Environmental Health Sciences, North Carolina.

Rodbell has attempted to show at the molecular level how cells respond to such chemical signals as hormones and neurotransmitters. It had been shown by Earl Sutherland in 1957 that hormones, also known as 'first messengers', do not actually penetrate into the cell but rather stimulate the production of a so-called second messenger, cAMP (cyclic adenosine monophosphate). But, Rodbell asked, how does the binding of a hormone to its receptor stimulate the production of cAMP?

The process proved to be quite complex. In the late 1960s Rodbell found that at least two other factors, referred to as an amplifier and a transducer, were essential. The first extra factor, the amplifier, was needed to initiate the production of cAMP. It was identified as the enzyme AC (adenylate cyclase), which converted the energy-rich molecule ATP (adenosine triphosphate) into the second messenger cAMP. For the second extra factor, the transducer, Rodbell found that no reaction would occur without the presence of a complex energy-rich molecule GTP (guanine triphosphate). The GTP reacted in some way with the AC to initiate cAMP production. If either were absent the cell simply would not respond to such external stimuli as insulin or adrenaline.

For his work on what later became known as *G proteins*, Rodbell shared the 1994 Nobel Prize for physiology or medicine with Alfred GILMAN.

Rohrer, Heinrich (1933–) *Swiss physicist*

Born at Buchs in Switzerland, Rohrer was educated at the Federal Institute of Technology, Zurich, where he obtained his PhD in 1960. After two years' postdoctoral work at Rutgers, New Jersey, he returned to Zurich in 1963 to join the staff of the IBM Research Laboratory, Roschliken.

The conventional electron microscope developed by RUSKA in the 1930s could present a two-dimensional image only. Further, while atoms have a diameter of 1–2 angstroms (1 angstrom = 10^{-10} meter), electron microscopes could not resolve images below 5 angstroms. Consequently, the surface structure at the atomic level was beyond the range of any existing microscope. To overcome this limitation Rohrer, in collaboration with his IBM colleague, Gerd BINNIG, began work in 1978 on a scanning tunneling microscope (STM).

In the STM a fine probe passes within a few angstroms of the surface of the sample. If a positive voltage is applied to the probe, electrons can move from the sample to the probe by the tunnel effect, and a current can be detected. This current is sensitive to distance from the surface; a slight change in distance will produce a significant change in current. Consequently, in theory at least, a feedback mechanism should be able to keep the probe at a constant distance from the surface, or, in other words, trace the surface's contours. If the tip is allowed to scan the surface by sweeping through a path of parallel lines, a three-dimensional image of the surface can be constructed.

Inevitably practice proved less straightforward than theory. A major difficulty was to eliminate vibration. As the magnification required was of the order of 100 million, any interference would grossly distort the image produced. The microscope was suspended on springs and placed in a vacuum, and further vibrations were dampened by resting the microscope on copper plates positioned between magnets. If the copper plates begin to move an eddy current will be induced by the magnetic field and the interaction between current and field will, in turn, damp the motion of the plates. Vibration was so reduced as to allow a vertical resolution of 0.1 Å; the lateral resolution, depending upon the sharpness of the probe, was initially no better than 6 Å.

The STM has proved useful in the study of the surfaces of semiconductors and metals and has also been applied to biological samples such as viruses. For their work in this field Rohrer and Bining shared the 1986 Nobel Prize for physics with Ruska.

Romer, Alfred Sherwood (1894–1973) *American paleontologist*

Romer, who was born at White Plains, New York, and educated at Amherst College and Columbia University, established his reputation with a PhD on comparative myology (musculature), which remains a classic in its field. The impetus for subsequent paleontological fieldwork and research came with his appointment as associate professor in the University of Chicago's department of geology and paleontology, where he was able to study the collections of late Paleozoic fishes, amphibians, and reptiles. Professor of biology at Harvard from 1934, Romer then became Harvard's director of biological laboratories (1945) and director of the Museum of Comparative Zoology (1946).

One of the major figures in paleontology since the 1930s, Romer spent the greater part of his career researching the evolution of vertebrates, based on evidence from comparative anatomy, embryology, and paleontology, and his work has had considerable influence on evolutionary thinking, especially with regard to the lower vertebrates. He paid particular attention to the relationship between animal form and physical function and environment, tracing, for example, the physical changes that occurred during the evolutionary transition of fishes to primitive terrestrial vertebrates. He made extensive collections of fossils of fishes, amphibians, and reptiles from South Africa and Argentina and from the Permian deposits in Texas. His best-known publication is *Man and the Vertebrates* (1933), subsequently revised as *The Vertebrate Story* (1959).

Römer, Ole Christensen (1644–1710)
Danish astronomer

Born at Aarhus, Denmark, Ole (or Olaus) Römer was professor of astronomy at the University of Copenhagen when Jean Picard visited Denmark to inspect Tycho Brahe's observatory at Uraniborg. Picard recruited him and Römer joined the Paris Observatory in 1671. In Paris, working on Giovanni Cassini's table of movements of the satellites of Jupiter, he noticed that whether the eclipses happened earlier or later than Cassini had predicted depended on whether the Earth was moving toward or away from Jupiter. Römer realized that this anomaly could be explained by assuming that the light from the satellite had a longer (Earth moving away from Jupiter) or shorter (Earth moving toward Jupiter) distance to travel. As Cassini had recently established the distance between the Earth and Jupiter, Römer realized that he had all the information needed to calculate one of the fundamental constants of nature – the speed of light. In 1676 he announced to the French Academy of Sciences that the speed of light was, in modern figures, 140,000 miles (225,000 km) per second. This value is too small but was an excellent first approximation. In 1681 Römer was made Astronomer Royal and returned to Copenhagen where

he designed and developed the transit telescope.

Röntgen, Wilhelm Conrad (1845–1923) *German physicist*

Röntgen, who was born at Lennep in Germany, received his early education in the Netherlands; he later studied at the Federal Institute of Technology, Zurich. After receiving his doctorate in 1869 for a thesis on *States of Gases*, he held various important university posts including professor of physics at Würzburg (1888) and professor of physics at Munich (1900). Röntgen researched into many branches of physics including elasticity, capillarity, the specific heat of gases, piezoelectricity, and polarized light. He is chiefly remembered, however, for his discovery of x-rays made at Würzburg on 8 November 1895.

In 1894 Röntgen had turned his attention to cathode rays and by late 1895 he was investigating the fluorescence caused by these rays using a Crookes tube. In order to direct a pencil of rays onto a screen, he covered a discharge tube with black cardboard and operated it in a darkened room. Röntgen noticed by chance a weak light on a nearby bench and found that another screen, coated with barium platinocyanide, was fluorescing during the experiment. He had already established that cathode rays could not travel more than a few centimeters in air, and as the screen was about a meter from the discharge tube he realized that he had discovered a new phenomenon. During the succeeding six weeks he devoted himself, feverishly and exclusively, to investigating the properties of the new emanations, which, because of their unknown nature, he called 'x-rays'. On 28 December 1895 he announced his discovery and gave an accurate description of many of the basic properties of the rays: they were produced by cathode rays (electrons) at the walls of the discharge tube; they traveled in straight lines and could cause shadows; all bodies were to some degree transparent to them; they caused various substances to fluoresce and affected photographic plates; they could not be deflected by magnetic fields. Röntgen concluded that x-rays were quite different from cathode rays but seemed to have some relationship to light rays. He conjectured that they were longitudinal vibrations in the ether (light was known to consist of transverse vibrations). Their true nature was finally established in 1912.

Röntgen's discovery immediately created tremendous interest. It did not solve the contemporary wave–particle controversy on the nature of radiation but it stimulated further investigations that led, among other things, to the discovery of radioactivity; it also provided a valuable tool for research into crystal structures and atomic structure, and x-rays were soon applied to medical diagnosis. Unfortunately their danger to health only became understood very much later; both Röntgen and his technician suffered from x-ray poisoning.

Although Röntgen was subjected to some bitter attacks and attempts to belittle his achievements, his discovery of x-rays earned him several honors, including the first ever Nobel Prize for physics (1901).

Rose, William Cumming (1887–1984)
American biochemist

Born in Greenville, South Carolina, Rose was educated at Davidson College, North Carolina, and at Yale, where he obtained his PhD in 1911. He taught at the University of Texas from 1913 to 1922, when he moved to the University of Illinois as professor of physiological chemistry; from 1936 until his retirement in 1955 he was professor of biochemistry there.

In the late 1930s Rose was responsible for a beautifully precise set of experiments that introduced the idea of an essential amino acid into nutrition, demonstrating its effect on both human and rodent diet. It had been known for a long time to nutritionists that rats fed on a diet in which the only protein was zein (found in corn), despite enrichment with vitamins, would inevitably die. Rose worked with the constituent amino acids rather than proteins; he still found, however, that whatever combination of amino acids he tried the rats died. However, if the milk protein, casein, was added to their diet the ailing rats recovered.

It was obvious from this that casein must contain an amino acid, not present in zein and then unknown, that was essential for life. Rose began a long series of experiments extracting and testing various fragments of casein until at last he found, in 1936, threonine, the essential amino acid that provided a satisfactory rodent diet when added to the other amino acids. Rose argued that if there was one essential amino acid there could well be others. Over several years he therefore continued to manipulate the rodent diet and finally established the primary importance of ten amino acids: lysine, tryptophan, histidine, phenylalanine, leucine, isoleucine, methionine, valine, and arginine, in addition to the newly discovered threonine. With these in adequate quantities the rats were capable

of synthesizing any of the other amino acids if and when they were needed.

In 1942 Rose began a ten-year research project on human diet. By persuading students to restrict their diet in various ways Rose eventually established that there are eight essential amino acids for humans: unlike rats we can survive without arginine and histidine. Since then, however, it has been suggested that these two amino acids are probably required to sustain growth in infants.

Ross, Sir Ronald (1857–1932) *British physician*

The son of an Indian Army officer, Ross was born in Almora, India. He originally wished to be an artist but his father was determined that he should join the Indian Medical Service. Consequently, after a medical education at St. Bartholomew's Hospital, London, Ross entered the Indian Medical Service in 1881.

Much of Ross's early career was spent in literary pursuits, writing poetry and verse dramas; he published some 15 literary works between 1883 and 1920. It was also during this first period in India that Ross developed his passion for mathematics. This was a lifelong interest and he published some seven titles between 1901 and 1921; in his *Algebra of Space* (1901) he claimed to have anticipated some of the work of A.N. Whitehead.

On leave in England in 1889, Ross took a diploma in public health and attended courses in the newly established discipline of bacteriology. He became interested in malaria and in 1894 approached Patrick Manson with a request to be shown how to detect the causative parasite of malaria, first described by Charles Laveran in 1880. With his guidance and encouragement, Manson turned out to be the major influence in Ross's scientific career; it was Manson who suggested to Ross that mosquitoes might be the vectors of malaria, and when Ross returned to India he spent the next four years researching this theory.

His first strategy, to try and demonstrate the transmission of the disease from mosquitoes to man, met with little success: attempts to infect a colleague with bites from a mosquito fed on malaria patients failed, possibly because the species he used was not a carrier of the disease. He therefore decided to study the natural history of the mosquito in more detail and by 1897 had succeeded in identifying malaria parasites (plasmodia) in the bodies of *Anopheles* mosquitoes fed on blood from infected patients. Ross then attempted to show what happened to the parasite in the mosquito and how it reached a new human victim. He decided to work with avian malaria and its vector *Culex fatigans*, giving him a control over his experimental subjects impossible to attain with man. By 1898 he had succeeded in identifying the *Proteosoma* parasite responsible for avian malaria in the salivary glands of the mosquito, thus proving that the parasite was transmitted to its avian host by the bite of the mosquito. Manson was able to report Ross's work to the meeting of the British Medical Association in Edinburgh and by the end of the year Italian workers under Giovanni Grassi had been able to show similar results in the *Anopheles* mosquito, the vector of human malaria.

In 1899 Ross resigned from the Indian Medical Service and accepted a post at the Liverpool School of Tropical Medicine, remaining there until 1912, when he moved to London to become a consultant. During this period he spent much time on the problem of mosquito control, advising many tropical countries on appropriate strategies.

For his work on malaria Ross was awarded the 1902 Nobel Prize for physiology or medicine.

Rossby, Carl-Gustaf Arvid (1898–1957) *Swedish–American meteorologist*

Rossby was born the son of an engineer in Stockholm and educated at the university there. In 1919 he joined the Geophysical Institute at Bergen, which at the time, under Vilhelm Bjerknes, was the world's main center for meteorological research. In 1926 he emigrated to America and was appointed professor of the first meteorology department in America at the Massachusetts Institute of Technology in 1928. After two years as assistant head of the Weather Bureau he became professor of meteorology at the University of Chicago in 1941.

Rossby carried out fundamental work on the upper atmosphere, showing how it affects the long-term weather conditions of the lower air masses. Measurements recorded with instrumented balloons had demonstrated that in high latitudes in the upper atmosphere there is a circumpolar westerly wind, which overlays the system of cyclones and anticyclones lower down. In 1940 Rossby demonstrated that long sinusoidal waves of large amplitude, now known as *Rossby waves*, would be generated by perturbations caused in the westerlies by variations in velocity with latitude. Rossby also showed the importance of the strength of the circumpolar westerlies in determining global weather. When these are weak, cold polar air will sweep south, but when they are strong, the normal sequence of cyclones and anticyclones will develop.

Rossby is credited with having discovered the jet stream. He also devised mathematical models to predict the weather which were simpler than those of Lewis F. Richardson. His school provided the 'dynamic meteorology' that allowed, with the coming of computers and weather satellites, the long-term prediction of weather.

Rosse, William Parsons, third earl of (1800–1867) *Irish astronomer and telescope builder*

The eldest son of the second earl of Rosse, William Parsons was born at York in England. He was educated at Trinity College, Dublin, and Oxford University, where he graduated in 1822. He was a member of parliament from 1822 until 1834, when he resigned to devote himself to science.

Rosse's main aim was to build a telescope at least as large as those of William Herschel. As Herschel had left no details of how to grind large mirrors, Rosse had to rediscover all this for himself. It was not until 1839 that he had made a 3-inch (8-cm) mirror; this was followed by mirrors of 15 inches (38 cm), 24 inches (61 cm), and 36 inches (91 cm) until, in 1842, he felt confident enough to start work on his 72-inch (183-cm) masterpiece. He was only successful on the fifth casting. It weighed 8960 pounds (4064 kg), cost £12,000, and became known as the 'Leviathan of Corkstown'. Its tube was over 50 feet (15 m) long and because of winds it had to be protected by two masonry piers 50 feet high and 23 feet (7 m) apart in which it was supported by an elaborate system of platforms, chains, and pulleys.

The giant reflector suffered, despite the cost and time, from two major defects. The climate of central Ireland is such that very few nights of viewing are possible during the year. Also, viewing (when possible), was restricted by the piers to a few degrees of the north–south meridian. Despite this Rosse made a couple of discoveries. He was the first to identify a spiral nebula and went on to discover 15 of them. He also named and studied the Crab nebula, which has been so important to contemporary astronomy. The telescope was finally dismantled in 1908. More than the individual discoveries made by Rosse, the Leviathan was important in the warnings it gave telescope builders. Good big mirrors were needed but they were by no means sufficient; in addition a good site and an adequate mounting were necessary.

Rossi, Bruno Benedetti (1905–1994)
Italian–American physicist

Rossi, born the son of an electrical engineer in Venice, Italy, was educated at the universities of Padua and Bologna. He first taught at the universities of Florence and Padua before emigrating to America in 1938. There he worked at Chicago and Cornell universities and in 1943 moved to Los Alamos to work on the development of the atom bomb. After World War II he was appointed, in 1946, to the chair of physics at the Massachusetts Institute of Technology where he remained until his retirement in 1970.

Rossi's main work was in the field of cosmic rays. These had first been detected by Victor Hess in 1911 but, by 1930, there was little agreement on their real nature; it was not even certain whether or not they were charged particles. To answer this question most physicists had been inconclusively searching for a variation in intensity with latitude.

Instead, in 1930 Rossi proposed an experimental arrangement that would search for any east–west asymmetry. Charged particles coming from outer space would be deflected by the Earth's magnetic field eastward if positively charged and westward if negatively charged. To detect them Rossi suggested that two or more Geiger counters be arranged pointing eastward with their centers arranged in a straight line. A similar arrangement should be set up pointing westward. Thus only particles coming from the direction along the axis of the counters would register simultaneously on both or all of them. In 1934 Rossi set up his counters in the mountains of Eritrea and found a 26% excess of particles traveling eastward, thus showing that the majority of cosmic-ray particles are positively charged.

Rossi was the author of several books, including *Cosmic Rays* (1964), which has been used by generations of physics students.

Rotblat, Joseph (1908–   ) *Polish–British physicist*

Rotblat was educated at the University of Warsaw. In 1939 he was appointed to a research fellowship at the University of Liverpool to work on neutron fission in the laboratory of James Chadwick. Like many other Europeans, he worked during World War II at Los Alamos on the development of the atom bomb. But unlike most other scientists as soon as it was clear in early 1945 that Germany was defeated and would be unable to produce a nuclear weapon in time, Rotblat felt unable to justify working any longer on the development of such weapons. He was also alarmed by the attitude of some of his senior colleagues. General Groves, for example, the head of the Manhattan Project, was overheard by Rotblat insisting that the real purpose of the bomb was to subdue Soviet Russia.

Consequently he resigned from Los Alamos, arousing the deep suspicion of the security officers who suspected him of being a Soviet agent, and returned to Liverpool in early 1945. He remained at Liverpool until 1950 when he was appointed professor of physics at Bart's Hospital Medical College, a position he held until his retirement in 1976. Rotblat's scientific work was mainly concerned with radiation medicine.

He did, however, concern himself with other matters. After the explosion of the H-bomb on Bikini atoll, the Atomic Energy Commission reported that the fallout from this and all other explosions was no more damaging to the individual than the exposure received from a single diagnostic x-ray. The announcement did nothing to reassure Rotblat. The Bikini bomb, he worked out independently, would have been much more dangerous than the authorities admitted. Further, he reasoned, chest x-rays screen only chests; nuclear bombs radiated the whole body including wombs, ovaries, and testicles.

Rotblat was determined not to let the matter rest. He drafted an appeal for peace, backed by Bertrand Russell and Albert Einstein among others, to be delivered to world leaders. He realized, however, that something more permanent and constructive was needed. Consequently he set about raising money to hold a series of conferences in which technical matters could be debated, authoritative proposals made, and contacts established between scientists from different disciplines and countries.

The American millionaire Cyrus Eaton offered to finance the first conference as long as it was held in the Nova Scotian fishing village of Pugwash, Eaton's birthplace. The first conference was held in 1957 and was attended by 22 scientists. Known as Pugwash conferences, ever since they have continued to be held around the world. Rotblat served as the Secretary-General of Pugwash from its inception until 1973. Since 1988 he has held the office of Pugwash President.

Rotblat was awarded the 1995 Nobel Peace Prize, an award he shared with the organization he helped to found, the Pugwash Conferences on Science and World Affairs.

The award was made, the Nobel committee announced, to mark the 50th anniversary of Hiroshima and Nagasaki and to protest against French nuclear tests in the Pacific.

Rous, Francis Peyton (1879–1970)
American pathologist

Rous was born in Baltimore, Maryland, and educated at Johns Hopkins University there, obtaining his MD in 1905. After working as a pathologist at the University of Michigan, he moved in 1908 to the Rockefeller Institute of Medical Research in New York, remaining there until his official retirement in 1945. Unofficially, Rous continued to work in his laboratory until his death at the age of 90.

In 1909 Rous began to investigate a particular malignant tumor of connective tissues in chickens – later to be known as *Rous chicken-sarcoma*. He ground up the tumor and passed it through a fine filter, extracting what would normally be accepted as a cell-free filtrate. On injection of this filtrate into other chickens, identical tumors developed. In 1911 Rous published his results in a paper with the significant title *Transmission of a Malignant New Growth by means of a Cell-free Filtrate*, significant because nowhere in the title (or even in the paper) does the expected term 'virus' occur.

It was well known by 1911 that only a virus could be present in such a filtrate, but Rous was unwilling to use the term for fear of offending his more senior colleagues. Scientists were reluctant to accept that cancer could be caused by viruses since the epidemiology of the disease was obviously different from that of such viral infections as influenza. Rous persisted with his work, however, and by the late 1930s it was widely accepted that a number of animal cancers were caused by viruses. In 1966 Rous was awarded the Nobel Prize for physiology or medicine for the discovery he had announced some 55 years earlier.

Rous also worked on the development of a number of culture techniques for both viruses and cells, techniques that have since become standard laboratory practice.

Rowland, Frank Sherwood (1927–)
American chemist

Born in Delaware, Ohio, Rowland was educated at Wesleyan University, Ohio, and at the University of Chicago, where he gained his PhD in 1952. After holding teaching posts at Princeton and Kansas, Rowland moved to the University of California, Irvine, in 1964 as professor of chemistry.

Shortly before Christmas 1973, Mario Molina took to Rowland, his postdoctoral adviser, some calculations suggesting that CFCs (chlorofluorocarbons), widely used in aerosol propellants, will rise to the upper atmosphere and destroy the ozone layer, located 8 to 30 miles above the Earth. As the layer protects us from harmful ultraviolet rays, its destruction could have disturbing consequences.

Rowland and Molina published their preliminary results in June 1974. They pointed out that in the lower atmosphere CFCs were relatively inert compounds. But at a height of about 25 kilometers in the stratosphere they begin to absorb ultraviolet radiation in the 1900–2250 angstrom range and decompose, releasing chlorine atoms which will attack ozone (O_3) atoms in a chain reaction:

$$Cl\cdot + O_3 \rightarrow ClO + O_2$$

$$ClO + O\cdot \rightarrow Cl\cdot + O_2$$

In the first part of the reaction a chlorine atom attacks an ozone molecule and forms chlorine monoxide and normal oxygen; in the second stage of the reaction, involving oxygen atoms, the chlorine is regenerated and is free to enter once more into the first reaction, destroying an ozone molecule in the process. The result is that a relatively small amount of CFC can destroy a large amount of ozone.

Rowland discovered that 400,000 tons of CFCs had been produced in the United States in 1973, and that the bulk of this was being discharged into the atmosphere. He calculated that at the then current production rate there would be a long-term steady-state ozone depletion of 7–13%. The CFC industry responded by pointing out there was no actual proof of Rowland's hypothesis. Further, they argued, even if the hypothesis was true, other atmospheric processes could offset the effects of the reaction. In 1974 it seemed that Rowland had found just such a process with the possible formation of chlorine nitrate ($ClONO_2$) in the atmosphere. Thus it seemed possible that the reaction:

$$ClO + NO_2 \rightarrow ClONO_2$$

would remove chlorine monoxide, leaving less chlorine to react with ozone. More detailed analysis revealed that chlorine nitrate might change the distribution of ozone in the atmosphere without significantly minimizing its depletion rate. The National Academy of Sciences published a report in September 1976 supporting the work of Rowland and Molina, and in October 1978 CFC use in aerosols was banned in the United States. Final confirmation came when Joe Farman discovered in late 1984 a 40% ozone loss over Antarctica.

For his work on CFCs Rowland shared the 1995 Nobel Prize for chemistry with Mario MOLINA and Paul CRUTZEN.

Rubbia, Carlo (1934–   ) *Italian physicist*

Born at Gorizia, Trieste, Rubbia was educated at the University of Pisa, where he obtained his PhD in 1958. After spending a year each at Columbia, New York, and Rome, he took up an appointment in 1960 at the European Laboratory for Particle Physics (CERN), Geneva, becoming its director-general in 1989. He has also held since 1972 a professorship of physics at Harvard.

Rubbia is noted for his work in high-energy physics using the considerable accelerator capacity of CERN. He set himself an ambitious target in the mid 1970s, namely, the discovery of the intermediate vector bosons. Forces operate by interchanging particles. Thus the electromagnetic force works by exchange of virtual photons. The weak interaction would, therefore, require a comparable particle; in actual fact three such particles would be needed, W^+, W^-, and Z^0. Further, as the weak force acts at distances below about 10^{-13} centimeters, and as the shorter the distance the larger the particle would have to be, the bosons would have to be massive, some 80 times bigger than a proton.

To produce such particles in an accelerator requires enormous energies and it was not expected that CERN would be able to obtain such energies for more than a decade. Rubbia proposed in 1976 that the existing super proton synchroton should be changed from a fixed-target accelerator to one producing collisions between beams of protons and antiprotons traveling in opposite directions. If feasible, and given that a particle's kinetic energy increases as the square of its velocity, much higher energies would be attained. As redesigned by his CERN colleague, Simon VAN DER MEER, the SPS produced energies of 540 billion electronvolts (540 GeV) – the equivalent of the 155,000 GeV achieved by striking a stationary target.

Rubbia faced two further problems: how to produce enough antiprotons, and how to recognize the W and Z particles. Antiprotons were produced by accelerating protons in the SPS and firing them at a metal target. A new detector, designed by Charpak, was built. To detect a W particle the experimenters looked for its characteristic interactions. They should see antiprotons collide with protons and emit a W particle, which in 10^{-20} second should decay into an electron and a neutrino. The experiment began in September 1982 and ran until December

6, leaving millions of collisions to analyze. Among them they found six possible W particles, five of which were accepted as genuine. The Z particle was subsequently discovered in May 1983.

Rubbia published the discovery of the W particle in January 1983 in a paper listing 130 coauthors. For their part in the discovery of the W and Z particles Rubbia and van der Meer shared the 1984 Nobel Prize for physics.

Rubin, Vera Cooper (1928–   )
American astronomer

Born in Philadelphia, Pennsylvania, Rubin was educated at Vassar, at Cornell, and at Georgetown University, Washington DC, where she obtained her PhD in 1954. Since 1965 she has worked at the Carnegie Institution, Washington DC, while also being an adjunct staff member of the Mount Wilson and Las Campanas observatories.

Rubin's main work has long been concerned with galactic rotation measurements and it has led to one of the more persistent problems of modern astronomy. She has concentrated on spiral galaxies and has measured the rotational velocities of the arms of the galaxy as their distance from the center increases. The velocities of the spiral arms are measured by determining their doppler shifts. That is light emitted from a body moving away from an observer will show a red shift, and a blue shift when emitted from a body moving toward the observer. The degree of spectral shift is proportional to the velocity of the source.

The initial assumption, based upon Kepler's laws, was that rotational velocity would decrease with distance. Thus the theoretical expectation was that: $v^2 = GM/r^2$ where G is the gravitational constant, M the attracting mass, and r the orbital radius. It is clear from the equation that as r increases, v will decrease. Rubin, however, found that the rotational velocity of spiral galaxies either remains constant with increasing distance from the center or rises slightly. The only possible conclusion, assuming the laws of motion, was that the figure for M was too low. But as all visible matter had been taken into account in assessing the mass of the galaxy, the missing mass must be present in the form of 'dark matter'. Rubin found similar results as she extended her survey. It seemed to her in 1983 that as much as 90% of the universe is not radiating sufficiently strongly on any wavelength detectable on Earth.

Rubin's work has presented modern astronomy with two major problems. Firstly to calculate the amount of dark matter in the universe and describe its distribution, and secondly to identify particles that make up the dark matter.

Earlier in her career, in collaboration with Kent Ford, Rubin made the extraordinary discovery that the Milky Way had a peculiar velocity of 500 kilometers per second quite independently of the expansion of the universe. When their results were published in 1975 they were met with considerable skepticism and it was assumed they had miscalculated the distances of the measured galaxies. However, later work by John Huchra and others in 1982 seems to have confirmed their measurements.

Rumford, Benjamin Thompson, Count (1753–1814) *American–British physicist*

Benjamin Thompson was the son of a farmer from Woburn, Massachusetts. He started his career apprenticed to a merchant but was injured in a fireworks accident and moved to Boston. In 1772 he married a rich widow and moved to live in Rumford (now Concord, New Hampshire). When the American Revolution broke out, he took the English side and spied for them. By 1775 the hostility of his countrymen toward him had grown to such a pitch that he was forced to sail to England, leaving his wife and daughter behind. Once in England, his opportunist nature quickly raised him to the position of colonial undersecretary of state but, with the end of the American Revolution, he moved to Bavaria.

Here he rose rapidly to high government administrative positions and initiated many social reforms, such as the creation of military workhouses for the poor and the introduction of the potato as a staple food. In 1790 he was made a count in recognition of his service to Bavaria, taking the name of his title from the town of Rumford, New Hampshire.

It was in Bavaria that he first became interested in science, when he was commissioned to oversee the boring of cannon at the Munich Arsenal. Rumford was struck by the amount of heat generated and suggested that it resulted from the mechanical work performed.

According to the old theory of heat, heat produced by friction was caloric 'squeezed' from the solid, although it was difficult to explain why the heat should be released indefinitely. Rumford, in his paper to the Royal Society *An Experimental Enquiry concerning the Source of Heat excited by Friction* (1798), suggested the direct conversion of work into heat and made quantitative esti-

mates of the amount of heat generated. It was suggested that the heat came from the lower heat capacity of the metal turnings, although Rumford could discount this by using a blunt borer to show that the turnings produced were not important. Another objection – that the heat came from chemical reaction of air with the fresh surface – was disproved by an experiment of Humphry Davy (1799) in which pieces of ice were rubbed together in a vacuum. The idea that heat was a form of motion replaced Lavoisier's caloric theory over the first half of the 19th century.

Rumford returned to London in 1798 and there began work on a series of inventions, including a kitchen stove, a photometer, and an oil lamp. He also advocated the standard candle for luminosity measurement. More lastingly, he established the Royal Institution of Great Britain (1800), introducing Davy as director. He went to France in 1804 and settled in Paris, where he married Lavoisier's widow. The marriage was unhappy and ended after four years (Rumford is said to have suggested that Lavoisier was lucky to have been guillotined). Rumford himself appears to have been a disloyal and unappealing character, although at the end of his life he left most of his estate to the United States.

Runcorn, Stanley Keith (1922–1995) *British geophysicist*

Runcorn was born at Southport in Lancashire, and was educated at Cambridge University. After working on radar during World War II he held teaching appointments at the University of Manchester (1946–50) and at Cambridge (1950–55), before being appointed in 1956 to the chair of physics at King's College, Newcastle, which became the University of Newcastle upon Tyne in 1963. He became Senior Research Fellow at Imperial College, London, in 1989.

Under the early influence of Patrick Blackett, Runcorn began research on geomagnetism. From detailed field surveys in both Europe and America they eventually able to reconstruct the movements of the North Magnetic Pole over the past 600 million years. Runcorn found that he obtained different routes for the migration depending on whether he used European or American rocks. Also, the European rocks always pointed to a position to the east of that indicated by the American rocks for the magnetic pole. From this evidence Runcorn argued, in his paper *Paleomagnetic Evidence for Continental Drift* (1962), that if the two continents were brought close to each other they could be so aligned that the magnetic evidence of their rocks pointed to a single path taken by the magnetic pole. This led Runcorn to become an early supporter of the newly emerging theory of continental drift.

Runcorn died in somewhat mysterious circumstances: he was found battered to death in a motel room in Los Angeles, where he had been attending a conference.

Rushton, William Albert Hugh

(1901–1980) *British physiologist*

Rushton, the son of a London dental surgeon, studied medicine at Cambridge University and University College Hospital, London. He worked in Cambridge from 1931 until 1968, being appointed professor of visual physiology in 1966. In 1968 he moved to the Florida State University, Tallahassee, to serve as research professor of psychobiology until his retirement in 1976.

Rushton studied the theory of nerve excitation until the early 1950s but changed to studying visual pigments following some work with Ragnar Granit in Stockholm. Rushton's novel technique was to shine light into the eye and measure the amount reflected back with a photocell. The effects of rhodopsin, the 'visual purple' of Willy Kuhne, could be discounted by working with the fovea, the retinal region of sharpest vision devoid of rhodopsin-containing rods. As the fovea is also deficient in blue cones, Rushton argued that by limiting pigment absorption measurements to this small area the properties of the red and green cones alone should be revealed.

By examining color-blind individuals, Rushton showed that red-blind defectives lack the red-sensitive pigment erythrolabe and that people who cannot distinguish between red and green lack the green-sensitive pigment chlorolabe.

Ruska, Ernst August Friedrich (1906–1988) *German physicist*

Born in Heidelberg, Germany, Ruska was educated at the Munich Technical University and at Berlin University, where he obtained his PhD in 1934. He worked in industry until 1955 when he became professor of electron microscopy at the Haber Institute, Berlin, a post he held until his retirement in 1972.

It had long been known that optical microscopes are limited by the wavelength of light to a magnifying power of about 2000, and the ability to resolve images no closer together than 2–3000 angstroms (1 angstrom = 10^{-10} meter). In 1927, however, G. P. THOMSON first demonstrated that electrons can behave like waves as well as like particles. The wavelength of the electron depends on its momentum according to de Broglie's equation $\lambda = h/p$. The higher the momentum of the electron, the shorter the wavelength. It should be possible to focus short-wavelength electrons and obtain better resolving powers.

In 1928 Ruska attempted to focus an electron beam with an electromagnetic lens. He went on to add a second lens and thus produced the first electron microscope; it had a magnifying power of about seventeen. Improvements, however, came quickly and by 1933 the magnifying power had been increased to 7000. Soon after he joined the firm of Siemens and began to work on the production of commercial models. The first such model appeared on the market in 1939. It had a resolution of about 250–500 angstroms.

For his work in this field Ruska shared the 1986 Nobel Prize for physics with BINNIG and ROHRER.

Russell, Bertrand Arthur William, third earl Russell (1872–1970) *British philosopher and mathematician*

Russell, who was born at Trelleck, England, was orphaned at an early age and brought up in the home of his grandfather, the politician Lord John Russell. He was educated privately before attending Cambridge University (1890), from which he graduated (1893) in mathematics. In 1895 he became a fellow and lecturer at Cambridge. His work after 1920 was mainly devoted to the development of his philosophical and political opinions. He became well known for his popularization of many areas of philosophy and also, in works such as *The ABC of Atoms* (1923) and *The ABC of Relativity* (1925), of the new trends in scientific thought. For his writings he was awarded the 1950 Nobel Prize for literature. He succeeded his brother to become the 3rd Earl Russell in 1931. Throughout much of his life Russell was an intense advocate of pacifism and during World War I he was imprisoned for expressing these views. Later, in the 1950s and 1960s, he became a central figure in the movements criticizing the use of the atomic bomb, leading demonstrations and mass sit-downs and becoming president of the British Campaign for Nuclear Disarmament in 1958.

At Cambridge Russell became interested in the relatively new discipline of mathematical logic in which he was to be a pioneer. With Guiseppe PEANO he was one of the few to recognize the genius of Gottlob FREGE and his new system of logic. In 1902 he wrote to Frege, presenting what is now known as *Russell's paradox*, and asking how Frege's system would deal with it. (Unfortunately, as Frege acknowledged, the system could not accommodate it.) The paradox is one of the paradoxes of set theory and rests on the (then ill-defined) notion of a set. Some sets are members of themselves (the set of all sets is an example because it is itself a set; the set of cats is not an example, as it is not itself a cat). Consider the set of all sets that are not members of themselves: is it a member of itself? If it is, it is not and vice versa. To avoid such paradoxes Russell formulated his logical theory of types. In 1903 he began his collaboration with A. N. Whitehead on their ambitious, if not entirely successful, project of placing mathematics on a sound axiomatic footing by deriving it from logic. This culminated in the publication of *Principia Mathematica* (1910, 1912, 1913), containing major advances in logic and the philosophy of mathematics.

Russell, Henry Norris (1877–1957)
American astronomer

Russell, the son of a Presbyterian minister, was born in in Oyster Bay, New York. A brilliant scholar at Princeton, he graduated in 1897 and obtained his PhD in 1899. He spent the period 1902–05 as a research student and assistant at Cambridge University, England, returning then to Princeton where he served as professor of astronomy from 1911 to 1927 and director of the university observatory from 1912 to 1947. He was also a research associate at the Mount Wilson Observatory in California (1922–42) and, after his retirement, at the Harvard and Lick observatories.

Russell's great achievement was his publication in 1913 of a major piece of research contained in what is now called the *Hertzsprung–Russell diagram* (H–R diagram). The same results had in fact been published earlier and independently by Ejnar Hertzsprung with little impact. Russell's work was based upon determinations of absolute magnitudes, i.e., intrinsic brightness, of stars by the measurement of stellar parallax. His measurement technique was developed in collaboration with Arthur Hinks while he was at Cambridge and involved photographic plates, then a fairly recent scientific tool. He found that values of absolute magnitude correlated with the spectral types of the stars. Spectral type was derived from the Harvard system of spectral classification as revised by Annie Cannon and indicated surface temperature.

A graph of absolute magnitude versus spectral type produced the H–R diagram and showed that the majority of stars lie on a diagonal band, now called the 'main sequence', in which magnitude increases with increasing surface temperature. A separate group of very bright stars lie above the main sequence. This meant that there could be stars of the same spectral type differing enormously in magnitude. To describe such a difference the now familiar terminology of 'giant' and 'dwarf' stars was introduced into the literature.

The most obvious feature of the diagram for Russell, however, was that it was not completely occupied by stars. This led him to propose a path of stellar evolution, which he put forward in 1913 at the same time as the diagram. He argued that stars evolve from hot giants, pass down the main sequence and end as cold dwarfs. The mechanism driving the change was that of contraction. The bulky giants of spectral type M contract and with the resulting rise of temperature move leftward in the diagram, gradually becoming B-type dwarfs. But at some stage the contraction and density become too great for the gas laws to apply and the star cools, slipping down the main sequence and evolving finally to an M-type dwarf.

By 1926, however, Arthur Eddington could talk confidently of the overthrow of the 'giant and dwarf theory'; it was too simple to fit the growing data on the distribution of mass and luminosity among the different spectral types of stars. Although Russell's evolutionary theory quickly fell from favor the H–R diagram has continued to be of enormous importance and the start for any new theory of stellar evolution.

Eclipsing binary stars, such as Algol, the 'winking demon', were also of great interest to Russell. He devised methods by which both orbital and stellar size could be determined and which became widely used. He also analyzed the variations in light output of a large number of eclipsing binaries, which again became invaluable to later researchers.

Another major line of research for Russell was his investigation of the solar spectrum, which began as a result of the publication in 1921 of the ionization equation of Meghnad SAHA. The Saha equation was tested and modified by Russell, using the solar spectrum, and was then used by him to calculate the abundance of the chemical elements in the Sun's atmosphere. He realized that the abundances in other stars could also be calculated from their spectra. He showed that the abundance of elements within the Sun itself could be found and in 1929 published the first reliable determination of this, demonstrating surprisingly that 60% of the Sun's volume was hydrogen. Although this was an underestimate, as Donald Menzel was later able to show that a figure of over 80% was more accurate, it did pose the problem as to why the Sun, and presumably other stars too, should contain so much hydrogen. The answer to this question was given in the version of the big-bang theory proposed by George Gamow.

Rutherford, Daniel (1749–1819) *British chemist and botanist*

Rutherford, the son of an Edinburgh physician, studied under William Cullen and Joseph Black at Edinburgh University and became a doctor of medicine in 1777. In 1786 he was made professor of botany and keeper of the Royal Botanic Garden at Edinburgh.

Rutherford was the first to distinguish between carbon dioxide and nitrogen. A thesis he wrote in 1772, *De aere fixo dicto aut mephitico* (On Air said to be Fixed or Mephitic), contains some of Joseph Priestley's later discoveries. In his experiment mice were allowed to breathe in a closed container. The fixed air (carbon dioxide) was absorbed by caustic potash. The remaining air, Rutherford pointed out, was not fixed but would not support life or combustion and he called it 'mephitic air'. He had in fact isolated nitrogen about the same time as Karl Scheele.

Rutherford, Ernest, first baron Rutherford of Nelson (1871–1937) *New Zealand physicist*

Rutherford, who was born at Nelson in New Zealand, was certainly the greatest scientist to emerge from that country; he can also fairly be claimed to be one of the greatest experimental physicists of all time. His career almost exactly spans the first great period of nuclear physics, a field he did much to advance and which he dominated for so long. This period stretches from the detection of radioactivity by Henri Becquerel in 1896 to the discovery of nuclear fission by Otto Hahn in 1938, the year after Rutherford's death. He came from a fairly simple background, the fourth of twelve children, the son of a man variously described as a farmer, wheelwright, and miller. He was educated at Canterbury College, Christchurch, and in 1895 won a scholarship to Cambridge University, England.

In New Zealand Rutherford had done some work on high-frequency magnetic fields. At Cambridge, working under J. J. Thomson, he first continued this research, and then in 1896 began to work on the conductivity of air ionized by x-rays. In 1898 he

moved to become professor at McGill University in Canada. This was a good appointment for Rutherford in two respects. McGill had one of the best-equipped physics laboratories in the world and, in particular, there was a good supply of the then very costly radium bromide. The other main gain for Rutherford in Montreal was the presence of Frederick Soddy, an Oxford-trained chemist with whom he entered into a most rewarding eighteen-month collaboration, from October 1901 to April 1903, during which time they produced nine major papers laying the foundations for the serious study of radioactivity.

When Rutherford began working on radioactivity at the end of the century little was known about it apart from the result of Pierre and Marie CURIE that it was not limited to uranium alone but was also a property of thorium, radium, and polonium. Rutherford's first important advance, in 1899, was his demonstration that there were two quite different kinds of emission, which he referred to as alpha and beta rays. The first kind had little penetrating power but produced considerable ionization while the beta rays (electrons) were as penetrating as x-rays but possessed little ionizing power. To find out exactly what they were took Rutherford the best part of a decade of careful experimentation but, long before he had the final answer, he had used their existence to work out with Soddy a daring theory of atomic transmutation. In 1900 Rutherford showed that a third type of radiation, undeflected by magnetic fields, was high-energy electromagnetic radiation. He called this radiation 'gamma rays'.

Rutherford also began to investigate the radioactive element thorium, which in addition to alpha, beta, and gamma rays also emits a radioactive gas that he called 'emanation'. He showed that the emanation decayed in activity at a particular rate, losing half its activity in a fixed period of time (the half-life). Rutherford and Soddy began an intensive investigation of thorium compounds and showed that a more active substance, thorium X, was present. They eventually came to the view that the emanation was produced from the thorium X, which in turn came from the original thorium. In other words, there was a series in which chemical elements were being changed (transmuted) into other elements. Rutherford and Soddy published their theory of a series of transformations in 1905. Rutherford later published a book with the title *The Newer Alchemy* (1937). Soddy went on to continue this work, eventually introducing the idea of isotopes.

Rutherford directed his attention to the

alpha radiation emitted in radioactive decay, proving that it consisted of helium atoms that have each lost two electrons. He continued to study alpha radiation, moving to the University of Manchester, England, in 1907. At Manchester Rutherford and Hans Geiger invented the Geiger counter in 1908. Here too Geiger and E. Marsden in 1910, at Rutherford's suggestion, studied the scattering of alpha particles passing through thin metal foils. The particles were detected by a screen coated with zinc sulfide, which gives brief flashes of light (scintillations) when hit by high-energy particles.

Geiger and Marsden found that most of the particles were deflected only slightly on passing through the foil but that a small proportion (about 1 in 8000) were widely deflected. Rutherford later described this as "quite the most incredible event that has ever happened to me in my life ... It was almost as incredible as if you fired a 15-inch shell at a piece of tissue paper and it came back and hit you." To make sense of the results, Rutherford published in 1911 a model of the atom in which he suggested that almost all the mass was concentrated in a very small region and that most of the atom was 'empty space'. This was the nuclear atom (although Rutherford did not use the term 'nucleus' until 1912). He also produced a theoretical formula giving the numbers of particles that would be scattered by a nucleus at different angles. The idea of the nuclear atom was developed further by Niels Bohr.

After the end of World War I, which Rutherford spent working for the Admiralty on sonic methods of detecting submarines, he moved in 1919 to take the Cavendish chair of physics and the directorship of the Cavendish Laboratory at Cambridge University. It was there that he announced in 1919 his third major discovery, the artificial disintegration of the nucleus. Following some earlier experiments of Marsden he placed an alpha-particle source in a cylinder into which various gases could be introduced. At one end of the cylinder a small hole was covered with a metal disk through which some atoms could escape and register their presence on a zinc sulfide screen. The introduction of nitrogen produced highly energetic particles, which turned out to be hydrogen nuclei (that is, protons). The implications were not lost on Rutherford who concluded that "the nitrogen atom is disintegrated under the intense forces developed in a close collision with the swift alpha particle, and that the hydrogen atom which is liberated formed a constituent part of the nitrogen nucleus."

Occasionally, it was later shown, "the alpha particle actually enters the nitrogen nucleus...breaks up...hurling out a proton and leaving behind an oxygen nucleus of mass 17." Rutherford had thus succeeded in bringing about the first transmutation, although when described in nuclear terms it seems a simple enough process. With James Chadwick he went on to show between 1920 and 1924 that most of the lighter elements emitted protons when bombarded with alpha particles.

By his work in 1911 and 1919 Rutherford had shown that not only does the atom have a nucleus but that the nucleus has a structure from which pieces can be knocked out and by which other particles can be absorbed. It was this work which virtually created a whole new discipline, that of nuclear physics. Rutherford received the Nobel Prize for chemistry in 1908.

Ružička, Leopold (1887–1976)
Croatian–Swiss chemist

Ružička was born in Vukovar, Croatia, the son of a cooper. He graduated in chemistry from the Karlsruhe Institute of Technology, in Germany, where he became assistant to Hermann Staudinger, following him to Zurich in 1912. In 1926 he was appointed professor of organic chemistry at the University of Utrecht but in 1929 he returned to the Federal Institute of Technology at Zurich to take up a similar chair.

Beginning in 1916 Ružička worked on the chemistry of natural odorants. While investigating such compounds as musk and civet he discovered a number of ketone compounds containing large rings of carbon atoms.

From the early 1920s Ružička also worked on terpenes. By dehydrogenating the higher terpenes to give aromatic hydrocarbons he was able to determine the structure of pentacyclic triterpenes. He also corrected the formulas of the bile acids and cholesterol proposed by Adolf Windaus and Heinrich Wieland. Ružička's theory that the carbon skeleton of higher terpenes could be seen as consisting of isoprene units proved a useful hypothesis in further work.

In the 1930s Ružička moved into the field of sex hormones. In 1931 Adolf BUTENANDT, with whom Ružička shared the 1939 Nobel Prize for chemistry, isolated 15 milligrams of the steroid hormone androsterone from 7000 gallons of urine. Androsterone is a male hormone secreted by the adrenal gland and testis, which when released at puberty causes the development of male secondary sexual characteristics. In 1934

Ružička succeeded in synthesizing it, the first of several such triumphs.

Rydberg, Johannes Robert (1854–1919) *Swedish physicist and spectroscopist*

Johannes Rydberg was born in Halmstad, Sweden, and educated at Lund University, where he received a PhD in 1879. The next year he started teaching mathematics there and stayed at Lund for the rest of his life, taking the chair of physics in 1901.

All of Rydberg's work arose from his interest in the periodic classification of the elements introduced by Dmitri Mendeleev. Rydberg's great intuition was that the periodicity was a result of the structure of the atom. His first research was into the relationship between the spectral lines of elements. In 1890 he found a general formula giving the frequency of the lines in the spectral series as a simple difference between two terms. His formula for a series of lines is:

$$\nu = R(1/m^2 - 1/n^2)$$

where n and m are integers. The constant R is now known as the *Rydberg constant*.

In the early 1900s Rydberg continued to work on the periodic table, reorganizing it, finding new mathematical patterns, and even casting it into spiral form. In the main his theoretical work was confirmed by Henry Moseley's discovery that the positive charge on the nucleus gave a better periodic ordering than the atomic weight.

Ryle, Sir Martin (1918–1984) *British radio astronomer*

Ryle, the son of a physician, was born at Brighton and studied at Oxford University. He spent the war with the Telecommunications Research Establishment in Dorset working on radar. After the war he received a fellowship to the Cavendish Laboratory of Cambridge University and in 1948 was appointed lecturer in physics. In 1959 he became the first Cambridge professor of radio astronomy, having been made in 1957 the director of the Mullard Radio Astronomy Observatory in Cambridge. Ryle was appointed Astronomer Royal in 1972 and in 1974 was awarded, jointly with Antony

Hewish, the Nobel Prize for physics. He was knighted in 1966.

It was mainly due to Ryle and his colleagues that Cambridge, after the war, became one of the leading centers in the world for astronomical research. He realized that one of the first jobs to be done was simply to map the radio sky. He therefore began in 1950 the important series of Cambridge surveys. The first survey used the principle of interferometry and discovered some 50 radio sources. The second survey in 1955 listed nearly 2000 sources, many of which turned out to be spurious. The crucial survey was the third one, the results of which were published in 1959 in the *Third Cambridge Catalogue* (3C). This listed the positions and strengths of 500 sources and has since become the definitive catalog used by all radio astronomers. The use of more sensitive receivers in 1965 enabled the 4C survey to detect sources five times fainter than those in the 3C and covered the whole of the northern sky; 5000 sources were cataloged. Finally, with the opening of two highly sensitive radio telescopes in 1965 and 1971, important areas of the sky are being surveyed in depth: a full survey would take over 2000 years.

The two new telescopes, the One Mile telescope and then the Five Kilometer telescope, operate by a technique developed by Ryle and called 'aperture synthesis'. A number of radio dishes are used to give a very large effective aperture, much larger than the aperture of a single dish, and hence produce very considerable resolution of detail in a radio map of an area of the sky. The dishes are mounted along a line, some fixed in position, some movable, and are used in pairs, at different distances apart, to form interferometers.

These telescopes and other equipment were used by Ryle and his colleagues to investigate pulsars, which were discovered at Cambridge by Antony Hewish and Jocelyn Bell, quasars, radio galaxies, and other radio sources. Ryle quickly appreciated that the distribution of radio sources throughout the universe had cosmological implications and that the number of sources found tended to support the evolutionary big-bang theory rather than the steady-state theory.

Sabatier, Paul (1854–1941) *French chemist*

Sabatier, who was born at Carcassone in southwest France, was a student at the Ecole Normale, Paris, and gained his PhD from the Collège de France in 1880. He became professor of chemistry at the University of Toulouse (1884–1930).

In 1897 Sabatier showed how various organic compounds could undergo hydrogenation, e.g., ethylene will not normally combine with hydrogen but when a mixture of the gases is passed over finely divided nickel, ethane is produced. Benzene can be converted into cyclohexane in the same way. Sabatier discussed the whole problem in his book *Le catalyse en chimie organique* (1912; Catalysis in Organic Chemistry), published the same year in which he was awarded the Nobel Prize for chemistry for his work on catalytic hydrogenations.

Sabin, Albert Bruce (1906–1993) *Polish–American microbiologist*

Sabin, who was born at Bialystok Poland, emigrated with his parents to America in 1921; he was educated at New York University, where he gained his MD in 1931. He later joined the staff of the Rockefeller Institute of Medical Research but in 1939 moved to the University of Cincinnati. Following war service with the U.S. Army Medical Corps, he was appointed (1946) research professor of pediatrics at Cincinnati, a post he held until his retirement in 1971.

It was clear to Sabin from the success of John Enders in growing polio virus in tissue culture that a vaccination against the disease was only a matter of time. Sabin already had experience in this field having worked on developing vaccines against dengue fever and Japanese B encephalitis. He therefore began work on the polio vaccine but, unlike Jonas Salk, he was determined to develop a live attenuated vaccine rather than a killed one.

By 1956, Sabin had developed a live virus, attenuated in monkey kidney tissue. It was impossible to persuade the American public to submit to the testing of another vaccine after the difficulties involved with the Salk campaign of 1954. Sabin therefore hit on the audacious idea of attempting to arouse the interest of the Russians and to persuade them to do his tests for him.

In 1959 Sabin was able to produce the results of 4.5 million vaccinations and show that they were completely safe. The vaccine also gave a stronger longer lasting immunity than Salk's vaccine and could be administered orally. Great Britain changed over to the Sabin vaccine as early as 1962 with most other countries following soon afterward.

Sagan, Carl Edward (1934–1996) *American astronomer*

Born in New York City, Sagan studied at the University of Chicago where he obtained his BS in 1955 and his PhD in 1960. He was a research fellow at the University of California, Berkeley, from 1960 to 1962 when he moved to the Smithsonian Astrophysical Observatory in Cambridge, Massachusetts, working at Harvard as lecturer then assistant professor. In 1968 he moved to Cornell where he was appointed director of the Laboratory for Planetary Studies and in 1970 became professor of astronomy and space science. Sagan's main work has been on virtually all aspects of the solar system. One major line of research has been on the physics and chemistry of planetary atmospheres and surfaces, especially of Mars. His other primary interest is the origin of life on Earth and the possibility of extraterrestrial life and he has done much to interest the general public in the new field of exobiology. In laboratory experiments simulating the primitive atmosphere of Earth, he and his colleagues have shown how a variety of organic molecules, such as amino acids, which are the building blocks of proteins, can readily be produced. The energy sources used in these syntheses have included ultraviolet radiation, which would have flooded the Earth's primitive atmosphere, and high-pressure shock waves. It was while working with C. Ponnamperuna and Ruth Mariner at NASA's exobiology division in 1963 that he showed how the fundamental molecule adenosine triphosphate, ATP, could have been produced. ATP is the universal energy intermediary of living organisms and without its presence it is difficult to see how life could have ever originated on Earth.

In 1984 Sagan coauthored, with R. Turco, O. Toon, T. Ackerman and J. Pollock, an influential paper, *Nuclear Winter: Global Consequences of Multiple Nuclear Explosions*, referred to since as the TTAPS paper. The authors argued that even a relatively small-scale nuclear bomb of 5000 megatons would create enough atmospheric smoke (300 million tons) and dust (15 million tons) to produce a temperature drop of 20–40°C, which would persist for many months. This prolonged nuclear winter would destroy much of the world's agriculture and industry. The impact of the paper on politicians and the public was dramatic.

The nuclear-winter argument itself was heavily criticized by scientists. "These guys don't know what they are talking about," commented Richard Feynman, and Freeman Dyson dismissed the paper as an "absolutely atrocious piece of science." The meteorologist S. Schneider pointed out that the TTAPS model was one-dimensional in that it represented only the vertical structure of the atmosphere and ignored the oceans and seasonal changes. It was, he concluded, "a first generation assessment whose conclusions would have to be modified," and claimed that it threatened more a 'nuclear fall' than a nuclear winter.

Sagan has written extensively on the results of planetary science. His *Cosmic Connection* (1973) introduced these results to a wider audience. His later works *The Dragons of Eden* (1977) and *Broca's Brain* (1979) have tried to do the same for recent advances in the theory of evolution and neurophysiology. In a further work, *Cosmos* (1980), based on a major TV series, Sagan charted the history of physics and astronomy. His later books include *Pale Blue Dot: A Vision of the Human Future in Space* (1994) and *The Demon-Haunted World* (1996).

Saha, Meghnad N. (1894–1956) *Indian astrophysicist*

Born the son of a small shopkeeper in Dacca (now in Bangladesh), Saha won a scholarship to the Government School there in 1905 but was expelled for participating in the boycott of a visit by the Governor of Bengal. He completed his education in Calcutta, at the Presidency College, where he obtained his MA in applied mathematics in 1915. After lecturing in mathematics and then physics at Calcutta's University College of Science (1916–19), he visited London and Berlin on a traveling scholarship. He returned to India in 1921 and from 1923 to 1938 taught at the University of Allahabad. In 1938 he moved to the chair of physics at Calcutta where he remained until his death.

Early in his career Saha became interested in both thermodynamics and astrophysics and this led to his work on the thermal ionization that occurs in the very hot atmospheres of stars. In 1920 he published a fundamental paper, *On Ionization in the Solar Chromosphere*, in which he stated his ionization equation. The absorption lines of stellar spectra differ widely, with some stars showing virtually nothing but hydrogen and helium lines while others show vast numbers of lines of different metals. Saha's great insight was to see that all these spectral lines could be represented as the result of ionization. He saw that the degree of ionization, i.e., the number of electrons stripped away from the nucleus, would depend primarily on temperature. As the temperature increases, so does the proportion of ionized atoms. The remaining neutral atoms will thus produce only weak absorption lines that, when the temperature gets high enough, will disappear entirely. But the singly, doubly, and even triply ionized atoms will absorb at different sets of wavelengths, and different sets of lines will appear in stellar spectra, becoming stronger as the proportions of these ions grow.

In later years Saha moved into nuclear physics and worked for the creation of an institute for its study in India, which was later named for him. He also devoted much time to social, economic, and political problems in India.

Sakmann, Bert (1942–) *German biophysicist*

Born in Stuttgart, Germany, Sakmann attended the universities of Tübingen and Munich, and gained his MD from the University of Göttingen. He became a research assistant at the Max Planck Institute of Psychiatry, Munich (1969–70), and subsequently spent two years as a British Council Fellow at the Biophysics Department of University College, London (1971–73). In 1974 he joined the Max Planck Institute for Biophysical Chemistry at the University of Göttingen, becoming head of the membrane physiology unit in 1983 and director in 1985. Two years later he was appointed professor in the department of cell physiology. In 1989 he moved to Heidelberg as director of the cell physiology department of the Max Planck Institute for Medical Research.

While working at Göttingen in the mid-1970s, in collaboration with the biophysicist Erwin NEHER, Sakmann developed the so-called 'patch-clamp' technique for studying ion channels in cell membranes. This, together with their descriptions of the biophysical properties of the channels, earned them the 1991 Nobel Prize for physiology or medicine.

Salam, Abdus (1926–1996) *Pakistani physicist*

Salam, who was born at Jhang in Pakistan, attended Punjab University and Cambridge University, where he received his PhD in 1952. From 1951 to 1954 he was a professor of mathematics at the Government College of Lahore, concurrently with a post as head of the mathematics department of Punjab University. From 1954 until 1956 he lectured at Cambridge and from 1957 to 1993 he was a professor of theoretical physics at the Imperial College of Science and Technology, London. He was largely responsible for the establishment in 1964 of the International Center for Theoretical Physics, Trieste, as an institute to assist physicists from developing countries. He was director of the center from its inception until 1994, dividing his time between there and Imperial College.

Salam's work was concerned with the theories describing the behavior and properties of elementary particles; for this he received the 1979 Nobel Prize for physics, shared with Sheldon GLASHOW and Steven WEINBERG. Although the three men did most of their work independently, they each contributed to the development of a theory that could take account of the 'weak' and 'electromagnetic' interactions. One of their predictions was the phenomenon of neutral currents and their strengths, which was first confirmed in 1973 at the European Organization for Nuclear Research (CERN) and later by other groups. A further prediction of the theory is that of the existence of 'intermediate vector bosons' with high masses. The discovery of a vector boson was reported in 1983 by two teams (comprising 180 scientists) working at the European Laboratory for Particle Physics near Geneva.

Salk, Jonas Edward (1914–1995) *American microbiologist*

Salk was born in New York City, the son of a garment worker. He was educated at the City College of New York and at New York University Medical School, where he obtained his MD in 1939. In 1942 he went to the University of Michigan where he worked as a research fellow on influenza vaccine under Thomas Francis. In 1947 he moved to the University of Pittsburgh, serving as professor of bacteriology from 1949 onward. Here Salk began the work that eventually led to the discovery of a successful polio vaccine in 1954. After this breakthrough Salk was invited in 1963 to become director of the Institute for Biological Studies at San Diego, California, known more simply as the Salk Institute – soon to emerge as one of the great research centers of the world.

Salk was not the first to develop a vaccine against polio for in 1935 killed and attenuated vaccines were tested on over 10,000 children. It turned out, however, that not only were the vaccines ineffective, but they were also unsafe and probably responsible for some deaths and a few cases of paralysis.

By the time Salk began his work in the early 1950s a number of crucial advances had been made since the 1935 tragedy. In 1949 John Enders and his colleagues had shown how to culture the polio virus in embryonic tissue. Another essential step was the demonstration, in 1949, that there were in fact three types of polio virus with the inconvenient consequence that vaccine effective against any one type was likely to be powerless against the other two.

Salk had to develop a vaccine that was safe but potent. To ensure its safety he used virus exposed to formaldehyde for up to 13 days and afterward tested for virulence in monkey brains. This, in theory, allowed a large safety margin, for Salk could detect no live virus after only three days.

To test its potency Salk injected children who had already had polio and noted any increase in their antibody level. When it became clear that high antibody levels were produced by the killed vaccine Salk moved on to submitting it to the vital test of a mass trial. Two objections were raised to this. One from Albert Sabin that killed vaccine was simply the wrong type to be used and a second, from various workers, who claimed to find live virus in the supposedly killed vaccine.

Despite such qualms Salk continued with the trial administering in 1954 either a placebo or killed vaccine to 1,829,916 children. The evaluation of the trial was put into the hands of Francis, who, in March 1955, reported that the vaccination was 80–90% effective. The vaccine was released for general use in the United States in April 1955.

Salk became a national hero overnight and plans went ahead to vaccinate 9 million children. However within weeks there were reports from California in which children developed paralytic polio shortly after being vaccinated. After a period of considerable confusion it became clear that all such cases involved vaccine prepared in a single laboratory.

After several days of almost continuous debate, the decision was taken to proceed and, by the end of 1955, 7 million doses had been administered. Further technical improvements were made in the production process. These safeguards would either eliminate any further cases of live vaccine or if a live virus did manage to penetrate all defenses it should make its presence known long before its use in a vaccine.

The courage shown by Salk in persisting with his vaccine was clearly justified by the results for the period 1956–58 – 200 million injections without a single case of vaccine-produced paralysis.

Samuelsson, Bengt Ingemar
(1934–   ) *Swedish biochemist*

Born at Halmstad in Sweden, Samuelsson was educated at the Karolinska Institute, Stockholm, where he gained his MD in 1961. He continued to work there until 1966, when he moved to the Royal Veterinary College, Stockholm as professor of medical chemistry. In 1972 he returned to the Karolinska Institute as professor of medicine and physiological chemistry.

Samuelsson has worked extensively on the hormonelike prostaglandins first identified by Ulf von Euler in the 1930s. With Sune Bergström in the 1950s he worked out the structure of several prostaglandins and went on to explore some of their physiological properties. Later work by Samuelsson and his colleagues indicated a relationship between prostaglandins and the chemicals involved in transmitting nerve impulses. He discovered the prostaglandin PGA_2, thromboxane, which causes blood vessels to contract and platelets to clump. A second prostaglandin, PGE_2, inhibits the release of norepinephrine, a neurotransmitter of the sympathetic nervous system, and thereby blocks the transmission of nerve impulses.

Samuelsson also worked out the structure of a number of prostaglandins. They were shown to be closely related and synthesized in the body from a number of polyunsaturated fatty acids. All prostaglandins were found to be 20-carbon carboxylic acids with a five-member carbon ring. They are divided into three series – PG_1, PG_2, and PG_3 – depending on whether they have one, two, or three double bonds. The different prostaglandins could be distinguished by the location of an oxygen atom or an hydroxyl group (OH). For his work on prostaglandins Samuelsson shared the 1982 Nobel Prize for physiology or medicine with John VANE and Sune BERGSTROM.

Sandage, Allan Rex (1926–   )
American astronomer

Born in Iowa City, Sandage graduated from the University of Illinois in 1948 and obtained his PhD in 1953 from the California Institute of Technology. He was on the staff of the Hale Observatories at Mount Wilson and Mount Palomar from 1952 when he began as an assistant to Edwin Hubble. He was professor of physics at Johns Hopkins University (1987–88) and is now on the staff of the Carnegie Observatories, Pasadena.

In 1960, using the 200-inch (5-m) reflecting telescope, Sandage in collaboration with Thomas Matthews succeeded in making the first optical identification of a quasar or quasi-stellar object. Quasars first came to the notice of astronomers when a number of compact, rather than extended, radio sources were detected by the Cambridge surveys of the radio sky carried out in the 1950s. Sandage and Matthews showed that 3C 48, a compact radio source discovered during the third Cambridge survey, was at the same position as a faint apparently starlike object. Sandage and others succeeded in obtaining spectra of 3C 48 that were found to be quite unlike those of any other star. The mystery of these strange new objects was partially cleared up by Maarten Schmidt in 1963 when he showed that the spectral lines of a quasar have undergone an immense shift in wavelength.

Sandage continued to work on quasars and in 1965 introduced a method of identifying them by searching at an indicated radio position for objects emitting an excessive amount of ultraviolet or blue radiation. He found that many ultraviolet objects, which he named blue stellar objects or BSOs, were not radio emitters but could be still classed as quasars because they had the characteristic immense red shift first detected by Schmidt. He speculated that these might be older quasars that had passed beyond the radio phase of their life cycle. It is now known that the vast majority of quasars are not radio sources.

Sanger, Frederick (1918–   ) *British biochemist*

Sanger, a physician's son from Rendcombe in England, received both his BA and his PhD from Cambridge University (in 1939 and 1943 respectively). He continued his research at the university and from 1951 until 1983 was a member of the scientific staff of the Medical Research Council. In 1955, after some ten years' work, Sanger established the complete amino-acid sequence of the protein bovine insulin. This was one of the first protein structures identified, and Sanger received the Nobel Prize for chemistry in 1958 in recognition of his achievement. Sanger's work enabled chemists to synthesize insulin artificially and generally stimulated research in protein structure.

In 1977 Sanger's team at the MRC laboratories, Cambridge, published the complete nucleotide (base) sequence of the genetic material (DNA) of the virus Phi X 174. This involves determining the order of 5400 nucleotides along the single circular DNA strand. Moreover they found two cases of genes located within genes. Previously it had been thought that genes could not overlap. Sanger's research required the development of new techniques for splitting the DNA into different-sized fragments. These are radioactively labeled and then separated by electrophoresis. The base sequence can then be worked out because it is known which base is located at the end of each fragment due to the specificity of the enzymes (the so-called restriction enzymes) used to split the DNA. Sanger was awarded the Nobel Prize for chemistry a second time (1980) for his work on determining the base sequences of nucleic acids.

Sarich, Vincent (1934–) American biochemist

Chicago-born Sarich was educated at the University of California, Berkeley, where he gained his PhD in 1967. He has remained at Berkeley, being appointed professor of biochemistry in 1981.

Sarich was struck by the range of dates, from 4 million to 30 million years ago, within which anthropologists of the early 1960s placed the origin of the split between the hominids and the great apes. He began work, in collaboration with his Berkeley colleague Allan Wilson, to see if there was a more precise method of dating using the genetic relationship between man and apes. They chose to work with proteins, which closely reflect genes, choosing the blood-serum protein, albumin. As man and apes diverged further from their common ancestor, their albumins would also have diverged and would now be recognizably different.

Serum samples from apes, monkeys, and man were purified and then injected into rabbits to produce antiserums. A rabbit immunized against a human sample (antigen) will also react to other anthropoid antigens, only not as strongly. As antigenic differences are genetically based, response differences will therefore measure genetic differences between species. Sarich chose to work with a group of proteins found in blood serum known collectively as the 'complement system'. Antigens tend to attract and fix some of the complement. The amount of complement fixed could be mea-

sured precisely. Thus differences in complement-fixation rates produced by the albumin of a human and a gorilla when injected into immunized rabbits would measure their immunological distance.

If it could be assumed that protein differences between species have evolved at a constant rate then immunological distance would also be a measure of evolutionary separation. It remained to calibrate the clock. Sarich and Wilson took as their base line the date 30 million years ago marking the separation between the hominoids and the old-world monkeys. Thereafter it was a relatively easy matter to turn immunological distance into dates.

The results were clear but surprising. *Homo*, on this scheme, separated from the chimps and gorillas only 5 million years ago. This was a bold claim to make in 1967 as orthodox opinion, argued for example by David Pilbeam, placed the split between hominids and hominoids closer to 15 million years. What is more they had the skull of *Ramapithecus*, dating from this period, to prove their point. Initially, therefore, Sarich's views were rejected out of hand by paleontologists. Slowly, however, Sarich made converts. He argued, "I know my molecules have ancestors, you must prove your fossils had descendants." They found it more and more difficult to do so. Consequently, when it became clear that *Ramapithecus* was the ancestor not of man but the orangutan, opposition to Sarich largely disappeared.

Saussure, Horace Bénédict de (1740–1799) Swiss physicist and geologist

Saussure was the son of an agriculturist. He was educated at the university in his native city of Geneva, graduating in 1759, and became professor of physics and philosophy at the Geneva Academy (1762–86).

He was the first to make a systematic and prolonged study of the Alps, his work being published in his classic *Voyages dans les Alpes* (1779–96; Travels in the Alps). He began as a disciple of Abraham Werner, accepting that the mass of the Alps had crystallized from the primitive ocean. However, 17 years of studying the convolutions and folds of the Alps led him to state in 1796 that such folds could only be produced by some force acting from below, or that they must have actually been laid down folded. Both alternatives preclude deposition by water. He was unwilling to decide in favor of the plutonist theories of James Hutton and thus to introduce fire as an agent, for he could recognize no sign of it.

He also collected considerable meteorological data and developed, in 1783, an improved hygrometer to measure humidity, using a human hair. He made the second ascent of Mont Blanc (1787) and at the summit took many scientific recordings. He also made nocturnal recordings and, in 1788, stayed for 17 days on the 11,000-foot (3358 m) summit of Col du Géant.

Schaefer, Vincent Joseph (1906–1993)
American physicist

Schaefer, who was born at Schenectady in New York, graduated from the Davey Institute of Tree Surgery in 1928. He was appointed as assistant to Irving Langmuir at the research laboratory of the General Electric Company in 1931 and remained there until 1954, becoming a research associate in 1938. In 1954 he was appointed director of research at the Munitalp Foundation, where he remained until 1959 when he was appointed to a chair of physics at the State University of New York, Albany. He retired in 1976.

In 1946 Schaefer was the first to demonstrate that it was possible to induce rainfall. Tor Bergeron had earlier argued that the presence of ice crystals in the atmosphere was a necessary precondition for the formation of rain. During World War II Schaefer had worked on atmospheric research and, more specifically, the problem of airplane wings icing up, and had discovered that he could produce a snow storm in the laboratory by dropping dry ice (solid carbon dioxide) into a container filled with a supercooled mist. In 1946 he seeded clouds over Massachusetts with dry ice pellets and produced the first man-made precipitation.

Following the success of this experiment the atmospheric research program known as Project Cirrus was established during which Bernard Vonnegut discovered the effectiveness of silver iodide as a cloud-seeding material.

Schally, Andrew Victor (1926–)
Polish–American physiologist

Schally, who was born at Wilno in Poland, left his native country for Britain in 1939. After graduating from the University of London, he worked at the National Institute for Medical Research from 1949 until 1952 when he moved to Canada. There he worked at McGill University, Montreal, obtaining his PhD in biochemistry in 1957, before joining the staff of Baylor University Medical School, Houston. In 1962 he became head of the endocrine and polypeptide laboratories at the Veterans Administration Hospital, New Orleans.

Like his great rival Roger GUILLEMIN,

Schally spent much of his early career trying to confirm the hypothesis of Geoffrey Harris on the existence and role of hypothalamic hormones. It was not in fact until he had been donated a million pig's hypothalami by a meat packer that, independently of Guillemin, he isolated some 3 milligrams of the thyrotropin-releasing factor in 1966.

He followed this in 1971 by detecting the luteinizing releasing factor, showing it to be a decapeptide and working out its sequence of ten amino acids thus permitting its synthesis.

For his work on the hypothalamic hormones Schally shared the 1977 Nobel Prize for physiology or medicine with Guillemin and Rosalyn YALOW.

Schawlow, Arthur Leonard (1921–)
American physicist

Born in Mount Vernon, New York, Schawlow was educated at the University of Toronto and worked at Columbia (1949–51) and at the Bell Telephone Laboratories (1951–61). He became professor of physics at Stanford University in 1961, retiring in 1991.

Schawlow is noted for his work on the development and use of lasers. He collaborated with Charles Townes in early work on maser principles and is generally credited as a coinventor of the laser. Although he did not share in Townes's Nobel award (1964), Schawlow did share the 1981 Nobel Prize for physics with Nicholaas BLOEMBERGEN for their (independent) research in laser spectroscopy. In particular, Schawlow, with Theodor Hänsch, has used tunable dye lasers for high-resolution spectroscopy.

Scheele, Karl Wilhelm (1742–1786)
Swedish chemist

Scheele, who came from a poor background in Straslund (now in Germany), received little schooling and was apprenticed to an apothecary in Göteborg when he was 14 years old. In 1770 he moved to Uppsala to practice as an apothecary. He met and impressed Torbern Bergman, the professor of chemistry there, and was elected to the Stockholm Royal Academy of Sciences in 1775. Also in 1775 he moved to Köping where he established his own pharmacy.

In 1777 Scheele published his only book, *Chemical Observations and Experiments on Air and Fire*. In this work he stated that the atmosphere is composed of two gases, one supporting combustion, which he named 'fire air' (oxygen), and the other preventing it, which he named 'vitiated air' (nitrogen). He was successful in obtaining oxygen in about 1772, two years before Joseph Priestley. He also discovered chlorine, manganese, barium oxide, glycerol, silicon tetrafluoride, and a long list of acids, both organic and inorganic, including citric, prussic, and tartaric acids. One further piece of work that had unexpectedly important consequences was his demonstration of the effects of light on silver salts.

Despite receiving many lucrative offers from Germany and England, Scheele remained at Köping for the rest of his life devoting himself to his chemical researches. Although his work must have suffered from his isolation, and he lost priority in many discoveries owing to delay in publication, he is still frequently referred to as the greatest experimental chemist of the 18th century.

Schiaparelli, Giovanni Virginio
(1835–1910) *Italian astronomer*

Schiaparelli was born at Savigliano in Italy. After graduating from Turin in 1854, he studied under Johann Encke in Berlin and Friedrich Struve in St. Petersburg. In 1860 he became director of the Brera Observatory, Milan, where he remained until he retired in 1900.

Schiaparelli worked mainly on the solar system, discovering the planetoid Hesperia in 1861. He contributed to the theory of meteors when he showed in 1866 that they follow cometary orbits. He also made careful studies of Mars, Venus, and Mercury. In 1877 Mars approached Earth at its nearest point, a mere 35 million miles. He observed what he called 'canali'. In Italian this means not 'canals' but 'channels,' but the word was mistranslated into English as the former, which led to much controversy. Schiaparelli himself was neutral as to their origin. He would not rule out that they were constructed rather than natural but nor would he conclude from their geometrical precision that they were buildings, for he pointed out that other examples of regularity, such as Saturn's rings, had not been man-made. It was other astronomers, such as Percival Lowell and Camille Flammarion, who made extravagant claims about the 'canals', not Schiaparelli.

After detailed observations of Venus and Mercury he announced that their period of axial rotation was the same as their sidereal period (the time taken to orbit the Sun, relative to the stars). Thus they would always keep the same face to the Sun. It was not until the early 1960s that this view was disproved, and then only by the use of sophisticated radar techniques.

Schiff, Moritz (1823–1896) *German physiologist*

Schiff, the son of a merchant from Frankfurt am Main, obtained his doctorate from the University of Göttingen in 1844. After working in the Frankfurt Zoological Museum, Schiff moved to Bern in 1854 as professor of comparative anatomy where he remained until 1863 when he was appointed to the chair of physiology in Florence. A campaign against vivisection forced Schiff to leave Florence in 1876 when he accepted the professorship of physiology at Geneva.

In 1856 Schiff demonstrated that removal of the thyroid gland in dogs and guinea pigs resulted in their death. He also showed, in 1885, that the effect could be postponed by grafting a piece of the gland elsewhere in the animal before its removal. The relief was however only temporary as the gland was absorbed by the body. Unfortunately Schiff's earlier work was unknown to surgeons like Theodor Kocher when, in the early 1870s, they began to perform thyroidectomies in humans, operations that often led to tragic ends.

Schiff had also worked in the 1850s on nervous control of the blood supply. By cutting the brainstem he was able to show the existence of special centers in the brain for the control of vasomotor nerves, nerves that narrow or widen blood vessels as the body's demand rises and falls. The same results were independently obtained by Claude Bernard.

Schimper, Andreas Franz Wilhelm
(1856–1901) *German plant ecologist*

Schimper was born at Strasbourg, which is now in France. He first became interested in natural history while on excursions with his father, Wilhelm Philipp, who was professor of natural history and geology at the University of Strasbourg. Andreas entered the university in 1874, obtained his doctorate in natural philosophy in 1878, and in 1880 earned a fellowship to Johns Hopkins University. He returned to Germany in 1882 and became lecturer and eventually professor at the University of Bonn (1886), where he remained until in 1898 he was appointed professor of botany at the University of Basel.

While at Strasbourg Schimper made an important study of the nature and growth of starch grains showing that they arise in specific organelles, which he named chloroplasts. However, it is to the study of plant geography and ecology that he made his most significant contributions. During travels to the West Indies in 1881 and 1882–83, Brazil (1886), Ceylon (Sri Lanka) and Java

(1889–90), and the Canary Islands, Cameroons, East Africa, Seychelles, and Sumatra (1898–99) with the *Valdivia* deep-sea expedition, he made ecological studies of tropical vegetation. His results led to publication of important papers on the morphology and biology of epiphytes and littoral vegetation, culminating with his masterpiece, *Pflanzengeographie auf physiologischer Grundlage* (1898; Plant Geography Upon a Physiological Basis), which relates the physiological structure of plants to their type of environment.

Schleiden, Matthias Jakob (1804–1881) *German botanist*

Schleiden was born at Hamburg and studied law at Heidelberg; he then returned to Hamburg to practice as a lawyer. However, he soon became fully occupied by his interest in botany and graduated in 1831 from the University of Jena, where he became professor of botany in 1839.

Instead of becoming involved in plant classification – the pursuit of most of his botanical contemporaries – Schleiden studied plant growth and structure under the microscope. This led to his *Contributions to Phytogenesis* (1838), which stated that the various structures of the plant are composed of cells or their derivatives. He thus formulated the cell theory for plants, which was layer eleborated and extended to animals by the German physiologist Theodor SCHWANN. Schleiden recognized the significance of the cell nucleus and sensed its importance in cell division, although he thought (wrongly) that new cells were produced by budding from its surface. He was one of the first German biologists to accept Darwinism.

Schmidt, Bernhard Voldemar (1879–1935) *Estonian telescope maker*

Schmidt, who was born on the island of Naissaar, in Estonia, received little education. After working in Gothenburg, Sweden, he went in 1901 to study engineering at Mittweida in Germany, near Jena. He set up his own workshop in 1904 in Mittweida and manufactured high-grade mirrors to be used in telescopes. He also built some reflecting telescopes, including one for the Potsdam Astrophysical Observatory, and set up his own observatory. In 1926 he moved to the Hamburg Observatory in Bergedorf. As a master craftsman he worked unaided even though he had lost his right arm as a boy. He was also an alcoholic and claimed to have his best ideas after prolonged drinking bouts. He died in a mental hospital.

His name is known to all astronomers as the designer of one of the most basic items of observatory equipment, the Schmidt telescope. This was built to overcome some of the penalties inherent in the design of the large parabolic reflectors like the Mount Wilson 100-inch (2.5-m) telescope. Parabolic mirrors are used rather than spherical ones in telescopes to correct the optical defect known as spherical aberration and thus allow the light from an object to be accurately and sharply focused. This accurate focusing only occurs, however, for light falling on the center of a parabolic mirror. Light falling at some distance from the center is not correctly focused owing to a different optical distortion in the image, known as coma.

This limits the use of parabolic reflectors to a narrow field of view and thus precludes them from survey work and the construction of star maps. Schmidt replaced the primary parabolic mirror with a spherical mirror, which though coma-free did however suffer from spherical aberration, thus preventing the formation of a sharp image. To overcome this fault Schmidt introduced a 'corrector plate' through which the light passed before reaching the spherical mirror. It was so shaped to be thickest in the center and least thick between its edges and the center. In this way a comparatively wide beam of light passing through it is refracted in such a way as to just compensate for the aberration produced by the mirror and produce an overall sharp image on a (curved) photographic plate.

Schmidt's first hybrid reflector/refractor was ready and installed in the Hamburg Observatory in the early 1930s. Observatories have since used the Schmidt telescope to photograph large areas of the sky. The whole sky has now been surveyed with these instruments and the results, which include the very faintest objects down to a magnitude of 21, are published in the Palomar Sky Survey and the Southern Sky Survey.

Schmidt, Ernst Johannes (1877–1933) *Danish biologist*

Schmidt was born at Jaegerspris in Denmark and became director of the Carlsberg Physiological Laboratory, Copenhagen. He is chiefly known for his discovery of the breeding ground and life history of the European eel in 1904. Schmidt attained this end by a careful compilation of statistics of the length of eel larvae (leptocephali) found at different points and at different times in the Atlantic. From these he was able to link together leptocephali of similar size, radiating from a central area, the smaller and younger nearer the center. The center of radiation, and the breeding ground of all European eels, proved to be the Sargasso Sea, near Bermuda. Schmidt also carried out research and produced publications on bacteria and the flora of the island of Ko Chang, Thailand.

Schmidt, Maarten (1929–) Dutch–American astronomer

Born in Groningen in the Netherlands, Schmidt graduated from the university there in 1949 and obtained his PhD in 1956 from Leiden University. After working at the Leiden Observatory from 1953 to 1959, he moved to America, taking up an appointment at the California Institute of Technology as a staff member of the Hale Observatories. He was made professor of astronomy in 1964 and also served as director of the Hale Observatories from 1978 to 1980.

Schmidt has investigated the structure and dynamics of our Galaxy and the formation of stars but he is best known for his research on quasars, or quasi-stellar objects. In 1960 Alan Sandage and Thomas Matthews identified a compact radio source, known as 3C 48, with a 16th-magnitude starlike object that was found to have a most curious spectrum. Soon, other optical identifications were made, including that of 3C 273 with a 13th-magnitude object that had an equally puzzling spectrum. These objects became known as quasars. In 1963 Schmidt was the first to produce a satisfactory interpretation of the spectrum of a quasar.

Schmidt realized that certain broad emission lines in the spectrum of 3C 273 were the familiar hydrogen lines but shifted in wavelength by an unprecedented amount. According to the Doppler effect, light emitted from a source that is moving away from an observer increases its wavelength, i.e., its spectral lines shift toward the red end of the spectrum. The faster an object is moving away, the greater the so-called red shift. Hubble had assumed that the red shift of the galaxies was explained by the Doppler effect: the galaxies were receding as the universe expanded and that as the velocity and hence the distance of a galaxy increased, its red shift increased accordingly. 3C 273 had an immense red shift. Assuming it to be a Doppler shift resulting from the expansion of the universe, Schmidt was amazed when he found that 3C 273 must be a billion light-years away. In that case, how could such a small source be visible at such an enormous distance? It would need to be as luminous as a hundred galaxies and it was by no means clear what physical mechanism could yield so much energy from such a compact source. Schmidt's work was soon confirmed by the red-shift interpretation of the spectra of other quasars; they all possessed unusually large red shifts. There arose a long debate as to whether the Doppler effect did explain the quasar red shift but it is now generally accepted that this is the case.

By the end of the 1960s many quasars had been discovered and their distribution mapped in the heavens. Schmidt realized that this allowed him to test the cosmological steady-state doctrine of Thomas Gold and others, which assumes that the universe on a large scale looks the same at all times and all places. He found, however, on examining the distribution of quasars and using the Doppler interpretation of their red shifts, that their numbers increase with distance and that they are indeed the most distant objects in the universe. Assuming that the big-bang rather than the steady-state theory is correct, they are also the youngest objects in the universe.

The discovery of the quasars with the problems they posed produced an enormous growth in astronomical research that led to the discovery of even stranger objects, such as pulsars, and the continued search for black holes. Huge black holes are indeed thought to be the source of the prodigious energy of quasars.

Schönbein, Christian Friedrich
(1799–1868) German chemist

Schönbein was born at Metzingen in Germany. After studying at the universities of Tübingen and Erlangen, he took up an appointment at the University of Basel in 1828, staying there for the rest of his life.

Many stories relate how he discovered nitrocellulose (guncotton) in 1846. In all of them a bottle in which he had been distilling nitric and sulfuric acids broke on the floor of the kitchen. In some stories, as he was forbidden by his wife to experiment in the kitchen, he is supposed to have panicked and wiped the mess up with his wife's cotton apron. In others he is unable to find a mop and uses the nearest thing to hand, his wife's cotton apron. Put to dry over the stove it flared up without smoke: Schönbein had discovered the first new explosive since gunpowder. (He was nearly anticipated in his discovery of guncotton: Théophile Pelouze had obtained an inflammable material in 1838 by treating cotton with nitric acid, but he failed to follow it up.)

Schönbein saw what a valuable commodity he had and quickly secured the appropriate patents on it. He gave exclusive rights of manufacture to John Hall and Sons in Britain but, unfortunately, their factory at Faversham blew up in July 1847, killing 21 workers. Similar lethal explosions occurred in France, Russia, and Germany. Its properties were too valuable to allow chemists to abandon it altogether: it was smokeless and four times more powerful than gunpowder; properly controlled it would make an ideal propellant. It was finally modified by Frederick Abel and James Dewar later in the century in the forms of Poudre B and cordite.

In 1840 Schönbein discovered ozone, the allotropic form of oxygen. Investigating the curious smell that seemed to linger around electrical equipment, he traced it to a gas (O_3) that he named after the Greek word for smell (*ozon*).

Schrieffer, John Robert (1931–)
American physicist

Born in Oak Park, Illinois, Schrieffer was educated at the Massachusetts Institute of Technology and the University of Illinois, where he obtained his PhD in 1957. After serving as a postdoctoral fellow in Europe at Birmingham and Copenhagen he worked at the University of Illinois from 1959 until 1962 when he moved to the University of Pennsylvania, Philadelphia, being appointed professor of physics there in 1964. He was professor of physics at the University of California, Santa Barbara (1980–91), moving to the Florida State University, Tallahassee, in 1992.

Schrieffer worked on superconductivity. In 1972 he was awarded the Nobel Prize for physics with John BARDEEN and Leon N. COOPER for their formulation in 1957 of the first successful theory of superconductivity, the BCS theory.

Schrödinger, Erwin (1887–1961)
Austrian physicist

Schrödinger, the son of a prosperous Viennese factory owner, was educated at both the gymnasium and the university in his native city, where he obtained his doctorate in 1910. After serving as an artillery officer in World War I, he taught at various German-speaking universities before he succeeded Max Planck as professor of physics at the University of Berlin in 1927.

Before long, however, Schrödinger's bitter opposition to the Nazis drove him, in 1933, into his first period of exile, which he spent in Oxford, England. Homesick, he allowed himself to be tempted by the University of Graz in Austria in 1936 but, after the Anschluss in 1938, he found himself once more under a Nazi government which this time was determined to arrest him. Schrödinger had no alternative but to flee. He was however fortunate in that the prime minister of Eire, Eamonn De Valera, himself a mathematician, was keen to attract him to a newly established Institute of Advanced Studies in Dublin. Working there from 1939 Schrödinger gave seminars that attracted many eminent foreign physicists (as well as the frequent presence of De Valera) until his retirement in 1956 when he returned to Austria.

Starting from the work of Louis de Broglie, Schrödinger in the period 1925–26 developed wave mechanics, one of the several varieties of quantum theory that emerged in the mid-1920s. He was deeply dissatisfied with the early quantum theory of the atom developed by Niels BOHR, complaining of the apparently arbitrary nature of a good many of the quantum rules. Schrödinger took the radical step of eliminating the particle altogether and substituting for it waves alone.

His first step was to derive an equation to describe the behavior of an electron orbiting an atomic nucleus. The de Broglie equation giving the wavelength $\lambda = h/mv$ (where h is the Planck constant and mv the momentum) presented too simple a picture for in reality, particularly with the inner orbits, the attractive force of the nucleus would result in a very complex and variable configuration. He eventually succeeded in establishing his famous wave equation, which when applied to the hydrogen atom yielded all the results of Bohr and DE BROGLIE. It was for this work that he shared the 1933 Nobel Prize for physics with Paul DIRAC.

Despite the considerable predictive success of wave mechanics, as the theory became known, there remained two problems for Schrödinger. He still had to attach some physical meaning to ideas of the nature of an electron, which was difficult if it was nothing but a wave; he also had to interpret the ψ function occurring in the wave equation, which described the wave's amplitude. He tried to locate the electron by constructing stable 'wave packets' from many small waves, which it was hoped would behave in the same way as a particle in classical mechanics. The packets were later shown to be unstable.

Nor was his interpretation of the ψ function as a measure of the spread of an electron any more acceptable. Instead the probabilistic interpretation of Max Born soon developed into a new orthodoxy. Schrödinger found such a view totally unacceptable, joining those other founders of quantum theory, Einstein and de Broglie, in an unrelenting opposition to the indeterminism entering physics.

In 1944 Schrödinger published his *What is Life?*, one of the seminal books of the period. Partly due to its timely publication it influenced a good many talented young physicists who, disillusioned by the bombing of Hiroshima, wanted no part of atomic physics. Schrödinger solved their problem by revealing a discipline free from military applications, significant and, perhaps just as important, largely unexplored. He argued that the gene was not built like a crystal but that it was rather what he termed an 'aperiodic solid'. He went on to talk of the possibility of a 'code' and observed that "with the molecular picture of the gene it is no longer inconceivable that the miniature code should precisely correspond with a highly complicated and specified plan of development." It is not surprising that such passages, written with more insight than that contained in most contemporary biochemical works, inspired a generation of scientists to explore and decipher such a code.

Schultze, Max Johann Sigismund
(1825–1874) *German zoologist*

Schultze was born at Freiberg in Germany. He was educated at the University of Griefswald, where his father was professor of anatomy, and the University of Berlin. After a brief period on the staff of the University of Halle he moved in 1859 to Bonn where he served as professor of zoology until his sudden death in 1874 from a perforated ulcer.

In 1861 Schultze, who had worked on the cellular structure of a wide variety of animals, published a famous paper in which he emphasized the role of protoplasm in the workings of the cell. Cells, he argued, were 'nucleated protoplasm' or 'the physical basis of life', the protoplasm and not the cell wall being the important constituent. This he illustrated by pointing out that some cells, for example those of the embryo, do not have bounding membranes.

In 1866 Schultze went on to formulate the so-called duplicity theory of vision. He had noticed that in diurnal birds the retina consisted mainly of cones but nocturnal birds possessed a retina with an abundance of rods. This led him to propose that cones must respond to colored light while rods should be more sensitive to black and white.

Schuster, Sir Arthur (1851–1934)
British physicist and spectroscopist

Schuster was the son of a Frankfurt textile merchant and banker who, unwilling to remain in the city after its annexation by Prussia in the wake of the 1866 war, moved with his family to Manchester, England. Schuster became a British citizen in 1875 and studied physics at Owens College, Manchester, and the University of Heidelberg where he obtained his doctorate in 1873. Schuster then spent the period 1875–81 at the Cavendish Laboratory, Cambridge, but returned to Manchester to serve first as professor of applied mathematics and from 1889 to 1907 as professor of physics. His somewhat premature retirement at the age of 56 was spent on his own research and the formation of the International Research Council, which he served as first secretary from 1919 to 1928.

Initially Schuster worked as a spectroscopist. In 1881 he refuted the speculation of George Stoney that spectral lines could be regarded as the harmonics of a fundamental vibration. This was done by a statistical analysis of the spectral lines of five elements in which he showed their random distribution. Somewhat discouraged by this result he turned to the study of the passage of an electric current through a gas.

In the 1880s he was the first to show that an electric current is conducted by ions. He went on to propose how the ratio between the charge and the mass of cathode rays could be calculated and in fact described the technique later used by J. J. Thomson in his determination of the charge on the electron. He further proposed, in 1896, that the new x-rays of Wilhelm Röntgen were in fact transverse vibrations of the ether of very small wavelength.

Schwann, Theodor (1810–1882)
German physiologist

Born at Neuss in Germany, Schwann was educated at the universities of Bonn, Würzburg, and Berlin where he obtained his MD in 1834. He worked with Johannes Müller in Berlin from 1834 until 1838 when he moved to Belgium, serving as professor of anatomy first at Louvain (1838–47) and thereafter at Liège until his death.

Schwann's first experiments at Berlin were on muscle contraction. He showed that the mechanism of contraction could be explained without invoking any vital principles – a marked departure from the teachings of Müller. This mechanistic philosophy was fruitfully developed by Schwann's successors at Berlin, Emil du Bois-Reymond and Hermann von Helmholtz. Schwann next conducted some experiments to disprove (again) the theory of spontaneous generation, which was enjoying a renaissance in the mid 1830s. One un-expected outcome of his experiments on putrefaction and fermentation was his dis-covery in 1836, independently of Cagniard de la Tour, that yeast is involved in fermen-tation. The same year Schwann also discov-ered the digestive enzyme pepsin.

His most memorable achievement how-ever is his *Mikroskopische Untersuchungen* (1839; Microscopical Researches) in which he first formulated, at the same time as Matthias Schleiden, the most important of all ideas in modern biology, namely that "cellular formation might be a widely ex-tended, perhaps a universal principle for the formation of organic substances."

In 1838 Schleiden had proposed that all plant tissue was composed of nucleated cells. Using the newly introduced achro-matic microscope Schwann went on to ex-amine a variety of tissues taken from several different animals. He surmised that fibers, ducts, etc., do not form directly from molecules but rather are built up from cells. The process of cell formation he saw as something like that of crystallization: cells were not formed from other cells but somehow condensed out of intercellular 'nutrient liquid'. One further radical mis-conception was that the cellular material, Schwann's cytoblastema, was devoid of structure.

Despite such errors the cell theory met with rapid acceptance. Improvements were soon made. Robert Remak first described cell division in 1841 and by 1855 Rudolf Vir-chow could issue the new dogma *omnis cellula e cellula* (all cells come from cells). The cytoblastema also came in for revision; renamed protoplasm, it was shown by Max Schultze in 1861 to have definite properties and a structure.

Despite these successes Schwann's work on fermentation was savagely criticized by leading chemists of the time, notably Jus-tus von Liebig and Friedrich Wöhler. A par-ticularly damaging paper by the pair was published in 1839 after which Schwann found it impossible to continue his career in Germany. In Belgium he conscientiously carried out his professional duties and in-vented some useful equipment for the min-ing industry. His brilliant contributions to physiology, however, virtually ceased. Not until Pasteur's work in the 1850s was Schwann vindicated.

Schwartz, Melvin (1932–) *American physicist. See* LEDERMAN, LEON MAX.

Schwarz, John Henry (1941–) *American mathematical physicist*

Born in North Adams, Massachusetts, Schwarz was educated at Harvard and the University of California, Berkeley, where he completed his PhD in 1966. After working at Princeton until 1972, he moved to the California Institute of Technology and was appointed professor of theoretical physics there in 1985.

In 1970 Yoichiro Nambu had proposed that elementary particles may not be parti-cles at all but could be vibrating rotating strings. Schwarz saw in this idea a way to explain the behavior of hadrons – i.e., parti-cles such as protons and neutrons, which respond to the strong nuclear force. Hadrons were known to be composed of quarks and, in the new model, the quarks could be seen as joined by stringlike con-nections. The theory required space to have 26 dimensions, the existence of a massless particle, and the presence of tachyons (par-ticles supposedly able to travel faster than light). More significantly, however, string theory had to compete with the more plausible account of hadrons proposed by Sheldon Glashow and others, known as quantum chromodynamics (QCD). Against competition from this source string theory withered away.

Schwarz, however, continued to work on string theory and in collaboration with Michael Green reduced the dimensions de-manded by early theories to ten. They also eliminated the need for tachyons. As for the massless particle, it seemed to possess precisely the properties demanded by Ein-stein's theory of general relativity for the carrier of the gravitational force, a fact that was of interest to cosmologists.

Further, the new theory carried other implications. It exhibited a deep symmetry, known as supersymmetry, which seemed able to unify two fundamentally different categories of particles: fermions and bosons. Bosons are not conserved and have an integral spin; fermions are conserved and have a spin of one half. Schwarz demonstrated how they could be seen as waves moving in a closed loop, with fermi-ons moving in one direction and bosons in the other direction.

The fact that the theory needs space–time to have ten dimensions rather than the four observed is explainable if the six 'extra' dimensions are extremely small, curled into six-dimensional balls with a diameter of about 10^{-35} meter.

Schwarz has published a full account of his work, in collaboration with Green and Ed Witten, in their book *Superstring Theory* (1987, 2 vols.).

Schwarzschild, Karl (1873–1916)
German astronomer

Schwarzschild was the son of a prosperous Jewish businessman from Frankfurt am Main. His interest in astronomy arose while he was at school and he had published two papers on binary orbits by the time he was 16. Following two years at the University of Strasbourg, he went in 1893 to the University of Munich, obtaining his PhD in 1896. He worked at the Kuffner Observatory in Vienna from 1896 to 1899 and after a period of lecturing and writing became in 1901 associate professor, later professor, at the University of Göttingen and director of its observatory. In 1909 he was appointed director of the Astrophysical Observatory in Potsdam. He volunteered for military service in 1914 at the beginning of World War I and was invalided home in 1916 with a rare skin disease from which he died.

Schwarzschild's practical skill was demonstrated by the instruments he designed, the measuring techniques he devised, and the observations he made. In the 1890s, while the use of photography for scientific purposes was still in its infancy, he developed methods whereby the apparent magnitude, i.e., observed brightness, of stars could be accurately measured from a photographic plate. At that time stellar magnitudes were usually determined by eye. He was then able to establish the photographic magnitude of 3500 stars brighter than magnitude 7.5 and lying between 0° and 20° above the celestial equator. He also determined the magnitude of the same stars visually, demonstrating that the two methods do not yield identical results. This difference between the visual and photographic magnitude of a star, measured at a particular wavelength, is known as its color index.

Schwarzschild also made major contributions to theoretical astronomy, the subjects including orbital mechanics, the curvature of space, and the surface structure of the Sun. In 1906 he published a paper showing that stars could not just be thought of as a gas held together by its own gravity. Questions of thermodynamics arise, concerning the transfer of heat within the star both by radiation and convection, that need a full mathematical treatment.

Einstein's theory of general relativity was published in 1916. While serving in Russia, Schwarzschild wrote two papers on the theory, which were also published in 1916. He gave a solution – the first to be found – of the complex partial differential equations by which the theory is expressed mathematically and introduced the idea of what is now called the *Schwarzschild radius*. When a star, say, is contracting under the effect of gravity, if it attains a particular radius then the gravitational potential will become infinite. An object will have to travel at the velocity of light to escape from the gravitational field of the star. The value of this radius, the Schwarzschild radius, SR, depends on the mass of the body. If a body reaches a radius less than its SR nothing, including light, will be able to escape from it and it will be what is now known as a 'black hole'. The SR for the Sun is 3 kilometers while its actual radius is 700,000 kilometers. The theoretical study of black holes and the continuing search for them has become an important field in modern astronomy.

Schwarzschild's son, Martin, also became a noted astronomer.

Schwinger, Julian Seymour
(1918–1994) *American physicist*

Schwinger, who was born in New York City, developed his prowess for mathematics and physics at an early age. At 14 he entered the City College of New York, but later transferred to Columbia University. He received his BA degree from Columbia at the age of 17 (1936) and his doctorate three years later. Moving to the University of California at Berkeley, he worked as a research associate under J.Robert Oppenheimer. In the war years (1943–45) he worked at the Metallurgical Laboratory of the University of Chicago and at the Radiation Laboratory of the Massachusetts Institute of Technology. In 1945 he joined the faculty of Harvard as an associate professor of physics, and the next year was made full professor, one of the youngest in Harvard's history. He became professor of physics at the University of California, Los Angeles, in 1972.

Schwinger's most notable contribution to physics was in the fusion of electromagnetic theory and quantum mechanics into the science of quantum electrodynamics (the foundations of which had been laid by Paul Dirac, Werner Heisenberg, and Wolfgang Pauli). During World War II, Schwinger, and others such as Richard FEYNMAN, Sin-Itiro TOMONAGA, and Frank Dyson, developed the mathematical formulation of quantum electrodynamics in a way that was consistent with Einstein's theory of relativity. The new theory led to a better understanding of the interactions between charged particles and electromagnetic fields and proved useful in measuring and explaining the behavior of atomic and subatomic particles. Schwinger, Feynman, and Tomonaga, who had conducted their work independently – Feynman at the California Institute of Technology and Tomonaga at the Tokyo Education University – were subsequently rewarded with the 1965 Nobel Prize for physics.

Schwinger also conducted significant research into the properties of synchrotron radiation, produced when a fast moving charged particle is diverted in a magnetic field. He was the author of *Particles Sources and Fields* (1970).

Seaborg, Glenn Theodore (1912–   )
American nuclear chemist

Born in Ishpeming, Michigan, Seaborg graduated in 1934 and gained his doctorate in 1937 at the University of California. He rose to become full professor in the Berkeley faculty in 1945.

Over the period 1948–58 Seaborg and his collaborators extended the periodic table beyond uranium (element 92) – hence the term 'transuranics' applied to artificial elements with atomic numbers higher than 92. Chief among his collaborators in the early days was Edwin McMILLAN (with whom he shared the Nobel Prize for chemistry in 1951), who with Philip Abelson had discovered the first transuranic element – neptunium (element 93) – in the spring of 1940. Neptunium was found to be a beta-particle emitter and it was thus expected that its decay product should be a transuranic element – the next in the series. In December 1940 Seaborg, McMillan, and their collaborators isolated element 94 – plutonium. It was realized that the transuranics formed a special series – the actinide transition series of elements, similar to the lanthanide series of rare-earth elements. Thus Seaborg and his coworkers were able to predict the chemical properties of further then-unknown transuranics and enabled them to be isolated. Seaborg's name is associated with the discovery or first isolation of a number of transuranics:

Element 93 neptunium 1940
Element 94 plutonium 1940
Element 95 americium 1944
Element 96 curium 1944
Element 97 berkelium 1949
Element 98 californium 1950
Element 101 mendelevium 1955
Element 102 nobelium 1958

It should be noted that all of these discoveries are correctly attributed to groups or teams of researchers and that attribution has been disputed in the past. In particular the first, unconfirmed, report of element 102 was in 1957 by an international group of physicists working at the Nobel Institute in Stockholm. The Berkeley team subsequently confirmed the discovery the next

year. Similar work to Seaborg's was done in the former Soviet Union by Georgii Flerov.

Another discovery with which Seaborg is associated is the isolation of the isotope uranium–233 from thorium (1941). This may be an alternative source of fuel for nuclear fission – a route to nuclear energy that is still relatively unexplored.

The work on elements was directly relevant to the World War II effort to develop an atomic bomb, and from 1942 until 1946 Seaborg was on leave to the University of Chicago metallurgical laboratory, where he was made head of the laboratory's chemical-separation section. It is said that he was influential in determining the choice of plutonium rather than uranium in the first atomic-bomb experiments.

Seaborg went on to become chancellor of the University of California from 1958 to 1962 and was then chair of the US Atomic Energy Commission until 1971. Element 106, synthesized in 1974, was named seaborgium in his honor.

Secchi, Pietro Angelo (1818–1878)
Italian astronomer

Secchi, who was born at Reggio in Italy, was a Jesuit who lectured in physics and mathematics. He spent some time abroad when the Jesuits were expelled from Rome, being at one time professor of physics at Georgetown University, Washington. He returned to Italy in 1849, becoming professor of astronomy and director of the observatory of the Roman College, which he rebuilt and reequipped.

He researched in stellar spectroscopy and his main work was done on spectral types. He introduced some order into the mass of new observations that was pouring in from the early spectroscopists. In 1867 he proposed four spectral classes. Class 1 had a strong hydrogen line and included blue and white stars; class 2 had numerous lines and included yellow stars; class 3 had bands rather than lines, which were sharp toward the red and fuzzy toward the violet and included both orange and red lines; finally, class 4 had bands that were sharp toward the violet and fuzzy toward the red and included red lines alone. These spectral types mark an important, and fairly straightforward, temperature sequence. Secchi's classification, as very much extended and modified by Edward Pickering and Annie Cannon, has become one of the basic tools of astrophysicists.

Sedgwick, Adam (1785–1873) *British geologist and mathematician*

Sedgwick was the son of the vicar of Dent

in England. He graduated in mathematics from Cambridge University in 1808, was made a fellow in 1810, and was elected to the Woodwardian Chair of Geology in 1818, a post he retained until his death. He was made president of the Geological Society in 1829.

In 1831 he began a study of the Paleozoic rocks of Wales, choosing an older region than the Silurian recently discovered by Roderick Murchison. In 1835 he named the oldest fossiliferous strata the Cambrian (after Cambria, the ancient name for Wales). This immediately caused a problem for there was no reliable way to distinguish the Upper Cambrian from the Lower Silurian.

Sedgwick formed a close friendship with Murchison. The two made their most significant joint investigation with their identification of the Devonian System from studies in southwest England in 1839. The partnership between Sedgwick and Murchison was broken when Murchison annexed what Sedgwick considered to be his Upper Cambrian into the Silurian. The bitter dispute between the two over these Lower Paleozoic strata was not resolved until after Sedgwick's death, when Charles Lapworth proposed that the strata should form a new system – the Ordovician.

Sedgwick's works included *A Synopsis of the Classification of the British Paleozoic Rocks* (1855). In 1841, largely due to Sedgwick, a museum now bearing his name was opened to house the growing geological collection. Sedgwick was, throughout his life, a committed opponent of Darwin's theory of evolution.

Seebeck, Thomas Johann (1770–1831)
Estonian–German physicist

Seebeck was born into a wealthy family in Tallinn, the Estonian capital, and moved to Germany at the age of 17. He studied medicine in Berlin and in 1802 received an MD from the University of Göttingen. More interested in science than medical practice, he was wealthy enough to be able to devote his time to scientific research. In the early years of the 19th century he moved to Jena, where he became acquainted with an important intellectual circle of scientists and philosophers. His subsequent researches made him one of the most distinguished experimental physicists of his day.

Seebeck made investigations into photoluminescence (the luminescent emission from certain materials excited by light), the heating and chemical effects of different parts of the solar spectrum, polarization, and the magnetic character of electric currents. His most important work however came in 1822, after he had moved to Berlin. His discovery of thermoelectricity (the *Seebeck effect*) showed that electric currents could be produced by temperature differences. Seebeck joined two wires of different metals to form a closed circuit and applied heat to one of the junctions; a nearby magnetic needle behaved as if an electric current flowed around the circuit. He called this effect 'thermomagnetism' (and later objected to the term thermoelectricity).

Sefström, Nils Gabriel (1787–1845)
Swedish chemist

Born at Ilsbo in Sweden, Sefström studied under Jöns Berzelius in Stockholm, graduating in 1813. He taught chemistry at the School of Mines from 1820. While there he was informed that the local steelmakers were able to predict whether iron ore delivered at the foundries would produce steel that was brittle or not. On investigation he found that they tested the ore by dissolving it in hydrochloric acid and if a black powder resulted the steel was likely to be brittle. Sefström investigated and found that what was important in the test was the presence or absence in the ore of a new element. In 1830 he isolated the new element, which he named vanadium after the Norse goddess Vanadis. This proved to be identical to the metal discovered by Andrès Del Rio in 1801 and named erythronium. Del Rio had been dissuaded that this was in fact a new element and had abandoned his claim.

Segrè, Emilio Gino (1905–1989)
Italian–American physicist

Segrè, who was born at Tivoli in Italy, studied at the University of Rome under Enrico Fermi and obtained his doctorate there in 1928. He worked with Fermi until 1936, when he was appointed director of the physics laboratory at Palermo. He was dismissed for political reasons in 1938 and moved to America where he worked at the University of California, Berkeley, from 1938 to 1972, apart from the years 1943–46, which he spent at Los Alamos working on the development of the atom bomb. He became a professor in 1945.

Segrè made a number of significant discoveries in his career. In 1937 he filled one of the gaps in the periodic table at atomic number 43 when he showed that some molybdenum that had been irradiated with deuterium nuclei by Ernest Lawrence contained traces of the new element. As the first completely artificial element they gave it the appropriate name, technetium. Segrè played a part in the detection of element 85, astatine, and also plutonium in 1940.

His main achievement however was the discovery of the antiproton with Owen CHAMBERLAIN in 1955, for which they shared the 1959 Nobel Prize for physics. Segrè calculated that producing an antiproton would require about 6 billion electron-volts (Bev), which could be provided by the recently constructed bevatron at the University of California. He therefore went on to bombard copper with protons that had been accelerated to 6 Bev, thus yielding a large number of particles. As only one antiproton was produced to about 40,000 other particles his next problem was to detect this rare event.

This was done by noting that the antiproton would travel much faster than the other particles and at such speeds it would give off Cherenkov radiation in certain media and could thus be detected. The few particles that produced this radiation could more easily be screened to see if any of them possessed the necessary properties. Before long Segrè had identified antiprotons at the rate of about four per hour. The work of the California group was soon confirmed by Italian physicists who began to detect the tracks of antiprotons on photographic plates.

Semenov, Nikolay Nikolaevich
(1896–1986) *Russian chemist*

Semenov was born in Saratov in Russia and educated at the University of Petrograd (now St. Petersburg). After working in various institutes in St. Petersburg he moved to Moscow University in 1944 as head of the department of chemical kinetics.

It was for work in this field that Semenov was awarded the 1956 Nobel Prize for chemistry, the first Russian to be so honored. He shared the prize with Sir Cyril HINSHELWOOD. His particular contribution was in the study of chemical chain reactions – an idea introduced by Max Bodenstein in 1913. Semenov investigated the idea of a chain reaction in the 1920s and was able to show that such reactions can lead to combustion and violent explosions when the chain branches, spreading with explosive rapidity. In 1934 he published a book on the subject, which was translated into English the following year, *Chemical Kinetics and Chain Reactions*.

Seyfert, Carl Keenan (1911–1960)
American astronomer

Seyfert was born in Cleveland, Ohio, and studied at Harvard where he graduated in 1933 and obtained his PhD in 1936. He worked at the McDonald Observatory in Texas from 1936 to 1940, the Mount Wilson Observatory in California from 1940 to 1942 and the Case Institute of Technology in Cleveland, Ohio from 1942 to 1946. Seyfert then moved to the Vanderbilt University in Tennessee as associate professor and where from 1951 until his death he was director of the Dyer Observatory.

In 1943, while observing at Mount Wilson, Seyfert discovered an unusual class of spiral galaxies that have since been named for him. Optically they presented a very small intensely bright nucleus; spectroscopically they had very broad emission lines indicating the presence of very hot gas moving at considerable velocities.

Since their discovery Seyfert galaxies have become even more puzzling as they are now recognized to be emitters of prodigious amounts of energy from a very compact area. Energy is released not just in the form of light but also as x-rays and radio and infrared waves. It is felt that they are related in some way to quasars, discovered in the 1960s, although possessing a less powerful source of energy.

Shannon, Claude Elwood (1916–   )
American mathematician

Born in Gaylord, Michigan, Shannon graduated from the University of Michigan in 1936. He later worked both at the Massachusetts Institute of Technology and the Bell Telephone Laboratories. In 1958 he returned to MIT as Donner Professor of Science, a post he held until his retirement in 1978.

Shannon's greatest contribution to science has been in laying the mathematical foundations of communication theory. The central problem of communication theory is to determine the most efficient ways of transmitting messages. What Shannon did was to show a precise way of quantifying the information content of a message, thus making the study of information flow amenable to exact mathematical treatment. He first published his ideas in 1948 in *A Mathematical Theory of Communication*, written in collaboration with Warren Weaver. The resulting theory found wide application in such wide-ranging fields as circuit design, computer design, communication technology in general, and even in biology, psychology, semantics, and linguistics. Shannon's work made extensive use of the theory of probability; he also extended the concept of entropy from thermodynamics and applied it to lack of information.

Shannon has also made important contributions to computer science. In his paper *A Symbolic Analysis of Relay and Switching Cir-*

cuits (1938) he drew the analogy between truth values in logic and the binary states of circuits. He also coined the term 'bit' for a unit of information.

Shapley, Harlow (1885–1972) *American astronomer*

Shapley came from a farming background in Nashville, Missouri. He began his career as a crime reporter on the *Daily Sun* of a small Kansas town when he was 16. He entered the University of Missouri in 1907 intending to study journalism but took astronomy instead, gaining his MA in 1911. He then went on a fellowship to Princeton where he studied under Henry Russell and gained his PhD in 1913. From 1914 to 1921 he was on the staff of the Mount Wilson Observatory in California. Finally Shapley was appointed in 1921 to the directorship of the Harvard College Observatory where he remained until 1952, also serving for the period 1922–56 as Paine Professor of Astronomy.

Shapley's early work, under Russell, on eclipsing binaries proved that the group of stars, known as Cepheids, were not binary but were single stars that changed their brightness as they changed their size. Cepheids were thus the first 'pulsating variables' to be discovered, the theory of the pulsation being supplied subsequently by Arthur Eddington.

Once at Mount Wilson, Shapley began to study Cepheids in globular clusters, huge spherical groups of closely packed stars. From this stemmed his fundamental work on the size and structure of our Galaxy. In 1915 he was able to make a bold speculation about the galactic structure. Using the relation between the period of Cepheids and their observed brightness, discovered in 1912 by Henrietta Leavitt, he was able to map the relative distances of clusters from us and from each other. To his surprise he found that they were widely and randomly distributed both above and below the plane of the Milky Way and appeared to be concentrated in one smallish area in the direction of the constellation Sagittarius. He argued that such a distribution would make sense if the Galaxy had the shape of a flattened disk with the clusters grouped around the galactic center. This required that the solar system be displaced from its accepted central position by a considerable distance.

Thus Shapley had found the general structure of the Galaxy but not its size. Here the Cepheids were of limited use as they could only provide a relative scale. Absolute distances could at that time only be determined for small distances. In order to calibrate his galactic structure Shapley needed to measure the distance of a few Cepheids. He used a statistical method pioneered by Ejnar Hertzsprung in 1913. Since the intrinsic brightness, or luminosity, of stars can be determined once their distance is known, Shapley's measurements allowed him to produce a quantified form of the relationship between Cepheid period and observed brightness, i.e., a period-luminosity relationship. This P-L relationship meant that a measure of the period of any Cepheid would reveal its luminosity and hence its distance and the distance of the stars surrounding it.

By 1920 Shapley felt that he had finally cracked the fundamental problem of the scale of the Galaxy. The Sun, he declared, was some 50,000 light-years from the center of the Galaxy while the diameter of the galactic disk could be perhaps 300,000 light-years. Actually Shapley's calculations were too generous as he was unaware of the interstellar matter that absorbs some of the light from stars and thus affects determinations of stellar brightness. Consequently his figures were later revised to 30,000 light-years for the distance to the galactic center and 100,000 light-years for the diameter.

Shapley was however less successful with his work on the scale of the universe. In 1920 he took part with Heber Curtis in a famous debate organized by the National Academy of Sciences at the Smithsonian in Washington. Using the brightness of novae in the Andromeda nebula, Curtis gave an estimate approaching 500,000 light-years for its distance and maintained that it was an independent star system. Shapley, misled by the measurements of Adriaan van Maanen, argued that this distance was far too great and that the Andromeda nebula and the other spiral nebulae lay within the Galaxy. It was left to Edwin Hubble to show, some years later, that Curtis had in fact underestimated rather than overestimated the distance of the Andromeda nebula and that it was in fact a separate star system.

Not the least of Shapley's achievements was his development of the Harvard Observatory into one of the major research institutions of the world. He introduced a graduate program and attracted a distinguished and much increased permanent staff. During his time there his interest turned to 'galaxies', as he called them, or 'extragalactic nebulae' in Hubble's terminology. Northern and southern skies were surveyed for galaxies and tens of thousands were recorded. In 1932 he produced a catalog, with Adelaide Ames, of 1249 galaxies, which included over a thousand galaxies brighter than 13th magnitude. In 1937 he published a survey of 36,000 southern galaxies. He also studied the Magellanic Clouds and identified the first two dwarf galaxies, the Fornax and Sculptor systems, which are members of the Local Group of galaxies.

Shapley wrote several books on astronomy and left an account of his scientific life in his informal *Through Rugged Ways to the Stars* (1969).

Sharp, Phillip Allen (1944–   )
American molecular biologist

Born in Falmouth, Kentucky, Sharp was educated at Union College, Kentucky, and the University of Illinois, Urbana, where he obtained his PhD in 1969. After spending short periods as a postdoctoral fellow at Caltech and Cold Spring Harbor Laboratory, New York, Sharp joined the Massachusetts Institute of Technology in 1974 and was appointed professor of biology in 1979.

Much early work in molecular genetics had been carried out on prokaryotes, cells that lack a nucleus. It was found that continuous stretches of DNA were converted into various proteins. The DNA was first transcribed into a continuous sequence of messenger RNA (mRNA), triplets of which coded for one of the amino acids from which proteins were assembled. It was automatically assumed that similar mechanisms would be found to operate in eukaryotic cells, cells with a nucleus.

In 1977, however, Sharp demonstrated that this assumption was baseless. Sharp worked with adenoviruses, the viruses responsible for, among other things, the common cold. He explored the process of protein production by forming double stranded hybrids of adenovirus DNA and mRNA. The hybrids were then displayed on an electron micrograph. To Sharp's surprise the mRNA hybridized with only four regions of DNA, and these were separated by long stretches of DNA looping out from the hybrid. The intervening loops, later to be termed 'introns' by Walter Gilbert, it was presumed, were later snipped off and the four remaining groups, 'exons' in Gilbert's terminology, would be spliced together to form the mature mRNA. This mature mRNA would then leave the cell's nucleus and serve as the template upon which proteins could be assembled.

Sharp's work was confirmed independently by Richard ROBERTS. The 'split genes' identified in adenoviruses by Sharp were quickly shown to be fairly standard in

eukaryotic cells. The phenomenon has proved highly puzzling. In some organisms as much as 90% of nuclear DNA is snipped away as introns and consequently seems to serve no purpose at all. Why there should be so much 'junk' DNA as it has sometimes been described remains a mystery.

For his discovery of split genes Sharp shared the 1993 Nobel Prize for physiology or medicine with Richard Roberts.

Sharpey-Schäfer, Sir Edward Albert
(1850–1935) *British physiologist*

Schäfer, the son of a city merchant in London, qualified in medicine at University College there in 1874. He joined the staff of the college and served as Jodrell Professor of Physiology from 1883 until 1899. He then moved to a similar chair at the University of Edinburgh where he remained until his retirement in 1933.

In 1896 Schäfer, working with George Oliver, discovered that an extract from the medulla of the adrenal gland produced an immediate elevation of blood pressure when injected into animals. The substance, adrenaline (epinephrine), was later isolated and crystallized by Jokichi Takamine in 1901. Schäfer also worked on pituitary extracts. He is further remembered in the field of endocrinology for his proposal that the active pancreatic substance in the islets of Langerhans should be called 'insuline', some eight years before its discovery by Frederick Banting and Charles Best.

Schäfer published two influential works: *Essentials of Histology* (1885) and *Endocrine Organs* (1916). He also founded the important *Quarterly Journal of Experimental Physiology* in 1898.

Schäfer had named one of his two sons Sharpey after his much admired anatomy teacher, William Sharpey, at University College. But after the tragic death of both his sons in World War I Schäfer changed his own name to the hyphenated Sharpey-Schäfer.

Sherrington, Sir Charles Scott (1857–1952) *British physiologist*

Sherrington, a Londoner by birth, was educated at Cambridge University and St. Thomas's Hospital, London, gaining his BA in natural science in 1883 and his MB in 1885. He then traveled to Europe to study under Rudolf Virchow and Robert Koch in Berlin. After lecturing in physiology at St. Thomas's Hospital, Sherrington was superintendent of the Brown Institute (1891–95), a veterinary hospital of the University of London. He then became professor of physiology, firstly at the University of Liverpool

(1895–1913) and then at Oxford University, holding the latter post until his retirement in 1935.

Sherrington's early medical work was in bacteriology. He investigated cholera outbreaks in Spain and Italy and was the first to use diphtheria antitoxin successfully in England, his nephew being the patient. During World War I he tested antitetanus serum on the wounded and also worked (incognito) as a laborer in a munitions factory. He then turned his attention to studies of the reflex actions in man, demonstrating their effect in enabling the nervous system to function as a unit and anticipating Ivan Pavlov in his discovery of the 'conditioned reflex'. Sherrington also did much work on decerebrate rigidity and the renewal of nerve tissue. For their work on the function of the neuron, Sherrington and Edgar ADRIAN were jointly awarded the Nobel Prize for physiology or medicine in 1932. Sherrington was knighted in 1922.

Shockley, William Bradford (1910–1989) *British–American physicist*

Shockley, born the son of a mining engineer in London, was educated at the California Institute of Technology and at Harvard, where he obtained his PhD in 1936. He started work at the Bell Telephone Laboratories in 1936. In 1963 he took up an appointment as professor of engineering at Stanford University.

Shockley is noted for his early work in the development of the transistor – an invention that has had a profound effect on modern society. He collaborated with John BARDEEN and Walter BRATTAIN in their work on the point-contact transistor (1947). The following year Shockley developed the junction transistor.

In semiconductors such as germanium and silicon the electrical conductivity is strongly affected by impurities. The germanium and silicon atoms have four outermost electrons and an impurity such as arsenic, with five outer electrons, contributes extra electrons to the solid. In such materials the current is carried by negative electrons and the conductivity is said to be n-type. Alternatively, impurities such as boron, with three outer electrons, have a different effect in that they introduce 'holes' – i.e., 'missing' electrons. An electron on an adjacent atom can move to 'fill' the hole, leaving another hole. By this mechanism electrical conduction is by movement of positive holes through the solid – the conductivity is said to be p-type.

Shockley experimented with junctions of p- and n-type material, showing how they act as rectifiers. He formed the first junction transistor of a thin layer of p-type material sandwiched between two n-type regions. This $n–p–n$ junction transistor could be used to amplify current. Shockley shared the 1970 Nobel Prize for physics with Bardeen and Brattain.

Shull, Clifford Glenwood (1915–) *American physicist*

Shull, who was born in Pittsburgh, Pennsylvania, was educated at the Carnegie Institute of Technology and New York University, where he obtained his PhD in 1941. He began as a research physicist working first for the Texas Company, from 1941 to 1946, and then with the Oak Ridge National Laboratory from 1946 until 1955, when he entered academic life as professor of physics at the Massachusetts Institute of Technology. He remained at the institute until his retirement in 1986.

Shull's main research interest has been in the diffraction of slow neutrons by crystals. Just as x-rays can be diffracted by a crystal lattice, neutron beams of suitable energy also show diffraction effects. In the case of x-rays, diffraction is mainly by the electrons in the atom, whereas in neutron diffraction the nuclei scatter the neutrons. From about 1946 onward Shull applied neutron diffraction to determining crystal structure, showing that the method could indicate the position of light atoms such as hydrogen (which are not detected by x-ray methods).

Shull also showed that an additional effect occurred in neutron diffraction – magnetic scattering by interaction of the neutron's magnetic moment with that of the atom. He demonstrated antiferromagnetism in manganese(II) oxide using this technique in 1949. He has subsequently done considerable work in 'magnetic diffraction' of neutrons and in other aspects of neutron interaction with matter. For his work on neutron diffraction Shull shared the 1994 Nobel Prize for physics with Bertram BROCKHOUSE.

Sidgwick, Nevil Vincent (1873–1952) *British chemist*

Sidgwick, who was born in Oxford, came from a distinguished intellectual family; both his father and an uncle were Oxford classicists and another uncle was a professor of moral philosophy at Cambridge University. He was educated at Oxford University obtaining first class degrees in both chemistry (1895) and classics (1897). After further study in Germany, during which he obtained his PhD in 1901 from

Tübingen, he returned to Oxford as a fellow and spent the remainder of his life there.

Sidgwick began his career working on organic compounds and in 1910 he produced *The Organic Chemistry of Nitrogen*, a classic text on the subject. In 1914 Sidgwick attended a meeting of the British Association in Australia and there he met Ernest Rutherford with whom he formed a lasting friendship. The meeting marked a turning point in his career; he became interested in atomic structure and tried to explain chemical reactions through this.

Sidgwick's theory was eventually published in 1927 in his *Electronic Theory of Valency*, which established his international reputation. The significance of his work was that it extended the idea of valency developed by Gilbert Lewis and Irving Langmuir to inorganic compounds, emphasizing the necessity of assuming the Bohr–Rutherford model of the atom. He introduced what he termed a coordinate bond in which, unlike the covalent bond of Lewis, both electrons are donated by one atom and accepted by the other. This explained the coordination compounds of Alfred Werner.

In his later years Sidgwick worked on his two-volume *The Chemical Elements and their Compounds* (1950), a massive work that attempted to demonstrate the adequacy of valency theory by showing that it applied to all compounds. The work took 25 years of Sidgwick's life and for it he was reported to have examined 10,000 scientific papers.

Siegbahn, Kai Manne Börje (1918–   )
Swedish physicist

Siegbahn, who was born at Lund in Sweden, was the professor of physics at the Royal Institute of Technology, Stockholm, from 1951 to 1954. He taught at the University of Uppsala from 1954 to 1984. Here he worked on the emission of electrons from substances irradiated with x-rays. Siegbahn's technique was to subject a specimen to a narrow beam of x-rays with a single wavelength (i.e., energy) and measure the energy spectrum of the ejected electrons by magnetic or electrostatic deflection. The spectrum shows characteristic peaks formed by electrons ejected from different inner energy levels of atoms. Moreover, the positions of these peaks depend to a slight extent on the way in which the atom is linked to other atoms in the molecule. These 'chemical shifts' allow the technique to be used as an analytical tool – Siegbahn has named it ESCA (electron spectroscopy for chemical analysis). He has also worked on the related

technique of ultraviolet photoelectron spectroscopy developed by David Turner.

Siegbahn is the son of Karl Manne Siegbahn, who won the Nobel Prize for physics in 1924. Kai Siegbahn was awarded the Nobel Prize in 1981.

Siegbahn, Karl Manne Georg (1886–1978) *Swedish physicist*

Siegbahn, who was born at Örebro in Sweden, was educated at the University of Lund, where he studied astronomy, mathematics, physics, and chemistry, obtaining his doctorate in 1911. In 1914 he turned his attention to the new science of x-ray spectroscopy. It had already been established from x-ray spectra that there were two distinct 'shells' of electrons within atoms, each giving rise to groups of spectral lines, labeled 'K' and 'L'. In 1916 Siegbahn discovered a third, or 'M', series. (More were to be found later in heavier elements.)

Through successive refinement of his x-ray equipment and technique, Siegbahn was able to achieve a significant increase in the accuracy of his determinations of spectral lines. This allowed him to make corrections to Bragg's equation for x-ray diffraction to allow for the finer details of crystal diffraction. Besides working with crystals, he performed x-ray spectroscopy at longer wavelengths using gratings. Here again his accurate measurements revealed discrepancies that were later shown to result from inaccuracies in the value assumed for the electronic charge.

In 1920 Siegbahn was made professor and head of the physics department at the University of Lund and in 1923 he moved to the University of Uppsala to become chairman of the physics department. In 1924 he received the Nobel Prize for physics, cited for "his discoveries and research in the field of x-ray spectroscopy," and the following year saw publication of his influential book *Spectroscopy of X-rays* (1925). In the same year Siegbahn and his colleagues showed that x-rays are refracted as they pass through prisms, in the same way as light.

When, in 1937, the Swedish Royal Academy of Sciences created the Nobel Institute of Physics at Stockholm, Siegbahn was appointed its first director. In the same year he became professor of physics at the University of Stockholm, retaining this post until his retirement in 1964. He was responsible for the building of accelerators, laboratory spectrometers, and other equipment at the Nobel Institute.

Siemens, Ernst Werner von
(1816–1892) *German engineer*

The son of a farmer from Lenthe in Germany, Siemens was the eldest of fourteen highly talented children, who included William Siemens. In 1834 he joined the Prussian army and spent three years in Berlin receiving a thorough training in science and mathematics. Afterward duties were so light as to allow him to pursue his growing interest in chemistry and electricity. From this work he derived his first invention, a new system of electroplating sold by his brother William in London for £1600 in 1843.

In 1847 Siemens founded, with Johann Halske (1814–90), the firm of Siemens and Halske, later to become one of the major industrial concerns in Europe. Initially Siemens hoped to move into the rapidly growing telegraphy business. In 1847 he built the Berlin–Frankfurt line, insulating the underground cables with the newly introduced gutta-percha. Unfortunately for Siemens the gutta-percha had been vulcanized and the copper wire and sulfur destroyed the insulation. Contracts were canceled and, for a time, Siemens found it necessary to work outside Germany. The period, nonetheless, gave Siemens time to experiment, refine, and improve on the basic principles of telegraphy. He was consequently selected to construct the telegraph line connecting London to Calcutta, a distance of 11,000 kilometers, which was completed in 1870.

Siemens's other main interest lay in power generation. The early electric generators were cumbersome machines using large steel permanent magnets and delivering very little power. In 1867 Siemens proposed to replace them with the self-activating dynamo. The permanent magnets were replaced by electromagnets and these were fed by a current obtained from an armature and commutator. Once the dynamo had been perfected it made possible the many manifestations of electric power – lighting, both domestic and public, transport, heating, cooling, and so on. The Siemens companies were well placed to take advantage of the commercial and industrial revolution created by the dynamo. Perhaps the clearest measure of the achievements of Siemens could once have been found in Berlin, where the suburb in which the firm's factories were located and where 120,000 men were employed was named Siemensstadt.

Siemens, Sir William (1823–1883)
British engineer

Born Carl Wilhelm in Lenthe, Germany, Siemens was the son of a tenant farmer and a younger brother of Ernst Werner Siemens. He was educated at Göttingen and first visited Britain in 1843 as an agent of his brother Ernst Werner. He settled in England shortly afterwards, becoming a naturalized citizen in 1859.

Siemens worked in two main areas, namely, heat and electricity. In the age of Joule he was aware of the potential value to be gained by conserving heat. Early attempts to redesign the steam engine proved impractical. More successful was his introduction, aided by his younger brother Friedrich (1826–1904), of the regenerator furnace (1856). In the Siemens furnace the hot combustion gases were not simply discharged into the air but used to heat the air supply to the chamber. The process was first used in the manufacture of steel by an open-hearth process known as the *Siemens–Martin process* (after the French engineer Pierre Blaise Emile Martin, 1824–1915) in the 1860s. It proved to be the first serious challenge to the Bessemer process and by the century's end had become the favored method of steel production. On the strength of this a steel foundry was opened at Landore, South Wales, in 1869. As it failed to prosper it was abandoned in 1888.

He was more successful with his work in electric telegraphy. Siemens designed the cable-laying ship *Faraday* for laying a new trans-Atlantic cable in 1874. He also worked on electric lighting and on the Portrush electric railway in Northern Ireland. He died suddenly from a heart attack in 1883. When, forty years before, he had first arrived in Britain his English had been so poor that he looked for legal advice from an undertaker. Since then, it was said of him, he made three fortunes: one he lost, one he gave away, and one he bequeathed to his brothers. The electrical unit of conductance, the *siemens*, is named in his honor.

Simpson, Thomas (1710–1761) *British mathematician*

The son of a weaver from Market Bosworth in Leicestershire, Simpson was largely self-educated. His mathematical interests were aroused when a peddler gave him a copy of the popular textbook, *Cocker's Arithmetic*. He left home early, for by 1724 he was reported to be in nearby Nuneaton, practicing as an astrologer. By 1735 he had arrived in London where he worked initially as a weaver but also as a part-time teacher of mathematics. He soon became well known through a series of popular textbooks among which were *A New Treatise on Fluxions* (1737) and his *Treatise of Algebra* (1745).

In 1743 he was appointed to the Royal Military Academy at Woolwich. He also served (1754–60) as editor of the *Ladies Diary* – a journal that sought to interest the "fair sex" in "Mathematicks and Philosophical Knowledge."

In mathematics he is best known for his formulation in 1743 of what has since been known as *Simpson's rule*, allowing the area under a curve to be approximated by using parabolic arcs.

Sitter, Willem de *See* DE SITTER, WILLEM.

Skolem, Thoralf Albert (1887–1963)
Norwegian mathematician

The son of a teacher, Skolem was born at Sandsvaer in Norway and educated at the University of Oslo. He joined the faculty in 1911 and was appointed professor of mathematics in 1938, a post he held until his retirement in 1950.

Skolem is best known for his work in mathematical logic, including his contribution to the proof of the *Lowenheim-Skolem theorem* and the construction of the *Skolem paradox*.

The Lowenheim theorem of 1915, as generalized by Skolem in 1920, simply states that any schema satisfiable in some domain is satisfiable in a denumerably infinite domain. Denumerably infinite domains, also known as countable domains, can be matched in a one–one correspondence with the domain of natural numbers. Clearly the natural numbers are denumerably infinite, as are the even numbers and the rational numbers. There are in fact just as many even numbers as natural numbers, as can be seen from the correspondences set out below:

2 4 6 8 10 12 14 16 ...
1 2 3 4 5   6   7   8 ...

There are, however, domains, such as the domain of the real numbers, which cannot be put into such a correspondence with the natural numbers. Such domains are nondenumerably infinite.

Skolem pointed out in 1922 that this result leads to a new paradox in set theory. There are sets, the set of real numbers for example, which are nondenumerable. Yet, by the Lowenheim-Skolem theorem, they must be satisfiable in a denumerably infinite domain. Skolem proposed to defuse the paradox by claiming that notions such as nondenumerability have no absolute meaning, but can only be understood within the confines a particular axiomatic system. Thus a set may be nondenumerable within a system and denumerable outside. Consequently, the paradox will fail to arise.

Skou, Jens Christian (1918–) *Danish biologist*

Skou was educated at the University of Copenhagen. In 1946 he joined the staff of the Institute of Physiology, Aarhus University, where he served as professor of biophysics from 1978 until his retirement in 1988.

Skou has sought to understand how the energy-rich adenosine triphosphate (ATP) molecule fuels cellular activities. It had been established by Peter MITCHELL that a greater concentration of ions was normally found on one side of the cell's membrane. How the ions were transported across the membrane, however, remained a mystery. Skou suspected that the process was mediated by an enzyme. In 1957, working with crab nerve cells, Skou found an enzyme in the cell's membranes that appeared to pump sodium out of cells while transporting potassium within, a process since referred to as the Na^+/K^+ pump. The enzyme, known as sodium-potassium-ATPase, proved to be the first of many ATP-based enzymes responsible for transporting molecules through cellular membranes.

For his discovery of the Na^+/K^+ pump Skou shared the 1997 Nobel Prize for chemistry with Paul BOYER and John WALKER.

Slipher, Vesto Melvin (1875–1969)
American astronomer

Born in Mulberry, Indiana, Slipher graduated from the University of Indiana in 1901 and obtained his PhD there in 1909. He spent the whole of his career from 1901 to 1952 at Percival Lowell's observatory in Flagstaff, Arizona, being made acting director on Lowell's death in 1916 and director in 1926.

Slipher was basically a spectroscopist. One of his major achievements was to determine the rotation periods of some of the planets by spectroscopic means. Thus in 1912, in collaboration with Lowell, he found that the spectral lines at the edge of the disk of Uranus were displaced by an amount corresponding to a speed of 10.5 miles (16.8 km) per second. Knowing the circumference it was easy to work out the rotation period as 10.8 hours. Although still the accepted figure, it is now thought that this rotation period could be considerably longer. Slipher also produced comparable data for Venus, Mars, Jupiter, and Saturn and showed that Venus's period was much longer than expected.

Slipher also studied the matter lying between the stars in our Galaxy. Like Johannes Hartmann he concluded in 1908 from his spectroscopic research that there must be gaseous material lying between the stars. He also studied the spectra of the luminous nebulae in the Pleiades cluster of stars and proposed in 1912 that they were illuminated by starlight reflected off dust grains. This was an early indication of the presence of solid material in nebulae and other interstellar clouds.

Slipher's most important achievement however was his determination of the radial velocities of spiral nebulae by the measurement of the displacement of their spectral lines. Such measurement relies on the Doppler effect by which the wavelength of light from an object moving away from an observer will be lengthened, i.e., shifted toward the red end of the spectrum, while light from an object moving toward an observer will have its wavelength shortened, i.e., moved toward the blue end of the spectrum. Thus by measuring the change in wavelength, known as the Doppler shift, the velocity of the moving object can be determined easily.

Slipher's work produced two surprising results. The first was the immense speed of the Andromeda nebula (galaxy), which he first successfully measured in 1912. He found it to be moving toward the Earth with a velocity of nearly 300 kilometers per second, which was then the greatest velocity ever observed. Secondly, by 1917 he had obtained the radial velocities of 15 spiral nebulae of which it would have been thought that roughly half would be receding while the other half would be approaching. But he found that 13 out of the 15 were receding. What was equally significant was their velocity, which in many cases exceeded that of the 300 kilometers per second of the Andromeda nebula. Many astronomers questioned these findings. At that time there was considerable controversy over whether the spiral nebulae were part of our Galaxy or lay far beyond it as independent star systems. Slipher's work was, in retrospect, evidence both for the extragalactic hypothesis, since the velocities of the spiral nebulae were too great for them to be members of the Galaxy, and for the expanding universe, which was first proposed by Alexander Friedmann in 1922 and later shown to be correct by Edwin Hubble.

Smalley, Richard Errett (1943–)
American chemist

Born in Akron, Ohio, Smalley was educated at Michigan University and at Princeton where he obtained his PhD in 1973. After spending the period from 1973 to 1976 at the James Franck Institute, Chicago, Smal-

ley moved to Rice University, Houston, and was appointed professor of chemistry in 1981.

In 1981 Smalley devised a procedure to produce microclusters of a hundred or so atoms. The technique is to vaporize the metal by a laser. The released atoms are cooled by a jet of helium and condense into variously sized clusters. In 1985 a visiting British chemist, Harry Kroto, persuaded Smalley to direct his laser beam at a graphite target. Smalley knew that an Exxon group had already used graphite and produced carbon molecules with an even number of atoms. At first Smalley was reluctant to repeat this work but he was eventually persuaded. They soon had spectroscopic evidence for the presence of an apparently large, stable molecule of sixty carbon atoms – now known as buckminsterfullerene.

Smith, Hamilton Othanel (1931–)
American molecular biologist. See NATHANS, DANIEL.

Smith, Henry John (1826–1883) *British mathematician*

Dublin-born Smith studied at Oxford and had a great interest in classics – it was only after a good deal of hesitation that he chose mathematics as a profession instead. He remained in Oxford in various capacities for most of the rest of his life. In 1860 he became Savilian Professor of Geometry there.

Smith's main work was in number theory and his greatest contribution was his development of a general theory of n indeterminates, which enabled him to establish results about the possibility of expressing positive integers as sums of five and seven squares. This achievement ought to have won Smith the prestigious prize offered in 1882 by the French Academy for their mathematical competition. However Smith, a notably unambitious man, did not enter and the prize was in fact given to Hermann Minkowski. When it was discovered that Minkowski had made use of crucial results published by Smith, the French Academy hastened to transfer the prize to Smith, but as he had unfortunately died in the meantime his fame was only posthumous. Smith also worked on the theory of elliptic functions.

Smith, John Maynard *See* MAYNARD SMITH, JOHN.

Smith, Michael (1932–) *Canadian biochemist*

Born in the Lancashire coastal town of

Blackpool, Smith was educated at the University of Manchester where he obtained his PhD in 1956. He moved soon after to Canada working initially as a postdoctoral fellow at the University of British Columbia, Vancouver. From 1961 until 1966 Smith served with the Fisheries Research Board of Canada, Vancouver, but returned to the University of British Columbia in 1966 and was appointed professor of biochemistry in 1970.

In 1978 Smith introduced a basic new technique known as 'site specific mutagenesis' into molecular biology. In order to establish the function of a particular protein or gene, it had long been an established procedure to induce a mutation in the gene and observe the consequences. Thus if changes to a gene prevented an organism from making a particular enzyme, then it was reasonable to conclude that the gene controlled some part of the production of that enzyme. The difficulty with this approach was that the available mutagens, radiation and chemicals, produced random and multiple mutations. The precise effects of a single mutant gene could seldom, therefore, be distinguished from the other consequences of the mutagens.

Smith demonstrated how to introduce specific mutations into genes. He worked with a single strand of viral DNA. A short segment of complementary DNA differing at a single site was assembled and allowed to bind to the original viral DNA. The second strand was then completed in the normal way and the double-stranded DNA inserted into the viral genome. The virus would develop with normal and mutated versions of the gene which would in turn produce normal and mutated proteins. When the different protein molecules were compared, the role of the initial mutation would become apparent.

The new technique has been widely used in protein chemistry and molecular biology. Smith himself has used it to investigate the role of cytochrome c in cellular respiration, and myoglobin in oxygen storage.

For his work in this field Smith shared the 1993 Nobel Prize for chemistry with Kary MULLIS.

Smith, William (1769–1839) *British surveyor and geologist*

Smith was born in Churchill, England, the son of the village blacksmith. He was educated at local schools and in 1787 began work with the surveyor who had been commissioned to make a survey of his parish. This was at the time of the great canal boom and Smith soon found himself fully employed conducting surveys for proposed canals. He was also regularly employed to report on coal deposits in different parts of the country while making his canal surveys. During this work he traveled considerable distances throughout Britain.

From his surveying and observation of rock strata Smith formulated very clearly two basic principles of geology for which he is often known as the father of British geology. As early as 1791 he had noted that certain strata, wherever they occurred, all contained the same invertebrate fossils and that different strata could be distinguished by a difference in their fossil content. Previously geologists had relied upon the nature of the rocks to identify and discriminate between strata. This could work well in some favored cases but, in general, was far from reliable. Smith's other major theory was the law of superposition, which simply states that if one layer of sedimentary rocks overlays another then it was formed later, unless it can be shown that the beds have been inverted.

Smith never managed to produce a major book on the geology of Britain although he did publish two small pamphlets: *Strata Identified by Organized Fossils* (1816) and *Stratigraphical Systems of Organized Fossils* (1819). His major productions were instead in the field of maps. In 1815 he produced the first geological map of England and Wales. This was published in 15 sheets at a scale of 5 miles to the inch. During the period 1819–24 he published a series of geological maps of 21 counties. The plates were still being used to produce maps as late as 1911.

Smith seems to have received little recognition and reward during his early life; he was forced to sell his collection of fossils to the British Museum to overcome his financial difficulties. However, in the 1830s he began to receive the recognition he deserved. In 1831 the Geological Society of London awarded him their first Wollaston medal and in 1835 he received an honorary LLD from Dublin.

Smoot, George Fitzgerald III
(1945–   ) *American astrophysicist*

Born at Yukon in Florida, Smoot was educated at the Massachusetts Institute of Technology where he took his PhD in physics in 1970. He moved to the University of California, Berkeley, in 1971 as a research physicist and in 1974 was appointed team leader for the differential microwave radiometers on board the Cosmic Background Explorer Satellite (COBE).

In 1965 Penzias and Wilson had discovered the cosmic background radiation. Initially it appeared to be perfectly isotropic, exactly the same whatever part of the universe it came from. Theorists found it difficult to account for such uniformity, and experimentalists began to wonder if it really was as uniform as it appeared.

The first disproof of isotropy came in 1977 from observations taken on board a high-flying U2 plane. The dipole anisotropy, as it was called, was small and was connected with the position of the Milky Way. Clearly further work was called for. After a number of delays, COBE was launched in 1989. Three instruments were carried. The differential microwave radiometer would measure differences in radiation from two points in the sky and could pick out differences between them of 1 part in 100,000. Also, a photometer measured the absolute brightness of the sky and searched for diffuse infrared radiation from the early universe. Finally, an interferometer measured the spectrum of the background radiation from 1 centimeter to 100 micrometers.

As the results emerged Smoot saw within the assumed uniformity 'islands of structure'. A year was spent checking the reliability of the data – prizes were offered to anyone on the team who could identify a significant flaw. Finally the material was checked against a list of all the systematic errors ever noted during the years of preparation. After four papers describing the initial results had been revised more than a hundred times, Smoot was ready to go public.

The results seemed to show that there were bright spots in the universe, 30 millionths of a degree warmer than the average temperature. This was precisely the result predicted by the inflationary model of Alan Guth. It might also be possible, Smoot considered, to find in the ripples in the radiation the galactic clusters that populate the universe. Smoot has published a valuable popular account of the COBE mission in his *Wrinkles in Time* (1993).

Snell, George Davis (1903–1996)
American geneticist

Snell was born in Bradford, Massachusetts, and educated at Dartmouth and Harvard, where he obtained his doctorate in 1930. After brief appointments at Texas, Brown, and Washington University, St. Louis, he joined the staff of the Jackson Laboratory, Bar Harbor, Maine, in 1935 and remained there for his entire career, retiring finally in 1969.

Early in his career, while at the University of Texas, Snell was the first to show that x-rays can cause mutations in mam-

mals, by his demonstration that x-rays induce chromosome translocations in mice. His main work concerned what he called the major histocompatibility complex. It had been known since the 1920s that although skin grafts between mice are generally rapidly rejected they survive best when made between the same inbred line. Snell's coworker Peter Gorer showed in 1937 that this was due to the presence of certain histocompatibility antigens found on the surface of mouse cells and since known as the H-2 antigens. In the 1940s Snell began a detailed study of the system.

His first task was to develop inbred strains of mice through backcrossing, genetically identical except at the H-2 locus. After much effort he was able to show that the H-2 antigens were controlled by the genes at the H-2 complex of chromosome 17, described by him as the major histocompatibility complex (MHC).

It was for this work that Snell shared the 1980 Nobel Prize for physiology or medicine with Jean DAUSSET and Baruj BENACERRAF.

Snell, Willebrord van Roijen (1580–1626) *Dutch mathematician and physicist*

Snell, who was born at Leiden in the Netherlands, received his initial training in mathematics from his father, who taught at Leiden University. He traveled widely in Europe, visiting Paris, Würzburg, and Prague, and among the celebrated scientists he met were Johannes Kepler and Tycho Brahe. Once he had returned to Leiden, Snell published a number of editions of classical mathematical texts. On the death of his father (1613) Snell succeeded him as professor of mathematics at the university.

He was involved in practical work in geodesy and took part in an attempt to measure the length of the meridian. In this project he was one of the first to see the full usefulness of triangulation and published his method of measuring the Earth in his *Eratosthenes Batavus* (1617; The Dutch Eratosthenes). In 1621 Snell discovered his famous law of refraction, based on a constant known as the refractive index, after much practical experimental work in optics. Snell did not, however, publish his discovery and the law first reached print in Descartes's *La Dioptrique* (1637; Dioptrics). However, Descartes had arrived at the law in a totally different way from Snell and made no use of practical observation.

Snyder, Solomon Halbert (1938–   ) *American psychopharmacologist*

Snyder was born in Washington DC and educated at Georgetown University. After receiving his MD in 1962 he moved to the National Institute of Health, Bethesda, Maryland, as a research associate. He later (1965) joined the staff of Johns Hopkins where he has served since 1970 as professor of psychiatry and pharmacology.

Many drugs, hormones, and neurotransmitters are effective at very low concentrations. The synthetic opiate etorphine produces euphoria and relieves pain in doses as low as one ten-thousandth of a gram. It was inferred from this that for such small doses to be effective they must bind to highly selective receptor sites. Snyder, in collaboration with C. Pert, began the search for such receptor sites using radioactively labeled opiates. By 1973, despite many complications, they were able to report the presence of receptors in the mammalian limbic system, a primitive region in the center of the brain associated with the perception and integration of pain and emotional experiences. To identify the receptors Snyder, working with Candice Pert, developed the widely used technique of 'reversible ligand binding'. Brain tissue was exposed to opiates labeled with radioactive isotopes. These were quickly washed away. The assumption was that, in low concentrations, opiates would first bind tightly to receptors. The opiates which would normally bind loosely with other tissue would be washed away. The binding sites could then be identified by locating the radioactive isotopes.

The implications of such a discovery were far-reaching for it is clear that opiate receptors had not evolved to await the isolation of morphine. The alternative is that there must be natural morphinelike substances in the brain that bind at these sites. Within a few years the first such enkephalins or endorphins, as they were named, were discovered by J. Hughes and Hans Kosterlitz.

In more recent work Snyder has claimed to have identified a new kind of neurotransmitter, namely, the unlikely and highly toxic nitric oxide (NO). In 1987 it had been discovered that NO diffused from blood-vessel walls causing adjacent muscles to relax and the vessels to dilate. Snyder set out to find if NO was made in the brain. He found NO present bound with iron in an enzyme, cyclic guanosine monophosphate (cGMP). NO acts in an unusual way by initiating a three-dimensional change in the shape of the enzyme. Snyder has also suggested that nitric oxide in the brain could be involved in changes connected with learning and memory processes. He has proposed that carbon monoxide may also belong to this novel class of neurotransmitters.

In another breakthrough in 1987 Snyder succeeded in cultivating *in vitro* human cerebral cortex tissue. For some unknown reason neurons, which do not normally divide, taken from a child undergoing an operation have continued to divide. "They have all the properties of neurons," Snyder emphasized, "they do everything that neurons do." Snyder has speculated that it might in the future be possible to implant such neurons in badly damaged brains.

Sobrero, Ascanio (1812–1888) *Italian chemist*

Born at Casal in Italy, Sobrero began by studying medicine but changed to chemistry, attending the universities at Turin, Paris, and Giessen. He became professor of chemistry at Turin in 1849, staying there until his retirement in 1882.

In 1846 – the year that Christian Schönbein discovered nitrocellulose – Sobrero discovered an even more powerful explosive, nitroglycerin. By slowly stirring drops of glycerin into a cooled mixture of nitric and sulfuric acids he produced a new but unpredictable explosive. Unlike Schönbein, Sobrero showed no desire to exploit the commercial value of his discovery. As it was liable to explode on receiving the slightest vibration there seemed to be no way to develop it, and its liquid nature made it difficult to use as a blaster. It was not utilized until 1866, when Alfred Nobel mixed it with the earth kieselguhr to produce a compound that could be transported and handled without too much difficulty. In this form – dynamite – it was used extensively in the great engineering programs of roads, railroads, and harbors of the late 19th century.

Soddy, Frederick (1877–1956) *British chemist*

Soddy, born the son of a corn merchant in the coastal town of Eastbourne, was educated at the University College of Aberystwyth and Oxford University. After working with Ernest Rutherford in Canada and William Ramsay in London, Soddy took up an appointment at Glasgow University in 1904. He moved to take the chair of chemistry at Aberdeen University in 1914 where he remained until 1919 when he accepted the post of Dr. Lee's Professor of Chemistry at Oxford.

Soddy's work was quite revolutionary in that he succeeded in overthrowing two deep assumptions of traditional chemistry. The first arose out of his period of collaboration with Rutherford, from 1901 to 1903. Together they established that radioactive elements could change into other elements through a series of stages.

Soddy's next major achievement was to make some kind of sense of the bewildering variety of new elements that had been found as decay products of radium, thorium, and uranium. The books of the period refer to such strange entities as mesothorium, ionium, radium A, B, C, D, E, and F, and uranium X. Such entities were clearly distinct for they had markedly different half-lives. But what they were and, more significantly, where they fitted in the periodic table were difficult questions. There were gaps in the periodic table but far too few to accommodate so many new elements. One further difficulty soon forced itself on chemists. Attempts to separate thorium from radiothorium by Otto Hahn in 1905 and radium D from lead by Georg von Hevesy a few years later had failed, as had numerous other attempts to separate various radioactive elements by chemical means.

Finally Soddy made the bold claim that the reason such substances could not be separated was because they were in fact identical. Consequently some kind of modification of the periodic table was called for. In his view (1913) "it would not be surprising if the elements...were mixtures of several homogeneous elements of similar but not completely identical atomic weights." He called such chemically identical elements, with slightly differing atomic weights, isotopes (from the Greek words meaning in the same place). He could thus assert that both radium D and thorium C were in fact isotopes of lead. Radium D has a half-life of 24 years and an atomic weight of 210 while thorium C has a half-life of 87 minutes and an atomic weight of 212; but, although they have different half-lives and slightly differing weights, they were both chemically indistinguishable as lead.

Until the discovery of the neutron by James Chadwick a complete understanding of this enormously fruitful idea was not available to Soddy. All he could propose, somewhat vaguely, as an explanation was different numbers of positive and negative charges in the nucleus. As yet, nobody seemed to suspect the existence of a neutral particle, without a charge.

He did, however, go on to explain the transformation of atoms by his displacement law. In this, the emission of an alpha particle, a helium nucleus of two protons and two neutrons, lowers the atomic weight by four while the emission of a beta particle, an electron, raises the atomic number by one. Given these rules Soddy could show how, for example, uranium and thorium could both decay, by different paths, to different isotopes of lead (Casimir Fajans independently suggested the same law).

Despite the award of the 1921 Nobel Prize for chemistry for his work on the origins and nature of isotopes, Soddy became disillusioned with science and his place in it. After 1919 Soddy took no further part in creative science. He wrote a good deal, mainly in the fields of economic and social questions, which raised little interest or support. On the issue of energy, however, he was remarkably perceptive. As early as 1912 he could comment that "the still unrecognized 'energy problem' ... awaits the future," continuing with the by now familiar refrain of our profligate use of hydrocarbons, "a legacy from the remote past," and concluding with what he saw as our only hope, atomic energy, which "could provide anyone who wanted it with a private sun of his own."

Solvay, Ernest (1838–1922) *Belgian industrial chemist*

Solvay was born at Rebecq-Rognon in Belgium. As the son of a salt refiner and the nephew of a manager of a gas plant, he was introduced at an early age to the techniques and problems of the chemical industry. He devised several methods for purifying gases but is best known for the ammonia–soda process named for him.

For most of the 19th century soda was produced by the Leblanc process. This had a number of disadvantages: it produced toxic hydrochloric acid fumes and also a number of expensive and irrecoverable waste products. As early as 1811 Augustin Fresnel had proposed an ammonia–soda process. However, although chemists succeeded in the laboratory, when they tried to translate their results onto an industrial scale they invariably ended up like James Muspratt, who lost £8000 in the period 1840–42. Solvay was the first to solve the engineering problems of the process. He later confessed that he was completely ignorant of all these earlier failures, adding that he would probably never have tried if he had known.

In 1861 Solvay took out his first patent for soda production and in 1863 set up his first factory at Charleroi, in partnership with his brother. The process involved mixing brine with ammonium carbonate, which produced sodium carbonate and ammonium chloride. The sodium carbonate yielded soda on being heated and the ammonium chloride, when mixed with carbon, regenerated the ammonium carbonate the process started from. Solvay's innovation was to introduce pressurized carbonating towers.

The system was soon adopted throughout the world and by 1900 95% of a greatly increased world production of soda came from the Solvay process. The price of soda fell by more than a half in the last quarter of the 19th century.

Solvay is also remembered for financing the great series of international conferences of physicists starting in 1911, in which much of the new nuclear and quantum physics was discussed.

Somerville, Mary (1780–1872) British astronomer and physical geographer

Mary Fairfax, as she was born in Jedburgh, Scotland, was the daughter of a naval officer. She received precisely one year of formal education before her marriage in 1804 to a cousin who was a captain in the Russian navy. After his death in 1807 she married another cousin, W. Somerville, an army physician, in 1812.

Somerville was unique in 19th-century British science because she was an independent female. Virtually all other women participated in science as the wife or sister of a husband or brother whom they assisted and sometimes went on to make some small contribution of their own. Her interest in science began when as a young girl she first heard of algebra and Euclid and satisfied her curiosity as to the nature of these subjects from books she purchased. She certainly received no encouragement from her father nor was her first husband much more sympathetic. She was more fortunate with her second husband, who encouraged and assisted her.

Living with her husband in London from 1816 she soon became a familiar and respected figure in the scientific circles of the capital. Her first significant achievement was her treatise on the *Mécanique céleste* (Celestial Mechanics) of Pierre Simon de Laplace. She was persuaded to undertake this difficult task by John Herschel and in 1831 750 copies of *The Mechanism of the Heavens* were published. The work was a great success and was used as a basic text in advanced astronomy for the rest of the century.

She followed this in 1834 with her *On the Connexion of the Physical Sciences*, a more popular but still serious work. In this she suggested that the perturbations of Uranus might reveal the existence of an undiscovered planet. Somerville was of course denied such obvious honors as a fellowship of the Royal Society as a result of her work.

She was, however, granted a government pension of £300 a year in 1837.

From 1840, because of the health of her husband, she moved to Europe living mainly in Italy. It was there that she produced her third and most original work, *Physical Geography* (1848). It was widely used as a university text book to the end of the century, although overshadowed by the *Kosmos* (Cosmos) of Friedrich von Humboldt, which came out in 1845.

She produced her fourth book, *On Molecular and Microscopic Science* (1869), at the age of 89 and was working on a second edition when she died.

When a hall was opened in Oxford in 1879 for the education of women it was appropriately named for her and was to produce sufficient talent to refute her own belief that genius was a gift not granted to the female sex.

Sommerfeld, Arnold Johannes Wilhelm (1868–1951) German physicist

Sommerfeld, the son of a physician, was born in Königsberg (now Kaliningrad in Russia) and educated at the university in his native city. He later taught at Göttingen, Clausthal, and Aachen before being appointed to the chair of theoretical physics at the University of Munich in 1906.

In 1916 Sommerfeld produced an important modification to the model of the atom proposed by Niels Bohr in 1913. In Bohr's model an atom consists of a central nucleus around which electrons move in definite circular orbits. The orbits are quantized, that is, the electrons occupy only orbits that have specific energies. The electrons can 'jump' to higher or lower levels by either absorbing or emitting photons of the appropriate frequency. It was the emission of just those frequencies that produced the familiar lines of the hydrogen spectrum. Increasing knowledge of the spectrum of hydrogen showed that Bohr's model could not account for the fine structure of the spectral lines. What at first had looked like a single line turned out to be in certain cases a number of lines close to each other. Sommerfeld's solution was to suggest that some of the electrons moved in elliptical rather than circular orbits. This required introducing a second quantum number, the azimuthal quantum number, l, in addition to the principal quantum number of Bohr, n. The two are simply related and together permit the fine structure of atomic spectra to be satisfactorily interpreted.

Sommerfeld was the author of an influential work that went through a number of editions in the 1920s, *Atombau und*

Spektrallinien (Atomic Structure and Spectral Lines).

Sondheimer, Franz (1926–1981) *British chemist*

Sondheimer was born at Stuttgart in Germany but moved with his family to Britain in 1937. He was educated at Imperial College, London, where he obtained his PhD in 1948. After serving as a research fellow with Robert Woodward at Harvard from 1949 to 1952 he spent a brief period as associate director of chemical research with Syntex in Mexico City before being appointed in 1956 professor of organic chemistry at the Weizmann Institute, Rehovoth, Israel. In 1964 Sondheimer returned to Britain where he held a Royal Society research professorship first at Cambridge and from 1967 at University College, London.

In 1952, while with Syntex, Sondheimer collaborated with Carl Djerassi in the synthesis of an oral estronelike compound, the precursor of the contraceptive pill. In the 1960s Sondheimer deployed his synthetic skills on the annulenes, monocyclic hydrocarbons with alternating double and single bonds like the familiar benzene ring. Such molecules were important in theoretical chemistry following the formulation in 1931 by Erich Hückel of his rule claiming that compounds with monocyclic planar rings containing $(4n + 2)\pi$ electrons should be aromatic. The rule obviously held for benzene ($n = 1$).

In 1956 Sondheimer and his colleagues discovered a relatively simple way to synthesize large-ring hydrocarbons and by the early 1960s they had produced annulenes with 14 and 18 carbon atoms, $n = 2$ and $n = 4$ respectively. 14–annulene is a highly unstable compound, which is not planar because of the positions of the hydrogen atoms on the molecule. 18–annulene has a planar ring obeying the Hückel rule and does have aromatic properties. The group also synthesized 30–annulene – a planar compound ($n = 7$). In 1981 while a visiting professor at Stanford, Sondheimer was found dead in his laboratory beside an empty cyanide bottle. He had apparently been suffering from depression.

Sosigenes (*c.* 1st century BC) *Egyptian astronomer*

Nothing seems to be known about Sosigenes apart from his design of the Julian calendar. By the time of Julius Caesar the Roman calendar was hopelessly out of alignment with the seasons. The Romans had traditionally had a lunar 12-month calendar of 355 days. To bring it into phase with the solar year an intercalary (inserted) month of 27 days was supposed to be added every other year to a reduced February of 23 or 24 days. In theory this should have produced a year of 366¼ days, which would have proved inaccurate in the long run but should have been controllable by skipping an intercalation whenever the discrepancy became too uncomfortable. For whatever reason the practice had not been followed and to cure the confusion Caesar felt in need of expert foreign advice. He called in Sosigenes, an Alexandrian Greek from Egypt. To restore the situation to normal he introduced two intercalary months between November and December totaling 67 days and one of 27 days after February producing the famous year of 'ultimate confusion' of 445 days in 46 BC. To ensure that harmony would continue he introduced what was the basic Egyptian year of 365 days plus a leap year every four years. This is in fact eleven minutes too long but it is a tribute to Sosigenes that it lasted for 1500 years before being modified.

Spallanzani, Lazzaro (1729–1799) *Italian biologist*

Spallanzani was born at Scandiano in Italy and educated at the Jesuit College, Reggio, before leaving to study jurisprudence at Bologna University. While at Bologna he developed an interest in natural history, which was probably encouraged by his cousin, Laura Bassi, who was professor of physics there. After receiving his doctorate he took minor orders and a few years later became a priest, although he continued to pursue his researches into natural history.

Spallanzani's most important experiments, published in 1767, questioned John Needham's 'proof' 20 years earlier of the spontaneous generation of microorganisms. He took solutions in which microorganisms normally breed and boiled them for 30 to 45 minutes before placing them in sealed flasks. No microorganisms developed, demonstrating that Needham's broth had not been boiled for long enough to sterilize it. Opponents of Spallanzani asserted, however, that he had destroyed a vital principle in the air by prolonged boiling. While conducting these experiments, Spallanzani showed that some organisms can survive for long periods in a vacuum: this was the first practical demonstration of anaerobiosis (the ability to live and grow without free oxygen).

In 1768 he submitted papers to the Royal Society on his findings concerning the regeneration of amputated parts in lower animals, and on the strength of this was elected a fellow of the Royal Society. In the same year Maria Theresa of Austria appointed Spallanzani to the chair of natural history at Pavia, which at that time was under Austrian dominion, and here he remained until his death. He was also in charge of the museum at Pavia and made many journeys around the Mediterranean collecting natural-history specimens for the museum.

Spallanzani's research interests covered a wide area and during his career he made important contributions to the understanding of digestion, reproduction, respiration, and blood circulation, as well as sensory perception in bats. He also (in 1785) managed to accomplish the artificial insemination of a dog.

Spedding, Frank Harold (1902–1984)
American chemist

Spedding was born at Hamilton, Ontario, in Canada and educated at the University of Michigan and Berkeley where he obtained his PhD in 1929. After working at Cornell from 1935 to 1937, he moved to Iowa State University, where he remained for the rest of his career. He was appointed professor of chemistry in 1941 and director of the Institute of Atomic Research from 1945 to 1968.

In 1942, at the request of Arthur Compton, Spedding and his Iowa colleagues devised new techniques for the purification of the uranium required urgently for the development of the atomic bomb. Their method reduced the price of uranium from $22 per pound to $1 per pound.

After the war Spedding put his new skills to separating the lanthanide elements, an extremely difficult task because of the similarity of their physical and chemical properties. The technique used on uranium, and later successfully applied to the lanthanides, was that of ion-exchange chromatography. A simple example is seen when hard water is allowed to percolate through a column of the mineral zeolite; calcium ions are absorbed by the mineral, which releases its own sodium ions into the water – in effect, an exchange of ions. In the late 1930s more efficient synthetic resins were introduced as ion exchangers.

Spedding passed lanthanide chlorides through an exchange resin that differentially absorbed the compounds present, thus allowing them to be separated. As a result, for the first time, chemists could deal with lanthanoids in substantial quantities.

In 1965 Spedding published, with Adrian Daane, an account of his work in his *Chemistry of Rare Earth Elements*.

Spemann, Hans (1869–1941) *German zoologist, embryologist, and histologist*

Spemann, who was born at Stuttgart in Germany, worked for a time in his father's bookshop there before graduating in zoology, botany, and physics at the universities of Heidelberg, Munich, and Würzburg. He was first an assistant, then a lecturer, at the Zoological Institute of Würzburg (1894–1908) before becoming professor at Rostock (1909–14). He was then successively associate director of the Kaiser Wilhelm Institute of Biology, Berlin (1914–19), and professor of zoology at Freiburg (1919–35).

Spemann's concept of embryonic induction, based on a lifetime's study of the development of amphibians such as newts, showed that certain parts of the embryo – the organizing centers – direct the development of groups of cells into particular organs and tissues. He further demonstrated an absence of predestined organs or tissues in the earliest stages of embryonic development; tissue excised from one part of the embryo and grafted onto another part will assume the character of the latter, losing its original nature. Spemann's highly original work, for which he received the Nobel Prize in 1935, paved the way for subsequent recognition of similar organizing centers in other animals groups. It is elaborated in *Experimentelle Beiträge zu einer Theorie der Entwicklung* (1936; Embryonic Development and Induction).

Sperry, Roger Wolcott (1913–1994) *American neurobiologist*

Sperry, who was born in Hartford, Connecticut, studied psychology at Oberlin College and zoology at the University of Chicago, where he obtained his PhD in 1941. He worked at Harvard, the Yerkes Primate Center, and at Chicago before he moved to the California Institute of Technology in 1954 as professor of psychobiology where he remained until 1984.

Sperry worked on the hemispheres of the brain. Architecturally the brain consists of two apparently identical halves constructed in such a way that each half controls the opposite side of the body. The language center of the human brain is located in most people in the left side alone. The two cerebral hemispheres are far from distinct anatomically, with a number of bands of nervous tissue (commissures) carrying many fibers from one side to the other. In the early 1950s Sperry set out to find how a creature would behave if all such commissures were severed resulting in a 'split brain'. To his surprise he found that monkeys and cats with split brains act much the same as normal animals. However, where learning was involved the creatures behaved as if they had two independent brains. Thus if a monkey was trained to discriminate between a square and a circle with one eye, the other being covered with a patch, then, if the situation was reversed the animal would have to relearn how to make the discrimination.

He also studied a 49-year-old man whose brain had been 'split' to prevent the spread of severe epileptic convulsions from one side to the other. He found that, though normal in other ways, the patient showed the effect of cerebral disconnection in any situation that required judgment or interpretation based on language. Sperry's work immediately posed the problem of whether there is any comparable specialization inherent in the human right-hand brain. This topic is receiving much attention.

Sperry also performed some equally dramatic experiments on nerve regeneration in amphibians. Although in mammals a severed optic nerve remains permanently severed, in certain amphibians such as the salamander it will regenerate. Sperry wondered if the nerves regenerate along the old pathway or whether a new one is formed. He found that whatever obstacles were placed before the nerve fiber it would invariably, however tortuous the path might be, find its way back to its original synaptic connection in the brain. This was shown most convincingly when, after severing the optic nerve, Sperry removed the eye, rotated it through 180° and replaced it. When food was presented to the right of the animal it would aim to the left, thus clearly showing the fibers had made their old functional connection. Sperry shared the 1981 Nobel Prize for physiology or medicine with David HUBEL and Torsten WIESEL.

Stahl, Franklin William (1910–)
American molecular biologist. See MESELSON, MATTHEW STANLEY.

Stahl, Georg Ernst (1660–1734)
German chemist and physician

Stahl was the son of a protestant minister from Ansbach in Germany. He studied medicine at Jena, graduating in 1684, and in 1687 was appointed physician to the duke of Sachsen-Weimar. He moved to Halle in 1694 where he became professor of medicine in the newly founded university. In 1716 he became physician to the king of Prussia.

Stahl developed phlogiston from the vague speculations of Johann Becher into a coherent theory, which dominated the chemistry of the latter part of the 18th cen-

tury until replaced by that of Antoine Lavoisier. Phlogiston was the combustible element in substances. If substances contained phlogiston they would burn and the fact that charcoal could be almost totally consumed meant that it was particularly rich in phlogiston. When a metal was heated it left a calx (a powdery substance) from which it was deduced that a metal was really calx plus phlogiston. The process could be reversed by heating the calx over charcoal, when the calx would take the phlogiston driven from the charcoal and return to its metallic form. It seemed to chemists that for the first time ever they could begin to understand the normal transformations that went on around them and the theory was the first rational explanation of combustion. It is no wonder that Stahl's theory was eagerly accepted and passionately supported.

As principles in addition to phlogiston Stahl accepted water, salt, and mercury. He also adopted the law of affinity that like reacts with like. However there were difficulties with the theory for it seemed that, to explain some interactions, phlogiston must have no weight or even negative weight for the bodies that gain it, far from becoming heavier, sometimes become lighter.

Stanley, Wendell Meredith (1904–1971) *American biochemist*

Stanley, who was born in Ridgeville, Indiana, gained his doctorate in chemistry from the University of Illinois in 1929 and then traveled to Munich to work on sterols. On his return to America he joined the Rockefeller Institute for Medical Research in Princeton, New Jersey, where he began research with the tobacco mosaic virus (TMV).

Stanley was impressed by John NORTHROP's success in crystallizing proteins and applied Northrop's techniques to his extracts of TMV. By 1935 he had obtained thin rodlike crystals of the virus and demonstrated that TMV still retained its infectivity after crystallization. Initially this achievement met with skepticism from many scientists who had thought viruses were similar to conventional living organisms and thus incapable of existence in a crystalline form. In 1946 Stanley's research was recognized by the award of the Nobel Prize for chemistry, which he shared with Northrop and with James SUMNER, who had crystallized the first enzyme.

During World War II Stanley worked on isolating the influenza virus and prepared a vaccine against it. From 1946 until his death he was director of the virus research laboratory at the University of California.

Stark, Johannes (1874–1957) *German physicist and spectroscopist*

Born at Schickenhof in Germany, Stark was educated at the University of Munich where he obtained his doctorate and began his teaching career in 1897. Between 1906 and 1922 he taught successively at the universities of Göttingen, Hannover (where he first became a professor), Aachen, Griefswald, and Würzburg. At this point his academic career came to an end. He first tried to start a porcelain industry in northern Germany but the years following World War I were not generous to new businesses. Despite the award of the Nobel Prize for physics in 1919 his attempt to return to academic life was not successful and he had been rejected by six German universities by 1928.

This was due to his general unpopularity and because he had become somewhat extreme in his denunciation of quantum theory and the theories of Albert Einstein as being the product of 'Jewish' science. Thus Stark, like Philipp Lenard, began to drift into Nazi circles and in 1930 joined the party. Unlike Lenard, who was content merely to rewrite the history of physics in the Aryan mode, Stark made a real bid for the control of German science. In 1933, although he was rejected by the Prussian Academy of Science, he succeeded in obtaining the presidency of the Imperial Institute of Physics and Technology, which he tried to use as a power base in his attempt to gain control of German physics. His attempt brought him into conflict with senior politicians and civil servants at the Reich Education Ministry, who saw him as too erratic and disruptive a force to be of much use to them, and consequently forced his resignation in 1939. Stark's final humiliation came in 1947, when he was sentenced to four years in a labor camp by a German de-Nazification court.

Stark first observed (1905) a shift of frequency in the radiation emitted by fast-moving charged particles (i.e., a Doppler effect). His other main scientific achievement was his discovery in 1913 of the spectral effect now known as the *Stark effect*, which won him the Nobel Prize. In this, following Pieter Zeeman's demonstration of the splitting of the spectral lines of a substance in a magnetic field, Stark succeeded in obtaining a similar phenomenon in an electric field. This is a quantum effect but Stark, although an early supporter of quantum theory, began to argue, with typical perversity, against the new theory as evidence for it mounted.

Starling, Ernest Henry (1866–1927) *British physiologist*

A Londoner by birth, Starling studied medicine at Guy's Hospital, London, where he obtained his MB in 1889 and eventually became head of the department of physiology. In 1899 he moved to University College, London, to become Jodrell Professor of Physiology, a position he held until his death.

In 1896 Starling introduced the concept of the *Starling equilibrium*, which tried to relate the pressure of the blood to its behavior in the capillary system. He realized that the high pressure of the arterial system is enough to force fluids through the thin-walled capillaries into the tissues. But as the blood is divided through more and more capillaries its pressure falls. By the time it reaches the venous system the pressure of the fluid in the surrounding tissues is higher than that of blood in the venous capillaries, allowing much of the fluid lost from the arterial side to be regained. In theory the two systems should be in a state of equilibrium. In reality the system is complicated by the hydrostatic pressure of the blood and the osmotic pressure arising from the various salts and proteins dissolved in it.

In 1915 Starling formulated the important law (*Starling's law*) stating that the energy of contraction of the heart is a function of the length of the muscle fiber. As the heart fills with blood the muscle is forced to expand and stretch; the force with which the muscle contracts to expel the blood from the heart is simply a function of the extent to which it has been stretched. The curve that relates the two variables of the heart – pressure and volume – is known as *Starling's curve*.

Starling's best-known work was his collaboration with William Bayliss in the discovery of the hormone secretin in 1902. The normal pancreas releases a number of juices into the duodenum to aid in the process of digestion. By cutting all the pancreatic nerves and noting the continuing secretion of the pancreatic juices Starling and Bayliss showed that the release of the juices was not under nervous control. They concluded that a chemical, rather than a nervous, message must be sent to the pancreas through the blood when food enters the duodenum. They proposed to call the chemical messenger secretin. For the general class of such chemicals Starling proposed, in 1905, the term 'hormone', from the Greek root meaning to excite. Thus endocrinology – a major branch of medicine and physiology – had been created.

It was widely known before the outbreak

of World War I that Starling and Bayliss had been the strongest of the candidates for the Nobel Prize for physiology and medicine. However, as no awards were made during the war they missed out completely; the prizes after 1918 were awarded for more recent work. As for honors from his own country, Starling was far too outspoken about the incompetent direction of the war even to be considered.

Stas, Jean Servais (1813–1891) *Belgian chemist*

Stas, who was born at Louvain in Belgium, trained initially as a physician. He later switched to chemistry, serving as assistant to Jean Dumas before being appointed to the chair of chemistry at the Royal Military School in Brussels in 1840. He had to retire in 1869 because of trouble with his voice through a throat ailment and became instead commissioner of the mint, but retired from this in 1872.

Stas was well known in his time for his extremely accurate determination of atomic weights. At first he supported William Prout's hypothesis that the weight of all elements is an exact multiple of that of the hydrogen atom. All his early measurements seemed to agree with this theory, but as his work progressed he seemed to be getting more and more fractional numbers and this turned him into the most articulate and damaging opponent of Prout. His work laid the foundations for the eventual formation of the periodic system.

Stas also carried out chemical analysis on potato blight and nicotine poisoning.

Staudinger, Hermann (1881–1965) *German chemist*

Staudinger, was born in Worms, Germany, the son of a philosophy professor; he was educated at the universities of Darmstadt, Munich, and Halle where, in 1903, he obtained his doctorate. He taught at the University of Strasbourg, the Karlsruhe Technical College, and the Federal Institute of Technology in Zurich before taking up an appointment at the University of Freiburg in 1926, where he remained until his retirement in 1951.

In 1922 Staudinger introduced the term 'macromolecule' into chemistry and went on to propound the unorthodox view that there was no reason why molecules could not reach any size whatever. He argued that chain molecules could be constructed of almost any length in which the atoms were joined together by the normal valence bonds. Innocuous as such a view may now

sound, at the time it was considered very strange and, by some, quite absurd.

The accepted view, the aggregate theory, regarded molecules in excess of a molecular weight of 5000 as aggregates of much smaller molecules joined together by the secondary valence (nebenvalenzen) of Alfred Werner. Staudinger argued for his theory at length at a stormy meeting of the Zurich Chemical Society in 1926 in front of his most important critics. Within a few years the issue would be decisively settled in favor of Staudinger by the development of the ultracentrifuge by Theodor Svedberg. Consequently Staudinger was awarded the Nobel Prize for chemistry in 1953.

Stebbins, George Ledyard (1906–   ) *American geneticist*

Born in Lawrence, New York, Stebbins studied biology at Harvard where he obtained his PhD in 1931. After working at Colgate University he moved to Berkeley in 1935 and to Davis in 1950, where he established the department of genetics, holding the chair until his retirement in 1973.

In his *Variation and Evolution in Plants* (1950) Stebbins was the first to apply the modern synthesis of evolution, as expounded by Julian Huxley, Ernst Mayr, and others to plants. In collaboration with Ernest Babcock, Stebbins also studied polyploidy – the occurrence of three or more times the basic (haploid) number of chromosomes. When an artificial means of inducing polyploidy was developed Stebbins applied it to wild grasses and in 1944 managed to establish an artificially created species in a natural environment. He also used the technique to double the chromosome number of sterile interspecific hybrids and in so doing created fertile polyploid hybrids. Fertility tends to be restored in polyploid hybrids because the two different sets of chromosomes from the parent species will each have an identical set to pair with at meiosis and so the formation of gametes is not disturbed. Polyploids have proved extremely useful in plant-breeding work. Knowledge of naturally occurring polyploid systems has also helped greatly in understanding the relationships and consequently in classifying difficult genera such as *Taraxacum* (the dandelions).

Stebbins also studied gene action and proposed that mutations that result in a change in morphology act by regulating the rate of cell division in specific areas of the plant.

Stefan, Josef (1835–1893) *Austrian physicist*

Stefan was educated in his native Klagenfurt and at the University of Vienna. In 1863 he became professor of mathematics and physics at Vienna University and remained there for the rest of his life.

Stefan's wide-ranging work included investigations into electromagnetic induction, thermomagnetic effects, optical interference, thermal conductivity, diffusion, capillarity, and the kinetic theory of gases. However, he is best remembered for his work on heat radiation in 1879. After examining the heat losses from platinum wire he concluded that the rate of loss was proportional to the fourth power of the absolute temperature; i.e., rate of loss = σT^4. In 1884 one of his students, Ludwig Boltzmann, showed that this law was exact only for black bodies (ones that radiate all wavelengths) and could be deduced from theoretical principles. The law is now known as the *Stefan–Boltzmann law*; the constant of proportionality, σ, as *Stefan's constant*.

Stefan was a good experimental physicist and a well-liked teacher. During his lifetime he held various important positions, including *Rector Magnificus* of the University (1876) and secretary (1875) then vice-president (1885) of the Vienna Academy of Sciences.

Stein, William Howard (1911–1980) *American biochemist. See* MOORE, STANFORD.

Steinberger, Jack (1921–) *American physicist. See* LEDERMAN, LEON MAX.

Steno, Nicolaus (1638–1686) *Danish anatomist and geologist*

The son of a goldsmith, Steno was educated in his native city of Copenhagen before beginning his travels and studies abroad in 1660. While studying anatomy in Amsterdam he discovered the parotid salivary duct, also called *Stensen's duct* after the Danish form of his name. Other important anatomical findings included his realization that muscles are composed of fibrils and his demonstration that the pineal gland exists in animals other than man. (René Descartes had considered the pineal gland the location of the soul, believing that both were found only in man.)

Steno obtained his medical degree from Leiden in 1664 and the following year went to Florence, where he became physician to the grand duke Ferdinand II. In the field of geology he made important contributions to the study of crystals and fossils. His observations on quartz crystals showed that, though the crystals differ greatly in physical appearance, they all have the same angles between corresponding faces. This led to the formulation of *Steno's law*, which states that the angles between two corresponding faces on the crystals of any chemical or mineral species are constant and characteristic of the species. It is now known that this is a consequence of the internal regular ordered arrangement of the atoms or molecules.

Steno's geological and mineralogical views were expressed in his *De solido intra solidum naturaliter contento dissertationis prodromus* (1669; An Introductory Discourse on a Solid Body Contained Naturally Within a Solid). The curious title refers to the solid bodies we refer to as fossils found in other solid bodies. Steno was particularly concerned with the common Mediterranean fossils known at the time as 'glossipetrae' (tongue stones), thought by some to have fallen from the sky and by others to have grown in the earth like plants. They were triangular, flat, hard, and with discernible crenellations along two sides.

In 1666 Steno was presented with the head of a giant shark. He was immediately struck by the close similarity between the glossipetrae and sharks' teeth. In attempting to understand this correlation Steno formulated two important principles to explain how solids form in solids. By the first, an ordering rule, it proved possible to tell which solidified first by noting which solid was impressed on the other. As glossipetrae left their imprint in the surrounding rocks they must have been formed first. Therefore it made no sense to suppose that they grew in the strata.

Steno's second rule proclaimed that if two solids were similar in all observed respects then they were likely to have been produced in the same way. It followed that the similarity between the glossipetrae and sharks' teeth revealed them as fossilized teeth, a revolutionary claim at the time. But *Steno's rules* offered more than an explanation of glossipetrae; they in fact offered a novel way of interpreting the fossil record, one which would be followed increasingly by later geologists.

Steno was brought up a Lutheran but converted to Catholicism in 1667, taking holy orders in 1675. In 1677 he was appointed Titular Bishop of Titopolis (in Turkey), catering for the spiritual needs of the few Catholics surviving in Scandinavia and Northern Germany.

Stern, Curt (1902–1981) *German–American geneticist*

Born at Hamburg in Germany, Stern received his PhD in zoology from the University of Berlin in 1923. He spent two years as a postdoctoral fellow with T. H. Morgan at Columbia before being appointed *Privatdozent* at the University of Berlin in 1928. Stern returned to America as a refugee from Nazi Germany in 1933 and settled first at the University of Rochester, serving as professor of zoology from 1941 until 1947. He then moved to the chair of zoology and genetics at the University of California, Berkeley, from which post he retired in 1970.

Stern, in 1931, was the first geneticist actually to demonstrate the phenomenon of crossing over in the chromosomes of *Drosophila*. That crossing over did occur had been assumed and widely used by Morgan and his school since about 1914. It was, however, only when Stern managed to get flies with a pair of homologous chromosomes that were structurally markedly different from each other at both ends that experimental support could be produced. (Normally chromosomes that pair together are structurally identical.) Stern knew that the longer chromosome (long–long) carried the genes AB while the shorter chromosome (short–short) carried the genes A^1B^1. Cytological examination of the offspring revealed that those carrying the genes AB^1 or A^1B had long–short and short–long chromosomes respectively, showing that crossing over had indeed occurred. In the same year comparable evidence was provided by Harriett Creighton and Barbara McClintock from their work with maize.

Stern later worked on problems concerned with genetic mosaics and demonstrated that crossing over can occur in the somatic (nonreproductive) cells as well as the germ cells. He also produced the widely read textbook *Principles of Human Genetics* (1949).

Stern, Otto (1888–1969) German–American physicist

Stern, who was born at Sohrau (now in Poland), was educated at the University of Breslau where he obtained his doctorate in 1912. He joined Einstein at the University of Prague and later followed him to Zurich (1913). After teaching at a number of German universities he was appointed an associate professor of theoretical physics at Rostock in 1921. He later moved (1923) to the University of Hamburg as professor of physical chemistry, but resigned in opposition to Hitler in 1933 and emigrated to America, where he took up an appointment with the Carnegie Institute of Technology at Pittsburgh. He retired in 1945.

Stern's main research came from his work with molecular beams of atoms and molecules (beams of atoms traveling in the same direction at low pressure, with no collisions occurring within the beam). Using such beams it is possible to measure directly the speeds of molecules in a gas. In 1920 Stern used a molecular beam of silver atoms to test an important prediction of quantum theory – namely, that certain atoms have magnetic moments (behave like small magnets) and that in a magnetic field these magnets take only certain orientations to the field direction.

The phenomenon is known as space quantization, and it could be predicted theoretically that silver atoms could have only two orientations in an external field. To test this, Stern with Walter Gerlach passed a beam of silver atoms through a nonuniform magnetic field and observed that it split into two separate beams. This, the famous *Stern–Gerlach experiment*, was a striking piece of evidence for the validity of the quantum theory and Stern received the 1943 Nobel Prize for physics for this work.

Stern used molecular beams for other measurements. Thus he was able to measure the magnetic moment of the proton by this technique. He also succeeded in demonstrating that atoms and molecules had wavelike properties by diffracting them in experiments similar to those of Clinton J. DAVISSON on the electron.

Stevin, Simon (1548–1620) Flemish mathematician and engineer

Stevin was also known as Stevinus, the Latinized form of his name. Born in the city of Bruges, he worked for a time as a clerk in Antwerp, eventually working his way up to become quartermaster of the army under Prince Maurice of Nassau. While in this post he devised a system of sluices, which could flood the land as a defense should Holland be attacked.

Stevin was a versatile man who contributed to several areas of science. Mathematics owes to him the introduction of the decimal system of notating fractions. This system was perfected when John Napier invented the decimal point. Stevin helped to popularize the practice of writing scientific works in modern languages (in his case Dutch) rather than Latin, which for so long had been the traditional European language of learning. However such was the hold of the old ways that Willebrord Snell thought it was worthwhile to translate some of Stevin's work into Latin. To hydrostatics he contributed the discovery that the shape of a vessel containing liquid is irrelevant to the pressure that liquid exerts. He also did some experimental work in statics and in the study of the Earth's magnetism.

Stokes, Adrian (1887–1927) Anglo-Irish bacteriologist

Stokes, whose father worked in the Indian Civil Service, was born at Lausanne in Switzerland and educated at Trinity College, Dublin, where he obtained his MD in 1911. After serving in the Royal Army Medical Corps during the war, in which he was awarded the DSO, he returned to Dublin in 1919 as professor of bacteriology but soon moved to London, where in 1922 he became professor of pathology at Guy's Hospital.

In 1920 Stokes visited Lagos to study yellow fever. He was anxious to test the suggestion of the Japanese bacteriologist Hideyo Noguchi that yellow fever was caused by the bacillus *Leptospira icteroides*, but it was not until his second visit to Lagos in 1927 that he made the vital breakthrough.

Stokes succeeded, for the first time, in infecting an experimental animal (the rhesus monkey) with the disease. He went on to show that while he could pass yellow fever from monkey to monkey there was no evidence that Noguchi's bacillus was also transmitted. But before he could proceed further Stokes, who was daily handling infected monkey blood, contracted the disease and joined the growing list of bacteriologists who had fallen victim to the virus.

Stokes, Sir George Gabriel (1819–1903) British mathematician and physicist

Stokes was born at Skreen (now in the Republic of Ireland) and studied at Cambridge, remaining there throughout his life. In 1849 he became Lucasian Professor of Mathematics, but he found it necessary to supplement his slender income from this post by teaching at the Government School of Mines in London. He held his Cambridge chair until his death aged 84. He was the member of parliament for the university and among his many honors were a baronetcy conferred on him in 1889.

Stokes was equally interested in the theoretical and experimental sides of physics and did important work in a wide area of fields, including hydrodynamics, elasticity, and the diffraction of light. In hydrodynamics he derived the formula now known as *Stokes's law*, giving the force resisting motion of a spherical body through a viscous fluid. Among Stokes's other fields of study was fluorescence – one of his experimental discoveries was the transparency of quartz to ultraviolet light. He was also much interested in the then influential concept of the ether as an explanation of the propagation of light. Stokes became aware of some inherent difficulties with the concept, but rather than rejecting the whole idea of an ether he tried to explain these problems away by using work he had done on elastic solids, though naturally enough problems arose with his own ideas.

Stokes was perceptive in his views of other physicists' work. For example, he was among the first to appreciate the importance of the work of James Joule and to see the true meaning of the spectral lines discovered by Joseph von Fraunhofer.

Stoney, George Johnstone (1826–1911) Irish physicist

Stoney, the son of an impoverished landowner, was born at Oakley Park (now in the Republic of Ireland) and educated at Trinity College, Dublin. After graduation in 1848 he worked as an assistant to the astronomer, Lord Rosse, at his observatory at Parsonstown until 1853 when he was appointed professor of natural philosophy at Queen's College, Galway. However, from 1857 onwards Stoney worked as an administrator, first as secretary of Queen's University, Belfast, and finally, from 1882 until 1893, as superintendent of civil service examinations.

Stoney is best known for his introduction of the term 'electron' into science. Although he is reported to have spoken of "an absolute unit of electricity" as early as 1874, his first public use of the term in print was in 1891 when he spoke of "these charges, which it will be convenient to call electrons" before the Royal Society of Dublin.

He did however make more substantial contributions to science than this and in early spectroscopy his work was of considerable significance. He began, in 1868, by making a crucial distinction between two types of molecular motion. There was the motion of a molecule in a gas relative to other molecules, which Stoney was able to exclude as the cause of spectra. There was also internal motion of a molecule, which according to Stoney produces the spectral lines. He went on to tackle, with little real success, the difficult problem of establishing an exact formula for the numerical relationship between the lines in the hydrogen spectrum. This problem was solved by the quantum theory of Niels Bohr.

Störmer, Horst L. (1949–　) German–American physicist

Störmer was born in Frankfurt-am-Main, Germany, and gained his PhD in physics in 1977 from Stuttgart University. From 1992 to 1998 he was supervisor of the Physical Research Laboratory, Bell Laboratories, where he studied the fractional quantum Hall effect. In 1998 he moved to Columbia University, New York. In 1998 Störmer shared the Nobel Prize for physics with Robert LAUGHLIN and Daniel TSUI, for their discovery and explanation of a new form of quantum fluid with fractionally charged excitations.

Strabo (c. 63 BC–c. AD 23) *Greek geographer and historian*

Strabo, who was born at Amaseia (now Amasya in Turkey), traveled to Rome in 44 BC and remained there until about 31 BC. He visited Corinth in 29 BC and in about 24 BC sailed up the Nile.

Although the historical writings of Strabo, including his *Historical Sketches*, in 47 books, have been almost entirely lost, his *Geography*, in 17 books, has survived virtually intact. This major geographical work is an important source of information on the ancient world. In it Strabo accepted the traditional description of the Earth as divided into five zones with the *oikoumene*, or inhabited part, represented as a parallelogram spread over eight lines of latitude and seven meridians of longitude. Where he excelled, however, was in the field of historical and cultural geography and he gave a detailed account of the history and culture of the lands and people of the Roman Empire and of such areas as India, which lay beyond the dominion of Augustus. In this he quoted much from the earlier Greeks, including Eratosthenes, and Artemidorus.

Strabo, not content merely to describe the lands of the civilized world, also wished to understand its enormous diversity. He rejected the simple climatic determinism that he attributed to the Stoic Poseidonius, arguing in its place for the role of institutions and education. Despite the value of this work Strabo seemed to exercise little influence until Byzantine times.

Strassmann, Fritz (1902–1980) *German chemist*

Strassmann was born at Boppard in Germany and educated at the Technical University at Hannover. He taught at Hannover and at the Kaiser Wilhelm Institute before being appointed to the chair of inorganic and nuclear chemistry at the University of Mainz in 1946. In 1953 he became director of chemistry at the Max Planck Institute.

In 1938 Strassmann collaborated with Otto Hahn on the experiment that first clearly revealed the phenomenon of nuclear fission.

Strömgren, Bengt Georg Daniel (1908–1987) *Swedish–Danish astronomer*

Elis Strömgren, father of Bengt, was an astronomer of distinction who served as director of the Copenhagen Observatory. His son was born at Gothenburg in Sweden and studied at the University of Copenhagen. After obtaining his PhD there in 1929 he joined the staff and was appointed professor of astronomy in 1938. He succeeded his father as director in 1940. He later moved to America, serving from 1951 to 1957 as professor at the University of Chicago and director of the Yerkes and McDonald observatories. He was a member of the Institute for Advanced Study, Princeton, from 1957 until 1967, when he returned to Copenhagen as professor of astrophysics.

In the 1930s and 1940s Strömgren engaged in pioneering work on emission nebulae – huge clouds of interstellar gas and dust shining by their own light. He showed that they consist largely of ionized hydrogen, H II to the spectroscopist. If hot young stars were embedded in uniformly but thinly distributed neutral hydrogen, then the emission by them of ultraviolet radiation would virtually ionize the gas completely. To meet this condition the stars would need a surface temperature of some 25,000 kelvin. At a certain distance from the star, the *Strömgren radius*, the emitted photons of radiation would no longer possess sufficient energy to ionize the hydrogen, leading to a sharp boundary between ionized and cooler nonionized regions. Strömgren showed that this distance would depend on the density of the hydrogen and the stellar temperature.

A typical example of the process described by Strömgren is to be found in the Orion nebula. Later work has however shown that there are three types of emission nebulae, two of which are produced by different mechanisms.

Struve, Friedrich Georg Wilhelm von (1793–1864) *German–Russian astronomer*

Struve, who was born at Altona in Germany, moved to Dorpat in Latvia in 1808 in order to escape conscription into the Napoleonic army then in control of Germany. He took a degree in philology in 1811 before becoming professor of astronomy and mathematics in Dorpat in 1813. In 1817 he became director of the Dorpat Observatory, which he equipped with a 9.5-inch (24-

cm) refractor that he used in a massive survey of binary stars from the north celestial pole to 15°S. He measured 3112 binaries – discovering well over 2000 – and cataloged his results in *Stellarum Duplicium Mensurae Micrometricae* (1837; Micrometric Measurements of Double Stars).

In 1835 Czar Nicholas I persuaded Struve to set up a new observatory at Pulkovo, near St. Petersburg. There in 1840 Struve became, with Friedrich Bessel and Thomas Henderson, one of the first astronomers to detect parallax. He chose Vega, a bright star with a larger-than-normal proper motion and soon established a parallactic measurement (that was, however, too high).

Struve founded a dynasty of astronomers that is still in existence. He was succeeded by his son Otto at Pulkovo, his grandson Hermann became director of the Berlin Observatory, and his great-grandson, Otto Struve, became director of the Yerkes Observatory in Wisconsin.

Struve, Otto (1897–1963) *Russian– American astronomer*

Struve, who was born at Kharkov in Russia, came from a long line of distinguished astronomers, being the great grandson of its founder Friedrich Georg von Struve. His father was the professor of astronomy and director of the observatory at the University of Kharkov and he had two uncles who were directors of German observatories. His studies at the university were interrupted by World War I but he finally graduated in 1919. Called up again in 1919 after the revolution, he ended up destitute in Turkey in 1920. Following a journey of some difficulty he finally arrived in America in 1921 where he attended the University of Chicago, obtaining his PhD in 1923. He worked at the Yerkes Observatory, serving as director from 1932 to 1947 as well as professor of astrophysics at Chicago for the same period. He played an important role in the founding of the McDonald Observatory on Mount Locke in Texas and the planning of its 82-inch (2.1-m) reflecting telescope, then the second largest in the world. He served as McDonald's first director from 1939 to 1950. Struve moved to a less demanding position at the University of California at Berkeley in 1950 but agreed in 1959 to become the first director of the National Radio Astronomy Observatory at Green Bank in West Virginia. Forced to resign in 1962 owing to ill health, he died shortly after.

Although Struve spent much of his time in administration and organization, he was able to conduct some major observational work. He made spectroscopic studies of binary and variable stars, stellar rotation, stellar atmospheres, and, possibly most important, of interstellar matter.

One of the problems facing astronomers at the beginning of the century was whether there was any interstellar matter and if so, did it significantly absorb or distort distant starlight. This was no trivial question for the answer could make nonsense of many accounts of the distribution of stars. In 1904 Johannes Hartmann had argued for the presence of interstellar calcium by pointing out that the calcium spectral lines associated with the binary system Delta Orionis did not oscillate with the other spectral lines as the stars orbited each other. This work was extended by Vesto Slipher in 1908 and 1912.

Struve produced evidence on the next crucial point as to whether the interstellar matter was diffuse and pervasive or only local and associated with individual star systems. In 1929, in collaboration with B.P. Gerasimovic, he showed that it exists throughout the Galaxy. This work was also done independently by John Plaskett. In 1937 Struve discovered the presence of interstellar hydrogen, in ionized form, which though much more prevalent than calcium was initially more difficult to detect.

Sturgeon, William (1783–1850) *British physicist*

Sturgeon's father, a shoemaker of Whittington, England, has been described as an "idle poacher who neglected his family." Seeing little future as an apprentice cobbler Sturgeon enlisted in the army in 1802. While serving in Newfoundland his interest in science was aroused while watching a violent thunderstorm. Finding that no one seemed able to explain satisfactorily to him the cause and nature of lightning, he started reading whatever science books were available. This led him to the study of mathematics and Latin. When he left the army in 1820 he had acquired a considerable amount of scientific knowledge and skill. He began to write popular articles, joined the Woolwich Literary Society, and must have so impressed his associates that a move was made to find him a more suitable job than the shoemaking he was being forced back into. Thus in 1824 he was appointed to a lectureship in experimental philosophy at the East India Company's Royal Military College at Addiscombe.

In 1840 he moved to Manchester as the superintendent of the Royal Victoria Gallery of Practical Science. In 1836 he began the publication of the *Annals of Elec-*

tricity, the first periodical of its kind to be issued in Britain.

After various further appointments as an itinerant lecturer he was awarded a government pension of £200 a year for his services to science. His collected papers, *Scientific Researches*, were published in 1850.

Sturgeon made several fundamental contributions to the new science of electricity. The cell devised by Alessandro Volta had certain inherent weaknesses – any impurity in the zinc plates used caused erosion of the electrode. In 1828 Sturgeon found that amalgamating the plate with mercury made it resistant to the electrolyte. More important was his construction in about 1821 of the first electromagnet. Following the work of François Arago he wound 16 turns of copper wire around a one-foot iron bar, which, when bent into the shape of a horseshoe, was powerful enough to lift a weight of 9 pounds when the wire was connected to a single voltaic cell. He demonstrated his magnets in 1825 in London. More powerful ones were soon built by Joseph Henry and Michael Faraday.

In later years Sturgeon also made improvements to the design of the galvanometer, inventing the moving-coil galvanometer in 1836. In the same year he introduced the first commutator for a workable electric motor (1836).

Sturtevant, Alfred Henry (1891–1970) *American geneticist*

Born in Jacksonville, Illinois, Sturtevant graduated at Columbia University in 1912 and continued there, working for his PhD under the supervision of T. H. Morgan. His thesis dealt with certain aspects of fruit fly (*Drosophila*) genetics, the research being conducted in the famous 'fly room' at Columbia.

During this period Sturtevant developed a method for finding the linear arrangement of genes along the chromosome. This technique, termed 'chromosome mapping', relies on the analysis of groups of linked genes. His paper, published in 1913, describes the location of six sex-linked genes as deduced by the way in which they associate with each other: it is one of the classic papers in genetics.

Sturtevant later discovered the so-called 'position effect', in which the expression of a gene depends on its position in relation to other genes. He also demonstrated that crossing over between chromosomes is prevented in regions where a part of the chromosome material is inserted the wrong way round. This had important implications for genetic analysis. Although employed by the Carnegie Institution in 1915, Sturtevant continued working at Columbia until 1928. He then moved to the California Institute of Technology, where he was professor of genetics and biology until his death. He wrote many important papers and books and was one of the authors of *The Mechanism of Mendelian Heredity* (1915).

Suess, Eduard (1831–1914) *Austrian geologist*

Suess, born the son of a businessman in London, was educated at the University of Prague. He began work, in 1852, in the Hofmuseum, Vienna, before moving to the University of Vienna in 1856 where he became professor of geology in 1861. Besides being an academic Suess served as a member of the Reichsrat (parliament) from 1872 to 1896. He was responsible for the provision of pure water to Vienna by the construction of an aqueduct in 1873 and the prevention of frequent flooding by the opening of the Danube canal in 1875.

His major work as a geologist was his publication of *Das Antlitz der Erde* (1883–88), translated into English as *The Face of the Earth* (5 vols., 1904–24). This was not a particularly original work but acquired significance as being the great synthesis of the achievements of the later 19th-century geologists, geographers, paleontologists, and so on. He also published, in 1857, a classic work on the origin of the Alps.

Suess was the first to propose the existence of the great early southern continent, Gondwanaland. He was impressed by the distribution of a fern, *Glossopteris*, present during the Carboniferous period. It was found in such widely scattered lands as Australia, India, South Africa, and South America. Suess therefore proposed that these lands had once formed part of one great continent, which he named for the Gonds, the supposed aboriginal Indians.

Sumner, James Batcheller (1877–1955) *American biochemist*

Sumner, a wealthy cotton manufacturer's son from Canton, Massachusetts, was educated at Harvard, where he obtained his PhD in 1914. In the same year he took up an appointment at the Cornell Medical School where, in 1929, he became professor of biochemistry.

Despite having lost an arm in a shooting accident at 17, Sumner persisted in his desire to become an experimental chemist. In 1917 he began his attempt to isolate a pure enzyme. He chose for his attempt urease, which catalyzes the breakdown of urea into ammonia and carbon dioxide and is found in large quantities in the jack bean. After much effort he found, in 1926, that if he dissolved urease in 30% acetone and then chilled it, crystals formed. The crystal had high urease activity. Moreover Sumner's crystals were clearly protein and however hard he tried to separate the protein from them he always failed. He was therefore forced to conclude that urease, an enzyme, was a protein. However, this ran against the authority of Richard Willstätter who had earlier isolated enzymes in which no protein was detectable. In fact, protein was in Willstätter's samples, but in such small quantities as to be undetected by his techniques.

Consequently little attention was paid to Sumner's announcement and it was only when John NORTHROP succeeded in crystallizing further protein enzymes in the early 1930s that his work was properly acknowledged. In 1946 for "his discovery that enzymes can be crystallized" he was awarded the Nobel Prize for chemistry jointly with Northrop and Wendell STANLEY.

Sutherland, Earl (1915–1974) *American physiologist*

Born in Burlingame, Kansas, Sutherland was educated at Washington University, St. Louis. After serving in World War II as an army doctor he returned to St. Louis but in 1963 moved to Vanderbilt University, Tennessee, as professor of physiology. In the year before his death Sutherland joined the University of Miami Medical School in Florida.

In 1957 Sutherland discovered a molecule of great biological significance – 3,5-adenosine monophosphate, more familiarly known as cyclic AMP. At that time he was working with T. Rall on the way in which the hormone adrenaline (epinephrine) effects an increase in the amount of glucose in the blood. They found that the hormone stimulated the release of the enzyme adenyl cyclase into liver cells. This in turn converts adenosine triphosphate (ATP) to cyclic AMP, which then initiates the complex chain converting the glycogen stored in the liver into glucose in the blood. The significance of this reaction is that adrenaline does not act directly on the molecules in the liver cell; it apparently needs and 'calls for' what soon became described as a 'second messenger', cyclic AMP.

Sutherland went on to show that other hormones, such as insulin, also used cyclic AMP as a second messenger and that it was in fact used to control many processes of the cell. For his discovery of cyclic AMP

Sutherland was awarded the 1971 Nobel Prize for physiology or medicine.

Svedberg, Theodor (1884–1971) *Swedish chemist*

Svedberg, born the son of a civil engineer in Fleräng, Sweden, was educated at the University of Uppsala, where he obtained his doctorate in 1908. He spent his whole career at the university, becoming a lecturer in physical chemistry in 1907, a professor (1912–49), and finally, in 1949, director of the Institute of Nuclear Chemistry.

In 1924 he introduced the ultracentrifuge as a technique for investigating the molecular weights of very large molecules. In a suspension of particles, there is a tendency for the particles to settle (under the influence of gravity); this is opposed by Brownian motion, i.e., by collision with molecules. The rate of sedimentation depends on the size and weight of the particles, and can be used to measure these.

Svedberg applied this to measuring the sedimentation of proteins in solution, using an ultracentrifuge that generated forces much greater than that of the Earth's gravitational field. Using this, he could measure the molecular weights of proteins and was able to show that these were much higher than originally thought (hemoglobin, for instance, has a molecular weight of about 68,000).

Apart from confirming the claim made by Hermann Staudinger for the existence of giant molecules, Svedberg's invention also settled one further question. The same protein invariably yielded the same weight thus implying that they did have a definite size and composition and were not, as Wilhelm Ostwald had earlier maintained, irregular assemblies of smaller molecules. For his work on the ultracentrifuge Svedberg was awarded the Nobel Prize for chemistry in 1926.

Svedberg was less successful with the inference he drew from his measurements of protein molecular weights. He thought that the molecular weight of egg albumin formed the basic protein unit of which all the other proteins were multiples. Following later research by crystallographers in the 1930s this view was disproved.

Swammerdam, Jan (1637–1680) *Dutch naturalist and microscopist*

Swammerdam, an Amsterdam apothecary's son, studied medicine at Leiden University, graduating in 1667. However he never practiced and instead devoted his life to microscopical studies of a widely varying nature. His most important work, namely the discovery and description of red blood corpuscles in 1658, was completed before he went to university. He later demonstrated experimentally that muscular contraction involves a change in the shape but not volume of the muscle. He also studied movements of the heart and lungs and discovered the valves in the lymph vessels that are named for him.

Swammerdam is also remembered for his pioneering work on insects. He collected some 3000 different species and illustrated and described the anatomy, reproductive processes, and life histories of many of these. This work, together with his system of insect classification, laid the foundations of modern entomology. Swammerdam's *Biblia naturae* (Book of Nature), published long after his death (1737–38), still stands as one of the finest one-man collections of microscopical observations.

At the theoretical level Swammerdam developed a new argument in support of the preformationist position, the view that organisms are born already formed. His argument, first presented in his *Historia insectorum* (1669; Account of Insects), was based upon the nature of insect metamorphosis. At first sight it might appear that the metamorphic process supported the alternative view of development, epigenesis, the claim that organisms develop gradually and in sequence. Swammerdam, however, revealed a different picture when, with the aid of a microscope, he succeeded in identifying structures belonging to butterflies in pupae and caterpillars. The caterpillar, Swammerdam insisted, was not changed into a butterfly, rather grew by the expansion of parts already formed. Nor does the tadpole change into a frog; it becomes a frog "by the infolding and increasing of some of its parts." In proof of his position Swammerdam would display a silkworm to his critics, peel off the outer skin, and display the rudiments of the wings within.

In the same work Swammerdam added one more piece of evidence against the claim that organisms can generate spontaneously. Insects found in plant galls, he pointed out, developed from eggs laid therein by visiting flies.

Sylvester, James Joseph (1814–1897)
British mathematician

Born in London, Sylvester studied mathematics at Cambridge but was not granted his BA degree since he was a practicing Jew. The relevant statute was later revoked and Sylvester was granted both his BA and MA in 1871. He was widely read in a number of languages and was a keen amateur musician and a prolific poet. Feeling unable to keep an academic post as a mathematician Sylvester worked first in an insurance company and later as a lawyer. In 1876 he went to America to become the first professor of mathematics at Johns Hopkins University. He became the first editor of the *American Journal of Mathematics* and did much to develop mathematics in America. He returned to England in 1883 to become Savilian Professor of Geometry at Oxford University.

Sylvester's best mathematical work was in the theory of invariants and number theory. With his lifelong friend the British mathematician Arthur Cayley, he was one of the creators of the theory of algebraic invariants, which proved to be of great importance for mathematical physics.

Synge, Richard Laurence Millington
(1914–1994) *British chemist. See* MARTIN, ARCHER JOHN PORTER.

Szent-Györgyi, Albert von (1893–1986) *Hungarian–American biochemist*

Szent-Györgyi, who was born in the Hungarian capital Budapest, studied anatomy at the university there, obtaining his MD in 1917. He continued his studies in Hamburg, Groningen, and at Cambridge University where he received his PhD in 1927. He also spent some time at the Mayo Clinic, Minnesota, before returning to Hungary as professor of medical chemistry at the University of Szeged. In 1947, however, he emigrated to America becoming director of the Institute for Muscle Research at the Marine Biological Station, Woods Hole, Massachusetts.

Szent-Györgyi, a highly original and productive biochemist, first became widely known in the late 1920s for his work on the adrenal glands. In the usually fatal condition Addison's disease, where the adrenal glands cease to function, one symptom is a brown pigmentation of the skin. Szent-Györgyi wondered if there was a connection between this and the browning of certain bruised fruits, which is due to the oxidation of phenolics to quinole. Some fruits, notably citrus, do not go brown because they contain a substance that inhibits this reaction. Szent-Györgyi isolated a substance from adrenal glands, which he named hexuronic acid, that also turned out to be present in nonbruising citrus fruits known for their high vitamin C content. He suspected he had finally succeeded in isolating the elusive vitamin but was anticipated in announcing his discovery by Charles King, who published his own results two weeks earlier. The main reason for Szent

Györgyi's delay was the problem of supply. However when he began work in Szeged, with its paprika milling industry, he found a rich supply of the vitamin in Hungarian paprika and was soon able to confirm his suppositions and further investigate the action of the vitamin in the body.

Szent-Györgyi also studied the uptake of oxygen in isolated muscle tissue and found that he could maintain the rate of uptake by adding any one of the four acids – succinic, fumaric, malic, or oxaloacetic. This work was extended by Hans Krebs and led to the elucidation of the Krebs cycle. For his studies into "biological combustion processes" Szent-Györgyi was awarded the 1937 Nobel Prize for physiology or medicine.

In addition to such work Szent-Györgyi became widely known for his studies into the biochemistry of muscular contraction. It was known that the contractile part of muscle was made mainly from the two proteins, actin and myosin. In 1942, in collaboration with Ferenc Straub, Szent-Györgyi showed that the two proteins can be encouraged to form fibers of actomyosin which, in the presence of ATP, the cell's energy source, will contract spontaneously. Just how the combining of the two proteins can lead to muscular contraction was a question pursued and illuminated by Hugh Huxley.

Szilard, Leo (1898–1964) *Hungarian–American physicist*

Szilard, the son of an architect, studied engineering in his native city of Budapest before moving to the University of Berlin where he began the study of physics and obtained his doctorate in 1922. He remained there until 1933 when, after spending a few years in England working at the Clarendon Laboratory, in Oxford, and at St. Bartholomew's Hospital, London, he emigrated to America in 1938. After the war Szilard moved into biology and in 1946 was appointed to the chair of biophysics at the University of Chicago, where he remained until his death. He became a naturalized American in 1943.

Szilard was one of the first men in the world to see the significance of nuclear fission and the first to bring it to the attention of Roosevelt. In 1934, after hearing of the dismissal of the possibility of atomic energy by Ernest Rutherford, he worked out that an element that is split by neutrons and that would emit two neutrons when it absorbed one neutron could, if assembled in sufficiently large mass, sustain a nuclear chain reaction. Szilard applied for a patent, which he assigned to the British Admiralty to preserve secrecy.

When in 1938–39 he heard of the work of Otto HAHN and Lise MEITNER on the fission of uranium he was well prepared. After quickly confirming that the necessary neutrons would be present Szilard, fearing the consequences that would ensue from Hitler's possession of such a weapon, decided that the only sound policy was for America to develop such a weapon first. To this end he approached Albert Einstein, with whom he had worked earlier and who commanded sufficient authority to be heard by all, and invited him to write a letter to the President of the United States. This initiated the program that was to culminate in the dropping of the atomic bomb on Hiroshima six years later. During the war Szilard worked on the development of the bomb and, in particular, worked with Enrico Fermi on the development of the uranium–graphite pile.

If Szilard was one of the first to see the possibility and necessity to develop the bomb he was also one of the earliest to question the wisdom and justice of actually using it against the Japanese. He was the dominant spirit behind the report submitted by James Franck to the Secretary of War in 1945 forecasting the nuclear stalemate that would follow a failure to ban the bomb.

Although his early reputation was based on his work in physics he moved, after the war, into molecular biology. Szilard took his new subject seriously, attending classes at the Cold Spring Harbor laboratories in 1946. He was soon to develop a high degree of competence, designing an important new instrument, the chemostat, formulating new theories on the aging process, and stimulating Jacques Monod in his work on the operon and the repressor.

Takamine, Jokichi (1854–1922)
Japanese–American chemist

Takamine was born at Takaoka in Japan, the son of a physician. Although brought up along traditional lines, he nevertheless received a modern scientific education at the Tokyo College of Science and Engineering, where he graduated in chemical engineering in 1879. After two years' training at Anderson's College, Glasgow, he returned to Japan in 1883 and entered the government department of agriculture and commerce. In 1887 he left to establish the first factory for the manufacture of superphosphates in Japan.

In 1890, having married an American, he settled permanently in America. He set up a private laboratory and in 1894 produced Takadiastase, a starch-digesting enzyme, which had applications in medicine and the brewing industry.

It had been demonstrated in 1896 that an injection of an extract from the center of the suprarenal (adrenal) gland causes blood pressure to rise rapidly. In 1901 Takamine managed to isolate and purify the substance involved – adrenaline (epinephrine). This was the first isolation and purification of a hormone from a natural source.

Tamm, Igor Yevgenyevich (1895–1971) *Russian physicist. See* CHERENKOV, PAVEL ALEKSEYEVICH.

Tansley, Sir Arthur George (1871–1955) *British plant ecologist*

Tansley was born in London. Having found his school science teaching "farcically inadequate," he attended lectures at University College, London, where he received his first proper tuition in botany from Francis Oliver. In 1890 he went to Cambridge University and on graduation returned to London as Oliver's assistant.

In the following years Tansley's thinking was greatly influenced by two major books, *Ecological Plant Geography* (1895) by E. Warming and *The Physiological Basis of Plant Geography* (1898) by Andreas Schimper. These – together with his travels in Ceylon, Malaya, and Egypt – stimulated his interest in different vegetation types.

In 1902 Tansley founded *The New Phytologist*, a journal designed to promote botanical communication and debate in Britain. In 1913 he founded and became the first president of the British Ecological Society and four years later founded and edited the *Journal of Ecology*. These activities, and his ecology courses at Cambridge, played a large part in establishing the science of ecology.

After World War I Tansley turned to psychology and resigned from Cambridge in 1923 to spend time studying under Sigmund Freud in Austria. In 1927 he became professor of botany at Oxford University, a position held until his retirement in 1937. He continued to exert much influence, however, becoming president of the Council for the Promotion of Field Studies in 1947 and chairman of the Nature Conservancy Council in 1949, both bodies that he had helped to create. Probably his most important book, *The British Islands and Their Vegetation* (1939), was also published after his retirement.

Tarski, Alfred (1902–1983) *Polish–American mathematician and logician*

Tarski served as a professor at the university in his native city of Warsaw (1925–39). In 1942 he joined the staff at the University of California and became professor there in 1949 and research professor at the Miller Institute (1959–60).

Tarski worked on set theory and algebra and is noted as one of the pioneers in the study of formalized logical systems as purely algebraic structures. He emphasized the difference between the metalanguage, used to talk about these structures, and the formal language whose syntax formed the system being studied. His famous paper *The Concept of Truth in Formalized Languages* (1935) was one of the foundation stones of model theory and has had a profound influence both in logic and the philosophy of language.

Tartaglia, Niccoló (1500–1557) *Italian mathematician, topographer, and military scientist*

Tartaglia was born Niccoló Fontana but as a boy he suffered a saber wound to his face during the French sack of Brescia (1512), his native city; this left him with a speech defect and he adopted the nickname Tartaglia (Stammerer) as a result. Tartaglia began his studies as a promising mathematician, but his interests soon became very wide-ranging. He held various posts, including school teacher, before he eventually became a professor of mathematics in Venice where he stayed.

Tartaglia is remembered chiefly for his work on solving the general cubic equation. He discovered a method in 1535 but did not publish it. Incautiously he revealed his new method to his friend the mathematician Girolamo Cardano, who published it in *Ars magna* (1545; The Great Skill). This, not surprisingly, was the end of their friendship and led to a violent controversy. Tartaglia eventually lost the quarrel and with it his post as lecturer at Brescia in 1548.

Tartaglia's other chief mathematical interests were in arithmetic and geometry. The pattern now known as 'Pascal's triangle' appeared in a work of Tartaglia's. His geometrical work centered on problems connected with the tetrahedron and he helped further the diffusion of classical mathematics by making the first translation of Euclid's *Elements* into a modern European language. His chief published work was the three-volume *Trattato di numeri et misure* (1556–60; Treatise on Numbers and Measures), an encyclopedic work on elementary mathematics. Apart from these mathematical activities Tartaglia made notable innovations in topography and the military uses of science, such as ballistics.

Tatum, Edward Lawrie (1909–1975)
American biochemist

Tatum, who was born in Boulder, Colorado, studied chemistry at the University of Wisconsin, where his father was professor of pharmacology. He obtained the BA degree in 1931, then undertook research in microbiology for his master's degree, conferred the following year. His PhD was more biochemically oriented and after receiving his doctorate he worked as a research assistant in biochemistry for a year. He studied bacteriological chemistry at Utrecht University from 1936 to 1937 and on returning to America was appointed research associate at Stanford University.

His early experiments at Stanford concentrated on the nutritional requirements of the fruit fly, *Drosophila melanogaster*, but in 1940, in collaboration with George BEADLE, he began working on the pink bread mold, *Neurospora crassa*. They irradiated the mold with x-rays to induce mutations and were then able to isolate a number of lines with different nutritional deficiencies. These lines needed special supplements to the basic growth medium to enable growth

to continue as normal. When a mutant mold was crossed with the normal wild-type mold, the dietary deficiency was inherited in accordance with expected Mendelian ratios. Such studies established that genes act by regulating specific chemical processes. During World War II this work was of use in maximizing penicillin production, and it has also made possible the introduction of new methods for assaying vitamins and amino acids in foods and tissues.

In 1945 Tatum moved to Yale University where he extended his techniques to yeast and bacteria. Through studying nutritional mutations of the bacterium *Escherichia coli*, he and Joshua LEDERBERG were able to demonstrate, in 1946, that bacteria can reproduce sexually. Following this work, bacteria have become the primary source of information on the genetic control of biochemical processes in the cell.

Tatum returned to Stanford in 1948 and in 1957 joined the Rockefeller Institute for Medical Research. In 1958, together with Beadle and Lederberg, he received the Nobel Prize for physiology or medicine in recognition of the work that helped create the modern science of biochemical genetics.

Taube, Henry (1915–   ) *American inorganic chemist*

Taube, who was born in Saskatchewan, Canada, moved to America in 1937 and became naturalized in 1942. He was educated at the University of Saskatchewan and the Berkeley campus of the University of California, where he gained his PhD in 1940. After working at Cornell University (1941–46), Taube moved to Chicago and in 1952 was appointed professor of chemistry, a post he held until 1962 when he accepted a comparable appointment at Stanford, California.

As a leading inorganic chemist Taube has succeeded in developing a range of experimental techniques for studying the kinetics and mechanism of inorganic reactions, in particular electron-transfer reactions. Transition metals such as iron, copper, cobalt and molybdenum form coordination compounds of a type first described by Alfred Werner. In a typical coordination compound a metal ion is attached to a number of ligands, such as water or ammonia. It was thought that the ligands would keep the ions apart and inhibit electron transfer between ions. Taube showed experimentally that ligand bridges form between interacting complexes, thus allowing electrons to be transferred.

For his work in this field Taube was awarded the 1983 Nobel Prize for chemistry.

Taylor, Brook (1685–1731) British mathematician

Born in Edmonton, near London, Taylor studied at Cambridge University, and was secretary to the Royal Society during the period 1714–18. He made important contributions to the development of the differential calculus in his *Methodus incrementorum directa et inversa* (1715; Direct and Indirect Methods of Incrementation). This contained the formula known as *Taylor's theorem*, which was recognized by Joseph Lagrange in 1772 as being the principle of differential calculus. The *Methodus* also contributed to the calculus of finite differences, which Taylor applied to the mathematical theory of vibrating strings.

Outside mathematics Taylor was an accomplished artist and this led him to an interest in the theory of perspective, publishing his work on this subject in *Linear Perspective* (1715). *Taylor expansions* are named for him.

Taylor, Joseph Hooton (1941–) American astrophysicist

Born in Philadelphia, Taylor was educated at Haverford College, Pennsylvania, and at Harvard, where he gained his PhD in astronomy in 1968. He moved to the University of Massachusetts, Amherst, in 1969 and was appointed professor of astronomy in 1977, a post he held until 1980 when he was elected professor of physics at Princeton.

In 1974 Russell HULSE, a research student of Taylor, while working at the Arecibo Radio Telescope in Puerto Rico, discovered a binary pulsar. The pulsar orbited its invisible companion with a period of 7.75 hours, and rotated about its axis every 0.05903 seconds. Taylor and Hulse continued to observe the pulsar and to establish the details of its orbital behavior as precisely as possible.

Taylor also saw that the pulsar could provide an important observational test of Einstein's theory of general relativity. In 1916 Einstein had argued that an accelerating mass should radiate energy in the form of gravitational waves. Any such energy radiated by Hulse's pulsar, 16,000 light years away, would be so weak by the time it reached Earth as to be undetectable. In fact, so far no direct reproducible evidence has been obtained for the existence of gravitational waves, despite the experiments of Joseph Weber carried out since the 1960s.

Taylor realized there was another way for the gravitational waves to be detected. Any system radiating gravitational waves will be losing energy. This loss of energy will cause the pulsar and its companion to approach closer to each other and a consequent decrease in the pulsar's orbital period. The orbital shrinkage would amount to only 3.5 meters a year, too small to be detected; a decrease of 75 millionth of a second per year in the orbital period, however, should be detectable. After four years careful observation and analysis Taylor announced in 1978 that he had detected just such a decrease in the orbital period. "Hence 66 years after Einstein predicted the existence of gravitational waves," Taylor concluded, "an experiment has been done that yields clear evidence for their existence." For his discovery of this evidence Taylor shared the 1993 Nobel Prize for physics with Hulse.

Taylor, Richard (1929–) Canadian physicist. See FRIEDMAN, JEROME ISAAC.

Teisserenc de Bort, Léon Philippe (1855–1913) French meteorologist

Teisserenc de Bort worked as chief meteorologist for the Central Meteorological Bureau in his native city of Paris from 1892 until 1896, when he opened his own meteorological observatory at Trappes, near Versailles.

In 1902 he put forward his conclusions on the atmosphere. Early balloonists had established that temperature decreased with height by about 6°C per 330 feet (100 m). Using unmanned instrumented balloons Teisserenc de Bort found that above an altitude of 7 miles (11 km) temperature ceased to fall and sometimes increased slightly. He named this upper part of the atmosphere the stratosphere, because he thought that the different gases would lie in distinct strata as, without temperature differentials, there would be no mechanism to disturb them. The lower part of the atmosphere he named the troposphere (Greek: 'sphere of change') as here, with abundant temperature differentials, constant change and mingling of atmospheric gases occurred.

The phenomenon was explained by E. Gold in 1909 by reference to cooling of rising air in the troposphere and the absence of convection currents in the stratosphere.

Teller, Edward (1908–) Hungarian–American physicist

The son of a lawyer, Teller was born in the Hungarian capital Budapest. Having attended the Institute of Technology there, he continued his education in Germany at the universities of Karlsruhe, Munich, Leipzig (where he obtained his PhD in 1930), and Göttingen. He left Germany when Hitler came to power in 1933. After a short period in Denmark and London, he emigrated to America where in 1935 he took up an appointment as professor of physics at George Washington University. During the war he worked in the theoretical physics division at Los Alamos on the development of the atom bomb, resuming his academic career in 1946 at the University of Chicago. Teller moved in 1953 to the University of California at Berkeley, where he remained until his retirement in 1975.

Teller is often referred to as the 'father of the hydrogen bomb'. Insofar as he made the initial proposal in 1942, worked longest on the project, and campaigned most vigorously for its completion, the description is accurate. If, however, the phrase is taken to mean that the bomb exploded in 1951 was Teller's own design, the description is misleading.

From the mid-1940s Teller was working with three possible bomb designs, A, B, and C. By 1947 it was clear that B would fail and that C, though viable, would produce too small an explosion to be worthwhile. Research effort was therefore concentrated on design A which required horrendous amounts of calculation; these were carried out by the mathematician Stanislaw Ulam. In 1950 President Truman, following the Russian atomic bomb explosion, ordered the program to be speeded up. At this point Ulam revealed that option A was hopeless, requiring such massive amounts of tritium to be virtually unworkable. At this point Teller found himself, after nearly a decade of intensive and costly research, without any viable design or idea in response to the President's urgent call.

By early 1951 Ulam and Teller had worked out a fourth and effective method, the origin of which remains a matter of dispute. The basic problem of the early designs was that the bomb would fly apart under the explosion of the fission device before the fusion material was sufficiently compressed. Ulam's solution was to use x-rays from the fission device to produce compression waves long before any shock waves could strangle the planned thermonuclear reaction. While Hans Bethe attributes the idea to Ulam, Teller has claimed the credit for himself, insisting that "Ulam triggered nothing."

After the successful explosion of the first thermonuclear device in 1951 Teller moved to the Livermore laboratories, which were performing research for the Atomic Energy Commission. Shortly afterward, loyalty hearings were held against Oppenheimer. Teller, despite much pressure from the scientific community, decided to testify against him and although he did not accuse Oppenheimer of disloyalty, still less of treason, he did complain that "his actions frankly appeared to me confused and complicated...I would personally feel more secure if public matters could rest in other hands." In the charged atmosphere of the 1950s this contributed to the withdrawal of Oppenheimer's security status and to the ostracism of Teller by many of his old friends and colleagues. For ten years Teller was neither invited to nor visited Los Alamos.

Teller continued to be a powerful figure in American science after his retirement from Berkeley in 1975. In 1984, for example, he advised Washington that the influential paper of Carl Sagan and his colleagues on the dangers of a nuclear winter was far from convincing. At Livermore he worked on and campaigned vigorously for the Strategic Defense Initiative (SDI), better known as 'Star Wars'. The key ingredient of SDI was the x-ray laser, which would supposedly destroy enemy missiles in space. Teller had to face charges against the program from Hans Bethe that it was "unwieldy, costly, easily countered, destabilizing, and uncertain." Despite these and other charges, and despite a tendency for supporters of the SDI to promise more than they could ever hope to deliver, Teller's support for the project never wavered. He published a forthright defense of the program in his book *Better a Shield than a Sword* (1987). However, in 1993 the project was abandoned amid accusations that test results had been distorted. The SDI department was renamed the Ballistic Missile Defense Organization and it now researches ways of eliminating enemy missiles nearer the ground.

Temin, Howard Martin (1934–1994)
American molecular biologist

Born in Philadelphia, Pennsylvania, Temin studied biology at Swarthmore College and at the California Institute of Technology, where he obtained his PhD in animal virology in 1959. He worked at the University of Wisconsin from 1960 onward, serving as professor of oncology there from 1969 until his death from lung cancer.

There are two classes of viruses, those with DNA and those with RNA genes. The former replicate by transforming their DNA into new DNA and transmit information from DNA through RNA into protein. The latter class of viruses replicate RNA into RNA and transmit information directly into protein without the need for DNA. That is, all such reactions fitted into the general sequence DNA to RNA to protein, the so-called Central Dogma of molecular biology. In the early 1960s Temin discovered a curious feature of the RNA Rous chicken sarcoma virus (RSV): he found that it would not grow in the presence of the antibiotic actinomycin D, a drug known to inhibit DNA synthesis. Temin realized that this might mean the RSV replicated through a DNA intermediate, which he called the provirus. That is, Temin was proposing the sequence RNA (of the RSV) to DNA (provirus) to RNA (replicated RSV) which, while not actually excluded by the Central Dogma, was not implied by it either.

If such a reaction did take place then it would certainly require the presence of an enzyme capable of transcribing RNA into DNA. It was not until 1970 that Temin identified the enzyme (discovered independently by David BALTIMORE) known variously as reverse transcriptase or RNA-directed DNA polymerase. It was for this work that Temin shared the 1975 Nobel Prize for physiology or medicine with Baltimore and Renato DULBECCO.

Tesla, Nikola (1856–1943) *Croatian–American physicist*

Tesla was born at Smiljan in Croatia, at that time within the Austro–Hungarian empire. He studied mathematics and physics at the University of Graz and philosophy at Prague. In 1884 he emigrated to America where he worked for Thomas Edison for a while before a bitter quarrel led to his resigning and joining the Westinghouse Company. After his invention of the first alternating current (a.c.) motor in 1887 he left to set up his own research laboratory.

Most commercially generated electricity at that time (including that of Edison) was direct current (d.c.). Tesla saw some fundamental weaknesses in the d.c. system: it required a commutator and needed costly maintenance. The main advantage of a.c. was that, with transformers, it was easier and cheaper to transmit very high voltages over long distances. Tesla's invention was soon taken up by Westinghouse and led to intense competition with Edison and the other d.c. users. Edison was not beyond suggesting that a.c. was inherently dangerous and when in 1889 the first criminal was electrocuted, Edison proposed that being 'westinghoused' would be a good term to describe death by the electric chair.

In 1891 the transformer was first demonstrated at the Frankfurt fair when it was shown that 25,000 volts (alternating) could be transmitted for 109 miles (175 km) with an efficiency of 77%. The a.c. system soon replaced d.c. electricity, which was confined to specialized uses.

Thales (*c.* 625 BC–*c.* 547 BC) *Greek philosopher, geometer, and astronomer*

It is with Thales that physics, geometry, astronomy, and philosophy have long been thought to begin. However, little is known of the first supposed identifiable 'scientist' apart from the fact that he was born at Miletus, now in Turkey, and a number of anecdotes that clearly originate in folklore.

Thus he is traditionally supposed to have acquired his learning from Egypt, an implausible claim when the modest mathematical skills of sixth-century Egypt are contrasted with the supposed achievements of Thales. To him is even attributed a proof of the proposition that the circle is divided into two equal parts by its diameter, a theorem not to be found in Euclid some 300 years later. It is also reported by the historian Herodotus that Thales gave a prediction of a solar eclipse in 585 BC.

The remaining claim for Thales rests on his introduction of naturalistic explanations of physical phenomena in opposition to the customary understanding of nature in terms of the behavior of the gods. Hence the importance of his claim that everything is water, perhaps the first recorded general physical principle in history.

Theiler, Max (1899–1972) *South African–American virologist*

Theiler, the son of a physician from Pretoria in South Africa, was educated at the University of Cape Town; he received his MD in 1922 after attending St. Thomas's Hospital, London, and the London School of Tropical Medicine. The same year he left for America to take up a post at the Harvard Medical School. In 1930 Theiler moved to the Rockefeller Foundation in New York, where he later became director of the Virus Laboratory and where he spent the rest of his career.

When Theiler began at Harvard it was still a matter of controversy whether yellow fever was a viral infection, as Walter Reed had claimed in 1901, or whether it was due to *Leptospira icteroides*, the bacillus discovered by Hideyo Noguchi in 1919. Theiler's first contribution was to reject the latter claim by showing that *L. icteroides* is responsible for Weil's disease, an unrelated jaundice.

Little can normally be done in the development of a vaccine without an experimental animal in which the disease can be studied and in which the virus can spread. The breakthrough here came in 1927 when Adrian Stokes found that yellow fever could be induced in Rhesus monkeys from India. Within a year Stokes and Noguchi had both died from yellow fever and did not witness Theiler's next major advance. As monkeys tend to be expensive and difficult to handle, researchers much prefer to work with such animals as mice or guinea pigs. Attempts to infect mice had all failed when Theiler tried injecting the virus directly into their brains. Although the animals failed to develop yellow fever they did die of massive inflammation of the brain (encephalitis). In the course of this work Theiler himself contracted yellow fever but fortunately survived and developed immunity.

Although, he reported in 1930, the virus caused encephalitis when passed from mouse to mouse, if it was once more injected into the monkey it revealed itself still to be functioning and producing yellow fever. Yet there had been one crucial change: the virus had been attenuated and while it did indeed produce yellow fever it did so in a mild form and, equally important, endowed on the monkey immunity from a later attack of the normal lethal variety. All was thus set for Theiler to develop a vaccine against the disease. It was not however until 1937, after the particularly virulent Asibi strain from West Africa had passed through more than a hundred subcultures, that Theiler and his colleague Hugh Smith announced the development of the so-called 17-D vaccine. Between 1940 and 1947 Rockefeller produced more than 28 million doses of the vaccine and finally eliminated yellow fever as a major disease. For this work Theiler received the 1951 Nobel Prize for physiology or medicine.

Theophrastus (c. 372 BC–c. 287 BC)
Greek botanist and philosopher

Theophrastus, who was born at Eresus on Lesbos (now in Greece), attended the Academy at Athens as a pupil of Plato. After Plato's death he joined Aristotle and became his chief assistant when Aristotle founded the Lyceum at Athens. On Aristotle's retirement Theophrastus became head of the school. The school flourished under him and is said to have numbered two thousand pupils at this time.

Of Theophrastus's many works, his nine-volume *Enquiry into Plants* is considered the most important. This is a systematically arranged treatise that discusses the description and classification of plants and contains many personal observations. A second series of six books, the *Etiology of Plants*, covers plant physiology. Theophrastus appreciated the connection between flowers and fruits and, from his description of germination, it is seen that he realized the difference between monocotyledons and dicotyledons.

Many of Theophrastus's pupils lived in distant regions of Greece and he encouraged them to make botanical observations near their homes. This practice probably helped him to conclude that plant distribution depends on soil and climate. Theophrastus was the first to invent and use botanical terms and is often called 'the father of scientific botany'.

Theorell, Axel Hugo Teodor (1903–1982) *Swedish biochemist*

Theorell, who was born at Linköping in Sweden, received his MD from the Karolinska Institute in Stockholm in 1930. However, he did not pursue a career in medicine because of a polio attack. Instead, he became assistant professor of biochemistry at Uppsala University (1932–33, 1935–36), spending the intervening years with Otto Warburg at the Kaiser Wilhelm Institute in Berlin.

Theorell found that the sugar-converting (yellow) enzyme isolated from yeast by Warburg consisted of two parts: a nonprotein enzyme (of vitamin B_2 plus a phosphate group) and the protein apoenzyme. He went further to show that the coenzyme oxidizes glucose by removing a hydrogen atom, which attaches at a specific point on the vitamin molecule. This was the first detailed account of enzyme action.

Theorell studied cytochrome c (important in the electron-transport chain) and was the first to isolate crystalline myoglobin. His research on alcohol dehydrogenase resulted in the development of blood tests that may be used to determine alcohol levels.

In 1937 Theorell became director of the biochemistry department of the Nobel Medical Institute, Stockholm, and in 1955 received the Nobel Prize for physiology or medicine.

Thiele, Friedrich Karl Johannes (1865–1918) *German chemist*

Born at Ratibor (now Racibórz in Poland), Thiele studied mathematics at the University of Breslau but later turned to chemistry, receiving his doctorate from Halle in 1890. He taught at the University of Munich from 1893 to 1902, when he was appointed professor of chemistry at Strasbourg.

In 1899 Thiele proposed the idea of partial valence to deal with a problem that had been troubling theoretical chemists for some time. The structures produced by August Kekulé in 1858 and 1865 had revolutionized chemical thought but had also produced major problems. Double bonds in chemistry usually indicate reactivity but Kekulé's proposed structure for benzene, C_6H_6, contained three double bonds in its ring and yet benzene is comparatively unreactive. Thus it tends to undergo substitution reactions rather than addition reactions.

Thiele proposed that, when double and single bonds alternate, a pair of single bonds affect the intervening double bond in such a way as to give it some of the properties of a single bond. Given the ring structure of benzene, this occurs throughout the molecule and so neutralizes the activity of the double bonds. The same argument cannot be used with double bonds in a carbon chain for there the ends of the chain will be open to addition. Thiele's problem could not be completely solved until the development of quantum theory. Thiele's ideas are similar to the later concept of resonance structures – intermediate forms of molecules with bonding part way between conventional forms.

Thomas, Edward Donnall (1920–)
American physician

Thomas was born at Mart in Texas and educated at the University of Texas, receiving his BA in 1941 and MA two years later. In 1946 he was awarded his MD by Harvard University. He worked at the Peter Bent Brigham Hospital, Boston, from 1946, eventually specializing in hematology. After two years as a research associate with the Cancer Research Foundation at the Children's Medical Center, Boston (1953–55), he moved to the Mary Imogene Bassett Hospital as hematologist and assistant physician. In 1956 he became associate clinical professor of medicine at the College of Physicians and Surgeons, Columbia University, and from 1963 until 1990 he served with the University of Washington Medical School in Seattle as professor of medicine.

Although primarily a clinician rather than a research scientist, Thomas was instrumental in gaining new insights into how the body's immune system rejects tissue transplants. His expertise in hematology and cancer biology enabled him to develop the technique of bone-marrow transplantation to treat patients suffering from leukemia or other cancers of the blood. This involves the transfer of bone-marrow cells from a healthy donor to the bone marrow of the patient, so that the patient can resume production of healthy white blood cells to replace the cancerous cells.

In experiments using dogs, Thomas demonstrated the importance of matching donor tissue and the recipient's tissue as closely as possible, so as to minimize the risk of rejection of the transplanted tissue. He also showed that by treating the recipient with cell-killing drugs, it was possible to avoid another of the pitfalls associated with tissue transplantation, namely, the graft-versus-host reaction. This occurs when immune cells belonging to the donor and transferred with the transplant recognize the host's tissues as foreign and start to attack them.

Under Thomas's leadership the University of Washington Medical School became the preeminent North American center for bone-marrow transplants, where physicians from all over the world came to learn the technique. For his work Thomas was awarded the 1990 Nobel Prize for physiology or medicine, jointly with Joseph MURRAY.

Thompson, Sir D'Arcy Wentworth
(1860–1948) *British biologist*

Thompson studied medicine at the university in his native city of Edinburgh, where he was greatly influenced by Charles Thomson, who had recently returned from the Challenger Expedition. In 1884 he became professor of biology (subsequently natural history) at University College, Dundee. In 1917, when he became senior professor, Thompson published *On Growth and Form*, in which he developed the notion of evolutionary changes in animal form in terms of physical forces acting upon the individual during its lifetime, rather than as the sum total of modifications made over successive generations – the latter being the traditional credo postulated by Darwinists. In a later edition (1942), however, Thompson admitted the difficulty of explaining away the cumulative effect of physical and mental adaptations, which can scarcely be accounted for in the experience of one generation. In addition to such theoretical work, Thompson was much involved in oceanographic studies, as well as fisheries and fur-seal conservation in northern Europe. He was one of the British representatives on the International Council for the Exploration of the Sea, from its foundation in 1902. He was also interested in classical science, publishing works on the natural history of ancient writers, including an edition of Aristotle's *Historia Animalium* (1910;

History of Animals) and accounts of Greek birds and fishes.

Thomson, Benjamin See RUMFORD, BENJAMIN THOMSON, COUNT.

Thomson, Sir Charles Wyville (1830–1882) British marine biologist

Thomson was born at Bonsyde in Scotland and educated at Edinburgh University; his first academic posts were as lecturer in botany at Aberdeen University (1850–51) and Marischal College (1851–52). He was then appointed to the chairs of natural history at Cork (1853) and Belfast (1854–68). From 1870 he was professor of natural history at Edinburgh University.

Thomson is chiefly remembered for his extensive studies of deep-sea life, and particularly of marine invertebrates, in which he came to specialize. He made a number of oceanic expeditions to various parts of the world. In 1868–69 he led two deep-sea biological and depth-sounding expeditions off the north of Scotland, discovering, at a depth of some 650 fathoms, a wide variety of invertebrate forms, many of them previously unknown. To explain the variations in temperature that occurred at great depths he postulated the existence of oceanic circulation. After a further expedition to the Mediterranean (1870), Thomson published *The Depths of the Sea* (1872), in which he described his researches and findings. This culminated in his appointment as scientific head of the Challenger Expedition to the Atlantic, Pacific, and Antarctic oceans (1872–76), during which soundings and observations were made at 362 stations in a circumnavigation of some 70,000 miles. Using temperature variations as indicators, Thomson produced evidence to suggest the presence of a vast mountain range in the depths of the Atlantic – the Mid-Atlantic Ridge. His findings were later confirmed by a German expedition in 1925–27. Knighted on his return from the Challenger voyage, Thomson began preparation of the expedition's scientific reports – a work that eventually ran to 50 volumes – but had to resign in 1881 due to ill health. Thomson also wrote a general account of the expedition in *The Voyage of the Challenger* (1877).

Thomson, Sir George Paget (1892–1975) British physicist

George Thomson was the son of J. J. Thomson, the discoverer of the electron. He was born in Cambridge and educated at the university there, where he taught (1914–22). He was then appointed to the chair of physics at Aberdeen University. Thomson moved to take the chair of physics at Imperial College, London, in 1930. He remained there until 1952 when he returned to Cambridge as master of Corpus Christi College, a position he held until his retirement in 1962.

His early work was in investigating isotopic composition by a mass spectrograph method. In 1927 he also performed a classic experiment in which he passed electrons through a thin gold foil onto a photographic plate behind the foil. The plate revealed a diffraction pattern, a series of concentric circles with alternate darker and lighter rings. The experiment provided crucial evidence of the wave–particle duality of the electron. Thomson shared the 1937 Nobel Prize for physics for this work with Clinton J. DAVISSON who had made a similar discovery independently in the same year.

During World War II Thomson was chairman of the 'Maud committee' to advise the British government on the atom bomb. (The name of this committee arose from a telegram message that Niels Bohr had managed to convey to England shortly after the German invasion of Denmark. To assure his friends of his well-being he instructed: "Please inform Cockroft and Maud Ray, Kent," which was mistakenly interpreted as a secret message to 'make uranium day and night'; Maud Ray was Bohr's former governess.) It was this committee that, in 1941, gave the crucial advice to Churchill that it was indeed possible to make an effective uranium bomb and elicited from him the minute: "Although personally I am quite content with existing explosives, I feel that we must not stand in the path of improvement."

Thomson, Sir Joseph John (1856–1940) British physicist

Thomson, who was born in Manchester, entered Owens College (later Manchester University) at the age of 14. After studying engineering and then the sciences, he won a scholarship to Trinity College, Cambridge University. He graduated in 1876 and remained a member of the college in various capacities for the rest of his life. After graduating he worked at the Cavendish Laboratory under John Rayleigh, whom he succeeded as Cavendish Professor of Experimental Physics in 1884. As professor, Thomson built up the Cavendish Laboratory as a great and primarily experimental research school. Thomson was succeeded as professor in 1919 by his student Ernest Rutherford.

Thomson's most brilliant and famous scientific work was his investigations into cathode rays, in which he is considered to have discovered the electron. Using a highly evacuated discharge tube he calculated the velocity of the rays by balancing the opposing deflections caused by magnetic and electric fields. Knowing this velocity, and using a deflection from one of the fields, he was able to determine the ratio of electric charge (e) to mass (m) of the cathode rays. Thomson found that the ratio e/m was the same irrespective of the type of gas in the tube and the metal of the cathode, and was about a thousand times smaller than the value already obtained for hydrogen ions in the electrolysis of liquids. He later measured the charge of electricity carried by various negative ions and found it to be the same in gaseous discharge as in electrolysis. He thus finally established that cathode rays were negatively charged particles, fundamental to matter, and much smaller than the smallest atoms known. This opened up the way for new concepts of the atom and for the study of subatomic particles. Thomson announced his discovery of a body smaller than the hydrogen atom in April 1897.

His later researches included studies of Eugen Goldstein's canal rays, which he named positive rays. These studies gave a new method (1912) of separating atoms and molecules by deflecting positive rays in magnetic and electric fields. Ions of the same charge-to-mass ratio form a parabola on a photographic plate. Using this arrangement, Thomson first identified the isotope neon-22. This work was taken up by Francis W. Aston, who later developed the mass spectrograph.

Thomson's treatises were widely used in British universities. His *Conduction of Electricity Through Gases* (1903) describes the work of his great days at the Cavendish; his autobiography, *Recollections and Reflections*, was published in 1936. He was awarded the 1906 Nobel Prize for physics for his work on the conduction of electricity through gases, and was knighted in 1908.

Thunberg, Carl Per (1743–1828)
Swedish botanist

Thunberg, who was born in Jönköping in Sweden, studied medicine at Uppsala University, graduating in 1770. While there he went on botanical collecting trips for his teacher Linnaeus. After a year's study in Paris he accepted an invitation to make a plant-collecting trip aboard a Dutch merchant ship bound for Japan. By April 1772 Thunberg had completed the first stage of the journey with his arrival in Cape Town, South Africa. He remained there for three years, during which time he made three excursions into the interior on which he collected over 3000 species of plants. About a third of these were new to science. On two of his trips he was accompanied by the British plant collector Francis Masson.

In March 1775 Thunberg sailed on to Japan, arriving at Nagasaki in August. Restrictions imposed on the movements of foreigners at that time prevented him from making long botanical excursions. However, with the aid of some young Japanese physicians whom the traders employed as interpreters, Thunberg was able to obtain species of Japanese plants in exchange for his knowledge of modern European medicine. In December 1776 he left Japan and visited Java, Colombo (Sri Lanka), Cape Town, and London before reaching Sweden in March 1779. On his return Thunberg took up his appointment as botanical demonstrator at Uppsala University and in 1784 he succeeded Carl von Linné (the younger) as professor of botany, a post he held until his death.

Thunberg's time as professor was mainly occupied with writing about his extensive collections. In 1784 he published his *Flora Japonica*, describing 21 new genera and several hundred new species of Japanese plants. His works on floras of the Cape colony include *Prodromus Plantarum Capensis* (1794–1800; Foreword to the Plants of the Cape) and the more important *Flora Capensis* (1807–23; Flowers of the Cape), completed with the help of the German botanist Joseph Schultes. His shorter works include writings on *Protea*, *Oxalis*, *Ixia*, and *Gladiolus*.

Tinbergen, Nikolaas (1907–1988)
Dutch–British zoologist and ethologist

Tinbergen was born in The Hague, the Dutch capital, and educated at Leiden University, where he gained his doctorate in 1932 for a thesis on insect behavior. Soon after he joined a Dutch meteorological expedition to East Greenland. The results of his Arctic year observing huskies, buntings, and phalaropes were later described in his *Curious Naturalists* (1958). In 1936 Tinbergen was appointed lecturer in experimental zoology at Leiden. Contact with Konrad LORENZ in 1937 led to an early collaboration. Tinbergen's work, however, was interrupted by the war. He refused to cooperate with plans to Nazify Leiden University and was consequently imprisoned in a concentration camp from 1942 to 1944. Although he was appointed a full professor by Leiden in 1947, Tinbergen chose to move to Oxford in 1947 to escape administrative duties. Here he took up the more junior post of lecturer in animal behavior. Tinbergen remained in Oxford until his retirement in

1974, having been appointed professor in animal behavior in 1966. He became a naturalized British subject in 1954.

Tinbergen demonstrated that ethology was basically an observational and experimental science. Unlike Lorenz, who tended to work with a large number of pets, Tinbergen worked with animals in their natural setting. Much of his early work dealt with identifying the mechanisms by which animals found their way around. How, for example, does a digger wasp recognize its burrow? In a few simple experiments with nothing more elaborate than a handful of pine cones, Tinbergen was able to show that the wasps were guided by the spatial arrangement of landmarks at the nest entrance. He also studied the social control of behavior in his work on the mating habits of sticklebacks.

Much of this work was brought together in his classic text, *The Study of Instinct* (Oxford, 1951). In his other major work, *The Herring Gull's World* (London, 1953), Tinbergen began by recognizing the diversity of behavioral signals found in different species of gulls. Such a diversity had as much an evolutionary origin and history as more obvious anatomical features. Tinbergen set out to recover some of this history.

In his later years Tinbergen attempted to apply some of the principles of ethology to problems in human behavior. In particular, he worked with autistic children, publishing his results in *Autistic Children* (1983), a book he wrote in collaboration with his wife.

For his achievements in the field of animal behavior Tinbergen shared the 1973 Nobel Prize for physiology or medicine with Lorenz and FRISCH. His brother Jan Tinbergen had been awarded the Nobel Prize for economics four years earlier.

Ting, Samuel Chao Chung (1936–)
American physicist

Although born at Ann Arbor, Michigan, Ting was educated at primary and secondary schools in China; he subsequently moved to Taiwan and returned to America to study at the University of Michigan. At Michigan he gained his bachelor's, master's, and doctoral degrees in the six years 1956–62.

His interest in elementary-particle physics, which was to lead to his sharing the Nobel Prize for the discovery of a significant new particle, took him to the European Organization for Nuclear Research (CERN) in Geneva (1963) and then Columbia University, New York (1964), where he became an associate professor in 1965. In 1966 Ting was given a group leader post at DESY, the German electron synchrotron project at Hamburg, and in 1967 joined the Massachusetts Institute of Technology; he was appointed professor of physics there in 1969.

Working at Long Island, New York, on the Brookhaven National Laboratory's alternating-gradient synchrotron, Ting and his collaborators performed experiments in which streams of protons were fired at a stationary beryllium target. In such an experiment a particle was observed that had a lifetime almost 1000 times greater than could be expected from its observed mass. Announcement was made in a 14-author paper in the *Physical Review Letters* in 1974. The discovery was made independently and almost simultaneously by Burton RICHTER and his colleagues some 2000 miles away at the Stanford Linear Accelerator Center. Ting called the new particle J, Richter named it psi (ψ); it is now known as the J/psi in recognition of the simultaneity of its discovery. Confirmation came quickly from other high-energy physics laboratories and a whole family of similar particles has since been created and detected.

Ting and Richter were very quickly honored for their discovery by the award, jointly, of the 1976 Nobel Prize for physics. By 1976 Ting was directing three research groups, at Brookhaven, CERN, and DESY.

Tiselius, Arne Wilhelm Kaurin (1902–1971) *Swedish chemist*

Tiselius was born in Stockholm, Sweden, and educated at the University of Uppsala, where he became the assistant of Theodor Svedberg in 1925. He obtained his PhD in 1930 and his whole career was spent at Uppsala where, in 1938, a special research chair in biochemistry was created for him, which he occupied until 1968.

Tiselius's doctoral thesis was on electrophoresis – a method of separating chemically similar charged colloids. An electrical field is applied to the sample, and particles with different sizes migrate at different rates to the pole of opposite charge, enabling them to be detected and identified. The method was not initially very successful but by 1937 Tiselius had made a number of improvements to the apparatus. Using the technique on blood serum Tiselius confirmed the existence of four different groups of proteins – albumins and alpha, beta, and gamma globulins. Tiselius also conducted work on other methods for the separation of proteins and other complex substances in biochemistry including chromatography (from 1940) and partition and gel filtration (from the late 1950s).

In 1948 he was awarded the Nobel Prize for chemistry for his work on electrophoresis and other new methods of separating and detecting colloids and serum proteins. After the war Tiselius played an important role in the development and organization of science in Sweden, serving (1946–50) as chairman of the Swedish Natural Science Research Council.

Tizard, Sir Henry (Thomas) (1885–1959) *British chemist and administrator*

Tizard, who was born at Gillingham in Kent, was the son of a naval officer who served as the navigator on the *Challenger* voyage. Barred from a similar career by an eye accident, Tizard instead went to Oxford University where he studied chemistry under Nevil Sidgwick. After spending a year in Berlin working under Walther Nernst, he returned to Oxford in 1911 to take a fellowship. It was in Berlin that he first met and became friendly with Frederick Lindemann, who was later to become his principal opponent for positions of power in British scientific government circles.

Tizard spent World War I in the Royal Flying Corps working on the development of bomb sights and the testing of new planes. After the war he realized, as he put it in his unpublished autobiography, that he "would never be outstanding as a pure scientist." Having developed a taste for the application of science to military problems, he took the post of assistant secretary at the Department of Scientific and Industrial Research (DSIR) in 1920 with specific responsibility for coordinating research relevant to the needs of the armed forces. In 1929, largely for financial reasons, Tizard accepted the position of rector of Imperial College, London, where he remained until 1942.

Tizard quickly established a reputation for having an expert and practical knowledge of service needs. He had the rare ability to distinguish between a crankish, totally unsound, idea and one that, though strange and new, was basically sound and could find practical military application. Thus it was that Tizard backed the young Frank Whittle in the development of jet propulsion of aircraft in 1937 and also Barnes Wallis in 1940 in his development of the bouncing bomb.

But, above all else, it was Tizard's support for the development of radar that will be remembered. In 1934 the Air Ministry set up the Committee for the Scientific Survey of Air Defence, under the chairmanship of Tizard. This was the famous 'Tizard committee', which, in 1935, decided that radar was a workable means of air defense and should receive top priority.

The decision was not taken without dissent. In particular, Lindemann, then Churchill's scientific adviser, while recognizing the potential of radar, did not agree with the overriding priority demanded for it by Tizard and his associates. There was a further disagreement between the two men in that Lindemann advocated mass bombing of Germany while Tizard proposed instead (in 1942) a more balanced bombing policy with adequate aircraft being committed to the Battle of the Atlantic.

As a chemist Tizard's most significant work was on the ignition of gases in the internal combustion engine. He was editor of *Science of Petroleum* (1938), a standard multivolume work on the subject. He was knighted in 1937.

Todd, Alexander Robertus, Baron (1907–1997) *British biochemist*

Todd graduated from the university in his native city of Glasgow in 1928 and spent a further year there on a Carnegie Scholarship before going to the University of Frankfurt, Germany. He received doctorates from both Frankfurt (1931) and Oxford (1933) universities and in 1934 joined the medical faculty at Edinburgh University where he began work on thiamine (vitamin B_1). He continued this research at the Lister Institute of Preventive Medicine, London, and worked out the structure and synthesis of thiamine.

In 1938 Todd became professor of chemistry at Manchester University and continued vitamin studies on vitamins E and B_{12}. He also isolated the active principle from *Cannabis*, extracting the compound cannabinol from cannabis resin.

Todd transferred to Cambridge in 1944 to become professor of organic chemistry, a post he held until his retirement in 1971. At Cambridge he synthesized all the purine and pyrimidine bases that occur in nucleic acids (DNA and RNA) and found their structures. This was an important development in the understanding of the structure of the hereditary material and verified the formulae that Phoebus Levene had suggested for the nucleotide bases. Todd also synthesized various coenzymes related to these compounds, e.g., flavin adenine dinucleotide (FAD), and synthesized the energy-rich compounds adenosine diphosphate and triphosphate (ADP and ATP) so important in energy transfer in living cells.

The 1957 Nobel Prize for chemistry was awarded to Todd for these contributions to biochemistry and the understanding of the gene. Todd was knighted in 1954, raised to the British peerage as Baron Todd of Trumpington in 1962, and from 1975 to 1980 was president of the Royal Society. He also published an account of his busy life in his autobiography *A Time to Remember* (1983).

Tombaugh, Clyde William (1906–1997) *American astronomer*

Tombaugh came from a poor farming background in Streator, Illinois; although he never went to college he managed to teach himself enough of the basic observational skills to be taken on by the Lowell Observatory in Flagstaff, Arizona, in 1929. He transferred to New Mexico in 1955 and served as professor between 1965 and 1973.

Percival Lowell had begun his search for a planet lying beyond the orbit of Neptune in 1905 and this search continued at the Lowell Observatory after his death. Tombaugh was given the job of systematically photographing the sky along the ecliptic where it was thought any trans-Neptunian planet would be found. He used a specially designed wide-field telescope and for each region took two long-exposure photographs separated by several days. He then examined the pairs by means of a blink comparator, an instrument that allows two plates to be alternately observed in rapid succession. Any object that has moved against the background of the stars in the interval between the two exposures will appear to jump backward and forward. Methods were therefore devised for distinguishing asteroids and other moving bodies from the sought-for planet. After a year's observation Tombaugh was able to announce on 13 March 1930 the detection of the new planet, later named Pluto, at a point agreeing closely with the position predicted by Lowell.

The question arose as to whether there were any further trans-Neptunian planets. Consequently Tombaugh continued the search but, although he examined 90 million star images and discovered 3000 asteroids, no other new planet was detected. It is likely that Tombaugh has the honor of discovering the final planet of the solar system.

Tomonaga, Sin-Itiro (1906–1979) *Japanese theoretical physicist*

Tomonaga, who was born at Tokyo in Japan, graduated from Kyoto University in 1929 and then went to work in his native city. He remained there for the rest of his academic career, becoming professor of physics in 1941 and president of the university in 1956.

He was one of the first to develop a consistent theory of relativistic quantum electrodynamics. The problem at the time was that there was no quantum theory applicable to subatomic particles with very high energies. Tomonaga's first step in forming such a theory was his analysis of intermediate coupling – the idea that interactions between two particles take place through the exchange of a third (virtual particle), like one ship affecting another by firing a cannonball. Between 1941 and 1943 he used this concept to develop a quantum field theory that was consistent with the theory of special relativity. However, World War II prevented news of his work from reaching the West until 1947, at about the time that Richard FEYNMAN and Julian SCHWINGER published their own independent solutions to the same problem. All three shared the Nobel Prize for physics for this work in 1965.

Tonegawa, Susumu (1939–   ) *Japanese immunologist*

Tonegawa was born at Nagoya in Japan and educated at Kyoto University and the University of California, San Diego. He worked at the Basle Institute for Immunology from 1971 and in 1981 was appointed professor of biology at the Center for Cancer Research and Department of Biology of the Massachusetts Institute of Technology.

Working at Basle in collaboration with Niels Jerne and Nobumichi Hozumi, Tonegawa revealed how the immune system is capable of generating the enormous diversity of antibodies required so that whatever the nature of the invading organism or 'foreign' tissue a suitable antibody is available to bind specifically to it. This implies that the immune system's antibody-producing cells – the B-lymphocytes – can potentially manufacture billions of different antibodies; yet, even in humans, these cells carry only about 100,000 genes on their chromosomes.

Working with mouse cells, Tonegawa showed that during the development of the antibody-producing cell, the genes coding for antibody are shuffled at random, so that in the mature cell a cluster of functional genes is formed specific to that cell. Each individual mature cell thus produces its own specific antibody. This potential diversity is amplified by the fact that each antibody molecule comprises four protein chains, all with a highly variable terminal region. Hence the diversity of antibodies is a consequence of the huge numbers of lymphocytes present in the body, each with its own combination of functional antibody-producing genes. In recognition of the significance of his discovery Tonegawa was awarded the 1987 Nobel Prize for physiology or medicine.

Torricelli, Evangelista (1608–1647)
Italian physicist

Born at Faenza in Italy, Torricelli was educated at the Sapienza College, Rome. His *De motu* (1641; On Movement) attracted the attention of Galileo who invited him to come to Florence to work and live with him. After the death of Galileo in 1642 Torricelli was appointed professor of mathematics in Florence, where he remained until his death.

He had been introduced by Galileo to the problem of why water, in the duke of Tuscany's well, could not be raised higher than 30 feet (9 m). Dissatisfied with earlier explanations, he used Galileo's earlier demonstration that the atmosphere has weight to offer a more satisfactory account. He argued that as the atmosphere has weight, it must also have pressure that can force water up a pipe but only until the weight of the water produced an equivalent counterpressure. 30 feet of water was equal to the pressure exerted by the atmosphere.

Torricelli realized that he could test this argument by substituting mercury for water. A tube of mercury inverted over a dish – given that mercury is 14 times heavier than water – should be supported by the atmosphere to only one-fourteenth the height of an equivalent amount of water. This was confirmed by his pupil Viviani in 1643. Torricelli noticed that over time there was a variation in the height of the mercury in the tube, and reasoned that this was due to variations in the pressure of the atmosphere. This led to his construction of the barometer in 1644. The vacuum above the mercury in a closed tube is called a *Torricellian vacuum* and the unit of pressure, the *torr*, was named in his honor. Torricelli also made advances in pure mathematics and geometry, in particular in his calculations on the cycloid.

Townes, Charles Hard (1915–   )
American physicist

Born in Greenville, South Carolina, Townes was educated at Furman and Duke universities in his home state and at the California Institute of Technology, where he obtained his PhD in 1939. He worked at the Bell Telephone Laboratories (1939–47) before he took up an appointment at Columbia University, New York, where he became a full professor in 1950. He moved to the Massachusetts Institute of Technology in 1961 and then served as professor of physics at the University of California at Berkeley from 1967 until 1986.

In 1953 Townes designed the first maser (microwave amplification by stimulated emission of radiation). The maser works on the realization in quantum theory that molecules can only adopt a certain number of discrete characteristic energy states and that in their movement from one energy level to another they emit or absorb precisely determined amounts of radiation. Townes knew that the ammonia molecule (NH_3) could occupy one of two energy levels, the difference between them equaling a particular energy of a photon.

The question Townes went on to ask is, what happens if the ammonia molecule absorbs the photon of the appropriate frequency while it is at its higher energy level? Albert Einstein had answered the question in 1917 and shown that the molecule would fall to its lower state emitting a photon of the same frequency. There would then in fact be two photons of the right frequency to repeat the process and produce four photons. This is a rapid and powerful amplification producing a narrow beam of radiation with a single frequency. In this case the radiation emitted would have a frequency of 1.25 centimeters and thus fall in the microwave band, hence the name maser.

In any normal sample of ammonia only a few of the molecules would be in the higher energy state. Townes's problem was to devise a technique for the separation of molecules of the higher energy level ('population inversion') and he did this using a nonuniform electric field; molecules in the higher state were repelled and focused into the resonator while those in the lower state were attracted to it. By 1953 Townes had a working model of a maser.

Masers quickly found use in atomic clocks, receivers in radio telescopes, and numerous other uses. The maser led to the development of the laser, where light is amplified rather than microwave radiation and which was known in its earlier days as an 'optical maser'. Townes, in fact, published a paper with A.L. Schawlow in 1958 showing the theoretical possibility of the laser. He was, however, beaten in the race to construct it by Theodore Maiman in 1960.

For his work on the maser Townes shared the 1964 Nobel Prize for physics with the

Russians Nicolai BASOV and Aleksandr PROKHOROV, who had independently produced a maser in the Soviet Union in 1955.

Townsend, Sir John Sealy Edward
(1868–1957) *Irish physicist*

Townsend, the son of a professor of civil engineering from Galway (now in the Republic of Ireland), was educated at Trinity College, Dublin. In 1895 he took advantage of a change in the Cambridge examination statutes and, together with Ernest Rutherford, entered the Cavendish Laboratory as one of the first two non-Cambridge graduates. There they worked as research students of J. J. Thomson. In 1900 Townsend moved to Oxford as the first Wykeham Professor of Experimental Physics, a post he retained until his retirement in 1941.

In 1898 Townsend achieved his first major scientific success when he measured the fundamental unit of electric charge (the charge of the electron). The previous year Thomson had reported the discovery of the electron, whose mass he estimated at about 1/1000 that of the hydrogen atom. Townsend, working with gases released by electrolysis, was able to form charged clouds of water droplets and, by measuring the rate of fall of a water drop in the cloud, he could calculate the charge on each drop. More accurate work of this type was done by Robert Millikan in 1911.

Townsend's main work however was on, to take the title of his important book, *Electricity in Gases* (1915). He formulated a theory of ionization by collision, showing that the motion of electrons in an electric field would release more electrons by collision. These in turn would release even more electrons, and so on. This multiplication of charges, known as an avalanche, allowed him to explain the passage of electric currents through gases where the electric field was thought to be too weak.

Townsend was knighted in 1941.

Trembley, Abraham (1710–1784) *Swiss zoologist*

Trembley was born at Geneva in Switzerland. In the uprising of 1733, however, his father Jean, a leading politician and soldier, was driven from office and into exile. The fall in the family's fortune forced Trembley to seek employment. He moved to Holland in 1733 and served as tutor to the children of various noblemen. While working for Count Bentinck he read the *Mémoires* of René Réaumur, which so stimulated him that he began to observe nature himself. During the next few years

he made a number of discoveries which were to astound Europe.

At first he worked on parthenogenesis in aphids. Though he achieved some interesting results the work was basically derivative, having already been carried out by Réaumur and Charles Bonnet. At the same time he was studying polyps or, in modern terminology, hydra, of the species *Chlorohydra viridissima*. They were assumed to be plants but one day in the summer of 1740 Trembley observed them to move their 'arms'. At first he assumed that the movement was caused by currents in the water. When he swirled the jar around, expecting to see the hydra sway with the vortex, he noted that they suddenly contracted to a point, their tentacles seeming to disappear in the process. As the water calmed, the polyps stretched and once more revealed their tentacles. He was still unsure, however, whether they were plants or animals. There was, he realized, a simple procedure he could carry out to resolve the dilemma. If they were animals, then they would surely die if cut into two; plants would continue to grow.

In late 1740 he divided a number of polyps transversely. To his surprise he found that within a few days the two parts had not merely grown, but had developed into two perfect polyps: the tail grew a head, and the head a tail. He published his results in his *Mémoires...à l'histoire d'un genre de polypes d'eau douce* (1744; Memoirs on the Natural History of Freshwater Polyps). Polyp samples were also dispatched to scholars and institutions throughout Europe. Some, particularly vitalists, found Trembley's work difficult to accept. What happened to the animal's soul? Was that also divided into two? Others saw it as evidence for the oneness of nature, the 'Great Chain of Being', with the polyp being the link between plants and animals. Embryologists saw in the polyp conclusive proof against the preformationists who claimed that embryos were minute but preformed individuals. These and other issues were endlessly debated throughout the century, and Trembley's polyps became the best-known invertebrates in Europe.

Trembley himself had little more to contribute to science. He left his post with Bentinck in 1747. Thereafter he traveled around Europe, engaged in some kind of diplomatic activity for Britain, for which he received a pension of £300 per annum for life, and wrote a number of books on education, politics, and philosophy.

Trumpler, Robert Julius (1886–1956)
Swiss–American astronomer

Trumpler was the son of an industrialist. He studied at the university in his native city of Zurich in Switzerland (1906–08) and then at the University of Göttingen in Germany, where he obtained his PhD in 1910. After spending four years with the Swiss Geodetic Survey he emigrated to America in 1915, where he worked first at the Allegheny Observatory near Pittsburgh before moving to the Lick Observatory in California in 1919. He remained there until his retirement in 1951, also holding from 1938 to 1951 a professorship of astronomy at Berkeley.

Trumpler's most important work was his discovery in 1930 of conclusive evidence for interstellar absorption. He had examined over 300 open clusters of stars and found that remote clusters seemed to be about twice the size of nearer ones. He could find no observational error nor could he believe that he was witnessing a real phenomenon. He did, however, appreciate that this could be due to the presence of an absorbing medium occurring between the clusters and the observer on Earth. Trumpler assumed correctly that the quantity of absorbing medium increased with distance so that this would cause more distant clusters to appear fainter and would lead to an overestimate of their distance and size. For nearby objects only a small correction would be needed but for distant ones it could be quite considerable. He went on to estimate the effect of the absorbing medium, which was interstellar dust, on the dimming of the received light as 0.2 of a magnitude per thousand light-years. This means that the brightness of a star is decreased by interstellar dust by a factor of 1.208 for every thousand light-years that the starlight travels toward Earth. This had far-reaching implications for the work of such astronomers as Harlow Shapley who had been working on the size and structure of our Galaxy. It forced him to reduce the scale of his model by a factor of three.

Trumpler was also involved in 1922 in a test of Einstein's general theory of relativity. Einstein had predicted the amount by which starlight would be bent when it passed close to the Sun's limb. Trumpler assisted W. W. Campbell of the Lick Observatory to make the relevant measurements at Wallal in Australia during the total solar eclipse of 1922. The value they obtained for the deflection, 1.75 ± 0.09 seconds of arc, was much more accurate than the value Arthur Eddington had found in 1919 and was very close to Einstein's prediction of $1''.745$.

Tsui, Daniel C. (1939–   ) *Chinese–American physicist*

Tsui was born in Henan in China, and gained his PhD in physics in 1967 from the University of Chicago, USA. In 1998 he became professor at Princeton University, where he studied the fractional quantum Hall effect. In 1998 he shared the Nobel Prize for physics, with Robert LAUGHLIN and Horst STÖRMER, for their discovery and explanation of a new form of quantum fluid with fractionally charged excitations.

Tsui, Lap-Chee (1950–   ) *Chinese–Canadian molecular biologist*

Tsui was born at Shanghai in China and educated at the Chinese University, Hong Kong, and at the University of Pittsburgh, where he obtained his PhD in 1979. He joined the staff of the Hospital for Sick Children, Toronto, in 1980 and has continued to work there while also holding (since 1990) a professorship of medical genetics at the University of Toronto.

In 1989, in collaboration with his Toronto colleagues Jack Riordan and Francis Collins of the University of Michigan and against strong competition, Tsui announced that he had located the cystic fibrosis gene. Cystic fibrosis (CF) is caused by a recessive gene widely distributed among Caucasians; about 1000 children with CF are born in the United States each year. The disease affects secretory epithelia and, until recently, patients tended to die from lung infections and heart failure in their twenties.

When Tsui arrived in Toronto in 1980 new techniques were being proposed which, if effective, should allow defective genes to be identified. The procedure, introduced by Ray White and his colleagues, involved identifying an appropriate RFLP (restriction fragment length polymorphism), i.e., a fragment of DNA for use as a genetic marker to locate the site of the defective gene. The difficulty was that the human genome contains 3 billion base pairs of DNA; it was, therefore, a very remote possibility that any genetic marker would be within a reasonable distance of the CF gene. The chances would, however, be much improved if it was known on which chromosome the gene was sited. This was established as chromosome 7 by a Massachusetts biotechnology firm, Collaborative Research Inc (CRI), in 1985.

Thereafter it was a matter of using the available probes to focus on the area in which the gene could be found. By 1989 it had been narrowed to 300,000 base pairs. Further work demonstrated that the defective gene encoded a membrane protein of 1480 amino acids and has been dubbed the CF transmembrane conductance regulator

(CFTR). Tsui and his colleagues have shown that a loss of one amino acid one third of the way along the gene is responsible for 68% of cases of CF. He has continued to search for the mutations responsible for the other cases and has also sought to understand at the molecular level variations in the severity of the disease.

Tsvet, Mikhail Semenovich (1872–1919) *Russian botanist*

Tsvet, who was born at Asti in Italy, entered Geneva University in 1891 and followed courses in physics, chemistry, and botany. In 1896, having presented his thesis on cell physiology, he moved to the biological laboratory at St. Petersburg, where he began working on plant pigments.

Before Tsvet started applying chemical and physical methods to pigment analysis it was thought that only two pigments, chlorophyll and xanthophyll, existed in plant leaves. Following established procedures, Tsvet soon demonstrated the existence of two forms of chlorophyll. However, the isolation of pigments became a much simpler matter once he had developed, in 1900, the technique of adsorption analysis. By 1911 Tsvet had found eight different pigments.

His technique involved grinding leaves in organic solvent to extract the pigments and then washing the mixture through a vertical glass column packed with a suitable adsorptive material (e.g., powdered sucrose). The various pigments traveled at different rates through the column due to their different adsorptive properties and were therefore separated into colored bands down the column. Tsvet first described this method in 1901 and in a publication of 1906 suggested it should be called 'chromatography'.

The technique is extremely useful in chemical analysis, being simple, quick, and sensitive, but it was not much used until the 1930s. Tsvet died when only 47 from overwork and the stress of the war, during which he was frequently transferred from one institute to another. He thus did not live to see the fruits of the wider application of chromatography in the hands of such scientists as Richard Kuhn.

Turing, Alan Mathison (1912–1954) *British mathematician*

Turing, who was born in London, saw little of his parents in his early years. His father served in the Indian Civil Service before retiring in 1926; thereafter they lived in France to eke out a small pension. Turing was educated at Cambridge University, where he gained a fellowship at King's College in 1935. He spent the period from 1936 to 1938 at Princeton. During this time he published one of the most significant mathematical papers of the century, *On Computable Numbers* (1937).

He began by describing a hypothetical universal computer, since known as a *Turing machine*. It consists of an infinite length of tape divided into cells, a movable scanner/printer capable of reading the tape, printing, erasing, moving to the left and right, and halting. In each cell the tape has a symbol taken from a finite set of symbols (in a simple case 0 and 1). The control unit of the machine can be in one of a finite set of internal states (states S_1, S_2, S_3, etc.). The machine has a 'program', which is a set of groups of five symbols. For example, one set of five symbols might be $S_1 01XS_2$, where X is R, L, or N. This is interpreted as meaning that the machine is in state S_1 (the first symbol of the five) and reading 0 (the second symbol). In this state it replaces the 0 by 1 (third symbol). If $X = R$ it moves to the next cell on the right, if $X = L$ it moves to the next on the left, and if $X = N$ it does not move (it halts). Finally it goes into state S_2. The program, which can be used to do calculations, consists of a set of such quintuples (e.g., $S_1 00RS_1$, $S_1 10RS_2$, $S_2 01RS_3$, etc.).

Turing went on to define a set of integers N as computable if there was a Turing machine which, given any number m as input, will halt on 1 if m is a member of N, and halt on 0 otherwise. Using a variant of Cantor's diagonal argument Turing proved, echoing earlier work by Kurt Gödel and Alonzo Church, that some sets of integers are not computable.

Soon after the outbreak of war in 1939 Turing joined the government Code and Cypher School at Bletchley Park, Buckinghamshire. The Germans were known to be using a coding device called 'Enigma'. The basic model looked like an electric typewriter; the keyboard (input) was connected to the typed output by three rotors which changed position after each letter. This was equivalent to a polyalphabetic system with a periodicity of $26^3 = 17,576$. The military version of Enigma added a number of complications. The positions of the rotors could be changed, increasing the periodicity to 105,456. Further improvements increased the periodicity to over a trillion. The Germans felt that the military Enigma was 'very close to practical insolvability'.

Turing, along with a motley collection of mathematicians, linguists, and chess grandmasters, worked initially on the naval version of Enigma. The key innovation was the development of a computer, known as a

'Bombe', to handle the vast amounts of traffic. The name derived from the fact that early models designed by Polish analysts ticked very loudly. The Bombe allowed numerous possible solutions to be quickly checked against traffic and eliminated. By March 1940 they were reading some of the traffic and finding that it consisted of nursery rhymes sent as practice transmissions. By June 1941 they were reading operational naval traffic. This, however, was not the end of Turing's work. In early 1942 the German navy adopted a new Enigma system and added a fourth rotor to its design. The sinking of Allied shipping rapidly increased. The breakthrough came in December 1942. The Germans were transmitting weather reports daily by Enigma machines using only the first three rotors. Cribs of the weather reports were provided rapidly from other sources. It was therefore only necessary for the Bombes to work through the 26 possibilities of the fourth rotor to decipher fully encrypted traffic. By the new year Allied shipping could once more be diverted away from known U-boat positions. Shortly after this Turing left Bletchley Park for nearby Hanslope Park where he worked for the rest of the war on speech encipherment. Few individuals can have contributed so much to the war effort, or have saved so many lives, as Turing. In 1946 he was awarded an OBE for his services.

Turing was reluctant to return to Cambridge and a career in pure mathematics. Consequently he accepted a position at the National Physical Laboratory working on the design of a new computer, ACE (Automatic Computing Engine). He moved to Manchester University in 1948 to undertake similar work on the development of MADAM (Manchester Automatic Digital Machine).

During this period Turing produced two influential papers. In his *Computing Machinery and Intelligence* (1950) he challenged his critics to specify how computers could be distinguished from intelligent human beings. In the imitation game the interrogator posed questions to two 'individuals' A and B; he was asked to determine from their written replies which answer came from a computer. Both can of course lie. The *Turing test*, as the procedure is now called, has been cited as a way of testing machine intelligence and still causes debate and experiment. Turing himself was in no doubt that one day computers would be able to think.

Turing's other paper, *The Chemical Basis of Morphogenesis* (1952), concerned the generation of form. How can an assemblage of cells develop, as with the case of a starfish, a five-fold symmetry? Or how does a sphere of cells, in the process of gastrulation, form a groove at a specific point? He argued that it was possible for differences in chemical concentration to develop, even though the original situation had a uniform concentration. Turing's original model was mathematical. Chemists have, however, since found that there are systems, namely reaction–diffusion models, which mimic Turing's 'morphogens'.

Before he could develop his ideas further Turing committed suicide. He was homosexual and, for the times, fairly open about his life. A friend of a casual pick-up had stolen a few items of no great value from Turing's house and Turing reported the theft to the police. The culprit was arrested and in the course of investigations it was revealed that Turing had been sexually involved with a 19-year-old man. He was charged with gross indecency. Reluctantly he allowed himself to be persuaded to plead guilty and the court placed him on probation on the condition that he undergo hormone treatment. Although he seemed to find the process no more than irritating, and although his job remained secure, to the surprise of his family and friends he took his own life in 1954 by eating an apple dosed with cyanide.

Tuve, Merle Antony (1901–1982)
American geophysicist

Born at Canton in South Dakota, Tuve gained his BS degree in electrical engineering in 1922 from the University of Minnesota. He held posts at Princeton (1923–24) and Johns Hopkins (1924–26), receiving his PhD from the latter in 1926. From 1926 he was a staff member of the department of terrestrial magnetism of the Carnegie Institution of Washington.

Tuve is known principally for his techniques of radio-wave exploration of the upper atmosphere. In 1925 Tuve and Gregory Breit at Carnegie conducted some of the first experiments in range-finding using radio-waves in which they measured the height of the ionosphere. They transmitted a train of pulses of waves and determined the time each pulse took to return to Earth. Thereafter, pulse-ranging became the standard procedure for ionospheric research and laid the foundation for much of the later work on the development of radar.

In 1926 Tuve investigated long-range seismic refraction – the effect of different materials in the Earth's crust on the propagation of a seismic disturbance. He went on to construct an 'upper-mantle velocities map' of America, which has been found to accord with theories of isostasy – a hydrostatic state of equilibrium in the distribution of materials of varying density in the Earth's interior.

During World War II Tuve worked for the Office of Scientific Research and Development, developing the 'proximity fuse', which stopped the 'buzz bomb' attacks on Britain and Antwerp, among other projects. He returned to Carnegie in 1946 to become director of the department of terrestrial magnetism, a position he held up to 1966.

As well as seismic refraction and range-finding, Tuve also made studies of artificially produced beta and gamma rays, transmutations of atomic nuclei, and artificial radioactivity. He was for nine years editor of the *Journal of Geophysical Research*.

Twort, Frederick William (1877–1950)
British bacteriologist

Twort, a doctor's son from Camberley in Surrey, qualified in medicine in 1900 and after various appointments in London hospitals became professor of bacteriology at London University. His most important discovery was made during an attempt to grow viruses in artificial media: he noticed that bacteria, which were infecting his plates, became transparent. This phenomenon proved to be contagious and was the first demonstration of the existence of bacteria-infecting viruses. These were later called 'bacteriophages' by the Canadian bacteriologist Felix d'Herelle, who discovered them independently.

Twort was also the first to culture the causative organism of Johne's disease, an important intestinal infection of cattle.

Tyndall, John (1820–1893) *British physicist*

Tyndall was born at Carlow (now in the Republic of Ireland) and after leaving school began work as a draftsman and civil engineer in the Irish Ordnance Survey. He later became a railway engineer for a Manchester firm. His drive for knowledge caused him to read widely and attend whatever public lectures he could. In 1847 he became a teacher of mathematics, surveying, and engineering physics at the Quaker school, Queenwood College, Hampshire.

The following year Tyndall entered the University of Marburg, Germany, to study mathematics, physics, and chemistry; after graduating in 1850 he worked in H.G. Magnus's laboratory in Berlin on diamagnetism. He was appointed professor of natural philosophy at the Royal Institution in 1853 and became a colleague and admirer of Michael Faraday; he succeeded Faraday as director of the Royal Institution in 1867 and held this position until his retirement in 1887.

Tyndall's activities were many-sided. His chief scientific work is considered to be his researches on radiant heat; these included measurements of the transmission of radiant heat through gases and vapors published in a series of papers starting in 1859. But he is perhaps better known for his investigations on the behavior of light beams passing through various substances; he gave his name to the *Tyndall effect* – the scattering of light by particles of matter in its path, thus making the light beam visible – which he discovered in 1859. Tyndall elucidated the blue of the sky following the work of John Rayleigh on the scattering of light. He also discovered the precipitation of organic vapors by means of light, examined the opacity of the air for sound in connection with lighthouses and siren work, demonstrated that dust in the atmosphere contained microorganisms, and verified that germ-free air did not initiate putrefaction.

Tyndall was especially noted in his day as a great popularizer of science and advocate of scientific education, rather than as a great scientist. Among his many books for the nonspecialist the famous *Heat Considered as a Mode of Motion* (1863), the first popular exposition of the mechanical theory of heat, went through numerous editions. He was a member of the 'X' Club, a group of prominent British scientists formed to ensure that the claims of science and scientific education were kept before the government of the day. He also helped to inaugurate the British scientific journal *Nature*. In 1872 and 1873 he undertook public lecture tours in America, giving the proceeds to a trust set up to benefit American science.

Tyndall died in 1893, accidentally poisoned by his wife with an overdose of chloral hydrate. "You have killed your John," he is alleged to have told her shortly before he died the following day. Louisa Tyndall lived another 47 years.

Uhlenbeck, George Eugene (1900–1988) *Dutch–American physicist.* See GOUDSMIT, SAMUEL ABRAHAM.

Ulam, Stanislaw Marcin (1909–1986)
Polish–American mathematician

The son of a lawyer, Ulam was educated at the polytechnic in his native city of Lwow, Poland, where he completed his doctorate in 1933. Ulam quickly developed a reputation as an original mathematician and in 1936 he was invited to visit the Institute for Advanced Study, Princeton, for a year. He decided to remain in the United States and spent the period from 1937 to 1940 at Harvard before being appointed professor of mathematics at the University of Wisconsin. He became a naturalized American citizen in 1943.

At the same time Ulam was invited to work on the development of the atom bomb at Los Alamos, New Mexico, and he remained associated with Los Alamos until 1967. Here he worked on the theory of nuclear reactions. When neutrons are released in a reactor some scatter, some are absorbed, others escape or collide, etc. The actual process is too complex for analytical calculation. If, however, the fate of a practical number of neutrons is followed, and if at each branch one outcome with a suitable probability is selected, it is possible to derive a reasonably accurate mathematical model of the process. Ulam's technique, which is known as the 'Monte Carlo method' (after the casino), is a widely used numerical method in many different fields.

After the war Ulam worked with Teller on the development of the hydrogen bomb. He served as research adviser to the director of Los Alamos from 1957 to 1967, when he was appointed professor of mathematics at the University of Colorado, Boulder, a post he held until his retirement in 1977. He left an account of his life in his *Adventures of a Mathematician* (New York, 1976).

Ulugh Beg (1394–1449) *Persian astronomer*

Ulugh Beg was a grandson of Tamerlane. He was born at Soltaniyeh (now in Iran) and succeeded to the throne in 1447 but was killed by his rebellious son two years later. He began building an observatory at Samarkand in 1428. He was himself an observer and published planetary tables and a catalog of stars in 1437. They were published in Europe in 1665. The observatory was said to have had a gnomon for measuring the elevation of the Sun as high as the dome of St. Sophia in Byzantium (180 feet).

Urey, Harold Clayton (1893–1981)
American physical chemist

Urey, born the son of a teacher and lay minister in Walkerton, Indiana, was educated at the universities of Montana, where he studied zoology, and California, where he obtained a PhD in chemistry (1923). After a year at the Institute of Theoretical Physics in Copenhagen, he began his teaching career at Johns Hopkins in 1924. In 1929 he moved to Columbia University, remaining there until 1958 when he became a professor at the University of California.

He is best known as the discoverer of deuterium – the isotope of hydrogen containing one proton and one neutron in its nucleus. This followed the accurate measurement of the atomic weights of hydrogen and oxygen by Francis W. Aston and the discovery of oxygen isotopes by William Giauque.

To obtain deuterium Urey used the fact that it would evaporate at a slightly slower rate than normal hydrogen. He took some four liters of liquid hydrogen, which he distilled down to a volume of one cubic centimeter. The presence of deuterium was then proved spectroscopically. Urey went on to investigate differences in chemical-reaction rate between isotopes. During World War II he was in charge of the separation of isotopes in the atomic-bomb project. Urey's research also led to a large-scale method of obtaining deuterium oxide (heavy water) for use as a neutron moderator in reactors.

His interest in isotope effects in chemical reactions gave him the idea for a method of measuring temperatures in the oceans in the past. It depended on the fact that the calcium carbonate in shells contains slightly more oxygen-18 than oxygen-16, and the ratio depends on the temperature at which the shell formed.

For his discovery of heavy hydrogen Urey received the 1939 Nobel Prize for chemistry.

Vallisneri, Antonio (1661–1730) Italian physician and biologist

Born at Trassilico, near Modena in Italy, Vallisneri studied medicine at Bologna under Marcello Malpighi and at Reggio where he obtained his MD in 1684. After practicing medicine in Reggio, Vallisneri was appointed to the chair of medicine at the University of Padua in 1700 where he remained until his death.

Francesco Redi in 1668 had performed a famous experiment proving that the maggots in rotten meat were not spontaneously generated but arose, in the normal manner, from eggs laid by flies. He did however spoil the force of his argument by conceding that the larvae found in galls, for which he could find no eggs, were spontaneously generated. In 1700 Vallisneri plugged this gap in his *Sopra la curiosa origine di molti insetti* (On the Strange Origin of Many Insects) in which he reported detecting eggs of the insects in plant galls.

In 1715 Vallisneri published *Origine delle fontane* (Origin of Fountains), which threw much light on another longstanding problem. Many ancient and medieval authorities were convinced that springs and rivers originated in the sea, and consequently the source of artesian wells, such as those at Modena, presented a problem. By exploring the local mountains, Vallisneri found that the rain and melting snow ran into fissures and formed subterranean rivers. Such rivers, passing under Modena at high pressure, would readily produce 'fontane' if deep enough shafts were sunk.

As a biologist and anatomist Vallisneri also produced a number of treatises on such unfamiliar animals as the ostrich (1712) and the chameleon (1715). His studies of a group of aquatic plants led to the genus *Vallisneria* being named for him.

Van Allen, James Alfred (1914–) American physicist

Van Allen was born at Mount Pleasant, Iowa. After graduating from the Iowa Wesleyan College in 1935 he went on to the University of Iowa, where he gained his PhD in 1939. His subsequent career took him to the Carnegie Institution of Washington (1939–42), as a physics research fellow in the department of terrestrial magnetism, and to the applied physics laboratory at the Johns Hopkins University (1942 and 1946–50). In 1951 Van Allen returned to the University of Iowa as a professor of physics and head of the department of physics and astronomy, retiring in 1990.

During the war years (1942–46) he served as an ordnance and gunnery specialist and combat observer with the US Navy and developed the radio proximity fuze, a device that guided explosive weapons, such as antiaircraft shells, close to their targets and then detonated them. He also gained considerable expertise in the miniaturization of electronics and rocket controls, which he later put to use in the scientific exploration of the Earth's upper atmosphere.

After the war Van Allen was able to use German V–2 rockets for atmospheric studies and was associated with the development of the Aerobee sounding rocket. He also used rocket–balloon combinations that could carry small rockets to higher altitudes. In the years 1949–57 he organized and led several scientific expeditions (to Peru, the Gulf of Alaska, Greenland, and Antarctica) to study cosmic rays – highly energetic particles arriving from space. The direction of all this work led to the launching in January 1958 of America's first satellite, Explorer I (as part of a major International Geophysical Year series of experiments), which carried experiments designed to measure cosmic rays and other energetic particles. Unexpectedly high radiation levels were found in certain regions of the Earth's atmosphere – so high that the satellite's Geiger counters jammed. This observation was contrary to the observation of the first Russian satellite, Sputnik I, launched five months earlier, and gave impetus to further satellite exploration. Subsequent observations by a succession of satellites (Explorer, Pioneer, Sputnik, Mechta, Lunik) have shown that the Earth's magnetic field traps high-speed charged particles in two zones girdling the Earth, with the greatest particle concentration above the equator. One zone lies roughly 600–3000 miles (1000–5000 km) above the Earth's surface; the other is 9000–15,000 miles (15,000–25,000 km) above the equator, curving down toward the magnetic poles. These regions were later to be named the *Van Allen belts*. The particles in the belts are electrons and protons (as suggested by F. Singer early in 1957) originating in cosmic-ray collisions or captured from the 'solar wind' of particles that streams out from the Sun. In 1958 a controversial experiment, known as 'Project Argus', was carried out – also as part of the International Geophysical Year. This involved the detonation of three small nuclear bombs, at altitudes over 300 miles (480 km) over the South Atlantic Ocean, to inject very energetic particles into the upper atmosphere. These were subsequently found to have been captured in the Van Allen belts.

Van Allen has produced over 200 scientific papers, has received a great number of scientific awards, and has been a member of several US governmental committees concerned with space exploration.

Van de Graaff, Robert Jemison
(1901–1967) *American physicist*

Born in Tuscaloosa, Alabama, Van de Graaff studied engineering at the University of Alabama, gaining his BS in 1922 and his MS in 1923. He enrolled in 1924 at the Sorbonne in Paris where he was inspired by the lectures of Marie Curie to study physics. In 1928 he obtained a PhD from Oxford University for research into the motion of ions in gases. It was during these studies that he conceived of an electrostatic generator that could radically improve on existing types, such as the Wimshurst machine, by building up electric charge on a hollow insulated metal sphere. A year later he returned to America and started working as a research fellow at Princeton. In 1931 he moved to the Massachusetts Institute of Technology as a research associate, serving as associate professor of physics from 1934 until he resigned in 1960.

While at Princeton he constructed, in 1931, the first model of his generator, now known as the *Van de Graaff generator*. The charge was carried to the hollow sphere by means of an insulated fabric belt and once transferred could accumulate on the outer surface of the sphere, leading ultimately to potentials of 80,000 volts. This was eventually increased to over a million volts.

At MIT Van de Graaff developed the generator for use as a particle accelerator. This *Van de Graaff accelerator* used the generator as a source of high voltage that could accelerate charged particles, such as electrons, to high velocities and hence high energies. It was thus to be a major tool in the developing fields of atomic and nuclear physics. One of Van de Graaff's aims was to explore the possibility of uranium fission and to try to create elements with larger atoms than uranium.

In collaboration with John Trump, an electrical engineer, he adapted the generator to produce high-energy x-rays, which could be used in the treatment of cancer. The first x-ray generator began operation in a Boston hospital in 1937. During World War II Van de Graaff was director of the radiographic project of the Office of Scientific Research and Development in which the generator was developed for another use: the examination of the interior structure of heavy ordnance by means of x-rays.

In 1946 Trump and Van de Graaff formed the High Voltage Engineering Corporation to market Van de Graaff accelerators and x-ray generators to hospitals, industry, and scientific research establishments. Van de Graaff was director and chief physicist and in 1960 left MIT to work there full time as chief scientist.

Van de Hulst, Hendrik Christoffel
(1918–) *Dutch astronomer*

Van de Hulst studied at the university in his native city of Utrecht where he obtained his PhD in 1946. He spent two years at the University of Chicago as a postdoctoral fellow (1946–48) then took up an appointment at the University of Leiden. Following several years at different universities in America he became professor of astronomy at Leiden and director of the Leiden Observatory.

In the German-occupied Netherlands a group of astronomers began to think about the implications of Grote Reber's discovery of radio emission from the Milky Way. Jan Oort, then director of the Leiden Observatory, wondered whether the emission was merely a uniform noise or could the equivalent of the absorption and emission lines of light be detected. In 1944 van de Hulst came up with the answer.

He proposed that hydrogen atoms, which occur in diffuse but widespread regions in interstellar space, can exist in two forms. In ordinary hydrogen the proton and its orbiting electron spin in the same direction. There is a very small chance that the electron will spontaneously flip over and spin in the opposite direction to the proton and in the process emit radiation with a wavelength of 21 centimeters, i.e., at a frequency of 1420.4 megahertz. Although emission from a single atom is a very rare event, there is such an abundance of hydrogen in the universe that the process should be taking place with sufficient frequency to be detectable.

It was not, however, until 1951 that van de Hulst's proposal was confirmed: the 21-centimeter hydrogen line emission was detected at Harvard by Edward M. Purcell and Harold Ewen who used equipment specially built for the purpose. It has since proved a crucial tool for the investigation of the distribution and movement of neutral hydrogen in our own Galaxy and in other spiral galaxies. Since the hydrogen lies in the spiral arms and since the 21-centimeter emission passes unimpeded through the dust that prevents optical observation, this has led to a greatly increased knowledge of galactic structure.

It was also felt that if intelligent life did exist outside the solar system and wished to communicate with other civilizations, then it would be highly rational to transmit signals at the hydrogen-emission wavelength of 21 centimeter. Although much expensive telescope time has been spent listening on this wavelength, nothing has been heard that does not come from hydrogen itself.

Van de Kamp, Peter (1901–) *Dutch–American astronomer*

Van de Kamp, who was born at Kampen in the Netherlands, studied at the University of Utrecht, obtaining his PhD in 1922. He emigrated to America in 1923 and, after appointments at the Lick Observatory (1924–25) and the University of Virginia (1923–24, 1925–37), became director of the Sproul Observatory and professor of astronomy at Swarthmore College, Pennsylvania. Following his retirement in 1972 he became research astronomer there.

In the 1960s van de Kamp found strong evidence for a new celestial phenomenon: planets orbiting stars other than the Sun. Since 1937 he had been studying the motion of Barnard's star, a nearby red star with a very large proper motion of 10.3 seconds of arc per year. By 1969 he was able to state that the star was oscillating very slightly in position about a straight line and that this wobbling motion was caused by an unseen companion. This companion was orbiting Barnard's star in about 25 years and was only about 1.5 times the mass of Jupiter. As this is too small a mass for a star, van de Kamp concluded that it was a planet. After further calculations he said that it was more likely that there were two planets, both of a similar mass to Jupiter, one orbiting in about 12 years and the other in 26 years.

This was not the only search for planets. In 1943 K. A. Strand claimed that he had detected a planetary body in the binary star 61 Cygni. His evidence was not as good as van de Kamp's however, although more recent observations indicate a planet about eight times the mass of Jupiter orbiting the brighter component of 61 Cygni in 4.8

years. There are other stars that have also shown perturbed motions from planet-sized companions.

The planets belong to stars that are relatively close. It is unlikely that this is merely coincidental and consequently van de Kamp and others concluded that planetary systems are likely to be widespread. Such a conclusion implies that some form of life may be present outside the solar system.

Van der Meer, Simon (1925–) *Dutch engineer and physicist*

Van der Meer was educated at the Gymnasium in his native city of The Hague and at the Technical University, Delft, where he gained his PhD in 1956. He immediately joined the staff at the European Organization for Nuclear Research (CERN) and remained there until his retirement in 1990.

In 1979 the Nobel Prize for physics was awarded to Sheldon Glashow and two colleagues for their unification of the electromagnetic and weak forces. Although the neutral currents predicted by the theory were detected in 1973, it still remained to discover the charged W^+ and W^- and the neutral Z^0 bosons whose existence was a consequence of the theory. As the masses of the particles were about 80 times that of the proton, the energy required for their production outstripped the capacity of any existing accelerator. In 1978 Carlo Rubbia, a colleague at CERN, asked van der Meer if there was any way to conjure such high energies from the existing accelerators.

CERN's SPS (Super Proton Synchroton) could deliver about 450 billion electronvolts (450 GeV). One possible solution would be to convert the SPS into a colliding-beam machine, that is, protons and antiprotons would be accelerated, stored separately, and then induced to collide with each other head-on. Proton–antiproton collisions, it was calculated, with an energy of 270 GeV per beam were equivalent to a beam of 155,000 GeV hitting with a stationary target.

The problem facing van der Meer was how to concentrate the beams. Protons normally repel each other, as do antiprotons, and, consequently, charged particle beams tend to spread out in space. To maximize the colliding power of the beams van der Meer somehow needed to focus them. He proposed to use the technique of 'stochastic cooling', first described by him in 1972 as a way of reducing random motion in the beam. To achieve this the exact center of the beam was calculated and correcting magnetic fields were applied by a system of 'kickers' placed around the ring. By this means particles out of line were nudged back into position. The system was successfully tested in May 1979 and was used in 1983 to create the W and the Z particles. Van der Meer shared the 1984 Nobel Prize for physics with Rubbia for this work.

Van der Waals, Johannes Diderik
(1837–1923) *Dutch physicist*

Van der Waals was born at Leiden in the Netherlands. He was largely self-taught in science and he originally worked as a school teacher. He later managed to study at the University of Leiden, having been exempted from the Latin and Greek entrance requirements. In 1877 he became professor of physics at the University of Amsterdam.

Van der Waals studied the kinetic theory of gases and fluids and in 1873 presented his influential doctoral thesis, *On the Continuity of the Liquid and Gaseous States.* His main work was to develop an equation (the *van der Waals equation*) that – unlike the gas laws of Robert Boyle and Jacques Charles – applied to real gases. The Boyle–Charles law, strictly speaking, applies only to 'ideal' gases, but can be derived from the kinetic theory given the assumptions that there are no attractive forces between gas molecules and that the molecules themselves have zero volume.

Since the molecules do have attractive forces and volume (however small), van der Waals introduced into the theory two further constants to take these properties into account. Initially these constants had to be specific to each gas since the size of the molecules and the attractive force between them is different for each gas. Further work by van der Waals yielded the law of corresponding states – an equation that is the same for all substances. His valuable results enabled James Dewar and Heike Kamerlingh-Onnes to work out methods of liquefying the permanent gases.

In 1910 van der Waals was awarded the Nobel Prize for physics for his work on the equation of state. The weak electrostatic attractive forces between molecules and between atoms are called *van der Waals forces* in his honor.

Vane, Sir John Robert (1927–   )
British pharmacologist

Vane studied chemistry at the University of Birmingham and pharmacology at Oxford, where he obtained his DPhil in 1953. He then worked at the Royal College of Surgeons, serving as professor of experimental pharmacology from 1966 until 1973, when he moved to the Wellcome Foundation as director of research and development. In 1985 Vane left Wellcome to serve as director

of the William Harvey Research Institute, St. Bartholomew's Hospital, London. He was knighted in 1984.

Vane has worked on hormonelike substances, the prostaglandins, first observed by Ulf von Euler in the 1930s. In the 1960s he began to explore their physiological roles. He extracted in 1969 a substance from the lung tissue of rats sensitive to an allergen. As it caused rabbit aortas to contract it was named 'rabbit aorta contracting substance' (RCS). He also found that RCS caused blood platelets to clot. It was later shown by Bengt Samuelsson that RCS contained the prostaglandin PGH_2 as an active ingredient. But Vane had earlier shown that the effects of RCS could be inhibited by aspirin and other antiinflammatory drugs. This allowed Vane to propose a mechanism for both the effects of aspirin and prostaglandins. Aspirin, he argued, reduced pain, inflammation, and fever by blocking the action of prostaglandins which, at least in some cases, seemed to produce precisely these effects. For his work in this field Vane shared the 1982 Nobel Prize for physiology or medicine with Samuelsson and Sune Bergstrom.

He has also worked on the pharmacological effects of adrenaline (epinephrine) and edited the CIBA Foundation symposium on the subject, *Adrenergic Mechanisms* (1960). He was awarded the 1982 Nobel Prize for physiology or medicine (with Sune Bergstrom and Bengt Samuelsson).

Van Maanen, Adriaan (1884–1946)
Dutch–American astronomer

Van Maanen, who was born at Sneek in the Netherlands, studied at the University of Utrecht, where he obtained his doctorate in 1911. He worked at the University of Groningen from 1909 to 1911 when he moved to America. After working briefly at the Yerkes Observatory he took up an appointment in 1912 at the Mount Wilson Observatory in California, where he remained for the rest of his career.

Van Maanen specialized in measuring the minute changes in position of astronomical objects over a period of time, from which he could determine their proper motion and parallax. These objects included stars, clusters of stars, and nebulae. Between 1916 and 1923 he produced a number of measurements of spiral nebulae from which he calculated their rotation rate. This was at the time of the controversy between astronomers as to whether such nebulae were island universes in their own right or part of our own Galaxy. Van Maanen's results were therefore of considerable significance, for whether one can detect rotation in a distant body and measure its rate of rotation partly depend on the distance of the object from the observer. The rotation of about 0.02 seconds of arc per year that he obtained from a number of nebulae over a period of seven years seemed to be indisputable evidence against the emerging view that such objects as the Andromeda nebula were really separate remote star systems. This was certainly the view that Harlow Shapley took in 1920 as he could see no reason to doubt the work of van Maanen, his close friend, who was known to be a careful and competent observer.

Van Maanen's work was, however, incompatible with the growing body of measurements produced by Edwin Hubble, also at Mount Wilson. These suggested that nebulae like Andromeda were as much as 800,000 light-years away, at which distance it was inconceivable that any internal motion should be detectable. As no one, including van Maanen himself, had any idea where he had gone wrong, his work became something of a curiosity and tended to be ignored. Other astronomers, like Knut Lundmark in 1923, failed to reproduce his results while in 1935 van Maanen was able to detect a displacement only about half that found in the 1920s. When in the same year Hubble also reported failure to detect the rotation, it became widely accepted that there was some unknown instrumental or personal error in van Maanen's work.

It is unlikely to have been an instrumental error as Hubble used the same instruments while a later computer analysis of his work has revealed no major computational errors. This only leaves unconscious personal error and recent work has shown that a systematic error of only 0.002 millimeter in the measurements of points on photographic plates would be sufficient to produce his results. The same systematic error also occurred in his work on the strength of the solar magnetic field, which he considerably overestimated.

He did however discover the second white dwarf, since named *van Maanen's star*, with a density some 400,000 times that of the Sun.

Van't Hoff, Jacobus Henricus (1852–1911) *Dutch theoretical chemist*

Van't Hoff was born at Rotterdam in the Netherlands, the son of a physician. He studied at Delft Polytechnic and the University of Leiden before going abroad to work with August Kekulé in Bonn (1872) and with Charles Adolphe Wurtz in Paris (1874), where he met Joseph-Achille Le Bel. In 1878

he was appointed to the Amsterdam chair of chemistry where he remained until moving to the University of Berlin in 1896.

In 1874 van't Hoff published a paper entitled *A Suggestion Looking to the Extension into Space of the Structural Formulas at Present Used in Chemistry*, which effectively created a new branch of science – stereochemistry. The problem began with the discovery of optically active compounds. Louis Pasteur later established the asymmetry of crystals of tartaric acid: some would rotate polarized light to the right and others to the left. This was explained by the actual asymmetry of the crystal: the crystals were mirror images of each other. Pasteur thought that the molecules themselves were asymmetric but could offer no proof. This would explain the further problem of the optical activity of noncrystalline solutions. Van't Hoff solved these problems and offered an account of molecular asymmetry by concentrating on the structure of the carbon atom, newly established by Kekulé. He announced (1874) that the four chemical bonds that carbon can form are directed to the corners of a tetrahedron. With this structure, certain molecules can have left- and right-handed isomers, which have opposite effects on polarized light. It also explained why certain isomers do not occur.

Van't Hoff's account of molecular structure was attacked by Hermann Kolbe but a similar theory was put forward simultaneously by Joseph-Achille Le Bel, independently of van't Hoff. Despite the hostility, his ideas were soon vindicated by Emil Fischer's researches into sugars in the 1880s.

Major contributions were also made by van't Hoff to the thermodynamics and kinetics of solutions. Many of these results are reported in his book *Etudes de dynamique chimie* (1884; Studies in Chemical Kinetics). He had the central insight in 1886 that there is a similarity between solutions and gases provided that osmotic pressure is substituted for the ordinary pressure of gases, and derived laws for dilute solutions similar to those of Robert Boyle and Joseph Gay-Lussac for gases. This fundamental result could be used to determine the molecular weight of a substance in solution.

In 1901 van't Hoff was awarded the first Nobel Prize for chemistry.

Van Vleck, John Hasbrouck (1899–1980) *American physicist*

Van Vleck was born at Middletown, Connecticut, and educated at the University of Wisconsin, where he graduated in 1920. Moving to Harvard University he gained his master's degree (1921) and his doctorate

(1922) and stayed for a further year as an instructor. From Harvard he went to the University of Minnesota, where he became a full professor in 1927, returned to Wisconsin in 1928, and then went back to Harvard in 1934.

Van Vleck is regarded as the founder of the modern quantum mechanical theory of magnetism. His earliest papers were on the old quantum theory, but with the advent of wave mechanics pioneered by Paul Dirac he began to look at the implications for magnetism in particular. In the field of paramagnetism he introduced the concept of temperature-independent susceptibility, now known as *Van Vleck paramagnetism*. He also made calculations of molecular structure that shed new light on chemical bonding and he developed ways of describing the behavior of an atom or an ion in a crystal. Another important contribution of Van Vleck was to point out the importance of electron correlation – the interaction between the motion of electrons – for the appearance of local magnetic moments in metals.

During World War II Van Vleck worked on radar, showing that at about 1.25-centimeter wavelength water molecules in the atmosphere would lead to troublesome absorption and that at 0.5-centimeter wavelength there would be a similar absorption by oxygen molecules. This was to have important consequences not just for military (and civil) radar systems but later for the new science of radioastronomy.

In 1977, together with Nevill MOTT and Philip ANDERSON, he shared the Nobel Prize for physics for "fundamental theoretical investigations of the electronic structure of magnetic and disordered systems." (Anderson was once a student of Van Vleck's at Harvard.) Van Vleck's work on electron correlation was mentioned specifically for the central role it played in the later development of the laser.

Varmus, Harold Eliot (1939–   )
American microbiologist

Born at Oceanside, New York, Varmus was educated at Amherst College, Harvard, and at Columbia University, where he studied medicine. After working at the Presbyterian Hospital, New York (1966–68), he joined the National Institutes of Health, Bethesda, as clinical associate (1968–70) before moving to the Department of Microbiology at the University of California at San Francisco. He was appointed full professor in 1979.

In the 1970s, working in collaboration with Michael BISHOP, Dominique Stehelin, and Peter Vogt, Varmus made a crucial

breakthrough in our understanding of cancer. The Rous sarcoma virus, which causes cancer in chickens, was known to have a particular gene (called an 'oncogene') associated with its cancer-causing capability. Varmus and his colleagues prepared a molecular probe for this gene – a fragment of DNA with a base sequence complementary to the gene and capable of pairing with it – and demonstrated that the gene was present in the cells of normal chickens.

This showed for the first time that viral oncogenes are derived from genes of the virus's host, incorporated into the genetic material of the virus in a modified form. This breakthrough led to the discovery of a large number of similar cellular genes, subsequently termed 'proto-oncogenes', that acted as a source of oncogenes. The key to understanding how viral oncogenes transform a normal cell into a cancerous one thus lies in determining how their equivalent proto-oncogenes function in normal cells. Several roles have been elucidated for these genes, principally the regulation of cell growth, division, and differentiation. Interference or disturbance in these processes, as may occur in the presence of an oncogene, could lead to uncontrolled cell proliferation, as in cancer.

The results of Varmus's work were published in 1976 and opened the door to a major new field in cancer research. For this work Varmus and Bishop were jointly awarded the 1989 Nobel Prize for physiology or medicine.

Vauquelin, Louis Nicolas (1763–1829)
French chemist

The son of a farm laborer from Saint-André d'Hebertot in France, Vauquelin began work as an apprentice to a Rouen apothecary. He became a laboratory assistant to Antoine-François Fourcroy (1783–91), with whom he later collaborated. Vauquelin became a member of the French Academy of Sciences in 1791 and professor of chemistry in the School of Mines in 1795. In 1799 he wrote *Manuel de l'essayeur* (An Assayer's Manual), which led to his being appointed assayer to the mint in 1802 and professor of chemistry at the University of Paris in 1809.

Vauquelin is best known for his discovery of the elements chromium and beryllium. In 1798, while working with a red lead mineral from Siberia known as crocolite, he isolated the new element chromium – so called because its compounds are very highly colored. Martin Klaproth made a similar discovery shortly afterward. In the same year Vauquelin also isolated a new element in the mineral beryl. It was initially called glucinum because of the sweetness of its compounds, but later given its modern name of beryllium. He was the first to isolate an amino acid: asparagine from asparagus.

Vavilov, Nikolai Ivanovich (1887–1943) *Russian plant geneticist*

Having graduated from the Agricultural Institute in his native city of Moscow, Vavilov continued his studies firstly in England under William Bateson and then in France at the Vilmoren Institution. Back in Russia he was appointed, in 1917, both professor of genetics and selection at the Agricultural Institute, Voronezh, and professor of agriculture at Saratov University. Three years later he took over the directorship of the Bureau of Applied Botany, Petrograd (now St. Petersburg), which later became the All Union Institute of Plant Industry. The institute flourished under Vavilov's leadership, becoming the center for over 400 research institutes throughout the Soviet Union. In 1929 he became the first president of the Academy of Agricultural Sciences.

During the years 1916–1933 Vavilov led several plant-collecting expeditions to countries all around the globe. The purpose was to gather material of potential use in crop-breeding programs, particularly the wild relatives and ancestors of cultivated plants. He was highly successful in this, his collection numbering some 250,000 accessions by 1940. This was the first large-scale attempt to conserve and utilize the immensely valuable genetic resources upon which crop improvement relies.

A second important consequence of these travels was Vavilov's observation that the genetic diversity of crop relatives is concentrated in certain areas that he termed 'gene centers', postulating that these correspond to regions where agriculture originated. The theory and the exact number of centers have since been modified but the recognition of such areas is an invaluable aid to other plant hunters. He also found certain regularities between unrelated genera in such centers, described in *The Law of Homologous Series in Variation* (1922).

Vavilov's excellent work was gradually stifled by the intrusion of politics into Soviet biology in the 1930s. His belief in the advances in genetics made by Mendel and T. H. Morgan brought him into conflict with the government-backed Trofim Lysenko, who was returning to a Lamarckian view of inheritance. The 1937 International Congress of Genetics, due to be held in Moscow in view of the strides made in Soviet genetics under Vavilov, was canceled by the Ly-

senkoists. Vavilov was arrested in 1940 while plant collecting and died three years later in a Siberian labor camp.

Today Vavilov is recognized in his own country as an outstanding scientist, the Vavilov Institute being named in his honor.

Vernier, Pierre (c. 1580–1637) *French mathematician*

Born at Ornans in France, Vernier was educated by his father, a scientist, and became interested in scientific instruments. He was employed as an official with the government of Spain and then held various offices under the French government.

In 1631 Vernier invented the caliper named for him, an instrument for taking very precise measurements. The principle of the vernier scale is described in his book *La Construction, l'usage, et les propriétés du quadrant nouveau de mathématique* (1631; The Construction, Uses, and Properties of a New Mathematical Quadrant), which also contained some of the earliest tables of trigonometric functions and formulas for deriving the angles of a triangle from the lengths of its sides.

Vesalius, Andreas (1514–1564) *Belgian anatomist*

Vesalius, born the son of a pharmacist in Brussels, Belgium, was educated at the universities of Louvain, Paris, and Padua, receiving his MD from the last in 1537. He was immediately appointed professor of anatomy and surgery at Padua where he remained until 1543 when, at the age of 28, he joined the Hapsburg court. Here Vesalius successively served as physician to the Emperor Charles V and King Philip II of Spain. For reasons unknown, he left their service sometime after 1562 and died while on a pilgrimage to the Holy Land.

Vesalius thus completed his anatomical researches in the short period between 1538, when he produced his six anatomical plates the *Tabulae sex* (Six Tables), and 1543 when his masterpiece, *De humani corporis fabrica* (On the Structure of the Human Body) was printed in Basel. With this work he gained the reputation of being the greatest of Renaissance anatomists.

The work generally followed the physiological system of Galen and repeated some traditional errors; for example, he described the supposed pores in the septum of the heart despite confessing his inability to detect them. Other parts, such as the female generative organs, were treated inadequately because of a lack of the appropriate cadavers. However Vesalius's main innovation was to insist on conducting, personally, dissections on human cadavers, which taught him that Galenic anatomy was not to be treated unquestioningly.

The work of Vesalius was of considerable significance in marking the departure from ancient concepts. The *Fabrica* presented in a single, detailed, comprehensive, and accessible work (superbly illustrated, probably at the Titian school in Venice), a basis for following generations of anatomists to compare with their own dissections. It has been said that only after Vesalius did medicine became a science.

Viète, François (1540–1603) *French mathematician*

Viète, who was born at Fontenay-le-Comte in France, is also known by the Latinized form of his name, Franciscus Vieta. He was educated at Poitiers where he studied law and for a time he practiced as a lawyer. He was a member of the *parlement* of Brittany but because of his Huguenot sympathies he was forced to flee during the persecution of the Huguenots. On Henry IV's accession, however, he was able to hold further offices and became a privy councillor to the king. He put his mathematical abilities to practical use in deciphering the code used by Spanish diplomats.

Viète's chief work was in algebra. He made a number of innovations in the use of symbolism and several technical terms still in use (e.g., coefficient) were introduced by him. His work is important because of his tendency to solve problems by algebraic rather than geometric methods. By bringing algebraic techniques to bear on them Viète was able to solve a number of geometrical problems. A particularly long-standing problem – formulated by the Greek geometer Apollonius of Perga – namely, how to construct a circle that touches three given circles, was solved in this way by Viète.

Viète's major work is contained in his treatise *In artem analyticem isagoge* (1591; Introduction to the Analytical Arts) and among other advances in algebra that it contains are new and improved methods for solving cubic equations. Among these are techniques that make use of trigonometric methods. Viète also developed methods of approximating the solutions to equations.

Vine, Frederick John (1939–1988) *British geologist*

Vine was educated at Cambridge University. After a period in America teaching at Princeton University (1965–70) he returned to Britain becoming reader (1970) and pro-

fessor of environmental science (1974) at the University of East Anglia.

In 1963, in collaboration with his supervisor **Drummond Hoyle Matthews** (1931–1997), Vine produced a paper, *Magnetic Anomalies over Ocean Ridges*, which provided additional evidence for, and modified, the sea-floor spreading hypothesis of Harry H. Hess, published in 1962. The fact that magnetic reversals had occurred during the Earth's history had been known since the work of Matonori Matuyama in the 1920s and B. Brunhes earlier in the century. Vine and Matthews realized that if Hess was correct, the new rock emerging from the oceanic ridges would, on cooling, adopt the prevailing magnetic polarity. Newer rock emerging would push it further away from the ridge and, intermittently, as magnetic reversals occurred, belts of material of opposing magnetic polarity would be pushed out.

From examining several ocean ridges in the North Atlantic, Vine and Matthews established that the parallel belts of different magnetic polarities were symmetrical on either side of the ridge crests. This provided crucial evidence for the sea-floor spreading hypothesis. Correlation between the magnetic anomalies of ocean ridges in other oceans was also established.

Vinogradov, Ivan Matreevich (1891–1983) *Soviet mathematician*

Vinogradov, who was born at Milolyub (now Velikiye Luki) in Russia, held a number of posts at various institutions in the Soviet Union. Initially he taught at the University of Perm (1918–20) until appointed professor of mathematics at the Leningrad Polytechnic Institute. In 1925 he became a professor at Leningrad State University and in 1932 was appointed chairman of the National Committee of Soviet Mathematicians of the Soviet Academy of Sciences. From 1934 he was professor of mathematics at Moscow State University.

Vinogradov has been preeminent in the field of analytical number theory, i.e., the study of problems posed in purely number-theoretic terms by means of the techniques of analysis. He published several books, chiefly on various aspects of number theory, which include *A New Method in the Analytical Theory of Numbers* (1937) and *The Method of Trigonometric Sums in the Theory of Numbers* (1947).

One of his most outstanding achievements was his solution in 1937 of a problem of Christian Goldbach's (not to be confused with Goldbach's famous conjecture about even numbers and primes, which is still undecided). Vinogradov showed that every sufficiently large odd natural number is a sum of three primes.

Virchow, Rudolf Carl (1821–1902)
German pathologist

The son of a merchant from Schivelbein (now Świdwin in Poland), Virchow graduated in medicine from the Army Medical School, Berlin, in 1843. He then worked at the Charité Hospital in Berlin where he wrote a classic paper on one of the first known cases of leukemia. In 1849 he moved to Würzburg as professor of pathological anatomy. He returned to Berlin in 1856 as director of the university's Institute of Pathology, where he remained until his death.

In 1858 Virchow published *Die Cellularpathologie* (Cellular Pathology), in which he formulated two propositions of fundamental importance. The first, consciously echoing the words of William Harvey: "Omne vivum ex ovo" (All life is derived from an egg), declared "Omnis cellula e cellula" (Every cell is derived from a preexisting cell). Others, such as John Goodsir, had already advanced such ideas but Virchow differed in applying them to pathology, his second major thesis being that disease was a pathological cellular state. The cells are the 'seat' of disease, or, disease is simply the response of a cell to abnormal conditions. This by itself immediately generated the immense research program of collecting, examining, and classifying different types of cells and noting their variety and development, both normal and abnormal.

Virchow consequently had little time for the emerging germ theory of disease, which later in the century would sweep all other theories out of the way. In fact after 1870 Virchow tended to pursue interests other than pure science. Dissatisfied not only with the new germ theory but also with the theory of evolution, which he tried to have banned from school curricula, Virchow seemed more interested in archeology and politics than science.

Thus Virchow encouraged his friend Heinrich Schliemann in his determination to discover the site of Homer's Troy and actually worked on the dig at Hissarlik in 1879. In politics he was a member of the Reichstag from 1880 to 1893 and, as a leading liberal, was a bitter opponent of Bismarck who went so far as to challenge him to a duel in 1865.

Virchow was also widely known for founding, in 1847, the journal *Archiv für pathologische Anatomie* (Archive of Pathological Anatomy), which he continued to edit for 50 years.

Virtanen, Artturi Ilmari (1895–1973)
Finnish chemist

Virtanen was educated at the university in his native city of Helsinki, where he obtained his PhD in 1919, and at the universities of Zurich and Stockholm. He worked from 1921 to 1931 as director of the Finnish Cooperative Dairies Association Laboratory and from 1924 at the University of Helsinki where, in 1931, he became director of the Biochemical Institute.

In 1945 Virtanen was awarded the Nobel Prize for chemistry for his method of fodder preservation. This AIV method, as it became known, named for his initials, was designed to stop the loss of nitrogenous material in storage. By storing green fodder in an acid medium he hoped to prevent spoilage and still retain nutritious fodder. After much experimentation he finally found that a mixture of hydrochloric and sulfuric acid was adequate as long as its strength was kept within certain precise limits. Specifically, this demanded a pH of about four. In 1929 Virtanen found that cows fed on silage produced by his method gave milk indistinguishable in taste from that of cows fed on normal fodder. Further, it was just as rich in both vitamin A and C.

Viviani, Vincenzo (1622–1703) *Italian mathematician*

Viviani, who was born at Florence in Italy, was an associate and pupil of Galileo, although his chief interest was in mathematics rather than in physics. After the condemnation of Galileo's ideas by the Catholic Church it was unsafe for Viviani to pursue his work on Galileo's mathematics. Accordingly Viviani devoted himself to the thorough study of Greek mathematics, in particular geometry, and in this field of work he achieved wide fame. In 1696 he was elected a fellow of the Royal Society of London. Viviani was particularly interested in trying to reconstruct lost sections of works by ancient Greek mathematicians, such as the missing fifth book of Apollonius's *Conics*. He also published Italian translations of the works of classical mathematicians including Euclid and Archimedes. He was an associate of the physicist Evangelista Torricelli and collaborated with him in his work on atmospheric pressure and in the invention of the mercury barometer.

Vleck, John Hasbrouck van *See* VAN VLECK, JOHN HASBROUCK.

Vogel, Hermann Karl (1842–1907)
German astronomer

Born at Leipzig in Germany, Vogel began as an assistant at the observatory there. He later directed a private observatory and finally moved to Potsdam to work in the new astrophysical observatory, of which he became director in 1882. He was one of the earliest astronomers to devote himself almost exclusively to spectroscopy. His first discovery came in 1871 when he showed that the solar rotation could be measured using spectroscopic Doppler effects, obtaining identical results to those achieved using sunspots as markers.

In 1890 he came across some unusual stellar spectra – in particular that of the variable star Algol. He found that some stars seemed to be both advancing and receding, for their spectral lines periodically doubled showing both a red and a blue shift. He correctly interpreted this as indicating a binary system with two stars so close together that they could not be separated optically, with one star advancing and one receding. When one star is eclipsed by its companion just one spectra will be visible, but as the other emerges the spectral line will appear to double only to disappear again in the next eclipse. Such systems are known as eclipsing binaries.

Volta, Count Alessandro Giuseppe Antonio Anastasio (1745–1827) *Italian physicist*

Volta, who was born at Como in Italy, grew up in an atmosphere of aristocratic religiosity with almost all his male relations becoming priests. However, Volta decided early that his life's work lay in the study of electricity and, by the age of 24, had developed his own version of Benjamin Franklin's electrical fluid theory. In 1774 he started teaching physics at the gymnasium in Como, where, a few months later, he invented the electrophorus – a device for producing electric charge by friction and, at the time, the most efficient way of storing electric charge. On the strength of this invention he was promoted, in 1775, to the position of professor of physics at Como and, three years later, took up a similar appointment at Pavia University. Here, stimulated by the experiments of his friend Luigi Galvani, he started investigating the production of electric current. In 1795 he was appointed rector of Pavia but his work was disturbed by the political upheavals in Lombardy at the time. The state was oscillating between French and Austrian control in the Napoleonic campaigns and in 1799–1800 the Austrians closed the university.

Volta chose this time to make public his great discovery that the production of electric current did not need the presence of animal tissue, as Galvani and others had supposed. Volta produced the famous *voltaic pile*, consisting of an alternating column of zinc and silver disks separated by porous cardboard soaked in brine. This instrument revolutionized the study of electricity by producing a practical source of current, leading almost immediately to William Nicholson's decomposition of water by electrolysis and later to Humphry Davy's discovery of potassium and other metals by the same process.

In 1800 Napoleon returned in victory to Pavia, reopened the university, and invited Volta to Paris to demonstrate his pile. He awarded Volta the medal of the Legion of Honor and made him a count. In his honor the unit of electric potential (or potential difference or electromotive force) was called the volt.

von Euler, Ulf Svante (1905–1983)
Swedish physiologist

Von Euler was the son of Karl von Euler-Chelpin, Nobel Prize winner in 1929. He was born in the Swedish capital of Stockholm and educated at the Karolinska Institute, where he obtained his MD in 1930. He taught there from 1930 onward becoming, in 1939, professor of physiology. In 1966 von Euler was elected to the powerful position of president of the Nobel Foundation, which he held until 1975.

In 1906 the idea that nerve cells communicate with each other and the muscles they control by the release of chemicals was first proposed by Thomas Elliott. Since then there had been much searching for the elusive neurotransmitters and it was not until 1946 that von Euler succeeded in isolating that of the sympathetic system and showed it to be noradrenaline (norepinephrine). For this work von Euler shared the 1970 Nobel Prize for physiology or medicine with Julius Axelrod and Bernard Katz.

Von Euler had earlier, in 1935, discovered a substance in human semen showing great physiological potency. As he assumed it came from the prostate gland he named it 'prostaglandin'. It later turned out that prostaglandins could be found in many other human tissues; however, his deduction that they were fatty acids has since been confirmed.

von Kármán, Theodore (1881–1963)
Hungarian–American aerodynamicist

The son of a distinguished educationist, von Kármán studied engineering at the Polytechnic in his native city of Budapest. After graduating in 1902 he taught at the Polytechnic until 1906 when he moved to Göttingen, where he completed his PhD in 1908. At about this time his interest in aeronautics was aroused when he saw Henri Farman fly a biplane in Paris. He pursued his new interests further at Göttingen when he was asked to help Ludwig Prandtl design a wind tunnel for research on airships. Von Kármán continued to work in aeronautics and in 1912 he was invited to establish and direct a new institute of aerodynamics at the University of Aachen. Here he remained until 1930, apart from the war years spent in Austria working at the Military Aircraft Factory, Fischamend. In 1930, unhappy with political conditions in Germany, he moved to the California Institute of Technology to set up and direct another new institute, the Guggenheim Aeronautic Laboratory at Pasadena, California. He became a naturalized American in 1936.

Von Kármán remained director of the Guggenheim Laboratory until 1949. During this time he contributed to many branches of aeronautics and encouraged work on jet propulsion, rockets, and supersonic flight. At von Kármán's insistence the world-famous Jet Propulsion Laboratory was set up in 1938 and he served as its director until 1945. He also served as a consultant to the US Army Air Corps from 1939 onward. After his retirement from Pasadena he organized the Advisory Group for Aeronautical Research and Development to provide NATO with technical advice.

Among his many contributions to aerodynamics, von Kármán is probably best known for his discovery in 1911 of what have since been called *Kármán vortices* – the alternating vortices found behind obstacles placed in moving fluids. The basic idea was drawn to his attention by a graduate student in Prandtl's laboratory. He had been asked to measure the pressure distribution around a cylinder placed in a steady flow. But, the student found, the flow refused to move steadily and invariably oscillated violently. Prandtl insisted the fault lay with the student who had not bothered to machine circular cylinders. Von Kármán would enquire of the student daily how the flow was behaving and was daily given the sad reply that the flow still oscillated. Eventually von Kármán came to see that the student had stumbled upon a genuine effect. Over a weekend he calculated that the wake should indeed separate into two periodic vortices. Further, there is a symmetric arrangement of vortices which is unstable; only an asymmetric arrangement of vortices persists when the conditions are changed.

Von Kármán went on to demonstrate that above a certain velocity v, where d is the cylinder's diameter, vibrations will be induced with a frequency v/d cycles per second. It was precisely these vibrations which were induced in 1940 in the Tacoma Narrows suspension bridge when v exceeded its critical velocity of 42 mph.

von Laue, Max Theodor Felix (1879–1960) *German physicist*

The son of a civil servant, von Laue was born in Pfaffendorf, Koblenz, and educated at the universities of Strasbourg, Göttingen, Munich, and Berlin, where he obtained his doctorate in 1903. He worked in various universities before his appointment as professor of theoretical physics at Berlin University in 1919. He remained there until 1943 when he moved to Göttingen as director of the Max Planck Institute.

Although von Laue began his research career working on relativity theory, his most important work was the discovery of x-ray diffraction in 1912 for which he was awarded the 1914 Nobel Prize for physics. From this discovery much of modern physics was to develop and, some forty years later, the new discipline of molecular biology was to emerge.

Von Laue put together two simple and well known ideas. He knew that x-rays had wavelengths shorter than visible light; he also knew that crystals were regular structures with their atoms probably lined up neatly in rows. Thus, he concluded, if the wavelength of x-rays was similar to the interatomic distance of the atoms in the crystal, then x-rays directed onto a crystal could be diffracted and form a characteristic and decipherable pattern on a photographic plate.

He passed the actual experimental work to two of his students, Walter Friedrich and Paul Kipping, who first tried copper sulfate (1912), which yielded a somewhat unclear pattern. When they changed to zinc sulfide they almost immediately obtained a clear photograph marking out the regular and symmetric arrangement of the atoms in the crystal.

Vonnegut, Bernard (1914–   ) *American physicist*

Born in Indianapolis, Indiana, Vonnegut was educated at the Massachusetts Institute of Technology, where he obtained his PhD in 1939. After working in the Research Laboratory of the General Electric Company under Vincent Schaefer (1945–52), he moved to the

Arthur D. Little Company and remained there until 1967, when he was appointed professor of atmospheric science at the New York State University, Albany.

In 1947, while with the General Electric Research Laboratory, Vonnegut made a major advance in the rain-making techniques developed by Schaefer, when he found that he obtained much better results with silver iodide crystals for cloud seeding than the dry ice used by Schaefer.

Von Neumann, John (1903–1957)
Hungarian–American mathematician

John (originally Johann) Von Neumann was born in Budapest, Hungary, and studied at the University of Berlin, the Berlin Institute of Technology, and the University of Budapest, where he obtained his doctorate in 1926. He was *Privatdozent* (nonstipendiary lecturer) at Berlin (1927–29) and taught at Hamburg (1929–30). He left Europe in 1930 to work in Princeton, first at the university and later at the Institute for Advanced Study. From 1943 he was a consultant on the atomic-bomb project.

Von Neumann may have been one of the last people able to span the fields of pure and applied mathematics. His first work was in set theory (the subject of his doctoral thesis). Here he improved the axiomatization given by Ernst Zermelo and Abraham Fraenkel. In 1928 he published his first paper in the field for which he is best known, the mathematical theory of games. This work culminated in 1944 with the publication of *The Theory of Games and Economic Behavior*, which Von Neumann had coauthored with Oskar Morgenstern. Not all the results in this work were novel, but it was the first time the field had been treated in such a large-scale and systematic way.

Apart from the theory of games Von Neumann did important work in the theory of operators. Dissatisfied with the resources then available for solving the complex computational problems that arose in hydrodynamics, Von Neumann developed a broad knowledge of the design of computers and with his interest in the general theory of automata became one of the founders of a whole new discipline. He was much interested in the general role of science and technology in society and this led

to his becoming increasingly involved in high-level government scientific committees. Von Neumann died at the relatively early age of 54 from cancer.

von Ohain, Hans Joachim Pabst
(1911–   ) American aeronautical engineer

Born at Dessau in Germany, von Ohain took his PhD in aerodynamics at Göttingen in 1935. He immediately joined the Heinkel Aircraft Company at Rostock. It had long been apparent to engineers that if planes were to fly faster they would have to fly higher and so benefit from the lower air resistance. But in a thinner atmosphere propellers and piston engines worked badly. The dilemma, von Ohain realized, could be resolved if turbojets were used. Thus in 1935, four years after Frank WHITTLE, von Ohain took out his first patent on the gas-turbine jet engine.

Backed by Ernst Heinkel (1885–1958) he began to work on the He 178. In September 1937 a hydrogen-fueled bench model produced a 250-kilogram thrust. The plane was ready for its test flight, the first jet flight ever, in August 1939 just before the outbreak of World War II, when it reached a top speed of about 350 miles per hour. Whittle's first jet, the Gloster E28/39 prototype, had its maiden flight in 1941.

Heinkel went on to develop the He 280 powered by two von Ohain engines. By this time, however, Heinkel had lost the confidence of the Nazis and the contract to develop a jet fighter was awarded to Messerschmitt. The Me 262, powered by Junkers-built jet engines, entered service in late 1944 with a top speed of 550 mph. Although 1,430 were built, only about 400 actually saw combat and they arrived too late to influence the war's outcome.

Despite this von Ohain found himself in great demand when peace came and in 1947 he began work for the U.S. airforce on the design of a new generation of military jets at the Wright-Patterson base, where he remained until 1975. After a further spell as chief scientist at the Aero-Propulsion Laboratory, von Ohain retired in 1979.

In 1991 he shared with Whittle the Draper Prize – the engineering equivalent of the Nobel Prize – for their independent invention of the jet engine.

Waage, Peter (1833–1900) *Norwegian chemist. See* GULDBERG, CATO MAXIMILIAN.

Waals, Johannes Diderik van der *See* VAN DER WAALS, JOHANNES DIDERIK.

Wagner-Jauregg, Julius (1857–1940) *Austrian psychiatrist*

Wagner-Jauregg was born at Wels in Austria and educated at the University of Vienna, where he gained his MD in 1880. Finding it difficult to obtain an academic post in orthodox medicine, he turned to psychiatry in 1883 and in 1889 succeeded Krafft-Ebbing as professor of psychiatry at the University of Graz. In 1893 he returned to Vienna as director of the Psychiatric and Neurological Clinic, where he remained until his retirement in 1928.

In 1917 he proposed a new treatment for general paralysis of the insane (GPI), then a relatively common complication of late syphilis. As early as 1887 he had noticed that rare cases of remission were often preceded by a feverish infection, suggesting that the deliberate production of a fever could have a similar effect. Consequently, in 1917 he inoculated nine GPI patients with tertian malaria – a form of malaria that gives a two-day interval between fever attacks. He later reported that in six of these patients extensive remissions had taken place. It was for this work that Wagner-Jauregg received the Nobel Prize for physiology or medicine in 1927. Although therapeutic malaria inoculations were used in the treatment of GPI for some time, demand for them ceased with the discovery of penicillin.

Wagner-Jauregg also proposed in 1894 that cretinism, a thyroid deficiency disease, could be successfully controlled by iodide tablets.

Waksman, Selman Abraham (1888–1973) *Russian–American biochemist*

Waksman, who was born at Priluki in Russia, emigrated to America in 1910; he graduated from Rutgers University in 1915 and obtained his American citizenship the following year. He studied for his doctorate at California University, receiving his PhD in 1918, and then returned to Rutgers, where he became professor of soil microbiology in 1930.

A new area in the science of soil microbiology was opened up with the discovery by René Dubos, in 1939, of a bacteria-killing agent in a soil microorganism. This stimulated renewed interest in Fleming's penicillin and, with the value of penicillin at last established, Waksman began a systematic search for antibiotics among microorganisms. In 1943 he isolated streptomycin from the mold *Streptomyces griseus* and found that it was effective in treating tuberculosis, caused by Gram-negative bacteria. This was a breakthrough as previously discovered antibiotics had proved useful only against Gram-positive bacteria. This work gained Waksman the 1953 Nobel Prize for physiology or medicine; he donated the prize money to a research foundation at Rutgers.

Waksman isolated and developed many other antibiotics, including neomycin. From 1940 until his retirement in 1958 he was professor of microbiology and chairman of the department at Rutgers; from 1949 he also held the post of director of the Rutgers Institute of Microbiology.

Walcott, Charles Doolittle (1850–1927) *American paleontologist*

Walcott was born into a poor family in Utica, New York State, and educated in the public schools there. He began work as a farm laborer and took to collecting the trilobites he found scattered around the farm, some of which he sold to Louis Agassiz. In 1876 he became assistant to the New York state geologist. He moved to the US Geological Survey in 1879 as a field geologist and by 1894 had risen to be its director. In 1907 he accepted the important post of secretary of the Smithsonian Institution, a position he held, along with a number of other offices in scientific administration, until his death in 1927.

Walcott specialized in the Cambrian, the period 550 million years ago when multicellular organisms first appeared. In this field he is best known for his discovery in 1909 of the much discussed Burgess Shale fossils. The shale lies 8000 feet high in the Rockies on the eastern border of British Columbia. Within two strata he found thousands of fossils representing 120 species of marine invertebrates. Further, while most fossils preserve only such hard parts as shells, bones, and teeth, the Burgess specimens by some geological fluke had preserved their soft tissues.

Walcott shipped his material back to Washington. Between 1910 and 1912 he published a few preliminary reports on the "abrupt appearance of the Cambrian fauna." His initial view that his specimens were early forms of modern groups remained unchallenged. Walcott himself was too concerned with administering American science to have time to reconsider his early ideas. It was not until the 1970s when Harry Whittington began to review Walcott's specimens that it was appreciated that another, more radical, view was possible. Walcott's story is vividly told in S. J. Gould's popular work *Wonderful Life* (1989).

Wald, George (1906–1997) *American biochemist*

Born in New York City, Wald was educated at New York University and at Columbia where he obtained his PhD in 1932. After spending the period 1932–34 in Europe, where he worked under Otto Warburg in Berlin and Paul Karrer in Zurich, he returned to America where he took up an appointment at Harvard. Wald remained at Harvard for the whole of his career, becoming professor of biology in 1948 and emeritus professor in 1977.

Wald did fundamental work on the chemistry of vision. In 1933 he discovered that vitamin A is present in the retina of the eye, and thereafter tried to find the relationship between this vitamin and the visual pigment rhodopsin. The first clue came from the constitution of rhodopsin. It was found to consist of two parts: a colorless protein, opsin, and a yellow carotenoid, retinal, which is the aldehyde of vitamin A. Wald was now in a position to work out the main outlines of the story.

Rhodopsin is light sensitive and splits into its two parts when illuminated, with the retinal being reduced further to vitamin A by the enzyme alcohol dehydrogenase. In the dark the procedure is reversed. What was further needed was some indication of how the splitting of the rhodopsin molecule could somehow generate electrical activity in the optic nerve and visual cortex. Part of the answer came from Haldan HARTLINE and Ragnar GRANIT who shared the 1967 Nobel Prize for physiology or medicine with Wald.

Wald speculated that since retinal is a carotenoid pigment, and such pigments are also found in plants, then it is possible that the phototropic responses of plants may rely on a similar mechanism.

Wald later became widely known for his opposition to the Vietnam War.

Walden, Paul (1863–1957) *Russian–German chemist*

The son of a farmer from Cēsis (now in Latvia), Walden was educated at Riga Polytechnic, where he studied under Wilhelm Ostwald. Having become professor of chemistry in 1894, he remained at the polytechnic until the Russian Revolution, when he moved to Germany. From 1919 to 1934 he served as professor of chemistry at the University of Rostock.

In 1896 Walden found that if he took a sample of malic acid that rotated polarized light in a clockwise direction and allowed it to react in a certain way, then on recovery it would be found to rotate polarized light in a counterclockwise direction. The actual reaction involved first combining the malic acid with phosphorus pentachloride to give chlorosuccinic acid. This converts back into malic acid under the influence of silver oxide and water but the malic acid has an inverted configuration. Such inversions later became a useful tool for studying the detail of organic reactions. *Walden inversions*, as they are called, occur when an atom or group approaches a molecule from one direction and displaces an atom or group from the other side of the molecule.

Walden also worked on the electrochemistry of nonaqueous solutions and formulated *Walden's rule*, which relates conductivity and viscosity in such solutions. In later life he turned to the history of chemistry on which topic he is notable for having regularly lectured at the University of Tübingen while well into his nineties.

Walker, John Ernest (1941–   ) *British molecular biologist*

Walker was educated at Oxford University, gaining his DPhil in 1969. In 1974 he joined the staff of the Medical Research Council at the Molecular Biology Laboratory, Cambridge.

In the 1970s Paul BOYER had proposed a theoretical model by which the enzyme ATP-synthase operating in mitochondria could catalyze the production of the adenosine triphosphate molecule (ATP), the main source of cellular energy. The model was partially verified by Walker in 1994. He determined the structure of the enzyme, first by low-resolution electron microscopy and eventually, using x-ray crystallography, constructed a three-dimensional model of the enzyme.

For his contribution to this field Walker

shared the 1997 Nobel Prize for chemistry with Paul Boyer and Jens Skou.

Wallace, Alfred Russel (1823–1913)
British naturalist

Wallace, who was born at Usk in Wales, received only an elementary schooling before joining an elder brother in the surveying business. In 1844 he became a master at the Collegiate School, Leicester, where he met the entomologist Henry Bates. Wallace persuaded Bates to accompany him on a trip to the Amazon, and they joined a scientific expedition as naturalists in 1848.

Wallace published an account of his expedition in his *A Narrative of Travels on the Amazon and River Negro* (1853). In 1854 he traveled to the Malay Archipelago, where he spent eight years and collected over 125,000 specimens, a journey described in his *Malay Archipelago* (1869). In this region he noted the marked differences between the Asian and Australian faunas, the former being more advanced than the latter, and proposed a line, still referred to as *Wallace's line*, separating the two distinct ecological regions. He suggested that Australian animals are more primitive because the Australian continent broke away from Asia before the more advanced Asian animals evolved and thus the marsupials were not overrun and driven to extinction. This observation, together with a reconsideration of Thomas Malthus's essay on population, led him to propose the theory of evolution by natural selection. He wrote an essay entitled *On the Tendency of Varieties to Depart Indefinitely from the Original Type*, which he sent to Darwin for his opinion. On receipt, Darwin realized this was a summary of his own views and the two papers were jointly presented at a meeting of the Linnaean Society in July 1858.

Wallace continued to collect evidence for this evolutionary theory, making an important study on mimicry in the swallowtail butterfly and writing pioneering works on the geographical distribution of animals, including his *Geographical Distribution of Animals* (2 vols., 1876) and *Island Life* (1880). He was also an active socialist, having been introduced to the ideas of the reformer Robert Owen at an early age, and he campaigned for land nationalization and women's suffrage.

In addition to his scientific and political pursuits, Wallace also participated in many of the more dubious intellectual movements of the 19th century. He supported spiritualism, phrenology, and mesmerism. He testified in 1876 on behalf of Henry Slade, a professional medium, charged on evidence submitted by Ray Lankester with being a "common rogue." His views on these matters led Wallace to disagree with Darwin on the evolution of man. Man's spiritual essence, Wallace insisted, could not have been produced by natural selection. "I hope you have not murdered our child," Darwin commented. Wallace also campaigned persistently against the practice of vaccination. He published a pamphlet in 1885 claiming British and US statistics showed it to be "both useless and dangerous." He testified in a similar manner before a Royal Commission in 1890 and published his evidence in a pamphlet, *Vaccination, a Delusion* (1895).

Throughout his career Wallace never held an academic appointment and after 1848 no appointment of any kind. He hoped to live on the sale of specimens collected during his Amazon and Malay expeditions. Unfortunately, however, the bulk of the Amazonian material was lost at sea, while funds gathered from the sale of his Malay collection were squandered in unwise investments and expensive disputes with builders. Wallace was therefore forced to earn his living by writing and lecturing. The award of a civil list pension of £200 a year from 1880 greatly eased Wallace's financial burdens.

Wallace also published a spirited account of his life in *My Life* (London, 1905).

Wallach, Otto (1847–1931) *German chemist*

Born at Königsberg (now Kaliningrad in Russia), Wallach studied at Berlin and at Göttingen, where he obtained his PhD in 1869. After a period in industry in Berlin he moved to Bonn (1870), becoming August Kekulé's assistant and later (1876) professor of chemistry. He remained at Bonn until 1889, when he moved to a similar chair at Göttingen.

When Wallach began to give regular classes in pharmacy he became interested in essential oils – oils removed from plants by steam distillation with wide uses in medicine and the perfume industry – and started research into determining their molecular structure. This study led to what was to become his major field of research, the chemistry of the terpenes.

These had hitherto presented considerable difficulties to the analytic chemist. Wallach succeeded in determining the structure of several terpenes, including limonene, in 1894. His greatest achievement, however, was his formulation of the isoprene rule in 1887. Isoprene, with the formula C_5H_8, had been isolated from rubber in the 1860s by C. Williams. Wallach showed that terpenes were derived from isoprene and therefore had the general formula $(C_5H_8)_n$; limonene is thus $C_{10}H_{16}$. Terpenes were of importance not only in the perfume industry but also as a source of camphors. It was also later established that vitamins A and D are related to the terpenes.

Wallach published 126 papers on the terpenes – work for which he was awarded the Nobel Prize for chemistry in 1910.

Wallis, John (1616–1703) *English mathematician and theologian*

Born at Ashford in Kent, Wallis was educated at Cambridge University (1632–40), obtaining his MA in 1640. His early training was in theology and it was as a theologian that he first made his name. He took holy orders and eventually became bishop of Winchester. He moved to London in 1645 where he became seriously interested in mathematics and in 1649 he was appointed to the Savilian Chair in Geometry at Oxford University.

Wallis's most celebrated mathematical work is contained in his treatise the *Arithmetica infinitorum* (1655; The Arithmetic of Infinitesimals). In this work he gave an infinite series expression for π. Generally the treatise took the development of 17th-century mathematics a significant step nearer Newton's creation of the infinitesimal calculus. Wallis was one of the first mathematicians to introduce the functional mode of thinking, which was to be of such importance in Newton's work. He also did notable work on conic sections and published a treatise on them, *Tractatus de sectionibus conicis* (1659; Tract on Conic Sections), which developed the subject in an ingeniously novel fashion. His writings were certainly read by Newton and are known to have made a considerable impact on him. Before Newton, Wallis was probably one of the most influential of English mathematicians.

Wallis wrote a substantial history of mathematics. His other interests included music and the study of language. He was active in the weekly scientific meetings that eventually led to the foundation of the Royal Society in 1662. During the English Civil War he was a Parliamentarian and put his mathematical talents to use in decoding enciphered letters.

Walton, Ernest Thomas Sinton (1903–1995) *Irish physicist*

Walton, who was born at Dungarvan in Ireland, studied at the Methodist College, Belfast, where he excelled at mathematics and science. In 1922 he entered Trinity College, Dublin, graduating in mathematics and experimental science in 1926.

In 1927 he went to Cambridge University on a research scholarship and worked in the Cavendish Laboratory under Ernest Rutherford. It was here that he performed experiments, together with John COCKCROFT, with accelerated particles. The experiments were to lead to the two men sharing the 1951 Nobel Prize for physics for "their pioneer work on the transmutation of atomic nuclei by artificially accelerated atomic particles," more commonly known as "splitting the atom."

In 1934 Walton gained his PhD from Cambridge and returned to Dublin as a fellow of Trinity College. He was appointed Erasmus Smith Professor of Natural and Experimental Philosophy in 1946 and was elected a senior fellow in 1960. In 1952 he became chairman of the School of Cosmic Physics of the Dublin Institute for Advanced Studies, where he remained until retiring in 1974.

Warburg, Otto Heinrich (1883–1970) *German physiologist*

Warburg, who was born at Freiburg im Breisgau in Germany, was the son of Emil Warburg, a distinguished professor of physics at Berlin. Otto was educated at the University of Berlin, where he obtained his PhD in 1906, and at Heidelberg, where he gained his MD in 1911. He joined the Kaiser Wilhelm Institute for Biology in 1913, attaining professorial status in 1918, and in 1931 became director of the Kaiser Wilhelm Institute for Cell Physiology, renamed after Max Planck following World War II. Here Warburg remained in charge until his death at the age of 86.

When the human body converts lactic acid into carbon dioxide and water it consumes oxygen. In the early 1920s Warburg began to investigate just how such aerobic metabolism works. To do this he designed, in 1923, the *Warburg manometer*, which is used to measure the rate of oxygen uptake by human tissue. It was clear to Warburg that such a reaction could only take place at normal temperatures with the aid of enzymes but, because of the tiny amounts involved, such enzymes would be impossible to isolate by orthodox analytical techniques. He suspected the respiratory enzymes to be the cytochromes discovered a decade earlier and consequently set out to explore their nature by noting which substances affected the rate of oxygen uptake. He first noted that intercellular respiration was blocked by hydrogen cyanide and by carbon monoxide. This suggested to Warburg that the respiratory enzymes contained iron on the analogy that carbon monoxide acts on hemoglobin by breaking the oxygen–iron bonds. Support for such a supposition was derived from the similarity between the spectrum of the carbon monoxide–hemoglobin complex and that of the carbon monoxide–respiratory enzyme complex.

Warburg also studied the metabolism of cancerous cells and in 1923 discovered that malignant cells use far less oxygen than normal cells and can in fact live anaerobically. This extremely interesting observation led him to speculate that cancer is caused by a malfunction of the cellular respiratory system. He advocated that cancer might be prevented by avoiding foods and additives that impair cellular activity and by ensuring a high level of respiratory enzyme in the body by taking plenty of iron and vitamin B.

Warburg also worked on other enzyme systems, particularly the flavoproteins, or yellow enzymes, active in cellular dehydrogenation. He found that the coenzyme flavin adenine dinucleotide (FAD) is the active part of flavoproteins and later demonstrated that nicotinamide is similarly the active part of nicotinamide adenine dinucleotide (NAD$^+$). Following these discoveries he showed that in alcohol fermentation a hydrogenated form of NAD$^+$ (NADH$_2$) reacts with acetaldehyde to give NAD$^+$ and ethyl alcohol.

For his contributions to biochemistry, Warburg was nominated three times for the Nobel Prize for physiology or medicine, in 1926, 1931, and 1944, although he only actually received the award in 1931.

Warming, (Johannes) Eugenius Bülow (1841–1924) *Danish botanist*

Warming was born on the island of Manö in the Frisian islands. He studied botany at Munich and later became professor of botany at Stockholm (1882–85) and at Copenhagen (1885–1911).

In 1895 he published his book *Plantesamfund* on plant ecology and is regarded as one of the founders of the subject.

Wassermann, August von (1866–1925) *German bacteriologist*

Wassermann, who was born at Bamberg in Germany, was educated at the universities of Erlangen, Vienna, Munich, and Strasbourg, where he graduated in 1888. From 1890 he worked under Robert Koch at the Institute for Infectious Diseases in Berlin, becoming head of the department of therapeutics and serum research in 1907. In 1913

he moved to the Kaiser Wilhelm Institute, where he served as director of experimental therapeutics until his death.

Wassermann is best remembered for the *Wassermann test* (or *reaction*), which he introduced in 1906 for the diagnosis of syphilis. The test depends upon an infected person producing in his or her blood the antibody to syphilis, which will combine with known antigens, such as beef liver or heart, to form a complex. The test is regarded as positive by the ability of the complex to fix complement, the serum protein discovered by Jules Bordet in the 1880s. The test is still widely used as a diagnostic tool.

Watson, James Dewey (1928–) *American biochemist*

Watson entered the university in his native city of Chicago at the early age of 15, graduating in 1947. He obtained his PhD (1950) for studies of viruses at the University of Indiana and continued this work at the University of Copenhagen. In Copenhagen he realized that one of the major unsolved problems of biology lay in identifying the structure of the nucleic-acid molecules making up chromosomes. In 1951 he moved to the Cavendish Laboratory in Cambridge, England, to study the structure of DNA.

Early in 1953 Watson and Francis CRICK published a molecular structure of DNA having two cross-linked helical chains (*General Implications of the Structure of Deoxyribonucleic Acid*). They arrived at this by considering possible geometric models, which they based on two independent sets of experimental work: the x-ray crystallography of Maurice WILKINS and Rosalind Franklin at King's College, London, and the earlier work of Ernst Chargaff, which had established the relative quantities of the organic bases present in the nucleic acids. Watson and Crick were able to show that certain organic bases linked the chains together by hydrogen bonds.

The model explains the three basic characteristics of heredity. It shows how genetic information can be expressed in the form of a chemical code; it demonstrates the way in which genes replicate themselves – when the two chains separate each can serve as a template for the synthesis of a new chain; and finally it provides an explanation of how mutations occur in genes, in terms of changes in the chemical structure of DNA. Watson, Crick, and Wilkins shared the Nobel Prize for physiology or medicine for this work in 1962.

Watson left Cambridge in 1953 for the California Institute of Technology. From 1955 to 1968 he worked at Harvard, becoming professor of biology in 1961. Here he continued to study the genetic code. In 1968 he became director of the Cold Spring Harbor Laboratory, New York, where he concentrated effort on cancer research. The same year he published *The Double Helix*, an informal, highly personal, and somewhat controversial account of the discovery of the structure of DNA. He retired in 1993.

Watson, Sir William (1715–1787)
British physicist, physician, and botanist

Watson, the son of a London tradesman, was apprenticed to an apothecary from 1731 to 1738. After working for many years at that trade, Watson was made a licentiate of the Royal College of Physicians. This was later followed in 1762 with an appointment as physician to the Foundling Hospital.

Watson had a great interest in natural history and was instrumental in introducing the Linnaean system of botanical classification into Britain. He is, however, mainly remembered for his account of the nature of electricity. This was based on a series of experiments with the Leyden jar, discovered by Pieter van Musschenbroek in 1746. Watson not only improved the device by coating the inside of it with metal foil but also realized that the pattern of discharge of the jar suggested that electricity was simply a single fluid or, as he termed it, an 'electrical ether'. Normally bodies have an equal density of this fluid so that when two such bodies meet there will be no electrical activity. If, however, their densities are unequal the fluid will flow and there will be an electric discharge. That is, electricity can only be transferred from one body to another; it cannot be created or destroyed. Such a theory was also developed with greater depth at about the same time by Benjamin Franklin and was to emerge as the orthodox position by the end of the century.

Watson also made an early and unsuccessful attempt in 1747 to measure the velocity of electricity over a four-mile (6.4-km) circuit. Although it appeared to complete its journey in no time at all Watson sensibly concluded that it probably traveled too fast to be measured.

Watson-Watt, Sir Robert Alexander
(1892–1973) *British physicist*

Watson-Watt was born Robert Watt at Brechin in Scotland. The Watson part of his name came from his mother's family and the hybrid Watson-Watt was adopted in 1942 on receipt of his knighthood. He was the son of a carpenter and was educated at the University of St. Andrews. After graduating in 1912 he immediately joined the faculty but found his academic career disrupted by World War I. He spent much of the war working as a meteorologist at the Royal Aircraft Establishment, Farnborough, attempting to locate thunderstorms with radio waves.

He remained in the scientific civil service after the war and in 1921 was appointed superintendent of the Radio Research Station at Slough. In 1935 he was asked by the Air Ministry if a 'death ray' could be built – one capable of eliminating an approaching enemy pilot. Watson-Watt asked a colleague to calculate how much energy would be needed to raise a gallon of water from 98°F to 105°F at a distance of a mile, i.e., a significant rise in body temperature. He advised the Ministry that the energy needed outstripped the available technology.

Watson-Watt also pointed out that Post Office engineers had noted interference in radio reception as aircraft flew close to their receivers. Interference of this kind, he suggested, could perhaps be used to detect the approach of enemy aircraft. In 1935 he submitted an important paper, *The Detection of Aircraft by Radio Methods*, to Tizard at the Ministry. Watson-Watt was normally a man, it was said, who could never say in one word what could be said in a thousand. This time, however, the report was terse and to the point. Tizard asked for a demonstration. In February 1935 the BBC short-wave transmitter at Daventry was successfully used to identify the approach of a Heyford bomber eight miles away.

Tizard moved quickly. Watson-Watt was invited to set up a research station at Bawdsley in Suffolk to develop radio detection and ranging; the acronym 'radar' was first recorded in use in the *New York Times* in 1941.

The principles behind radar are relatively simple. Radio waves are reflected strongly off large objects such as airplanes. The difficulty was that very little, something of the order of 10^{-12}, of the transmitted signal would be picked up by the receiving antennae. Both high transmitting power and high amplification would therefore be needed. Watson-Watt assembled a talented team at Bawdsley and by the outbreak of World War II an operational chain of eight stations, known as 'Chain Home', defended Britain's eastern and southern coasts. They operated in the high-frequency bands and required very visible 360-foot-high transmitters and 240-foot-high receivers.

Watson-Watt left Bawdsley in 1938 for the Air Ministry and the post of director of communication development. His main task was to make radar workable, to ensure that it was acceptable to the RAF and that they could actually operate the new equipment. He also had to arrange for the manufacture of the relevant transmitters, receivers, and electron tubes.

He finally left the civil service in 1945 to set up as a consultant. He was also invited to give evidence before the Royal Commission on Inventors on behalf of his colleagues and himself. After speaking for six days Watson-Watt was awarded £52,000 for his work on radar.

Watt, James (1736–1819) British instrument maker and inventor

The son of a Clydeside shipbuilder and house builder, Watt was born in Greenock, Scotland. At the age of 17 he started a career in Glasgow as a mathematical-instrument maker. Through his shop, opened in 1757, he met many of the scientists at Glasgow University.

In 1764 it occurred to Watt that the Newcomen steam engine, a model of which he had been repairing, wasted a great deal of energy by dissipating the latent heat given up by steam condensing to water. The solution was to build an engine with a separate condenser, so that there was no need to heat and cool the cylinder at each stroke. In 1768 Watt entered into partnership with John Roebuck, who had established an iron foundry, to produce the steam engine but his duties as a land surveyor, taken up in 1766, left him little time to develop this and Roebuck went bankrupt in 1772. A second partnership (1775) with Matthew Boulton proved more productive although it took Watt until 1790 to perfect what became known as the *Watt engine*.

This engine, throughout its various stages of improvement, was one of the main contributors to the Industrial Revolution. Early reciprocating versions were used for pumping water out of Cornish copper and tin mines. A rotating engine with the sun-and-planet gearing system invented by Watt in 1781 was used in flour mills, cotton mills, and paper mills. An automatic speed control mechanism, the centrifugal governor invented in 1788, was another improvement.

Watt made a great deal of money from the sale of his engines and became accepted into the scientific establishment. He retired from the business of steam-engine manufacture in 1800 and spent his time traveling, working as a consultant, and working on minor inventions in his workshop at home. Watt was the first to use the term horsepower as a unit of power and the *watt*, a unit of power, was named for him.

Weber, Ernst Heinrich (1795–1878) German physiologist and psychologist

Weber was the eldest of three brothers who all made important contributions to science. He was born at Wittenberg in Germany and became a professor at the University of Leipzig in 1818, a position he held until his death.

Weber is best known for his work on sensory response to weight, temperature, and pressure. In 1834 he conducted research on the lifting of weights. From his researches he discovered that the experience of differences in the intensity of sensations depends on percentage differences in the stimuli rather than absolute differences. This is known as the just-noticeable difference (j.n.d.), difference threshold, or limen. The work was published in *Der Tastsinn und das Gemeingefühl* (1851; The Sense of Touch and the Common Sensibility) and was given mathematical expression by Weber's student Gustav Theodor Fechner as the *Weber–Fechner* law.

Weber is regarded as a founder of experimental psychology and psychophysics. He also conducted important anatomical work.

Weber, Joseph (1919–) American physicist

Born in Paterson, New Jersey, Weber graduated from the US Naval Academy in 1940 and served in the Navy until 1948, when he joined the faculty of the University of Maryland, College Park. He completed his doctorate at the Catholic University of America, Washington DC, in 1951 and was appointed professor of physics at Maryland in 1959, a post which he held for the remainder of his career.

Einstein's general theory of relativity predicts that accelerated masses should radiate gravitational waves. Like electromagnetic waves, these should carry energy and momentum and should be identifiable with a suitable detector. For gravitational waves, this would be an object of large mass with a method of detecting any disturbance of it. In 1958 Weber began the design and construction of just such a device. By 1965 he had built a solid aluminum cylinder detector, 3 feet in diameter and weighing 3.5 tons. Bonded around the cylinder were a number of piezoelectric crystals, which generate a voltage when the bar is compressed or extended. Weber claimed that his instruments could detect deformations corresponding to 1 part in 10^{16}, a difference of about 1/100th the diameter of an atomic nucleus.

Weber was aware of the problems involved in this kind of design. To rule out causes other than gravitational – acoustic, thermal, seismic, etc. – he suspended the cylinder in a vacuum. More significantly he built a second detector 600 miles away from Maryland at the Argonne National Laboratory in Chicago, and only recognized coincident readings as evidence for gravitational waves. He reported the first coincident readings in 1968. He also noted, in 1970, that such readings reached a peak when the cylinders were both oriented in the direction of the galactic center.

Unfortunately, although there were several attempts to replicate Weber's work in the 1970s, none proved successful. Work has, however, continued with more sensitive antennas. Supercooled niobium rods have been installed at the European Laboratory for Particle Physics in Geneva, at Stanford, and at the Louisiana State University for a three-way coincidence experiment. Despite recognizing 60–70 events a day, none have yet conclusively proved to be coincidental.

Weber, Wilhelm Eduard (1804–1891)
German physicist

Weber was the son of a professor of divinity and brother of the noted scientists Ernst Heinrich Weber and Eduard Friedrich Weber, both of whom worked in anatomy and physiology. He was born in Wittenberg in Germany and studied physics at Halle, where his early research concerned acoustics. He obtained his PhD in 1826 for a thesis on reed organ pipes. He remained teaching at Halle until 1831 when he was made professor of physics at Göttingen on the recommendation of the mathematician Karl Friedrich Gauss.

Some of Weber's research was done in collaboration with his brothers. Thus in 1824 he published work on wave motion with Ernst, and in 1833 he and Eduard investigated the mechanism of walking. However, most of his academic life was spent working with Gauss. In 1833 they built the first practical telegraph between their laboratories to coordinate their experiments on geomagnetism. In 1837 Weber lost his post for opposing the new king of Hannover's interference with the State constitution. Nevertheless, he stayed in Göttingen for a further six years until he was appointed professor at Leipzig. Here, he improved the tangent galvanometer invented by Hermann von Helmholtz and built an electrodynamometer suitable for studying the force produced by one electric current on another.

His main work was the development of a system of units that expressed electrical concepts in terms of mass, length, and time.

Gauss had previously done this for magnetism. Since force was expressed in these dimensions, he was then able to find his law of electric force. The principle was not very satisfactory because it did not conserve energy, but with it Weber publicized the view that matter was made up of charged particles held together by the force. This inspired the direction that physics took in the latter half of the century. The units of Gauss and Weber were adopted at an international conference in Paris in 1881. The unit of magnetic flux (the *weber*) is named in his honor.

In 1849 he returned to his post in Göttingen and collaborated with R. H. A. Kohlrausch in measuring the ratio between static and dynamic units of electric charge. This turned out to be the speed of light; this unexpected link between electricity and optics became central to James Clerk Maxwell's great development of electromagnetic field theory.

Wegener, Alfred Lothar (1880–1930)
German meteorologist and geologist

Wegener, who was born in Berlin, was educated at the universities of Heidelberg, Innsbruck, and Berlin, where he obtained his doctorate in astronomy in 1905. In 1906 he went on his first meteorological research trip to Greenland and, on his return (1908), was appointed to a lectureship in astronomy and meteorology at the University of Marburg. After World War I he moved to a special chair of meteorology and geophysics at the University of Graz, Austria, in 1924. He made further expeditions to Greenland, where he died on his fourth visit.

In 1915 Wegener produced his famous work *Die Enstehung der Kontinente und Ozeane* (translated as *Origin of Continents and Oceans*, 1924), in which he formulated his hypothesis of continental drift. In this he proposed that the continents were once contiguous, forming one supercontinent, Pangaea, which began to break up during the Mesozoic Era and drifted apart to form the continents we know today.

To support his theory Wegener produced four main arguments. He first pointed to the obvious correspondence between such opposite shores as those of Atlantic Africa and Latin America. An even better fit was evident if the edges of the continental shelves were matched instead of the coastlines. Secondly he argued that geodetic measurements indicated that Greenland was moving away from Europe. This supported his third argument that a large proportion of the Earth's crust is at two separate levels, the continental and the ocean floor, and that the crust is made of a lighter granite floating on a heavier basalt. His final argument was that there were patterns of similarities between species of the flora and fauna of the continents.

Wegener's theory at first met with considerable hostility. However, in 1929 Arthur Holmes was able to suggest a plausible mechanism to account for continental movement and this, together with advances in geomagnetism and oceanography, was to lead to the full acceptance of Wegener's theory and the creation of the new geophysical discipline of plate tectonics after World War II.

Wegener's meteorological works include *Die Klimate der Geologischen Vorzeit* (1924; Climates in Geological Antiquity) published in association with his father-in-law, Wladimir Köppen.

Weierstrass, Karl Wilhelm Theodor
(1815–1897) *German mathematician*

Weierstrass, who was born at Ostenfelde in Germany, spent four years at the University of Bonn studying law to please his father. After abandoning law he trained as a school teacher and spent nearly 15 years teaching at elementary schools in obscure German villages. However, he found time to combine his mathematical researches with his school teaching and in 1854 he attracted considerable favorable attention with a memoir on Abelian functions, which he published in Crelle's journal. The fame this work brought him resulted in his obtaining a post as professor of mathematics at the Royal Polytechnic School in Berlin and he soon moved on to the University of Berlin.

Weierstrass's work on Abelian functions is generally considered to be his finest, but he made numerous other contributions to many other areas of mathematics. He was one of the first to make systematic use in analysis of representations of functions by power series. He was a superb and very influential teacher, an excellent fencer, and, unlike many mathematicians, he intensely disliked music. His work in 'arithmetizing' analysis led him into a fierce controversy with the constructivist Leopold Kronecker, who thought that Weierstrass's widespread use of nonconstructive proofs and definitions was unsound.

It is to Weierstrass together with Augustin Cauchy that modern analysis is indebted for its high standards of rigor. Weierstrass gave the first truly rigorous definitions of such fundamental analytical concepts as limit, continuity, differentiability, and convergence. He also did very important work in investigating the precise conditions under which infinite series converged. Tests for convergence that he devised are still in use.

Weil, André (1906–1998) *French mathematician*

Weil studied at the Ecole Normale Supérieure in his native city of Paris and at the universities of Rome and Göttingen. He held teaching posts in many countries, including posts at the Aligarh Muslim University in India and at the universities of Strasbourg, São Paulo in Brazil, and Chicago. In 1958 he moved to the Institute for Advanced Study at Princeton, where he has been professor emeritus since 1976.

Weil's mathematical work centered on number theory, algebraic geometry, and group theory. He proved one of the central results in the theory of algebraic fields. His publications include *Foundations of Algebraic Geometry* (1946).

The religious philosopher and mystic Simone Weil, who died in 1943, was his sister.

Weinberg, Steven (1933–) *American physicist*

Born in New York, Weinberg was educated (as was Sheldon Glashow) at the Bronx High School of Science, at Cornell, and at Princeton, where he gained his PhD in 1957. Following appointments at Columbia (1957–59), Berkeley (1959–69), the Massachusetts Institute of Technology (1969–73), and Harvard (1973–83), he was appointed professor of physics at the University of Texas, Austin.

In 1967 Weinberg published a paper, *A Model of Leptons*, which proposed a unification of the weak and electromagnetic interactions since known as the 'electroweak theory'. In modern particle physics forces operate through the interchange of particles: the electromagnetic force by interchanging photons, and the weak force by the interchange of the W and Z bosons. The claim that the forces had been united into a single force would imply that photons and bosons belonged to the same family of particles. But it is only too clear that this could not be the case; the photon was virtually massless, while the bosons were even more massive than the proton.

The difference was explained by Weinberg in terms of spontaneous symmetry breaking (SSB). At the extremely high temperatures present shortly after the big bang photons and bosons would have been indistinguishable. At some point during the cooling the initial symmetry was spontaneously broken, and during this breakage some particles acquire different properties. Weinberg likens the process to what happens when a piece of iron is cooled below a temperature of 770°C. Below this point the material becomes ferromagnetic and a magnetic field pointing in some unpredictable direction can appear, spontaneously breaking the symmetry between different directions.

The question of the origin of the mass of the bosons remained. Weinberg proposed that the Higgs mechanism, described by Peter Higgs in 1964, though hypothetical, would suffice. As a consequence of Weinberg's theory the existence of 'neutral weak currents' was predicted. It has previously been supposed that weak interactions invariably involved a transfer of electric charge carried by the bosons W^+ and W^-. In electromagnetic interactions the photon is exchanged setting up a neutral current. The weak interaction should be able to proceed in the same way with the transfer of the neutral boson Z^0. Neutral weak currents were first observed in 1973, and the bosons of the electroweak theory were detected by Carlo Rubbia at the European Laboratory for Particle Physics in 1983. It was for this work that Weinberg shared the 1979 Nobel Prize for physics with his schoolmate from the Bronx, Sheldon GLASHOW, and with Abdus SALAM.

Weinberg has also worked in the field of cosmology, publishing in 1972 a substantial treatise on the subject, *Gravitation and Cosmology*. This was followed by *The First Three Minutes* (1977), an extremely popular account of the three minutes following "about one hundredth of a second after the beginning when the temperature had cooled to a mere hundred thousand million degrees Kelvin."

In a later work, *Dreams of a Final Theory* (1993), Weinberg argued that in today's theories we are already beginning to catch glimpses of the outlines of a final theory. Whether or not the glimpses are of shadows or something more substantial, Weinberg suggests, depends upon whether the US Government goes ahead and constructs the 8-billion-dollar Superconducting Super Collider in Ellis County, Texas. When complete and running the SSC should be sufficiently powerful to reveal the Higgs boson.

Weismann, August Friedrich Leopold (1834–1914) *German biologist*

Born at Frankfurt am Main, Weismann studied medicine at Göttingen, graduating in 1856. He took several temporary jobs before joining the medical faculty of the University of Freiburg in 1863.

In his early work Weismann made much use of the microscope, but failing eyesight forced him to abandon microscopy for theoretical biology. His microscopic observations, especially those on the origin of the germ cells of hydrozoans, were nevertheless put to good use in the formulation of his theory of the continuity of the germ plasm, which he published in 1886 (English translation, 1893; *The Germ-Plasm: A Theory of Heredity*). Weismann had noted that germ cells can be distinguished from somatic cells early in embryonic development, and from this he visualized the protoplasm of the germ cell (germ plasm) as being passed on unchanged through the generations and therefore responsible for inheritance. Although the body might be modified by environmental effects, the germ plasm – well protected within it – could not be. This insulation of the germ plasm from environmental influences – the so-called *Weismann barrier* – is one of the fundamental tenets of modern Darwinian theory. Weismann himself argued strongly against the Lamarckian theory of the inheritance of acquired characteristics. His publication *Studies in the Theory of Descent* (1882) contained a preface by Darwin.

Weismann closely followed Edouard van Beneden's work on meiosis (reduction division of cells) and arrived at the correct explanation for this process – that a reduction division is necessary to prevent chromosome numbers doubling at fertilization. Weismann became director of the new museum and zoological institute built at Freiburg and remained at the university until his retirement in 1912.

Weizsäcker, Baron Carl Friedrich von (1912–) *German physicist*

Weizsäcker, who was born at Kiel in Germany, studied at the universities of Berlin, Göttingen, and Leipzig, obtaining his PhD from Leipzig in 1933. Between 1933 and 1945 he taught successively at the universities of Leipzig, Berlin, and Strasbourg. In 1946 he returned to Göttingen as director of physics at the Max Planck Institute where he remained until 1957, when he was appointed professor of philosophy at Hamburg. In 1970 he moved to Starnberg as director of the Max Planck Institute on the Preconditions of Human Life in the Modern World, a post he occupied until his retirement in 1980.

Weizsäcker proposed solutions to two fundamental problems of astrophysics. In 1938 he tackled the problem of how stars like the Sun can continue to radiate colossal amounts of energy for billions of years. Independently of Hans Bethe, he proposed a chain of nuclear-fusion reactions that could proceed at the high temperatures occurring in the dense central cores of stars. In this sequence, called the 'carbon cycle', one carbon nucleus and four hydrogen nuclei, or protons, undergo various transformations before ending the cycle as one carbon nucleus and one helium nucleus. The process involves the release of an immense amount of energy that is eventually radiated from the star's surface mainly as heat, light, and ultraviolet radiation. As the stars are rich in hydrogen, it was now clear that they could continue radiating until their core hydrogen was consumed.

In 1944 Weizsäcker proposed a variation of the nebular hypothesis of Pierre Simon de Laplace to account for the origin of the planets. Beginning with the Sun surrounded by a disk of rotating gas he argued that such a mass would experience turbulence and break up into a number of smaller vortices and eddies. Where the eddies met, conditions were supposed to be suitable for planets to form from the continuous aggregation of progressively larger bodies. The system did not, however, explain the crucial point of how the planets managed to acquire so much angular momentum, a property that is conserved and cannot just be created out of nothing. Modifications and additions later proposed by Hannes Alfvén and Fred Hoyle on this issue used forces generated by the Sun's magnetic field as the means of transmitting momentum and won a fair amount of support for the theory.

Weller, Thomas Huckle (1915–   )
American microbiologist

Born in Ann Arbor, Michigan, Weller was educated at the University of Michigan, where his father was professor of pathology, and at Harvard, where he gained his MD in 1940. After serving in the US Army Medical Corps from 1942 until 1945 Weller worked with John Enders at the Children's Medical Center, Boston. In 1954 he returned to Harvard as professor of tropical public health, becoming professor emeritus in 1985.

In 1948 Weller, in collaboration with Franklin Neva, succeeded in growing the German measles (rubella) virus in tissue culture. They later went on to grow and isolate the chickenpox virus in a culture of human embryonic muscle and skin. With ENDERS and Frederick ROBBINS, Weller successfully applied the same method to the culture of poliomyelitis virus. By making adequate supplies of polio virus available to laboratory workers, this opened the way for the development of a successful polio vaccine.

For this work Weller shared the 1954 Nobel Prize for physiology or medicine with Enders and Robbins.

Werner, Abraham Gottlob (1750–1817) *German mineralogist and geologist*

Werner was born in the traditional mining town of Wehrau, which is now in Poland. Most of his ancestors had worked in some position or other in the industry and his father was inspector of the iron foundry at the town. He began work as an assistant to his father before entering the new Freiberg Mining Academy in 1769. He studied at the University of Leipzig (1771–75) before returning to teach at the Freiberg Mining Academy. There he established his neptunist views on the aqueous origin of rocks and attracted a considerable following.

Werner's neptunian theory explained the surface of the Earth and the distribution and sequence of rocks in terms of a deluge, which had covered the entire Earth including the highest mountains. The rock formations were laid down when the flood subsided in a universal and specific sequence. The first layer consisted of primitive rocks, such as granite, gneiss, and slates, and contained no fossils. The next strata (the transitional) consisted of shales and graywacke and contained fossilized fish. Above this were the limestones, sandstones, and chalks of the secondary rocks and then the gravels and sands of the alluvial strata. Finally, after the waters had completely disappeared, local volcanic activity produced lavas and other deposits.

However, this fivefold scheme, while no doubt applicable in Werner's region of Saxony, presented great difficulties outside the area. There was much that Werner could not explain, such as where the enormous flood had gone to and the presence of large basalt tracts in Europe, which were found in areas free of volcanoes. For many years Werner's theories eclipsed those of the plutonists, led by James Hutton, who emphasized the origin of igneous rocks from molten material. But as knowledge of the strata of Europe increased it became clear that there were too many regions in which Werner's sequence bore no relation to reality.

Yet neptunism certainly had its attractions, with Werner's disciples distributed throughout Europe. The advantages of the theory were that it was theologically acceptable, it was simple, and it showed how the Earth could be formed in the short time available.

Werner was also a mineralogist and he constructed a new classification of minerals. There was a major split among 18th-century mineralogists as to whether minerals should be classified according to their external form (the natural method) or by their chemical composition (the chemical method). Werner finally adopted, in 1817, a mixed set of criteria by which he divided minerals into four main classes – earthy, saline, combustible, and metallic.

Werner, Alfred (1866–1919) *French chemist*

Werner was born the son of an ironworker at Mulhouse in France. He was educated at the University of Zurich, where he gained his PhD in 1890. After a year in Paris working with Marcellin Berthelot he returned to Zurich, where he was appointed professor of chemistry in 1895.

In 1905 Werner produced a work, later translated into English as *New Ideas on Inorganic Chemistry* (1911), which was to revolutionize inorganic chemistry and earn him the Nobel Prize for chemistry in 1913. Although the ideas introduced by August Kekulé had contributed greatly to organic chemistry, attempts to apply his valence theory to inorganic molecules were much less successful. Many metals appeared to show variable valence and form complex compounds.

Werner proposed distinguishing between a primary and a secondary valence of a metal. The primary was concerned with binding ions, while the secondary valence applied not only to atoms but also to molecules, which can have an independent existence. Certain metals, such as cobalt and platinum, were capable through their secondary valences of joining to themselves a certain number of atoms or molecules. These were termed by Werner 'coordination compounds' and the maximum number of atoms (or 'ligands' as he called them) that can be joined to the central metal is its coordination number. This led Werner to make very detailed predictions about the existence of certain hitherto unsuspected isomers. He managed to resolve optical isomers of an inorganic compound in 1911.

West, Harold Dadford (1904–1974) *American biochemist*

West was educated at the University of Illinois, Urbana, graduating in 1925 and gaining his PhD in 1927. After working initially at Morris Brown College, Atlanta, he moved to Meharry Medical College, Nashville, in 1937. West spent his entire career at Meharry serving as professor of biochemistry from 1938 until his retirement in 1973, apart from a break between 1952 and 1963, when he held the position of college president.

Although West worked in a number of fields and conducted research on the biochemistry of various bacilli, the B vitamins, and antibiotics, he is best known for his studies of the amino acids. In particular it was West who first synthesized the essential amino acid threonine.

Weyl, Hermann (1885–1955) *German mathematician*

Born at Elmshorn in Germany, Weyl studied at Göttingen, where he was one of David Hilbert's most outstanding students. He became a coworker of Hilbert, who influenced his particular interests and his general outlook on mathematics. Weyl taught at the Federal Institute of Technology in Zurich from 1913, and this too had a decisive influence in directing his mathematical interests through the presence there of Albert Einstein. In 1930 he returned to Göttingen to take up the chair vacated by Hilbert. With the Nazis' rise to power in 1933, Weyl, with many other members of the Göttingen scientific community, went into exile in America. Weyl found a post at the Institute for Advanced Study in Princeton along with other exiles, such as Einstein and Kurt Gödel.

Weyl's mathematical interests, like those of Hilbert, were exceptionally wide, ranging from mathematical physics to the foundations of mathematics. He worked on two areas of pure mathematics: group theory and the theory of Hilbert space and operators, which, although developed for purely mathematical purposes, later turned out to be precisely the mathematical framework needed for the revolutionary physical ideas of quantum mechanics. Weyl also wrote a number of books on the theory of groups and he was particularly interested in symmetry and its relation to group theory. One of his most important results in group theory was a key theorem about the application of representations to Lie algebras. Weyl's work on Hilbert space had grown out of his interest in Hilbert's work on integral equations and operators. The theory of Hilbert space (infinite-dimensional space) was recognized by Erwin Schrödinger and Walter Heisenberg in the mid-1920s as the necessary unifying systematization of their theories of quantum mechanics.

Weyl's contact with Einstein at Zurich was responsible for an interest in the mathematics of relativity, and especially Riemannian geometry, which plays a central role. Weyl initiated the whole project of trying to generalize Riemannian geometry. He himself worked chiefly on the geometry of affinely connected spaces, but this was only one of many generalizations that resulted from his work. Weyl also did similar work on generalizing and refining the basic concepts of differential geometry. All this work was to be of importance for relativity. Weyl's views on relativity were expounded in his book *Raum-Zeit-Materie* (1919; Space-Time-Matter).

Weyl, like his teacher Hilbert, was always interested in the philosophical aspects of mathematics. However, in contrast to Hilbert, his general attitude was similar to that of L. E. J. Brouwer with whom he shared constructivist leanings developed from work in analysis. Weyl expounded his philosophical ideas in another book, *Philosophy of Mathematics and Natural Sciences* (1949). Unlike Brouwer, however, Weyl was less rigorous in avoiding nonconstructive mathematics, and doubtless his interest in physics contributed to this.

Wheatstone, Sir Charles (1802–1875)
British physicist

After a private education in his native city of Gloucester, Wheatstone began business in London as a musical-instrument maker (1823). His early scientific researches were in acoustics and optics and his contributions were numerous. Thus he devised a 'kaleidophone' to illustrate harmonic motions of different periods; he suggested a stereoscope (1838) that, using two pictures in dissimilar perspective, could give the appearance of solidity; he showed that every Chladni figure was the resultant of two or more sets of isochronous parallel vibrations; and he demonstrated how minute quantities of metals could be detected from the spectral lines produced by electric sparks.

Perhaps his most important work, however, was to produce, with William Cooke, the first practical electric telegraph system. In 1837, in conjunction with the new London and Birmingham Railway Company, Cooke and Wheatstone installed a demonstration line about one mile long. Improvements rapidly followed and, with the needs of the railroads providing the impetus and finance, by 1852 more than 4000 miles of telegraph lines were in operation throughout Britain. Wheatstone constructed the first printing telegraph (1841) and a single-needle telegraph (1845). He made contributions to the development of submarine telegraphy and to dynamos. The *Wheatstone bridge*, a device for comparing electrical re-

sistances, was not invented by Wheatstone but brought to notice by him.

Wheatstone was appointed professor of experimental philosophy at King's College, London, in 1834 and was knighted in 1868. At his death he held about 40 awards and distinctions. He was prolific in his inventions and had an extraordinary ability to turn his theoretical knowledge to practical account.

Wheeler, John Archibald (1911–)
American theoretical physicist

Born in Jacksonville, Florida, Wheeler was educated at Johns Hopkins University, where he obtained his PhD in physics in 1933. After spending the period 1933–35 in Copenhagen working with Niels Bohr, he returned to America to take up a teaching position at the University of North Carolina. In 1938 he went to Princeton, where he served as professor of physics from 1947 until his move to the University of Texas in 1976 to become professor of physics. He retired in 1986.

Wheeler has been active in theoretical physics. One of the problems tackled by him has been the search for a unified field theory. His earlier papers on the subject were collected in 1962 in his *Geometrodynamics*. It was here that he introduced the geon (gravitational–electromagnetic entity), with which he aimed to achieve the unification of the two fields. He also collaborated with Richard Feynman in two papers in 1945 and 1949 on the important concept of action at a distance. They formulated a problem that arises when it is accepted that such action cannot take place instantaneously. If X and Y are at rest and one light-minute apart, then any electromagnetic signal emitted by X will reach Y one minute later. This is described by saying X acts on Y by a retarded effect. But by Newton's third law, to each action there corresponds an opposite and equal reaction. This must mean that from Y to X there should also be an advanced effect acting backward in time. Feynman and Wheeler demonstrated how the advance wave could be eliminated from the model to account for the fact that the universe displays only retarded effects.

Wheeler also made important contributions to nuclear physics. With Niels Bohr he put forward an explanation of the mechanism of nuclear fission. He joined the Los Alamos group exploring the possibility of producing an explosive device using heavy hydrogen in 1949–50. Wheeler has provided a popular account of his work in his *Journey into Gravity and Spacetime* (1990); he has also published his autobiography, *At Home in the Universe* (1993).

Whipple, Fred Lawrence (1906–)
American astronomer

Born in Red Oak, Iowa, Whipple graduated from the University of California in Los Angeles in 1927 and obtained his PhD from Berkeley in 1931. He then moved to Harvard where he became professor of astronomy in 1945, Philips Professor of Astronomy in 1950, and director of the Smithsonian Astrophysical Observatory from 1955 until his retirement in 1973.

He described his research as centering on "physical processes in the evolution of the solar system" and produced in this field a much admired work, *Earth, Moon and Planets* (1941 and many subsequent editions).

Whipple is also well known for his work on comets. In 1950 he proposed an icy-nucleus model in which he described the nucleus of a comet as a 'dirty snowball', made from a mixture of water ice and dust, plus carbon dioxide, carbon monoxide, methane, and ammonia ices, and only becoming active when passing close to the Sun. The main advantage of this model is that it can account for such distinctive features of comets as their orbital motion. It had been long known that some comets, such as Encke's, persist in returning earlier than Newtonian theory would predict while others, such as Halley's, arrive over four days later than expected. Whipple proposed that solar radiation would cause the ices on the outside of the cometary nucleus to evaporate, leaving a thin insulating layer of dust particles, and that this would set up a delayed jet reaction. The radiation has the effect of pushing further out those comets that are rotating in the same direction as their orbit. This will increase their orbit and delay their return. The radiation will produce a drag force on those comets rotating counter to their orbit, causing them to drift in toward the Sun, reducing their period and thus hastening their return.

As there should be no preferred direction of rotation, Whipple predicted that about half the comets should appear to be retarded and half accelerated in their orbit, an effect since confirmed.

Whipple, George Hoyt (1878–1976)
American physician and physiologist

Whipple, born the son of a physician in Ashland, New Hampshire, was educated at Yale and Johns Hopkins University, where he obtained his MD in 1905. After working at the University of California he moved in 1921 to the University of Rochester, where he served as professor of pathology until his retirement in 1955.

Whipple began his research career by working on bile pigments but went on to study the formation and breakdown of the blood pigment, hemoglobin, of which bile pigments are the breakdown products. To do this he bled dogs until he had reduced their hemoglobin level to a third, then measured the rate of hemoglobin regeneration. He soon noted that this rate varied with the diet of the dogs and by 1923 reported that liver in the diet produced a significant increase in hemoglobin production.

It was this work that led **George Minot** (1885–1950) and **William Murphy** (1892–1987) to develop a successful treatment for pernicious anemia and earned all three men the Nobel Prize for physiology or medicine in 1934.

Whiston, William (1667–1752) *British mathematician and geologist*

Whiston, the son of a parish priest from Norton in England, was educated at Cambridge University, where he came to the attention of Isaac Newton. He was selected, on Newton's recommendation, to succeed him as Lucasian Professor of Mathematics (1703) and to edit his *Arithmetica universalis* (1707; Universal Arithmetic). In 1710 he was dismissed from the university for his unorthodox religious belief in the Arian heresy, after which time he supported himself by giving public lectures on popular science.

Whiston's chief scientific work, *A New Theory of the Earth* (1696), was praised by Newton and by John Locke. In this Whiston followed the tradition recently established by Thomas Burnet in attempting to explain biblical events, such as the Creation, scientifically. The Flood, he believed, was caused by a comet pasing close to the Earth on 28 November 2349 BC. This put stress on the Earth's crust, causing it to crack and allow the water to escape and flood the Earth.

Whitehead, Alfred North (1861–1947)
British mathematician and philosopher

Whitehead, who was born at Ramsgate on the south coast of England, obtained his PhD from Cambridge University in 1884. For the next few years he taught there and met Bertrand Russell, who was one of his students and with whom he was later to collaborate. Whitehead was one of a growing section of philosophers of science who criticized the deterministic and materialistic views prevalent in 19th-century science. The main theme of this critique was that scientific theories were patterns derived from our way of measuring and perceiving the world and not innate properties of the underlying reality. While in Cambridge his mathematical work reflected this viewpoint, developed in his book *Treatise of Universal Algebra* (1898), which treated algebraic structures as objects worthy of study in their own right, independent of their relationship to real quantities. In 1910 he published, with Russell, the first volume of the vast *Principia Mathematica* (Mathematical Principles) which was an attempt, inspired by the work of Gottlob Frege and Guiseppe Peano, to clarify the conceptual foundations of mathematics using the formal methods of symbolic logic.

Whitehead then moved to London, where he taught at University College and later became professor at Imperial College. Here he developed his action-at-a-distance theory of relativity, which challenged Einstein's field-theoretic viewpoint but never gained wide acceptance. In 1924 he emigrated to America and worked at Harvard, developing his antimechanistic philosophy of science and a system of metaphysics, until he retired in 1937.

Whittington, Harry Blackmore
(1916–   ) *British geologist*

Whittington was born at Handsworth in Yorkshire. After gaining his PhD from the University of Birmingham, he spent the years of World War II teaching in the Far East, first at the University of Rangoon, Burma, and for the rest of the war at Ginling College, West China. He returned to Birmingham in 1945 but moved to Harvard as curator of vertebrate paleontology at the Museum of Comparative Zoology. In 1966 Whittington left America for the post of Woodward Professor of Geology at Cambridge, a position he held until his retirement in 1983.

Since the early 1960s Whittington has devoted the bulk of his time to the study of the Burgess Shale fossils, discovered and described by C. D. Walcott earlier in the century. He made two expeditions to the site in 1966 and 1967 and recruited two assistants, Derek Briggs and Simon Conway Morris, to help him reexamine the entire collection.

Whittington's first report, published in 1971, was devoted to *Marella splendens*, identified by Walcott as a trilobite, a primitive and long-extinct arthropod. Whittington, after four years' work on several thousand specimens, found too many uncharacteristic trilobite features to be happy with Walcott's classification. He compromised by calling it *Trilobitoidea* (trilobite-like). His suspicion that many of Walcott's arthropods had been wrongly classified were increased when Whittington next looked at the subject of his 1975 monograph, *Opabinia*. As he could find no jointed appendages it was clear to Whittington that *Opabinia* could not be an arthropod. What its affinities were, however, remained uncertain.

By the time he came to deal in 1985 with *Anamalocaris* he could state confidently that it was no arthropod but "the representative of a hitherto unknown phylum." Whittington and his colleagues went on to identify ten invertebrate genera "that have so far defied all attempts to link them with known phyla."

Whittington's labors thus presented a dramatic new picture. The Cambrian is now seen as a period in which many new complex species suddenly appear. Further, relatively few of these seemingly advanced groups lasted beyond the Cambrian. The full significance of Whittington's work has yet to be worked out.

Whittle, Sir Frank (1907–1996) *British aeronautical engineer*

Whittle, the son of a mechanic from Coventry in the English Midlands, joined the Royal Air Force as an apprentice in 1923. He was trained at the RAF College, Cranwell, and Cambridge University, where he studied mechanical sciences (1934–37).

While still a student at Cranwell, Whittle had expressed his prediction that there would soon emerge a demand for high-speed high-altitude aircraft. He recognized the inadequacies of the conventional airscrew to meet these needs and took out his first patent for the turbojet engine in 1930. He gained little government backing but with the assistance of friends he formed, in 1936, the company Power Jets. By the following year, his first engine, the W1, was ready for testing. With the advent of World War II government funds were rapidly awarded to develop this and the jet engine was fitted to the specially built Gloster E28/39 aircraft. It made its first flight on 15 May 1941 and by 1944 was in service with the RAF.

For his work Whittle was made a fellow of the Royal Society in 1947, knighted in 1948, and awarded a tax-free gift of £100,000 by the British government. He left the RAF in 1948 and served as a consultant with the British Overseas Airways Corporation (1948–52), the Shell Group (1952–57), and Bristol Siddeley Engines (1961–70). In 1977

Whittle accepted the post of research professor at the US Naval Academy, Annapolis.

Wieland, Heinrich Otto (1877–1957)
German chemist

Wieland was born in Pforzheim, Germany, the son of a chemist in a gold and silver refinery. He was educated at the University of Munich where he obtained his PhD in 1901. After teaching at the Munich Technical Institute and the University of Freiburg, Wieland succeeded Richard Willstätter in 1925 as professor of chemistry at the University of Munich, a post he retained until his retirement in 1950.

In 1912 Wieland began work on the bile acids. These secretions of the liver had been known for the best part of a century to consist of a large number of substances. He began by investigating three of them: cholic acid, deoxycholic acid, and lithocholic acid, finding that they were all steroids, very similar to each other, and all convertible into cholanic acid.

As Adolf Windaus had derived cholanic acid from cholesterol, an important biological sterol, this led Wieland to propose a structure for cholesterol. For his contributions to steroid chemistry Wieland was awarded the 1927 Nobel Prize for chemistry.

After 1921 Wieland worked on a number of curious alkaloids including toxiferin, the active ingredient in curare, bufotalin, the venom from toads, and phalloidine and amatine, the poisonous ingredients in the deadly amanita mushroom.

Wien, Wilhelm Carl Werner Otto
Fritz Franz (1864–1928) *German physicist*

The son of a farmer from Gaffken in Eastern Europe, Wien studied mathematics and physics for a brief period in 1882 at the University of Göttingen. Having recommenced his studies in 1884 at the University of Berlin, he received a doctorate in 1886 for a thesis on the diffraction of light. At various times he considered becoming a farmer but after his parents were forced to sell their land he decided on an academic career in physics. In 1890 he joined the new Imperial (now Federal) Institute for Science and Technology in Charlottenburg, Berlin, as assistant to Hermann von Helmholtz, under whom he had studied. From 1896 to 1899 he worked at the technical college in Aachen and in 1900 was appointed professor of physics at the University of Würzburg. In 1920 he became professor at the University of Munich.

Wien was highly competent in both theoretical and experimental physics. His major research was into thermal or black-body radiation. In 1893 he showed that the wavelength at which the maximum energy is radiated from a source is inversely proportional to the absolute temperature of the source. Thus in heating an object it first glows red hot, emitting most of its energy at the wavelengths of red light; as the temperature is increased, the wavelength at which maximum energy is emitted becomes shorter, and the body becomes white hot. This behavior is known as *Wien's displacement law*. In 1896 Wien derived a formula, now known as *Wien's formula*, for the distribution of energy in black-body radiation for a whole range of wavelengths. Its importance for future research lay in the fact that although successful at short wavelengths it disagreed with experiments at longer wavelengths. The discrepancy, which is sometimes known as the 'ultraviolet catastrophe', highlighted the inadequacies of classical mechanics and inspired Max Planck to develop the quantum theory. Wien was awarded the Nobel Prize for physics in 1911 for his discoveries regarding the laws governing the radiation of heat.

Wien also studied the conduction of electricity in gases and, while teaching in Aachen, confirmed that cathode rays consisted of high-velocity particles (1897) and were negatively charged (1898). In addition he showed that canal rays were positively charged particles. He later conducted research into x-rays.

Wiener, Norbert (1894–1964) *American mathematician*

Born in Columbia, Missouri, Wiener was a child prodigy in mathematics who sustained his early promise to become a mathematician of great originality and creativity. He is probably one of the most outstanding mathematicians to have been born in the United States. Such was Wiener's precocity that he took his degree in mathematics, from Tufts University, at the age of 14 in 1909.

Throughout his life Wiener had many extramathematical interests, especially in biology and philosophy. At Harvard his studies in philosophy led him to an interest in mathematical logic and this was the subject of his doctoral thesis, which he completed at the age of 18. Wiener went from Harvard to Europe to pursue his interest in mathematical logic with Bertrand Russell in Cambridge and with David Hilbert in Göttingen. After he returned from Europe, Wiener's mathematical interests broadened but, surprisingly, he was unable to get a suitable post as a professional mathematician and for a time tried such unlikely occupations as journalism and even writing entries for an encyclopedia. In 1919 Wiener finally obtained a post in the mathematics department of the Massachusetts Institute of Technology, where he remained for the rest of his career.

After his arrival at MIT Wiener began his extremely important work on the theory of stochastic (random) processes and Brownian motion. Among his other very wide mathematical interests at this time was the generalization of Fourier's work on resolving functions into series of periodic functions (this is known as harmonic analysis). He also worked on the theory of Fourier transforms. During World War II Wiener devoted his mathematical talents to working for the military – in particular to the problem of giving a mathematical solution to the problem of aiming a gun at a moving target. In the course of this work Wiener discovered the theory of the prediction of stationary time series and brought essentially statistical methods to bear on the mathematical analysis of control and communication engineering.

From here it was a short step to his important work in the mathematical analysis of mechanical and biological systems, their information flow, and the analogies between them – the subject he named 'cybernetics'. It allowed full rein to his wide interests in the sciences and philosophy and Wiener spent much time popularizing the subject and explaining its possible social and philosophical applications. Wiener also worked on a wide range of other mathematical topics, particularly important being his work on quantum mechanics.

Wieschaus, Eric (1947–   ) *American biologist*

While working in the late 1970s in the European Molecular Biology Laboratory, Heidelberg, Wieschaus collaborated with Christiane Nüsslein-Volhard on a study of the genetic factors producing segmentation in the fruit fly *Drosophila melanogaster*. Flies were exposed to mutagenic chemicals and thousands of their larval descendants examined to see if particular types of mutants emerged. Their work, published in 1980, established 15 mutant loci that radically altered the segmental pattern of the *Drosophila* larvae. It allowed the main development sequences to be marked out – to show, in effect, how the embryo becomes increasingly segmented. At first the gap genes divide the embryo into its main regions. Pair-rule genes then subdivide these regions into segments and, finally, polarity genes mark out repeating patterns in each

segment. This has proved to be especially significant as it is suspected that the same development pattern may be found in other organisms. It has even been suggested that Waardenburg's syndrome, a rare disease in humans that leads to deafness and albinism, is caused by mutations in the human version of the pair-rule gene.

Wieschaus shared the 1995 Nobel Prize for physiology or medicine with his collaborators NÜSSLEIN-VOLHARD and Edward LEWIS.

Wiesel, Torsten Nils (1924–   ) *Swedish neurophysiologist*

Wiesel, who was born at Uppsala in Sweden, obtained his MD from the Karolinska Institute, Stockholm. He moved to America shortly afterward, working first at Johns Hopkins before moving to Harvard (1959), where he was appointed professor of neurophysiology in 1974. In 1983 he moved to Rockefeller University, New York, where he served as head of the neurobiology laboratory.

Since his arrival in America Wiesel has been engaged upon a most productive investigation with David HUBEL, into the mammalian visual system. Their 20-year collaboration led to the formulation of the influential hypercolumn theory. Wiesel and Hubel received the 1981 Nobel Prize for physiology or medicine for their work, sharing the prize with Roger Sperry. Wiesel has gone on to investigate the chemical transmitters involved in the nerve cells of the visual system.

Wigglesworth, Sir Vincent Brian (1899–1994) *British entomologist*

Born at Kirkham in England, Wigglesworth was educated at Cambridge University and at St. Thomas's Hospital, London. He subsequently held posts as lecturer in medical entomology at the London School of Hygiene and Tropical Medicine and as reader in entomology at the universities of London and Cambridge. He was director of the Agricultural Research Council Unit of Insect Physiology at Cambridge (1943–1967) and from 1952 was Quick Professor of Biology. Wigglesworth's main line of research was in insect physiology, much of his work being done using the bloodsucking bug *Rhodnius prolixus*. He carried out research on hormonal stimulation in insect ecdysis (molting of the cuticle), glandular growth and reproductive secretions, external stimuli perception (e.g., heat receptors on antennae, and body hairs), and insects' perception of time, due to metabolic rate and daily rhythm. His most important publications are *The Physiology of Insect Metamorphosis*

(1954), *The Control of Growth and Form* (1959), and *The Principles of Insect Physiology* (1939; 6th edition, 1965).

Wigner, Eugene Paul (1902–1995)
Hungarian–American physicist

Born the son of a businessman in Budapest, Hungary, Wigner was educated at the Berlin Institute of Technology, where he obtained a doctorate in engineering in 1925. After a period at Göttingen he moved to America in 1930 and took a part-time post at Princeton. He became a naturalized American citizen in 1937 and in 1938 was appointed to the chair of theoretical physics. Wigner remained at Princeton until his retirement in 1971 apart from leave of absence when he served at the Metallurgical Laboratory, Chicago (1942–45), and at Oak Ridge as director of the Clinton Laboratories (1946–47).

Wigner made many fundamental contributions to quantum and nuclear physics. He did some early work on chemical reactions and on the spectra of compounds. In 1927 he introduced the idea of parity as a conserved property of nuclear reactions. The basic insight was mathematical and arose from certain formal features Wigner had identified in transformations of the wave function of Erwin Schrödinger. The function $\Psi(x,y,z)$ describes particles in space, and parity refers to the effect of changes in the sign of the variables on the function: if it remains unchanged the function has even parity while if its sign changes it has odd parity. It was proposed by Wigner that a reaction in which parity is not conserved is forbidden.

In physical terms this meant that a nuclear process should be indistinguishable from its mirror image; for example, an electron emitted by a nucleus should be indifferent as to whether it is ejected to the left or the right. Such a consequence seemed natural and remained unquestioned until 1956 when Tsung Dao Lee and Chen Ning Yang shocked the world of physics by showing that parity was not conserved in the weak interaction.

In the 1930s Wigner made major contributions to nuclear physics. Working particularly on neutrons he established early on that the nuclear force binding the neutrons and protons together must be short-range and independent of any electric charge. He also with Gregory Breit in 1936 worked out the *Breit–Wigner formula*, which did much to explain neutron absorption by a compound nucleus. Wigner was involved in much of the early work on nuclear reactors

leading to the first controlled nuclear chain reaction.

Wigner shared the 1963 Nobel Prize for physics with Maria Goeppert MAYER and J. Hans JENSEN for "systematically improving and extending the methods of quantum mechanics and applying them widely."

Wildt, Rupert (1905–1976) *German–American astronomer*

Wildt was born in Munich, Germany, and studied at the University of Berlin, obtaining his PhD there in 1927. After a period of teaching at Göttingen he emigrated to America in 1934 and worked at various institutions including the Mount Wilson Observatory (1935–36), Princeton University (1937–42), and the University of Virginia (1942–46). In 1948 he took up an appointment at Yale University where he served as professor of astrophysics from 1957 until his retirement in 1973.

Wildt worked in stellar spectroscopy, theoretical astrophysics, and geochemistry, but his main interest lay in planetary studies. Since much of his work was done before the start of the space program it is not surprising that many of his speculations have since been rejected. Thus his claim that the Venusian clouds contained formaldehyde (CH_2O) formed under the influence of ultraviolet rays has not been confirmed by space probes.

He was, however, successful in his identification in 1932 of certain absorption bands observed by Vesto Slipher in the spectrum of Jupiter as being due to ammonia and methane. He also, in 1943, proposed a model of the constitution of Jupiter based on its density of 1.3 arguing that it consisted of a large metallic rocky core surrounded by ice and compressed hydrogen above which lies a thick layer of atmosphere. Saturn, Uranus, and Neptune were thought to have a similar constitution, but more recent models, together with the Pioneer and Voyager space flights, have suggested that the giant planets are made mainly of hydrogen in various forms with much smaller cores than Wildt proposed.

Wiles, Andrew John (1953–) *British mathematician*

The son of a theology professor, Wiles was educated at Cambridge University, where he gained his PhD in 1980. He immediately took up an appointment as professor of mathematics at Princeton.

Wiles worked on the most famous of all mathematical problems, namely, 'Fermat's last theorem' (FLT). Pierre Fermat claimed in 1637 that he had proved that there are no numbers $n > 2$ such that:

$$a^n + b^n = c^n$$

It was, of course, well known that where $n = 2$ there were many solutions to the equation as when $a = 3$, $b = 4$, and $c = 5$. Fermat had merely stated the theorem, as was his custom, in the margins of a book, in this case the *Arithmetica* of Diophantus. He simply added that there was insufficient room in the margin to record the details of the proof.

As over the years all Fermat's other marginalia have turned out to be accurate and proofs found, mathematicians were optimistic that the one unproved proposition – the last theorem – would also succumb. Yet 300 years later not only had no proof been found, but mathematicians seemed unaware in which direction a proof could be found. They could, of course, simply show the proposition to be false by finding an $n > 3$ which does satisfy the equation. But that was going to be no easy matter either, for it had been shown that any such number n must be very large – by 1992 all exponents up to 4 million had been tested and failed.

An alternative approach was suggested by some work in 1954 on elliptic curves by the Japanese mathematician Yutaka Taniyama. An elliptic curve is a set of solutions to an equation relating a quadratic in one variable to a cubic in another as in:

$$y^2 = ax^3 + bx^2 + cx + d$$

The Taniyama conjecture asserts that associated with every elliptical curve was a function with certain very precise specific properties. The German mathematician Gerhard Frey argued in 1985 that the Taniyama conjecture had important implications for Fermat's last theorem. He demonstrated that any possible solution to the theorem would give rise to a class of elliptical curves, referred to as *Frey curves*, which could not satisfy the conditions of the Taniyama conjecture. Thus a proof of the Taniyama conjecture would show that there could be no solutions to Fermat's last theorem.

In 1986 Wiles set out to show that Frey curves could not exist. Seven years later he had established a 200-page proof, which he revealed to the public for the first time at a mathematical conference in Cambridge, England, in 1993. Although Wiles's proof made headline news around the world it soon became evident that gaps still existed. After a further year the gaps had been eliminated and the 200-page paper had been accepted for publication.

Wilkes, Maurice Vincent (1913–)
British computer scientist

Wilkes was born at Dudley in Worcestershire, and educated at Cambridge University. After working on operational research during World War II, he returned to Cambridge where he was appointed professor of computing technology in 1965, a post he held until his retirement in 1980.

In 1946 Wilkes attended a course on the design of electronic computers at the Moore School of Electrical Engineering at the University of Pennsylvania. Here Wilkes learned of the direction modern computers would have to follow. Earlier models, such as the Moore School's ENIAC, were really designed to deal with one particular type of problem. To solve a different kind of problem thousands of switches would have to be reset and miles of cable rerouted. The future of computing lay with the idea of the 'stored program', as preached by John von Neumann at the Moore School.

Consequently Wilkes returned to Cambridge to begin work on EDSAC (Electronic Delay Storage Automatic Computer). In order to store a program, the computer must first have a memory, something lacking from ENIAC and earlier devices. Wilkes chose to adopt the mercury delay lines suggested by J. P. Eckert to serve as an internal memory store. In a delay tube an electrical signal is converted into a sound wave traveling through a long tube of mercury with a speed of 1450 meters per second. It can be reflected back and forth along the tube for as long as necessary. Thus assigning the number 1 to be represented by a pulse of 0.5 microsecond, and 0 by no pulse, a 1.45-meter-long tube could retain 1000 binary digits.

EDSAC came into operation in May 1949, gaining for Wilkes the honor of building the first working computer with a stored program; it remained in operation until 1958. The future, however, lay not in delay lines but in magnetic storage, and EDSAC soon became as obsolete as ENIAC.

Wilkes provided a lively account of his work in his *Memoirs of a Computer Pioneer* (1985).

Wilkins, John (1614–1672) *English mathematician and scientist*

Born at Fawsley in Northamptonshire, Wilkins was educated at Oxford University, graduating in 1631. He was a parliamentarian during the English Civil War and became warden of Wadham College, Oxford University. In 1659 he was appointed master of Trinity College, Cambridge University.

After the Restoration he lost his post but regained favor to become bishop of Chester.

Wilkins's chief contribution to the development of science was his part in founding the Royal Society. His influence can be traced back to his student days at Oxford when he collected around him a lively group of philosophers and scientists who later became founder members of the society in 1662. His own writings covered a wide range of fields and although he had a certain amount of mathematical knowledge he was more a practical scientist. His *Discovery of a World in the Moon* (1638) is a fantasy in which he speculated about the structure of the Moon. A later semimathematical work, *Mathematical Magick*, deals with the principles of machine design and in it Wilkins argued that perpetual motion is a theoretical possibility. One nonscientific interest to which Wilkins devoted much time was his project of devising a universal language.

Wilkins, Maurice Hugh Frederick

(1916–) *New Zealand–British biophysicist*

Wilkins was born at Pongaroa in New Zealand. After graduating in physics from Cambridge University in England in 1938, he joined John Randall at Birmingham University to work on the improvement of radar screens. He received his PhD in 1940 for an electron-trap theory of phosphorescence and soon after went to the University of California, Berkeley, as one of the British team assigned to the Manhattan project and development of the atomic bomb. The results and implications of this work caused him to turn away from nuclear physics and in 1945 he began a career in biophysics, firstly at St. Andrews University, Scotland, and from 1946 at the Biophysics Research Unit, King's College, London.

The same year that Wilkins joined King's College, scientists at the Rockefeller Institute announced that genes consist of deoxyribonucleic acid (DNA). Wilkins began studying DNA molecules by optical measurements and chanced to observe that the DNA fibers would be ideal material for x-ray diffraction studies. The diffraction patterns showed the DNA molecule to be very regular and have a double-helical structure. The contributions of Wilkins's colleague, Rosalind Franklin, were especially important in showing that the phosphate groups are located on the outside of the helix, so disproving Linus Pauling's theory of DNA structure.

Wilkins passed on his data to James WATSON and Francis CRICK in Cambridge who used it to help construct their famous molecular model of DNA. For their work in elucidating the structure of the hereditary material, Wilkins, Watson, and Crick were awarded the 1962 Nobel Prize for physiology or medicine.

Wilkins went on to apply his techniques to finding the structure of ribonucleic acid (RNA). From 1955 he was deputy director of the Biophysics Research Unit and from 1963 he was professor at King's College, firstly of molecular biology and from 1970 of biophysics. He retired in 1981.

Wilkinson, Sir Geoffrey (1921–1996)

British inorganic chemist

Wilkinson was born at Todmorden in Yorkshire, and educated at Imperial College, London; after spending World War II working in North America on the development of the atomic bomb, he finally obtained his PhD in 1946. He later worked at the Massachusetts Institute of Technology and at Harvard, before being elected to the chair of inorganic chemistry at Imperial College, a post he held from 1956 until 1988. He was knighted in 1976.

Wilkinson is noted for his studies of inorganic complexes. He shared the Nobel Prize for chemistry in 1973 with Ernst FISCHER for work on 'sandwich compounds'. A theme of Wilkinson's work in the 1960s was the study and use of complexes containing a metal–hydrogen bond. Thus complexes of rhodium with triphenyl phosphine $((C_6H_5)_3P)$ can react with molecular hydrogen. The compound $RhCl(P(C_6H_5)_3)_3$, known as *Wilkinson's catalyst*, was the first such complex to be used as a homogeneous catalyst for adding hydrogen to the double bonds of alkenes (hydrogenation). This type of compound can also be used as a catalyst for the reaction of hydrogen and carbon monoxide with alkenes (hydroformylation). It is the basis of industrial low-pressure processes for making aldehydes from ethene and propene.

Williams, Robert R. (1886–1965)

American chemist

The son of a Baptist missionary, Williams was born at Nellore in India and educated at the universities of Ottawa, Kansas, and Chicago. He began his career in government service, serving as chemist to the Bureau of Science in Manila before returning to America, where he worked at the Bureau of Chemistry in the agriculture department until 1918. He then moved into industry, working first for Western Electric before joining the Bell Telephone Laboratories in 1924, where he directed the chemistry laboratory until 1945.

With considerable single-mindedness Williams, early in his career, set himself the task of isolating the cause of beriberi. As early as 1896 Christiaan Eijkman had shown that it was a deficiency disease while Casimir Funk had demonstrated that the vitamin whose absence caused the disease was an amine. Beyond that nothing was known when Williams began his work in the Philippines.

Working mainly in his spare time, in 1934 he managed to isolate, from several tons of rice husks, enough of the vitamin, B_1, to work out its formula. In 1937 he succeeded in synthesizing it.

His brother Roger, also a chemist, discovered pantothenic acid, another important vitamin in the B complex.

Williams, Robley Cook (1908–)
American biophysicist

Williams, who was born in Santa Rosa, California, received a PhD in physics from Cornell University in 1935 and then went on to teach astronomy at the University of Michigan, transferring to the physics department in 1945. He remained there until 1950, when he transferred to a lecturing post in the biochemistry department at the University of California, Berkeley. In 1964, when a department of molecular biology was established at Berkeley, Williams became its chairman.

As an astronomer Williams worked on the estimation of stellar surface temperatures. Military research during World War II turned his attention to electron microscopy, and an insight drawn from his knowledge of astronomical techniques led to a fruitful collaboration with the crystallographer Ralph Wyckoff. The early electron microscopes were transmission microscopes, i.e., the beam of electrons passes through the sample, giving a two-dimensional image. Working with Ralph Wyckoff at Michigan, Williams developed a technique of preparing specimens so that they could be observed with reflected beams of electrons. The technique involves depositing metal obliquely on the specimen. This effectively 'casts shadows' and creates a vivid three-dimensional effect in the image.

Williams turned to the study of viruses, using his shadowing technique, and made important contributions to an understanding of viral structure. In 1955 (in collaboration with Heinz Fraenkel-Conrat) he achieved, with the tobacco mosaic virus, the first reconstitution of a biologically active virus from its constituent proteins and nucleic acids.

Williamson, Alexander William
(1824–1904) *British chemist*

Williamson's father was a clerk in the East India Company in London. After his retirement in 1840 the family lived on the Continent, where Williamson was educated. He studied at Heidelberg and at Giessen (under Justus von Liebig), where he received his PhD in 1846. He also studied mathematics in Paris. In 1849 he took up the chair of chemistry at London University, a post he occupied until 1887.

Between 1850 and 1856 Williamson showed that alcohol and ether both belong to the water type. Type theory, developed by Charles Gerhardt and Auguste Laurent, was based on the idea that organic compounds are produced by replacing one or more hydrogen atoms of inorganic compounds (which form the types) by radicals. Using the correct formula for alcohol (which he had recently established) Williamson represented the water type as: H_2O (water); C_2H_5OH (alcohol); $C_2H_5OC_2H_5$ (ether), where the H of water is progressively replaced by C_2H_5.

A further contribution to chemical theory was his demonstration (in 1850) of reversible reactions: two substances, A and B, react to form the products X and Y, which in turn react to produce the original A and B. Under certain conditions the system could be in dynamic equilibrium, when the amount of A and B reacting to form X and Y is equal to the amount of A and B produced by X and Y. He is remembered for what is now known as *Williamson's synthesis*, a method of making ethers by reacting a sodium alcoholate with a haloalkane.

Willstätter, Richard (1872–1942)
German chemist

Willstätter was the son of a textile merchant from Karlsruhe in Germany. He was educated at the University of Munich, receiving his PhD in 1894 for work on cocaine. He was professor of chemistry in Zurich from 1905 to 1912, when he left to work in the Kaiser Wilhelm Institute in Berlin. In 1916 he succeeded Adolf von Baeyer to the chemistry chair at Munich. He resigned in 1924 in protest at the growing anti-Semitism in Germany but remained in his homeland until he felt his own life was no longer safe, going into exile in Switzerland in 1939.

His early work was mainly on the structure of alkaloids – he managed to throw light on such important compounds as cocaine, which he synthesized in 1923, and atropine. In 1905 he began work on the chemistry of chlorophyll. By using the chromatographic techniques developed by

Mikhail Tsvet, he was soon able to show that it consists of two compounds, chlorophyll a and b, and to work out their formulas. One of the significant features he noted was that chlorophyll contains a single atom of magnesium in its molecule, just as hemoglobin contains a single iron atom. He also investigated other plant pigments, including the yellow pigment carotene and the blue pigment anthocyanin. His work on chlorophyll was justified in 1960 when Robert Woodward succeeded in synthesizing the compounds described by his formulas and came up with chlorophyll.

Willstätter was less successful with his enzyme theory. In the 1920s he claimed to have isolated active enzymes with no trace of protein. His views were widely accepted until protein was restored to its rightful place in enzyme activity by the work of John Northrop in 1930.

For his work on plant pigments Willstätter was awarded the Nobel Prize for chemistry in 1915.

Wilson, Allan Charles (1934–1991)
New Zealand biochemist

Born at Ngaruawakia in New Zealand, Wilson was educated at the University of Otago, Dunedin, and at Washington State University before completing his PhD in 1961 at the University of California, Berkeley. After working at the Weizmann Institute in Israel and at universities in Nairobi, Kenya, and Harvard, he returned to Berkeley serving as professor of biochemistry until his death from leukemia in 1991.

In 1967, in collaboration with Vincent Sarich, Wilson, following the work of Emile Zuckerandl, argued that molecular clocks could reveal much about the early history of the human race. Against the opposition of paleontologists they claimed that the divergence between man and the great apes began only 5 million years ago. Their view seems to have prevailed.

In the 1980s Wilson sought to challenge the paleontologists once more, this time on the issue of the emergence of modern humans. While anthropologists favored a date of 1 million years, Wilson's work suggested a time no later than 200,000 years ago.

He chose to work with mitochondria, the cellular organelles which convert food into energy. Like a cell nucleus, mitochondria also contain DNA. It encodes, however, only 37 genes as opposed to the 100,000 of nuclear DNA. Further, mitochondrial DNA evolved rapidly and regularly and, surprisingly, it is inherited from the mother alone. It follows, Wilson pointed out, that "all human mitochondrial DNA must have had an ultimate common female ancestor." Where and when, he went on to ask, could she be found?

Wilson adopted the parsimony principle that subjects are connected in the simplest possible way. That is, the fewer differences found in mitochondrial DNA, the closer they were connected. Mitochondria from 241 individuals from all continents and races were collected and analyzed. The tree constructed had two branches, both of which led back to Africa.

What was the date of this 'African Eve' as she was quickly dubbed by the press? Wilson measured the ratio of mitochondrial DNA divergence between humans to the divergence between humans and chimpanzees. The ratio was found to be 1:25 and, as human and chimpanzee lineages diverged 5 million years ago, human maternal lineages must have separated by 1/25 of this time, namely, 200,000 years ago. Wilson's hypothesis, first presented in 1987, has provoked considerable opposition.

Wilson, Charles Thomson Rees (1869–1959) *British physicist*

Charles Wilson was the son of a sheep farmer from Glencorse in Scotland, but his father died when he was four and Charles and his mother moved to Manchester. He was educated there and started to specialize in biology but moved to Cambridge University to study physics. There he started work with J. J. Thomson.

Wilson began experiments to duplicate cloud formation in the laboratory by letting saturated air expand, thus cooling it. He found that clouds seemed to need dust particles to start the formation of water droplets and that x-rays, which charged the dust, greatly speeded up the process. Inspired by this, he showed that charged subatomic particles traveling through supersaturated air also formed water droplets. This was the basis of the cloud chamber, which Wilson perfected in 1911 and for which he received the Nobel Prize for physics in 1927. The cloud chamber became an indispensable aid to research into subatomic particles and, with the addition of a magnetic field, made different particles distinguishable by the curvature of their tracks.

Wilson, Edmund Beecher (1856–1939) *American biologist*

Wilson, born the son of a judge in Geneva, Illinois, was educated at Yale and Johns Hopkins where, in 1881, he gained his PhD. After further training abroad at Cambridge, Leipzig, and Naples he returned to

America and taught for some years at the Massachusetts Institute of Technology and Bryn Mawr College. In 1891 Wilson moved to Columbia where he spent the rest of his career, serving as professor of zoology from 1894 until his retirement in 1928.

In his *Cell Development and Inheritance* (1896) Wilson stressed the importance of the cell theory, hoping that its application to the problems of development and heredity would lead to advances in these areas. He did important work on the concept of cell lineage, studied internal cellular organization, and investigated the part played by the chromosomes in the determination of sex. It was in Wilson's department that the science of genetics really became established through the work of T. H. Morgan and Hermann Muller.

Wilson, Edward Osborne (1929–)
American entomologist, ecologist, and sociobiologist

Wilson, who was born in Birmingham, Alabama, graduated in biology from the University of Alabama in 1949 and obtained his PhD from Harvard in 1955. He joined the Harvard faculty the following year, becoming professor in 1964 and curator of entomology at the Museum of Comparative Zoology in 1971.

Much of Wilson's entomological work was with ants and other social insects and was comprehensively surveyed in his massive *Insect Societies* (1971). He has also worked on speciation and with William Brown introduced the term 'character displacement' to describe the process that frequently takes place when closely related species that have previously been isolated begin to overlap in distribution. The differences that do exist between the species become exaggerated to avoid competition and hybridization.

Wilson collaborated with Robert MacArthur in developing a theory on the equilibrium of island populations from which emerged their *Theory of Island Biogeography* (1967). To test such ideas Wilson conducted a number of remarkable experiments with Daniel Simberloff in the Florida Keys. They selected six small mangrove clumps and made a survey of the number of insect species present. They then fumigated the islands to eliminate all the 75 insect species found. Careful monitoring over the succeeding months revealed that the islands had been recolonized by the same number of species, thus confirming the prediction that "a dynamic equilibrium number of species exists for any island."

It was, however, with his *Sociobiology* (1975) that Wilson emerged as a controversial and household name. He argued that "a single strong thread does indeed run from the conduct of termite colonies and turkey brotherhoods to the social behavior of man." Using the arguments of William Hamilton and Robert Trivers, Wilson had little difficulty in showing the deep biological and genetic control exercised over many apparently altruistic acts in insects, birds, and mammals. He also proposed plausible mechanisms to explain much of the social behavior and organization of many species. Many believe, however, that he is on very shaky ground when he extends such arguments to human social evolution. Wilson has continued to produce a large number of popular, personal, and technical works. Among these are a work on ecology, *The Diversity of Life* (1992); his Pulitzer prize-winning *The Ants* (1988, written in collaboration with B. Hölldobler); and his revealing autobiography, *Naturalist* (1994).

Wilson, John Tuzo (1908–1993)
Canadian geophysicist

Born in Ottawa, Canada, Wilson was educated at the University of Toronto and at Princeton, where he obtained his PhD in 1936. After working for the Canadian Geological Survey (1936–39) and war service, he was appointed professor of geophysics at the University of Toronto (1946) where he remained until his retirement in 1974.

Wilson did much to establish the new discipline of plate tectonics during the early 1960s and was the first to use the term 'plate' to refer to the rigid portions (oceanic, continental, or a combination of both) into which the Earth's crust is divided. In 1963 he produced some of the earliest evidence in favor of the sea-floor spreading hypothesis of Harry H. Hess when he pointed out that the further away an island lay from the mid-ocean ridge the older it proved to be.

His most significant work, however, was contained in his important paper of 1965, *A New Class of Faults and their Bearing on Continental Drift*, in which he introduced the idea of a transform fault. Plate movement had been identified as divergent, where plates are being separated by the production of new oceanic crust from the mid-ocean ridges, and convergent, where plates move toward each other with one plate sliding under the other. Wilson realized a third kind of movement was needed to explain the distribution of seismic activity and the way in which the ocean ridges do not run in continuous lines but in a series of offsets joined by the transform faults. Here the plates slide past each other without any creation or destruction of material.

Wilson replied to critics of the plate tectonics theory, such as Vladimir Belousov, in his *A Revolution in Earth Science* (1967).

Wilson, Kenneth G. (1936–)
American theoretical physicist

Wilson was educated at Harvard and Cal Tech where he gained his PhD in 1969. He taught at Cornell University from 1963, serving as professor of physics there from 1970 to 1988, when he moved to a similar post at Ohio State University, Columbus.

Wilson received the 1982 Nobel Prize for physics for theoretical work on critical phenomena in connection with phase transitions. He first applied his methods to the problem of ferromagnetic materials. Above a certain temperature, known as the Curie point, such materials become paramagnetic. This behavior results from the individual magnetic moments of the atoms. In the ferromagnetic state numbers of individual atoms 'couple' together so that their spins are aligned, and there is a resulting long-range interaction over a region of the solid. Above the critical point (the Curie point) this long-range order breaks down. Wilson's achievement was to develop a theory that could apply to the system near the critical point.

He did this using an idea first suggested by Leo Kadanoff. He took a block of atoms and calculated the effective spin of the block, then took a number of blocks and calculated the value for the larger block, and so on. The method involves a mathematical technique known as renormalization.

Using such methods Wilson could go from the properties of individual atoms to properties characteristic of many atoms acting together, and the resulting theory could be applied to properties other than magnetism. Thus it can be used for the critical state observed in the change between liquid and gas and to changes in alloy structure. Wilson is now applying his methods to the strong forces between nucleons.

Wilson, Robert Woodrow (1936–)
American astrophysicist

Wilson studied initially at Rice University in his native city of Houston, where he gained his BA in physics in 1957; he went on to obtain his PhD from the California Institute of Technology in 1962. He joined the Bell Laboratories, Holmdel, New Jersey, in 1963 and served as head of the radiophysics research department from 1976 to 1990.

It was at the Bell Laboratories that he and his coworker Arno PENZIAS found the first evidence in 1964 of the cosmic microwave background radiation, which is now widely interpreted as being the remnant radiation from the 'big bang' creation of the universe several billion years ago. The two men were jointly honored with the 1978 Nobel Prize for physics, which they shared with Pyotr L. KAPITZA for his (unrelated) discoveries in low-temperature physics.

Wilson is continuing his astrophysics work with Penzias, looking for interstellar molecules and determining the relative abundances of interstellar isotopes.

Windaus, Adolf Otto Reinhold
(1876–1959) *German chemist*

Windaus studied medicine at the university in his native city of Berlin and at Freiburg University, where he changed to chemistry under the influence of Emil Fischer. After holding chairs in Freiburg and Innsbruck he became, in 1915, professor of chemistry at Göttingen, where he remained until his retirement in 1944.

In 1901 Windaus began his study of the steroid cholesterol, a compound of considerable biological significance. Over the years he threw considerable light on its structure and in 1928 was awarded the Nobel Prize for chemistry for this work and for showing the connection between steroids and vitamins.

It was known that cod-liver oil prevents rickets because it contains vitamin D. It was also known that sunlight possesses antirachitic properties and, further, that mere exposure of certain foods to sunlight could make them active in preventing rickets. Clearly something in the food is converted photochemically into vitamin D but nobody knew what.

As vitamin D is fat soluble, the precursor of vitamin D (the provitamin) was not surprisingly found to be a steroid. In 1926 Windaus succeeded in showing that the provitamin is present as an impurity of cholesterol, ergosterol, which is converted into vitamin D by the action of sunlight.

Winkler, Clemens Alexander (1838–1904) *German chemist*

Winkler was born at Freiberg in Germany and studied at the School of Mines there. He was later appointed to the chair of chemical technology and analytical chemistry at Freiberg in 1871.

In 1885 a new ore – argyrodite – was discovered in the local mines. Winkler, who had a considerable reputation as an analyst, was asked to examine it and to his surprise the results of his analysis consistently came out too low. He discovered that this was due to the presence of a new element, which, after several months' search, he isolated and named germanium after his fatherland. The properties of germanium matched those of the eka-silicon whose existence had been predicted in 1871 by Dmitri Mendeleev. Winkler's discovery completed the detection of the three new elements predicted by Mendeleev nearly 20 years before.

Wislicenus, Johannes (1835–1902)
German chemist

Wislicenus was born in Klein-Eichstadt, Germany, the son of a Lutheran pastor who was forced to flee Europe in 1853 because of his political views. Wislicenus accompanied his father to America, where he attended Harvard until returning to Europe in 1856. He continued his education at Halle and at Zurich, where he was appointed professor of chemistry in 1870. In 1872 he moved to Würzburg, where he stayed until he succeeded Adolph Kolbe as professor of chemistry at the University of Leipzig (1885).

In 1872 Wislicenus showed that there were two forms of lactic acid having the formula $CH_3CH(OH)COOH$. One, derived from sour milk by Carl Scheele in 1870, was optically inactive; the other, discovered by Jöns Jacob Berzelius in 1808, was active. Wislicenus suggested that this was caused by different arrangements of the same atoms in space producing different properties in the compounds. Wislicenus's findings and similar work led Jacobus van't Hoff and Joseph Le Bel to establish the new discipline of stereochemistry a few years later. Wislicenus went on to study 'geometrical isomerism' – the existence of isomers because of different arrangements of groups or atoms about a double bond in the molecule.

Witten, Ed(ward) (1951–) American
mathematical physicist

Witten was born in Baltimore, Maryland. Having graduated from Brandeis College, Massachusetts, in 1971 with a degree in history, he intended to pursue a career in journalism. However, after working on George McGovern's 1972 presidential campaign, he realized that he was ill-suited to the world of political journalism and returned to university to study physics at Princeton. After completing his PhD in 1976 Witten remained at Princeton, where he was appointed professor of physics – a post he occupied until 1987 when he moved to the Institute for Advanced Study.

Witten has worked mainly in the development of string theory. In the 1960s Yoichipo Nambu and others had shown that elementary particles could be treated as strings of a certain kind, but it was soon shown that the theory only worked satisfactorily in 26 dimensions. A more ambitious theory of superstrings was promoted by Mike Green and others in the 1970s. When Witten came across the theory in 1975 he saw that it could throw light on what he termed "the single biggest puzzle in physics," namely, how to unify general relativity, which deals with gravity and space, with quantum mechanics, which explains events at the nuclear level. The realization in 1982 that superstring theory demanded the presence of gravity in its working was, for Witten, "the greatest intellectual thrill of my life." In the early 1980s Witten ruled out string theories in 11 dimensions derived from models based on the approach of Theodor Kaluza and Oskar Klein. Further, he argued that a number of mathematical anomalies would emerge in spaces with two, six, or ten dimensions. In 1984, however, Green and John Schwarz were able to show that, under certain special assumptions, a theory of ten dimensions could be developed that avoided the anomalies and explained the existence of particles with a built-in handedness (termed chirality).

Witten then began work showing how, in a ten-dimensional universe, the hidden extra six dimensions could be compacted and how they could interact with particles in detectable ways. He has sought for an analysis, based on geometric foundations, and has attempted to develop a topological quantum-field theory that gives due regard to the fundamental geometrical properties of matter. Witten's work is important in pure mathematics as well as in physics. In 1990 he was awarded the Fields Medal (regarded as the mathematics equivalent of a Nobel prize).

Some critics, including the Nobel laureate Sheldon Glashow, have objected that Witten's work has nothing to do with physics and is merely mathematical, while being impenetrable at the same time. Witten has replied that the theory has not been fully worked out yet and that it may well be many years before a precise description of nature can be offered. He has described string theory as "a 21st-century theory that has dropped by accident into the 20th century." Glashow replied:

"Please heed our advice that you too are not smitten;
The book's not finished, the last word is not Witten."

Wittig, Georg (1897–1987) *German organic chemist*

Born in Berlin, Germany, Wittig was educated at the university of Marburg. He worked at Braunschweig (1932–37), at Freiburg im Breisgau (1937–44), and at Tubingen (1944–65). In 1965 he became director of the Chemical Institute at Heidelberg, a post he held until his retirement in 1967.

Wittig worked extensively in organic chemistry, in particular on the chemistry of carbanions – negatively charged organic ions such as $C_6H_5^-$. In this work he discovered a class of reactive phosphorus compounds of the type $(C_6H_5)_3P{:}CH_2$. Such compounds (known as ylides) are able to replace the oxygen of a carbonyl group C=O by a CH_2 group, to give C=CH_2. This reaction, known as the *Wittig reaction*, is of immense importance in the synthesis of certain natural compounds, such as prostaglandin and vitamins A and D_2. Wittig also discovered a useful directed form of the aldol condensation. He was awarded the Nobel Prize for chemistry in 1979.

Wöhler, Friedrich (1800–1882) *German chemist*

Wöhler, who was born at Eschersheim near Frankfurt, acquired from his father, the master of horse of the crown prince of Hesse-Cassel, an interest in mineralogy – he actually met the aged poet Johann Wolfgang von Goethe, another devotee, in the shop of a Frankfurt mineral dealer. He began training as a physician at Marburg and Heidelberg but was persuaded by Leopold Gmelin to change to chemistry. After a year in Sweden with Jöns Jacob Berzelius he taught chemistry in Berlin and Cassel before his appointment to the chair of chemistry at Göttingen (1836), where he remained for the rest of his life.

Wöhler's most famous discovery occurred in 1828, when he synthesized crystals of urea while evaporating a solution of ammonium cyanate. He wrote excitedly to Berzelius, "I must tell you I can prepare urea without requiring a kidney of an animal, either man or dog." The significance of his achievement was that urea is an organic substance, which it was hitherto thought could be synthesized only by a living organism. If the constituents of a living body can be put together in the laboratory like common salt or sulfuric acid then there is apparently nothing left to distinguish the living from the nonliving. For this reason Wöhler's work is frequently cited as marking the death of vitalism, although at the time Wöhler was probably more concerned with the chemical reactions involved.

However, it was not seen by Wöhler's contemporaries as having that significance. Just because one substance had been synthesized, no one was prepared to claim that all organic substances could be so created. Justus von Liebig, who knew Wöhler's work well and collaborated with him over a long period of time, was a vitalist and vitalism was too complex and deep-seated an idea to disappear as a result of one experiment. Wöhler's work was more important in opening up whole new dimensions of biochemistry, stimulating work on the chemistry of digestion, respiration, growth, and reproduction.

Wöhler made other contributions to organic chemistry. In 1832, in collaboration with Liebig, he showed that the benzoyl radical (C_6H_5CO) could enter unchanged in a series of compounds: the hydride, chloride, cyanide, and oxide. Thus organic chemistry became, for a time, the chemistry of compound radicals. With the theories of Berzelius, this approach led to a great increase in the knowledge of organic compounds without a corresponding understanding of their chemistry.

In fact organic chemistry became so confusing that Wöhler returned to inorganic chemistry. In later years he tended to concentrate on the chemistry of metals, in particular the production of pure samples of some of the less common metals. He succeeded, at great expense, in obtaining pure aluminum (1827) and beryllium (1828).

With Liebig he was partly responsible for the discovery of isomerism. In 1823, while working in the laboratory of Berzelius, he prepared silver cyanate; at the same time Liebig produced silver fulminate, a compound with very different properties. To their surprise they found both compounds had identical formulas. Berzelius named the phenomenon 'isomerism'.

One final achievement of Wöhler was the creation of one of the first great teaching laboratories of Europe at Göttingen. From the 1830s nearly all creative chemists of the 19th century spent some time at Göttingen; students came not just from the Continent but also from America and Britain. The tradition persisted until the time of Hitler.

Wollaston, William Hyde (1766–1828) *British chemist and physicist*

Wollaston, the son of a clergyman from East Dereham in Norfolk, was educated at Cambridge University, England, where he graduated in 1788. He practiced as a physician before moving to London (1801) to devote himself to science, working in a variety of fields, including chemistry, physics, and astronomy, and making several important discoveries, both theoretical and practical.

Wollaston made himself financially independent by inventing, in 1804, a process to produce pure malleable platinum, which could be welded and made into vessels. He is reported to have made about £30,000 from his discovery, as he kept the process secret until shortly before his death, allowing no one to enter his laboratory. Working with platinum ore, he also isolated two new elements: palladium (1804), named for the recently discovered asteroid Pallas, and rhodium (1805), named for the rose color of its compounds. In 1810 he discovered the second amino acid, cystine, in a bladder stone.

In optics Wollaston developed the reflecting goniometer (1809), an instrument for the measurement of angles between the faces of a crystal. He also patented the camera lucida in 1807. In this device an adjustable prism reflects light from the object to be drawn and light from the paper into the draftsman's eye. This produces the illusion of the image on the paper, allowing him to trace it. Wollaston was a friend of Thomas Young and a supporter of the wave theory of light. One opportunity he missed occurred when, in 1802, he observed the dark lines in the solar spectrum but failed to grasp their importance, taking them simply to be the natural boundaries of colors. He missed a similar chance in 1820 when he failed to pursue the full implications of Hans Oersted's 1820 demonstration that an electric current could cause a deflection in a compass needle. Although he performed some experiments it was left to Michael Faraday in 1821 to discover and analyze electromagnetic rotation. Wollaston was successful in showing that frictional and galvanic electricity were identical in 1801. In 1814 he proposed the term 'chemical equivalents'.

Wolpert, Lewis (1929–) *British embryologist*

Wolpert, who was born at Johannesburg in South Africa, trained initially as an engineer at the University of Witwatersrand. After working as an engineer in Britain and Israel, Wolpert's interests turned to biology and he began to study for a PhD in embryology at King's College, London. He taught there from 1958 until 1966, when he was appointed professor of biology at the Middlesex Hospital Medical School. From 1987 he has worked at University College, London.

Wolpert has worked mainly on the problem of pattern formation in biological development. How is it, for example, that the same differentiated cells – muscle, cartilage, skin, connective tissue – arrange themselves as legs in one place and arms in another. Francis Crick proposed in 1970 that patterns could be produced through the action of a 'morphogen', a substance whose concentration throughout the field could be sensed by individual cells. Wolpert illustrated the mechanism with his flag analogy.

Imagine a line of cells capable of turning blue, red, or white. What simple mechanism could generate the pattern of the French tricolor? One way would be to have a chemical whose concentration, while fixed at one end of the line, decreased along the line. Cells could respond to a certain concentration of the morphogen and turn blue, red, or white accordingly.

Wolpert found that in such a system it should be possible to specify some 30 different cell states along a line of about 100 cells. The limiting factor was the accuracy with which cells can identify thresholds of concentration.

Wolpert identified a second positional system, one dependent upon time. Wing growth in chicks, for example, is mainly due to cell multiplication at the tip of the limb in a region known as the 'progress zone'. The cells learn their position by responding to the length of time they remain in the progress zone. Thus the cells which stay in the progress zone the shortest time form the humerus, and those that stay in the longest develop into digits.

Much recent work in developmental biology was described by Wolpert in his *The Triumph of the Embryo* (Oxford, 1991), material that was originally presented in his 1986 Royal Institution Christmas Lectures. Wolpert has also taken it upon himself to speak for science in such works as his *The Unnatural Nature of Science* (London, 1993), against what he sees as increasingly philistine attacks from journalists and politicians against the aims and methods of modern science.

Woodward, Robert Burns (1917–1979) *American chemist*

Born in Boston, Massachusetts, Woodward was educated at the Massachusetts Institute of Technology, obtaining his PhD in 1937. His whole career was spent at Harvard where, starting as a postdoctoral fellow in 1937, he became Morris Loeb Professor of Chemistry in 1953.

In 1944 Woodward, with William von Eggers Doering, synthesized quinine from the basic elements. This was an historic moment for it was the quinine molecule that William Perkin had first, prematurely, attempted to synthesize in 1855.

Woodward and his school later succeeded in synthesizing an impressive number of molecules, many of which are important far beyond the field of chemistry. Thus among the most important were cholesterol and cortisone in 1951, strychnine and LSD in 1954, reserpine in 1956, chlorophyll in 1960, a tetracycline antibiotic in 1962, and vitamin B_{12} in 1971. The work on the synthesis of B_{12} led Woodward and Roald Hoffman to introduce the principle of conservation of orbital symmetry. This major theoretical advance has provided a deep understanding of a wide group of chemical reactions.

He received the Nobel Prize for chemistry in 1965. Woodward's death in 1979 deprived him of a second Nobel award, namely, the chemistry prize awarded to his colleague Hoffmann in 1981 for their work on orbital theory.

Wright, Sewall (1889–1988) *American statistician and geneticist*

Born in Melrose, Massachusetts, Wright graduated from Lombard College in 1911; he gained his master's degree from the University of Illinois the following year and his doctorate from Harvard in 1916. He then worked as senior animal husbandman for the US Department of Agriculture and began his researches into the population genetics of guinea pigs. His first work aimed to find the best combination of inbreeding and crossbreeding to improve stock, this having practical application in livestock breeding. From this he also developed a mathematical theory of evolution.

His name is best known, however, in connection with the process of genetic drift, which is also termed the *Sewall Wright effect*. He demonstrated that in small isolated populations certain forms of genes may be lost quite randomly, simply because the few individuals possessing them happen not to pass them on. The loss of such characters may lead to the formation of new species without natural selection coming into operation. Wright held professorial positions at the University of Chicago and Edinburgh University and was emeritus professor at the University of Wisconsin.

Wright, Orville (1871–1948) *American aeronautical engineer. See* WRIGHT, WILBUR.

Wright, Wilbur (1867–1912) *American aeronautical engineer*

The sons of a bishop in the United Brethren Church, Wilbur Wright was born in Millville, Indiana, and his brother **Orville**

Wright was born in Dayton, Ohio. Neither brother received more than a high-school education. They had, however, shown a certain inventiveness and an interest in things mechanical. They were the kind of boys who having seen a woodcut in a magazine would immediately make their own woodcut. Thus on leaving school they first experimented with printing, publishing the weekly *West Side News* for over a year. By 1892 they had lost their interest in printing and decided instead to open a bike shop in which they not only sold and repaired bikes but made them themselves.

They later reported that their interest in flight had been stimulated by reading in 1896 of the death of the German engineer Lilienthal in a gliding accident. They first devoured the available literature describing the machines and flights of Lilienthal, Samuel Langley, and others. Above all they were struck by the lack of control mechanisms in the early machines. The early designers had merely sought to maintain equilibrium, but the Wrights saw that flying meant directing and upsetting equilibrium in a carefully controlled manner. A specific control mechanism was suggested to them by observing the flight of pigeons, and how they maintained their balance by twisting their wing tips. A comparable effect could be achieved in a plane by warping the wings' ends. But how could this be produced? The answer came to Wilbur when, while fiddling with a narrow rectangular box, he noted how easily the ends could be twisted in opposite directions.

The principle was incorporated in a biplane kite which they tested in 1900 on the sandhills at Kitty Hawk, North Carolina. A larger kite was tested in 1901 and in 1902 further data was collected from trials in a wind tunnel constructed by the brothers. One result of this work was the installation of a vertical tail on the 1902 glider. At this point they considered converting their kite-glider to a powered aircraft. Characteristically they designed and built their own 12 horsepower model and fitted two propellers with a diameter of 8.5 feet. Wilbur piloted the first flight on 14 December 1903 but induced a stall; during the second flight, on 17 December, Orville covered 120 feet at an average speed of 7 miles per hour. The plane, known as 'the Flyer', was damaged in a later flight that day and was never flown again; it was later placed as a permanent exhibit at the Smithsonian, Washington DC.

The brothers continued to work on their design and only when completely satisfied with a new version of the Flyer were they prepared to demonstrate powered flight to the public. Wilbur first flew publicly near

Le Mans in France in August 1908, and Orville a few days later at Fort Meyer, Virginia.

In 1909 they set up the Wright Company, with considerable financial backing, to build versions of the Flyer. They also received license fees from European manufacturers. Much of their time, however, must have been spent in patent disputes which dragged on in one form or another until 1928. Wilbur died from typhoid fever in 1912. Orville sold the business in 1915 for a sum said to be $1.5 million, while remaining as a consultant for $25,000 a year. Much of his later life was spent ensuring the contribution of the Wright brothers to the early history of aviation was properly recognized. He died of a heart attack in 1948.

Wrinch, Dorothy (1894–1976) *British–American mathematician and biochemist*

Wrinch was born at Rosario in Argentina and educated at Cambridge University, where she held a research fellowship from 1920 to 1924. She then taught physics at Oxford until 1939, when she moved to America to take up an appointment as lecturer in chemistry at Johns Hopkins University. In 1942 she moved to Smith College, remaining there until her retirement in 1959.

In 1934 Wrinch tackled the important problem of identifying the chemical carriers of genetic information. In common with other scientists at that time, she argued that chromosomes consisted of sequences of amino acids; these were the only molecules thought to possess sufficient variety to permit the construction of complex molecules. She proposed a model of the gene in the form of a T-like structure with a nucleic-acid stem and a sequence of amino acids as the cross bar.

In actual fact there were many such models in the 1930s. If it was not accepted that genes were made from specific sequences of amino acids then it became very difficult to see what they could come from. The trouble with all these models was that the experimentalists quickly found serious defects in them. Thus W. Schmidt in 1936 was able to show that Wrinch's model was incompatible with the known optical properties of nucleic acid and the chromosomes. The first suggestion that there might be an alternative to the protein structure of the gene came with the famous experiment of Oswald Avery in 1944.

Wu, Chien-Shiung (1912–   ) *Chinese–American physicist*

One of the world's leading experimental physicists, Wu, who was born in Shanghai, China, gained her BS from the National Central University of China before moving to America in 1936. Here she studied under Ernest O. Lawrence at the University of California, Berkeley. She gained her PhD in 1940, then went on to teach at Smith College, Northampton, Massachusetts, and later at Princeton University. In 1946 she became a staff member at Columbia University, advancing to become professor of physics in 1957.

Her first significant research work was on the mechanism of beta disintegration (in radioactive decay). In particular, she demonstrated in 1956 that the direction of emission of beta rays is strongly correlated with the direction of spin of the emitting nucleus, showing that parity is not conserved in beta disintegration. This experiment confirmed the theories advanced by Tsung Dao Lee of Columbia and Chen Ning Yang of Princeton that in the so-called 'weak' nuclear interactions the previously held 'law of symmetry' was violated. Yang and Lee later received the Nobel Prize for physics for their theory, and the discovery overturned many central ideas in physics.

In 1958 Richard Feynman and Murray Gell-Mann proposed the theory of conservation of vector current in beta decay. This theory was experimentally confirmed in 1963 by Wu, in collaboration with two other Columbia University physicists.

Wu's other contributions to elementary-particle physics include her demonstration that the electromagnetic radiation from the annihilation of positrons and electrons is polarized – a finding in accordance with Dirac's theory, proving that the electron and positron have opposite parity. She has also undertaken a study of the x-ray spectra of muonic atoms. More recently she has become interested in biological problems, especially the structure of hemoglobin.

Wurtz, Charles Adolphe (1817–1884) *French chemist*

Wurtz was educated at the university in his native city of Strasbourg. He worked under Justus von Liebig in Giessen and under Jean Dumas in Paris. In 1853 he was appointed professor of chemistry at the Ecole de Médicine until he moved to the chair of organic chemistry at the Sorbonne in 1874.

Wurtz contributed to the development of the type theory of Charles Gerhardt and Auguste Laurente by introducing the ammonia type in 1849. He synthesized ethylamine from ammonia and constructed his ammonia type by substituting the carbon radical C_2H_5 for one or more of the hydrogen atoms in ammonia (NH_3). He thus produced the series ammonia (NH_3); ethylamine ($C_2H_5NH_2$); diethylamine (($C_2H_5)_2NH$); triethylamine (($C_2H_5)_3N$). Other types were added by Gerhardt.

In 1855 Wurtz developed a method of synthesizing hydrocarbons by reacting alkyl halides with sodium (still known as the *Wurtz reaction*). With Rudolf Fittig he developed a similar reaction for synthesizing aromatic hydrocarbons. In 1860 Wurtz was involved, with August Kekulé, in initiating the first conference of the International Chemical Congress at Karlsruhe. He was also involved in the Couper tragedy. In 1858 Archibald Couper had apparently anticipated Kekulé in working out the structure of the carbon atom and asked Wurtz to present his paper to the Académie des Sciences. Wurtz delayed and Kekulé published. When Couper remonstrated with Wurtz he was expelled from Wurtz's laboratory. Couper had a breakdown on his return to Scotland and never did any serious chemistry again.

Wurtz was a prolific author, his *La Théorie atomique* (1879; Atomic Theory), being his best-known work.

Wyckoff, Ralph Walter Graystone
(1897–1994) *American crystallographer and electron microscopist*

Wyckoff was born in Geneva, New York, and graduated from Hobart College. He obtained his PhD from Cornell in 1919. Between 1919 and 1938 Wyckoff worked first in the Geophysical Laboratory, New York, and then at the Rockefeller Institute before transferring to the Lederle Laboratories in 1938. He then worked at the University of Michigan (1943–45) and the National Institute of Health (1945–59). He was appointed to the chair of physics and microbiology at the University of Arizona in 1959.

While at the Rockefeller Institute Wyckoff purified various viruses, including that causing equine encephalomyelitis, using an ultracentrifuge. The pure preparations of encephalomyelitis virus were used to develop a killed-virus vaccine which proved effective against the epidemic that was affecting horses in America. This success led to a program for producing typhus vaccine.

In 1944 Wyckoff entered into an unusual and profitable collaboration with the astronomer-turned-biophysicist Robley Williams. Wyckoff was using the electron microscope to photograph viruses but found, as did other virologists of the time, that the amount of information conveyed about the size and shape of the virus was strictly limited.

Wyckoff discussed with Williams the problem of determining the size of a speck of dust that had fallen onto a specimen and been photographed with it. To an astronomer the solution was obvious, for it is a standard procedure to measure the heights of lunar mountains from the length of the shadow cast by them and knowledge of the angle of the incident light source. The problem was to make viruses cast shadows. They placed the specimen in a vacuum together with a heated tungsten filament covered with gold. This vaporized and coated the side of the specimen nearest the filament, leaving a 'shadow' on the far side.

This technique of 'metal shadowing' opened a new phase in the study of viruses allowing better estimates to be made of their size and shape, as well as revealing details of their structure.

Wynne-Edwards, Vero Copner
(1906–) *British zoologist*

Wynne-Edwards, who was born in Leeds, graduated in natural science from Oxford University in 1927. After leaving Oxford in 1929 he taught zoology at Bristol University (1929–30) and at McGill University, Montreal (from 1930). He returned to Britain in 1946 and served as professor of natural history at Aberdeen University until his retirement in 1974.

In 1962 Wynne-Edwards published his *Animal Dispersion in Relation to Social Behaviour*, one of the most influential zoological works of the postwar years. Much of it became known to a wider public through the popular writings of Robert Ardrey. In it he put the strongest possible case for group selection, the view that animals sacrifice personal survival and fertility to control population growth, that is, for the good of the group as a whole. They behave, in fact, altruistically.

Thus for Wynne-Edwards all such animal behavior as territoriality, dominance hierarchies, and grouping in large flocks (epideictic behavior) were simply devices for the control of population size. Such views stimulated a strong reaction, forcing his opponents to develop alternative accounts of altruism and population control in as much depth as his own.

It was from this dispute that theorists such as William Hamilton and Robert Trivers began to develop the concepts that emerged as one of the strains of sociobiology developed by Edward O. Wilson.

Yalow, Rosalyn Sussman (1921–)
American physicist

Yalow was born in New York City and educated at Hunter College and at the University of Illinois, where she obtained her PhD in nuclear physics in 1945. Since 1947 she has worked at the Veterans Administration Hospital in the Bronx as a physicist and, since 1968, she has also held the post of research professor at the Mount Sinai School of Medicine.

In the 1950s, working with Solomon Berson, Yalow developed the technique of radioimmunoassay (RIA), which permits the detection of extremely small amounts of hormone. The technique involves taking a known amount of radioactively labeled hormone, together with a known amount of antibody against it, and mixing it with human serum containing an unknown amount of unlabeled hormone. The antibodies bind to both the radioactive and normal hormone in the proportions in which they are present in the mixture. It is then possible to calculate with great accuracy the amount of unlabeled hormone present in the original sample; using this technique, amounts as small as one picogram (10^{-12} g) can be detected.

This technique enabled Roger GUILLEMIN and Andrew SCHALLY to detect the hypothalamic hormones; Yalow, Guillemin, and Schally shared the Nobel Prize for physiology or medicine in 1977.

Yang, Chen Ning (1922–) *Chinese–American physicist*

Yang, who was born the son of a mathematics professor at Hefei in China, graduated from the National Southwest Associated University in Kunming and received an MSc from Tsinghua. A fellowship enabled him to travel to America, where he studied for his PhD at the University of Chicago, under Enrico Fermi. After teaching at Chicago he joined the Institute for Advanced Study, Princeton, becoming professor of physics in 1955. In 1965 he was appointed Einstein Professor of Physics and director of the Institute of Theoretical Physics at the State University of New York, Stony Brook.

Yang collaborated with Tsung Dao LEE, and in 1956 they made a fundamental theoretical breakthrough in predicting that the law of conservation of parity would break down in the so-called weak interactions. Their startling prediction was quickly confirmed experimentally, by Chien-Shiung Wu, and in 1957 Yang and Lee were awarded the Nobel Prize for physics.

Yang has also made other advances in theoretical physics. In collaboration with R. L. Mills he proposed a non-Abelian gauge theory – also known as the *Yang–Mills theory* – a mathematical principle describing fundamental interactions for elementary particles and fields. Yang has also made contributions to statistical mechanics.

Young, Thomas (1773–1829) *British physicist, physician, and Egyptologist*

Young, who was born at Milverton in southwest England, was a child prodigy. He could read with considerable fluency at the age of 2 and by 13 he had a good knowledge of Latin, Greek, French, and Italian. He had also begun to study natural history and natural philosophy and could make various optical instruments. A year later he began an independent study of the Hebrew, Chaldean, Syriac, Samaritan, Arabic, Persian, Turkish, and Ethiopic languages. When he was 19 he was a highly proficient Latin and Greek scholar, having mastered many literary and scientific works including Newton's *Principia* and *Opticks* and Antoine Lavoisier's *Traité élémentaire de chimie* (Elementary Treatise on Chemistry).

In 1793 Young began a medical education, studying first at St. Bartholomew's Hospital, London, and then at the universities of Edinburgh (1794), Göttingen (1795), and Cambridge (1797). In 1800, after receiving a considerable inheritance, he set up a medical practice in London; this practice, however, never really flourished. In 1801 he was appointed professor of natural philosophy at the Royal Institution. Although his lectures were erudite, and remarkable for their scope and originality, they were not successful. In 1803 Young resigned his post. From then until his death he held various medical appointments and several offices related to science.

Young's early scientific researches were concerned with the physiology of the eye. He was elected a fellow of the Royal Society in 1794 for his explanation of how the ciliary muscles change the shape of the lens to focus on objects at differing distances (accommodation); in 1801 he gave the first descriptions of the defect astigmatism and of color sensation.

Young's most lasting contribution to science was his work in helping to establish the wave theory of light. Between 1800 and 1804 he revived an interest in this theory and gave it strong support. He compared the ideas of Newton and Christiaan Huygens on the nature of light, criticizing the corpuscular theory for its inadequacy in explaining such phenomena as simultaneous reflection and refraction. He introduced the idea of interference of light, which he explained by the superposition of waves – a principle that he applied to a range of optical phenomena including Newton's rings, diffraction patterns, and the color of the supernumerary bows of the rainbow. In his best-known demonstration of interference he passed light first through a single pinhole, then through two further pinholes close together; the light then fell upon a screen and gave a series of light and dark bands. The apparatus is known as *Young's slits*. Young's views were very badly received in England, where opposition to Newton's corpuscular theory was unthinkable.

From about 1804 Young devoted himself more to medical practice and the study of philology, especially the decipherment of hieroglyphic writing. He made very important contributions to the latter field and, independently of Jean François Champollion, helped in translating the text of the Rosetta Stone. His interest in optics was revived in about 1816 by the work of François Arago and Augustin Fresnel. In a letter to Arago he suggested that light might be propagated as a transverse wave (in which the vibrations of the medium are perpendicular to the direction of propagation). This allowed polarization to be explained on the wave theory and gave a satisfactory explanation of the known optical phenomena. The decisive test on the nature of light came later when its speed in the air and water could be accurately measured. Young's other scientific contributions included researches into sound, capillarity, and the cohesion of fluids. Because he gave a physical meaning to the constant of proportionality (E) in Hooke's law, E is called *Young's modulus*.

Yukawa, Hideki (1907–1981) *Japanese physicist*

Yukawa was born Hideki Ogawa at Kyoto in Japan, the son of the professor of geography at the university there; he assumed the name of his wife, Sumi Yukawa, on their marriage in 1932. He was educated at the university of Kyoto and at Osaka, where he joined the faculty in 1933 and where he completed his doctorate in 1938. In the following year Yukawa was appointed professor of physics at Kyoto University, a position he continued to hold until his retirement in 1970.

Yukawa was concerned with the force that binds the neutrons and protons together in the nucleus. At first sight, any nucleus containing more than one proton should be unstable since positively charged particles repel each other; squeezing a number of positively charged protons into the nucleus of an atom should generate powerful repulsive forces. The obvious answer is that there must be another, attractive, force that operates only at short range and holds the nucleons together. Such a force became known to physicists as the 'strong interaction'.

Yukawa sought to find the mechanism of the strong force and used the electromagnetic force as an analogy. Here the interaction between charged particles is seen as the result of the continuous exchange of a quantum or unit of energy carried by a 'virtual particle' – in this case the photon. So, just as electrons and protons interact by exchanging photons, the nucleons interact by exchanging the appropriate particle. Yukawa could predict its mass from quantum theory as the range over which a particle operates is inversely proportional to its mass. The massless photon is thus thought to operate over an infinite distance; as the strong force operates over a distance of less than 10^{-12} cm it must be mediated by a particle, Yukawa predicted, with a mass of about 200 times that of the electron.

Yukawa made his prediction in 1935 and when two years later Carl Anderson found signs of such a particle in cosmic-ray tracks physicists took this as supporting Yukawa's hypothesis and named the particle a mu-meson (now called a muon). However, although the muon had the appropriate mass it interacted with nucleons so infrequently that it could not possibly be the nuclear 'glue'. Yukawa's theory was saved, however, by the discovery in 1947 by Cecil Powell, once more in cosmic-ray tracks, of a particle with a mass of 264 times that of the electron and of which the muons were the decay product. The pi-meson, or pion as it became known, interacted very strongly with nucleons and thus filled precisely Yukawa's predicted role.

For this work Yukawa was awarded the Nobel Prize for physics in 1949, the first Japanese person to be so honored.

Z

Zeeman, Pieter (1865–1943) *Dutch physicist*

Born at Zonnemair in the Netherlands, Zeeman studied at Leiden University and received a doctorate in 1893. This was for his work on the Kerr effect, which concerns the effect of a magnetic field on light. In 1896 he discovered another magnetooptical effect, which now bears his name – he observed that the spectral lines of certain elements are split into three lines when the sample is in a strong magnetic field perpendicular to the light path; if the field is parallel to the light path the lines split into two. This work was done before the development of quantum mechanics, and the effect was explained at the time using classical theory by Hendrik Antoon LORENTZ, who assumed that the light was emitted by oscillating electrons.

This effect (splitting into three or two lines) is called the *normal Zeeman effect* and it can be explained using Niels Bohr's theory of the atom. In general, most substances show an *anomalous Zeeman effect*, in which the splitting is into several closely spaced lines – a phenomenon that can be explained using quantum mechanics and the concept of electron spin.

Zeeman was a meticulous experimenter and he applied his precision in measurement to the determination of the speed of light in dense media, confirming Lorentz's prediction that this was related to wavelength. Also, in 1918, he established the equality of gravitational and inertial mass thus reconfirming Einstein's equivalence principle, which lies at the core of general relativity theory.

Zeeman and Lorentz shared the 1902 Nobel Prize for physics for their work on magnetooptical effects.

Zeno of Elea (c. 490 BC–c. 430 BC) *Greek philosopher*

Zeno was born at Elea (now Velia in Italy) and in about 450 BC accompanied his teacher, Parmenides, to Athens. There he propounded the theories of the Eleatic school and became famous for his series of paradoxes and his invention of dialectic.

Little survives of Zeno's written work and this only in other authors' writings. He proposed that motion and multiplicity are unreal (thus supporting Parmenides's theo-

ries) since assumption of their existence gave rise to contradictory propositions. One of the most famous arguments against plurality and motion is that of Achilles and the tortoise: if the tortoise is given a start in a race against Achilles, when Achilles reaches the tortoise's starting position, the tortoise will have advanced a small way to a new position. Endless repetition of this argument means that Achilles can never overtake the tortoise.

Zeno's paradoxes remained unresolved for about 20 centuries, in fact until the advances in rigor of mathematical analysis (to the development of which these paradoxes may be said to have contributed). These advances included the study of convergent series (infinite series with a finite sum), the invention by Gottfried Leibniz and Isaac Newton of calculus, and Georg Cantor's theory of the infinite in the 19th century.

Following his return to Elea Zeno died while joining a coup against the tyrant Nearchus.

Zernike, Frits (1888–1966) *Dutch physicist*

Zernike, who was the son of mathematics teachers at Amsterdam in the Netherlands, studied at the university there, obtaining a doctorate in 1915. In 1913 he became assistant to the astronomer Jacobus Kapteyn at the University of Groningen, where he remained until his retirement in 1958, becoming professor of theoretical physics in 1920 and later of mathematical physics and theoretical mechanics.

Zernike's interest centered around optics and, more particularly, diffraction and in 1935 he developed the phase-contrast microscope. This uses the fact that light passing through bodies with a different refractive index from the surrounding medium has a different phase. The microscope contains a plate in the focal plane, which causes interference patterns and thus increases the contrast. For instance, it can make living cells observable without killing them by staining and fixing. The method of phase contrast also allows the detail in transparent objects or on metal surfaces to be observed.

Ziegler, Karl (1898–1973) *German chemist*

Ziegler was born at Helsa in Germany, the son of a minister. He received his doctorate from the University of Marburg in 1923 and then taught at Frankfurt, Heidelberg, and Halle before becoming director of the Max Planck Institute for Coal Research in 1943. In 1963 he was awarded the Nobel Prize for chemistry with Giulio NATTA for their discovery of Ziegler–Natta catalysts.

One of the earliest plastics, polyethylene, was simply made by polymerization of the ethylene molecule into long chains containing over a thousand ethylene units. In practice, however, the integrity of the chain tended to be ruined by the development of branches weakening the plastic and endowing it with a melting point only slightly above the boiling point of water.

In 1953 Ziegler introduced a family of catalysts that prevented such branching and produced a much stronger plastic, one which could be soaked in hot water without softening. The catalysts are mixtures of organometallic compounds containing such metallic ions as titanium and aluminum. The new process had the additional advantage that it requires much lower temperatures and pressures than the old method.

Zinkernagel, Rolf (1944–) Swiss immunologist

Zinkernagel qualified as an MD at the University of Basle in 1970. He moved to the Australian National University, Canberra, where he gained his PhD in 1975. Zinkernagel returned to Switzerland in 1979 to work at the University of Zurich. In 1992 he was appointed head of the Department of Experimental Immunology.

While in Canberra, when still a graduate student, Zinkernagel worked with Peter DOHERTY on the role of T lymphocytes and major histocompatibility complexes in fighting infection. For their work in this field they shared the 1997 Nobel Prize for physiology or medicine.

Zinn, Walter Henry (1906–) Canadian–American physicist

Born at Kitchener in Ontario, Canada, Zinn moved to America in 1930 and received a PhD from Columbia University four years later. He continued research there in collaboration with Leo Szilard, investigating atomic fission. In 1938 he became a naturalized American citizen.

A year later, Zinn and Szilard demonstrated that uranium underwent fission when bombarded with neutrons and that part of the mass was converted into energy according to Einstein's famous formula, $E = mc^2$. This work led him, during World War II, into research into the construction of the atomic bomb. After the war Zinn started the design of an atomic reactor and, in 1951, he built the first breeder reactor. In a breeder reactor, the core is surrounded by a 'blanket' of uranium–238 and neutrons from the core convert this into plutonium–239, which can also be used as a fission fuel.

Zozimus of Panopolis (born c. 250) Greek–Egyptian alchemist

Little seems to be known about the life of Zozimus except that he was born at Panopolis (now Alchmon in Egypt). He is best known for his writings – a 28-volume encyclopedia of chemical arts. Zozimus showed how alchemy had progressed since the time of Bolos of Mende, a hellenized Egyptian who lived in the Nile Delta. Sulfur, mercury, and arsenic were essential ingredients in this alchemy, mercury being alluded to variously as 'divine dew' or 'Scythian water'. The main aim was the preparation of gold from base metals and its success depended on the production of a series of colors, usually from black to red, yellow, white, black, green, and finally purple. Although the search for the philosopher's stone had not yet begun Zozimus refers to 'the tincture', a substance the alchemists believed to exist, that could instantly transform base metals to gold.

Zsigmondy, Richard Adolf (1865– 1929) Austrian chemist

The son of a Viennese doctor, Zsigmondy was educated at the universities of Vienna and Munich, where he acquired his PhD in 1890. After periods at the University of Graz and in a glass factory in Jena, in 1908 he became professor of inorganic chemistry at the University of Göttingen, where he remained until his death.

Zsigmondy's first interest was in the chemistry of glazes applied to glass and ceramics. Studies on colored glasses led him into the field of colloids, first distinguished and named by Thomas Graham. Little advance had been made since Graham's time as it was not clear how to study them; the conventional microscope was not powerful enough to detect the particles. In 1903 Zsigmondy remedied this when, in collaboration with Henry Siedentopf, he invented the ultramicroscope in which the particles were illuminated with a cone of light at right angles to the microscope. Although still too small to be seen the particles would diffract light shone on them and therefore appeared as disks of light against a dark background. The particles could be counted, measured, and have their velocity and path determined. Zsigmondy published his work in this field in his book *Kolloidchemie* (1912; Colloidal Chemistry). In 1925 he was awarded the Nobel Prize for chemistry for his work on colloids.

Zwicky, Fritz (1898–1974) *Swiss–American astronomer and physicist*

Zwicky, who was born at Varna in Bulgaria, studied at the Federal Institute of Technology, Zurich, where he obtained his BS in 1920 and his PhD in 1922. He moved to America in 1925, working at the California Institute of Technology and the Mount Wilson and Palomar Observatories until his retirement in 1968. He was associate professor of theoretical physics from 1929 to 1942 and professor of astrophysics from 1942 to 1968.

Zwicky worked in various fields of physics, including jet propulsion and the physics of crystals, liquids, and gases. He is, however, better known for his astronomical research. In 1936 he began an important search for supernovas. These are celestial bodies whose brightness suddenly increases by an immense amount as a result of a catastrophic explosion. They had been observed over several centuries in our Galaxy and one had been detected in the Andromeda galaxy as long ago as 1885. But when Edwin Hubble showed in 1923 that the Andromeda galaxy was about 900,000 light-years away, the question arose as to how anything could appear so bright over such a vast distance.

Zwicky worked out their frequency as about three per millennium per galaxy. Although many have passed unobserved in our Galaxy, five supernovas have been reported since AD 1000, including one in 1054 that produced the Crab nebula, Tycho's star in 1572, and Kepler's star in 1604. Zwicky also showed that supernovas characteristically have an absolute magnitude of -13 to -15, which makes them up to 100 million times brighter than the Sun.

In 1932 Lev Landau introduced the concept of a neutron star into astronomy and in 1934 Zwicky and Walter Baade suggested that these compact superdense objects might be produced in the cores of supernovas. This was later developed by Robert Oppenheimer, G. M. Volkoff, and others in 1939 into an important theory of stellar evolution.

In more recent years Zwicky and his colleagues carefully studied both galaxies and clusters of galaxies. One result of this work is the so-called *Zwicky catalog*, which gives the positions and magnitudes of over 30,000 galaxies and almost 10,000 clusters lying mainly in the northern-hemisphere sky.

Zworykin, Vladimir Kosma (1889–1982) *Russian–American physicist*

Born at Mouron in Russia, Zworykin studied electrical engineering at Petrograd (now St. Petersburg), graduating in 1912. During World War I he served as a radio officer in the Russian army. He moved to America in 1919 and joined the Westinghouse Electric Corporation in 1920. He did graduate research at Pittsburgh University, receiving a PhD in 1926. In 1929 he joined the Radio Corporation of America. Zworykin made a number of contributions to electron optics and was the inventor of the first electronic-scanning television camera – the iconoscope.

The first such device was constructed at Westinghouse in 1923. The principle was to focus an image on a screen made up of many small photoelectric cells, each insulated, which developed a charge that depended on the intensity of the light at that point. An electron beam directed onto the screen was scanned in parallel lines over the screen, discharging the photoelectric cells and producing an electrical signal.

Zworykin also used the cathode-ray tube invented in 1897 by Karl Ferdinand Braun to produce the image in a receiver. The tube (which he called a 'kinescope') had an electron beam focused by magnetic and electric fields to form a spot on a fluorescent screen. The beam was deflected by the fields in parallel lines across the screen, and the intensity of the beam varied according to the intensity of the signal. In this way it was possible to reconstruct the electrical signals into an image. In 1923 an early version of the system was made and Zworykin managed to transmit a simple picture (a cross). By 1929 he was able to demonstrate a better version suitable for practical use.

Zworykin also developed other electron devices, including an electron-image tube and electron multipliers. In 1940 he invited James Hillier to join his research group at RCA, and it was here that Hillier constructed his electron microscope.

NOBEL PRIZES

Physics

1901	W. Röntgen (Ger)	1944	I. Rabi (USA)		A. Bohr (Den)
1902	H. Antoon Lorentz	1945	W. Pauli (Austria)		B. Mottelson (Den)
	(Neth)	1946	P. Bridgman (USA)	1976	B. Richter (USA)
	P. Zeeman (Neth)	1947	Sir E. Appleton (UK)		S. Ting (USA)
1903	A. Becquerel (Fr)	1948	P. Blackett (UK)	1977	P. W. Anderson (USA)
	P. Curie (Fr)	1949	H. Yukawa (Jap)		Sir N. F. Mott (UK)
	M. Curie (Fr)	1950	C. Powell (UK)		J. H. van Vleck (USA)
1904	Lord Rayleigh (UK)	1951	Sir J. Cockcroft (UK)	1978	P. L. Kapitsa (USSR)
1905	P. Lenard (Ger)		E. Walton (Ire)		A. A. Penzias (USA)
1906	Sir J. J. Thomson (UK)	1952	F. Bloch (USA)		R. W. Wilson (USA)
1907	A. A. Michelson (USA)		E. Purcell (USA)	1979	S. L. Glashow (USA)
1908	G. Lippmann (Fr)	1953	F. Zernike (Neth)		A. Salam (Pak)
1909	G. Marconi (It)	1954	M. Born (UK)		S. Weinberg (USA)
	K. Braun (Ger)		W. Bothe (Ger)	1980	J. Cronin (USA)
1910	J. Van Der Waals (Neth)	1955	W. Lamb, Jr. (USA)		V. Fitch (USA)
1911	W. Wien (Ger)		P. Kusch (USA)	1981	K. Siegbahn (Swed)
1912	N. G. Dalen (Swed)	1956	W. Shockley (USA)		N. Bloembergen (USA)
1913	H. Kamerlingh Onnes		J. Bardeen (USA)		A. Schawlow (USA)
	(Neth)		W. Brattain (USA)	1982	K. G. Wilson (USA)
1914	M. Von Laue (Ger)	1957	Tsung-Dao Lee (China)	1983	S. Chandrasekhar (USA)
1915	Sir W. Bragg (UK)		C. N. Yang (China)		W. Fowler (USA)
	Sir L. Bragg (UK)	1958	P. A. Cherenkov (USSR)	1984	C. Rubbia (It)
1916	no award		I. M. Frank (USSR)		S. van der Meer (Neth)
1917	C. Barkla (UK)		I. Y. Tamm (USSR)	1985	K. von Klitzing (Ger)
1918	M. Planck (Ger)	1959	E. Segrè (USA)	1986	E. Ruska (Ger)
1919	J. Stark (Ger)		O. Chamberlain (USA)		G. Binnig (Ger)
1920	C. Guillaume (Swtz)	1960	D. Glaser (USA)		H. Rohrer (Switz)
1921	A. Einstein (Switz)	1961	R. Hofstadter (USA)	1987	A. Müller (Switz)
1922	N. Bohr (Den)		R. Mössbauer (Ger)		G. Bednorz (Ger)
1923	R. Millikan (USA)	1962	L. D. Landau (USSR)	1988	L. M. Lederman (USA)
1924	K. Siegbahn (Swed)	1963	J. H. D. Jensen (Ger)		M. Schwartz (USA)
1925	J. Franck (Ger)		M. G. Mayer (USA)		J. Steinberger (Ger)
	G. Hertz (Ger)		E. P. Wigner (USA)	1989	H. Dehmelt (USA)
1926	J. Perrin (Fr)	1964	C. H. Townes (USA)		W. Paul (Ger)
1927	A. H. Compton (USA)		N. G. Basov (USSR)		N. Ramsey (USA)
	C. Wilson (UK)		A. M. Prokhorov (USSR)	1990	J. Friedman (USA)
1928	Sir O. Richardson (UK)	1965	J. S. Schwinger (USA)		H. Kendall (USA)
1929	Prince L. de Broglie (Fr)		R. P. Feynman (USA)		R. Taylor (Can)
1930	Sir C. Raman (India)		S. Tomonaga (Jap)	1991	P. De Gennes (Fr)
1931	no award	1966	A. Kastler (Fr)	1992	G. Charpak
1932	W. Heisenberg (Ger)	1967	H. A. Bethe (USA)	1993	R. Hulse (USA)
1933	P. A. M. Dirac (UK)	1968	L. W. Alvarez (USA)		J. Taylor (USA)
	E. Schrödinger (Austria)	1969	M. Gell-Mann (USA)	1994	B. Brockhouse (Can)
1934	no award	1970	H. Alfvén (Swed)		C. Shull (USA)
1935	Sir J. Chadwick (UK)		L. Néel (Fr)	1995	M. Perl (USA)
1936	V. Hess (Austria)	1971	D. Gabor (UK)		F. Reines (USA)
	C. Anderson (USA)	1972	J. Bardeen (USA)	1996	D. M. Lee (USA)
1937	C. Davisson (USA)		L. N. Cooper (USA)		D. D. Osheroff (USA)
	Sir G. P. Thomson (UK)		J. R. Schrieffer (USA)		R. C. Richardson (USA)
1938	E. Fermi (It)	1973	L. Esaki (Jap)	1997	S. Chu (USA)
1939	E. Lawrence (USA)		I. Giaever (USA)	1998	R. B. Laughlin (USA)
1940	no award		B. Josephson (UK)		H. L. Störmer (USA)
1941	no award	1974	Sir M. Ryle (UK)		D. C. Tsui
1942	no award		A. Hewish (UK)		
1943	O. Stern (USA)	1975	J. Rainwater (USA)		

Chemistry

1901	J. V. Hoff (Neth)	1941	no award	1974	P. J. Flory (USA)
1902	E. Fischer (Ger)	1942	no award	1975	J. W. Cornforth
1903	S. Arrhenius (Swed)	1943	G. de Hevesy (Hung)		(Austral)
1904	Sir W. Ramsay (UK)	1944	O. Hahn (Ger)		V. Prelog (Switz)
1905	A. von Baeyer (Ger)	1945	A. Virtanen (Fin)	1976	W. M. Lipscomb (USA)
1906	H. Moissan (Fr)	1946	J. Sumner (USA)	1977	I. Prigogine (Belg)
1907	E. Buchner (Ger)		J. Northrop (USA)	1978	P. Mitchell (UK)
1908	Lord Rutherford (UK)		W. Stanley (USA)	1979	H. C. Brown (USA)
1909	W. Ostwald (Ger)	1947	Sir R. Robinson (UK)		G. Wittig (Ger)
1910	O. Wallach (Ger)	1948	A. Tiselius (Swed)	1980	P. Berg (USA)
1911	M. Curie (Fr)	1949	W. Giauque (USA)		W. Gilbert (USA)
1912	V. Grignard (Fr)	1950	O. Diels (Ger)		F. Sanger (UK)
	P. Sabatier (Fr)		K. Alder (Ger)	1981	K. Fukui (Jap)
1913	A. Werner (Switz)	1951	E. McMillan (USA)		R. Hoffmann (Pol)
1914	T. Richards (USA)		G. Seaborg (USA)	1982	A. Klug (UK)
1915	R. Willstätter (Ger)	1952	A. Martin (UK)	1983	H. Taube (USA)
1916	no award		R. Synge (UK)	1984	R. B. Merrifield (USA)
1917	no award	1953	H. Staudinger (Ger)	1985	H. Hauptman (USA)
1918	F. Haber (Ger)	1954	L. C. Pauling (USA)		J. Karle (USA)
1919	no award	1955	V. du Vigneaud (USA)	1986	D. Herschbach (USA)
1920	W. Nernst (Ger)	1956	N. Semeyonov (USSR)		Y. Tseh Lee (USA)
1921	F. Soddy (UK)		Sir C. Hinshelwood (UK)		J. Polanyi (Can)
1922	F. Aston (UK)	1957	Sir A. Todd (UK)	1987	D. Cram (USA)
1923	F. Pregl (Austria)	1958	F. Sanger (UK)		J. Lehn (Fr)
1924	no award	1959	J. Heyrovsky (Czech)		C. Pedersen (USA)
1925	R. Zsigmondy (Austria)	1960	W. Libby (USA)	1988	J. Diesenhofer (Ger)
1926	T. Svedberg (Swed)	1961	M. Calvin (USA)		R. Huber (Ger)
1927	H. Wieland (Ger)	1962	J. C. Kendrew (UK)		H. Michel (Ger)
1928	A. Windaus (Ger)		M. F. Perutz (UK)	1989	S. Altman (USA)
1929	Sir A. Harden (UK)	1963	G. Natta (It)		T. Cech (USA)
	H. von Euler-Chelpin		K. Ziegler (Ger)	1990	E. Corey (USA)
	(Swed)	1964	D. M. C. Hodgkin (UK)	1991	R. Ernst (Switz)
1930	H. Fischer (Ger)	1965	R. B. Woodward (USA)	1992	R. Marcus (Can)
1931	K. Bosch (Ger)	1966	R. S. Mulliken (USA)	1993	K. Mullis (USA)
	F. Bergius (Ger)	1967	M. Eigen (Ger)		M. Smith (USA)
1932	I. Langmuir (USA)		R. G. W. Norrish (UK)	1994	G. Olah (USA)
1933	no award		G. Porter (UK)	1995	P. Crutzen (Neth)
1934	H. Urey (USA)	1968	L. Onsager (USA)		M. Molina (Mex)
1935	F. Joliot-Curie (Fr)	1969	D. H. R. Barton (UK)		F. Rowland (USA)
	I. Joliot-Curie (Fr)		O. Hassel (Nor)	1996	H. Kroto (UK)
1936	P. Debye (Neth)	1970	L. F. Leloir (Arg)		R. Curl (USA)
1937	Sir W. Haworth (UK)	1971	G. Herzberg (Can)		R. Smalley (USA)
	P. Karrer (Switz)	1972	C. B. Anfinsen (USA)	1997	P. D. Boyer (USA)
1938	R. Kuhn (Ger)		S. Moore (USA)		J. E. Walker (UK)
1939	A. Butenandt (Ger)		W. H. Stein (USA)		J. C. Skou (Den)
	L. Ruzicka (Switz)	1973	E. Fischer (Ger)	1998	W. Kohn (USA)
1940	no award		G. Wilkinson (UK)		J. A. Pople (USA)

Physiology or Medicine

1901	E. von Behring (Ger)	1909	E. Kocher (Switz)	1919	J. Bordet (Belg)
1902	Sir R. Ross (UK)	1910	A. Kossel (Ger)	1920	A. Krogh (Den)
1903	N. R. Finsen (Den)	1911	A. Gullstrand (Swed)	1921	no award
1904	I. Pavlov (Russia)	1912	A. Carrel (Fr)	1922	A. V. Hill (UK)
1905	R. Koch (Ger)	1913	C. Richet (Fr)		O. Meyerhof (Ger)
1906	C. Golgi (It)	1914	R. Bárány (Austria)	1923	Sir F. G. Banting (Can)
	S. Ramón y Cajal (Sp)	1915	no award		J. J. R. MacLeod (UK)
1907	A. Laveran (Fr)	1916	no award	1924	W. Einthoven (Neth)
1908	P. Ehrlich (Ger)	1917	no award	1925	no award
	I. Metchnikov (Russia)	1918	no award	1926	J. Fibiger (Den)

Physiology or Medicine (continued)

1927	J. Wagner-Jauregg (Austria)	1958	G. W. Beadle (USA)		A. V. Schally (USA)
1928	C. Nicolle (Fr)		E. L. Tatum (USA)	1978	W. Arber (Switz)
1929	C. Eijkman (Neth)		J. Lederberg (USA)		D. Nathans (USA)
	Sir F. Hopkins (UK)	1959	S. Ochoa (USA)		H. Smith (USA)
1930	K. Landsteiner (USA)		A. Kornberg (USA)	1979	A. M. Cormack (USA)
1931	O. Warburg (Ger)	1960	Sir F. MacFarlane		G. N. Hounsfield (UK)
1932	E. D. Adrian (UK)		Burnet (Austral)	1980	G. Snell (USA)
	Sir C. Sherrington (UK)		P. B. Medawar (UK)		J. Dausset (Fr)
1933	T. H. Morgan (USA)	1961	G. von Békésy (USA)		B. Benacerraf (USA)
1934	G. R. Minot (USA)	1962	F. H. C. Crick (UK)	1981	R. Sperry (USA)
	W. P. Murphy (USA)		J. D. Watson (USA)		D. Hubel (USA)
	G. H. Whipple (USA)		M. Wilkins (UK)		T. Wiesel (Swed)
1935	H. Spemann (Ger)	1963	Sir J. C. Eccles (Austral)	1982	S. K. Bergstrom (Swed)
1936	Sir H. H. Dale (UK)		A. L. Hodgkin (UK)		B. I. Samuelson (Swed)
	O. Loewi (Ger)		A. F. Huxley (UK)		J. R. Vane (UK)
1937	A. Szent-Györgyi (Hung)	1964	K. Bloch (USA)	1983	B. McClintock (USA)
1938	C. Heymans (Belg)		F. Lynen (Ger)	1984	N. K. Jerne (Den)
1939	G. Domagk (Ger)	1965	F. Jacob (Fr)		G. J. F. Köhler (Ger)
1940	no award		A. Lwoff (Fr)		C. Milstein (UK)
1941	no award		J. Monod (Fr)	1985	J. Goldstein (USA)
1942	no award	1966	C. B. Huggins (USA)		M. Brown (USA)
1943	H. Dam (Den)		F. P. Rous (USA)	1986	S. Cohen (USA)
	E. A. Doisy (USA)	1967	H. K. Hartline (USA)		R. Levi-Montalcini (It)
1944	J. Erlanger (USA)		G. Wald (USA)	1987	S. Tonegawa (Jap)
	H. S. Gasser (USA)		R. A. Granit (Swed)	1988	J. W. Black (UK)
1945	Sir A. Fleming (UK)	1968	R. W. Holley (USA)		G. B. Elion (USA)
	E. B. Chain (UK)		H. G. Khorana (USA)		G. H. Hitchings (USA)
	Lord Florey (Austral)		M. W. Nirenberg (USA)	1989	M. Bishop (USA)
1946	H. J. Muller (USA)	1969	M. Delbrück (USA)		H. Varmus (USA)
1947	C. F. Cori (USA)		A. D. Hershey (USA)	1990	J. Murray (USA)
	G. T. Cori (USA)		S. E. Luria (USA)		E. Thomas (USA)
	B. Houssay (Arg)	1970	J. Axelrod (USA)	1991	E. Neher (Ger)
1948	P. Müller (Switz)		Sir B. Katz (UK)		B. Sakmann (Ger)
1949	W. R. Hess (Switz)		U. von Euler (Swed)	1992	E. Fischer (USA)
	A. E. Moniz (Port)	1971	E. W. Sutherland, Jr.		E. Krebs (USA)
1950	P. S. Hench (USA)		(USA)	1993	R. Roberts (USA)
	E. C. Kendall (USA)	1972	G. M. Edelman (USA)		P. Sharp (USA)
	T. Reichstein (Switz)		R. R. Porter (UK)	1994	A. Gilman (USA)
1951	M. Theiler (S Af)	1973	K. von Frisch (Ger)		M. Rodbell (USA)
1952	S. A. Waksman (USA)		K. Lorenz (Ger)	1995	E. Lewis (USA)
1953	F. A. Lipmann (USA)		N. Tinbergen (Neth)		C. Nüsslein-Volhard
	Sir H. A. Krebs (UK)	1974	A. Claude (USA)		(Ger)
1954	J. F. Enders (USA)		C. de Duve (Belg)		E. Wieschaus (USA)
	T. H. Weller (USA)		G. E. Palade (Belg)	1996	P. Doherty (Austral)
	F. Robbins (USA)	1975	D. Baltimore (USA)		R. Zinkernagel (Switz)
1955	A. H. Theorell (Swed)		R. Dulbecco (USA)	1997	S. B. Pruisner (USA)
1956	W. Forssmann (Ger)		H. M. Temin (USA)	1998	R. F. Furchgott (USA)
	D. Richards (USA)	1976	B. S. Blumberg (USA)		L. J. Ignarro (USA)
	A. F. Cournand (USA)		D. G. Gajdusek (USA)		F. Murad (USA)
1957	D. Bovet (It)	1977	R. S. Yalow (USA)		
			R. Guillemin (USA)		

INDEX

absolute zero 296
accommodation (eye) 246
acetylcholine 121, 293, 344
acetylene 48
acids and bases 19, 48, 128, 207
actinium 129
actinometer 147
actinomycin D 516
action at a distance 41, 331
acylation 194
Addison's disease 76, 296, 449, 510
adenosine diphosphate (ADP) 96
adenosine triphosphate (ATP) 67, 179, 332, 340, 408
adenoviruses 487
adiabatic demagnetization 212
adrenal glands 76, 296, 318
adrenaline 318, 487, 512
adrenocorticotrophic hormone (ACTH) 228
aerodynamics 541
age of rocks 263
age of the Earth 237, 287
age of the universe 25
AIDS 31, 201, 384
aircraft 570
alchemy 207, 403
algebra 8, 88
algebraic geometry 222
algorithm 8
alizarin 423
all-or-none law 5, 351
alpha rays 467
alternation of generations 263
altimeter 85
aluminum 91, 137, 236
Amalthea 34
amatol 456
americium 483
amino acid 385, 524
ammonia 64, 231
ammonia–soda process 496
analytical engine 26, 84
analytical geometry 174
anesthesia 282, 345, 387
angina 54
angiography 154
animal behavior 348, 521, 572
anthrax 303, 416
anthropic principle 90
antibiotics 135, 148, 183
antibodies 82, 153, 317, 524
anticyclones 202
antiferromagnetism 398

antihistamine 66, 96, 142, 485
antimatter 142
antiseptic surgery 341
antitoxins 301
aperture synthesis 469
argon 444, 447
aromaticity 271
arteries 199
artificial intelligence 381, 422, 528
artificial radioactivity 255, 287
aspirin 534
asteroids 300, 426
astigmatism 574
asymmetric carbon atom 326, 416
atherosclerosis 219
atmosphere 367
atomic bomb 3, 21, 60, 95, 223, 246, 311, 411, 511
atomic clocks 442, 524
atomic number 387
atomic pile 176
atomic theory 122, 164, 216, 256, 334
atomic weights 21, 49, 86, 150, 295, 322, 375, 407, 438, 452, 502
aurora borealis 15, 52
Australopithecus 124, 286, 324
background radiation 140, 217, 268, 420, 422, 493
bacteria 107
bacteriophages 133, 139, 529
barbituric acid 29
barium 128
barometer 11, 264, 415, 524, 539
BCS theory 33, 109, 288
benzene 48, 271, 295, 346, 349, 382, 518
beriberi 156, 162, 563
berkelium 483
beryllium 536
beta blockers 54
beta decay 176, 328, 417, 571
bevatron 96
big-bang theory 7, 81, 139, 203, 217, 230, 243, 268, 332, 422
bile acids 558
bilharzia 359
bilirubin 180
binary stars 6
binoculars 316
binomial theorem 402, 410
biosynthesis 56

birefringence 298
black-body radiation 139, 352, 428, 558
black holes 97, 242, 421, 482
bleaching 98
blood circulation 236, 357
blood groups 317
blood pressure 256, 392, 487
blood transfusions 126, 317
body humors 199
bomb calorimeter 48
boranes 341
boron 76, 128
bromine 30
Brownian motion 76, 157, 424
bubonic plague 139
buckminsterfullerene 120, 272, 310, 492
buffer solutions 399
Burgess Shale fossils 543, 557
butterfly effect 347
calcium 128
calcium pump 434
calculus 92, 330, 336, 356, 401, 546
calculus of variations 47, 314
calendar 498
californium 483
caloric 366, 436
calorimeter 69
canals (on Mars) 15, 351, 476
cancer 53, 178, 221, 260, 272, 288, 384, 462
capillary action 241
capillary system 309
carbolic acid 342
carbon cycle 51, 553
carbon dioxide 54, 93, 114, 234, 247
cardinal number 192
carotene 292
carotenoids 311
cartography 372
catalysis 49, 143, 280, 338, 413, 470, 576
catastrophism 39, 62, 353
cathode rays 219, 333
cathode-ray tube 577
cavity magnetron 445
cell division 395
cell formation 481
cell theory for plants 477
cellular metabolism 162
celluloid 415
Central Dogma 31, 516
central limit theorem 362
central nervous system 186, 396

Cepheid variables 25, 252, 325, 486
Ceres 426
cerium 49
cesium 80, 300
chain reaction 196, 287
chain reaction (chemical) 485
chaos theory 348
charm 209, 215
chemical bonding 418
chemical equilibrium 58, 326
chemical kinetics 170, 259
chemical symbols 49
chemotherapy 155
chernozem 144
chimpanzees 221
chlorine 48, 128
chlorofluorocarbons (CFCs) 117, 350, 383, 462
chlorophyll 140, 151, 421, 564, 570
cholera 139, 303
cholesterol 56, 100, 113, 123, 219, 570
chromatography 362, 527
chromium 301, 536
chromosome mapping 508
chromosomes 91, 184, 368, 386
chronometer 109, 239
cine camera 394
cinematography 154
circulation of the blood 95, 199, 240
climate 306, 315, 364
cloud chamber 55, 215, 564
cobalt 71
COBE 494
COBOL 267
cocaine 193
codon 115
coenzymes 169, 238, 307, 340, 353
cold fusion 183
collective unconscious 289
colloids 193, 224
color 402
color blindness 122, 233, 246, 369
color index 482
color photography 340
combustion 437
comets 52, 63, 145, 162, 188, 200, 234, 269, 298, 374, 382, 411, 432, 556
communication theory 485
complementarity principle 59
complex numbers 135
computer-aided tomography (CAT) 113, 267, 359
computers 21, 26, 27, 186, 527, 561
conditioned reflexes 418, 488
conic sections 15, 136, 546
conservation of energy 253, 367

constellations 168
continental drift 43, 55, 79, 264, 284, 465, 550
continuum hypothesis 105
contraceptive pill 143, 428, 498
coordinate geometry 136
coordination compounds 554
Copenhagen interpretation 59, 169
Copernican system 71, 110
cordite 2, 138, 479
Coriolis force 161
corpuscular theory 16
correspondence principle 59
corticotrophic releasing factor (CRF) 228
cortisone 142, 247, 296, 570
cosmic rays 12, 23, 55, 65, 96, 107, 254, 379, 462
cosmological constant 159
covalent bond 336, 345
cowpox 284
CP conservation 116, 181
Crab nebula 218
crepe ring 61, 321
Creutzfeldt-Jakob disease (CJD) 199, 439
critical state 85
Cro-Magnon man 321
crown ethers 114, 330, 420
cryptands 330
crystallography
crystalloids 224
cubic equation 88, 410, 513
curium 483
cybernetics 559
cyclic AMP 509
cycloid 277
cyclotron 95, 287, 324
cytosine 99
dark nebulae 34
dating techniques 61, 336
DDT 391
decimal point 504
deficiency disease 156
Deimos 102, 236
deoxyribonuclease 406
determinants 283
deuterium 410, 530
diabetes 32, 267
didymium 22, 387
differential equations 121, 142, 308
diffraction of light 27
diffusion 224
digestion 38, 311
dinosaurs 10, 13, 30, 359
diphtheria 39, 301
dipole moments 130
dissociation 20, 138
DNA 20, 23, 115, 191, 204, 213, 251, 259, 334, 547, 562
double refraction 35, 403
double stars 50, 376
dyes 423

dynamite 405, 495
dysprosium 104, 327
ear 33, 40
earthquakes 80, 330, 376, 380, 383, 410, 454
Earth (magnetism) 72, 161, 316, 363
Earth (rotation) 248
Earth (shape) 102
echolocation 226, 318
eclipsing binaries 540
EDSAC (Electronic Delay Storage Automatic Computer) 561
electric cell 124
electricity generation 154, 203, 490
electric light bulb 319
electric motor 173, 248
electric relay 248
electrocardiogram (ECG) 160
electrochemistry 49, 128
electroencephalogram (EEG) 44
electrolysis 174
electrolytes 20, 130
electromagnet 248, 508
electromagnetic induction 248
electromagnetic waves 252, 343, 366
electromagnetism 11, 16, 206, 295, 333, 408
electron 346, 505, 519
electron diffraction 128, 130, 161
electron microscope 258, 302, 465, 563, 572
electron-transfer reactions 361, 513
electron-transport chain 96
electrophoresis 521
electroplating 415
electrostatic generator 532
electroweak theory 215, 257, 472, 551
ellipse 15
endocrine glands 87
endothelium-derived relaxing factor (EDRF) 279, 392
ENIAC 22
Enigma 527
enkephalins 307, 495
entropy 61, 104, 366, 485
enzymes 78, 179, 238, 308, 376, 509, 517
epilepsy 44, 98
EPR experiment 159
equation of state 534
equipartition of energy 61
erbium 387
Erlangen Programm 301
ESCA 489
escapement 279
estrogen 8
ethanol 48

ether 320, 347, 377
ether (compound) 345, 387
eudiometer 93
eugenics 202
eukaryotes 361
evolution 36, 62, 125, 144, 232, 276, 307, 314, 367, 545
exobiology 470
expanding universe 159, 195, 270, 332
explosives 1, 405
extra terrestrial intelligence 146
extrovert 289
eye 229
fermentation 85, 416, 481
ferrimagnetism 398
ferrocene 180
ferromagnetism 119
fertilizers 323, 338
field-emission microscope 389
field-ion microscope 389
firedamp 128
fixation of nitrogen 52, 231
fixed-point theorem 75
flash photolysis 406, n434
flavin adenine dinucleotide (FAD) 307, 547
fluorine 383
fluxions 331, 402
food chains 161
foot-and-mouth disease 344
four-color problem 15
Fourier analysis 142, 166, 242, 342, 346
fractals 358
francium 423
frontier orbital theory 196
front (weather) 54
fullerenes 272, 310
fundamental theorem of algebra 206
gadolinium 198, 361
Gaia 350
galactic rotation 411, 429
galaxies 209, 271
Galaxy 250, 338, 411, 486,
gallium 327
galvanization 203
galvanometer 160, 203, 550
game of life 108
game theory 367, 397, 542
gamma globulin (IgG) 434
gamma rays 467
gas 247
gas laws 99
gasoline 45
gastric juice 447
gel filtration 522
general theory of relativity 137, 153, 158, 216, 526
genes 286, 480
genetic code 72, 299, 404, 548
genetic engineering 17, 67, 327
genetic fingerprinting 284

genetics 37, 144, 181, 286, 371, 390
geochemistry 219
geodesy 494
geometry 167, 257, 301
geosyncline 123
germanium 567
germ theory (of disease) 303, 539
glaciation 96, 100, 134, 230
glycogen 46, 101, 111
glycolysis 111
Gondwanaland 150, 508
gonorrhea 399
gout 260
G proteins 457
gravitation 243, 401
gravitational constant 68, 140, 142, 245, 435
gravitational waves 514, 549
Great Attractor 271
Great Wall 209, 271
greenhouse effect 20, 450
Green Revolution 63
group theory 202, 209, 288, 302
guanine 99
guncotton 1, 456
gunpowder 323
hafnium 255
Hall effect 302, 321, 506
Halley's comet 102
hardness (of minerals) 383
heat 436, 464, 529
heat engines 103
heat radiation 503
heavy water 287
heliocentric system 78
helium 283, 343
helium II (He II) 291, 317
helium-3 412, 452
helium-4 328
hemoglobin 46, 180, 425
hemophilia 233
Henry Draper Catalogue 87
hepatitis B 57
heredity 138, 202, 306, 354
Hertzian waves 343, 433
hidden variables 58
Higgs boson 328
histamine 51, 121
histocompatibility antigens 222
HIV (human immunodeficiency virus) 202, 385
holmium 104
holography 198
Homo erectus 325
Homo habilis 324, 325
hormones 87, 228, 267, 501, 512
host–guest chemistry 114, 330
Hovercraft 105
Human Genome Project 264
humoral theory 165

hydrogen 93
hydrogenation 470, 562
hydrogen bomb 9, 51, 311, 412, 515
hydrometer 278
hygrometer 11, 124, 475
hyperbola 15
Hyperion 321
hypertension 54, 256
hypotension 256
hypothalamus 254
hysteresis 169
Iapetus 91
Icarus 25
ice ages 4, 5, 20, 96, 115, 124, 170
Iceland spar 403
iconoscope 577
ideal gas 206
immune system 43, 153, 370, 393
immunoglobulin 153
imprinting 348
incompleteness proof 216
indeterminacy principle 59
indigo 29, 100
inert gases 35
inferiority complex 4
inflationary universe 230
influenza 189, 222, 500
infrared spectroscopy 263
inheritance 181, 233, 286, 354, 371
inoculation 284
insecticides 391
insulin 2, 32, 51, 356, 373
integrated circuit 262, 299, 407
intelligence 83
interference microscope 275
interference of light, 574
interferometer 377
interferon 281
intermediate vector boson 463, 472
internal-combustion engine 121, 404
interstellar matter 240, 272, 283, 429, 491, 507, 526
introvert 289
intuitionism 75, 306
invar 228
iodine 114, 207
ion-exchange chromatography 85
ionosphere 16, 72, 360
iridium anomaly 9
irrational numbers 131, 441
isomerism 49, 337, 568
isomorphism 382
isoprene 280, 546
isostasy 6, 151, 435
isotopes 21, 60, 245, 496
jaundice 247
Java man 148
jet engine 542, 557

jet stream 460
Jodrell Bank 350
J/psi particle 215, 453, 521
jumping genes 285, 368
Jupiter 200
kaleidoscope 73
kaons 116, 209
kinetic theory 98, 104, 116, 288, 345, 349, 366
krypton 444
kurchatovium 312
kuru 199
lac repressor 213
lanthanum 387
large-number coincidences 142
lasers 57, 356, 438, 442, 475
laser trap 106, 426
latent heat 54
law of large numbers 431
law of mass action 48, 229, 326
law of octaves 400
law of triads 143
laws of chemical combination 123
laws of motion 401
lead-chamber process 207
Leblanc process 393
leptons 215
leukemia 260, 518
levers 17
Leyden jar 393, 406
lighthouses 122, 192
lightning conductors 433
limit (in mathematics) 17, 92
linear accelerator 263, 324
liquefaction of gases 85, 138, 290, 427
liquid air 339
liquid crystals 211
liquid-drop model 442
lithium 49
lock-and-key hypothesis 180
logarithms 74, 396
logic 19, 62, 192, 216, 257, 419, 465, 491, 512
longitude 182, 239, 362
low temperatures 212, 290, 345, 426, 427
LSD 74, 570
Lucy 286
macromolecules 502
Magellanic Clouds 252, 325
magic bullets 155
magic numbers 217
magnetic resonance imaging 359
magnetic reversals 170, 244, 450, 538
magnetic storms 98
magnetic variables 27
magnetism 213
magnetohydrodynamics 7
main-sequence stars 252

major histocompatibility antigens 144
malaria 322, 359, 459
Manhattan project 95, 96, 150
manometer 10, 85
many-worlds interpretation 169
Mars 15
masers 36, 57, 356, 438, 442, 444, 524
mass spectrograph 20, 135, 520
matrices 94
matrix mechanics 64, 245
melanism 298
mendelevium 372, 483
Mendel's laws 113
meningitis 66
Mercury 15
metallurgy 6, 274
meteorites 101
meteorology 202; see also weather
meteors 476
method of exhaustion 168
method of indivisibles 92
metric system 132, 314
microorganisms 149
microprocessor 262
microscopes 241, 264, 329, 403
microsomes 103, 131
Mid-Atlantic Ridge 170, 519
midwife toad 290
Milky Way 60, 250
mimicry 103
Miranda 311
Mischmetal 22
mitochondria 414
mitosis 184
Mizar 365
MKK classification 293
Moho 383
molecular-orbital theory 139, 333, 391
molecular weights 24, 86
Moon 126, 147
morphine 114, 456
mosquitoes 322, 359, 459
multiple sclerosis 43
muon 13
muscle 148, 258, 267, 276, 480
myoglobin 297, 425
naphthalene 48
natural selection 125, 129, 144, 181, 238, 371, 419
navigational aids 122
nebulae 269, 273, 374
nebular hypothesis 319
neodymium 22, 104, 387
neomycin 543
neon 444
neoprene 89
Neptune 6, 16, 50, 57, 334
neptunian theory 553
neptunium 3, 369, 483
Nereid 311

nerve cells 220
nerve fibers 166, 205, 311
nerve growth factor 106, 335
nervous system 204, 318
neuron 443
neurotransmitters 24, 540
neutrinos 29, 51, 127
neutron 65, 95
neutron diffraction 74, 161, 488
neutron stars 256, 273, 577
niacin 218
nicotinamide adenine dinucleotide (NAD) 307
nicotinic acid 162
niobium 160
nitric oxide see nitrogen monoxide
nitrocellulose 478
nitrogen cycle 48
nitrogen monoxide 279, 392, 495
nitroglycerin 405, 495
nitrous oxide 128, 247, 437
non-cooperative games 397
nonequilibrium thermodynamics 410, 437
non-Euclidean geometry 61, 159, 206, 342
noradrenaline 24, 540
novae 120
nuclear energy 496
nuclear fission 232, 405, 511
nuclear magnetic resonance (NMR) 56, 166, 358, 440
nuclear transformations 105
nuclear transmutations 233
nuclear winter 117, 470
nucleic acids 91, 378
nucleons 245, 263
number theory 142, 165, 175, 206, 239, 257, 380
nutation 69
Nylon 89
ocean currents 161, 176
ocean temperature 365
octet theory 336
omega minus 209
oncogenes 53
one-fluid theory (of electricity) 191
one gene–one enzyme hypothesis 38
open-hearth process 490
operons 135, 283, 384
ophthalmoscope 246
optical activity 52, 351, 424
optical pumping 293
optical rotatory power 351
oscilloscope 72
osmosis 138, 344
oxidative phosphorylation 382, 408
oxygen 212, 437, 475
ozone 14, 117, 479
ozone layer 384

pair production 55
Pangaea 550
pangenesis 19, 125
paper chromatography 362
parabola 15
parallax 50, 69, 247, 298, 507
parallel postulate 61, 168, 342
paramagnetism 318, 536
parity 116, 329, 560, 571, 573
particle accelerator 533
patch-clamp technique 398, 471
pellagra 162, 197, 218
pendulum clock 277
penicillin 95, 135, 183, 185, 262
peptide synthesis 45, 372
perceptrons 381
perihelion of Mercury 140, 335
periodic table 319, 372, 375, 387, 400, 439, 496
period-luminosity relation 25, 270, 325
pernicious anemia 556
perturbations 319, 497
phages 16, 106, 133, 139, 251, 352
phagocytes 145
phase-contrast microscope 575
phase transitions 566
phenol–formaldehyde resins 28, 29
phenolphthalein 29
pheromones 83
philosopher's stone 247
phlogiston 45, 322, 345, 500
Phobos 102, 236
Phoebe 427
phonograph 154
phonons 317
photochemistry 147
photoelectric effect 157, 332, 379
photography 121, 152, 404
photometry 65
photons 157
photosynthesis 85, 140, 279, 376
pi 18, 316, 339, 546
piezoelectricity 119
Piltdown man 294
pion 13, 328
pitchblende 117
plankton 248
plant ecology 547
plant pigments 310
plate tectonics 551, 565
Pluto 351
plutonium 369, 483
pneumonia 23, 66
pocket calculator 299
polarimetry 52
polarization of light 16, 73, 298
polarography 256

Polaroid 316
polio 31, 163, 317, 472
pollination 86
polonium 118
polyethene (polythene) 397, 576
polymerase chain reaction (PCR) 392
polymers 89, 185, 211, 371, 576
polyploids 56, 502
polypropene 397
positrons 12, 55, 96, 141
potassium 128, 207
Poudre B 2, 479
praseodymium 22, 104, 387
preformationism 19
prime number theorem 231, 342
probability 47, 306, 320, 431
Procyon 50
progesterone 143, 428
projective geometry 136, 302
proper motion (of stars) 237
prostaglandins 45, 473, 534
protactinium 232
proteins 14, 49, 418
protein synthesis 69, 261
protoplasm 441
Prutenic Tables 71
psychiatry 4, 193, 289
pterodactyl 120
Ptolemaic theory 440
Pugwash Conferences 462
pulsars 42, 217, 255, 273, 469
purine bases 99
pyrimidine bases 99
quantum electrodynamics 151, 177, 482, 523
quantum theory 58, 59, 64, 142, 159, 169, 170, 177, 243, 245, 258, 288, 305, 417, 428, 433, 479
quarks 171, 195, 209, 215, 328, 395, 398
quartic equation 88
quasars 81, 350, 473, 478
quasicrystals 422
quaternions 212, 238
quinine 421, 423
quintic equation 2
rabies 281, 417
radar 9, 445, 522, 548
radiation laws 428
radiation sickness 119
radioactivity 39, 117, 232, 370
radio astronomy 11, 283, 350, 411, 447, 469
radiocarbon dating 146, 337
radioimmunoassay 573
radio transmission 16, 72, 131, 433
radio waves 252, 343, 360
radium 60, 118
rainbow 574
rainfall 44, 475, 542
recombinant DNA 44, 67

red shift 270, 273
relativity 157, 347, 381
relaxation techniques 155
resonance 280
respiration 151, 233, 256, 323, 357, 437
restriction enzymes 17
retrovirus 31
RFLP 526
rhenium 405
rhesus factor 318
rheumatoid arthritis 247, 296
rhodopsin 311, 465, 544
rho-meson 263
ribonuclease 9, 14, 385, 406
ribosomes 69
rickets 197, 215, 566
RNA 8, 334, 562
rockets 194, 531
rosaniline dyes 180
R–S system 436
rubber 89, 545
rubidium 80, 300
Rudolphine Tables 297
Salvarsan 155
samarium 327
sandwich compounds 180
Saturn 236, 366, 456
scandium 104
scanning tunneling microscope 457
scarlet fever 66
Schrödinger equation 141
scintillation counter 263
scrapie 439
scurvy 109, 197
sea-floor spreading 170, 253, 450, 538
sedimentation 509
seismograph 380
selenium 49
semiconductors 72, 488
serotonin 74
set theory 216
sex hormones 8, 83
sexual behavior 299
shell model 58, 217, 442
sickle-cell hemoglobin 280
siphons 249
Sirius B 4, 50, 102
sleeping sickness 77, 155, 359
slide rule 413
smallpox 279, 284
sociobiology 238, 565
sodium 92, 128, 207
sodium carbonate 496
sodium pump 261
solar eclipse 153, 283
solar prominences 343
solar spectrum 14, 192, 272, 283, 569
solar system 7, 57, 176, 319
solar wind 532
sonar 41, 318
sound 406, 409
space–time 158, 290, 381, 481

SPEAR 424
spectroheliograph 235
spectroscopy 14, 31, 80, 253, 300
speed of light 91, 182, 187, 458
speed of sound 135, 205
speedometer, 26
spermatozoa 97
spin 141, 223, 417
spiral galaxies 338, 463, 485
spiral nebulae 120, 352
split genes 455, 487
spontaneous generation 107, 447, 498
staining techniques 303, 443
stars 11, 87; see also stellar
statistical mechanics 61, 212
steady-state theory 217, 268
steam engine 249, 549
steamships 77
steel 50
stellar distances 252
stellar magnitudes 61, 325
stellar spectra 4, 147, 188, 365, 471
stellar structure 97
stereochemistry 436, 567
steroids 143, 247
stethoscope 313
strangeness 209
stratosphere 514
streptomycin 543
string theory 290, 396, 481
strong interaction 177, 574
strontium 128, 265
strychnine 421, 456, 570
substitution theory (in chemistry) 150, 322
sugars 244
sulfa drugs 66, 145
sulfuric acid 98, 207, 393
Sun 201, 214, 453; see also solar
sunglasses 316
sunspots 16, 146, 235, 316, 343, 364
superconductivity 13, 33, 39, 90, 101, 109, 290, 317, 345, 363, 370, 389, 479
superfluids 13, 291, 317, 328, 412, 452
supernova 120, 577
superphosphates 323
superstring theory 567
supramolecules 330
synchrocyclotron 369
synchrotron radiation 411
syphilis 63, 155, 405, 543
syringe 415
tantalum 160
tau particle 424
technetium 373, 405
telegraphy 1, 40, 154, 244, 248, 282, 360, 490, 550, 555

telephone 40, 154
telescopes 200, 225, 235, 255, 264, 340, 402, 460, 477
television 30, 72, 577
tellurium 301
temperature scale 94, 447
terbium 387
terpenes 424, 468, 546
testosterone 83, 143
tetanus 39, 301
tetracyclines 148
thallium 116
thermionic emission 452
thermionic tube 131, 154, 184
thermochemistry 48
thermocouple 326
thermodynamics 89, 104, 212, 289, 295, 366, 399
thermoelectricity 484
thermometer 171, 447
thiamine 426
thorium 49, 60
three-body problem 53, 314, 431
thulium 104
thymine 99
thymus gland 378
thyroid gland 296, 476
time zones 1
Titan 311
titanium 225, 301
tobacco mosaic virus 37, 189, 406, 500
topology 75, 302, 382, 431
torsion balance 68, 93, 113, 164, 376
trade winds 231
transactinide elements 185
transfinite set theory 87, 105
transformer 516
transfusion 126
transistors 33, 72, 299, 488
transmissible spongiform encephalopathy 439
transmutation 546
transpiration (in plants) 235
transplantation 89, 127, 144, 392
transuranic elements 3, 483
triangulation 494
tricarboxylic acid cycle 309
trigonometry 259
tritium 410
Triton 321
troposphere 514
tuberculosis 155, 303
tungsten 133
tunnel effect 167, 211, 457
tunnel diode 167
two-fluid theory (of electricity) 148, 191
type theory (in chemistry) 211, 322, 563
typhus 404

ultracentrifuge 509
ultramicroscope 425, 576
ultramicrotome 275
Umbriel 321
uncertainty principle 245
unified field theory 159, 555
uniformitarianism 275, 353
upsilon particle 328, 424
uranium 117, 135, 301, 369
Uranus 3, 50, 250, 334, 351
urea 568
uridine triphosphate 332
vaccines 40, 222, 404, 417, 472, 517
valence 1, 190, 336, 408, 489
vanadium 49, 134, 484
varve-counting 146, 208
vasomotor system 46
vasopressin 151
vectors 212, 238, 295
Vega 61, 147
Venus 267
viruses 37, 163, 281
vision 544
vitamin A 292, 311
vitamin B_2 292, 311
vitamin B_6 311
vitamin B_{12} 167, 186, 262, 570
vitamin C 244, 449
vitamin D 566
vitamin E 292
vitamin H 151
vitamin K 123
vitamins 27, 197, 215, 244, 267, 368, 426
volcanoes 137, 228
vulcanization 415
wave mechanics 130, 479
wave–particle duality 58, 59, 130, 519
wave theory of light 16, 192, 345, 569, 574
weak interaction 328, 560
weather forecasting 1, 44, 347, 452
weather mapping 202
wind scale 38
W particle 463
xenon 35, 444
x-ray crystallography 46, 242, 292, 346
x-ray diffraction 70, 130, 262, 292, 297, 541
x-ray fluorescence 34
x-rays 34, 333, 458, 494
x-ray spectroscopy 489
x-ray tomography 113
yellow fever 222, 406, 505, 516
ytterbium 361
zero 8
zirconium 301
Z particle 463